BEHIND THE BLUE LAMP

SCOTLAND YARD'S POLICE STATIONS 1829-2020

Alan Moss, David Swinden and Peter Kennison

Blue Lamp Books

First Edition published 2021.

Copyright © Alan Moss, David Swinden and Peter Kennison 2021

The right of Alan Moss, David Swinden and Peter Kennison to be identified as the authors of this work has been asserted in accordance with the Copyright, Designs & Patents Act 1988.

All rights reserved. No part of this book may be reprinted or reproduced or utilised in any form or by any electronic, mechanical or other means, now known or hereafter invented, including photocopying and recording, or in any information storage or retrieval system, without the prior permission in writing of the publishers.

Unless otherwise stated, images are from the authors' collection. Whilst every effort has been made to credit all images to the appropriate source/copyright holder, the author apologises for any oversight, which we would be happy to correct in future editions.

ISBN: 978-1-914277-23-8 (hardcover)
ISBN: 978-1-914277-24-5 (softcover)

Published by Blue Lamp Books,
an imprint of Mango Books

www.MangoBooks.co.uk

18 Soho Square
London W1D 3QL

All photographs, images, illustrations and maps have been reproduced by kind courtesy of the Metropolitan Police Historic Collection, with the exception of the following:

John Barrett page 267 (image 1); Ken Batson 48(1), 463(3); Linda Clark 335; D. Collett 402; Jeff Cowdell 27, 453(3&4), 455(1), 461, 470(2), 472(1); Betty Donaldson 266(2); Jack Edwards 141(1); Essex Police Museum 302(1); Chris Forester 229, 341, 381; Mike Fountain 184; I. French 207-209; London Borough of Hillingdon Library 213; London Borough of Hackney Archives 169-170; Janice Horne 193(3); Julian Jephcote 38(1), 68-70, 127, 128, 182(1), 194-195, 244, 252(1), 324-325, 328, 329(2), 336(1), 338, 354(3), 391, 401; Dee Jupp 408; Peter Kennison 8-11, 12(1), 13(1)-14, 18, 23, 29-31, 43, 44(1), 46(1), 47(1), 48, 49(3), 52, 56-57, 60, 62(3), 65-66, 68, 71-72, 74(2), 113, 115, 118-119(1), 120-121, 122, 127(1), 128, 129(1)-130, 131, 132(1&3)-133, 135, 136(1), 140(2), 142(1&2), 143(2), 151-152(3), 153, 154-156, 158, 160, 168, 170, 171-173, 175-176, 185, 196, 202(1), 204(1&2), 206, 210, 212(3), 214(1), 215(1), 218, 219(1), 221(2), 223-224(3), 226(2), 227(1)-228, 230, 232, 234-235, 243, 249, 252(3), 255(1), 256(1&3)-257, 259(1), 260-261, 263(1)-264(1), 266, 269(2), 272-273(1), 275(2), 279, 281(2), 284(1&2), 286, 295, 301(2), 302, 304(1), 310(1), 314(1), 316, 319-320(1), 320(3)-321, 322(2), 327(1), 332-333, 336, 340(1), 341(2), 342(2), 343, 344(1), 350, 355-356, 358(1), 360, 364, 365(1), 366(1), 371, 372(2), 378, 380, 382, 390, 394, 395, 399, 400(1), 409(1), 410(1), 411(2), 413, 416-417, 420(1), 421, 422(1), 423, 424-425, 426-429(1), 432-433, 433(2), 434(2), 435(4), 436, 437(1)-438(3), 440-442, 443(1), 444, 445(1), 447(1), 449(2&3), 450(1&3), 451(1), 452(4), 453, 454-455, 458(1), 459(1), 459(3), 460(1&3), 461(1), 462(2&4), 463(1), 467, 471(4), 473-474(1); Chris Lordan 250, 322(3), 362(2); *Bacon's Maps* 271(1), 292(1); *Dawson's Map 1837* 475; *Stamford Map 1866* 476; *Bacon's map 1910* 478; *Geographia 1933* 481; *Metropolitan Police Map 1965* 482; *Morden Messenger* 277(2); Alan Moss 63, 78(1), 102-103, 146, 294(1), 296(2), 336(2), 346(1), 389(2); National Archives 40, 109, 314; George Plumb 425(1), 452(1), 469(1); Peter Straighton 337; David Swinden 49(1), 61, 65-66, 90, 98, 138, 143(1), 154, 184, 191, 194, 203, 212(1), 213(1), 214, 228(1), 228(2), 235(1), 259, 262, 271, 288, 295, 306, 329(1), 351, 352, 358, 371(1), 379, 396, 448, 450, 456(3), 457(1), 462; Neil Watson 189, 190-192, 387, 388-389; Victor Legender Wilkinson 263, 459(2), 461(4), 462(1), 463(3&5), 464(3).

Contents

Foreword i
Introduction iii

1. The Metropolitan Police District 1
2. Some Aspects of Metropolitan Police History 5
3. London Boroughs and their Police Stations 17
4. Gazetteer of Police Buildings and Stations Past and Present 37
5. Thames Division 419
6. The Royal Dockyards Divisions 424
7. Police Uniforms, Badges and Equipment 447
8. Police Ranks 458
9. Women Police 466
10. Metropolitan Police Divisions: A History 1829-2019 475

Appendix A – Warrant Numbers allocated by year 485
Appendix B – Section Houses 487
Acknowledgements 489

Index 491

Foreword

CRESSIDA DICK
Commissioner of Police of the Metropolis

This book describes, in one volume, the complete history of Metropolitan Police stations, how they came to be built, and how they were replaced. It also contains many personal stories of individual officers who served and sometimes lived 'behind the blue lamp'. There are chapters describing the uniforms they wore and some of the historical context of policing's development since Sir Robert Peel introduced the Metropolitan Police in 1829.

Designing and providing police stations, many of them of significant architectural interest, came under the sometimes overlooked remit of a succession of Chief Architects and Surveyors working for the Receiver of the Metropolitan Police District and the Home Secretary; their modern equivalents are the Property Services Directorate and the Mayor's Office for Policing and Crime. So as well as reflecting changes in policing, this book also acts as a tribute to the loyal and diligent efforts of the members of police staff who have ably supported the policing of London over the years.

In its earliest days, the Metropolitan Police Service was the only single public body with a jurisdiction covering the London area (outside the City of London itself). London itself was far smaller in Victorian times. As local authorities developed, the relationship between them and the Met has changed and some areas on the outskirts of London have been transferred to other police forces along with their police stations. The management structure of the MPS has also changed periodically as policing needs have changed, and understanding how former Divisions and other groups of police stations have been organised from Scotland Yard has sometimes been a very complex business. This book sets out the changes that have taken place.

Behind the Blue Lamp will undoubtedly act as a valuable historical resource for many years to come, particularly for those who need to understand how the Met was organised in Victorian times and how it is different today.

Some things have not changed, however. The officers who ventured out to patrol the streets of London from their first rather basic police stations in 1829 may not have had the offices, equipment and technology of today, but they set the standards of determination, bravery and public service to uphold the law and keep London safe that our current men and women share as an essential part of policing London in the 21st century.

Introduction

This book combines into one volume the contents of three earlier books: *Behind the Blue Lamp: Policing North and East London* by Peter Kennison and David Swinden (2003); *More Behind the Blue Lamp: Policing South and South-East London* by David Swinden, Peter Kennison and Alan Moss (2011) and *Discovering More Behind the Blue Lamp: Policing Central, North and South-West London* by Peter Kennison, David Swinden and Alan Moss (2014).

Since these three books were published there have been many changes in the Metropolitan Police Service (MPS), not least in relation to the number of traditional police stations open to the public, so we have taken the opportunity of updating the information as much as we can. For those who find the organisation of the MPS difficult, we have described the latest organisation of Basic Command Units (BCUs) and how they relate to local authority areas. We have also included a chapter of how police divisions have changed over the years.

The basic principle of the book remains unchanged. We set out the history of the police stations operated by the Metropolitan Police since its formation in 1829 and relate these buildings to local communities and the officers who served – and sometimes lived – in those police stations and section houses. The architecture of the stations shows interesting developments over the course of 190 years, and the internal accommodation has also changed at various points to make provision for features such as waiting rooms, control rooms, custody suites and other technological or policing developments.

In our earlier books we described various features of policing in various places throughout the books, using individual police stations or officers as examples of wider issues. In this volume we have collected much of this more generalised history into a Chapter Two. It is not intended as a comprehensive history of the MPS, but it does explain a number of issues to help the reader understand how things have changed. The very brief histories of the communities for each local authority area and their police stations have been pulled together in Chapter Three. This then means that the main gazetteer of police stations in Chapter Four is organised alphabetically, regardless of where they are located in the Metropolitan Police District (MPD).

Police stations no longer in the MPD or part of BCUs appear in the gazetteer, with a reference explaining, the county (eg Surrey) to which they were transferred.

Chapter Seven is about uniforms, equipment and badges of rank, and collates all the information that was published across the three preceding books.

The MPS is probably the largest employer in London, and over the years many people's ancestors have served in the organisation. We believe it is important to reflect the changes that have been made in relation to those buildings that have meant so much to individuals and communities, and to record the largely unsung work done by members of the civil staff who have worked in difficult circumstances to design, build, maintain and replace them in the never-ending chase to keep up with operational needs from tight budgets.

We have not included all the police support buildings that have existed over the years, nor the large number of married quarters and section houses that have formed part of the MPS estate. Within the memory of many of us, the Receiver for the Metropolitan Police District acted as the landlord of a vast property portfolio, much of it owned freehold; the operator of both a very significant and varied motor vehicle fleet and also a significant multiple-site catering facility; and provider of large, complex technological systems that had to be used from sites all over London. Specialist suppliers have been used for many functions since 1829, and modern financial considerations have meant changes to how public bodies regard ownership of freehold and other property, but commercial contracts for the supply of services are still an important aspect of support for the MPS, now the responsibility of the Mayor's Office for Police and Crime.

This book is unashamedly historical in its outlook and aims to describe some of what went on behind the walls of police stations and what life may have been like for the officers who served in them. It is based on the local police station serving its local community, and we hope that this principle will apply for many years to come.

Alan Moss, David Swinden and Peter Kennison

April 2020

About the Authors

ALAN MOSS, a Classics graduate from Durham University, served as a Metropolitan Police officer for 30 years, retiring as a Chief Superintendent in 1997. He has worked abroad in police training and consultancy, was involved in planning for a Metropolitan Police museum at Bow Street, has co-authored a number of books about policing history with Keith Skinner, has made a number of TV appearances about policing history and operates a website about the history of London policing at www.historybytheyard.co.uk

DAVID SWINDEN MSC., DMS., PgDip (History) retired from the Metropolitan Police as a Superintendent in 1994. His 36 years' Police service was spent in north and east London and at New Scotland Yard. He also carried out police consultancy projects in the USA, Uganda and Gibraltar. After retiring from the Police service he became a senior lecturer in Human Resources Management at the University of East London, and was responsible for a number of educational programmes worldwide.

PETER KENNISON BA, MA, PhD has been a practitioner and academic for over 35 years. He joined the Metropolitan Police in 1970 and over a career spanning nearly three decades he served on five Police divisions in north and east London, the Police Training School at Hendon, and in the Complaints Investigation Branch (CIB3) at New Scotland Yard. His interests include policing (including its historical context), child protection and community safety. Peter is now fully retired having been a senior lecturer in Criminology at the Universities of Middlesex and Brighton.

Chapter 1.
The Metropolitan Police District

The chart below sets out the London boroughs, their main police stations and how they relate to the structure of Basic Command Units (BCUs) introduced in 2018-19. The two letter codes for each BCU is shown on their officers' uniform epaulettes. Other places policed now or in the past follow after the list of the London boroughs and City of Westminster:

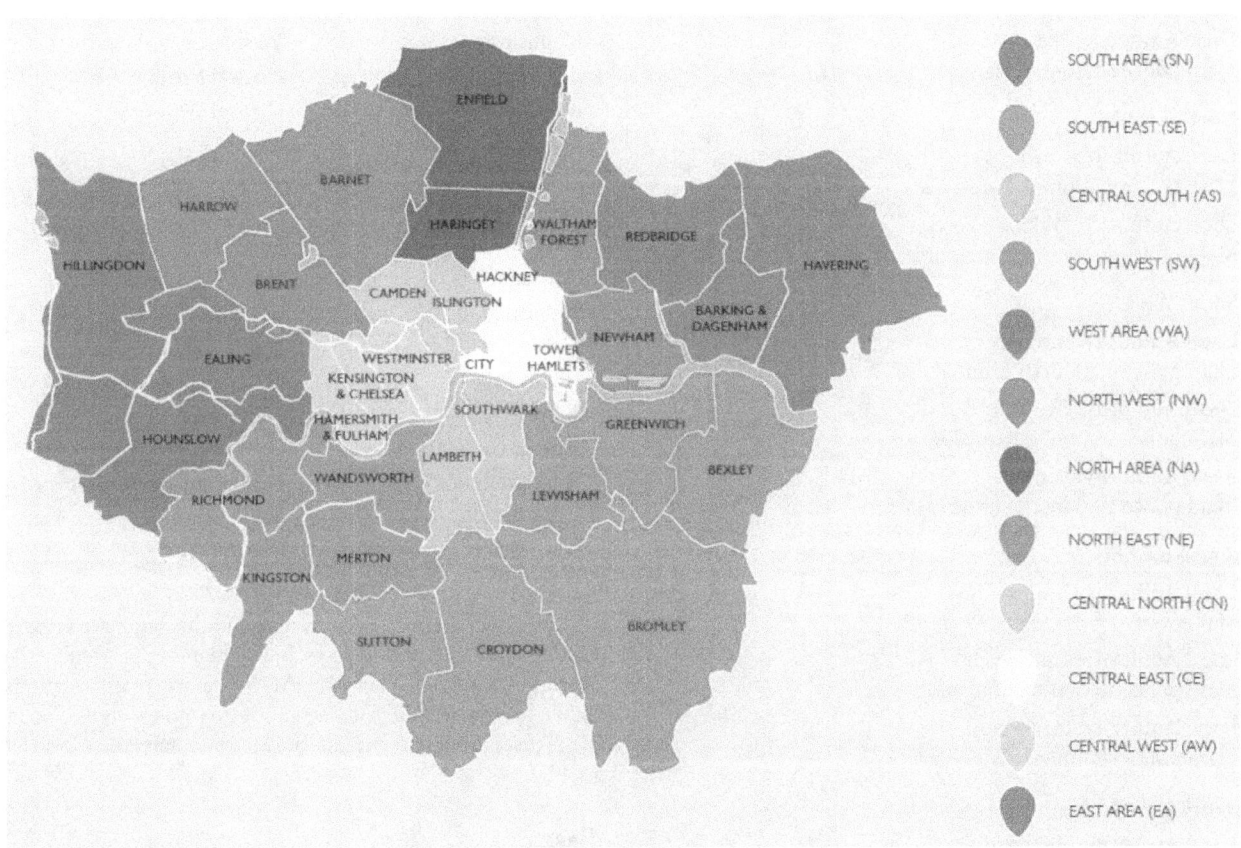

Courtesy Metropolitan Police Service

Central East CE

Local Authority: Hackney
Main police station(s): Stoke Newington

Local Authority: Tower Hamlets
Main police station(s): Bethnal Green

Central North CN

Local Authority: Camden
Main police station(s): Kentish Town

Local Authority: Islington
Main police station(s): Islington

Central South AS

Local Authority: Lambeth
Main police station(s): Brixton

Local Authority: Southwark
Main police station(s): Walworth

Central West CW

Local Authority: Kensington & Chelsea
Main police station(s): Kensington, Notting Hill

Local Authority: Hammersmith & Fulham
Main police station(s): Shepherds Bush

Local Authority: City of Westminster
Main police station(s): Charing Cross

East Area EA

Local Authority: Barking & Dagenham
Main police station(s): Dagenham

Local Authority: Havering
Main police station(s): Romford

Local Authority: Redbridge
Main police station(s): Ilford

North Area NA

Local Authority: Enfield
Main police station(s): Edmonton

Local Authority: Haringey
Main police station(s): Tottenham

North West NW

Local Authority: Barnet
Main police station(s): Colindale

Local Authority: Brent
Main police station(s): Wembley

Local Authority: Harrow
Main police station(s): Harrow

North East NE

Local Authority: Newham
Main police station(s): Forest Gate

Local Authority: Waltham Forest
Main police station(s): Chingford

South Area SN

Local Authority: Bromley
Main police station(s): Bromley

Local Authority: Croydon
Main police station(s): Croydon

Local Authority: Sutton
Main police station(s): Sutton

South East SE

Local Authority: Bexley
Main police station(s): Bexleyheath

Local Authority: Greenwich
Main police station(s): Plumstead

Local Authority: Lewisham
Main police station(s): Lewisham

South West SW

Local Authority: Kingston
Main police station(s): Kingston

Local Authority: Merton
Main police station(s): Wimbledon

Local Authority: Richmond
Main police station(s): Twickenham

Local Authority: Wandsworth
Main police station(s): Lavender Hill

West Area WA

Local Authority: Ealing
Main police station(s): Acton

Local Authority: Hillingdon
Main police station(s): Hayes

Local Authority: Hounslow
Main police station(s): Hounslow

By alphabetical order, local authorities are therefore policed as follows:

Local Authority	Area
Barking & Dagenham	East Area EA
Barnet	North West NW
Bexley	South East SE
Brent	North West NW
Bromley	South Area SN
Camden	Central North CN
Croydon	South Area SN
Ealing	West Area WA
Enfield	North Area NA
Greenwich	South East SE
Hackney	Central East CE
Hammersmith & Fulham	Central West CW
Haringey	North Area NA
Havering	East Area EA
Harrow	North West NW
Hillingdon	West Area WA
Hounslow	West Area WA
Islington	Central North CN
Kensington & Chelsea	Central West CW
Kingston	South West SW
Lambeth	Central South AS
Lewisham	South East SE
Merton	South West SW
Newham	North East NE
Redbridge	East Area EA
Richmond	South West SW
Southwark	Central South AS
Sutton	South Area SN
Tower Hamlets	Central East CE
Waltham Forest	North East NE
Wandsworth	South West SW
Westminster	Central West CW

Some police stations described within this book are outside the remit of London boroughs, but were once operated by the Metropolitan Police Service (MPS) before reorganisations either transferred them to neighbouring police forces, or in some cases brought them into the Metropolitan Police District (MPD).

Essex

In 1965, some parts of Essex covered by the current London Boroughs of Havering and Barking & Dagenham were transferred to the MPD when a major local government reorganisation created the Greater London Council and London boroughs. Epping, Chigwell and Waltham Abbey were transferred to Essex in 2000 to coincide with the formation of the Greater London Authority and the Metropolitan Police Authority.

Police stations
- Chigwell
- Debden
- Limes Farm
- Loughton
- Waltham Abbey

Hertfordshire

Similarly, Broxbourne, Cheshunt, Hertsmere, South Mimms, Radlett and Welwyn Hatfield were transferred to Hertfordshire in April 2000.

Police stations
- Aldenham
- Bushey
- Elstree
- Potters Bar
- Radlett
- Goffs Oak

Kent

Knockholt was policed by Kent County Constabulary from 1857 as part of their Sevenoaks division, but was policed by the Metropolitan Police from 1947 until 1969 when it reverted back to Kent. Biggin Hill was transferred to the MPS in 1947 and has remained within the MPD, since it now forms part of the London Borough of Bromley.

Police station
- Knockholt

Surrey

Parts of Surrey such as Elmbridge and Spelthorne were also transferred from the MPS to Surrey Constabulary from April 2000.

Police stations
- Epsom
- Ewell
- Esher
- East Molesey
- Staines
- Banstead

Airports

Responsibility for policing Heathrow Airport was transferred to the Metropolitan Police on 1 November 1974 when it became a Division in its own right, comprising Heathrow and parts of West Drayton and Staines. Along with London City Airport, It is now policed by MPS officers from SO18 Aviation Security and Airport Policing.

Police station
- Heathrow

Marine policing

Policing of the London Docks and the River Thames started in 1798, well before the Metropolitan Police was established, when the crime situation was described as:

"....there were no fewer than 10,000 thieves, footpads, prostitutes and pilferers at work on the jetties, quays that lined the riverside and that the plunder and pillage represented an annual loss of over half a million pounds."

With the formation of the Metropolitan Police in 1829 the River Police became a division of the MPS. The first station to open near the Thames was Wapping, followed by an office at Greenwich which had an establishment of one hundred constables. Police were recruited not only to stem the tide of crime on the river, but also to deal with the frequent robberies on the roads leading into the metropolis and thefts in the dockyards at Deptford and Woolwich.

The division extended practically through the whole navigable area of the River Thames. This stretched from Teddington Lock in the west to Dartford Creek, Kent and Rainham, Essex in the east.

Police stations
- Barnes
- Erith
- Waterloo Pier
- Wapping

HM Dockyards

Policing of the Royal Dockyards, at Woolwich within the MPD but also at Chatham, Devonport, Portsmouth, Pembroke and Rosyth, was undertaken by the Metropolitan Police for some periods in history, described in further detail in Chapter Six.

Headquarters Buildings, Training Establishments, Sports Clubs and Section Houses

Within our gazetteer of police stations in Chapter Four we have included some, but not all, of the other buildings that will have made an impact on the lives of officers behind the blue lamp. Examples are Great Scotland Yard, that once contained a police station, Peel House in Regency Street, Hendon Training School, The Warren sports club and Ambrosden House section house.

Chapter 2.
Some Aspects of Metropolitan Police History

This book is primarily about the police stations of the Metropolitan Police Service, and acts as a historical reference for the buildings in which police have been accommodated. But behind the blue lamp invariably displayed on the fronts of those buildings lie an interesting series of historical features, including how the Metropolitan Police has been organised, and some of the characters who served in the police stations.

Policing London before 1829

The Metropolitan Police Act that established the Service received its royal assent on 19th June 1829. At the time, policing in London consisted of a number of local watchmen, sometimes operating from watch houses, supplemented by the magistrates at seven police offices which had been established under the Middlesex Justices Act 1792. Each of these, the forerunners of our modern magistrates courts, had three stipendiary magistrates and six constables.

The offices outside Westminster were at Hatton Garden, Worship Street (Finsbury), Lambeth Street (Whitechapel), Shadwell (later at Marylebone High Street) and Union Hall, Southwark, whilst Westminster had Great Marlborough Street and Queen's Square. The most famous additional and eighth office was at Bow Street, from where the Bow Street officers and patrols operated. There was a Receiver appointed to raise money from parishes to fund these offices.

The Receiver for the Metropolitan Police District

The first ever appointment to the Metropolitan Police was also a Receiver, when Home Secretary Sir Robert Peel appointed John Wray on 7th July 1829 to perform a similar function for the New Police. It was John Wray's job to finance, accommodate and supply the new organisation, and the fact that over 1,100 new police officers were recruited, fitted with uniforms and then started to patrol London's streets by 25 September that year, ten weeks after his appointment, was an enormous achievement.

Therefore, in legal terms, it was the Receiver for the Metropolitan Police District who bought and sold police stations rather than the police Commissioners. From 1829 until June 2000, when the Metropolitan Police Authority started its life, the financial and support arrangements of the Police Authority were formally the responsibility of the Home Secretary, but arrangements were established by Sir Robert Peel so that there was a clear demarcation between the Commissioners, who took responsibility for the operations and discipline of the new police force, and the Receiver, who organised the finance, buildings, equipment and ancillary support. So all police stations were in fact the property of the Receiver, whose legal status was a *corporation sole* as provided for in the Metropolitan Police (Receiver) Act 1861.

The Receiver had the power to levy rates from the local authorities within London for the Metropolitan Police, for the Inner London Magistrates' Courts Service, and later for the Inner London Probation Service. This legal status for a public servant was a convenient and efficient method of operating at the time, and it is doubtful if any other method could have raised so many resources in the short time between the passage of the Metropolitan Police Act through Parliament in June 1829, and the first officers of the new force recruited from 21 September of that year who started their first patrols on 25 September. For many years, the Metropolitan Police was the only public body that had jurisdiction on a London-wide basis.

John Wray was a barrister by profession and throughout his tenure as Receiver he also held the position of Resident Director of the University Life Assurance Society. He retired in 1860 at the age of 78 years. Never a man to become involved in detailed financial records, bureaucracy or written memoranda rather than oral communication, his departure caused some concern at the Home Office when they were unable to locate the personal bond for £9,000 Wray had given when he took up his post.

John Wray appointed a firm of solicitors, Lyons, Barnes & Ellis, to conduct property and other business on behalf of the Receiver. Various changes in title of the firm occurred over the years, until they became Winckworth & Pemberton in 1978. Separately, by 1874 a legal advisor to the Commissioner, James Davis, was appointed, later being succeeded in 1887 by Messrs Wontner & Son. In 1935 Lord Trenchard brought most of the Met's legal business in-house, creating the Solicitor's Department.

Legal issues would have arisen in relation to contracts and buildings, but operationally it was the criminal law that governed prosecutions. Commissioner Sir Richard Mayne was also a barrister, and therefore had a legal background to direct criminal investigations until he died in post in 1868. (The office of Director of Public Prosecutions was not instituted until 1879.)

For police buildings, initially Joseph Morris surveyed premises, and in 1842 Richard Fletcher was appointed as the first permanent Surveyor of the Police Establishment, being replaced the following year by Charles Reeves who took responsibility for what had become 125 buildings within the Metropolitan Police District. Reeves started the process of properly designing police stations. Until 1845, Fletcher and Reeves may well have reported to the Surveyor General of Prisons who seems to have had overall responsibility for all the buildings used by the police.

In 1853 Colonel Paschal started the Executive Branch with the rank of Chief Inspector. The post, which included responsibility for the Public and Hackney Carriage Offices, was later held by a Superintendent, some of whom (eg Kittle, Harris, Cutbush) became prominent figures at Scotland Yard.

The London County Council (1889-1965) and its successor the Greater London Council (1965-1986) did not have direct responsibility for the Metropolitan Police.

The post of Receiver was made redundant in 2000 when the Metropolitan Police Authority came into being along with the Greater London Authority and took over the role of police authority for the Metropolitan Police from the Home Secretary. Police and Crime Commissioners were elected in November 2012 to replace police authorities, and at that stage the arrangements for London also changed so that the Metropolitan Police Authority was replaced by the Mayor's Office for Policing and Crime.

Fire and Ambulance Services

The watchmen who had operated before Peel's New Police were responsible for preventing crime, but also for raising the alarm for fires and calling out the time. With the advent of formally-constituted police forces, the responsibility for dealing with fires fell back on to the Fire Societies who provided fire-fighting equipment on behalf of their subscribing members.

In 1835 the London Fire Engine Establishment was formed, and in October that year there was a call for the police to be put in charge of fighting fires after a large conflagration at Millbank Penitentiary.

The Metropolitan Police acted as firemen at the British Museum in 1860, and there were comprehensive instructions for police fire brigades employed at Royal Navy dockyards, where the Metropolitan Police undertook policing responsibilities from 1860 until 1934.

The Metropolitan Fire Brigade began life in 1866. Responsibility for the provision of a fire-fighting force later became a formal local authority responsibility. In some cases the fire and police stations were located in adjoining premises, particularly outside London where there was a closer relationship of both services with the local authority. The clear demarcation between the police and fire services of today therefore had origins of a much less straightforward situation.

Hand ambulances, effectively flat-bed handcarts, were used by the police from 1860; it was not until 1915 that the Fire Service was authorised to open a number of motor ambulance stations. The Metropolitan Police had run a small horse ambulance service for the sick from 1884. The hand ambulances were made by Bischoffsheim, and comprised a stretcher 2.7 metres (9 feet) long mounted on an axle with two large wheels and a smaller wheel at the front. Although sometimes used to transport sick people, their main purpose became the carriage of drunken and violent prisoners, and they eventually passed out of use in 1938. Police stations of that time would often feature an ambulance shed.

London Boroughs

Since 1965 London boroughs have shared boundaries with Metropolitan Police divisions. Sometimes, as in the case of Bexley, one borough equated with one division. P Division at one time comprised the Boroughs of Lewisham and Bromley; in other boroughs, like Lambeth or Southwark, a borough even comprised three or four police divisions. This was because the police workload did not equate with the population and other criteria that defined a viable London borough.

In 1999 police divisions were reorganised to match boroughs more precisely, partly because of the introduction of the Greater London Authority and the Mayor of London. Police command structures were then varied, according to the workload of each borough, and were no longer consistent with each other across the Metropolitan Police as a whole. Police divisions had been referred to as 'Operational Command Units' for several years before this, reflecting a national policing trend, and then became known as 'Borough Command Units', or simply 'Boroughs'.

In 2018-19, a time of severe budget restraints, Borough Command Units were combined together to become twelve 'Basic Command Units', a term used elsewhere in the country for what were known once as divisions. The shoulder numbers worn by uniform officers were then changed so that they would read CN123 or EA456, for example, the two letters corresponding to their Basic Command Unit, as described in the Chapter One.

Design of Police Stations

The rapid expansion of the Metropolitan Police required the urgent provision of a large number of stations throughout London. In many cases living accommodation was also provided for police officers. Under the Receiver's guidance there developed a considerable property estate.

In 1881 a comprehensive survey into the Metropolitan Police estate examined 176 buildings, 158 of which were police stations and 18 section houses provided for the accommodation of single officers. 74 were owned freehold; the remainder were leased. At the time there were 99 purpose-built police stations, 50 houses that had been adapted for police station use and 27 houses that had not been altered at all. 95% of single officers and 3.5% of married men lived in police stations or section houses at the time.

Police stations could be a mixture of operational rooms and private living quarters. This was not always a happy combination. In the case of 45 stations, families had to pass through the charge room or other parts of the station to gain access to their quarters or to reach washing facilities, and there were complaints from families whose daughters had to live in close proximity to single men. Of the 176 police stations, thirteen (8%), mostly in central London, accommodated 50 or more officers, 26 (16%) had 20-49 officers, 29 (18%) had more than ten, whilst 80 stations – just over half – had fewer than ten officers in residence.

The 1881 survey found there was rarely any space for more than one case or prisoner to be dealt with at any one time, and there was no waiting room for the public at all in 143 of the 158 stations.

There was an innovation at Bethnal Green station where the public could see the inspector *without* having to use the charge room, and gradually station offices developed which separated prisoners from the public's access points. Later, when station officers, often sergeants, were required to deal with prisoners, they would walk from the station office to the adjoining charge room, from where there would be direct access not only to the cells, but also to a surgeon's room where the police doctor could examine any ill or injured prisoners or police officers.

On the outskirts of the Metropolitan Police District police stations were similar to many rural police stations that, outside London, were the home of the local constable. The premises would have the outward appearance of a conventional house, but would sometimes be equipped with a small cell, a police sign, notice board, communications equipment and a reception area for callers who would not infrequently be dealt with by the constable's wife. This typical pattern of rural policing could not be sustained for towns and cities, where the police stations needed to be larger, with more cells, bigger charge rooms, and offices for clerical staff.

In central London early police stations provided accommodation for single police officers on the upper floors and sometimes a flat for the superintendent or other senior officers in charge. There was therefore a ready means for regular 24-hour supervision by the officer in charge, notwithstanding that a busy station would mean that they would be kept permanently busy. In a disciplinary climate that would be regarded as harsh by today's standards, the officers in charge of a police station would never be able to advance any argument with their more senior officers that they had been unable to fulfil a responsibility because of being 'off duty'. The expansion of office staff gradually took over the upstairs accommodation that had originally been intended for officers living above the station. Snooker rooms, once a common feature in police stations, have also become offices.

The library was a feature of police stations of this period, and was provided as a means of recreation, education and somewhere to sit for officers not on duty. A mess for officers was also provided, often in the basement, and the 1881 report found that at Bromley the men would frequently socialise in the rather unhealthy climate of the basement, rather than in the better ventilated libraries. Provision of catering facilities was in itself a major operation, undertaken under the overall responsibility of the Receiver. Until relatively recently it was typical for relatively small stations to have a canteen, sometimes staffed for limited hours, but nowadays these facilities are confined to the very largest stations, and police officers may sometimes be seen taking refreshments in local cafés. The Metropolitan Police Catering Service has a history marked by its ability to service an enormous number of outlets in police stations, HQ buildings, courts and section houses on a day-to-day basis, but also to provide food for large-scale public order events, some of them planned, including the Notting Hill Carnival, some spontaneously occurring like the Iranian Embassy siege.

By 2012 the estate, managed on a day-to-day basis by the Metropolitan Police Service's Property Services Department, comprised over 600 operational buildings and 1,116 residential properties, used by 42,000 police officers and staff and valued at c.£1.7billion.

In the period of public expenditure restraint from 2010 there has been a very considerable programme of disposing of police stations and other property, and this has been reflected in the details of this book. Some police functions, for instance custody facilities for prisoners and radio communications systems, have been centralised and proposed for contracting out to private companies, and this has had a radical effect on police patrolling bases and stations.

Budgetting

The Metropolitan Police accounts for the year 1884/85 indicate that a total of £10,159 was stopped from the pay of police officers for lodging on police premises, whilst the equivalent arrangement for officers employed in Her Majesty's Dockyards amounted to £1,814. In that year the expenditure of the Metropolitan Police totalled £1,378,407. The pay of inspectors, sergeants and constables amounted to £987,947 that year, by far the largest item of expenditure (72% of the total). £760 (0.1%) was spent on rattles, truncheons, whistles, revolvers and belts etc; £66,110 (4.8%) on uniform and clothing, £13,839 (1%) on horses, stabling, saddles and carts, and £50,464 (3.7%) on the purchase, building, repairs and alteration of police stations.[2]

The overall budget in 2011-12 was £3.69 billion (£3.26 billion in 2017-18).

Police Ranks

Clues about the historical duties of Superintendents appear in Police Orders. On 29 January 1835 it was directed that Superintendents should sign the Occurrence Book in red ink for the date and time they had visited stations; a later order on 14 January 1850 clarified that this procedure was not required more than once in 24 hours. Superintendents had to deal with the cases of discipline defaulters no later than 7.00am each morning, and an order for 11 November 1848 dictated that any superintendent arriving late at the Commissioner's office with his morning report would miss their turn and wait until the last division had been dismissed.

The rank of station sergeant had been introduced in 1875, and was a position of some status within the force. These officers wore four stripes on their uniform, and three stripes and a crown from 1921, as may be recalled by those who remember the uniform worn by Jack Warner playing George Dixon in the 1955-76 television series *Dixon of Dock Green*. The rank, mid-way between sergeant and inspector, was only used in the Metropolitan Police, and occupied a point in national pay scales that arguably prevented the progression of senior sergeants. In 1972 the Metropolitan Police started to phase out the rank, and this process was finally complete in January 1980 when the last serving station sergeant in the Metropolitan Police, William Palmer, retired from Highbury Corner Magistrates' Court.

The job of a patrolling police officer has changed dramatically, particularly since the advent of motorised patrolling has removed the necessity for walking many miles each day. Safer neighbourhood bases are premises providing a local base from which officers can patrol without their needing to visit the main police station. They are often in fairly prominent positions, but provide only very limited access for dealing with public enquiries.

Charge Rooms and Custody Suites

The charge room was where the inspector, later the station officer, would investigate the evidence of police and private witnesses and decide on the charge to be faced by the prisoner. The room was also used at the time for accident cases where a doctor would examine the injured person. When the Metropolitan Police was formed in 1829, the police officers who arrested a suspect would often simply take them before a magistrate who, at that time, would have taken on the responsibility for much more investigation of the offence and the prisoner's culpability. In those early days the legal system was much simpler, but harsh by today's standards. It was not until 1836 that a barrister was allowed to address the jury on behalf of a prisoner accused of a felony, for instance. There was no Court of Appeal to review a judge and jury's decisions until 1907.

After the Police and Criminal Evidence Act of 1984, the post of custody officer was created for sergeants who dealt with prisoners. They acquired more formalised legal and procedural

1   Metropolitan Police Surveyors' Records 1881.
2   Metropolitan Police. Appropriation Account 1884-5.

responsibilities, and it then became unrealistic to combine these duties with those of station officer. The charge room then became known as a custody suite. This will typically have interview rooms with tape-recording facilities for prisoners, interview rooms for suspects with their legal representatives, closed-circuit TV systems, automated fingerprint equipment, and computerised custody record systems. It is no longer possible for police officers to arrest a suspect and have the charge processed at a local community police station. Cells for prisoners, once a feature of nearly every station, are now restricted to far fewer police stations, sometimes one per Basic Command Unit, or little more than twelve in the whole of the Metropolitan Police District. Travelling time for police officers and witnesses has increased accordingly, and some aspects of running custody suites are considered for contracting out to private companies.

All prosecutions are now subject to being recorded on files, with statements and other paperwork going through the Crown Prosecution Service. It is therefore hardly surprising that much more office space was required to accommodate the additional staff for these processes. A CID office from the 1960s would typically run with support staff consisting only of a clerk and a typist, but these were replaced by a fully-staffed criminal justice unit responsible for supervising and processing court papers, the notification (referred to within the Police Service as being 'warned') of police officers and private witnesses of the dates when they were required to attend court, liaison with the Crown Prosecution Service, and reporting court results.

Detectives' Accommodation

Police stations have not always provided accommodation for detectives. Until 1842 there were no official detectives in the Metropolitan Police. It was in that year that a small detective branch was formed, and the first officer in charge, Nicholas Pearce, a Bow Street Foot patrole who joined in 1825, had an office at Gardner's Lane Police Station. Detectives were not employed on local divisions until the Criminal Investigation Department was formed in 1877. The paperwork, procedures and protocols involved in major investigations were far less demanding in Victorian times, notwithstanding that the death penalty was frequently the result of a murder conviction.

In 1864, for instance, London was pre-occupied with the search for Franz Müller. He had killed a chief bank clerk, Thomas Briggs, on 9 July 1864 on a Highbury-bound North London Railway journey, the first murder in Britain to have been committed on a railway train. Müller had accidentally left his hat in the compartment however, and, in an age when all men wore hats, had put on Mr Briggs' hat by mistake instead of his own. The hat left at the scene of the crime showed a distinctive style of stitching where it had been altered to make it lower. It transpired that Müller was a German tailor by trade. The murderer had also exchanged Mr Briggs' watch chain at a jeweller's shop and had given the box from this shop to the child of his landlord. Müller was identified as the culprit from this evidence, but he had already left the country for America. One of the early detectives, Inspector Richard Tanner from Scotland Yard, applied to the chief magistrate at Bow Street Magistrates' Court to commence one of the first extradition proceedings. Tanner set off on a steam ship, overtook the sailing ship on which Müller was a passenger, and arrested him in New York. Müller was brought back to stand trial at the Old Bailey and was executed in November 1864.[3]

Sometimes police stations have accommodated specialist squads of detectives on their upper floors.

Occupational Health

The post of Chief Medical Officer was created in 1830, and in 1899 there was concern about the high rate of suicides among officers, with some commentators blaming the harsh discipline and insensitive handling of junior officers. The modern police service has a significant Occupational Health Service that concerns itself with the mental as well as physical health of MPS staff.

Gallantry

Until 1909, when the King's Police Medal (KPM) was instituted after the infamous incident known as the Tottenham Outrage, there was no medal available for recognising police officers' bravery apart from the Albert Medal (replaced in 1940 by the George Cross). Of 226 KPMs awarded up until 1940 to Metropolitan Police officers, 33 (15%) were for saving or attempting to save a life from drowning, whilst 26 (12%) were for going into houses or other buildings that were on fire. A large group of 41 (18%) were for dealing with runaway horses, but the largest number were the 63 officers (28%) recognised for their courage in incidents involving firearms.

A cluster of three medals with the King's Police Medal, left, together with the 1911 Coronation Medal centre and the 1935 Jubilee Medal right

For many years officers, many of whom would have used revolvers after serving in the armed forces, would have booked out the police revolvers under the watchful eye of the station officer, and then responded to an incident with the best courage and initiative they could muster. The training is much more sophisticated these days, partly because of the development of a specialist Firearms Branch within the Metropolitan Police, who monitor each time a gun is used by police.

The first known recorded use of a firearm by the Metropolitan Police occurred on 18 February 1887 when PC Henry Owen, an officer serving on P Division, fired six shots from his revolver into the air in Keston village to awaken the inhabitants of a house which was on fire after the officer's shouting, hammering on the door and blowing of his whistle had failed to rouse them from their slumber. Six months later, PC Owen (warrant number 52206) had left the service, suffering from general debility at 42 years of age. He was awarded an annual pension of £29 12s 10d (£29.64).

The Houses of Parliament were the scene of great gallantry in 1885, when Constable William Cole became the only

Metropolitan Police officer ever to have been awarded the Albert Medal in gold. He removed a Fenian bomb from Westminster Hall, and was badly injured when it exploded. The practice of militant Irish Republicans of leaving bombs in London has been frequently repeated over the years. The famous Detective Inspector Robert Fabian was awarded a King's Police Medal for dismantling an IRA bomb in Piccadilly in wartime 1940, but the increasing sophistication of these lethal devices led to the deployment from Cannon Row of a distinguished and brave group of Explosives Officers.

Originally recruited to deal with the paraphernalia of criminals intent on blowing open the doors of safes, their role became intimately bound up with counter terrorism operations of the 1970s. Roger Goad, awarded a posthumous George Cross, was killed whilst defusing a bomb in Kensington Church Street in 1976. Kenneth Howorth, a recipient of the George Medal, was killed whilst dealing with an IRA bomb in Oxford Street in 1981. Donald Henderson, Geoffrey Biddle and Peter Gurney were all awarded George Medals, and Derek Pickford a Queen's Gallantry Medal, for their outstanding courage in defusing bombs designed to kill and maim innocent Londoners. Their courage, and that of other explosive officers, has been an awe-inspiring contribution to the safety of London and the conviction of terrorists.

The George Cross has been awarded to Metropolitan Police officers on only five occasions, including the case of Roger Goad mentioned above. The George Medal, also instituted in 1940, has been awarded on 139 occasions, 81 of which were for wartime bravery. After a period from 1992 of the medal not being awarded to anybody from the Metropolitan Police Service, the actions of off-duty PC Charlie Guenigault were recognised in 2018 after he had confronted terrorists in an incident at London Bridge on 3 June 2017.

The George Cross, left, and the KPFSM, right

The British Empire Medal has been awarded to Metropolitan Police officers for bravery on at least 112 occasions, and the Queen's Gallantry Medal, instituted in 1974, on 54 occasions.

Police officers and civil staff from the Metropolitan Police, and indeed other Forces, served in the armed forces in wartime, and some were awarded gallantry medals during their war service. Many officers joined the RAF during WWII, and there are also may examples of wartime medals being awarded in the Great War of 1914-18.

Charles William Riseboro, for instance, was born at Sheringham in Norfolk in 1894. He was employed as a porter for the Metropolitan and Great Northern Railway and later joined the Metropolitan Police (warrant no. 104874) in February 1915. At nearly 5ft 11in tall he commanded a solid presence and so was initially posted to F Division, where he stayed until 1929 when he was transferred to X as a detective.

PC Riseboro being presented with his Distinguished Flying Medal

During the First World War, men of a certain age including police officers were expected to join the colours; in fact women would openly castigate young police officers who had not joined up. Riseboro put in an application to fight for King and country and in January 1917 he transferred to HM Forces, being posted to Palestine. No. 187480 CW Riseboro was a Sergeant Mechanic in the Royal Air Force (RAF) that had been formed in April 1918. What happened next saw Riseboro, as an NCO, display courage and devotion to duty whilst flying on active operations against the enemy. It was whilst an observer flying dangerous missions over enemy territory that he was awarded the Distinguished Flying Medal (DFM) for service in Palestine – a particularly rare event. Of the 104 DFMs awarded during 1918/19, this was the only one identified as being awarded for service in Palestine. His award was announced in the *London Gazette* on 3 June 1919. In the picture above he is receiving his medal from the Commissioner Brigadier General Sir William Horwood at Kensington Police Station, together with other war veterans of various police divisions who displayed meritorious and courageous service. The canteen had been prepared for the award ceremony and the Divisional Superintendent J. Cameron was also present.

The Distinguished Flying Medal

3   *The Scotland Yard Files*, Alan Moss & Keith Skinner (2006).

The Distinguished Flying Medal was instituted on 3 June 1918. It was the other ranks' equivalent to the Distinguished Flying Cross, which was awarded to commissioned officers and warrant officers (WOs could also be awarded the DFM), although it ranked below the DFC in order of precedence, between the Military Medal and the Air Force Medal. Recipients of the Distinguished Flying Medal were allowed to use DFM after their name. In 1993 the DFM was discontinued, and since then the Distinguished Flying Cross has been awarded to personnel of all ranks.

Constable Riseboro's medal group of DFM, British War and Victory Medals were sold at auction on 29 March 2000 for £1,650.[4] PC Riseboro married around the same time as his award and had two children. He was an active police officer, although he did not get on well initially with learning First Aid as he failed his examination four times during his service. On the other hand he passed his educational exams 2nd class in 1921, and in July the following year was promoted to sergeant, staying on F Division. He was well thought of by his senior officers, and was not involved in any disciplinary matters. In 1929 he transferred as a detective sergeant 2nd class to X Division and later 1st detective sergeant in March 1936. He failed his 1st class educational examinations, which meant he was precluded from inspector rank. He had 16 commendations, one involving a case of murder in 1937. He retired in March 1942 after just over 27 years' service aged 47 years, on a pension of £208 14s (£208.70) per year. He was awarded an exemplary certificate of conduct from the Commissioner for his service. He died aged 63 years in February 1958.

Metropolitan Police Minstrels

In entertainment activities regarded as harmless in those days, the Metropolitan Police Minstrels troupe was founded in 1872 by ten police officers from A Division, including James Olive (later Sir James and Deputy Commissioner) who became associated with it for over 50 years. They were set up to raise money for police charities including the Orphanage and Convalescent Home, and in their 60-year timespan (1872 until 1933) they raised £250,000. The troupe gave standard 'Nigger Minstrel' entertainment, with singers and musicians in black evening dress and blacked-up faces (now considered offensive to black people) giving performances involving banjos, guitars, trumpets, tambourines and ensembles who sang popular ballads, songs and negro spirituals.

Metropolitan Police Minstrel troupe at Fulham Military Hospital, 1915

In the picture above a selection of the Minstrels entertain the troops at Fulham's military hospital during WWI. Clearly they helped cheer up the injured troops. Here they are not in performance dress, and there was a chance to raise much-needed funds for their charities. Postcards were prepared for sale to mark such occasions.

It was typical for police divisions to run their own bands in Victorian times, and there was a central band for the Metropolitan Police which would play, for instance, at Highbury stadium at half time at Arsenal football matches, sometimes accompanying a fine singer named PC Alexander Morgan. The band had a busy schedule of events at schools and other community events but became civilianised in the 1980s and finally abolished.

The Metropolitan Police Orphanage

The Orphanage that was beneficiary of the Minstrels' fundraising was referred to in the 1870 Annual Report of Superintendent Griffin of R Division:

'The men generally appear to be well satisfied with their present condition, and having received an increase of pay, they very willingly gave up the weekly leave, for the one day in a fortnight. Every man in the Division subscribes to, and I believe feels proud of, the Metropolitan Police Orphanage.'

The Metropolitan and City Police Orphanage arose from the harsh conditions of service for police officers of the time. If a constable died from injuries he received in the course of duty, his widow would normally receive an annuity of £15 plus £2 10s 0d for each child. It was about 50 years later that widows' pensions were introduced, and the welfare system which later developed within the Service was unknown at the time. In January 1870 a committee of five superintendents had considered the Commissioner's proposal for 'a widows and orphans fund and an orphanage of small size for children who have lost both parents'. The Orphanage was established at Strawberry Hill as a result of this, and a subscription of 1d per week, later 3d, was levied on all officers to support the scheme. Within ten years it had become clear that no building could adequately house all the orphans, and widows were then given direct grants to support children who remained living at home. The Orphanage closed its doors in 1937, by which time 2,807 boys and girls had been accommodated, and 5,194 widows supported by grants for 10,000 children. A hundred and fifty years after Sir Edmund Henderson's initiative, the Metropolitan and City Police Orphans Fund still operates today from its base at 30 Hazlewell Road, Putney, London SW15 6LH.[5]

Leave

Around 1870 Commissioner Sir Edmund Henderson had achieved a rise in pay for his officers, but to compensate their rest days were reduced to one per fortnight instead of one day's leave per week. An increase of 400 officers had been approved, and the Commissioner calculated that by the increased recruitment, and the reduction of leave for serving officers, 1,231 officers could be provided towards the 1,442 that he had stated to be necessary to protect the public in 1869.[6] For a period in the 1970s leave was awarded, but the need for patrolling resources was met by officers being rostered to work rest days automatically. These were known as 'additional rest days' (ARDs) and 'further additional rest days' (FARDs). In due course, routinely worked overtime was ended as financial constraints outweighed the importance of maintaining patrolling strength.

Fixed Points

In the 1870s a system of fixed points where the public could

Metropolitan Police Training School, Peel House SW1 circa 1910

expect to see a police officer was introduced, being generally acknowledged to work well. These fixed points at strategic locations no doubt added considerably to the tradition of a beat officer invariably being available to the public. In the days before telephones, the public would rush to that point to call an officer when they required one. Today's more mobile patrolling officers are not predictably at one point, but are invariably seen when responding to a call or engaged on specific duties.

Traffic Congestion

The origins of traffic congestion in London are not new. In a report on London's traffic in 1903[7] it was found that the streets of London had suffered from

'the manner of growth, which was, for centuries, totally unregulated by the control of any central authority. Hence there is an absence of plan in the construction and arrangement of streets; and, in addition, no adequate provision has been made to meet growing needs. Apart from a few exceptions, the streets in London are as narrow and irregular as they were a hundred years ago.'

The Commissioner was given legal power under the 1839 Metropolitan Police Act to make regulations for preventing obstruction in the streets, and much as the police would have preferred to have concentrated on dealing with crime and disorder, dealing with traffic congestion, regulations, taxis and buses rapidly developed into a police responsibility because the Metropolitan Police was the only body with a jurisdiction that ran across the whole metropolis.

In 1919 the four departments of Scotland Yard were reorganised so that B Department, under the command of Mr Frank Elliott, took responsibility for all traffic matters.

One of the stalwarts in the new department was Superintendent Arthur Bassom, who, along with a Mr Suffield Mylius of the civil staff, was awarded the title of Traffic Advisor. Superintendent Bassom took charge of matters concerning summonses for traffic offences, maintaining an index for stolen motor vehicles and an index of motoring convictions, and the Public Carriage Office that regulated and licensed taxis, buses, and their drivers. Bassom became known as the 'father of traffic policing' and was only the third officer to be promoted to Chief Constable from the lower ranks of the service. He had been transferred to the Public Carriage Office in 1887, and had taken an interest in the mechanics of the new motor omnibuses introduced a decade later. He had acquired an international reputation by the time of his retirement in 1925, and was the driving force behind the development of the rigorous test of London knowledge demanded as a condition of a licence for taxi drivers. He was awarded an OBE in recognition of his contribution to the management of traffic matters in a crucial period in London's development.[8]

The vehicle fleet of the Metropolitan Police in 1919 comprised 35 vehicles, including 11 two-seater Fords for the use of superintendents on outer divisions such as R (Greenwich). In 1940 there were 1,260 vehicles, and by 1995/96 some 4,500 Metropolitan Police vehicles travelled 83 million miles and

4   Private correspondence with Richard Hayes.
5   www.met-cityorphans.org.uk/history.php and *The Official Encyclopedia of Scotland Yard* by Martin Fido and Keith Skinner (1999).
6   Report of the Commissioner of Police of the Metropolis, 1870. C 358.
7   Quoted in *History of the Traffic Department of the Metropolitan Police* by Chief Inspector K. Rivers.
8   *The Official Encyclopaedia of Scotland Yard*, Martin Fido and Keith Skinner (2000).

A class of recruits at Peel House in the 1920s

A final practical exercise prior to passing out from Peel House circa 1920s

used 14 million litres of fuel annually.⁹ Today, there are about 5,000 vehicles travelling nearly 47 million miles annually.

Training

Peel House was the location for much of the training of police recruits, located not far from Scotland Yard. Freeholds to land were purchased in 1904 and 1910 in Regency Street and Causton Street SW1, on which was built a recruit training establishment for officers which was named Peel House. The block also had married quarters for police officers who found it difficult to obtain affordable housing in central London. The five blocks of flats were Gladston House, Harcourt House, Douglas House, Matthews House and Ridley House, providing accommodation for 54 families. When completed, this training school consisted of classrooms, an entertainment hall, a section house and six sets of married quarters for teaching staff and their families.

Between 1829 and 1907 recruits had been posted to division after two weeks' foot drill, followed by a period of accompanying an experienced constable and then, armed with an Instruction Book, learning on the beat as they went along. In the early twentieth century Commissioner Sir Edward Henry decided to improve this system, and Peel House became the centre for much-improved training. After passing a revamped selection procedure including an educational test, recruits undertook a residential course of instruction at Peel House. This included lessons in police duty, but also general education, physical training, self-defence (added in 1908) and First Aid.

In the picture top left recruits are being given practical instruction in stopping a member of the public, questioning and arrest. In this scenario a man has been stopped and detained for suspected unlawful possession of a bicycle.

Notice all the potential police officers are required to provide their own clothes, as they did not get fitted for uniforms until the end of training. Here the station sergeant is restraining his suspect using a hold which reduces chance of escape or assault on the officer by the person detained.

In the picture top right a class of recruits are being tested on licensing matters at the end of their course as part of their final assessment before being posted to division. There were a variety of scenarios that recruits would be put through as part of their final test. In the example shown, a constable has been called into licensed premises, probably by the licensee who has a drunk and incapable man on his premises. Notice the Inspector to the right with his clipboard assessing not only the constable, but also the instruction given by the Station Sergeant.

The picture below shows the dining hall at the Peel House in about the 1920s. Recruits probably sat at the tables in alphabetical order according to the class they were in.

By 1909 Peel House was extended as it was already too small. During World War One part of the complex was handed over to Dominion troops to use as a club for the duration, but by 1918 some sections of the building were reclaimed for training Metropolitan Women Police Patrols. Post-war expansion saw a site taken into service in Aldwych called 'Eagle Hut' where

Peel House Training School Staff 1911

The dining hall at Peel House

Bush House now stands. In 1923 Peel House started to run Staff College courses for senior overseas police officers as well.

By 1927 the basic training course was lengthened to ten weeks, and the following year pre-promotion courses for constables and sergeants aspiring for higher rank were introduced. On its temporary closure in 1939 it soon re-opened to help train the 12,000 war reserve volunteers who had enlisted.

In 1937 Superintendent F. Smith was in charge of the training school with Sub-Divisional Inspectors S.M. Ogden and H.S. Glasby in support.

For a short period in 1940, additional premises were used for War Reserve officers at the Holy Trinity Church School Mayfield Road, Dalston. Later in the war, in 1941, training also took place at Grey Coat School, Grey Coat Place SW1.[10]

In 1946, Hendon – or 'Peel House II' as it was sometimes termed at the time – was re-opened for basic training and operated together with Peel House in Regency Street. With the running of both training schools (and its satellites), a little gentle rivalry occurred with competitions in all aspects of sport, First Aid and other games between the two. After World War Two Peel House also provided senior officer non-residential training courses.

The *Training School Magazine* was started in January 1953 and the editorship ten years later belonged to Chief Superintendent J.J. Miller MBE with its Treasurer being T. G. Wall. This magazine was produced to inform interested parties of what was happening in the training environment, and had a very wide circulation considering that many Commonwealth countries sent their more senior police officers on the Overseas Police Course and CID for training at Hendon. As such, many of these found their way into police libraries around the world.

In the 1960s other courses were run at Peel House, including those for probationer constables, traffic wardens and also promotion courses for uniform branch constables. The Royal Park Keepers course trained 16 men and women in 1963. This was designed to assist them in their daily duties in the parks,

A boxing class at Peel House

where they could exercise the legal powers of a constable.

The Metropolitan Police organised many sporting activities, overseen by the Metropolitan Police Athletic Association (MPAA). The clubs would enter competitions including cross-country, table tennis, rugby and lifesaving. In fact sport has, until recently, been positively encouraged by senior officers so as to maintain general fitness but also to focus on group participation and teamwork. Senior officers would take a personal interest and would select and encourage officers of particular sporting prowess in their divisions. Being good at sport at the Training School could be to an officer's advantage.

One notable sportsman was Sergeant Harry Mallin, one of the Metropolitan Police heroes and premier sportsmen, who joined the police in 1915 having previously been a storekeeper. He was posted initially on E Division, and then within two years was transferred to the 6th Division or Rosyth Dockyard, where he was allowed to train as a boxer. During his service he spent time on the training school staff and in administration roles at Commissioner's Office (CO) having passed the sergeant's examination in 1924. He trained constantly, often in duty time, and is shown opposite with all his cups and prizes in boxing. He opened his account as a 28-year-old (he was ABA champion of 1919 and 1920) and won the Olympic middleweight title at Antwerp in 1920 by out-pointing Lt. Joseph Cranston of the US army. In a hard-fought final, Mallin won on points to take the gold medal. He successfully (and with much controversy) defended his gold medal in Paris four years later. Sergeant Mallin is also seen as a referee in the gymnasium at Peel House. The boxing group would meet up most evenings and go through their fitness and training regimes. Whilst he was perhaps the greatest athlete the Metropolitan Police has had, he was beset with injury worries which were probably the reason he never turned to professional boxing.

Mallin's left leg had been injured badly during the First World War and was always a source of aggravation to him, which perhaps explains why he was often photographed wearing leg coverings or trousers. His leg was amputated in later life.[11] He stayed single all his life and remained in the service for a very long time until 1952 when, on age limit, he retired having completed 37½ years' service aged 60. Whilst his police service was untypical, as he only gained practical policing experience on J Division in 1945, his impressive display of medals, cups and prizes for boxing made him a role model for aspiring police officers. As such, he was a recruiting

9 Report of the Commissioner of the Metropolis, 1995-6.
10 Metropolitan Police Orders dated 24th November 1941.
11 Private correspondence 21st November 2012.

sensation for the police. After his retirement Mallin lived until 1969 and died at Lewisham.

Another character associated with Peel House was Sir George Abbiss, who had been born in 1884 at Hitchin and died in 1966. He was the second officer to rise through the ranks to become Assistant Commissioner of Scotland Yard. Originally a gardener, he joined the Metropolitan Police in 1905 and was an ordinary constable, later a sergeant and station sergeant before being promoted to inspector in 1919. In 1920 he was made MBE and in 1932 OBE, before being appointed Assistant Commissioner and retiring in 1946.[12] In 1936 as George Abbiss OBE (later knighted) he became the Assistant Commissioner D Department with a responsibility for the training of recruits, a subject in which he took a deep interest.

Assistant Commissioner George Abbiss

In the picture above, Abbiss is shown in a light suit at the front centre of a class of recruits who have successfully completed their training prior to being posted to division.

Abbiss was an approachable person who had risen up the ranks from constable, and understood the nature of being a well-balanced police officer. He had a nice nature, possessed a good sense of humour which was absent in most senior officers of the time, and would even autograph the class photographs for the students. The class photographs (of which Abbiss is often sat front centre) were in fact taken up until the 1990s by the official police Metropolitan Police photographer, Messrs T. H. Everitts of Annerley Road SE19.

Superintendent (warrant no. 118329) 'Tommy' Wall joined the Police in April 1929 and was posted to N Division. He was a real character, tough and uncompromising and feared by recruits when he later took charge at Peel House. Thomas

George Wall was born, the son of a gas inspector, in Cardiff on 16 August 1909 and was formerly a transport worker. He soon came to attention after making notable arrests and was commended by the Commissioner on no less than five occasions. He passed the promotion examination to sergeant in 1938 and transferred to G Division, and within a short time was transferred as station sergeant 16 to N division in 1945. He was married and had a son. Some five years later, as inspector, he was sent for the first time to the Training School. Whilst Tommy Wall was a stern disciplinarian there was also a compassionate side to him for those who asked his help. He was a member of the Salvation Army and was often seen in his Army uniform in his spare time, giving his services for the greater good. Such were his talents he became a staff officer on A Division in September 1954 and three months later, as chief inspector, moved to staff officer on C Division. Sadly, in the interim his wife died. Between 1955 and 1963 he rose through the superintending ranks to chief superintendent and was awarded a Queen's Police Medal for distinguished service in 1961. Whilst still serving aged 57 years and qualified for a pension, he developed stomach cancer and died in service after 38 years in the Metropolitan Police. His pension was never paid as his wife had pre-deceased him. His rival and opposite number at Hendon was Superintendent Arthur Buchanan. Training schools came under the heading of D3 Department, whilst buildings, cadets and dogs were the responsibility of Chief Superintendent Philip R. Broad in D2.

In 1974 Peel House closed for training purposes when there was less need to maintain so much capacity to increase the number of police officers, and the staff were transferred to Hendon.

Women Police Training

Male and female officers did not mix for training in the earliest days. The women's social study course was carried out at Aybrook Street Section House in Paddington where single women were later resident.

Aybrook Street section house, circa 1923

The picture above shows the section house in about 1923. The early days of women police in the Metropolitan Police were overshadowed by the disbanding of the Women Police Volunteers – a Geddes Committee recommendation following economies of police expenditure. Such was the outrage in Parliament that a compromise was reached to retain some twenty female officers as a nucleus, but with full powers of arrest. In 1948 the section house in Aybrook Street was named after Miss Dorothy Peto, an early senior female officer, and replaced Wandsworth section house as the training school for

Women Police tug of war circa 1920s

women.[13]

In 1918 women were initially housed in Beak Street section house, where they commenced training for the first time. Aybrook Street section house was erected between 1908-9 for the Metropolitan Police and was designed by J. Dixon Butler. It is an austere building reflecting something of the influence of C.R. Mackintosh. The walls are of grey brick above a base of brown glazed bricks, and there are plain stone surrounds with cyma-moulded labels to the arched doorway and the three-light windows of the ground storey. A large segmental bowed window, divided by stone mullions and transoms, lights the staircase.[14] In later years Aybrook Street accommodated Management Services Department. Women police were notably supportive of First Aid competitions.

The National First Aid competition very often took place in London at Central Hall, Westminster SW1 in early February each year and the Training School always provided a team. The trophy was the Parsons Shield. The Metropolitan Police First Aid competition challenged for the 'Vivian Rogers' First Aid Trophy and eliminations took place within the four districts. The top two teams in each district were selected to compete in April each year; competitors were not allowed to take part in 'service time' and each team paid one shilling to enter.[15]

In the picture above women police are involved in a tug of war with another women police team (probably in Hyde Park) showing if the men can do it then so can they.

12 www.flickr.com/photos/hillview7/2957298019/in/photostream/#comments accessed 18th November 2012.
13 www.metpolicehistory.co.uk/1946-to-date.html accessed 27th November 2012.
14 www.british-history.ac.uk/report.aspx?compid=41469#s5 accessed 16th November 2012.
15 Metropolitan Police Orders dated 18th February 1949.

Chapter 3.
London Boroughs and their Police Stations

When the Metropolitan Police boundary was extended to cover the Barnet area in 1840, the responsibility for supervision fell to the senior officers of the Metropolitan Police's S or Hampstead Division. The divisional headquarters and administration moved from Albany Street Police Station to High Street, Highgate during 1840 when S Division became the largest police division in terms of area covered. From this time on, the other S Division stations were Stone Bridge, Willesden; Edgware Road, 8 mile stone; 52 Albany Street, Regents Park; Junction Place, Kentish Town 1 Heath Street, Hampstead; 52 Salisbury Street, Portman Market; Phoenix Street, Somers Town; High Street, Chipping Barnet; High Street, Bushey and South Mimms.[16]

The S Division was shaped rather like a wedge, with its apex located in the centre of the metropolis and its outer edges bordering the county of Hertfordshire. The policing of the division evolved, expanded and became more complex as greater numbers of people moved to the suburbs to find work. Gradually, as travel and transport became easier and cheaper, sleepy villages soon became overwhelmed with traffic, people and crime.

Administratively, Barnet borough was created in 1965 from the former urban districts of Chipping Barnet and East Barnet, both previously in Hertfordshire, the urban district of Friern Barnet, and the boroughs of Finchley and Hendon, previously in Middlesex.[17] These changes in local authority boundaries caused police borders to be re-aligned with them, and changes to police areas and divisions resulted.

By 2011 Barnet borough had become one of the larger boroughs of the Metropolitan Police, with a population of over 331,000 people and 157,000 households covering some 34 square miles. Within Barnet there are inner city and town centre areas as well as leafy suburbs and swathes of countryside. Barnet enjoys a diverse multi-cultural population, spread across the borough.

The London Borough of Barnet is presently served by four police stations: Barnet, Colindale, Golders Green and Whetstone. There are also 21 Safer Neighbourhood Teams who help prevent crime and deal with community problems. Response teams operate on a 24-hours-a-day basis, and deal with emergency calls; Criminal Investigation Department (CID) officers and forensic teams investigate crimes and bring criminals before the court. All this work is undertaken for the Barnet community with the express aim of keeping Barnet Borough one of the safest in London.[18]

The Borough of Barnet

The borough is crossed by three main roads from London to the north. On the western boundary, the Edgware Road, Watling Street or A5, is part of a major Roman route. The main medieval route was put through further east, and runs through Finchley, Whetstone, Chipping Barnet and Hadley. It was once the Great North Road or A1, but after a bypass was built in the 1920s it became the A1000. The M1, the next generation of main roads, also opened through the borough in 1966.

The first railway through the borough was the Great Northern main line running up through Friern and (New) Barnet, which opened in 1850. New Barnet began to develop as a new suburb near the station during the 1860s.

Railways arrived in Barnet in the 1860s: the Midland mainline through Hendon and Mill Hill and Great Northern Railway (GNR) suburban lines through Finchley to Barnet and to Edgware via Mill Hill.

London had always expanded in rings, and since areas closer to London were not yet developed, these lines stimulated very little change. By the end of the century the inner rings were full and it was this area's turn. A new underground line to Golders Green opened in 1907 and a brand new suburb developed simultaneously. Development stopped during the First World War, but in the 1920s the line was extended through Hendon to Edgware and again the building of new housing spread concurrently.[19]

Barnet Fair

Chipping Barnet was founded around 1100 to take advantage of the new main road. It was granted a market in 1199 ('chipping' means market) and a fair in 1588. The fair became so famous that 'Barnet' became cockney rhyming slang for hair (Barnet Fair = Hair). Having the fair in Barnet became very lucrative for business and provided opportunities for making money. This brought the benefits of employment, but it also drew in crime, disorderly conduct and drunkenness.

In 1758 John Tomlinson, the Lord of the Manor of Barnet, was granted permission to change the dates of the fairs from June to April for the first one and from October to September for the second, due to it being better for business. Animals were driven from all over the country to the Barnet fairs, with cattle from Scotland, cows from Devon and ponies from Wales.

The September cattle fair was held in fields near Wood Street until 1909, and various fields around the town were used for herding and displaying the livestock. In September 1834 it was reported in *The Times* that the Barnet Fair was the largest cattle market in all of England, with up to 40,000 animals on offer and £100,000 being taken in trade on the first day.

---

16 *Kelly's Directory*, 1840.
17 www.barnet.gov.uk/index/leisure-culture/local-history-heritage.htm#chip accessed 2nd November 2011.
18 met.police.uk/Site/barnetaboutus?scope_id=1257246650510 accessed 29th December 2011.
19 www.barnet.gov.uk/index/leisure-culture/local-history-heritage.htm#chip accessed 2nd November 2011.

It was necessary from the early days of the fair to ensure order was kept, and police officers were posted each year to keep the peace. The picture below shows eight police officers posing before a crowd, and a donkey at the Barnet horse fair in about 1908. Notice how the police officers were in the habit of carrying walking sticks.

A group of police officers pose at the Barnet Fair with a donkey in about 1908

By the mid-18th century Barnet fair had become associated with horseracing, and races were held on the last three days of the event. The course they ran on was where the present High Barnet station is now. The last race held there was The Barnet Stakes on 6 September 1870. But the fair carried on and the animals kept coming, usually to the land opposite High Barnet station.[20] In the 17th century there was a briefly famous spa near Chipping Barnet which was visited by Pepys.[21]

Police Stations
- Aldenham Police (Station)
- (Chipping) Barnet Police Station
- Borehamwood Police station
- Bushey Police Station
- Colindale Police Station
- East (New) Barnet Police station
- Elstree Police Station
- Finchley Police Station
- Golders Green Police Station
- Hendon Police Station
- Hendon – The Peel Centre
- Mill Hill Police Station
- Potters Bar Police Station
- Radlett Police Station.
- Shenley Police Station
- (South) Mimms Police Station
- West Hendon Police Station
- Whetstone Police Station

London Borough of Bexley

Part of R Division (1839-1985/86)

Bexleyheath Division (RY) (1985/86)

Part of No 4 Area (South East) (1985/86-2018/19)

Part of South East Basic Command Unit (SE) (from 2018/19)

Bexley village (nowadays known as Old Bexley) has origins going back to the Domesday Book, and was included in an earlier charter dating from 814AD.[22] In the early 1820s the Bexley vestry consulted with neighbouring parishes to set up a nightly foot and horse patrol because of an increase in crime, and in 1825 the presence of a constable (a Mr Viner)[23] was recorded as being insufficient to stop indecent exposure and gambling on the heath. When the Metropolitan Police was formed in 1829 Bexley was unaffected, because it was outside the new police boundary which had originally been set at seven miles from Charing Cross. The nearest Police division to Bexley was R or Greenwich Division, formed in February 1830.

The area now covered by the London Borough of Bexley was then very clearly rural Kent in its nature. Although well outside the jurisdiction for the policing arrangements set up for the capital city, the London to Canterbury Roman road, Watling Street, did pass nearby across uninhabited heath land where the only building was a coaching inn called The Golden Lion. The nature of this lonely road was the cause of some anxiety to travellers, not least because of the problems caused by highwaymen. One such highwayman, John Popham, preyed on travellers, but in later life turned to the good, and apparently even became Lord Chief Justice from 1592 to 1607.[24]

For the new Metropolitan Police London itself was the priority, but the problem of highwaymen in and around Bexley had already been part of the operations of the Bow Street Horse Patroles that were originally started in 1763 and re-instituted in 1805. The Bow Street men apparently had patrols based at Shooters Hill, Welling[25] and on Bexley Heath.[26]

In 1836, Bow Street's operations were amalgamated with the new Police, and the need to carry on protecting travellers may have been part of the reason for a Parliamentary Act of 1839 extending the Metropolitan Police District to take in Welling, East Wickham, Bats Well, Erith, Crayford, Bexley and Blandon. The problem continued to some extent for some years: in 1877, for instance, Superintendent Baxter reported on a serious highway robbery on Blackheath where the two thieves had escaped at the time, but were afterwards arrested at Portsmouth and given seven years' penal servitude at the Central Criminal Court.[27]

The new police arrangements also included Bexley New Town, now known as Bexleyheath. The heath land had been 'enclosed' through two Acts of Parliament in 1812 and 1814, and by 1837 there were 170 cottages and 100 houses in this 'new town'.[28]

In 1866 the railway reached Bexleyheath, followed in due course by other lines running to Dartford. Main roads such as the A2 and A20 also had their impact on what is now a London borough without an obvious historic, commercial 'hub', but containing large suburban areas of housing, including part of Thamesmead, Little Heath, Bostall, Picardy, Belvedere, Lessness, Erith, North End, Slade Green, Barnehurst, Sidcup, Foots Cray and North Cray.

The first police station in the area was a house in Bexleyheath, opened in 1840, followed by Erith in 1847. Local authority arrangements also evolved over the years for an area that was in Kent, but also part of an expanding London. Old Bexley was a local government urban district in north-west Kent from 1894. It became a municipal borough in 1935 and then a London Borough in 1965 when it was combined with Crayford Urban District Council, Erith municipal borough, and the Sidcup part of Chislehurst and Sidcup Urban District. At this point, Bexleyheath Police Sub-Division, later Division, attained the same external boundaries as its local authority, and remained part of R Division. Sidcup, Erith and Belvedere were sectional (or sub-divisional) stations.[29]

Police Stations
- Belvedere Police Station (RB)
- Bexleyheath Police Station (RY)
- Erith Police Station (RE)

- Sidcup Police Station (RS)
- Welling Police Office

The London Borough of Brent

Part of S Division (1839-1865)

Part of X Division (1865-1965)

Part of Q Division (1965-1985/86)

Part of No 7 Area (1985/86-1993/94)

Part of No 2 Area (North West) (1993/94-2018/19)

Part of North West Basic Command Unit (NW) (from 2018/19)

The London Borough of Brent is divided by the River Brent into two major parts; Willesden and Wembley. In 1965, these two separate districts were joined to form a new London borough. It covers an area of 17 square miles (44 square kilometres), with a population of 263,464 people.[30]

The borough started as a collection of villages and farms surrounded by fields and woods. It was transformed into a London suburb by the arrival of the railways and extensive house-building in the 19th and early 20th centuries.

Brent takes in much of Kilburn. The main thoroughfare running northwest –southeast is Kilburn High Road, part of the modern A5, which forms the boundary between the Boroughs of Brent and Camden.

Currently, Wembley Police Station is the only one in the London Borough of Brent open to the public 24 hours per day.

Police Stations
- Harlesden Police Station (named Willesden until 1896)
- Kilburn Police Station
- Kingsbury Police Station
- Wembley Police Station
- Chalkhill Police Station
- Willesden Green Police Station

London Borough of Bromley

Part of P and R Divisions (1840-1965)

Part of P Division (1965-1985/86)

Part of No 3 Area (1985/86-1993/94)

Part of No 4 Area (South East) (1993/94-2018/19)

Part of South Area Basic Command Unit (SN) (from 2018/19)

Bromley, now a large part of the south-eastern suburban section of the Metropolitan Police District, was firmly part of rural Kent when the Metropolitan Police was formed in 1829. Gradually the rural watch houses were taken over by more formal policing arrangements as London problems expanded, and the small villages grew to become part of the urban sprawl. Successive police and local authority re-organisations have also complicated the story of policing the London – Kent borders.

Before the advent of the Metropolitan Police in 1829, the hundred of Bromley and Beckenham had a lock-up cage for prisoners in Widmore Lane (now Road) Bromley,[31] and a brick-built structure at Church Hill, Beckenham that displayed an engraved notice 'Live and Repent' above its door.[32]

To the south, St Mary Cray and St Paul's Cray were part of the hundred of Ruxley. There were stocks and a lock-up in the parish of St Nicholas Chislehurst, whilst Farnborough village used the local workhouse at Locks Bottom as a place of detention. West Wickham, Downe and Keston also had stocks.

Even Bromley was a small place at that time, with buildings clustered around what is now Market Square, and no development apparent in what is now Bromley South. The surroundings were definitely rural. The boundaries of the Metropolitan Police District were determined by the isolated but strategic points along turnpike roads, which travellers passed on their journeys towards London itself. On 13 January 1840 the parish of Bromley came within the jurisdiction of the Metropolitan Police, as part of Greenwich or R Division.[33]

Two-letter station codes that are often used for stations had their origins in the telegraph system. From September 1867 they were a two-letter short form of the station's name, but this was revised in March 1936 so that the first of the two letters would always match the division. The station codes for Bromley therefore started with the letter P, reflecting that they came under P Division.

The letter shown on a police officer's uniform along with a divisional number (eg P123) was the letter of the division for many years, but after a 1985 Force Organisation and Management Review under Commissioner Sir Kenneth Newman the two letters of the divisional code started to appear on uniforms.

One may also see photographs of officers between 1870 and 1913 with two letters, the second being 'R'. This referred to a Reserve pool of officers attached to each division who had been specially selected for duties when required and for public order and ceremonial events. They received extra money for this responsibility. An officer from P Division with this status would therefore wear the letters 'PR' during this period.

Bromley is geographically by far the largest of the new London boroughs, and in 2015 the population was just over 324,900 people.

Police stations
- Beckenham Police Station (PB)
- Biggin Hill Police Station (PH)
- Bromley Police Station (PR)
- Chislehurst Police Station (PC)
- Farnborough Police Station (PF)
- Knockholt police station (PT)
- Orpington police station (PN)
- Penge Police Station (PG)
- St Mary Cray Police Station (PM)
- West Wickham police office
- The Metropolitan Police (Hayes) Sports Club

20 www.barnet4u.co.uk/barnet%20history/barnetfair.html accessed 4th November 2011.

21 www.barnet.gov.uk/index/leisure-culture/local-history-heritage.htm accessed 2nd November 2011.

22 'A Brief History of Bexley' by John Acworth at www.bag.org.uk/Education/education.htm

23 Bernard Brown.

24 'A Brief History of Policing Bexleyheath', by George Palmer.

25 'A Short History of Bexleyheath Police', compiled by Acting Police Sergeant Bernard Brown.

26 TNA MEPO 2/25.

27 *Report of the Commissioner of Police for the Metropolis for the year 1877.* C 2129.

28 'The History of Bexleyheath' by Father Michael Jones at www.stjvianney.net/bexleyheath.html.

29 Metropolitan Police Orders, 6th August 1964.

30 2001 Census.

31 Brown, B. (1997) 'Back to the Drawing Board – Law and Order in Bromley. Bygone Kent', 2/97.

32 Brown, B (1997) 'Lock, Stock and Barrel. Bygone Kent'.

33 Brown, B. (1997) 'Back to the Drawing Board – Law and Order in Bromley. Bygone Kent', 2/97.

The London Borough of Camden

Parts of E, F and (from 1830) S Divisions (1829-1869)
Parts of E and S Divisions (1869-c.1910)
Parts of E, D, S and Y Divisions (c.1910-1933)
Parts of C, E, D, N and S Divisions (1933-1965)
E Division (1965-1985/86)
Part of No 7 Area (1985/86-1993/94)
Part of No 2 Area North West (1993/94-2018/19)
Part of Central North Basic Command Unit (CN) (from 2018/19)

The Borough of Camden lies in the centre of London. The southern part borders the City of Westminster to the west, and the City of London to the east. The eastern borough boundary adjoins Islington, whilst to the west is Brent. The boroughs of Barnet and Haringey run along the northern edge of the Borough. It is an area of immense contrasts, and includes the exclusive residential districts of Hampstead and Highgate, the youthful energy of Camden Town, the graceful squares of Bloomsbury and inner city areas of Kings Cross and Somers Town. About 200,000 people either work in or travel through this Borough each day.[34]

In terms of policing, today's London Borough of Camden and its parishes have, over the years, been located variously within the police boundaries of E, Y and S Divisions. However, Camden is perhaps best recognised as being on E Division. This division was formed on 29 September 1829 using the men of the 5th and 6th Companies. In those early days, the division was responsible for the parishes of St. Andrew and St. George the Martyr, St. Giles and St. George and Bloomsbury (which it shared with neighbouring F Division), part of St. Marylebone and St. Pancras south of the Euston Road.[35]

In 1829 there were two police stations located on E Division. These were at George Street, St. Giles and King's Cross, Battlesbridge.[36] The first superintendent in charge of the division was William Skene. He died of cholera on 26 August 1832 while still serving.[37] Inspector William E. Grimwood of the Bow Street Foot Patrole was appointed in the same rank to the Metropolitan Police on 29 September 1829 and stationed at George Street.[38] Grimwood succeeded him on 27 August 1832 holding the post until 12 April 1849, when he too died in service.[39] The division suffered from the cholera epidemic which swept through the Thameside Divisions in August 1832, claiming the lives of many police officers.[40] Grimwood was assisted by four Inspectors: John Rawley, promoted in 1835; Edward Bell, promoted in 1835; Gregory Dudley, promoted in 1840, and Henry Maude. Rawley had joined the division in 1841.[41]

In 1840, S or Hampstead Divisional headquarters was at 52 Albany Street, Regents Park with Superintendent John Carter in charge. The division was responsible for Somers Town Police Station from 1845, which was located at 10 Phoenix Street, Kentish Town, situated in Junction Place, and St. Johns Wood Police Station which was located at 52 Salisbury Street, Portman Market.

By 1845 there had been a number of alterations and additions to station strengths. There were two police stations on E Division located at Clarks Buildings, High Street, St. Giles and Hunter Street, Brunswick Square.

In 1850 the officer in charge of E or Holborn Division was Superintendent Frederick George Foxall, who was appointed on 13 April 1849 and remained in post until 26 January 1856, when he resigned on pension.[42] Four inspectors – namely

Superintendent James J. Thomson, E Division

Roger Harvard, William Clement, Edward Durgan and Richard Checkley – assisted him.[43] By 1855 Gregory Dudley had replaced Roger Harvard as inspector.[44] Superintendent Foxall was succeeded by Superintendent S. Hannant, who was in charge from 9 February 1856 until 20 February 1857, when he transferred to take charge of C Division. Nassau Smith O'Brian took over from him on 20 February 1857 until 31 August 1863, when he also transferred to C Division.[45]

By 1888 the total strength of the division had risen to 515. This consisted of Richard W. Steggles, Divisional Superintendent, who was located at Bow Street, 17 inspectors, 50 sergeants and 447 constables.[46]

E Division was considered small for a division, and consisted of Bow Street, Tottenham Court Road and Hunter Street. In 1877, E or Holborn Division had one Superintendent, James J. Thomson (pictured above), nine inspectors (John Clifford (Chief Inspector), James Dutchess, John Cook, George Cruise, Henry Wood (Chief Inspector), William De. Maid, William Mee, Edmund Arnold and Henry Aunger), 46 sergeants and 437 constables. The Detective Branch consisted of one sergeant and eight constables. Commenting on the state of the Detective force within his division, the Divisional Superintendent stated in his Annual Report of 1871 that he would "gladly double the strength if he could."[47]

The strength of E Division in 1879 was one superintendent, 34 inspectors and 558 sergeants and constables. Bow Street Police Station was the Divisional Headquarters. There were a further twelve Divisional Superintendents until 1953.[49]

Police Stations

- Albany Street Police Station
- Gray's Inn Road Police Station
- Hampstead Police Station

- Holborn Police Station
- Hunter Street Police Station
- Kentish Town Police Station
- St. John's Wood Police Station (formerly Portland Town Police Station)
- Somers Town Police Station
- West Hampstead Police Station

The London Borough of Croydon

Part of P Division (1839-1865)

Part of W Division (1865-1921)

Part of Z Division (1921-1965)

Z Division (1965 – 1985/86)

Part of No 4 Area (1985/86-1993/94)

Part of No 4 Area (South East) (1993/94-2018/19)

Part of South Area Basic Command Unit (SN) (from 2018/19)

The London Borough of Croydon is the southernmost of London's boroughs and one of the largest, with a population of around 340,000 people. Much of the 34 square miles of the borough is urban and the town of Croydon itself is large, with many tall buildings and business premises. The main London to Brighton Road passes through the centre of Croydon, and the town has its own tram service.

Croydon, and the area surrounding it, was originally policed by the first Division of Bow Street Horse Patrols in 1827.[50] Local policing for what was a small town had been in the hands of a beadle, who was responsible for being 'vigilant in clearing the streets of vagrants and beggars' since the end of the eighteenth century. Croydon Improvement Commissioners found that the parochial Police were somewhat inefficient, and had established its own Police Force in the town as early as July 1829. The Metropolitan Police was not established until September that year, and did not extend as far as Croydon until 1840.

The new Croydon Police consisted of three men appointed to patrol the town. These men were referred to as 'Patrols' or 'Privates', never as 'Policemen'. Their uniform was blue pantaloons, blue coat and red waistcoat, which they had to provide themselves. Each was armed with a pistol and a cutlass; they also had a staff or truncheon bearing the King's Arms and the words 'Croydon Police'. This small Police Force was modelled on the Bow Street Runners, who had withdrawn their services to Croydon when the new Police Force had been introduced.[51]

In December 1829 Richard Colman, a former Bow Street Runner, was appointed Sergeant. The Privates were each paid one guinea (£1.05) a week and Colman received an extra nine shillings (45p); two weeks later William Smith, the Assistant Overseer of the Poor, was appointed Superintendent. The Metropolitan Police took over the policing of Croydon in January 1840.[52]

The Police in the London Borough of Croydon currently operate from Croydon, which is open every day for 24 hours.

Police Stations

- Addington Police Office/New Addington Police Station
- Croydon Police Station
- Kenley Police Station
- Norbury Police Station
- Sanderstead (Hamsley Green) Police Station
- South Norwood Police Station
- Thornton Heath Police Station

The London Borough of Ealing

Part of T Division (1830-1865)

Parts of T and X Divisions (1865-1965)

T Division (1965-1985/86)

Part of No 6 Area (1985/86-1993/94)

Part of No 2 Area (North West) (1993/94-2018/19)

Part of West Area Basic Command Unit (WA) (from 2018/19)

Ealing, the fourth largest London Borough, borders Hillingdon to the west, Harrow and Brent to the north, Hammersmith and Fulham to the east, and Hounslow to the south.

The London Borough of Ealing was created in 1965 with the reorganisation to the structure of London Boroughs. It merged the municipal boroughs of Ealing, Southall and Acton.

The borough has a population of over 300,000 and is divided into seven districts. They are Ealing, Hanwell, Acton, Southall, Greenford, Perivale and Northolt. There were four main police stations – Greenford, Southall, Ealing and Acton.

Over 40% of the local population are from a non-white ethnic group, with 16.5% having origins in India. 31.0% of the population of Ealing was born outside the European Union (EU), compared to 6.9% nationally and 21.8% across London. Only Newham and Brent have a greater proportion of residents born outside the EU.[53]

Police Stations

- Acton Police Station
- Ealing Police Station
- Greenford Police Station
- Hanwell Police Station
- Norwood Green Police Station
- Southall Police Station

---

34 *Municipal Year Book 2000 and Public Services Directory Vol. 2.* Newman Books (1999) and Publicity literature for the London Borough of Camden.

35 *The John Back Archive* (1975). Metropolitan Police Museum, Charlton.

36 *Directory for the Return of Mops, 1st July 1832.* Metropolitan Police Museum, Charlton.

37 *Curator's List of Divisional Superintendents.* Metropolitan Police Museum, Charlton.

38 *The John Back Archive* (1975). Metropolitan Police Museum, Charlton.

39 Ibid.

40 TNA MEPO 4/2.

41 'The Police and Constabulary List of 1844' (1990), Monograph No. 3 The Police History Society.

42 Ibid.

43 *Kelly's Directory*, 1850.

44 *Kelly's Directory*, 1855.

45 *Curator's List of Divisional Superintendents*, Metropolitan Police Museum, Charlton.

46 *Commissioner's Annual Report for 1888.*

47 *The Commissioner for the Metropolis Annual Report of 1871.*

48 *Dickens's Dictionary of London*, 1879

49 *Curators' List of Divisional Superintendents*, Metropolitan Police Museum, Charlton.

50 TNA MEPO 2/25.

51 Hobbs, D.C.H. 'The Croydon Police (1829-1840)', *Journal of the Police History Society* pp66-79.

52 Ibid.

53 2001 Census.

The London Borough of Enfield and Broxbourne District Council

Part of N Division (1839-1865)
Part of Y Division (1865-1886)
Parts of N and Y Divisions (1886-1933)
Part of Y Division (1933-1985/86)
Part of No 1 Area (1985/86-1993/94)
Part of No 3 Area North East (1993/94-2018/19)
Part of North Area Basic Command Unit (NA) (from 2018/19)

The London Borough of Enfield is situated twelve miles to the north of the centre of London. Prior to 1850, vestries governed both Enfield and Edmonton. The Vestry originated as an annual meeting of Parishioners, usually held at Easter, to elect the Churchwardens for the coming year. Enfield was an area where royal visitors came to enjoy hunting and riding in the woods of Enfield Chase. Enfield has been a market town since 1303.[54]

The area also has a rich industrial heritage, and for more than 200 years the eastern perimeter of the borough was the hub of the capital's manufacturing industry. The area was dominated by the bulk of the Royal Small Arms factory, which produced the Lee Enfield rifle. During World War I Enfield saw a lot of bombardment from Zeppelins and Gotha bombers in their attempt to destroy the Enfield factory together with the gunpowder works not far away. The defence of these establishments was paramount and, as a result, two German Zeppelin airships were destroyed at Potters Bar and Cuffley by British fighter pilots.

In 1965, as a result of the London Government Act of 1963 Enfield, Edmonton and Southgate merged into the London Borough of Enfield.[55] The Borough of Enfield includes Cheshunt, Edmonton, Enfield Town, New Southgate, Ponders End (Enfield Highway), Southgate and Winchmore Hill.[56] A former Metropolitan police station at Goffs Oak, located within Broxbourne District Council Area, is included in this volume.

Police Stations
- Cheshunt Police Station
- Edmonton Police Station
- Enfield Police Station
- New Southgate Police Station
- Ponders End/Enfield Highway Police Station
- Southgate Police Station
- Winchmore Hill Police Station
- Goffs Oak Police Station (Broxbourne District)

Epping Forest District Council

Part of N Division (1839-1886)
Part of J Division (1886-1985/86)
Part of Part of No 1 Area (1985/86-1993/94)
Part of No 3 Area North East (1993/94-2000)
Essex Police (from 2000)

The Epping Forest District Council area of 131 square miles extends out in a fan-shape from the edge of the Greater London area, north along the Lea Valley and the length of Epping Forest.[57] It stretches as far as the River Stort and the town of Harlow, then north east along the Roding Valley.

In April 2000 the Metropolitan Police handed over the policing of Chigwell, Loughton and Waltham Abbey to the Essex Constabulary. However, the policing of these areas by the Metropolitan Police reaches back some 160 years, and their past is worth recording.

The Metropolitan Police retained the old Claybury Police Station, now known as Claygate House, at Woodford Bridge in April 2000. It is located in the London Borough of Redbridge, but the strong links with Chigwell Police station, and the fact that it is only a few yards outside of Epping District Council Area, has dictated its position in this book.

The stations and offices shown within Epping Forest District Council Area are Chigwell/Claybury, Debden, Hainault, Limes Farm, Loughton and Waltham Abbey.

Police Stations
- Chigwell and Claybury Police Stations
- Debden Police Office
- Hainault Police Office
- Limes Farm Police Office
- Loughton Police Station
- Waltham Abbey Police Station

London Borough of Greenwich

Part of R Division (1830-1985/86)
Part of No 3 Area (1985/86-1993/94)
Part of No 4 Area (South East) (1993/94-2018/19)
Part of South East Basic Command Unit SE (from 2018/19)

Greenwich is made up of the two old boroughs of Greenwich and Woolwich. Until 1965, Woolwich included a strip of land to the north of the Thames called North Woolwich, which now forms part of Newham (see the London Borough of Newham). In 1981 the population of Greenwich was 211,840. Together with Deptford, the London Borough of Greenwich is bound up with Britain's naval and military past, and early development was concentrated along its northern boundary, the River Thames. To the west Greenwich is adjoined to Lewisham; Bromley lies to the south, and Bexley to the east. Between 1800 and 1813 the villages of Deptford, New Cross, Blackheath, Greenwich and Woolwich saw considerable population increases, but it took longer for the villages of Plumstead, Charlton, Shooters Hill, Eltham and Lee to expand. By 1851 Greenwich had seen a rise in Irish immigration totalling nearly 10%, whilst up to 1991 an influx of people from India amounted to nearly 5% of the population.

In 1738 the New Cross Turnpike Trust extended their improved road system from Blackheath to the notorious Shooters Hill and on to Dartford Town via Crayford. Further improvements in 1781 altered the route so that it would go through Nettlebed Bottom. This area had become relatively lawless, with highwaymen, footpads and housebreakers operating along the isolated roads and thoroughfares after dark, and inhabitants of the villages lived in constant fear of attack by the thieves and bandits. A plan was conceived in 1763 to introduce Horse Patrols to deal with the threat of highway robbery; however these patrols were not instituted until 1805. The Bow Street Horse Patrol or Foot Patrol was established along the main routes to Dover.[58] The original plan was for the Horse Patrol to be stationed at turnpikes, but this was rejected. These patrols were regarded as a success since there were a number of innovations introduced as well. The Horse Patrol was allowed to pass through all turnpikes free of charge, with the sole exception of Hyde Park Turnpike. Turnpike keepers were paid to hand out pamphlets about crime to travellers, and horns were also issued to them, to help alert 'the Patrol' in the event of a traveller being robbed.[59] The Horse Patrol often stayed close to the turnpikes because the keepers would have information about people and suspects passing through the

Constables, sergeants and the Inspector of R Division during the Dock Strike 1912

area. The turnpike keepers were occasionally paid for their information, especially when robbers or highwaymen were caught. Bow Street Magistrate John Fielding tried to get police offices established next to turnpikes, but this also proved unsuccessful.

From the start of Sir Robert Peel's administration in 1829, the New Police presence in Greenwich and Woolwich continued to grow in importance, indicated by the rise in the number of naval and military establishments which spread out along the south side of the River Thames. The importance of making munitions and armaments for the wars, and its close proximity to the centre of London, also made this a rapidly-growing residential area.

With the growth of population and increased urbanisation came the expansion of the Police in London. The Metropolitan Police Service extended to 700 square miles, with a complement of some 4,500 officers and men,[60] radiating 15 miles from Charing Cross. Greenwich fell within the 6-mile band from central London.

The allocation of divisional policing boundaries during Victorian times meant that Greenwich and Woolwich became part of a very large R Division, stretching from Deptford to St. Mary Cray. Officers would have been required to patrol the parks of Greenwich and Southwark, and man one of the three fixed points on the Division. These were located at the village centre of Blackheath, the Broadway, Greenwich, the High Street, Deptford and Lower Road, Deptford.

Since 1829 many Police Stations within R Division and the areas of Woolwich and Greenwich have both opened and closed. Nowadays, Greenwich borough has just four stations: Greenwich (RD), Woolwich (RW), Plumstead (RP) and Thamesmead (RA).

During various times of unrest, including coal and dock strikes, R Division sent serials of police officers to maintain law and order. The photograph above shows just such a serial sent in 1912 to police the Dock Strike, with the inspector seated in between his sergeants. These are ordinary police officers from the division, probably drawn from all the stations, whilst the inspector is likely to have been the reserve inspector located at Blackheath Road. R Division had also sent a contingent to police the Tonypandy coal strike in South Wales in 1910.

Police Stations

- Abbey Wood Police Station
- Eltham Police Station
- East Greenwich Police Station
- Greenwich Police Station
- Plumstead Police Station
- Shooters Hill Police Station
- Thamesmead Police Station
- Westcombe Park Police Station
- Woolwich Police Station

54 *Municipal Year book 2000 and Public Services Directory Vol. 2,* Newman books (1999), and publicity literature for the London Borough of Enfield.
55 Metropolitan Police Orders, 6th August 1964.
56 Op cit.
57 Epping Forest District Council publicity material.
58 Brown, B. (1997) 'Nothing to do with Reggie and Ronnie - Law and Order in the Crays' in *Bygone Kent,* Vol. 18. no. 9.
59 Priggle, P. (unknown), *Hue and Cry.*
60 *The Police and Constabulary List 1844*, Parker, Furnival and Parker Whitehall, London.

The London Borough of Hackney

Part of N Division (1830-1886)
Part of J and N Divisions (1886-1933)
Parts of G, J and N Divisions (1933-1965)
G Division (1965-1985/86)
Part of No 2 Area (1985/86-1993/94)
Part of No 3 Area North East (1993/94-2018/19)
Part of Central East Basic Command Unit (CE) (from 2018/19)

There had always been a proud tradition of policing in Hackney Borough even before the introduction of the New Police in 1829. Old Hackney Town had had an efficient system of parochial police, which consisted of horse patrols and Parish constables who took their duties seriously. The Lighting and Watch Trustees of the Parish, who had a responsibility for ensuring the Parish constables performed efficiently also ensured that gas lamps were adequately maintained. The Trustees, who had been responsible for the police since 1763, took pride in reporting the fact that in 1828 night time robberies had been completely eradicated from the borough.[61]

A team of four Inspectors assisted by 26 constables of the evening patrol and 30 constables of the night patrol kept order. Additionally, eight Parish constables were responsible for inns, shops and the serving of warrants. This force was so efficient that Hackney was one of only two petitioners who voted against the New Police Bill when it was proposed.[62] Prior to the formation of the uniformed police, the charge made to Hackney ratepayers to pay for constables and watchmen in the last year of operation was £3,380. When the new Metropolitan Police rate was announced the rate fell to £3,164.[63] This was a substantial saving, and was probably made to appease the parishioners.

By the 1830s Hackney was fast developing into a fashionable residential area for the professional and clerical classes. The local population doubled between 1841 and 1861 to 81,000; however, by 1881, it had risen again to 163,000.[64] By the 1880s, development in Hackney had reached Seven Sisters Road, and some parts of the borough around Hackney Fields, Hackney Wick and along the flooded stretches of the River Lea were attracting the lower classes.[65]

The largest parish was Hackney, which contained the hamlets of Homerton, Clapton, Dalston and Shacklewell. In this time, the only development was the construction of Stoke Newington High Street, which was the main route to Cambridge. Road development also took place in the quiet hamlets of Clapton, Homerton, Hackney and Dalston.[66] Between these hamlets were fields, market gardens, pastures, watercress beds and brick fields.[67] This meant that the small hamlets were growing into small towns connected by main roads that ran through farmland.

With the coming of the railway in 1850, the area became heavily populated and the rich businessmen moved out of their large houses and moved further into the countryside.

The London Borough of Hackney was formed in 1965. It stretches from Bishopsgate in the south to Stamford Hill in the north, and from the River Lea in the east to Islington in the west. Hackney Borough contains the former boroughs of Shoreditch, Stoke Newington and Hackney. Each of these names has their origins in Anglo-Saxon times.[68] Now the area is vibrant and culturally diverse, with people from Africa, the West Indies, Turkey, Cyprus and the Indian subcontinent.[69] At the southern end of Hackney Borough the boundary borders the City of London which is policed by a separate police force.[70]

The policing of Hackney Borough has, since the late 1960s, often attracted significant attention from academics, politicians and the press, alleging insensitive policing. Attention has also focused on the care and custody of prisoners, especially those drawn from minority ethnic groups. Hackney and Stoke Newington share an important place in police history where from the very early days police sought to become accepted by the population.[71]

Police Stations
- City Road Police Station
- Dalston Police Station
- Hackney Police Station
- Hoxton (Kingsland Road) Police Station
- Old Street Police Station
- Stoke Newington (Kingsland) Police Station
- Victoria Park Police Station

London Borough of Hammersmith and Fulham

Part of T Division (1839-c.1863)
Parts of T and V Divisions (c.1863-1865)
Part of T Division (1865-1888)
Parts of T and X Divisions (1888-1909)
Parts of B and T Divisions (1909-1933)
Parts of B and F Divisions (1933-1965)
F Division (1965-1985/86)
Part of No 6 Area (1985/86-1993/94)
Part of No 1 Area (Central) (1993/94-2018/19)
Part of Central West Basic Command Unit (CW) (from 2018/19)

The London Borough of Hammersmith and Fulham is one of the smallest boroughs by area, and forms part of Inner London. The borough was formed in 1965 by the merging of the Metropolitan Boroughs of Hammersmith and Fulham. It was known as the London Borough of Hammersmith until being renamed in 1979. The two boroughs had been joined together previously as Fulham District from 1855 until 1886.

The new Metropolitan Police commenced responsibility for the policing of both Hammersmith and Fulham from May 1830.

Police stations
- Fulham Police Station (also known as Walham Green, South Fulham)
- North Fulham Police Station
- Hammersmith Police Station
- Shepherds Bush Police Station

The London Borough of Haringey

Part of N Division (1830-1865)
Parts of N and Y Divisions (1865-1965)
Y Division (1965-1985/86)
Part of No 1 Area (1985/86-1993/94)
Part of No 3 Area (North East) (1993/94-2018/19)
Part of North Area Basic Command Unit (NA) (from 2018/19)

The Borough of Haringey is situated in the centre of north London and is surrounded by six other boroughs. To the south lie Camden, Islington and Hackney; to the east lies Waltham Forest and to the west is Barnet. Enfield runs along the northern boundary.

The London Borough of Haringey was formed in 1965 when the former councils of Tottenham, Wood Green and Hornsey merged. Tottenham and Hornsey were ancient parishes dating from before the Norman Conquest. Wood Green, which was formally part of Tottenham, emerged as a separate district in 1885. The name 'Haringey' is the medieval form of the modern name Hornsey.[72]

Police Stations
- Highgate Police Station
- Hornsey Police Station
- Muswell Hill Police Station
- St. Ann's Road Police Station
- Tottenham Police Station
- Wood Green Police Station

The London Borough of Harrow

Parts of S and T Divisions (1839-1865)
Parts of S and X Divisions (1865-1933)
Part of X Division (1933-1965)
Part of Q Division (1965-1985/86)
Part of No 7 Area (1985/86-1993/94)
Part of No 2 Area (North West) (1993/94-2018/19)
Part of North West Basic Command
Unit (NW) (from 2018/19)

At the time of the founding of the Metropolitan Police, the area of Harrow was a rural outpost outside of London. The small villages of Pinner, Stanmore, Edgware and Harrow Weald were in the district, whose only sizable settlement was Harrow on the Hill.

Harrow on the Hill had become notable due to the presence of the famous Harrow School which sits at the very top of the hill, facing towards London. The school has been attended by hundreds of famous men since it was established in 1572 by John Lyon. Eight prime ministers are former Harrow pupils, including Sir Winston Churchill and Sir Robert Peel himself.

In the early part of the 19th century the area was patrolled by the 3rd Division of the Bow Street Horse Patrol, which had been set up in 1805. The S or Hampstead Division was extended in 1840 to include Edgware, where a station house was taken on the Edgware Road by the 8-mile stone adjoining the turnpike gate. This initially had two sergeants, fourteen constables and a horse patrol located there.

Over the last century, the London Borough of Harrow has had four police stations to cover the policing needs of the district. They have been at Edgware, Pinner, Wealdstone and Harrow. West Street Police Station was the original 'Harrow Police Station' since Victorian times, before it was replaced in 1963 by the present Harrow Police Station.

The district of Harrow grew with the coming of the railway which had the effect of killing off the coaching industry, considering that Harrow was exactly one day's drive to Holborn. The London to Birmingham Railway from Euston cut through the borough, with its first local station being Harrow (now Harrow & Wealdstone) which opened in 1837. A station at Hatch End was opened in 1844. Later still, the Metropolitan Line from London reached Harrow on the Hill in 1880, and progressed to Pinner in 1886.

Following the coming of the railway to Harrow, Pinner Police Station was closed and the officers there moved to Harrow in 1842. By 1865 the increase in population saw the need for a police reorganisation, and Harrow was to become part of the new X or Paddington Division. Edgware Police Station remained in the S or Hampstead Division.

In 1872/73 telegraph communication was being introduced across the Metropolitan Police and was installed at Edgware, which was given the code 'EG'. Soon after the system was extended to include Harrow, which became 'HW'. Pinner did not get its telegraph until the new station opened in 1899, and their designation became 'PI'.

London and its environs continued to grow steadily northwards towards Harrow and new rail lines and new stations sprang up into the first quarter of the 20th century. Industry began to develop in the area and factories (such as a large one for Kodak) were built, particularly in Wealdstone which helped the area to grow. This also meant there was a considerable increase in the need for more police officers and police buildings to cope with the construction of new streets and houses as people migrated into the suburbs.

On 1 December 1933 Wealdstone Police Station moved from S or Hampstead Division to become part of X or Kilburn Division.

On 1 April 1965 the old county of Middlesex was abolished and the GLC was formed, resulting in the creation of the London Borough of Harrow. At the same time, Edgware (QE) moved from S Division to the new Q or Wembley Division. Harrow (QA), Pinner (QP) and Wealdstone (QW) also moved to Q Division. Harrow Police Station is now the only 24 hour operational station in the borough.

Police Stations
- Edgware Police Station
- Pinner Police Station
- Harrow (West Street) Police Station
- Harrow (Northolt Road) Police Station
- Wealdstone Police Station

The London Borough of Havering

Part of Essex Police (until 1965)
Part of K Division (1965-1985/86)
Part of No 2 Area (1985/86-1993/94)
Part of No 3 Area (North East) (1993/94-2018/19)
Part of East Area Basic Command Unit (EA) (from 2018/19)

This borough is situated at the most easterly point of all the London Boroughs. To the north and east it is bordered by the Essex countryside. To the south there is a three-mile frontage on the River Thames, and to the west are the boroughs of Redbridge and Barking & Dagenham. It is one of the largest London Boroughs, and 50% of it is Green Belt Land. The name 'Havering' originates from the picturesque village of Havering-atte-Bower, where at one time there had been a royal palace.

---

61 *The Victorian County of Middlesex* (1995), p112.
62 F.H.W. Shepherd, *London 1808-70: The Inferno Men* (1971), p35; 10 Geo. IV, c.44.
63 Ascoli, D. (1979) *The Queen's Peace*. Hamish Hamilton, London.
64 Hunter, M. (1981) 'The Victorian Villas of Hackney' (The Hackney Society).
65 Inwood, Stephen (1998) *A History of London*, p584.
66 Ibid, p583.
67 Ibid.
68 *The Municipal Year Book 2000 and Public Services Directory Vol 2*.
69 www.hackney.gov.uk/history/data/potted.htm accessed 7th February 2000.
70 The London Borough of Hackney promotional material.
71 Ibid.
72 *The Municipal Year Book 2000 and Public Service Directory. Vol.2*. and publicity literature for the London Borough of Haringey.

However, the London Borough of Havering was created in 1965 with the merger of the Borough of Romford and Hornchurch Urban District Council. In the same year the Metropolitan Police took over the responsibility for the Essex police buildings and for the 139 officers attached to them, covering Romford, Collier Row, Harold Hill, Plough Corner, Hornchurch, Rainham and Upminster.

The only police station presently open to public in the London Borough of Havering is at Romford.

Police Stations
- Collier Row Police Station
- Harold Hill Police Station
- Hornchurch Police Station
- Plough Corner Police Station
- Rainham Police Station
- Romford Police Station
- Upminster Police Station

The London Borough of Hillingdon (incorporating Spelthorne & Heathrow Airport)

Part of T Division (1830-1865)

Parts of T and X Divisions (1865-1985/86)

Airport Division formed 1974, transferring from British Airports Authority Constabulary

Part of No 6 Area (1985/86-1993/94)

Part of No 5 Area (West) (1993/94-2018/19)

Spelthorne was transferred to Surrey in 2000

Heathrow Airport transferred to Specialist Operations (SO18) in 2002, by 2018/19 becoming part of Aviation Policing

Hillingdon became part of West Area Basic Command Unit (WA) (from 2018/19)

Originally set up in 1805 to patrol the radius of 16 miles around London, the Bow Street Horse Patrol kept watch up and down the main highways to the west from London. Prior to the appearance of the New Police, the area was described as 'the flattest and most bleakest in Middlesex'. It was the haunt of highwaymen who preyed upon the travellers on the main Exeter Mail Coach Road (the Staines Road) and who would often rob the toll-house itself at Bedfont, near the Horse & Groom public house.[73]

The Staines Road in the south of the parish was turnpiked in 1727.[74]

There was a toll-house opposite the New Inn, and also a side-bar at the end of the New Road. Bedfont toll-house was situated between the 15th and 16th milestones. Two of these stones, dating from 1843, can be seen today outside Bedfont Library (12 miles) and Bedfont Service Station (13 miles to Hyde Park Corner).[75]

Before the Bow Street patrols, highwaymen were sometimes pursued by soldiers from the cavalry barracks on Hounslow Heath. A station consisting of a double cottage with stabling was established at Bedfont in the High Street as part of the 3rd Division of the Bow Street Horse Patrol.[76]

Before the railway came to Feltham in 1848, the village clustered around St. Dunstan's Church. Amongst the gravestones in the churchyard is that of William Wynne Ryland (d.1783), a forger. This was a crime taken very seriously in those days, and Ryland was one of the last criminals to be hanged on the public gallows at Tyburn (now Marble Arch).[77]

Feltham was a village and a parish in the Staines district of Middlesex. The village is located on the Richmond Extension railway near the Longford river, 4¼ miles north east of Staines. It has a station on the railway and a post office under the Hounslow postal district, London West. Feltham has been described as a pleasant suburb, with many ornate dwellings, situated 13 miles from central London and two miles south of Heathrow Airport.[78]

There is evidence of arrests being made by Bow Street officers for murders and highway robberies as early as 1799, although one murder committed in 1802 on Mr Steele was unsolved until 1807.[79]

Police Stations
- Ashford and Ashford Police Cottages
- Harlington Police Station
- Harefield Police Station
- Hayes and Gould's Green Police Stations
- Hillingdon and Uxbridge Police Stations
- Northwood Police Station
- Ruislip Police Station
- Staines Police Station (and Spelthorne)
- Shepperton Lock Police Station
- Stanwell Police Station
- Sunbury Police Station
- West Drayton Police Station

Heathrow Airport Division SO18

Heathrow Airport is situated on the south end of the London Borough of Hillingdon, on a parcel of land that is designated part of the Metropolitan Green Belt. The airport is surrounded by the built-up areas of Harlington, Harmondsworth, Longford and Cranford to the north, and by Hounslow and Hatton to the east. To the south lie East Bedfont and Stanwell, while to the west Heathrow is separated from Colnbrook in Berkshire by the M25 motorway.

Although located within the London Borough of Hillingdon, Heathrow Airport is not currently incorporated into one of the MPS boroughs but instead sits independently as an entity of its own, as SO18 Aviation Security since 2007. SO18 are responsible for both Heathrow and London City Airport.

Heathrow is an airport owned by the British Aviation Authority (BAA), currently handling in excess of 68 million passengers and 450,000 aircraft movements per year. There are over 80,000 staff working within the airport (as a comparison, the town of Wigan in northern England has a population of just over 80,000). Additionally, over 12 million other visitors and more than 20 million vehicles travel through the airport each year. Terminal 5 was opened in March 2008, after the longest Public Inquiry that sat for 524 days and concluded eight years after the initial application for Government approval. The Inquiry cost £80m, heard 700 witnesses and generated 100,000 pages of transcripts.[80]

Originally Heathrow was a hamlet in the parish of Harmondsworth, and consisted of a small number of cottages on the edge of Hounslow Heath.

'Hounslow Heath was once an oak forest that spread its green boughs from Staines to Brentford, and there is an old tradition that the last wolf in England, killed centuries ago, was hunted down at Perry Oaks in that neighbourhood.'[81]

Prior to the existence of any police station in the area, there was still a need for the forces of law and order to maintain peace on Hounslow Heath. Once part of the extensive Forest of Middlesex, and now largely buried beneath the runways of London Airport, Hounslow Heath was for more than 200 years

Left: Ministry of Civil Aviation Constabulary Helmet Plate Badge
Middle: Ministry of Civil Aviation Constabulary Inspector Cap Badge 1948-66
Right: British Airports Authority Constabulary Cap Badge

the most dangerous place in Britain. Between the 17th and early 19th centuries, the Heath occupied perhaps 25 square miles. No-one was really certain where its boundaries lay, and no-one cared, for it was a tract of country to be crossed as quickly as possible.

Though Hounslow itself was not large, it was, after London, the most important of coaching centres. Across the Heath ran the Bath Road and the Exeter Road, along which travelled wealthy visitors to West Country resorts and courtiers travelling to Windsor. All provided rich pickings for highwaymen lurking in copses bordering the lonely ways. Claude Duval (Du Val, Duvall or Duvail) was a highwayman who had been born in France in 1643 but moved to England in 1660 to pursue his 'career' as a highwayman. Duval was eventually captured and executed in 1670 for his crimes, but was remembered for his success at seducing his female victims as much as the notoriety of his crimes. He was known as a 'true gentleman of the road'. He stopped a woman's coach on Hounslow Heath in which there was a booty of £400, but only took one hundred, allowing "the fair owner to ransom the rest by dancing 'a coranto' with him on the Heath."[82]

The hamlet of Heathrow was beset by highwaymen, so in 1805 the Bow Street Horse Patrols were introduced for 'the suppression of highwaymen, footpads and housebreakers'. Horse Patrol stations were established at Bedfont, Hounslow, Harlington Corner and Colnbrook, and these were integrated into the Metropolitan Police in 1837.[83]

The Metropolitan Police area was extending further out from the centre of London. The hamlet of Heath Row became part of the Metropolitan Police District in 1840 as the old T or Paddington Division was extended from the boundary set at Brentford in 1830 to Staines. By 1849 a sectional police station had been opened in Stanwell village to police the local area. In 1857, another station was opened on the Staines Road at Bedfont and took over from the nearby horse patrol station. In 1865 Hattons Road, Harlington was chosen as the site for a new station, which was moved to a new site on the Bath Road in 1890.[84]

In 1919 the first commercial flight from London to France left Hounslow Aerodrome, a former Great War aerodrome. At that time the first record occurred of police officers being stationed at Hounslow Aerodrome – an increase in the complement of T District by one sergeant and nine constables – was noted, whose presence was commensurate with the use of aircraft. However, Hounslow Aerodrome was closed in 1920, as operations were moved to the London Croydon Airport.

In 1925 a Royal Air Force pilot, Norman MacMillan, was forced to land his plane on a piece of flat land in the area. His appraisal of the land as being suitable for an airfield was noted by Fairey Aviation. In 1929/30 Fairey Aviation bought several plots of land. British aero engineer and aircraft builder Richard Fairey paid the Vicar of Harmondsworth £15,000 for a 150-acre plot on which to build a private airport to assemble and test aircraft. Complete with a single grass runway and a handful of hastily-erected buildings, Fairey's Great West Aerodrome was created from humble beginnings.[85]

During World War II the Government requisitioned land in and around the ancient agricultural village of Heath Row, including Fairey's Great West Aerodrome, in order to build RAF Heston, a base for long-range troop-carrying aircraft bound for the Far East. An RAF-type control tower was constructed and a 'Star of David' pattern of runways laid, the longest of which was 3,000 yards long and 100 yards wide.[86] In 1944 the hamlet of Heath Row was demolished to make way for the new airport as part of the war effort. As the airport (known then as the Great Western Aerodrome) began to expand, the families who lived in the area were relocated.

During the war the Air Ministry Constabulary were responsible for airports and stations. Following the conclusion of the conflict the RAF no longer needed the airport, so the site was transferred to the Ministry of Civil Aviation. The airport was officially opened for commercial operations in May 1946. The first aircraft to take off from Heathrow after the war was a Starlight (a converted Lancaster), which flew to Buenos Aires. The early passenger terminals were primitive indeed and consisted of

'ex-military marquees which formed a tented village along the Bath Road. The terminals were primitive but comfortable, equipped with floral-patterned armchairs, settees and small tables containing vases of fresh flowers. To reach aircraft parked on the apron, passengers walked over wooden duckboards to protect their footwear from the muddy airfield. There was no heating in the marquees, which meant that during winter it could be bitterly cold, but in summer when the sun shone, the marquee walls were removed to allow a cool breeze to blow through.'[87]

73 Brown, B. (1997). 'Policing Old Feltham'. Metropolitan Police Museum.
74 'Act for repairing road from Hounslow Heath to Basingstone', I Geo. II, Stat. ii, c. 6.
75 Brown, B. (1997). 'Policing Old Feltham'. Metropolitan Police Museum.
76 Brown, B. (1997). 'Policing Old Feltham'. Metropolitan Police Museum.
77 www.hounslow.info/libraries/local-history-archives/discover-hounslow/#fel accessed 24th December 2012.
78 Ibid.
79 *The Job*, 14th January 1983, p13.
80 www.guardian.co.uk accessed 22nd May 2007.
81 *All the Year Round*, 1868.
82 www.flageolets.com/biographies/duval and www.stand-and-deliver.org.uk/highwaymen/claude_duval.htm, both accessed 20th March 2012
83 www.scribd.com/doc/57482167/Heathrow-The-Lost-Hamlet.
84 John Back Archive (1972).
85 www.heathrowairport.com/about-us/company-news-and-information/company-information/our-history accessed 24th February 2013.
86 www.heathrowairport.com/about-us/company-news-and-information/company-information/our-history accessed 25th February 2013.
87 www.heathrowairport.com/about-us/company-news-and-information/company-information/our-history accessed 24th February 2013.

The policing of Heathrow fell to the Ministry of Civil Aviation Constabulary from 1948 – two years after flights commenced – although during any major incident the Metropolitan Police always took overall command.

By 1954 the name changed again to the Ministry of Transport and Civil Aviation Constabulary, although uniform buttons still contained the initials MCA. All this just meant that tunics and coats remained the same, but headgear badges and plates were changed.

The British Airports Authority was established in 1965 by the Airport Authority Act 1965, and on 1st April 1966 the new British Airports Authority Constabulary took on responsibility for operating London Heathrow, London Gatwick and London Stansted airports.[88]

This occurred at the same time as Terminal 3 was built, Terminal 2 having been constructed in 1955. The change of administration was seen as an opportunity to partially reform old working methods, and then-novel innovations were introduced such as report forms with tick-boxes, an index card system and dictation machines for detectives.[89] In December of that year the strength of the force stood at 201.[90]

In 1965, at the formation of the Greater London Council (GLC), Heathrow ceased to be part of Middlesex and was incorporated into the GLC. It is now part of the London Borough of Hillingdon, although the postal address is in Hounslow. In 1969 the Chief Constable, Major W. Ronnie, was awarded the Queen's Police Medal.[91] The police strength at the time stood at 326, of which 28 were women.[92]

BAAC constables were sworn in under section 10 of the Airport Authority Act 1965.[93] They were all attested before a justice of the peace (or a sheriff in Scotland), and had "the powers and privileges and [were] liable to the duties and responsibilities of a constable" on all the aerodromes owned or managed by BAA.[94] They also enjoyed their powers when following (pursuing) a person from such an aerodrome, if they couldn't have arrested them on the aerodrome,[95] although they were not a Home Office force and subject to their supervision.

BAA had the power to sack or suspend constables, and were vicariously liable for their actions whilst on duty. In April 1971 R.M. Carson was appointed as Chief Constable of the BAAC.[96]

The policing of Heathrow by the constabulary ceased in 1974, when with the exception of the Chief Constable and his deputy the remainder transferred into the Metropolitan Police. The same thing had happened with the Dockyard officers of Chatham, Portsmouth, Devonport and Pembroke when the Metropolitan Police took control of them in the 1860s, and the old dockyard officers merged with the Metropolitan Police.

Police Stations
- Heathrow Airport Police Station (ID)
- Heathrow Police Station, Polar Park

The London Borough of Hounslow

Part of T Division (1830-1985/86) (also part of X Division in approximately 1888)

Part of No 5 Area (1985/86-1993/94)

Part of No 5 Area (South West) (1993/94-2018/19)

Part of West Area Basic Command Unit (WA) (from 2018/19)

The name Hounslow first appeared in the Domesday Book as *Honeslauu*, a combination of the Old English words for hounds and hill. A year before the signing of the Magna Carta the Friars founded the Priory of Holy Trinity in Hounslow, their first permanent home in England. They built a hospice for travellers and the sick, and a chapel. The chapel survived the transition to lay ownership at the Dissolution, until it was replaced by the new Holy Trinity Church in the 19th century. The ownership of the manor and the estate passed through many hands, though from 1704 till 1820 it was held by the Bulstrode family.[97]

By 1650 there were 120 houses in the town, and many of them were either inns or alehouses catering for travellers. The development of regular coach services in the 18th century benefitted the town; it was usually the first stop from, or the last stop into, London. At the turn of the 19th century there were stables for 800 horses, and 150 coaches passed through the town each day. In a town so dependent on coach traffic, the opening of the railways in the 1830s and 1840s caused a depression, though the arrival of the suburban line in 1850 encouraged the development of South Hounslow as a high-class residential area.[98]

For most of its history the town has been divided between the parishes of Isleworth and Heston – the parish boundary was the middle of the main road. The two vestries found it hard to agree on improvements to the town, so in the 19th century a body of local philanthropists including Dr Frogley the surgeon, Dr Benson the curate of the chapel, Mr Henry Pownall, Mr Farnell of the Isleworth Brewery, Dr Joseph Banks and James Clitherow took it upon themselves to raise money for a new chapel, the town school and the town hall.

Since Heston and Isleworth united in an Urban Sanitary District in 1875 with Hounslow as its centre, the area has developed through an Urban District Council and Borough Council to the present London Borough of Hounslow.[99]

On 10th May 1830 the 16th Company of the newly-formed Metropolitan Police came into existence when men of Kensington or T Division marched into the parishes of Chiswick and Brentford. Station houses were established at Front Street, Old Brentford and Market Place.[100]

In November 1912 William Edward Fitt (warrant no. 72486), before he transferred to T Division, became Superintendent of J Division. And it was here that he formed a close relationship with Major Manners as Commander and later Deputy Commander Jerborough-Bonsey, the J Division Metropolitan Police Special Constabulary (MSC) Commander.

The role played by the police in the UK, but particularly the Metropolitan Police, by the MSC from 1914 through the war years, and then later as the MSC Reserve from 1919 onwards progressing into the 1920s and 30s, cannot be underestimated. Fitt was transferred to T Division in November 1916, where he remained in charge until April 1919 when he retired on pension. William Fitt's son Percy, as we shall see, also had an association with the MSC on both J and T Divisions, as later he became the T Division full-time paid staff officer Sub Inspector at Hammersmith.

Superintendent Fitt and his MSC Head Commander W.C.E. Gibson, and later Commander George Gentry OBE, were located at Hammersmith and worked together regarding the day-to-day running of the division. Gentry from Isleworth had joined the MSC as a constable, but because of his connections quickly came to the attention of the Home Office. Gentry was a very wealthy coal merchant and was secretary of the Coal Merchants Federation of Great Britain. He co-ordinated with the Home Office, became advisor to the various Government officials and coal controllers who dealt with the distribution side of the coal trade throughout the country, until the de-control of the trade. Because of his managerial ability he quickly gained promotion, so that he became Assistant

Edward Fitt Superintendent, T Division

Commander George Gentry OBE

Commander of T Division by 1919.

Inspector Percy Fitt worked to Commandant McAdam (warrant no. 011905), who was taken on full pay in September 1939 when the war started. He was assisted by Commander Roe, who also went on pay at the same time as his colleague.

Police Stations
- Bedfont Police Station
- Brentford Police Station
- Chiswick Police Station
- Feltham Police Station
- Hounslow Police Station
- Isleworth Police station

The London Borough of Islington

Part of N Division (1830-1865)

Parts of N and Y Divisions (1865-1933)

Parts of G and N Divisions (1933-1965)

N Division (1965-1985/86)

Part of No 1 Area (1985/86-1993/94)

Part of No 2 Area (North West) (1993/94-2018/19)

Part of Central North Basic Command Unit (CN) (from 2018/19)

This inner London Borough lies with the Boroughs of Haringey to the north, Camden and Hackney to the west and east, and the City of London to the south. The borough consists of a number of what were once separate villages, the best-known being Clerkenwell, Highbury, Barnsbury, Holloway and the Angel. In 1965 the Metropolitan Boroughs of Finsbury and Islington were merged to form the London Borough of Islington.[101]

Today, Islington is described as a melting pot of race, religion and social classes. It is home to numerous personalities, from actors, artists and crafts people to journalists and politicians.

There were six principle police stations within the London Borough of Islington, listed below.[102]

Police Stations
- Caledonian Road Police Station
- Highbury Vale Police Station
- Holloway Police Station
- Islington Police Station
- Kings Cross Road Police Station
- Upper Holloway Police Station (aka Archway Police Station)

88 en.wikipedia.org/wiki/Airport_policing_in_the_United_Kingdom accessed 2nd May 2012.

89 'Crime and Security at British airports' in *Flight International*, 15th April 1971. Retrieved 27th May 2011.

90 Ibid.

91 'In the Birthday Honours list' in *Flight International*, 26th June 1969. Retrieved 26th May 2011.

92 'Crime and Security at British airports in *Flight International*, 15th April 1971. Retrieved 27th May.

93 Airports Authority Act 1965.

94 Ibid.

95 Ibid.

96 'British Airports Authority' in *Flight International*, 8th April 1971. Retrieved 27th May 2011.

97 brentfordandchiswicklhs.org.uk/local-history/places/the-history-of-hounslow-town accessed 15th December 2012.

98 Ibid.

99 Ibid.

100 www.bhsproject.co.uk/section4.shtml#60 accessed 15th December 2012.

101 *The Municipal Year Book 2000 and Public Services Directory Vol.2*, Newman Books (1999).

102 www.discover-islington.co.uk accessed 7th February 2000.

Royal Borough of Kensington and Chelsea

Parts of B, T and V Divisions (1829-65)
Parts of B and T Divisions (1865-86)
Parts of B and F Divisions (1886-1965)
B Division (1965-1985/86)
Part of No 6 Area (1985/86-1993/94)
Part of No 1 Area (Central) (1993/94-2018/19)
Part of Central West BCU (CW) (from 2018/19)

Kensington and Chelsea have been policed by a number of divisions over the years, the various reorganisations taking place as London has changed and developed. When the Metropolitan Police was first formed in September 1829, the second of the six companies formed was B (then Westminster) Division and policed part of the parish of St Luke's Chelsea. For a few months it formed part of the external boundary of the Metropolitan Police District, until T (Kensington) and V (Wandsworth) Divisions were formed on 13th May 1830.

In those early years the World's End part of Chelsea was policed by V Division. Gradually, with the influx of people from the country urbanisation took place, which saw the boundary pushed further out from the centre of London.

It was not until 1st April 1886, when many of the inner London divisions were re-aligned, that B Division became known as Chelsea Division. The new B Division headquarters were then taken over from T (Kensington), whilst B Division's Rochester Row Police Station passed to A (first Whitehall, then Westminster) Division. In the early days of T Division the Commissioner's residence was located in Old Brompton Road, so this provided an extra pressure for the Divisional Superintendent.

Fixed points had been introduced throughout London in 1871, not only to provide help unblock some of the more congested roads but also to give the public a dedicated location where they could find a police officer most times of the day and night. On T Division these were located (usually at junctions) at Hammersmith Road outside West Kensington Gardens, Holland Road at the junction with Holland Villas, Fulham High Street, and Tregunter Road.[103]

Notting Hill, Notting Dale and Kensington stations were transferred from F to B Division under the local government reorganisation of April 1965, while Gerald Road was transferred to A Division. Fulham (formerly Walham Green) went to F Division.[104]

Police stations
- Chelsea
- Kensington
- Notting Dale
- Notting Hill
- Walton Street

Other building
- Adam & Eve Mews

The Royal Borough of Kingston on Thames

Part of V Division (1839-1985/86)
Part of No 5 Area (1985/86-1993/94)
Part of No 5 Area (South West) (1993/94-2018/19)
Part of South West Basic Command Unit (SW) (from 2018/19)

The second division of the Bow Street horse patrol was responsible for Kingston in 1827.[105] Originally set up in 1805 to patrol a radius of 16 miles around London to combat the frequency of highway robberies, the officers patrolled North Cheam, Croydon, Sutton, Merton, Wimbledon, Robin Hood Hill, Kingston and Ditton Marsh, which were all far beyond the Metropolitan Police District at that time. The horse patrol stations were situated on Robin Hood Hill, Kingston Market and Ditton Marsh, and by October 1836 had been under the jurisdiction of the Metropolitan Police as part of V or Wandsworth Division. The policing of the Kingston area before the 1820s was carried out and supervised by the various vestries and parish authorities. There was a fairly efficient police within the Surrey parishes, and these consisted of sworn constables (including those of the Bow Street horse patrol), beadles and head-boroughs who would patrol during the day and night by rota.

Qualification for appointment into the horse patrol included previous horse experience, often in the cavalry regiments. Men should be aged over 35 years, and at least 5ft 5in tall. They were paid four shillings a day, and had to be in uniform at all times when out on duty. The horse patrol was well armed with a truncheon, cutlass and belt with a certain number of them carrying pistols.[106]

The area was not included within the Metropolitan Police until 1839, when Kingston, Hook and Chessington formed part of the inner district of V or Wandsworth Division. As the boundary of the MPD was extended the mounted officers, under Inspector Dowsett, became full time members of V Division.[107] In January 1840 these areas came under the jurisdiction of the Metropolitan Police when the force boundary was extended to its present limits. Another 13 sergeants and 101 constables were added to the division, new V Division stations being opened at Kingston, Epsom, Hampton, Sunbury and Richmond (the Surrey Constabulary not coming into existence for another decade).[108]

The division also took in Epsom, Hampton, Sunbury, Princes Street, Richmond and High Street, Mortlake,[109] where there were police stations or houses.

Further extensions to the Metropolitan Police area occurred in 1865, with new divisions W, X and Y formed and others re-organised. The new W or Clapham Division was formed with its HQ at Brixton Police Station. No fewer than two inspectors, eight sergeants and 71 constables were transferred to the new division from V Division, along with Tooting and Clapham Police Stations.[110] Superintendent Edward Butt, who was then in charge at Wandsworth, oversaw the decrease when Chelsea (and Inspector Pitt Tarlton) was transferred from W to T Division,[111] and Clapham (and Inspector William Bushnell) transferred from V to W Division.

The five inspector stations on V were now reduced to three, these being Wandsworth, Kingston and Richmond. All the stations in Middlesex — Sunbury, Hampton, Twickenham, Chelsea and Fulham — were transferred from V or Wandsworth Division to the T or Kensington Division. These stations excepting Kingston were closed to the public when sergeants or acting sergeants were patrolling.

Special duties included one sergeant as divisional clerk, one sergeant and three constables in charge of the police van and horses, one constable as superintendent's groom, two constables at Wandsworth Police Court, one constable at Cremorne Gardens, three constables at Kew Gardens, one constable at Strawberry Hill House and six constables at Hampton Court Palace.[112]

The policing of the division evolved, expanded and became more complex as greater numbers of people moved into the suburbs to find work. Gradually, as travel and transport became easier and cheaper, sleepy villages soon became overwhelmed with traffic, people and crime.

Furthermore, an electricity supply was created in Kingston in 1893 and Victoria Hospital was built in 1897. By 1841 Kingston upon Thames had a population of over 8,000 people. Meanwhile, in 1838 the railway reached Kingston. The railway led to the rapid growth of the area, and by 1901 the population of Kingston was 37,000. In the early 19th century Surbiton was a little hamlet, then it boomed: by the 1880s it had a population of over 10,000 people.[113]

Kingston upon Thames was made an urban district council in 1894, and the Borough of Kingston was formed in 1936. The Guildhall was built in 1935. Meanwhile, from 1875 horse-drawn buses (and from 1906 electric trams) ran in the streets of Kingston. Buses replaced them in 1931. Kingston by-pass was built in 1927. Eden Walk Shopping Centre first opened in 1979, and the Bentall Centre was built in 1987/92.

In 2011 the population of Surbiton, Ewell, Epsom and Kingston upon Thames was 147,000.[114]

In 2019 the Borough of Kingston was served from one central station at 5-7 High Street Kingston, New Malden Police Community Office and Millbank Police Community Office. There are also sixteen Safer Neighbourhoods Teams, who are there to prevent crime and deal with community problems. Response teams were available 24 hours a day to deal with emergency calls.

Only the police stations of Ewell, New Malden, Kingston and Surbiton are covered in this volume.

Police Stations
- Ewell Police Station
- Kingston Police Station
- Surbiton (Tolworth) Police Station
- New Malden Police Station

The London Borough of Lambeth

Parts of L, P and V Divisions (1830-1865)

Parts of L, P and W Divisions (1865-1921)

Parts of L, W and Z Divisions (1921-1932)

Parts of L, M and Z Divisions (1932-1965)

L Division (1965-1985/86)

Part of No 4 Area (1985/86-1993/94)

Part of No 5 Area (SW) (1993/94-2018/19)

Part of Central South Basic Command Unit (AS) (from 2018/19)

The London Borough of Lambeth is a borough which forms part of what is known as Inner London. It measures seven miles north to south, and about two and a half miles east to west, an area of around 10.5 square miles. It was created in 1965 by the merger of the Metropolitan Borough of Lambeth with parts of the Metropolitan Borough of Wandsworth, namely Clapham and Streatham.[115] It forms one of the most densely populated inner London boroughs, with a population of around 270,000.[116]

At the northern end of the borough are the Central London districts of the South Bank and Lambeth which have a developing tourist economy, while at the very south of the borough are the leafy suburbs of Gipsy Hill, Tulse Hill, West Dulwich and West Norwood. In between the two are the built-up and inner-city districts of Brixton, Herne Hill, Stockwell and Kennington, which are each at different stages of gentrification and have elements of suburban and urban settlement, while Vauxhall and South Lambeth are central districts being redeveloped with high-density business and residential properties. Streatham is located between suburban London and inner-city Brixton, with the partly suburban and partly built-up areas of Streatham Hill and Streatham Vale.[117]

The Metropolitan Police first came to L (Lambeth) Division in February 1830. The 10th Company took over the role of policing from the parishes of St. George's Lambeth, St. George's Southwark, Christchurch, Blackfriars and St. Mary Newington, and also used three of the former parish Watch Houses at St. Johns (Waterloo Bridge Road), Christchurch (Blackfriars) and High Street, Lambeth (eventually given up by police in 1858 when Kennington Lane Police Station was opened).

Christchurch Watch House (1819-1932)

The Watch House at Christchurch, shown above, situated in the grounds of the church of the same name by Collingwood Street just off Blackfriars Road, was passed into the ownership of the Receiver by Act of Parliament. This station came with another adjoining building made of brick and slate, and had two cells and a charge room. Shown as a station on L Division, it had a constable in charge. It was retained as a station until 1869, although it did not pass out of the ownership of the Police until at least 1871,[118] as records show it was painted and ameliorated regularly until that date. The building appears to have been there still in 1888.[119]

---

103 *Commissioner's Annual report for the Metropolitan Police 1871.*
104 Bernard Brown, *The Job*, 15th May 1987.
105 TNA MEPO2/25.
106 Wade, J. (1829). *A Treatise on the Police and the Crimes of the Metropolis.* Patterson Smith, New York (reprinted 1972).
107 TNA MEPO 2/76.
108 Tim Lambert (2011). 'A Brief History of Kingston upon Thames' at www.localhistories.org/kingston.html accessed 25th January 2011.
109 *Kelly's Directory*, 1841.
110 Brown, B. 'When Victor Bowed out' in *Police Review*, 29th October 1985.
111 Ibid.
112 Ibid.
113 Tim Lambert (2011). 'A Brief History of Kingston upon Thames' at www.localhistories.org/kingston.html accessed 25th January 2011.
114 Ibid.
115 Lambeth Archives History.
116 www.lambeth.gov.uk. accessed 25th February 2008.
117 Ibid.
118 Metropolitan Police Surveyor's Records, Charlton.
119 *Bacon's Atlas*, 1888.

The parish Watch House, built in 1819, stood in the churchyard until its demolition in 1932. It was a plain brick building of two storeys, divided by a slightly projecting stone string course and with a simple stone cornice. The building had three bays, the centre one being slightly recessed. The two end bays had flat stone pediments. A stone tablet inscribed "Christ Church Watch-House. MDCCCXIX," formerly over the central doorway, was preserved and stood in the garden adjoining the present rectory.

Superintendent Maurice G. Dowling was placed in charge of the Division by 1833.[120] As the accommodation at these Watch Houses was not fit for the officers, two properties were acquired for the housing of police officers; one at 12 Walcott Place (now 149 Kennington Road) and the other at 9 Kennington Cross. The old Watch House in Waterloo Bridge Road was soon replaced in 1836 by one at 58 Tower Street (now Morley Street).[121] The Tower Street property was leased from Miss Helen Orchard from Christmas 1836 to Michaelmas 1884, at an annual rent of £35. She charged an additional £30 per year for that part of the premises containing the cells.[122]

Since 1830 there have been a number of different police stations at various locations in the borough. In this volume we look at those which have operated in the current London Borough of Lambeth since that time, namely Brixton, Clapham, Kennington Lane, Kennington Road, Knights Hill, Norwood/Gipsy Hill and Streatham.

In 1994 Kennington Police Station became the new headquarters of the Vauxhall Division.

Currently, there are six stations policing the London Borough of Lambeth. These are at Brixton, Gipsy Hill, Kennington, Cavendish Road, Clapham and Streatham. The future of the last three stations is the subject of discussion.

The Senior Management Team operates from the new office building called Frank O'Neill House, at 43-59 Clapham Road. The building is named after Police Constable Frank O'Neill, who was fatally stabbed whilst on duty in October 1980. It was opened by the Commissioner Sir John Stevens, QPM, DL and Kathie O'Neill and family in October 2004.[123]

Police Stations
- Brixton Police Station
- Balham / Cavendish Road Police Station
- Clapham Police Station
- Knights Hill or Lower Norwood Police Station
- Norwood/ Gipsy Hill Police Station
- Streatham Police Station

The London Borough of Lewisham

Part of P Division (1839-c.1910)

Parts of P and R Divisions (c.1910-c.1950)

Part of P Division (c.1950-1985/86)

Part of No 3 Area (1985/86-1993/94)

Part of No 4 Area (South East) (1993/94-2018/19)

Part of South East Basic Command Unit (SE) (from 2018/19)

The London Borough of Lewisham was created in 1965 and comprises the three old administrative parishes of St. Mary Lewisham, St. Margaret Lee and St. Paul Deptford. In 1900 Lewisham and Lee were combined to form the Metropolitan Borough of Lewisham. Also in 1900, the parish of St. Paul became the Metropolitan Borough of Deptford. In 1996 the old Royal Dockyard at Greenwich was transferred to Lewisham.[124]

The borough is bordered on the east by the London Borough of Greenwich; the London Borough of Bromley lies to the south and the London Borough of Southwark to the west. The River Thames runs along its northern boundary.

In 2001 the population of the borough was estimated as over 305,000 in 2019.

In May 1830 the Metropolitan Police, known as the 14th Company (R) or Greenwich Division, took over parts of Kent and the parishes of Bermondsey and Rotherhithe. Those police stations which at one time or other were still in the London Borough of Lewisham are covered in this volume.

Police Stations
- Brockley Police Station
- Catford and Southend Village Police Stations
- Deptford Police Station
- Lee Road Police Station
- Lewisham Police Station
- Sydenham Police Station

The London Borough of Merton

P Division (1841-1842)

V Division (1842-1993)

Borough of Merton OCU (1993-2018/19)

South West (SW) BCU (together with Kingston and Richmond) (from 2018/19)

Located within this borough are Mitcham, Merton and Morden, whose names originate from Anglo Saxon times and mean 'big home' or 'big place', 'the farm by the pool', and 'the hill by the marsh'. The area is of significant historical interest, since King Ethelred was killed at the Battle of Mereton in AD 871 during clashes with rival Saxon groups. Wimbledon village was first established by Wynnman, a Saxon leader. During the Doomsday survey in 1086, the Archbishop of Canterbury owned the Manor of Mortlake, which mentioned Merton and Morden, although Wimbledon was excluded. By the 13th Century Wimbledon became the centre of the Manor, but when the estate passed into the hands of Archbishop Cranmer in 1536 Henry VIII ordered him to give the estate to his Chief Minister, Thomas Cromwell, in exchange for land at Canterbury. Henry dissolved the monastery, which had been established in the area in 1117, and used the stone to build Nonsuch Palace at Ewell.

In 1553 the Manor passed out of Royal hands into the control of Richard Garth, and over the next 200 years the borough became the property of farmers, city merchants and businessmen, who built fine houses throughout the district. The most influential of these families were the Cecils, with Sir William later becoming Lord Burghley, moving to Wimbledon in 1550 and setting up home in the Old Rectory (still located in Church Road). His son Thomas, Earl of Exeter, built the Manor House in 1588 and entertained Elizabeth I and James I there. The area became a fashionable place to live, especially as a country retreat. In 1801 Admiral Lord Nelson purchased Merton Place, a house and 70 acres of ground, where he resided with Lady Hamilton and her husband Sir William, who died in 1803.

Industries had strung up along the River Wandle and 1803 saw the arrival of the Surrey Iron Railway, which passed between Wandsworth and Croydon to serve those industries. South of the railway new houses were being built in what was called New Wimbledon. In 1838 Wimbledon Station was opened on the London to Southampton Railway, with the Wimbledon to Croydon line opening in 1858, and the Southampton line in 1871. The Fire Brigade was established in Wimbledon in 1880.

In 1867 John Innes (today of potting compost fame) brought land in the area, although it was not until 20 years after his death and with monies bequeathed that houses in the roads of Poplar, Kenley, Erridge and Circle Gardens were built. Later the John Innes Horticultural Institute was founded, in 1910 moving to Hertfordshire in 1953 and later to Norwich.

The Victorian designer William Morris set up craft, fabrics, furniture, stained glass and tapestry industries in Merton in the 1880s. Morris's friend Arthur Liberty took over old premises along the River Wandle and developed hand-printed fabrics, which became world-renowned. From a population of 4,387 in 1831 rising to 29,606 in 1911, the area saw an explosion in numbers of people moving into the area.

A large number of houses, both terraced and semi-detached, were built in the area to accommodate the influx of people, although the Wimbledon Common area continued to attract the wealthy for which the larger mansions were built. In 1864 the 5th Earl Spencer, who was then Lord of the Manor, attempted to enclose the Common and convert the windmill into six small cottages. This was not a popular move on his part, upsetting the locals, who after a seven year fight saw the passing of both the Wimbledon and Putney Commons Act which protected the commons forever.

In 1907 Lord Baden Powell penned *Scouting for Boys* at Mill House next to the windmill. Earlier, in 1868, the All England Croquet Club, later to become the All England Lawn Tennis and Croquet Club, was founded in Worple Road but later moved to a site in Church Road in 1922.

One of the largest manufacturers in the area, situated on the Lombard Road Factory Estate, was Lines Bros Ltd. Formed in 1919 by the three Lines Brothers under the Triang Toys brand, they employed 4,000 people. Large building works were being undertaken prior to the Second World War. For example, the development of the St. Helier Estate between 1928 and 1936, part of which lies within the borough, saw 9,068 council houses built for about 40,000 people at a cost of £4,000,000. Two hospitals in Mitcham were opened: the Wilson in 1928, and the Cumberland in 1937. At the same time the Library, the Baths Hall and the Majestic Cinema were developed in Mitcham, and the Odeon in Morden. The Royal cinema in Wimbledon Broadway (now the Odeon) was opened in 1933, and Wimbledon Stadium in 1928. The Town Hall was built in 1931.

In 2019 the records show that although Merton is one of the smaller London boroughs, with a population of approximately 206,000, it has a surprisingly diverse community and has one of the fastest-growing black minority ethnic communities in London. Merton, for example, is home to one of the largest mosques in western Europe.

Merton is divided into three sectors that cover the areas of Wimbledon, Mitcham and Morden. These localities provide an interesting mix of communities with differing social, economic, educational and policing needs. Wimbledon Village has some of the most expensive residential properties in the whole of London, while parts of Mitcham figure significantly in deprivation indices. There has been a positive history of Police/community working, which is being developed further through the advent of Safer Neighbourhood policing.

Police Stations
- Mitcham Police Station
- Morden Police Station
- Wimbledon Police Station (and Merton)

The London Borough of Newham

Part of K Division (1839-1985/86)
Part of No 2 Area (1985/86-1993/94)
Part of No 3 Area (North East) (1993/94)
Part of North East Basic Command Unit (NE) (from 2018/19)

Prior to the formation of the Greater London Council in 1965, which led to the creation of the London Borough of Newham, the area had been divided into the County Boroughs of East Ham and West Ham. Until then, each borough had its own Fire and Ambulance Service. Policing was separate, and the local police enjoyed an excellent working arrangement with the other local emergency services.

The Borough is surrounded by the River Lea and the Borough of Tower Hamlets to the west, the River Roding and the boroughs of Redbridge and Barking & Dagenham to the east, the River Thames to the south and Waltham Forest to the north. The Newham residents form the communities of Beckton, Custom House, Cyprus, East Ham, Plaistow, Canning Town, North Woolwich, Manor Park, Forest Gate, Stratford and West Ham.[125]

There were two police divisions, H and K, which had previously covered the London Borough of Newham. In 1890, for example, K Division consisted of Barking, Barkingside (so called because it was located on the Barking side of Epping Forest), Bethnal Green, Bow Road, Dagenham, Great Ilford, Isle of Dogs, Limehouse (Pigot Street), North Woolwich, Plaistow, West Ham Lane, Chadwell Heath and Canning Town.

Police Stations
- Canning Town Police Station
- East Ham Police Station
- Forest Gate Police Station
- North Woolwich Police Station
- Plaistow Police Station
- West Ham Police Station

---

103 *Commissioner's Annual report for the Metropolitan Police 1871.*
104 Bernard Brown, *The Job*, 15th May 1987.
105 TNA MEPO2/25.
106 Wade, J. (1829). *A Treatise on the Police and the Crimes of the Metropolis*. Patterson Smith, New York (reprinted 1972).
107 TNA MEPO 2/76.
108 Tim Lambert (2011). 'A Brief History of Kingston upon Thames' at www.localhistories.org/kingston.html accessed 25th January 2011.
109 *Kelly's Directory*, 1841.
110 Brown, B. (1985). 'When Victor Bowed out' in *Police Review*, 29th October.
111 Ibid.
112 Ibid.
113 Tim Lambert (2011). 'A Brief History of Kingston upon Thames' at www.localhistories.org/kingston.html accessed 25th January 2011.
114 Ibid.
115 Lambeth Archives History.
116 www.lambeth.gov.uk accessed 25th February 2008.
117 Ibid.
118 Metropolitan Police Surveyor's Records, Charlton.
119 *Bacon's Atlas*, 1888.
120 *Robson London Directory*, 1833.
121 Brown, B. 'A Brief History of the Vauxhall Division', July 1997.
122 TNA MEPO 4/234.
123 *The Post*, 20th October 2004.
124 www.ideal-homes.org.uk/lewisham. accessed 3rd October 2007.
125 *Municipal Yearbook* (2000); *Newham Book* (1999) vol. 2, and *The Public Services Directory*.

The London Borough of Redbridge

Part of K Division (1839-c.1910)
Parts of J and K Divisions (c.1910-1985/86)
Part of No 1 Area (1985/86-1993/94)
Part of No 3 Area (North East) (1993/94-2018/19)
Part of East Area Basic Command Unit (EA) (from 2018/19)

Three other London boroughs surround Redbridge. Waltham Forest is to the west, Havering lies to the east, and the borough of Barking and Dagenham covers the south and southeast corner. The County of Essex runs along the northern edge. In 1965 the London Borough of Redbridge was formed when Ilford and Wanstead & Woodford, and small parts of Dagenham and Chigwell, joined together. The name 'Redbridge' was derived from an old red (brick) bridge which spanned the River Roding, which runs through the Borough.

Prior to the Local Government reorganisations in 1965, the local authorities were much smaller and were called urban district councils. The complexities of policing and the locations of stations and other facilities meant that very often Local Authority Areas did not match with police boundaries. This caused severe problems over the years as both police and council areas have expanded and contracted, although borough-based policing came into effect in the Metropolitan Police on 1st April 2000. This has now aligned the police boundary to that of the local authority.

The tradition of the police has always been one of reflection, especially in terms of organisation. Therefore, when stations, senior officers and other resources could be better located, this was often done to improve effectiveness and better use of resources.

The stations within Redbridge discussed in this volume include Barkingside, Chadwell Heath, Ilford, Wanstead and Woodford. However, only Ilford Police Station is now open to the public.

Police Stations
- Barkingside Police Station
- Chadwell Heath Police Station
- Ilford Police Station
- Wanstead Police Station
- Woodford Police Station

The London Borough of Richmond-upon-Thames and Elmbridge

Part of V Division (1839-1865)
Parts of T and V Divisions (1865-1965)
Esher brought into the MPD 1946
Part of T Division (1965-1985/86)
Part of No 5 Area (1985/86-1993/94)
Part of No 5 Area (South West) (1993/94-2018/19)
Cobham and Esher transferred to Surrey 2000
Part of South West Basic Command Unit (SW) (from 2018/19)

Mounted patrols were introduced by John Fielding, the Bow Street magistrate, to deal with the plague of highwaymen infesting the metropolitan area's turnpikes. The plan was so successful that the original horse patrol of eight men was strengthened to more than 50 in 1805. The Bow Street horse patrol could then provide protection on all main roads within 20 miles of Charing Cross. Their scarlet waistcoats, blue greatcoats and trousers and black leather hats and stocks were the first uniform issued to any police force in the world.[126]

In 1827 the second division of the Bow Street horse patrol was responsible for Kingston.[127] The area was not included within the Metropolitan Police until 1839, when Kingston, Hook and Chessington formed part of the inner district of V Division.[128] When the Metropolitan Police boundary was extended to cover the Richmond area in 1840, the responsibility for supervision fell to the senior officers of the Metropolitan Police of V or Wandsworth Division. The extension of the Met for the division also took in Epsom, Hampton, Sunbury, Princes Street, Kingston, and High Street, Mortlake.[129]

In 1837 the second division of the Bow Street horse patrol, under the command of Inspector Dowsett, was amalgamated with the Metropolitan Police as part of the Mounted Branch attached to V Division. But in January 1840 these geographical areas also came under the jurisdiction of the Metropolitan Police when the force boundary was extended to its present limits. Another 13 sergeants and 101 constables were added to the division, new V Division stations being opened at Kingston, Epsom, Hampton, Sunbury and Richmond (the Surrey Constabulary not coming in existence for another decade).

Further extensions to the Metropolitan Police area occurred in 1865, when a number of new divisions were formed (W, X and Y) and others reorganised.[130] This affected Superintendent Edward Butt at Wandsworth Police Station (the divisional headquarters) significantly, when Chelsea Station (with Inspector Pitt Tarlton) was removed to T Division and Clapham Station (with Inspector William Bushnell) to W Division.

The Municipal Borough of Richmond was incorporated by Royal Charter in 1890. In 1892 its boundaries were enlarged to include the parishes of Kew, Petersham and a portion of Mortlake, and again in 1933 with the addition of Ham Common and village.[131]

In 1965 the Borough of Richmond was merged with the Municipal Borough of Twickenham, on the other side of the Thames and previously in Middlesex, to form the new London Borough of Richmond.[132]

In 2011 the Borough of Richmond on Thames was served by three police stations; Twickenham, Richmond and Teddington. The Borough has a number of Safer Neighbourhoods Teams who are there to prevent crime and deal with community problems. Response teams are available 24 hours a day to deal with the emergency calls; CID officers and forensic teams investigate crimes and bring criminals before the court. All this work is undertaken for the residents of the borough of Richmond with the express aim of keeping the borough one of the safest in London. The following histories include the police stations at Barnes, Cobham, Ditton, East Molesey, Esher, Ham, Hampton, Kew, Long Ditton, Richmond, Twickenham and Teddington but also the Police Orphanage at Strawberry Hill, Twickenham.

Police Stations
- Barnes Police Station
- Cobham Police Station
- Ditton Police Station (also known as Thames Ditton and Long Ditton)
- East Molesey Police Station
- Esher Police Station
- Ham Police Station (Office)
- Hampton Police Station
- Kew Police Station
- Richmond Police Station
- Teddington Police station

- Twickenham Police station

Other Buildings
- The Metropolitan and City Police Orphanage
- Imber Court

London Borough of Southwark

M Division (1829-1830)

Parts of M, P and R Divisions (1830-1886)

Parts of L, M and P Divisions (1886-1921)

Parts of M and P Divisions (1921-1932)

Parts of L and M Divisions (1932-1965)

M Division (1965-1985/86)

Part of No 3 Area (1985/86-1993/94)

Part of No 4 Area (South East) (1993/94-2018/19)

Part of Central South Basic Command Unit (AS) (from 2018/19)

The London Borough of Southwark was created in 1965 of the Metropolitan Boroughs of Southwark (which in turn was made from an amalgamation of the ancient parishes of Christ Church, St. Saviour, St. George the Martyr and St. Mary Newington), Bermondsey (which comprised the parishes of St. Thomas, St. John, Horselydown, St. Mary Bermondsey and St. Mary Rotherhithe) and Camberwell, which had the same boundaries of the parish of that name dedicated to St. Giles. Camberwell parish was huge, and also comprised the districts of Peckham, Nunhead and Dulwich.

Today the borough is one of great contrasts: prosperity in its south, pockets of deprivation in Peckham and Walworth; ethnic diversity throughout. It has part of the cultural heart of London on its riverside and, in Tate Modern, its Jubilee Line stations and Peckham Library, modern buildings of international importance.[133]

In February 1830 the 11th Company of the Metropolitan Police known as M (Southwark) Division took over the parishes of St. Saviour, St. Thomas, St. Olaves, St. John Horselydown, part of the parishes of Christchurch, Blackfriars, St. George-the-Martyr, St. Mary Newington and St. Mary Magdalene Bermondsey. There were two police stations to cover this area, one at Guildford Street, a former Watch House, and the other at 4 (and 5) Southwark Bridge Road.[134] The latter station had been built between 1814 and 1819, and was still in operation until 1845.[135] The parish watch house, built in 1819, stood in the churchyard until its demolition in 1932.

Many of the old police stations do not meet current policing requirements and in 2020 Walworth Police Station was the only station in the Borough open to the public.

Police Stations
- Camberwell Police Station
- Carter Street/ Walworth Police Station
- Grange Road Police Station (Bermondsey)
- North Dulwich, East Dulwich and West Dulwich Police Stations
- Peckham Police Station
- Rodney Road Police Station
- Rotherhithe Police Station
- Southwark/Stones End Police Station
- Tower Bridge Police Station

London Borough of Sutton

P Division (1847-1865)

W Division (1865-1965)

Z Division (1965-1993)

Borough of Sutton (1993-2018/19)

Area South BCU (with Croydon and Bromley)

The London Borough of Sutton covers nearly 17 square miles and borders the London Boroughs of Croydon to the east and Merton to the north. The remaining part of the Borough is bounded by the county of Surrey. The borough is largely a 20th century creation, especially along the seemingly monotonous northern stretches, but is nonetheless described as an area with a great deal of charm. The river Wandle runs through the northern part, and attracted early industries and rural retreats. There are plenty of worthwhile buildings surviving in Cheam, Carshalton and Beddington.[136]

Police Stations
- Banstead Police Station (now Surrey Constabulary)
- Carshalton Police Station
- Epsom Police Station (now Surrey Constabulary)
- Sutton Police Station
- Wallington Police Station
- Worcester Park Police Office

The London Borough of Tower Hamlets

Part of H and K Divisions (1830-1886)

Parts of H, J and K Divisions (1886-1933)

H Division (1933-1985/86)

Part of No 2 Area (1985/86-1993/94)

Part of No 3 Area (North East) (1993/94-2018/19)

Part of Central East Basic Command Unit (CE) (from 2018/19)

Tower Hamlets is one of the smallest boroughs in London. The River Thames forms the southern boundary of the borough, with eight miles of river frontage, and to the west lies the City of London.

In earlier times, the area between the River Lea and the Tower of London became a charge of the Constable of the Tower, and in time the hamlets and small villages contained therein became known as the Tower Hamlets. In the 1830s the Borough of Tower Hamlets was formed to cover these seventeen hamlets and parishes situated east of the City.

126 www.met.police.uk/mountedbranch/history.htm accessed 22nd February 2012.
127 TNA MEPO 2/25.
128 TNA MEPO 2/76.
129 *Kelly's Directory* 1841.
130 Brown, B. 'When Victor Bowed out' in *Police Review* 29th October 1985.
131 library.wellcome.ac.uk/assets/wtl039768.pdf accessed 31st January 2012.
132 Ibid.
133 www.idealhomes.org.uk accessed 29th December 2005.
134 Brown, B. 'The Metropolitan Police in the County of Surrey' in *Police History Society Journal* (1994).
135 *Kelly's Directory* 1840-46.
136 Pevsner, N and Cherry, B. (1983). *London. 2: South*. Penguin, Harmondsworth. p637.
137 Tower Hamlets official guide.
138 *The Municipal Year Book* 2000. Newham Books, and *Public Services Directory* Vol.2.
139 Police Orders, 11th January 1864.

In 1899, as the population increased, flood prevention work along the River Thames meant that more land became available on which housing could be built. The parishes became independent Boroughs of Stepney, Poplar and Bethnal Green. These boroughs later merged, in 1965, to become the London Borough of Tower Hamlets.

The area has seen constant changes. In the 17th and 18th centuries the Huguenots from France settled there, bringing their silk weaving skills. Poverty in 18th century Ireland brought in labourers, who built the docks. Later, Jewish families became traders in the area. More recently the Bangladeshi settlers have contributed to the richness of life in the borough.

Policing this part of east London has not been an easy task, since most of London's commercial trade came up and down the Thames. The ships unloaded at docks which stretched from Stepney and Tower Bridge in the west, to Limehouse and the Isle of Dogs in the east. Smaller ships transferred cargoes to warehouses along small rivers such as the River Lea. Where there were docks, wharves and warehouses, there was crime.

The Thames Division was formed in 1798 to combat the high levels of crime on the river. High volumes of commercial trade created ever-increasing opportunities for crime with the Thames Division, the Dockyard Police and the Metropolitan Police left not only to police the river, but also the docks, bonded warehouses and wharves.

Police history has shown that tact and forbearance are required in good measure to police sensitive situations, not only in London itself but also in dockland areas, where from time to time different disputes occurred such as dock strikes, industrial action and political demonstrations.

Prior to the formation of the Met, Wellclose Square – situated between Ratcliffe Highway in the south and Cable Street in the north – acted as the Stepney Parish police office.

One of the first H or Whitechapel Division Metropolitan Police stations was situated at 8 Denmark Street, Ratcliffe Highway, St. Georges in the East. To the south was Ratcliffe Highway, and to the north Cable Street. In 1849 the station was vacated and the police moved to Chapel Yard, Spital Square, next to Bishopsgate Street. By 1864 the Denmark Street Station was retained for the housing of police officers and occupied by two families, each paying between 2 shillings and 2 shillings and six pence a week.

Leman Street had been built in the meantime. It had a strength of three inspectors, 28 sergeants and 109 constables. Chapel Yard was smaller, with two inspectors, eight sergeants and 78 constables. Both these stations housed prisoners, and were charging stations.

A sub-divisional station called London Docks also existed on H or Whitechapel Division, manned by two inspectors of Thames Division, one sergeant and 16 constables from H Division. Of the sixteen, eleven operated by day whilst one sergeant and five constables took the night shift.

The first officer in charge of H Division was the unfortunate Superintendent D. Herring, who took command from 10th February 1830 until he died just a few months later in June 1830. The post of Superintendent was an unlucky one at this time, as the incoming officer in charge – Robert Hunter – also died, after four years in office. He was at the station from July 1831 until March 1835.

Originally some of the stations were located on K or Stepney Division, but boundary changes over the years together with the growth of east London and the Metropolitan Police have made revision necessary. Therefore, on occasions stations have alternated between G, H, and K Divisions. Police divisions tended to be formed radiating from the centre of London, and being wedge shaped. This often meant that a central inner London station was the headquarters for the division, although this was not the case in later years.

By 1888 such was the expansion of the Metropolitan Police that the Division boasted 30 inspectors, 44 sergeants and 473 constables. Superintendent Thomas Arnold was the officer in charge and was located at the headquarters at Leman Street, Whitechapel.

By 1994 there were two sub-divisions within the Borough of Tower Hamlets. These consisted of Limehouse sub-division (comprising Bow, Poplar, Limehouse and the Isle of Dogs) and Whitechapel, which was formed in the same year with the amalgamation of Bethnal Green and Leman Street Divisions.

The stations represented in the Borough of Tower Hamlets in 2004 were Commercial Street, Leman Street, Arbour Square, Shadwell, Limehouse, Bow, Poplar, Isle of Dogs, Thames Blackwall, Thames Wapping and Bethnal Green.

Since that time there has been a shift in the number of operating police stations in the Borough. As of 2019 there are twenty Safer Neighbourhood units, one for each ward in the Borough. There is a police station in Bethnal Green (situated at 12 Victoria Park Square), a police office on Brick Lane, and Limehouse Police Station (27 West India Dock Road; no public access station, counter closed).

Chapter 4.
Gazetteer of Police Buildings and Stations Past and Present

Abbey Wood Police Station

London Borough of Greenwich

Abbey Wood Road (1912-1926)

R Division (1912-1926)

In 1906 the Receiver of the Metropolitan Police purchased a freehold site on Abbey Wood Road and a police station was built there in 1912 of brick and slate and, though small by normal standards, it also included a yard.[140] It only existed as a police station for a short time, and was probably used for other purposes, as normal policing in the area seems to have been covered by stations at Plumstead and Belvedere.

In 1925 Abbey Wood Police Station was attached to R Division, located at the junction of Abbey Wood Road and Conference Road. It was a busy junction, with the tram depot opposite and Abbey Wood Railway Station behind that in Harrow Manor Way. This road led to a powder magazine, which was situated next to the Thames for ease of transport.

Abbeywood Police Station 1912-1926

There were also police buildings further down that road, as the general area was mostly set aside for munitions production. These police buildings would also have ensured greater security for the nearby gunpowder magazines and the rifle and artillery ranges on neighbouring Plumstead Marshes. By the mid-1920s it was felt that there was some duplication of policing responsibilities for the area, so Abbey Wood Police Station was closed in December 1926. The quarters and offices were retained for administrative purposes and for a time became a Traffic Warden Centre.

In the 1950s Abbey Wood became a boomtown, with both industry and more housing arriving in the area which then became known as the Abbey Wood Estate. Little further building took place there until the 1960s, when the newly-formed Greater London Council, mindful of the need for more housing, took over the marshland which had recently been vacated by the military and commenced a huge development which was later named Thamesmead, this name being chosen after a competition in the now-defunct *Evening News*.[141]

With the demise of the GLC in 1986 the town was handed over to a private company called Thamesmead Town Limited, which created concern amongst the local community by introducing higher rents whilst at the same time reducing services. The police station was sold and is in private hands as of 2019.

Acton Police Station

The London Borough of Ealing

High Road, Acton (1845-1864)

Acton Hill, Acton (1864-1972)

250 High Street, Acton (1972 to Present)

T Division (1830-1865)

X Division (1865-1933)

T Division (1933-1965)

X Division (1965-1985/86)

Ealing Division / OCU (1985/86-1993; 2 area NW 1993-2018/19)

Basic Command Unit West Area (WA) (2018 to Present)

Acton was included in the new Metropolitan Police district in 1829. In 1832 one Samuel Lloyd is described as the Sergeant at Acton.[142] The next reference to policing in Acton is that police broke up a riot at the Kings Arms in 1837.

By 1845 there was a police station in Acton, at or near a site in High Road. The building was described as a station house owned by Mr Clewo of Acton. Police had a yearly tenancy that was given up after a notice to quit on Lady Day 1853. The building was described as a very old brick and tile house, with a small yard and washhouse with copper and sink.[143] Police may then have renegotiated the lease for a further three years, from 24th June 1853.

In the 1870s Acton was populated by many poorer people. Land owned by the British Land company provided houses which did not sufficiently attract the middle classes. Instead, by 1872 there were sixty laundries on the South Acton estate, which was an essential Victorian service, but these were often run by women with a reputation for hard drinking. Otherwise, there was a slaughterhouse and a number of factories for the manufacture of fertiliser from bone crushing.[144] Such was the

140 Metropolitan Police Surveyor's Records 1912.
141 www.idealhomes.suberbiainfocus.org accessed on 4th March 2008.
142 *Pigots Directory* of 1832.
143 Metropolitan Police Surveyors' Book 1845 p143.
144 Weightman, G and Humphries, S. (1983) *The Making of Modern London*. Sidgwick and Jackson, London p142.

nature of the area to be policed.

The next police station in Acton was on Acton Hill in 1862,[145] another converted house. The existence a police station in prior to 1864 was shown in the 'Distribution of the Force' published in Police Orders in 1864.[146]

In 1863 Police Constable William John Davey was shot in the head and killed at his home in Avenue Road, Acton by a man he was investigating for theft of some wood.[147]

Acton formed part of T or Kensington Division, with a total strength of one police sergeant and eleven police constables. The inspectors and station sergeants on duty at Hammersmith Police Station were detailed to patrol Acton, Ealing and Chiswick on horseback.[148]

Three new divisions were formed in 1865; W or Clapham, X or Paddington, and Y or Highgate.[149] Acton then came under the jurisdiction of X's Exterior Districts with Hanwell, Hillingdon, Harefield, Harrow and Willesden, Greenford and Ruislip. The Inner Districts were Paddington, Notting Hill and Harrow Road. Inspector Eccles was placed in charge of the Division as an Acting Superintendent.[150]

In May 1872 there was an enquiry from Henry George Briggs of Brighton asking whether the Commissioner intended to renew the lease of Acton Police Station. Home Office approval was given to renew the lease for 14 years at £50 per annum. In 1878 there were two sergeants, Frederick Savage and Jesse Smith, and ten police constables shown as based at Acton Police Station.[151]

Approval was granted by the Home Office in 1879 for the purchase of property at a sum not exceeding £1,500, and the freehold for the land was purchased for the sum of £1,400.[152]

In 1881 a Metropolitan Police report on the station described it as an ordinary dwelling-house with cells built in the yard. It was entirely occupied by married people; a married police inspector and three married police constables. The quarters were reported as being too small, and urgent work was recommended such as sorting out the cess pool and adopting a 'dry earth' system for cells and privies; as well as to install heating and provide oil lamps to the cells. There was no communication bell from the cells. Improved ventilation and daylight within the cells was needed.

It was also recommended the married quarters part of the station be separated from the administrative areas. Finally, there should be a supply of purer water to the police station.[153]

By 1886 there were two inspectors, William Ellison and Thomas Mules, and three police constables recorded at Acton Station,[154] and by 1890 the strength had grown to having two inspectors, two sergeants and 37 constables.[155]

The new Acton Police Station, designed by Metropolitan Police Surveyor John Butler, was built in 1894 at a cost of £3,225.

The address was shown as 250 High Street.[156] It was described locally as being 'plain to the verge of ugliness'.[157] The new station was handed over, and married quarters occupied on 2nd July 1894.[158] There were also stables for horses, which in the 1920s were converted into spaces for motor vehicles whilst some of the married quarters were converted into a CID Office.[159]

In that year the station was under the command of Sub-Inspector Alfred Newnham, assisted by two sergeants and 30 constables.[160]

By 1911 the police inspectors were Frederick Instance and Archibald Watson. They were assisted by Station Police Sergeants Percy McCullock and Charles Butt.[161]

In 1911 Sergeant Thomas King Cheeseman was living in three rooms in the Police Station at 250 High Street, Acton with his wife Laura and four children.[162]

Acton Police Station 1894-1972

Six years later, in 1917, Inspector Instance, who had been stationed at Acton, retired from the Police service and he was presented with a canteen of cutlery by his Superintendent, James Olive. He was thanked for his service to the people of Acton. Among those colleagues present were Police Inspectors Watson and Brennan, and Station Police Sergeants Hutchins and Brown.[163]

In 1920 Police Constable James Kelly was shot three times and fatally wounded while pursuing an armed burglar he disturbed at Acton.[164]

In 1933, the reorganisation of divisions north of the Thames

The front door into the old Acton Police station

resulted in Acton becoming a sub-divisional station of T or Ealing Division, with Brentford as the sectional station.[165]

Another piece of land was purchased in 1949, on the west side of the station at a price of £400; this was an extension for the CID and Metropolitan Police Special Constabulary (MSC).

Yet more land was needed, and in 1955 a site was purchased at 2 Lexden Road from London Transport for the sum of £35,000. This site had originally been used by the London General Omnibus Company for stabling horses for the horse-trams, and had been taken over by the London Transport Tram company and subsequently used as a tram depot.[166]

The London Government Act 1963 caused a revision of boundaries aligning police and local authority boundaries, and as a result Acton became a sectional station with Ealing Sub-Division as part of X Division.[167]

In 1972 a new sectional police station for Acton (XA) was taken into operational use at 6.00am on Monday, 10th July. The postal address of 250 High Street, W3 and telephone numbers remained unchanged.[168] The cost of the new station was approximately £175,000.[169]

The new Acton Police Station was built behind the old 1894 station, which was pulled down and a car park and gardens replaced it. It was hoped at the time that the old blue police lamp from outside the old station would be transferred to the new station.[170] Whilst clearing the rubble in front of the new police station, an old brick well was discovered. It was still filled with water, and situated underneath the CID office in the old station. It appears to have been covered up when the old police station was built in 1894. It is thought a large house previously built on this site in the early 18th century was occupied by a Miss Margaret Gainsborough, daughter of the famous painter.[171]

Acton Police Station 1972 to present

In 1990 Police Constable Ashley Day was killed when the area car in which he was operator crashed responding to an alarm at Acton.[172]

At the time of writing, the police station is the only one in the London Borough of Ealing that is open to the public 24 hours each day.

Addington Police Office/ New Addington Police Station

The London Borough of Croydon

Overbury Crescent, Addington (1962-1977)

Addington New Road, Addington (1977-2013)

P Division (1840-1865)

W Division (1865-1921)

Z Division (1921-1985/86)

No. 4 Area (1985/86-1993/94)

No. 4 Area (SE) 1993/94-2013)

The village of Addington was separated from Croydon by woodland of the Ballards Plantation around Coombe Lane and the golf course, formerly the grounds of Addington Palace.[173]

Records show that when the Metropolitan Police District was extended in 1840, Addington was attached to Croydon Police Station, on P Division; it had the strength of one constable who was privately lodged. The local magistrates heard charges in their own homes.[174]

In 1865, Croydon – including the Addington area – was transferred to W Division.[175] In 1921, Z or Croydon Division was formed, to which the Addington area was transferred.

By 1957 consideration was being given for a small temporary building to be erected in the area of New Addington to enable Police on duty to take refreshment instead of having travel around six miles to Croydon Police Station. It was intimated that the building should be manned to deal with minor Police duties. When approached, the Town Planning Officer was not in favour of reserving a site for a temporary Police Station unless a permanent structure would be developed within ten years.[176]

The following year Police received a number of complaints about damage, hooliganism and the inadequate policing in the area. In addition, the council estate had expanded and therefore the workload had increased. Eventually, in 1960 a site in Overbury Crescent was selected for the erection of Police married quarters and a Police office,[177] designated (ZA),

145 Oates, J. Dr. *Policing the Past*. London Borough of Ealing Library
146 Metropolitan Police Orders dated 11th January 1864.
147 www.met.police.uk/history/remembrance2 accessed 28th September 2012.
148 J. Back archive circa 1975.
149 Metropolitan Police Orders dated 28th October 1865.
150 J. Back archive circa 1975.
151 *Kelly's Directory for Middlesex* 1878.
152 J. Back archive circa 1975.
153 Metropolitan Police Condition of police stations report 1881.
154 *Kelly's Middlesex Directory* 1886.
155 British History on-line accessed 16th July 2012.
156 MP List of Police Stations 1912.
157 Oates, J. Dr. *Policing the Past*. London Borough of Ealing Library 2012.
158 Metropolitan Police Orders dated 30th June 1894.
159 Oates, J. Dr. *Policing the Past*. London Borough of Ealing Library 2012.
160 *Kelly's Middlesex Directory* 1894.
161 *Kelly's Middlesex Directory* 1911.
162 1911 Census.
163 *Acton Gazette*, 14th December 1917.
164 www.met.police.uk/history/remembrance3 accessed 28th September 2012.
165 Metropolitan Police Orders dated 28th November 1933.
166 J. Back archive.
167 Metropolitan Police Orders dated 6th August 1964.
168 Metropolitan Police Orders dated 7th July 1972.
169 J. Back archive.
170 *Acton Gazette & Post*, 20th July 1972.
171 *Acton Gazette & Post*, 21st September 1972.
172 www.met.police.uk/history/remembrance4 accessed 28th September 2012.
173 Pevsner, N and Cherry, B. (1983) *London 2. South*. Penguin, Harmondsworth p203.
174 MEPO 2/76.
175 Metropolitan Police Order dated 28 October 1865.
176 J. Back Archive 1975.
177 LB 806.

Addington Police Office, Overbury Crescent 1962-77

was opened on 23 February 1962.[178]

By 1966 the existing Police office was inadequate to cope with the increased operational business, and the cramped conditions in which the officers were obliged to work impaired efficiency. It was suggested that a site be found for the erection of a new Police station. The City Centre Service Station, Kent Gate Way, was closing down and the freehold land adjoining the petrol station was purchased in March 1976. In the meantime the Croydon Natural History and Scientific Society had requested permission to make archaeological investigations before the site was developed. It was believed that Addington had been a medieval village that had existed in Saxon times. Permission was granted, but unfortunately nothing of importance was found. It was suggested that any material might have been disturbed at the time that the service station, with its petrol tanks, was constructed.[179]

The old Police office in Overbury Crescent closed in September 1977 when a new Police station was opened in Addington Village Road, Croydon.[180] The station was closed in 2013 and sold.

Albany Street Police Station

London Borough of Camden OCU (1993-2018)
104 Albany Street, Regent's Park (1866-1960)
60 Albany Street, Regent's Park (1960 to present)
S Division (1832-1933)
D Division (1933-1965)
E Division (1965-1985/86)
Kentish Town Division / OCU (1985/86-2018)
Central North BCU (2018 to Present, together with Islington)

A police station existed as far back as 1832 and was situated at Albany Street, Regent's Park, London. Albany Street was the headquarters station for S or Hampstead Division. By 1836 the Divisional Superintendent was John Carter, and he was assisted by five inspectors who were in charge of the five divisional stations.

Details of the old station are sketchy, except that the address was shown as Albany Street, Regents Park, and was leased from Mr. C. Gore, Her Majesty's Commissioner of Woods. The lease was for 80 years, although details of costs are unknown.

By 1864 the Police force at Albany Street was recorded as being located on S Division.[181]

In the same year Superintendent Loxton stated, in a special report, that the station was no longer suitable for police purposes. It was once the watch house to the Crown estate, and therefore had insufficient space for an increase in police numbers. In an emergency, he suggested, the Duty Officer had to send to Somers Town and Portland Town (later renamed St. Johns Wood) for re-enforcements. In the report Loxton judged the site as suitable for the construction of a new station together with residential accommodation for up to thirty single officers.[182]

A preliminary report on the estimated costs for a new building was in the region of £3,400, although the actual cost when completed was £4,134. The second police station for the area was opened in August 1866 at Albany Street, Regent's Park.[183] In 1871 Albany Street Police Station was shown as being connected to the direct telegraph network located at Scotland Yard. In 1881 there were 43 single constables resident at the station.[184]

In 1882 Albany Street was recorded as being a sub-divisional station on S Division.

Records show that Albany Street Police Station was soon afterwards Divisional Headquarters for S Division, located at 104 Albany Street, Regent's Park, NW1. The site had been leased from the Commissioners of Her Majesty's Woods and Forests for 99 years from 1896, with a ground rent of £150 paid annually. This was a large station, with a superintendent's office and dressing room, chief inspector's office, harness room, divisional clerk's office, superintendent's store, inspectors' office, lobby, charge room, matron's room, six cells, CID office, recreation room, library and mess room. In the basement there were a variety of rooms including a canteen, lamp store and drying room.[185] The stables and section house accommodation for eighteen single constables were located not far away, at 62 Little Albany Street. The horses were housed in a three-stall stable block, with two coaching sheds attached.[186]

The station telegraphic code was Sierra Delta (SD).[187] A house at 27 Clarence Gardens was also leased for police use from the same vendors, and was granted in 1896.[188] New married quarters and a section house opened in November 1897,[189] with accommodation for one married Inspector and 33 single men.

Albany Street Police Station 1866-1960

Albany Street Sub-Division was enhanced in 1898 when Portland Town was integrated to form one division called Albany Street Sub-Division.

The cost of the new section house was £6,002, and the station was altered substantially by W.H. Lascelles and Co. Builders of 121 Bunhill Row, EC in 1900 at a cost of £4,968.[190]

Re-organisation of the divisions north of the River Thames in 1933 meant that Albany Street was transferred from S or Hampstead to D or Marylebone Division.[191]

In 1934 the station was significantly enlarged and assigned the status of Divisional Headquarters for D Division. The section house was converted into married quarters in 1949.

In the 1950s the question of building a new station was considered, and permission was granted by St. Pancras Borough Council, who purchased the old police station site for £45,000. Land was purchased at 60 Albany Street where a modern Divisional Headquarters for D Division, including the sub-divisional station, was built. It opened for police business at 6.00am on Monday, 20th August 1960. Force orders reported that the telephone numbers would remain the same, as would the telegraphic code (which had been changed in the 1930s to correspond with the divisional boundaries we know today) to Delta Delta (DD).

Albany Street Police Station 1960 to present

Albany Street was designed with ample space in mind; it was much larger than the station it replaced. It was built with two floors above ground, perhaps with a view to place the Divisional Headquarters, their staff and administration there in the future.

A revision of police boundaries occurred in 1963, when the Local Government re-organisation also took place. Albany Street changed from D to E Divisional Headquarters in April 1965, and was located within the London Borough of Camden.

In April 1999 Albany Street became the Borough Police Headquarters, and at this time was open 24 hours a day, 7 days a week.[192]

In 2013 the station was closed to the public but retained by the police as a base.[193]

Aldenham Police (Station)

Summerhouse Lane, Watford

Bow Street Horse Patrol Station (1830-1841)

Metropolitan Police S Division (1841-1930)

The District of Aldenham is at the outer extremity of the Metropolitan Police, situated between Watford Junction and Radlett.

Colonel W. Stuart of Aldenham Abbey, Watford, local land owner and lord of the manor, owned a small cottage in the village near Roundbush. The cottage was situated on the east side of the road (now called Summerhouse Lane, Watford) south of the triangle and not far from the almshouses situated across the road.

The Metropolitan Police rented the cottage, originally paying £10 per year rent but rising to £15 10s in 1912 and £23 18s in 1922.

The accommodation consisted of a two-stall stable, a wood and coal shed and a privy. This was not a police station for the purposes of taking and holding prisoners as there were no cells or a charge room for these purposes. This was a station where a constable was in charge. It appears to have been formerly a Bow Street horse patrol station. Any prisoners would have been taken to Barnet Police Station by the arresting officer.

When the constable was out on his patrol it was common for his wife to take messages on police business for her husband from people who would call at the cottage.

The owner was required to pay the rates and carry out repairs. On the first floor were three rooms, whilst the ground floor had two rooms. The accommodation was used to house a married constable and his family. The cottage was still occupied in the 1930s.

Ambrosden House Section House

City of Westminster

A Division (1886-1973)

1 Ambrosden Avenue, SW1P 1QD

Ambrosden House (also referred to on occasions as Westminster Section House) accommodated single and married officers under one roof, providing the area with police officers who could walk to work at nearby Rochester Row. Purpose-built, it was an imposing building situated at the corner of Ambrosden Avenue and Francis Street, and the building still stands today.

The section house was purchased freehold in 1886, and its address was 1 Ambrosden Avenue, Westminster SW1. In December 1927 it was closed and the residents moved out whilst the building underwent substantial refurbishment. The Metropolitan Police sold the block of flats and they are now in private ownership. This was a building over six floors, and was located near to the Roman Catholic cathedral. Originally it had rather spartan sleeping arrangements, with occupants residing in cubicles which were small, noisy and draughty.

During the 1927 refurbishment those large rooms with cubicles had the partitions removed and furnished single bedrooms were developed in their place. The section house

178   Metropolitan Police Orders dated 23rd March 1962.
179   LB 807.
180   PO 26 August 1977.
181   Metropolitan Police Orders dated 11th January 1864.
182   The John Back Archive (1975).
183   Metropolitan Police Orders dated 21st August 1866.
184   PRO Census Records 1881.
185   Metropolitan Police Surveyor's Manifest (1882).
186   Ibid.
187   Metropolitan Police General Orders 1893.
188   Ibid.
189   Metropolitan Police Orders dated 5th November 1897.
190   Op cit.
191   Metropolitan Police Orders dated 28th November 1933.
192   www.met.police.uk/contact/phone.htm dated 13th March 2002.
193   MPD (2018) MOPAC – Police station closures broken down by year.

was not far away from the Windsor Castle public house, which meant a change of scenery and time to relax for many residents when off duty.

The building had drying rooms, a canteen, snooker room and a dart board, so there was always recreational activity. The section house employed a number of wardens, who maintained security and were responsible for the Book 92 to record times when officers were absent from their duties, and also the booking in an out of visitors. These wardens were also responsible for early morning calls to residents so that officers were in time for parade a quarter of an hour before 6.00am on early turn, 2.00pm late turn and 10.00pm for night duty. In the early 1950s an elderly ex-serviceman was the night duty warden, and he had to trudge up the five floors to wake those who had signed in the book at reception for a call.

There were periodic inspections by the local inspector and section sergeant, who would call at the section house and sign the occurrence book held in the reception office. They would then check the visitors book to ensure that non-resident police officers were not on the premises and absent from their beat.

Ambrosden House had few facilities for parking motor cars:

'...except outside on the street. However whilst car ownership by single officers was limited, a number did have motor cycles which were kept safely near the kerb outside. The section house also had fire escape facilities that exited at the rear gate leading on to the pavement. It was always claimed that female giggles were never to be heard in this all male environment.'[194]

The section house was shut and sold in 1973 as part of a review into section house accommodation.[195]

Arbour Square Police Station and Thames Police Court

The London Borough of Tower Hamlets

K Division (1842-1880) (Arbour Street East, Stepney)

H Division (1880-1889) (East Arbour Street)

H Division (1923-1985/86)

Bethnal Green Division (1985/86-1993/94)

Whitechapel OCU HT (1993/94-2000)

Tower Hamlets OCU (2000-2018/19)

Central East OCU (from 2018/19)

Tower Hamlets OCU (1993-1999)

3 Area NE (1999-2005)

This station was perhaps one of the more important stations of London's East End. In 1840 it was decided to remove Thames Police Court from Wapping Police Station, and a search was made to find a suitable location not far away. On 17th July 1841 the Home Office approved a request from the Receiver of the Metropolitan Police to purchase the leasehold of a site in the Commercial Road, E1 owned by the Mercers Company.[196] This was located at Arbour Street, Stepney just north of Commercial Road. The site was to be used to build a court with a police station attached.

The 61-year lease cost £25 per annum, and commenced on 25 March 1841. A loan had been secured from the University Life Company by the Receiver for the sum of £4,986 0s 6d, with which to build the new police station. This attracted an annual charge of £311 12s 6d.[197] The documents do not state for how long the loan was secured.

The new Arbour Square Police Station, together with stables, was built on the site at a cost of £4,143. On the first floor of the station accommodation was provided for nineteen constables, whilst above the stables three rooms were set aside for the married sergeant and his family.

Instructions had been passed from the Home Secretary directing the Commissioner of the Metropolis to move Thames Police Court to the new building which had been built in Arbour Square, Stepney,[198] commencing business in December 1842.[199]

The address of the new Thames Court was Arbour Street East,[200] Stepney, and the station next door became known as Arbour Square Police Station. This was a station of sufficient importance, to be supervised by an Inspector.[201]

Records show that there were two courts in operation in 1844 in the east end of London; Stepney Street and Thames Court. Stepney Street, which had been instituted in November 1840, was headed by the principle magistrate, George Chapple Norton.[202]

Arbour Square Police Station, East Arbour Street 1889-1923

In 1844 the superintendent in charge of Arbour Square Police Station was Edward Young, who had been promoted in 1836. Superintendent Young was head of the Division, and was assisted in his supervisory duties by two inspectors, William R. Garde – promoted in 1832 – and Anthony Rutt, who was promoted in 1837.[203]

In 1844 two magistrates sat daily, except for weekends, from 10.00am until 5.00pm. Records show that the magistrates at Thames Police Court were William Ballantine of 89 Cadogan Place, off Eaton Square, and William J. Broderip of 2 Raymond Buildings, Grays Inn. The clerk was Edward William Symonds.

Thames Police Court boundaries were fixed by order of the Council, dated 10th December 1842, and included the eastern entrance of the London Docks, to Fox's Lane, High Street Shadwell, Ratcliff Highway, Cannon Street, Cannon Street Road, Whitechapel Road, Mile End Road, Grove Road, and along the Eastern Counties Railway to the River Lea, then to the River Thames and back to the eastern entrance of the London Docks.[204]

In 1864 the police station strength at Arbour Square was three inspectors, fifteen sergeants and 120 constables. One inspector, five sergeants and fifty constables remained at the station as A Division Reserve, on standby for emergency use. Two sergeants and 24 constables worked the day shift, whilst four sergeants and 42 constables worked night duty.[205]

Records showed Arbour Square Police Station as becoming the Divisional Station on K or Stepney Division.

Boundary alterations in 1880 transferred a section of K Division, including Arbour Square and the whole of Shadwell Sub-Division, located south of the Mile End Road, to H or

Whitechapel Division. In effect, this meant the transfer in strength of nine Inspectors, seventeen sergeants and 157 constables.

Although Bow Police Station was the Divisional Station for K or Stepney Division, the name and status were altered to Bow Division which now included Arbour Square and Shadwell. The cost of these boundary alterations involved an expenditure of £135, which the Home Office paid for.[206]

Superintendent Thomas Arnold, Divisional Superintendent of H Division for 18 years

Superintendent Thomas Arnold (shown above) resided at 14A Arbour Square East with his wife Mary and their six children.[207] Superintendent Arnold was the Divisional Superintendent from 14 November 1874 until 31 January 1893, when he retired on pension.[208]

As the area developed and new streets and houses were built, the address of the station also changed and in 1884 it was recorded as Arbour Street East, Stepney.[209]

Police horse drawn van collecting prisoners from the Thames Court for transportation to prison

On 4 August 1888 the Home Office authorised the Receiver to spend £7,500 to purchase the freehold for the Police court and station from the Mercers Company. The transactions for the purchase of both were completed in March 1889 at a cost of £7,350. Like the station, the address of the Police court also changed and was shown as Charles Street, Stepney[210] Not only was the Receiver responsible for the purchase of the court building, he was also required to pay the yearly rates.

The picture bottom left shows the daily prison van collecting prisoners from Arbour Square Police Court for transportation to Holloway, Pentonville, Brixton and Wandsworth Prisons. It was taken about 1912, and shows a sergeant and constable helping with prisoner security.

In November 1920 building work was authorised to upgrade the court and police station. Whilst alterations to the police station were being carried out, police business was transferred to the Court building which was designated a temporary police station. The cost of the work amounted to £66,000. The police station came into service on 22 December 1923, and the court was finished in January 1925.

On 13 October 1930 Arbour Square and Shadwell Sub-Divisions were amalgamated, making the latter a sectional station of Arbour Square which retained its Sub-Divisional status.[211]

Arbour Square became the Divisional Headquarters for H Division in 1934. It was extensively refurbished again in 1936.[212] It was shown as having seven sets of married quarters, but was reduced to six to accommodate the administrative functions of its newly-acquired Divisional standing.

On 19 July 1944 Arbour Square Police Station was badly damaged by a V1 flying bomb, which injured some 18 people.[213] As a consequence, the administrative functions were transferred to Shadwell Police Station in King David Lane (latterly a police section house), although an office was maintained at the station to deal with public enquiries. Six sets of married quarters had to be vacated. This was one of ten police stations badly damaged. The Divisional Superintendent transferred his office to Leman Street Police Station. Three months later, on 9 October 1944, the station was re-opened,

194 Stoner, M. (2011) 'Home Service' *London Police Pensioner* 141 - June p17.
195 *Commissioner's Annual Report* 1973.
196 John Back Archive (1975).
197 Metropolitan Police Surveyors Records.
198 John Back Archive (1975).
199 The Police and Constabulary List 1844, Parker, Furnivall and Parker, Military Library Whitehall.
200 The names of streets and numbers of addresses in the area changed from time to time. The court and the station have been given differing addresses like Arbour Square, East, Arbour Street or East Arbour Square.
201 Metropolitan Police General Orders 1873.
202 The Police and Constabulary List 1844, Parker, Furnivall and Parker, Military Library Whitehall.
203 Ibid.
204 Ibid.
205 Metropolitan Police Orders dated 11th January 1864.
206 Metropolitan Police Surveyor's Records.
207 Census Records 1881.
208 Metropolitan Police Service Records.
209 Metropolitan Police Orders dated 20th June 1884.
210 Ibid.
211 John Back Archive (1975).
212 Police Stations – erection dates via Metropolitan Police Museum.
213 Howgrave-Graham, H.M (1947) The Metropolitan Police at War. HMSO.

Bomb damage at Arbour Square Police Station in 1944

although with reduced status as a Sub-Division, and the temporary station at Shadwell was closed at the same time.

Leman Street station retained Divisional Headquarters status until July 1947 when it was transferred to Arbour Square once more, until the new Leman Street station was opened in March 1970.

The 1965 Local Authority boundary revisions created the London Borough of Tower Hamlets, within which Arbour Square was designated a sub-divisional station of H Division, with its sectional station being Bow Road Police Station. The picture below shows Arbour Square substantially rebuilt and extended.

During re-organisation in 1986, all the former divisions which were known as Districts reverted back to the title Division. This meant that Leman Street Division, on which Arbour Square had sub-divisional status, became a division of 2 District, with the District Headquarters being above the station at Leman Street.

Arbour Square Police Station 1923 (rebuilt 1944) to 1999

In 1999 Arbour Square station was still a designated charging station for prisoners, albeit with limited public opening hours, from 6.00am until 10.00pm daily.[214]

The station was finally closed to the public later that year, and in 2005 sold at auction to Bernard Construction Ltd (Stepney). The building has since been converted into residential accommodation.[215]

Ashford and Ashford Police Cottages

In 1891 43-year-old Police Constable James Potterill (warrant 49552) lived at 3 Alpha Cottages, Ashford in Middlesex, with his wife Elizabeth and their four children. Potterill had joined the London police in 1868, and he retired in 1893 from T Division. In the same year Constable Henry Bassett (warrant 57060) and his family lived at York Cottages, Ashford. Bassett had joined in 1873 but resigned after 20 years, in 1893. Sergeant Edward Kemp, his wife and family lived in Staines Road, Ashford.

The freehold to the property in Feltham Road, Ashford, was purchased by the Receiver for a total of £305 in August 1903. This was not a police station, but simply accommodation to house married officers and their families. These cottages were located on T Division, and included numbers 61 and 63 Feltham Road which were purchased together with plots of land at Nos. 39, 40, 41, 42, 43 and 44. The land formed part of the Chestnut Field estate, whose owners included Mr. J. Collins and others. Also situated on the purchased land were some houses and cottages whose state of repair was unknown.

The site remained dormant for a while before authority was given for Police officers to make use of and cultivate the land, before any building works commenced without paying any rates to the council. The Council adopted Chestnut Road in the meantime, and the rates for No. 61 were £72 19s 10d. Two further cottages were purchased in 1906 and cost £834 12s. The two cottages were occupied by two constables and their families, and the rent was 7s 6d weekly. In 1934 the cottages were still being occupied by police families.

Balham/Cavendish Road Police Station

London Borough of Lambeth
47 Cavendish Road, SW12 (1891-2013)
W Division (1891-1965)
L Division (1965-1985/86)
Clapham Division (1985/86-1993/94)
Vauxhall OCU (1993/94-2018/19)
Central South Basic Command Unit AS (from 2018/19)

Land was sought in Balham on which to build a police station in the late 1880s because there was a demand for police due to a growth in population. A sectional station was built and occupied for operational purposes in August 1891 and attached to the divisional station, which was situated at Brixton at the time. It was designed by John Dixon Butler, the Metropolitan Police Surveyor. Balham also had a section house for single police officers, a two-storey building situated at the rear.[216] The rear access gate provided the entrance into the station yard. What can also be observed from the picture below between the section house and the station are the stables, which were a separate building with a hay loft and arched windows to the front. The bowed front office window to the front of the building also afforded a good observation point to see who was coming up and down the main road. The call sign in 1893 for telegraphic purposes was Bravo (BB).

In 1912 Balham Police Station was situated on W Division at 47 Cavendish Road SW, the freehold having been purchased in 1888. An ambulance shelter had been built in Station Road,[217] with a hand cart referred to as a hand ambulance. The hand ambulance was not only used for the transportation of sick or injured people, but also for drunken prisoners as well. These would be strapped to the cart, allowing for the proper security of a prisoner who might escape, and to prevent them from further injury to themselves.

Balham and Battersea Park Road Police Stations were both sectional station of Clapham, which was the sub-divisional station. In the 1880s there had been an increase in funding from the government, due in part to help the police cope with the influx of people into the metropolis. The police sought to recruit more police officers, and increases in constable numbers resulted in additional sergeants and Inspectors as well. For example, an inspector was placed in charge of each police station and a sub-divisional inspector located at the sub-divisional stations. The Clapham Sub-Divisional Inspector was James Janes, who was a frequent visitor to Balham checking duty states, ledgers, charge sheets, the refused charge book, lost and cab property returns and all other books.

Balham Police Station (Cavendish Road from 1965) 1891-2013

In the 1920s the station also had a set of married quarters above the station, but when Brixton was removed to L Division and Balham became the divisional headquarters, these rooms became administrative offices.[218] The accommodation above the stables was also converted for administrative functions. The station was refurbished in 1939 and the address remained as 47 Cavendish Road.[219]

By 1937 Cavendish Road was the principle station of the new and reformed W or Tooting Division, with Superintendent Ballantyne in charge.[220] The station transferred its divisional function, administration and staff to the new station in Mitcham Road, SW17 in 1939.

Balham was a station situated on W or Tooting Division, and in 1960 was a sub-divisional station with call sign Whiskey Hotel (WH). Superintendent F.C. Brown was in charge.[221] It had always been known as Cavendish Road Police Station by the local residents.

With the introduction of the London boroughs in 1965 Balham found itself on the boundary of two London boroughs, that of Wandsworth and Lambeth. It was just inside Lambeth, and so the station became part of L Division.

The station closed in June 1973 for operational purposes but instead became a traffic warden centre until 1984. In 1977 local residents wanted to have their station re-opened with police officers instead of wardens, but this effort failed.[222] However, in 1984 the public got their wish and the station reopened, but then in January 1996 it reverted to a police office instead.[223]

By 2001 Cavendish Road was still situated within the London Borough of Lambeth, part of L Division with call sign Lima Charlie (LC). It became a non-charging station where no prisoners were housed, but was still in use in 2001 as housing administrative offices for various divisional functions.[224] The headquarters station was located at Brixton, where in 2000 the now-famous Borough Commander was Brian Paddick, later Liberal candidate for Mayor of London.

In 2013 the station counter was closed to the public. In 2019 the freehold site and buildings remain in the possession of the Metropolitan Police, and are used for operational purposes although still closed for public access.[225]

Banstead Police Station

High Street, Banstead
Metropolitan Police (1853-2000)
Surrey Constabulary (2000 to Present)
P Division (1853-1865)
W Division (1865-1965)
Z Division (1965-1985/86)
Epsom Division (1985/86-1993)
London Borough of Sutton OCU (1993-2018/19)
South Area BCU SN (from 2018/19)

Banstead is a village with a police station located about a mile-and-a-half north of the Epsom Downs branch of the London to Brighton railway.[226]

The first police station in Banstead was a building purchased in 1852, on the north side of High Street in front of Buff House. It was fitted out and opened in 1853.

In 1864 Banstead was shown as a station on P (Camberwell) Division. It was a sectional station and formed part of Carshalton Sub-Division along with Mitcham, Sutton and Carshalton stations. The strength was one sergeant, eleven constables and one horse. The horse was ridden by the sergeant, who performed twelve hours' duty daily from 9.00am to 9.00pm. The station ground comprised of one section divided into two beats, six by day and six at night. The station was under the supervision of the inspector from Carshalton.[227]

In 1865 three new Divisions were formed: W or Clapham, X or Paddington, and Y or Highgate. Banstead was one of several stations transferred to form the new W Division.[228]

Discipline in the Police was harsh in those early days, and many officers were either dismissed or retired early from the Force. In 1877 one young officer, 22-year-old, Police Constable Joseph Stevens, found himself before the Epsom Magistrates for being "unlawfully guilty of a violation of duty in his office of Constable in the parish of Banstead". Whatever he did cost him his job and 21 days' imprisonment.[229]

The address of the station in 1884 was High Street, Banstead.[230]

In 1891 the census revealed that Police Constable James Childs, his wife Adelaide Elizabeth and their two daughters were living at the station; there were also three single constables living in the building.[231] Inspector Thomas Flynn was shown

---

214   *Police and Constabulary Almanac* 1998.
215   MPS (2019) Freedom of Information request – MPS station closures broken down by year.
216   Metropolitan Police Surveyor's records 1912.
217   Ibid.
218   Metropolitan Police Surveyor's records 1924.
219   Ibid.
220   *Police and Constabulary Almanac* 1937.
221   *Police and Constabulary Almanac* 1960.
222   *South London Press*, 11th March 1977.
223   Brown, B. 'A Brief History of Vauxhall Division'. July 1997
224   *Police and Constabulary Almanac* 2001.
225   MPS (2019) Metropolitan Police Assets.
226   *Kelly's Directory* 1891 p1164.
227   Police Order dated 11th January 1864.
228   Police Order dated 28th October 1865.
229   Old Banstead. 'Off Beat' April 2000.
230   Police Order dated 20th June 1884.
231   Census 1891.

in charge of the station in 1891, and he was responsible for ensuring that everything ran smoothly. He was also the supervisor in charge of three sergeants and 14 constables.²³² Flynn was replaced in 1893.

A communication was received on 4 October 1901 from the Secretary of State sanctioning the purchase from a Mr Lambert of a site proposed for the building of a new police station, almost opposite the old station, at a cost of £250. The freehold site was purchased on 2 May 1902.²³³

Banstead Police Station 1906 to present

The new Banstead Police Station was opened for business in July 1906. There was accommodation for one married sergeant, three married constables and six unmarried men.²³⁴

In 1960 Banstead Station was closed at night from 10.00pm for an experimental period. The officers normally employed were posted to outside duties on the night relief. Incoming telephone calls to Banstead were diverted to Sutton Police Station.²³⁵ In 1964 Banstead Police Station reopened at night.²³⁶

In 1965 the local authority boundaries were changed in London, and Banstead (ZB) was designated a Sectional Station of Epsom (ZP) Sub-Division, situated in the local authority of Banstead, Surrey.²³⁷

In April 2000 Banstead Police Station was transferred to Surrey Police when the Metropolitan Police District Area was realigned. Banstead was one of the Metropolitan Police stations transferred to County Authorities. In 2015 the station was considered for disposal, but this was delayed for operational reasons.

Barking Police Station

The London Borough of Barking and Dagenham

83 North Street, Barking (1849-1910)
4 Ripple Road, Barking (1910-2002)
6 Ripple Road, Barking (2002-2014)
K Division (1840-1985/86)
Dagenham Division & OCU (1985/86-2000)
Barking & Dagenham OCU (2000-2018/19)
East Area BCU EA (from 2018/19)

A watch house was erected near the Whalebone crossroads in 1643 to protect the constable and watchmen as they looked out for highwaymen and footpads on the [Chadwell] Heath. It was 1837 before a night watch was established in Barking.²³⁸ Prior to 1840, and the introduction of the Metropolitan Police to the town, there were two old-style police officers who worked from Vine Cottage in Tanner Street.²³⁹ Barking Police Station should not be confused with Barking Road Police Station, which is nearer Canning Town and Plaistow than Barking old town.

Barking Police Station Lamp

The first Barking Police Station was built on land bought in 1848 for £144. This new purpose-built station house was erected in 1849 in North Street, at the cost of £942.²⁴⁰ By 1864 there were two sergeants and eleven constables at the station²⁴¹ which was small, with a charge room and two cells, which were frequently insufficient for the needs of the station. A two-stall stable was also erected, with a hayloft above. The officers of the station could rest in the mess room or the library, both situated on the ground floor.²⁴²

The station had a total of eleven constables and two sergeants in 1864. A mounted officer and his horse were also located there.²⁴³ Instructions were also given that the inspector from Ilford Police Station should make periodic visits to the station to ensure the officers were correctly carrying out their duties.²⁴⁴

In 1881 Thomas Lamb, 50-year-old from Aldworth near York, was the inspector in charge of the station. He resided there with his 41-year-old wife Mary and their 17-year-old son. The station's six single constables lived in the section house.²⁴⁵

The photograph right was taken at Calverts Photographers near Barking Police Station, and shows Constable 420K William Cook dressed in the 1875 uniform with a helmet having a black star pattern plate. The picture was taken before the end of 1901 as the helmet plate bears the Victorian crown. Cook was born at Bromley-by-Bow in Middlesex, and his previous occupation was shown as hammerman in an iron foundry. Records also show he was 5ft 11 inches tall, and had joined the Force on 9 May 1892 at the age of 23 years. His warrant number was 77645, and after initial training he was posted to E Division as PC 278E. The training of constables took place at Kennington Lane Section House, as Peel House²⁴⁶ in Pimlico did not open until 1907.²⁴⁷ This was a barracks and school of instruction where recruits had to undertake a course lasting between three to five weeks.²⁴⁸ Within a year Constable Cook had transferred to K Division, but on 18 January 1902 he died suddenly.²⁴⁹ Death in service is a sad event at any time, not only for relatives but also for colleagues. This would, under normal circumstances, result in a police funeral, paid for by the police service and attended by all of his family, friends and fellow officers.

Constable 420K William Cook

By 1890 two inspectors, Thomas Dixon and George Allen, three sergeants and 26 constables were posted to the station.²⁵⁰

In 1892 more building work created accommodation for six single police officers. They were each charged one shilling[251] a week for their lodging. The station call sign was Bravo Kilo (BK) in 1893.[252]

In 1891 an inspection of the station found that the sewer was leaking into the station's water supply from underneath the kitchen. Urgent work was completed to correct the fault. The well and cesspool were cut off, and arrangements were made with the South Essex Water Company to lay on and supply mains water. The cells and rooms were also lit.[253] The picture below shows Barking Police Station in 1872. The gas-lit station lamp above the front door was issued in 1861, and had blue glass.[254] The constable standing outside is wearing the 'coxcomb' helmet, which was phased out in 1870 in favour of a Home Office six-panel helmet and star pattern plate.[255]

The station was lit with oil lamps and candles. Gradually, as the local population increased the small local police station was no longer sufficient for policing, and arrangements were made to purchase land and build a new station nearby. By 1898 the station strength was increased to two inspectors, six station sergeants, twelve sergeants and eighty-seven constables.[256]

was sold in 1911 for £400.

Barking Police Station, 4 Ripple Road, Barking 1910-2014

In 1924 two sets of married quarters were built, together with section house accommodation for 21 unmarried men, each paying one shilling a week rent. The cost of the married quarters amounted to 8/6d and 5/6d a week rent respectively.[258] There was extensive refurbishment in 1926 when the section house accommodation was rebuilt. The new section house was opened later the same year. The station was refurbished in 1936.[259]

Barking became synonymous with the event of race walking, as every police officer in the Metropolitan Police will testify. Barking Sub-Division hosted the annual Barking to Southend road walk later organised by the Metropolitan Police Athletic

Barking Police Station, 83 North Street, Barking 1849-1910

In 1906 the freehold title on land to build a new police station was purchased from Mr. J.W. Glenny at a cost of £825. This land was situated in Ripple Road. Negotiations to purchase the land appeared to be difficult, as the threat of compulsory purchase was made against the owner under legislation. These powers were never invoked, because the sale of the land was concluded in favour of the Receiver. This may have been due to the fact that Mr. Glenny also owned adjacent property, and did not favour a busy police station next door. An agreement was made for a seven-foot brick wall (later revised to five feet) to be built between the two properties within three months of purchase.

Barking was a station located on K or Bow Division, although the headquarters was not in Bow but at 27 West India Dock Road, Limehouse.[257]

Building work commenced in 1908 at 4 Ripple Road, Barking. By September 1910 the station had opened for business. Interestingly, the Receiver was also responsible for paying tithe rent charge on the site, which was "part of a field of 3 acre wood and 27 perches" to the Vicars of Barking and a lay impropriator (a person with a claim on the land), amounting to a total of £1 3s. The old station in North Street

232 *Kelly's directory* 1891 p1164.
233 LB 682.
234 Metropolitan Police Order dated 23rd July 1906.
235 Metropolitan Police Order dated 11th November 1960.
236 Metropolitan Police Order dated 28th August 1964.
237 Metropolitan Police Order dated 6th August 1964.
238 Metropolitan Police K District Handbook.
239 J. Frogley (1894) *History of Barking*.
240 MEPO 2/26.
241 Metropolitan Police Orders dated 11th January 1864.
242 John Back collection (1975).
243 Metropolitan Police Orders 11th January 1864.
244 Ibid.
245 Census records 1881.
246 Leeson, B (1934) *Lost London*. Stanley Paul, London.
247 Fido, M and Skinner, K (1999) *The Official Encyclopaedia of Scotland Yard*. Virgin, London.
248 Op cit.
249 Metropolitan Police Divisional Records.
250 *Kelly's Directory* 1890.
251 www.eh.net/hmit. Accessed 11th May 2002.
252 Metropolitan Police General Orders 1893.
253 R.L. Pearson, A. McHardy, and T. Bond – Report on the conditions of Metropolitan Police Stations (1981).
254 Fido, M and Skinner, K (1999) *The Official Encyclopaedia of Scotland Yard*. Virgin, London.
255 Taylor, M. and Wilkinson V. (1989) Badges of Office Hazell and Co, Henley on Thames.
256 Op cit.
257 *Police and Constabulary Almanac* 1907.
258 Metropolitan Police Surveyor's Records (1924).
259 Metropolitan Police Surveyor's Records (undated).

Association. The competition and prestige of winning this race meant that all stations entered teams of young officers in the hope of success. This event was originally the idea of a famous police sportsman, Walter C. Batson. The first road walk took place in 1921, and it was an annual event until the 1980s, when it was considered too dangerous to stage because of the increase in traffic.

Deputy Commander Walter Batson 1919-64

Mr Batson was not only an exceptional sportsman but also a successful police officer, rising to the old rank of Deputy Commander in 1953. Mr Batson was born on 16 May 1899, and joined the police in September 1919. He was promoted to Sergeant in August 1928 and to Station Sergeant in November 1930. Promotions quickly followed, and he became Inspector in 1935, Chief Inspector in 1937 and Superintendent in 1944. He became the J Divisional Superintendent and Deputy Commander in 1953. He was a founder member of the Metropolitan Police Athletic Association (MPAA) and its first Hon. Secretary. He won the ten-mile police championships in 1925, 1926 and 1927, and also the Barking to Southend race in 1927. He received the King's Police Medal in 1950, the OBE in 1957 and the Swedish Gold medal in 1963. This was presented by King Olaf of Sweden himself, for Mr Batson's outstanding contribution to sport. Mr Batson retired in 1964 after 44 years police service, and died in 1984.

The enamelled medal shown below was awarded by the Metropolitan Police Athletic Association to all participants of the event. The medal was made of gold at first but later, because of cost, participants were honoured with silver medals instead.

Records show that in 2002 the address of the station had changed. The address was shown as 6 (not 4) Ripple Road, Barking.

In June 2014 the Barking Police Station was closed and sold for £925,000.[260] It is being redeveloped for retail and residential space (2018). A front office counter was opened in 2014 at the Barking Learning Centre at 2 Town Square.

Barkingside Police Station

The London Borough of Redbridge
Cranbrook Road (1872-1964)
1 High Street (1964-2017)
K Division (1840-1965)
J Division (1965-1985/86)
Barkingside Division (1985/86-2000)
Redbridge OCU (2000-2018/19)
East Area BCU EA (from 2018/19)
Basic Command Unit East Area (EA) (2018 to Present)

Barkingside Police Station Lamp

There was a station listed in 1864 at Barkingside as part of K Division.[261] In 1869, after pressure from the local residents for their own police station, the freehold of the Mossford Arms, a beer house with grounds at the junction of High Street and Church Road, was purchased from Mr. L Ingram. The building was formally the vicarage to the nearby Holy Trinity Church. After conversion into a police station the building opened in 1872.[262] The address was shown as Cranbrook Road, Barkingside and was under the supervision of a sergeant.[263]

In 1881 the population of Barkingside was over 2,000 people,[264] and in 1890 there were two inspectors, James Dickson and Thomas Saunders and 18 constables at the station.[265]

In 1900 two mounted officers were allocated to the station

Above left: The ten Batson Medals starting at left with the MBE and the Order of St. John of Jerusalem. The medal second from the right is the Police Long Service medal instituted in 1951. The medals are arranged in order.

Above right: Metropolitan Police Athletic Association Medal awarded to participants of the Barking to Southend road walk. This medal is dated 1938.

and a stable was erected in the yard.²⁶⁶ By 1939 there was a need to find additional accommodation to assist with overcrowding in the old police station. A bungalow across the road was rented to house the canteen, Special Constabulary and a lecture room.²⁶⁷

Barkingside Police Station, Cranbrook Road, Barkingside 1872-1964

In 1962 a pre-fabricated timber building was used as a temporary police station until the new one was built.²⁶⁸ This was used until 1964.

Mossford Cottage, The Forge and No. 2 Upper Cranbrook Road were purchased and demolished, and the new police station was erected on the now enlarged site. Station reception duties at Barkingside were performed from a portakabin near the old front entrance, where members of the public were seen.²⁶⁹ The address of the new police station was now 1 High Street, Barkingside and it opened for business in September 1964.²⁷⁰

Barkingside Police Station, 1 High Street, Barkingside 1964-2017. Below can be seen the extension opened in 1993

There was then a need to further expand the accommodation and deal with some structural problems within the building. The basement was also subject to flooding. The police purchased and eventually demolished the old cottages in Mossford Green situated between the police station and the recreational ground. This gave the station additional ground space for parking and expansion. Plans were made to add additional office space and a much-needed communications centre to the station. The building work commenced in 1991, when the senior staff and administration moved to the nearby (and recently-vacated) Chigwell Police Station. Chigwell had been used as the Area Headquarters, however they had transferred to the newly-built Edmonton Police Station. The new extension to Barkingside Police Station in effect doubled the size of the station, and was eventually opened in May 1993.

One of the last officers in charge of the division before Borough policing was implemented was Chief Superintendent Sidney Mackay. On promotion he transferred to Barkingside on 2 June 1989. It was one of the largest police divisions in the Metropolitan Police District at the time. Barkingside Division included Woodford, Chigwell, Loughton, Debden, Limes Farm, Hainault and Waltham Abbey. Chief Superintendent Mackay had a long and distinguished career, having served at a number of stations which included Bow Street. Together with other senior officers he retired from the police in 1995, at a time when there were financial incentives for them to do so. This coincided with re-organisation that involved cutting by half the superintending ranks of the force.

Chief Superintendent Sidney Mackay with his daughter, Constable Nina Mackay

260   Metropolitan Police Information Rights Unit accessed 25th January 2019.
261   Brown, B. (1993) Private correspondence, 22nd September 1993.
262   John Back Archive (1975) Metropolitan Police Museum, Charlton.
263   Metropolitan Police General Orders 1873.
264   Census records 1881.
265   *Kelly's Directory* 1890.
266   Metropolitan Police Surveyor's records (undated).
267   Ibid..
268   John Back Archive (1975) Metropolitan Police Museum, Charlton.
269   Elliott, B. (1993) *A History of the Police Stations of J Division 1886-1986*.
270   Metropolitan Police Orders 4th September 1964.

Chief Superintendent Mackay's daughter Nina tragically gave her life in 1997 when she was stabbed whilst attempting to detain a man during a search of a house in Newham. She was attached to the Territorial Support Group at the time. Her name appears on the Metropolitan Police Roll of Honour.[271]

In April 2000 the re-organisation of the Metropolitan Police into borough-based Operational Command Units (OCUs) reduced the status of this station and saw Chigwell, Loughton and Waltham Abbey removed from its area of responsibility. The borough headquarters was established at the newly-built Ilford Police Station.

Barkingside station was closed to the public in 2017 but it is still used for police purposes.

Barnes Police Station

London Borough of Richmond

Lonsdale Road (1892-1976)

102 Station Road (1976-2014)

V Division (1841-1985/86)

Richmond upon Thames Division /OCU (1985/86-1993/94)

Twickenham OCU (1993/94-2000)

Richmond upon Thames OCU (2000-2018/19)

South West BCU SW (from 2018/19)

Barnes Police Station was shown as a station on V or Wandsworth Division in 1841. There were no charging facilities and no space for cells at the cottage brought into use for police purposes. There was one sergeant, one acting sergeant and 15 constables. There were four day beats and ten night beats. There were also no stabling facilities for horses. The inspector at Richmond was expected to patrol the area and to visit each station to see that everything was in good order.[272]

In 1878 a cottage belonging to W. Lowther MP was rented at £25 per year for the purposes of a police station. The freehold to land was purchased by the police in 1887 for £575 and a station was rebuilt, at a cost of £4,038, on the site. This consisted of a police station and one set of married quarters. The section house can be seen on the photograph below, with the coal bunker leaning against it.

Rear access to Barnes Police station circa 1908, and below station yard showing the dog kennel and parade room

Barnes Police Station 1892-1976

The inspector's office was on the ground floor with a charge room, waiting room, store and two cells. There was also a larger association cell (often used for drunks) and a parade shed outside in the yard. On the first floor was a mess room, recreation room, bathroom, lavatory and a locker place, where the private property of police officers could be secured. At the back of the station, also on the ground floor, was a kitchen, scullery, boot room, drying room, clothes room, brushing room and a place to store paraffin lamps. In the basement was a coal cellar, coke cellar, seven water closets and a urinal. In the section house lived eight single constables who paid one shilling a week rent. This was deducted from their weekly pay.

In 1887 the Receiver sold a strip of land at the front of the station for £100 to the Mortlake District Highways Board for the purposes of road widening. There was a condition that the Board would make good the road and footways in an area known as 'The Jews Garden'.

In 1900 neighbours overlooking the station gave up their right to light to the Receiver, providing one shilling a year was paid to them.

One of the notable inspectors at Barnes was Sub Inspector William Feaver (warrant 54066), who by the time he retired in 1896 had spent over eight years at Barnes. His leaving celebration, held at the Bulls Head in Barnes, was attended by friends and colleagues including the police band, with Mr C.E. Morley making the presentation of a substantial cheque for £55 18s 2d. Mr Morley gave a short speech indicating this was a pleasant duty for him, and that he hoped the inspector would have many more years of life to enjoy his retirement. The inspector responded with thanks to those who contributed to this handsome present.[273]

In 1898 a strange incident occurred to a constable at Barnes who was patrolling near Kew Bridge, which clearly demonstrates the dangers of police work. Constable 411V Wear was walking his beat between Kew and Mortlake just before midnight in August when he detected a man in the bushes. He aimed a gun at him and shot the officer in the chest. The assailant made off, leaving the officer bleeding profusely on the ground. The bullet had passed through the body to the left of the heart, and once PC Wear was discovered he was rushed to Richmond hospital where he was critically ill. It was believed that Wear had discovered a potential burglar who was in the process of breaking into one of the isolated houses nearby. There was no real description of the suspect as this happened so quickly, and no-one was ever arrested for these crimes. However, later in the year, Constable Wear was presented with a testimonial in the shape of a silver cruet set by the Pioneer Sick and Provident Society (Mortlake) to commemorate his recovery.[274]

In 1907 the Conservators of the River Thames gave the Receiver permission to build a mooring above Barnes bridge to take a police launch for a nominal amount of one shilling annually.[275]

In 1924 the address of the station was shown as 371 Lonsdale Road, SW13.[276] There was correspondence in 1927 asking the Receiver if there were any objections to an advertisement noticeboard being placed on the flank wall of an adjoining building – the Bulls Head Public House. No objection was raised, and the boarding was erected.[277]

A property was also used in Barnes High Street for the purposes of repairing police motor vehicles, being rented from Sir Henry Lowther. The premises had originally been rented for £143 per annum from 1920, but were purchased from in 1930 for £3,593 15s[278] and its use as a police garage continued.

In May 1976 the New Barnes Police Station was opened. The old station was put up for sale and eventually sold for redevelopment, which was completed in 2004. The site now consists of a mixture of commercial and residential properties.[279]

Barnes Police Station 1976-2014

In March 2014 Barnes Police Station and the freehold site was sold for £10.005M to Berkeley Homes (Central London) Ltd.[280] A neighbourhood office was opened in Lowther Primary School on Stillingfleet Road, Barnes, to help cover the loss of the police station.[281]

Battersea Police Station

The London Borough of Wandsworth
118 Bridge Road (1861-1911)
112-118 Battersea Bridge Road (1907-2014)
V Division (1861-1923)
L Division (1923-1932)
W Division (1965-1985/86)
Battersea Division / OCU (1985/86-2013)
Borough of Wandsworth OCU (1993-2014)

The first records relating to situating a police station in Battersea came in 1858, when Superintendent Fenn of V Division reported that a piece of land near The Castle public house was available and suitable for erecting a police station. In February 1859 the Metropolitan Police Surveyor, Charles Reeves, recommended the purchase of the freehold land for £300. With the transaction completed, a new station was erected on the site.

Named Battersea Bridge Road Station, it was taken into service by V Division in January 1861[282] and was a sergeant-designated station. Situated at the corner of Battersea Bridge Road and Hyde Road (later Hyde Lane), this was a standard two-storey brick-built police station that cost £2,911 14s to build, including £700 worth of alterations. Upstairs was a Section House of five rooms for 13 single constables and one sergeant, who resided with his family in separate rooms.[283] The basement contained a kitchen and a mess room, where the constables could relax or take their refreshments.

Battersea Police Station 1861-1911

The station strength in 1864 was four sergeants and 20 constables. Of the four sergeants, two supervised the day duty shift whilst the remaining two were responsible for the night duty. Two of the sergeants (one by night and the other by day) were also required to ride one of the two horses stabled at the station, with the inspector or sergeant from Wandsworth patrolling Battersea, Merton and Tooting. The remaining

271 Martin Fido and Keith Skinner (1999) *The Official Encyclopedia of Scotland Yard*.
272 Metropolitan Police Special Police Orders 1864.
273 *The Police Review and Parade Gossip*, 24th July 1896.
274 *The Police Review and Parade Gossip*, August 19th and December 23rd 1898.
275 Surveyors' Records.
276 Metropolitan Police Surveyors' Records 1924.
277 Metropolitan Police Surveyors' Records.
278 Metropolitan Police Surveyors' Records 1924.
279 www.goddardmanton.com/projects/selected_projects.php?title=Barnes%20Police%20Station accessed 16th February 2012.
280 MPS (2018) Freedom of Information request – Land and property sold by the MPS for more than £1M.
281 MPS (2018) Freedom of Information request – MPS assets.
282 Metropolitan Police Orders dated 5th January 1861.
283 Metropolitan Police Surveyor's Records 1860.

sergeant was to stay in the station. Battersea was a charging station, with cells and records show that Merton and Tooting did not have such facilities and prisoners would have to be taken to the main station.[284]

In 1868 it became a sub-divisional station in its own right, and Inspector Samuel Egerton was sent from Wandsworth (the sub-divisional headquarters) to take charge of Battersea Bridge Road.[285] Egerton would have supervised his four sergeants (in 1864) to ensure that all the beats were covered 24 hours a day by the 20 constables. Duties would be planned in advance, and Battersea was split into two sections and had six day and 14 night beats. More police officers were allocated to the night duty shift in order to man the beats, and the times were determined by 'lighting up time' which was published in advance by Scotland Yard each year. There was little margin for error in terms of manning the beats since they matched exactly the numbers of constables available, so sickness meant sometimes that more than one beat would have been allocated to an individual constable or even covered by the mounted sergeant. Directions were given that sergeant(s) on duty at Battersea were not to leave the station.[286]

Metropolitan Police surveyors inspected the station in 1881 and reported that it was occupied by one single sergeant and 13 single constables, and that

'This station was originally designed for occupation by married officers. It is now wholly occupied by single men. The site is low, and subject to be flooded; the basement is damp, and it is therefore totally unfit for occupation.'[287]

The Commissioner appointed inspectors on division to inspect local common lodging houses and report annually to him. In Battersea the poorer classes were mainly concentrated in Little Europa Place, Currie Street, Ponton Road, Southampton Street West and Latchmere Grove. The inspector, after visiting the designated common lodging houses, would supply a report to the superintendent covering the conditions of the water supply, ventilation, privy accommodation and overcrowding.[288]

There were nine stations on the division, four covered by inspectors and five by sergeants. The station address at Battersea was shown as 118 Bridge Road, Battersea,[289] and its call sign for the telegraph which was connected to Scotland Yard was Bravo Sierra (BS).[290] Above the station lived Inspector Albany J. Ollett, his wife and their five children. Next to them was a section house containing five single constables.[291]

Battersea Bridge Road was built with three cells, but by 1888 these were considered insufficient due to the large numbers of prisoners being arrested and application was made for a further two cells.[292] A much larger association cell (drunk tank) and another cell were added. This showed that the numbers of prisoners were increasing and that insufficient space was available to house them. There were two stations in Battersea itself, the other being located on W Division and called Battersea Park Road.

By 1907 the address had changed to 112-118 Bridge Road, SW, with the purchase of some adjacent properties. Such was the state of the old station that since 1901 the drains would over-flow and flood the basement whenever there was a downpour or if the Thames flooded, causing sewerage to seep in. This led to a number of officers contracting diphtheria and typhoid fever. The gas lamps were also criticised, as many were faulty and some were dangerous.[293] Battersea Police Station became a passing station for the Public Carriage Office, which for a short period was responsible for the supervision of taxi drivers in London. Because the taxi business was on the increase a more permanent site was selected, so the passing station was moved from Battersea to another station.

In 1907 a new, much larger station was built on the site by F.G. Minter, Contractors of Putney, together with a section house and one set of married quarters.

Battersea Police Station, 112-118 Battersea Bridge Road, 1907-2014

In September 1914 Constable 78886 George Johnson was on his patrol near a railway line when he was accidentally knocked down by a passing train, dying from his injuries.[294] A service funeral was held and many of his friends and colleagues were there. The Divisional Superintendent and his deputy also attended, as these events were paid for by the Police if the circumstances of the accident occurred on duty.

During the First World War aerial bombardment from German zeppelins and other aircraft caused the anti-aircraft battery to respond, but one unexploded shell hit Grosvenor Road railway bridge at Queen's Road,[295] with devastating effect.

The picture below shows the rear yard and back entrance to the station lit by a gas lamp fashioned in the typical police station lamp style.

The rear entrance to the police station showing a station lamp with white glass

In 1921 Wandsworth Sub-Division was shown as a station on L Division, although in 1932 it was transferred back to W Division when the boundaries on 4 District were revised.[296]

Records show that the section house was closed for renovation between March 1926 and July 1929, and then opened again for a short period. The section house was vacated again by residents in January 1932[297] and probably used as a temporary station whilst Battersea Police Station itself underwent improvement shortly afterwards in 1934. Because of its importance at the time, Lavender Hill (WL) was the Sub-Divisional station, with Battersea (WA) and Nine Elms (WN) as sectional stations. In charge at Lavender Hill was Sub-Divisional Inspector F. Nichols.[298] But this was not to remain like this, and whilst the station remained on W or Clapham Division by 1966, Superintendent H.G. White was in charge with WL and WN now as sectional stations.[299]

During the Second World War many stations were kept open, surrounded with sand bags and guarded by War Reserve constables. The duty shifts at most stations were also augmented by War Reserve constables, who would help to replace those officers who had left the Police to join the Colours. Many of the reserve were retired police officers who returned to duty until the end of the war. WRC Ernest Frank Hunt was killed by a flying bomb attack in 1944.[300]

In 1965 local authority boundaries were revised, and this meant changes in policing areas. Following these, Battersea was shown as a sub-divisional station with Putney and Tooting on W or Tooting Division.[301]

Battersea Police Station was vacated and put up for sale in 2013, and by January 2014 it had been sold for development for £6M.[302]

Beak Street Section House

40 Beak Street W1F 9RQ (1910-1999)

A new section house, designed by J Dixon Butler, was built near West End Central at 40 Beak Street W1 in 1909/10 and taken into use on 22 August 1910 for 88 unmarried officers from Great Marlborough Street and Vine Street Police Stations, with the rent being assessed at 1 shilling per week. It was at Beak Street shortly after Christmas 1918 where the first group of Women Metropolitan Police officers began their training.

Beak Street Section House 1910-1999

Many officers will have remembered the small cubicles, with partitions stopping well short of ceiling height, that comprised the personal living space here and in many other section houses of the period. The building also accommodated offices and other functions at various times. Recruitment candidates were interviewed here, including after the Second World War.

Records state that the building re-opened as a section house on 16 December 1957, with room for 75 officers and 13 junior cadets. Offices for the administration of central traffic process functions were located here for a period, and the newly-formed Diplomatic Protection Group had a temporary base here. When the section house had closed because of the standard of accommodation for single officers being raised, officers attended Beak Street for assessment centres and resettlement courses. The building was put up for sale at the end of 1998.

Beckenham Police Station (PB)

London Borough of Bromley

A cottage (1843-1882)

27 High Street (1882-2010)

Lait House Unit GO3C, Albermarle House,
  Albemarle Road, Beckenham (2010 to present)

R Division (1839-1865)

P Division (1865-1985/86)

Beckenham Division (1985/86-1993/94)

Bromley & Orpington OCU (PY) (1993/94 -2018/19)

South Area (SN) BCU (from 2018/19)

In September 1833, Alderman Wilson applied for Beckenham to be covered by the Metropolitan Police because of the number of robberies that were occurring in the area.[303] A diary held in Bromley Central Library refers to a loaded blunderbuss being recovered in a haystack near to Eden Cottage, perhaps indicating an intention to attack a Mr Oakley who used to travel home that way at 10.00pm each night.[304] One sergeant and seven constables were duly posted there as the result of the Metropolitan Police Act 1839, and a police station was taken into use from Midsummer 1843. It was described as a 'common brick, tile and slate built house with a two-stall stable, two cells and a wash house in the yard, with a garden behind occupied jointly by the sergeant and men'. The landlord was a Mr C. L. Wilson of The Cedars, Beckenham.[305]

In January 1864 Beckenham was part of R (or Greenwich) Division, with ten constables and two sergeants who

284 Metropolitan Police Special Order dated 1864.
285 Metropolitan Police Orders dated 13th July 1868.
286 Metropolitan Police Orders dated 11th January 1864.
287 Metropolitan Police Surveyors Report 1881 MEPO 2/234.
288 Metropolitan Police Annual Report 1874.
289 Metropolitan Police Orders dated 20th June 1884.
290 Metropolitan Police General Orders 1893.
291 Census 1881.
292 Receiver's List 1888.
293 LB 684 and MEPO 2/578.
294 Metropolitan Police Roll of Honour dated 2002.
295 Reay, W. T. (1919) *The Specials*. Heineman, London.
296 Metropolitan Police Orders dated 1st January 1932.
297 Metropolitan Police Surveyor's Records 1924.
298 Districts and Divisions 1937.
299 Metropolitan Police List 1966.
300 The Metropolitan Police Roll of Honour dated 2002.
301 Metropolitan Police Orders dated 6th August 1964.
302 MPS (2018) Freedom of Information request – Police station closures broken down by year.
303 *South London News* 11 October 1970, 'A Police Station's History'.
304 Back, John 1975. Beckenham Police Station Metropolitan Police Heritage Centre.
305 Back, John 1975. Beckenham Police Station Metropolitan Police Heritage Centre.

patrolled either on foot or on horseback. In October 1865, a reorganisation of boundaries transferred these officers away from their R Division inspector at Lewisham to become part of P Division (Camberwell). Instructions were given that the Lewisham inspector was to patrol the areas of Beckenham, Sydenham, Bromley and Farnborough. He was not to perform station duty as his time would be spent moving between the stations, where he would sign the occurrence book on each visit.

The station strength was one sergeant who would patrol the stations on a horse and who would supervise the twelve night duty constables. An acting sergeant would supervise the four day duty constables, and post them to their beats.[306] The constables would meet the sergeant at pre-arranged times and locations on their beats. Failure to rendezvous would cause alarm and concern for the missing officer's safety.

In 1876 the Metropolitan Police Surveyor reported that the station well had been contaminated by nearby cesspools, and recommended that it be connected to the nearby water mains.[307] By 1881, Beckenham station was described as 'an old dilapidated cottage'. The bedrooms were 'damp and ill-ventilated'. The cells in the yard were also damp, and the roof said to be dangerous. Beckenham and seven other buildings were found to be 'dilapidated, unsatisfactory and unsuitable for the purpose they have to serve'.[308]

In September 1882 the freehold of a site at 27 (renumbered in 1934 as 45) High Street, Beckenham) was purchased, where a new station was taken into use on 25 May 1885. The land had been bought for £950, and the building costs had amounted to £4,022 12s 1d. The new building incorporated an inspector's office, charge room, waiting room and a store on the ground floor, along with two cells and a larger association cell. There was also a day room, mess room, kitchen, scullery, a clothes room and scullery.

Beckenham Police Station 1882-2010

A hay-loft was provided over the two-stall stable in the yard, along with a parade shed, where officers were inspected before going out on patrol.[309]

Because accommodation was part of the remuneration of police officers, the residential parts of the police station were assessed separately from the operational part of the building. In November 1878, for instance, the inspector's accommodation at Beckenham was rated as 4s 9d per week.[310]

The station code in 1893 was 'BC', and this was not altered until the 1930s during a general re-organisation by Commissioner Lord Trenchard.[311]

In 1929 Beckenham Urban District Council increased the height of the wall at the back of Beckenham station yard as part of a development to provide flats for firemen.[312]

In 1964 Beckenham was shown as a sectional station with Penge and Bromley sub-divisions on P Division.[313] Beckenham was part of Southend Village (Catford) sub-division in 1932, but from 1 April 1965 both Penge and Beckenham became part of Bromley sub-division when boundaries were changed to become aligned with the new London borough boundaries.[314] Further re-organisation of internal boundaries took place in 1974.[315] The station closed in 2010 to be replaced by an office at Albermarle House, Albemarle Road Beckenham.

Bedfont Police Station

The London Borough of Hounslow
Staines Road, Bedfont
T Division (1868-1932)

In 1807 the parish constable was Edmund Betts, low-born as he could not read or write but who would serve summonses at 4d a time.[316] Parish constables were usually appointed yearly, but those who did not want the job would sub-contract the employment, often to the cheapest bidder. By 1834 the parish constable had changed to a school teacher whose responsibility was to ensure that the cage at Feltham had enough straw on the floor. He was required to purchase 'a truss of straw' and claim the cost of 10d back from the vestry.[317]

The local court heard some cases from Bedfont. In 1837, for instance, during the Ascot Races two men took over the toll house, refusing to pay the toll and locking the toll keeper up. He remained there for a while until the horse patrol arrived and set him free. When one of the assailants appeared on his return from the races he was identified to the police, arrested and prosecuted.[318]

In 1872 a man who was begging in High Road, Feltham had been given a sovereign by the magistrate but continued to beg and was brought before the justice and sentenced to one month's hard labour.[319] A regular occurrence (and often a dangerous one) along the main Staines road was that drivers of small carts would fall asleep at the reins. For this, a man was fined 10 shillings. Most accidents that occurred on the roads were caused by the drivers of small carts and their reckless or irresponsible use. A driver falling asleep meant that a horse could be spooked by other vehicles or people, and runaway carriages were a fairly frequent and dangerous occurrence.

A man arrested at the Railway Arms public house for being drunk and disorderly was being taken back to the station when his friend tried to rescue his mate from custody. The friend even resorted to throwing stones at the officer's helmet. Both were sentenced to 14 days' imprisonment.[320]

On 13 January 1840 the parish of Feltham became part of the T Division (or 16th Company) policed from Staines, although the Bow Street horse patrols (now part of the Metropolitan Police) continued to have a station at Bedfont until Lady Day 1887, separate from the police station. The horse patrol station situated in the Staines Road, Bedfont was rented from Mr Francis Newborn of Bedfont for the annual sum of £28. There were three sets of married quarters there where constables would live, and they each paid one shilling a week rent.[321] The horse patrol station acted as the principal police station in the area until the new one was built in 1866.

The horse patrol station was still in use in 1881, and was described as 'two semi-detached cottages on the roadside' which were occupied by two constables and their families. Regular complaints were made from them as the cesspool leaked, providing unhygienic odours in the yard at the rear.³²² The horses were housed to the side of each building and had a hay loft for the storage of equipment and fodder.

The pair of cottages of the Bedfont horse patrol station

Not all the new recruits were of the calibre desired, such as Constable John Moore, who in January 1842 was dismissed 'for entering the police service under an assumed Christian name, having been previously in custody for pot-stealing'.³²³

The parish of Feltham then comprised 2,620 acres and a population in 1851 of 1,109 people, but ten years later it was 1,837, spread throughout some 306 homes. The increase of population arose partly from the facilities of railway communication with London, and partly from the establishment of industrial and Welsh schools.³²⁴ In 1854 an industrial school was built in Feltham, opening in 1859 as the more respectable-sounding Middlesex Industrial School, but was in fact a Reformatory for 1,000 boys aged between 7-14 years connected with crime sentenced from one to three years in lieu of transportation. In 1910 this became the second borstal in the UK, and today it is a prison and young offenders' institution.

Land on which to build Bedfont Police Station had been purchased by the Receiver from Mr George Daws for £360 in June 1866. Construction of a new purpose-built police station commenced later the same year, and was completed for occupation on Christmas Eve 1868. The new station was erected adjoining The Load of Hay public house, at a cost of £2,185.³²⁵ It had a charge room and three cells, and was an inspector-designated station with an inspector's office situated on the ground floor. There was also a general wash house on the ground floor store and three coal cellars. In the yard was a three-stall stable with hay loft.

Bedfont Police Station 1868-1932

The inspector was allowed five rooms to rent at the station, which cost him 6s 6d per week. There was a slight revision of the sub-divisional boundary upon the opening of a new station at Hatton(s) Road, Harlington in September 1870.³²⁶ There were three horses located at Bedfont in the stables,³²⁷ and they had to patrol the 22 square miles of the sub-division.

Living at Bedfont Police Station in 1871 was Hackney-born 37-year-old constable William Andrews, his wife Susan and their family. Andrews had recently witnessed a change of senior officer in charge at Bedfont Police station, when Inspector George Bush became the officer in charge of the sub-division although he did not live at the police station. Instead, he lived at no. 57 with his wife and three children.

By 1878 Bush was no longer there, and most likely had retired from the service. Next door was Sergeant John Laver with his wife and three children. The police wives and families were a close community and helped each other out with chores, or when there were problems.

Further along the road, at 117, was Sergeant Charles Salter who lived with his wife and family. Constable Frederick Farley from Mile End, who was widowed, lived at 116 with his four children, his 16-year-old niece helping out by looking after the children.³²⁸

A line up of the Bedfont police in the 1880s

306 Metropolitan Police Special Police Orders 1869.
307 Metropolitan Police Surveyor's records 1878.
308 Metropolitan Police Surveyor's records 1881.
309 John Back (1975) Beckenham police station. The Metropolitan Police Heritage Centre.
310 Metropolitan Police Surveyor's Records 1881.
311 Metropolitan Police General Orders 1893.
312 John Back (1975) Beckenham police station. The Metropolitan Police Heritage Centre.
313 Metropolitan Police Orders 6th August 1964.
314 John Back (1975) Beckenham police station. The Metropolitan Police Collection, Charlton.
315 Metropolitan Police Orders 12th July 1974.
316 *The Job*, 14th January 1983 p13.
317 Ibid..
318 Ibid..
319 Ibid..
320 Ibid..
321 Metropolitan Police Surveyor's Records, London.
322 Condition of Police Stations 1881.
323 Brown, B. (1997) 'Policing Old Feltham'. Metropolitan Police Museum.
324 John Marius Wilson (1870-72) *Imperial Gazetteer of England and Wales*.
325 Metropolitan Police Surveyor's Records, London.
326 Brown, B. (1997) 'Policing Old Feltham'. Metropolitan Police Museum.
327 Metropolitan Police Surveyor's Records, London.
328 Census 1871.

By December 1872 Bedfont was considered to be important enough to be connected to the new telegraph system, and was given the identification station code letters 'BE'.[329] The telegraph enabled quick communication between Scotland Yard and the station. Sergeants were trained to use the telegraph initially, but later reserve constables took over the task. The address was shown as Staines Road, Bedfont and along this road lived other police officers and their families.

In 1881 Warwickshire-born Joseph Hughes (warrant no. 46722) was the inspector in charge of Bedfont Police Station, where he lived above the station with his wife Ann and their two children. The address was shown as 66 Staines Road, Bedfont and also resident were two married constables, Joseph Webb with his wife and their two children, together with John Bluekwill and his wife.[330]

Tragedy struck Hughes, who was a busy officer and held in high esteem, whilst in 1882 returning from Sunbury court when he was thrown from his horse and killed.[331] There were no witnesses to the accident, and the startled horse was grazing nearby.[332] His police service funeral was attended by most of the station and members of the whole of T Division were present, before Hughes was buried in the churchyard at St. Mary's Church, Bedfont. A headstone was purchased by the police of T Division as a mark of the respect and esteem in which that Inspector Hughes was held. The inspector's quarters at the station were vacated within a short while, rendering the family not only fatherless but also homeless. Ann would have received a lump sum of money from the insurance scheme her husband had paid into together with a gratuity from the police, which would tide her over.

Even at the newly-built Bedfont station its well in the yard was found to be polluted, and this was meant to supply fresh drinking water to the inspector and two constables and their families. Instructions were given to sink a new well to provide suitable drinking water.[333] At this time the police in general were constantly aware that drunkenness was a problem amongst the constables, and they often chose to drink 'fermented near beer', which provided a suitable and safer alternative to polluted water.

Also living at Bedfont in 1881 was 38-year-old Inspector William Barrett from Sidmouth, with his wife Sarah and three children.[334] Barrett is shown below on his horse, whilst on his patrol. He was stationed at Bedfont police station where he remained until he left in 1894 on retirement.

Inspector Barrett of Bedfont from 1881 to 1894 on his horse patrol

In 1884 there was room for one married inspector and two married constables residing at the station, although this was rather cramped. The surveyors replaced the polluted well by having pipes laid by the local water company for the supply of fresh water.[335]

In 1892 Sub-Divisional Inspector James Morsley (warrant no. 49647) was the officer in charge of the station, which then had a strength of four sergeants and 20 constables.[336] Morsley resigned on pension in May 1894.[337] Taking over from him was Sub-Divisional Inspector 55187 Frederick Foster, who only remained for a short while; until May 1898. Foster, from Deal in Kent, had been posted to T Division and lived in Hammersmith in 1891 with his wife and two children. He had already been stationed at Bedfont for some time as an inspector, and received promotion on Morsley's resignation. In due course Foster's position was taken by Sub-Divisional Inspector 65779 Henry Herwin, who lived at the station with his wife Caroline and their son and four daughters. Herwin remained for ten years, retiring on pension in July 1907 and is shown in the centre of the group pictured below, and inset.

Coronation celebrations at Bedfont Police Station in 1902

Sergeant John Neville and his wife and family lived in Victoria Road, Staines in 1901. Sergeant George Sallows and his wife and seven children lived in George Street, Staines in the same year. At the same time Sergeant Richard Chamberlain, his wife and four children lived in London Road, Staines, and Station Sergeant Edward Hagarty, his wife and family lived nearby in Argyle Cottages, where a number of other police families were resident such as Sergeant Albert Kidd, his wife Jane and their four children.

As the areas of Staines, Feltham, Ashford and Bedfont were rapidly expanding due to the influx of people and the building of houses, it was necessary to re-organise policing arrangements for the Spelthorne area. As such, in January 1907 Bedfont sub-division was renamed the Staines sub-division, with the unfortunate Inspector Mott being dismounted upon his transfer to the latter station. At that time the urban district of Feltham consisted of 1,790 acres and now had a population of 5,315. In 1908 Harry Smith took over as Sub-Divisional Inspector of the new Staines sub-division, even though he was located at Bedfont.

Bedfont had two sectional stations, located at London Road, Staines and Bath Road, Harlington. There were 150 men and nine horses attached to the sub-division. The pay for the stations was brought on a Wednesday by the Sub-Divisional Inspector on a horse, but later this was replaced by a pony and trap. When motorcycle combinations were introduced the sub-divisional inspector would carry out the same duty using a motorcycle and the divisional clerk would use the sidecar.

One police officer out on patrol recalled that he saw his inspector riding his horse and saw him ride up the steps to The Hounds public house (now The Bulldog at Ashford), order and drink a pint of beer whilst still astride the horse and then reverse down the steps and continue his patrol.

A police telephone box was installed in 1904 between Bedfont Police Station and the fixed point at the junction of Hanworth Road and High Street, Feltham. Here a constable was stationed continuously day and night in all weathers, until replaced by the new Dr Who TARDIS-style box which appeared during the 1930s.[338] There were five such police boxes in Feltham, at the following locations:

T8   Hatton Cross, Great South West Road/Hatton Road
T9   Staines Road/Hounslow Road
T10 Hanworth Road, Front of Urban District Council Offices
T11 Staines Road, Old Bedfont Police Station
T12 Ashford Road/Lower Sunbury Road. Lower Feltham

Up until 1908 Bedfont was a sub-division without responsibility for any other areas, however it acquired Harlington and Staines as sectional stations by 1910.[339] In 1908 Sub-Divisional Inspector Harry Smith was in charge of the sub-division, a post he held until 1915.[340] The following is a brief extract from the writings of Inspector Smith, on his posting to Bedfont in 1908:

Sub Divisional Inspector Smith

'After a course of equitation I was in 1908 appointed as Sub-Divisional Inspector (mounted) in charge of what is known as Staines Sub-Division. This comprised an area of some 40 square miles with three stations, over 100 men, and nine horses and with occasional charge of the adjoining Sub-Division of Hampton with four stations and 150 men. This entailed long and arduous hours of duty.'

Inspector Smith stayed at Bedfont until 1915 when he retired on doctor's advice and joined the Volunteer Home Defence. It was whilst serving with them that he was awarded the bronze medal of the Royal Society for the Protection of Life from Fire and also the Meritorious Service Medal for saving the life of a flying officer from his crashed and burning plane whereby he himself sustained injury. It was about this period that the large Feltham marshalling yards were built, mainly by prisoners of war.[341]

Hanworth Park House, originally the home of Lord Lafone, was used as a hospital for injured troops returning from the war, and many local ladies helped out at the hospital during this time. St. Anthony's Catholic Orphanage was at Bedfont, and St. Theresa's was a home for inebriate women near the Crown and Sceptre. Ashford hospital was at this time a workhouse, and this was in fact what it was originally built for.

In 1931 the districts of Bedfont and Feltham were being policed from Harlington police station.

The town's magistrate's court was built as a town hall in 1903 when the growing town of Feltham became separated from the Rural District of Staines to become an Urban District in its own right.

Constable Jimmy Payne at Bedfont in 1921 recalled;

'There were two beats at the Station at this time and they were set 12 hour beats designed to be covered in a regular way, but as the officers only did an 8 hour day they had to be covered as best they could. One should remember that a lot of the roads were long and only lead to a single farm. Also at this time there were only four or five men on the street at one time, one of these was posted to a fixed post at the High Street, junction with Bedfont Lane. There were no Police Cars at this time in this area. There were some police boxes however, one of these was in the High Street near Wilton Parade. Communications were a little old fashioned by today's standards. Bedfont had a direct (telephone) line to Staines and communication with Harlington was by way of Telegraph. Internal despatches were carried by the mounted men until about 1925 when the good old bikes took over.'[342]

In 1930 the neighbouring villages of Bedfont and Hanworth were incorporated into the Urban District of Feltham.[343]

Dead bodies were dealt with and removed by Police using a hand-ambulance, and this was sometimes also used to convey persons from as far as Stanwell to Hounslow hospital.[344]

Oil lamps were carried by the Police during the hours of darkness and these were covered by a shutter when not in use, or in rainy weather. When the cape was being worn one can imagine the smell that came from the uniforms. Refreshments were taken out on the street wherever you happened to be at the appointed time; tea was carried in a small container with a meths burner underneath and brewed up on the roadside. There was no refreshment period for men on night duty. It is remembered by several officers that when walking out to Bedfont they found that the walking was very hard, with many tracks and unmade roads to walk along.

Houses in the Bedfont area could be brought from about £400, and there are several ex-officers who took the plunge in buying their own house, often not in the reach of many families, who had to rely on rented accommodation. Pay at this time had increased to about £3 per week, which apparently was not too bad for the time.[345]

In the early 1920s there was a footpath known as Lovers' Lane, across the High Street at the junction of Manor Lane which ran to the airpark opposite. This was closed to the public when the War Department built the houses on what is

329 Brown, B. (1997) 'Policing Old Feltham'. Metropolitan Police Museum.
330 Census records 1881.
331 www.rollofhonour.org/forces/england/metropolitan/metropolitan_roll_1829-1899.htm accessed 5th January 2013.
332 *Pall Mall Gazette*, 28th November 1882.
333 Condition of Stations 1881.
334 Census records 1881.
335 Condition of stations survey 1884.
336 *Kelly's Hertfordshire and Middlesex Directory* 1894.
337 Ibid.
338 Brown, B. (1997) 'Policing Old Feltham'. Metropolitan Police Museum.
339 *Kelly's Directory* 1910.
340 Ibid..
341 'Local History of Police: Bedfont and Feltham' (date and author unknown), London.
342 Ibid.
343 www.hounslow.info/libraries/local-history-archives/discover-hounslow/#fel accessed 24th December 2012.
344 'Local history of Police: Bedfont and Feltham' (date and author unknown), London.
345 Ibid.

now the junction of Elmwood Avenue. This caused an uproar amongst the residents, and a local businessman named Parker supplied a very large crowd with pieces of wood and iron, resulting in the breaking down of the wall, and once opened the road remained that way.

Receiving gratuities from local businessmen in line with instructions needed to be reported to the Commissioner, and whilst it was accepted that local people wanted to show their appreciation this should be done by supporting a charity like the orphanage at Twickenham. In line with this policy, in 1932 the then Commissioner Viscount Byng stopped the Bedfont Police from receiving an annual gift from Mr. David Waring of either tea or tobacco at Christmas time.

At 6.00am on Monday, 16th November 1932 the Police facilities at Bedfont old station were withdrawn and transferred to Feltham, which would be a Sectional Station of Staines Sub-Division. However this produced a local outcry, and calls for the station to be reinstated. As soon as war was declared Bedfont opened again.

Just prior to the WW2 Constable Walter Woods at Bedfont was awarded the King's Police Medal for bravery after rescuing two men from a fume-filled sewer in Uxbridge Road.

At the outbreak of the war a further four sergeants and 56 constables, who were either Specials or War Reserves, reported for duty but the numbers soon dwindled as many were called up for active service. At this time, regular serving officers could only volunteer as air crew.[346]

In Hatton Road recreation ground during the war an anti-aircraft unit (AAU) had been built, consisting of four 3.7AA guns, and later a Bofors gun was added. This is well remembered by everyone in the area especially, when they opened up on the enemy above. Several landmines were reported to have landed in the area during the war, and a 'doodle-bug' landed in Florence Road. The only bomb to land on the Allied Estate in Lower Feltham fell right outside the house of a police officer.[347]

Police officers, whether they were re-engaged pensioners, War Reserve or full-time paid Special Constables would be called out to unexploded bombs when they were reported, and one consequence of having an AAU nearby was occasionally their shells failed to explode and returned to earth, often providing fatal consequences to inquisitive young boys seeking mementoes from the aerial battles overhead.

The station was pulled down in 1952 to make way for a block of police flats. In the revision of boundaries which took place on 1st April 1965[348] Feltham, which took over the policing of Bedfont, was shown then as a sectional station of Hounslow Sub-Division.

In 1973 a new sectional police station for Feltham opened and this replaced Bedfont. The old temporary station at Feltham was replaced with a new, but very cube-like, unimaginative building, that became operational at 6.00am on Monday, 8th October, the address being 34 Hanworth Road.[349] With the formation of Airport Division, certain other boundary changes took place with T Division.

In 2013 a Safer Neighbourhoods Unit was based in Bedfont.

Belgravia Police Station

202-206 Buckingham Palace Road (1993 to Present)
No. 8 Area (1993)
No. 1 Area (Central) (1993-94)
Belgravia Division / OCU (1993/94-2018/19)
Central West Basic Command Unit from 2018-19

Opened in 1993 as newly-built police station, Belgravia became the headquarters of the policing of South Westminster, covering the areas of the former Bow Street, Cannon Row, Charing Cross, Rochester Row and Gerald Road stations. Gerald Road and Rochester Row divisions had amalgamated on 1st October 1989. The station was built in just over two years and cost about £7m.[350]

Belgravia Police Station from 1993, 202-206 Buckingham Palace Road

It was to Belgravia Police Station that Eric Joyce, Labour MP for Falkirk, was taken after a disturbance in the Strangers Bar in the Houses of Parliament in February 2012. Mr Joyce later pleaded guilty to assault and provides an example of how junior police officers are sometimes called to arrest and deal with offenders regardless of their position in life.

Members of Parliament have been found indulging in dishonourable behaviour a number of times. Horatio Bottomley MP was the Liberal member for Hackney South from 1906 to 1912. He commenced publication of John Bull, a patriotic journal. He started the John Bull Victory Bond Club, a forerunner of premium bonds, and had a great talent in persuading people to spend their money on the bonds. A mixture of fraud and mismanagement resulted in the collapse of the scheme, his conviction for fraud, a sentence of seven years' imprisonment and his expulsion from Parliament. In 1972 Reginald Maudling, the Conservative Home Secretary, resigned when the Metropolitan Police commenced fraud investigations against John Poulson, a bankrupted property developer and architect whom Maudling had assisted to win contracts.

Officers in the nearest operational police station to the Houses of Parliament are likely to reflect, more than most, upon the importance of separating politics from the operation of the criminal law. This principle, perhaps set out most explicitly in the Police Act 1964 that dealt with the separate roles of Chief Officers, Police Authorities and the Home Secretary, will no doubt continue to give food for thought, particularly since 2012 when elected Police Commissioners have taken over the role of Police Authorities outside London.

In 2019 Belgravia acted as the base for Westminster's operational response teams.

Belvedere Police Station (RB)

London Borough of Bexley
33 (renamed 15 in 1931) Woolwich Road, Belvedere
(1881-1968)
2 Nuxley Road, Belvedere (1968-2018)
R Division (1864-1985/86)
Bexleyheath Division / OCU (1985/86-2000)
Bexley OCU (2000-2018/19)
South East BCU SE (from 2018/19)

In August 1878 R Division's Superintendent H Baynes submitted a report about a police station for Lessness Heath. Police Orders of 8th October 1881 indicate that from that date the new premises were taken into police use, the address being 33 Woolwich Road, Belvedere.[351]

The cost of the land had been £275, and the station itself £3,386. The ground floor of the new station comprised a waiting room, charge room, three cells, a store and a lamp room, and there was also a mess room, kitchen, and a brushing room where officers could maintain their uniforms. A right of way was negotiated over a private road leading into Albert Road, one of the legal details that often had to be negotiated for developing such premises.

An Inspector Andrew Meering (who joined on 29th August 1864, warrant no. 45200) was transferred to take charge of the new station, with two other inspectors, two sergeants and one acting sergeant. A Mounted Branch officer joined them on transfer from Blackheath Road, Greenwich.

Andrew Meering had himself been posted to mounted duty earlier in his career on M (Southwark) Division as a sergeant in 1869. Police Orders of 3rd December 1879 announced that he had been given a reward of £1 in connection with a case he had worked on. At this time such monetary rewards were frequent, sometimes originating from a grateful victim of crime after approval by the Commissioner. The rewards from the Police Fund appear to have been balanced by monetary punishments for poor discipline.

Belvedere Police Station 1881-1968

Superintendent Meering finished his service as the officer in charge of J Division (Bethnal Green), and retired on an annual pension of £266 15s 4d on 1st March 1895.[352] He had finished as one of 32 superintendents within the Metropolitan Police, aged 49. The physical nature of the job in the lower ranks was reflected by the fact that only two constables and sergeants still serving at the end of 1895 had managed to serve more than thirty years, having joined before 1864.[353]

The living accommodation for officers who lived at the new Belvedere station was assessed for rent purposes as 3s 6d per week for inspectors, 2s per week for sergeants and 1s per week for constables. These sums of money were in effect the rent charged to police officers for their accommodation.

The rear of the police station, showing a garden where fruit and vegetables were cultivated for the families living in the station accommodation

In October 1921, Bexley became the sub-divisional headquarters in place of Belvedere, causing it to be renamed as Bexley sub-division. Sub-Divisional Inspector Frederick Lummus took command there, at the rate of pay of 96 shillings (£8) per week.[354] He had originally been a groom from Ampthill, Bedfordshire who had joined the Metropolitan Police on 20th November 1899 (warrant no. 85747) at the age of 22, and had served initially on M Division (Southwark). He had been promoted to sergeant in 1905, station sergeant in 1909, inspector in 1912, and sub-divisional inspector in March 1919. When he retired in November 1924 after serving three years at Bexley he was awarded a pension of £262 11s per year.[355]

By 1931 the station was located on R or Greenwich Division, and its postal address had varied to 15 Woolwich Road, Belvedere in Kent.[356]

From April 1958 until 26th July 1965 Belvedere was a police station that closed at night.[357] In 1959 a site for a new police station was identified 200 yards away, opposite All Saints Parish Church at the corner of Nuxley Road with Woolwich Road, where an empty Church of England school had been due to be demolished and replaced by four houses. In due course the new police station opened on that site, on 13th May 1968.[358]

346 'Local History of Police: Bedfont and Feltham' (date and author unknown).
347 Ibid.
348 Metropolitan Police Orders dated 6th August 1964.
349 Metropolitan Police Orders dated 5th October 1973.
350 Belgravia Police Station – Commemorating the Official Opening. Metropolitan Police.
351 National Archives MEPO 5/51 (394).
352 Pension certificate. National Archives MEPO 21/24.
353 Commissioner's Annual Report 1895 Table No 7.
354 Metropolitan Police Orders dated 10th March 1919.
355 National Archives refs: Pension Certificate – MEPO 21/55; Certificate of service MEPO 4/418.
356 *Kirchner's Police Index* 1931.
357 Metropolitan Police Orders dated 1st April 1958 and 23rd July 1965.
358 Correspondence LB 532/-/0 and LB 532/67/1.

Belvedere Police Station 1968-2018

The former school on the site and its church connections was ironic; the older Belvedere station was referred to by some as 'the chapel on the hill' because of prayer meetings held by officers posted there.[359]

The new station contained police station offices, a CID suite, a charge room, two detention rooms, three cells, a writing room and a meal room with facilities for cooking meals. The cost of the new building was £70,000. The exterior was faced with dark brown bricks to blend in with surrounding buildings, and had an oil-fired central heating system. The architects were J. Innes Elliott, with Mr S.J. Hanchet from the Chief Architect and Surveyor's Department in charge for the Metropolitan Police.

Belvedere remained under the command of an Inspector when a reorganisation in 1965 created Chief Inspector or Inspector units for police stations in the outer parts of the Metropolitan Police District.[360] In 1999 there were reduced opening hours at the station due to a shortage of civil staff. The station closed and was being developed for alternative use in 2018. The Station was sold to Homeland London Ltd for £1.230M on 28th March 2018.[361]

Bethnal Green Police Station

243 Bethnal Green Road (1840-1860)

Church Street, Bethnal Green (1860-1894)

458 Bethnal Green Road (1894-1998)

12 Victoria Park Square (1998-2018/19)

K Division (1840-1860)

J Division (1894-1933)

H Division (1933-1985/86)

Bethnal Green Division (1985/86-1993/94)

Whitechapel Division / OCU (1993/94-2018/19)

Tower Hamlets OCU (1993-2018/19)

Basic Command Unit Central East (CE) (with the London Borough of Hackney) (2018/19 to present)

The history of Bethnal Green and its division is an interesting if not complex example, because planners made errors when considering how the local area was going to be policed. Records show permission was granted to build a police station on a plot of land at 243 Bethnal Green Road in December 1860. The freehold to this land was purchased in 1860 for £1,400, and the construction of the station cost £2,660.

When the station was built it was a fine example of a Victorian police station house, which could provide living accommodation for fourteen single constables who resided in the section house. Additionally, the station also provided quarters for a married constable and his family, who were allocated three rooms, and a married Inspector and his family who resided in four rooms. The inspector was probably the chief officer in charge of the station. In 1868 reference was made to the purchase of a portion of freehold land and the cost of building a police station for £9,000 at 458 Bethnal Green Road. The sale was finalised in 1869. According to records, Bethnal Green was shown as a station on K Division with a strength of one inspector, nine sergeants and 66 constables.[362]

However, the building of such a station did present rather a problem as there appear to have been two police stations in Bethnal Green, albeit they were on different divisions.[363] The Orders stated "The police of H Division are to take up and occupy the new police station at Church Street Bethnal Green on the 9th January".[364] This is strange, as Church Street is the Shoreditch end of Bethnal Green, whilst the other station is located near the junction with the Great Cambridge Road at the other end of the Bethnal Green Road. Research indicates that there was a station at the Church Street site, because the K Divisional Superintendent makes mention of the fact in his Divisional account published in the Commissioner's Annual Report of 1871. The Bethnal Green Road of today was only half its length in 1860, with the Shoreditch end being called Church Street. The Church Street Police Station was located on the south side of the road opposite Turville Street, between Club Row and Swan Street.[365]

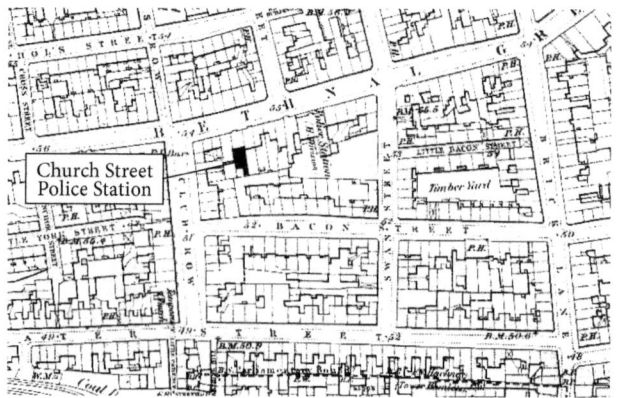

Site of the second Bethnal Green Police Station (1872)

Superintendent White said:

"A new station has been built, and is now occupied, situated in Church Street, Shoreditch. This is very commodious and much enhances the comfort of the men".[366]

Therefore, not only were there two police stations in Bethnal Green in 1871, but they were situated along the same road and were within one mile of each other. This was not the only planning error, because Hoxton Police Station (on N Division)[367] was situated just round the corner from the Church Street station.

In 1873 Bethnal Green was designated a station with an inspector in charge.[368] A revision of the divisional boundaries took place in 1886, altering the status of Bethnal Green Police Station to Divisional Headquarters responsible for Bethnal Green, Dalston, Hackney, Leytonstone, Woodford, Wanstead, Loughton, Chigwell and Barkingside. Supervision by the superintendent from Bethnal Green was essential, and this explains the presence of a stable at the rear of the station for lodging the horse, as this was the preferred mode of transport at the time.

The officer in charge of the station in 1881 was Inspector William Quigley, who resided at the station with his wife Sophia.[369] The Divisional Superintendent in 1888 was James

Keating, and he had control over 38 inspectors, 56 sergeants and 522 constables – a total 612 officers.[370]

In February 1894 the new station at Bethnal Green was completed and opened for business.[371] A section house also opened at the same time, with accommodation for 24 single men and one set of married quarters for the inspector.[372] In 1917 an administration section was completed at the new police station, and was occupied in June of the same year. It appears a third set of married quarters was added, with two sets of accommodation.

Bethnal Green Police Station, 458 Bethnal Green Road 1894-1995

The records show that Bethnal Green Police Station was located at 458 Bethnal Green Road, and it consisted of a station and a section house together with three sets of quarters. The section house is shown to occupy a site at the rear of the station, where it would appear that there was also a stable at the rear.[373] Bethnal Green lost its Headquarters status when in 1933 it became a sectional station of Bow Police Station after being transferred from J to H Division. During the Second World War an entrance was made in the yard of the police station to provide access to an air raid shelter belonging to the British United Shoe Machinery Company. The entrance was blocked up in 1948.

The Aliens Registration office was located on Bethnal Green Police Station area at Ainsley Street, Bethnal Green, and it remained there until 1951 when it moved to Piccadilly Place, W1. The office dealt with foreign seamen deserters.

Local Authority Boundary revisions in 1965 meant that Bethnal Green became a sectional station to Commercial Street Sub-Division, with Arbour Square as the Divisional Headquarters. However, by 1967 Sub-Divisional status was resumed when Leman Street Police Station shut for rebuilding. By this stage there were signs that the old station was no longer suitable for modern day policing, and plans were made to build a new modern station.

There is a detached police office located at 25 Brick Lane which is open to the public Sunday to Fridays, 10.00am to 6.00pm.[374]

In January 1994 the Divisions of Leman Street and Bethnal Green merged to become Whitechapel Division, without any revision of boundaries. In November 1995 both stations at Leman Street and Bethnal Green closed permanently, and all officers and functions transferred to the new station located at 12 Victoria Park Square E2.

Bethnal Green Police Station 12 Victoria Park Square, 1995 to present

The new station retained Bethnal Green as its title, with the code letters HT as its call sign.[375] In 2002 the records showed the name of the station as Bethnal Green – Tower Hamlets Borough Headquarters. The station is open 24 hours a day, 7 days a week.[376]

As of 2019 this was the only station left open for public access in Tower Hamlets.[377]

Bexleyheath Police Station (RY)

London Borough of Bexley

House opposite Twelfth Milestone (1840-1855/58)

28 Broadway, Main Road, Bexleyheath (1855/58-1907)

57 Broadway (1907-1994)

2 Arnsberg Way, Bexleyheath (1994 to present)

R Division (1840-1985/86)

Bexleyheath / Bexley Division / OCU (1985/86-2018/19)

Part of SE Basic Command Unit (2018-19)

The Bow Street horse patrol had established what could arguably be described as Bexleyheath's first police station, but the first Metropolitan Police building at Bexleyheath was opened in 1840. It was not purpose-built, but took the form

359 Bernard Brown, private correspondence.
360 Metropolitan Police Orders dated 16th March and 23rd July 1965.
361 Information rights MPS – Stations closed and sold for over £1M 2088-2018.
362 Metropolitan Police Orders dated January 1864.
363 Ordnance Survey Map, London Sheet 51 Shoreditch 1872.
364 Metropolitan Police Orders dated 6th January 1871.
365 Ordnance Survey Map, London Sheet 51 Shoreditch 1872.
366 Commissioner's Annual Report 1871.
367 Ordnance Survey Map, London Sheet 51 Shoreditch 1872.
368 Metropolitan Police General Orders 1873.
369 Census Records 1881.
370 *Dickens's Dictionary of London* (1888) pp197-99.
371 Metropolitan Police Orders dated 7th February 1894.
372 Ibid.
373 Metropolitan Police Surveyor's Records 1924.
374 www.met.police.uk/contact/phone.htm accessed 23rd March 2002.
375 Metropolitan Police Orders dated January 1994.
376 www.met.police.uk/contact/phone.htm accessed 23rd March 2002.
377 MPS station closures since 2010. Information Rights Unit MSP accessed 6th May 2019.

of a new house rented from a John Franklin for £28 a year, located opposite the Twelfth Milestone[378] (by the current Civic Centre). A sergeant was in charge, with nine constables.

There had been proposals from December 1839 to erect a new police station complete with cells to accommodate prisoners from Bexley and North Cray, and eventually this station superseded the 1840 house and became the third police station, built on the new High Road into Kent. The cost of the land had been £330 in 1852, and the building itself cost £1,452. Some records indicate that it opened in 1855,[379] but the Surveyor's Property Register[380] states 'Erected in 1858'.

Bexleyheath Police Station 1855/58-1907

The building featured a charge room, reserve room, mess, kitchen and two cells, whilst the first floor comprised a loft. The station's address became 28 Broadway, Main Road, Bexleyheath, but the building was eventually sold in February 1908 after the police station had been replaced.

The inspector in charge was based some miles away, at Shooters Hill. He was not designated for a particular station, but took overall charge of Shooters Hill, Bexley and Erith. In March 1865 the sub-division was enlarged, when it took in Eltham section from Lee sub-division, and in 1881 the sub-divisional headquarters was transferred to Belvedere.[381]

After 50 years, Bexleyheath's 1855 station had become inadequate. In fact a survey in 1881 revealed the inspector and his family to be living in a small wash-house or scullery, into which a water closet opened. There was much urgent work to be done to improve the sanitation and ventilation, including the need to cure a smoky chimney in the mess room. In due course a new site was found at the corner of the Broadway and Highland Road (also referred to as Dover Road) for Bexleyheath's fourth station. The land for the site was bought freehold by the Receiver in 1904 for £1,200. The new station was built for £8,187 and taken into use on 7th October 1907.[382]

The new premises were much larger than its predecessor. There was an inspector's office, and with the charge room were four cells, two of which were for women, a room for the matron who would supervise female prisoners, four cells and an association cell. A day room was provided for officers separate from the mess room, space for food lockers, a kitchen and a scullery. On the first floor was a library for the benefit of officers living at the station who needed somewhere for leisure pursuits. There were two sets of married quarters and accommodation for eleven unmarried men. It would be another decade before women police officers were first recruited.

Bexleyheath Police Rifle Club Winners 1913/14

The early twentieth century was marked by significant social and sporting activities on the part of police officers. Pictures from Bexley Central Library show the Bexley Rifle Club in 1913-14 with their trophies. Senior officers encouraged competition, especially with reference to accurate shooting and the advent of World War I.

The photograph below shows an R Division band playing, probably at a local sports day where officers took part in athletics, including tug of war.

The R Division police band with Superintendent shown without an instrument and with his hands on his hips

In July 1912 a list of police boxes were connected to the station by telephone, with locations at Wickham Lane (Welling), Mottingham Lane, Kidbrooke Green, Crayford and Bexley High Street, by the railway station.

By 1924 the Crayford area also hosted a box at Slade Green by Crayford Bridge. Police officers were given keys that would open the entrance door of these kiosks, and would use the telephone inside to send and receive messages from the police station, or as a convenient point for meeting the

Bexleyheath Police Station 1907-1994

sergeant or another constable. A light on the top of the boxes would flash when the station needed to contact patrolling officers. There was a small desk on which officers could write reports, and it would be possible for a police officer to keep a prisoner detained there until transport arrived to take them to the station. A telephone link to the police station was also available for public use.

The chain of boxes across the Metropolitan Police District was completed by 1937, supplemented in some central London locations, by police posts that performed similar, but more limited functions. By the late 1960s the increasing availability of domestic telephones, the introduction of personal radios and the greater use of motorised patrolling for police officers made these landmarks redundant. Despite their eventual removal, the image of the police box has been maintained in the public's imagination by the TARDIS time machine featured in the TV programme Doctor Who. An experimental modern version, equipped with CCTV, was installed near Earls Court in 1997.

The tendency to interchange the names of Bexley and Bexleyheath was resolved in Police Orders of 30th June 1961 when the name of the police station formally became Bexleyheath Police Station. The address was originally number 57, later 39, Broadway, Bexleyheath, Kent.

Finally, on 26th April 1994 the fifth police station for Bexleyheath opened at 2 Arnsberg Way, Bexleyheath to replace the one opened in 1907.[383]

Bexleyheath Police Station 1994 to present

In 2019, Safer Neighbourhood Teams based on council wards used fewer independent bases. Barnehurst, Bexleyheath, Crayford, Crook Log and West Heath ward units operated from Bexleyheath Police Station. Belvedere, Erith, Slade Green & Northend, and Northumberland Heath wards used Pier Road, Erith. East Wickham and Falconwood & Welling units used Bellegrove Road, Welling. Thamesmead East were based at Limestone Walk, Thamesmead, whilst the premises at Marlowe House Sidcup accommodated the units for Blackfen & Lamorbey, Blendon & Penhill, Longlands, Sidcup and St Mary's & St James.

Biggin Hill Police Station (PH)

London Borough of Bromley

Westerham Hill (Kent Police) closed in 1947

195 Main Road (1970-1999)

192-194 Main Road (2000 to present)

P Division (1947-1985/86)

Orpington Division (1985/86-1993/94)

Bromley & Orpington OCU (PY) (1993/94-2018/19)

South Area (SN) BCU (2018/19 to present)

The history and development of the farmland and countryside around the Aperfield estate took on a new impetus with the arrival of the Royal Air Force at Biggin Hill, particularly in World War II. The local authority was Orpington Urban District, which was policed by the Metropolitan Police, but Biggin Hill was policed by Kent Constabulary. The area was intended for transfer to the Metropolitan Police as early as 1932, but this was delayed by World War II; the transfer of 17 square miles finally took place on 1st April 1947. At this time Kent's Biggin Hill Police Station, probably a police house at Westerham Hill, was closed.

Biggin Hill Police Station

In 1966 plans began to be made for a police office to serve the rapidly-expanding housing developments in the area.

The Home Office approved the purchase of 195 Main Road, Biggin Hill as a police office, which duly opened on 29th June 1970 as part of the St Mary Cray sub-division on P Division, but closed around 1999. By August 2006 the house at 195 Main Road was due to be sold, and had been replaced by alternative premises a few hundred yards away at 192 Main Road, perhaps reflecting a trend towards using former retail premises rather than residential property. The office was then opened Monday-Friday 10.00am to 12.00 noon, staffed by volunteers rather than police staff with that arrangement regularly reviewed.

Borehamwood Police Station

Elstree Way, Borehamwood

S Division (1841-1985/86)

Barnet Division (1985/86-1993/94)

Barnet & Hertsmere OCU (1993/94-2000)

Barnet OCU (2000-2018/19)

North West BCU (from 2018/19)

The population in the Borehamwood area increased from 9,000 in 1945 to an estimated 22,000 in 1955, and the Commissioner first started to consider locating a police station there in 1949. The London County Council encouraged the Commissioner to increase the police presence, and in 1955 it was decided that a temporary pre-fabricated police station be erected on a site in Elstree Way Borehamwood purchased from the British and Dominions Film Co-operation Ltd.

378 Bernard Brown, private correspondence.
379 MEPO 2/76 and 5/26 (152); LB 534/-/0.
380 Surveyor's Property Register 1858, Metropolitan Police Historic Collection.
381 Metropolitan Police Orders dated 10th March 1865.
382 MEPO 2/649; LB 534/-/0 and Police Orders 5th October 1907.
383 Police Notices 14/94 of 6th April 1994.

Borehamwood Police Station, with officers posing outside their temporary base (1956)

This station was given the station code SR, and in March 1957 the temporary station was occupied for police purposes.[384] Contractors tendered for the building of the more permanent station, and the winning builders were Yeomans.

Between 1957-58 the new police station, situated also at Elstree Way, Borehamwood was erected.[385] The station at Shenley was closed on the same day in 1959 as this new station was opened, and the staff and business were transferred to Borehamwood which became a sectional station attached to Barnet Sub-Division.

The construction of the new Borehamwood Police Station in Elstree Way, shown from the rear

The station at Borehamwood was still located at Elstree Way, within the borough of Aldenham, Hertfordshire in 1967, but this time it had been removed from Barnet and was a sectional station of West Hendon Sub-Division instead.[386] In the meantime, a much larger new station was built in Elstree Way and replaced the temporary pre-fabricated station, which was closed.[387] The station code changed from (SR) to (SD) in July 1971 when the divisional headquarters at Golders Green was moved to Borehamwood whilst extensive building work was undertaken.[388]

Borehamwood Police Station 1959 to present

In 2000 the station and its area was transferred to Hertfordshire Police.

Bow Road Police Station

Devons Lane, Bromley (1845-1860)
1 Bow Road, Bromley-by-Bow (1860-1903)
111 Bow Road, Bromley-by-Bow (1903-1993)
K Division (1845-1965)
H Division (1965-1993)
Tower Hamlets OCU (1993-2018/19)
Basic Command Unit Central East (CE) (with the London Borough of Hackney) (2018/19 to present)

Bow Road Police Station Lamp

In 1845 a rented station and section house were located in Devons Lane, Bromley (by Bow). The building was owned by Mr. C.J. Robbins of High Street, Bromley, who rented the property annually to the Receiver of the Police. It consisted of an old brick and slate building, with a charge room and two cells. At the rear was a small yard. It was given up in 1860 and no longer used for police purposes.

Details were published that Bow was a designated station of K or Stepney Division.[389] Prior to this, records show that on 8th October 1831 H or Stepney Division had two stations, probably both old watch houses, located at 8 Wentworth Place and Newby Place, near Poplar Church.[390] Section houses to house single policemen were shown located at Arbour Square, Devons Lane, Bromley by Bow, and in Three Colt Street.

In 1840 Bow Police Station was used as a charging station for stations on K Division, and officers were authorised to cross the Divisional boundary from Stratford and Leytonstone stations in order to bring their prisoners for processing to appear at the Petty Sessions sitting at Lambeth Street Police Court off Commercial Road.

In 1859 the Receiver of the Metropolitan Police leased land in the Bow Road for ninety years from the Rev. G. J. Driffield, Rector of Bow. A ground rent of £20 per year was payable, with a further £8 per year payable on land located at the rear of the station. Its exact position was 116B Bow Road E3, immediately opposite Fairfield Road. The station was built in 1860 at a cost of £2,294 4s 9d, and insured for £1,500 at the Law Office by the Receiver. Accommodation for thirteen constables was provided on the second floor, whilst the married inspector resided in three rooms on the first floor.[391]

Records show that in 1862 Bow Police Station was situated at the back of the High Street, opposite Bow Railway Station and Fairfield Road. It was flanked by three public houses, namely The Bowry's Arms, The Bird in Hand and The Sailmakers Arms. Another station called Mile End Old Town was also shown on K Division in a place called Hickfield, not far from the workhouse in a road we know today as Devons Road.[392]

In 1865 the Receiver purchased freehold land in the Mile End Road, not far from Bow Police Station, for the purposes of building a section house specifically for single constables. The land and dwelling cost £2,500 and comprised of basement, ground, first and second floors. In the basement were washing, cleaning and boot rooms, and a kitchen locker room and coal cellar. The ground floor housed a library, a mess room and two further locker rooms. There was space for 22 single officers, who paid 1s per week rent.

Bow Road Police Station 1860-1903

During 1880 there was a boundary revision of the divisions of G, H, K and Y.[393] It stipulated that Bow was to become the new Divisional station for K Division, and that this status had now been removed from the previous headquarters of Stepney. The division of Stepney was now transferred from K to H Division. Records show that in 1881 the Divisional Superintendent George Turner resided not far from Bow Police Station, at 19 Tomlins Grove where he lived with his wife and three children. Turner became Divisional Superintendent in June 1876 and retired on pension in October 1887. The address of the station in 1881 was 1 Bow Road, Bromley. Records show there were thirteen single officers living above the station[394] at the time.

The address of the new station was published in 1884 as being Bow Road, Bromley-by-Bow. Even today the station can still be seen, as there is a preservation order on the building. In 1887 alterations were made to the station including the building of new cells, at a total cost of £895.[395]

Occasionally an event takes place about which both police and public should feel rightly proud. Such an event took place on Bow Sub-Division on 29th August 1894. Its officers, friends and acquaintances gathered at the Bromley Vestry Hall to commemorate the heroism of four members of the public who had rendered assistance to the police when they had had violent prisoners. The gathering was presided over by the Magistrate Mr W. Hunter who, at the request of Sub-Divisional Inspector Causby, wished to present Mr Arthur Chambers, Mr J. Sobey, Mr J.D. Collins and Mr D.P. Collins with ivory-handled Malacca walking sticks complete with inscribed silver collars as a token of their appreciation. Superintendent Wells made a speech and then presented the gifts amid vigorous applause. It is always nice for police officers to know that policing by consent means that they can rely on members of the public in time of difficulty.[396]

The Metropolitan Police reviewed its building stock in the early 1900s and considered that Bow Police Station was no longer suitable for modern-day policing. They viewed a number of sites for the new station and found a suitable freehold site for a station being offered by Lord Tredegar at 111, 113, 115 and 117 Bow Road, at the corner of Addington Road. Home Office approval was given for the purchase and accordingly a new station was completed for occupation on 20th July 1903.

Bow Road Police Station 1903 to present

The station was built with a section house to accommodate 40 single police officers, who were required to pay rent of 1/-

384 Metropolitan Police Orders dated 26th February 1957.
385 Ibid.
386 Metropolitan Police Orders dated 6th August 1964.
387 Metropolitan Police Orders dated 5th July 1968.
388 Metropolitan Police Orders dated 9th July 1971.
389 Metropolitan Police Orders dated 11th January 1864.
390 Metropolitan Police Surveyor's Records.
391 Metropolitan Police Property Book.
392 Ordnance Survey Maps 1862.
393 Metropolitan Police Orders dated 15th May 1880.
394 Census Records 1881.
395 Metropolitan Police Property Book.
396 *Police Review* magazine, August 1894.

per week each. There was also room for a married inspector, who paid rent of 5/6d per week, and one married constable paying 3/- rent per week.

During the demonstrations and window smashing in 1913 one prisoner at Bow Road was suffragette Sylvia Pankhurst, who was detained in the cells.

In 1915 new married quarters and a section house were built in Violet Road, Bow Common. The section house was built to house 60 unmarried officers. Additionally, there were a set of married quarters and a room for one unmarried sergeant.

In 1938 the stable block at the rear of the station was completed. These stables were the largest in the Force at the time. The stables could house twenty horses, although there were only about fourteen mounted officers.

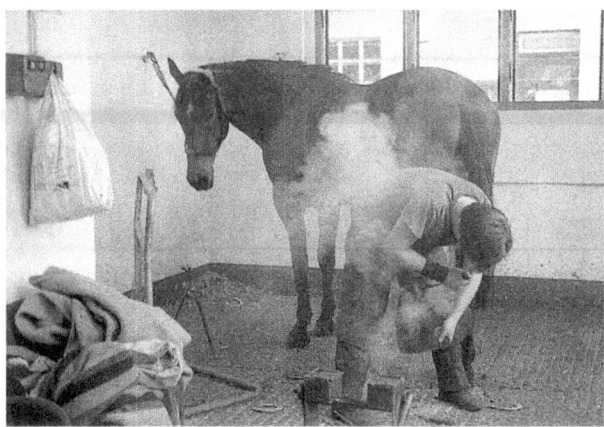

The Farrier shoeing horses in the stables at Bow Road Police Station circa 1970

The station suffered a direct hit by a German bomb during the Second World War. The damage was quickly repaired and the station returned to full operational duties. The stable block was emptied and the horses were housed elsewhere temporarily in case the glass roof collapsed after the attacks.

During the 1933 re-organisation, Bow Road was transferred from K or East Ham Division to H or Whitechapel Division. The police boundary changes of 1965, in line with Local Authority Boundary revisions, saw the transfer of Bow Road as designated sectional station of Arbour Square Sub-Division.

By 1968 the Mounted Branch at Bow Road had grown an establishment of one inspector, one station sergeant and twelve constables.[397] There was also a full-time farrier, Thomas Melody, who was responsible for the fully fitted forge. The farrier was responsible for shoeing up to 60 horses a month.[398]

In 2002 the 99-year-old police station at Bow Road appeared empty and boarded up, but records show that it had limited opening times to the public.[399]

In 2009 Bow Road Police Station, its stables and police accommodation became listed. In 2013 the front counter was shut down and in 2019 the station was closed to the public, but was still retained together with the section house for use by the police.[400]

Bow Street Police Station

Old watch house at St Paul's church, Covent Garden
(1829-1832)
33-34 Bow Street (1832-1881)
27-28 Bow Street (1881-1992)
F Division (1832-1869)
E Division (1869-1965)

C Division (1965-1985)

Bow Street started its road to fame in the history of maintaining law and order in 1739, when Thomas de Veil occupied a house at No 4, on the west side, and began work as London's first notably honest magistrate. In 1749 the police office was opened;[401] later Henry and Robert Fielding took over as magistrates and established permanent officers employed as constables by the court to investigate complaints of crime and to execute warrants. In 1803 no. 3 was acquired to extend no. 4.[402] Later there were uniform foot patrols organised from the court, and in 1763 the Bow Street horse patrol was commenced, although it only lasted a year through lack of funding.[403] Later, in 1805, these patrols were re-introduced and they extended their operations throughout what is now Greater London. The complexities of these Bow Street principal officers, runners and 'patroles' are explained in *Policing from Bow Street* by Peter Kennison and Alan Cook (Mango Books 2019).

But this was not the first Metropolitan Police base for this area, as the watch house in Covent Garden by St. Paul's Church was originally chosen and adapted at an early date but went on to cause John Wray, the Receiver, much consternation. The watch house stood in an empty space near to the church and according to Superintendent Thomas of F Division, it was an ideal site for his headquarters. But there were complaints from parishioners about the drunks 'recovering from drunken orgies' who abused them from the watch house's basement on their way to church on Sundays. A furious row broke out between the two parties, and despite Supt. Thomas begging Joint Commissioner Charles Rowan to ignore the complaints, the Bishop of London was dragged into the argument. A temporary (but unsightly) wooden annex was erected on the side of the watch house, which added to the parishioners' concerns. It was stated that the watch house was situated on consecrated ground and as a result the Commissioner asked

Bow Street Police Station 1831-1881

Bow Street Police Station and Court 1880-1992

Wray to investigate. Wray reported that the parishioners' calls were appropriate, and that a new station in Bow Street should be sought in the vicinity.[404] It was then that Bow Street became the centre of policing for the area by the Metropolitan Police.

In 1832[405] the police therefore moved to 33-34 Bow Street, opposite the court, on the east side of the road, into a brick and slate-built house leased from the Duke of Bedford by the Receiver for 61 years from midsummer 1831.[406] There was a yard at the rear, nine cells, a charge room, a mess, and a kitchen in the basement. The advent of the new police station made it unnecessary to keep the controversial old watch house by the portico of St Paul's church, Covent Garden. Bow Street became the new headquarters of the Met's F Division (Covent Garden), with the station taking responsibility for policing from the City of London boundary down to Trafalgar Square, and up to St Giles.

In October 1869 Bow Street became the divisional headquarters of E Division when E and F Divisions were combined. There was therefore no F Division until April 1886, when a new F (Paddington) Division was formed.

The replacement for 33-34 Bow Street was the now disused police station and court further north at number 27-28 Bow Street. Plans were first discussed in 1876 and a new building, designed by Sir John Taylor of the Office of Works, was completed towards the end of 1880 with the house at 33-34 being retained for a period as a section house, and eventually disposed of when accommodation became available at Clark's Buildings, George Street. The fine stone façade, opposite the Opera House, has led to the building being listed (Grade II). It is one of the few examples in London of a police station and court being built together, and was famous for its lamps not being in the traditional police station blue colour. The story is that when police station blue lamps were introduced in 1861, Queen Victoria objected to this reminder of Windsor Castle's Blue Room, in which Prince Albert had died that same year, confronting her each time she went to the Royal Opera House.[407] If the story is true it would naturally have related to 33-34 Bow Street, and would somehow have been translated into the design of the new station nearly twenty years later.

There had been section house accommodation at 7 Ricketts Place, Strand that had 22 rooms and was given up in 1845. 82 Charing Cross Road was also a section house from 30 November 1886. In 1901 it housed 129 unmarried constables, seven single sergeants and a married Sub-Divisional Inspector by the name of Hayers, who lived there with his wife and son.[408] By July 1916 it was occupied by the Victoria League Soldiers' Club at a nominal rent.

397 The H Division Handbook 1968/69.
398 Ibid.
399 www.met.police.uk/contact/phone.htm accessed 23rd March 2002.
400 MPS station closures since 2010. Information Rights Unit MSP accessed 6th May 2019.
401 Bow Street Police Station timeline (Dave Allen).
402 Ibid.
403 Ibid.
404 Browne, Douglas, C. (1956) *The Rise of Scotland Yard*. Harrap and Co, London p88.
405 Bow Street Police Station timeline (Dave Allen).
406 The Property Register also refers to a lease from Christmas 1832 for 41 years.
407 Fido, M. and Skinner, K (1999) *The Official Encyclopedia of Scotland Yard*. Virgin London.
408 Census records 1901.

In 1920 the station had temporary buildings for an Aliens Registration Office (ARO), which then moved to the station's basement in 1925 when a section house on the upper floors was closed. A gate in the railings by the modern Martlett Court was provided to give access direct to the basement. Later, in 1965, the ARO moved to Vine Street, then premises above Holborn Police Station and, from 1999, to Borough High Street with a new name of Overseas Visitors Records Office.

Bow Street became part of C Division in 1965 when there were also many boundary changes to make police divisions co-terminous with local authority boundaries. In 1989 Bow Street and Cannon Row were amalgamated to form Charing Cross Division, operating from that station (CX). On 5th October 1992 at 6.00am Bow Street police station was closed, but later used temporarily whilst West End Central was refurbished. In 2019 a hotel was planned for the building, with a small museum in the cell block.

Bow Street is a famous police station, and several cases reflected its high-profile name. In 1961 'Identikit' was used for the first time in the murder of Elsie Batten at 22 Cecil Court WC2, on Bow Street's ground.[409] In October of the same year a WH Smith van caught fire and Constable Cawdwell ran and saved the driver from burning to death.[410] In 1973 Constable Michael Whiting QPM was killed after clinging to a car that had driven off as he was questioning the occupants.[411] In 1984 a Bow Street officer, Constable Yvonne Fletcher, was killed in St. James's Square by shots fired from the Libyan People's Bureau during a demonstration against the regime of Colonel Gaddafi; the case created enormous controversy after the 'diplomats' were allowed to leave the Embassy and the case is still open today after tireless campaigning by Yvonne Fletcher's colleague John Murray.[412] In 1991 Detective Constable James Morrison QGM was stabbed to death whilst off duty near Aldwych whilst chasing a suspect.

A station with keen footballers, Bow Street won their section of the sub-divisional football league in 1967 but were beaten in the final by Hammersmith. At the same time Norwell Roberts became the first black police officer in the Metropolitan Police and served at Bow Street.[413]

In 1985, although Bow Street was replaced by the new Charing Cross police station, the magistrates' court continued to be used until its last case was heard on 14th July 2006. A plan to open the building as a police museum was outlined, but the Metropolitan Police Authority declined to support the scheme, quoting legal reasons.

Brentford Police Station

The London Borough of Hounslow
60 High Street (1830-1869)
42 High Street (1869-1966)
The Half Acre (1967-1993)
T Division (1830-1985/86)
Chiswick Division (1985/86-2000)
Hounslow Borough OCU (2000-2013)

New Brentford was a narrow strip of land between the River Brent and Half Acre, and research into the history of crime in Brentford taken from ledgers shows some intriguing entries. A somewhat unusual one appears in the record for 1634:

'Paid Robert Warden (a smith by trade) the Constable which he dispurs'd for conveying away the witches 11s 0d.'[414]

Brentford had long been associated with witches. Falstaff, in the Merry Wives of Windsor, disguised himself as the old fortune-telling Fat Woman of Brentford, whom Master Ford swore was a witch. However, the witches taken away by Robert Warden were no doubt of more humble origin. Typically such women were old and poor, and the victims of the gossiping slander of neighbours who accused them of bringing sickness to both men and beasts.[415]

The ripples of the Industrial Revolution reached Brentford in the early 19th century with the opening of the Grand Junction Canal. Breweries, mills and other industries began to displace the previous agricultural economy. The coming of the railways, the opening of Brentford Dock, the waterworks, gas works and factories increased noise and pollution, changing the character of New Brentford. With the development of more sophisticated forms of transport Brentford grew into a thriving market town and became the county town of Middlesex, now no longer a county.

Brentford market square circa early 1800s

Land at New Brentford for a cage, stocks and whipping post was sought in 1720. A cage was to be built or rebuilt in 1753; a watch box for the Beadle was to be set up near the market house and a new stocks provided in 1787.[416] At Brentford the cage stood on the corner of Ferry Lane and High Street in 1839.[417]

The first Brentford police station was situated on the eastern corner of Town Meadow:

'The building was early C18, with 3 bays and consisted of house, stable and yard. Prior to its use by the Police, Lawrence Rowe, who ran a local soap works business, bought this property (complete with its own wharf) in 1799.'[418]

Brentford Police Station 1813-1830 (photograph 1897)

A report in The Times of 19th July 1831 stated that a constable of the T Division stopped two boys in possession of an ass which they confessed they had stolen in the neighbourhood of Oxford and had travelled all that distance without being stopped despite the presence of Bow Street horse patrols which had been set up in 1805 and were based in Hounslow.[419] Although rural in nature, Chiswick and Brentford suffered with traffic congestion with no fewer than 50 stage coaches which passed though the towns daily en route to the southwest.

In the Tythe map of Front Street, Brentford[420] above the police station marked 36 is a short distance to no. 49 – the lock up house or cage where prisoners were kept. The station possessed a yard and stable behind.

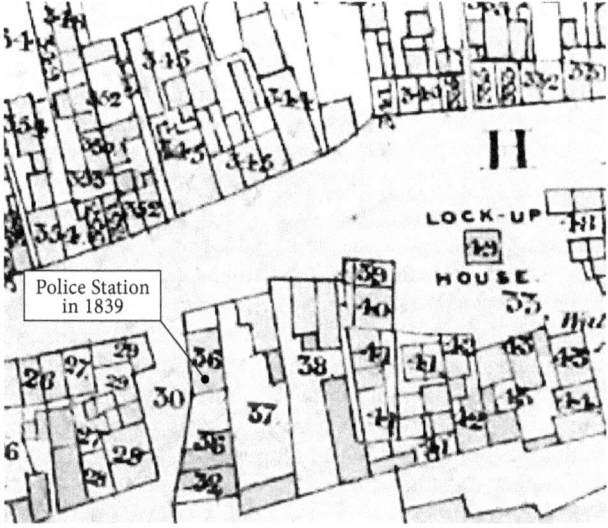

Brentford Police Station 1830-1869

On 13th January 1840 T or Kensington Division was extended west of Brentford up to the Buckinghamshire county boundary. All arrests made in the parishes of Isleworth, Hounslow, Heston, Hanwell, Greenford, Perivale, Norwood and Alperton were taken to Brentford police station.[421]

The station address in 1836 was Front Street, Old Brentford near the cage and was a station on T or Kensington Division under Superintendent David Williamson.[422]

In the 1839/41 tithe return (mentioned above) the owner Thomas and L. Rowe is recorded as renting a 'house, stable & yard'[423] to the Metropolitan Police as a station house. Access to a yard was a fundamental requirement for police officers as it was essential to house horses for transport and to patrol the main routes.

And so the Metropolitan Police moved into the Brentford area. When the first Brentford police station was built here in 1830 the main thoroughfare was called 'Front Street' rather than 'High Street' it's later name. The station also had a covered passage way, washhouse at extreme rear, a water closet; three store sheds at rear; side gateway entrance, and a cellar in the basement.[424] The cells for holding prisoners were also located in the basement.[425]

In due course the station address became 60 High Street, Old Brentford and in 1841 Inspector Cortney Henry Marquard and five constables lived there, two having small families living with them. Marquard had joined as a constable in April 1830 with promotion to inspector in 1834. He was recognised for his leadership skills in Brentford by the Commissioners who in 1845 promoted him to Superintendent of K or Stepney Division. One wonders how impressed he was being posted from a semi-rural location into the depths of the East End of London where he stayed until 1852.[426] The East End was the most difficult area to police in London with its levels of crime and assaults on police officers. Marquard was discharged by the Medical Officer as being 'used up' (a term later replaced with 'worn out'), with a gratuity of £150 having only completed 22 years. He had not completed the usual 25 years' service[427] which would have qualified him for a pension. By 1844 Brentford had become 'an inspector station' meaning that the highest rank supervising the police station area of Brentford was an Inspector[428] with Marquard being its first incumbent. In 1841 Marquard was assisted by 30-year-old police Sergeant James Levy who lived at the station with his wife and two children.[429] Constable John Duckett and his family also lived there.[430]

William Brown was the inspector in charge in 1851 and resided there with two sergeants and three constables. In 1853 Thomas Bristow was sergeant of police living in Brookshot Road, Old Brentford, with sergeant James Oxley Turner living in Orchard Road.[431] Charles Cox started working there in 1862. The station moved to 42 High Street in 1869. In 1987 the cells were still evident in the building and by 2003 the station had become a solicitor's office. Constable Joseph Jacobs who resided in Ealing Lane was also attached to the station in 1851.

In July 1861 there are complaints to the vestry of the 'annoyance to which the inhabitants are subjected by persons standing about in the streets and obstructing the footpaths

409 Bow Street Police Station timeline (Dave Allen).
410 Ibid.
411 Ibid.
412 Ibid.
413 Ibid.
414 brentfordandchiswicklhs.org.uk/publications/the-journal/journal-8-1999/law-and-order-in-new-brentford/ accessed on 15th December 2012.
415 Ibid.
416 Baker et al (1982) *The History of the County of Middlesex* Vol 7.
417 Ibid.
418 Ibid.
419 www.chiswickw4.com/default.asp?section=info&link=police/history.htm accessed 18th December 2012.
420 Courtesy of the London Metropolitan Archives.
421 www.chiswickw4.com/default.asp?section=info&link=police/history.htm accessed 18th December 2012.
422 *Kelly's Directory* 1836.
423 www.bhsproject.co.uk/section4.shtml#60 accessed 15th December 2012.
424 Ibid..
425 Ibid..
426 *Kelly's directory* for 1845 to 1851.
427 Metropolitan Police pension registers 1840 to 1848.
428 Kelly's Directory 1844.
429 Census records 1841.
430 Ibid.
431 1853.

thereof and by the obscene, blasphemous and immoral language which are so shamefully and indecently prevalent in the streets of the township at all hours of the day and night.' Sergeant 42T Charles Blake from Southwold in Suffolk, his wife Mary and two sons and a daughter lived at the police station in 1861. Blake was ten years older than his wife whom he had met locally, but displayed a lack of ability as a sergeant and had been reported a number of times to the Superintendent. He was placed on report but it was decided by the Commissioner that he had taken sufficient steps to come up to standard. But things did not go well for Charles in 1868 as he had by then been demoted to constable and sent to urban Stepney from rural Brentford as punishment. By 1872 he had been medically retired as being 'worn out' by the police doctor. Constables Edward Hitchcock and Frederick Forman were also stationed at Brentford at the time.[432]

Brentford Magistrates' Court 1850-2011

The Brentford Vestry minutes in 1863 recorded that

'During the 19th century powers had been stripped away from the vestry and given to a variety of elected boards and councils. Policing had become the responsibility of police commissioners in 1829 and an Act of 1839 allowed JPs to create a county force of chief and petty constables. The rough and ready systems that had proved adequate in the past were being transformed into a modern industry'[433]

Police Orders show that Brentford was a station of T Division in 1864.

Originally built in 1850 as a town hall when Queen Victoria was only 31, the building which became the court building and stands in Market Place off London Road was used for Brentford's first library and other Victorian social gatherings such as vegetable shows. By 1891 the building was fully bought out by Middlesex County Council to be used full-time as a magistrate's court. The police officers of the district were frequent visitors often taking their prisoners there to appear before the magistrate. This was never used as a police station although it did have a police room.

Brentford Magistrates' court shut in 2011 after 161 years[434] and is likely to become a public house.

Inspector Tarling lived at the police station with his wife Anne and five children. The conditions were cramped and space at a premium. Constable Charles Pontin and his wife, constable John Bucks and his wife, constable Philip Vaughn and his wife and 15 single constables all resided there. In July 1867 the Police Surveyor recommended purchase of the site and the Home Office approved the transaction in August 1867.[435] By 1881 Tarling had retired and become the licensee of the Red Lion public house situated opposite the police station at 318 High Street.

The duties of all officers of the police were published in 1868. At Brentford there was only one inspector at this time (Tarling) who was responsible for patrolling only. His job specifically excluded him from duty at the police station and he was to supervise on horseback the sections of Hounslow, Staines, Isleworth, Heston and Stanwell section – where there was no police station. The beats were split into two sections – the day beats and the night beats. There were two sergeants at the station. One sergeant and six constables covered the days beats whilst the other sergeant and 12 constables patrolled by night. There were two horses stabled at Brentford, one for use by the Inspector and the other for a constable to patrol on.[436]

On 21st January 1867, Superintendent T Division Robert Beckerson reported that Inspector James Tarling had found a suitable site for a new station in Main Street near the Church at the township of New Brentford close to the town hall. Main street was later named High street. A new three-storey police station with basement was built in 1869 at a cost of £5,674. 44p (£7,000 including land) and to be occupied on 28th September,[437] and the police of T Division moved to the new Station at Brentford on this day. The station had six cells and the building is no longer standing. The boundaries of Bedfont, Brentford and Hampton Sub-Divisions were altered in 1890.[438] Brentford became one of nine new purpose built police stations to have been built in the two years prior to 1870.[439] The population of Brentford at the time was 11,091.

Brentford Police Station 1869-1966

Early in the 20th century Mrs Mary Ann Cox (1869-1954) was matron at the police station and employed to search female prisoners. In 1894 she married Charles William Cox (1869-1950) at St. Paul's Church. He worked as a potter in the Bull Lane Pottery, Pottery Road, making chimney pots. Mary and family lived in New Road and then at several addresses

A retirement celebration group c1906 in the station yard of Brentford Police Station

in Ealing Road not far from the station. There were several members of the Cox family living on Brentford High Street from 1841, including a John Cox from Northamptonshire at the police station in 1891 where he was a police sergeant.[440] Charles Cox joined Brentford police force (as Police Constable 187T) and lived with his wife and family in Town Meadow Road. This was convenient since, Brentford police station (where he served) was then situated at 60 High Street at the junction with Town Meadow, Brentford. Cox died at Kew bridge in 1870 when he accidentally drowned.[441]

The numbering of the High Street took place in 1876 and the police station was allocated no. 42. However there appears to be an extra property between the police station and the George IV public house at no. 50 which may account for later references to no. 43a and no. 45a.[442] These may have been used as police living accommodation.[443] In 1881 Sub-Divisional Inspector John Rowling (warrant no. 47987) was the officer in charge and he resided at the station with his wife Mary Ann and their two children. Rowling, an ardent Cornishman from St. Columb, joined the police in January 1867 and retired in March 1892. They were still resident at the station in 1891 but Rowling had died by 1901 and his wife had moved back to Cornwall in the meantime. His place was taken by inspector John Oran Mumford (warrant no. 54453). Mumford, born 1851 in London, joined the Metropolitan Police in 1871 and took over at Brentford from March 1892 until 1897 when he was retired on pension. He lived in the married quarters at the station with his wife Catherine and Minnie his daughter. On retirement he moved to 14, Lateward Road, Brentford.[444]

The following report appeared in the *Police Review* in 1897:

"RETIREMENT OF AN INSPECTOR. *Having completed upwards of twenty-five years' service in the Metropolitan Police Force, Sub-divisional Inspector Mumford has retired on a pension. Mr. Mumford came to Brentford in 1891, on the retirement of Sub-divisional Inspector ROWLING, his immediately preceding appointment having been at Albany Street in the S Division. During his residence in Brentford, Inspector Mumford has gained the respect and esteem of the general body of the residents alike by his genial and kindly bearing and by the efficiency with which he has discharged the onerous duties of his position. Mr. Mumford intends, we understand, to enter into business in Brentford.*"

In fact Mumford did indeed stay in Brentford once he retired because he took over the George IV Public House situated at 50 High Street, on the corner of Goat Wharf until 1899 when he died in Brentford Cottage Hospital. As licensee he would be well aware of his responsibilities as he would have closely supervised all the licensed establishments in his area when he was the inspector. In the 1913 directory a Mrs C. Mumford is listed at the George IV although her daughter then aged 20 had pre-deceased her in 1905.[445] Joseph B. Hart had taken over by 1920. The public house was situated right near the police station and was a place that off duty police officers would go to and be in comfortable surroundings with the ex-police inspector and his wife in charge.

The picture above shows an officer wearing plain clothes without a hat receiving his ornamental time piece for completing 25 years' service. Sub-Divisional Inspector Edwin Digby, in charge of Brentford, is sat on his horse to the back left of the group, facing away from the camera. Divisional Superintendent James Powell is seated in the front row wearing plain clothes and a bowler hat. Powell, as the chief officer of the division, would often officiate at retirement celebrations where it would be incumbent on him to 'say a few words' about the outgoing officer's service and contribution.

432   Census records 1861.
433   brentfordandchiswicklhs.org.uk/publications/the-journal/journal-8-1999/law-and-order-in-new-brentford. 'Law and Order in New Brentford', David Shavreen accessed 15th December 2012.
434   www.hounslowchronicle.co.uk/west-london-news/local-hounslow-news/2011/12/14/brentford-s-historic-court-could-become-a-pub-109642-29952587 accessed 18th December 2012.
435   John Back Archive circa 1975.
436   Metropolitan Police Special Police Order 1868.
437   Metropolitan Police Orders dated 28th September 1870.
438   Metropolitan Police Orders dated 18th July 1890.
439   Metropolitan Police Commissioner's Annual Report 1870.
440   www.bhsproject.co.uk/families_cox.shtml accessed 15th December 2012.
441   Metropolitan Police Commissioner's Annual Report 1870.
442   www.bhsproject.co.uk/section4.shtml#60 accessed 15th December 2012.
443   Ibid.
444   www.bhsproject.co.uk/families_mumford.shtml accessed 22nd December 2012.
445   Ibid.

From 1897 until 1908 Sub-Divisional Inspector Edwin Digby was in charge of the station and lived there with his wife Emily and their two sons. Digby had been promoted from E or Holborn Division in 1896. Also resident at the station were Constable William Clayden with his wife and family, Constable John Seaman and his wife and in the section house were 20 single officers. These were Constables Charles Anderson, Goodman Proops, Ernest Wachter, Thomas Rimmington, Frank Potter, Herbert Cottage, George Smith, William Hope, William Farrer and Henry Rudling, Arthur Rickens and Charles Gaylor, Fred Burchell, Wallace Sturrock, James Willie, Joseph Harwood, Henry Nock, James Duguid, Edward Smith, and David Thomas.[446]

In the same year Digby was assisted by nine sergeants and 34 constables. Brentford was the sub-divisional station with Hounslow, Isleworth, and Norwood Green all sectional stations. Digby had retired to the local area and moved to 70 Hamilton Road, Brentford where he resided with his wife, his two sons and daughter.[447] In 1908 Sub-Divisional Inspector Richard Wallis.[448] took his place and in turn his place was taken in 1914 by Charles Richardson.[449]

Brentford Police Station was a one of a number of places designated under the Royal Humane Society for the receiving of dead bodies, apparently drowned, where drags and other apparatus were kept. Other storage locations included the public houses in Brentford.[450]

There were problems with the drainage at the station in early 1903 which caused some discomfort and complaint by the inhabitants. Works were carried out by the Surveyors who not only improved the sanitary conditions but in the single men's accommodation partitions were set up between the beds giving some degree of privacy on the part of the occupants.[451]

In 1910 the police station at no. 42 was owned by the Receiver of the Metropolitan Police and valued at £4,410. Richard Wallis, in 1910, and Thomas Faulkner, in 1913 were the sub-divisional inspectors at the police station.

Police Orders dated 30th December 1916 stated that the Sub-Division would comprise of the stations of Brentford and Chiswick, with Brentford the sub-divisional station. Brentford did not escape enemy action World War One; bombs fell on 29th January 1918 demolishing a house in White Star Road and the houses either side being severely damaged. Eight people were also killed at Brentford water works. Special constable P. Bentley tried to rescue people from a partly demolished building, removing a dead body and won a commendation for his actions.[452]

Special Constable Frederick Tickner

Frederick Tickner, a local boat builder and foreman joined the Metropolitan Police Special Constabulary at the start of the war to supplement the regular police officers being called up and was posted to Brentford police station. He is seen at left standing in front of the bricks at Goat Wharf. Research shows the cap badge is that of the Metropolitan Special Constabulary and this suggests he volunteered to be a Special Constable during World War One. Special Constables often had no uniform provided but were issued with armlets, whistles and truncheons, and later on, badges. Frederick recalled some of his experiences whilst a special constable. He saw a German Zeppelin follow the river up to Brentford and bombed the town, the damage being most severe in Green Dragon Lane and Walnut Tree Road. He also wrote that the Vestry Hall Brentford was used as a County Court until the new building in Alexandra Road was built.[453] Once the war was finished the area returned to normality but there was a feeling that a permanent reserve of Special Constables should remain after 1919.

The stables at the rear of the station were converted into a District Traffic Garage and re-occupied in 1932. In 1937 a site on which to build a police station was purchased freehold in Ealing Road, Brentford. Because of the impending situation in Europe and the likelihood of war plans were temporarily shelved and the site was rented out to Alpha Romeo Co. Ltd for 21 years commencing in 1944 on an annual rent of £100.[454] In the same year Brentford was classified as a sectional station to Acton Sub-Division, call sign TB.

It was not long before preparations were being made to go to war again and the police special constabulary reserves were increased to support local policing. However this time the methods of wreaking havoc changed with the delivery of bombs not only coming from heavy bombers but also via new remote technology, Rocket, flying bomb and bombing raids severely affected Brentford. During the World War Two a V1 Rocket hit 63 Claypons Avenue, Brentford at 15.20 hours on the 12th July 1944 causing considerable damage including some houses in Ealing Road. The blast resulted in George Forgan and his sister being trapped in the rubble, but luckily they were pulled out quickly and not harmed.[455] Police were quickly on the scene of any bombing or damage caused from aerial bombardment. They would quickly secure the area, rescue victims, recover bodies and search for unexploded munitions. Any of the injured would be conveyed to the medical stations or hospitals for treatment. Dead bodies would be conveyed to the mortuary. Until families were informed of the damage, police would remain on scene to protect property from looters.

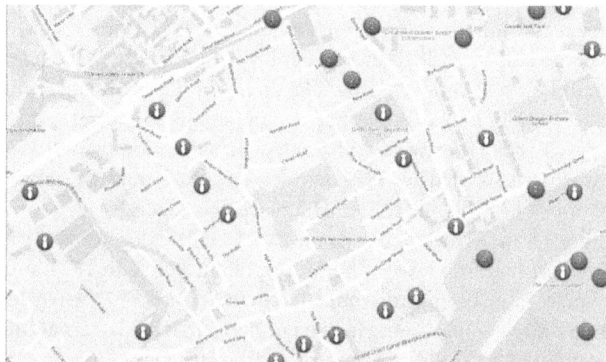

Map of Brentford showing clusters and single bombs dropped

Brentford's fortunes were rather mixed when it came to bombs falling during German air raids between 7th October 1940 and 6th June 1941. Two bombs fell in Brentford High Street, one quite close to the police station. Also Syon Lane, Beech Avenue, Somerset Road, Barnhurst Road were hit causing damage and injury but six fell harmlessly into the Thames.[456]

A revision of boundaries took place on the 1st April 1965 to align with local authorities and Brentford was shown as a sectional station to Chiswick as the sub-divisional station. Later, until 1963 when the re-building of Chiswick was completed, Brentford became the sub-divisional headquarters.⁴⁵⁷ The vestry hall was on the Half Acre corner with St Paul's Road and was demolished in the 1960s to make way for a new police station.

The design of the Brentford Police Station lamp shown right.

The *Police Review* of 1st July 1966 reported that the £400,000 new station would comprise police station and section house within the eleven floor tower block with accommodation for 98 single officers, each with their own room. The station would replace the existing Brentford police station in the High Street reverting to a sectional station with the opening of the new Chiswick sub-divisional station on 27th March 1972. The old station was shut for day- to-day policing in 1967 after the new station became operational. The public were directed to the new station whilst the Metropolitan Police retained the old building for use as administrative offices. In December 1969 the old station was pulled down and workmen found several artefacts of interest such as an 1865 warrant and a badly made counterfeit half sovereign believed to have belonged to a prisoner who hid it in the cell where he was kept.⁴⁵⁸

Brentford Police Station 1967-2013

The plush new Sub-Divisional Police Station for Brentford on T Division was built at The Half Acre, Brentford was taken into operational use at 6.00am on 4th July 1967.⁴⁵⁹ It closed in 2013, vacated and put up for sale. In March 2015 it was sold for £9M to a developer.⁴⁶⁰

Brixton Police Station

The London Borough of Lambeth

Watch Houses at Waterloo Bridge Road; Christchurch, Blackfriars

High Street, Lambeth (1829-1858)

Brixton Road, Brixton (1858 to Present)

L Division (1830-1865)

W Division (1865-1932)

L Division (1932-1985/86)

Brixton Division / OCU (1985/86-2018/19)

Central South BCU AS (from 2018/19)

In April 1830 the new Metropolitan Police (13th Company – Camberwell Division) arrived to police the parishes of St. Giles Camberwell, St Mary Newington, St Mary Lambeth, St George-the-Martyr Clapham and the small hamlets of Penge and Hatcham.⁴⁶¹ The three Police Stations to cover this new area were Park House, East Lane, Walworth; Camberwell Green; and Brixton Washway;⁴⁶² so called due to the flooding by the local River Effra at high tide.⁴⁶³

In December 1831 there was an early reference to Police in Brixton when the Brixton Wall Stables were leased from a Mr Elden on an annual lease of £9. The old Station in Brixton Road was the former old Watch House, located on P Division.⁴⁶⁴ It had some 16 rooms, a 5-stall stable, and 6 cells. In 1845 it was stated that the Station needed cleaning, had rain and damp coming through the roof, and was seriously in need of painting. The Watch House was vacated at Christmas 1858.⁴⁶⁵

In the 1830s, with the arrival of gas for the lighting of lamps, parish authorities followed the lead given by the City of Westminster by asking the owners of public buildings to put a gas lamp on the outside of them. There was no proper street lighting at the time and Police Stations placed a gas lamp on the outside of their premises. The main gas pipe ran along the road named Brixton Hill and past the Police Station; gas was supplied at no cost to the Police Force. In 1851 a dispute arose as to who should pay for the gas when further gas pipes were being laid along Brixton Road, The pipe to the gas lamp outside the Police Station was disconnected from the main supply pipe and attached to the paying meter that recorded gas burnt inside the station.⁴⁶⁶

The lamps outside the Police Stations were white glass until 1861 when each Superintendent was told to requisition for three pieces of blue glass to be placed in the front and sides of each lamp.⁴⁶⁷ There were only two Police lamps outside Police Stations in the Metropolitan Police Districts which used white glass. The first was outside the old Bow Street Police Station which did originally display a blue lamp but when Queen Victoria was visiting the Royal Opera House she noticed the blue lamp opposite and objected to it. The reason for her decision appears to be related to the fact that Prince Albert had died in the Blue Room at Windsor Castle. The other Police Station was at Northwood where in 1911 a blue lamp was placed outside the new Police Station without planning permission. The local authority demanded that it be removed and a white lamp later replaced it.

446 Census records 1901.
447 Census records 1911.
448 *Kelly's Ealing Hanwell, Brentford and Hounslow Directory* 1911
449 *Kelly's Ealing Hanwell, Brentford and Hounslow Directory* 1914
450 Ibid.
451 The Report of the Commissioner of the Metropolis of the Year 1904.
452 Reay, W. T. (1919) *The Specials. How They Served London*. Heineman, London
453 www.bhsproject.co.uk/memories_fatickner.shtm accessed 10th January 2013.
454 Police Property list 1947.
455 www.bhsproject.co.uk/mem_gforgan.shtml accessed 23rd December 2012.
456 bombsight.org/#15/51.4830/-0.3038 accessed 23rd December 2012.
457 Metropolitan Police Orders dated 6th August 1964.
458 *Brentford and Chiswick Times*, 23rd December 1969.
459 Metropolitan Police Orders dated 1st July 1967.
460 www.hounslow.gov.uk/police_stations accessed 19th December 2012.
461 MPS (2018) Freedom of Information department – Police stations Closures broken down by year.
462 Brown, B. *Police History Society Journal* 1994.
463 *Post Office Directory* 1838.
464 Brown, B. *Police History Society Journal* 1994.
465 MEPO 5/3 (10/8).
466 Metropolitan Police Surveyor's Records, Charlton.
467 MEPO 5/25 (142/1).

In 1852 a freehold site was purchased in Brixton but it then took until September 1857 for the Home Office to approve the plans for a new Police Station to be built on that site. It was agreed that £3590 could be spent on the project.[468] The new Police Station was designed by Charles Reeves, the Metropolitan Police Surveyor, and opened in 1858.[469] The design of the building, which actually cost only £2974 to build, was very like other Police buildings at the time. It was built of stock brick and slate, was five bays wide, had a two-bay extension to the south, it was three storeys high on a semi-basement and formerly had a mansard roof. There were sixteen rooms and six cells. It had an Engine house, dust and dung pits and a large drill ground. A pound at the rear was also purchased for £400. It was painted outside in 1861. Accommodation was provided for one married inspector at a cost of £11 1s per year.[470]

The doorway was altered later in the refurbishment in 1909.[471] The picture below shows officers appearing from the yard of the station and marching out to their beats just prior to a shift change. They are marching in single file and will fall out when they reach their beats which they were not allowed to leave unless for a very good reason. The officer had to make a note in his pocket book whenever he was absent from his beat. His pocket book was submitted to the sergeant prior to going off duty and if it was judged by the supervisory officer to have been a frivolous absence it may have made himself the subject to disciplinary proceedings. It was not uncommon for sergeants to disbelieve their constables.[472]

Brixton Police Station 1858-1909

By 1864 the total number of officers at the station was two Inspectors, eight sergeants and 77 constables. There were also three horses stabled there. One to be ridden by either of the two inspectors and one to be ridden by either of the two sergeants when on duty alternately at Peckham and Brixton Police Stations.[473]

In 1865 there was a reorganisation of Police boundaries and Brixton was transferred to W (Croydon) Division and became the Divisional Office where Inspector D Fraser took charge as an Acting Superintendent.[474] Four years later in 1869 W Division had one superintendent, nine inspectors, 40 sergeants and 343 constables. In addition it also became the Headquarters of No. 4 District with District Superintendent Captain H. Baynes in charge.[475] By 1879 W Division, and its nine Stations, was under the command of Superintendent William Wiseman.[476]

A report in 1881 described Brixton Police Station as an important station on an ample site. It made comment that one of the sleeping rooms was very badly ventilated. At the time there were 24 single Constables living in the station.[477] In 1884 the address of Brixton Police Station was shown as 367 Brixton Road, Brixton.[478] As time went on the accommodation at the station became very cramped and extensive alterations were necessary. Work started in 1905 and was completed by 1909.[479] The new refurbished Station and the Section House were taken into occupation in July 1909 and provided accommodation for 31 single men.[480]

Brixton Police Station, 1909-1959

The picture above shows the Station with the new extension to the right of the main entrance built in keeping with the rest of the building and now spread over the four floors.

Constable 130 O (not W Division) was George Applegate, born on 1st August 1855. In 1881 he was a single man residing in a Section House located at Plumstead Royal Arsenal (official quarters), Plumstead, Kent, and came from Standerwick in Somerset. George had retired on 1st April 1901 as 62WR Division on a pension of £108 having joined the Metropolitan Police on 19th April 1875.

Constable Applegate was originally PC 186W, but transferred to the Reserve with pay on 1st October 1890. He married Ann from Beauleigh in Hampshire in about 1883, was a Brixton Police Officer and all their three children (all boys) were born there. In fact Applegate was the Groom responsible for the horses at Brixton and therefore a most trusted and respected Police Officer from the senior Officer's point of view. He was a retired pensioner who had been kept on reserve. Records show that he re-joined for

Constable George Applegate

7 days on 10th June 1902 and 28 days on 5th August 1902. The latter was the Coronation of King George VII. Queen Victoria had died on 22nd January 1901 but the Coronation was not held until some 19 months later. Applegate joined for 7 days for rehearsals to the Coronation, carrying on with his role as Groom responsible for the horses

O Division was not a recognised geographical division but was used by Scotland Yard (CO) and issued to supplement Force strengths for re-engaged pensioners. Re-engaged pensioners were used at both of the Jubilee celebrations in 1887 and 1897. In 1897 103 former inspectors, 113 ex-sergeants and 570 ex-constables received clasps to their 1887 Jubilee Medal, whilst six ex-inspectors, two ex-sergeants and 38 ex-constables were awarded the actual medal.

The picture right shows Superintendent West MBE of W Division, based at Brixton. Supt. West, shown in full dress uniform, was awarded his honours in recognition of long and loyal service especially through the war years. He retired in 1921.

The photograph below shows the Brixton Section of the Metropolitan Police Special Constabulary, who had paraded in the yard to show off the Transport Section. These are all part-time unpaid Police Officers who used their own vehicles to patrol the street and sound the alarm whenever Zeppelins or German bombers were on a raid.

Superintendent West MBE

Metropolitan Police Special Constabulary Brixton Motorised Patrols

During the war the Specials would watch from the top of the Station for lights in the sky. Brixton was badly hit on a number of occasions because the German aircraft would follow either the road (main route into London) or the railway line. Special Constables would be despatched from the Station on motorised patrols, as shown in the picture below, to warn people to put their lights out or pull the blackout curtains. Failing to do so would render them liable to prosecution The 'All Clear' would be sounded by whistles and Special Constables would display a placard stating 'ALL CLEAR'.

By 1928 Brixton Police Station was just one of eleven Police Stations under the command of Superintendent Charles H. Clark.[481]

Once again, in 1932, Police boundaries changed and Brixton was transferred from W Division to L Division but continued to be the District Headquarters.[482]

The picture at the top of the following column shows the Senior Officers of W Division in 1914 just prior to the war. We see Superintendent West shown in the centre with his Chief Inspector on his left together with Detective Inspector Berrett, fourth from the left, who later went on to become a famous Scotland Yard Detective. He chronicled his experiences in a book published in the 1930s.

Senior Police officers of W Division c1914

There was again a need to increase the size of Brixton Police Station due to lack of space, and in 1937 the freeholds of Nos. 2 and 4 Gresham Road were purchased. Later a small piece of freehold land was purchased in Canterbury Crescent.[483] With the commencement of World War II in September 1939 some work on Police buildings was suspended.

On the night of 8/9 October 1940, whilst Superintendent M Purbrick was in charge, a bomb fell on Nos. 6 and 8 Gresham Road and damaged the police station.[484] Later in April 1941 the Station was badly damaged by a parachute mine and incendiaries. The Fire Brigade were quickly on the scene but were unable to save the roof of the Station from being completely burnt. The siren on top of the Station was left hanging dangerously from a chimney stack and the basement of the building was flooded with water to the depth of about four feet,[485] but there were no casualities.[486] The Station was closed and business was transferred to Nine Elms Police Station at 147 Battersea Park Road.

Subsequently a new Police Station, designed by J. Innes Elliot, Metropolitan Police Surveyor, was erected on the same site, taken into use in 1959 and continued to be the No. 4 District Headquarters, L Division Headquarters and Brixton Sub-Divisional Station.[487] The new Police Station building won a Civic Trust Award in 1961.[489]

When the new local authority boundaries were put in place in 1965, Brixton Police Station remained within the London Borough of Lambeth.[490]

468 Metropolitan Police Orders dated 4th February 1861.
469 MEPO 5/26 (156).
470 LB440.
471 Metropolitan Police Surveyor's Records, Charlton.
472 www.british-history.ac.uk accessed 9th October 2007.
473 Metropolitan Police Orders dated 11th January 1864.
474 Metropolitan Police Orders dated 28th October 1865.
475 MEPO 2/37.
476 *Post Office Directory* 1879.
477 Metropolitan Police Surveyor's Report 1881.
478 Metropolitan Police Orders dated 20th June 1884.
479 MEPO2/902.
480 Metropolitan Police Orders dated 17th July 1909.
481 *Post Office Directory* 1928.
482 Metropolitan Police Orders dated 1st January 1932.
483 LB 440.
484 Ibid.
485 Brown B. *The Job*, 5th February 1988.
486 'The Metropolitan Police at War'. HMSO 1947.
487 Metropolitan Police Orders dated 5th January 1959.
488 www.urban75.org/brixton/history/police. Accessed 14th March 2008.
489 Metropolitan Police Orders dated 6th August 1964.
490 LB511.

Brixton Police Station 1959 to present

The District Headquarters eventually moved out of Brixton Police Station in 1977 to 173/183 Lordship Lane, SE22, the new East Dulwich Police Station.[495] The horses based at Brixton also moved to new stables at East Dulwich.[491]

In April 1981 there occurred what is known as the 'Brixton Riots'. This incident ended with the injury of many Police Officers and civilians and a substantial amount of damaged property. At the time, there had been a large increase in street robbery and police started an operation which resulted in a significant number of black youths being stopped and searched on the streets of Brixton. There was strong resentment of police actions in the area and this led to civil unrest and violence on the streets. The riots led to 299 Police Officers and at 65 civilians being injured, 61 private vehicles and 56 police vehicles damaged or destroyed, 28 premises were burned, and another 117 damaged and looted. There were 82 arrests for various offences. Both the Police and the Community were to learn, from the experience, valuable lessons for the future.[492]

In July 1987 Brixton Station was visited by the Prince and Princess of Wales. The royal couple were shown around by Chief Superintendent Richard Monk, and they unveiled a plaque to mark the major extension and modernisation of the Station, which has been on its present site for almost 130 years.[493]

Currently the Front Counter of Brixton Police Station is open every day.

Brockley Police Station

The London Borough of Lewisham
4 Howson, Brockley (1883-2013)
P Division (1883-1985/86)
Lewisham Division / OCU (1985/86-2018/19)
South East BCU SE (from 2018/19)

In April 1880 the District Police Superintendent, Captain H Baynes, suggested that if a Police Station at Brockley was considered, the accommodation should consist of quarters for one married Officer (either an Inspector or a Sergeant), ten single men, three cells, an office and a charge room. He further suggested that it should be situated no more than 600 yards south of Brockley Lane Railway Station on the London, Chatham and Dover Railway.[494]

After inspection a site at the corner of Howson and Kneller Roads was considered suitable. The freeholders were the Governors of Christ's Hospital and the lessee was Mr I W Webb. Home Office approval was given in February 1881 for the lease to be purchased and in May 1882 approval of a Tender for the work was accepted.[495]

The new Police Station, designed by John Butler, Metropolitan Police Surveyor, was opened in December 1883 and Inspector Jewell was transferred from Lewisham to Brockley Police Station to take charge[496] The address of the station was shown as 4 Howson Road, Brockley.[497] In August 1899 the freehold of the property was obtained under the Compulsory Purchasing powers for the sum of £300.[498]

In 1891 the England Census showed an Inspector Harry Croft living at the Station with his wife Elizabeth and four children. Also that night there were ten Constables 'lodging' there. The address was shown as 2&4 Howson Road. One of the constables was named Charles Dickens, aged 25 years; was he named after the famous Charles Dickens who died in 1870? An interesting point to consider when looking at the census data is to see in which part of the country the officers were born. Whilst the inspector was born in Sussex the ten constables came from Bedfordshire (2), Kent, Lincolnshire, Hampshire (2), Somerset, Surrey, Dorset and one from Aberdeen, Scotland. This was an interesting mixture of people from different areas of Britain.[499]

Brockley Police Station 1883-2013

In 1960 it was decided to close the Station at night. This was to allow Officers who were normally employed there on the night shift to be posted to outside duties. A telephone connected to the Sub-Division Station was installed in a pillar by the front door of the Station for use by the public and Police.[500] The Station reopened at night from July 1965.[501]

When police boundaries were aligned to the new local authority boundaries in 1965 then Brockley, as a Sectional Station together with Deptford, became part of the Lewisham Sub-Division on P (Catford), Division.[502]

In 2003 with the closure of Brockley Police Station and the staff being moved to the new Lewisham Police Station the local authority considered adding Brockley Police Station to the list of Locally Listed Buildings in Lewisham. The report included the following comments:

"The station was built at the same time as the surrounding residential streets, which is contrast to later police stations, which were fitted into existing streetscapes. The building survives in its original layout with the sergeant's family quarters upstairs; offices on the round floor; the canteen in the Kneller Road wing and the cells in the opposite wing. Elements of the plain interior survive and include a small number of panelled doors and timber partitions. The station is surrounded by a yard with its original six foot wall and substantial gate posts. The two storey building is built of red brick in the neo-Georgian style with six-over-six pane sash windows. Portland stone rusticated door cases and stone lintels. The ground floor is in rusticated brick and the building is topped by a slate hipped roof and highly

decorative chimney stacks and terracotta pots."[503]

In 2003 the future of the Station was under threat. Many of the older Police Stations were in urgent need of repair and do not lend themselves easily to receiving new technology and increases in support staff. Some Stations did not comply with the disability discrimination rules because their structure did not easily convert to give proper access to disabled persons. The Metropolitan Police indicated that Stations should be disposed with if they are not "fit for purpose". Brockley Police Station was one of those buildings, and in 2013 it was closed to the public and the following year sold for £2,050,000.[504]

Bromley Police Station (PR)

London Borough of Bromley

Bromley Common, near Gravel Road (c.1835-1840)

Middle Row, Market Place (c.1840-1865)

Market Square, Bromley (1865-1915)

Widmore Road, Bromley (1915-2003)

High Street, Bromley BR1 1ER (2003 to Present)

R Division (1840-1865)

P Division (1865-1985/86)

Bromley Division PR (1985/86-1993/94)

Bromley & Orpington OCU (PY) (1993/94-2018/19)

South Area (SN) BCU from (2018/19)

Two officers of the Bow Street horse patrols were stationed on Bromley Common in 1805 to protect travellers from highwaymen. Bromley parish had a population of 4,000 and its own constable, and so tried to form its own town police in 1835; the tithe map for December 1839 shows a cottage rented to Police by Robert Booth Latter on Bromley Common near the modern junction with Gravel Road, a location which would have been well-situated for protecting travellers from highwaymen. Nevertheless, Bromley was taken over by R or Greenwich division of the 'new' Metropolitan Police on 13 January 1840. The new arrangements brought in two sergeants (one of them on horseback) who were responsible for four constables in Bromley, two in the parish of Hayes, and two in West Wickham. Bromley's police station in 1845, and probably for a few years beforehand, was a brick-built house in Middle Row, Market Place on a yearly lease from Mr Marsden, a brewer from Lewisham. The building had no yard or back entrance, but did have five rooms and a charge room, and acted as the Bromley police headquarters until about 1862, by which time the population had increased to over 5,000, partly assisted by the arrival of the new railway stations now known as Shortlands and Bromley South.

Bromley Police Station, The Old Market Square, 1840-1865

In 1865 Bromley acquired the status of a police sub-division, with responsibility for Beckenham, Farnborough, Sidcup and St Mary Cray. New premises, part of a new site containing the town hall, were leased from Lady Day (25 March) 1865 for 99 years from Mr. Coles Childs Esq. This was for the purpose of a police station and section house and formed part of P Division. It contained a charge room and library. There were also two cottages although the inspector resided in the station with his family for a rent of five shillings per week or £13 per year. A constable paying rent of 3s per week was allowed one of the cottages whilst a sergeant rented the other cottage for 3s 6d rent per week.

James Linvell transferred from Lewisham to take charge and lived in the new police station, which contained a charge room, library, three cells and a store on the ground floor. Bromley's establishment of constables was increased to 18 in 1869 when it was supervised by a substantive sergeant and an acting sergeant. The Lewisham Inspector would pay periodic visits to the station and patrol the area on horseback. Ten years later, when the third railway station (now Bromley North) was built, the station strength was increased to 29. Bromley's station code in 1893 was BM.

Bromley Police Station, Market Square, 1865-1915

By 1912 two extra rooms in the town hall were rented for police purposes, and there were two police cottages known as Nos. 1 and 2 Market Square. The landlord was Mrs Coles Child, and her agent was E. Britten Holmes from Bromley Palace estate office.

During WWI, on 15 March 1915, the police station was given up, but the two police cottages were retained, the rent reducing from £150 to £30pa. This was because the new Widmore Road station was then taken into use under the command of Sub-Divisional Inspector Vincent Coster, Inspector Clement Burton, a Station Sergeant, eight Sergeants and 70 Constables. The freehold on the Widmore Road site had been purchased in 1910 and was described in the property records of 1924 as a 'Station, Section House and two sets of quarters'.

491 *South London Press*, 27th September 1977.
492 www.met.police.uk/history/brixton_riots accessed 9th April 2008.
493 *The Job*, 10th July 1987.
494 Back, J. (1975) The Metropolitan Police Historical Collection.
495 MEPO 5/52.
496 Metropolitan Police Orders dated 14th December 1883.
497 Metropolitan Police Orders dated 20th June 1884.
498 Back, J. (1975) The Metropolitan Police Historical Collection.
499 Census 1891.
500 Metropolitan Police Orders dated 8th July 1960.
501 Metropolitan Police Orders dated 6th July 1964.
502 Metropolitan Police Orders dated 6th August 1964.
503 www.2lewisham.gov.uk/161 accessed 11th November 2005.
504 Metropolitan Police Information Rights Unit 22nd October 2017 accessed 25th January 2019.

The rear of Bromley's no. 2 Police Cottage had a stable for two horses, a harness room, store sheds and an ambulance shed. The cottage itself was let for three years from 1916 to Bart Cooper and eventually sold in May 1935 to HG Dunn and Sons Ltd. The Army (Eastern Command) occupied the old police station next to the town hall for six months from January 1917. Then the Bromley detachment of the 7th battalion of the Kent Volunteer Regiment was allowed to use the premises until the end of the war.

In 1921, Bromley police were involved in a serious incident when PCs Charles Hall and Jack Lewis were issued with revolvers to try to arrest four armed Sinn Fein fugitives. A short gunfight ensued between the officers and one of the terrorists as they decamped from a taxi in Bromley, and all four terrorists were arrested. The two officers were awarded the King's Police Medal for bravery (KPM), a medal that had been instituted twelve years earlier after the 1909 Tottenham Outrage, a running chase and gunfight with two anarchists who had undertaken an armed robbery.

On 1 January 1932 Bromley Sub-Division acquired St Mary Cray and Chislehurst police stations from R Division. It lost Beckenham and Penge to Southend (Catford) Village sub-division, only to regain them in the later reorganisation of 1965. Bromley was completely refurbished and repainted in 1937 on the instructions of the Surveyor's Department after 17 years' constant use 24 hours a day.

Bromley Police Station, Widmore Road, 1915-2003

In 1958 a Bromley officer, PC Henry Stevens (died 2018), became the second of only five officers from the Metropolitan Police ever to receive the highest possible civilian gallantry award, the George Cross. The officer was covering the back door of a house in Bromley where a break-in was reported, and gave chase to an armed man who ran away through the garden. As PC Stevens gained on him and shouted that he was a police officer the man pulled his gun and shot the officer at very close range in the face, breaking his jaw. Despite this, the officer caught up with him, seized and disarmed him. The prisoner broke free, but PC Stevens caught him again, and before collapsing, kept hold of the prisoner's jacket that gave clues leading to the man's arrest.

Widmore Road station was closed and converted into flats under a £120m 25-year Private Finance Initiative (PFI) contract resulting in a new police station and borough headquarters that was completed in 2003 at Bromley South. This contract included the provision of catering, reception, and maintenance staff for the building. The PFI system of financing, encouraged by the government of the day, made a break from the previous trend to own the freehold of sites and to contract out the building work direct.

Bromley Police Station, High Street, Bromley, 2003 to present

The new police station, in High Street, Bromley, is vastly bigger than its predecessors, reflecting the fact that more support staff and facilities are accommodated in such police stations in the 21st century. It was a borough police headquarters when it was opened in 2003 and in 2018-19 became part of the South Area Basic Command Unit that also included the London boroughs of Croydon and Sutton.

Bushey Police Station

The London Borough of Barnet
High Street, Bushey (1841-1993)
S Division (1841-1985/86)
Barnet Division SA (1985/86-1993)
Borough of Barnet OCU (1993-2000)

The Metropolitan Police extended its boundary to encompass the parish of Bushey in 1840. A police station was shown in the High Street, Bushey, Hertfordshire in 1841 when a suitable building was purchased.[505] The station was considered a suitable station for a sergeant to be in charge and in 1855 the sergeant in charge was Zachariah Hollier.[506]

Bushey Police Station 1840-1884

There was sufficient room above the station to house a married officer (most likely the sergeant and his family) costing the occupant 5/- per week.[507] During the 1860s the station manpower consisted of one sergeant, one acting sergeant and fifteen constables. Four constables were posted to day beats and ten constables to the night shift each week. There was a floating constable who would fill in for absences, sickness or would be used as reserve officer and retained at the station for prisoner transport etc.[508] The picture on the previous page shows the original police station, now a private residence called 'Church View House'; the first police station in Bushey opened in 1840, which remained in service until 1884 when the building was given up.

The station call sign for the telegraph published in Police orders in 1893 was Bravo Hotel (BH) but by the 1926 it changed[509] to Sierra Uniform (SU) and its status was that of a sectional station of Edgware.

Bushey Police Station 1884-2000

Bushey Police officers taken in the station yard c.1900

The picture above shows the station strength at Bushey Police Station taken in the yard at the rear in about 1900. The two police officers in charge were station sergeants who wore four chevrons on each forearm rather than the three worn by sergeants. Notice there is not one clean shaven officer amongst them perhaps a help when getting ready for the day shift.

The freehold title to land located at 43 Clay Hill, Bushey, Hertfordshire was purchased by the Receiver in 1876[510] on which to build a replacement police station.[511] By 1884 the new station was completed with 2 sets of married quarters and opened.

This new substantial station is shown at the top of the following column. By 1881 an Inspector had taken charge of the station as large numbers of police officers were recruited. Up until 1881 a sergeant had been in charge.

A police fixed point box was located on land owned by the London and North West Railway outside New Bushey Railway station in 1912. A police (hand) ambulance shelter was also situated there.[512]

In 1914 the station at Bushey was located at Sparrows Herne area of the village, with one Station Sergeant Tom Allinson in charge. He was supported by one other station sergeant, two sergeants, two acting sergeants and 22 constables.[513]

In 1929 Bushey was a sectional station to Barnet police station. In 1947 the station was shown to have one set of married quarters above the station where the Inspector would mostly reside.

In 2000 Bushey Police station was transferred to Hertfordshire Constabulary following government decisions to make the boundaries of the Metropolitan Police coincide with the Greater London Authority and institute the Metropolitan Police Authority to replace the Receiver.

In 2010 the residents of Bushey were informed by the Hertfordshire Police that their station was likely to close due to the high maintenance costs and the need to save money.

Caledonian Road Police Station

The London Borough of Islington
470 Caledonian Road (1855-1992)
Y Division (1840-1958)
N Division (1958-1985/86)
Kings Cross Road Division (1985/86-1992)

The original station in Caledonian Road was built on a plot of land purchased from a local landowner, a dairyman named Mr. Pocock. It cost £2,526 in 1855. The Police purchased the freehold for the sum of £1,040 in 1866. There have been two stations named Caledonian Road Police Station, both of which have been located on the same piece of land. The land was situated near the corner of Georges Road and Caledonian Road.

In 1864 the strength of the station was shown as two inspectors, six sergeants and 50 constables.[514] There was also a mounted constable and horse located at the station. It was a station where charges were taken, and police officers paraded for duty.

The cost of building the station was £2,515. The ground floor consisted of the Inspectors' office, charge room, library, three cells, five stalls for horses and three toilets. In the basement there was a mess kitchen with cooking facilities, a lavatory and

505   *Kelly's Law Directory* 1841 p877.
506   *Kelly's Directory* 1855.
507   Metropolitan Police Orders dated 4th February 1871.
508   Metropolitan Police Special Police Orders 1869.
509   Metropolitan Police General Orders 1893.
510   Metropolitan Police Surveyor's Records 1912.
511   Metropolitan Police Surveyor's Records 1912 p28.
512   Metropolitan Police Surveyor's Records 1912 p30.
513   *Kelly's Directory* 1914.
514   Metropolitan Police Orders dated 11th January 1864.

six coal vaults. On the ground floor there were three cells for detaining prisoners.[515]

The station also contained accommodation for police officers and their families. One married inspector lived on the first floor in a set of rooms, whilst 20 unmarried constables lived together in dormitories on the second floor. The main reason for the location of the station was to be close to the new Metropolitan Cattle Market.

Due to its proximity to the market it became a very important station, with Islington's markets and public houses requiring strict supervision by the police. It is interesting to note that since July 1865 there had been 159 police officers removed from street duties in the Metropolitan Police District to be solely employed in connection with the Cattle Plague Act. The effect of the Act meant that no cattle could be moved for a distance of more than 500 yards except with a Licence from the Commissioner of Police.[516] During the three years since the introduction of legislation in 1866, 20,720 licences were granted by Police in order that 301,526 head of cattle could be moved out of London.[517] From 24th March 1866 Police had been posted day and night at every road around the Metropolis, forming a complete cordon to prevent cattle being moved.

Police officers were also posted to railway stations and wharves. They were required to watch infected districts especially the transportation of manure, which was possibly infected. The Commissioner reported that after three and a half years of this responsibility had been not only a drain on the Metropolitan Police Fund, but also on the available strength of his men.

In 1873 Caledonian Road was designated a station on Y Division under the command of an Inspector.[518]

In 1881 the Station Inspector was Edward Wilkes, a 39-year-old from Rousham near Oxford. He resided there with his wife Fanny. There were 22 single police officers resident at the station. The address was published as 470 Caledonian Road, Islington.[519]

The policing of the Metropolitan cattle market at Caledonian Road was the cause of a great injustice. The market was always the subject of letters to the Commissioner regarding its regulation and control, possibly because of the disruption and chaos which descended on the area.[520]

Policing market areas could be a demanding and testing duty for police officers. Sub-Divisional Inspector Robert Ruff[521] was responsible for markets at Caledonian Road, and also the taverns, inns and other licensed premises in the vicinity. These premises could remain open during market hours, normally when other public houses were shut. This was to allow market workers, herdsmen and drovers the chance for refreshment. It created difficulties because locals purporting to be cattle drovers tried to drink in these establishments.[522]

When two Caledonian Road constables arrested two local men for drinking at one of the establishments, the inspector released them without making an official entry in the Occurrence Book.[523] The Commissioner, Sir Edward Bradford, had received a number of letters of complaint from outraged members of the public regarding the drinking of local people. One anonymous letter pointed out the inspector's decision to release local suspects for drinking during market hours. An investigation concluded that the inspector, who was highly thought of and had nearly 25 years' exemplary police service, should face a discipline hearing. At the hearing he was found guilty, reduced in rank to constable and transferred half-way across London, as was usual. He was so shocked that he was too

ill to commence work, and he appealed to the Home Secretary to be reinstated. The irony was that he needed to complete just six months' more service before he could retire on full inspector's pension. His appeal failed.[524] This underscores the fact that discipline in the police was harsh and often unjust.

In 1894 a cottage at the rear of the station was purchased for the purpose of housing an inspector and his family. He paid five shillings and sixpence a week.

A new police station was built in 1917 on the same site at 470 Caledonian Road, N7.[525] The station was scheduled for a re-fit and was updated in 1937.[526]

Caledonian Road Police Station 1917-1992

In 1958 it was transferred to N Division. The communication code for Caledonian Road was NC (November Charlie). In the early 1970s Caledonian Road was a sub-divisional station of Islington, and the Area Car November 2 was stationed there. The size of the yard and facilities at the station also allowed for the Special Patrol Group (SPG) to be stationed there until they were disbanded in 1985.

Caledonian Road Police Station was finally closed in 1992. Police officers had served the community for over 145 years from this station. Today it is known as Anguilla House, and has been sold and converted into apartments.

Camberwell Police Station

London Borough of Southwark
Camberwell Green (1833-1898)
Church Street, Camberwell (1898-2013)
P Division (1833-1932)
L Division (1932-1965)
M Division (1965-1985/86)
Carter Street Division (1985/86-1993/94)
Walworth Division / OCU (1993-2013)

The old Watch House in Camberwell was used by Police and situated in Camberwell High Road near The Joiner's Arms public house.[527] It contained a small charge room with two cells leading off from it.

In 1833 Camberwell Green was one of the police stations on P Division and was under the command of Superintendent Alexander McLean. The station was one of those where police constables were in attendance at all times.[528]

The station was passed over from the Parish Authorities to the Metropolitan Police by Act of Parliament, with the Surveyors noting that the station was renovated in 1846.[529]

In April 1852 the Home Office considered the purchase of a freehold site for a police station and county court, but the asking price of £4,500 was thought exorbitant so they looked elsewhere. In November 1857 an application was made to the Home Office to rent a house, owned by a Mr John Flower, next to Camberwell Police Station on a lease for 50 years for £100 per annum. Authority was given, with the proviso that the proprietor constructed cells to plans approved by the Commissioner and Surveyor.[530] When the work was finished there was a reserve room, charge room, kitchen and reserve cell with accommodation for a sergeant and two constables.[531]

In 1864 Camberwell Police Station is shown as being on P Division and attached to Walworth Sub-Division (Carter Street). There were two police sergeants and five constables attached to the station.[532]

With a revision of Police boundaries in 1865 P (Camberwell) Division consisted of the following stations: Camberwell (sometimes known as Camberwell Green Police Station), Walworth, Peckham, Norwood, Sydenham, Lewisham, Beckenham, Bromley and Farnborough. Inspector D. Fraser was temporarily in charge as Acting Superintendent.[533]

By 1879 the Camberwell Division was headed by Superintendent Thomas Butt, assisted by Chief Inspector James Davis.[534] In fact Butt was still in post in 1889, although based at Peckham Police Station. By 1881 the Chief Inspector at the station on the night of the national census was James Perry who was living at the station with his son, 14-year-old James Jr. One sergeant and 28 constables were also living in the accommodation.[535] The Division now had a total strength of 726 officers, made up of 44 inspectors, 68 sergeants and 613 constables.[536]

A report in 1881 described it as follows:

"This is one of the old watch houses. The area is very cramped. It is occupied by some married people, who have all to pass through the charge room in coming and going. The accommodation was occupied by two married inspectors."[537]

In 1889 the premises were enlarged at a cost of £579.[541]

In 1893 new premises were considered, and the existing police station is quoted as being 'two old houses adapted for Police purposes at the corner where two roads intersect'.[542]

On 7th March 1894 a freehold site at 22 Church Street, Camberwell, was purchased for £4,000 from Mr Humbert, the land having originally been owned by the Metropolitan Board of Works. The question arose about the Right of Way to the

Camberwell Police Station 1898-2013

Camberwell Police Station 1833-1898

In 1884 the address of the station was shown as Camberwell Green.[538] The freehold of the property was purchased in 1887.[539] In the 1891 census one single sergeant, Joseph Daniel and 18 single constables were residing at the police station. There was also one prisoner in custody, a local bricklayer/labourer.[540]

515	John Back Archive (1975).
516	*Commissioner's Annual Report* 1869.
517	Ibid.
518	Metropolitan Police General Orders 1873.
519	Census 1881.
520	John Back Archive (1975).
521	In 1881 Sergeant Robert Ruff, his wife Eleanor and four children resided at 7 Grange St. Shoreditch, London (Census 1881).
522	The *Police Review* and Parade Gossip 4th May 1894 p209.
523	Ibid.
524	Ibid.
525	Metropolitan Police Surveyor's Records, dated 1924.
526	Metropolitan Police Surveyor's Records, undated.
527	MEPO 5/23 (128) (1).
528	*Robson's London Directory* 1833.
529	Metropolitan Police Surveyor's Records.
530	MEPO 5/26 (154).
531	Metropolitan Police Surveyor,s Records.
532	Metropolitan Police Orders dated 11th January 1864.
533	Metropolitan Police Orders dated 28th October 1865.
534	*Post Office Directory* 1879.
535	Census 1881.
536	*Police Almanac* 1889.
537	1881 Report.
538	Metropolitan Police Orders dated 20th June 1884.
539	John Back Archive (1975).
540	Census 1891.
541	Ten Year Report 1884-1893.
542	LB 442.

rear, and eventually the sum of £60 was paid in compensation to the Trustees of the Camberwell Green Congregation Chapel for a piece of land in Wren Road; the stipulation being that only the Police Authorities would have access to the right of way.[543]

The new police station, designed by John Dixon Butler the Metropolitan Police Surveyor, was opened for business in June 1898 together with the married quarters and section house at the station. The lodging assessment was for one married inspector at 5s 6d per week, one married constable at 3s per week and 24 single constables at 1s per week each.[544] The building was described as follows:

"The new building is a handsome edifice built of red brick and white granite. The base is of glazed brick."[545]

Retirement ceremony of Camberwell officers in 1912

The picture above shows the retirement in 1912 of three officers at Camberwell, who each received a nice carriage clock in appreciation for their long service.

Apparently, the new station was opened without an imposing ceremony by Inspector Fox and his men. A few days later a dog, without a muzzle, ran into the station through open door and claimed the honour of being the first 'run-in'.

The old station at Camberwell Green had been sold and was demolished to make way for a railway station on the proposed branch of the City and South London Electric Railway to Camberwell, Peckham and Dulwich.[546]

In October 1917 Police Constables Jesse Christmas and Robert Melton accompanied Police Inspector Frederick Wright into buildings that had been bombed in a Zeppelin raid in Camberwell. Ten people were killed and 18 were trapped in the debris. The officers cut a hole in the floor and dropped into the basement to search for survivors in spite of a fire raging above them and the risk of wreckage collapsing on them. For their gallant efforts in rescuing thirteen people that night Inspector Wright was awarded the Albert Medal and Constables Christmas and Melton both received the King's Police Medal.

The medals shown bottom left are, from left to right, the KPM, the 1911 Coronation medal and lastly the 1935 Jubilee medal. The Albert Medal is awarded to those who endangered their own lives. The standard set for the award is that the chances of death are greater than the chance of survival, although some have said that the chances of survival had to be negligible.[547]

In 1932 another police boundary reorganisation was made and Camberwell and Peckham police stations were transferred from P to L Lambeth Division.[548]

Behind the station and just a short walk away was the Metropolitan Police Nursing Home, situated at 113 Grove Park Road. The picture below shows police officers recuperating in the garden of the nursing home. Originally called 'Inglewood', the nursing home was bought in 1927 and was followed two years later by the purchase of 114 Grove Park Road for use by nursing staff.

Metropolitan Police Nursing Home

In 1933 the Metropolitan Police took over the responsibility for the licensing of drivers and conductors of trams, trolley vehicles and coaches, also cab drivers in the Metropolitan Police District and the new Metropolitan Traffic Area. This Branch was known as the Public Carriage Office. Camberwell was No. 7 Passing Station, but it is noted that it ceased to be so when the building (which was only a hut) was moved to Lambeth.[549]

In 1934 it was proposed to reconstruct the station elsewhere and extend the section house to provide accommodation for 100 men; twenty years on it was still just a proposal, but it was decided that the station was situated at a focal point and therefore it should remain where it was.[550]

In 1954 the Dixon Committee proposed that Camberwell should remain a Sectional Station with a new Sub-Division of L consisting of Peckham, Camberwell and East Dulwich. The question of the section house was once more mooted, and this was resolved by the purchase of a site at Clapham.[551]

Another reorganisation of boundaries in 1965 saw Camberwell (MC) find itself as a Sectional Station to Carter Street (MC) on M Division.[552]

L-R: The KPM, 1911 Coronation and 1935 Jubilee medals

In September 1970 Camberwell Police Station became a 24-hour Police Office.[553] In 1976 work on a £100,000 conversion of the former section house behind Camberwell Police Station was completed.[554]

In 2004, the station had been closed for three years, and residents, businessmen and politicians were united in their desire to see it opened again. The Borough Commander, Chief Superintendent Ian Thomas, said that with the cost of staffing and arranging disabled access reaching an estimated £400,000 it would be difficult for it to be reopened. He would research this issue and submit detail to the Metropolitan Police Authority.[555]

Camberwell Police Station was closed to the public in 2019 but retained for operational purposes.[556]

Canning Town Police Station

London Borough of Newham

46 Lansdowne Road E16 (1888-1938)

K Division (1840-1938)

Canning Town is situated on the south side of Barking Road, and lies to the north of the Victoria Docks. Today the Barking Road is called the A13, and the first indication the motorist receives that Canning Town is near is when the road rises over what is now known as the Canning Town Flyover.

The first station serving the area was built closer to the Victoria Docks than it was to the centre of Canning Town itself. Barking Road Police Station was situated not far from Canning Town, at the junction with Newham Way and Butcher's Road (eastside). Butcher's Road was originally called New Barn Street; a section of which still exists today to the north of the Newham Way (A13).[557]

At the beginning of 1886 a freehold site was purchased by the Receiver of the Metropolitan Police at a cost of £800. The land used for the station and nearby housing was taken from reclaimed marshland known as Plaistow Marsh, situated south of Becton Road.[558] The new station was called Canning Town and opened in 1888 at 46 Lansdowne Road, Tidal Basin, E16.[559]

At the time of purchase Canning Town was shown as a station on K Division. This appears to have been a large station, which had four public rooms on the ground floor. These were the Inspector's office, the charge room, the store and the public waiting room.[560] The station appears to have been a busy one, because it was built with five cells which perhaps reflects the levels of crime in the area. The constables paraded for duty in the yard where a parade shed had been constructed. Additionally, there was a hand ambulance shed located in the yard, which housed the Bishoffen hand ambulance used for the conveyance of drunken prisoners, ill or sick people and dead bodies. On the first floor there was a mess room, day room, food locker room, bathroom and lavatory. The cooking took place in the kitchen next to the scullery on the ground floor.[561] On the second floor there were two large rooms which housed eleven constables.

In 1888 the station was demolished and the impressive station shown pictured in the opposite column was built.[562]

In 1917, during the height of the war, there was a major incident in this area which attracted a large amount of attention but little publicity, and became known as the Silvertown Explosion. A chemical factory site in Crescent Wharf, West Silvertown, between Canning Town and North Woolwich, was used for the production of munitions for the war effort. It was not an ideal site as it was situated next to a wood yard to the west and an oil depot to the east. Also in the vicinity were substantial residential accommodation, the Tate and Lyle sugar refinery, and a paint works. All this added up to an accident waiting to happen.[563]

Canning Town Police Station 1888-1938

On the morning of 19th January 1917, a massive explosion occurred and 73 people lost their lives, including 13 women and 17 children. Two people were reported missing, believed killed in the tragedy; 170 persons were injured, and 60-70,000 properties were damaged.

One brave police officer, Constable George Greenhoff, was seen rescuing people from the fire and warning others to keep away from the vicinity, as the chemical factory contained quantities of TNT.[564] Later he was caught by the full force of an explosion and died in hospital of his injuries two days later. His widow and eight-year-old son Edward later accepted the King's Gallantry Medal, a posthumous award for his bravery. Edward Greenhoff himself later joined the Force and served 27 years before retiring in 1955.[565]

543 Ibid.
544 Metropolitan Police Orders dated 10th & 20th June 1898.
545 *Police Review and Parade Gossip*, 17th June 1898.
546 Local Press Report 1898 – publisher unknown.
547 www.historybytheyard.co.uk/gallantry accessed 23rd March 2008.
548 Metropolitan Police Orders dated 1st November 1932.
549 MEPO 2/5359.
550 LB 442.
551 Ibid.
552 Metropolitan Police Orders dated 6th August 1964.
553 Metropolitan Police Orders dated 28th August 1970.
554 *South London Press*, 27th January 1976.
555 *Southwark News*, 5th February 2004.
556 MPS (2019) FOI request. Station closures broken down by year.
557 *Master Atlas of Greater London* (1998).
558 *Bacon's London Atlas 1888*.
559 John Back Archive (1975).
560 Ibid.
561 Metropolitan Police Surveyors Records 1924.
562 Ibid.
563 John Back Archive (1975).
564 Fido, M. and Skinner, K. (1999) *The Official Encyclopaedia of Scotland Yard*. Virgin Press. p109.
565 John Back Archive (1975).

This incident was entirely the result of an unfortunate set of circumstances rather than good military precision by the German fighting machine. Special constables had been sent from Canning Town and North Woolwich to help with the situation, and were quickly followed by re-enforcements from East Ham and Forest Gate. Regular constables were supplied from Bow, Poplar, Limehouse and East Ham. They helped the firemen deal with the flames, carry out the dead and attend to the injured and homeless. They also helped to secure the huge number of damaged properties. Special constables assisted, and supported the regular officers for sixteen days after the event, during some of the coldest days for some time. The homeless slept in partly-constructed shelters in the area and were helped by the goodwill of the constables and specials who attended.[566]

One of the major problems facing new police officers, many of whom have come from outside London, is accommodation. The Metropolitan Police have, since the very earliest times, been conscious of the need for clean and adequate dwellings for police officers and their families not only for health reasons but also in case of corrupt practice. The highly regulated nature of policing ensured that approval to live at certain locations was given by senior officers, to avoid problems like criminal or problem neighbours. The police made a conscious decision to build both married and single officers' quarters, in the process making them the largest London landlord.

A need was identified at the turn of the 20th Century for more quarters, and various premises were selected to cater for this. It was to this end that Canning Town Police Station was designed to have sufficient space, and work in April 1911 and provided accommodation for 35 unmarried men at the station.[567]

Canning Town Police Station remained operational until closing in June 1938, when all business and other policing functions were transferred to Plaistow Police Station.[568]

A new police office for Canning Town was opened in Tarling Road in 1989. By 2002 the office, which was located in a parade of shops which had all ceased trading, was no longer in use and was closed.

Cannon Row Police Station

City of Westminster
1 Cannon Row (1902-1985)
Victoria Embankment (1985-1992)
A Division (1902-1985/86)
Cannon Row Division (1985/86-1993)

This small street off Bridge Street, opposite the Houses of Parliament and sometimes spelled Canon Row, was once the place where the canons of St Stephen's Chapel in the Palace of Westminster had their lodgings. The police station was built between 1898 and 1902, and designed by J. Dixon Butler with R. Norman Shaw as consultant because it effectively became an extension of the New Scotland Yard buildings. The redevelopment of King Street provided the opportunity for the police to acquire a site in Cannon Row, backing on to New Scotland Yard. A new station was duly built by Messrs E Lawrence and Sons at a cost of £36,468, and finally taken into use on 21 July 1902. This convenient location, adjacent to Scotland Yard, brought fame to Cannon Row, not only because of its central location but also because the famous Scotland Yard detective squads would tend to bring their high-profile prisoners there. The building contained married quarters for two inspectors and two constables, with accommodation for a further 96 single officers.

The building was constructed from granite, Portland stone and red brick, with a slate roof. The style was an amalgam of Flemish and English Baroque sources, continuing Shaw's original New Scotland Yard theme. The design included an L-shaped plan with screen wall to a courtyard. There were four storeys and an attic main block with a two-storey range in parallel fronting Cannon Row and a five-storey east wing. The building had some notable architectural features which led to it becoming a listed building.

Cannon Row Police Station 1902-1985

In 1935, the section house at Cannon Row was closed and the accommodation converted for use as offices. Cannon Row was used by the Metropolitan Police until May 1985 when the police moved to a new Cannon Row police station converted from the Curtis Green building, which later became a base for the Diplomatic Protection Group in 1992. The Curtis Green building became New Scotland Yard in November 2016.

The officer in charge of A Division at Cannon Row had the privilege and responsibility of having responsibility for the officers policing Buckingham Palace and the Houses of Parliament. Until the establishment of specialist branches to undertake these roles in the 1980s, Cannon Row's remit, like that of King Street before it, extended to maintaining the policing presence for the Palace of Westminster and the royal residences.

Modern policing tends to bring stories of security scares every so often, but there has not been anything recently to compare with the action of John Bellingham on 11th May 1812. Spencer Perceval, the Tory Prime Minister, was walking through the lobby of the House of Commons to attend a committee examining the problem of the recession when he was accosted by Bellingham who had fallen into debt after having been imprisoned in Russia. The security of the Houses of Parliament was far less strict in those days, and Bellingham had been able to lay in wait, armed with a pistol, and murder the Prime Minister, whom Bellingham appeared to blame for his personal situation. Bellingham was detained by unarmed bystanders and given into custody.

Superintendent Creswell Wells was a famous officer of the Metropolitan Police who joined in February 1871 (warrant no. 52767) and retired after 46 years' service in November 1916 after his health had started to fail. He also had to bear the loss of one of his sons in WWI. Holding the prestigious position as the senior officer in charge of A Division, he was decorated a number of times by the King.

Wells, originally from Bosham in West Sussex, was first

posted to D (Marylebone) Division and lived in the police section house in Wellbeck Street, Marylebone in 1871 as a single man aged 20 years. In March 1877 he was made a 1st Class Constable on V (Wandsworth) Division. Later, as an Inspector at Wandsworth Police Station, in 1881 he resided in West Hill, Wandsworth with his wife Fanny and their four children. Inspector Wells then moved to K (Stepney) Division 1885. By 1891 he was a Chief Inspector on E (Holborn) Division, only to return to K by 1893 as the Superintendent in charge. He stayed there until 1908 when he was selected to take charge of the higher-profile A Division. Wells presided over the militant suffragette demonstrations and was instrumental in ensuring that sufficient officers were on duty to cope with the disturbances. He was particularly upset by suffragettes stabbing his officers' horses with hat pins, which meant that many were arrested and brought before the courts. Wells monitored all the suffragette marches, incidents, demonstrations and protests. He was present at court to supervise the prosecutions and to report back to the Commissioner and more senior officers.

Superintendent Creswell Wells

Mrs Pankhurst under arrest in Victoria Street on 13 February 1908

Wells held his responsibilities of protecting Buckingham Palace, Parliament, the House of Lords and the Prime Minister's residence 10 Downing Street very seriously indeed. Anyone attempting to over-run any of these was subject of arrest and prosecution on his orders. In 1909, three suffragettes who wished to speak with the Prime Minister outside his residence refused to move when Wells had asked them to. There were a further 150 members of the League who supported them. Wells was left with little choice but to have the three arrested, and the 150 supporters moved on. This caused some disquiet amongst the gathering crowd but was ably dealt with by Wells and his men. In 1910 his officers arrested suffragettes in Downing Street for obstruction, and he appeared before the court to justify their arrests.

In January 1911 Wells was awarded an MVO for his contribution to the security and safe-keeping of King Edward VII. Appointment to the Royal Victorian Order recognised distinguished personal service to the Sovereign, the reigning monarch of the Commonwealth realms, any members of their family or any of their viceroys. Established in 1896, its motto is Victoria, alluding to the founder of the order, Queen Victoria. Admission remains the personal gift of the monarch. The Royal Victorian Medal can be awarded at three different levels.[569]

Wells was always regarded 'as a first-rate officer, a well-known and popular figure, and a very nice man'. When a prosecuting solicitor reported to Wells that he had left his wristwatch in the men's wash room at Bow Street Court and that the attendant had denied any knowledge of the item, Wells immediately left their lunch table at the Gaiety restaurant and returned the lawyer's wrist watch without disclosing how he had managed avert an embarrassing incident.[570]

Much of Wells' duties were performed on horseback. He was an accomplished horse rider, and had the services of a groom at Cannon Row to care for his horses. Wells would ride in full ceremonial uniform at events such as Trooping the Colour, and would have his horse transferred to race meetings such as Goodwood, Ascot and Kempton Park, where he would also take charge of policing and the King's security.

Wells was also responsible for the arrangements for the state funeral of Edward VII in May 1910. The King was laid in state in Westminster Hall and thousands of people were shepherded into the hall to file past the coffin. Wells was responsible for the good order of the people wishing to pay their respects and police arrangements.

Senior officers of A Division, with Superintendent Creswell Wells wearing a helmet

Early in 1917, a few short months after his retirement, Creswell Wells was found dead at home. There was a full service funeral held at Tooting cemetery, which was attended by Sir Edward Henry, the Commissioner, and other representatives from the Metropolitan Police to mark the end of his distinguished life.

On a happier note his son Sidney George Wells, who had joined the police at Bow Street in 1914, was doing well with his new police career, becoming a Sergeant by 1919, Station Sergeant at Albany Street in 1925 and three years later Inspector at Kentish Town. In 1933 he became Sub-Divisional Inspector at Marylebone Lane, Chief Inspector and then Superintendent at the new Traffic Branch, New Scotland Yard in 1945. Like his father he excelled at organisation and management, which was

566   Reay, Col. W. T. (1920) *The Specials*, Billing and Sons Guildford.
567   Metropolitan Police Orders dated 3rd April 1911.
568   Metropolitan Police Orders dated June 1938.
569   en.wikipedia.org/wiki/Royal_Victorian_Order accessed 5th August 2012.
570   Dornford Yates (2001) '*As Berry and I Were Saying.*' House of Stratus.
571   Jones A.E. *An Illustrated Directory of Old Carshalton*. Published by the Author, date unknown.

recognised by the King and other foreign royals on state visits by the award of a number of important medals, including the MBE in 1949 and the King's Police and Fire Service Medal for distinguished service in the 1953 Coronation awards.

Riding horses on duty is not without risk. Chief Inspector Frederick Rivett had been transferred to Cannon Row on promotion in 1916, replacing Chief Inspector Joseph Short. This rising star, who was set for higher rank, came off his horse three years later in similar fashion to Sir Robert Peel on Constitution Hill and broke his neck. The recently promoted James Powell, who had replaced Wells as Superintendent, soon had to arrange a full service funeral for his unfortunate deputy.

*Cannon Row Police Station 1985-1992.
The former Curtis Green Building, Victoria Embankment and New Scotland Yard since November 2016*

After 1985 the station at 1 Cannon Row closed, and was replaced by refurbished accommodation in the Curtis Green building that had originally been designed as an extension to New Scotland Yard but had been taken over in 1939 by the War Office at the outbreak of WW2 before the Metropolitan Police could make use of it. In due course the building reverted back to police use. After serving as the 'new' Cannon Row, it became a base for the Diplomatic Protection Group for a period when territorial policing for this part of central London was reorganised so that Charing Cross Police Station accommodated the officers previously serving at Cannon Row and Rochester Row. The Curtis Green building was given a major refurbishment before replacing the Metropolitan Police's Broadway headquarters and continuing the title New Scotland Yard in November 2016.

Carshalton Police Station

London Borough of Sutton
Pound Lane Carshalton, Surrey (1848-1920)
P Division (1848-1865)
W Division (1865-1920)

The first Metropolitan Police station built in Carshalton was at the junction of Pound Street and West Street, next door to an old wooden-slated house called Wandle Lodge. It was built on the site of the "Cage for erring humans and a pound for straying animals".571 The station was opened in 1848 and was the first one in the area to have a base for a horse patrol. It was a sergeant station on P or Camberwell Division.572 A Carshalton at the time was the largest and most important village between Croydon and Ewell.

Carshalton Police Station 1848-1920

In 1865 it was a Sergeant supervised station on P or Camberwell Division. In October 1870 the supervising Police Sergeant was George Robins, aged 46, rode his Police horse from Carshalton to Wimbledon, and tragic circumstances occurred. He stopped at an inn and spoke to someone in the stable about his horse when suddenly the horse kicked the officer in the chest and he died immediately. He was interred in Carshalton Church, with over 100 officers attending the funeral. Sergeant Robins left a wife and a number of children.573

In 1892 Inspectors Rowbottom and Holdaway were in charge of the station.

It served the community until it was demolished in 1920, when Carshalton came under the new police station at Wallington. At the start of the 20th Century Carshalton had over 50 constables and policed Wallington; when the new station was built the staff moved over to Wallington.

When Carshalston Police Station was demolished the site was laid out with turf and flowers, and enlarged later when Wandle Lodge was demolished.

Carter Street/Walworth Police Station

London Borough of Southwark
Apollo Buildings, East Street (1830-1844)
Carter Street (1856)
292 Walworth Road (1884-1993)
12-28 Manor Place (1993 to Present)
P Division (1830-1886)
L Division (1886-1921)
M Division (1921-1932)
L Division (1932-1965)
M Division (1965-1985/86)
Carter Street (Walworth from 1993) Division / OCU (1985/86-2018)
Basic Command Unit Central South (AS) (2018 to present)

In P Division there was a Section House called Apollo Buildings situated in East Street, Walworth. This was a traditional brick and tile building, which was rented from Mr. H. Davis on a yearly tenancy. The Section House also had a three-stall stable. This was given up in 1844.

The Receiver, John Wray, often travelled all over London on horseback looking for suitable premises in which he could house his constables, and in May 1856 he leased a house and grounds in Carter Street, known as Walworth House, for a term of 26¼ years expiring in June 1882, for use as a Police station.[574] The premises were owned by a Mr Gedge, and had originally been occupied by him as his private residence. The rent was £80 per year. When the premises were taken, six cells were erected and other works carried out, including a three-stall stable/coach house,[575] under the supervision of Charles Reeves, Metropolitan Police Surveyor, and involved an outlay of about £600. Accommodation was provided for one inspector and 30 single constables,[576] and in March 1856 the station was opened.

On 9th November 1860, at about 1.00pm, two persons called at Carter Street/Walworth Police Station. The Station Officer, Police Sergeant 18P, ascertained that the two gentlemen were from the London, Chatham and Dover Railway, and had called for the purpose of measuring a proposed line for the railway. They stated that the 'Station House' would have to come down. The Railway Company would require 13 perches of ground at the end of the station yard, and the line would be open to traffic within the space of two years. In November 1861 the Receiver sold his leasehold interest in the strip of land at the rear of the Police Station site to the Railway Company for the sum of £300, for the erection thereon of part of the viaduct to carry the railroad. A proviso in the agreement was that Police would have the use of the space under the arches.[577]

In 1869 Carter Street Police Station was part of Camberwell Division, of which Superintendent Edward Payne was in charge, based at Carter Street. The Division comprised of four inspector police stations: Bromley; Clockhouse, Peckham; Gipsy Hill and Norwood. There were also five sergeant police stations, at Camberwell Green, Beckenham, Farnborough, Rushey Green, Lewisham and Sydenham.[578]

In July 1869 the Secretary of State at the Home Office, on the recommendation of the Commissioner, agreed that a room at each police station be regarded as a recreation room in which smoking would be allowed. Expenditure was also agreed on the purchase of a miniature billiard table for each division, and games such as 'Draughts, Dominoes, Backgammon, Singlesticks, and Boxing Gloves for each principal Section House'. Carter Street received the billiard table and other stations on the division just the games.[579]

At an auction held on 26th June 1875 the Receiver's agent purchased the freehold of the residue of the lease of 1856 for £3,710.[580]

In 1879 Carter Street was under the command of Superintendent Thomas Butt on P (Camberwell) Division.

Superintendent Butt, warrant no. 38649, joined the Police on 16th January 1860 and retired in 1892 after 32 years' service.[581]

In 1881 a major report was prepared on the condition of Metropolitan Police stations. Each station visited was in need of work to improve the sanitary conditions in which the policemen were working. Carter Street was described as:

Superintendent Thomas Butt

'a fine open site. The buildings consist of an old residence with cells (5) &c, added to it. The basement is low and unhealthy. The bedrooms seem crowded, and the occupation not arranged for the comfort of the men'.[582]

The accommodation was occupied by one single sergeant and 29 single constables. On the night of the 1881 census there were six prisoners detained at the station – two unemployed females and four males. Two of those were unemployed, one was a bricklayer and the other a bookmaker.[583]

The accommodation at the station was unsatisfactory and major refurbishment took place, but it was obvious that a new station would have to be built.[584] It is interesting to note that the report referred to the station as 'Walworth, Carter Street', as did the *Post Office Directory* of 1879.

In 1884 the address of the station was recorded as 292 Walworth Road, SE17,[585] and was located on P Division.

In 1886 Carter Street Police Station was transferred to L Division. In 1891 Superintendent J. Brannan was in charge of the division, together with six Police Inspectors: A. Waddell, J. Porter, G. Dunleavy, C, Branwhite, H. Powell and W. N. Race.[586] The telegraphic code or code signals for Carter Street was Charlie Whiskey (CW).[587]

Carter Street Police Station, 292 Walworth Road, 1910-1993

572 *Post Office London Directories* 1847.
573 *Sutton Journal*, 20th October 1870.
574 John Back Archive (1975).
576 Ibid.
577 Ibid.
578 *Police Almanac* 1869.
579 Metropolitan Police Orders dated 15th July 1889.
580 John Back Archive (1975).
581 MEPO 4/339.
582 1881 Report.
583 Census 1881.
584 Surveyor's Report 1881.
585 Metropolitan Police Orders dated 20th June 1884.
586 *Kelly's Sydenham, Norwood and Streatham Directory* 1891.
587 Metropolitan Police General Orders 1893.

In the early 1900s it was decided to rebuild the station to suit the growing requirements of the district, and there was much discussion with the Home Office before they would approve the cost of a new police station at Carter Street. The Home Office was concerned about the increase in cost of new stations. The Metropolitan Police Surveyor, John Dixon Butler, was required to make a detailed report tabulating the cost of materials necessary to build the station, together with the costs, per cubic feet, of the thirteen police stations built between 1882 and 1903.[588] Eventually a new station, designed by Butler, was built and opened in June 1910. Lodging assessment for Carter Street Police Station was established as 9s 6d per week for married quarters and 1s per week each for 50 unmarried men.

James Ford was the Sub-Divisional Inspector from 1899 until 1903, when he was succeeded by Frederick Spencer in 1904, who in turn was followed by Francis Rolf (1905-07), John Collins (1908-11), Frederick Wright (1911) and Francis Odell (1914-19). Odell, shown in the picture below, was famous since he was the recipient of the RHS bronze award for saving life, a rare event for an inspector. He is shown, together with his medals on both sides of his chest, seated second from the left together with his three inspectors and five sergeants.

HRH Queen Mother with Commissioner Sir John Nott-Bower and Constable Musto

In 1956 Carter Street was visited by HRH The Queen Mother as part of her duties as patron for the London Gardens Society. The competition winner would receive the ultimate prize: the Lady Byng Trophy for Best Police Station Garden. Police Constable Musto had tended the garden with a small group of other Police volunteers for some time, and told the Queen Mother that he had done so for 31 years.

It was reported that

'she was surprised to see such a nice garden in such a busy area; it's a little paradise'.[593]

The Queen Mother signed the Police Station's Occurrence Book in red ink, a very rare event indeed, but this led to an investigation because by the next day someone had torn the page from the book. This action caused a great deal of concern and consternation, since this amounted to theft of Police property by an insider – a police officer or member of the civil staff. The local Complaints Department carried out a thorough investigation, but after many months of interviewing they got nowhere. The page could not be found, and only resurfaced in the 1980s along with other correspondence.

Inspector Francis Odell and colleagues at Carter Street Police Station

In 1921, during an internal revision of boundaries the police station was transferred from Lambeth Division (L) to Southwark Division (M).[589] Superintendent Henry M. Mann was in charge of Southwark Division, which at the time consisted of Carter Street, Deptford, Grange Road, Rodney Road, Rotherhithe and Tower Bridge stations.[590]

Nine years later, in 1932, Carter Street returned to L Division as a result of the closing of Kennington Lane and Rodney Road Police Stations.[591]

A communication from the London County Council dated 13th March 1950 was received at the station informing the Metropolitan Police that, as of 1st July, the portion of Carter Street in which the police station was situated would be renamed Carter Place. The Commissioner was approached to see if the station name could be changed from Carter Street to Walworth Police Station, but he felt that there should be no change.[592]

The front of Carter Street Police Station shows a well-kept garden, which was tended by a group of police officers in their spare time. There was a Police Garden competition instituted which prompted a fierce rivalry amongst officers, especially senior officers, who would brag about their divisional attainments in all sorts of sports.

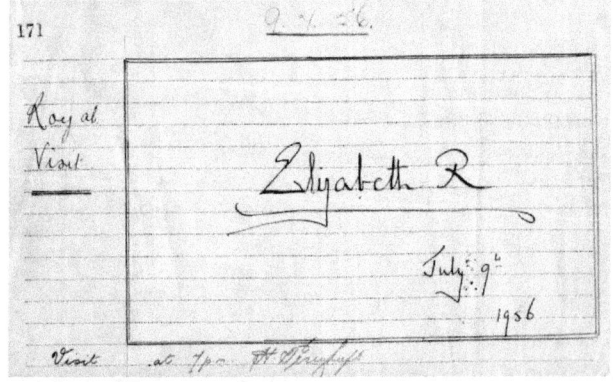

Entry in Carter Street Police Station Occurrence Book, July 1956

Another change of Police boundaries occurred in 1965 and Carter Street (MS) was designated a Sub-Divisional Station of M Division, with Camberwell (MC) as its Sectional Station, both situated on the new London Borough of Southwark.[594]

By the 1990s the old Carter Street Police Station had become too small for Police purposes. The old buildings did not adapt well to the modern technology being used in the Police service, and the increase of Police personnel meant that there was an urgent need to build a modern, much larger, police station.

The author of many books on the humorous side of policing, the late Harry Cole served as a police constable for 30 years at the old Carter Street Police Station. He said:

"It always had a reputation as a violent station, which was nonsense really. It was a very happy station to work at".[595]

In November 1993 the new police station replacing Carter Street was opened at 12-28 Manor Place, Walworth,[596] named Walworth Police Station. The £4.3 million new station took three years planning and two years to build. The new red brick building is twice the size of the old station, with 4,200 sq m of floor space compared with 1,600 sq m. Before the new Walworth Police Station was built the land had been occupied by a liquor warehouse, which had to be demolished to make way for the new station.[597] An archaeological dig was made on the site before the go-head was given for development in an effort to trace historical artefacts from the Manor House which was originally situated near to the site, however nothing was found.

Walworth Police Station is open 24 hours each day.

Catford and Southend Village Police Stations

London Borough of Lewisham

Catford Hill (1892-1927)

333 Bromley Road, Southend Village (1927-2017)

P Division (1892-1985/86)

Catford Division (1985/86-2000)

Lewisham Division / OCU (2000-2017)

The first police station in Catford was acquired as a freehold site on June 1888 from the Trustees of the late Major John Forster's estate. It was a few minutes walk from Catford Bridge Railway Station on the main Perry Hill Road leading to Lower Sydenham.[598]

The new station, designed by John Butler, Metropolitan Police Surveyor, was built and opened March 1892.

Catford Police Station 1892-1927

Four Station Sergeants, one Section Sergeant and four constables (one Acting Sergeant) were posted to the new station.[599] It slowly increased in importance, and by 1899 Sub-Divisional Inspector George Smith and Inspectors Harry Knighton and John Cathcart were attached to the station.[600] By 1903 Smith had been replaced as Sub-Divisional Inspector by William Phillips.[601]

Mr Robert John Collie of St. George's Lodge, Catford, was appointed Divisional Surgeon to the Police of P Division, and covered Catford Police Station.[602]

Catford was originally a Sub-Divisional Station but in 1905 lost that status, being replaced by Lewisham. This meant that Sub-Divisional Inspector W. Fraser, Inspectors Charles Lane and William Austin, Section Sergeants Frederick Dyer and Ernest Coombs were all transferred from Catford to Lewisham.[603]

In March 1913 the Town Clerk of the Borough of Lewisham informed Police that Catford Police Station, situated at the junction of Catford Hill and Rathfern Road, was to be known as 128 Catford Hill.[604]

In due course a new police station was needed. Two houses were purchased, one known as The Elms and the other The Limes,[605] and converted for Police purposes at 333 Bromley Road, Southend Village. It was taken into occupation and business commenced in November 1927. It was to be known as Southend Village Police Station, and was situated some way away from the displaced old Catford Police Station. The old Catford Station later became the Metropolitan Police Engineer's Depot.[606]

In 1932 Southend Village Police Station became a Sub-Divisional Station, with Penge and Beckenham having Sectional Status.[607]

Catford Police Station 1940-2017

In early 1936 it was found that due to an increase workload larger premises were needed, but the present site was

588 HO 45/9999/A47675.
589 Metropolitan Police Orders dated 24th February 1921.
590 *Police Almanac* 1930.
591 Metropolitan Police Orders dated 1st January 1932.
592 John Back Archive (1975).
593 *Daily Mail*, 10th July 1956.
594 Metropolitan Police Orders dated 6th August 1964.
595 Annette Butler. *The Job*, 7th January 1994.
596 Metropolitan Police Orders dated 24th November 1993.
597 *The Job*, 7th January 1994.
598 MEPO 5/502.
599 Metropolitan Police Orders dated 15th March 1892.
600 *Kelly's Lewisham, Brockley & Catford Directory* 1899.
601 *Kelly's Directory* 1903.
602 Metropolitan Police Orders dated 16th March 1892.
603 Metropolitan Police Orders dated 14th December 1905 and MEPO 2/905.
604 John Back Archive (1975).
605 Covenants 24th January 1927. Lewisham Archives A93/4/12/55.
606 Metropolitan Police Orders dated 15th November 1927 and L.B.506.
607 Metropolitan Police Orders dated 1st January 1932.

considered too small for expansion. Messrs Wates had acquired land from the Forster Estate and offered the Police a corner site. The Police agreed to purchase the site, but the London Council refused to approve the layout of the estate as planned by Messrs. Wates. Eventually a revised site was offered, and the freehold was purchased in November 1936 from the Forster Estate Development Company.[608] In January 1940 the new Catford Police Station opened at Bromley Road, Southend Village,[609] with Superintendent W. Collins placed in charge.[610] His command of P Division now contained the following police stations: Catford, Lewisham, Brockley, East Dulwich, West Dulwich, Sydenham, Beckenham, Penge, Bromley, Farnborough, Chislehurst and St. Mary's Cray.

By 1965 Catford (PD) Police Station was not only the P Divisional Headquarters, but also the Sub-Divisional Station with Section Stations at Lee Road (PE) and Sydenham (PS).[611]

The station was closed to the public in 2017.[612]

Chadwell Heath Police Station

The London Borough of Redbridge

High Road, Chadwell Heath, Essex (1892-1969)

14 Wangey Road, Chadwell Heath (1969-2000)

K Division (1840-1965)

J Division (1965-1985/86)

Ilford Division / OCU (1985/86-2017)

Chadwell Heath Police Station Lamp

In 1840 Chadwell Heath was shown as a station on K Division, situated on the outer district. It had a station strength of one sergeant and three constables,[613] who all lodged privately. All prisoners were transported to Ilford Police Station[614] for charging, and were remanded to the Petty Sessions at Ilford.

The exact location of Chadwell Heath Police Station was unknown, except it was a station without cells and no charges were taken there.[615] It is strongly suspected that the old watch house in the centre of the village was used as a police station before the purchase of a purpose-built police station house.[616] The records show that in 1873 Chadwell Heath was designated a station of K Division (West Ham), and had a sergeant in charge. The division was a large one, covering fifty square miles. The Divisional Superintendent needed to travel from his base at Stepney (Arbour Square) for supervision purposes.[617]

The station strength was one sergeant and seven constables.[618] There were no senior ranks at Chadwell Heath, so further supervision originated from Ilford Police Station. An Inspector and a Section Sergeant would supervise (sometimes across divisional boundaries) a large area which included Ilford, Barking, Dagenham, Loughton, Woodford, Wanstead, Chadwell Heath, Barkingside, Chigwell and East Ham. This would be achieved on horseback, as there were two sergeants at Ilford who would share the station horse for this purpose.

In 1880 arrangements were made for the lease of land in the Romford Road from the owner Mr. Thomas Hearn of Chadwell Heath, Essex, for an annual rental of £20. The landlord was required to pay the rates, and was also responsible for the insurance in case of fire. The building could only be used for police business and for no other purpose.

In 1881 a new station was to be occupied for a short period by police, with accommodation for a married sergeant who occupied four rooms at the station.[619] The address of the station was published as Romford Road, Chadwell Heath.[620]

In 1889 a parcel of land became available, at the corner of the High Road and Station Lane, Chadwell Heath, on which to build a new police station. This site was where old stocks once stood for the public humiliation of offenders. The freehold land was purchased from Mr. Pritlove for £400, and over the next two years a station was built on the site.[621] Meanwhile, Chadwell Heath was being policed by Sergeant Gibson and eight constables.[622] The station was completed and ready for occupation in December 1892.[623] In 1931 Chadwell Heath was described as a sectional station of Ilford Sub-Division.[624] The picture below was taken in 1911.

Chadwell Heath Police Station, High Road, 1892-1969

In January 1938 Inspector 112439 Thomas Hill, his wife and two children took up occupancy of the married quarters above Chadwell Heath Police Station. He soon became involved in the community issues at Chadwell Heath and Ilford. Inspector Hill was born in Deptford in South East London. He joined the Metropolitan Police Service in 1923 at the age of 23, and served on inner police divisions as a Constable, Sergeant and Station Sergeant. On promotion to Inspector, in 1936, he was posted to E Division. He then came to Ilford Sub-Division, on K Division, in 1938. Sadly, he died in May 1953, just six months before he reached his thirty years service and his pension.[625] He was a well-liked and respected officer during his fifteen years on Ilford Sub-Division and his colleagues sorely missed him. His family (although compensated with a death in service award) had to leave the married quarters and find private accommodation.

Inspector Thomas Hill c.1936

By the late 1950s there were doubts that the old Chadwell Heath Police Station could continue to perform adequately as a police station, and instructions for the purchase of new land to build a modern police station were issued to the Surveyor's Department. A substantial piece of land became available a short distance away from the old station in Wangey Road and Cedar Park Gardens, just off the High Road.

In 1961 negotiations to purchase this land were undertaken, and by 1962 the land had become the property of the Metropolitan Police.[626] Meanwhile, the Traffic Police used the old station until 1978. It then remained empty until 1981, when the property was sold to a local building company called Harts.[627] It is now licensed premises called The Eva Hart, named after a survivor of RSS *Titanic* who died recently and had lived locally.

In the meantime there was a re-organisation of boundaries which coincided with a Local Authority revision of boundaries. As a consequence Chadwell Heath and Ilford, located on K Division, were transferred to J Division with effect from April 1965. Records show that both Wanstead and Chadwell Heath were section stations to Ilford Sub-Division.

The new station was built at 14 Wangey Road, Chadwell Heath and became operational in December 1969.

Chadwell Heath Police Station, 14 Wangey Road, 1969-2000

In April 2000 Chadwell Heath Police Station joined with Ilford, Wanstead, Barkingside and Woodford to become part of the Borough of Redbridge Police Division. Chadwell Heath became a non-operational police station in 1997. The property was eventually sold.

Chalkhill Police Station

The London Borough of Brent
1 Ken Way, Wembley (1997-2017)
Wembley OCU

In 1997 plans were passed by Brent Council for a 'community police station' to be built on the land to the north-west side of Ken Way, Chalkhill Estate, Wembley, Middlesex, HA9 9DS. This building was eventually built, and owned, by the local authority. It became known as the 'police station' and was responsible for policing the Chalkhill Estate. In more recent times it has become one of the twenty one Safer Neighbourhood Teams offices in the borough and officers there are known as the Welsh Harp Team. In 2017 the Local Authority closed the station as part of austerity measures along with proposals to close other police stations in the borough.

Charing Cross Police Station

Agar Street, London WC2N 4JP from 1992
Charing Cross Division (1992-2018/19)
Part of Central West Basic Command Unit (c.2018 to Present)

The former Charing Cross Hospital in Agar Street, designed by Decimus Burton, was refurbished for use as a police station and officially opened by the Queen in December 1992. It replaced both Bow Street and Cannon Row police stations. The number of police officers required at these, and indeed other central London stations, reduced dramatically with the advent of computerised traffic management systems. Charing Cross was designed with a large number of cells so that it could cope with arrests arising from demonstrations in central London. It also became a base for part of the Diplomatic Protection Group.

Charing Cross Police Station 1992 to present

Charing Cross is, of course, famous for its railway station, where many thousands of people arrive into central London each day without any problem or controversy. Every so often, however, something extraordinary happens.

On 6th May 1927 a man, looking as if he might have been a soldier, arrived in a taxi and deposited a trunk at the station's left luggage office, leaving in the same taxi. After a while, the trunk began to smell, and a police officer was called before the trunk was opened. The contents turned out to be various parts of a murdered woman.

608	LB 506.
609	Metropolitan Police Orders dated 1st January 1940.
610	*Police and Constabulary Almanac* 1940.
611	Metropolitan Police Orders dated 6th August 1964.
612	Metropolitan Police Information Rights Unit 10th June 2018, accessed 25th January 2019.
613	John Back Archive (1975).
614	In the early days the station was referred to as 'Little Ilford Police Station' by Senior Officers and those responsible of issuing of Police Orders.
615	Elliott, B. (1993) *A History of the Police Stations of J Division 1886-1986*.
616	John Back Archive (1975).
617	Metropolitan Police General Orders 1873.
618	Elliott, B. (1993) *A History of the Police Stations of J Division 1886-1986*.
619	Metropolitan Police Orders 24th March 1881.
620	*Kelly's Directory* 1884.
621	Elliott, B. (1993) *A History of the Police Stations of J Division 1886-1986*.
622	*Kelly's Directory* 1890.
623	Metropolitan Police Orders dated 4th December 1892.
624	*Kirchner's Police index* (1931). Police Review Publishing.
625	Metropolitan Police Records.
626	Elliott, B. (1993) *A History of the Police Stations of J Division 1886-1986*.
627	Ibid.

Over the years we have become used to calling in the CID to make sense of distasteful and perplexing situations like these. Their professionalism and skill are great assets for the life and safety of London, and on this occasion it was Detective Chief Inspector George Cornish who started a murder enquiry.

Some items of clothing had laundry marks, perhaps more common then than nowadays, and the police traced them to a Mrs Holt, who was found to be alive, well and living in Chelsea. Mrs Holt had had ten female servants in the previous two years, and all but one was accounted for, a Mrs Rolls. The detectives then traced a Mr Rolls and established that the victim had once been living with him, her real name being Minnie Bonati, a prostitute. A shoeblack had picked up the left luggage receipt after it had been thrown from the taxi window, and the taxi driver was then traced. The taxi had taken his fare to 86 Rochester Row, where a John Robinson had a second-floor office, working as an estate agent. At his lodgings, a telegram was found that led to a Mrs Robinson, who had believed that she was John Robinson's legal wife, unaware that he had committed bigamy at their wedding. Mrs Robinson became just as anxious to trace him as the police, and took George Cornish to meet him at a pub in Walworth, where John Robinson was arrested. Robinson denied any knowledge of the crime, was not picked out at an identification parade, and the murder enquiry was in danger of stalling. But George Cornish asked for a grimy duster found in the trunk to be washed and examined more carefully – it revealed the word 'Greyhound', creating a link with the hotel where Robinson had been staying. A renewed search of his offices also revealed a blood-stained match, and this led Robinson to confess.

This case occurred before the Metropolitan Police Forensic Science laboratory had been established in April 1935, but the case did enjoy the expert attentions of pathologist Sir Bernard Spilsbury who had first come to public attention with the Dr Crippen investigation in 1910.

Another forensic science connection to Charing Cross was the gun shop in nearby Agar Street owned by Edwin Churchill, where detectives would often call for an opinion about firearms. Edwin, assisted by his nephew Robert Churchill, gave expert evidence in the 1903 Moat Farm murder case in Essex where Samuel Dougal had shot Camille Holland, demonstrating the distance from which a gun would need to have been fired to have inflicted a head injury. Robert Churchill helped his uncle by test-firing bullets into sheep heads, and eventually developed an encyclopaedic knowledge of firearms. In later years he regularly gave evidence as an expert witness alongside Bernard Spilsbury, and was one of the first people to use a comparison microscope to confirm or disprove, from tiny rifling marks, that bullets had been fired from the same gun barrel.

A conference room at the station is dedicated to the memory of detective Constable James Morrison QGM, who was stabbed to death whilst off duty and chasing a suspect at Aldwych WC2 in 1991.

In 2019 Charing Cross was the only station in Westminster to feature a public counter open 24 hours a day.

Chelsea Police Station

Royal Borough of Kensington and Chelsea
4 Union Place (pre-1830)
1-2 Milman's Row (1830-1852)
Strewan Place / King's Road (1852-1897)
385-9 King's Road SW10 (1897-1939)
2 Lucan Place SW3 3PB (1939 to present)
V Division (1830-1865)
T Division (1865-1886)
B Division (1886-1985/86)
Chelsea Division (1985/86-1993/94)
Part of Brompton OCU (1993/94-2018/19)
Part of Central West BCU (2018/19 to present)

An early section house stood at 4 Union Place, Chelsea, which may have had an earlier life as a watch house before 1830 when the Metropolitan Police started patrolling in this area. It was brick and tile built, with ten rooms and a yard at the back that was shared, along with a solitary water closet, with the neighbouring house. Another section house existed at Exeter Buildings, Brompton, but it was given up in 1851.

In 1836, a police station existed in Worlds' End at Milman's Row, later Milman's Street. This road, where the former Gorges House once stood, ran from King's Road down to the river. Milman's Row was built up on its east side with rows of terraced cottages in 1836. On the west side were two brick and tile-built houses at numbers 1-2 which served as the police station and section house. They were rented, and described as being old in 1845, but there were eleven rooms on the first floor, a yard to the rear and two cells.

One of the officers living at Milman's Row in 1846 was 30-year-old PC 54V Robert Woolgar. He had been born in the Isle of Wight, had nine years' service, and lived above the police station with his dressmaker wife Ann and their 5-year-old son. One May Saturday afternoon he was called to a dreadful incident on Battersea Bridge when 24-year-old Eliza Clark had walked to the middle of the bridge and thrown her three children into the river. The officer was in time to stop the mother jumping in after her children, but only one child was rescued alive. The incident had occurred at about 3.00pm and, in a reflection of the rapid speed of justice of the day, by 5.00pm Mrs Clark was in Westminster police court. She had been subject to domestic violence from her husband, a journeyman painter, and later told the court that he had been a good husband and father, when sober. She had been obliged to pawn her petticoat and sell other clothing to buy food when he had been out of work. Eliza Clark was charged with the murder of her daughter, who had hit her head on the river bed and drowned, but the jury at the Old Bailey found that she was not mentally responsible for her actions and she was detained 'during Her Majesty's pleasure'.[628]

A plot of land was leased from Lord Cadogan in Strewan Place, Chelsea from Christmas 1850. Strewan Place was effectively part of the adjoining King's Road, and the Receiver thereby gained control of a useful corner plot. A police station and section house were built for £1,500 in 1852. This was described as a substantial brick and slate building with a day room, charge room and three cells.

London was increasing in size rapidly at that time, and World's End was beginning to lose the validity of its name. The Metropolitan Police was conscious of the risk of its patrolling strength being diminished by increased demands, and in 1855 a B Division report indicated that since 1849 44 streets, four

Chelsea Police Station, 383-389 King's Road, 1897-1939. Demolished 1984

squares, and 1,860 houses had been added to the division, with another 199 in the process of construction. The average length of their night duty beats had increased from 1,100 yards to 2,000 yards in that time, despite 15 new beats being formed.

Arguments over the adequacy of resources are not new. The Superintendent estimated that four extra sergeants and 20 constables would be needed to keep up the level of protection that had been given in 1849.[629] Some of the B Division beats were covered by the Reserve Force, which had been established with six inspectors, 30 sergeants and 300 constables on 24th August 1848. This body of officers were selected to be ready to deal with public order problems and ceremonial events. These sergeants and constables would display the letter R on their uniform after the letter of their division (eg BR) and, for some periods of time, they would receive extra pay.

The amount of property in police possession in World's End increased when Earl Cadogan's estate leased premises to the Receiver at 389 King's Road. Adjoining houses at 383-387 were then also purchased, and the freehold bought in 1892 for £2,750. Enlargement works were undertaken at a cost of £7,352 and the resulting new police station, covering the entire corner plot, was taken into use on 9th August 1897.

The 1897 Chelsea Police Station was closed when the new B Division headquarters were taken into use at 2 Lucan Place at 6.00am on Sunday, 6th August 1939.

The outbreak of the Second World War in 1939 ensured that the station and its officers were kept at full stretch. Within the Metropolitan Police District there were 1,900 cases of war damage to police stations, 124 of them being regarded as 'serious'. B Division was hit by 24 V1 flying bombs and one V2 rocket during the war. A total of 5,000 members of the Special Constabulary enrolled for war service as full-time officers at the beginning of the War, and of those who did not become full-time officers 6,000 joined the Armed Forces. The strength of the Metropolitan Police was supplemented by re-engaged police pensioners and war reserve officers, but thousands of regular officers were released to the Armed Forces. Part-time Specials were used extensively; often after they had performed a full day's work at their normal jobs.[630] The value of having a substantial body of relatively experienced officers available for emergencies was thereby plainly demonstrated.

One traumatic event to occur at Chelsea involved the arrest of Günther Podola in 1959. Podola had been a member of the Hitler Youth movement, and escaped to Canada from East Berlin in 1952. He was deported to West Germany in 1958 after being sentenced to prison for burglary in Canada, and later came to England with the intention of promoting himself as a gangster. On 7th July 1959 he broke into a flat in Roland Gardens, South Kensington, stole money and some passports, and then wrote to the victim in an attempt to blackmail her.

These cases have always been difficult to investigate, but when Podola telephoned her using an alias to make arrangements for a payment of $500 to be made, the victim cleverly kept Podola on the telephone for long enough for the call to be traced. Detective Sergeant Sandford from Chelsea rushed to a telephone box in Thurloe Street near South Kensington underground station with his colleague DS Raymond Purdy to arrest Podola whilst the suspect was still talking on the telephone.

Podola broke away and escaped to a block of flats in Onslow Square, where the officers caught up with him in the entrance hall. Suddenly, the situation escalated. John Sandford saw Podola pull out a gun, shoot Raymond Purdy at point blank range, and then run off. Despite his desire to catch the suspect, John Sandford remained to give what assistance he could to his dying colleague, and telephoned Chelsea for assistance. Detective Superintendent David Hislop and DCI Bob Acott rushed to the scene and a full-scale murder hunt ensued.

627 www.woolgar.org/timespdf/times072.pdf
628 MEPO 2/26.
629 'The Metropolitan Police At War' HMSO 1947.
630 *Death on the Beat*, Dick Kirby, Pen and Sword 2012.

Chelsea Police Station, 3 Lucan Place, from 1939

Raymond Purdy's widow had been given her dead husband's personal possessions, but within these there was an address book that she did not recognise. This appeared to belong to the suspect, and it provided the clue to his identification. One of the addresses belonged to 'Little Jack', the owner of a shop where, a few days earlier, Podola had attempted to sell a stolen tape recorder, and had been stopped and questioned by two 'aides to CID'. Because the tape recorder had not then been recorded as stolen, the officers had, reasonably, not arrested Podola, but the details they had recorded in their pocket books enabled the investigating team to identify him as having been in Canada, and they obtained a copy of his photograph and fingerprints.

Podola was then traced to the Claremont House hotel in Kensington. When the officers tried to enter his room they thought they heard the click of a gun being cocked the other side of the door, but nevertheless charged the door open, knocking Podola across the other side of the room in the process. After a trial at the Old Bailey Podola was executed on 5th November 1959.[631]

Chelsea Police Station became part of Central West BCU in 2018/19.

Cheshunt Police Station

Broxbournet District Council Essex
101 Turners Hill, Cheshunt, Enfield, Middlesex
N Division (1862-1865)
Y Division (1865-1886)
N Division (1886-1933)
Y Division (1933-1985/86)
Enfield Division / OCU (1985/86-2000)
Transferred to Essex Police 2000

In September 1861 the Home Office allocated £250 for the building of a police station in Cheshunt. It would appear that the police used the old watch house in Turners Hill, Cheshunt until suitable land could be found to build a new station. Therefore the first station to take the name Cheshunt Police Station appears to have been the old watch house, because records show in 1864[632] Cheshunt Police Station as being part of N or Islington Division, prior to the building of any new station. Along with a number of other stations, Cheshunt was transferred to the new Y or Highgate Division in October 1865 upon its formation.

It was reported that the old watch house was most unsuitable for policing purposes, and that effort should be made to find an alternative site and premises for a new station. In May 1869 the Metropolitan Police Surveyor reported that a suitable piece of land had been found in Turner's Hill, opposite the old watch house. The freehold to the land was purchased from the owner, Mr. Cox, for £600 in 1870. The building on the site cost £900, and consisted of a two-storey building with a 50ft frontage. This was in need of conversion for police purposes. Messrs. Hill and Son completed this work at a cost of £738. Once completed the ground floor had a charge room, a reserve room, a washing room, two cells, a two-stall stable, two water closets and two coal sheds. The section house above provided accommodation for four constables, a married sergeant and a married inspector.

Superintendent Walker, the Divisional Superintendent for Y or Highgate Division reported on 4th June 1872 that the new station at Cheshunt "was now complete and ready for occupation this day".

A revision of divisional and station boundaries took place in August 1886. Cheshunt reverted back to N or Islington Division, only to be transferred back some years later as a sectional station of Enfield Sub-Division in July 1933.

The next boundary revisions occurred as a result of the Local Government re-organisation in 1964, and saw Cheshunt designated as 'YC' and remaining as a sectional station of Enfield Sub-Division. The station was located within the Cheshunt area of Hertfordshire.

Cheshunt Police Station 1872-1968

At about the same period, negotiations were in hand to purchase and build a new station in Cheshunt, the old site being unsuitable, awkward in shape and not situated centrally. A site was found 200 yards away on the opposite side of the road from the old station at 101-117 Turner's Hill, and was purchased by the Metropolitan Police for £50,000 in February 1964. The site was cleared ready for building.

Tenders were invited for a two-storey modern police station with access from the front, and to include car parking places at the rear. The station would be faced in brick, contain proper load-bearing walls and wood-framed windows, with the boundary walls to have blue flint brickwork. Builders Messrs. David Chaston Ltd won the contract, and building work commenced in July 1966 and continued until March 1968.

Police Orders recorded the opening as such:

"A new sectional station for Cheshunt (YC) at 101, Turners Road, Cheshunt, will be taken into operational use at 6am 1st April 1968, when the existing station will be closed."[633]

In the entrance lobby of Cheshunt Police Station is a small cabinet which contains the original watch house stone and reproductions of some of the old Watch Committee activities. The old blue police station lamp, which stood outside the old station, was refitted outside the new building. The station contains a front office reception area, three cells and two detention rooms. There is a garage at the rear for two cars and motorcycles, together with parking space for a further twelve vehicles.

Cheshunt Police Station 1968-2000

The police station was transferred to Hertfordshire Constabulary in April 2000.[634]

Chigwell and Claybury Police Stations

Epping Forest District Council
Chigwell Cottages (1875-1900)
Woodford Bridge (1900-1976)
24 Brook Parade, High Road, Chigwell (1976-2000)
N Division (1840-1886)
J Division (1886-1985/86)
Barkingside Division (1985/86-2000)
Essex Police (2000 onwards)

Claybury Police Station Lamp

In 1840 Chigwell Police station strength was shown as one sergeant and four constables. The sergeant was recorded as a mounted officer, and all five officers were shown as being lodged privately. In rural areas it was normal for the sergeant to live at the station house, which was usually a private house, whilst the constables lived nearby also in private rented accommodation.

Supervision was undertaken from Ilford Police station, where the officer in charge was an inspector and it was the place to take prisoners for safe-keeping and charging. The petty sessions were also held at Ilford, so it was a simple task to escort them to court from the station. Some three constables were also shown stationed at Lamborne (End) and lodged privately.[635]

In January 1864 Chigwell Police Station was described as having with no cells, and being a place where no charges were taken.[636] By this time the authorised strength had increased to one sergeant and eight constables, however it appears that one constable was also used as an acting sergeant, allowing for supervision of both the day and night shifts. Two constables paraded for day duty and four constables for the night shift,[637] There was no further increase in strength to replace the acting sergeant.

Further supervision of Chigwell continued from Ilford Police Station, which was on a neighbouring division. Chigwell was a station on N Division whilst Ilford was on K Division.[638] The Inspector had considerable responsibility, which necessitated him covering the stations at Ilford, Barking, Dagenham, Loughton, Woodford, Wanstead, Chadwell Heath, Barkingside and East Ham. This was a huge area in those days to supervise, and was probably completed by horse. The instruction concluded that one horse was to be ridden by two sergeants alternately at Ilford Police Station.[639]

The Commissioner had issued instructions in December 1864 for the building of a number of Police station houses. Within this instruction Superintendents were required to make an effort and obtain sites for these new stations, and Chigwell was one station specifically mentioned.[640]

In 1865 three new Divisions were formed: W for Clapham, X for Paddington and Y for Highgate. Chigwell is shown on N or Islington Exterior Division, and also on K or Stepney Green Exterior Division as being sergeant's houses only.

In 1871 the newly-acquired Woodford Police Station became the Sub-divisional station for the others located at Wanstead, Chigwell, Loughton and Waltham Abbey. It appears that the sergeant was removed to Waltham Abbey, because records in 1873 indicate that Chigwell as it was called was a constable station.[641]

A cottage at Woodford Bridge, owned by Mrs. P. McAvoy, was found and later leased by the Metropolitan Police for use as Chigwell Police Station. Accordingly, when the adjoining cottage became available with stable and loft in 1875,[642] Mrs. E. McAvoy offered this to the police. It appears that the offer was accepted with an annual rental of £20 for each cottage. The exact location of this station was unknown, but it appears to be on the same site as the current building.

Both cottages were known as Chigwell Cottage. In 1875 it was reported that the new Police station at Chigwell should be occupied forthwith and 'that rent in the sum of 3s per week should be paid by the occupying married constable' for four rooms.[643] Over the years the cottages deteriorated, and conditions were unhealthy. During an inspection by the Metropolitan Police Chief Surgeon he described the station as 'two small ordinary cottages with a poor stable rented in neighbours' outhouse'. The cottages were shown as being occupied by one married sergeant and one married constable. He recommended that the cottages should be pulled down, and a purpose-built station erected in its place.[644]

The address in 1884 was recorded as Woodford Bridge, Chigwell, but it was called Chigwell Cottage. The lease was renewed yearly with an option of a three-month notice to quit on either side. The Receiver paid for all repairs and taxes. The ground floor space included a charge room, a reserve room, one water closet and a coal shed. Use of a stable was also provided, however this was given up in 1884.[645]

In 1886 Chigwell was transferred from N or Islington Division with the formation of the new J or Bethnal Green Division. On 23rd March 1900 a new Police station at Claybury was opened and replaced Chigwell, which started a 70-year

631 Metropolitan Police Orders dated 11th January 1864.
632 Metropolitan Police Orders dated 29th March 1968.
633 www.met.police.uk/enfield/history.htm accessed 15th May 2002.
634 Metropolitan Police Surveyor's records (undated).
635 Metropolitan Police Orders dated 11th January 1864.
636 Ibid.
636 Ibid.
637 Ibid.
638 Metropolitan Police Orders dated December 1864.
639 Metropolitan Police General Orders 1873.
640 John Back Archive (1975).
641 Metropolitan Police Orders dated 9th August 1875.
642 Report on the conditions of the Metropolitan Police Stations, 1881.
643 Metropolitan Police Surveyors records (undated).
644 Metropolitan Police Orders dated February 1900.
645 *Kelly's Directory of Essex* 1898.

gap when Chigwell Police station ceased to exist, although officers covered the Chigwell Area.[646]

The Metropolitan Police purchased the freehold site in 1892, and work soon began to build a new station at the location. Claybury Police Station was completed in 1900 and was the first purpose-built station for the area. It was built at the fork in the road where Chigwell Road and Manor Road meet and contained stables for horses and cells to hold prisoners, in addition to two sets of married quarters.

In 1898 Sergeant Hankerville was the sergeant in charge of Woodford Bridge Police Station, as it was referred to then.[647] In 1907 Claybury was a sectional station of Woodford on J or Hackney Division,[648] and in addition to the station itself it had two sets of quarters, probably for the sergeant-in-charge and his family.[649] Later, the address was shown as High Road, Claybury,[650] however this was later changed to Manor Road, Woodford Bridge, Essex. After 1900 telegraphic codes were issued to stations to help with communication. Claybury had 'CL' as its telegraphic code. In 1937 all stations received standardised station codes to assist operators of telegraphic equipment in order to facilitate the identification of not only individual stations, but also of their division as well. Claybury, being a station on J Division, was allocated the code 'JY'. In the same year Claybury was refurbished, and a number of improvements were made to modernise the station.

Claybury Police Station, Manor Road, Chigwell, 1900-1976

A review of police areas as result of the Local Authority boundary revisions in 1965 found that Claybury Police Station was wrongly situated, so instructions were given for the purchase and building of a new station at Chigwell.

Chigwell was shown to have an ambulance shelter some distance from the station, located at the Rector's House in Chigwell Row, with the agreement that for this service 2/6d per year was paid.[651]

Instructions were issued that the new station, at 24 Brook Parade, High Road, Chigwell will be taken into use, and on 12th January 1976 and that the present Claybury Sectional Station should close.[652]

Claybury was still in use by the police but not as an operational police station. It had been for some time the area dogs' section headquarters, known as Claygate House, although the property has now been sold.

Force re-organisations caused Chigwell to become the headquarters station for J Division when the divisional suite and staff transferred from Leyton Police Station on 30th December 1975.[653]

The new station at Chigwell was built to a high specification and considerable cost since senior officers and area headquarters staff were to be housed there. In 1989 the Area Headquarters and their staff moved once more, to Edmonton Police station where purpose built accommodation was prepared for them.

Chigwell Police Station, 24 Brook Parade, High Road, Chigwell, 1976-2000

Further reorganisation and border realignment in April 2000 meant that Chigwell Police station was transferred to Essex Police. The station was surplus to requirements, and has been shut down and sold off.

Chingford Police Station

London Borough of Waltham Forest
Kings Head Hill, Chingford, Essex (1888 to present)
N Division (1840-1933)
J Division (1933-1985/86)
Chingford Division / OCU (1985/86-2018)
Basic Command Unit, East Area (NE) (2018 to present)

Chingford Police Station Lamp

Chingford Police Station has had a long and chequered career. In 1837 the Bow Street Horse Patrol operated locally, being based at Enfield and Loughton with responsibility for patrolling Chingford. When the Horse Patrol was integrated into N Division of the Metropolitan Police in 1839, Chingford was allocated two constables from Waltham Abbey from a strength of four sergeants and 13 constables.[654]

Records tell us that on 31st December 1864 the Commissioner directed, with immediate effect, the Divisional Superintendent for N or Islington Division, in co-operation with the Metropolitan Police Surveyor, to make every effort to find a suitable site for the location and building of a new police station at Chingford.

Before this time Chingford was policed from Sun Street Police Station, Waltham Abbey. Police officers usually worked from their homes, and were scattered about the parish. In 1873 the station was designated a constable-only station.[655]

In 1874 a memorandum from the Commissioner of Police to the Receiver[656] requested a report from the police surveyor on the suitability of a plot of land owned by Mr. Charles Alcock. The land available was on the hill at Chingford, not far from the railway station. This land fronted the highway, behind the old Lockup, and had a side road. It was available for sale at £250. The surveyor commented that it was most suitable in every way for the building of a police station. The Commissioner recommended to the Home Office in January 1875 that the land should be purchased with a view to building a police station on the site. The Home Office duly approved this purchase, and the freehold was secured in June of the same year.[657]

There appears to have been no urgency to build a station at the location because the site remained vacant until 1887, except perhaps for the "old watch house" and the stable built in 1881. The stable was added at a cost of £495 in order to stable the horse ridden by the Divisional Superintendent. The horse was used to inspect the division and the Superintendent had to travel from Islington to the Divisional Headquarters station located some distance away. N Division stretched even further out to Loughton and Waltham Abbey, making the job of supervision by the Superintendent a difficult and arduous task. A married sergeant resided above the stables, occupying five rooms at a weekly cost of 4/- rent.

In May 1882 the police at Chingford were present when Queen Victoria opened up Epping Forest to the people of London. By 1871 the Corporation of London had purchased some 6,000 acres of forest land which, whilst private in nature, came within the newly-constituted Epping Forest Act 1878 allowing access by the public. The Queen arrived at Chingford Railway Station by train and was conveyed by carriage to High Beech, where she planted a sapling oak, which did not survive. Apparently, seventeen divisions supplied officers to police the event with 1,529 police officers involved in ensuring the security of the Queen during her visit. The three-and-a-half mile route from Chingford Station by way of Ranger's Road, Fairmead, had police officers at intervals of between two and twenty yards. It was estimated that half a million people welcomed the Queen to the forest, with ten thousand of them being officially entertained by the Lord Mayor of London at temporary accommodation set up on Queen's Green. The Queen arrived late at 4.05pm and returned to Windsor at 5.30pm. This was a costly affair for the Police Commissioner, as the Secretary of State instructed the Receiver to give the officers employed on the Queen's visit an extra day's pay.[658]

With the formation of J or Bethnal Green Division, Chingford was re-affirmed as remaining on N Division.[659]

Permission was granted by the Home Office to build a new police station on the hill at Chingford in 1886, with building work commencing the following. The new station cost £1,869 and was completed for occupation in March 1888.[660] With the building of a new station came the authorisation of an increase in staff and an alteration in the boundary for the station. The enhancement included two Divisional Inspectors and two Sub-Inspectors. The boundaries of Enfield Highway and Walthamstow were altered in consequence of the opening of the new station.

The Police and the Fire Brigade usually worked together at the scenes of fires. If a police officer rendered assistance to the Fire Brigade at the scene of a fire he could receive a cash reward.[661] In 1900 there was a fire in Station Road and Constable Wiggins, attached to Chingford Police Station, gave assistance to the Brigade. On reporting a fire to the Brigade the reward was ten shillings, whilst rendering assistance was a further five shillings, which he claimed.

An incident which attracted significant attention in Chingford in 1912 was the mysterious death of a local councillor and member of the Stock Exchange, Mr. Piers N. Holmes. Chingford Station Sergeant Edward Maber was assigned to investigate the matter, and visited the scene of the suspicious death at Chingford Lodge (now renamed 'Kilgreana') at Chingford Green. He found the deceased in bed holding a five-chambered revolver, and from this he concluded that Mr. Holmes had taken his own life. Ultimately suicide was the verdict of the Coroner, and in those days it was a criminal offence for someone to take or attempt to take his/her own life.[662]

Chingford Police Station 1888 –1977

During the First World War Mr. R. Bullock OBE was the Divisional Commander of the Chingford Special Constabulary. In 1917 Police Sergeant Francis Breed was shown as the officer in charge of the station, with a compliment of 38 constables. He served until 1922.[663]

In 1924 an additional strip of land was purchased for £160 at the rear of the station. As a consequence of this purchase, the station was enlarged to ensure greater efficiency. In 1930 a change occurred in how fires should be notified to the particular emergency service. Previously notifications by the public had been given to the police, but now this responsibility passed to the local fire brigade, bypassing the police. This system altered on 21st July when the new fire station, which had been built in the Ridgeway next to the Town Hall, took over responsibility for fire warnings.[664]

646 *Kirchner's Almanac* 1907.
647 Metropolitan Police Property records 1924.
648 Metropolitan Police Property records 1912.
649 Metropolitan Police Property records 1924.
650 Metropolitan Police Orders dated 30th December 1975.
651 Ibid.
652 Elliot, B (1992). *History of the Police Stations of J Division 1886-1986*, p5.
653 Metropolitan Police General Orders 1873.
654 Metropolitan Police Commissioners Memorandum dated 15th December 1874.
655 Elliot, B (1992). *History of the Police Stations of J Division 1886-1986*, p5.
656 Metropolitan Police Orders dated 23rd May 1882.
657 Metropolitan Police Orders dated 26th June 1886.
658 Metropolitan Police Orders dated 12th March 1889.
659 Rider, G. (1987) *Chingford Police – Law and Order 1504-1987*.
660 Ibid.
661 Ibid and Reay, Col. W. T. (1920) *The Specials*, Billings, Guildford, Surrey p71.
662 John Back Archive (1975).
663 Metropolitan Police Orders dated May 1932.
664 Metropolitan Police Surveyor's Records.

In 1932, as part of the Force re-organisation, Chingford was transferred from Walthamstow Sub-Division to Enfield Highway Sub-Division. A further status change a year later transferred Chingford to J or Hackney Division, but kept it as a sectional station of Walthamstow Sub-Division.[665]

During the mid 1930s police telephone boxes appeared at major traffic junctions in Chingford. They were originally made of concrete painted blue, and contained a single telephone which was connected by secure private line to Walthamstow Police Station.

Metropolitan Police Box c.1955

Around this time Chingford Police received its first motorised transport – a police car for patrolling the Walthamstow and Chingford area.

Between 1860 and 1938 a hand ambulance was used at most police stations to transport ill, injured or drunken people. The 'barrow', as it was called, was a heavy three-wheeled vehicle, purpose-made for the Metropolitan Police. The ambulance on Chingford Division was situated behind the police box on the corner of New Road opposite the Prince Albert.[666]

Towards the end of the 1950s and early '60s the Metropolitan Police began to modernise by making officers more mobile. Previously pedal cycles and patrol motorcycles had been used. The motorcycles were usually a single 500cc Triumph twin, Norton 500c or BSA Bantam solo motorcycle. They were allocated to individual stations. The Metropolitan Police issued the Velocette LE light motorcycle, a water-cooled 198cc motorbike from 1959 to police stations for the purpose of speedier response to calls for assistance. Some of the "Noddy" motorcycles, as they were called, were fitted with a Force radio transmitter so that they could remain in contact with the station or New Scotland Yard. They lasted until the early 1970s when they were withdrawn.[667]

Personal radios and unit beat 'Panda' cars were issued to Chingford Division in 1968. The Pandas were Morris Minor 1000cc saloon motor vehicles, and were issued to replace the ageing 'Noddy' bike. With the advent of the personal radio, which was issued to each officer on duty outside the station, came the demise of the police telephone box. Mobile communications meant that the fixed telephone boxes could be removed, as they were now out of date. They were phased out over a period of time.[668]

During the 1965 boundary changes there was no change in status or responsibility, except that the new Division was located with the London Borough of Waltham Forest.

Chingford Police Station was extended in 1971/72, although it was still woefully inadequate for its task. The police considered building a new station soon after the extension was completed. Tenders were invited for a four-storey building of reinforced concrete pillars surrounded by brickwork and blocks. Costain's won the contract, and authority was granted at a cost of £700,000, however final completion cost the police some £200,000 more. It was built with a basement and allowed for further vertical extension later if necessary.[669] The building took two years to build, but on completion was surrounded in controversy. Speculation had indicated that the re-organisation of the Metropolitan Police District might have meant that Chingford lose its police station, however in reality this was not the case.

On completion of the new building Chingford replaced Walthamstow as the Sub-Divisional headquarters. The new station became operational on 10th January 1977, but was officially opened by the Minister of State for the Home Office, Lord Harris of Greenwich, on Friday, 23rd September 1977. On the following two days the station was open to the public and many visitors took the opportunity to look around the station.

Chingford Police Station 1977 to present

On 29th November 1991 Sergeant Alan King was stabbed to death in Higham Hill Road, E17 when he went to apprehend a suspect.[670] The killer was captured, later convicted of his murder and sentenced to life imprisonment. A monument was unveiled by the film director Michael Winner of the Police Memorial Trust during a ceremony as a tribute to Sergeant King at the place where he gave his life.

In 1999 Chingford Police Station was renamed Waltham Forest Police Station, and became the Borough Headquarters. The newly-appointed Borough Commander and administrative staff were relocated to the station.

In 2020 the station was still operational and is open to the public 24 hours a day seven days a week.[671]

(Chipping) Barnet Police Station

High Street, Chipping Barnet (1841-1915)

26 High Street, Chipping Barnet (1915-1977)

26 High Street, Barnet (1977-1993)

S Division (1841-1985/86)

Barnet Division (1985/86-1993)

Borough of Barnet OCU (1993-2018)

North West NW BCU (together with Brent and Harrow, 2018 to present)

Evidence of a police presence in the village of Chipping Barnet (now called High Barnet), on the Great North Road, can be traced back to 1841 when a station situated in the High Street was occupied for police purposes as part of S or Hampstead Division, with Divisional Superintendent John Carter in charge.[672]

Annual rental for two cottages at 47 and 48 Barnet Road (later Barnet Lane), originally the Bow Street horse patrol cottages, were taken over by the Metropolitan Police in 1845. These consisted of standard brick and tile cottages, with a small garden and stable in each. Each had four rooms and a coal cellar. The cottage was rented from Mr. Anderson of Anderson Cottages, Finchley for £10 per year, with the cost of the stable being an additional £5. When taken over by the Metropolitan Police they were in a sad state of repair and needed renovation, which were immediately carried out, but the premises were given back to the landlord in 1849[673] and vacated by police.

It was felt that because of its position Chipping Barnet Police Station was an important enough station for an inspector to be in charge. Accordingly, the first senior officer in charge was Inspector Samuel Evans between 1841-45 (having been promoted to Inspector on 30th March 1832), residing there with his wife and six children. Also billeted at the station was 34-year-old constable Thomas Webb. Evans joined the Metropolitan Police as one of the very first police officers (warrant no. 784), attested on 21st September 1829.

Because of the exceptional leadership skills displayed by Evans (including the supervision of the Barnet horse fairs) he was recommended for promotion to Superintendent and was transferred to M Division in June 1845. Such was the exacting role of a superintendent that Evans retired on pension as 'worn out' just four years later, in October 1849.[674]

The Divisional Superintendent would make unannounced visits to each station on the Division on horseback. At the top of the following column is a picture of Superintendent Loxton of S Division, 1855-1867, taken in about 1865. He is seated on his dappled grey mount on Hampstead Heath, wearing the new uniform and helmet introduced in 1865.

Loxton's predecessor in 1845 was Inspector George Billers, who was well known to Samuel Evans as they had both joined the police together on the same day in 1829. Billers, a Londoner from Kentish Town, took charge of the station[675] and stayed in post until 1855, when he retired on pension.[676] Billers had been promoted to Inspector in 1840, and then posted to Somers Town Police Station before being transferred to leafy Barnet.

In 1863 a new police station was brought into service, shown above. Barnet Police Station and section house for single police officers was occupied in June 1863 as a station on S or Hampstead Division.[677] The station, which was designed over four floors cost £2,084 and consisted of an Inspector's office, waiting room, four cells, water closets and urinals. In the yard were stables and a hay loft, together with a free-standing parade shed where the constables would muster for parade before being posted to their patrols. Also downstairs in the basement was a library, mess room, kitchen, food locker, drying room and three coal cellars. Upstairs on the first floor was a bathroom and residential accommodation.

Superintendent Loxton of S Division c.1865

The section house accommodation for single police officers comprised space for six constables who paid 1 shilling each per week, whilst the married quarters were charged at 5/6d per week.[678] The station was allocated the call sign of Bravo Alpha (BA) for telegraphic purposes in 1871.[679]

The police station at Barnet was purposely situated on the main route north, which saw a rise in traffic heading in and out of London as methods of transport evolved and horse-drawn vehicles were gradually replaced by motorised and mechanical vehicles.

Gradually, as more people came into London to find work from the countryside, the suburbs began to expand in terms of transport with the building of new roads and houses. This expansion also increased the need for more police officers and stations. The consequences of this were the need on occasions to re-balance police station and divisional boundaries. Such a re-organisation occurred in 1889 when a new sub-division was formed. The boundaries of Hampstead, Barnet and Edgware were altered and a new sub-division of Finchley was formed, which Barnet was a part.[680]

Sergeant Alfred Tuckwell was shown in the 1871 census at residing at 163 South Mimms Road with his wife and child.[681]

665 Rider, G. (1987) *Chingford Police – Law and Order 1504-1987*.
666 Ibid.
667 Ramsey W. G. (1986) *Epping Forest Then and Now*. p86.
668 Mead, B. (undated) Welcome pack Chingford Division.
669 www.met.police.uk/a/your-area/met/waltham-forest/chingford-green/?introducingyoursaferneighbourhoodsteam=nearestpolicestations accessed 23rd October 2020.
670 *Kelly's Law Directory* 1841.
671 Metropolitan Police Surveyor's Records.
672 List of Superintendents of Divisions 1829-1953.
673 *Kelly's Law Directory* 1855.
674 Ibid.
675 Metropolitan Police Orders dated 20th June 1863.
676 Metropolitan Police Orders dated 4th February 1871.
677 Metropolitan Police Orders dated 12th December 1871.
678 Metropolitan Police Orders dated 6th December 1889.
679 Census 1871.
680 *Kelly's Directory* 1875.
681 Metropolitan Police Orders dated 4th February 1871.

Barnet Police Station, High Street, Chipping Barnet, 1863-1915

He was the Station Sergeant at the local Barnet Police station in 1875.[682] One married Inspector resided there with his family, whilst a further six single constables also lived above the station. The inspector and constables contributed towards their living accommodation, with the inspector paying 5/6d and the constables one shilling per week.[683]

In 1871 a review was undertaken of police accommodation as there was a lack of affordable and clean housing in London. Apart from the Metropolitan Police being the largest London employer at this time, it was soon to become the largest landlord. And so began an audit of police buildings and living areas which considered housing conditions, cleanliness, sanitation and disease.

The duties of the inspector were clearly set out, with strict instructions that he should patrol the area on horseback and was not to be posted to duty at the station itself. Because Barnet was an outlying station, supervision of the constables fell to the patrolling inspector. Sergeant Tuckwell was to remain at the station at Barnet, dealing with day-to-day inquiries and processing of prisoners for court. Tuckwell was one of two sergeants attached to Barnet, each working a 12-hour shift (one by day and the other by night). The sergeants would rotate their duties to ensure neither was permanent days or nights, but there was also an acting sergeant who would cover for the substantive sergeant for 12 hours in every 24 hours whilst he was away from the station. The inspector was responsible for patrolling the sectional stations of (South) Mimms, Shenley and Whetstone. Shenley had no cell space, so prisoners were transferred to Barnet either by trap, or accompanied by the arresting officer on foot. There were also no cells at Mimms although Whetstone did have cells for prisoners.[684] There were two horses stabled at Barnet.

The Barnet Fair

The Barnet Fair, or Costermongers Fair as it was colloquially known, was policed from Barnet Police Station and by the 1870s it had become the most popular fair in the country with great opportunities to make money both legally and illegally. Large numbers of people meant that there a chance to have a good time, especially with betting and drinking.

In 1859 the horse fair was held on land to the east of the railway, between Potters Lane and the Meadway, and by 1929 development saw the fair move across Barnet Hill to fields to the south of Bedford Avenue. Two years later it moved to a field adjoining Pricklers Hill.[685]

In 1874 *The Barnet Press* reported that 20 plain-clothes detectives, four sergeants and 44 constables from London were brought in to be on duty at the fair. This probably did not work very well, as in 1888 there was a serious attempt to close down the fair on the grounds that it had become a nuisance. Serious disorder had been narrowly avoided by the strong presence of police, but local businessmen got together a petition that stated:

'It has been ascertained that an average of over 20,000 persons attend Barnet on each fair day and expenditure in the town and neighbourhood alone is estimated at upwards from £10,000 to £12,000 among tradesmen and farmers.'[686]

The April fair had ceased in 1881 which left the September fair, and this took place in the area around Wood Street. Later this became part of Barnet Common. The matter of rowdiness was referred to the Home Secretary, who decided that there were insufficient reasons to close the fair and the local people were pleased with the outcome. So the fair continued at High Barnet.

The code signal for Barnet for the telegraph was Bravo Alpha (BA) in 1871, although during the 1930s this would be altered under the new Trenchard re-organisation.[687]

In 1873 Barnet Police Station was one of five Inspector Stations on S or Hampstead Division, with Albany Street being the headquarters station.[688] The other stations were Portland Town (St John's Wood), Hampstead and Edgware (Whitchurch Lane).

In 1881 Thomas Cole, aged 36 years from Farnham in Surrey, was the Inspector in charge at Barnet and he lived above the station with his wife and family. There were nine single constables also living there, in what was termed the section house.

By the 1880s space at the station was becoming cramped, as the Divisional Superintendent indicated in 1888 when he requested the need of an additional three cells to be added to the four already in existence.[689] Sub-Divisional Inspector Robert Nutt took over from Cole in 1890, with three sub inspectors, five sergeants and 38 constables.[690] Nutt, from Ollerton in Yorkshire, lived at the police station at 23 High Street, Barnet with his wife and five children in 1891. In the section house at the time were single constables William Turner, Tom Webber, Ernest Randall, Albert Holmes, William Todd, Truman Ellis, Arthur Woolmore, John Houndsome (who had married and moved to Shenley by 1901) and Edwin Robbins.

Instructions were issued that land should be purchased in Barnet, and a police station built there for a sum not exceeding £1,200. Surveyors Messrs. E. Ryde and Sons reported that on 23rd December 1898 they had settled negotiations for the purchase of land at £1,150 plus costs. Messrs. Ellis and Ellis (solicitors) completed the purchase of land at Chipping Barnet, and as a result the freehold title to land located at 26 High Street, Chipping Barnet was purchased by the Receiver in May 1899.[691]

The continued increase in the local population raised concerns that the station and its facilities were already becoming too small, so further negotiations commenced to acquire an adjacent piece of land (Nos. 28, 30 and 32 High Street, Barnet) to be added to the station. Negotiations with the owners, the Leather-sellers Company, were slow and eventually the purchase of this land was finalised in 1908[692] for the sum of £1,800.[693] Plans were redrawn and builders obtained, but the start of WWI delayed the progress of the station. As a result, the police station and three sets of married quarters were rebuilt on the site and opened in February 1916.[694] The cost of renting the two married quarters was set at 10s per week. Inspector Thomas Browning, his wife Clara and their five daughters were living at the station in 1901.[695]

Resident at the old station in 1911 was the Sub-Divisional Inspector 74035 Albert Tom Wilkinson from Pickering in Yorkshire, who resided at the station with his wife and three teenage children. Also resident, in the section house above the station in a dormitory, were nine single constables: Charles Jenkins, Arthur Meadon, Henry Racey, William Artherton, Ellis Cooper, Thomas Jasper, Gray Herbert, Charles Yallop and Arthur Cloughton (warrant no. 97854).[696]

The photograph below, showing Inspector Wilkinson (with flat cap) seated to the right of Superintendent Thomas Williams (in plain clothes centre, front), was taken in the yard at Barnet Police station in 1910.

Superintendent Williams, Inspector Wilkinson and men at Barnet in 1910

In the meantime, and given the increased tensions in Europe with the impending arms race with Germany, arrangements were made to give police officers practice in shooting firearms. By July 1912 the Receiver agreed with the War Office to lease the miniature rifle range located at the Barracks, Barnet on an annual rental of £2.[697]

By 1914 Sub-Divisional Inspector Herbert Grace was in charge of the station, and he was supported by Inspector Arthur Smitheram. There was also one station sergeant, nine section sergeants, 45 constables and one officer from the Criminal Investigation Department.[698]

In 1925 the Sub-Divisional Inspector was O. Webb and the divisional code was changed to Sierra Bravo (SB).[699] The following year there was a further re-organisation of station and divisional boundaries.

The Barnet Fair continued to be challenging for police, due to the large crowds and transport problems. Whilst clearing a path through the crowds to allow a heavily-laden lorry out of the fair late one Saturday night, Constable 112399 James Warrender Thomson KPM of 37 Mays Lane, Barnet was struck and killed by a lorry.[700] There were three other fatalities all from the same family, together with four people who were injured and taken to hospital.

The accident happened when the lorry, heavily laden with cement bags, was about to pass a stationary tramcar just as a motor car drew out from an open space. A collision occurred and the lorry mounted the footpath, which was crowded with people. Police Constable Thompson, who was directing traffic nearby, saw the danger. He rushed to the footpath and, flinging out his arms, pressed the crowd back from the path of the lorry. Many people were saved from death or injury by the policeman's action. He himself was struck down and received multiple injuries, from which he died soon afterwards in hospital. Thompson won the King's Police Medal for gallantry posthumously in 1936 and the medal was received from the Prince of Wales by Mrs Thompson. PC Thompson, who was married, with three children, had been in the police force about 15 years.[701]

Barnet Police Station 1915-1977

In 1926 the sub-divisions of Finchley, Golders Green, Hendon and Barnet Sub-Divisions were policed from the stations of Barnet, Whetstone, South Mimms and Shenley.[702] Further re-organisation took place north of the Thames in 1933, when Barnet Sub-Division was re-shaped to absorb Potters Bar as well. This was part of remodelling of the larger divisional boundaries which saw Potters Bar move into S Division from Y Division.

Because of tensions in Europe, precautions were taken to ensure that the country was prepared in the event of war. Air raid warning centres were set up, and dedicated telephone lines were laid between police stations. The dedicated line

682 Metropolitan Police Special Police Orders 1869.
683 Ibid.
684 www.barnet4u.co.uk/barnet%20history/barnetfair.html accessed 4th November 2011.
685 Metropolitan Police Orders dated 19th December 1871.
686 Metropolitan Police Special Orders 1873.
687 Metropolitan Police Surveyor's Records 1899.
688 *Kelly's Directory* 1890.
689 Copyhold of the Manor of Chipping Barnet and East Barnet cited in Back, J. (1975) 'Barnet Police Station'.
690 Metropolitan Police Surveyor's Records 1912.
691 Back, J. (1975) 'Barnet Police Station'.
692 Metropolitan Police Surveyor's records 1912.
693 Census 1901.
694 Census 1911.
695 Metropolitan Police Surveyor's Records 1924.
696 *Kelly's Directory* 1914 and 1915.
697 Metropolitan Police Divisional Map 1926.
698 Metropolitan Police Roll of Honour.
699 *The Times*, 9th September 1935.
700 Metropolitan Police General Orders dated 31st May 1926.
701 Metropolitan Police Surveyor's Book Folio 152.
702 Back, J. (1975) 'Barnet Police Station'.

between Potters Bar and Barnet police stations was laid in 1936, with the local authority being responsible for damage during installation and for removal after when it was no longer needed.[703]

In 1965 local authority boundary changes occurred and the station code was changed again, this time to Sierra Alpha (SA). In due course the officer in charge became a Sub-Divisional Inspector, but this rank was abolished in favour of a sub-divisional superintendent by the 1950s.

Concerns were raised in the 1960s that the station was no longer suitable for policing purposes as it was too small. Estates Branch with Surveyor's Department considered that the station should be rebuilt and enlarged, so a programme of work was instituted to commence in 1967/68 but this was postponed in favour of a compromise. A nearby house at 2 Park Road was purchased for £8,000 in January 1969 to act as additional accommodation for administrative functions, and to act as a temporary police station whilst renovation and refurbishment took place at the old station.[704]

Police boundaries were revised again following the change of boundaries relating to Local Authorities under the Local Government Act 1964. Barnet was now designated as being located on S Division within the London Borough of Barnet (SA), together with Whetstone, South Mimms, Potters Bar (losing Shenley). Chief Inspector F. Brokenshire and Superintendent A.M.F. Bundock were in charge in 1966.[705]

The station was eventually rebuilt in 1972 when the sub-divisional office moved its functions to Whetstone (ST), but during the building works the station reverted to sectional station status.[706] The works took four years to complete, with the station being brought back into service in 1976 when it reverted back to sub-divisional status with Whetstone again becoming a sectional station.

Within a year the local police were inviting members of the public to attend two open days when the station at Barnet threw its doors open to people who were interested to see the daily workings of a busy rebuilt police station.

On 15th and 16th April 1977 the station was open from 6.00pm daily for a display of equipment. Commander S Division Stan Squire held a reception for the mayor of Barnet and local dignitaries including the new Police Commissioner Sir David McNee. Other police branches were represented, including Mounted Branch, Dog Section, Careers Section, the CID and Thames Division.[707]

Barnet Police Station 1977 to present

In 2002 Barnet was a station within Barnet Borough and was open to the public from 6.00am until 10.00pm daily. This was a station where prisoners were detained and charged for court until 2007. As of 2019 the station is still open and in the possession of the Metropolitan Police.[708]

Chislehurst Police Station (PC)

London Borough of Bromley
Cottage at Chislehurst Hill (1888-1893)
27 High Street (1893-1999)
Temporary building, car park on High Street (1999-2007)
1A High Street (2007 to present)
R Division (1839-c.1925)
P Division (1925-1985/86)
Bromley Division (1985/86-1993/94)
Bromley & Orpington OCU (PY) (1993/94)
South Area (SN) BCU (2018/19 to present)

Policing the area prior to the introduction of the Metropolitan Police had taken the form of the Bow Street horse patrol in 1805 when stations at Sidcup and Bromley Common had been brought into use. The village of Chislehurst possessed a lock-up and stocks near the Bull's Head public house for housing of prisoners prior to removal to the station house at Foots Cray.

In October 1873 a new Chislehurst section was formed from part of the former Sidcup territory, the station comprising two cottages at the top of Chislehurst Hill (now Old Hill) that were converted to provide a cell, a magistrates' room and a lobby on the ground floor, and a day room on the first floor.

The cottages were leased from Mr Thomas Townsend of 9 Glenrose, Chislehurst Common, and living accommodation was provided for a married inspector. The magistrates' room was not used as such after 1884. The local police were particularly busy in January 1873 and July 1879 for two funeral processions, marking the deaths of the Emperor Napoleon and the Prince Imperial Louis Napoleon who had lived at Camden House, Chislehurst.

In 1888 the freehold of premises in West Chislehurst High Street was bought for £800 from a Mr Owen Edwards, and the new police station, costing £3,453 16s 8d, started operations on 24th June 1893. This year also saw Police Orders give the station telegraphic code as 'CT' when it was confirmed as a station on R Division.

Chislehurst Police Station 1888-1893

Fire-fighting equipment was kept in a temporary shed from 1896, for which Chislehurst Urban District Council paid five shillings a year rent, and a more permanent structure, which effectively became a fire station, was built in 1910. When a motor fire tender was placed in the new structure, the Receiver for the Metropolitan Police District made new financial proposals and the council withdrew their equipment from the shed.

Notification was received in 1927 from the Urban District that the station was to be numbered 27 High Street as from

19th May.

The premises included an inspector's office, a charge room, a waiting lobby, two cells, an association cell for more than one prisoner, an ambulance shed and a lamp room. Simple oil lamps were issued to officers from the inception of the Metropolitan Police, supplied initially by Thomas Joyce and Son who cleaned and trimmed their wicks daily for a charge of 5½d per lantern. The oil of the lamps made them hot, smelly and dirty, and required a leather guard to protect the officer's uniform. Eventually they were replaced in 1920 by an electric lamp powered by an accumulator invented by George Wooton, who became the Metropolitan Police Chief Engineer from 1930 until 1935.

Mottingham Lane, once the local main route to London, was relieved of much of its traffic by the opening of the Sidcup bypass in 1924, and the police station was then able to concentrate on protecting the large houses in the area. Chislehurst became part of the Bromley sub-division of P Division on 1st January 1932, and part of St Mary Cray sub-division from 1st April 1965.

A site was purchased for a new police station at 3 High Street, Chislehurst in 1964, but it was leased to the local authority for use as a car park and the new police station was not built. The station had been the subject of night-time closures since 1961, but under re-organisation in July 1974 24-hour policing was resumed.

Chislehurst Police Station 1893-1999

Sector policing was introduced in February 1993 when the area was renamed Chislehurst and Petts Wood Section. The old police station was closed in 1999. The public were served by a temporary wooden building located in the car park until 2007, when new premises at 1A High Street were opened as a Safer Neighbourhood Unit for the Chislehurst, and North Chislehurst and Mottingham sectors. The base comprised a reception office, and accommodation for officers who patrol by foot and cycle.

Chiswick Police Station

London Boroughs of Hounslow, Richmond on Thames,
  Urban Districts of Staines and Sunbury of Thames
Chiswick Field Road, Turnham Green (1850-1884)
210 High Road, Chiswick (1884-1965)
T Division (1850-1933)
F Division (1933-1965)
T Division (1965-1985/86)

Chiswick Division / OCU (1985/86-2018/19)
Borough of Hounslow OCU (1993-2018/19)
West Area WA BCU (together with Ealing and Hillingdon, 2018/19 to present)

Hounslow Heath, to the west of Brentford, became a natural training ground for the military, and its proximity led to the development of Brentford and Chiswick. The increased traffic in and out of the capital both by road and river brought an increase in population to the area along the routes, not always of the most desirable kind since highwaymen and women were a common hazard to the newly-developing stage coach service.

The Star and Garter Inn at Kew Bridge became one of many coaching inns along the way. Chiswick, Isleworth and Osterley were the sites of some of the most magnificent house-building, together with estates consisting of parkland and formal gardens. In the present day they are open to the public, preserving a very necessary green area. The region prospered and the villages expanded with small family housing for the estate workers and the small retail shops stretching along the increasingly busy roads.[709]

This general trend of the expansion and merging of boundaries continued and the region continued comfortably and unspectacularly. Roads were steadily improved, the railway arrived, horse-drawn trams gave way to trolley buses. There were some Victorian terrace house developments in common with most other areas, but despite the innovations the essential character of the four original communities was retained.[710]

Although the river traffic and associated commerce has declined since World War Two, the waterfront retains its importance in the life and development of this part of Hounslow Borough as it is the leisure and recreational aspects of this oldest asset which is ripe for exploitation and can only serve to enhance the reputation of Brentford and Chiswick as a desirable place to live and work – something it seems it has always enjoyed.[711]

Chiswick did not possess a police station at that time and was policed from Hammersmith and Shepherds Bush, although there were stables at Turnham Green for the Bow Street horse patrol. Brentford was to be the western extent of the Metropolitan Police District (MPD) until about 1840. Although somewhat rural in nature, Chiswick and Brentford had its traffic problems even then, as no fewer than 50 stagecoaches passed through the towns daily, to the southwest, nine coaches a day to Bristol alone, with the Star and Garter Hotel at Kew Bridge being an important coaching hostelry.[712]

Tollgates were erected at Brentford and Isleworth near Busch Corner, which added to the congestion, but were finally removed in July 1872. Prosperity came to Brentford in the form of the Grand Junction Canal, which opened in November 1794 as far as Uxbridge.[713]

703 Metropolitan Police List 1966.
704 Metropolitan Police General Orders dated 13th October 1972.
705 Metropolitan Police Press Release 7th April 1977.
706 MPS (2019) Freedom of information request – MPS Assets.
707 John Back Archive 1975.
708 Brown, B. (1991). 'A Brief History of Brentford and Chiswick' (unpublished monograph).
709 Ibid.
710 Ibid.
711 John Back Archive 1975.
712 Ibid.
713 Ibid.

In 1840 further development commenced with the coming of the London and South Western Railway, who opened a line from Waterloo with stations at Chiswick, Kew Bridge and Brentford. In January 1869 the company opened stations at Bedford Park (now Turnham Green) and Brentford Road (now Gunnersbury), while the Great Western Railway had opened a branch to Brentford from the Southall direction in May 1860. This closed during the last war. Like the canal companies, the railways had their own police forces. The London & South Western Railway became part of the Southern Railway Police in 1923, both companies coming under the British Transport Commission Police in 1948. The British Transport Police were formed in 1962. Finally the District Railway opened a station called Acton Green (now Chiswick Park) in July 1879, bringing yet another police force.[714]

Chiswick and Brentford were stations both connected to the telegraph system in December 1872, the identification codes being 'CK' and 'BR' respectively.

The first horse-trams appeared on the streets in March 1882, running between Shepherds Bush and Young's Corner, owned by the West Metropolitan Tramway Co. and were extended to Kew Bridge in December that year. They were replaced by electric trams in April 1901 and extended through Brentford to Hounslow that July.[715]

In Police Orders of 1864 Chiswick was shown as a station of T or Kensington Division. In November 1869 a report by Superintendent Fisher spoke of a piece of land for sale which was suitable on which to build a police station near The Windmill public house on the south side of Great Western Road, Chiswick High Road at the corner of Windmill Lane.[716]

A second police station opened in January 1870 replacing the original 1850s structure at Chiswick Field Road, Turnham Green, an area which was to become London's first garden suburb in 1876. This building was a temporary measure pending the opening of a purpose built station in the High Street in December 1872.[717]

In February 1884, following the creation of a new Shepherds Bush sub-division, the Chiswick sub-divisional boundary was revised, the strength at the at time being three inspectors, five sergeants and 61 constables.

Home Office approval was received in June 1870 for the purchase of a site at Turnham Green. In the meantime Police Orders in January 1870 shows a temporary new station being brought into use until the new building was constructed. The entry reads:

'The Commissioner approves of the temporary police station in Chester Terrace, Chiswick Field Road, Turnham Road, being occupied by police from the 25th inclusive.'

Chiswick Police Station 1884-1963

Police Orders of 22nd February 1884 recorded Chiswick as a Sub-Divisional Station of T Division,[718] while another Orders on 20th December that year stated that a portion of the new police station at Chiswick was occupied and that possession of the old station was given up.

One of the more notable senior officers to take charge of Chiswick Sub-Division was Sub-Divisional Inspector David Rawlings (warrant no. 55889), who transferred there in 1888 and remained until he retired in 1898. A rare pen picture of Rawlings highlights his special leadership and detective qualities. A native of Danbury in Essex, in 1867 Rawlings went to sea and travelled all over the world. On his return in 1872 he joined the police and once the preparatory class was finished he was sent to Old Street Police station on G or Shoreditch Division. After only eight months he was transferred to Rochester Row on B or Chelsea Division, where he soon came into favour with his superiors being seconded to special duties at the Army and Navy stores in Victoria Street, Westminster. With this special duty he was promoted to 1st Class constable on the top rate of pay.

Sub-Divisional Inspector David Rawlings

In 1879 he was promoted to sergeant and transferred to Southwark on M Division, where he only remained for a short time as his seniors on B Division wanted him back. Whist there he was rewarded with another special duty and was placed in charge of the police staff at the Fisheries Exhibition at South Kensington. Such was the success of this exhibition and police arrangements that he was rewarded with a purse of money which the Commissioner allowed him to keep.

He was placed in charge of another exhibition in 1884, and on its successful conclusion Rawlings was promoted to Inspector and sent to Fulham Police station on T Division. It was whilst at Fulham that he investigated and arrested a man named Tucker who had murdered his wife. Tucker was sentenced to death and Rawlings was commended by the trial judge, Mr Justice Hawkins. A fire occurred at Favart Road where a family was trapped. Without thought to his own safety, Rawlings entered the building and, one by one, brought the family to safety. For this act of bravery and selflessness he was rewarded with a certificate on vellum from the Society for the Protection of Life from Fire and two guineas, also receiving a reward of one guinea from the Commissioner for his promptitude. In 1888 he was again recognised for his leadership skills and example when he was further promoted to sub-divisional inspector and moved to Chiswick.

At Chiswick he brought a notable burglar to justice, supervised and also featured prominently in a case of manslaughter in the district. Apart from his normal duties and other cases he took charge of the police arrangements at an industrial dispute at the Thorneycroft factory in 1897. Through his leadership and guidance he was able to defuse the tensions in the strike, which passed off peacefully. He was also considered popular amongst the local population, possessing firmness and even temper. He was also well-liked and respected amongst his men and especially the younger constables, who would often receive guidance and advice for their future careers.

Rawlings also favoured sporting activities, where he became involved in charitable activities between the police and the Fire Brigade donating monies raised to local and other good causes. On retirement he received a 1st Class certificate of service plus an annual pension of £126 6s 8d. Chiswick local tradesmen presented him with an illuminated address on vellum, a purse containing £110 and a gold watch. His wife Mary also was included, and she received a purse of money as well. His colleagues presented him with a silver cruet set, and the sergeants and constables gave him a liqueur stand.[719] Rawlings, then aged 48-years-old, could not have been in particular good health as his wife Mary was widowed in 1901, living on her own means and without any children in Glebe Street, Chiswick.

When Rawlings retired his replacement was Sub-Divisional Inspector William Cheyney (warrant no. 66050), who was promoted from A or Whitehall Division. Cheyney resided at Chiswick Police Station with his wife Barbara and their three children.[720] Cheyney remained at Chiswick until 1907, when he retired on pension.

Sub-Divisional Inspector Arthur Copping (warrant no. 75231) from Suffolk was in charge in 1911 and resided at the station with his wife Louisa and their son and three daughters.[721] Also present and living at the station were six single constables living in the section house. Copping remained there until 1917, when he retired from T Division.

In 1912 there was a fixed point box situated in Grove Park, Chiswick on land owned by Chiswick Urban District Council. These were to be manned for 24 hours a day, and could be a place for a member of the public to find a constable should the need arise. These are not to be confused with the Dr Who TARDIS-type police box which was introduced later in the 1920s and 1930s.

The introduction of the T Division Specials saw a large contingent being enrolled at Chiswick, where Chief Inspector G. Gentry worked together with SDI Copping to cover the stations duties.[722] There were at least 250 Specials posted to Chiswick, the largest and keenest group in the division.

The rear of Chiswick Police station taken c.1908

During the Great War, in 1917, Chiswick became a mere sectional station to Brentford and was supplemented by a contingent of T Division Special Constabulary made up of employees of the London General Omnibus Co. from Turnham Green depot in Belmont Road. During the same year postal code numbers were introduced, eg Chiswick W4.[723]

Three bombs dropped on Chiswick High Road on the night of 29th January 1918, injuring five people and causing damage to surrounding properties but also smashing the gas and water mains.[724] This was part of a raid that also did substantial damage to Brentford and Isleworth on the same night. Chiswick specials were good at first aid, and some 94 held first aid certificates. This prompted the senior officers to make arrangements with the District Council for an ambulance station where the manpower was provided by the police and the lorry and equipment by the council. Over 700 regulars from T Division were sent to the armed services.[725]

Chiswick Police Station in 1919 dressed up in celebration of the ending of WW1

The narrow streets of Brentford were at last bypassed in 1924 by the opening of the Great West Road, however the section between South Ealing Road and Boston Road was not completed until June 1926, and its extension over the Chiswick flyover much later, in September 1959. Up until June 1931 a police station existed at Isleworth, and when it closed in the same year Chiswick became a sub-division again with Shepherds Bush as a section to it. Brentford, meanwhile, became a sectional station of Hounslow sub-division together with Norwood Green, at the same time temporary workshops were opened at Brentford to ease the workload at Barnes Garage but closed in December 1939.

An entry in Police Orders of 28th May 1931 read:

'The following re-arrangement of Sub-Divisions will take effect on the 1st June. Chiswick Sub- Division to be comprised of Chiswick as the Sub-Divisional Station and Shepherds Bush as its Sectional Station.'

In July 1931 a new railway station opened at Syon Lane due to a new housing development.[726]

714 Brown, B. (1991). 'A Brief History of Brentford and Chiswick' (unpublished monograph).
715 Ibid.
715 Ibid.
716 The *Police Review and Parade Gossip*, 14th April 1899.
717 *Kelly's Directory* 1891-1901.
718 Census 1911.
719 Reay, W. (1919) *The Specials: How They Served London*. Heineman, London. p86.
720 Brown, B. (1991). 'A Brief History of Brentford and Chiswick' (unpublished monograph).
721 Reay, W. (1919) *The Specials: How They Served London*. Heineman, London. p86.
722 Ibid.
723 John Back Archive circa 1975.
724 Metropolitan Police Orders dated 28th November 1933.
725 www.paranormaldatabase.com/hotspots/W4.php accessed 22nd December 2012.
726 *Kirchner's Police Index* 1931.

In the re-organisation of the divisions north of the Thames on 1st December 1933,[727] Chiswick was transferred from T to F Division.

The police station is said to be haunted by the ghost of Mrs Abercrombie, who was murdered by her son-in-law in 1792. When not pacing about the ground floor she is apparently seen on the upper floors.[728] The station was located at 210 High Road, Chiswick in 1931, and was a sectional station of Brentford Sub-Division on T Division.[729]

A rather amusing speeding case was heard at Brentford Magistrates' Court during this period, when evidence was given in defence to the effect that the new traffic patrols had lured drivers into speeding by causing them to overtake the slow-moving police vehicle which was disguised as a fruiterer from the vast Brentford fruit market, displaying a large board to the rear reading 'BANANAS 3 for 2d'.[730]

Chiswick ceased to be part of T Division in December 1933 (the same year that Chiswick Bridge opened) and passed to F Division, where it was to remain for over 30 years.[731] In Police Orders of 5th July 1933 mention is made of a new Sub-Divisional Station to be opened on 8th July at Shepherds Bush. Chiswick was to become a sectional station and form part of the new Shepherds Bush sub-division.[732]

The division has public order commitments within its own boundary, with the presence of Brentford Football Club, established in 1889, and the annual boat race run over the present stretch of the Thames since 1864. Between 1923 and 1928, a police sports day was a regular local event and was held at the Polytechnic Sports Ground in Cavendish Road, Brentford. These events were very popular with the public, and the local bus route was specially extended from Chiswick railway station to cater for the crowds.[733]

In Police Orders of 5th July 1963 mention is made of a new sub-divisional station to be opened on 8th July at Shepherds Bush. Chiswick was to become a sectional station, and form part of the new Shepherds Bush Sub-Division.[734]

Chiswick Police Station 1963 to present

During the large-scale revision of boundaries in 1965 Chiswick returned to T Division as a sub-divisional station, with Brentford as its sectional station.[735] Pending the rebuilding of Chiswick, Brentford became the sub-divisional station and headquarters of the sub-division.

On 1st April 1965 the GLC came into existence and created the new London Borough of Hounslow, replacing the old borough of Brentford and Chiswick, and at this point Middlesex ceased to be a county.

The site for the new Chiswick Police Station was found on the site of the old fire station at 209/211 Chiswick High Road, and it was purchased on 16th March 1967.

Police Orders in March 1972 announced:

'A new sub-divisional station for Chiswick (TC) at 205/211, Chiswick High Road will be taken into operational use at 6am on Monday 27th March when the existing Chiswick Station will be closed and Brentford (TB) will revert to sectional status'.

In 1972 a new purpose-built police station was opened at Chiswick.

When the Metropolitan Police abolished Districts in April 1986, T District as it had been known since 1980 ceased to exist, and Chiswick became a division which included Brentford as part of a new No. 5 or South West Area.[736]

It is now over 160 years since the New Police first extended to Chiswick and Brentford, but the Metropolitan Police continue to give service to the community.

In 2012 Chiswick Police Station was open 24 hours a day, seven days a week, and detained and charged prisoners for court.[737] It was feared at that time that because of cutbacks Chiswick Police Station was likely to close[738] in favour of a more user-friendly shop front or office at the Town Hall, but in 2018 the station was still in use and occupied by the Metropolitan Police.[739]

City Road Police Station

London Borough of Hackney
4-6 Shepherdess Walk (1901-1993)
G Division (1961-1985/86)
Hackney Division (1985/86-1993/94)
Shoreditch & Hackney OCU (1993/94-2018/19)
Central East (CE) BCU (together with Tower Hamlets, 2018/19 to present)

City Road Police Station Lamp

In 1899 a sizeable portion of land became available in Shepherdess Walk on the old site of the Grecian Theatre,[740] which was bounded by Nile Street and City Road. The site was purchased from the Bishopsgate Foundation.[741]

The Metropolitan Police Surveyor considered the site suitable for a police station, and negotiations commenced for the freehold purchase of the land from the owners.

The sale was finally agreed in November 1899 and ownership of the land passed to the Metropolitan Police. The site was made ready and a new station was soon built.

Police Orders of 1901 reported:

"...the new Police Station in City Road is to be taken into occupation by Police, and business commenced therein by 19th instant. The lodging assessment will be:- 1 Married Inspector at 5s 6d per week, 30 single constables at 1s per week. The Police Station at Old Street will be vacated on the 13th instant."[742]

A substantial station was built at the front of the plot in Shepherdess Walk, not in City Road itself, although the station took the name of the nearest main road. At the rear of the station a section house was built in Shepherdess Place N1, which accommodated 30 single officers.

Problems occurred with access to the section house, because the Metropolitan Police did not own the right of way, so

City Road Police Station 1901-1961

access was negotiated with the Governors of the Bishopsgate Foundation for the annual sum of 10s. The police also leased two buildings, one at 16 Nile Street to Mr. David Hazel for the annual sum of £155 rent for 84 years, and the other at 7 Shepherdess Place for the rent of £170 to the Turret Button company (later the Autostop Safety Razor Company and then Gillette Industries).

Arrangements for the transfer and re-negotiation in respect of the lease with Autostop Razor in December 1926 for the sum of £18,500. The leasehold title passed to Gillette Industries Ltd in June 1931. The address of the station was recorded at the time as being 4 and 6 Shepherdess Walk, Shoreditch.

A larger and better-equipped section house was built at City Road in 1911 with space for 102 single officers. One single inspector and a married officer and his family also resided there.[743] The section house was renamed Shepherdess Walk Section House.[744] In line with policy to provide affordable housing for its officers, the police purchased a freehold site in 1920. Located in Ironmonger Row, between Lever Street and Old Street, the site included some 30 sets of married quarters which were called Warren Buildings.[745]

In 1931 G or Finsbury Division consisted of three police stations. These were Kings Cross, Old Street and City Road. The division had a strength of 672 police officers.[746] Kings Cross Road Police Station was the Divisional Headquarters, although on a revision of boundaries City Road Police Station took over when the former station was transferred to E or Holborn Division during the 1930s.

Records show that a police ambulance shelter for the hand-ambulance was located at Rosemary Branch Bridge over the Regents Canal in the London Borough of Shoreditch.[747] Experience had shown that having the ambulance site near the canal helped to save people's lives if they fell into the water, because they could be taken quickly to hospital.

In 1932/33 extensive reconstruction work began at the old station. This included the permanent closing of the old section house and conversion of the ground floor into stables. Reconstruction work on the old station began immediately. It was completed by August 1933, and designed to accommodate the increased administrative functions on becoming the Divisional Headquarters. The stables were taken into service at the same time. In the interim the Borough of Shoreditch had purchased the land in Shepherdess Place from the Governors of the Bishopsgate Foundation, which included the right of access. The land was turned over for general public use, and the annual cost of 10 shillings for access to the rear of the station lapsed.

In 1939 it was decided to rebuild the police station on the original site. Police business carried on using temporary accommodation in the section house. The station reopened for business in August 1940,[748] but on 15th October a large bomb fell on the Shepherdess Walk Section House, caused half the building to be demolished.[749]

The start of WWII meant plans for a new station were shelved, and the old station was re-occupied in August 1940. It took another twenty years before a new station was finally built on the site.

In 1960 the old station was demolished[750] to make way for a new modern police station, which was also to include sufficient space for the Divisional Headquarters and their staff. A new station was built at City Road, on the same site and whose call sign was Golf Delta (GD). It was taken into service in January 1961.[751]

The boundary changes of 1965 due to the Local Authority revisions showed City Road as the G Divisional headquarters and Sub-Divisional station, with Old Street (GS) having sectional status. Old Street station was closed in 1973[752] when the court took over responsibility for the building.

In 1968 there was further restructuring, which replaced the existing 23 divisions and their sub-divisions, and divided them

727 Brown, B. (1991). 'A brief History of Brentford and Chiswick'. (unpublished monograph).
728 Ibid.
729 Ibid.
730 Ibid.
731 John Back archive circa 1975.
732 Metropolitan Police Orders dated 6th August 1964.
733 Brown, B. (1991). 'A brief History of Brentford and Chiswick'. (unpublished monograph).
734 www.hounslow.gov.uk/police_stations accessed 23rd December 2012.
735 www.hounslowchronicle.co.uk/west-london-news/local-hounslow-news/2012/12/21/sham-consultation-about-chiswick-police-station-closure-criticised-109642-32475108 accessed 28th December 2012.
736 MPS (2018) Freedom of Information request – MPS Assets.
737 John Back Archive (1975).
738 Ibid.
739 Metropolitan Police Orders 17th August 1901.
740 Metropolitan Police Orders 2nd December 1911.
741 Metropolitan Police Orders 17th August 1912.
742 Metropolitan Police Surveyor's Records 1924.
743 *Bacon's Atlas* 1926.
744 Metropolitan Police Surveyors' Records 1924.
745 Metropolitan Police Orders 16th August 1940.
746 John Back archive (1975) also 'The Metropolitan Police at War' (1947). HMSO.
747 Ibid.
748 Metropolitan Police Orders 27th January 1961.
749 Metropolitan Police Orders 6th July 1973.
750 Fido, M. and Skinner, K. (1999) *The Encyclopedia of New Scotland Yard*, Virgin Press. p78.
751 Ibid p 71.
752 B. Brown. (1996). 'Policing old Hackney', in *Peeler* magazine.

between eight districts, each sub-divided into eight divisions. This left City Road Police Station on G Division, still with the status of Divisional Headquarters.[753]

In 1986 Sir Kenneth Newman, the Metropolitan Police Commissioner, restructured the police by creating eight Areas rather than four Districts, and removing Commanders from having direct responsibility for a division. This meant that a Commander had operational responsibility for a number of divisions within the Area. Divisions became the basic unit for policing.[754] City Road Police Station lost its Divisional HQ status, and this was transferred to a station of 2 Area based at Chigwell Police Station.

In 1990 27-year-old Constable Lawrence Brown was shot dead in Pownall Road. A tribute to his devotion and courage is marked in stone at the place where he fell, a gesture instigated by the film producer Michael Winner.[755]

Shoreditch (City Road) Police Station 1961 to present

In 1995 the Service went through another restructuring exercise which reduced the Areas to 5 from 8, and this meant that Leman Street ceased as Area HQ, when City Road Police Station became attached to 3 Area (North East) Headquarters located at Edmonton Police Station.

A further change occurred in 1998 when the five Areas were reduced to three, although this meant no change for City Road, which by now had changed its name to Shoreditch Division.[756]

In 2019 the station was retained for operational purposes by the Metropolitan Police.[757]

Clapham Police Station

The London Borough of Lambeth

Old Town, Clapham Common (1830-1847)

Smedley Street, Clapham (1847-1907)

51 Union Grove (1907-2013)

L Division (1846-1985/86)

Clapham Division (1985/86-1993/94)

Vauxhall OCU (1993/94-2013)

In May 1830 the Metropolitan Police arrived in the parish of Clapham. The station house was in the former parish watch house in Old Town, Clapham Common.[758]

In 1845, the Home Office gave authority to rent a plot of land near Lark Hall Lane on a 78-year lease to allow the building of a new police station, which opened in March 1846. The ground rent at the time was £16.[759] Records in 1847 mention that the old watch house at Clapham Common, near the New Church, was no longer required for Police purposes,[760] This Police building was one of the three on the Wandsworth Division, the other two being The Plain, Wandsworth, and 1&2 Millman's Row, Chelsea.[761]

By 1865 W Division consisted of the following stations: Clapham, Brixton, Streatham, Croydon, Sanderstead, Carshalton, Mitcham, Sutton, Banstead and Tooting.[762] The total number of Police Officers on W Division was 296, all ranks.[763] In 1879 W Division was under the command of Superintendent William Wiseman, and William Mason was his deputy.[764]

In 1881 a report stated that the accommodation had been originally built for two married men, but at this stage it was occupied by one single sergeant and 21 single constables. The report also made comment that the kitchen was too small, and that the ablution room could only be reached by passing through the mess room.[765] Not much had changed by 1891, when the census in April that year showed 18 single officers residing at the police station. This included Police Sergeant George Saich and seventeen constables.[766] It is interesting to note that five of the constables were born in Norfolk.

In 1884 records show the address of the station as Smedley Street, Clapham.[767] By 1893, part of Norwood and Penge Sections had been transferred from P to W Division.[768]

The freehold of the site was purchased in 1898 from the Reverend George Ferris Whidbourne for £434. Later, in 1903, extra land and buildings were purchased at 56 Union Grove, 27 Smedley Street and 49&51 Union Grove in order to enlarge the station. This land was under Trust of the will of a Richard Allen.

In March 1905 a letter was sent to the London County Council from John Dixon Butler, Metropolitan Police Surveyor, stating that he was intending to rebuild Clapham Police Station following the existing building lines.[769]

The Receiver bought the freehold of these properties and offered to pay an annuity on 49&51 Union Grove, but in 1920 an agreement was reached for a payment of a lump sum of £200 instead.[770] The new enlarged Clapham Police Station, designed by Butler, reopened for business in 1907.[771]

Clapham Police Station 1907-2013

A further reorganisation of Police boundaries in 1921 meant that Clapham and Battersea Park Road (Nine Elms Police Station) were transferred to L Division.[772] By 1930, L or Lambeth Division consisted of five stations: Clapham, Battersea, Kennington Road, Lavender Hill and Nine Elms. All the officers were under the command of Superintendent

Ernest Brind, who was based at Kennington Road Police Station.[773]

In 1994 Clapham Police Station was amalgamated with Kennington Road Police Station to form the new Vauxhall Division. The front counter was closed to the public in 2013, and the property was sold in 2014 for £4,500,000.[774]

Clark's Buildings
(later George Street Police Station)

London Borough of Camden

9-12 Clark's Buildings (1845-1874)

George Street (c.1865-c.1895)

E Division

Clark's Buildings was situated in the area of St. Giles southwest of Bloomsbury, in the Rookeries; it ran north from St Giles High Street towards (but not quite reaching) Church Lane, running parallel with and west of Dyott Street. It was too far south to be immediately affected by the development of New Oxford Street in the 1840s, although it had become more overcrowded as displaced residents of streets cleared for this development flooded into the area.[775]

1863 map showing the location of Clark's Buildings Police Station

The original watch house at George Street, St Giles was replaced in 1843 by four separate brick and slate buildings at 9-12 Clark's Buildings, leased from 25th March 1843 and enjoying a large yard at the back. There were four cells, warmed and ventilated, and 34 rooms without a scullery, a charge room and offices. It was recorded as an Inspector's station and seems to have been renamed as George Street, St Giles by 1865, and sometimes as George Street Bloomsbury. It may well have been replaced by Tottenham Court Road, built in 1900.

In 1860 Henry Mayhew described a visit to St Giles' rookery,[776] which acquired infamy for its cramped, insanitary slum dwellings where crime and poverty, villains and prostitution were prevalent. Locations like these (sometimes also known as 'stews') were called rookeries by analogy to the untidy, multiple, noisy nests of rooks. Slum clearance schemes transformed the area. The area was immortalised by Hogarth's picture of Gin Lane, and had apparently been the source of the plague that affected London in 1665.

The plan drawings at the top of the next column show the side elevation plans for the police station at Clark's Buildings. It shows a substantial three-storey L-shaped purpose-built police station with basement.

By 1886 the address had acquired an extra letter 'e', as in

Clarke's Buildings. In April 1893 it was announced that the tenancy, probably for part of the premises, had been relinquished, but a new section house for an inspector and 45 constables was announced in Police Orders of 9th March 1896, apparently replacing the accommodation at 33-34 Bow Street.[777] Clarke's Buildings were sold to Charing Cross Hospital for £14,000 on 31st January 1939.

Cobham Police Station

Elmbridge; The London Borough of Richmond (1993-2000)

91-93 Portsmouth Road KT1 1JJ (1947-2012)

Surrey Constabulary (c.1850s-1947)

V Division (1947-1985/86)

Kingston Division / OCU (1985/86-2000)

Surrey Police (from 2000)

Cobham is a village about four miles south east of Weybridge and the same distance south west of Esher. The parish is bounded on the north by Walton, Esher, Thames Ditton, and a corner of Kingston; on the south east by Stoke D'Abernon; on the south by Little Bookham, Effingham and East Horsley; on the south-west by Ockham; on the west by a corner of Wisley and by Walton – thus touching ten other parishes.[778]

753 Op cit p71.
754 MPS Information Rights Unit (2019) MPS Assets.
755 Brown, B. A' Brief History of the Vauxhall Division.' July 1997.
756 MEPO 5/34 (214).
757 John Back Archive (1975).
758 *Post Office London Directory* 1838.
759 Metropolitan Police Orders dated 28th October 1865.
760 MEPO 2/26.
761 *Post Office Directory* 1879.
762 Metropolitan Police Surveyor's Report 1881.
763 Census 1891.
764 Metropolitan Police Orders dated 20th June 1884.
765 Metropolitan Police Orders dated 13th February 1893.
766 London Metropolitan Archives: GLC/AR/BR/22/026347.
767 LB446.
768 Metropolitan Police Orders dated 10th August 1907.
769 Metropolitan Police Orders dated 24th February 1921.
770 *Police Almanac* 1930.
771 www.met.police.uk/Information Rights Unit Accessed 25th January 2019.
772 *Journal of the Statistical Society of London*, vol. XI, March 1848.
773 Henry Mayhew. *A Visit to St Giles Rookery and Its Neighbourhood.*
774 Metropolitan Police Orders dated 7th April 1893.
775 www.british-history.ac.uk accessed 2nd March 2012.
776 Brown, B. (1999) 'Policing Old Esher'.
777 Ct. R. of Cobham.
778 '1851-1951 A Short Centenary History of the Surrey Constabulary', Biddles, Guildford.

It was usual in rural villages to have parish lock-ups, cage or stocks where drunken or violent individuals needed on occasions to be placed temporarily, however Cobham seemed to go against the trend. In 1824 the overseers of Cobham parish were fined by the Court-Leet for not having a cage or stocks for the detention of prisoners. It was agreed that a cage be built at the south end of the village, near the alms houses on The Tilt. It was not proceeded with, however, and a further resolution adopted for a building of an octagon plan with a domed ceiling to be built on the old common, near the Royal Oak Tavern[779] instead.

The lord of the manor had a view to keep the peace. Constables and tithing-men were elected for the tithings of Street Cobham, Church Cobham, and Downeside, together with one pinder and one ale-taster.[780] There was a paid Surrey Constabulary constable residing in Cobham in the 1850s.[781]

During the summer of 1859 Constable Allen Mason, aged 30, who had been stationed at Cobham for some years, sustained a ruptured blood vessel in the lungs caused during a violent assault by a deserter whom he was trying to arrest and died as a result of his injuries. The Surrey Comet newspaper commented that Constable Mason was 'greatly respected both by the inhabitants and the members of the Force'.[782] His funeral was attended by many police officers, as is typical at official police funerals.

The road through Cobham (now the main A3) was becoming busy, and there were reports in 1896 regarding the furious riding by light locomotives and motor cars. Calls from police reported that all vehicles should be fixed with some identifying features like an index mark. Also, reports of reckless cycling at Pains Hill and Hartar Hill, Cobham were made to the Chief Constable, who ordered Sergeant Fletcher from Esher to investigate. Later the sergeant was knocked down and seriously injured in trying to prevent the furious riding of bicycles.[782]

During the 1920s the Metropolitan Police had introduced police (Dr Who type) telephone boxes and telephone posts across London. When Cobham came into the Metropolitan Police District, arrangements were made for police call box V71 to be situated in the village. This took place on 1st December 1948, and the box, containing a telephone but not an air raid warning siren,[783] was sited at the junction of Fairmile Lane (on the east side) and Green Lane Cobham. The box was removed on 21st October 1970.

In 1931 Cobham was a sectional station of Hersham Division of the Surrey Constabulary, with a sergeant in charge,[784] and in 1937 it was part of Woking Division, with Superintendent J. H. White in charge.[785]

In 1947 there were boundary changes, and Cobham (VC) joined the Metropolitan Police on V or Wandsworth Division, becoming a sub-divisional station of Kingston. In 1955 Superintendent D. C. Horsley at Kingston was in charge of the sub-division,[786] with Surbiton, East Molesey and Esher. In 1960 he had been replaced by Superintendent E.J.E. Tickle.[787]

By 1965 Cobham (VC) was a sectional station of Esher (VH).[788] The station had limited opening times and was shut from 10.00pm until 6.00am daily, although this was soon to change.

Experienced Sergeant Desmond Randall, who had served at Barnes, Esher and Epsom, was the officer in charge of the station in 1971. He had been posted there in 1964 when the station reverted from being open 16 hours a day as a section of Epsom. He was responsible for supervising 14 constables, and records show that at the time Cobham was open to the public 24 hours a day, seven days a week.[789] The home beat system of policing was also introduced in 1971.

Cobham was responsible for four Surrey villages: Cobham, Downside, Oxshott and Stoke D'Abernon. Constable John Wallace covered Stoke D'Abernon, while Constable Patrick Lynch patrolled Oxshott. Both the constables lived in their villages, and were known as 'residentials'. Constable Jenner, who retired on ill health grounds in 1968 and was the residential for Oxshott before Constable Lynch, was an experienced and well-respected officer who was greatly appreciated by the community, so much so that when he retired he was presented with a gift of £714 raised for his retirement fund by the local people.[790]

Cobham Police Station 1947-2000

Advertisements for a station cleaner were placed in a number of newspapers and the job was given to a local lady. These ladies (and sometimes gentlemen), who would also be telephone exchange operators at bigger stations, often formed the backbone of the station and remained in the local area when others police officers had moved on. In Cobham's case it was Florence Bundy[791] who ensured the station was kept clean and tidy. From time to time she would also make the tea, answer enquiries by members of the public at the front counter when the station officer was temporarily engaged, and cook a fried breakfast for the station staff. They were a consistent feature of the 'nick' being much valued and part of the police family. Many a new young recruit, miles away from home and coming to London, would seek advice from such ladies. It was a sad day when computerisation and the outsourcing of cleaning services made them redundant.

Constable Bob Powell was Cobham's dog handler in 1971. His dog Kim71 was a very good police dog and had won the Frederika Shield in the Metropolitan Police dog trials in the same year.[792] Constable Powell also lived in the community, and lived with his family in purpose-built police house. The back garden also housed the dog kennel, and whilst this was a working dog they were often part of the family when 'off duty'. Dog handlers had a dog van which they kept at home when not on duty, if no other dog handler was patrolling for use in an emergency call out. If near a police station they would keep the van at the station instead. The dog handler had to ensure the fitness of his/her dog at all times, which meant daily exercise and training. The dog had to be fed in accordance with police regulations, where a mixture of biscuit and tinned meat was measured out daily for the animal. Handlers were often called out to search premises or land where people had been seen committing crime and making off.

Detective Sergeant Harold (Ben) Dover was in charge of the crime books and was responsible for supervising and investigating the offences reported to police at Cobham.[793] Because Cobham was a good class residential area burglary was (and probably still is) a problem in Cobham, and it was his job to ensure that offenders were caught and brought before the courts. The main A3 ran through Cobham, and at Fairmile the road was so treacherous to motorists that it became known as 'Murder mile'. Although planned in 1938, the main Esher and Cobham bypass was not built until the 1970s, and the planned re-routing would ease traffic problems in the area.

Cobham Police Station was located at 91-93 Portsmouth Road, Cobham, Surrey.

Up until the year 2000 it was open on Tuesday, Thursday and Friday between 10.00am-12.00noon, and closed Mondays, weekends and Bank Holidays. In 1998 Cobham (VC) was located on 5 Area and did not have authorised cell space, so it could not detain prisoners or operate as a charging station because it was not a Police and Criminal Evidence Act 1984 (PACE) designated station. The officer in charge was Borough Commander Superintendent W. Wilson.[794]

Under new boundary revisions between the Metropolitan Police and Surrey Constabulary in 2000, Cobham Police Station was returned to Surrey.

In 2004, under the auspices of the Surrey Police, a team of 20 volunteers kept the front desk of the station open for four days a week. Whilst in the control of the Metropolitan Police the station had been shut, but now in the hands of the Surrey Constabulary it had remained open.

An evaluation into police buildings and establishment considered Cobham as unsuitable for its purpose, and it was decided to sell the building in 2009, as Surrey Police Authority considered its ageing estate. Front counter services ceased in April 2011 and a mobile police station replaced services usually administered from the old police station.[795]

In May 2012 Cobham Free School, purchased the old police station for educational purposes.

Colindale Police Station

London Borough of Barnet

Grahame Park Way, London NW9 5TW

Borough of Barnet OCU (1997-2018)

North West NW BCU (together with Brent and Harrow, 2018 to present)

Around 1990 plans were laid to co-ordinate the policing arrangements in Barnet and to replace some worn out stations. This would allow for a much larger, modern multi-functioning, state-of-the-art station that could also act as an Area Headquarters. The intention was to replace Hendon, West Hendon and Mill Hill with a 'super station' to be named Colindale,[796] situated between all those stations.

The site for the new Colindale police station and No. 2 Area Headquarters was purchased from the Ministry of Defence on 25th April 1991. The police station design was suggested as being in keeping with its surroundings such as the former Hendon airfield, the adjacent Battle of Britain museum and the listed control tower.[797]

Tenders were invited from a number of building companies, and the winning bidder commenced construction in March 1995. The building was completed in January 1997, costing £8.8 million. It consists of a 6,500 sq m building, with four storeys of accommodation broken down into two wings with a rotunda in the middle to house both the station office and reception area.[798]

The building was meant to offer staff all the benefits of a safe and efficient working environment, while providing accommodation that was to establish 'the image of a modern police building'. The rotunda was extensively glazed at ground and third floor levels to 'reinforce the building's prominence during the day and night'. The ground floor contains the custody suite and offices associated with day-to-day policing. The station has the largest custody suite of any station in the borough, with 17 cells and four detention rooms.

The building also houses an Area control room which can be used to control major incidents including large-scale public order events anywhere in north west London. The rest of the building is made up of large open-plan cellular offices. The building was designed to give it a great degree of flexibility, and to cater for changes in operational and legislative needs. Provision for staff and visitors with special needs and disabilities was also been included throughout.[799]

Colindale Police Station 1997 to present

The station at Colindale opened in 1997. Their was another police stations front counter situated nearby at Simpson Hall, Aerodrome Road (the old cadet centre less than half a mile away from Colindale). West Hendon police station was being refurbished and so their front counter responsibilities had been transferred to Simpson Hall in the meantime until the new front office was completed.

In 2019 the station is open for operational purposes and still in the possession of the Metropolitan Police.[800]

779 blog.old-and-bold.info//?s=cobham accessed 2nd March 2012.
780 Ibid.
781 Site Locations for Metropolitan Police Telephone boxes and telephone posts for V Division.
782 *Kirchner's Guide* 1931.
783 *Police and Constabulary Almanac* 1937.
784 *Police and Constabulary Almanac* 1955.
785 *Police and Constabulary Almanac* 1960.
786 Metropolitan Police Stations 1965.
787 *The Job*, 1st January 1971.
788 Ibid.
789 Ibid.
790 Ibid.
791 Ibid.
792 *Police and Constabulary Almanac* 1998.
793 www.elmbridgeguardian.co.uk/news accessed 2nd March 2012.
794 MPS Station closures Reduced Opening 1997-2000.
795 'Colindale – A modern building for the 21st Century'. *The Job*.
796 Ibid.
797 Ibid.
798 MPS (2019) Freedom of information request – MPS Assets
799 Brown, B. (1990) 'Romford Police : The Anniversary of a Change in the Romford Record', Romford and District Historical Society.
800 Woodgate, J. (1985) *The Essex Police*, Lavenham, Suffolk. p138.

Collier Row Police Station

The London Borough of Havering
22 Collier Row Lane, Romford (1936-2008)
Essex Police (1936-1965)
K Division (1965-2008)

Collier Row Police Station Lamp

In 1841 there were two constables posted to Collier Row and Havering (-Atte-Bower, as we know it today.) This situation remained the same, certainly until 1851.[801] At Collier Row there were Constable 31 James Parslow, who had joined on 26th August 1841 and who had previously been a painter born in Kingston, Surrey,[802] and Constable 30 Jonathon Birdseye, who had joined a month later than his colleague.[803] Constable Parslow remained at Collier Row for some time,[804] eventually transferring to Romford Town Centre. It was decided to establish new beats in this area to cope with the growth of the population in the village. Supervision of the area was undertaken by the Inspector, who was stationed at Romford,[805] In 1900, due to divisional boundary changes, Collier Row became a station within Brentwood division.[806]

Records show that in 1931 this area was policed from Romford (South Street) Police Station,[807] although cottages in the area had police officers and their families in residence. In 1930 the population of Collier Row was estimated at 3,000 people, and it was a rapidly growing residential area.[808] The station strength remained at two constables. There was a proposal by the surveyor to purchase four further houses in the area.[809]

When the Metropolitan Police arrived in 1965 they found that the station was one of the few which had a beer cellar, as the building was originally an off-licence. A spring flowing under the building frequently caused flooding of the basement.[810] It was suspected that beer was brewed on the premises because of the abundant supply of fresh spring water.

Collier Row Police Station 1936-2008

The station was shut in 1968 together with Plough Corner, however a petition of 1,000 signatures from the local residents saw it reopen, albeit under limited opening times. The station had no cells or charging facilities.

Collier Row had been taken out of service under borough-based policing implemented in April 2000.[811] The station was finally closed, vacated and sold in 2008.[812]

Commercial Street Police Station

29 Church Street, Spitalfields (1829-1844)
Church Passage, Spitalfields (1844-1876)
160 Commercial Street, Shoreditch (1876-1970)
H Division (1829-1933)
G Division (1933-1965)
H Division (1965-1970)

The first Commercial Street Police Station was a watch house situated in Spital Square at the junction with Lamb Street, and behind St. Mary's Church. This was known as Spitalfields Watch House because it covered that area.[813] It was probably an original watch house handed over in 1829, but was still in use in 1862. It was usual to post two inspectors to each station, one being responsible for taking charges, complaints and calls for assistance in the station, whilst the other would supervise the constables and sergeants on their beats.[814] The two inspectors were Joseph Lewis (promoted to Inspector in 1835) and Henry Harris (promoted to Inspector in 1836).[815] Inspector Lewis was the senior of the two and was in charge of the station. This station was the divisional headquarters, and housed the Superintendent.

Former Spitalfields watch house, Spital Square

On 1864 a site was purchased from the Commissioners of Works for the police at the corner of Fleur de Lis Street and Commercial Street. A large new police station was planned, built by Messrs. Lathey Brothers to the design of Frederick H. Caiger, Surveyor for the Metropolitan Police. It then had a three-storey frontage, to Commercial Street only.[816] It was ready for business by March 1876.[817]

The payment for weekly lodging at the station for one inspector was 5s 6d, one sergeant was 4s, and 50 constables at 1s. The cost of one shilling a week rent for single constables had remained the same amount since it was instituted in 1829.[818] Commercial Street station has been described as "a sombre palazzo, has an arcaded ground storey of stone and three well-defined storeys of red brick with widely spaced windows".[819]

In 1881 there were 48 constables resident in the section house part of the station, which at the time of recording also held five prisoners.[820] Also lodged at the station was a hard-working detective who was suddenly thrust into the public eye during the controversial serial murder inquiry involving Jack the Ripper. He was Frederick George Abberline, who lived at the station with his wife, Emma who was ten years his junior. Abberline was from Blandford in Dorset, and had been married to Martha Mackness in 1868 only for her to die of tuberculosis two months later. He married Emma Beament in 1876, the marriage lasting more than 50 years until his death in 1929. From 1878 until 1887 Abberline was a local Inspector on H Division. He was promoted in 1887 to Inspector 1st Class and transferred to Central Office, Scotland Yard, and seconded back to H Division to lead the Ripper inquiry on the ground. He was promoted Detective Chief Inspector in 1890, retiring on pension in 1892 and going to work for the Pinkerton Detective Agency as their European agent.[821]

Commercial Street Police Station 1876-1970

Police Orders in 1884 show the address of the police station as 160 Commercial Street, Shoreditch.[822] Because of the odd-shaped corner plot on which it stood, officers who worked at the station gave it the fond nickname 'Comical Street'.

In 1907 the accommodation at the premises was altered to give two sets of married quarters and room for 39 unmarried men[823] when an extra storey was added.

By November 1911 the building had been enlarged to accommodate up to 100 single men, still paying rent at 1s per week. These living quarters at the station were known as Commercial Street Section House,[824] but in 1912 it was renamed Aldgate Section House.[825]

In 1933 the station was transferred to G Division, however in 1964 Commercial Street rejoined H Division and became a sub-division of Leman Street.[826]

In 1967 staff had to move from Leman Street (HD) as the old station was being pulled down. The operational staff moved temporarily to Commercial Street. Bethnal Green and Commercial Street Divisions amalgamated. In 1968 the Special Constabulary on H Division totalled 60 officers of all ranks. Woman Special Sergeant Miss M.R. Mounce was stationed at Commercial Street, in charge of the detachment of constables.[827] The station remained operational until March 1970, when a new police station was opened at 74 Leman Street. Today converted to flats, the building is now called Burhan Uddin House.

Croydon Police Station

The London Borough of Croydon

North End Road (1843-1895)

Fell Road (1895-1980)

71 Park Lane (1980 to present)

P Division (1843-1865)

W Division (1865-1921)

Z Division (1921-2018)

Basic Command Unit South Area (SN) (2018 to present)

When the Metropolitan Police District was extended in 1840 Croydon is shown not only as a station where charges were taken, but also being responsible for policing the Outer District, which included Beddington, Carshalton, Sutton, Cheam, Banstead, Woodmarston, Coulsdon, Worlingham, Farley, Sanderstead, Addington, Chipstead and Chelsham. It was designated P or Camberwell Division, and had the strength of one inspector, three sergeants and 29 constables. There were also three mounted sergeants. The officers stationed at Croydon were accommodated in a section house, whilst elsewhere the officers were privately lodged. Petty Sessions were held every Saturday, and a list of the names of the magistrates is included in documents at the National Archives.[828]

A substantial brick and slate station and section house was rented in the High Street Croydon. It comprised a charge room, kitchen, magistrate's room and three cells. In the yard was a 5-stall stable. The premises, at 13 North End, Croydon[829] were leased from Mr Townley of 3 Arlington Place, Kensington, for a period of 99 years from March 1841. Accommodation above the station consisted of two rooms for one inspector, at a yearly rent of £15 12s.[830] The rent payable on the lease was

801 Essex Record Office Q/Apr. 1 – Distribution List.
802 Ibid.
803 Woodgate, J. (1985) *The Essex Police*, Lavenham, Suffolk. p179.
804 Ibid.
805 *Kirchner's Police Index* (1931).
806 *Essex County Constabulary – Police Stations and Police Houses Booklet* (c.1930) Essex Police Museum, Police Headquarters, Springfield, Chelmsford, Essex.
807 Ibid.
808 *The Job*, 10th May 1968.
809 www.met.police.uk/contact/phone.htm accessed 3rd February 2002.
810 Information rights unit, MPS, police stations closed since 2010. Accessed 10th June 2019.
811 *The H Division Handbook* 1968/69.
812 Metropolitan Police General Orders 1829.
813 *The Police and Constabulary List* 1844. Furnivall, Parker and Furnivall, London.
814 www.british-history.ac.uk/survey-london/vol27/pp256-264 accessed 8th May 2019.
815 Metropolitan Police Orders dated 23rd March 1876.
816 Metropolitan Police General Orders 1829.
817 www.british-history.ac.uk/survey-london/vol27/pp256-264 accessed 8th May 2019.
818 Census 1881.
819 Begg, Fido and Skinner (1999) *Jack the Ripper A-Z*. p8.
820 Metropolitan Police Orders dated 20th June 1884.
821 Metropolitan Police Orders dated 5th January 1907.
822 Metropolitan Police Orders dated 11th November 1911.
823 Metropolitan Police Orders dated 17th August 1912.
824 *The H Division Handbook* 1968/69.
825 Ibid.
826 MEPO 2/76.
827 Metropolitan Police Surveyor's Records 1912.
828 Ibid.
829 *The Police and Constabulary List* 1844. p3.
830 Ibid p2.

quite high due to the fact that the owner, one James Townley, advanced the sum of £1,719 to build the station and needed repayment of the loan.

Croydon Police Station opened in 1841 at George Street, Croydon, with Inspector John Collier in charge (Collier had been promoted to Inspector in 1837).[831] Superintendent Andrew McLean was in charge of the Division which was located at Park House, Walworth.[832] the station was considered too small.

The station needed rebuilding and enlarging to accommodate the growth of Croydon's population and the demands on policing the town. The new station reopened in 1849 on a site where the Drummond Centre (now Primark) now stands. It consisted of four cells, a quiet/library room, four basement cellars and four stables. A new site in Katherine Street was offered as a possible site but was declined. A sum of £950 was found for improvements to the existing station instead.[833] The new further enlarged station was situated in George Street but also named North End situated at no. 9 (later 13 North End).

By 1851 Inspector W.H. Shaw was in charge of the station and in command of over 100 men, whose duties extended beyond Croydon. These included the Parishes of Addington, Beddington, Carshalton, Coulsdon, Mitcham, Merton, Morden, Sutton, Streatham, Sanderstead, Warlingham, Wallington and Woodmansterne.[834]

Croydon had a famous resident in the 1850s; this was none other than Richard Mayne, one of two Joint Commissioners appointed in 1829 on the formation of the Metropolitan Police, who resided in the Addiscombe area of the town. The local Inspector would have been aware of this, and Mayne without doubt would have paid visits to the station.[835] Croydon Sergeant George Thoburn resided at 30 Adelaide Street, whilst another Sergeant, Thomas Prendergast, lived in Bell Yard.

Croydon Police Station 1843-1895

In 1864 Croydon is shown as being on P or Camberwell Division, with strength of one inspector, six sergeants and 50 constables. There was stabling for five horses. One horse would be ridden alternately by two sergeants on station duty.[836]

The following year, the Force in that area created three new Divisions – W or Clapham, X or Paddington and Y or Highgate. Croydon was transferred to W Division.[837]

By 1869 Superintendent William Wiseman was in charge of W Division. There were five stations, each having an Inspector in charge: Brixton, Carshalton, Clapham. Croydon and Streatham. Sergeants were in charge of Banstead, Mitcham, Sutton and Tooting. At a meeting of the Croydon Local Board of Health held at the Town Hall on Tuesday 3rd January 1871 it was resolved:

"That in the opinion of this Board the Police arrangements in Croydon are of an inadequate nature and are not commensurate with the large amount contributed to the Police rate of the Parish, and that the Clerk be instructed to communicate with Colonel Henderson on the subject in the confident expectation that no time will be lost in providing a remedy for so unsatisfactory a position".

District Superintendent Baynes, in a memo to the Commissioner dated 10th January 1871, refutes the above motion.

In March 1871 Superintendent Wiseman of W Division requests an augmentation of four constables for the division for better protection of Croydon.[838] It was felt that Croydon was an important enough centre to require an officer of more senior rank, and in 1878 Chief Inspector William Mason and Inspector Charles Hunt were shown to be in charge at 6 North End.[839] This was probably because of the growing size of the town and the busy nature of the courts.

By 1881 an inspection of all Metropolitan stations revealed that the Croydon station was far too small for the amount of work carried out. There were also comments that the site was too small for expansion. In addition, the quarters at the station housed one married inspector, one single sergeant and 19 single constables, and the inspection made comment that living quarters of the single and married people were all mixed up.[840]

By 1889 Superintendent Stephen T. Lucas was in charge of W Division, whose strength was 38 inspectors, 72 sergeant and 584 constables – a total establishment of 695 officers and men.[841]

Although the police station was renovated in 1873/74 there was still a need for larger premises. In 1890, Croydon Corporation sold some of the land in central Croydon that it had purchased from the London, Brighton and South Eastern Railway to the Metropolitan Police Receiver.[842] As the new building was going to be next to the Municipal Buildings, Croydon Corporation insisted that the same stone was to be used as that of other buildings in the vicinity.[843] In 1891, just prior to the change, Chief Inspector Andrew Webb was shown in charge of the station at 13 North End.[844]

The freehold title to Fell Road, Katherine Street, was purchased in 1892 and included a subway under Fell Road that was maintained by the Receiver of the Metropolitan Police.[845] In the meantime, the North End station was vacated and the premises sub-let. In fact, the Police were making profits from the old station which they had rented to Messrs. Kennard Brothers in 1912 for £307 a year, while their ground rent and rent charges only came to £118 annually.[846] This carried on until at least 1924 at the same rental rate.[847]

The new police station, designed by John Butler at a cost of £12,000, opened in Fell Road, Croydon in September 1895,[848] some 22 years after the previous building was considered inadequate. The station had an Inspector's Office, charge room, parade room, matron's room, drying room, four cells, quiet room, library, mess room and bathroom. In addition there were three stables and an ambulance shed. There was also accommodation for a married inspector and 20 single constables.

Croydon Police Station 1895-1980

The old police station continued serving the public, first as Wilson's Tea Rooms and finally as Kennard's.[849] Frederick Bonner became the first Sub-Divisional Inspector (SDI) for Croydon followed by William Lemmey until 1898 when Samuel Parlett took over, and then Frank Chinn in 1902. By 1905 Chinn had transferred to Clapham as SDI.

Inspector William Lemmey retired from Croydon Police Station in September 1898 due to ill health. The Superintendent from W Division, Mr Lucas, made a presentation to the Inspector of a 'handsome liquor stand' given as a mark of respect from the officers and colleagues in the division.[850]

In a letter from the Commissioner to the Home Office dated July 1920 it was recorded that there was to be the formation of a new division on the south side of the Thames which would be known as the Z or Croydon Division. The Commissioner said:

"The question which was under discussion in the year 1913 was not proceeded with in consequence of the outbreak of the war, has now, owing to the ever increasing population and more exacting duties of Police, and from the point of view of efficiency become one of importance and urgency. It is proposed to vary the present boundaries and establishments of all the Division south of the Thames with a view, as far as possible, to equalising the area and personnel of each. The W Division in particular, will be considerably reduced, and the new Division, to a large extent, will embrace what is now part of the Division.

The new Z Division will be divided into three Sub-Divisions. Headquarters to be at Croydon. Croydon Sub-Division to be Croydon and Kenley Stations. Thornton Heath Sub-Division to be Thornton Heath and South Norwood Stations. Gipsy Hill Sub-Division to be Gipsy Hill and Knights Hill Stations. (Knights Hill closed in 1930) It will be within the knowledge of the Secretary of State that the residents of Croydon have agitated for many years past for a re-organisation of the Police arrangements within the Borough, and general satisfaction will doubtless be given by making Croydon the chief Station of the new Division".

The Home Office sanctioned the formation of Z Division in a letter to the Commissioner dated 9th October 1920.[851]

The new Division came into being on 28th February 1921,[852] and with its introduction suitable police officers were transferred in from other divisions. For example, the picture right shows Station Sergeant 84862 Harold Brewer (PS 2Z), who was the most senior sergeant and who had been transferred from W Division on 24th February 1921. It was the same year that station sergeants were given a crown to wear above their stripes rather than a fourth stripe. Brewer remained on Z Division until he retired in February 1924.

Station Sergeant Harold Brewer

By 1928 Superintendent James Wilson was in charge of Croydon Division and under his command was Croydon Sub-Divisional Station and its Sectional Station at Kenley (Godstone Road), Norbury Sub-Divisional Station (London Road, Norbury) and two Sectional Stations, those of South Norwood (82 High Street) and Thornton Heath (Parchmore Road).

Also included in the division at that time was Gipsy Hill Sub-Division, with Knight Hill as the Sectional Station.[853] By 1939, Superintendent H.C. Quincey was in charge of the division in addition to the above stations of Streatham, Gipsy Hill and Wallington.[854]

In 1944, towards the end of the Second World War, the town of Croydon was subjected to attacks by flying bombs. Some 20,000 women and children were evacuated, but still many people were killed or injured. One such incident in 1944 led Inspector William James Holloway to enter, at great risk, the debris of a house demolished by a Flying Bomb and rescue three people. For his "courage, perseverance and devotion to duty" he was awarded the British Empire Medal.[855]

In 1952, Police Constable Sidney George Miles was shot and killed on the roof of a warehouse near the Croydon Bus Station, while he and other officers were giving chase to two local youths who were suspected of being on the getaway from

831 'Croydon Police Station' by PC 872A Jephcote (1982).
832 *The Croydon Directory* 1851, p156.
833 Ibid p54.
834 Police Order 11th January 1864.
835 Police Order 28th October 1865.
836 MEPO 2/139.
837 *Kelly's Directory* 1878, p2169.
838 Metropolitan Police Report 1881.
839 *Police Almanac* 1889.
840 Metropolitan Police Historical Collection.
841 Notes by Chief Inspector Delaney 1982.
842 *Kelly's Directory* 1891 p1239.
843 Metropolitan Police Surveyor's Records 1912.
844 Ibid p35.
845 Metropolitan Police Surveyor's Records 1924.
846 Police Order 30th August 1895.
847 'Croydon Police Station' by PC 872A Jephcote (1982).
848 *The Police Review and Parade Gossip*, 30th September 1898. p466.
849 MEPO 5/127.
850 Police Order 24 February 1921.
851 *Post Office Directory* 1928.
852 *Post Office London Directory* 1939.
853 Metropolitan Police Historical Collection.
854 Ibid.
855 *The Official Encyclopedia of Scotland Yard*, 1999.

an armed robbery. Detective Constable Frederick Fairfax was shot in the shoulder.[856] Police Constable Miles was awarded the King's Police and Fire Services Medal (KPFSM).

This medal was only awarded posthumously for Gallantry from 1950 until 1954. Detective Constable Fairfax was awarded the George Cross, which is the highest non-military gallantry ward, sometimes known as the civilians' Victoria Cross. Fairfax received his award because he walked unflinchingly towards the two youths, who continued to fire the weapon until the gun was empty. It has only been awarded to five Metropolitan Police officers.[857]

The King's Police Medal was one of the older awards, instituted in 1909 by King Edward VII but discontinued in 1954 when separate medals for Police and for Fire Service were substituted. Although titled the King's Police Medal, it could be awarded to members of the Fire Service, and was awarded to Police or Fire personnel who perform 'acts of exceptional courage and skill, or who had exhibited conspicuous devotion to duty'.[858]

Constable Sislin Fay Allen

In May 1968 Mrs Sislin Fay Allen, a nurse at Croydon's Queens Hospital, became Britain's first black policewoman. She started work at Croydon Police Station in a blaze of publicity, so much so that she remained on indoor duty throughout her first week to avoid being photographed or interviewed on the beat.[859]

She said, "On the selection day there were so many people there, the hall was filled with the young men. There were ten women and I was the only black person."

After taking a set of exams and a stringent medical, Sislin Allen was told she had passed and would start work at Croydon's Fell Road Police Station.

"I can remember one friend said, 'Oh they wouldn't accept you, they don't accept black people in the force,' and so I said, 'Well my dear, I've got news for you,' and I showed her the letter. The first day on the beat in Croydon was daunting, but it wasn't too bad because I went out with an officer. People were curious to see a black woman there in uniform walking up and down, but I had no problem at all, not even from the public. On the day I joined I nearly broke a leg trying to run away from reporters. I realised then that I was a history maker. But I didn't set out to make history; I just wanted a change of direction."[860]

There were less than 600 Women Police Officers working in the Metropolitan Police at that time.

In 1969 the District Police Commander and his staff moved from the station into the old Town Hall opposite, and in 1977 they were joined by the Chief Superintendent of Croydon and the Juvenile Bureau.[861]

A new police station had been proposed and discussed locally since at least 1967, and it was to be situated at 70 Park Lane in front of the law courts. Consultations were slow, and a date in 1972 was discussed but the proposed construction was put back in time as building priorities changed. Originally it was proposed that the building would include an eleven-storey section house, but that was abandoned because there were only a handful of unmarried men and women serving in the area.[862] There was also a view that the vast cost of building single persons' quarters was not cost-effective, and that it would be better for single officers to make their own living provisions.

Croydon Police Station 1980 to present

The building was designed by J.I. Elliot, Metropolitan Police Chief Architect, who had used a facade with horizontal brick bands.[863] Work on the new police station began in January 1974 when private houses on the site were demolished. The five-storey building cost £2.25million. At the time of opening it would house 250 police officers, 100 traffic wardens and 35 civil staff. There is a 3-storey car park and recreational facilities at the station, together with a small arms firing range in the basement.[864]

The new District Headquarters and Police Station at Croydon was opened by HRH Prince Charles on 6th March 1980 at 71 Park Lane, replacing the old Police Station in Fell Road, which was demolished in 1980.[865] The vacant site was incorporated into Queen's Gardens.[866]

The opening of the new station was the first time that His Royal Highness had performed the opening ceremony of a Metropolitan Police station. Among the guests attending was the Home Secretary Mr William Whitelaw, Metropolitan Police Commissioner Sir David McNee and the Mayor of Croydon, Councillor P. Bowness. The station code was 'ZD'.

Currently, Croydon Police Station is the Borough of Croydon Police Headquarters and is open 24 hours a day.

Dagenham Police Station

The London Borough of Barking and Dagenham
Bull Street, Dagenham, Essex (1840-1851)
Rainham Road South, Dagenham (1851-1961)
561 Rainham Road South, Dagenham (1961 to Present)
K Division (1840-2018)
Basic Command Unit East Area (EA) (2018 to Present)

Dagenham was first policed in 1840 by the Metropolitan Police, from a shop in Bull Street. Dagenham was shown on the outer District of K Division and had a station strength of one sergeant and five constables.[867] All the officers at the station were housed privately,[868] and lodged near the station. This became the first police station in the area. It was not for another ten years that arrangements were made for the building of a proper police station in Dagenham. Prisoners who were charged and detained without bail would be transported, often handcuffed and on foot, to Ilford Police Station where they would travel by horse-drawn police van to prison. Charges were taken at Dagenham, and persons would appear before the Petty Sessions at Ilford on the first and third Saturday of each month.[869]

Surveyors for the Metropolitan Police found a plot of land which appeared suitable for a police station, which had a freehold title that could be purchased. Arrangements and contracts were made, and the building of the police station commenced in 1850 on Rainham Road South at the junction of Shafter Road, Dagenham, at a cost of £949. The land had been purchased from Mr. John Jarrow for an additional £100.

There was accommodation on the first floor for one married sergeant (later an inspector) and four unmarried constables. The station was not equipped with a gas supply (this was not fitted until January 1906), and the occupants had to rely on oil lamps and coal for its lighting and heating. Furthermore there was no sewage system, and effluent was emptied from the cesspool once a year.[870] There was a charge room and cells in which to house prisoners. There was also a parade room for constables to report for duty.[871]

In 1846 Constable George Clark was found murdered at Dagenham. This 20-year-old had recently been posted to Dagenham from Arbour Square Police Station, and was settling into the routine of police work. His sergeant, William Parsons, was a man who liked a drink, as did most of the men under his command. Constable Clark was a man of strict morals, and was keen to save his fellow officers from the evils of the demon drink. This must have caused irritation among the men.

The lower class inhabitants in the area did not like the new police system. They much preferred the unsuspicious and lazy constables of the old Parish system. Barking, an adjacent village, had long been the centre for smuggling activities, which meant that active policemen were not welcome.

On 1st July 1846 Constable Clark started his night duty shift at 9.00pm, and was paraded as usual by Sergeant Parsons. At 1.00am he was met by Sergeant Parsons, who arranged to meet him again at 3.00am. This was the last time he was seen alive. He never turned up at 3.00am, or returned to Dagenham station house at 6.00am at the end of his shift. Later that day he was not found sleeping in the station house where he should have been. A search was ordered, but it was not until two days later that his body was found, a quarter of a mile off his beat, on farmland belonging to a Mr. Page. Constable Clark had a fatal stab wound to the throat, the back of his head had been beaten in and his head had been scalped.

Inspector Richardson and Sergeant Parsons worked on the enquiry, but when there was no quick conclusion the Commissioners became concerned and ordered the newly-formed Detective Department to take over the case. In a very short time Dagenham, in the words of one resident, was crawling with the detective force. Two of the department's inspectors, three of the six sergeants and the celebrated detective of the day, Nicholas Pearce, recently promoted to Superintendent of F Division, appeared on the scene.

Later three arrests were made at Woolwich. However there was no evidence other than that they were in possession of white gloves usually worn by a policeman, and that a woman had overheard a conversation suggesting that two of the men had murdered a constable.

Dagenham Police Station, High Road, Dagenham 1851-1961

Meanwhile a sensation had been caused at the Coroner's hearing, where the farmer's wife, Mrs. Page, suggested that Sergeant Parsons had not been on duty on the night of the murder, because he was ill. She had been told this by one of the constables on the day the body was found, yet no less than six people, including Sergeant Parsons, denied this allegation on oath. In fact it transpired that Parsons and some of the other constables had been drinking whilst Clark was out on his beat.

---

856 cfa.vic.gov.au accessed 23rd March 2010.
857 *Croydon Advertiser*, 17th May 1968.
858 www.blackhistorymonthuk.co.uk/uni/first_in_the_force.html accessed 25th March 2010.
859 NSY Press Release dated 5th March 1980.
860 *Croydon Advertiser*, 14 May 1971.
861 Pevsner, N and Cherry, B. (1983) *London. 2: South*. Penguin, Harmondsworth.
862 NSY Press Release dated 5th March 1980.
863 Brown B. 'The Warren' 1982.
864 Ibid.
865 MEPO 14.
866 Metropolitan Police Asset Management Plan. November 2007.
867 TNA 'Distribution of men on K Division 1840'.
868 Ibid.
869 Ibid.
870 Metropolitan Police Surveyor's records (undated).
871 Metropolitan Police Orders 11th January 1864.

One of the constables, Abia Butfoy, who had said Parsons was well, went to London to see the Commissioners. He told them that he and others had lied on oath. He also told them that Sergeant Parsons had not been on duty that night. When the body was discovered Sergeant Parsons took him to one side and told him that, if asked, both of them had rendezvoused on Butfoy's beat between midnight and 1.00am.

The murder was re-investigated and the Coroner returned a verdict of murder by persons unknown, and made comments about perjured evidence by police officers in his court. The Commissioners considered their next move. They suspended Sergeant Parsons, Butfoy and four constables, pending inquiry.

The police were not popular but the case attracted little attention outside Dagenham. The three lesser culprits, including Butfoy, were dismissed from the Force, whilst Sergeant Parsons and two constables remained suspended. During further enquiries the three were kept as virtual prisoners within the station house. The guarding became lax and Sergeant Parsons and one of the constables escaped and went on the run. A poster was put up offering a £50 reward for the apprehension of the two escapees, and three weeks later the constable was arrested in Lincolnshire.

A year after the murder the two constables stood trial for perjury, were found guilty and sentenced to seven years' transportation. Sergeant Parsons was never found, rather like the murderer of Constable Clark. There was a final twist when, some twelve years after the murder, a woman came forward and implicated her own late husband and another man. At the hearing, after the arrest of a man named Blewett, her evidence was discredited, and the man was acquitted.[872]

In 1864 there was one sergeant and eight constables posted to the station.[873] In 1874 the sergeant in charge was Frederick Stratford. These men were supervised by an inspector who patrolled and supervised police stations at Ilford, Barking, Dagenham, Loughton, Woodford, Wanstead, Chadwell Heath, Barkingside, Chigwell and East Ham.[874]

Concern had been raised regarding the activities of constables and sergeants whilst off duty away from the station. At that time, as drinking water could be contaminated in many cases people drank beer because it was fermented. This led to off-duty hours being spent in local public houses. The concerns of senior officers were further heightened when constables and some sergeants became indebted to the Landlord of a public house who provided free drink. Whilst drinking on duty was forbidden by police rules, off-duty hours were a different matter. The recruiting policy was to select non-Londoners as it was felt that they were more honest and that Londoners were, in many cases, naturally inclined to crime.

The Commissioner was pressed to introduce billiard tables and games rooms into police stations and section houses in order that recreation could be spent under the watchful eye of supervising officers, a method which ensured against drunkenness and contributed towards good behaviour.

In July 1896 instructions were issued to K Division that a recreation room should be created in each station and section house.[875] Barking and Dagenham stations were issued with draughts, dominoes, backgammon and single sticks (or pick-up sticks), whilst the principle section house on the division received a set of boxing gloves.[876] This perhaps explains the fact that even today snooker and boxing is still taken very seriously by many police officers. The principle station on the division, Arbour Square, received a miniature billiards table.[877]

The officers playing billiards in the picture below are in training at Peel House Pimlico circa 1910.

The Billiard Room, Peel House, Pimlico

The billiards tables soon found favour amongst the Superintendents, who reported to the Commissioner that:

"The various articles supplied by the Commissioner for the amusement of the Police continue to be highly appreciated by them; no irregularity of any description has arisen in consequence of their use; and I venture respectfully but strongly to recommend and increase of billiard tables for the happiness of the single men. I would suggest that all stations where 30 single men (or upwards) reside, or to which 100 men are attached, that a billiard table should be supplied." [Superintendent W. F. Green, N Division].

In 1881 John Durley, aged 38 years, was the inspector in charge of the station. Durley was from Whitchurch in Buckingham, and he resided at the station with his wife Maria and their three sons. Also there were four single constables and a nurse. The nurse was called Hester Purkiss, and she was probably there to look after their eight-month-old son Joseph Durley. It was also likely that Maria Durley and the nurse would cook and clean for the station, which also meant providing meals for the prisoners.[879]

The old Dagenham Police Station was used until 1937, when it was refurbished.[880] Once re-opened for business it remained in continuous use until 1961, when a new station was built on the other side of the Railway Bridge at 561 Rainham Road South. It took eighteen months to build.

The main entrance has a natural Portland stone floor and marble walls. It was one of the first Metropolitan Police stations to have a reading/rest room with armchairs and reading material.

The old station was sold and became a betting office.

Police Constable 711K Wilfred Adams

The picture left is of Wilfred John Adams, who was born on 16th May 1889 at Morse in Gloucestershire. Prior to joining the Metropolitan Police he was a collier. He became a Constable, warrant no. 99949, on 20th March 1911 aged 21 years. He served on K Division as Constable 711 K until 3rd April 1929, when he transferred and became Constable 751 of T Division. Constable Adams was given a Commissioner's Commendation in July

1919 'for promptitude with another officer at the scene of a fire'. He had a son, who was born in 1926. He left the service in March 1936 and lived until 1952. On leaving the service he was awarded an exemplary 'certificate of service', indicating that his disciplinary record was outstanding.

In 1957 Dagenham Police Station (KG) was a sectional station of East Ham (KD) Sub-Division, which was also the Headquarters of K Division. The officer in charge of the Division in 1960 was Superintendent W. J. Merchant, and the Divisional head was Chief Superintendent Arnold Lockwood,[881] who had been promoted from Leman Street Sub-Division.[882]

Prior to the 1960s information and intelligence about local criminals was usually passed to other officers by word of mouth. The flow of information was inefficient, and there was a need for recording and greater accuracy. In 1967 Constable Nevil 'Spike' Hughes (BEM) thought up a new system to collate this information. He progressed the idea without funding or equipment. Originally nicknamed 'SPYKANEDY' (Spike and Eddy) after Constable Hughes and his colleague Constable Eddy Gurney (BEM), who helped refine the process, the collator system was born.[883]

Introduced first at Carter Street Police Station, it was soon developed across the whole of the Metropolitan Police Service. At Dagenham a collator was appointed and a room was found to house the information in filing cabinets. Only police officers and members of the civil staff were allowed in this room, and visitors were excluded. The system brought together data, including maps, criminal records, vehicle registrations and other information likely to be of assistance in the investigation of beat crimes. The place where the information was held was called the Collator's Office, however it has been renamed the Local Intelligence Office manned by the Local Intelligence Officer. Constables Hughes and Gurney were both deservedly awarded British Empire Medals for their innovation.[884]

Dagenham Police Station, 561 Rainham Road South, 1961 to present

In 2002 Dagenham Police Station was recorded at 561 Rainham Road South, Dagenham, Essex, and was the Barking and Dagenham Borough Police Headquarters. The station is open to the public 24 hours a day 7 days a week.[885]

As a result of Electoral boundary changes in the mid 1990s the policing of Marks Gate changed. This meant that Barkingside Police gave up this remote site located on the north side of the A12, midway between Barley lane and Whalebone Lane. Because of the remote nature of the station to Marks Gate it was decided to locate a detached police office on the Estate called Marks Gate Police Station. The station is near the border with the London Boroughs of Redbridge and Havering at 78 Rose Lane, Romford, Essex. The police office was closed in 2013,[886] although the building is still used for police purposes.

Dalston Police Station

The London Borough of Hackney
6 Caroline Terrace (1845-1871)
41 (39) Dalston Lane (1871-1933)
39-41 Dalston Lane (1933-1991)
N Division (1845-1886)
J Division (1886-1933)
G Division (1933-1985/86)
Stoke Newington Division (1985/86-1991)

Dalston Police Station Lamp

The Parish watch house was originally situated on the east side of Stoke Newington High Street, just south of Shacklewell Lane and opposite Robinson's Place.[887] This building backed onto Alvington Crescent, next to Kingsland Independent Chapel. The watch house remained there until 1880s, although it was no longer used for police purposes. It was probably given up in 1845 when the new Dalston Police Station was first occupied.

The new station was taken into service at 6 Caroline Terrace, Dalston in 1845, rented from Samuel Culff of Median House, Median Road, Clapton[888] for £40 per annum. It consisted of a brick and slate building which included a station and section house, and was located on N or Islington Division.

A new station at Dalston was taken into service in September 1871.[889] Records dated 1873 show that this was designated as a station with a sergeant in charge.[890] New leases had been negotiated in 1870 for three years at £40 rent per year, and again in 1880 for 31 years[891] at £100 rent per annum. The building was very small and appears not to have had any cells, although there was a charge room. There were first and second floors which housed a married sergeant and his family, and six single constables. During this time the address of the station changed to 39 instead of 41 Dalston Lane.

Instructions were given that a new sub-division should be formed. Dalston Police Station was created with a strength of two inspectors, eight sergeants and 91 constables.[892] Both

872 Cobb, B. (1961) *Murdered on Duty*, W. H. Allen, London.
873 Metropolitan Police Orders 11th January 1864 and Metropolitan Police Surveyor's Records (undated).
874 Metropolitan Police Orders 11th January 1864.
875 Metropolitan Police Orders 15th July 1896.
876 Ibid.
877 Ibid.
878 Commissioner's Annual Report 1871.
879 Census 1881.
880 Metropolitan Police Surveyor's Records.
881 *The Police and Constabulary Almanac* 1960.
882 *The Police and Constabulary Almanac* 1957.
883 Fido, M and Skinner, K (1999) T*he Official Encyclopaedia of Scotland Yard*. Virgin, London. p252.
884 Ibid.
885 www.met.police.uk/contact/phone accessed 3rd February 2002.
886 Metropolitan Police Information Rights Unit 22nd March 2017, accessed 25th January 2019.
887 *Stanford's London Suburbs* February 1862 – Margate, Kent.
888 Metropolitan Police Surveyor's Records.
889 Metropolitan Police Orders dated 7th September 1871.
890 Metropolitan Police General Orders 1873.
891 John Back Archive (1975).
892 Metropolitan Police Orders dated 3rd March 1878.

Kingsland and Hackney Sub-divisions were split to become Stoke Newington, Dalston and Hackney. Records also show that two Inspectors were shown stationed at Dalston Police Station at this time. They were Inspector Overy and Inspector Jenkins.[893]

In 1882 Constable George Cole was patrolling in Dalston when he disturbed a man attempting to illegally enter a dwelling. In the process of being arrested the burglar produced a gun and shot the officer in the head. Constable Cole died of his injuries.[894]

The Home Office approved the acceptance of tenders in order to build a new police station[895] in Dalston Lane. In 1883 the land was leased for a period of 99 years. The cost of the building was borne by the Metropolitan Police and not the owner of the land. Restrictions were placed on the Receiver which determined the relative disruption to the neighbouring area and conditions under which the station could operate. For example, he was required to paint the outside of the building every three years and the inside every seventh year. He was also required to build a police station within eighteen months of the removal of any building on the site, and to clear the ground within three months of 14th September 1883. Any premises built must be either a police station or a private dwelling house. The station was built in 1884 on the original site and cost £5,004.[896] Once built, the large house next door was incorporated into the premises.

In August 1886 the Metropolitan Police formed J or Bethnal Green Division, which meant a revision of boundaries with Dalston transferring from N to J Division.[897]

The picture below is of Dalston Police Station circa 1906, situated to the right of the larger building, which had also been leased and was used as a section house[898] for single constables and sergeants. A constable is standing in the foyer of the police station.

The Metropolitan Police Surveyors decided in the early 1900s that a new station should be built on the existing site, together with a much larger section house. To build the section house required the purchase of further land adjoining the old station. Accordingly, in 1910 the Receiver acquired a site in Ramsgate Street, at the rear of the station, on which a section house for 50 single men was built. This opened in June 1913.[899] Land in the area was scarce so it was decided to demolish the old station and rebuild it on the same site, at the cost of £4,283. The new station opened in June 1914, and included two sets of married quarters.[900]

Dalston Police Station 1914-1991

The freehold for the station was purchased from the owners in 1923. In 1933 there was another re-organisation with Dalston transferring from N to G Division. This meant that Dalston was a sectional station of Islington Sub-Division, with City Road becoming the Headquarters station for G Division.

The photograph right shows a young officer, Constable 737 N Joseph Ernest Richardson, taken by a Dalston photographer in 1928. PC Richardson probably lived at the back of Dalston Police Station in the section house. It is also likely that he was attached to the station. Born in 1904 in Sheffield, on leaving school became a turner. He served in the army from 7th August 1923 until 9th January 1928 and on 13th February 1928 joined the Metropolitan Police.[901]

Police Constable 737N Richardson

In the 1930s London saw the rise of Fascism. The British Fascist Movement, led by Sir Oswald Mosley, had a significant effect on the Metropolitan and City of London Police, particularly in the policing of political demonstrations. Mosley was allowed to be protected by his own uniformed black-shirted and booted guards. Demonstrations were commonplace in the East End, often leading to violence and disorder.[902] High numbers of police officers regularly paraded for duty to keep the peace and provide a 'thin blue line' between the demonstrators and their attackers. The picture below shows police officers parading at the back of Dalston Police Station ready to travel to police the latest Black Shirt march in the East End. You will notice that the officers are

Dalston Police Station 1871-1914

Several serials of police at Dalston Police Station in 1936 preparing to travel to police the Black Shirt demonstrations

smartly dressed, and have been instructed to parade with rolled capes. The police cape provided protection in the event of rain or inclement weather.

The 1965 local government re-organisation caused police boundaries to be revised, and with effect from April 1965 Dalston became a sectional station of Hackney Sub-Division. In 1962 a substantial section of land was purchased by the police at 175-189 Balls Pond Road and 202 Southgate Road N1, on which to build a new modern purpose-built station.[903] However a combination of events, together with a lack of finance, caused the police to shelve any ideas of building the station. The site was used for parking vehicles and as a vehicle test site.[904] This has now been sold to a developer who has built luxury flats on the site.

By the late 1970s Dalston became a sectional station to Stoke Newington Sub-Division, and ceased to take prisoners. All prisoners were dealt with instead at Stoke Newington Police Station. The station was closed in 1991, when all police work was transferred to Stoke Newington Police Station, where a far larger, more modern station had been built.

By 2002 the situation had changed and Dalston was provided with an operational police station. It was called Dalston Cross as it is located at the rear of The Kingsland Shopping Centre in Kingsland High Street. It is open every other Monday, then Tuesday-Saturday from 10.30am to 5.30pm, although these times might vary occasionally.[905] This was a front counter in the Shopping Centre and by 2010 its was no longer present and had been closed.[906]

Dean Street Police Station

6 Dean Street (1830-c.1838)

C Division (1830-c.1838)

In 1830, 6 Dean Street was an operational police station that was central to the parish of St Anne's, Soho.[907] A 'List of Police Stations where Charges are taken in the Metropolitan Police District where police constables are at all times' was published in 1836 showing that C or St James's Division had two police stations, one at Little Vine Street, Piccadilly and the other on Dean Street, Soho. By 1838 Dean Street station was no longer in use.[908] The station may have been occupied by B Division in 1832,[909] but the premises were later relinquished by the police.

It was, however, a good site for a police station, especially as Soho developed as a vibrant and diverse centre. The Admiral Duncan public house in Old Compton Street, a few doors down from the junction with Dean Street, became the centre of a bomb outrage in April 1999 when David Copeland, an English neo-Nazi militant, planted a number of nail bombs in various parts of London aimed against gay, Bangladeshi and black communities. His nail bombs killed three people and injured 129. A paranoid schizophrenic working alone, Copeland was sentenced to life imprisonment with a recommendation that he serve at least 50 years, a reminder that bombs are not always the weapon of organised terrorist groups.

Debden Police Office

Epping Forest District Council

Barrington Green, Debden, Essex

J Division (1970-2000)

Essex Police (2000-2015)

In 1970 the first of three new police offices were opened on Barkingside Division on the Debden Estate in Essex. Others were planned for Hainault and Limes Farm.[910] This was in line with the policy of building police offices where larger communities were located. The photograph below shows a purpose-built police office designed to be opened at particular times to deal with enquiries from the public.

Debden Police Office

The office was built without cells or other facilities for prisoners. Until 2000 any arrests were taken to Barkingside Police Station. Today they are taken to an Essex Police Station at Loughton or Epping.

The Debden Estate was a Greater London Council estate, which had developed following the Second World War and

893 John Back Archive (1975).
894 www.policememorial.org.uk/Forces/Metropolitan/metroll.htm accessed 12th March 2002.
895 Ibid.
896 Metropolitan Police Surveyors records (undated).
897 Metropolitan Police Orders 22nd July 1886.
898 John Back Archive (1975).
899 Metropolitan Police Orders 28th June 1913.
900 Metropolitan Police Orders 27th June 1914.
901 Metropolitan Police Service Records.
902 Fido, M. and Skinner, K. (1999) *The Encyclopedia of New Scotland Yard*, Virgin Press.
903 John Back Archive (1975).
904 Ibid.
905 www.met.police.uk/contact/phone.htm accessed 12th March 2002.
906 Freedom of Information Request (2017) Metropolitan Police.
907 From a picture donated by Bernard Brown.
908 *Kelly's Directory* 1838
909 Private correspondence with Mr Ken Butler.
910 *The Job*, 20th November 1970.

was designed to re-house families from London.[911] The station call sign was JE. The police office was transferred to Essex Police in 2000 and was later closed and sold. It is now a private residence.

Deptford Police Station

The London Borough of Lewisham

Prince Street, Deptford (1855-1912)

114 Amersham Vale, Deptford (1912-2005)

P Division (1855-2005)

The town of Deptford, having derived its name from 'Depeford', a deep ford across the River Ravensbourne and situated at the mouth of what is now known as Deptford Creek, is located just four miles from London Bridge.[912] This area was at one time also known as West Greenwich, situated in the Hamlet of Hatchem.[913] The ferry crossing was replaced with a bridge in 1805/06 and this allowed access to Greenwich and beyond. The Bow Street Horse Patrol operated in Deptford from 1805 from the Station at Rushey Green.[914]

Records show that between 1830 and 1832 there was a station at Lucas Street, Rotherhithe, which was one of two police stations or watch houses on R Division. The other station was Rose Cottage in Greenwich Road.[915]

In 1839 Police Constable William Aldridge died from a fractured skull after he was stoned by a mob during an arrest in Deptford. He was not the only officer to die in the streets of Deptford during those early days. In 1846 PC James Hastie of R Division died from extensive head injuries following a disturbance in the street in Deptford. He died in the execution of his duty having been beaten by several men.[916]

It wasn't until the 1850s that the Home Office agreed to fund the purchase of a police station in Deptford, although the estimated cost was expected to be very high.[917] In 1855 a station was brought into service in Prince Street, and records show that it had an 80-year lease from the landlord, W. J. Evelyn, from 1855 until 1935 at £12 per annum.[918] Originally a sergeant was in charge of the station, but later an inspector became responsible; it was a Sectional Station to Blackheath Road.[919]

In 1855/56 Deptford became another suburb of the metropolis and was absorbed into Greenwich District of the new Metropolitan Board of Works.[920]

Deptford Police Station was located at 13 Prince Street and quite often a Station was situated near to toll gates. Deptford was no exception, as there was one in Evelyn Street at the junction with Prince Street and just yards from the station. Tolls were abolished in October 1865, much to the joy of the local population, although the bridge toll on the Creek swing bridge remained until March 1880.[921]

In 1864 Deptford Sub-Division was formed as part of R Greenwich Division.[922] and it would appear that the status of the station was enhanced from that supervised by a sergeant to an inspector station. The station strength showed that it had a complement of two inspectors, four sergeants and 27 constables.[923] The Police officers at the station could not have failed to notice the increased hardship amongst the local population, due in part because of the closure of Deptford dockyard in March 1869, although the opening of the Foreign Cattle Market in 1871 would have brought many jobs back to the area.[924]

Records show that by 1873 Deptford had been connected by telegraph to Commissioners Office, 'CO' at Scotland Yard.[925]

Deptford Police Station 1855-1912

There were six cells located at the station, but in a review of accommodation in 1881 the Surveyor reported that four more cells were required. He also found that the coal allocation per man was insufficient in 42 stations he had visited.[926]

The station had 13 police officers residing in the Section House in 1881. It was situated a short distance from the Foreign Cattle Market, and had the cricket ground and racing path to the north, with Evelyn Street to the south. The 1881 census also shows that a number of officers lived near the station in Prince Street, with Inspector Thomas Turk and his family living at No. 32. Turk had lived at the station since his promotion in 1871 and remained there until 1888.[927]

In 1888 Police Constable Thomas Dean drowned in the Surrey Canal at Deptford whilst patrolling his beat on a foggy night. Tragically, deaths similar to this were not uncommon among those officers policing riparian divisions and dockyards.[928]

By 1889 Deptford ceased to be a part of Surrey or Kent, and from April that year was administered by the London County Council (LCC).[929]

The old station was deemed no longer fit for purpose, so a new station in the area was planned. A site was compulsorily purchased in July 1907 from Mr William Evelyn of Wotton, near Dorking in Surrey. It was located at 114 and 116 Amersham Vale and 28 and 30 Napier Street, and records show that the tenants and leaseholders were duly compensated by the Police.[930] Tenders were invited to build and equip the new station, and the bid by Messrs W. Lawrence and Son was accepted.[931]

The station was built in a rough area consisting of bad housing, poverty and disease, and was rife with crime. The Divisional Superintendent at the time commented that:

'The conditions of the inhabitants round about was very poor, casual and in chronic want. It was a resort of bad characters, and many crime of a serious nature happened occasionally in the district and were to be expected.' [932]

The Divisional Surgeon also added to the debate by commenting on the growth of diseases, especially tuberculosis and influenza, which were caused by bad air circulation, lack of sun light, below ground level rooms and over-crowding.[933]

The new station was designed by John Dixon Butler, son of the previous Metropolitan Police Surveyor, John Dixon, and opened in February 1912. It contained accommodation for 30 single officers in the Section House, and there was also one set of married quarters located there. These were usually kept for the inspector in charge and his family.[934] The new station was situated between New Cross Road and Edward Street, not far from New Cross railway station. The front entrance was in Amersham Vale, whilst the rear entrance was in Napier Street.

Deptford Police Station 1912-2005

There had been moves before the Great War to reorganise station boundary areas, especially since Deptford Police Station was in the Borough of Greenwich whilst the opposite end of Princes Street was in the Borough of Deptford, but these revisions were delayed until the war ended. Accordingly, boundary revisions in south London in 1921 transferred Deptford from R (Greenwich) Division to M (Lewisham) Division.[935]

By 1931 Deptford was shown as a Sub-Divisional Station on M (Southwark) Division, and its address was listed as 116 Amersham Vale, Deptford, with Rotherhithe at 23 Paradise Street being a Sectional Station.[936] Further reorganisations of the Force took place with Borough boundary changes in the mid-1960s, and were introduced on 1st April 1965. Deptford was shown as a Sectional Station with Brockley on Lewisham or P Division.[937] The station telegraphic code was revised at the same time to 'PP' from 'MF'.

Internal boundaries were reviewed in the 1970s regarding P Division, with some alterations being made to Deptford Section Station and Brockley being reduced to the status of a Police Office. With the demise of the GLC in April 1985, P District was abolished and officers returned to having a single letter 'P' on their shoulders.

In 1994 further re-organisation of the MPD into eight Areas placed Deptford under Three Area (South East), although not long after this it became, following the reduction to five areas, Four Area (South East) instead.[938]

The new Deptford Police Station, built with public and private funding, was situated at 114-116 Amersham Vale. In 2005 the station was closed to the public and the building sold.[939]

Ditton Police Station (also known as Thames Ditton and Long Ditton)

The London Borough of Richmond

Ferry Road, Ditton (1855-1933)

V Division (1855-1933)

Thames Ditton is situated on a busy thoroughfare of the Portsmouth Road, some two miles south-west of Kingston. In the 1850s the area was developing and there was a need for a police station in the area. The Metropolitan Police therefore purchased the freehold title to a site in Ferry Road, Thames Ditton in 1855[940] from Mr Clarkson and Mr Avery, at a cost of £350.[941]

Surveyors drew up plans to build a station and suitable builders were employed for the purpose. The purpose-built station cost £978 7s to construct in 1856, and had three cells and two stables. Sergeant Robert Mittall was placed in charge of the station and lived upstairs with his family.[942] Although closed since December 1933, this fine building still stands in Ferry Road.

Two single constables lived on the first floor in a large room, two more lived on the second floor and a further two on the third floor, for which they paid one shilling each per week. On the ground floor there was an inspector's office, lobby, charge room, parade room and three cells. There was also a three-stall stable and loft in the yard. Also on the ground floor was a store, mess room, kitchen and pantry, whilst on the first floor there was a library[943] where off duty police officers could rest, read and smoke.

911 *The Job*, 20th November 1970.
912 Brown, B. (1998) 'Up the Creek – Or Policing Old Deptford'.
913 Ibid.
914 Ibid.
915 Metropolitan Police Return of Mops (1832).
916 National Police Officers Roll of Honour 2002.
917 MEPO 5/29 (174).
918 MEPO 4/234.
919 Brown, B. (1998) 'Up the Creek – Or Policing Old Deptford'.
920 Ibid.
921 Ibid.
922 Metropolitan Police Orders dated 18th April 1859.
923 Metropolitan Police Orders dated 11th January 1859.
924 Brown, B. (1998) 'Up the Creek – Or Policing Old Deptford'.
925 Metropolitan Police General Orders 1873.
926 Metropolitan Police Surveyor's Records 1881.
927 Kelly's directories 1871 – 1888
928 www.metcbb.co.uk accessed 5th November 2009.
929 Brown, B. (1998) 'Up the Creek – Or Policing Old Deptford'.
930 LB460.
931 MEPO 2/686
932 Ibid.
933 Ibid.
934 Metropolitan Police Orders dated 3rd February 1912.
935 Metropolitan Police Orders dated 24th February 1924.
936 *Kirchner's Police Index* 1931 p118.
937 Metropolitan Police Orders dated 12th July 1964.
938 Brown, B. (1998) 'Up the Creek – Or Policing Old Deptford'.
939 Metropolitan Police Information Rights Unit 19th November 2017, accessed 25th January 2019.
940 Metropolitan Police Surveyor's records 1912.
941 Metropolitan Police Surveyor's Registers.
942 *Kelly's Directory for Surrey* 1855.
943 Metropolitan Police Surveyor's Records.

Thames Ditton Police Station 1855-1933

In 1891 the status of the station had been upgraded, and an inspector was placed in charge. Inspector William Aldridge was the first such officer in charge, and he was supported by two sergeants and 20 constables.[944]

The photographs below show the station's rear yard and garden. It was usual for the occupant, whether it was the constable, sergeant or inspector and family, to cultivate the garden in order to provide fresh vegetables for the kitchen. The picture was taken in about 1906, and as we can see, the senior officer who was in residence was keen on his runner beans. Sometimes, if the land was not used, the reserve constable would tend the garden and grow produce for the benefit of all.

Above: Thames Ditton Police Station garden and (below) the rear yard and dog kennels in 1908

It was often the vogue – and not against Force orders – to dress the station with ivy, as we see below, to cover the bare London-brick face of the walls. To the right of the main building one can see the cell block area, which has bars added to prevent prisoners escaping.

In 1910 the single men vacated the section house and were relocated elsewhere, while the rooms were set aside for a married family to occupy at a rather expensive cost of 6s 6d per week. The station address changed to Long Ditton by 1924, and consisted of a station and one set of married quarters situated above.[945]

Thames Ditton was a sub-division of Kingston in 1931. A police call telephone box, Box V51, was erected on 16th March that year at the junction with Weston Green Road and Ember Court Road, in the centre of the road on the double pier of the railway bridge. The box provided a refuge for a patrolling constable either to phone into the station, take a meal or smoke break. It was removed on 23rd October 1970.[946] Box V69, with air raid warning sirens, was erected on Portsmouth Road, 20 yards west of Thorkhill Road. It was removed on 16th October 1970.[947]

During the First World War an army light biplane made a forced landing and came down at Thames Ditton. Special Constable George John Wiley went to assist from the station but collapsed and died whilst trying to help.[948]

A review of police station stock under Lord Trenchard suggested that the station was no longer considered suitable for its original purpose, so Ditton was closed as a station in December 1933.[949] A month earlier instructions had been issued that all police business previously undertaken at Ditton was now to be transferred to Kingston, whilst all details of telegraph codes for the station were to be deleted from the manuals.

Ditton was put up for sale and in September 1936 sold to Mr. Frederick Vernon Worthy for £1,200. On the side of the old building Surrey County Council have placed a plaque marking Ditton out as a building of special interest.

North Dulwich, East Dulwich and West Dulwich Police Stations

North Dulwich

The London Borough of Southwark
North Dulwich (1864-1884) exact address unknown)
P Division (1864-1884)

In the mid-1700s a Watch House stood close to the junction of Calton Avenue and Dulwich Village, and attached to it was a lock-up. During building works in the 1920s an inscribed stone dated 1760 was found, bearing the following description,

*'It is the sport of a fool to do mischief
To thine own wickedness, shall correct thee'*[950]

With the increase in crime local residents formed the 'Dulwich Patrol', to be armed with cutlasses and pistols, and by 1812 had introduced horse patrols. Wooden Watch Boxes were set up near the Fox on the Hill and near Dulwich College.[951] The police station had been described previously in 1854 as a

'small brick message at the end of Boxall Row erected c.1810 by Charles Druce for the purposes of the Mounted Police on Patrol.'[952]

The station and section house was rented by the Metropolitan Police in North Dulwich, on P Division, and owned by Mr William Sawyer of Dulwich. This was a traditional brick-and-slate house which was rented from 29th September 1864 until 22nd September 1889 for an annual rent of £42. The Receiver was required to pay all other taxes.[953]

In February 1868 a public meeting was held in Dulwich College to discuss the issue of the lack of policing in Dulwich. As a result North Dulwich Police Station was opened in March 1872 at Wellington House, again owned by William Sawyer, in Red Post Hill and almost next door to the North Dulwich Railway Station which had opened in 1866 on the London Brighton Railway.

A Metropolitan Police Report in 1881 described North Dulwich Police Station as

"A small cottage to which considerable additions have made. The lease expires in eight years. More space is required." The building was occupied by one married Inspector and one married Constable.[954]

East Dulwich

The London Borough of Southwark
97 Crystal Palace Road (1884-1977)
173-183 Lordship Lane (1977-2013)
M Division (1884-1985/86)
Peckham Division (1985/86-2013)

In the 1880s North Dulwich Police Station needed replacing as it had become too small for the number of Police Officers now needed to police the increasing population. In June 1881 Mrs Taite of 'Rose Bank', Crystal Palace Road, at the corner of Upland Road, East Dulwich, offered her house for use as a Police Station.[955] The premises were taken on an 85 year lease from 1883. The cost of adapting the property, under the supervision of John Butler, Metropolitan Police Surveyor, was £1800.[956]

The new Station at 97 Crystal Palace Road was ready for use in May 1884. At the same time Police Inspectors Pride and Pearn were transferred from North Dulwich to East Dulwich Police Station.[957] The freehold for the building was later purchased for £1550 plus costs in August 1899.[958]

East Dulwich Police Station 1884-1977

On the night of the National Census in 1891 a Police Inspector John Flanagan and his wife May and five of their children were recorded as living at the Police Station.[959] Flanagan had been a P Division Inspector since 1885, having been promoted from Station Sergeant at the time when greater numbers of Inspectors were needed.

As early as 1959 it was realised that a new larger Police Station was needed. Accommodation was so cramped that in 1972 a two-storey prefabricated administrative building had to be crane-lifted into the yard behind the Station to give room for Constables to write their reports and to provide a separate interview room.[960]

The site at 173/183 Lordship Lane, and 77/85 Whatley Road, East Dulwich, was purchased for the accumulative sum of £40,000 between the years 1962 and 1963.[961] It was still some time before the new Station was built.

In 1965 with the formation of the London Borough of Southwark, East Dulwich and West Dulwich became Section Stations to Peckham Division.[962]

Work on the new East Dulwich Police Station eventually started in 1975[963] and was finally opened in September 1977. It was built with stables for twelve horses.[964] The new station also served as the Area Four Headquarters (London at that time was divided into four areas each having a Deputy Assistant Commissioner in overall charge).

East Dulwich Police Station 1977-2013

East Dulwich Police Station was closed in 2013 and the premises were sold in 2014 for £6.4M.[965]

944 *Kelly's Directory* 1891.
945 Metropolitan Police Surveyor's Records 1924.
946 Site Locations for Metropolitan Police Telephone boxes and telephone posts for V Division.
947 Ibid.
948 The Metropolitan Police Roll of Honour www.policememorial.org.uk, accessed 12th March 2002.
949 Metropolitan Police Surveyor's Records 1924.
950 Green B. *Dulwich – A History*. College Press (2002) 2ed. p.32.
951 Ibid.
952 'Estates Terrier' (1854) in Darby, William. *Dulwich – A Place in History*. William Darby, London. 1967 p.69.
953 Metropolitan Police Surveyor's Records.
954 Surveyor's Report 1881.
955 MEPO5/53 (427).
956 Ten Year Report.
957 Metropolitan Police Orders dated 7th May 1884.
958 LB510.
959 Census 1891.
960 *South London Press*, 29th July 1975.
961 LB511.
962 Metropolitan Police Orders dated 6th August 1964.
963 *South London Press*, 29th July 1975.
964 Metropolitan Police Orders dated 2nd September 1977.
965 Metropolitan Police Information Rights Unit 22nd October 2017, accessed 25th January 2019.

West Dulwich

The London Borough of Southwark
134 Thurlow Park Road (1887-1978)
M Division (1887-1978)

The London Chatham & Dover Railway Company was extending the railway through Dulwich, and acquired from the Governors of Alleyns College of Gods Gift, Dulwich, land which included that is now known as 134 Thurlow Park Road. After building the railway the land alongside West Dulwich Railway Station, which opened in 1863 (originally Lower Knights Hill Station), appears to have been surplus to requirements. In 1868 it was offered back to the Governors of Alleyns College, who declined to accept it.

It was eventually sold by the Railway Company in July 1870 to Arthur Ashwell of Beresford Street, Camberwell, for £920. The house 'Fairfield' was built on the site. The buildings and grounds, which included a vinery, hot house, stable and a shop, which was let at 7 shillings a week, were sold by Ashwell to the Receiver of the Metropolitan Police in December 1885 for the sum of £2,400. To the east of the property, between the land bought by the Receiver and the Railway, was a public footpath to Crystal Palace.

Just over a year later the additional building work under the supervision of John Butler, the Metropolitan Police Surveyor, was completed and the building opened as a Police Station. There were four floors. The basement contained the stores, parade room and WCs. The ground floor contained the public entrance, charge room, writing lobby, Inspector's Office, two cells, CID Office and Recreation Room. The two upper floors became Police accommodation later, in 1924.[966]

West Dulwich Police Station 1887-1978

The large parcel of land beyond the police station was laid out into lawns and gardens. It also contained a water fountain.[967]

In 1887 West Dulwich Police Station was opened.[968] These premises had been adapted as a police station at a total cost of £3,067.[969] The bulk of the cost, £2,400, was for the purchase of the freehold. The address was shown as 134 Thurlow Park Road, West Dulwich, next to West Dulwich Railway Station.

The National Census on 5th April 1891 shows thirteen constable in residence that night.[970]

In 1969 there was public disquiet over the proposed partial closure of West Dulwich Station. Local senior police officers wanted the whole of Dulwich to be a composite Police Area when it introduced a new unit beat policing system.[971] When West Dulwich was closed, telephone calls would be diverted to East Dulwich. The station became a Police Office in September 1969.[972]

In 1974 it was decided that the police station should be closed. Part of the building was then leased to the Metropolitan Police Trading Service (MPTS), who had vacated their premises at 222/224 Borough High Street. In September 1976 the large garden at the rear of the site was sold by the Receiver to the London Borough of Southwark for £2,250.[973]

West Dulwich Police Station was eventually closed on 28th April 1978.[974] In March 1980 the remaining land and old police station were sold to the MPTS for £18,900.[975] The premises are now known as Stephen Barrett House after a Police Sergeant/Federation member/Board member of the MPTS who had died. Part of the property is rented to the British Transport Police Federation.

Ealing Police Station

The London Borough of Ealing
Near Uxbridge Road, Ealing (1837-1877)
5 High Street, Ealing (1877-1967)
67-69 Uxbridge Road, Ealing (1967-2017)
T Division (1836-1865)
X Division (1865-1933)
T Division (1933-1965)
X Division (1965-1985/86)
Ealing Division / OCU (1985/86-2017)

Before the formation of the Metropolitan Police, there had been an earlier police presence in Ealing in 1805, when Lord Sidmouth set up mounted horse patrols.[976]

The Ealing Cage adjoined the engine house near the church in Ealing, and there was a need for a police station in the town. On 27th July 1836, a letter was received from the Home Office authorising the police force to take on premises in Ealing near to the Uxbridge Road. The premises belonged to a Mr Samuel Grinsdell, who leased them to the Receiver at a rent of £52 10s per annum.[977] The lease was for 21 years from Christmas 1837. It was described as an old brick and tiled house, with a large scullery with copper sink and convenience and two comfortable cells. It had rooms in the basement, together with a coal cellar. There was stabling for two horses and it had a small garden at the rear.[978]

In Police Orders dated 11th January 1864 Ealing was designated as a station on T or Kensington Division.[979] In October 1865 the formation of X Division was announced, and many stations were transferred to the new Division.[980] It was not until December of that year that Ealing became part of X or Paddington Division, the boundaries between T and X Division having been altered.[981]

Prior to 1865 when X Division was formed, in February 1862 an X Division was specially created to police the International Exhibition which was opened at South Kensington on 1st May 1851. The division was commanded by Superintendent Durkin, who was seconded from F Division. The division was disbanded in December 1862 when the exhibition was finally closed.[982]

By 1875 the population had grown to such an extent that it was decided to erect a new and larger station at Ealing. The estimated cost was put at £3,410. A freehold site was purchased at 5, The High Street, and building work commenced.[983] The new Ealing Police Station was opened in January 1877.[984] The construction of the new building was designed and supervised by John Butler, the Metropolitan Police Surveyor, and was described as a red brick building with stone dressing and an attractive feature of the High Street. Carved in the stone lintel above the front door was the word 'POLICE'.[985] The accommodation was for one married inspector and two married constables. At the same time the name of Hanwell Sub-Division was changed to Ealing Sub-Division.

Ealing Police Station 1877-1967

In 1881, on the night of the census, there were three police families living at the police station at 5 High Street, Ealing; Police Constable Thomas Paterson, his wife Emma and their young baby daughter, Police Constable Carlos Jordon with his wife and two daughters, and Inspector George Wills with his wife and son. Wills is an interesting person, having been born on the island of St. Helena and being classified as a British subject and allowed to join the Force. In 1861 he had been a young constable at Stones End Police Station, Southwark.[986]

In 1886 the police station was under the command of Inspector George Willis,[987] and Superintendent Thomas Foinett was in charge of X Division. By 1894 the station was under the command of Sub-Divisional Inspector Alfred Newnham, and his superior was Superintendent James Cuthbert at Kilburn.[988] Below is a picture of Ealing Station yard.

A section house attached to Ealing, accommodating 30 single constables, was opened in August 1913.[989] The freehold for the land was purchased in 1911, and the address was 1-6 Baker's Lane, Ealing.[990]

In 1911 X Division was one of the largest Divisions under the command of Superintendent James Olive. It consisted of four sub-divisional stations of Ealing: Harlesden, Craven Park, Harrow and Uxbridge. There were six sectional stations at Acton (250 High Street), Hanwell (169 Uxbridge Road), Kilburn (38 Salusbury Road), Southall (North Road), Willesden Green (High Road) and finally Wembley (Harrow Road).[991]

In 1911 Sub-Divisional Inspector Henry Andrews was living at Ealing Police Station in five rooms with his wife Ellen and five children.[992] He had taken over command from David Richards.[993]

In 1912 the Ealing police were saddened at the sudden death of one of their officers. Inspector Alfred Edward Deeks collapsed and died after dispersing boys causing a nuisance outside a chapel in West Ealing.[994]

In 1922 Ealing Police (as part of X Division), along with many other police divisions, undertook Ju Jitsu self-defence training to help combat the many injuries received on duty. This training took place under Capt. Leopold MacLagan. The successful class is shown in the picture below with their teacher.

The Ju Jitsu class of Capt. Leopold McLagan circa 1922

On 1st December 1933 a reorganisation of divisions north of the Thames took place.[995] Ealing was transferred from X to T or Ealing Division, and it became the divisional headquarters. At the same time, a new sub-division was created which was known as Ealing sub-division with sectional stations at Southall and Norwood Green. Superintendent C. Adams was the officer in charge of the division.[996] The station was modernised in 1936,[997] and by 1937 Superintendent R.C. Hannaford was in charge.

966 MPTS Documents.
967 Ibid.
968 Metropolitan Police Orders dated 24th December 1886.
969 Ten Year Report.
970 Census 1891.
971 *West London News*, 13th June 1969.
972 *Lewisham Boro' News*, 11th September 1969.
973 LB 522.
974 John Back Archive (1975).
975 MPTS Documents.
976 *County Times and Gazette*, 4th February 1972.
977 John Back Archive (1975).
978 Metropolitan Police Surveyors' Book 1845 p 145.
979 Metropolitan Police Orders dated 11th January 1864.
980 Metropolitan Police Orders dated 28th October 1865.
981 Metropolitan Police Orders dated 26th December 1865.
982 John Back Archive (1975).
983 John Back Archive (1975).
984 Metropolitan Police Orders dated 2nd January 1877.
985 *County Times and Gazette*, 4th February 1972.
986 Census 1861 and 1881.
987 *Kelly's Directory of Middlesex* 1886.
988 *Kelly's Directory of Middlesex* 1894.
989 Metropolitan Police Orders dated 30th July 1913.
990 MP List of Police Stations 1912.
991 *Kelly's Directory* 1911.
992 Census 1911.
993 *Kelly's Directory* 1911.
994 www.met.police.uk/history/remembrance3 accessed 28th September 2012.
995 Metropolitan Police Orders dated 28th November 1933.
996 *Kelly's Directory* 1933.
997 *County Times and Gazette*, 4th February 1972.

During the Second World War many officers lost their lives on the streets of London. One such case was the death in 1940 of War Reserve Constable Arthur Wilfred White, who was killed by the explosion of a bomb during an enemy air raid at Ealing.[998]

After the war in 1949 another death occurred when Police Constable Albert Victor Hawkins was fatally injured while cycling to duty at Ealing Magistrates' Court when he crashed in fog.[999]

In 1961 the Home Office authorised the purchase of the freehold interest of 67-69 Uxbridge Road, Ealing for the erection of a new station at the cost of £75,000.

Riding solo motorcycles was a dangerous affair at any time, but more particularly at night. At Ealing in 1963 another police officer sadly died whilst on duty, when Police Constable Brian Bernard Joseph Holden was fatally injured while on lightweight motorcycle patrol at night when struck by a car at Ealing.[1000]

These motorcycles were 200cc Velocettes, known as 'Noddy bikes', but were efficient in policing the streets of London. Co-author of this book David Swinden, whilst a constable at West Ham Police Station in the 1960s, rode these motorcycles over a number of years. Part of his beat covered the industrial and derelict area of Stratford, now the transformed 2012 Olympic Park.

In 1965 the reorganisation of the police boundaries[1001] to coincide with the new London Boroughs meant that Ealing once more joined X Division, with Acton as its sectional station both situated in the London Borough of Ealing. The new station was built and opened on 4th July 1966.[1002] At the same time the old police station and section house at 5 High Street closed. This old station was not sold until 1970, and was used by the BBC on many occasions when filming location shots for the long-running and very successful television series *Dixon of Dock Green*.

Above: The rear yard and front gate to the old Ealing Police Station, and (below) the new station

Police Constable Piara Singh Kenth

In 1969 Ealing Police Station received the first Indian policeman in the Metropolitan Police. Police Constable Piara Singh Kenth, a Sikh, was living in West Ealing.[1003]

In 1972 the old Ealing Police at High Street Ealing was pulled down after 166 years on the site. A car park replaced the police station, until the site was incorporated into the new town centre redevelopment.[1004]

As far back as 2006 there were whispers that Ealing Police Station might close. In 2010 Ealing Council also expressed concerns that the Metropolitan Police were intending to sell or mothball Norwood Green Police Station. However, just to show that the station at Ealing was still open, they held an open day on 2nd October 2011.[1005] By 2012 the station closure was still under consideration,[1006] and still had not been resolved although in July the Mayor of London agreed that in principle Ealing was to be sold off.[1007]

In 2017 the police station was closed to the public.[1008]

Earlsfield Police Station

522 Garratt Lane (1914-1993)
V Division (1914-1920)
W Division (1920-1993)
Borough of Wandsworth OCU (1993-2018/19)
SW BCU with Richmond, Kingston and Merton (2018/19 to present day)

In the early 1900s Sir Edward Henry, the Commissioner, had been lobbied by the residents of Earlsfield for a police station to be built. As a result, the Receiver enquired into the possibility of purchasing a suitable site, which was on the corner of Garrett Lane and Weybourne Street, Wandsworth. Negotiations commenced in 1912 to buy the freehold title from the owners, Mrs E.E. Hardman and Mr A.E. Boyce,[1009] which resulted in the station being built in 1914.

The address was shown as Garrett Lane, Earlsfield, but later in 1931 it was shown as a Sub-Divisional Station, with Wandsworth Common and Balham being Sectional Stations.[1010] The station was allocated to V or Wandsworth Division. It was built with married quarters and a Section House attached. The development of the new Sub-Division caused a revision of the boundaries to Wandsworth, Battersea, Wimbledon and Kingston Sub-Divisions in 1914.[1011] The Section House had been built to accommodate 33 single officers at a nominal weekly rent of 1s each; the married

Earlsfield Police Station 1914 to present

quarters were charged at 10s per week.

The station was refurbished in 1937, which meant that in addition to being completely re-painted, various building works and extensions would have been planned and carried out. In the same year Earlsfield was a sectional station to Balham (Cavendish Road) (WD), whilst Wandsworth Common (WC) was the other sectional station.[1012]

The London County Council informed the Metropolitan Police in 1945 that a change of street numbering was required, and allocated No. 522 Garratt Lane to the police station and No. 520 to the married quarters.[1013]

In 1920, apparently ahead of further revisions of boundaries and the creation of the Z or Croydon Division, saw Earlsfield transferred to W or Brixton Division.[1014]

In 1960 Earlsfield was still located on W Division, with call sign Whiskey Foxtrot (WF) and being supervised from Balham where Superintendent F.C. Brown was in charge. Further Local Authority boundary alignments in 1964 saw Earlsfield reduced in status to Sectional Station on Tooting Sub-Division.[1015] By 1966 the station at Tooting (Mitcham Road) continued as the Sub-Divisional station with Earlsfield retaining its status of sectional station.[1016]

The station was closed in 1998 for operational purposes,[1017] although it remained in the possession of the police for use as offices.

In 1999 Earlsfield Police Station was used as a base by officers of the Area Major Investigation Pool (AMIP), and for local sector officers for meetings of the local Sector Working Group and, as necessary, for the storage of lost or stolen motor vehicles.

By 2010 the station was still operated by the Metropolitan Police Service, but as a building used for administrative purposes in housing the Earlsfield Safer Neighbourhood Team.[1018] In 2018 the station was still in the possession of the Metropolitan Police.[1019]

East (New) Barnet Police Station

The London Borough of Barnet

2 Edward Road, East Barnet (1884-1932)

Y Division (1884-1932)

The freehold to a piece of land was purchased in East Barnet in 1874 by the Receiver. Although it was not until 1883 that a police station was built on the site, opening a year later. The station address was shown as 2 Edward Road, East Barnet,[1020] taking up a large plot of land that bordered Margaret Road, New Barnet. There was a confusion over the title of the station whilst it was called East Barnet because it was in fact closer to New Barnet with the train station being under a quarter of a mile away.

The accommodation included housing for two families, one married inspector and a married constable.[1021] The station itself was manned by one inspector, three sergeants and fifteen constables.

East Barnet Police Station 1884-1932

Because of its position, East Barnet was a sectional station together with Potters Bar and Southgate to the Sub-Divisional station of Enfield. Unlike most other stations in Barnet, who were situated on S or Hampstead Division, East Barnet was located on Y or Highgate Division. In 1890 there was station strength of one inspector, three sergeants and 15 constables.[1022]

998 www.met.police.uk/history/remembrance3, accessed 28th September 2012.
999 Ibid.
1000 www.met.police.uk/history/remembrance4 accessed 28th September 2012.
1001 Metropolitan Police Orders dated 6th August 1964.
1002 Metropolitan Police Orders dated 1st July 1966.
1003 *Middlesex County Times*, 31st October 1969.
1004 *County Times and Gazette*, 4th February 1972.
1005 content.met.police.uk/Event/Ealing-Police-Open-Day accessed 20th November 2012.
1006 philtaylor.org.uk/2006/11/ealing-police-station-no-shock-shock accessed 20th November 2012.
1007 snipelondon.com/scoop/london-police-stations-to-be-sold-off-admits-boris accessed 20th November 2012.
1008 Metropolitan Police Information Rights Unit 10th June 2018, accessed 25th January 2019.
1009 LB686.
1010 *Kirchner's Police Index* 1931.
1011 Metropolitan Police Orders dated 27th August 1914.
1012 Districts and Divisions 1937.
1013 LB686.
1014 Metropolitan Police Orders dated 24th February 1921.
1015 Metropolitan Police Orders dated 6th August 1964.
1016 Metropolitan Police List 1966.
1017 Metropolitan Police Authority Committee reports accessed 15th February 2009.
1018 www.earlsfieldhub.co.uk/viewtopic.php?f=7&t=90 accessed 29th January 2010.
1019 MPS (2018) Freedom of Information request – MPS assets.
1020 Metropolitan Police Surveyor's Records 1912 and 1924.
1021 Metropolitan Police Hygiene Inspection Report 1880.
1022 *Kelly's Directory* 1890.

The station call sign for the telegraph published in Police Orders in 1893 was Echo Bravo (EB), but by the 1920s these were changed.[1023]

In charge of the station was Station Sergeant George Jewell who was assisted by two section sergeants and 15 constables[1024] In 1899 the officer in charge of the Division was flamboyant Superintendent Louis Vedy who paid periodic visits.

In 1914 Station Sergeant Joseph Thompson of Y Division, Section Sergeant William Norris, Detective Constable Ernest Milner, two Acting Sergeants – George Sharplin and Henry Barton – and 18 constables were attached to the station.[1025]

During WW1 East Barnet was allocated a squad of special constables to make up for the call-up of regular officers to the colours.[1026]

The end of the Great War was subsequently marked each year by ceremonies which included the police setting off maroons or small explosions in the station yard at the eleventh hour, on the eleventh day of the eleventh month. The photograph below shows this happening in the yard at East Barnet, being supervised by the station sergeant in charge. The constable on the bicycle displayed the 'take cover' signs that were used during the war itself.

November 1919: Setting off the maroons in celebration of World War One ending

The building remained in service as a police station up until 1932.[1027] Its future was discussed, and as a result, during the Trenchard restructuring programme, the old station became residential accommodation for three families until at least 1947,[1028] although it was later sold.

By 1985 the former East Barnet Police Station was in a sad state of repair, having been vacated and left in a derelict state. Today the building has long since been demolished and the plot is now home to the Barnet Service and Tuning Centre.

East Greenwich Police Station

The London Borough of Greenwich
2 Park Row (1849-1902)
Trafalgar Road (Trafalgar Road) (1902-1962)
R Division (1849-1962)

There was a Station House with a sergeant in charge at East Greenwich from 1849 when the Receiver rented land at 2 Park Row from Lewis Glenton of Pageot Cottage, Blackheath, initially for 21 years.

The premises appeared to be not up to standard, as there was a stipulation it should be occupied only when thoroughly repaired. The rent was reviewed yearly and cost the Receiver £63 per annum.[1029] Later, in 1873, the Freehold was purchased for £1,000.

It was described as a substantial brick and slate built house having some 14 rooms over three floors, which included a charge room, kitchen scullery, three cells and a 2-stall stable. It required maintenance, but had been kept clean and decorated.

Surveyor's records show that it was redecorated and painted in 1853, and was then usually redecorated every four years. The station also provided accommodation at that time for four married constables and one single constable.[1030] It was surveyed in 1850 to consider its suitability to remain a police station, and was kept in service.

In 1867 the records show that a married inspector occupied three rooms on the second floor at a cost of 3s per week. Rent generated at the time to defray the cost of the building amounted to £31 4s per annum.[1031]

Police Orders of January 1864 referred to East Greenwich (Park Row) Police Station for the first time, when it was shown as a station on R or Greenwich Division with strength of four sergeants and 19 constables.[1032] Two of the sergeants, who were called Station Sergeants, did not leave the station and had to work 12-hour shifts. Inspectors and sergeants from Greenwich Police Station supervised the East Greenwich area.

By 1874 permission had been obtained from the Home Office by the Divisional Superintendent, James Griffin, for a freehold site to be purchased, since the old station was no longer fit for its purpose. In 1881 substantial work was required to bring the existing station up to a satisfactory level of health and cleanliness. It was reported that this was an old house with poor administrative accommodation, and had a water supply that was insufficient for the station's needs. It must have been very uncomfortable to live and work there, since the surveyors when commenting on the sewers, sinks, sewer pipes and gas mains[1033] suggested work to be carried out urgently.

Living there at the time under such conditions was the Superintendent of the Division, Christopher H. McHugo, a 44-year-old Irishman from Galway, with his wife and eleven children. There were not many stations that could accommodate such a large family, and he would have pressed

East Greenwich Police Station 1873-1902

for better conditions. McHugo had been well thought of by senior officers when he became the R Divisional Superintendent in January 1879, after being promoted from being Chief Inspector at Y or Hampstead Division. Promotion to Superintendent in nine years was indeed rapid for McHugo, as he had been promoted to the rank of Reserve Inspector in 1870 when it was created for S Division at a better rate of pay. McHugo was selected from all the Divisional Inspectors for this prestigious new position.[1034] He remained in charge for 20 years until he resigned on pension in April 1899. Even in retirement his contribution was recognised, when the Secretary of State granted McHugo an annual allowance of £25[1035] in addition to his pension.

For communication purposes East Greenwich had call sign Papa Alpha (PA).[1036] Instructions were given to find land nearby on which to build a new station, and in the meantime the Park Row site (now numbered 23) was sold to Mr J.P. Crosby for £450, somewhat of a loss considering the Metropolitan Police had originally paid £1,000 for the site in 1873.

In 1881 a site premises in Lower Woolwich Road (now Bridge Terrace and Aldeburgh Street) was leased from Henry and Alfred Walker (Builders) of Greenwich for £41 per annum.[1037] Plans were drawn up to build a station, but the railway company purchased the land, which meant another site had to be found.

New premises were found at the junction of Park Row and Trafalgar Road, and were purchased on 22nd April 1902. The premises had been previously called The Good Duke Humphrey Hall and Coffee Tavern.[1038] The cost to the police was £8,250.

East Greenwich officers on duty during the 1926 General Strike

Wells, aged 51, and a War Reserve Constable.[1041] As a result of the damage to the police station the headquarters returned to Blackheath Road.

East Greenwich Police Station showing War damage in 1941

Trafalgar Road was very unfortunate, as a V2 rocket hit it on 8th July 1944 and five people were injured. However, after that only skeleton staffs were left behind to man the token police office, the remainder being transferred back to Blackheath Road. Some fourteen regular and auxiliary R Division officers

East Greenwich Police Station 1902-1962

The picture on the top of the following column shows R Division in the yard at East Greenwich during the 1926 General Strike. The most senior officer, the Station Sergeant, is seated, whilst the rest of the mobile unit parade at the rear of their van.

Instructions were given for the relocation of the Divisional Headquarters for R Division to East Greenwich just three months before the outbreak of the Second World War.[1039] As with the First World War, and because of their military significance, Greenwich, Woolwich and the locality became the focus of German bombers, flying bombs and rockets. Between June 1940 and July 1941 the Blitz, as it was known, caused widespread damage in the area.

On the evening of 10th/11th May 1941 six 1,000-pound bombs blew up most of Trafalgar Road, severely damaging the police station[1040] and killing Reserve Police Inspector Arthur

1023 Metropolitan Police General Orders 1893.
1024 *Kelly's Directory* 1894.
1025 *Kelly's Directory* 1914.
1026 Col. W. T. Reay (1919) *The Specials: How They Served London*.
1027 *The Police and Constabulary Almanac* 1919, 1929 and 1932.
1028 The Police Property List 1947 MEPO 4/133.
1029 MEPO 5/53(425).
1030 Metropolitan Police Surveyor's Records.
1031 Metropolitan Police Surveyor's Records.
1032 Metropolitan Police Orders dated 11th January 1864.
1033 Report on the Conditions of the Metropolitan Police Stations 1881, p64.
1034 Metropolitan Police Orders dated 2nd July 1870.
1035 *The Police Review and Parade Gossip*, April 24th 1899.
1036 Metropolitan Police General Orders 1893.
1037 Metropolitan Police Surveyor's Records.
1038 Metropolitan Police Surveyor's Records.
1039 Brown, B. (2001) 'Romeo- Law and Order in Old Greenwich' (part 2 1900-2000) in *Bygone Kent* Vol. 22 No 3.
1040 Ibid.

were killed during enemy air raids in the war,[1042] and between June 1944 and March 1945 no fewer than 241 V1s and 92 V2s landed on R Division.[1043]

East Greenwich Police Station showing War damage in 1941

East Greenwich Police Station was shut for police purposes in 1962 at the same time as Blackheath Road. The current Greenwich Police Station, situated on Royal Hill, opened in May 1962 and consolidated policing in Greenwich.[1044]

East Ham Police Station

The London Borough of Newham
East Ham Gate, East Ham (1864-1904)
4 High Street South, East Ham (1904-2013)
K Division (1864-2013)

East Ham Police Station Lamp

In 1864 a police station existed at East Ham from which two sergeants and eight constables patrolled.[1045] This station had no cell accommodation, so prisoners were taken to either Plaistow Police Station or another station if closer. The station, which was probably a pair of cottages, was shown as being located at East Ham Gate, East Ham.[1046]

According to the 1881 census Inspector Mark Veronne, aged 45 years from Newton in Suffolk, and his wife Anne resided at the station, along with four unmarried constables.[1047]

In 1901 enquiries were made to purchase land in East Ham on which to build a new station, as the older one was considered unsuitable for continued use, and in November 1904[1048] this opened in High Street South, East Ham. The station had accommodation for one married inspector, one married constable and ten unmarried constables.

The picture right shows Constable 166K Sidney Charles Clackett, who joined the Metropolitan Police in April 1912 at the

Constable 166K Sidney Charles Clackett

age of 22 years. His initial posting after Training School was to K Division, although it is unclear from records at which station he served. Clackett was born at St. Lawrence in Kent on 8th September 1890 and took up market gardening prior to joining the police. He was 5 feet 9 inches tall. He was a married man and had a son, who was born in September 1926. He stayed on K Division until 26th July 1915, when he transferred to Woolwich Arsenal where he became Constable 121 Dockyard Police. He stayed there until 22nd July 1923 when he transferred back to K Division. PC Clackett was of good character, and appears not to have been involved in any disciplinary matters. In 1935 the Commissioner commended him for his diligence in offences involving licensing, betting and gaming in the streets. He retired at the age of 46 years on 4th April 1937 with just over 25 years' exemplary police service. He died on 15th April 1965 aged 75 years.[1049]

In 1937 East Ham Police Station was reconstructed at the cost of £40,000, although much of the existing frontage was left intact. In addition, at a further cost of £30,000, they built a new police section house for 90 single men. It was named after Assistant Commissioner Sir Norman Kendall. It was occupied from 1940 when section houses at Canning Town, Forest Gate, West Ham and North Woolwich were closed. It was also the official home of co-author Superintendent Swinden, who lived there as a young constable between 1958 until 1963.

East Ham Police Station 1904-2013

From time to time divisions and also stations formed tug of war teams, which would compete against each other and also outside teams. Successful teams would be entered for the National Police Championships, or the Commonwealth or Olympic Games if they were good enough. Over the years a number of police teams have been very successful at winning medals for their country in these events. The K Division team shown below was one such team. The photograph also shows their trainers and managers. Notice that the qualification for the team seems to be the wearing of a moustache!

Metropolitan Police K Divisional Tug of War team c1910

Prior to 1937 East Ham became the Divisional Headquarters, and the Divisional Superintendent was also responsible for the operational running of East Ham Sub-Division. T.W.C. Aylett was the officer in charge,[1050] but by 1957 Superintendent H. Timmins had operational control of the Sub-Division whilst Chief Superintendent A.H. Thompson was the officer in charge of K Division.[1051]

In 2001 East Ham was shown as an operational station open 24 hours a day, 7 days a week, where charges were taken and prisoners housed.[1052] This changed the following year, and prisoners were taken to nearby Forest Gate Police Station.

The East Ham Police station was finally closed in 2013. Both the station itself and the Norman Kendall Section House at the rear were sold in February 2014 for the sum of £3,350,000.[1053] As of 2019 the Section House has been demolished, although the old police building is intact.

East Molesey Police Station

The London Borough of Richmond

1 Walton Road (1902-1993)

V Division (1902-1993)

The London Borough of Richmond OCU (1993-2000)

Surrey Constabulary (2000 to Present)

When it was established that a police station was needed at East Molesey, suitable premises were found at 1 and 2 Rothsay Villas. But because it was not purpose-built, the building was in need of adaptation. The buildings were owned by Mr Bowers on a mortgage, and No. 2 had an occupant with an interest (believed to be a sitting tenant), so careful negotiations were undertaken by surveyors for the purchase. In 1900 these cottages, now addressed in Bridge Road, were purchased for £550. Additional land adjacent was also purchased, for £1,500, whilst the sitting tenant's interest was purchased for £70. A covenant attached to the deeds established that the minimum worth of any houses to be erected on the site was £200, or £300 for a pair of buildings, so surveyors had to be mindful to build a substantial station.

The freehold title to premises at 1 Walton Road, East Molesey was purchased in 1900 by the Receiver, and a police station was built in 1903 together with two sets of married quarters[1054] at a cost of £3,334. In August 1902 the rental costs for the married quarters were assessed. A married constable and his family occupied the married quarters on the ground floor at a cost of three shillings per week. A married sergeant lived in the married quarters which were rooms on the ground and first floor would pay four shillings a week.

In 1908 the lodging assessment was raised to 3s 6d and 4s 6d respectively. Originally Mr Bowers, the previous owner, had negotiated with Messrs Kerrison and Sons for an advertising hoarding to be erected on the side of the building at an annual cost of £12. Permission was granted in 1913 by the Receiver to East Molesey Urban District Council for a fire alarm box connected to the fire station to be fitted to the railings of the station.

A Police call telephone Box V51, with air raid warning siren, was erected on 16th March 1931 at the junction with Walton Road (south side) and Langton Road, East Molesey. It was removed on 23rd October 1970.[1055] East Molesey is shown as being a sub-division of Kingston in 1931.

By 1957 there was only one set of married quarters in use at the station, whilst the other rooms were used for administrative purposes. The call sign for the station was Victor Echo (VE).

East Molesey Police Station 1902-2000

In 2000, when East Molesey reverted to the Surrey police area, the Police station was transferred to Surrey Constabulary.[1056]

Edgware Police Station

The London Borough of Harrow

Watling Street, Edgware (1840-1851)

Whitchurch Lane, Edgware (1851-1993)

S Division (1840-1976)

Q Division (1876-1993)

Borough of Harrow OCU (1993-2018/19)

North West (NW) BCU with Barnet and Brent

(2018/19 to Present)

A police station existed in Edgware at 8-mile Stone in 1842. This was probably at the toll gate in Edgware Road (known at the time as Watling Street). The station was part of S or Hampstead Division, under the charge of Superintendent John Carter.

Prior to the building of the first Edgware Police Station, the area was policed by various local officials. In 1828 Great Stanmore had a single Parish constable, Francis Chapman, who was assisted by four 'headboroughs' (deputy constables), and the old system ran parallel with the introduction of the New Police.

By 1829 they had printed notices cautioning boys from the parish from assembling in the town to the annoyance of the public and in breach of the public peace. A beadle was

1041 Metropolitan Police Roll of Honour at www.policememorial.org.uk, accessed 12th March 2002.
1042 Brown, B. (2001) 'Romeo- Law and Order in Old Greenwich' (part 2 1900-2000) in *Bygone Kent* Vol. 22 No 3.
1043 Ibid.
1044 'History of Greenwich' at intranet.aware.mps/BOCU_eh/Greenwich accessed on 5th March 2008.
1045 Metropolitan Police Orders dated 11th January 1864.
1046 *Dickens's Dictionary of London* 1879.
1047 Census 1881.
1048 Metropolitan Police Orders dated 26th November 1904.
1049 Metropolitan Police Service Records.
1050 *Police and Constabulary Almanac* 1937.
1051 *Police and Constabulary Almanac* 1957.
1052 *Police and Constabulary Almanac* 2001.
1053 www.met.police.uk/ Information Rights Unit 21st January 2018, accessed 25th January 2019.
1054 Metropolitan Police Surveyor's Records 1924.
1055 Site Locations for Metropolitan Police Telephone boxes and telephone posts for V Division.
1056 Metropolitan Police Authority (2000) Police Station opening hours Committee; MPA Reports 9th November.

appointed in 1834 at 7 shillings a week, and his role was to keep order and prosecute people for vagrancy as well as maintaining order in beer houses and preventing disorder on the Sabbath day.

The local stocks, which had been first mentioned in 1639, were moved to the workhouse yard in 1819. A cage built for imprisoning offenders was also situated at the Great Stanmore Workhouse. The Stanmore district became part of the Metropolitan Police District in 1842, though parish constables and headboroughs continued to be appointed till the 1860s.

Courts in the area were mostly held in Edgware from about 1551. They were usually held in a room of an inn such as The Crane, later renamed The Chandos Arms in Watling Street (later Edgware Road), or the Abercorn Arms on Stanmore Hill. The house next to the Chandos Arms belonging to the brewer Thomas Clutterbuck, joined to the inn by cellars and passageways, became the first proper court of justices in 1850. By 1913 it was replaced by the new court in the Hyde, Hendon.[1057]

The building on the right is the court house in High Street, Edgware and to the left is the Chandos Arms Public House. The photo is thought to be a Victorian wedding party

Land was sought on which to build a police station on Whitchurch Road in the village of Edgware, and Mr Andrew Jordan sold the Receiver, John Wray, a suitable plot for £80. The first known police station in Edgware was thus built in 1848 at a cost of £582.[1058] The building contained a charge room, three cells, a 3-stall stable, two water closets and a coal shed. The station had one inspector, three sergeants and 21 constables, and they were required to patrol Bushey as well.[1059] Edgware had a sergeant in charge until 1861, when it was considered important enough for an inspector to take over.[1060]

Edgware was originally part of S or Hampstead Division, and in 1889 it became part of Finchley Sub-Division. In 1892 new land was acquired adjacent to the old station as there were plans to build to build a better and bigger purpose-built station on site. A new station was built, while the original building was converted into married quarters.[1061]

The station in Edgware was opened for business on 19th May 1892 and immediately the building was occupied by a married inspector who paid 5s 6d a week rent. Further land was acquired which cost £250 for another building in 1889, while the alterations had cost an additional £1,693.[1062]

In 1894 Edgware became a Sub-Divisional station, with sectional stations at Bushey and Elstree. This meant the station and area was big enough for a Sub-Divisional inspector to take charge of the Sub-Division.[1063] The station was built with a waiting lobby, Inspector's office, charge room, two cells and an association cell (often referred to as the 'drunk tank'). In the yard was a place to store oil lamps, two coal cellars, a 3-stall stable (with hay loft), ambulance store, parade shed and an Inspector's store.[1064] The area of Whitchurch Lane where the station was situated was known locally as 'Poor Lane',[1065] probably as the alms houses were located there as well.

Above: Edgware Police Station, Whitchurch Lane, 1848-1932 and Below, Front entrance

In 1901 Sub-Divisional Inspector (warrant no. 66383) Stephen W.T. Gifford (often misspelt Giffard) lived at the station with his wife and family. The station was small and he had recently been posted to Edgware, where he was in overall charge.[1066] Gifford, from Kennington, joined the police in 1882 and remained in charge at Edgware for six years until 1907, when his place was taken by Sub-Divisional Inspector Cundell.[1067] Gifford had been an Inspector on D or Marylebone Division in 1891, when he was newly-promoted and residing in a block of flats at 54 Miles Buildings, Lintern Street, Marylebone. Both Gifford, his wife and family must have been relieved to be moving out into the country from the smoky and built up conditions of Marylebone.

Court Sergeant Hubert Hale (warrant no. 67645) from Gloucestershire retired in 1907 at the same time as his Inspector. He had resided in the courthouse situated not far from the police station, with his wife and two daughters.[1068]

The area around the station had quite a narrow lane, as can be seen in the photograph above, and because the main thoroughfare was restricted on 13th April 1927 the Receiver was served with a notice of compulsory requirement for the police station by the Local Authority. This gave the receiver an opportunity to redevelop the station as it was to be demolished

Edgware police line up c1920s

due to road widening, and the Receiver was to be compensated with £2,000.

An article in the *Hendon and Finchley Times* of 10th February 1928 gave an insight into the station's loss:

"No-one, least of all the police, I imagine, will regret the news that the dismal old police station is to be pulled down. It is certainly a depressing place to visit, and must give the hump to those that work there." [1069]

Below is the plan of the 1931 Edgware Police Station, taken from the Metropolitan Police Architect's drawings. The architect was G. MacKenzie Trench. The new station was constructed by Messrs Patman and Fotheringham. Trench made sure that there were two separate entrances, one into the station for business whilst the other enabled access to the living quarters, both married and single officers' accommodation. Keeping these two areas separate was an essential feature of police station design.

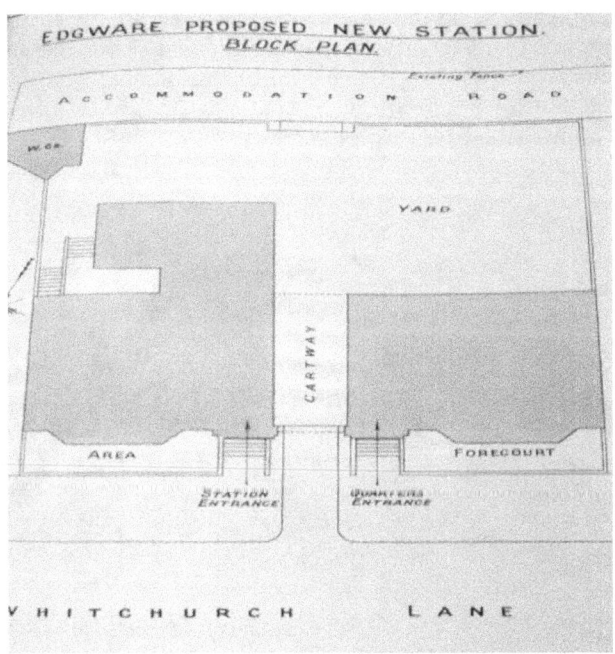

Plan of the 1931 Edgware Police Station by Architect G. MacKenzie French

Edgware Police Station comprised three storeys and a basement, and most importantly it had a yard which could be accessed through a central arch. There was a back door to the yard which could be accessed on foot only. In the picture below, taken in about 1920, the Sub-Divisional Inspector is flanked by his two colleagues and the total strength of the station.

The new station was open for business on 6th June 1932, and the following year was given Sub-Divisional status, with Elstree and Bushey as sectional stations.

Edgware Police Station 1931 to present

On 1st April 1965, Q Division was formed and Edgware moved from S Division, being given the station code 'QE'.

By 1976 Sergeant Dennis Harris was in charge, with six constables who patrolled the area. The station was reduced to office status with Pinner in the same year. The Crime Prevention department was also located at Edgware, with Constable John Rogers stationed there.

In 2012 Edgware Police Station remained a police building, but had been closed to the public for many years. It had been used as a base for the Child Protection Team. A report for Harrow Council described the station as 'an imposing but appealing building, built in mock-Dutch style with modernist, angular details on an otherwise traditional form'.[1070]

As of 2019, while retained for operational purposes by the Metropolitan Police and a base for the Safer Neighbourhood Team, the station was closed as a public contact point, and the Child Protection Team no longer operate there.

1057 *Stanmore Past* by Eileen M. Bowlt.
1058 Metropolitan Police Property Register p154.
1059 Edgware Police Station History. Metropolitan Police Archives.
1060 *Kelly's Directory* 1861-1900.
1061 *Harrow Highways* Volume 8 by R.S. Brown, 1978.
1062 Metropolitan Police Surveyor's Records p154.
1063 *Kelly's Directory* 1894.
1064 Metropolitan Police Surveyor's Records.
1065 Harrow Division Athletic & Social Club Anniversary Souvenir Programme 1829-1979; Met Police 150th anniversary.
1066 *Kelly's Directory* 1902.
1067 *Kelly's Directory* 1908.
1068 Census 1901.
1069 Harrow Division Athletic & Social Club Anniversary Souvenir Programme 1829-1979; Met Police 150th anniversary.
1070 Edgware High Street Conservation Area Appraisal www.harrow.gov.uk; www2.harrow.gov.uk/documents/s15569/Edgware%20High%20Street%20Conservation%20Area%20-%20Appx.pdf.

Edmonton Police Station

The London Borough of Enfield
Church Street Edmonton (1840-1867)
320 Fore Street, Edmonton (1867-1916)
320 Fore Street (new Building) (1916-1989)
462 Fore Street (1989 to Present)
N Division (1840-1865)
Y Division (1865-1886)
N Division (1886-1933)
Y Division (1933-1985/86)
Edmonton Division / OCU (1985/86-2018/19)
North Area BCU NA (from 2018/19)

Edmonton Police Station Lamp.[1072]

In the early 1800s Edmonton had a population of 9,627 and was still a very rural place. The village itself was located around Fore Street, Silver Street and Water Lane (Angel Road), whilst Lower Edmonton was centred around the village green (Edmonton Green) and situated at the junctions with Fore Street, Church Street and Hertford Road.[1071]

The Metropolitan boundary extended its limit in 1840 to take in the village of Edmonton.

The old Edmonton watch house was situated in Church Street, opposite Old Saints Church and where Winchester Road is now. It was surrendered by the local Parish authorities to the Metropolitan Police in October 1840 at a cost of £100, paid over a four-year period.[1073] The watch house, sometimes referred to as the station house, was designated as part of N or Islington Division. This was the Area Headquarters, responsible for supervision of those divisions within its area.

The station house was handed over to the Receiver of the Metropolitan Police in September 1852. The building was described, in 1845, as being substantial and built of brick and tile, containing four cells and a charge room.[1074] The station had the use of two stables, one in Lower Edmonton and the other in Upper Edmonton.[1075] They were rented from Mr. George Sanderson on a yearly rental. In September 1853 both stables were used by the Metropolitan Police, who were then responsible for the rent.

Edmonton Fire Brigade outside the Police Station in Church Street in 1870

The very first officer in charge was Sergeant John Harrison, who also resided as tenant at the station house. Harrison had been promoted to the rank from 1st Class Constable in January 1840, and posted to Edmonton watch house. Records show that Sergeant Harrison resided at the station with his wife Betty and their three children. Harrison had been born in Cothill, Berkshire on 18th March 1811, and was recruited into the Metropolitan Police on 12th May 1835.[1076] His warrant number was 10640 and, after joining, he was posted to N or Islington Division. It appears that the family lived in Islington as he married his wife Betty there in 1837.

Gradually, as the divisional boundaries were extended more police officers were required to police them. In June 1854 Harrison was further promoted to Inspector, and it appears he was transferred from the station. No further information is available, but it is possible that with the growth of the New Police extending into the constabularies he took the opportunity to move to the country.[1077]

The population of Edmonton started to grow with the development of public transport, especially with the Great Eastern Railway Company building stations at Angel Road and Edmonton Green.

Three new divisions were formed, and Edmonton was included as part of the new Y Division.[1078]

The station strength was two sergeants and ten constables with supervision by the Inspector coming from Enfield Highway (Ponders End) Police Station.[1079] The Commissioner approved PS47 Parsons to be employed on Station Duties at Edmonton as from 27th April 1864.[1080]

A freehold site, on which to build a new station, was purchased in May 1865 from Mr J.H. Grimley for the sum of £400. The site was purchased at 320 Fore Street, Edmonton, and not only was a station to be built but also stables and a section house for single men were to be included. The ground floor contained a charge room, three cells, a 2-stall stables, an Inspector's Room, day room and two coal sheds. The first floor provided accommodation for an inspector, a married sergeant and eight constables.[1081] The building costs were £1,907. The old watch house was retained until May 1867, when it was handed back to the parish authorities.[1082]

Edmonton Police Station 1867-1916

In 1881 the station was called Lower Fore Street Police Station, with Inspector Henry Hopkins in charge. He resided there with his wife and daughter. The single constables section house was full at the time of the census.[1083]

In August 1886 a new Division of J or Bethnal Green was formed, and Edmonton transferred from Y to become a Sub-Division of N Division once more.[1084]

In July 1897 Edmonton Police Station was struck by lightning during a storm.[1085]

A new parade shed was built in 1903 together with improved drainage, at a cost of £436. In 1905 a new section house was built at a cost of £3,093, and in 1907 five more cells were added, together with a waiting room at a cost of £2,000.

In March 1916 a new station was completed for occupation on the site of the old 1867 building.[1086] As previously mentioned, Mr. John Dixon-Butler, Architect and Surveyor for the Metropolitan Police from 1895-1920, designed and built the station to a formula which had been used in over 200 police stations. Dixon-Butler built in the Queen Anne-style, showing impressive structure including red brick and white stone facings. The design of these magnificent buildings was influenced by two factors; his father, who was a Metropolitan Police architect before him, and Richard Norman Shaw, the architect who designed New Scotland Yard.

Edmonton Police Station 1916-1989

The Section House at the rear of the station was retained, and two sets of married quarters were built within the new station. Officers from Edmonton helped swell the ranks of the Metropolitan Police Centenary Parade in Central London on May 25th 1929. They joined the Divisional Superintendent C. Pearce (from Stoke Newington), together totalling 240 constables.[1087]

In 1933 a further re-organisation of the divisional boundaries resulted in Edmonton being transferred again from N to Y Division.

During the Second World War a bomb exploded on the parade shed, causing severe damage to both the shed and accompanying section house kitchen. Constable W.H. Richards, who was on duty on 2nd October 1940, took the force of the blast as he was walking across the yard, and later died of his injuries in hospital. The section house was closed until after the war and re-opened, after refurbishment, in 1951.

With the advent of Local Authority boundary changes in 1965, Edmonton, Southgate and Enfield were joined together within the London Borough of Enfield. The population of Edmonton steadily increased to over 100,000 in 1951 then gradually declined.

From 1890 until the early 1920s station sergeants would have been identified wearing four strips on each arm. In the early 1920s one stripe was replaced with a Tudor crown, which was worn above the remaining three stripes. The rank as such was phased out in 1972, however Edmonton's last station sergeant was Station Sergeant 129790 Eric Varney, who retired from the Police service on 5th September 1976.

In 1979 a new system of message handling was introduced on Y Division, and together with other pilot sites Edmonton Police Station took part in trials relating to the new computer-aided dispatch system. Gradually the success of this system ensured that it spread over the whole of the Metropolitan Police District. Edmonton's call sign was YE, with its sectional stations Winchmore Hill being YW and Southgate YS.

The station at Edmonton was considered far too small to cope with the building of a computer complex within its walls so a Portakabin was constructed in the station yard, and stayed there for ten years. The Portakabin coped well, and proved just how robust it was until the high winds of the 1980s caused damage to the cabin when a tree fell on it. Four more Portakabins were placed beside it as the pressure for office space built up.

It had been recognised in 1972 that the station was far too small for modern policing requirements, so plans were made to build a new station. By 1986 it was also recognised that the police service was changing and that restructuring was required, with New Scotland Yard losing some of its autonomy. With these moves came the creation of eight Areas, with Edmonton being the flagship of the new 1 Area and the devolvement of responsibilities to Deputy Assistant Commissioners. 1 Area North became the sixth largest police area in Britain.[1088]

A large plot of land was purchased at 462 Fore Street Edmonton N9, just south of Edmonton Green on which to build a station and Area Headquarters.

The modern new station with six floors was completed at a cost of £6.5 million, and was taken into service in 1989. The first two floors and the basement belonged to the station, whilst the top four floors were given over to Area Headquarters staff. The old station could not be demolished because of a preservation order, but was sold to a developer who converted it into private flats.

Princess Diana formally opened the station for business in July 1990. There were a number of other guests including the Commissioner Sir Peter Imbert, ACTO Geoffrey McLean, ACMS Peter Winship, Director of Property Services Department Mr Trevor Lawrence and members of the local community including the Mayor and Mayoress of Enfield.[1089]

1071 Elmes, E. Constable (1990) Pamphlet on 'Edmonton Police' produced to commemorate the opening of the new Edmonton Police Station.
1072 Ibid, p1.
1073 Metropolitan Police Surveyor's Manifests and John Back Archive (1975)
1074 Ibid.
1075 Census 1841.
1076 Census 1851.
1077 Elmes, E. Constable (1990) Pamphlet on 'Edmonton Police'.
1078 Metropolitan Police Orders dated 28th October 1863.
1079 Metropolitan Police Orders dated 28th January 1864.
1080 Metropolitan Police Orders dated 27th April 1864.
1081 John Back stated there was no record of occupation in respect of Edmonton Police Station given in police orders.
1082 John Back Archive (1975).
1083 Census 1881
1084 Metropolitan Police Orders dated 22nd July 1886
1085 *Police Review*, 30th July 1897.
1086 Metropolitan Police Orders dated 3rd March 1916.
1087 Metropolitan Police Centenary Celebration Programme 1929.
1088 www.met.police.uk/enfield/history.htm accessed 13th March 2002.
1089 Metropolitan Police News Release dated 3rd July 1990.

The station was open to the public for two days after the Royal visit. Edmonton Police Station was the only station the Princess ever opened.

The new station assumed the call sign of the old Edmonton station, Yankee Echo (YE).

The following officers were Chief Superintendents in charge of the Edmonton Division from dates shown during the period 1965 to 1998:[1090]

- Ch. Supt. Mackinnon: 1st April 1965
- Ch. Supt. Hunt: 1st April 1968
- Ch. Supt. Brokenshire: 17th November 1969
- Ch. Supt. Morris: 31st August 1971
- Ch. Supt. Thornton: 1st September 1976
- Ch. Supt. Martin: 3rd September 1979
- Ch. Supt. Dickinson: 24th March 1980
- Ch. Supt. Markham: 28th April 1980
- Ch. Supt. Williams: 10th September 1984
- Ch. Supt. O'Connor: 26th January 1987
- Ch. Supt. Pearce: 23rd October 1989
- Supt. Waring/Supt. Vincent: 1st April 1992
- Ch. Supt. Searle: 1st July 1992
- Supt. Watson (later Ch. Supt): 1998 [1091]

The advent of Borough-based policing and a realignment of policing boundaries on 1st April 1999 meant that certain sections of the Area Headquarters would cease to exist or would be transferred. The officer in charge now has responsibility for the whole of Enfield Borough. Enfield Division lost some of its ground to Hertfordshire under the revision of boundaries. The Borough Commanders, as they are now called, hold the substantive rank of Superintendent 1st Class, although they wear the rank of Chief Superintendents (a Tudor crown and star), which was phased out in 1995. The purpose of this is to show seniority.[1092]

Edmonton Police Station 1989 to present

In 2019 Edmonton remained in the possession of the Metropolitan Police for operational purposes.[1093]

Elstree Police Station

London Borough of Barnet
Cottage, High Street, Elstree (1869-1893)
Barnet Lane (1893-1971)
S Division (1869-1893)
S Division (1893-1971)

Several of the roads in Elstree have interesting histories. Deacons Hill Road was created in the 19th century by the owner of Deacons Hill House in Barnet Lane to provide easier access to the railway station, which was opened in 1868. Other roads, including Barnet Lane, Furzehill Road, Shenley Road, Allum Lane and Theobald Street, were created as a result of the Enclosure Act of 1776, whereby the 684 acres of Borehamwood Common were divided up amongst various landowners, including the Church, and in return new roads were laid out which were to be sixty feet wide including verges.[1094]

Originally, in 1853 a small cottage (possibly a gatehouse) on the Aldenham Abbey Estate (now Aldenham Park) was used as a police station. It was situated near the main road now known as Elstree Hill, immediately opposite Allum Lane.[1095]

A cottage was rented by the Metropolitan Police in High Street, Elstree in 1869 from Mrs Cornelia Willis, who lived near the Green Dragon public house in Elstree. The building was surveyed by the Receiver and considered to be well-constructed, and agreement was reached that the annual rent should be £15.[1096] To defray the costs, the Receiver rented out rooms above the station to a serving officer and his family. Calculated at a rate of 6d per 50 square feet, this cost the occupant 3s 3d per week.[1097]

Whilst the cottage was adequate enough for the purposes of policing, it was essential in these outlying areas for the constables to have access to transport. As a result, stables were rented from Alderman John Bailey of Elstree Hall, Elstree at an annual cost of £10.[1098] The station was opened in November 1869 and was designated a station on S Division.[1099]

When the station was given up in June 1892, the freehold was purchased to an address in Barnet Lane, Elstree and a new station was brought into service on 24th June 1893.[1100] This station was situated on the north side of Barnet Lane between Sumner Grove and Fortune Lane, Elstree. The building consisted of a new station with one set of married quarters above. There were also two sets of married quarters behind the station.[1101]

In 1914 the officer in charge of the station was Station Sergeant Henry Lewis, and he was assisted by two sergeants, one acting sergeant and 12 constables.[1102]

The telephone exchange at Elstree had just 97 subscribers in 1924. The police were even reluctant to be connected in the early days, in case it encouraged the public to 'phone in crime reports'! (a feeling some older policemen shared about the 999 system).[1103]

The station call sign for the telegraph published in Police Orders in 1893 was Echo Echo (EE), but by the 1926 this was changed[1104] to Sierra Lima (SL) when it was a sectional station of Edgware.

During WW1 Elstree Police Station was an Air Raid observation post along with Barnet Police Station, due to their elevated position. Special constables would be posted to the roof and made observations regarding any bombing by German planes or Zeppelins and report their positions via telephone to Scotland House (located in another building at Scotland Yard), where the reports were collated and action taken to send the alert to anti-aircraft batteries and search light stations, or the fire brigade or police units for their attendance.

These observation posts were also there to see if the population were complying with the Blackout and keeping their curtains closed so as not to alert a passing foreign plane to a likely target. On seeing a light in any house, a police unit, normally on a cycle, would be dispatched and pay the owner a visit, getting the light hidden.

In 1965, when the local authority boundaries were altered, Elstree retained the same station code but moved to being a sectional station of West Hendon (SW).

As few members of the public were using the station, it closed at night from 10.00pm on 31st July 1960 for an experimental period of six months, and the station officer, usually a constable, was posted to outside duties on night duty. In a pillar at the front of the station a telephone was installed which had a dedicated line to the divisional station. Incoming telephone calls to the station were diverted to Edgware Police Station.[1105] Following a revision of local authority boundaries Elstree (SL) was designated a sectional station of West Hendon (SW)[1106] in October 1964.

The photograph below taken in the 1960s shows Constable Ivan Bracey tending to the garden at the front of the station.

Elstree Police Station 1893-1971

By 1968 the status of the station was downgraded further when it became a police office with limited opening hours and incorporated into Borehamwood (SB).[1107]

The station closed on 30th August 1971, but Elstree Rural District Council became interested in the building for providing residential accommodation for four families. The long-term future for the building was for it to be demolished to provide higher-density housing.[1108]

Eltham Police Station

The London Borough of Greenwich

Blunts Cross (1839-1865)

172 High Street (1865-1939)

Well Hall Road (1939-1993)

R Division (1839-1993)

Borough of Greenwich OCU (1993-2018)

South East (SE) BCU (together with Bexley and Lewisham) (2018 to Present)

The area of Eltham became part of the first Bow Street Horse Patrol Divisions in 1827,[1109] although the area had been patrolled since 1820 from their station which was situated on Shooters Hill.

The Horse Patrols were introduced by Sir Richard Ford, Chief Magistrate at Bow Street in 1805, and were incorporated into the Metropolitan Police in 1836. These were armed horsemen in cavalry cloaks, blue coats and trousers, and red waistcoats. They patrolled the main highways and thoroughfares of the Metropolis, giving confidence to the travellers, often with the cry 'Bow Street Patrol'.[1110] A prisoner lock-up was situated in Eltham, and in 1827 the First Division of the Bow Street Horse Patrol began patrolling the area.[1111]

Watch Houses, which were built by and belonged to the Parish, had been taken over by the Metropolitan Police under an Act of Parliament at the introduction of the New Police in 1829. These also included Watch Houses that fell into the Metropolitan Police area later as the boundary of the Met was extended, and this is what occurred in 1839 when Eltham was included.

Eltham was shown to have a Watch House called 'Blunts Cross', built by the Parish in 1745[1112] not far from the present Blunts Road, and had an established strength of one sergeant and seven constables in 1839.[1113] Eltham Watch House was built between Elm Terrace and Pound Place, including a cage situated on the other side of the road that was used for stores, lost dogs and property.

It had long been felt in the area that the old watch house was worn out and no longer fit to be used. A new Station House was needed, and correspondence passed between Commissioner Sir Richard Mayne and the Chief Surveyor, granting permission for a new police station to be created in Eltham. Final Home Office permission was granted on 2nd March 1863.[1114] However, ownership of the Cage was in dispute between the Police and the original landlords, the Fifteen Penny Society, who insisted that 'since it had not been used since 1858 it should be returned'. The Police challenged their Trustees' ownership claims, but it was later proved, in meeting minutes taken in September 1745, that the Society

---

1090 Elmes, E. Constable (1990). Pamphlet on 'Edmonton Police'.
1091 *The Police and Constabulary Almanac* 1998.
1092 Fido, M. and Skinner, K. (1999) *The Encyclopaedia of Scotland Yard*. Virgin Press, London.
1093 MPS (2019) Freedom of Information request – MPS Assets.
1094 www.elstreeborehamwood-tc.gov.uk/joomla15/town-history.html accessed 6th January 2012.
1095 Metropolitan Police Map 1853.
1096 Metropolitan Police Surveyor's Records.
1097 Metropolitan Police Orders dated 4th February 1871.
1098 Metropolitan Police Surveyor's Records.
1099 Metropolitan Police Orders dated 15th November 1869.
1100 Metropolitan Police Orders dated 23rd June 1893.
1101 The Police Property List 1947, MEPO 4/133.
1102 *Kelly's Directory* 1914.
1103 www.elstreeborehamwood-tc.gov.uk/joomla15/town-history.html acccessed 6th January 2012.
1104 Metropolitan Police General Orders 1893.
1105 Metropolitan Police Orders dated 29th July 1960.
1106 Metropolitan Police Orders dated 6th August 1964.
1107 Metropolitan Police Orders dated 1st November 1968.
1108 *Barnet Times*, 4th January 1973.
1109 MEPO 2/25.
1110 Moylan, J. F. (1929), *Scotland Yard*. Puttnams, London p 210.
1111 'History of Greenwich' on intranet.aware.mps/BOCU_eh/Greenwich accessed 5th March 2008.
1112 Hadaway, D. 'Early Days of Policing', *Kentish Times*, 4th July 1985.
1113 John Back Archive 1975.
1114 MEPO 5/36 (250).

was the Trustee of the land. The Police did not rush to return the property though, and this finally occurred in January 1875.[1115]

Because Eltham was a minor station and only supervised by a sergeant, instructions were given that further supervision would be undertaken by the inspector at Lee (Road), who carried out patrols on horseback. The mounted sergeant at Sidcup also provided supervision, patrolling on horse or foot for at least nine of the 24 hours.[1116]

In 1870 surveyors' records note that Eltham was a station on R Division, built in 1865 at a cost of £1,925 7s, but the land on which the station was built was leased from the Office of Woods and Forests at a ground rent of £15 3s 6d per annum.

The station occupied a large corner plot situated on the southern side of the High Road, at the junction with Victoria Road. The premises consisted of a basement, ground and first floor, and contained a charge room, three cells and a two-stall stable. There was also a drying closet, store, scullery and coal cellar. Accommodation for eleven single constables was shown above the station on the first floor where, in two rooms, the station inspector also resided with his wife and family.

Eltham Police Station 1865-1939

The resident inspector was John Pryke, aged 31 years, who lived there with his family,[1117] paying the weekly sum of 3s 6d for rent. The address was recorded as 172 Eltham Street, Eltham,[1118] although by 1898 this became 172 High Street,[1119] changing again to 172 High Street, Eltham before 1939.[1120]

The rear yard of Eltham Police Station in 1911

To improve upon the cramped living conditions a re-assessment of space allocation took place in 1885. The review decided to allocate five rooms for the married inspector, but increased the rent to 5s 6d per week. The Section House still showed eleven constables residing, each paying 1s per week rent.[1121] The sergeant paid the rent for the station and was given an allowance for the cost of the charge room, which was a public room.

In the picture below, Inspector 69265 Thomas Hill is shown on patrol when he was an Inspector on D or Marylebone Division, in about 1903. Hill became the Sub-Divisional Inspector on R Division in 1905, responsible for Lee Road, and he was a frequent visitor to Elham since this was one of his Sub-Divisional stations. An accomplished rider, he shows that he is prepared for all weathers; note the riding cape, which is rolled at the front part of the saddle. Both he and his companion are in possession of sabres. The station had a groom to keep the horses in top condition and, judging by the photograph he did an excellent job. Hill retired in 1909.

Sub-Divisional Inspector Thomas Hill in 1903

There was an expansion in the Eltham area where houses were built or found for munitions workers during the First World War, and the growth of the workforce continued up to the Second World War and beyond. This increase in local population caused problems for policing, which meant that as new communities sprang up the needs of the police were reassessed and new stations considered.

In 1931 the building was over 50 years old and not really suitable anymore as a Police station. Land on which to build a new station,[1122] which was originally part of the Sherard Hall estate, had been purchased in Well Hall Road in 1921 from Mr Archibald Tarry. The old station was closed at 6.00am on Sunday, 12th March 1939, and business was moved to the new station, an Art Deco building, at Well Hall Road near the junction of High Street.[1123] The new station, whilst not on the High Street, was situated just inside Well Hall Road.

During the 1930s Commissioner Lord Trenchard instigated considerable organisational change and improvements to the Metropolitan Police in a variety of ways. Improvements in communications commenced in June 1934 with the introduction of a wireless car scheme on each of the four Sub-Divisions, and the call signs allocated were 5R for Blackheath Road, 6R for Eltham, 7R for Woolwich and 8R for Bexleyheath. These communications are still in use today, using the phonic alphabet introduced in 1956. Following on from this, November 1934 saw the advent of the familiar blue Dr Who-style Police Boxes.[1124] By November 1937 the famous 999 call system was also introduced. To improve railway communications and ease the growth of the travelling commuter, new railway stations were built at Albany Park (1935) and Falconwood (1936).[1125]

Eltham Sub-Division was being broken up in 1959 when it became a Sectional Station, and by the summer of 1968 Eltham (RM) was transferred to Greenwich Sub-Division. The Divisional Headquarters moved from Greenwich to Eltham, now (RD), although it remained as a Sub-Divisional Station in October 1984. Eltham also became a Traffic Headquarters for TDR, and later the upper floors served R District, 3 Area, 4 Area, SE Area and finally South Area before being transferred to Marlowe House, Sidcup, in 1996.

Eltham Police Station 1939 to present

The building was subsequently occupied by RM Sector, the Finance Unit, the Quality Performance Review Unit, the Training Department and a variety of business units including SO1(4) and SCG (South),[1126] and as of 2019 the station was still in the possession of the Metropolitan Police.[1127]

Enfield Police Station

The London Borough of Enfield

22 The Town Enfield (1840-1873)

33 London Road Enfield (1873-1965)

41 Baker Street, Enfield (1965 to Present)

N Division (1857-1873)

Y Division (1873-1993)

Borough of Enfield OCU (1993-2018)

North Area NA BCU (together with Haringey)

(2018 to Present)

The first reference to a police station at Enfield was shown in Police Orders of 1857, and Enfield Town Police Station, as it was then called, was part of N or Islington Division. Later, with the formation of Y or Highgate Division,[1128] Enfield Town was transferred to the new division.

The first station in Enfield was situated at 22, The Town, Enfield, Middlesex, right next to the market place. It was originally the Beadle's house, and was called the Vestry Office. The police occupied it until 1873, when it was considered too small for police purposes and handed back to the vestry. Within its confines stood a central house with two cages either side. These were quite substantial and secure rooms. At the rear was an enclosed yard with a privy at the end. The plan is shown at the top of the following column, whilst the picture shows the officers of Enfield outside the old station in 1873 shortly before vacating the building. The old station is still in use today and is now occupied by the Enfield Parochial Charity.[1129]

In 1867 land was purchased at the junction of London Road and Cecil Road for the building of a new police station. The Police Surveyor estimated the cost of building a new station at £3,500, and tenders were invited from a number of builders for this task. The contract was awarded to Messrs. Lathey Brothers of Battersea Park, London at £2,690. The new police station was built and ready for occupation in December 1873.

The new station was built with a charge room, an office, a store, a drying room, a mess, a brushing room, a lavatory, three cells, a 4-stall stable and two water closets on the ground floor. The first floor provided the residential accommodation. A married sergeant and his family occupied one room, whilst the remainder were occupied by six constables.

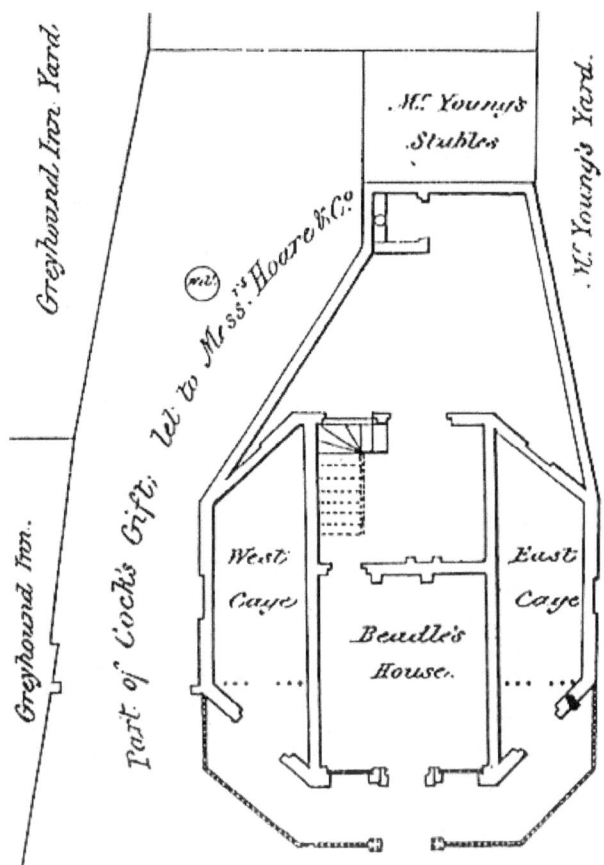

Above: Enfield Police Station Plan 1840, and Below, Enfield Police Station 1840-1873

1115   MEPO 5/23 (128).
1116   Metropolitan Police Special Order 1864.
1117   Census 1881.
1118   Metropolitan Police Orders dated 20th June 1884.
1119   Premises in the occupation of the Metropolitan Police 1898, Surveyor's Department.
1120   John Back Archive 1975.
1121   Metropolitan Police Surveyor's Records.
1122   LB 544.
1123   Metropolitan Police Orders dated 1st March 1939.
1124   Brown, B. (2001) 'Romeo- Law and Order in Old Greenwich' (part 2 1900-2000) in Bygone Kent Vol. 22 No 3.
1125   Ibid.
1126   Greenwich-History of Greenwich intranet.aware.mps/BOCU_eh/Greenwich accessed on 5th March 2008.
1127   MPS Information Rights Unit (2019).
1128   Metropolitan Police Orders dated 28th October 1865.
1129   Sykes, R. (1988) *History of the Enfield Parochial Charity*.

Enfield Police Station 1873-1965

Police Orders indicated that the stables for mounted officers were ready for occupation before completion of the police station in July 1873, and was supervised by a sergeant.[1130]

In 1881 George Head was the inspector in charge of Enfield Police Station. He resided at the station with his wife Annie and their seven children. There were six constables at the station, and a 'live-in' domestic servant aged thirteen years.[1131]

Records show that in 1889 the boundaries of Kentish Town, Upper Holloway, Holloway, Hornsey and Enfield Sub-Divisions were to be revised, and that this would create a new sub-division called Wood Green Sub-Division.[1132]

Enfield Division Special Constable 1920

The picture on the left shows a smartly-dressed member of the Metropolitan Police Special Constabulary with duty armlet and merit stripe during the 1st World War. The photograph was taken in Enfield, so it is probable that he was attached to Y Division at Enfield Police Station. Special constables wore flat hats with their own bronze cap badge. A Special Constabulary officer's cap badge was silver and more ornate.

The photograph right is of special interest, because it is of Constable 26YR Henry John Halford, who spent 20 years of his service at Enfield. Born in St. Pancras in the County of Middlesex in 1867, he joined the Metropolitan Police on 18th February 1889 as Constable 392Y (warrant no. 74235). His previous trade was that of a cab driver. Later in his service, and whilst at Enfield, he was granted Reserve status with extra pay. Constable Halford has four medals, which are the 1887 Jubilee medal and 1897 bar, the 1901 Coronation medal and the 1911 Coronation medal, which means that he saw duty at these events. In 1913, when the Metropolitan Police abolished Reserve status, Constable Halford was issued with the number 1031Y instead. He retired on pension with £69 11s 6d per annum in February 1915.

Constable 26YR Henry John Halford

On 5th October 1917 the Urban District Council of Enfield wrote to the Metropolitan Police informing them that the address of Enfield Town Police Station was 33 London Road, Enfield.

1931 records show that Enfield Police Station was a Sub-Divisional station of Y or Highgate Division, with sectional stations of East Barnet, Potters Bar, Southgate and Winchmore Hill.

The re-organisation in 1933 changed this picture, and Enfield was shown as a sub-divisional station of Wood Green Division, and Southgate, Enfield Highway and Cheshunt were now included as its sectional stations.[1133]

Improvements in 1936 cost £462, but by 1939 the old Victorian police station was considered inadequate for present-day policing needs. The Receiver of the Metropolitan Police purchased about an acre of land located on a site known as Oak House, Baker Street, Enfield for £5,850 on 21st June 1939.

The land remained empty for the next six years, not least because of the outbreak of the Second World War in 1939, and not until 1963 did the building of the new station finally get underway. The builders were Messrs. F.R. Hipperson and Son of Dagenham, who tendered at a cost of £124,244 and completed the work in March 1965.[1134]

Enfield Police Station 1965 to present

Enfield was designated a sub-divisional station when the new Local Authority boundary changes occurred in 1965. The station code became YF, with Enfield Highway (later called Ponders End) being YI and Cheshunt becoming YC. Force Orders showed the new station located at 41 Baker Street, Enfield.

In 2019 the station remained in the possession of the Metropolitan Police for operational purposes.[1135]

Epsom Police Station

The London Borough of Sutton
Epsom Watch House (1839-1855)
Ashley Road, Epsom, Surrey (1855-1963)
Church Street, Epsom (1963-2000) transferred to the
  Surrey Constabulary
V Division (1839-1921)
W Division (1921-1963)
Z Division (1963-1993)
The London Borough of Sutton OCU (1993-2000)

The picture below shows the Watch House in the centre of Epsom before the Metropolitan Police arrived in the area, with stocks situated to the front, next to the pond.

Old Watch House, Stocks and Pond in Epsom

The papers dealing with the extension of the Metropolitan Police District in 1839 showed Epsom forming part of the V or Wandsworth Division. It would seem that six constables and one sergeant (mounted) were responsible for policing Morden, North Cheam and Malden, Ewell and Epsom. At this time the population of Epsom was about 3,200.[1136]

A Deed of Conveyance signed by the Secretary of State for a freehold site was received from the Home Office on 15th June 1852. Home Office approval was granted on 21st February 1855 for the building of a police station at Epsom at a cost of £917.[1137] The station was built at the corner of Ashley Road and Ashley Avenue.[1138]

In 1864 Epsom was shown as being still attached to V Division, with the strength of two sergeants and eleven constables. The inspector at Kingston was not posted for duty at a station, but had to patrol and have supervision of Kingston, Ditton, Epsom, Hampton and Sunbury. The Patrol Sergeants were each to perform nine hours out of every 24 on horse or foot, and have care of his horse. The stations, with the exception of Kingston, were closed when sergeants or acting sergeants were patrolling.[1139]

Epsom Police Station 1857-1963

In 1878 Henry Haynes was the sergeant in charge of the station; it did not become an Inspector-designated station until the following year. Haynes, who lived at the station, was supported by one other sergeant and 17 constables.[1140]

The station at Epsom was a V Division station in 1891, shown as being located in Ashley Road. Inspector Charles Pearn was in charge, with three sergeants and 22 constables attached to the station. There were another five inspectors posted there: A. Wilson, W. Knights, J. Godden, A. Hill and W. Knott.[1141]

In June 1919 two Canadian soldiers were arrested for disorderly conduct and placed in the cells at Epsom. As a result of these arrests 400 soldiers marched on the station from their camp, causing damage to property on the way. On arrival at the station, intent on releasing the two detained soldiers, they created havoc by smashing windows, fittings and furniture. Inspector Pawley lived above the station with his wife and children. During the riot a number of police officers suffered injuries, including Station Sergeant 87V Thomas Green, Warrant No. 80417, who died from his wounds. He is buried in Epsom Cemetery.[1142] The picture below shows his funeral procession passing Epsom Railway Station on its way to the cemetery. The Z or Croydon Division was formed in 1921, and this caused a large revision of boundaries. The stations of Earlsfield, Wandsworth Common, and Epsom were transferred from V to W or Brixton Division.[1143]

The funeral of the late Station Sergeant Green in 1919

In 1937 it was proposed to rebuild the station on the existing site, and a private architect was instructed to prepare plans. These had reached an advanced stage by 1939, but the outbreak of World War II prevented any work being done. The architect, however, reported that in his opinion the site was too small and irregular for the type of station required.

In July 1944 the first floor of the station was demolished by enemy action, a V1 flying bomb. The ground floor was so severely damaged that temporary accommodation was sought at Worple Lodge on Ashley Road, Epsom[1144] until the ground floor was rebuilt, with indications that work would be completed by the end of 1946.[1145] However, by 1953 the first floor had still not been rebuilt.[1146]

In 1953 Surrey County Council offered the Police a site for a new station within the civic amenities called The Silver Birches. In this development it was hoped to incorporate a Welfare Clinic, Ambulance Station and Library. In 1955 the owner decided not to sell the site and was not prepared to negotiate, so the question of compulsory purchase powers was

1130 Metropolitan Police General Orders 1873.
1131 Census 1881.
1132 Metropolitan Police Orders dated 4th May 1889.
1133 'Enfield Station History', J. Back archive (1977).
1135 Ibid.
1135 MPS (2019) Freedom of Information request – MPS Assets.
1136 MEPO 2/76.
1137 MEPO 5/26 (153 -155).
1138 LB 689.
1139 Metropolitan Police Order dated 11th January 1864.
1140 *Kelly's Directory* 1878 p2217.
1141 *Kelly's Directory* 1891.
1142 Metropolitan Police Orders dated 20th June 1919, 28th July 1919 and 5th June 1920. Also MEPO 2/1962 and MEPO 3/331.
1143 Metropolitan Police Order dated 24th February 1921.
1144 Metropolitan Police Order dated 17th November 1944.
1145 Metropolitan Police Order dated 29th January 1946.
1146 LB 689 and 'Met Police at War' (HMSO).

discussed. Eventually the owner decided to sell part of the site to the Police for the purpose of building a station. The price was agreed, authorised by the Home Office on 4th February 1960, and the freehold purchased on 25th May 1960.[1147] Epsom Police Station was built and became operational in July 1963.[1148]

Epsom Police Station 1963-2016

The change in local authority boundaries meant that Epsom was transferred to Z or Croydon as a Sub-Divisional Station.[1149] The Divisions of Epsom and Sutton were amalgamated into one Division called Epsom, whilst Sutton, now designated a Sub-Division, retained its prisoner processing and charging facilities.[1150]

In April 2000 Epsom Police Station was transferred to Surrey County Constabulary when the Metropolitan Police District Area was realigned. Epsom was one of nineteen Metropolitan Police Stations transferred to County Authorities.[1151]

The station was sold for re-development in 2016 with a complete demolition of the site and a proposal for 29 residential units to be built as part of the plans.

Erith Police Station (RE)

London Borough of Bexley
Back Lane (later 103 Bexley Road), Erith (1847-1908)
22 High Street, Erith (1908-2000)
R and Thames Divisions

In 1847 a new police station, including a section house for single officers, was built at Erith at a cost of £583 17s 2d. The address was in Back Lane, later designated as 103 Bexley Road, Erith.[1152] The land was leased for 99 years, the landlords being recorded as John Williams of Denbigh and Sir H. Wheatly of St James' Palace, and later as Frederick Arthur Kelsey of Park Hill, Bexley.[1153]

The police strength at Erith was shown in Police Orders of 11th January 1864 as two sergeants, ten constables and one mounted sergeant. In 1870 Sergeants Henry Wilson and Joseph Bond were in charge, with 17 constables.[1154]

There were six night beats and two day beats in Erith in 1861. The substantive sergeant was responsible for the night duty parading at published times along with seven constables. The acting sergeant was responsible for two day duty constables.[1155] The inspector from Shooters Hill would pay periodic visits to Erith on horseback and provide an additional level of supervision often during the day duty whilst the acting sergeant was present.[1156]

A picture taken in Erith in 1865 with police officers either end of the group

The picture above was taken in 1865 when the uniform changed. The most senior rank at the station was often a sergeant, however in the picture the day duty sergeant shown extreme left was a responsible constable who was selected to become an acting sergeant, and had two chevrons instead of the normal three for substantive sergeants. The acting sergeant has the new cox-comb helmet, whilst his constable shown extreme right still has the old-style top hat.

The Commissioner's annual reports contained individual accounts of the activity on each division for the period, and for 1869, the Superintendent was able to report that:

'Very few events of importance happened in this extensive district... no serious accidents, loss of life or riot occurred... Only one murder was committed (in Rotherhithe)... there was only one serious burglary... and only three cases of highway robbery' The report then continued, *'Only three sheep were stolen on the Division; detection did not follow in [any] case, owing to the exposed and unfrequented places whence they were taken; one, there is little doubt, was taken in a boat to a ship lying in the Thames. Great facilities are afforded for this kind of felony, as numbers of sheep are grazed in marshes and fields at a considerable distance from the public paths and roads, and to watch them, the Police have to cross fields and endeavour to count them, night and morning, a duty more properly belonging to a shepherd or watchman, but I find farmers prefer an occasional loss to paying a watchman.'*[1157]

Erith Police Station 1847-1908

During 1871 the Commissioner reported that throughout the Metropolitan Police District 619 fires had occurred that had required the attendance of a total of 16,950 officers (165 superintendents, 667 inspectors, 1,760 sergeants and 14,358 constables).

Superintendent Charles Digby of R Division reported that in early 1871, a volunteer fire brigade was established at Erith:

'It is composed principally of young gentlemen of the neighbourhood, and has already done good service by prompt attendance and energetic action at fires.' [1158]

Later in his report he described how an explosion had occurred on the brig 'Ruth', lying at anchor in the Thames off Erith. The cargo of paraffin, oil and rosin caught fire, exploded, and burnt the ship to the water line, seriously damaging two other ships nearby, but nobody was killed and only one of the seven crew on board at the time was injured.

This temptation for seafarers to acquire a source of fresh food as they passed down the river was part of the reason for Thames Division officers also being stationed in the area, initially using the cutter 'Spray' as their floating base. She had been purchased on 21st June 1878 for £110 and with repairs needed in the sum of £90, but by 1891 the cutter had become dilapidated and was run aground in the August of that year to prevent her from sinking. In December the lighthouse at the end of Ballast Wharf was rented at 24 shillings per month from John Parish & Co for storage of equipment, rather than as an office or station, and the 'Spray' was repaired and sold.

By 1891 therefore, both land-based and river-based officers had serious problems with accommodation. The Superintendent suggested that the Thames officers should be transferred to Hammersmith because there was no longer a problem with sheep stealing. This caused much controversy and objection by riverside businesses, who were then assured that river patrols from another police ship, the 'Royalist', would patrol their area. The real answer to the problem, however, was to give Thames Division officers accommodation within a new police station planned for the area.

In a report dated 10th April 1900 the sub-divisional inspector complained that the administrative portion of Erith station consisted of only one room measuring 13ft by 11ft 6in (4x3.5 metres). Although formally recorded as a charge room, this one space had to serve as a parade room, charge room, office and place where members of the public would be attended to, as well as where the 30 sergeants and constables paraded for duty in inclement weather. There were also two cells, two water closets and two stalls for horses, no doubt all subject to being used for other purposes because of the lack of space.

Properties at 59-64 Crayford Road were purchased, but the site was considered too far from the Thames for the river-based officers to use it, and eventually the freehold of another site at 22 High Street, Erith, next to the river, was bought in 1905.[1159] The new station also had a base for the Thames Division officers, which had its own designated call sign UE in 1966. The Crayford Road houses were eventually sold in August 1927 for £1,000, well below the £2,500 purchase price in 1902.

The plot of land at 22 High Street was on the site of a large house once owned by a John Snow, who organised illegal gaming on the premises and forfeited his house for building it without planning permission. In 1872 the house was replaced by three homes, some shops and a slaughterhouse. These were demolished in order for the police station to be built,[1160] and this was duly opened on 16th November 1908.[1161] The old station building was eventually sold to a Mr F.A. Stone on 18th July 1921.

The riverside location was not without difficulty at times. In 1937 it was reported that members of the public were using the landing steps for gaining access to the river, from where

Erith Police Station 1908-2000

boatmen were running river trips. The public had started to use the station toilets indiscriminately, so locks were fitted, and notices displayed banning unauthorised access.[1162] Thames Division retained Erith as a River Police base until 1978.

An Erith Special Constable in the station yard, demonstrating a mobile air raid warning system in WWI

In 1973 plans were drawn up for a new police station for Erith, but they were met with controversy at the Local Authority's planning committee, where some councillors were reported as having considered that the modern design was more in keeping with 'a power station or a factory'.[1163]

This was a reflection on the fact that police stations have developed public expectations and images over the years.

1147 LB 689.
1148 Metropolitan Police Order dated 26th July 1963.
1149 Metropolitan Police Order dated 6th August 1964.
1150 Metropolitan Police Order dated 28th December 1979.
1151 MPA Report 6.
1152 Metropolitan Police Order dated 20th June 1884.
1153 Metropolitan Police Property Register, 1845.
1154 George Palmer.
1155 Metropolitan Police Special Orders 1861.
1156 Ibid.
1157 Report of the Commissioner of Police for the Metropolis 1869.
1158 Report of the Commissioner of Police for the Metropolis 1871.
1159 John Back archive.
1160 George Palmer.
1161 Metropolitan Police Orders dated 16th November 1908.
1162 John Back archive.
1163 *Police Review,* 22 February 1974, and *Erith and Crayford Observer,* January 1974.

The style of red brick and stone of the 1908 Erith station, as also seen at Bexleyheath in 1908 and Sidcup in 1906, exuded a sense of solid warmth, conservative respectability and approachability, important factors in the relationship between the police and the public.

The proposed replacement police station was never built, and its predecessor was eventually sold for redevelopment as housing. Erith was a sectional station of Bexleyheath sub-division in the 1960s.

Erith police station was shut in 2000 and was converted into residential dwellings.

Erith Safer Neighbourhood Unit 2019

In 2009 at Safer Neighbourhood Team base was located at 70 Galleon Close, Erith. A flat was rented to enable officers to patrol locally without the need to go to the nearest conventional police station, but it was not available for any form of front counter service for the public. A base was later introduced at Pier Road, Erith.

Esher Police Station

The London Borough of Richmond (Elmbridge)
Surrey Constabulary (transferred to the Metropolitan Police in 1947)
113 High Road Esher (1947-1993)
V Division (1947-1993)
The London Borough of Richmond OCU (1993-2000)
Transferred to the Surrey Constabulary 2000

When the Metropolitan Police District was extended from its original seven-mile radius in January 1840 this part of the V or Wandsworth Division included only the parishes of Long Ditton, Thames Ditton, East and West Molesey, together with the hamlets of Ember, Weston and Claygate, the latter having been enclosed two years earlier and creating an ecclesiastical parish in 1841 separated from the civil parish of Thames Ditton.[1164]

The Surrey County Constabulary had still a decade to wait before it came into being and, like most of the county, each parish had its own constables (normally unpaid). Parish constables continued in their office as late as 1872. Both Cobham and Esher were important stops on the route of the Southampton stagecoaches as they were on the Portsmouth turnpike road, a system that was soon to fall into decline after the opening in May 1838 of the London and Southampton Railway between Nine Elms and Woking Common with intermediate stops at Kingston (now Surbiton) and at Ditton Marsh (now Esher).[1165]

The Bow Street horse patrols had established a station at the latter, described as being 'Near Esher' in a small double cottage taken on a yearly lease under the charge of Inspector David Cornwell (warrant no. 15498). Cornwell had been a patrol since 1822 and retired from the Metropolitan Police in October 1852 after they had been absorbed into the London force.[1166]

The location of the former Metropolitan/Surrey force boundary between 1851 and 1947 can be found by the former toll-house at Kempton (Farm) Park, and elsewhere in the form of a white coal-post bearing the City of London crest.[1167]

The Metropolitan Police stations were under the command of Station Sergeant (SPS) James Whitmore (East Molesey) and Station Sergeant Willie Tilby (Ditton), who wore four chevrons instead of the sergeants' three until these were replaced in 1921 by three chevrons and a crown.[1168]

Two notable events in 1929 were the opening of the Metropolitan Police Sports Club at Imber Court and the opening of the Kingston bypass. An important piece of legislation passed between the wars was the Surrey Review Order 1933, whereby Esher and Dittons UD was renamed Esher Urban District, and enlarged to include the Moleseys, the Dittons, Stoke and Cobham.

On 1st April 1947 Esher Police Station was in the Surrey Joint Police Force Area, but under Section 16 of the Police Act 1964, deferred by WWII, the parishes of Esher, Stoke D'Abernon and Cobham, all in Esher Urban District Council, were transferred into the Metropolitan Police District. The area acquired from the Surrey Police approximately 18 square miles. The change-over took place at 6.00am on 1st April 1947, and Esher and Cobham became Metropolitan Police Stations. The area served by Esher (VH) and Cobham (VC) Stations became the Esher Section of Kingston Sub-Division, V Division.[1169]

The Surrey Police also allowed officers who served at the stations to remain and transfer into the London force if they wished. As a result, ten sergeants, 34 constables, one detective sergeant and a detective constable transferred. In October that year Dr. J. Stanley Whitton Sandcroft of The Green, Esher was appointed by the Metropolitan Police as the first dedicated divisional surgeon for Cobham and Esher.[1170]

The county police station at Oxshott was not used operationally by the Met, so to compensate a Dr Who-type police telephone box (No V70) was erected in the High Street, more familiar on the streets of London than in rural Surrey.

The station call sign was 'VE' in 1957. Between August and December 1960 both Cobham and Esher police stations were closed at night as an experiment, only to be re-opened 24 hours a day in April 1965. Esher was replaced by the present modern-looking building in December that year, which until January 1980, along with East Molesey, was placed under the Surbiton sub-division in lieu of Kingston.[1171]

In December 1964 a new sectional police station opened at Esher (VH) replacing the old Surrey Constabulary station acquired in 1947.

The old Esher UD was replaced by the present Borough of Elmbridge in April 1974, but still part of the MPD.

Estates Branch, in a memorandum to the Receiver in December 1959, stated that Esher, a Sectional Station of Kingston Sub-Division, was transferred to the Receiver by the Surrey Standing Joint Committee in 1947. The Branch reported that the present station, which was originally a public house, was likely to be scheduled for demolition to enable Esher High Street to be widened. It was suggested that a new site be found, and in any case owing to the inadequacy of the existing premises, a new station would be necessary whether the High Street was to be widened or not.

One of Dixon Committee (Surrey Police Authority Review of police station stock) proposals was that Esher should remain a sectional station. The inter-departmental committee, which had recently concluded a review of police stations, recommended that Esher station should be scheduled for rebuilding during 1961/63 and it was included in the provisional building programme for 1962/63.

Esher Police Station 1960-2000

Freehold premises adjacent to the existing station known as Belvedere House, High Street, Esher were purchased as a site for a new station on 13th July 1960 for the sum of £11,000. The Secretary of State had authorised a re-organisation of the Force designed to relate police boundaries to the new local authority boundaries created by the London Government Act, 1963. The new local authority and police boundaries were introduced on 1st April 1965. Esher (VH) was designated a sectional station of Surbiton (VS) sub-division situated in the local authority Area of Esher, Surrey:

'A new Sectional Police Station for Esher, V Division, at 113 High Street, Esher, will be taken into operational use at 6am on 7th December (1967). The telephone numbers will remain unchanged.' [1172]

From 1st February 1980, V District was reduced from three to two Divisions when Kingston and Esher Divisions were amalgamated. The new division of Kingston incorporated New Malden, Esher, Cobham, Surbiton and East Molesey Sub-Divisions, and there was no change to the Sub-Divisional Boundaries.[1173]

In 2000 Esher became a station subject to boundary changes and was transferred to the Surrey Constabulary.[1174]

Ewell Police Station

Although there was an intention to build a police station in Ewell village which led to the purchase of the freehold title to land shown as a vacant site in London Road in 1907, the start of building procedures upset local people and led to disquiet amongst the residents. By 1912 the project met with significant local resistance, resulting in a covenant being placed on the title deeds that a wall not less than 4ft 6ins tall should be erected along the south-west and north-west boundaries of the site. This led to police surveyors rethinking the proposed building, eventually deciding to abandon the idea. A station was not built and in 1927 detailed negotiations took place to sell the site to Major Vernon for £500, the final sale being completed in 1930.

Farnborough Police Station (PF)

London Borough of Bromley
429 Crofton Road, Locksbottom, Farnborough (1867-1987)
P Division (1867-1987)

Originally part of R Division when the Metropolitan Police District was extended in 1840, Farnborough was an area full of market gardens producing food for the local population and for sale in London. It is said that Sir Robert Peel, who died in 1850, had friends who lived at Farnborough Lodge who lobbied him to build a police station in the area because of problems with highwaymen.

Farnborough was policed in 1864 by a sergeant and two constables by day, and a sergeant and five constables by night. One of the sergeants was mounted on horseback, and was required to patrol for nine hours daily and to take care of his horse. In October 1865 a major re-organisation of the outer parts of the Metropolitan Police resulted in Farnborough being transferred from R (Greenwich) to P (Camberwell) Division.

In August 1867 two freehold properties at Locks Bottom were bought for £750, becoming the police station that remained operational. They were described in the 1881 survey as 'two country cottages in a healthy position', which had a charge room, two cells and a 2-stall stable. The walls were damp, however.

Farnborough Police Station 1867-1987

In the 1930s Farnborough Police Station was shown as a sectional station to Bromley sub-division. It became part of St Mary Cray sub-division on P Division on 1st April 1965 until its closure on 1st July 1987.

1164 Brown, B. (1999). 'Policing Old Esher'.
1165 Ibid.
1166 Ibid.
1167 Ibid.
1168 Ibid.
1169 Metropolitan Police Orders dated 14th March 1947.
1170 Brown, B. (1999). 'Policing Old Esher'.
1171 Ibid.
1172 Metropolitan Police Orders dated 4th December 1967.
1173 Metropolitan Police Orders dated 1st February 1980.
1174 Metropolitan Police Authority (2000) Police Station opening hours Committee.

Feltham Police Station

The London Borough of Hounslow
34 Hanworth Road (1952-1971)
T Division (1952-1993)
London Boroughs of Hounslow, Richmond on Thames, Urban Districts of Staines and Sunbury of Thames (1965-1993)
Borough of Hounslow OCU (1993-2018/19)
West Area WA BCU together with Ealing and Hillingdon (2018/19 to Present)

In 1932 the Chief Constable in charge of D2 branch, Mr G. Abbiss, later to become Sir George Abbiss, reported that he was doubtful whether it was politic at that time to close down the police stations of Bedfont and Sunbury without providing a suitable replacement in the area. He commented that as Staines sub-division was one of the largest in No.1 District and that Staines station itself was situated on the extreme western boundary of the Metropolitan Police District, it would not be a wise move. He suggested that if the stations were closed then a new police station should be found in the Feltham area.

The two stations were closed on 1st June 1932 as a measure of re-organisation and economy, but a room remained open for public visits until a replacement was found. In the meantime, Bedfont was not sold and remained as living quarters for police officers and their families,[1175] although an office was manned by a local constable who lived at the station.

Frequent representations were made by the two local authorities, Sunbury and Feltham Urban District Councils, that a station should be provided in the area. The Commissioner considered the matter in 1937 and came to the conclusion that it was indeed desirable to build a station at Feltham.[1176]

Prior to WWII plans were made by the police to locate a police station in Feltham, and many sites were examined. Eventually two parcels of land were purchased in 1939 and 1940 at Auckland House, 34 Hanworth Road, and a frontage to Ashfield Avenue[1177] on which to build a purpose-built station on the site used during the war as the headquarters of the local Home Guard unit. However, because of the war and the general lack of funds, immediate plans were shelved. In the meantime policing of Feltham continued to take place from nearby Bedfont.

In September 1951 a single-storey temporary pre-fabricated building previously used as a canteen for the Festival of Britain was purchased by the Receiver and re-used from 1952 as the first Feltham police station.[1178]

Feltham Police Station 1952-1971

With the ending of hostilities and the restriction on new building in the post-war years the site was not developed until 1952 with the closing of the Police room at the old Bedfont Police Station. The situation had by now become serious, and the Commissioner asked for accommodation to transact essential police business at Feltham.[1179]

The picture below shows Feltham as a temporary office in 1953, with its prize garden being carefully tended.

The garden at the front of the temporary Feltham Police Station being lovingly tended

In the meantime, the nearby Heathrow Airport continued to expand and plans were made to build a purpose-built new modern station in Feltham. There was a further revision of the Feltham boundary in November 1974 when Staines was transferred to the new Heathrow Airport sub-division.

In 1955 Feltham was 'TF' on Staines sub-division, with the address of Ashfield Avenue, Feltham. In 1957 Feltham station was 'TG' and a sectional station, together with both Hampton and Harlington, part of Staines sub-division on T Division. In 1971 a three-storey flat-roofed police station was erected on the site and the pre-fabricated building removed.

In the revision of boundaries in conjunction with the local authorities and the setting up of the GLC on 1st April 1965, Feltham is shown as a sectional station of Hounslow sub-division,[1180] with Chief Inspector Hudson taking responsibility for the station. In the photograph below the Chief Inspector surveys the mountain of equipment needed to move to the new station.

Feltham's Chief Inspector prepares himself with the task of moving to the new station

At 6.00am on Monday 8th October 1973 the new sectional police station at Feltham was opened and became fully operational, the postal address being 34 Hanworth Road, Feltham.[1181]

With the formation of the new Airport Division in 1975 certain boundary changes took place within T Division, and these were covered by Metropolitan Police Orders dated 31st

October 1974 and 1st July 1975.

Feltham's green and pond still provide a focal point for the High Street today. The Old Red Lion public house stands beside the green, a fortunate survivor of the redevelopment of the town that occurred in the mid-1960s.

Under the borough-based policing policy of the 1990s Chiswick and Hounslow Divisions, with the exception of Spelthorne but including Feltham, were amalgamated, thereby returning virtually to the former T District system in use since 1829.[1182]

Feltham's centre was rebuilt during 2005 and 2006 as mixed-development, including flats, a hotel, new shops, a new library and medical centre, and an Asda superstore. Proximity to Heathrow Airport makes Feltham an important interchange for West London's bus and rail networks, and a hotel chain has taken over and converted one of Feltham's prominent 1960s office blocks for use as a hotel.[1183]

Feltham Police Station 1971-2012

In 2012 the police station situated at 34 Hanworth Road shut its front counter and public inquiries were diverted to Chiswick Police Station. The station was retained as part of a patrol base.[1184] As of 2019 the station was still in use for operational purposes.[1185]

Finchley Police Station

Cottages at Finchley (1872-1889)

Ballards Lane, Finchley (1889-1967)

Ballards Lane (new building) (1967-2014)

S Division (1872-1993)

Borough of Barnet OCU (1993-2014)

The constable, or headborough, was a duty performed for a period of twelve months without payment from the 16th century onwards in Finchley. The Vestry records show that three headborough and three constables were elected for the East End, and three headborough and three constables were elected for the North End of Finchley Parish, making twelve men in all.[1186] Between 1801 and 1861 the population of Finchley rose threefold, from 1,500 to 4,900 people.

The Bow Street horse patrol patrolled the Great North Road, adjoining common land, woods and the leas of Finchley between 1805 and 1851.

The Metropolitan Police did not extend its boundaries to take in Finchley until 1840. The Hampstead or S Division came into being on 12th February 1830, and its strength was recorded as one superintendent, four inspectors, twelve sergeants and 190 constables, but as far as is known they did not patrol the Finchley district until much later.[1187]

Two cottages with stabling from the original horse patrol were transferred to the Metropolitan Police in 1845. These were located at 49 and 50 Whetstone Road, Finchley Common, the property of Mr. Joseph Bourton of Willesden who rented them out for £15 each per year. These buildings consisted of brick and slate and were in a good state of repair having been renovated in 1844. There was a large garden to the rear with good stabling, a four-room wash house and a large water closet. There was also a good clean water supply, which was important in those days in order to maintain health and keep infection away.[1188]

The 3rd Division of the Bow Street Horse Patrol comprised Hanwell, Hillingdon, Harrow Road, Hendon, Highgate, Edgware and Whetstone.[1189] Its officers included No. 45 Joseph Higgs, No. 46 Robert Broffam, No. 47 Thomas North and No. 48 Samuel Collard, who resided at the Finchley station. Joseph Higgs' patrol was a routine carried out each day. He either patrolled, rode or walked the New Finchley Road for a distance of five-and-a-half miles, Barnet Road to Grand Junction gate twice a day and the fourth and fifth milestone four times. Broffam's beat overlapped that of Higgs in that he patrolled, walked or rode Finchley New Road, Barnet Road, to Grand Junction gate for a distance of five-and-a half miles twice per day whilst patrolling from the second to the fourth milestone four times per day. Patrol No. 47 North walked, rode or patrolled the Barnet Road from Wellington Bar to Whetstone Gate for four miles twice a day and from the sixth to the eighth milestone four times per shift. Patrol 48 Collard was required to ride, walk or patrol the Barnet Road from Wellington Bar to Barnet Gate, a distance of five-and-a-half miles, and between the eighth and ninth milestone four times per day.[1190]

The cottages were given up at Christmas 1851.[1191] Police numbers were small in Finchley during the 1840s, and whilst no accurate figures exist there were probably one sergeant and three constables.

The Vestry, concerned with crime in their area, often requested the Commissioners for more police officers to patrol the area, but these requests were declined due to lack of available numbers.[1192] In 1866 the Vestry even sought to sweeten their request by offering Sir Richard Mayne land free of charge next to Holy Trinity Church, in Church Lane, but this was turned down as unsuitable land on which to build a police station.

1175 Brown, B. (1997), 'Policing Old Feltham'.
1176 Ibid.
1177 *The Police List* 1947.
1178 www.metpolicehistory.co.uk/1946-to-date.html accessed 23rd December 2012.
1179 Brown, B. (1997), 'Policing Old Feltham'.
1180 Metropolitan Police Orders dated 6th August 1960.
1181 Metropolitan Police Orders dated 5th October 1973.
1182 Brown, B. (1997), 'Policing Old Feltham'.
1183 www.hounslow.info/libraries/local-history-archives/discover-hounslow/#fel accessed 24th December 2012.
1184 Brentwood and Feltham closed for good this weekend' in *Hounslow, Heston and Whitton Chronicle*, 28th August 2013.
1185 MPS (2018) Freedom of Information request – MPS Assets.
1186 Martin, S (1970) *The Policing of Finchley Through the Ages*.
1187 Ibid.
1188 Metropolitan Police Surveyor's Records.
1189 Martin, S (1970) *The Policing of Finchley Through the Ages*.
1190 Ibid.
1191 Ibid.
1192 Ibid.

There were also a pair of stocks in Finchley which originated in 1575. They remained there until 1815 and stood on a site near the Church and the village cage or lockup, built nearby in 1815 in a position near the new public library. This was near to the reputed position of a plague pit.

In the period 1854-59 143 people had been arrested and placed in the village cage or lockup. In February 1860 Sir Richard Mayne wrote a letter to the Clerk of the Vestry saying:

'...the Supt. of the Division reported that the Finchley Cage was required by police, it being the only lockup within 3 miles, and that in the last 5yrs 143 persons had been locked up, and that it was required more than ever.' [1193]

During this period the local police sergeant resided in a cottage opposite the Manor Cottage Tavern, and he had constructed a special coal bunker into which he would fling the drunken men to sober up before being taken to court.[1194] The village cage situated to the east side of the council offices in Hendon Lane continued to be used until 1906, because it was a perpetual cause of annoyance to the local population who were always complaining of the foul language used by its inmates. There was evidence to suggest that the cage was also a secure place to locate dead and unclaimed bodies prior to post mortem and burial.

After 1866 one of the lower rooms of a tall brick house in the Broadway was used as a police office, and this would appear to be 355 Regents Park Road. The building was later turned into shops and occupied by Messrs Williams, Sportswear. It was pulled down in 1964, and the site is now occupied by Winston House.

There is evidence to suggest that a police station existed in Hendon Lane and may have been known as Ballards Lane, as it was often the case to name the station after the road, lane or highway it was situated on. The station was located between the old King of Prussia public house and the Post Office, this being next to St Mary's School (known then as the National School), and it appears to be facing Lichfield Grove, from 1874 onwards, until it moved to its present site in Ballards Lane in 1888.

In 1872 a new cottage was leased from Mrs Ann Woods of Church End, Finchley for £26 per year until 1893. This was located at 7 or 9 Regents Park Road, Church End and consisted of a charge room on the ground floor and three rooms on the first floor which served as the inspector's married quarters.

By the early 1880s the cottage/station was described as 'modern' but it had cramped conditions, no place to accommodate prisoners and cell space was urgently required. It did house a married inspector and his family but was considered no longer fit for purpose. Recommendations were made to the Home Office for a new station to be found elsewhere when funds were available.[1195] The occupant appears to be Inspector Benjamin Ellis, his wife Sophia and their four children.[1196]

In 1885 Finchley was designated an Inspector's station.[1197] It was given up in 1889, together with the old cage which was given back to the parochial authorities.[1198]

The sum of £2,400 was paid for the freehold purchase of land formally called Wentworth Lodge in Ballards Lane, Church End, Finchley in 1886. Arrangements were made by surveyors for builders to tender for a contract to build the new station. The planners had to be mindful of the chapel next door, whose trustees were concerned that the newly-built station would block out light through the main window. The trustees argued that they had a right to light, and wished to enforce this right on the Receiver. The same right to light was expressed by the owner of the photographic shop with a glass roof on the other side of the station site.

A new station costing £3,759 was erected and included two cells, association cell (later known colloquially as the 'drunk tank'), inspector's office, waiting room, store and two sets of married quarters. In the yard there was an ambulance shed, parade shed, and a three stall stable with hay loft. To ensure the boiler fires were working in colder weather there were three coal sheds and a coke shed. Also on the ground floor were urinals and a toilet, whilst on the first floor there was a bathroom.[1199] The married inspector had six rooms at the station, which cost him £14 6s to rent yearly, whilst the married constable paid half that, with one less room. These amounts, calculated weekly, would be deducted from their pay which they would receive at 2.00pm on a Wednesday. The new station was occupied in 1889.[1200]

The following is an entry from the *Finchley Brochure* of June 1905:

'The parish is exceptionally well policed and forms part of S Division, under Supt. Dodd of Albany Street, and SDI Leech and at Finchley there are 2 SPSs J. Warne and A. Sutherland and 120 men. There are several mounted patrols in the district and the CID is represented by DS Francis Pike.' [1201]

Finchley Police Station 1893-1967

The use of cycles was gradually being introduced to travel around the division, and were taking over from horses which required greater maintenance. So in 1910 there were alterations to the station that increased the accommodation at a cost of £274, whilst a cycle shed was erected in the yard at a cost of £20 5s. Next to the station in 1914 was a car showroom, which had previously been a chapel but later converted. When Detective Constable George Knell retired in 1914 he took over the showrooms, altered the layout and converted it into a billiard hall.[1202]

Surplus land was sold to Mr S.L. Day for £1,900 in 1924, and negotiations with Mr R. Payne for additional land adjacent to the station at a cost of £50 were completed in the same year.[1203] The police took possession of the land purchased.

An elder of Finchley recalled that there was a constable named Gray (most likely to be Constable William Gray, warrant no. 64393, of S Division 1880-1901) who was portly and unable to give chase because of his size. As a boy he would stand with his mates on the opposite side of the road waving and sing the popular tune of the day, 'Good Bye Dolly Gray', and run off when the good officer gave chase. But Gray always got them in the end, with a clump round the ear,[1204] often with his gloves which were weighted in the ends with something heavy like thimbles or threepenny coins. Often the police officers would wait near the schools for the children to be released and those unsuspecting pranksters would receive their comeuppance with a flick that could not be reported back to their parents for fear of another thick ear from them.

The station call sign for the telegraph published in Police Orders in 1893 was Foxtrot Yankee (FY), but by the 1920s these were changed to Sierra Foxtrot (SF).[1205] In 1907 Finchley Police Station was an important station with a Sub-Divisional Inspector in charge as part of S or Hampstead Division,[1206] remaining so until the 1930s.

Special Inspector Scott of Finchley, 1917

Inspector Robert Ruff was stationed at Finchley from 1907 until he retired on pension in 1910. He retired with an exemplary record and a first-class certificate for good service. Born at Maldon in Essex, he was educated at Billericay and left school to work in the building industry in his native town. Joining the Metropolitan Police in 1885 he was first posted to Hunter Street on E Division. Becoming Superintendent's clerk within two years of joining earned him recognition, and on the resignation of his superintendent his skills as clerk were required at Blackheath Road. In the meantime he studied for his sergeant's examination which he passed very quickly. On promotion to Inspector in 1901 he discovered he was not a well man, but he also had to care for his ailing wife who needed country air away from the smog of London. On application to his superintendent he was transferred to a healthier location. Ruff had commendations for good arrests of thieves and restraining runaway horses. As sport was a central feature of the police and encouraged by senior officers, Ruff was a good athlete and won prizes at cricket, cycling rowing and punting. He also played cricket to a good standard for the Metropolitan Police central cricket club against outside teams.[1207] Ruff supported his 45-year-old Sub-Divisional Inspector John Cundell, from Cambridgeshire, who resided at the station with his wife and three teenage children.

Special Inspector Alderton, Finchley 1917

In 1924 surplus land from the site was sold to Mr S.L. Day for the sum of £1,900, but in the same year adjacent land was purchased from Mr. R.W.T. Payne for £50. Next to the station were married quarters located at Wentworth Lodge, Wentworth Park, Finchley, a building originally purchased in 1886.

During the 1914-18 war the Specials who helped local police in their duties were without a headquarters and it was decided to use a large house opposite the police station named Willow Lodge. The ground today is used by the Victoria Bowling Club, and part of the grounds and garden of Willow Lodge is now The Ridgeway. A drawing of Willow Lodge as the Special Constabulary headquarters is shown below.

Willow Lodge - Finchley Special Constabulary HQ 1915

Experiences in WWI made people vigilant to the dangers of fascist aggression in Europe. In the late 1930s arrangements were put in place in the event of war, and a number of publications had been prepared and published by His Majesty's Stationery Office (HMSO) to aid the public, police and other agencies. All constables and reserve staff, including special constables, were issued with certain additional publications in order to make them conversant with special arrangements.

1193 'The History of Ballards Lane' by C.O. Banks, printed in the *Finchley Press* of 1927/8 C/603/LF*vol.1.pages 20/21).
1194 Ibid, bk.l folio 9264.
1195 Metropolitan Police Hygiene Inspection Report of Police Premises 1880, p70.
1196 Census 1881.
1197 *Kelly's Directory* 1885.
1198 Metropolitan Police Surveyors Records.
1199 Ibid.
1200 Fletcher, J. (1972) Briefing note. Metropolitan Police Estates Management Department.
1201 *The Finchley Brochure* 1905.
1202 'The History of Ballards Lane' by C.O. Banks, printed in the *Finchley Press* of 1927/8 L942/191 LM402.
1203 Metropolitan Police Surveyor's Records, 1924.
1204 Martin, S. (1970) 'The Policing of Finchley Through the Ages'.
1205 Metropolitan Police General Orders 1893.
1206 *Kirchner's Police Almanac* 1907.
1207 *The Police Review and Parade Gossip*, 5th August 1910.

Metropolitan Police Special Constabulary (MPSC) were well organised in Finchley during the war. Large numbers of men who did not qualify for war service and stayed at home volunteered to be special constables, such was the enthusiasm for joining the war effort.

These volunteers were supervised in the main by ex-military gentlemen, especially at Finchley, and in S Division in general. Each special constable was required initially to attend the station each evening once they had returned from work to then complete four hours' duty.

However, it was soon realised that this was too much to ask and the norm became three times a week. Many of the WWI specials stayed on until the 1920s as camaraderie had been built up amongst the men and officers. Central to the leadership was Chief Inspector Cross, who is shown in the front centre of the picture below. Cross remained until he became Acting Assistant Commander in the same period.

Finchley Special Constabulary 1926

In 1936 Air Raid Precautions Handbook No. 1 on Personal Protection against Gas was issued. This was not a confidential document, as it was also for general public use.

However by 1939 the Metropolitan Police issued War Duty Hints, which was confidential. On receipt of the orange-coloured booklet the recipient wrote their name, division, divisional number and station in the front, and then familiarised themselves with the contents. It contained the general instructions in wartime in terms of police organisation and equipment. Arrangements for air raid precautions, anti-gas safeguards, air raid warnings and police action in the event of an air attack are only some of the contents.[1208]

Sub-Divisional Inspector Trott

The Sub-Divisional Inspector at the time was Thomas George Trott (warrant no. 87731), shown left. Trott had joined the police in August 1901 and retired in 1927, a year after this picture was taken.

In 1937 the station code was Sierra Foxtrot (SF), and its importance had been reduced to that of sectional station to Golders Green.

The Police and Fireman (War Service) Act 1939 suspended the right to retire on pension other than through medical grounds or with the Commissioner's consent. In the meantime the ranks of the police were swelled by the police reserve (retired police pensioners under 58 years of age), who volunteered to return because of a national emergency; special constables; Women's Auxiliary Police Corps; and War Reserves (full-time paid or part-time unpaid), consisting of selected and suitably-qualified members of the public. The War Reserve joined or rejoined the force, whilst their colleagues and younger police officers went to the armed forces. All the War Reserve wore the same uniform as the ordinary personnel, but with 'W.R.' on their epaulettes. Their duties were the same as their colleagues, and they were senior to special constables who only did specific duties.

A group of S Division officers who sounded the All-Clear after an air raid

In 1930 the divisions and sub-divisions were revised. The status of Finchley was reduced in favour of Golders Green when the sub-divisional administration and Sub-Divisional Inspector were transferred. The following order was issued:

'Finchley will, from 1st September, be known as Golders Green Sub-Division and Sub-Divisional Inspector Spruces will be transferred to Golders Green Station, which will be the Sub-Divisional Station.' [1209]

There were many incidents of brave conduct by serving police officers. In 1943 Tom Alec Page, a War Reserve Constable on patrol in Finchley's Lyndhurst Gardens, challenged an armed soldier whom he came across breaking into a house. The soldier tried to escape by running away, but the constable chased after him and when the soldier was in danger of capture he turned and aimed his rifle at Page, shooting him in the leg. Whilst on the floor injured, the soldier hit the officer in the face with the rifle butt, causing further injury. Later the soldier was apprehended and Page was rewarded for his bravery. He was awarded the King's Police and Fire Service Medal by the King at Buckingham Palace.[1210]

There were concerns that the old station was too small and inadequate for the policing of the area. WWI had seen that special constables had to be housed away from the station in a house opposite, so even then the squeeze on space was problematic. The outside toilets with their exposed pipes would freeze up and often burst, causing police officers to use the facilities in the park opposite.

The flats above the station were empty and cell space was given over to the CID, so when the pipes in the living space burst in the bad winter of 1963 detectives would walk around inside with umbrellas up – a very inadequate situation. Moves were being made in the Surveyor's department to upgrade the station.

In October 1965 a pre-fabricated building was erected in the yard with access from Grunieson Road and the Finchley staff were transferred there. The divisional staff had been moved to Golders Green in the meantime during the refurbishment period and, once completed, the staff would return. The old station was then demolished and a new more modern one erected in its place.

The new station now comprised luxury centrally-heated inside space, with plush offices, a billiard and darts room, a modern restaurant, a briefing rather than a parade room, a writing room, and at the back a block of married quarters. Also inside was a CID office, women police office, and a dedicated room for the special constabulary. In the yard was a purpose-built cycle shed with a rack for at least twelve cycles.[1211]

Finchley Police Station 1967-2014

Due to the building works the address of the station was altered to 5 Gruneison Road, and was shown as a sectional station of Golders Green (SD). Gruneison Road was the next left turning past the old police station, which was being demolished, indicating that the entrance had been removed from the High Road for reconstruction and refurbishment of the old station. By 1967 the address had reverted back to Ballards Lane, Finchley, when the new station had been completed and staff returned.

In the 1960s Chief Inspector Clelland was in charge here, whilst Superintendent M.J. Byrne was in overall charge of the Sub-Division.[1212] Superintendent Byrne supervised the transition from the old to the new station, and ensured the smooth running of the division.

The Youth and Communities section was housed at Finchley Police Station and covered the area of Barnet and Hertsmere. In charge were Chief Inspector John Oliver and Inspector Good. Superintendent Simon Humphrey was in charge of the sub-division in 1998.

In 2012 Finchley Police Station was still open to the public but a decision was taken to put the station up for sale and vacate the staff. In 2014 the freehold site was sold for £5.5M[1213] to developer Fizzy Finchley LLP.[1214]

Forest Gate Police Station

The London Borough of Newham
444 Romford Road (1888-1992)
350-360 Romford Road (1992 to Present)
K Division (1888-2018)
Basic Command Unit North East (NE) (2018 to Present)

Forest Gate Police Station Lamp

The policing of Forest Gate before 1855 was carried out by means of police patrols from the Night Watch Houses in Angel Lane, Stratford. During the 1880s the area expanded rapidly as a dormitory region, like so many other areas of London. With the influx of large numbers of people into the rural outskirts came the need to have greater numbers of police officers and its own police station.

After 1855 the policing of Forest Gate had been carried out from West Ham Police Station. The Divisional Superintendent George Turner had for some time been put under great pressure from the local people to have a greater presence in the area. The local Parish Safety Committee reported:

"The roaming about the streets of gangs of louts and vagabonds, the throwing of bricks and brick bats by them at the windows of properties, careless of the safety of tender ladies therein." [1215]

Large sums of money were collected from local inhabitants towards the cost of a new station. These local people lived in the more affluent area, situated north of the Romford Road, and centred mainly around Windsor Road.[1216] Accordingly, arrangements were made to search for available land on which to build a police station and the Home Office authorised the purchase of a site at Forest Gate in 1884. After a failed negotiation for this site another was soon found at a place called Manor Waste. The Lord of the Manor of West Ham was

Forest Gate Police Station 1888-1992

1208 'Metropolitan Police War Duty Hints', March 1939.
1209 Metropolitan Police Orders dated 29th August 1930.
1210 *London Gazette*, 1943.
1211 *The Job*, 19th January 1968, p2.
1212 Metropolitan Police List 1965.
1213 MPS (2019) Freedom of information request – Police station closures broken down by year.
1214 MPS (2018) Land and property sold for over £1M in the last ten years.
1215 Parish Safety Committee Reports 1855.
1216 'West Ham Police Station' (1970) author unknown.

Forest Gate Police Station 1992 to present

approached and was asked to give up the Waste in exchange for consideration money of £20 and costs amounting to £11 10s. He agreed to the sale of the land under these circumstances and the land was purchased on a leasehold basis. The freehold was finally purchased on 16th November 1886, at a further cost of £900. The cost of building the station was £3,341.[1217]

The first Police station at Forest Gate was erected at 444 Romford Road, opening in May 1888. The area to be policed covered the districts of Forest Gate, Manor Park and part of Plaistow. Records show that not only a station was built, but also a section house for ten single constables paying one shilling a week, and one set of married quarters, where four shillings a week rent was paid.[1218] With the opening of the new building came a re-organisation of the surrounding station areas. West Ham and Ilford were altered to accommodate the new sub-division.

The authorised strength of the station was two inspectors, two sub-inspectors, four sergeants and 69 constables. The first officer in charge of the new sub-division was Inspector Death. Joseph Death was then aged 41 years and was from Barking in Essex. In 1881 he resided in Cable Street, Shadwell with his wife Eliza, who was from Colchester in Essex. They did not have any children.[1219]

In 1910 the strength of the station was two inspectors, nine sergeants and 94 constables.[1220] The new station was shown as a sub-divisional station of Bow Road Police Station, the Divisional Headquarters.

The picture above shows a serial of ten constables from Forest Gate Police Station on duty at the Coronation of King George V in June 1911. They have dressed in ceremonial uniforms plus white gloves, and paraded at the photographers to commemorate the issue of the coronation medal. Sometimes the medals were not issued until a year after the event. The medal was designed by Sir Bertram MacKennal M.V.O.,

A group of constables from Forest Gate showing their medals from the Coronation in 1911

A.R.A., and was struck in silver and suspended from the ribbon by a silver ring swivelled on the claw affixed to the top of the medal.

The section house, which was attached to the station, was closed in May 1926 when the additional space was absorbed for offices. In 1962, following the publication of the Deller Report on re-organisation it was recommended that Forest Gate should be shut, the ground be split in half and that policing should revert back to Ilford and West Ham. Needless to say, these recommendations were shelved. By 1965, following local Government re-organisation on station areas Forest Gate became a sectional station of West Ham and had the station code of 'KF'.[1221]

Further Force re-organisation during 1985 saw West Ham and Forest Gate become a Division of the newly-established 2 Area (east). Although a small two-storey building, it remained an operational police station for longer than really necessary until a new building was opened in 1992.

The site, at 370 Romford Road, had been purchased by the Metropolitan Police from the London Borough of Newham and a suitable police station building was designed by the Property Services Department at Scotland Yard. Construction of the station by Bernard Sunley and Sons Ltd commenced at an estimated cost of £7 million. Plaistow became the Divisional headquarters of Newham (north) and Plaistow was headquarters for Newham (south). West Ham Police Station took over the role as office for the Borough Chief Superintendent Ivan L.A. Brown.[1222]

The new station was built at the corner of Romford Road and Green Street and was opened for police business in June 1992. In September 1992 the Rt. Hon. Kenneth Clarke, QC, MP Secretary of State for the Home Department, conducted the official opening. Also present were the Metropolitan Police Commissioner Sir Peter Imbert, the Mayor of the London Borough of Newham, Bill Chapman, the Receiver Mr. Graham Angel, Assistant Commissioner Robert Hunt and Property Services Department Director Trevor Lawrence. The opening ceremony attracted over 200 people as well as a number of other local dignitaries and schoolchildren.[1223]

The established strength of the station is shown as superintendent, three chief inspectors, twelve inspectors, 45 sergeants, 240 constables and 52 members of the civil staff. The officer in charge of the station was Superintendent (later Chief Superintendent) David Solman.[1224]

In 1998 the officer in charge of the station was Superintendent Barry Vincent and his deputy was Superintendent Dave Almond.[1225] Records show that in the same year the Borough Headquarters were located at Stratford Police Station,[1226] but by 2002 they had been transferred to Forest Gate.[1227]

As of 2019 the station was open 24 hours a day, seven days a week.

Fulham Police Station (also known as Walham Green, South Fulham)

London Borough of Hammersmith and Fulham

Lewis's Yard (behind the George Inn), Fulham Road,
  Waltham Green (1830-1863)
520 Fulham Road (1863-1914)
Heckfield Place (1914-2016)
V Division (1830-1863)
T Division (1863-1909)
B Division (1909-1965)
|F Division (1965-2016)

Before looking at details of the stations, it is worth mentioning that Fulham has been policed by two main police stations since the Metropolitan Police assumed the responsibility for policing the area in 1830.

Prior to 1862 the first police station was known as Walham Green Police Station. When the new police station was built in 1863 it became known as Fulham Police Station and the address was 520 Fulham Road, Walham Green. It became known as South Fulham Police Station in 1887 when North Fulham Police Station was opened.

In the 1890s, after buying extra land the police station was extended. A new police station opened in 1914 on a site opposite the old station, with the address now being Heckfield Place. At this stage the name of the station was changed from South Fulham back to Walham Green. Then in 1960 the name was again changed back to Fulham Police Station. In 1992 the station was substantially extended.

The first police building in Fulham was at Walham Green. It was described as a section house, and many such places were often also used as police station houses. The first police station at Walham Green was situated in the corner of Lewis's Yard which was behind the George Inn in Fulham Road.[1228] The owner of the property was a Mr Thornton of Walham Green. The building was described as a common brick and tile house with a yard at the back. It had a coal cellar, dust hole and water closet. It contained five rooms and had a scullery. This remained a rented building until the new police station was built in 1863,[1229] at which point the premises were given up.

The inspector and the sergeants from Chelsea were required to patrol the section of Fulham on horseback. The station strength in 1861 was three sergeants, one acting sergeant and 24 police constables. There were six day beats and 16 night beats. Two sergeants were required to remain in the station at all times whilst one mounted sergeant and one section sergeant supervised and patrolled the station area.[1230] The station was a sectional station to Chelsea on V or Wandsworth Division.

The owner of the second Walham Green station was Captain Cotton of Fulham, who leased the premises from 1862 for 60 years and charged an annual rent of £25. Even though the land was rented, the building was erected by the Commissioner and technically was owned by the Metropolitan Police. Later the land was purchased either voluntarily or by compulsory purchase.

In June 1863, police were instructed to take charge and to occupy the new Station and Section House at 520 Fulham Road,[1231] at the junction that later became Heckfield Place. It was henceforth to be known as Fulham and not Walham Green, as the previous station had been before June 1863, forming part of V or Wandsworth Division.[1232] The cost of the new building was £2,116.[1233] With the formation in 1865 of the three new Divisions – W, X and Y – Fulham was transferred to the T or Kensington Division.[1234]

In 1881 a report on Fulham Police Station stated that 'the station is somewhat arranged to the convenience of the married Police Inspector, who resides there.' At the time of the inspection the station was occupied by a married inspector and six single constables.[1235]

In 1884 Fulham was a sub-divisional station of T Division.[1236] The following year the police paid £350 for land at the rear of

---

1217 John Back Archive (1975).
1218 Metropolitan Police Surveyor's Records.
1219 Census 1881.
1220 'West Ham Police Station' (1970); author unknown.
1221 John Back Archive (1975).
1222 Open day publicity material June 1992.
1223 Ibid.
1224 Ibid.
1225 *Police and Constabulary Almanac* 1998.
1226 Ibid.
1227 www.met.police.uk/contact/phone.htm accessed 6th May 2002.
1228 'A Potted History of Fulham and Hammersmith Police' – Met Police Heritage collection.
1229 Metropolitan Police Surveyor's Book p165.
1230 Special Metropolitan Police Orders 1861.
1231 Metropolitan Police Orders dated 20th June 1863.
1232 John Back Archive circa 1975.
1233 Metropolitan Police Surveyor's Book.
1234 Metropolitan Police Orders dated 28th October 1865.
1235 Metropolitan Police Report on condition of Police Stations 1881.
1236 Metropolitan Police Orders dated 22nd February 1884.

the station. An agreement was reached with the owners of the land on which the station was built that a further £900 was to be paid for the freehold of the property in 1890.[1237]

In 1887 there was the sad case of Constable Robert McGraw, who unfortunately died from a fractured skull after being kicked by his police horse in Fulham Police Station stables.[1238]

When North Fulham Police Station opened in 1887, Fulham Police Station became known as South Fulham Police Station.

In 1909 there was a re-arrangement of the boundaries between T and B Divisions. The Fulham sub-division comprising the stations of North Fulham and South Fulham were transferred and became part of B or Chelsea Division.[1239]

The national census of 1911 shows the married quarters at South Fulham Police Station being occupied by a number of police families. One of these was Sergeant Charles Francis Hancox at No. 5 Police Quarters.

He and his wife Lucy were living in four rooms with their two teenage children.[1240] The station was described as having a section house and one set of married quarters.

The picture below shows the line-up of South Fulham with their Sub-Divisional Inspector Frederick May in the centre. See Borough Police Station for more on this officer. This photograph was taken in 1912 when the previous year's Coronation Medal was issued.

South Fulham contingent taken with SDI May in the centre in 1912

During 1911, land at the rear of numbers 522-534 Fulham Road was purchased for the erection of a new police station, in Heckfield Place. This station was opened for business on 30th March 1914[1241] and replaced the old station opposite.

There was no formal opening ceremony of the new station, but Superintendent John B. Kitch escorted a number of local dignitaries around the station.

Fulham (Waltham Green) Police Station, opened in 1914

Chief Inspector George Shervington (warrant no. 74004), Sub-Divisional Police Inspector Emerick (who took over from May) and Police Inspectors Reeves and Thursby were also in attendance.[1242] The name of the station was changed at the express wish of the then Commissioner, Sir Edward Henry, from South Fulham to Walham Green.[1243]

The new station was five storeys together with a basement, and was built of red sand-faced bricks with a Portland stone dressing. It had oak front doors and large windows throughout the building. The building contractor for the building was Messrs John Garlick and Co. of Sloane Street, and was built to the designs of John Dixon Butler, the Metropolitan Police Surveyor. At the time, this new building was considered to be one of the most modern police stations in London and was erected at the cost of £1,200. The station now had accommodation for 38 single police officers under the charge of bachelor Sergeant Edhouse. At the rear of the station was a large yard, accessed although a large arched gateway. The yard contained a parade shed, and stables for up to six horses. The number of police officers operating from the new station in 1914 was two inspectors, four station sergeants, ten sergeants and 120 constables together with two mounted patrols.[1244]

By 1919 B Division was under the command of Superintendent Ernest Bacchus. At Fulham Police Station, Sub-Divisional Inspector George Wilcox was in charge, and was assisted by Inspectors G. Bonnyman and John Thursey.[1245] In 1928 Walham Green Police Station was still shown on B Division and was at this time under the command of Superintendent William Crayfourd.[1246]

Superintendent Bacchus B Division

The regulation of public carriage vehicles, including taxi cabs in London was passed to the Metropolitan Police in 1850. The original Public Carriage Office (PCO) was situated in an annexe to New Scotland Yard called the Bungalow. It moved to 109 Lambeth Road in 1919. The PCO moved to 15 Penton Street, Islington in 1966, and then to Southwark in 2010. There were a number of 'Passing Stations' throughout the Metropolitan Police area for testing vehicles and drivers. No. 4 Passing Station of the PCO which had been at North Fulham Station was transferred to the old Fulham Police Station site in October 1938. It remained there until October 1966 when, with the other passing stations, it moved to Penton Street, Islington.[1247] The PCO then moved to Southwark in 2010 and is now known as the London Taxi and Private Hire Office[1248] as part of Transport for London.

A sad happening occurred in 1958 when Superintendent Thomas George James collapsed and died in the police car taking him to duty at Walham Green.[1249]

Once again there came a change of name for the station.[1250] As of 1st January 1960 Walham Green Police Station became known as 'Fulham', and the telegraphic code changed from 'BW' to 'BF'.

On a large-scale revision of boundaries on 1st April 1965 to match the local authority boundaries,[1251] Fulham changed Divisions yet again and this time became a sub-divisional

Station of F Division. A further revision of boundaries between Hammersmith and Fulham sub-divisions took place in 1975.[1252]

In May 1992 the Commissioner, Sir Peter Imbert, opened the refurbished Fulham Police Station. Work to extend and refurbish the building took almost four years to complete, at the cost of £4.5M.[1253]

Fulham Police Station 1914-2016 (extended 1992)

Also in 1992 ex-Constable Ken Walker was presented with a commendation, by Deputy Assistant Commissioner Alan Fry, to mark his retirement after 44 years' service at Fulham Police Station. He had joined the Police in September 1947 after four years in the Parachute Regiment, during which he took part in the Normandy invasion. During his service he had received two Commissioner's commendations and retired as a constable in 1960. He returned the following day to take up the post of Administrative Officer at the station.[1254]

In 1992 Heckfield Place was extended next to the station as the picture above shows. Fulham Police station code was 'FF' in 1992, and was a Divisional Station under the charge of Chief Superintendent R.A.S. Johnson with Superintendent M. Schuck in support.[1255]

In 2016 the front counter was closed to the public. Later that year the police station was sold for £20M.[1256]

Gardiner's Lane Police Station

City of Westminster

2 Gardiner's Lane (1830-1850)

A Division (1830-1850)

Probably the first police station on A or Whitehall Division that was not part of the Scotland Yard complex was at 2 Gardiner's Lane, a short road that ran west from King Street towards St James's Park, perhaps a few yards south from where the modern King Charles Street runs.

Gardiner's Lane was a brick and tile building, without a yard, leased by Receiver John Wray from midsummer 1830. It was vacated by the police in 1850, by which time King Street Police Station had been taken into use. Gardiner's Lane had five rooms and, on the ground floor, an office and charge room, two unventilated cells and stabling for three horses. At one point it was used by the detective branch, which was formed in 1842.

A note in the property register states: 'Dustbins and men's cupboards wanting... with other conveniences for the detective force'.

Modern police officers would probably recognise equivalent shortfalls in accommodation when a squad has to be set up urgently, but at least they would have had the consolation implicit in another note: 'Drain to sewer clean and healthy. Ventilation good'.

The 1841 census shows six police officers living in Gardiner's Lane, three of whom were married and parents of young children.

In May 1842, Queen Victoria was riding down Constitution Hill in her carriage when she was shot at by John Francis. Constable 53 William Trounce of A Division was on the scene and arrested him, but not without some additional intervention from Colonel Charles Arbuthnot, the Queen's equerry, who ordered that the prisoner be taken to Buckingham Palace. From there, more conventional police procedures followed, and it was to Gardiner's Lane Police Station that the prisoner was later taken and charged with high treason. This incident was one of a series of attacks on Queen Victoria and formed part of the arguments for the establishment of a detective branch. Nicholas Pearce, the first Detective Inspector, had his office at this police station.

Gerald Road Police Station

City of Westminster

1-2 Roberts Buildings (1829-1845)

5 Cottage Road (1845-1885)

5 Gerald Road (1885-1993)

B Division (1829-1965)

A Division (1965-1985/86)

No 8 Area (1985/86-1993)

The first police station, known variously as Roberts Buildings, Ebury Square or Elizabeth Place, comprised a house leased on a yearly tenancy, with two cells, a charge room, a reserve room, mess, kitchen and two bedrooms. It was noted that it was 'in need of thorough repair. The men have no lockers. Drainage very imperfect.' Nos. 1 and 2 Roberts Buildings were two small cottages used as section houses.

In 1845 the station was replaced by new premises at 5 Cottage Road, renamed as Gerald Road forty years later in 1885. The building was rented on a 78-year lease at an annual rent of £170 12s 9d from Miss Minnis, who apparently lived at number 14. In 1848 it was described as 'new and substantially brick and slate built with charge and reserve rooms, four cells and a section house'. It was later described as having seven cells, an association cell and an ambulance shed. This would have housed a hand ambulance, a common means of

1237 Metropolitan Police Surveyor's Book.
1238 met.police.uk/history/remembrance2 accessed 17th October 2012.
1239 Metropolitan Police Orders dated 31st March 1909.
1240 Census 1911.
1241 Metropolitan Police Orders dated 21st March 1914.
1242 *Fulham Chronicle*, 3rd April 1914.
1243 John Back Archive 1975.
1244 *Fulham Chronicle*, 3rd April 1914.
1245 *Kelly's West Kensington and Fulham Directory* 1919.
1246 *Post Office Directory* 1928.
1247 John Back Archive circa 1975.
1248 www.tfl.gov.uk accessed January 2013.
1249 met.police.uk/history/remembrance2 accessed 17th October 2012.
1250 Metropolitan Police Orders dated 29th December 1959.
1251 Metropolitan Police Orders dated 6th August 1964.
1252 Metropolitan Police Orders dated 24th October 1975.
1253 *The Job*, 29th May 1992.
1254 Ibid.
1255 *Police and Constabulary Almanac* 1992.
1256 Metropolitan Police Information Rights Unit 21st January 2018, accessed 25th January 2019.

Gerald Road Police Station 1885-1993

conveying ill or injured people to hospital before the advent of the London Ambulance Service and the later general introduction of motor ambulances.

The station telegraph code was originally 'CR', then 'BG', and later, when it became part of A Division in 1965, 'AL'. In 1891 the Metropolitan Police purchased the next door premises, at no. 3, from Canon Fleming, the vicar of St Michael's church in Chester Square and the freehold of both premises. Extension work was undertaken between 1892 and 1894 and the whole building was extensively reconstructed in 1925. An annexe in adjoining first floor premises of Elizabeth Street was acquired in 1981 and the station eventually closed, replaced by Belgravia Police Station in 1993.

One famous Gerald Road incident occurred in August 1909 when two officers arrested two drunken men for disturbing the residents, particularly a Mrs Costa, in Warwick Street, Pimlico. It later transpired that the prisoners were Mrs Costa's husband and their lodger who had, noisily, been trying to persuade her to let them in to the house by 'knocking at the door and pulling the doorbell without lawful excuse' – then an offence under the Metropolitan Police Act.

The inspector on duty was Inspector John Syme (warrant no. 79972), who had joined the Metropolitan Police in October 1894 and had risen rapidly through the ranks. In 1896 he was appointed to clerical duty in the offices of the Commissioner, and was promoted in 1899 and 1901, becoming a Clerk Sergeant – a very responsible position. In 1907 he had been transferred to V or Wandsworth Division and not long after, in 1908, he was promoted to Inspector and transferred to B Division. John Syme investigated the circumstances of the arrest, and decided not to charge the men. This then required an entry to be made in the Refused Charge Book, at a time when officers were very likely to be formally disciplined if they had made an arrest which did not justify a charge. The Sub-Divisional Inspector berated the two constables, and then Inspector Syme defended the two officers by arguing that they should not be disciplined because the two drunks had not revealed the true facts to the officers before their arrest. Syme was fair, but very pedantic. His senior officers thought that he was too close to his junior officers and transferred him to another station. Syme complained. Matters escalated. Syme was suspended, reduced in rank to Station Sergeant, appealed to the Home Office, threatened to write to his MP, but was then treated as 'impossibly insubordinate' and was dismissed.

What was originally a trivial matter became far worse, as Syme's obsession increased and the situation escalated out of control. Syme was dismissed for approaching the Home Secretary, Winston Churchill, to appeal against his reduction to Sergeant and compulsory transfer for alleged insubordination. On 28th June 1911 the Central Criminal Court tried Syme for sending a threatening letter to murder Alfred Reed. On 4th July he was sentenced to six months' imprisonment without hard labour.[1257]

From this the 'Police Union' was founded in 1913 by the now ex-Inspector John Syme. From the outset, the Commissioner, Sir Edward Henry, made it clear that the union was an illegal body, and warned that any man found to belong to it would be dismissed. During World War One, Special Branch officers and military police raided union meetings and any policemen caught in the net were promptly dismissed and drafted into the army.[1258]

Ex Inspector John Syme on an advertising postcard explaining his plight

In March 1914, Syme was charged with publishing a defamatory libel, entitled 'Fighting Officialdom: A Three Years' battle against Police and Home Office Persecution', concerning the Commissioner of the Metropolitan Police, Sir Edward Henry. The trial R v Syme took place before the High Court of Justice, King's Bench Division, from 9th to 16th July 1914. He was sentenced to eight months' imprisonment, and on 29th July the Court of Criminal Appeal dismissed his appeal. Syme continued campaigning for an inquiry into his dismissal.

Syme gave up his quest in 1940 when he informed the Home Office that he had finished his campaign, and he died in 1945. In the meantime the Police Union became a recognised body as the Police Federation Staff Association.

The union's biggest obstacle to progress was actually John Syme himself, who had become so obsessed with his fight that he was becoming more unwell. Twice during the Great War he went to prison, once for threatening to kill the Prince of Wales, and then for criminally libelling Sir Edward Henry in a *Police Review* article. John Syme pursued his grievance for many years afterwards, including throwing stones at 10 Downing Street and organising a prototype police union.

When it was known in 1977 that Gerald Road Police Station might close, the vicar of St Peter's church, Eaton Square composed the following special prayer in verse:

Visit, we beseech thee, Lord
The station down at Gerald Road.
Drive far, we pray, the hostile snares
That come from Scotland Yard (upstairs)
And let thine angels dwell therein,
To keep the manor free from sin.

Accept each detainee's contrition
And guard it, Lord, from demolition.
Thus blest, it may yet with us stick;
Our very own, Saint Peter's nick!

It eventually closed in 1993.

Goffs Oak Police Station

Broxbourne District Council

In 1895 the police erected two adjoining cottages in Goffs Lane, at the junction of Newgate Street Road. They were built as a result of pressure from Lady Meux of Theobalds, who was suffering from poachers on her land.

In November 1896[1259] two police officers and their families occupied the buildings. One was a sergeant who paid four shillings a week, the other a constable who paid three shillings a week, for their accommodation. In addition, one side of the building also contained a police office entered through a lobby. There was also one cell.

Goffs Oak Police Station

During the 1930s it was decided to convert the police office into a living room for the police house, whilst the lobby was made into a police box for use by the public. Police continued to patrol the area, and then on 1st April 1965, due to an increase in population and work, a police office was opened in the building. This time the ground floor front room on the opposite end of the building was used as an office. The officers used the kitchen at the rear, and upstairs was left empty.[1260]

The police station closed on 31st October 1972 and the property reverted back to two separate police houses.

Golders Green Police Station

The London Borough of Barnet
69 Finchley Road, Golders Green (1914-2014)
S Division (1914-1993)
Borough of Barnet OCU (1993-2014)

On 21st July 1910 Superintendent Williams of S Division reported on the availability of a plot of land suitable as a site for a new police station in the main (Finchley) road at Golders Green. The site could be obtained freehold for £1,080. The Receiver decided against this particular site, but purchased a larger area opposite for £1,330 on 9th March 1911.[1261]

On 25th March 1911 the Receiver wrote a memorandum to the Commissioner on whether it was prudent to erect a small station at Golders Green bearing in mind the phenomenal rate at which the neighbourhood was growing. He recommended a much larger station should be built now rather than later, and that work should commence by the summer of 1912. On 3rd June 1911 the Secretary of State for the Home Department agreed to this proposal and approved the building of a large first class town station with a section house for not less than 25 officers instead of a cottage-type station.

On 12th August 1912 the Home Office authorised the acceptance of the tender submitted by Messrs J. Grover and Sons for the building of the police station. A station, section house and married accommodation for one family was built on the site, and on 24th September 1913 the Receiver notified the Commissioner that the station at Golders Green would be ready for occupation on 27th October 1913.

The new police station was taken into service on 3rd November, when the lodging assessment was fixed as follows:

'Married quarters (1 set) at 10s 6d per week and 27 unmarried men paying at one shilling each per week.'

Golders Green Police Station 1913-2014

Consequent upon the opening of the new police station at Golders Green, the boundaries of Finchley and Hampstead sub-divisions were revised.[1262] There was a change in status for the station when in August Finchley sub-division was altered

1257   Ibid.
1258   policecommunitysupportofficer.com/phpBB2/viewtopic.php?t=12389 accessed 15th August 2012.
1259   Metropolitan Police Orders dated 8th December 1896.
1260   Histed, Graham, Constable 531(YF). Unpublished report on Goffs Oak Police (undated).
1261   John Back Archive.
1262   Metropolitan Police Orders dated 31st October 1913.

from 1st September, to be known as Golders Green Sub-Division, and Golders Green enhanced its status to become the sub-divisional station.[1263]

Upon re-organisation of the divisions north of the Thames which took place on Friday, 1st December 1933, Golders Green remained a sub-divisionals of S or Hampstead Division, with Finchley as its Sectional Station.[1264]

In 1924 the location of the station was 7 St. George's Parade Finchley Road, NW11, however this was later changed to 1069 Finchley Road, Golders Green, NW3 (Temple Fortune) in 1930 when it was a sectional station of Finchley.

In 1933 it was given divisional status after a re-organisation of the divisions (part of the Trenchard re-structuring) which saw Albany Street transfer to D Division. Offices had been converted and a garage built as the building was made ready for the transfer of Superintendent Arthur Annis and his divisional support staff.[1265] The station code was then Sierra Delta (SD). Finchley remained S Division Headquarters until 1962, when Superintendent C.J. Dace was in charge of the sub-division,[1266] until 1966 when Dace moved to the Divisional office.

Taking over from Dace in 1966 was Superintendent M.J. Byrne with Chief Inspector D. Clelland as deputy, whilst the Divisional Superintendent was Chief Superintendent L.R. Balm.[1267]

A further re-organisation, this time involving the whole Force, occurred with the view of making the 'police boundaries co-terminous with those of the new local authorities.' This was a direct result of the passing of the London Government Act 1963. Golders Green, which was now the divisional headquarters of S Division, remained a sub-divisional station with Finchley still as its Sectional Station in the new London Borough of Barnet.[1268] The division was also part of No. 2 District, under the command of Commander R.E. Rogers MBE.

By the 1970s the 60-year-old station was in serious need of updating given the advances in technology and the need for computerisation. This meant that from 9.00am on 12th July, the divisional suite and staff (which included the senior officers as well) were moved into temporary accommodation at Borehamwood Police Station whilst extensive building work was carried out at Golders Green. Whilst the divisional suite was accommodated at Borehamwood the station code was changed to 'SD', whilst the new code for Golders Green became 'SG'.[1269]

The Finchley Press reported that this massive and costly facelift to the station at Temple Fortune would extend its life by a further 15 years, with improvements being made to the office areas and cell accommodation. It was reported that this was a far cheaper option than building a new station.[1270]

In 1990 the system of policing was changed at Golders Green and Finchley. Out went the four-relief system with the traditional inspector, three sergeants and up to 30 constables, and in came beat-based teams that became a forerunner to Safer Neighbourhood teams which exist today.[1271] Inspector Terrence Matthews, the author of an evaluation into beat policing at Golders Green, was placed in charge of the four beats of Cricklewood, Golders Green, Garden Suburb and East Finchley and the station itself. Each beat had four dedicated constables attached to it.

In November 2010 a new Safer Neighbourhoods base was opened at 61 Golders Green Road, which formed the base for the Safer Neighbourhood Teams (SNTs) of Golders Green and Childs Hill.[1272]

In 2014 the Golders Green Police Station freehold site was sold for £5.312M to a developer.[1273]

Grange Road Police Station (Bermondsey)

London Borough of Southwark
Watch House, Abbey Street (Junction of Bermondsey Street) (1829-1883)
67-69 Upper Grange Road, Bermondsey (1883-1940)
M Division (1829-1940)

Bermondsey Parish Church Watch House, at the junction of Abbey Street and Bermondsey Street, was built in 1820. By 1850 the property was recorded as being owned by Mr J. Greenwood of Arthur Street West, City, EC. The rental was £20 per annum for a period of 70 years.[1274]

The 1881 report into Metropolitan Police station commented:

"This station is not yet occupied, except by one married constable. It consists of two ordinary dwelling houses which it is proposed to adapt for police purposes. There appears to be vacant ground in rear of the houses, which it might be well to acquire as the freehold of the houses has been bought, and the yard space may be found too small." [1275]

Bermondsey's second police station opened in October 1883, and although known as the Grange Road Sub-Division it was actually situated at 67-69 Upper Grange Road (now Dunton Road). The building had been adapted under the supervision of John Butler, Metropolitan Police Surveyor. The total cost was £4,560, of which the freehold was £2,200.[1276] The new station had four inspectors, six sergeants and 66 constables. The L Division Special Constable shown right is dressed in a 5-button tunic, traditional flat cap with waterproof cover and duty armlet. The photograph was taken in about 1920.

L Division Special Constable

Bermondsey (Grange Road) Police Station 1883-1940

In 1935 the police station at 67 Upper Grange Road, was

renamed Dunton Road Police Station.

Dunton Road Police Station received a direct hit from a bomb during the Blitz, injuring seven people, and closed on 19th September 1940. All operations were transferred to Tower Bridge Police Station.[1277]

It was reported in 1974 that the old Watch House building was being used as a meeting place for local Boy Scouts.[1278]

Gray's Inn Road Police Station

London Borough of Camden

27 Gray's Inn Road (1898-1965)

E Division (1898-1965)

In December 1897 the *Police Review* commented on the opening of a new station in Grays Inn Road in the following terms:

"Another new station, which is nearly ready for business, is the handsome building in Gray's Inn Road. A noticeable feature in connection with these latest additions to our public offices is the acceptable innovation in the style of architecture. The outward appearance of the majority of the Metropolitan Stations is by no means pleasing even to an uncritical eye." [1279]

The freehold to this site was purchased in 1895, and plans were drawn up to build a new police station at the location shown as 27 Grays Inn Road. It was soon erected, and opened in January 1898[1280] in Gray's Inn Road just opposite Holborn Town Hall. The three-storey red brick building eventually provided accommodation for nearly 100 constables on the newly-created Holborn Section.

On the ground floor there was a spacious charge room on one side and the inspector's office at the other. On the first floor was the police officers' mess room and on the upper floor the dormitories, with sleeping accommodation for the single men. Inspector Miller, of Hunter Street Police Station, was in charge. The address of the station was shown as 27 and 29 Grays Inn Road, London WC1. The station closed in 1965 when operational policing was transferred to the new Holborn Police Station, and the old police station became a traffic warden centre.

Gray's Inn Road Police Station 1898-1965

In 1999 the old station was opened for operational purposes during the refurbishment of Holborn Police Station, which had temporarily closed. Once Holborn was finished Grays Inn Road Police was put up for sale and sold privately. As of 2019 it was the home of Matrix Chambers Barristers' quarters set up by Cherie Blair in 2000.

Great Marlborough Street Police Station

19-20 Great Marlborough Street (1829-1940)

C Division (1829-1940)

The court began its famous role in dispensing justice in London's West End under the 1792 Middlesex Justices Act when in 1793 21 Great Marlborough Street was adapted for use as one of the public or police offices created by the Act. The premises also covered ground to the rear, in Marlborough Mews (now Ramillies Place).

The Metropolitan Police undertook operations from Great Marlborough Street from 1829, but in 1856 the Receiver took a lease on the house at No. 20 and let it out, but used the ground at the rear to extend the police station.

A 1910 photograph of 19-20 Great Marlborough Street

1263 Metropolitan Police Orders dated 29th August 1930.
1264 Metropolitan Police Orders dated 28th November 1933.
1265 Metropolitan Police Surveyor's records 1924.
1266 *The Police List* 1962.
1267 *The Police List* 1966.
1268 Metropolitan Police Orders dated 6th August 1964.
1269 Metropolitan Police Orders dated 9th July 1971.
1270 *Finchley Press*, 7th January 1972.
1271 The Annual Report of the Golders Green and Finchley Division 1990
1272 intranet.aware.mps/corporate/newarchive2010/11november210/sntbases.
1273 MPS (2019) Freedom of information request – Police station closures broken down by year.
1274 MEPO4/234.
1275 Surveyor's Report 1881.
1276 Ten Year Report Jan 1884 – Dec 1893.
1277 Bernard Brown personal correspondence.
1278 *South London Press*, 4th June 1974.
1279 *Police Review*, December 1897.
1280 Metropolitan Police Orders dated 22nd January 1898.

Great Scotland Yard looking west toward Whitehall, with the Metropolitan Police Office entrance on the left, and the A Division police station behind railings on the right

The freeholds were purchased in 1892 and a new police station was built at No. 20. No. 19 was bought from the Elwes family in 1912 and a new building, replacing numbers 19, 20 and 21, was designed by J.D. Butler and built by Patman and Fotheringham the following year.

Like Bow Street, the new building boasted a distinguished stone frontage shared by the court and police station, and continued as a bustling, busy court until its final closure in 2006.

The court heard many cases involving famous people, including John Lennon and Yoko Ono (cannabis possession, 1968), Mick Jagger and Marianne Faithfull (cannabis possession, 1969) and Keith Richards (drugs possession and unlicensed firearms, 1973). Early in his career, Charles Dickens reported on the stream of characters that passed through the court, and it was here that Oscar Wilde began his infamous case against the Marquess of Queensbury that ended in Wilde's downfall.

According to a London newspaper, one of the court's famous magistrates, Mr St. John Harmsworth, once acquitted a political demonstrator on the basis that his egg throwing was 'a time-honoured tradition of British political life'. Many call girls marked the occasion of his retirement by sending him cards, acknowledging his fair sense of justice; he responded by writing off many of their fines!

On Jubilee night 1887 Elizabeth Cass, a 23-year-old seamstress new to London, went out to watch the celebrations but became separated from her companions, and started to wander a rather circuitous route around the Oxford Circus area. PC Bowden Endicott started to observe her movements, including apparently approaching three different gentlemen, and then arrested her for disorderly conduct. She was duly charged with behaviour amounting to soliciting for prostitution, and was let off with a warning by the magistrate. Mme. Bowman, Elizabeth Cass's employer, wrote furious letters of protest to the Commissioner, Sir Charles Warren, who then held a formal inquiry to determine whether any action should be taken against Constable Endacott. The case continued to cause controversy, even to the extent of being debated in Parliament. The evidence of Endacott and the character of Elizabeth Cass were both put under great scrutiny, with the case encapsulating the fears of Victorian police critics who feared that police officers would either blackmail prostitutes or harass innocent, respectable women.[1281] Later, Sir Howard Vincent informed the 1908 Royal Commission that Miss Cass had been pregnant at the time and had led an immoral life, factors that may have led the champions against PC Endacott to have espoused her cause with less enthusiasm.

Policing from Great Marlborough Street ceased when West End Central police station was opened in 1940.

Great Scotland Yard

City of Westminster

Palace Place, Great Scotland Yard (c.1850-1889)

A Division

Access to Great Scotland Yard was through an arch from the east side of Whitehall just south of The Clarence public house that still stands today. The original headquarters of the Metropolitan Police was 4 Whitehall Place, the back entrance of which was in Great Scotland Yard. The *Morning Post* of 8th October 1829 reported 'A new station-house for the Metropolitan Police has been opened in Great Scotland yard opposite the Marshalsea Court, Whitehall.' This can be seen on the extreme left of the picture left.

The building seen on the right with a clock on its façade was the Marshalsea court house. Originally set up to have jurisdiction over the Sovereign's travelling court, Marshalsea Court was also linked with the Palace Court created by King Charles II, and this in turn may have been the reason why these buildings on the north side of Great Scotland Yard became known as Palace Place. Marshalsea prison, which remained located in Southwark after the court house moved from King Street Southwark to Great Scotland Yard, became well known in later years for incarcerating people for debt, as happened with Charles Dickens' father. When the court was abolished in 1849 the building seems to have been taken over by the Metropolitan Police and is marked as an A Division station on the 1871 Ordnance Survey map.

After the Metropolitan Police moved to New Scotland Yard on Victoria Embankment in 1889 the area was redeveloped. A substantial building was erected that included the site of the police station and became an Army Recruiting Depot. This building was in turn converted to a hotel in 2019. The square erection to be seen to the left of the police station was a water cistern that was subsequently incorporated into a new building, erected in 1874, that accommodated the Public Carriage Office on its ground floor, and CID officers on the floor above. It was subsequently the subject of a bomb attack by Fenians in 1884.

The Public Carriage Office building in Great Scotland Yard 1874-1880. It seems also to have been referred to as the Police Central Office

Greek Street Police Station

58 Greek Street (1829-c.1832)

C Division (1829-c.1832)

Greek Street runs north-south from Tottenham Court Road towards Leicester Square and Chinatown. No. 58 Greek Street was occupied by C Division in 1829, and had been turned over to the police from the parochial authorities for use as a police station. Originally erected in 1733, the station house was situated in front of the local water pump where people would gather. The premises were subject of much alteration over the years, and its ground floor, like many premises in the area, is now a restaurant. The station was no longer in use by 1832[1282] as other more suitable premises were found.

Greenford Police Station

The London Borough of Ealing

21 Oldfield Road (1896-2013)

T Division (1829-1865)

X Division (1865-2013)

Prior to new cottages being built in 1896, it appears that a room in a sergeant's house was used as a police office. Greenford is mentioned in Police Orders of 11th January 1864 as designated as part of T Division.[1283] There were no cells in the accommodation, but charges were taken there. The strength was one sergeant and nine constables, and the inspector at Hanwell was not posted for duty at a station but had to patrol and supervise Hanwell, Harrow and Greenford.[1284]

Mention was made as follows of Greenford Police Station in 1881: 'The police pay only a portion of the rent of a cottage in the village, which was occupied by an inspector.'[1285]

Due to the formation of three new Divisions – W or Clapham, X or Paddington and Y or Highgate – Greenford became annexed to the Exterior Districts of X Division.[1286] In 1872 there was a report from District Superintendent Robert Walker about Hanwell Sub-Division stating that there was a house to let at Greenford Green that was suitable for police purposes. This apparently was not taken up, because in 1889 another mention is made that new premises were needed as the sergeant, whose house the room was used as a police office, had retired. Arising out of this, a portion of land was bought (freehold) from Mr Bishop for £300 in 1892, next door to the White Hart public house in Oldfield Lane.

In 1894 constable Frederick Owen was the acting sergeant at Greenford police station.[1287]

Subsequently, new cottages were taken into occupation for police on 12th October 1896 at a cost of £1,740.[1288] The station was known as "The Police Station, Oldfield Lane". This was changed in 1936 to read 21 Oldfield Lane,[1289] later Oldfield Road.

Greenford Police Station 1896-2013

1281 Fido, M. and Skinner, K (1999) *The Official Encyclopedia of Scotland Yard*. Virgin, London.
1282 Return of Mops (1832) Metropolitan Police.
1283 Metropolitan Police Orders 11th January 1864.
1284 J. Back archive c1975.
1285 Metropolitan Police Condition of Police Stations 1881.
1286 Metropolitan Police Orders dated 28th October 1865.
1287 *Kelly's Directory of Middlesex* 1894.
1288 Metropolitan Police Orders dated 10th October 1896.
1289 J. Back archive c1975.

In 1911 there were two police families living at Greenford Police Station. The first was Police Sergeant Peter Sherwood, his wife Eliza and their two sons. They occupied five rooms in the station. The other occupant was Police Constable William Bowler Lowe, his wife Harriet and their two children, who occupied four rooms.[1290]

Also in 1911 there was a James Hitchcock, an 83-year-old retired sergeant living at Holly Cottage, Northolt Road, Greenford with his wife Jane Ann Hitchcock. When completing the census form he could only make his mark, and he got Police Sergeant Sherwood, mentioned above, to countersign his census form. One of the conditions stipulated when joining the Metropolitan Police was that you were required to read and write. It may be that James Hitchcock, at 83-years-old, was too frail to sign the for himself. When he retired from the police in 1881 he became the publican of the White Horse public house, Greenford. He was born in Northolt, and in 1871 had been living with his family in Kensington.[1291]

The London Government Act 1963 aligning police to local government boundaries was introduced on 1st April 1965. Greenford (XG) was shown as a sub-divisional station, but a footnote added 'Pending rebuilding of Greenford sub-divisional Station, the sub-divisional Headquarters will be Southall.'[1292]

In 1974 the high quality of the garden at Greenford was recognised and it won an award under the annual police garden competition.

Greenford Police Station garden being tended by Constable Norman Chatland

There was a later revision of boundaries on X Division, and Greenford Police Station reverted to police office status in 1977.[1293]

In 2013 the police station was closed to the public,[1294] but as of 2019 it was still retained for other operational purposes.[1295]

Greenwich Police Station

The London Borough of Greenwich
Rose Cottage, 1 Orchard Lane (1829-1836)
Blackheath Road (1836-1962)
31 Royal Hill (1962-1993)
R Division (1829-1993)
Borough of Greenwich OCU (1993-2018)

There have been at least four police stations built in the Greenwich area over the past 200 years, namely in Greenwich Road, Blackheath Road, Parkway and Trafalgar Road.

A Cage was erected to house prisoners in 1822 in Greenwich Road, on the corner of Cut-throat Lane.[1296] When the new Police were formed there in 1829, a Watch House called Rose Cottage was taken over in Greenwich Road. There was one other station on R Division, and this was located in Lucas Street, Rotherhithe[1297] (now called Cathay Street), but its actual address was 23 Paradise Street.[1298]

Dominating the area is the Royal Naval College (formally the Royal Hospital, moved from Portsmouth in 1873) and the Royal Hospital School behind it. Premises at 2 Queen Elizabeth's Row, Greenwich, shown as a detached office of the R Division[1299] next door to the Alms Houses and opposite Greenwich Railway Station, were offered to the Police prior to 1832. In February 1834 the Home Office recommended that the premises, which were owned by a Mr Wright, were suitable as a police station and should be leased at £40 per annum.[1300]

Inspector Francis M. Mallalieu, who was promoted to Superintendent in 1835, took command of R Division and briefly had his Divisional Headquarters at this station prior to its move to Blackheath Road. The Greenwich Police Station address was shown as 1 Orchard Lane, Greenwich.[1301] The Inspector in charge of the Sub-Division at the time was James Douglas, who had been promoted to Inspector in 1840.[1302]

In 1840 the boundary of Greenwich Division consisted of the parishes of Greenwich; St. Nicholas, Deptford; part of St. Paul's Deptford, in the county of Kent; Lewisham and Lee in Kent; Rotherhithe; that part of St Pauls, Deptford, in Surrey; and the hamlet of Hatcham.[1303] Because the Division covered a large area with semi-rural villages, and to enable them to patrol and supervise the division, the superintendent and inspectors were trained in the art of horsemanship. As travelling by horse and cart was the normal mode of transport at that time, it was common for people to be experienced in riding horses.

Blackheath Road Police Station, Greenwich 1836-1910

In 1836 the Home Office approved another police station, called Greenwich – Blackheath Road, as they considered the old station in Greenwich Road no longer fit for purpose. The new premises had been leased from Mr Thomas Pocknell for 50 years at an annual rent of £200, and there was a requirement to insure the premises for £4,000. The station was positioned along a busy thoroughfare running from New Cross Road, over Deptford Bridge and towards Blackheath Hill Railway Station. Located on the north side of the road, the station was positioned between Greenwich Road and Egerton Road on the edge of Deptford New Town.

Before separate Dockyard Police were formed it was the responsibility of R Division to provide security and post police officers there on duty. The Police and Constabulary List of 1844 shows that Inspector James Douglas, who had been promoted in 1840, was in charge of Blackheath Road Station, Greenwich. Improvements in communication in 1844 saw Blackheath Road Station linked to Scotland Yard by telegraph. Superintendent T.W. Baxter[1304] was in charge of the Division at this time. A published list in 1898 shows Greenwich to have the code Romeo Delta (RD).[1305]

Policing in Victorian times could be a dangerous occupation, with R Division being an especially difficult area. For example, in 1852 Sergeant Joseph Rendall died of injuries which he received during an accident while on duty on Greenwich Division,[1306] and a number of officers had also been killed on the Division under mysterious circumstances. Sergeant Arthur Gaynor died of head injuries in 1879; Sergeant William Bacon drowned whilst on duty at Greenwich coal wharves in 1881, and Constable Edwin Cousins died of injuries received in 1886. Constable Frederick Arnup died of a stroke whilst on duty in 1899, and Constable Richard Crabb died of spinal injuries in 1900.[1307]

A revision of boundaries in 1864 introduced a number of new Divisions, mirroring growth in the general population of London.[1308] This led to the establishing of W Division, and meant that Greenwich Division was reduced in area to make it a more equal and manageable size.

In 1864 the station strength was two inspectors, two sergeants, one acting sergeant, eleven day duty and 28 night duty constables, and a number of A Division Officers who were kept on reserve at the station. These included one inspector, two sergeants and nine constables. The station had ten beats, and stables for thirteen horses. There were two horses for supervision, one to be ridden by the superintendent, and the other for the use of the two inspectors on day and night duty, each riding the horse alternately. Five horses were available for the van, which was used to transfer prisoners from court to prisons.[1309]

By 1869 land had been leased in Blackheath Road from the estate of Thomas Pocknell of George's Place, Exeter, initially for five years but later extended until 1944. A building and stables were present and later refurbished, with extensive work being done to the existing building and a new section house, for the accommodation of 37 single constables, was built. Firearms were issued to stations, because occasionally criminals would take weapons with them to commit a crime. Adams breech-loading revolvers and ammunition were supplied to Metropolitan Police Divisions. Divisional Headquarters were issued with ten revolvers in August 1868, later supplemented with a further eleven weapons in January 1869, bringing the total number held on R Division to 39 firearms. Some ten rounds of ammunition were issued with each firearm.[1310]

As the area expanded it was necessary that security was required at vulnerable premises containing property so, as docks were being built to supply London's huge appetite, police officers were sent there on duty. In 1869 R Division supplied a total of four constables to the Surrey Commercial Docks.

The Commissioner sanctioned recreation and games rooms in July 1869, and these were places where off duty officers could smoke. He paid for a billiard table and games such as draughts, dominoes, backgammon and single sticks, as well as boxing gloves for their entertainment and exercise.

Billiard tables were generally reserved for Headquarters Stations like Blackheath Road, so the other R Division Stations – Rotherhithe, Deptford, Woolwich, Shooters Hill, Bexley, Eltham and Lee just received the games.[1311] The introduction of these measures helped to ensure that single officers remained in the station during their off duty hours and stopped them from getting bored, frequenting public houses, drinking too much, incurring debts or fraternising too much with the locals, who were perceived as villainous. Alcoholism was a problem at the time, since people often would drink beer rather than trust the water. The Divisional Superintendent commended the use of recreation rooms, and in 1871 suggested in his annual report to the Commissioner that a billiard table ought to be introduced at all stations where police reside.[1312]

Cattle plague was a problem in 1870, and farmers and drovers would herd their cattle to market by driving them along the main roads into the capital. Cattle drovers were required to stop at Police-manned posts on the boundary of any Division where the cattle would be inspected for signs of disease.

Outer-lying Divisions and other locations had checking points like railway stations, wharves or boundary points. R Division had eight boundary posts which were manned day and night by 24 constables.[1313] With the opening of the New Foreign Cattle Market at Deptford Dockyard (owned by the City of London Corporation) it meant a reduction in the numbers of police officers employed for cattle plague duty on the boundary roads.[1314]

Later, in 1871, a new set of six stables were added to the six which were already present, costing in total £890 9s. In addition to the new stables a harness room, loft, a cart house and a van house were also added, all located in the grounds of the station. The van was for the transfer of prisoners from the adjacent courthouse to the prisons. Alterations to the section house and station in 1877 cost the sum of £1,854 11s, and a range of public and private rooms were located beneath the section house.

1290 Census 1911.
1291 Census 1871, 1881 and 1911.
1292 Metropolitan Police Orders dated 6th August 1964.
1293 Metropolitan Police Order dated 26th August 1977.
1294 Metropolitan Police Information Rights Unit 19th November 2017, accessed 25th January 2019.
1295 MPS (2019) Freedom of Information – MPS police stations closed since 2010.
1296 John Back Archive (1975).
1297 Register for the Return of Mops from Cleaners, dated 1st July 1832.
1298 Chris Lordon, *History of Rotherhithe* (2008).
1299 Metropolitan Cleaning records dated August 1832.
1300 John Back Archive (1975).
1301 *Post Office London Directory* 1838.
1302 *The Police and Constabulary List* (1844).
1303 Order of Greenwich Council 3rd October 1840, cited in *The Police and Constabulary List* (1844).
1304 *Post Office Directory* 1879.
1305 Metropolitan Police General Orders 1893.
1306 Metropolitan Police Roll of Honour at www.policememorial.org.uk accessed 12th March 2002.
1307 Ibid.
1308 Metropolitan Police Orders dated 28th October 1865.
1309 Metropolitan Police Orders 11th January 1864.
1310 Metropolitan Police Orders dated 28th January 1869.
1311 Metropolitan Police Orders dated 15th July 1869.
1312 *Report of the Commissioner of the Metropolis* 1871.
1313 *Report of the Commissioner of the Metropolis* 1870.
1314 *Report of the Commissioner of the Metropolis* 1871

The rear yard of Blackheath Road Police Station in 1911

Somewhat strangely, the prisoners who were kept at the station were taken upstairs to three cells, which were allocated on the first floor. This is odd since it was usual for prisoners to be housed in cells on the ground floor since these were set in concrete foundations thus making escape more difficult, while determined prisoner in an upstairs room could seek an escape by taking up floorboards. At some later stage the three cells were increased to five and a 'drunk-tank', called here an 'association cell', was added. The association cell allowed for the retention of a number of prisoners together during raids or for drunken prisoners.

Greenwich continued to be the Divisional Station of R Division in 1873, covering a large area of south London and remaining important enough to have an inspector in charge. Other Inspector Stations included Woolwich (William Street) Lee Road, Shooters Hill, Rotherhithe (Paradise Street) and Prince Street, Deptford. Sergeants were placed in charge at East Greenwich (Park Row), Eltham, St Mary Cray, Sidcup, Bexleyheath, Erith and Deptford (Foreign Cattle market). Greenwich was one of the largest stations on the Division and it was often the way that the most senior officers would also reside there, however the incumbent superintendent resided at East Greenwich Station instead.

Trams were introduced in 1871 between East Greenwich and Canal Bridge and between Deptford Bridge and Blackheath Hill.[1315] These changes in transport added to the general traffic travelling along the main roads of the Division, making Police road traffic duty more complex.

In 1881 Police Sergeant Donald Walters, a married man who came from Caithness in Scotland, was shown resident at the station. Records do not show if his wife resided with him. On the night of the census not only those on duty but also those who were resident at the section house and prisoners in the cells were counted. This totalled some 31 police officers,[1316] although the allocation was 33 single officers, which by 1883 had been revised down to 28 beds.[1317]

In 1882 a CID office was created on the first floor of the old stable block attached to the station; originally this was part of the section house that accommodated four single constables. There were six rooms of various sizes used on the first floor to house single officers in a section house. The annual rent was £225; however this was defrayed as section house charges amounted to £93 12s pa. Police officers who were resident were allocated a certain square footage of space for themselves, as it was recognised that more space improved conditions of health and hygiene. Because of this the allocation was increased to 600 sq ft per officer in February 1883.[1318]

A notification in Police Orders in 1884 indicated that the station was allocated a postal address of 4 Blackheath Road, Greenwich.[1319] By the start of the twentieth century the Division covered 60½ square miles from the Thames to Chislehurst and the Crays.[1320] Extra cells had been added to the station in February 1888, and at the same time the section house allocation was revised down to 26 beds.[1321] Increases in station strengths and re-organisation of areas often took place, and Deptford and Blackheath Road Sub-Divisions merged in January 1898. The new Sub-Division was called Blackheath Road, and Police Orders showed that Deptford lost its Sub-Divisional Inspector whilst the Sub-Division gained an additional inspector.[1322] Freehold was purchased in 1899 for £9,000 from Edward Pocknell, and this was proportioned as £2,800 for the court and £6,200 for the station.[1323]

Permission to build a new station in Blackheath Road was approved by the Home Office and completed in 1910, with new married quarters being brought into service a year later.[1324] This also included a court building. The cost of lodging was 11s 6d per week (one set of married quarters), 5s per week (one set of married quarters, one unmarried sergeant's quarters at 2s per week, and 51 single constables still paid only 1s per week each.

Sub-Divisional Inspectors (Greenwich):

John Jackson: 1893-5
Walter Lee: 1895-1905
William Crostan: 1905-08
Thomas Hill: 1908-09
Arthur Pullen: 1911-17

In 1914 R Division was described as "an area of London with closely packed towns, many villages and great stretches of smiling countryside".[1325] The outbreak of war saw the Special Constabulary quickly established under the leadership of Major Bradford Atkinson at Blackheath Road, with units at Westcombe Park, Woolwich, Plumstead, Belvedere, Bexley, Erith, Sidcup, Lee Road, Chislehurst and St. Mary Cray.[1326] There were 32 vulnerable points on the Division, and it needed every man to cover these places. These included water works, railways, power stations, railway tunnels and telephone exchanges. Soon Major Atkinson was recalled to the Army, and his place was taken over by Commander R.G.J. Rawlinson from Lee Road. He struck up a good relationship with Divisional Superintendent A.D. Smith, who was often seen in the front passenger seat of his private motor-car visiting the vulnerable points, often at considerable speed.[1327]

The Divisional strength in 1915 was 985 regular men, which by 1918 had reduced to 726 because many more men went to fight the enemy. One of the problems for the Commander was maintaining the strength of the Specials, and 597 men left to join the forces. The death rate on the Division was fortunately low, even though many of the Special Constables travelled long distances at great risk of bombing by Gotha bombers, biplanes, and airships. Many Specials used their own transport like their Commander, and bought petrol even though it was in short supply.[1328]

The picture below shows Greenwich Police Court and Police Station in Blackheath Road in about 1907. The station is situated on the left, and the Inspector is standing by the front entrance. Greenwich Police Court and Station was designed and built by the Receiver, and like the one illustrated was adjacent to the station. Operationally this made for ease of transport for prisoners, and often when the courts shut for the day any remaining prisoners would be securely transferred next door.

Anti-German feeling spread, with people breaking the windows of shops and attacking likely suspects, with the main troubles occurring in Deptford, Greenwich, Woolwich and Plumstead. The Specials supplemented the ranks of the

Greenwich Police Station and Court (right), Blackheath Road 1910-1962

regulars to stem the angry uprising and their contribution was recognised when the Commissioner issued a letter thanking those who took part.

The Special Constabulary also played a significant part in mapping where the bombs fell each day and night, and gathering evidence of injuries, death and damage. Each Division was required to complete a log of events, and the information was recorded centrally. This was so that the Government could assess the death toll, aggregate the cost of the damage and set about the repair. Additionally, the authorities would minimise the publicity by placing restrictions on the reporting on the death toll and damage, thereby ensuring that the enemy would not capitalise on their attacks.

Bombing raids over London between 1914 and 1918 showed that 83 bombs were dropped on Greenwich, and such was in the inaccuracy seven fell in Greenwich Park and Blackheath.[1329] Many bombs fell along main roadways and in towns where lights could be found. The Police strictly enforced the Blackout Regulations, and people who failed to comply were initially warned and thereafter prosecuted.

During the First World War, whilst on duty at Greenwich Station Sergeant William James Wheller took his own life in 1917 as a result of injuries he had earlier received earlier.[1330] It was said that he was insane at the time, which was probably written on his death certificate to help relatives since it was at the time a criminal offence to commit suicide.

Blackheath Road Constable Leonard Dunn, shown on the following page, has an interesting record. He joined the Police Service in January 1920 with warrant number 108747. Born in the East End of London, he was a fitter's mate who had seen service in the Royal Navy during the war from September 1917 until May 1919.

He is wearing the Police Long Service Medal (instituted in 1951), and British War Medal for his service in the Royal Navy during the First World War.

On 1st April 1929 he was posted as PC656 R Division to Blackheath Road, where he remained for the rest of his service. He lived in Plumstead High Street with his wife and three children. The photograph was taken between 1936 and 1938, when the new helmet plate was introduced. He served over 33 years, and retired in 1953 with a Certificate of Service that showed his conduct to have been exemplary.

1315 *Report of the Commissioner of the Metropolis 1871.*
1316 Census 1881.
1317 Metropolitan Police Surveyor's Records.
1318 Ibid.
1319 Metropolitan Police Orders 20th June 1884.
1320 Brown, B. (2001) '"Romeo" – Law and Order in Old Greenwich (Part 2 1900-2000)' in *Bygone Kent* Vol. 22 No. 3 March edition.
1321 Metropolitan Police Surveyor's Records.
1322 Metropolitan Police Orders dated 28th January 1898.
1323 Metropolitan Police Surveyor's Records.
1324 Metropolitan Police Orders dated 8th December 1911.
1325 Reay, W. T. (1920) *The Specials.* Heineman, London.
1326 Ibid.
1327 Ibid.
1328 Ibid.
1329 Clout, H. (1997) *The Times London History Atlas*, Times Books, London.

Constable Leonard Dunn c1953

This is somewhat strange, since Dunn had been disciplined four times during his service. His most serious violation occurred during the Second World War. One morning in May 1942, as he was trying to sleep after coming off night duty, a cat in a neighbouring garden was making a lot of noise, preventing him from sleeping. Dunn took his Police issue revolver, aimed at the cat, fired and killed it – making sure he got his sleep. The neighbour, unsurprisingly, complained at the Police Station. Dunn originally denied shooting the cat to his Sergeant, which got him into even more trouble. He was disciplined by the Divisional Superintendent for the offence of discreditable conduct for killing the cat and reprimanded, whilst lying to the Sergeant cost him one day's pay. Dishonesty was treated harshly, whilst killing the cat deserved just a telling off! Dunn retired aged 55, living a further six years, and died in August 1959. In the early days, because of the nature of the job, police officers did not live long in retirement.[1331]

In 1921 there were a number of divisional boundary changes with the formation of Z or Croydon Division. Deptford Police Station was transferred from R to M or Southwark Division, and the boundary of Blackheath Road was altered.[1332] In 1928 the Superintendent in charge was Alfred J. Barrett.[1333] The address of the new police station was 7 Blackheath Road, Greenwich.[1334]

Such was the general condition of the Police those officers who were suffering from poor health or injuries could be pensioned off by the Chief Medical Officer if they could no longer perform the daily responsibilities of a police officer. This was the case in 1933, when Constable Albert Earnest Packer was pensioned from the Police and died shortly after from injuries received during an assault in 1932.[1335]

Police boxes introduced in 1934 were located on the Sub-Division at Tunnel Avenue, Box No. R2; Shooters Hill Road, at the junction with Dartmouth Terrace, Box No. R7; Tranquil Avenue, Blackheath, Box No. R19; together with two posts, one in the Blackwall tunnel, Box No. R40 and Tunnel Approach, Box No. R40A.[1336]

During the early part of WWII Greenwich and Woolwich became the front line for German air attacks, where the dock areas and munitions works were the main targets. It was later in the war when the worst of the damage was caused to the area, as Hitler launched his vengeance weapons – the V1 'doodlebugs' and V2 rockets. This caused devastation and panic, killing 9,200 people and injuring a further 22,000 others in London. Some 82 doodlebugs fell in Woolwich alone, whilst 73 hit Greenwich. In total Greenwich and Woolwich were hit by over 40 V2s.[1337] Croydon suffered worst of all the boroughs, with a total of 140 doodlebugs exploding in its area.[1338]

A bomb killed Special Constable Leonard Francis Clarke whilst he was guarding a disabled enemy aircraft downed at Woolwich in 1940, and Constable James Frederick Tottey was also killed by a bomb as he left his home to assist during an air raid in 1941.[1339] Also in 1940, the police station in Greenwich was struck, killing Special Sub-Inspector Herbert Linkins, Special Constable Ronald Lewis, Special Sergeant George Martin and Constable William Locke.[1340]

The station was still in service after the war and there were signs that it was no longer fit for its purpose. But that wasn't apparent until an inspection visit by Assistant Commissioner D Department in 1951 to Greenwich Police Station left the Chief Officer disturbed, since many of the section house rooms were being used for Police operational purposes. Clearly, the station had outlived its purpose so he gave instructions for a new site to be found in the vicinity of the Town Hall as soon as possible. Later that year a new site was found for a Divisional Headquarters and police station in Greenwich, but because of post-war economics there was no rush to build the station. It wasn't until May 1962 that the new station was completed and opened for operational purposes at 31 Royal Hill, Greenwich to replace East Greenwich and Blackheath Road Police Stations.[1341]

Greenwich Police Station 1962-2018

With the station were built eighteen sets of married quarters at Gloucester Circus, Greenwich.[1342] Maurice Drummond Section House also closed at the same time for refurbishment.

There are a number of officers attached to the Metropolitan Police who appear on the Roll of Honour and who died whilst stationed at Greenwich. In 1960 PC Leslie Edwin Vincent Meehan was mortally wounded when he was run over by a vehicle he had stopped and which then had driven off with the Officer clinging to the side.[1343]

The section house finally closed in July 1995 and was leased out, although the firing range in the basement was still in use.[1344] This became a Headquarters Station, and housed the District Commander and staff who were responsible for M, P and R Divisions, although the Divisional staff used to managing day-to-day operational policing of Greenwich were based at Eltham Police Station.[1345]

Blackheath Road was one of four Stations to pilot the Team Policing system in what was an exercise in saturation policing. The 'Aberdeen Scheme', as it was called (because it came from there), involved a sergeant who had the use of a wireless car who would ferry his officers and flood each area at a time during every shift. This became the forerunner to the Special Patrol Group introduced in 1965.

The London Government Act 1963 caused some boundary changes south of the Thames. Greenwich remained the Divisional Headquarters of R Division and a Sub-Divisional Station (RD), with Westcombe Park (RK) as its sectional station.[1346] By 1970 all the blue 'TARDIS' police boxes were being removed, although a red one remained near to Blackwall Tunnel southern approach entrance for some years after.[1347] Unit beat policing, the introduction of the Panda car and the personal radio heralded the demise of the police box.

Changes occurred with the demise of the GLC in 1984 when R District Office and Headquarters staff relocated to Eltham (RD), where it remained until 1999 when Borough based policing was introduced.[1348] Eltham was to remain as a Sub-Divisional Station.[1349]

Since April 1999 policing in London has become Borough-based, with boundaries for the Police following those of the local authority. Each Borough now has a Borough Commander in charge. From 2008 Greenwich housed the Criminal Justice Unit and the Crime Management Unit, as well as the South Area Telephone Switching Centre.

The old married quarters called Swanne House, situated behind the station, was in 2008 still used by a number of other administrative units.[1350]

The station site, together with Swanne House flats 1-18, fetched £11.45M purchased by London Square Developments in March 2018.[1351]

Hackney Police Station

The London Borough of Hackney

Jerusalem Square (1831)

Church Street (1832-1845)

1 Churchyard (1845-1886)

422 Mare Street (1886-1904)

2 Lower Clapton Road (1904-1993)

N Division (1831-1886)

J Division (1886-1965)

G Division (1965-1993)

Borough of Hackney OCU (1993-2014)

There have been a number of stations in the Borough of Hackney over the years. The original station house was situated in Jerusalem Square, Hackney Church Street, Hackney Old Town.[1352] The property in this area was demolished in 1906, and the road passing through it was named Vallette Street.[1353]

Site of the original Hackney Police Station in Jerusalem Square in 1831

The local census records of 1831 show that twelve police officers were resident there, together with Robert Messinger, the blacksmith. A number of police officers lived nearby in Jerusalem Passage. One such officer was Constable William Gillett, who joined the Metropolitan Police as the 999th applicant on 21st September 1829, being posted to N Division on 30th June 1830.[1354] Promotion was fast in those times, as he resigned as a Superintendent in July 1835.[1355] Also living nearby was Constable William Underwood, who was the 2,694th applicant to be accepted on 4th February 1830. He also became a Superintendent, in May 1831, resigning in April 1838.[1356] The officer in charge of Hackney Police Station in 1844 was shown as Inspector William D. Cooper, who was promoted in 1837.[1357] Hackney was shown as a station on N or Islington Division.

In 1845 a substantial brick and slate building was occupied at 1 Churchyard,[1358] Hackney Old Town, on the south side of St. John's Church Yard at the corner of what is now Mare Street.[1359] This was the second Hackney Police Station, and was designated with an Inspector in charge. The address of the building then was shown as Hackney Church Street, however it was later renamed and numbered as 422 Mare Street.[1360]

Records also indicate that the Receiver leased the land in 1848 from J.R.D. Lesson of Hackney for 99 years, and paid £20 per year ground rent for the property. The Receiver paid all the taxes, and insured the building with the Law Office for £1,700.

1330 Metropolitan Police Roll of Honour at www.policememorial.org.uk accessed 12th March 2002.
1331 Metropolitan Police Records.
1332 Metropolitan Police Orders dated 24th February 1921.
1333 *Post Office Directory* 1928.
1334 *Police and Constabulary Almanac* 1937.
1335 Metropolitan Police Roll of Honour at www.policememorial.org.uk accessed 12th March 2002.
1336 Brown, B. (2001) '"Romeo" – Law and Order in Old Greenwich' (part 2 1900-2000) in *Bygone Kent* Vol. 22 No 3.
1337 Clout, H. (1997) *The Times London History Atlas*, Times Books, London.
1338 Ibid.
1339 Metropolitan Police Roll of Honour at www.policememorial.org.uk accessed 12th March 2002.
1340 Ibid.
1341 John Back Archive (1975).
1342 Ibid.
1343 Metropolitan Police Roll of Honour at www.policememorial.org.uk accessed 12th March 2002.
1344 Section House Closure programme, Surveyor's Department (1997).
1345 'History of Greenwich' at intranet.aware.mps/BOCU_eh/Greenwich accessed 5th March 2008.
1346 John Back Archive (1975).
1347 Brown, B. (2001) '"Romeo" – Law and Order in Old Greenwich' (part 2 1900-2000) in *Bygone Kent* Vol. 22 No 3.
1348 'History of Greenwich' at intranet.aware.mps/BOCU_eh/Greenwich accessed 5th March 2008.
1349 Metropolitan Police Orders dated 15th October 1984.
1350 'History of Greenwich' at intranet.aware.mps/BOCU_eh/Greenwich accessed 5th March 2008.
1351 MPS Information Rights Unit (2019) Freedom of Information – Land and property sold by the MPS for over £1M.
1352 Census 1831.
1353 *Bacon's Atlas of London and Suburbs* 1926 by G.W. Bacon, London.
1354 Metropolitan Police Recruiting ledgers for the first 3,000 Metropolitan Police officers.
1355 Metropolitan Police Orders dated 17th July 1835.
1356 Metropolitan Police Recruiting ledgers for the first 3,000 Metropolitan Police officers.
1357 *The Police and Constabulary List* 1844. Parker, Furnivall and Parker, London.
1358 The Police station address at a later date changed from 1 Churchyard to Hackney Church Street.
1359 *Bacon's Atlas* 1888.
1360 Metropolitan Police General Orders 1873.

Hackney Police Station, 1 ChurchYard (later Mare Street) 1845-1904

In 1852, at a cost of £1,832 (including the leasehold for £850), substantial alterations were made to the existing building. These included a brick-dressed surround to the front of the ground floor, showing prominent arched windows either side of an arched front entrance. It had twenty rooms with four cells, a four-stall stable and five coal vaults. Some further alterations to the building were made in 1851. In 1891 the freehold lease was purchased.[1361]

The station was large and had a basement, ground, first and second floors. In the basement there was space for locker rooms, a scullery, a cooking room, a clothes room and four coal sheds. On the ground floor were a charge room, four cells, an Inspectors Office, a store, a drying room, a library, a parade room and three water closets. Outside there was a four stall stable for horses. The first and second floors provided cramped accommodation for 36 constables. There was also space for one married Inspector who rented three rooms. The freehold to these premises was obtained on 11th December 1891.

Records show that in 1864 Hackney Police Station had a total strength of two inspectors, eight sergeants, 83 constables and two Horse Patrols.[1362] The importance of Hackney Old Town Station was recognised early, and instructions were given that an Inspector should supervise the station.[1363]

Later, during restructuring in 1878, a new sub-division was formed. The Kingsland and Hackney division was split into three sub-divisions, namely Stoke Newington, Hackney and Dalston. Hackney Sub-Division's strength increased by a further three sergeants and 24 constables.

Thirty-six constables were shown as residing in the section house at the station in 1881.[1364] Senior officers were reassured to know that such large numbers of officers could be drawn on at a moment's notice to deal with any incident. In fact, since early times off duty men were informed that they could be called on at all times, and that they should prepare themselves to be available at the shortest notice.[1365] Records show that an inspector resided next to the police station in Mare Street. William J. Sherlock his wife and four children resided at 9 Churchyard, Hackney. He appears to have been the Inspector in charge of Mare Street Police Station in 1881. In 1883 he was promoted and transferred, becoming the Divisional Superintendent for G or Finsbury Division, based at King's Cross Road (Bagnigge Wells) Police Station.[1366] He stayed there until April 1885, when he was sixty years of age, and then he was transferred back to N Division.[1367]

Hackney Sub-Division was transferred to J Division in 1886 as part of further re-organisation,[1368]

On occasions in the past there have been glimpses of heroism and bravery. There has always been a long tradition of this in the British Police, and the police officers of Hackney were no exception. In July 1897, Constable Green of Hackney Police Station was awarded the Royal Humane Society's Bronze Medal for rescuing a woman from the River Lea whilst on duty near Lea Bridge.

In 1890, in conjunction with a number of further boundary changes, there was the creation of another sub-division called Victoria Park.[1369] These changes saw a revision of the supervisory staff of inspectors, to three inspectors and two sub-inspectors.

New police quarters for single men came into operation in April 1891 at the police station.[1370]

Instructions were also published merging Hackney and Victoria Park sub-divisions into one called Hackney sub-division. Victoria Park station remained open.[1371]

One of the last Inspectors in charge of the old Hackney station was Sub-Divisional Inspector Austin Askew. Born at Banbury in 1850, he joined the Metropolitan Police in 1871 having left the Life Guards as Corporal of Horse. He quickly rose through the ranks to take command of this very important station. He retired in September 1902. At this time, the Sub-Division could boast having the most number of recipients of the Royal Humane Society's medals for saving life from fire and drowning. At his retirement celebration held at Hackney Town Hall, the Mayor, Dr. F. Montague Miller JP, presented Inspector Askew with a gold watch and a cheque for £100 in recognition for his integrity, courtesy and efficiency.[1372]

Sub-Divisional Inspector Austin Askew of Hackney Police Station in 1902

In early 1900 arrangements were made for a new police station to be built to replace the old Victorian station. Accordingly, a large piece of land was acquired in March 1900 at 38 St. John's Church Road, Hackney, on the opposite side of the entrance (north side) to St. John's Churchyard. Originally an agreement had been reached with another buyer for the sale of the land, but on 27th April 1900 the owner, Miss Emily Isabella Clark, changed her mind and decided to sell the freehold to the Metropolitan Police instead. The cost of the purchase was not disclosed. Additionally, negotiations commenced with the owners for the acquisition of both 2 and 4 Lower Clapton Road. This was a site used by the Young Women's Christian Association. They demanded compensation as sitting tenants, and received an out of court settlement of £1,400 in 1902.

The Freehold of 34 St. John's Church Road and the leasehold of No. 36 were acquired on 9th May 1900. A considerable amount of money was spent obtaining a good site with plenty of space as re-organisation stipulated that Hackney was to become the Headquarters Station for J Division. The new station was built at the junction with Lower Clapton Road and St. John's Church Road, and was completed for occupation in October 1904.[1373] The call sign for the station was Hotel Kilo (HK).[1374]

The station provided accommodation for one married inspector and 30 unmarried constables. Records also show that its designation was altered from that of a sub-division of Bethnal Green to Hackney or J Division. Hackney Police Station was not only where normal police work was carried out, but it was also became the Divisional Headquarters where the Divisional Superintendent would be stationed.[1375]

Hackney Police Station 1904-2014

Henry Lovatt Ltd built the station, at a cost of £13,216. It was well fitted-out, and of considerable size. It was shown to have accommodation which included an Inspector's office, a charge room, two single cells for females, one large association cell or drunk tank, four single cells for males, a parade room and an ambulance shed. On the first floor the Divisional Headquarters staff were located. After the station was completed a stable block was built by Messrs. Jathey Brothers, at a cost of £1,075, and was occupied in 1905. The stable block consisted of a four-stall stable and horsebox, and situated on the floor above were married quarters occupied by a married sergeant and his family. New gates to the station were purchased because the old ones had been badly damaged during the building work. The Receiver purchased 34 and 36 St. John's Church Road and occupied by two married Inspectors.

The old Hackney Police Station located on the other side of the churchyard remained in service as a section house to accommodate single and married police officers until at least 1910.[1376] The senior officer in charge of the station was a Sub-Divisional Inspector.

A number of stations were designated to receive deceased persons, and at the back of the old Hackney station was a mortuary which still remains in use today. When the old station site was sold, the police retained the mortuary and Coroner's office.

In 1912 the Division was headed by Superintendent William E. Fitt who supervised the stations of J until November 1916, when he was transferred to south-west London. The photograph below shows Superintendent Fitt in ceremonial uniform with the sword of office. William E. Fitt joined the Metropolitan Police on 18th April 1887. His warrant number was 72486. The picture postcard clearly shows that he was awarded four medals; these were the 1887 Silver Jubilee medal, the 1897 Jubilee bar, 1901 Coronation medal and the silver 1911 Coronation medals. This meant that he was present at all these celebrations. The records also show that Superintendent Fitt retired on pension after 32 years of exemplary service.[1377] It is likely that the card was produced privately by friends or relatives of the superintendent as a mark of respect, after a long and distinguished career. He was a very powerful man, responsible for a sizeable section of East London that included the sub-divisions of Hackney, Bethnal Green, Barkingside, Claybury, Dalston, Leyton, Leytonstone, Loughton, Victoria Park and Wanstead. The total number of officers of the Division was also considerable, and by 1925 there were some 956 officers and men.[1378]

Superintendent Fitt of J Division in 1918

In May 1913 Metropolitan Police Surveyors purchased land and a building at 146 Mare Street, near Hackney Triangle, from the London County Council for £2,100. The purpose for this acquisition was to build a section house to accommodate single and married police officers. This was called Mare Street Section House, and was later renamed Ede House,[1379] after the Home Secretary J. Chuter Ede.

Hackney was J Division headquarters, and was shown as being on No.4 District. The division covered an area of 39 square miles, and spread as far north as Loughton and Epping Forest, as far west as Stoke Newington or N Division, and as far east as H Division or Whitechapel. Enrolment for the Special Constabulary commenced on 14th August 1914, and attestations before magistrates were taking place in court houses and police stations for some duration. Each Special Constable (SC) was required to take an oath, and was presented with a warrant card which showed his number and the signature of the magistrate.[1380]

1361 John Back Archive (1975).
1362 Metropolitan Police Orders dated 11th January 1864.
1363 *Police and Constabulary Almanac* 1864.
1364 Census 1881.
1365 *Metropolitan Police General Instructions* 1829 and 1871.
1366 Census 1881.
1367 John Back Archive (1975).
1368 Metropolitan Police Orders dated 3rd April 1878.
1369 Metropolitan Police Order s dated 30th August 1890.
1370 *Police Review,* July 1897.
1371 Metropolitan Police Orders dated 19th November 1894.
1372 *The Police Review and Parade Gossip*, 20th February 1903.
1373 Metropolitan Police Orders dated 10th October 1904.
1374 Metropolitan Police General Orders 1893.
1375 Metropolitan Police Surveyor's Records.
1376 John Back Archive (1975).
1377 Metropolitan Police Service Records.
1378 *Bacon's Atlas* 1926 published by G.W. Bacon, London.
1379 Metropolitan Police Surveyor's Estate Register (undated).
1380 Reay, Col. W.T. (1920). *The Specials*. Billing and Son, Guildford.

Hackney Special Constabulary c1914

The picture above, taken at the end of the station yard, shows the entire strength of Hackney Special Constabulary just after they were formed in August 1914.

There were eleven Special Constabulary stations on J Division, apart from Hackney. These were Barkingside, Bethnal Green, Buckhurst Hill, Claybury, Dalston, Hackney, Leytonstone, Leyton, Loughton, Wanstead and Woodford.[1381]

One of the major influences on the organisation and running of J Division Special Constabulary was Mr. H. Jerburgh-Bonsey, who is shown in the group picture second row from the front, kneeling at the extreme left, and wearing a bowler hat. He was a sergeant during 1914, but rose up the ranks to become a Commander and was later awarded the MBE. The picture right shows Commander Jerburgh-Bonsey in 1919 displaying his MBE.

Commander H. Jerburgh-Bonsey MBE

A number of members of the Special Constabulary were honoured in 1919 for valuable service to the Force.

In 1918 Detective Sergeant Charles Richard Lee, who had been pensioned from the Force, died of injuries he had received in the execution of his duty whilst attempting to arrest suspects in the street. Stationed at Hackney, Lee was retired and removed to hospital for treatment. However, he never recovered from the injuries which hastened his death.[1382]

After the First World War discontent rose within the Police Force over pay and conditions of service. Times were harsh, pay was low and discipline was strict. Many police officers voiced their concerns by demonstrating in Central London. The Police Protest Demonstrations, as they were called, took place on 4th May 1919, and officers from Hackney were involved. In the centre of the following photograph, which shows the demonstration, standing above and holding the banner is a contingent of Hackney Police officers in Hyde Park. In those days police officers could be paid up union members,

and Hackney J Branch were members of the National Union of Police and Prison Officers. The demonstration was peaceful, and was well-attended. Estimates of the numbers suggest that some 20,000 took part in the day of protest.

A contingent of Hackney Police voice their discontent in Hyde Park in 1919

Further boundary changes between J (Hackney) and K (Bow) took place in 1926. In 1933 a complete re-organisation north of the River Thames saw Hackney or J Division boundaries revised again, with the removal of both Dalston and Bethnal Green from J Division. The creation of new Local Authority Boundaries in 1965 saw a further revision of Police boundaries to ensure they were coterminous, with Hackney being transferred to G Division (GH) and becoming a sub-division of Dalston Police Station which had Sectional station status.

The picture on the top of the following column shows Constable 761J Cope, attached to Hackney Police Station. He joined the Metropolitan Police in 1918, at the end of the World War I. This photograph was taken in 1938, probably to show his two medals, the 1919 British War Medal and the 1937 Coronation Medal. It appears that Constable Cope took part in the 1937 Coronation, and was rewarded with the medal in recognition of this fact. Constable Cope retired in 1938 and received pension of £153 13s 5d.[1383]

Mare Street Section House (Ede House), which was situated on Hackney Division just south of Wells Street, was hit by a High Explosive bomb on 25th September 1940. The section house, which was in the course of construction, received considerable damage, but only one person was injured.[1384] It was intended that a new police station would be incorporated into the section house building, to enable the old station in Lower Clapton Road to be replaced. Additional land had been purchased in Tudor Road in 1936 to enlarge the site.[1385] These plans were put back by Hitler's bombing, and the section house was rebuilt after the war finished. Rebuilding work commenced in 1950,[1386] although it was decided, probably for economic reasons, not to include the station in the revised plans. When finished Ede House provided accommodation for 135 single officers.[1387] Also in 1940, a bomb during an air raid in Hackney killed War Reserve Constable Thomas Robert Pickett.[1388]

Constable 761J Cope

Surveyors for the police then decided that Hackney Police Station should be completely rebuilt on its present site at Lower Clapton Road, and create a police station in Mare Street. This re-building did not happen for some time, but substantial alterations to the front office, custody room and reserve room eventually took place in 1978. Ede House now belongs to a Housing Association for homeless single men.

Police officers at Hackney have had to deal with many difficult situations sometimes resulting in tragic circumstances for the officer. For example, in 1952 Sergeant Frederick Henry Keil was injured in the course of his duty, whilst stationed at Hackney. The injuries were to the officer's head, and it was found that he had developed a brain tumour. Sadly, within a short time the officer died from the effects of his injury and the tumour.[1389]

In 1957 another tragic incident occurred. This time it involved a very senior officer from Hackney Police Station. Superintendent Cornelius Carson collapsed and died when going to the assistance of a child who had become trapped in a fire at the police station.[1390] He is remembered, like so many others, in the Roll of Honour the citation reads:

'In the afternoon of 26th October 1957, a fire broke out in the basement of Hackney Police Station. Superintendent Carson assisted to extinguish the flames and was exposed to much smoke and fumes. On returning upstairs, he heard a child scream in the second floor married quarters above and he hurried immediately up the fire escape to her assistance. Before Superintendent Carson could take the child down, however, he collapsed on the fire escape, and he died on the way to the hospital.' [1391]

Other officers who gave their lives during WW2 are mentioned in the Roll of Honour including Police Constable Ernest George Emsley, who joined the RAF as a Sergeant Air Gunner. He was killed on active service off Grimsby on 24th April 1944.[1392]

Any person who had worked at the station would have been aware that there was a ghost. By the mid-1970s, when the co-author Peter Kennison was a sergeant there, the ghost was said to frequent the top floor administration section, and rumours circulated that a superintendent had shot himself in his office with a service pistol drawn from the station safe. In fact, the Divisional Detective Superintendent committed suicide in this way in February 1960, leaving a wife and daughter.[1393] It is assumed that the ghost is attributed to him.

In 1970, whilst on his way to work at Hackney Police Station, Sergeant David James Hems was killed whilst riding his motorcycle in a road traffic accident.[1394]

In 2001 the Borough Commander was Chief Superintendent Peter Robbins QPM,[1395] but his base was at Stoke Newington Police station.

In February 2014 this grand old police station was sold for £7.6M to Teuheedul Free School.[1396]

Hainault Police Office

Epping Forest District Council
182 Manford Way, Hainault (1970-2015)
J Division (1970-2000)
Essex Police (2000-2015)

The picture below shows Hainault Police Office, situated at 182 Manford Way, Hainault, Essex. It was built and opened in November 1970 on a new housing estate to deal with local enquiries by the new residents moving into the local area.[1397] It was transferred to Essex Police in 2000, and was sold in 2015 to a commercial organisation.

Hainault Police Office 1970-2015

1381 Reay, Col. W.T. (1920). *The Specials*. Billing and Son, Guildford.
1382 www.policememorial.org.uk/Forces/Metropolitan/metroll.htm accessed 12th March 2002.
1383 Metropolitan Police Service Records.
1384 Howgrave-Graham, H.M. (1947) *The Metropolitan Police at War*. HMSO.
1385 Metropolitan Police Surveyor's Estate Register (undated).
1386 John Back Archive (1975).
1387 Metropolitan Police Surveyor's Estate Register (undated).
1388 www.policememorial.org.uk/Forces/Metropolitan/metroll.htm accessed 12th March 2002.
1389 Ibid.
1390 Ibid.
1391 Metropolitan Police Roll of Honour dated 29th November 1957.
1392 Metropolitan Police Orders dated 12th May 1944.
1393 Metropolitan Police Death in Service Register 1960.
1394 www.policememorial.org.uk/Forces/Metropolitan/metroll.htm accessed 12th March 2002.
1395 *Police and Constabulary Almanac* 2001.
1396 MPS (2018) Freedom of Information request – Land and property sold by the MPS for over £1M.
1397 Elliott, B. (1993) 'A History of the Police Stations of J Division 1886-1986'.

Ham Police Station (Office)

London Borough of Richmond

18 Ashburnham Road, Ham (1972-1993)

V Division (1972-1993)

The London Borough of Richmond OCU (1993-1999)

On 2nd December 1929 a police telephone call box was erected in Ham, on the north-west corner of Ham Street and Lock Road. There was no police station in Ham at the time, and the box was the only connection with police in the area. Members of the public could contact Richmond Police Station by going to the box and making a call. Police officers out on patrol would make a pre-arranged call from the box on their rounds. Many were on cycles in these rural beats.

In the early 1970s the area of Ham needed a police office or station, and a site for the office in the grounds of Ham Clinic, Ashburnham Road was purchased by surveyors in November 1971.

An entry in Police Orders of 26th April 1972 reads:

'On Monday 29th April, a Police Office to be known as Ham Police Office will be opened at 18, Ashburnham Road, Ham, Richmond, Surrey. Its station code was (TH)'.

Ham Police Office 1972-1999

In the late 1990s the office was only open for an hour in the morning and evening, but due to staff shortages it frequently did not open at all.

In 1998 it was announced that the station was to close. The local community of Petersham and Ham were concerned at the removal of their station/office, and a campaign was introduced to try and prevent its closure. In the eyes of the local population the presence of a station adds to the notion of community in the same way as a school, railway station or hospital are closed. The police station, even if only open part-time, was a visible reassurance to the community. The community had been assured that the police presence locally, both on foot and in cars, would be kept up. Concerned that their nearest station was Richmond or Twickenham, it was suggested that it would take a considerable time to get to these places by car, particularly in the rush hour. The campaign consisted of public meetings, and even included a petition which collected many signatures and was handed in to Richmond Police Station to help prevent the shutting of the station.

This campaign was in vain, since in October 1999 the office and land came up for auction and was sold at Allsops, who were then the Receiver's agents for the disposal of police buildings and property.

Hammersmith Police Station

London Borough of Hammersmith and Fulham

Brook Green, Hammersmith (1833-1870)

Bridge Street (now called Queen Caroline Street) (1870-1940)

19 Brook Green Road (later called 226 Shepherds Bush Road) (1940 to Present)

T Division (1830-1933)

F Division (1933-2018)

Basic Command Unit Central West (CW) (2018 to Present)

In 1832 Home Office authority was given to find a site for a new police station at Hammersmith. The station was sited at Brook Green, roughly where the M-O. Valve Co. (Hammersmith) works were. The property was owned by Mr. W. Bird, and had been built on the site of the smith's old house.[1398] The property was held on lease from 25th March 1833 for a period of 30 years. The lease required police to pay all rates and taxes, except land tax and sewer rate. The Receiver was also required to keep the premises in good repair, and paint the outside every three years and the inside every seven years. The building was a substantially-built house of brick and slate, with a small yard at the rear. There was a good coach house with copper boilers, three cells and stabling for eight horses. It was later agreed to rent the station and three double cottages, plus one single cottage used as section house accommodation, for a further period of two years from Lady Day 1868, at a rent of £330 per annum. All were given up in 1870.[1399]

In 1842 the Reverend Edward Wakeham of Eagle House, Brook Green, Hammersmith, at the suggestion of Superintendent Williamson of T Division, made a present of upwards of 100 well-selected volumes of books to form the nucleus of a permanent library. The idea was to form a library at the station-houses for the instruction and amusement of the reserve part of the force, and when the men were off duty.[1400] This was followed up in 1843, when the London City Mission presented about 50 volumes of books to each London police station for the use of the men attached to it. The works consisted of sacred writings, selected sermons, sound theological and moral works, together with the biographies and travels of good religious and moral men. The works could either be read at the station houses, or taken home by the constable, under certain restrictions.[1401] Libraries were maintained at sub-divisional police stations well into the late 1960s.

Inspector James Morgan was shown in charge of the police station in 1845.[1402] In 1864[1403] Hammersmith was shown as a station on T Division.

In 1869[1404] a new police station was built at the cost of £6,415,[1405] on the site of Thatched Cottage, which was owned by two ladies. It was in Bridge Road, which was later renamed Queen Street and is now known as Queen Caroline Street. It stood where the entrance to the District & Piccadilly Station (Queen Caroline Street entrance) stands now.[1406] The land had been purchased at a cost of £3,200,[1407] but there was an outcry at the time from the vicar and churchwardens of St. Paul's Church as they thought it unseemly to have unsavoury characters such as drunks in the vicinity of the churchgoers.[1408]

The police station was probably designed by the Metropolitan Police Surveyor Thomas Sorby, but he left his position in 1868 and the deputy, Frederick Caiger, would have finished supervising the building.

In 1879 Hammersmith Police Station was still shown as being on T or Kensington Division, which had Superintendent William Fisher in command.[1409]

In 1881 there was a report published which looked at the condition of each of the Metropolitan Police stations. Hammersmith was described as 'a nearly new station'. However the report was critical of the charge room and the distance it was from the cells. The station had a basement mess, and a good stable in the yard. At the time of the inspection there were one married inspector, one single sergeant and 52 single constables living at the station.[1410]

In 1884 Hammersmith was shown as a sub-divisional station of T Division, and then in 1888 there was an alteration in the boundaries of Hammersmith and Shepherds Bush sub-divisions with the opening of Ravenscourt Park, Hammersmith.[1411] In 1889 part of T or Hammersmith Division transferred to X Division to provide better policing in the Ealing, Acton and Hanwell Districts.[1412]

In 1895 Chief Inspector P. Cronin of Hammersmith Police Station retired after 27 years' service. He had joined the Metropolitan Police in 1868, and had been posted to Stoke Newington. He was then specially selected for duty at the Exhibition of 1871 at South Kensington. He gained promotion, and eventually came to Hammersmith as a Police Inspector in 1885. During the years between 1887 and 1890 he had the entire control of police arrangements at the exhibitions at Earls Court, the Paris Hippodrome and Barnam's Show at Olympia. He was promoted to Chief Inspector in 1892. He was a prominent and enthusiastic member of Hammersmith Police Rowing Club, and was police band inspector for a long time. He was also a prominent figure in the concerts by the District put on for the benefit of the Police Orphanage.[1413]

In January 1896 Hammersmith Constable Harry Goddard returned to the station from Paris, France, where he had spent eighteen days at the Pasteur Institute being treated for a bite to his hand by a mad dog in the yard at the Hammersmith Police Station on Christmas Day 1895. Louis Pasteur had developed a vaccine for the treatment of rabies, and the divisional surgeon felt it necessary to send the officer to France for treatment.[1414]

By 1896 T Division was commanded by Superintendent Charles Hunt, with sub-divisional inspector James Boyle at Hammersmith Police Station assisted by Inspectors J. Lance, E. Harris, H. Ashwell, J. Scantlebury and T. Moffatt.[1415]

The rigours of police duty took its toll on the health of officers who died in service more frequently than in modern times. There were two such cases at Hammersmith Police Station in 1892, when Constable Ernest Ellis died from emphysema and pleurisy after 22 years' service. In 1900 this also happened to Constable Henry John Jiggins, who died from thoracic aneurism. His widow received a pension of £15 per annum, and £2 10s was paid yearly to each of the five children until they reached 15 years of age.[1416]

The F Division contingent at Earls Court for the 1904 Italian Exhibition

The Navy and Military Tournament was the world's largest military tattoo and pageant, held by the British armed forces annually between 1880 and 1999. The venue was originally the Royal Agricultural Hall in Islington but latterly moved to Earls Court, as the former venue was too small. In its later years it also acted as a fundraising event for leading forces charities, such as the Royal British Legion. In the picture below Chief Inspector Shervington (centre seated), SDI Littlejohns (centre left seated), two inspectors, three sergeants and 31 constables were specially chosen to carry out supervision of the tournament buildings and to ensure the event was as trouble free as possible. Littlejohns had been trained well by his old boss SDI May, who was an expert at policing exhibitions and large events like the Boat Race.

The Navy and Military Tournament Olympia circa 1907

In 1909 T Division lost Fulham Sub-Division to B or Chelsea Division in a revision of Divisional boundaries.[1417] New married quarters and a section house were taken into occupation in April 1911,[1418] and the station was reconstructed at a cost of £5,402[1419] in 1913.[1420]

Locals showed great interest in May 1914, when 230 boys and girls from the Metropolitan & City Police Orphanage arrived in Hammersmith on special tramcars. Headed by their band and the Orphanage banner, they marched up Hammersmith Road to Olympia to watch a rehearsal performance of the Royal Naval and Military Tournament.

1398 Notes at Hammersmith & Fulham Archives dated 15th October 2012.
1399 Metropolitan Police Surveyor's Book p.142.
1400 Notes dated 1842 at Hammersmith & Fulham archives, accessed 15th October 2012.
1401 *The Era* (London) 'The Synopsis', 26th February 1843. Issue 231.
1402 *Kelly's Directory* 1845.
1403 Metropolitan Police Orders dated 11th January 1864.
1404 Metropolitan Police Orders dated 15th November 1869.
1405 Metropolitan Police Surveyor's Book.
1406 Notes at Hammersmith & Fulham archives accessed 15th October 2012.
1407 Metropolitan Police Surveyor's Book.
1408 John Back Archive circa 1975.
1409 *Post Office Directory* 1879.
1410 Metropolitan Police Report on Condition of Police Stations 1881.
1411 Metropolitan Police Orders dated 7th June 1888.
1412 Metropolitan Police Orders dated 28th December 1889.
1413 *West London Observer*, 6th April 1895.
1414 *Fulham Chronicle*, 24th January 1896.
1415 *Kelly's West Kensington & Hammersmith Directory* 1896-97.
1416 met.police.uk/history/remembrance2 accessed 17th October 2012.
1417 Metropolitan Police Orders dated 31st March 1909.
1418 Metropolitan Police Orders dated 26th April 1911.
1419 Metropolitan Police Surveyor's Book.
1420 John Back Archive circa 1975.

The children were described as smart and having a well cared-for appearance. The girls, who were mostly taller than the boys, were neatly attired in blue dresses, with black coats and straw hats, with blue and red ribbons, whilst the boys wore black suits with dark blue caps with red stripes.

After the performance the children, headed by the T Divisional Band and accompanied by Sub-Divisional Inspector Walter Littlejohns and Inspector Grosch, marched to Hammersmith Police Station. They were received by Superintendent Powell, and the children enjoyed tea and cakes set out for them in the station yard.[1421]

Children from the Orphanage together with SDI Littlejohns (seated 2nd left), Chief Inspector Shervington (centre) and others in the yard at Hammersmith Police Station

In 1924 T Division was under the command of Superintendent William Newman. At Hammersmith Police Station, Sub-Divisional Inspector William Sergeant was in charge together with Detective Inspector William Gurney and Inspectors Charles Read, Thomas Taylor and George Harmon.[1422]

In 1928 the Superintendent in charge of T Division was Thomas Coombs.[1423]

In the 1933 reorganisation of the divisions north of the Thames, Hammersmith was transferred from T to F Division, and became the main station of that division.[1424]

In November 1939 the Section House at 3 Paddenswick Road, Hammersmith was taken into occupation after some reconstruction. It was now to be known as Ravenscourt House.[1425]

On 31st March 1940 Hammersmith Police Station at 1 Queen Caroline Street was closed, and business transferred to new premises at 19 Brook Green Road. This road was then renamed, and the police station address became 226 Shepherds Bush Road.[1426] The police station had been built on the site of Messrs Rogers Garage premises at 19-27 Brook Green Road.[1427] The site used to be a picturesque spot in Victorian days. Duckling's Nurseries, with the adjoining Laurel Cottage and King's Forage Yard, stood there for many years.[1428]

The new station took eighteen months to build and was designed by the London firm of architects, Messrs Farquharson and McMorran. A local artist, Mr. G. Kruger Gray of Addison Crescent, Hammersmith, designed the striking coat of arms over the main entrance. The walls of the entrance hall were covered with Portland stone, and the ceiling was of silver-grey Indian wood. There were four cells for male prisoners, and four cells for females. Behind the main building was built a stable block for twenty, with a harness room, forage store, sick box and a blacksmith's forge. There was also a garage for ten cars. Over the station there were married quarters for two resident officers.[1429] Architectural comment has been made of the unusual placing of the attic windows, which do not line up with the lower windows.[1430]

Hammersmith Police Station 1940 to present

The old police station at Queen Street was sold on 5th April 1940 to Mr H. Salmon for £27,000.[1431]

During the Second World War there were a large number of fatalities in London due to enemy aircraft during the air raids. Two War Reserve Constables at Hammersmith lost their lives. Simeon Oscar Glen and Arthur Needham Myers had both joined the Force in order to fill the gaps left at police stations when the regular policemen joined the armed forces. Both constables were killed by the explosion of a bomb during an enemy raid at Hammersmith.[1432]

The blue lamp outside Hammersmith Police station is over 100 years old, as it had been taken from Whetstone Police Station when it was pulled down in 1963. It was placed outside the building in 1965 when some alterations were made to the station.

The front entrance to Hammersmith Police Station

In 1965, when divisional boundaries were altered to coincide with the new local authority boundaries, Hammersmith remained the divisional station of F Division.[1433]

In 1975 Constable Stephen Andrew Tibble was riding his motorcycle off duty when he saw a man with a gun being chased by three plainclothes officers. Constable Tibble overtook him, dismounted and approached, whereupon the suspect, an IRA terrorist, shot him three times at close range and killed him. Tibble was posthumously awarded the Queen's Police Medal, which is only awarded for gallantry.[1434] In May 1992, when the refurbished Fulham Police Station (all part of the London Borough of Hammersmith and Fulham) was reopened, PC Tibble's parents attended the ceremony and unveiled a new plaque in memory of their son in the front office of the new-look station.[1435]

The police have not escaped being the victims of crime themselves: in 1987, a massive 16-stone bench was stolen from Hammersmith Police Station's foyer. It seems that the eight-feet long seat was carried out of the main entrance and along a busy road. The previous week two chairs were also stolen from the foyer.[1436] Sadly, this still happens at a number of police stations across the country. Police stations which are closed at night are particularly vulnerable, in spite of sophisticated alarm systems.

Hammersmith Police Station is one of 40 police buildings that English Heritage has classified as a Grade II listed building. Of the 40 buildings, 30 are police stations. There are many current and former Metropolitan Police stations being closed, and the buildings sold to developers either pulled down or refurbished as private living accommodation. Local communities forming action groups to keep these police stations open, and to keep policing at a local level, also seek to keep the old buildings instead of new development. Many police buildings blend into the local area and buildings around them. English Heritage, and local authorities, take an interest in buildings which are at risk and need to be preserved for their architectural qualities.

However, whilst local residents fight for the preservation of their local police stations English Heritage point out that over 350 Metropolitan Police stations were built between 1842 and 1900, and several are included in the Heritage List of Grade II buildings. Buildings need to be exceptional examples of Victorian police stations, in terms of design, and with clear architectural quality. Having selected 30 police stations, English Heritage feel that they have sufficient examples of London police stations on their list.[1437]

In 2016 the front counter of the Hammersmith Police Station was closed so that a £59 million refurbishment and expansion programme could commence. The work will include new custody cells, modern offices, improved horse stables and underground parking. The station is due to reopen in 2020. Meanwhile, the front counter facilities were temporary transferred to Shepherds Bush Police Station.[1438]

Hampstead Police Station

London Borough of Camden
Flask Walk, Holly Place (1829-1832)
1 Heath Street (1832-1868)
65 Rosslyn Hill (1868-1913)
26½ Rosslyn Hill (1913-1965)
S Division (1829-1965)
E Division (1965-1993)
London Borough of Camden OCU (1993-2014)

An imposing the first police station was built at Hampstead in the 1830s, and the old 'lock-up' fell into neglect and became a garden shed. In 1981 the Hampstead Plaque Fund erected a plaque on this Grade I-listed garden wall.[1439] From about 1730 there was also a lock-up in Flask Walk, which was used as temporary accommodation for suspected criminals until the magistrate was ready to deal with them.[1440] This was also the site of the village stocks and watchman's hut.

The first police station, known as the Old Watch House, was built in Holly Walk and was used from 1829 until 1834, although Metropolitan Police records show that in 1832 the address was Holly Place, Hampstead.[1441] This is now a private residence, and the old cells serve the present owners as a dining room. Buildings behind the Watch House in Hollyberry Lane are thought to have been the sergeant's house and stable.[1442]

Hampstead Police Station, Holly Place 1829-1834

1421 Press Cutting held in Hammersmith & Fulham archives dated 15th May 1914. Visited 15th October 2012.
1422 *Kelly's Hammersmith & Shepherds Bush Directory* 1924/25.
1423 *Post Office Directory* 1928.
1424 Metropolitan Police Orders dated 28th November 1933.
1425 Metropolitan Police Orders dated 22nd November 1939.
1426 Metropolitan Police Orders dated 28th March 1940.
1427 Hammersmith & Fulham Archives, accessed 15th October 2012.
1428 *West London Observer*, 10th May 1940.
1429 Ibid.
1430 Cherry. B & Pevsner N. *Buildings of England*. 1991.
1431 Metropolitan Police Surveyor's Book.
1432 met.police.uk/history/remembrance2 accessed 17th October 2012.
1433 Metropolitan Police Orders dated 6th August 1964.
1434 Fido M. & Skinner K. (1999) The Official Encyclopedia of Scotland Yard. Virgin, London.
1435 *The Job*, 29 May 1992.
1436 *The Sun*, 27th October 1987.
1437 'Wanstead Police Station' - English Heritage letter dated 28th September 2011.
1438 www.mylondon.news 29th May 2019, accessed 3rd July 2019.
1439 *The Job*, 11th September 1981.
1440 Wade, Christopher (unknown) 'Streets of Hampstead' published by the Camden History Society.
1441 'Directory for the Return of Mops', 1st July 1832.
1442 Wade, Christopher (unknown) 'Streets of Hampstead' published by the Camden History Society.

In 1834 the police leased larger premises at the bottom of Holly Hill, at the junction with Heath Street, where the clock tower building now stands.[1443] The station was not occupied until 1839, and was shown as a brick-built house with small yard with three cells, a three-stall stable and a charge room. It was leased from Mr. Cunnington of High Street, Hampstead, for a period of 21 years. The cost of redeveloping the new police station was shown as £62 17s 6d.[1444] By 1868 this building had been demolished, and rebuilt as a police fire station in the High Road.

In April 1865, permission was given for the police to look for and purchase a suitable site on which to build a station.[1445]

Additional land was purchased at a cost of £1,500 and £26 ground rent per annum. The cost of the new station was £5,363. The owners of the leased land were the Dean and Chapter of West Hampstead, who had permitted a 99-year lease. The building was of brick and slate and had 17 rooms, five cells and a four-stall stable. The new police station had been built on the same site opposite the Chapel, and opened for business in May 1868.[1446]

The station was located on S or Hampstead Division. The freehold to this site was purchased later, in 1909. In August 1868 Hampstead and West Hampstead sections were amalgamated to form Hampstead Sub-Division.

Hampstead Police Station 1868-1913

The new site was sufficiently large enough for a portion of the building to be used as a court, which the Receiver of the Metropolitan Police leased to the London County Council for twenty-one years with an annual ground rent payable of £150. The police purchased the freehold to land located at 24/26 Rosslyn Hill in 1909 for the sum of £6,250. Approval from the Home Office was sought in 1910 to build a new station.

Finally, the present police station and Magistrates' Court, at the corner of Downshire Hill, was opened in December 1913.[1447] There were two sets of married quarters and accommodation for 30 unmarried men. Around the time of the First World War alterations were made to the premises, with two sets of quarters being converted into a Special Constabulary office and a canteen. Curiously enough, today its correct postal address is 26½ Rosslyn Hill, Hampstead, NW3.

Furthermore, in 1913 there were boundary revisions between Golders Green, Finchley and Hampstead Sub-Divisions.

The old police station was eventually demolished and the site is now marked by a drinking fountain and a new development named Mulberry Close.[1448]

On 21st July 1915 Detective Constable Alfred Young KPM was fatally shot by Captain Richard Georges whilst the officer was attempting to execute a warrant. The official police funeral took place in Hampstead, near the station to which he was attached, and was attended by the Metropolitan Police Commissioner Sir Edward Henry and detachments of officers from every division of the force. Special Constables from Hampstead Division collected twelve guineas (£12 12s) for the officer's young son.[1449]

Hampstead Police Station 1913-2014

In July 1933 there were further boundary revisions which affected S Division, with changes between the surrounding divisions of J, Y and N followed by further revisions four months later.[1450]

Hampstead Police station attracted fame momentarily when, in 1955, Ruth Ellis was charged there with the murder of her lover, David Blakely – a crime, which saw her convicted and sentenced to death. She then became the last woman to be hanged in Britain.

In 1965 Hampstead left S Division and became part of E Division, when it was amalgamated with West Hampstead with the latter being its sectional station.

In 2014 Hampstead Police Station was sold for £14.105M to a private developer.[1451]

Hampton Police Station

The London Borough of Richmond

Hampton Village (1841-1848)

1 New Street (1848-1901)

Station Lane (1901-2015)

V Division (1841-1993)

The London Borough of Richmond OCU (1993-2015)

A horse patrol station was taken over by the Metropolitan Police from 1841 which was rented from Mr Kent of Castle House, Hampton and designated a station on V or Wandsworth Division. It consisted of a brick-and-tile house, which cost £16 16s per year to rent. Hampton was also designated a sergeant station, and as this officer was originally from the horse patrol his family also resided there with him. In the remaining part of the building three constables resided paying 1 shilling a week rent each. In general use was a kitchen, scullery and a stable in the yard. The building was given up and vacated in 1848,[1452] when it was no longer suitable for police purposes.

On 1st December 1846 the Home Office approved the building of a police station at Hampton,[1453] still within V or

Hampton Police Station 1848-1901. 1 New Street (now 12 Station Road), Hampton

Wandsworth Division.

As a result, land on which to build a police station in New Street, Hampton was rented for 60 years from Mrs E. Sawyers of Bushey Park on an annual rent of £10 from June 1847. The surveyors undertook to design a new station on the site which cost £879 2s 5d, and it was finished in 1848.

The substantial property consisted of an inspector's office, charge room, two cells and a reading room. Outside there was a hand-ambulance shed, urinals, and coal cellar, with a two-stall stable and hay loft. Because of a lack of running water, earth closets were also installed.[1454]

Upstairs there was accommodation for the married inspector and his family, who occupied five rooms which included bedrooms, a kitchen and scullery.[1455] The weekly rent for the inspector was 6s 6d, but this was reduced by one shilling in 1896 to 5s 6d. In 1853 it was cleaned and repainted, something which would be completed every three years until it was given up.

Policing in the area was not necessarily very quiet. When trouble broke out there needed to be a firm hand. The beer houses, some of which in the course of time were to become our public houses, were far from being the orderly places they appear today, and there were far too many reports of drunken fights breaking out.

In May 1864, Edward Danes, water bailiff of the Queen's River, Bushy Park, who lodged at the Star beer house, made an attempt on his own life by cutting his throat. He was unsuccessful and the wound was not serious, but the incident could scarcely have helped the already dubious reputation of the village.

In July 1864, there was a quarrel which developed into a full-scale riot between the Irish labourers who were engaged in laying down the railway and the locals. The trouble started in the Duke of Wellington, when, after refusing to pay for their beer, the Irish broke stools and windows. Mr Austin, the landlord, remonstrated with them and was knocked down and jumped on by four men who badly assaulted him, and he made a complaint to the magistrate.

More fighting broke out, and the Irish called reinforcements from their encampment which was close by. About twenty of them, armed with sticks and loaded with stones, set about the villagers, and there was a full-scale fight which lasted about half-an-hour. The unfortunate Mr Austin was again knocked

1443 Wade, Christopher (unknown) 'Streets of Hampstead' published by the Camden History Society.
1444 Metropolitan Police Surveyor's Manifest (1882).
1445 Op Cit.
1446 Metropolitan Police Orders dated 8th May 1868.
1447 Metropolitan Police Orders dated 28th November 1913.
1448 Wade, Christopher (unknown) "Streets of Hampstead" published by the Camden History Society.
1449 *Daily Graphic*, 21st July 1915.
1450 Metropolitan Police Orders dated July 1933.
1451 MPD (2018) MOPAC: Police station closures broken down by year.
1452 Metropolitan Police Surveyor's Registers.
1453 Metropolitan Police Orders dated 11th January 1864.
1454 Metropolitan Police Surveyor's Registers.
1455 Ibid.

down with half a brick, dragged into a ditch and brutally beaten with the butt end of a gun. Six policemen arrived, accompanied by Dr Holberton, and after tending the wounded, marched at the head of about fifty civilians to the encampment of the Irish in a field in Burton's Lane belonging to Mr Deacon to detain them, but they had already gone. What was left behind was immediately levelled to the ground and set fire to. A great search ensued, and four men were captured hiding behind hay ricks in Mr Deacon's farmyard. They were all injured, and had to be carried to the police station in a cart. A further search of tents in Mr Brice's meadows at Rectory Farm was to no avail, and the crowd dispersed.

At the petty sessions one of the prisoners was still so seriously hurt that he had to be carried to the bench, and the *Surrey Comet* reported that

'The case created a great sensation in court as it was quite a sight to see the bandages and plasters which had been applied to the wounds.' [1456]

In 1866 the landlord at The Star was charged with keeping a disorderly house after a brawl on his premises. Previous convictions of keeping a disorderly house, being open at unlawful hours and of assault were also mentioned. The constable who made the charge in this instance, doubtless incensed by having been told 'that no b—y policemen' were wanted on the scene, described how a crowd of eight or ten persons, male and female, were fighting. The landlord was said to have used 'the most disgusting language' and to have slammed the door in the constable's face. Despite the former's aggrieved declaration that he was in bed at the time in question and that his house was a well conducted one, the landlord, Charles Digby by name, was fined £4 with 14 shillings costs.

In 1868 Robert Rolfe, beer house keeper, was summoned for having his house open at 11.00am on a Sunday. His house backed on to the park, and access via a ladder was easy and presumably not obvious to passers-by in the road.[1457]

By 1867 re-organisation of the divisions saw Hampton transfer to T or Kensington Division, still as a sergeant station.[1458] However, by 1873 Hampton became an inspector-designated station for the first time since it came into being. Inspector George Steed took charge, but he did not live at the station. Steed, aged 31-years-old, resided with his wife and three daughters in Hammersmith. He remained in charge until 1877, when he was promoted to Chief Inspector and sent to K or Bow Division.

Inspector Edward Bullivent took over from Steed at Hampton, living not far away from the station in New Hampton, a short walk away. In 1881 Bullivent and his wife lived at 2 Pantile Close, Hampton,[1459] which seemed to be a favoured road for the occupation of police officers and their families. Bullivent remained there until about 1885 as Sub-Divisional Inspector, when he retired. He later died at Kingston in 1899.[1460]

There were alterations in the boundaries relating to the sub-divisions of F Division in 1890, and these were the Sub-Divisions of Bedfont, Brentford and Hampton.[1461]

In 1898 Sub-Divisional Inspector Edwin Carter Unsted (warrant no. 59080) was in charge of Hampton sub-division, and remained there until 1905 when he retired on pension and was replaced. Unsted, originally from Falmer near Brighton in Sussex, had joined the Metropolitan Police in 1875. In 1901 he resided at Castle Mail Cottage, Tudor Road, Hampton with his wife and seven children. Police Constable Mackintosh was on the sub-division at the time, and he became ill, falling blind and being partially paralysed. He was made to retire, and received a small annual grant in addition to a reduced pension. It fell to Unsted and his colleagues to look after Mackintosh, and as a result an appeal was made to the officers of the sub-division who raised £80. Unsted presented the money to Constable Mackintosh at a ceremony at Hampton.[1462]

In February 1901 the approval was given by the Home Office for building a new police station at Hampton. Hampton was at this time a sectional station of Kingston, a position it shared with Sunbury and Epsom.

Hampton Police Station 1901-2013

The freehold to a new site in Station Road, Hampton was purchased for £512 15s in 1901. The new purpose-built police station also comprised of a section house for single constables, and one set of married quarters. The administrative portion of the new police station at Hampton was taken into occupation by the police, and business commenced therein on 16th October 1905.[1463] The lease to the old station was surrendered in January 1906.

The rear aspect of Hampton Police Station c1908

The photograph above shows the rear aspect of the station and the huge amount of space purchased with the sale of this building plot. To the left is the stable block, complete with hay loft situated away from the station. Since often in older stations families of police officers occasionally lived above the stables, this was a welcomed beginning in situating stables away from main buildings where the odours were less offensive.

In 1907 Inspector John Henry Kempin (warrant no. 72741) was the Sub-Divisional Inspector at Hampton Police Station. He resided at the station with his wife Alice. No children lived with them. In the section house were nine single constables.[1464] Kempin joined the service in 1887, and remained in charge at Hampton until 1912 when he retired on pension.[1465]

In 1924 Hampton was shown as a station on T or Hammersmith Division.

Hampton Police Station dressed for the 1911 Coronation

Each station area is split into beats, which were either patrolled on foot, on a bicycle or by car. The beats at Hampton, which in 1932 was a station on T Division and a sub-divisional station of Twickenham, were patrolled by both constables and special constables (when available). Special constables would not patrol a regular officer's assigned beat. There were three priority patrol beats, four ordinary beats and three extra patrols.

The three priority beats were patrolled from 7.00am-3.00pm, 3.00pm-11.00pm and 7.00pm, creating an geographical overlap with ordinary beats. The constable was meant to patrol at a standard speed of about two-and-a-half miles an hour, with beat patrol one being two miles and 440yds long and set to take 54 minutes to complete.

On the ordinary beats the 2nd and 4th beats were cycle patrols. No. 1 beat was 6 miles 661 yards long, and was patrolled from 6.00am-2.00pm, 2.00pm-10.00pm and 10.00pm until 6.00am. No. 2 beat was a cycle beat 8 miles and 807 yards long; No. 3 beat was 11 miles and 1,026 yards long. Refreshment times were staggered throughout the beats at Hampton, and details were shown in the beat book. It was the responsibility of the section sergeants to complete the daily duty state which would show everyone at work and the duty to which they were assigned.

The inspector would sign at the bottom of the duty state when it was completed and checked by him. Refreshments times were just half an hour in those days, and were taken either at a police box or back at the police station.

The officer would either phone in from the box or report to the reserve officer that they were in the station/box for refreshments. If out on patrol, the constable would take sandwiches with him. The details of each beat were recorded in the beat book, which was kept in the station office for anyone who needed to familiarise themselves with the beats. From here, newly-posted constables, sergeants and inspectors would write out details of beats as the beat book held the latest instructions and changes.

A revision of boundaries took place on 1st April 1965 in conjunction with the local authorities and the formation of the Greater London Council (GLC). Hampton was designated as a sectional station of Twickenham Sub-Division.[1466] In 1965 the call sign for the station was Tango Romeo (TR), and had Superintendent Mulcahy MM in charge with Chief Inspector A.G. Meapham as his deputy.[1467] Hampton was a sub-divisional station, with Barnes being its sectional station.

In 1968 the existing station area of was incorporated into Teddington (TT) Section and Hampton Police Station reverted to the status of a police office on Monday 4th November.[1468]

Hampton Police Station closed in 2013.[1469] In January 2015, the station and traffic garage was sold for £5.4M to Pinnicle Hampton Station LLP.[1470]

Hampton Police Station yard c1970s

Hanwell Police Station

The London Borough of Ealing
High Street, Hanwell (1868-1886)
169 Uxbridge Road (1886-2012)
T Division (1839-1865)
X Division (1865-1933)

In 1837 the village of Hanwell was recorded as having only 164 houses, but the population in the area had increased due to a number of workmen brought in to construct the Great Western Railway which passed through the village. An early mention of police in Hanwell is made in 1838 when an 'affray' took place at the Coach and Horses Public House between excavators and labourers employed in the construction of the railway. The constables and horse patrols were attacked with 'great violence' by men and women using pickaxe handles and shovels. Nine persons were arrested, and each fined up to the sum of thirty shillings by the local magistrates.[1471]

Hanwell had a parish cage situated in the Halfacre. It was a small building about eight feet square, and was contiguous to the old fire engine house. The building fell into disuse and became a resting place for the road labourers' tools. It was pulled down in 1844 and the materials used to build the west wall of the churchyard.[1472]

In the Metropolitan Police Surveyor's book of 1845, Hanwell was described as 'Horse Patrol Station Nos. 32 & 33'. Hanwell

1456 www.stjames-hamptonhill.org.uk/History/B&G/1ChFace.htm accessed 16th February 2012.
1457 Ibid
1458 *Kelly's Directory* 1867.
1459 Census 1881.
1460 Death Records.
1461 Metropolitan Police Orders dated 18th July 1890.
1462 *Police Review and Parade Gossip*, 27th February 1903.
1463 Metropolitan Police Orders dated 16th October 1905.
1464 Census 1911.
1465 *Kelly's Directory* 1912.
1466 Metropolitan Police Orders dated 6th August 1964.
1467 Districts and Divisions 1965.
1468 Metropolitan Police Orders dated 29th October 1968.
1469 www.flickr.com/photos/61129021@N06/8250957130 accessed 26th October 2013.
1470 MPS (2018) Freedom of Information request: Land and property sold by the MPS for over £1M.
1471 Sharpe. M. Sir *Bygone Hanwell*, General Calendar 1924.
1472 Ibid.

was the 4th Division of the horse patrol provided by the Bow Street Runners and was used as a base for the patrols. See London Boroughs of Barnet and Kingston for more detail on these patrols. The building was 'a double brick, tile and slate built house with two large gardens, two stables and a cellar for coals to each house'. Recorded in the book as 'given up',[1473] but with no date given, the exact location of the building was also not known.

A further entry in the Metropolitan Police Surveyor's book shows that a property was on a yearly tenancy from a Mr Hall of Kingsland. This property is described as 'a common built brick and slate house with small garden and two stall stables with loft over', and contained four rooms and a scullery. It appears that this second building is different from the first, and seems therefore to be the first Metropolitan Police Station. This first station was finally given up on 24th December 1868.[1474]

In 1847 it was reported that a train derailed near Southall and Inspector Luxton of Hanwell Police attended the scene and removed two corpses from the wreckage.[1475]

Records show that in 1866 plans were in hand to rebuild the police station at Hanwell, but nothing happened.[1476]

By 1873 police lists show that the freehold of Hanwell Police Station at 169 High Street, Hanwell, was owned by the Receiver.[1477] This having been purchased from Mr Joseph and Eliza Palmer for £1800 in 1872.[1478] An inspector was posted as the officer in charge.

Hanwell Police Station 1868-1886

In a Metropolitan Police Report of 1881 Hanwell Police Station was described as;

'*Three old dilapidated cottages which have already been reported as totally unfit for the purpose of a police station. The sanitary conditions were very bad. These cottages should be replaced by a new station*'

It was occupied at the time by one married inspector and two married constables.[1479]

The rebuilding of Hanwell Police Station on the same site took place between 1884 and 1885 at a cost of £3,120 7s 5d.[1480] The new station opened on 26th January 1885.[1481]

In 1911 Constable Charles Lewis Scammell lived in three rooms with his wife Francis and two children at the police station at 169 Uxbridge Road, Hanwell. Also living there was Police Inspector Albert Edward Sellars, in four rooms with his wife Anne and three children.[1482]

The funeral depicted below seems to be that of Constable Percy Edwin Cook, en-route to Hanwell cemetery in January 1927. Cook bravely tried to rescue two workmen who had become overcome by poisonous gases in a high-tension chamber at Kensington. When both Cook and the workmen were found, all had perished. In the foreground a Metropolitan Police band leads the hearse and entourage, whilst many people look on.

A police funeral procession at Hanwell in the 1920s

Hanwell Police Station was closed from 18th November 1933 as a police station, but continued in use for other police purposes. A full-size police box was placed outside the station for public to have direct access to police as shown in the photograph below.

Hanwell Police Station 1886-2012

In 2007 mention was made of selling the property, but it was not until 2012 that the property was cleared out and made ready to sell.

Harefield Police Station

London Borough of Hillingdon

24 Rickmansworth Road, Harefield (1842-1974)

X Division (1842-1974)

A house in Rickmansworth Road, Harefield, owned by Mr Howe, was acquired in 1842 on a 21-year lease at £16 10s 0d per year. It was a newly-built brick and slate building, with a large garden, good scullery, coal hole and water closets, with a water supply from a well in the garden. The Receiver bought the freehold in October 1862, which included the adjoining cottage for £420.

The property was then converted at a cost of £410 to include an inspector's married quarters, two cells and two-stall stables. The cottage nearby was occupied by a constable and his family.[1483] In 1851 the two constables and their families living there were 29-year-old George Broughton and his wife Matilda. Next door was Charles Paine and his wife Emma. George and Matilda remained there for a further 20 years.[1484]

Harefield Police Station (cottages) 1862-1932

In a police report from 1881 Harefield Police Station was described as being 'two small cottages in a village, with new stables'. The water supply was polluted, and there was difficulty in disposing of the sewage. At the time of the inspection the buildings were occupied by one married inspector and one married constable.[1485]

In 1890 Harefield Police Station was on X Division as a sectional station to Uxbridge, and was being policed by Sergeant William Filbee and eight constables.[1486] Station Sergeant William Lay took charge before 1894, and he was assisted by one sergeant and eight police constables.[1487]

Harefield police cycle patrol c1908

In 1911 Police Sergeant George Grover, his wife Ellen and their three children were living in five rooms at the police station,[1488] while Constable John Albert Smith, his wife Agnes and their five children were living in five rooms in the Police Cottage, Harefield.[1489]

Harefield Police Station was closed in 1934 and the staff were transferred to Northwood and Ruislip Police Stations. After the station closed, it was used as two sets of married quarters. These premises which were erected in 1842, apparently with no proper foundations or damp-proof course, and during the last few years damp had started to seep in to the property.

The house was demolished in 1957 and four new police flats were erected. These flats were opened in 1958, and then in October 1966 it was decided to build a police office. This was built at the side of the flats.[1490] The address was 24 Rickmansworth Road, Harefield (XF).[1491] The police office closed in 1974.[1492]

Harefield Police Office, 2008

As of 2019 there is a police office situated at the gate office of Harefield Hospital, in Hill End Road, Harefield and a Safer Neighbourhoods unit for Harefield.

Harlesden Police Station (formerly named Willesden until 1896)

The London Borough of Brent
Stonebridge Willesden (1840-1860)
Craven Park Road (1860-1913)
76 Craven Park, Harlesden (1913 to Present)
S Division (1840-1865)
X Division (1865-1965)
Q Division (1965-1993)
London Borough of Brent OCY (1993-2018)
Brent (North West BCU) (2018 to Present)

The first Police Station in the area was established in 1840 in a small house in Stonebridge. It was a one of a terrace of properties known as 'Ivy Cottages' and in 1911, long after police vacated this building, it was being used as a greengrocer's shop. There were only two constables and they covered an area from Kilburn Lane to Harrow including Kilburn, Willesden Green, Cricklewood, Hendon and Kingsbury.[1493]

1474 Metropolitan Police Surveyor's Book as at 1845, p139.
1475 Metropolitan Police Surveyor's Book as at 1845, p141.
1476 Oates, J. Dr. 'Policing the Past' (2012).
1477 Charles Reeves, Metropolitan Police Surveyor, letter to Sir Richard Mayne, Commissioner, dated November 1866. MEPO file.
1478 Metropolitan Police List of Police Stations 1873.
1479 Metropolitan Police Surveyor's Register, p222.
1479 Metropolitan Police Condition of Police Stations 1881.
1480 Metropolitan Police Surveyor's Register, p222.
1481 Metropolitan Police Orders dated 24th January 1885.
1482 Census 1911.
1483 *Hillingdon Mirror* (unknown date) and Metropolitan Police Surveyor's Book, p158.
1484 Census 1851, 1861 and 1871.
1485 Metropolitan Police: Condition of Police Stations 1881.
1486 *Kelly's Middlesex Directory* 1890.
1487 *Kelly's Middlesex Directory* 1894.
1488 Census 1911.
1489 Ibid.
1490 Jephcote. J. 'Histories of Police Stations in Hillingdon' 1969.
1491 Metropolitan Police Orders dated 30th September 1966.
1492 Metropolitan Police Orders dated 23rd August 1974.
1493 *Willesden Chronicle*, 17th March 1911.

Willesden Police Station 1860-1913, Craven Park Road, Harlesden

In 1841 there were three policemen residing in Willesden according to the 1841 Census, but one was living at 'Railway Cottage' and may have been a railway policeman. The census in 1841 also shows there were two policemen living at Wood Lodge, Wembley.[1494]

In 1860 a police station was opened in Craven Park Road, at the junction of St. Mary's Road, Harlesden, with three Police Sergeants and four Police Constables. The cost of erecting the Police Station was £1132.

The land was leased from James Wright of Willesden, Middlesex, from Lady Day, 1860 for 99 years. Rental for the land was £10 per year with the Receiver paying the rates, taxes, repairs and the insurance.[1495] The police station had a charge room, inspector's office, store, three cells, two stalls, an ambulance shed, water closets, a cleaning shed and a stove. The freehold of the land was purchased by the Receiver in August 1899 for £440.[1496] Eventually it was sold to Middlesex Standing Joint Committee for £1350 on 31st July 1913.

Willesden was shown as being a police station on S or Hampstead Division in 1864,[1497] and was transferred to X Paddington Division in 1865.[1498] The station was called Willesden Police Station up until July 1896 when the new Willesden Green Station was opened and Willesden was renamed Harlesden Police Station.[1499]

Meanwhile, in 1879 Willesden was a Sectional Station on X Division under the command of Superintendent Hugh Eccles and Chief Inspector George Browning. They were assisted by ten Inspectors. X or Kilburn Division at this time covered a total of thirteen police stations.[1500]

In 1881 a report on the condition of all London police stations was critical of a number of issues. One in particular was that there were married quarters within the Station which were occupied by a married Police Inspector and a married Constable. The Inspector's kitchen was the Constable's washhouse.[1501]

In November 1900 an Inspector George Robert Hodder, (warrant no. 62839), who joined the Metropolitan Police in 1878, retired from the Force whilst serving at Harlesden. He came to Harlesden in 1896 to assist a Sub-Divisional Inspector Joseph Cooper whose workload had increased considerably.[1502] Inspector Sydney Smith was also stationed at Harlesden in 1899. Cooper moved to Harlesden as Sub-Divisional Inspector where he resided in 1891.[1503] When Cooper retired, aged 48 years old in 1901, he remained in Willesden living at 4, Leighton Gardens with his wife and four children who were all employed by then.[1504]

On the retirement of Inspector Hodder there was a glowing tribute to his contribution to the community in the local press, which said,

Inspector George Hodder

'…….Inspector Hodder will be a great loss to the district. During his service locally he had won the esteem of his fellow officers and men, but the regard of very many of the civil residents with whom his public work on the religious and temperance platform, as well as his professional duties, had brought him in contact. Mr Hodder was shrewd and capable in his office as second in command in the sub district and his qualities of tact and strict justice, tempered with good humour, made him many friends and few enemies. His Post Office service proceeding his Police duty rendered his retirement an earlier one than would otherwise have occurred, but whilst in the Police Service he won hearty praise from his superiors and more than one public commendation for saving life from fire in circumstances demanding great bravery and readiness of

action'.[1505]

On retirement Inspector Hodder became involved with the Police Pensioners Executive, the forerunner of the National Association of Retired Police Officers (NARPO). He was a founder member of the Retired Police Officers Association in 1910 and was elected its first Chairman. When this group became NARPO he was elected Chairman of that organisation. He was also actively involved with the Baptist Church and the Temperance Movement. He died in October 1932.[1506]

In the early 1900s plans were made to erect a new police station at Harlesden. A site was eventually found on the "West Ella" estate. In June 1909 a freehold parcel of land on this estate was purchased for £1,650 by Messrs Ryde and Sons acting for the Receiver at an auction of surplus properties owned by the Middlesex County Council. The site was situated on the south-east corner of the estate, i.e. Craven Park junction with Ella Road. The Home Office approved the purchase of the site, known as 'Fortune Gate', and returned the conveyance in October 1909.[1507]

There was a delay in developing the site because of restrictive covenants in the deeds which dated back to 1894. One of the covenants stated that 'no building or lot shall be used for any purpose which may be a nuisance or annoyance'. Counsel's opinion was sought and advised the Receiver to go ahead and build the police station. The erection of the station was authorised by the Metropolitan Police Act of 1886 which incorporated the Land Clauses Consolidation Act of 1845.[1508]

In 1894 the station was still called Willesden when Constable (warrant no. 48245) James W. Swaine, retired on pension as the oldest serving mounted police officer in the Metropolitan Police, having served 24 years of his 27 years' service at Willesden.[1509]

By 1911 the strength had increased to one Sub-Divisional Inspector, three Inspectors, 15 Sergeants, and 78 Constables. On the night of the census in 1911 Inspector William Perry his wife Esther and family together with a large number of single Constables were all shown as residing at the police station.[1510] That year Inspector William Dingle, (warrant no. 75042), then aged 44 years from Harlesden Police Station, resided at 4, Elynfield Road, Harlesden with his wife and five children in a 6-room house with two lodgers.[1511] Dingle had joined the police in 1889.

When the new station was opened in July 1913 the old police station was closed down and eventually demolished. Later, Willesden Magistrates Court was erected on the site.[1512]

The new station, designed John Dixon Butler, the Metropolitan Police Surveyor, was built and opened for business in July 1913.[1513] Harlesden then took over the responsibilities of the Sub Division and old Kilburn Police Station became a 'section house' and storage facility. The old building was reduced to rubble after an air raid in 1940 which killed a number of police staff – see Kilburn Police Station.

During World War 1, the war effort intensified, the fields of the Royal Agricultural Show Ground at Park Royal were taken over for war use, and munitions factories were built. The largest of these, in Acton Lane, employed seven thousand people, mainly women, including many mothers.[1514] Mrs S. Chambers of Winchelsea Road, Harlesden was a special war worker who worked in munitions during World War I. She was employed at the National Filling Factory No. 3 at Park Royal, Willesden and later as a packer of fuses for bombs and grenades. She was a good worker and also became a police woman at the filling factory. Tragically she met her death during an accident at the plant.

Harlesden Police Station 1913-2013

The women police were established by Margaret Damer Dawson and Mary Allen, and Mrs Chambers was one of the early police women who were needed by the Munitions Minister and the War effort. Chambers' work initially was to fill shells with gun cotton and nitro-glycerine (cordite).[1515] Both men and women on essential war work were issued with an "on war service" badge. The men wore it on their lapel, so that they would not be accused of being cowards because they were not in uniform. Women also wore it with pride, but as a brooch or hat pin.[1516] There were 140 men and 345 women employed at Park Royal. The workers were not pressed hard to do their work as the management wanted them to be slow and careful when handling the munitions so as to avoid accidents.

Sub-Divisional Inspector William Macmillan, (warrant no. 95809), (who had transferred from H or Whitechapel Division in 1909) was in charge of Harlesden up until 1915 when he was promoted to Chief Inspector and sent to F or Paddington Division. Macmillan, a Scotsman from Perthshire, was destined for higher office, became Superintendent of K or Bow Division in 1920[1517] and retired in July 1929.

1494 Census 1841.
1495 Metropolitan Police List of Police Stations 1873.
1496 MEPO 4/484.
1497 Metropolitan Police Orders dated 11th January 1864.
1498 Metropolitan Police Orders dated 28th October 1865.
1499 J. Back Archives circa 1965.
1500 *Post Office Directory* 1879.
1501 Report on Condition of Police Stations 1881.
1502 *Willesden Chronicle*, 29th May 1896.
1503 *Kelly's Directory* 1893.
1504 Census 1901.
1505 *Willesden Chronicle*, 2nd November 1900.
1506 The late Mike Fountain (Police historian and active member of the Friends of the Metropolitan Police Historical Collection) supplied all the information on his great grandfather, Police Inspector George Robert Hodder.
1507 J. Back Archives circa 1965.
1508 J. Back Archives circa 1965.
1509 *Police Review and Parade Gossip*, 19th January 1894.
1510 Census 1911.
1511 J. Back Archives circa 1965.
1512 Census 1911.
1513 Metropolitan Police Orders dated 8th July 1913.
1514 www.brent.gov.uk/museumarchive, accessed 19th June 2012.
1515 www.military-genealogy.com/viewRecord?product=nr&q accessed 19th June 2012.
1516 www.brent.gov.uk/museumarchive, accessed 19th June 2012.
1517 *Kelly's Directory* 1920.

By 1915 the police station was under the command of Sub-Divisional Inspector (warrant no. 79509) William Gilbert Grimmett and in addition to Inspector William Dingle, there were also George Barnett (warrant no. 85719) and later in 1916 (warrant no. 78770) Oliver Millard.[1518] Life at Harlesden must have suited Dingle since he remained there until January 1919 when he retired on pension after 30 years' service with an annual pension of £151 6s 5d. Grimmett later retired on pension from Harlesden in November 1921.

By 1928 Harlesden was designated a sub-divisional station of X or Kilburn Division with Willesden Green and Wembley as its sectional stations.

In the reorganisation of the Divisions north of the Thames in December 1933 Harlesden remained a sub-divisional station. The address, in 1938, of Harlesden Police Station was 76, Craven Park at the junction of High Road.[1519]

William George Gane, born 21st January 1911 in Harlesden, joined the War Reserve and was posted to Harlesden until October 1943 when he joined the Royal Navy. As a result of his police experience, he transferred to the Regulating Branch (naval police) in October 1944 as an acting Regulating Petty Officer (Master at Arms). He was discharged in August 1946 from service on the battleship HMS *Rodney*.[1520]

By 1955 Superintendent R. Linge was in charge of Harlesden Police Sub-Division.[1521]

In 1965 the Local Authority boundaries changed and Harlesden found itself as a Sub-Division on the newly formed Q Division. Its station code became 'QH' and its sectional stations were Willesden Green 'QL' and Kilburn 'QK'[1522]

Harlesden was now part of the London Borough of Brent. In 2012 the station address was 76, Craven Park and its opening hours 07:00 to 21:00, closed for breaks between 10:00 to 11:00 and 17:00 to 1800.[1523] In 2013 the front counter was closed to the public although the station remained in Police ownership to date.

Harlington Police Station

London Borough of Hillingdon

75 Bath Road, Harlington (1890-1973)

T Division (1830-1965)

The first police station at Harlington was a horse patrol station described as a house, held on a yearly tenancy of £30 from a Mrs Arabin Drayton.[1524] It consisted of a durable brick and slate property, with a stable for one horse and a garden at the rear. This station was given up in March 1870. Police then moved into another much larger property in Harlington owned by Mr William Hewett of Harlington, however it was not only regarded as a police station, but also used as a section house for single constables.[1525] Police occupied these premises from September 1870 until September 1873.

In 1886 police bought the freehold of a piece of land on the Bath Road for £350.[1526] This land also included the mineral rights to Cranford St. John and Cranford Le Mote. Luckily for the landscape, the police officers were not mining prospectors.[1527]

It is not clear which premises, if any, police occupied until the new police station was built and occupied in September 1890. The police station cost £2,714 to build.[1528] Accommodation at the new station allowed for the occupation of one married inspector at 5s and 6d per week, and one married constable at 3s a week living in the two adjoining police cottages.[1529] The station also included an ambulance shed that housed the heavy wooden handcart for the transfer of drunks, the sick or the dead.

In 1899 the police received notification from Lord Dawley, of nearby Dawley Manor, claiming that he had rights to the land and that police should vacate the station. A stern letter from the Metropolitan Police Receiver to Lord Dawley, stating the police held the freehold interest, soon put an end to his claim, leaving him in no doubt who was the law in Harlington.[1530]

Harlington Police Station 1890-1975

In 1911 Station Sergeant Fred Bristow, his wife Lily and their two teenage children were living in the Police Cottages, Bath Road, Harlington.[1531]

In 1930 Harlington Police Station was described as one of the 'country stations' of the Metropolitan Police, and was situated about three miles short of Berkshire and Buckinghamshire boundaries.

In the early days of the station's existence, before public transport and the amenities of banks were available, the Superintendent would ride from Hammersmith, with an escort of three mounted Police Constables, with the weekly pay for the officers at Harlington. Local inhabitants regarded this as a ceremonial occasion.

Invariably the Horse Guards on their way to Windsor would follow behind the Mounted Police.[1532]

The station closed at midnight and the constable, normally inside the station, would perform a short patrol in the vicinity. He carried the front door key to allow the patrolling station sergeant from Bedfont or sub-divisional inspector from Staines to sign the books, checking all was correct.

The rear entrance and yard of Harlington Police Station

In 1951 the address of the station was changed to 75 Bath Road, Harlington,[1533] and it was situated on the perimeter of the expanding main London Heathrow Airport.

Harlington Police Station could not survive with all the changes being made to Heathrow Airport and closed its doors on 8th November 1965. In 1967 the property was sold to the British Airport Authority, who by then had become the owner of all the surrounding land and buildings. The police station was later demolished.[1534]

In 1972 a plaque entitled 'Metropolitan Police 1890' from the former Harlington Police Station was placed in the courtyard of West Drayton Police Station. West Drayton and the surrounding district had previously been policed from Harlington.[1535]

Harold Hill Police Station

The London Borough of Havering

Gooshays Drive, Romford, Essex (1955-2011)

Essex Police (1955-1965)

Metropolitan Police (1965-2011)

In 1930 Harold Wood was expanding rapidly, and was estimated to have a population of 3,000 people. A house was rented by a constable (exact location unknown), and this also acted as the police station. There were no facilities for housing prisoners, so they were taken to the nearest divisional station at Romford. Two constables were attached to the area, but it was envisaged that further officers would be needed. The surveyor recommended the purchase of four further houses nearby.[1536]

The area around Harold Hill was developed in 1949. This major council housing development was also designed to accommodate overspill families from London. During the planning it was decided to build a modern police station, which was built in Gooshays Drive, Harold Hill,[1537] and opened in 1955.[1538] A new bus route was introduced to serve the large estate being built, and to provide direct transport to the Ford Motor Works at Dagenham.

Harold Hill Police Station 1955-2011

Harold Hill became a part of Romford Sub-Division, which also included Plough Corner, Collier Row and Rydal Mount, Havering. The other sub-division was Hornchurch.

The station was only open to the public between 10.00am and 6.00pm daily.[1539] The station was closed in 2011,[1540] and sold to a German High Street retailer who demolished the building and erected a supermarket in its place.

Harrow (Northolt Road) Police Station

The London Borough of Harrow

74 Northolt Road (1963 to Present)

X Division (1963-1965)

Q Division (1965-1993)

Borough of Harrow OCU (1993-2018/19)

North West (NW) BCU with Barnet and Brent (2018/19)

The current Harrow Police Station is a relatively modern building in South Harrow which replaced the old West Street Police Station as the main station for the borough in the early 1960s. West Street was an old Victorian building, in the oldest part of Harrow at the foot of Harrow-on-the-Hill, right next to the cricket fields of the famous Harrow School.

Less than half a mile away, the 'new' Harrow Police Station became operational at 6.00am on 30th September 1963. The station was constructed by Messrs Dove Bros Ltd of Islington, with the work commencing on 24th April 1962.[1541] Note the placement of the air raid siren on the roof. The old-looking building next door to the police station was later replaced by an office block, which now forms part of the 'extended' police station.

In 1936 the Commissioner had asked for consideration to be given for the acquisition of a new site in Harrow "on which a station might be built in a few years time to replace the present one."[1542] The old station in West Street was no longer suitable being very small and entirely inadequate to meet present-day requirements.

The site in Northolt Road had, in fact, originally been purchased in 1938 for the sum of £2,750, with plans for immediate building to commence. However, World War II was to halt the plans for a further 24 years. The site was let out to the GPO from September 1950 to December 1961 as a garage for their vehicles and for storing their cable drums.

In 1963, 'Plato' from the local newspaper reported the new stations opening under the headline "The Newcomers".[1543] It discovered an "air of gentle confusion," with "one detective entered a large office asking if anyone knew where the handcuffs were. It took several minutes to track them down." The reporter noted that the station was in possession of a full-size billiards table, and also that the building was fully up to

1518   *Kelly's Kilburn, Willesden and Cricklewood Directory* 1918/19.
1519   *Kelly's Kilburn and Willesden Directory* 1938.
1520   www.clanjackson.co.uk/genealogy/p14617.htm accessed 19th June 2012.
1521   Metropolitan Police List 1955.
1522   Metropolitan Police Orders dated 6th August 1964.
1523   content.met.police.uk/PoliceStation/harlesden accessed 13th June 2012.
1524   Metropolitan Police Surveyor's Book, p150.
1525   Ibid.
1526   *Hillingdon Mirror*, 19th June 1979.
1527   *West Drayton and District Local Historian*, September 1972, p10.
1528   Metropolitan Police Station List 1893.
1529   Metropolitan Police Orders dated 26th September 1890.
1530   *West Drayton and District Local Historian*, September 1972, p10.
1531   Census 1911.
1532   Metropolitan Police Heritage Centre Archive.
1533   Metropolitan Police Orders dated 3rd August 1951.
1534   *Uxbridge Gazette*, 5th May 1983.
1535   *West Drayton and District Local Historian*, September 1972, p10.
1536   Essex County Constabulary. 'Police Stations and Police Houses Booklet' (c1930) Essex Police Museum, Police Headquarters, Springfield, Chelmsford, Essex.
1537   *The Job*, 10th May 1968.
1538   Scollan, M. (1993). *Sworn to Serve*. Phillimore, Chichester. p134.
1539   www.met.police.uk/contact/phone.htm accessed 3rd February 2002.
1540   Information rights unit, MPS, police stations closed since 2010. Accessed 10th June 2019.
1541   Harrow Division Athletic & Social Club Anniversary Souvenir Programme 1829-1979. Met Police 150th anniversary.
1542   Harrow Police Station (Met Police Archives, author unknown).
1543   *Harrow Observer*, 3rd October 1963.

date and imaginatively designed. The cost of the building was reported to be £120,000.

Harrow Police Station under construction

Harrow was later to be designated the divisional code 'QA' via Police Orders of 8th August 1964. The new telephone number for the station was BYRon 1113.

In recent years Harrow Police Station has been struggling to cope with the demands of modern policing. The office building next door was incorporated into the station in the early 2000s. Extra 'portable' cells were also added. Plans for a new central police station has been discussed in recent years, but is currently on hold.[1544]

In 2019 the current station in Northolt Road is an operational 24-hour building, with a front counter service for public contact but with no custody or prisoner facilities. However, the station has now been amalgamated into the North West (NW) borough area, together with the stations at Wembley (Brent) and Colindale (Barnet).

Harrow Police Station 1963 to present

Harrow (West Street) Police Station

The London Borough of Harrow
Bottom end of West Street (1840-1865)
76 West Street (1865-1965)
74 Northolt Road (1965-2011)
T Division (1840-1865)
X Division (1865-1965)
Q Division (1965-1993)
Borough of Harrow OCU (1993-2011)

West Street Police Station was the first police building in the borough of Harrow. In 1842, Harrow Police Station had been leased for an annual rent of £30.[1545] Its exact location is unknown, but it is thought to be near the bottom of the hill in West Street. The 1851 census revealed the presence of a Sergeant James Cooper and four constables.[1546] It's probable that Sergeant Cooper's first child, Arthur, was born in the police station in 1850.[1547] The police station was listed in the 1850 guide 'Handbook for Visitors to Harrow on the Hill'[1548] as being at the bottom of the south side of West Street, next to a house in ruins, land and garden on land owned by George Beazley.

In June 1866 the local *Harrow Gazette* reported under the heading "Proposed New Police Station"5 that a new site was being considered for a replacement police building. The Commissioner was considering spending £3,000 on a new station. A site in Crown Street had been offered, and the paper suggested that the parish officers should make representations to Headquarters before the final decision was taken. Despite this encouragement from the local paper, later the same year the Receiver of the Metropolitan Police bought the freehold of West Street for £1,254.[1549]

By 1869 the need for a new building appeared to be pressing. A letter to the editor of the *Harrow Gazette* complained as follows:

'Sir, permit me through the medium of your paper to draw the attention of our Nuisances Authorities to the badly constructed and unhealthy cells for the confinement of prisoners at the Harrow Police Station, with a view to their making representation to the Commissioner of Police of the unfitness of these cells for the most depraved of our creatures. I believe the Inspector of Nuisances has only to make an inspection of the cells for them to be at once condemned. I am sir, yours obediently, HUMANITAS.'[1550]

Relief was almost at hand when the *Harrow Gazette* reported action by the police in their report of 25th May 1872:

"We are glad to see that the Commissioners of police have at last pulled down and removed the dilapidated cottages near their station, and we trust that this work of demolition will soon be followed by the erection of a new and suitable police station. The present station is neither ample nor decent. Considering the large amount paid for Police Rates by the parish of Harrow, (nearly £1,900 a year), we think we should have a respectable looking building as we see in other parishes of less importance. If the Commissioners could add a room in which the magistrates could occasionally meet to transact business, it would be very desirable, for it would tend to lessen offences, and save the parish still further expenses, incurred by the police in conveying prisoners to Hammersmith and other police courts."[1551]

On 9th November 1872, the *Harrow Gazette* reported more progress on the subject of the new station being erected 'above the cricket ground'.[1552] It described the previous station as "Little better than a village cage." The article went on, saying "The necessity for this building shows that Harrow is at least increasing in population, but, let us hope, not in crime."

West Street Police Station was finally finished in 1873.[1553] Police Orders of 31st October reported that police business would commence on 1st November. The building was designed by Mr R.H. Gager Esq,[1554] and the cost of the work £2,271.[1555] It was carried out by builders Messrs Fassnidge and Sons of Uxbridge. The same company was to build Pinner Police Station in 1899.

The locals were pleased with their new station, so much so that a party to celebrate the opening was held in private rooms in Crown Street in the room belonging to Mr J. Chapman. The *Harrow Gazette* reported in its 15th November 1873 edition that 70 guests attended the event.[1556] Toasts were made to Inspector George Wills and Sergeant Arnold. The station was described as "an ornament to that part of town." The health of

West Street Police Station 1865-1963

the clerk of works, Mr Holloway, and the foreman, Mr Grace, were also proposed. The following week's edition of the local paper described the building in great detail.[1557] The report mentioned the building being "of classic design", with a frontage of 40 feet, and that it was built of picked stock bricks with Doulton stone dressings. The building was "entered by a portico of Doulton stone." Three cells were present, which were "all warmed by Haydon's hot air apparatus". The officers enjoyed a reading room and a bathroom with a hot air closet for drying the men's clothes. The first floor was the private apartment for the sergeant in charge as well as the unmarried policemen. At the rear, a two-horse stable and an ambulance shed were erected. The only disappointment that the paper reported was that "No room has been provided for holding magistrates meetings in the new building, the present arrangements of taking cases to Edgware being both costly and inconvenient".

Harrow had originally been attached to T or Kensington Division, but in 1865 it transferred to X or Paddington Division. Another change to X Division was to follow in 1911, when Superintendent Olive submitted a report on 14th February suggesting that Harrow Sub-Division comprised of Harrow, Pinner, Greenford and Northwood Police Stations. Harrow was to change for a final time in 1965, to become part of the newly-formed Q Division.

West Street was to close as the operational station for Harrow on 30th September 1963, having become too small.[1558] The building remained in police ownership and has been used for various purposes since, such as Divisional Offices, traffic wardens and the Harrow Town Team. Sadly, along with lots of other Victorian buildings, the Met has been selling off small, cramped buildings not fit for 21st century policing, and West Street was finally sold to Harrow School in 2011 to be used as offices.[1559]

West Street officers were to deal with the first fatal motor car accident in Britain. On 25th February 1899, Daimler representative Mr Edwin Sewell was demonstrating a 6HP Daimler Wagonette car to five people on a journey from Westminster.[1560] After enjoying a lunch at the King's Head, Harrow, Mr Sewell was putting the car through its paces on Grove Hill when a rear wheel rim collapsed, causing the vehicle to crash. Mr Sewell, died at the scene within minutes, while one of his passengers, Major James Ritcher, was thrown from the vehicle and suffered such serious injuries that he died four days later without gaining consciousness in hospital. The

A West Street policeman surveys the damage and controls the crowds at Britain's first "FATACC" involving a motor car passenger death

1544 *Harrow Observer*, 6th January 2009.
1545 Harrow Division Athletic & Social Club Anniversary Souvenir Programme 1829-1979. Met Police 150th anniversary.
1546 1851 Census.
1547 Harrow: St Mary Parish Church Baptism Register for 1850.
1548 T. Smith. *Handbook for Visitors to Harrow on the Hill*.
1549 *Harrow Gazette*, 1st June 1866, and Metropolitan Police Property Register Sheet for West Street Police Station. Page 224.
1550 *Harrow Gazette*, January 1869.
1551 Ibid.
1552 *Harrow Gazette*, 9th November 1872.
1553 Metropolitan Police Orders dated 31st October 1873.
1554 West Street Police Station, 1st August 1970 (Harrow Civic Centre Archives, author unknown.
1555 Metropolitan Police Property Register Sheet for West Street Police Station.
1556 *Harrow Gazette*, 15th November 1873.
1557 *Harrow Gazette*, 22nd November 1873.
1558 Harrow Police Station (Undated history deposited in Harrow Archives, author unknown).
1559 *Harrow Observer*, 2nd November 2011.
1560 'The Archive Photographs Series – Harrow' by Brian Girling.

coroner's officer involved in this case was West Street acting Sergeant James Walter Pearce.[1561] The accident attracted a great crowd, and police from Harrow remained on the scene to secure the vehicle once people had been conveyed to hospital.

West Street Police Station c1960s. Note the 'Police' inscription above the main entrance, which has now been removed

A very notable West Street police officer was Sergeant 32X Charles Potter, who retired on 21st April 1902 with a pension of £87 16s 9d.[1562] He had a remarkable career, and was involved in some infamous cases. The *Harrow Gazette* recorded details of Potter's service, as well as his retirement at Harrow after 26 years' service.[1563] He joined the Metropolitan Police on 17th April 1876, coming from a police family as his grandfather had been the parish constable in Chappell in Essex, and his father a Superintendent in the Metropolitan Police. Three of his brothers were also policemen.

After arriving in London Potter was posted to Penge Police Station, where his first charge was for four people who were connected with the murder of Harriett Staunton. All four were convicted, and her husband and the husband's brother were sentenced to death. Both were later reprieved, but were given life sentences. The method of killing Mrs Staunton was by keeping her locked up and starving her to death. Sergeant Potter was present during the Trafalgar Square riots of 1887, as well as the dockyard strikes of 1888. In 1890 he was posted to Notting Dale Police Station, "in which rough district, was said to contain some of the worst characters in London". By 1895 Sergeant Potter was given his final posting to Harrow.

The other claim to fame that the good Sergeant could make was that he was the officer in charge of the only murder case where the defendant was a serving policeman who was convicted at the Old Bailey and later hanged at Newgate. It was known as the Wormwood Scrubs Tragedy,[1564] and involved Constable 385X George Samuel Cooke (warrant no. 73717) beating Maud Merton to death near the prison on 7th June 1893. Constable Cooke came from Ludham in Norfolk, and joined the force aged 22 years on 22nd June 1888 having previously been a fisherman.

The Old Bailey trial report[1565] gave details of the evidence against Constable Cooke. It recorded that he had served briefly on both L and A Divisions before being posted to Bow Street as Constable 130E. At about this time he became acquainted with Maud Merton, who was a prostitute who frequented the Strand. She later complained to the station inspector about Cooke's behaviour towards her, and he was subsequently transferred to Notting Dale on X Division.

Maud Merton's body was found with severe head injuries in the area where Constable Cooke had been on night shift, with witnesses reporting having seen Cooke with a female. On returning to his lodgings after his night shift PC Cooke was seen burying something in the garden. When the inspector dug up the garden he found a truncheon marked '857A'. Constable Cooke was interviewed, but denied the murder. He stated that he had bought the truncheon from a man named 'Black Dick' for sixpence, and that he had buried it as it was not his. Constable 857A, Henry Pomeroy, told the court that he had been lodging at Westminster Section House at the same time as Constable Cooke, when his truncheon had gone missing. Constable Cooke later confessed that he had not used the A Division truncheon, but had used his own X Division issue one to strike Maud Merton. He told officers that Merton had been following him and was annoying him, and that he "was in misery". He admitted hitting her three times with the truncheon, and keeping his foot on her neck for five minutes.

He said, "I felt nothing of killing her. I have been much happier since she has been dead". Cooke did not call any witnesses at the trial, at which he pleaded Not Guilty, but after hearing the evidence the jury convicted him of murder. The jury strongly recommended that Cooke should be shown mercy on the grounds of the provocation he received. The trial judge, Mr Justice Hawkins, was clearly unimpressed for the call for mercy in sparing Cooke's life. He told the prisoner that he would pass his plea for mercy to the Home Secretary. Mr Hawkins went on to describe the murder itself stating that "a peculiar atrocity has been manifested". He added that the act had been horribly cruel in response to her 'simply annoying him'. The blows to the head had been aggravated by his standing on her neck.

Hawkins told Cooke: "It is my painful duty to sentence you to die." As the sentence was passed by the black-capped judge, a woman in the gallery screamed out and then 'swooned'.

The *Illustrated Police News*[1566] reported that Cooke and his sweetheart had arranged to marry in the October. She was unaware of the existence of Maud Merton, and had discovered Cooke's arrest in the newspaper. She pawned her watch to bring comforts to her fiancé, and visited him in prison every day.

Cooke wrote to a police comrade on 26th June and lamented that he would no longer be able to share a half pint of 'bitter and Burton', and that he felt for his parents and for Nellie. He signed off, 'I remain your sincere friend, S. Cooke, HM Prison'.

An artist's impression of the forlorn-looking PC Cooke at West London Police Court

The trial took place on 7th and 8th of July 1893. On 10th July he was dismissed from the Metropolitan Police. Cooke's sweetheart had tried to secure a reprieve for him, but none was forthcoming. Cooke slept fitfully the night before the execution. In the morning he 'ate sparingly'. He expressed no sorrow for his crime, his only concern being that for his parents and sweetheart.

Though he looked haggard, he shook the hand of the chief warder and walked firmly to the scaffold, where a five feet drop awaited him. Mr

Billington performed the execution, which took place without a struggle. A huge crowd had assembled outside Newgate on the morning of 25th July 1893, when Cooke met his death at 9.00am. A black flag was raised above the 'Debtors' Door' to indicate the sentence had been carried out.

Police Orders[1567] summed up Constable Cooke's demise as follows: 'Convicted of unlawful murder at the Central Criminal Court sessions and sentenced to death. NO PAY'!

The census record of 1901 shows that Potter and his wife, niece and four constables resided at the station.[1568] These were Sergeant Charles Potter from Chappel in Essex, his wife Elenor, Florence Hull, a book-keeper, and William Hall, Arthur Shepherd, John Eaton, all constables.

Also retiring at the same time as Sgt Potter, on 21st April 1902, was Acting Sergeant James Walter Pearce, after 25 years' service. He also came from a police family, having three brothers also in the force. After serving his first year at Carlton Terrace Station, Harrow Road, he transferred to Harrow where he spent the next 24 years. In 1887 he spent three months in plain clothes, patrolling the grounds of Harrow School in an effort to prevent Irish terrorists blowing up the building.

The father of ten children, Sergeant Pearce must have been a popular man. The local newspaper reported that arrangements were afoot for a collection to be made in the district to present a testimonial to both good sergeants on the day of the Coronation in 1902. It was said that a collector would be visiting every house in the district soliciting subscriptions.[1569] Pearce retired on an annual pension of £57 8s 6d.[1570] A prominent article in the local newspaper, the *Harrow Gazette*, carried photographs of both the officers as well as a lengthy report of their service entitled 'The Police Retirements at Harrow'. The officers were both clearly well-regarded.

The Metropolitan Police Special Constabulary played a significant part on X Division and at Harrow during both World Wars. During WWI Harrow sustained the highest contingent of Specials, with 208. At Harrow was a fire squad (a mixture of MSC and temporary Fire Brigade) which was formed with the co-operation of Captain Leader, head of the Harrow Fire Brigade. The men were put through their drills and occasionally gave public displays. Numerous fires were attended by the Fire Squad, but their biggest and most dangerous test was on 25th November 1918 when 500 tons of coke caught fire at the local gas works.

Harrow Division Tug of War team winners 1920

Police sports days were a family event which allowed some the chance to excel. Tug of war was a feat of combined strength, and winners at these sport days were celebrated as the picture above shows. Tug of war was an Olympic sport from 1900 to 1920, when it was dropped. The picture below shows the Harrow Division police winners in 1920 of the combined F and X Division Sports Day. The officers are: Back row, left to right, Constables Hedges, Evans (Res), Creed, Rush (Res), Roots, Passmore and Sub-Divisional Inspector Cosgrove. In the front row, left to right, are Constables Crabtree, Winters, Mansell (Captain), Savage and Greenfield.

In 1957 Harrow was a station on X Division, with call sign 'XA'. It was a sub-divisional station with Superintendent W.J. Poole in charge, with Pinner, Wembley and Wealdstone all being sectional stations. Poole was still in charge in 1962.

By 1965 Superintendent A. Flett DFC had taken over the sub-division. With the amalgamations of the London Boroughs of Ealing and Hillingdon, Flett had been promoted to Chief Superintendent and placed in charge of X Division. The Boroughs of Harrow and Brent were now amalgamated on Q Division, and Harrow Police Station had the call sign 'QA', with Superintendent A. C. Stanley in charge and Chief Inspector H.W.C. Howell was his deputy.

Harrow had one sectional station; Pinner.[1571] The station continued as 'QA' until 1989, when it was no longer a station taking charges and detaining prisoners for court.

West Street as it looked in November 2011 following its sale to Harrow School

In 2011 the old station and grounds were sold to Harrow School for an undisclosed amount. The word 'POLICE' has been removed from the plinth above the front entrance. In 2019 the station was owned by John Lyon School and is currently used as offices.

1561 "Acting Sergeant Pearce" in *Harrow Gazette*, 26th April 1902.
1562 Metropolitan Police Pension Records.
1563 *Harrow Gazette*, 7th May 1898.
1564 *The Peeler*, No. 14, 2010/11 "Fortunately the only one?" by Terry Stanford.
1565 Old Bailey Online (www.oldbaileyonline.org) Case reference t18930626-621. Page 957, Ninth Session 1892-3.
1566 *Pall Mall Gazette*, 10th June 1893.
1567 *Illustrated Police News*, 15th July 1893.
1568 Census 1901.
1569 "Acting Sergeant Pearce" in *Harrow Gazette*, 26th April 1902.
1570 Metropolitan Police Pension Records.
1571 *Police and Constabulary Almanacs 1965-1969*.

Picture taken in 2003 outside West Street Police Station

The picture above shows the line up outside West Street Police Station and its officers in 2003, with Chief Superintendent Alex Fish of Harrow seated front row, second from right.

The following story illustrates the humorous side of policing. An amusing story involving Chief Superintendent Fish occurred before he retired. Contributor to this book, retired Metropolitan Police officer Neil Watson, and another officer at Pinner were called by a resident of a small block of flats where water was seen coming from a flat above. They knocked on the door of the but got no answer. The officers got into the flat and at first thought that the tank housing some tropical fish was leaking, as there was only two inches of water left.

Thus, to the amusement of officers on the night duty at Pinner listening on the radio, this incident became enshrined in Pinner folklore and rapidly became known as 'the Tropical fish emergency'. On seeking advice, the officers were told to take possession of the fish and remove them to London Zoo. However, happy to oblige they found suitable container and placed the fish inside. But due to a mix up by the Zoo staff the fish were placed in sea water and were later found dead. A complaint against the officers was made by the Zoo for bringing the fish to them in the first place. Fortunately, the officers were found to be completely blameless, but Harrow Police wrote to the Zoo, with the letter informing them of the results of the inquiry being signed by 'A. Fish'. Needless to say, Neil acquired the nickname 'Mr Fish'.

Harrow Road Police Station

City of Westminster
22 Carlton Crescent (later Terrace), Kensal New Town,
 Paddington (1859-1912)
325 Harrow Road (1912-c.2019)
D Division (1859-1865)
X Division (1865-1965)
D Division (1965-1985/86)
No. 8 Area (1985/86-c.1993)
No. 1 Area (Central) (c.1993–c.2018)
Central West Basic Command Unit (c.2018 to Present)

Harrow Road became one of the stations of D or Marylebone Division in 1859, however it was transferred to the new X or Kilburn Division under Superintendent Samuel Hughes in 1865, where it remained until it returned to D Division in 1965. Property at 22 Carlton Crescent (later Terrace) was leased in 1873, and then additional premises acquired over the years at 6, 12, 14 and 16 Woodfield Road.

Inspector John Mobley was one of the officers promoted to fill a vacancy in 1885, when he was posted to Harrow Road. Inspector Frederick Mitchell was the Sub-Divisional Inspector at Harrow Road in 1893; he remained in post until 1895, when he retired and was replaced by Inspector William Bell.[1572] With Inspector Mitchell was a Scot, Reserve Inspector Hugh Newlands, who was responsible for the mounted officers on reserve for X Division. Harrow Road was the principle station for the division and housed the many horses needed by the mounted reserve.

Harrow Road Police Station 1859-1912

It was important to have a police presence in the area as the fields either side of the newly-built toll road were rapidly being converted to dwellings and the local population was expanding. Land at 22 Carlton Crescent (later Terrace) situated between the Harrow Road and the Grand Junction Canal was obtained on lease from 1856 from Mr Charles Woodroffe of Harrow Road for an annual rent of £30. The lease was for 100 years. A station was erected on the site which was convenient for the Westbourne Green Road toll gate in the Harrow Road, the Lock Hospital and the Paddington workhouse at the bottom of Woodfield Road.

Additional premises were acquired over the years at 6, 12, 14 and 16 Woodfield Road, opposite the station. This became a substantial station with ground floor, three upper floors and a basement. By the 1900s the station was no longer suitable for policing purposes, and new premises were sought on which to build a modern purpose-built station. Land situated at the corner of Woodfield Road and Harrow Road was purchased. It was important that there should be access to the rear of the station, and that the station should be built on the main thoroughfare. A new police station and a section house for 60 officers was then built, and opened on 4th March 1912 with a postal address of 325 Harrow Road.

One famous officer located at the old Harrow Road Police Station was Inspector Charles Brown (warrant no. 71791), who was born in 1863 and joined the Metropolitan Police in 1888 when there was a recruiting drive. He lived until 1933, and died in Canada where he moved after retiring from the police. During his service he rubbed shoulders with royalty and saw service at race meetings, fairs, strikes and unrest. In 1905 Brown was earning 63 shillings a week as an Inspector of X Division, Kilburn.

In the picture below he is seen at Epsom Downs in 1909, when Minoru won the Epsom Derby. He is wearing his kepi, providing protection for King Edward VII as part of his duty as a Reserve Inspector. He was there as part of a large contingent of police officers drawn from all over the Metropolitan Police.

Inspector Charles Brown

Brown in masonic outfit

appears on the officer's helmet plate, in keeping with the design of helmets for this period.

In July 1912, just as officers would be moving to the new station in the Harrow Road, Brown retired on a pension of £121 15s, and left the police service at the age of 48 years with an exemplary record. Later that month he set sail and settled in Calgary, in Canada, with his wife Rose Ada. Brown had been a lifelong freemason during his police service, membership being seen by many officers as offering opportunities for self-improvement and companionship. The picture below shows him with the masonic regalia of his lodge in Calgary. He had joined Ashlar Lodge No. 28 on 25th March 1920, and served as Tyler (an outer guard doorkeeper role responsible for summonses to meetings, and for representing poor or distressed freemasons) from 1922 to 1932. He was re-elected in the autumn of 1932.

Charles Brown died on 10th January 1933 in a Calgary hospital after a period of ill-health, having drawn his pension for over 21 years, and was buried in Union Cemetery Calgary. He was given a masonic funeral service on 16th January 1933. His widow, Rose Ada, died on 10th June 1933 in Epsom, England, and is buried there. She and their daughter Maggie Rose had returned to England for a visit, but she had an accident on board the ship as it was nearing Southampton. During her treatment it was discovered that she had cancer, with little chance of survival. She was transferred to London and then to Epsom Cottage Hospital, where she died.

Charles Brown (arrowed) and King Edward VII at the Derby 1909

The Derby was a popular event with lots of ordinary people, however there were also teams of thieves who would prey on the racegoers, either through illegal gaming or just simple crime such as stealing or pickpocketing. The police were there to prevent offences from taking place.

Inspector Brown on duty on a ceremonial occasion

In 1908 Inspector Brown was photographed (as shown left) in uniform with an XR helmet plate, indicating his status as a reserve officer. Reserve officers were a formal grouping of officers who would be deployed on ceremonial and public order events for which, for some period of time, an extra allowance was paid, in Inspector Brown's case amounting to four shillings per week. Reserve officers wore a slightly better grade of uniform, and many were trained to ride horses in case of being required in an emergency. 'XR' duty

Constable William Harper

In 1900 constable William John Harper (warrant no. 86240) joined K (Stepney) Division, but by November he had been transferred to X Division residing at 28 Charlton Terrace, Paddington in the police section house situated upstairs. Harper was 21-years-old when he joined, and had been born in Rotherhithe, He was 5' 10" tall, and weighed 10st 10lbs. He had been in the 1st Middlesex Volunteer Engineers for two-and-a-half years, probably fighting in South Africa.

The character of the Harrow Road ground has been transformed by development since 1960 and the Westway overhead motorway, but its streets featured in the iconic 1950 film *The Blue Lamp*, which led to the famous TV series *Dixon of Dock Green* in which Constable George Dixon, played by Jack Warner, played an archetypal police officer character relating to the community in a manner which has come to

1572 *Kelly's Directories* 1880-1900.

symbolise a traditional and respectful excellence of public relations in British policing.

The origin of *The Blue Lamp* came from a letter to Commissioner Sir Harold Scott dated 6th May 1948, where Jan Read, who worked for J. Arthur Rank, sought the assistance of Scotland Yard in making an authentic film about policing. The plot that ended in the death of the police officer was based on the story of Constable Nat Edgar, who was murdered on duty in February 1948. It was during the search for Constable Edgar's killer that the phrase 'helping police with their enquiries' was first used.[1573]

By 2019 Harrow Road police station was reported to be up for sale.

Harrow Road Police Station 1912-c2019

Hayes and Gould's Green Police Stations

The London Borough of Hillingdon

Harlington Road, Gould's Green (1866-1902)

The original Hayes Police Station was a cottage on the Harlington Road, just north of Gould's Green, and was in use in 1866 as shown on the Ordnance Survey Map of that year.[1574] It was actually called Gould's Green Police Station. The property was leased, first from W.F. de Salis and later from Cecil de Salis, both of Dawley Court, Uxbridge. The rental was £9 per annum.[1575]

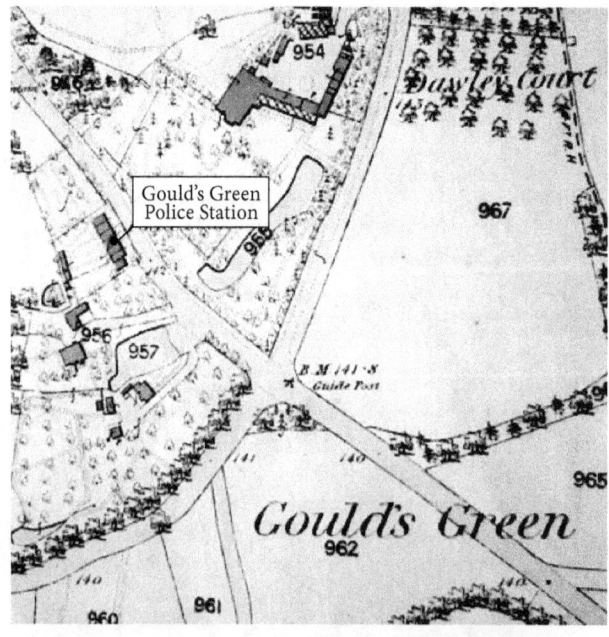

Early Victorian map of Gould's Green

A police report in 1881 described the property as 'a poor cottage, somewhat out of repair. The privy requires treatment'. The cottage was occupied by a married police constable.[1576] In 1894 this was Constable Walter Selman (warrant no. 76106), who had joined the police just four years before he occupied the cottage.[1577]

In 1898 Constable John Christie appears to have been responsible for the policing of Gould's Green,[1578] In the census of 1901 three years later, the officer is shown living with his wife Hannah and two children in Dawley Cottages, Gould's Green.[1579]

Gould's Green Police Station was vacated in December 1902.[1580]

By 1864 a Hayes Police Station had not yet been mentioned, and nor was it mentioned in 1865 when X Division was formed. Yet a report from the Police Surveyor at that time pointing out the dilapidation of the Police Office (a Sergeant's cottage in Bag Lane, Hayes), stated that the property had been rented from a Mr. Gurney at a rent of £9 per annum for many years.

Hayes Police Station 1870-1938

As a result of this report, property in High Road, Hayes was leased from Mr. Tilbury for £400 in February 1870. An additional £480 was spent converting it into a police station. The premises consisted, on the ground floor, of a charge room, two cells, two stalls, coal cellar, coke cellar, WC, urinal and a dry earth store. Part of the first floor of the station was occupied by the adjoining owner, an arrangement which had been in existence since 1871. The Home Office was aware of this unsatisfactory situation but continued to sanction this agreement as late as May 1892. The freehold of the property was later purchased in 1873.

Records confirm that the new Hayes Police Station was taken into occupation in September 1871,[1581] and later records in 1884 verify its address as High Road, Hayes.[1582]

In 1878 Hayes Police Station was being supervised by Sergeant Samuel Dolphin and nine constables.[1583] It was described in a police report in 1881 as a small cottage, with a stable and cells built in the yard. The well was polluted by drains which passed quite close to it. At the time it was occupied by one married inspector.[1584] In 1893 Hayes Police Station was held on an annual tenancy of £2 per annum.[1585]

The freehold of a new site for the present station in Uxbridge Road, at the corner of Morgan's Lane, Hayes, was purchased in 1911[1586] from a Mr. Phillips at a cost of £280, but WWI delayed its building. When it did become operational, on 19th June 1938, with one set of married quarters, it remained the most modern station in Middlesex until long after the Second World War.[1587]

A rare view of the front office to Hayes Police Station

Meanwhile, in July 1912 an agreement was reached with Hayes Urban District Council for them to use the police station yard in High Road for the storage of fire appliances for a yearly rental of five shillings. The agreement was terminated, and the fire appliances removed, in May 1928. Once the new station had been built, the property was sold to Middlesex County Council on 29th June 1938 for £2,400, in connection with the widening of Uxbridge Road.[1588]

The old police station was close, and all business was transferred to the new station in Uxbridge Road on 19th June 1938.[1589] The old Hayes Police Station, which was located on the north side of Uxbridge Road (formerly High Road, Hayes) opposite Angel Lane, was later demolished.

Hayes Police Station 1938 to present

In 1958 a notice from the then Hayes and Harlington Urban District Council required the station call sign (XY) to be numbered '755' Uxbridge Road.[1590]

In 1965, with the creation of the new London boroughs, Hayes became a Sub-Divisional Station in the new London Borough of Hillingdon. In 1966 freehold land adjoining the station at 1-5 Morgan's Lane was purchased by the Receiver.

With the formation of the Airport Division in 1974, the revision of police boundaries then placed Hayes as a sectional station to Ruislip Sub-Division.

In 1983 Police Constable John William Caplin died following the arrest of a violent shoplifter at Hayes, during which he was punched in the chest. He collapsed at the police station and died later the same day from heart failure.[1591] Once again, the hazards of policing are shown in this tragic case.

In 2013 the station was still open albeit with restricted opening hours for the station from Monday to Friday 9.00am until 9.30pm.[1592]

Heathrow Airport Division SO18

By David Little and Peter Kennison

The London Borough of Hillingdon

Heathrow Airport is situated on the south end of the London Borough of Hillingdon, on a parcel of land that is designated part of the Metropolitan Green Belt. The airport is surrounded by the built-up areas of Harlington, Harmondsworth, Longford and Cranford to the north, and by Hounslow and Hatton to the east. To the south lie East Bedfont and Stanwell, while to the west Heathrow is separated from Colnbrook in Berkshire by the M25 motorway.

Heathrow Airport is located within the London Borough of Hillingdon. Strangely, Heathrow Airport is not currently incorporated into one of the MPS Boroughs, but has sat independently as an entity of its own, as SO18 Aviation Security, since 2007. SO18 are responsible for both Heathrow and London City Airport.

Heathrow is an airport owned by the British Aviation Authority (BAA), and currently handles in excess of 68 million passengers and 450,000 aircraft movements per year. There are over 80,000 staff working within the airport (by way of comparison the town of Wigan in northern England has a population of just over 80,000). Additionally, over 12 million other visitors and more than 20 million vehicles travel through the airport each year. Terminal 5 was opened in March 2008, after the longest Public Inquiry that sat for 524 days and concluded eight years after the initial application

---

1573 Moss, A. and Skinner, K. (2006). *The Scotland Yard Files*. National Archives, Kew.
1574 Ordnance Survey Map 1/25000 Middx. Xiv 8, 12, 1866.
1575 Metropolitan Police Surveyor's Book p.225.
1576 Metropolitan Police Report: Condition of Police Stations 1881.
1577 *Kelly's Directory Middlesex* 1894.
1578 *Kelly's Directory Middlesex* 1898.
1579 Census 1901.
1580 Metropolitan Police Orders dated 5th February 1903.
1581 Metropolitan Police Orders dated 15th September 1871.
1582 Metropolitan Police Orders dated 20th June 1884.
1583 *Post Directory Middlesex* 1878.
1584 Metropolitan Police Report: Condition of Police Stations 1881.
1585 Metropolitan Police Station List 1893.
1586 X Division List of Police Stations 1924.
1587 *Hillingdon Mirror* (date unknown).
1588 Metropolitan Police Surveyor's Book.
1589 Metropolitan Police Orders dated 14th June 1938.
1590 X Divisional Report (date unknown).
1591 Metropolitan Police Book of Remembrance.
1592 content.met.police.uk/PoliceStation/hayes accessed 3rd March 2013.

Ministry of Civil Aviation Constabulary helmet plate badge

Ministry of Civil Aviation Constabulary Inspector cap badge 1948-1966

British Airports Authority Constabulary cap badge

British Airports Authority Constabulary helmet plate badge

for Government approval. The Inquiry cost £80m, heard 700 witnesses and generated 100,000 pages of transcripts.[1593]

Originally, Heathrow was a hamlet in the parish of Harmondsworth and consisted of a small number of cottages on the edge of Hounslow Heath, and was reported in All The Round in 1868 as follows:

'Hounslow Heath was once an oak forest that spread its green boughs from Staines to Brentford, and there is an old tradition that the last wolf in England, killed centuries ago, was hunted down at Perry Oaks in that neighbourhood.'[1594]

Prior to the existence of any police station in the area, there was still a need for the forces of law and order to maintain peace on Hounslow Heath. Once part of the extensive Forest of Middlesex, and now largely buried beneath the runways of London Airport, Hounslow Heath was for more than 200 years the most dangerous place in Britain. Between the 17th and early 19th centuries the heath occupied perhaps 25 square miles. No-one was really certain where its boundaries lay, and no-one cared, for it was a tract of country to be crossed as quickly as possible. Though Hounslow itself was not large, it was, after London, the most important of coaching centres. Across the heath ran the Bath Road and the Exeter Road, along which travelled wealthy visitors to West Country resorts and courtiers travelling to Windsor. All provided rich pickings for highwaymen lurking in copses bordering the lonely ways.

Claude Duval (Du Val, Duvall or Duvail) was a highwayman who had been born in France in 1643, but moved to England in 1660 to pursue his 'career' as a highwayman. Duval was eventually captured and executed in 1670 for his crimes, but was remembered for his success at seducing his female victims as much as the notoriety of his crimes. He was known as a 'true gentleman of the road'. He stopped a woman's coach on Hounslow Heath in which there was a booty of four hundred pounds but only took one hundred, allowing 'the fair owner to ransom the rest by dancing 'a coranto' with him on the Heath.'[1595]

The hamlet of Heathrow was beset by highwaymen, and in 1805 the Bow Street horse patrols were introduced for 'the suppression of highwaymen, footpads and housebreakers'. Horse patrols station were established at Bedfont, Hounslow, Harlington Corner and Colnbrook, and these were integrated into the Metropolitan Police in 1837.[1596]

The Metropolitan Police area was extending further out from the centre of London. The hamlet of Heath Row became part of the Metropolitan Police District in 1840, as the old T or Paddington Division was extended from the boundary set at Brentford in 1830 to Staines. By 1849 a sectional police station had been opened in Stanwell village to police the local area. In 1857 another station was opened on the Staines Road at Bedfont, taking over from the nearby horse patrol station. In 1865, Hattons Road, Harlington was chosen as the site for a new station, which was moved to a new site on the Bath Road in 1890.[1597]

In 1919 the first commercial flight from London to France left Hounslow Aerodrome, a former First World War aerodrome. At that time the first record occurred of police officers being stationed at Hounslow Aerodrome, an increase in the complement of T District by one sergeant and nine constables, was noted whose presence was commensurate with the use of aircraft. However, Hounslow Aerodrome was closed in 1920, when operations were moved to the London Croydon Airport.

In 1925 a Royal Air Force pilot, Norman MacMillan was forced to land his plane on a piece of flat land in the area. His appraisal of the land as being suitable for an airfield was noted by Fairey Aviation. In 1929/30 Fairey Aviation bought several plots of land. British aero engineer and aircraft builder Richard Fairey paid the Vicar of Harmondsworth £15,000 for a 150-acre plot on which to build a private airport to assemble and test aircraft. Complete with a single grass runway and a handful of hastily-erected buildings, Fairey's Great West Aerodrome was created from humble beginnings.[1598]

During World War II the government requisitioned land in and around the ancient agricultural village of Heath Row, including Fairey's Great West Aerodrome, to build RAF Heston, a base for long-range troop-carrying aircraft bound for the Far East. An RAF-type control tower was constructed and a 'Star of David' pattern of runways laid, the longest of which was 3,000 yards long and 100 yards wide.[1599] In 1944 the hamlet of Heath Row was demolished to make way for the new airport, as part of the war effort. As the airport (known then as the Great Western Aerodrome) began to expand, the families who lived in the area were relocated.

During the war the Air Ministry Constabulary were responsible for airports and stations. At the conclusion of the war, the RAF no longer needed the airport so the site was transferred to the Ministry of Civil Aviation and the airport was officially opened for commercial operations in May 1946. The first aircraft to take off from Heathrow after the war was a Starlight (a converted Lancaster), which flew to Buenos Aires.

The early passenger terminals were primitive indeed and consisted of

'ex-military marquees which formed a tented village along the Bath Road. The terminals were primitive but comfortable, equipped with floral-patterned armchairs, settees and small tables containing vases of fresh flowers. To reach aircraft parked on the apron, passengers walked over wooden duckboards to protect their footwear from the muddy airfield. There was no heating in the marquees, which meant that during winter it could be bitterly cold, but in summer when the sun shone, the marquee walls were removed to allow a cool breeze to blow through.' [1600]

The policing of Heathrow fell to the Ministry of Civil Aviation Constabulary from 1948 – two years after flights commenced – although during any major incident the Metropolitan Police always took overall command. By 1954 the name changed again to the Ministry of Transport and Civil Aviation Constabulary, although uniform buttons still contained the initials MCA. All this just meant that tunics and coats remained the same, but headgear badges and plates were changed.

The British Airports Authority was established in 1965 by the Airport Authority Act 1965, and on 1st April 1966 the new British Airports Authority Constabulary took on responsibility for operating London Heathrow, London Gatwick and London Stansted airports.[1601]

This occurred at the same time as Terminal 3 was built, with Terminal 2 having been constructed in 1955. The change of administration was seen as an opportunity to partially reform old working methods, and then-novel innovations were introduced, such as report forms with tick-boxes, an index card system and dictation machines for detectives.[1602] In December of that year, the strength of the force stood at 201.[1603]

In 1965, at the formation of the Greater London Council (GLC), Heathrow ceased to be part of Middlesex and was incorporated into the GLC. It is now part of the London Borough of Hillingdon, although the postal address is in Hounslow. In 1969 the Chief Constable, Major W. Ronnie, was awarded the Queen's Police Medal.[1604] The police strength at the time stood at 326, of which 28 were women.[1605]

BAAC constables were sworn in under section 10 of the Airport Authority Act 1965.[1606] They were all attested before a justice of the peace (or a sheriff in Scotland), and had "the powers and privileges and [were] liable to the duties and responsibilities of a constable" on all the aerodromes owned or managed by BAA.[1607] They also enjoyed their powers when following (pursuing) a person from such an aerodrome, if they could have arrested them on the aerodrome,[1608] although they were not a Home Office force and subject to their supervision. BAA had the power to sack or suspend constables, and were vicariously liable for their actions whilst on duty. In April 1971 R.M. Carson was appointed as Chief Constable of the BAAC.[1609]

The policing of Heathrow by the constabulary ceased in 1974, when with the exception of the Chief Constable and his deputy the remainder transferred into the Metropolitan Police. The same thing had happened with the Dockyard officers of Chatham, Portsmouth, Devonport and Pembroke, when the Metropolitan Police took control of them in the 1860s and the old dockyard officers merged with the Metropolitan Police.

Heathrow Airport Police Station (ID)

The area of Heathrow airport holds an important yet significant secret which affects all of us today. In 1783 General Roy, a Scottish Engineer, realised the military importance of knowing precisely where things were. In order to do so, he required a baseline and chose Hounslow Heath, the current location of Heathrow Airport. General Roy's men painstakingly measured out a distance of 27,404.01 feet, using rods and iron bars. Their measurement subsequently proved to be accurate to within two inches.

This baseline was to become the Ordnance Survey in 1791, used to this day[1610] on every single map surveyed and reproduced for them.

On 17th November 1967 a plaque was unveiled at Heathrow Police Station commemorating General Roy's first Ordnance Survey baseline in 1783. The plaque now stands immediately above the road tunnel that emerges from the middle of Terminal Island.

Terrorism

The biggest policing requirement in recent times at Heathrow has been the fight against terrorism. As one of the world's biggest transport hubs, Heathrow has in excess of 80 million visitors passing through each year. This number not only lends itself to an ideal opportunity for terrorists to pass through, but also creates an attractive target for terrorists.

Government concern around security at Heathrow Airport included the fact that this function was carried out by a non-Home Office police force. There were serious concerns whether they could cope and keep up-to-date with current firearms in the same way as the Metropolitan Police had done. It was the Metropolitan Police which was at the forefront of firearms training and policy, and in fact the BAA police received their training and reclassification from them.

In August 1967 the American Embassy in London had been machine-gunned. Nine months later the Spanish Embassy and the American Officers' Club in Lancaster Gate were both bombed. During the following year eight more bomb attacks followed, including one at Heathrow airport and another at the home of the Attorney-General. The reign of bombings continued throughout 1971, until members of what became known as the 'Angry Brigade' were arrested and convicted.

1593 guardian.co.uk, 22nd May 2007.
1594 *All the Year Round*, 1868.
1595 www.flageolets.com/biographies/duval and www.stand-and-deliver.org.uk/highwaymen/claude_duval.htm, both accessed 20th March 2012.
1596 www.scribd.com/doc/57482167/Heathrow-The-Lost-Hamlet.
1597 John Back Archive (1972).
1598 www.heathrowairport.com/about-us/company-news-and-information/company-information/our-history accessed 24th February 2013.
1599 Ibid.
1600 Ibid.
1601 en.wikipedia.org/wiki/Airport_policing_in_the_United_Kingdom accessed 2nd May 2012.
1602 'Crime and Security at British Airports' in *Flight International*, 15th April 1971. Retrieved 27th May 2011.
1603 Ibid.
1604 'In the Birthday Honours List' in *Flight International*, 26th June 1969. Retrieved 26th May 2011.
1605 'Crime and Security at British Airports' in *Flight International*, 15th April 1971. Retrieved 27th May 2011.
1606 Airports Authority Act 1965.
1607 Ibid.
1608 Ibid.
1609 British Airports Authority. *Flight International*, 8th April 1971. Retrieved 27th May 2011.
1610 'Map Addict' Mike Parker, 30th April 2009.

In September 1972 the Arab terrorist organisation 'Black September' launched its letter-bombing campaign in London, despatching 43 bombs over a four month period. The same month, in front of the world's media members of that organisation had attacked Israel's Olympic team taking several hostages at the close of the Munich Olympic Games. Following an unsuccessful rescue attempt by the West German police, all nine hostages were killed. A year earlier, the IRA had launched its Christmas 1971 bombing campaign in Ulster and the following month saw British para-troopers fire upon a crowd of unarmed demonstrators in Northern Ireland, killing 14 people. Amidst a growing profile of international terrorist activity, the IRA turned its attention to London, launching a bombing campaign there in March 1973. Mainland bombings continued throughout 1974, notably in Birmingham, Manchester and Guildford.[1611] In 1969/70 a number of incidents occurred involving the hijacking of commercial aircraft by terrorists such as Leila Khaled.

On 29th April 1974 it was announced in Parliament that

'... the Metropolitan Police should assume responsibility for the policing of London Airport – Heathrow... following the escalation of terrorist activity against civil aviation.'

The Home Secretary, Mr Roy Jenkins, stated

'dealing with terrorism could not satisfactorily be divided from other police work and the course suggested by the BAAC of making the Metropolitan Police responsible for dealing with terrorism while (sic) the BAAC retained responsibility for other Police functions was in the opinion of Ministers and the Metropolitan Commissioner unworkable.'[1612]

In 1974, as a result of the Policing of Airports Act, the Metropolitan Police assumed responsibility. Police Notice of 31st October 1974, Item 11 (Joined the Force) lists the officers who transferred from the British Airports Authority. On Friday, 1st November 1974, the new Airport Division of the Metropolitan Police came into being.

Police Orders published on 31st October 1974 contained the following entry:

'... in consequence of the above Orders, the Metropolitan Police will assume responsibility for the policing of Heathrow Airport... Two Chief Superintendents, six Chief Inspectors, 12 Inspectors, 47 Sergeants and 262 Constables (including CID officers) transferred from the BAAC to the MPS. Initially, the new Division also incorporated Staines and West Drayton, increasing in size in 1980 to include Sunbury.'[1613]

Airport District was formed as a 'single-Division District: District Code I, Heathrow Station ID... the staff levels remained almost the same', albeit they traded their old uniforms, hats, helmets and accoutrements with Metropolitan police issue. It also stated that 'Probationers will not be posted to Heathrow', an indication of the specialised nature of policing at the airport.[1614]

From 13th January 1986 police officers patrolling Heathrow Airport became routinely armed with Heckler and Koch machine guns.

The Metropolitan Police's internal newspaper, The Job, reported that, prior to the opening of Terminal Four, the Airport District – 'the Force's only one-station district' had launched 'a recruitment campaign to bring the number of officers up to the establishment of 330'. It also stated that officers based at Heathrow received more training than any others in the Metropolitan Police, in order to deal with the diverse incidents that they might be called upon to deal with. The article went on to describe the 'state-of-the-art' telephonic computer system originally designed for the Stock Exchange that had been fitted into the Communications and Major Incident Rooms. The system replaced telephones and directories', and enabled greater speed and efficiency when dealing with any incidents.[1615]

Heathrow Police Station 1974-2011. East Ramp, Heathrow Airport

There was concern that the division was somewhat top-heavy as far as senior officers were concerned. By 1991 the complement at Heathrow had changed to one chief superintendent (reduced by one), one superintendent, four chief inspectors (decreased by two), 14 inspectors (increased by two), 56 sergeants (increased by nine) and 365 constables (including CID Officers, and increased by 97). They were augmented by 14 Specials, 64 traffic wardens and 54 civilians. From these officers, each terminal had a team of permanent beat officers.[1616]

In 2007 Heathrow became an Operational Command Unit in its own right, as Aviation Security SO18. Airports, since the attack on New York's Trade Centre on 11th September 2001, have become terrorist targets, following the example, as early as 1939, of the Irish Republican Army (IRA), when they launched a campaign of bombing and sabotage against the civil, economic, and military infrastructure of the United Kingdom. In earlier years the main transport hubs were railways stations. As air transportation became more affordable for the masses the airports became more viable targets.[1617]

Sisters Dolores and Marion Price and nine others placed four car bombs in London on 8th March 1973. Ten of the team were apprehended as they attempted to leave Heathrow, and two bombs were defused.[1618]

On 21st December 1988, at about 6.25pm, just four days before Christmas, Pan-Am Flight 103 departed from Heathrow Airport with 243 passengers and 16 crew members. Just as they were preparing themselves for a relatively long flight to New York the plane blew up over the town of Lockerbie at about 7.03pm, killing all on board. This incident was to change the way that policing at a UK Airport was undertaken for all time.

In March 1994, the IRA launched a series of mortar attacks on Heathrow airport, partially paralysing the capital's main airport. During the first attack five mortars were fired into the airport grounds, but none detonated. The second attack, two days later, involved the firing of four mortars. Once again the mortars failed to detonate. The headlines in The Independent on 11th March 1994 read 'Heathrow Bombing: IRA exposes airport's vulnerability: Perimeter protection 'almost impossible''. Four mortars from a stolen red Nissan Micra car, registration number A274 TGK, had been fired from the car park, over Heathrow police station and the perimeter fence, and landed on a 20-metre wide apron at the edge of the 45-metre wide north runway. None exploded, although traces of high explosive, including Semtex, found later indicate that the damage could have been extensive.[1619]

The third and final attack on Sunday, 13th March 1994 caused the airport to close between 0800 and 1340 hours, despite the mortars failing to detonate yet again. The airport was again closed that evening after further coded warnings. The rationale for the Metropolitan Police taking over the policing of Heathrow in 1974 was being vindicated.

In February 2003, British troops were again deployed at Heathrow in support of the Metropolitan Police; not as a result of an IRA threat on this occasion, but in response to an heightened threat level from Islamic terrorists. Prime Minister Tony Blair personally authorised the use of 450 troops, with armoured vehicles, to back up more than 1,300 police officers. A suspected Islamist plot to fire a missile at an airliner prompted the largest security operation at Heathrow for a decade.[1620]

Both Police and Military at Heathrow Airport in 2003

In 1998 the address of Heathrow Police Station was recorded as East Ramp, Heathrow Airport, Hounslow, with OCU Commander Superintendent I. Hutcheson in charge. His deputy was Superintendent M. Calaminus.[1621] The station opening times in 2002/03 were 6.00am until 10.00pm.[1622] By 2007 the OCU Commander of Heathrow Airport was Chief Superintendent Jerry Savill, and his deputy was Superintendent Leigh Orwin.[1623]

The East Ramp Police station was decommissioned in 2011, and ceased to be used by police with the completion of the Polar Park complex.

Heathrow Police Station, Polar Park

The newest police station within the Metropolitan Police Service opened on 7th July 2011 at Polar Park, West Drayton, the new headquarters of Heathrow's Specialist Operations Aviation Command policing Heathrow Airport. Its opening hours were from 7.00am to 10.00pm daily. The station was opened by Commissioner Sir Paul Stephenson and Graham Speed, Independent member of the Metropolitan Police Authority with the responsibility for estates issues. The station was part of Specialist Operations Aviation Command SO18.

The station is designed to accommodate all of the specialist teams working at the airport, including baggage crime, human smuggling and all airport-related crime. It contains 30 custody cells, together with ancillary rooms for interviewing, medical examination and a state-of-the-art control room for dealing with major incidents. The station also boasts a 'silver suite' capable of coordinating and managing major incidents.

Heathrow Police Station 2011 to present

The commander of Heathrow who took over the new station was Chief Superintendent Bert Moore, who was very pleased with the new building having been five years in the planning and construction.

A Safer Neighbourhoods Team, Heathrow Villages, formed to offer a 'community and bespoke aviation policing (experience)' provides policing for the Terminals, much as Neighbourhood Policing Teams do for geographical boroughs elsewhere in the Metropolitan Police Service.[1624]

In 2011 the National Police Improvement Agency, in conjunction with the Association of Chief Police officers together with others, has developed a reference handbook on the guidance on the policing of airports following a risk assessment. This was led by the Policing and Crime Act 2009 (enacted in 2010) on a security planning framework, and has provided a proper contingency on the protection of airports.

The last major air accident involving Heathrow was BEA Flight 548, which crashed near Staines on 18th June 1972 soon after take-off, but there have been numerous emergencies and less serious incidents since, which have served to reaffirm the importance of good contingency planning and exercises.

1611 Squires, P and Kennison, P. (2010) *Shooting to Kill? Policing, Firearms and Armed Response*. Wiley Blackwell, Chichester.
1612 *Police Review*, 3rd May 1974.
1613 Metropolitan Police Orders dated 31st October 1974.
1614 Special Police Notice dated 28th November 1984.
1615 *The Job*, February 1986.
1616 *The Job* (1991).
1617 historyofwar.org/articles/concepts_terrortargets.html.
1618 news.bbc.co.uk/1/hi/uk/1201738.stm accessed 4th March 2001.
1619 *The Independent*, 11th March 1994 (located at www.independent.co.uk/news/uk/heathrow-bombing-ira-exposes-airports-vulnerability-perimeter-protection-almost-impossible--delay-in-closing-runway-defended-1428295.html).
1620 *The Telegraph*, 12th February 2003 (accessed at www.telegraph.co.uk/education/3307672/Troops-in-Heathrow-terror-alert.html).
1621 *Police and Constabulary Almanac* 1998, p39.
1622 Metropolitan Police Phone Directory 2002/03, located at www.met.police.uk/contact/phone.htm accessed 12th October 2003.
1623 *Police and Constabulary Almanac* 2007, p33.
1624 content.met.police.uk/News/New-police-station-at-Heathrow-unveiled/1260269186481/1257246745756 accessed 22nd March 2012.

The new Metropolitan Police Training School: The Peel Centre, Hendon c1974

Hendon: The Peel Centre

Peel Centre, Hendon (1974-2014)

In 1946 Hendon, or 'Peel House II' as it was termed at the time, was opened again after WWII for basic training, and operated together with Peel House in Regency Street. With the running of both training schools (and their satellites) a little gentle rivalry occurred, with competitions in all aspects of sport, first aid and other games between the two. After World War Two, Peel House apart from recruit training, also continued to offer senior officer non-residential training courses.

A Training School magazine was started in January 1963 under an operating committee from both schools, with editorship under Chief Superintendent J.J. Miller MBE. This magazine, produced to inform interested parties of what was happening in the training environment, had a very wide circulation considering that many Commonwealth countries sent their more senior police officers on the Overseas Police Course and for CID training. As such, many of these magazines found their way into police libraries around the world.

Also at Hendon was the Criminal Investigation Department (CID) Training School, a cadet school for young men aged 16 years (with an annex at Ashford in Kent called Kennington Hall) a wireless training school (later called the Communications School), a driving school and a forensic science laboratory, all located at the Hendon complex.

In the 1960s other courses were run at Peel House. These included courses for probationer constables and traffic wardens, and also promotion courses for uniform branch sergeants. The Royal Park 'keepers' course trained 16 men and women in 1963 from the Royal Parks Constabulary. This course was designed to assist them in their daily duties in the parks, where they enjoyed similar powers to a constable. The Cadet School also contributed to the magazine, and were keen competitors in sport taking part in boxing, wrestling (under SPS Blackwell), cross-country and canoeing competitions.

If there was a sport or activity, there was a force-level organised club (arranged within the rules of the Metropolitan Police Athletic Association). The clubs would enter competitions in sport organised for the Metropolitan Police and these included cross-country, table tennis, rugby and lifesaving. In fact sport has, until lately, been positively encouraged by senior officers so as to maintain general fitness and to encourage participation and teamwork. Senior officers of divisions, in banter between themselves, would often make remarks about their own sporting prowess amongst their colleagues. Team captains would go to Peel House and Hendon in order to ensure certain highly-regarded sports men and women were posted to their divisions.

In 1968 Peel House, at 105 Regency Street, SW1, was shut for training purposes and training was moved to Hendon. Extensive work was undertaken to modernise the site at Hendon, which included building a completely new training establishment with sufficient classrooms, a purpose-built courtroom, training roads, canteen facilities, sports facilities, residential accommodation, medical facilities, library and parking.

According to *Wikipedia*,

"The Peel Centre was redeveloped between 2014 and 2016. The new Peel House sits on the site of the old Metropolitan Police swimming pool. The three tower blocks, where officers used to stay during initial training, the old Peel House and Simpson Hall have now all been demolished and sold." [1625]

The part Peel Centre property was sold for £40M to Redrow Homes Ltd in October 2014.[1626]

The Driving School, Hendon

To say that you were trained to drive police vehicles at Hendon is a high accolade indeed, as the name is now synonymous with the best police driver training experience and as the premier driver training establishment, perhaps in the world.

In 1930 mobile police were introduced in London, known

as Traffic Patrols, originating from the introduction of the Road Traffic Act 1930. In order to ensure that drivers on the road were suitably qualified, a compulsory driving test was planned to come into operation in 1935 with voluntary testing (introduced by the Road Traffic Act, 1934), to avoid a rush of candidates when the test became compulsory a year later.

Mr. J. Beene was the first person to pass his driving test, at a cost of 7s 6d.[1627]

By 1st June 1935 compulsory testing (brought in for all drivers who had started driving on or after 1st April 1934) saw around 246,000 candidates applying to be tested. The pass rate was 63%, with 250 examiners (originally trained at Hendon Police Driving School) taking at least nine, and up to sixteen, half-hour driving tests a day. Examining staff also made all test bookings. Originally there were no test centres; examiners met candidates at a pre-arranged spot such as a car park or railway station. Anyone buying a driving licence was required to put 'L' plates on the car, and eventually to take a driving test to get their full licence. Driving tests were suspended in September 1939 for the duration of World War Two, and resumed once more on 1st November 1946. During the war examiners, who were also designated traffic officers, remained on their respective divisions, and some of their responsibilities included the supervision of fuel rationing.

As far as police officers abilities were concerned, the Police Driving School was established in 1935 by the then Commissioner, Lord Trenchard, who was concerned that many of his police drivers had no driving licence and that if they were to give evidence in court later about driving matters they ought to be able to show that they were suitably qualified as drivers to the required standard.

The school was established on a site (converted aircraft hangars) in Aerodrome Road, Hendon NW9 on S Division comprising the Training School, a sports ground, motor repair garages, a district garage and also included five sets of married quarters.[1628]

Previously the buildings had formed part of Hendon Country Club, a section of Hendon Aerodrome's club house and, albeit briefly, laboratories of Standard Cable and Wireless. By the end of 1933 the number of vehicles in use by the Metropolitan Police had risen to 585. Unfortunately, as the fleet grew in size so the number of accidents in which police were involved increased correspondingly. In the first few months of 1934 the accident mileage ratio rose to one accident for every 8,000 miles.

The high accident rate resulted in considerable adverse comment, both in the press and motoring journals and, as a result of this criticism, Commissioner Lord Trenchard arranged for the famous racing motorist, Sir Malcolm Campbell, to test a number of drivers from divisions. This difficult and strenuous test consisted of driving a squad or 'Q' car on normal patrol and on an emergency (999) call, both in heavy traffic and on the open road. Campbell also advised on necessary vehicles, garaging and equipment.

Despite the severity of the test and the high standard demanded, all the police drivers passed with flying colours and such was Sir Malcolm Campbell's praise that the ill-founded criticism was silenced. It could not, however, be denied that lack of experience and, in particular, inadequate training facilities were great handicaps in raising the standard of driving. For these reasons, in 1934 the setting up of the Metropolitan Police Driving School at Hendon was ordered.[1629]

The introduction of the Driving School caused very little comment, either locally or nationally. Few could have foreseen the impact which the teaching of the School would have on driving technique, not only in this country, but in other countries.

A sergeant takes the wheel of one of the first car simulators

Nevertheless, 'tall oaks from little acorns grow', and this is especially true of the Driving School, for the seed so firmly planted in 1934 has today grown into a strong tree, the branches of which stretch far and wide.[1630]

The first course for instructors was held in November 1934, attended by Inspector King, along with Police Constables Steele, Fowles, Jordon, Skeggs, McCullock and Thomas. Many of these instructors remained for the rest of their service, and some rejoined as civilian instructors when they retired. These men were the foundation stones on which the driving school was built, and their teaching has been perpetuated through the years by the current staff being responsible for the selection and training of future instructors.[1631]

The first course for students began on 7th January 1935, and on that day 21 young men, the forerunners of thousands, presented themselves for four weeks of instruction that included elementary motor mechanics and practical maintenance, in addition to driving. Eighteen instructional cars, including the Hillman '16', the Ford '14.9' and the Hillman '10' horse-power touring cars were allocated to the school. At the end of the first four days, which were spent in the classroom, the students were introduced to the principles of driving. All students were tested by the senior instructor before being allowed to drive on the public roads, and a system of routes was built up so that students graduated progressively from quiet country and suburban roads, through areas of heavier traffic, to the dense and crowded streets of inner London.

1625 en.wikipedia.org/wiki/Hendon_Police_College accessed 4th November 2019.
1626 MPS (2018) Land and property sold for over £1M in the last 10 years.
1627 uk.answers.yahoo.com/question/index?qid= 20071010084856AAeTJVH accessed 4th November 2012.
1628 Metropolitan Police Property List 1947.
1629 Chief Inspector WWR Fleming (1960s) *Police Driving School: A History of Police Transport and Driver Training with Additions by J Kirby.*
1630 Ibid.
1631 Ibid.

At the end of the first week, a second course of 21 students commenced training, and thus was founded the Elementary or Standard Car Wing, which to this day provides the basic training for all students. So outstanding were the results achieved from the training given to the students who attended the initial courses that the pattern of future instruction was made clear.[1632]

The first officer in charge of the driving school stayed for ten years, and established a firm grounding to the driving courses and set the standard for years to come. He was Chief Inspector A.T. King, who commenced on 7th January 1935 and remained until 17th September 1945. After the war, the level of authority and the changes in the rank structure meant that a Chief Superintendent was the head of the driving school. King's place was taken by Chief Superintendent W.M. Taylor MM, from 18th September 1945 until 31st December 1952.

Supporting the driving school as advisor for the Commissioner was Captain J.C. Byrne, who started on 7th January 1935 and remained in post until 19th December 1957.

One of the first advanced driving courses in 1935

In 1936 an Advanced Course of driving for Flying Squad, 'Q' Car and traffic patrol Car drivers were introduced. Early in 1937 the Commissioner appointed as his Civilian Advisor for the training of police drivers one of the most famous racing drivers of the day, Mark Everard Pepys, the sixth Earl of Cottenham, who had written widely on motoring.

Lord Cottenham, who in earlier years had been a member of both the Alvis and Sunbeam racing teams, approached his task with rare zest. His aim was simple: to bring to the technique of advanced driving a new standard of perfection.

To this end he personally trained six specially-selected instructors to give this training.

Briefly, his system was that by implementing a simple 'drill', or sequence of events, a driver would ensure that his vehicle was always in the right place at the right time, travelling at the right speed and in the correct gear. Thus, it was reasoned, a driver would be in complete control of any situation with which he might be faced.[1633] The success of Lord Cottenham's teaching can best be judged by results, for, whilst in 1934 the police vehicle accident rate was one accident to every 8,000 miles, by 1938 it had dropped to one accident to every 27,000 miles.

Lord Cottenham's stay with the Metropolitan Police was brief, as he left in 1938, but he developed new and improved standards of advanced driving based on 'defensive driving', and devised training programmes which still today lie at the heart of Hendon's courses. The impact of his teaching remains, and the system of driving which he initiated has resulted in a police vehicle mileage for each blame-worthy accident in 1982 of 26,108 miles for cars, 86,842 miles for motor cycles; proof, if proof were ever needed, that good driving pays handsome dividends in safety on the road.

The formal class photograph taken at the front of the Driving school

In 1946 Chief Superintendent Taylor and the Metropolitan Police Driving School (MDS) took part in annual driving competitions, particularly with the Bentley Drivers' Club (BDC), although occasionally other teams were invited. In 1964 Deputy Commander D.C. Macdonald was president of the MDS, and the BDC president was Stanley Sedgwick. This was a prestigious annual event held on the training roads at Hendon, where a purpose-built section was used. Held on a Sunday, and on occasions in conjunction with a gymkhana, it became a family day out, not only for police officers and their families, but also for invited guests, much needed entertainment especially after the recent long and costly war. In this competition of driving skills the best drivers of both clubs would be put forward to enter. The competition was for the Flying Wheel Trophy with the club gaining the lowest number of points retaining the trophy. The best individual driver in Event Six won the Harold Radford Trophy. Only members of the car clubs could enter. There were six events, with six drivers taking part in each team. Up until 1963, honours were even with both clubs having won on eight occasions each (one event was cancelled in 1955 due to the rail strike). This was a well-organised event, with the No. 2 District Sports Club at Hendon organising refreshments, and involving some other organisations such as the Royal Automobile Club, the Ministry of Transport, the Ministry of Works and local business and dignitaries. The prizes were presented in 1964 by the Assistant Commissioner, who was Andrew Way CMG.

Students receive instruction on traffic movement

In the mid-1950s the system of driving was published in *Roadcraft: The Police Drivers Manual*, published by HMSO at 3s 6d to help the driver realise

'the need for a high degree of physical and mental fitness in order to drive the car with a highest of standards of skill, safety and considerations for other user of the road.'

'The System', as it was called, was used whenever a hazard required a manoeuvre. A hazard is something which requires a change in speed, direction or both. The benefit of applying a systematic approach to driving was to reduce the simultaneous demands on the vehicle, and the driver's mental and physical ability. The system seeks to separate out the phases of a manoeuvre into a logical sequence of events so that the vehicle and the driver avoid being overwhelmed by having to do too much at the same time. For example, braking and steering at the same time places greater demands on the vehicle's available grip and, in the worst case, can lead to a skid.[1634]

Officers on the lightweight (Noddy) motorcycle course in the 1960s

A dummy is catapulted in front of a driver to test reactions

The Driving School also developed a traffic patrol wing to educate road users and reduce accidents. This included training for dealing with thoughtless parking, negligent driving, defective vehicles, and disregard for road signs because all these contributed to traffic accidents. This meant that 'TrafPols' could help prevent accidents and keep London's traffic flowing freely. Included in the courses were lectures on traffic law, covering diverse matters as Road Traffic Acts, Construction and Use Regulations, registration, licensing, driving licences, insurance, goods vehicles (and later Tachographs) steam rollers, street traders, road works, pedestrian crossings, road signs etc. Standard level courses were of four weeks' duration, whilst the advanced course lasted three weeks with examinations on vehicle examination, report writing on a fatal accident investigation (later accident reconstruction), general technical knowledge and traffic law.[1635]

In 1953 the Special Escort Group (SEG) of motorcyclists were formed in preparation for the visit of Marshal Tito, President of Yugoslavia. The group escorted the Queen at her Coronation, and has played regular and important roles during all State Visits. Members of the SEG are trained to a very high standard, including riding formations headed by 'Red Diamond', so-called because of the large red diamond affixed to the handlebars of the motorcycle.

In mid 1960s the programme included refresher, re-classification, instructors and special courses held as necessary. Approximately 2,000 students were trained each year, and 1,000 drivers were tested.

The training track at Hendon was called Cottenham Drive as a mark of respect for the Lord Cottenham legacy. In 1970 the Hendon Training Centre acquired the premises of an old sign-manufacturing business in Aerodrome Road, adjacent to the estate in front of Cottenham Drive, and built a skid pan. This site was converted into a fully multi-functional driving school, with its own petrol supply, washing bays and garages, as well as classrooms, workshops, canteen and assembly hall.[1636]

In 1999 the Driving School offered a comprehensive range of courses from basic driving instruction for cars and light and heavy motorcycles for provisional licence holders, through to advanced vehicle inspection and accident investigation. They maintained a range of vehicles from motor cycles to rigid HGVs and the 'Z' Wagon (a lorry that can hoist up illegally-parked cars). There were also a range of courses for instructors on the workings and inspection of lorries and HGVs, including their tachographs. Bespoke courses are also included for students particular work environment.

Today the school still retains its reputation for driving excellence and remains open except for the skid pan, which is no longer used.[1637]

The Detective Training School

By 1958 Hendon housed the Detective Training School then C7 Branch with Detective Chief Superintendent T. Barrett MBE in charge. In the 1960s it was decided to enlarge the site at Hendon with new classrooms, living accommodation, nursing home, a library and cadet school.

At the front the Peel Centre is the statue of Robert Peel originally sited in Cheapside in the City of London. It was moved to Hendon in 1974.

By 1974 the named changed on the opening of the Peel Centre, when the old buildings were demolished and a purpose-built complex was built.

The old Peel House in Regency Street then later housed the Personnel Department (later Human Resources), and continued to provide training for Civil Staff.

1632 Chief Inspector WWR Fleming (1960s) *Police Driving School: A History of Police Transport and Driver Training with Additions by J Kirby.*
1633 content.met.police.uk/Site/drivingschoolhistory accessed 4th November 2012.
1634 en.wikipedia.org/wiki/Roadcraf accessed 4th November 2012.
1635 Chief Inspector WWR Fleming (1960s) *Police Driving School: A History of Police Transport and Driver Training with Additions by J Kirby.*
1636 Fido, M. and Skinner, K. (1999) *The Official Encyclopaedia of Scotland Yard.* Virgin, London
1637 Private communication with author.

When the Empress State Building in Earls Court was taken over from the Ministry of Defence, the old Peel House in Regency Street was vacated and then sold to Bowater House of Knightsbridge in 2006. Bowater have applied to redevelop the site for affordable housing and high-end owner occupancy.[1638] The site's outward appearance is unchanged, because the company who sought permission was attempting to transfer the affordable housing element to another building while negotiations were still in hand. The building works were completed by 2010, when properties started coming onto the market. The picture below shows the intake of the Detective Training School, including students from Commonwealth countries' police forces.

The Metropolitan Police Cadet Corps

In 1948 the idea to introduce a police cadet system was accepted and buildings were planned on the Hendon Complex for a cadet school under the then Commissioner of the Metropolis, Sir Joseph Simpson. During the 1950s the Metropolitan Police had two types of police cadet. There was a junior cadet, who joined at 16½ years. These cadets received some initial training, and were then posted to a division. They spent a part of their week at college on academic studies, and the rest of the time they worked within the station. When they reached 18½ they became senior cadets and joined with direct entrants to the service at that stage. The senior cadets spent twelve weeks at Hendon Training School on a course identical to the constables' joining course. At the end of their training the senior cadets were posted to a police station and attached to court, traffic patrol, beat duties etc. At the age of 19 years they changed their uniform and were sworn in as constables. Normally they were then posted to a different police station.

The new cadet corps was formed in 1960 at its own school, located at the junction with Aerodrome Road and Colindale Avenue, being entirely separate from the Metropolitan Police Training School. These cadets were full-time paid members of the Metropolitan Police until they were old enough to join the regular force.

The buildings consisted of four low-level accommodation blocks, an administrative building with classrooms, the Simpson Hall and a gymnasium.

It was set up and run by the much-loved and respected Colonel Andrew Croft, the explorer, and as early as 1951 he was brought in to advise and head the new Metropolitan Police Cadet Corps. His aims were to promote citizenship, and to introduce the cadets to how the Police Service functioned, as well as develop leadership skills in young men (and later women). This saw young men aged between 16 and 17 years old, which in the first instance was meant as a career prior to National Service that could be rescued to policing afterwards.

Initially spending four weeks at Hendon, the cadets were posted to a division to undertake varying low key roles. They did, however, take part in the Coronation in 1953 when their numbers totalled 300. After 1968 a more rigorous programme of training commenced, heavily reliant on lectures on improving their educational qualifications in addition to preparing them for police duty.

There were many characters in the Metropolitan Police Cadets Corps. They included Sergeant Bill Bailey, the drill instructor at Hendon, whose legendary voice could be heard on the parade square. Another character was Station Sergeant William Henry Blackwell (warrant no. 125768), who joined the Training School in July 1951 and moved to the Cadet Corps in April 1966. Born in 1917 in Sheffield and being 6 ft tall, he was a strong, powerful man who had been a miner before he joined the Metropolitan Police in 1937. He was originally posted to H Division, and during the war became a corporal in the RAF between February 1942 and November 1945. Married with one child, he was seconded to the Home Office in July 1949 having passed all the examinations to Station Sergeant. When he retired from the force after 30 years' service in 1967 he accepted a civilian job at the Cadet School. He later became head of Physical Training at the Cadets' Centre at Grosvenor Hall, Ashford in Kent, where cadets undertook their second-phase training. He was a wrestling champion and taught the sport, always being on hand to demonstrate moves and holds. Even at 55 years of age he was a strong and fit man. The picture below shows Blackwell in the centre of the Grosvenor Hall Cadet wrestling team in 1971. Ex-Sergeant Blackwell died in July 2003 aged 86 years.

William Blackwell shown with his cadet wrestling team in 1971

Grosvenor Hall consisted of nearly 200,000 sq ft of educational, adventure, sports and recreational facilities within a fully secure 50 acre site. The site was later given up for training of police officers from the southern counties. In 2010 it was sold to provide educational facilities for children and young people. The cadets were disbanded in the late 1980s, and the cadet school at Hendon was shut in 1993. The picture below shows a drill class of the 'B' Course in 1976.[1639]

A drill class of 'B' course cadets in 1976

In June 1987 a Volunteer Cadet Corps was formed as a link between police and local communities in South Norwood as a pilot scheme. It was successful, and the scheme was gradually introduced on to other divisions. Now, after the introduction of borough policing, all of the 32 boroughs have at least one Voluntary Police Cadet unit.

Hendon Police Station

London Borough of Barnet
Unknown address (1844-1864)
4 Cowley Cottages New Brent Street (1864-1884)
S Division (1844-1993)
Borough of Barnet OCU (1993-1998)

Parish cages, pounds and lock-ups had been known in Hendon since the 13th century. In 1796 a cage for detaining prisoners was located at the junction of Bell Lane and Brent Street, Hendon.[1640]

By 1829 a watch house and stocks had been built at the same site. In 1888 a pound existed in the middle of Burroughs Lane and Church Lane[1641] (today The Burroughs and the Watford Way). The locally-appointed parish constable was responsible for Hendon up until 1840, when the Metropolitan Police District was extended. The boundary stretched to a radius of twelve miles from Charing Cross, taking in Edgware, Whitchurch, Finchley, Harrow, Great Stanmore and Hendon. The original watch house would have been transferred from the parish authorities to the control of the Metropolitan Police.

It was not until 1844 that a station or house was taken into service for police purposes by the Metropolitan Police, although this was a small station placed in the charge of a sergeant. It is likely that this was a horse patrol station.

Hendon was a station on S or Hampstead Division, and it remained a sergeant-designated station until 1881 when its status was upgraded and an inspector placed in charge. In 1864 No. 4 Cowley Cottages, New Brent Street (opposite the Congregational Schools and the junction with Bell Lane) was rented by the police,[1642] and they were still there in 1880. The cottages stood until 1959, when they were pulled down to make way for the Foster Estate.[1643]

In 1869 the station strength was one sergeant and one acting sergeant, with four constables on the day beats. During the night there was one sergeant and seven night constables. There were four day beats and six night beats, and one constable on reserve. Hendon was the sectional station to Hampstead and had no cells to house any prisoners, so they were transported to Hampstead often on foot or by horse and trap for processing. The two inspectors at Hampstead were instructed to supervise Hendon on horseback on rotation, twelve hours on duty and twelve hours off. This also worked for the horse, because it would be rested following twelve hours away from the station.[1644]

The inspector at Hampstead Police Station provided supervision, and a horse was his mode of transport in order that he would patrol the district and call in at the stations like Hendon.

Times were hard, with tours of duty lasting from 14-17 hours, seven days a week. On Sundays police officers were required to attend church in uniform. In 1868 respite came in the form of one day off a week, but this was later revised down a year later with this privilege being only two days per month instead. Great unrest amongst the police developed in 1872, with the police going on strike. This caused a very hard-nosed approach by the government, who arrested three of the ringleaders and imprisoned them, whilst dismissing 100 men from the service. Two weeks later the men were reinstated, and punished by being transferred to other divisions.

The area was changing though, with the influx of people and the development of transport and amenities. Modernisation had arrived with the opening of the Midland Railway in 1868 followed by horse-buses a year later, on a route from Brent Street to Praed Street, Paddington. In the meantime the parish vestry were in discussions regarding the sale of the lock and cage which was currently in the possession of the Metropolitan Police.

In October 1882 it was sold to Mr. Smart for £47 10s. The site was not forgotten, as a plaque was erected by the local authority to ensure its place in history.

A new station was erected in 1884, north of the junction of Brent Street with Brampton Grove.[1645] The station call sign for the telegraph published in Police Orders in 1893 was Hotel Bravo (HB), but by the 1920s this was changed[1646] to Sierra November (SN).

Hendon Police Station 1884-1998

Permission was given in 1915 for a fire escape shed to be erected in the station yard for use by the fire brigade, and annual rental of five shillings was paid by the local authority for this facility. The station address was changed to 133 Brent Street in 1921, which was notified to the police by the local authority.

Travelling to and from work for police officers working long hours was often hazardous. In 1928 Constable Samuel Henry Luscombe (warrant no. 96525) with 19 years' service was killed while cycling home after late turn duty at Hendon.[1647]

1638 transact.westminster.gov.uk/CSU/Planning%20Applications%20Committee/2006/09%20-%205%20October/ITEM%2001%20-%20Peel%20House,%20105%20Regency%20Street,%20SW1.pdf accessed 18th November 2012.
1639 www.friendsreunited.co.uk/drill-lesson-b-course-1976/Memory/7a599a97-892b-4bce-81a1-a0f000d9c0a4 accessed 27th November 2012.
1640 French, I. (1984) *Hendon Police*. Local police charity publication in aid of 2 Area Widows and Orphans.
1641 Bacon, G. W. (1888) *London and Suburbs*.
1642 French, I. (1984) *Hendon Police*. Local police charity publication in aid of 2 Area Widows and Orphans.
1643 Ibid.
1644 Metropolitan Police Special Orders 1869.
1645 Hendon Library.
1646 General Orders 1893.
1647 Metropolitan Police Roll of Honour.

The Birth of Aviation in Hendon

Hendon was also one of the most important pioneering centres of aviation. Claude Grahame-White (engineer, aircraft manufacturer and flying record holder) founded his airport there in 1910, and brought work to the area when he designed and built aeroplanes (and later motor cars) for the war effort, such as the successful XV. This caused the greatest impact to the station in the whole of its history. White created many of the buildings (like those of the current driving school and the old Hendon Training school) and workshops which housed many of the workers he employed. He also staged spectacular, crowd-pulling air displays. The airfield was requisitioned from him during WWI and was finally purchased for the RAF, which held annual pageants there until 1937. With the requisitioning of the airport and factories without compensation White sued the War Department, finally winning his action and receiving compensation in the early 1920s. Sadly, so disillusioned was White he shut his factories and sacked 400 workers, which caused severe unemployment in the area.

Chief Inspector Fitt and his capture Grahame White

White is remembered in the area because the Grahame Park Estate and Road are named after him. In the picture above White is shown together with Chief Inspector William Edward Fitt of S Division (later Superintendent J Division) in about 1912. White is dressed in driving or flying attire. During this time there were air shows, exhibitions, air races, illuminated flights and the construction of aeroplanes which drew huge crowds. For the police at Hendon, there was extra duty and aid to the Aerodrome every week.

Fitt lived in South Hampstead in 1911 with his wife and son Percy William Fitt, who later was a prominent senior officer of the Metropolitan Special Constabulary.[1648] Other nearby airfields and factories at Cricklewood, just across the Edgware Road, also lasted from the earliest pioneering days until the spread of housing. Apart from the early aircraft industry, the borough has never been heavily industrialised, but at the end of the 19th century significant concentrations of factories developed along the Edgware Road and at Barnet. Birt Acres was working for Elliot's photographic printing works in Barnet when he shot Britain's first moving picture there in 1895.[1649]

War Time 1939-45

After Hendon Aerodrome ceased its spectacular displays and aerobatics, instead the planes overhead were more likely to be flown by the Royal Air Force in practice for combat. Such was the case on 3rd September 1939, just as Neville Chamberlain was announcing that Britain was at war with Germany. A loud explosion was heard in Hendon, and the residents thought that Germany had started bombing raids. This later turned out to be untrue. In fact an RAF bomber was circling Hendon Aerodrome, intending to land when it ran into difficulties and plunged to earth crashing in Heading Street. Constable 928S Len Fry saw it disappear over Greyhound Hill before it exploded, killing all the crew in what were the first fatalities of World War Two.[1650]

The Metropolitan Police Driving School and Police College both shut for the duration. In the meantime Hendon was overwhelmed with applications for Aliens (non-Commonwealth citizens) to remain in the UK, and the station could not cope with long queues forming the length of the pavement outside. A temporary office was established in the CID office, but confiscated property was a problem as all aliens were required to give up their cameras. Spalding Hall in Victoria was taken over, where all the confiscated and labelled cameras were stacked from floor to ceiling.[1651] Over 13,900 cases of aliens wishing to stay in the UK were heard by a special court in Hendon. Suddenly applicants joined His Majesty's Forces or signed up for air raid precaution duties, so few turned up for court hearings on 4th September. In preparation for war the station was fitted with air raid protection shutters, and an air raid siren was placed on the roof.

Many local people joined the auxiliary police so larger numbers of police were coming on duty, usually averaging about thirty per shift. By 1942 the force had become so inflated that the Commissioner instructed that he was prepared to release men for service in the armed forces. Regular officers under 25-years-old and auxiliary officers under 30 years were told they may apply. Instructions were also issued that the regular Police officers under 25-years-old were no longer considered part of a reserved occupation.[1652] The age for volunteers for the armed services was raised to 26 years and there was no shortage of applications, which caused the Commissioner in May 1942 to stop any further applications except for pilot or radio observer.[1653]

On the night of 19th/20th September 1940 Hendon Police Station suffered bomb damage when a high incendiary bomb demolished the south-east corner of Victoria Street and Brent Street, smashing all the front windows and damaging the window frames.[1654]

By far the largest explosion occurred on 13th February 1941, when a 2,500 kilo land mine destroyed Ramsey Road, Borthwick Road, Ravenstone Road, York Road and Argyle Road. Eighty people were killed and 520 people injured, 148 seriously. It left 1,500 people homeless. Many police officers were commended for their tireless work and organization that day. SDI G.F. Payne and Sub-Inspector Orr were awarded the British Empire Medal. Special Inspector Gore (SN) and Special Constable Hite were awarded the George Medal.[1655]

Further personal tragedy struck Hendon when on 21st February 1941 Constable 603S Whellams (aid from Golders Green) was killed by an High Incendary bomb which fell in Brent View Rise. V1 and V2 rockets fell in Barnet and

Hendon, with the first one falling in Southfield Gardens on 27th July 1944.[1656]

Residential accommodation was being taken over in stations for essential administrative support as space became short. Following the war there was cause for celebration and street parties following both VE and VJ Days. Police and public relations were good, and police attended the celebratory firework display in Hendon Park on 8th June 1946.

The Police Training School re-opened in 1947, and the nearby driving School started training police drivers again. It was at the latter part of the war that Hendon received its first solo motorcycle – a Royal Enfield, which was well used.

Officers who had signed up for war service started returning to the station. Constable Jim Baldry drove the khaki-coloured Royal Enfield which was affectionately known as 'Bomber Brown'. Two riders per month per relief were deputed to ride Bomber Brown, and Constable Baldry's relief colleague 'Stormy' Winterflood was the other rider. The winter of 1947 was one of the severest of the century, and when riding the solo officers wore peaked caps, riding breeches, leather gaiters, leggings and an apron something described as being 'like a baby's nappy'.

In 1948 the Enfield was exchanged for a big machine – a 500cc Triumph. Constable Baldry had a lucky escape one day when he was answering an emergency call and travelling past Bell Lane and into Brent Street when he collided with a traffic patrol officer riding another solo motorcycle. His leather gaiters saved him from serious injury.

Building alterations were carried out at Hendon, with the married quarters being reduced to one unit of three bedrooms on the first floor and a living room on the top floor. A bathroom was added in 1952. Station Sergeant Oliver and his family occupied those quarters. The CID were moved from the small room in the front hallway on the ground floor upstairs to the first floor. CID officers in those days worked split tours of duty 9.00am-1.00pm and 6.00pm-10.00pm, and every other Sunday was taken as leave if duties permitted.[1657]

Constable Jock Cobban and Rinty 2

Police dogs were now being taken seriously as an aid to policing. The first two handlers at Hendon were Constable Jock Cobban and 'Rinty 2', followed by Constable 'Taff' Lindburn and 'Joe'.

The station general purpose (GP) car was issued in 1948, which was garaged in the old shed in Brampton Grove near the rear entrance to the station. The same year saw the introduction of the National Health Service, and people were much relieved because during the war there had been serious outbreaks of poliomyelitis.

On 9th February 1948 an Avro Anson taking off from Hendon crashed in the Edgware Road on top of a tram, killing the occupants of the plane and injuring nine people on the tram. Four hundred gallons of petrol cascaded down the Edgware Road, and there were calls at the time for flying out of Hendon to cease. Coupled with the difficulties of re-adjustment after the war, high inflation and low wages, the strength of the Metropolitan Police dropped from 18,600 in 1939 to 14,200 in 1946.[1658] Despite a 15% pay rise, even more officers left the service and life became very tough for those who remained.

On 28th April 1949 another plane taking off from Hendon crashed in the grounds of the Metropolitan Police Training School, narrowly missing the main buildings and killing all three people on board. This was not the worst plane crash to beset the Hendon section, as on 17th October 1950 a BEA Dakota on its way to Glasgow from Northolt crashed in Highwood Hill in a blazing inferno, killing 27 adults and a baby. The town hall was used as a mortuary, and officers from the station were faced with the difficulties of identification.

An individual and personal tragedy struck the station in April 1954, when Constable John Wren, who just completed a double tour on Sierra 7 'WT' (wireless telegraphy Morse code) car, felt ill at work and went home to his bed. Once at home he collapsed suffering from a heart attack and died. He was 44-years-old. A service funeral followed. Tragedy struck again when ex-Station Sergeant Raishbrook, who had retired from Hendon just three years before, was killed on a pedestrian crossing in October 1958.[1659]

Mrs Dangerfield (who lived in Dorberic House next to the station) campaign for women police officers at Hendon, started in 1936, finally bore fruit in 1954 when Women Police Constables (WPCs) Beryl Sewell and Eleanor Wilson (as they were called at the time) were posted to the station as the first women police.[1660] Mrs Dangerfield sold her house to the police in 1955, and Chapel Walk married quarters were soon constructed. Police Sergeant 79S Alfred Corden and his wife became the last residents to live above the station, and when they vacated their quarters in 1957 their quarters were converted into a police canteen.

One Hendon police officer who should be acknowledged was Constable 304S Jock Cobban, who was said to have been only the third officer since the formation of the force to not have had a single day's sick leave in 26 years' service.

Police officers, who often socialized with colleagues rather than with friends outside the police service, formed local social and athletic clubs. These clubs arranged children's parties at Christmas for the police children, where one of the police officers (with white beard if possible) would act as Father Christmas. In the case of Hendon it was John Whyte, who would arrive at the station in full Father Christmas outfit on his 'Noddy' police solo motorcycle, rather than using his reindeer. The children (those not frightened off of course) would sit on his knee and get a present from him.

1648 Census 1911.
1649 www.barnet.gov.uk/index/leisure-culture/local-history-heritage. htm#chip accessed 2nd November 2011.
1650 French, I. (1984) *Hendon Police*. Local police charity publication in aid of 2 Area Widows and Orphans.
1651 Ibid (p74).
1652 Metropolitan Police Orders dated 29th April 1942.
1653 French, I. (1984) *Hendon Police*. Local police charity publication in aid of 2 Area Widows and Orphans.
1654 Ibid (p77).
1655 Ibid (pp77-78).
1656 French, I. (1984) *Hendon Police*. Local police charity publication in aid of 2 Area Widows and Orphans.
1657 Ibid (p83).
1658 Ibid. (p84).
1659 Ibid.
1660 Ibid (p87).

Father Christmas arriving at the children's Christmas party in the form of Constable Whyte on his 'Noddy' motorcycle.

There were organised coach outings to the sea-side and other places like the races. One such trip from Hendon to Fowley Refinery in the New Forest saw the bus stop at every pub on the way back just to top up the radiator with water – a trip said by the social secretary, Constable 155S Johnny Howard, to have been 'the best ever'.[1661] The cricket team flourished during the post-war years, when the sub-divisional cup was won by Hendon who scored 239 against Lewisham Traffic Garage and then skittled out the opposition for 38. Often senior officers and sometimes even divisional superintendents would come to the ground to watch the matches, because it was great kudos for them to have a winning divisional team.[1662]

When there are errant police officers at stations and offences occur which defy explanation, then often the tight community of the police family becomes strained and many look at their neighbour with deep suspicion. During the late 1950s a police officer at Hendon was arrested and jailed for housebreaking offences, something which he admitted had lasted for over ten years. A collective sigh of relief came from the police family in what was described by some at Hendon police station as the blackest period in their history. It took some years to return to normality after this.

Constable Whyte with his national hammer-throwing trophy

One incident at Hendon was notable for its audaciousness. Constable 'Bunny' Warren (yes, the nicknames were as predictable as that) lost a prisoner (often a severe discipline offence) at court when he asked to the use the toilet. When Bunny went to find his prisoner who had been absent some time, he saw that the bars of the toilet had been sawn through, as it transpired the night before by an accomplice, and the prisoner was long gone.

Cowley Cottage, the scene for the first Hendon horse patrol station, was finally demolished in 1959 when the Foster Estate was built.

At that time there were four foot beat and three motorcycle beats at Hendon. The foot beats were Brent Street, Hendon Central, West Hendon and the Hyde. Time off would not be granted unless the four foot beats could be covered from the ten police officers available per shift.

The national hammer throwing champion for 1959 and 1960 was Constable 710S Jock Whyte of Hendon, shown above with his trophy, and the First Aid team won the Ralph Trophy twice as well, mirroring Jock's achievements. Constable Lindenbern's dog earned notoriety with 125 arrests to date, but also won the prestigious Black Knight Trophy in 1957 as Best Police Dog of the year.

1963 saw the demise of the station library, which passed into oblivion unnoticed except that the librarians (who were police officers doing it as part of their duties) lost their jobs.

Another major air crash occurred on the section in 1965, when a DC4 Air Liner mistook Hendon for Heathrow and actually landed there, to the concern of those on the ground.

Hendon was always being beset with problems relating to traffic accidents, especially since a number of main road carrying vast numbers of vehicles converge in the borough. Again in 1964, a lorry carrying 2,760 eggs crashed on the Great North Road shedding its load. Men were 'scrambled' from the station to attend. Another accident two months later occurred on the North Circular Road, when a heavy-lifting jib from a crane buckled and fell on a passing coach, killing seven people and injuring eight.[1663]

Imminent boundary changes in 1965 caused concern for many at Hendon, at a time when the all-black helmet plate was changed to silver or chrome. The boundary changes saw Hendon become a sectional station of the newly-built West Hendon Sub-Division, which now comprised West Hendon, Mill Hill, Borehamwood and Hendon. Hendon could not compete with the new spacious stations like West Hendon, and some felt that the closure of Hendon was near. Some officers put in for a transfer rather than be forced to move to another station, one of whom was the remaining female officer Constable Curl, who transferred off the division.

The first collator at Hendon was Constable 'Ginger' Marshall, whose office was on the first floor. The section was now divided into five home beats.

In 1973, during the blackout because of power cuts, the station reverted to candle power. Clip-on ties, designed to prevent officers being strangled, were issued to all officers in 1971.

In July 1977 the Queen Mother visited the station, whose front garden won a certificate in the London Garden Competition with the credit going to Constable 219S Gordon.

A station modernisation programme to upgrade the station was planned for Hendon in 1981. The cost was £50,000 and work was carried out by Linbrook and Sons of Enfield, commencing in 1982 in time for the centenary in 1984. The work was only just completed in time for the Open Day on 1st April 1984. Amongst the 2,000 visitors on that bitterly cold day, was the Metropolitan Police Surveyor, Mr. David Ratcliffe, who oversaw the work. All were pleased with the finished product. Gone were the outside toilets, and the canteen upstairs had been converted into a self-service catering unit. New toilets and a shower were also built, with central heating being provided to all floors. The fireplaces were all bricked up. Improvements were made to the communications suite, the front office and rear lobby.[1664]

The rear yard of Hendon in 1977 after renovation work

In 1998 the station was closed after 110 years' service, when the Metropolitan Police concentrated on occupying more modern stations. The building and its car park were sold at auction for £665,000. The occupants moved to the newly-built state-of-the-art Colindale Police Station, situated near the old Hendon Aerodrome site adjacent to the estate.[1665]

Highbury Vale Police Station

The London Borough of Islington
211 Blackstock Road, Islington (1910-2000)
Y Division (1840-1965)
N Division (1965-2000)

In 1888 Mr. Frederick Baker, who owned a parcel of land which he wished to sell, made an approach to the Commissioner of the Metropolis. The Commissioner was at the time seeking to buy a suitable plot on which to build a station. The land was located in Blackstock Road, opposite Myrtle Street (now known as Hurlock Street). The offer was considered but the plot of land was considered not only too expensive, but also not large enough for police requirements. Discussions between the Receiver and Commissioner concluded that there was no urgent need for a station at Highbury at this moment, so the matter was postponed.[1666]

In 1902 the residents of Highbury petitioned the Secretary of State, requesting that a police station be built on land owned by the London County Council. This was the same parcel of land considered in 1888, but with a change of ownership. The Metropolitan Police were not keen, as the land was considered small. However, suggestions were made that with the compulsory purchase of several houses in Canning Road backing onto the land, Police requirements would be satisfied. When approached, the London County Council did not want to sell the land but suggested an 80-year lease instead. A considerable amount of correspondence exchanged hands and the London County Council finally decided to sell the freehold after all, as the land was going to be used for a public purpose.[1667]

Accordingly, the site was bought for £2,250 in 1903, and compulsory purchase orders were served on the owners (British Equitable Insurance Company) of the houses located at 29, 31, 33, 37 and 39 Canning Road. One of the leaseholders was unhappy about the purchase, and claimed compensation of £4,100. A court case followed, with a jury assessing the compensation as £2,379, which was more than the cost of the original parcel of land. The site remained empty for over three years, presumably because of the court action for compensation. Finally, the Town Clerk of the Metropolitan Borough of Islington wrote to the Commissioner for the Metropolis following a resolution passed at a council session stating:

"That having regard to the distress prevalent in the borough owing to the unemployment the council respectfully urge His Majesty's Government to proceed with the erection of the proposed police station and officers quarters in Blackstock Road, at a cost of £80,000 (the site cleared nearly 3 years ago) at the earliest moment." [1668]

The police station was built shortly after the letter to the Commissioner and was ready for occupation in July 1910. The station was built with a section house for thirty unmarried men and two sets of married quarters (A former Metropolitan Police Commissioner, Sir Kenneth Newman, once lived at these premises). One set of married quarters cost 10/6d per week, whilst the other quarters were 9/- The address was shown as 211 Blackstock Road, Islington, N4.[1669]

Highbury Vale Police Station 1910-2013

The building of the new station caused a revision of the boundaries and the status of the surrounding stations. Police Orders showed that Highbury Vale was a sectional station of Stoke Newington Police Station. Further re-organisation of local authority boundaries introduced on 1st April 1965

1661 French, I. (1984) *Hendon Police*. Local police charity publication in aid of 2 Area Widows and Orphans.
1662 Ibid (p87).
1663 Ibid (p95).
1664 Ibid (p137).
1665 *Daily Mail*, 22nd May 1998, p62.
1666 John Back Archive (1975).
1667 Ibid.
1668 Minutes of Council meeting, December 1908.
1669 Metropolitan Police Orders dated 23rd July 1910.

removed Highbury Vale as a sectional station of Islington Police Station. However, a month a re-consideration saw Highbury Vale transferred to Holloway Police Station instead. Highbury Vale section house was re-opened after refurbishment on 7th September 1925.[1670]

A decision was taken to shut Highbury Police Station to the public, and this took place in January 2000.[1671] Two surveys had been completed which showed that on average the station was used by fourteen callers a day, and most of these were signing on bail or producing their motor vehicle documents.[1672]

The station building was still used for Police purposes, and officers paraded in the basement for match-day duty at Arsenal Football Club situated only 400 yards away. The building also provided a valuable resource as a place for briefings, planning and administrative work.[1673]

The buildings and land were sold in March 2013 to Indra Services for £3.850M.[1674]

Highgate Police Station

High Street, Highgate (1841-1849)

South Grove, later Highgate Grove (1849-1868)

Archway Road (1865-1993)

S Division (1841-1868)

Y Division (1865-1993)

The London Borough of Haringey OCU (1993-2014)

In 1849 a new police station was erected at 51 South Grove, Highgate for the sum of £1,475.[1675] A from the Home Office to the Receiver letter dated 14th February 1850 authorised him to re-surrender the old watch house to the Parish authorities at Highgate, as it was no longer required for Police Service as the new station was now open.[1676]

In 1863 an inspector and his horse were transferred from Kentish Town Police Station to Highgate.[1677] The station was shown located on S Division, and was referred to as Highgate Grove. It misleadingly reported that a sergeant supervised the station; however, instructions corrected this error and confirmed that there were two inspectors in charge.[1678] This was further confirmed with records showing that the station strength was two inspectors, six sergeants and 41 constables.[1679] There were twelve beats to patrol split between two shifts, night duty and day duty. Two sergeants and 14 constables covered the day duty, whilst two sergeants and 27 constables were responsible for the night duty shift.[1680] The two remaining sergeants covered the station duties between them. The station had cells, took charges and paraded police officers for duty.[1681] Supervision was carried out between the two inspectors, who took it in turns to ride the horse to ensure the men were carrying out their duties. The horse was stabled at the rear of the station.[1682]

By 1878 there were problems in the cell area of the station. Sewer gas was apparently leaking into the building. It is not certain whether this prompted the Home Office to look for a new site on which to build another police station.

There was a high turnover of police officers, who joined the force only to find the arduous conditions of service and the meagre pay caused them to resign. The picture above shows Constable 96Y William Rivers Sawyer (warrant no. 57621), aged 19 years, a gardener from Crayford in Kent. Sawyer stayed in the police for only a short while. He joined the Metropolitan Police on 23rd January 1874 and resigned on 11th June 1877. Sawyer would have left the police without any pension or other gratuity. Those who resigned before serving for 25 years left without a promise of financial support, even

Constable 96Y William Rivers Sawyer

if any injuries received on duty precluded them from further employment. They usually presented their case to the Commissioners, for it was at their discretion as to whether recommendations were made to the Home Secretary for the grant of a gratuity. The officer was awarded a certificate of conduct in lieu of any references, which would enable an ex-police officer to obtain further employment. Sawyer's certificate stated that his conduct was 'Good'. This was signed by Superintendent Edward Worells, the Divisional Superintendent. Sawyer returned to market gardening in Kent.

In 1886 the Divisional Headquarters for Y Division was established as Kentish Town Police Station, even though the name of the division was 'Highgate'.[1683] Facilities were introduced at Highgate Police Station in 1888 that allowed for the receiving of dead bodies, including those found in rivers, canals and waterways.[1684]

The 1891 census shows twelve constables being in residence at the station.[1685] On 21st February 1894 the officers and men of Highgate and Upper Holloway Police stations met in the Archway Tavern for their annual dinner. The dinner was attended by the guest of honour Mr. Frank Beal, Clerk to the Justices at Highgate Court, who listened to the vocal and instrumental music and then ended the evening with a speech and compliments to the Highgate Division.[1686]

The August Bank Holiday of 1897 was celebrated with the laying of a foundation stone for the new police court by Mr. R.D.M. Littler, QC, at Highgate. This was erected by the London County Council, near Highgate Police Station, at a cost of some £8,000, and was designed by the Metropolitan Police Surveyor John Dixon Butler.

On 15th October 1897 reports showed that a divisional Inspector had met with an accident, the result of which would incapacitate him for duty for some time. On 9th October Sub-Divisional Inspector Mountifield, of the Highgate and Upper Holloway Districts, had been returning from superintending the policing arrangements at an important football match at Caledonian Park when he crossed the Police Station yard at Upper Holloway, and, treading on some decayed leaves, fell heavily to the ground. His right side struck some iron railings, and he had to be assisted into the Station. Dr. Rattray, the Divisional Police Surgeon, was called, and found that the inspector was suffering from fractured ribs.[1687]

In 1898 the police paid £1,300 for a new site in Archway Road, Highgate,[1688] and the new station opened in January 1902.[1689] The building was modernised in 1936,[1690] with the station telegraph code signal 'HI'.[1691]

In the early 1930s, station telegraphic codes were revised and issued to stations based on the division and station name rather than the previous random format. Highgate changed to 'YH'.

In August 1944, during World War II, Highgate Police Station was seriously damaged by a V1 flying bomb. This was one of ten Metropolitan Police stations that were badly damaged. The adjoining Court House was demolished, and a set of married quarters had to be vacated. There were four people injured in the attack.[1692] Until the station was fully repaired in January 1945[1693] all business was transferred to Muswell Hill Police Station, Fortis Green.[1694]

Highgate Police Station 1902-1960

In 1957 Highgate was a sub-division of Hornsey under the supervision of Superintendent J.L. Sims-Kirby.[1695]

A new police station at 407-409 Archway Road, Highgate was erected on the same site at a cost of £49,088, and was opened in March 1960.[1696]

Highgate Police Station 1960-2014

In 2001 the station was still in use, but charges were no longer taken there. Despite having cell space available, prisoners were no longer detained at the station.[1697]

In 2014 Highgate Police station was sold to Bellway Homes Ltd for £3.575M.[1698]

Hillingdon and Uxbridge Police Stations

London Borough of Hillingdon

Kingston Lane, Hillingdon (1840-1871)

49 Windsor Street, Ruislip (1871-1988)

Warwick Place, Ruislip (1988-2017)

T Division (1840-1865)

X Division (1865-2017)

In 1838, prior to the arrival of the Metropolitan Police, the Uxbridge Voluntary Police Force was set up in the town workhouse at Uxbridge.[1699] For some months it was supported by voluntary subscriptions, and after a satisfactory trial of its worth, the Force was permanently established on 4th May in that same year and placed under the directions of the Commissioner of Paving. The force comprised Sergeant Superintendent William Winder and officers William Servant, Robert Minchinton and John Simpson.[1700]

During the setting up of the Metropolitan Police in 1829, many of the London Parish Vestries strongly objected to the increase of rates payable for this new service. The old system of parish constables was less expensive for the Parish. Once the Force was established in the inner parts of London and seemed to be successful the outer parishes then wanted their share of the Metropolitan Police.

The Commissioner received a letter dated 18th September 1839 from the residents of Hillingdon and Uxbridge requesting that the Metropolitan Police be extended out to their part of London. The letter[1701] addressed to the Home Secretary read as follows:

We, the undersigned Justices of the Peace acting for the division of Uxbridge in the county of Middlesex, also the undersigned inhabitants of the parish of Hillingdon and the town of Uxbridge and the vicinity, respectfully & earnestly beg your Lordship to be allowed to participate in the advantages and security offered by the recent Act of Parliament for the extension of the Metropolitan Police.

(signed) W. Wiseman J.P. B.P. Hodgson
T. Dagnall J.P. Curate of Hillingdon
Thomas T Clarke Jnr J.P.
And others

1670 Metropolitan Police Property Schedule 1924.
1671 www.islingtonfocus.com/articles/art030.htm accessed 27th May 2003.
1672 Ibid.
1673 Op cit.
1674 MPS (2019) Freedom of Information – Land and Property sold since 2010 for over £1M.
1675 John Back Archive (1975).
1676 Ibid.
1677 Metropolitan Police Orders dated 30th January 1863.
1678 Police and Constabulary Almanac 1864 and Metropolitan Police Orders dated 11th January 1864.
1679 Metropolitan Police Orders dated 11th January 1864.
1680 Ibid.
1681 Ibid.
1682 Ibid.
1683 John Back Archive (1975).
1684 *Dickens's Dictionary of London* (1888), p132-23.
1685 Census 1891.
1686 *Police Review*, February 1894.
1687 *Police Review*, October 1897.
1688 John Back Archive (1975).
1689 Metropolitan Police Orders dated 31st January 1902.
1690 Op cit. (J. Back).
1691 Metropolitan Police General Orders 1898.
1692 Howgrave-Graham, H.M. (1947) *The Metropolitan Police at War*. HMSO.
1693 Metropolitan Police Orders dated 2nd January 1945.
1694 John Back Archive (1975).
1695 *Police and Constabulary Almanac* 1957.
1696 John Back Archive (1975).
1697 *Police and Constabulary Almanac* 2001.
1698 MPS Information rights unit (2019) Land and property sold by the MPS for over £1M over the last 10 years.
1699 British History Online: Hutsons Recollections, visited 18th February 2013.
1700 *Lakes Uxbridge Appendix to the Almanacs* 1840.
1701 Letter dated 18 September 1839 held in Met Police Heritage Centre.

In January 1840 the Metropolitan Police extended cover to the outer areas of London, so Hillingdon and Uxbridge received their policemen.

A very substantial brick-and-slate house in Kingston Lane, Hillingdon was obtained on a 21-year lease from Michaelmas 1840 for use as a police station, initially to be known as Hillingdon and Uxbridge Police Station. The building had eight rooms including a scullery, three cells, stables for three horses, coal shed, dung pit and yards at the front and rear. This was an inspector's station, and remained so until 1871.[1702]

In 1842 the T Division was under the command of Superintendent David Williamson at Hammersmith, but Inspector Charles Otway was in charge of the Station House, assisted by Police Sergeants R. Roadnight and L. Monaghan.[1703] By 1843, Otway's place had been taken by Edward Cooke (warrant no.10679), who remained for some time, until 1857. Otway had been transferred to A or Whitehall Division. Cooke had joined in 1835, and promotion came early for him.

In 1851 Police Sergeant James Axley Turner, his wife Sarah and six single constables lived there. Also shown on the census record for that night are Police Inspector Charles Jeaks and Police Constable Joshua Turton, his wife Ann and their four children. The address shown is the 'Police Station House', near the turnpike in Kingston Lane, Hillingdon.[1704] Inspector Jeaks was still in charge of the station in 1853.[1705]

On the map (shown below) by the Local Board of Health in 1854, the police station is shown as a horse patrol station. Today the station long since gone, but the location is in present day Kingston Lane situated where Ivy Bridge Close now is. Stratford Bridge crosses the river at the point where Hillingdon Road meets Hillingdon Hill.[1706]

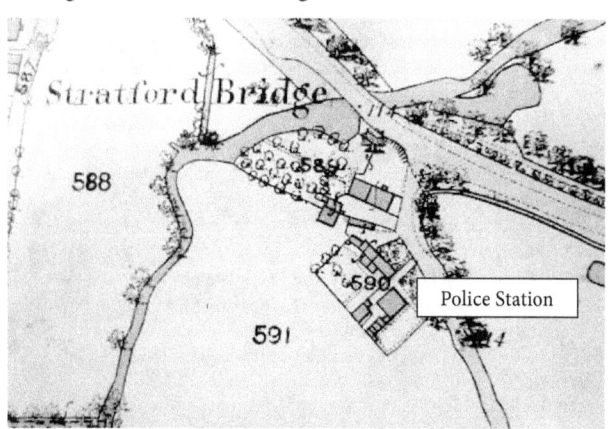

The horse patrol station at Stratford Bridge in 1854

Since the 1840s policing in the area was from Hillingdon Police Station, there being no police station at Uxbridge. In 1864 Hillingdon was a station on T or Kensington Division.[1707] Then in 1865 a new Division – X or Paddington Division – was formed, and Hillingdon was transferred from T to X.[1708]

In 1867 the X Division was commanded by Superintendent Hugh Eccles, who oversaw the purchase of the site in Uxbridge.

In 1866 a freehold plot of land owned by Mr George Baynham was purchased by the Receiver for £1,500 at 49 Windsor Street, Uxbridge for the erection of a new police station. It then took a number of years before the new station was completed at a cost of £2,870 and it was finally opened in September 1871 as Uxbridge Police Station.[1709] Included in the station were two sets of married quarters.

The new police station's actual construction had taken just five months, and was taken possession of by Inspector John Eames and Acting Inspector Bullivent. The building was described in the local newspaper in 1871 as an imposing structure, brick-built with stone facings and ornamental coping. It contained, on the ground floor, a charge room, reserve room, reading room for the single men, store room and three cells. On the first floor were the quarters of the acting inspector, and sleeping accommodation for five single men. There was also a suite of apartments for the inspector and his family. This was Inspector John Eames, his wife Jane and their two children. Also living there was Police Constable Ames Smith and his wife Fanny.[1710] The basement contained a mess room for the single men, a cook's kitchen, bath and washing rooms, and a drying closet. In the yard there was a four-stall stable.[1711]

Uxbridge Police Station 1871-1988

In February 1871, an adjoining piece of land occupied by a stable and dung pits was bought, again from Mr Baynham for £190.[1712]

In 1881 a Metropolitan Police report stated that the Uxbridge site was limited, but the station had been specially-constructed. The configuration of the accommodation needed revision, as the married men and single men's quarters were mixed. They also found the basement was damp. Living there were two married inspectors and five single constables.[1713] As a result of the above report, in 1882 one bed was removed from the section house above the station in order that every man might have 600 cubic feet of space. The water supply was from the Uxbridge Local Board, and was described as intermittent.[1714]

In the census of 1881 Inspector John Eames, his wife Jane and seven of their children were living at the police station. Inspector Joseph Capp and five constables were also there.[1715]

By 1887 the command of the division was in the hands of Superintendent G. Skeats.[1716]

In August 1889 William T. Wade (warrant no. 52942) was promoted to Sub-Divisional Inspector and put in charge of Uxbridge Sub-Division. He was assisted by James Phillips and Charles Whitlock, who were 3rd Class Inspectors. There were also six sergeants and 28 constables.[1717]

William Wade had joined the City of London Police after two years in the Army. In July 1870 he joined the Metropolitan Police, and

Sub-Divisional Inspector Wade

was posted to Bow Street Police Station. He then served at many different police stations in London as he rose through the ranks. He remained at Uxbridge for seven years until his retirement on 27th July 1896.[1718]

In 1893, at the police station described as in 'Ruislip Village', the following officers were stationed: Inspector Walter Weller and two constables William French and William Taylor (mounted).[1719]

Sub-Divisional Inspector Brownscombe

In 1903 Sub-Divisional Inspector Henry Brownscombe was in charge of Uxbridge Sub-Division and was medically retired from the Force as he had been partially blinded in an accidental shooting incident. He had been invited to a shoot on Lord Hillingdon's estate and had incurred the injuries. His retirement presentations were performed by Lord Hillingdon himself, who held himself responsible. He presented the officer with a gold watch and a cheque for £112. The inscription on the inner dome of the watch read:

"Presented to H.P. Brownscombe by the inhabitants of Uxbridge and neighbourhood as a mark of their esteem and regard and an acknowledgement of his faithful service as Sub-Divisional Inspector of the Metropolitan Police. Nov., 1903"

The inspector was also presented with a liqueur stand in an oak frame, mounted with silver, from the Captain and members of the Uxbridge Fire Brigade; an umbrella with ivory handle and travelling bag, from the Superintendent and Inspectors of X Division, and a clock in an early-English inlaid Chippendale case from the officers and men of the Uxbridge Sub-Division. The officer was obviously well-liked and had drawn much sympathy from both inside and outside of the police service.[1720]

In April 1911 Inspector William Daniels and his wife Sarah were living in five rooms, and six single Constables William O'Leary, George Thompson, Frederick Benner, George Sanderson, William Kentish and Robert Murton were living in five rooms in Uxbridge Police Station.[1721]

Uxbridge Police Station yard showing the old hand-ambulance and new mode of transport, the station van

The picture above, taken in the 1930s, shows the arrival of the new station van which replaced the hand ambulance on which drunks and sick or injured people would be transported. Dead bodies were also transported in this manner.

During the years 1937-39 talks were held with the Middlesex County Council and local Urban District Council on the question of building a new police station at Uxbridge.

There were plans for a new civic centre in the High Street, with a police station forming part of it. The war intervened and plans had to be shelved for the duration. Discussions resumed in 1958/59 but by that time the situation had completely changed. The price of land and building costs had soared, and so nothing happened.

A most unusual case that occurred in the area was that of the Russian master spies Peter and Helen Kroger, who turned their bungalow at 45 Cranley Drive, Ruislip into the headquarters for a spy ring which included Gordon Lonsdale, Harry Houghton and Ethel Gee. The house was raided by police with some of Britain's top spy catchers in the late 1950s. The Krogers were jailed for 20 years at the Old Bailey in March 1961. In 1969 they were exchanged in a deal with the Russians for Gerald Brooke. In 1977 local police went back to the bungalow to collect a radio transmitter used by the spies, which had been dug up in the back garden by the family then living there.[1722]

In 1965 the new London boroughs were created, and Uxbridge remained a Sub-Division Station on X Division in the new London Borough of Hillingdon.[1723]

Uxbridge Police Division was unaffected by the formation of the 'Airport Division' in 1974.[1724]

In August 1978 a portacabin was placed into the yard of Uxbridge Police Station for use as a temporary police station, prior to the station being closed for renovation and rewiring.[1725]

In 1983 Police Constable Frank Belienie was killed while on foot patrol when a car mounted the pavement and struck him at Hillingdon.[1726]

Planning permission was granted in 1984 for the building of a new police station at the junction of Harefield Road and Warwick Place, Uxbridge. The new £3 million building was built and on 20th May 1988 the Home Secretary, Douglas Hurd, opened the new police station. The station is known

1702 Met Police Heritage Centre Archives.
1703 *Lakes Uxbridge Appendix to the Almanacs* 1842.
1704 Census 1851.
1705 *Uxbridge Appendix to the Almanacs* 1853.
1706 Google maps.
1707 Metropolitan Police Orders dated 11th January 1864.
1708 Divisional Plan 'X' District. 'XR' Ruislip Division (undated).
1709 Metropolitan Police Orders dated 29th September 1871.
1710 Census 1871.
1711 *Middlesex and Bucks Advertiser*, 30th September 1871.
1712 Jephcote J. 'Histories of Police Stations in Hillingdon', 1969.
1713 Metropolitan Police: Condition of Police Stations 1881.
1714 Jephcote J. 'Histories of Police stations in Hillingdon', 1969.
1715 Census 1881.
1716 *Illustrated Uxbridge Almanac* 1887.
1717 *Kelly's Directory* 1890.
1718 *The Police Review and Parade and Gossip*, date unknown.
1719 *King's Uxbridge 'Gazette' Almanac* 1893.
1720 *The Police Review and Parade Gossip*, 11th December 1903.
1721 Census 1911.
1722 *Hillingdon Mirror*, 19th June 1979.
1723 Metropolitan Police Orders dated 6th August 1964.
1724 Metropolitan Police Orders dated 31st October 1974.
1725 *Uxbridge Gazette*, 31st August 1978.
1726 Metropolitan Police Book of Remembrance.

as the Hillingdon Borough Headquarters at Uxbridge Police Station.[1727]

The old station closed in 1988 and was converted into the Fig Tree, a licensed premises. Whilst the outside of the old station remain unaltered, the inside has greatly changed. There is no sign of there having been a police presence inside; even the cells were converted into toilets. The property has been listed by the Local Authority as a building of architectural interest.

Uxbridge Police Station 1988-2017

In 1992, just five years after the new police station opened, it was temporarily closed to install a divisional control room and to improve the custody suite. A 24-hour front counter service was available in portable offices next to the police station while the building work was in progress.

In 2017 it was decided to close the police station front counter[1728] prior to the property being sold, however by 2019 the station had been retained for police purposes.[1729]

Holborn Police Station

The London Borough of Camden

70 Theobalds Road, Holborn

E Division (1965-1993)

London Borough of Camden OCU (1993-2018)

Central North BCU (together with Islington) (2018 to Present)

One of the first stations in E or Holborn Division was located at George Street, St. Giles, and was an old Parish watch house. There was only one other station on the division, a strange-looking building in an area known as Battlesbridge, located in the centre of the carriageway at the junctions with New Road (later Pentonville Road), Grays Inn Road and Caledonian Road. In 1837 these premises were vacated in favour of a substantial brick building located in Hunter Street.

Another watch house was situated in Giltspur Street, Holborn. It had been built in 1791 and was attached to the church of St. Sepulchre, probably to prevent grave robbing.[1730]

A unit of E or Holborn Division with their Sergeant, c1910

The old building was not demolished immediately, but was converted into a public house, called the Omnibus Arms. The building was demolished in 1845, however some police officers still visited the old building whilst on duty for refreshment. PC John Robinson was dismissed from the Force for being drunk in the Eagle Street watch house (off Red Lion Square) after a drinking session at the old police station premises.[1731]

In the early 1960s local policing arrangements were reviewed, and plans were put in place for a large new police station to be built in Holborn. A suitable building plot was purchased which would not only accommodate the police station, but also several other departments transferred from New Scotland Yard.

In November 1965 a thirteen-storey building, with a total floor area of more than 110,000 square feet, was opened in Theobalds Road, Holborn. It was 155 feet tall, and was topped by a 75 feet wireless mast. This building, as well as being the new Holborn Police Station, also housed the Forensic Science Laboratory, relocated from New Scotland Yard, and the Aliens Registration Office, which transferred from Vine Street. The planned cost of construction was £80,000, and the builders were Laing Construction.[1732] The station code was shown as Echo Oscar (EO), and located at 70 Theobalds Road. When this building opened the nearby Grays Inn Road Police Station closed as an operational unit.

Holborn Police Station 1965 to present

Outside the new building hangs the 'hundred year old' blue lamp from the original Vine Street Police Station, which was situated off Piccadilly.[1733]

The Metropolitan Police Architects Department designed the building, whilst the Surveyor's Department invited tenders from reputable building companies to construct the station.

In 2002 it received an £8 million,[1734] and in 2019 Holborn Police Station was the Headquarters station, and was still open to the public.[1735]

Holloway Police Station

The London Borough of Islington

Bellefield House, Seven Sisters Road, Holloway (1845-1872)

Seven Sisters Road (1872-1874)

256 Hornsey Road (1874-1965)

284 Hornsey Road (1965-2017)

Y Division (1840-1965)

N Division (1958-2018)

The station at Holloway has often been referred to as Hornsey Road Police Station, confusing some observers that it was located in Hornsey, not on the road to it. Records show that the first police station in Holloway was set up in a house in Hornsey Road. The building was acquired in 1835 for an annual rent of £20, from a Samuel White who had used the building as an audit office.[1736]

In 1845 a brick-and-slate station house existed called Bellefield House, in Seven Sisters Road. It was rented from Mrs. Hannah Enkell of 4 Holloway Terrace, for £60 per year. It appears to have remained in service until 1872, when temporary accommodation was found nearby. A new temporary police station was also opened on 8th May 1871[1737] in Seven Sisters Road, staffed by one inspector, seven sergeants and 60 constables.[1738]

In 1874 a new police station was built at 256 Hornsey Road, some one hundred yards south of the present police station. The land for the station was purchased in 1873 at a cost of £1,700, and the building then erected for £3,592. It opened for business in January 1875.[1739] The ground floor was occupied by an Inspector's Office and two store rooms, four cells, a recreation room, a reserve room, a drying room and three WCs. In the basement there was a mess kitchen and cooking area, a washing room, brushing room, boot room, lamp room and four coal vaults. The first floor housed the married inspector and his family, and sixteen single constables occupied the second floor.

Holloway Police Station 1875-1965

In 1893 the telegraphic code for the station was published as Hotel Yankee (HY),[1740] however by 1960 this had become November Hotel (NH).[1741]

Discipline was very strict in the police, and to fail to turn up for duty without proper reason required severe action on the part of police supervisors. Absence without leave or absconding from the police force was a grave offence punishable before a court of law. In August 1897 Constable George Aubyn, attached to Holloway Police Station, failed to turn up for duty and was posted missing. He had hired a pony and trap, which he had failed to return, and had ridden it to Woking in Surrey. He was arrested on a warrant several days later when he gave himself up at the station. Inspector Joseph Davies, prosecuting, told the magistrate that Constable Aubyn had 18 months police service and had been dismissed from the service in consequence of his absence. Mr Bros, the magistrate, fined the officer £1 and stated that discipline must be maintained.[1742]

Only six stations out of fifteen on Y or Highgate Division were important enough to have Sub-Divisional Inspectors in charge of them. These were Kentish Town, Somers Town, Hornsey, Enfield, Caledonian Road and Holloway. The officer in charge of the police station at Holloway from 1897 until 1902 was Sub-Divisional Inspector Mountifield.[1743]

William Steggles Mountifield was born at Walton-on-the-Naze, Essex, in 1856, and joined the Metropolitan Police in 1877. In London he met and married Emily Oade, who was a year younger and was born at Gosport, Hampshire. In 1881 he was a constable living with his family (son Charles aged four, and Emily, three) at 31 Union Street, Clapham, Surrey.[1744] Gradually, over the years he rose through the ranks after coming to the attention of senior officers. Inspector Mountifield was indeed a character. Not only was he a strict disciplinarian, but he also understood the importance of sport and recreation in the police service. He was a competitive billiards player and a keen swimmer. The Hornsey Road swimming baths were situated next to the station, so swimming galas were a regular event. Mountifield was also Y Division's football representative for the Lady Bradford Challenge Cup, and was often seen supporting the Divisional Football Team. He commanded loyalty and respect.

In September 1899 he found Constable 566Y M'Kelvie drunk in full night duty uniform in Seven Sisters Road at 8.45am. The officer was off duty, and Mountfield walked back with him to his lodgings. Just outside the lodgings the constable became upset with Mountifield and assaulted him. The constable appeared at North London Court charged with assaulting the inspector. The case was heard by Mr. Fordham, who also listened to four witnesses supporting Mountifield.[1745] M'Kelvie

1727 *Uxbridge Gazette*, 18th May 1988.
1728 www.ruislipresidents.org.uk accessed 9th December 2017.
1729 MPS (2019) Freedom of Information Request – closure of Police stations since 2010.
1730 Kent, W (1937) *An Encyclopedia of London*. J.M. Dent. London.
1731 The John Back Archive (1975).
1732 *Police Review*, 23rd August 1963, p710.
1733 *Police Review*, 12th November 1965.
1734 *The Job*, 19th May 2000.
1735 uat01.nonlive.camden.pfiks.com/contact-police-stations accessed 31st October 2019.
1736 John Back Archive (1975).
1737 Metropolitan Police Orders dated 5th May 1871.
1738 John Back Archive (1975).
1739 Metropolitan Police Orders dated 22nd January 1875.
1740 Metropolitan Police General Orders 1893.
1741 *Police and Constabulary Almanac* 1960.
1742 *Police Review and Parade Gossip*, August 1897.
1743 *Police Review and Parade Gossip*, September 1902.
1744 Census 1881.
1745 *Police Review and Parade Gossip*, September 1899.

was sentenced to one month's imprisonment. The inspector was an active figure, so on a number of occasions he either won or came second in the station billiards competitions and veterans' swimming races.[1746]

In 1907 Holloway was shown as a station of Y or Highgate Division, with its Divisional Headquarters being located at Kentish Town.[1747] All prisoners charged with offences appeared at North London Court, Stoke Newington. This meant frequent visits by officers from Holloway to a court, which was open daily.

The 1907 Retirement photograph of a Holloway police officer after 25 years' service

The station was refurbished in 1911 when the section house accommodation was added,[1748] and was opened in February 1912.[1749]

Day trips in charabancs were often organised by the social clubs that grew up in police stations throughout the Metropolitan Police District during this time. Subscriptions paid weekly by the contributors towards the social club often meant that a trip to Brighton or Goodwood races (both very popular places of recreation in Edwardian England) required no further payment. The picture above shows a happy group of Holloway police officers outside the station prior to departure in 1921. These open-topped buses were susceptible to the elements, so suitable rain-ware was also carried.

Holloway Police Outing 1921

In 1941 a High Explosive bomb pierced the roof of the police station and exploded in the basement. Half of the building was demolished. Those killed in the incident were Sub-Divisional Inspector MacAlan Gibson (and his wife and their married daughter, Joyce Unwin), Inspector Leonard Clark, Station Sergeant 19N John 'Jack' Curry, Detective Sergeant Alick Stanley, Constable 377N James Rosen and Constable (War Reserve) Tom Killen. There were also five others injured. On 9th April 1941, Their Majesties King George VI and Queen Elizabeth visited the damaged Holloway Police Station and three other London police stations. At the station Their Majesties were able to talk to a number of representatives from other stations in the area, and all different ranks were assembled.[1750]

The destroyed police station at Holloway in 1941

During the 1939-45 War there were almost 1,900 reported cases of damage to police buildings in the Metropolitan Police District. Of these, some 124 received serious damage. Ten police stations were so badly damaged that they were either totally or partially abandoned. Some were reoccupied after extensive repairs.[1751]

After the war, one of the problems police faced were street gangs who would resort to fighting each other often with offensive weapons. Police Constable Raymond Henry Summers was on patrol in Holloway at night in 1958 when he came across a street gang fight and went to intervene. In the days before personal radios to raise the alarm were issued to individual police officers, officers walking their beats were on their own unless they were near a police box or telephone. During the fracas Summers was stabbed in the back with a thin-bladed knife, and died of his injuries.[1752] There was insufficient evidence to prosecute anyone in this matter, and subsequently no-one standing trial for the murder of a police officer.

In 1960 Holloway (telegraphic code 'NH') was shown as a station of N Division under the supervision of Superintendent G. Reay.[1753]

The complete Holloway Police Station building was later demolished, and the section house at the rear of the station yard was converted from living accommodation for single officers into a temporary police station, remaining so until 1965.

The original site of the demolished police station, when cleared, had a frontage of 48 feet and was 160 feet deep. This

Holloway Police Station 1965-2017

was considered too small for redevelopment, so a new location nearby had to be found. The present police station was built at 284 Hornsey Road, N7, a short distance away. Arrangements were made to design and build a new purpose-built modern station on the site, which opened on 19th July 1965. The new station was built without separate single officers' accommodation and married quarters. Separate buildings were constructed nearby to house the vast numbers of single officers who were joining the police. The nearest section house to Holloway was built in Canonbury, Islington and was called Olive House.

Holloway Police Station was closed to the public in 2017.

Hornchurch Police Station

The London Borough of Havering

74 Station Lane, Hornchurch (1955 to Present)

Essex Police (1955-1965)

K Division (1965-2018)

Basic Command Unit East Area (EA) (2018 to Present)

In 1841 there were two constables posted to Hornchurch. The Constabulary Act 1840 allowed distribution lists showing the location of the police force in Essex to be produced for the benefit and information of the Clerk for the Peace. They showed that in 1843 Constable 24 James Fowler (joined 23rd November 1840) and Constable 104 Uriah Fuller (joined 29th January 1841) were stationed at Hornchurch. Both constables had been transferred by May 1843.[1754] The distribution lists also showed that in early 1861 Constable 47 William Harrington (joined 4th May 1859) and Constable 145 Albert Ridley (joined 3rd March 1860) were stationed at Hornchurch.[1755]

In 1881 Constable George Wapling, his wife Eliza and their two children lived in Hornchurch village where he was the village constable.[1756]

In 1900, because of a revision of divisional boundaries, Hornchurch became a station within the division of Brentwood.[1757] Although there was a station in Hornchurch in 1931, located in a small terraced house in the High Street,[1758] the main policing of the area took place from Romford (South Street).[1759] One sergeant and two constables were stationed there. In essence, the house purchased for the sergeant and constable to live in, also acted as the police station.[1760] The population was estimated at 7,000, and recommendations were made to purchase four houses in the area as the neighbourhood was expanding rapidly.[1761]

The area around Hornchurch steadily grew. To the south the Royal Flying Corps Aerodrome had been built on Suttons Farm, Hornchurch, to combat the threat of German bomber and Zeppelin raids. In fact, the first three Zeppelins to be shot down in 1916 were all downed by pilots from Hornchurch. During the Second World War, the RAF pilots and crew from Hornchurch Aerodrome saw action against the German invaders during the Battle of Britain. The aerodrome was finally shut in 1962.[1762]

In 1930 two constables operated from their houses in Emerson Park, and one constable who was responsible for Gidea Park at Plough Corner.[1763]

In 1955 the Essex Constabulary built the station at 74 Station Lane, Hornchurch. The station was part of Hornchurch Sub-Division which included Emerson Park section and Harold Wood.

Hornchurch Police Station 1955-2013
(reopened 2018 for use by police)

This station (and Sub-Division) was transferred to the Metropolitan Police in 1965, along with Romford, Upminster, Harold Wood, Plough Corner and Rainham during boundary changes.

The station at Hornchurch is still operational at 74 Station Lane. It was sold in 2013[1764] to the London Borough of Havering who, under considerable pressure from local residents to keep the station open, then leased the property back to the Metropolitan Police for use by local police officers.[1765]

1746 *Police Review and Parade Gossip*, September 1902.
1747 *Kirchener's Almanac* 1907.
1748 Metropolitan Police Surveyor's Records.
1749 Metropolitan Police Orders dated 19th February 1912.
1750 Howgrave-Graham, H.M. (1947) *The Metropolitan Police at War*. HMSO.
1751 Ibid.
1752 www.policememorial.org.uk/Forces/Metropolitan/metroll.htm accessed 12th March 2002.
1753 *Police and Constabulary Almanac* 1960.
1754 Essex Record Office Q/Apr. 1: Distribution List.
1755 Essex Record Office Q/Apr. 12: Distribution List.
1756 Census 1881.
1757 Woodgate, J. (1985) *The Essex Police*. Lavenham, Suffolk.
1758 Brown, B. (1990) 'Romford Police: The Anniversary of a Change' in the *Romford Record*, Romford and District Historical Society.
1759 Ibid.
1760 *Essex County Constabulary – Police Stations and Police Houses* booklet (c1930) Essex Police Museum, Police Headquarters, Springfield, Chelmsford, Essex.
1761 Ibid.
1762 Brown, B. (1990) 'Romford Police: The Anniversary of a Change' in the *Romford Record*, Romford and District Historical Society.
1763 Op cit.
1764 Information rights unit, MPS, police stations closed since 2010, accessed 10th June 2019.
1765 www.romfordrecorder accessed September 2018.

Hornsey Police Station 1883-1915. Photograph taken c1890

Hornsey Police Station

The London Borough of Haringey
Hornsey village (1841-1865)
Crouch End Hill (1865-1876)
Hornsey Road, Holloway (1876-1915)
94 Tottenham Lane (1915-1936)
98 Tottenham Lane (1936-1993)
N Division (1841-1865)
Y Division (1865-1993)
Haringey OCU (1993-2018/19)
Basic Command Unit North Area (with the London Borough of Enfield) (2018/19 to Present)

Hornsey Police Station Lamp

According to records there has been a police station in Hornsey since 1841, however by 1864 the station was included as part of N Division.[1766] The station had a compliment of two sergeants and fifteen constables, along with one mounted constable and his horse.[1767] Further supervision was supplied from Tottenham, where the inspector resided. He was also in charge of Walthamstow and Tottenham. This was achieved on horseback, so supervisory officers in Victorian times had to be good horsemen.[1768] Charges could be taken at Hornsey, where there were cells for the detention of prisoners for court.[1769]

The 1890 photograph of Hornsey Police Station above shows it situated at the bottom end of Crouch End Hill near the Broadway, at the junction with Coleridge Road. It shows a substantial three-storey building with what appears to be accommodation on the third floor. In the distance is Christ Church. The station lamp situated outside the front of the station clearly shows a Victorian crown on the top. The current station lamp is shown above.

With the formation of the new Y Division in 1865, the interior divisions were shown as including Tottenham, Hornsey, Southgate, Enfield Town, Enfield Highway, Edmonton and Cheshunt. Inspector Webb was shown as the Acting Superintendent in charge of the division.[1770] A rather strange but tragic incident occurred in 1867, when Constable John Kennedy collapsed and died from the effects of sunstroke whilst patrolling his beat in Hornsey.[1771]

In 1881 a suitable parcel of land became available in Tottenham Lane, about a mile away from the original station. It was on a 100-year lease from the owner, the Rev. J. Jeakes, Rector of Hornsey.[1772] Ground rent of £30 per year was payable by the Receiver, who also had to insure the land and station with the Law Fire Office.[1773]

In 1883 a new station at Hornsey was completed, at a cost of £5,852. Supervised by an inspector, it had a charge room on the ground floor with two cells, a waiting room, Inspector's Office, a store, a day room, a mess room, a kitchen, a scullery, a clothes room, a drying room, a boot room and five water closets. On the first floor were a lavatory and a bathroom. Married quarters were also located on the first and second floors, housing one married inspector who occupied for five rooms and a pantry, whilst the married constable occupied four rooms and a pantry. Inspector George Carr was shown as the officer in charge of the sub-division, although he lived at Tottenham Police station.[1774] Apart from Hornsey and Tottenham, the Inspector was also responsible for Walthamstow. A horse was provided at Tottenham to enable the inspector to perform his supervisory duties.[1775]

In 1886 there was a revision of police boundaries, and Police Orders attributed Y or Kentish Town Division with Somers Town, Caledonian Road, Holloway, Highgate, Hornsey and Enfield. The stated strength of the division amounted to 49 inspectors, 67 sergeants and 768 constables. There were 22 horses also attached to the division. These figures were revised downwards after the boundary changes to 37 inspectors, 55 sergeants, 605 constables and 18 horses.[1776] In 1889 the introduction of Wood Green Division meant boundary changes to Hornsey division.

On 2nd October 1894 Police Sergeant Mortlock of Hornsey Police Station retired from the service after 26 years. A gathering of friends and relatives took place to commemorate the officer's retirement. Such occasions usually took place at the station, although they are also held in a hall or public house. Inspector King, in the absence of the Superintendent, made the retirement speech and the presentation of a marble time piece to the officer.[1777]

A retirement picture for three police pensioners together with their comrades and gifts

The photograph above is dated around 1906, and shows the ceremonial retirement photograph of three police officers from Y Division. They are in plain clothes in the centre, with their retirement gifts. Th retirees are unidentified, yet this is exactly what would have happened to Sergeant Mortlock, who would have been left with a similar photographic memento of his service with the Metropolitan Police. The social club would arrange for presents to be given to the officers, which in this case is a carved mantle clock for the man in the centre and carved figures for the other two officers. The official photograph was followed by a retirement party, which would have been attended by family, friends, and members of the community and work colleagues.

On 4th June 1897 the Royal Society presented Protection of Life from Fire Certificates and money grants to Constable 205Y Ernest Newman and Constable 384Y Patrick Connell, who rescued four people from a fire in a grocer's shop in Hornsey.[1778] The station telegraph signal was 'HE,'[1779] which changed in the 1930s to 'YR'.

Records show that in 1909 Hornsey Sub-Division was renamed Highgate Sub-Division under the supervision of Inspector Thomas, who subsequently transferred to Highgate Police Station.[1780]

Hornsey Police Station 1915-1936

In September 1912 the Receiver was able to purchase the freehold title to the land and station from the Rev. Bernard Spinks of Hornsey. Records show that at this time there was a police fixed-point box located on land belonging to Messrs. Huggins and Co. at Green Lanes, Hornsey.[1781] An ambulance shelter, containing a two-wheeled hand ambulance, was located in Hornsey Road on property belonging to Great Northern Railway Co.[1782] The address was recorded as 94 Tottenham Lane, Hornsey.[1783]

In February 1916 a new station was built in Tottenham Lane, together with a section house. The section house contained accommodation for 22 unmarried constables and one set of married quarters.[1784]

Gradually, as the roads in the area improved following the Great War, new methods of transport for police were tried. The introduction of pedal and motor cycles meant that large distances could be covered in a very short time. The Metropolitan Police needed to move with the times. Areas like Hornsey were still policed on horseback, but instructions were soon given for the authorisation of cyclists. Permission was given for a certain number of police officers at each station to use their own cycles on duty, for which they were entitled to an allowance. The use of cycles was particularly encouraged, especially for constables whose beats were some distance away from the station. At Hornsey, the authorised cyclists included Inspector William James Clarke. In 1922 Clarke was a station Inspector living and working at Hornsey Police Station. Before he joined the police service in 1904 he was a cycle mechanic.[1785] This was particularly relevant under the circumstances. Cycle racks were usually supplied in the station yard.

In 1933 boundary revisions north of the River Thames made Hornsey a sub-divisional station, with both Highgate and Muswell Hill being sectional stations.

The introduction of the police telephone boxes was extended to Hornsey Sub-Division on 1st April 1934. A number of police boxes were installed to allow for direct communication to adjoining stations and the divisional boundary. At the same time, a police van especially equipped with first aid apparatus (including a stretcher) was also issued to Hornsey Sub-Division.[1786] The telegraphic call sign for Hornsey was Yankee Romeo (YR) and the address shown as 98 (not 94) Tottenham Lane.[1787] The station was reconstructed in 1936.

1766 Metropolitan Police Orders dated 11th January 1864.
1767 Ibid.
1768 John Back Archive (1975).
1769 Metropolitan Police Orders dated 11th January 1864.
1770 *The Post Office Index* 1864.
1771 www.policememorial.org.uk/Forces/Metropolitan/metroll.htm accessed 12th March 2002.
1772 In 1881 the census records show James Jeakes was the widowed Rector of Hornsey aged 51 years residing in the High Street, Hornsey together with William and Jane Turner his coachman and servant.
1773 Metropolitan Police Surveyor's records.
1774 *Kelly's Directory of London* 1883.
1775 Metropolitan Police Orders dated 11th January 1864.
1776 Metropolitan Police Commissioner's Annual Report 1886.
1777 *Police Review*, October 1894.
1778 *Police Review*, June 1897.
1779 Metropolitan Police General Orders 1898.
1780 Metropolitan Police Orders dated 9th December 1909.
1781 John Back Archive (1975).
1782 Metropolitan Police Surveyor's records 1924.
1783 *Kitchener's Police Index* 1931.
1784 Metropolitan Police Orders dated 4th February 1916.
1785 Metropolitan Police Y Divisional Seniority Register.
1786 Metropolitan Police Orders dated 1st April 1934.
1787 Metropolitan Police Records 1978.

Hornsey Police Station 1936-2019

In 1999 Hornsey Police Station became part of a Borough-based policing initiative under the supervision of a senior Superintendent referred to as a Borough Police Commander. The station was shown as having full charging facilities at this time.[1788] In 2002 Hornsey police division formed part of Haringey Borough Policing Area, and the police station was open to the public 24 hours a day, seven days a week.[1789]

In 2019 Hornsey Police Station was still owned by the Metropolitan Police, but public access was now not available.[1790]

Hounslow Police Station

Montague Road, Hounslow (1887 to Present)

T Division (1887-1993)

Borough of Hounslow OCU (1993-2018/19)

West Area WA BCU (together with Ealing and Hillingdon) (2018/19 to Present)

There is evidence of settlement in the borough of Hounslow which pre-dates Roman Britain, more particularly at the eastern end, at the confluence of the Thames and the River Brent. Historically, Hounslow and Hounslow Heath have always been associated with the Army and things military. In medieval and Reformation times, armies were bivouacked on the heath prior to battle. The area gradually evolved into a training ground, with more substantial barracks being built. Until comparatively recently the present Hounslow West Underground Station was known as Hounslow Barracks, when it formed part of the old District railway. Two such barracks are still occupied by the army, in the form of the 10th Royal Signals Regiment and 1st Battalion Grenadier Guards.

Quite naturally, industries associated with the military grew up in the area and Hounslow once had a wide reputation for the quality of its sword making. In addition, there was a gunpowder mill in Hanworth for over two hundred years, which did not cease trading as such until 1925.

There is still a road in Hanworth called Powder Mill Lane, for obvious reasons. Other industries have gradually taken hold in the borough, and many of these became the targets for bombing in both world wars. Norwood had extensive brickworks, with acres of brick-cooling fields. Agriculture was quite important in the area, with extensive acreage given over to the production of wheat and fruit. It was not until 1955 that the last local orchards were ploughed under to provide more housing.

The beginnings of the aircraft industry are associated with the borough. Fighter aircraft were produced locally during the First World War, and there was a small commercial aerodrome at Heston. It is the place where Neville Chamberlain landed on his return from Germany, with his historic 'piece of paper'. Light- to medium-industry still flourished in the borough, much of it associated with servicing the nearby Heathrow Airport. Part of the reason is that the area is well served by major trunk roads and motorways, with such household names as Gillette, EMI and Del Monte foods all having extensive premises in the borough.

In 1864 Police Orders show Hounslow as being a station on T Division. A letter from the Home Office dated March 1885 authorised the purchase of a plot of land suitable for the site on which to construct a new purpose-built police station. In the meantime, plans were made and contracts advertised for builders to present their quotes to the police surveyors for the task. The building job got underway once a suitable piece of land in Montague Road, Hounslow was bought, in 1885. An entry in Police Orders stated that the new station at Hounslow would be ready for occupation about 15th March 1887.[1791] The front of the police station was actually in York Road.

Hounslow Police Station 1887-1965

In 1915 Inspector William Bingham was in charge at Hounslow, and he was responsible for the operational running of the station and its area to Sub-Divisional Inspector Charles Richardson at Brentford.[1792] Hounslow was a sectional station to Twickenham,[1793] and remained so for some time. There were a large number of vulnerable points to be protected on the division during war time. These included reservoirs, water works and gunpowder mills. These potential targets would wreak havoc to the infrastructure if anything was to happen to them.

The rear yard of the station in c1908

The following changes were made in 1916 to Sub-Divisions from the 1st January: Brentford Sub-Division would comprise the stations of Brentford and Chiswick and Hounslow Sub-Division the stations of Hounslow, Isleworth and Norwood Green, with the sub-divisional stations being Brentford and Hounslow respectively.[1794] Isleworth Station eventually was closed at 6.00am on Monday, 1st June 1931, and all business there transferred to Hounslow police station.[1795]

There had been a strong contingent of Metropolitan Police Special Constabulary at Hounslow since the First World War, and as previously mentioned one of them was Percy, the son of the T Division Superintendent Edward Fitt, who took his full part in the challenges of policing at the time.[1796]

The senior officers and sergeants of T Division receive their Coronation medals and certificates at Hounslow in 1937

In the picture above Percy Fitt is shown extreme left, having just helped distribute the 1937 Coronation medals to the Hounslow sergeants and inspectors of the sub-division's MSC who were on duty for the occasion. Percy Fitt (warrant no. 003750H) continued his service. In 1934 Commandants of Division were allowed to formalise their administration, and Fitt was put forward as a suitable candidate for the role of Staff Officer Inspector. Following a rigorous interview on police duty subjects, successful candidates awaited their promotion. These were salaried staff who held an equivalent Civil Service post, but without any opportunity to transfer across to the police service. His role was:

'to act for and on behalf of the Commandant and in accordance with his directions... he should have an intimate knowledge of his commandant's mind, and ideas in general, that he would be able to perform accurate judgement on what the commandant would do if present... and so issue such instruction as may be necessary.' [1797]

Staff Officer Sub Inspector Percy Fitt (right) at Hammersmith

In 1937 Percy was a Staff Officer Sub-Inspector to the officer in charge, and in 1939, at the outbreak of WWII, when staff officer roles were suspended, Fitt became a full inspector.[1798] In the picture above, Percy Fitt is on the right alongside his two senior officers, displaying his MSC Long service medal. The MSC medal is awarded for nine years' continuous service. In times of war, each year counted as double for awarding purposes.

Notice that on Sub Inspector Fitt's forearm there is also a star. This denotes that he joined the MSC in 1914, and the star was issued in recognition of the fact he was an early joiner. His two comrades do not have this, because they had joined the armed services and many of their medals show they had a distinguished service in WWI. Extra bars can be added to the long-service medal for further service or for recognition during war time. Inspector Fitt also has 'gorget patches' either side on his collar to show his status and rank. These patches originate from the British army, and consist of silver thread on a black background, rather similar to those worn by ACPO ranks of the police. No other member of the MSC has this distinction.

George V MSC Long Service Medal

Hounslow Police Station 1965 to present

1788 *Police and Constabulary Almanac* 1998.
1789 www.met.police.uk/contact/phone.htm accessed 12th March 2002.
1790 MPS Information rights unit (2019) MPS assets.
1791 Metropolitan Police Orders dated 29th December 1886.
1792 *Kelly's Hertfordshire and Middlesex Directory* 1915.
1793 Metropolitan Police List 1925.
1794 Metropolitan Police Orders dated 30th December 1916.
1795 Metropolitan Police Orders dated 28th May 1931.
1796 Reay, W. (1919) *The Specials*, Heineman, London.
1797 Pullen, H. G. (1981) *A Brief History of the Metropolitan Special Constabulary*.
1798 Metropolitan Police Special Constabulary Orders dated 2nd September 1939.

With the formation of the GLC on 1st April 1965, and the revision of police boundaries to coincide with those of the local authorities, Hounslow remained on T Division,[1799] but with a brand new police station at 5 Montague Road which was taken into operational use at 6.00am on 1st March 1965.[1800] On that date Hounslow became sub-divisional headquarters, and divisional headquarters for T Division.[1801] The officer in charge of the sub-division at this time was Superintendent C. Clarke, and the call sign for Hounslow station was 'TD'.

As a result of the formation of the Airport Division in 1974 certain boundary changes within T and X Divisions took place.[1802] Hounslow Sub-Division became Hounslow and Feltham sections. A further revision of boundaries took place between Airport and T Divisions in 1975.[1803]

In 2012 the station was open seven days a week, 24 hours a day. There were five Safer Neighbourhood teams operating in Hounslow.[1804]

As of 2019 Hounslow Police station was retained for operational purposes.[1805]

Hoxton (Kingsland Road) Police Station

London Borough of Hackney
Robert Street, Shoreditch (1832-1861)
Robert Street, Hoxton (1861-1880)
Kingsland Road, Hoxton (1880-1908)
N Division (1832-1880)
G Division (1880-1908)

In 1830, a year after the formation of the Metropolitan Police, G or Finsbury Division was formed and consisted of two stations located at Clerkenwell and Old Street.[1806] The eastern limit of the Metropolitan Police was N or Islington Division, which extended up to the banks of the River Lea at Hackney Marshes. Records show that the original Hoxton Police Station was located in Robert Street (now called Fanshaw Street), in the Parish of St. Leonards, Shoreditch,[1807]

Each station kept a Lamp Report book, which was a thick hardbound register into which reports of unlit, broken or defective gas lamps would be written. The parish authorities were responsible for lighting, repairing and maintaining these lamps, and whilst the officers were patrolling their beats they would note the various unlit lamps. The Lamp Report book for Hoxton Police Station began on 13th January 1836, when Constable 56G Edwin Ayland reported a defective lamp. The workmen responsible for the repairs would visit the station, inspect the Lamp Reports and repair the lamps. Between the 13th January and 16th February 1837 there were 22 reports.[1808] In those days police officers were responsible for lighting the lamps, calling the time and watching for fires, having taken on many of the functions of the old Parish Watch officers.[1809]

The officer in charge of the station in 1844 was Inspector John Tonge.[1810] Records for the year show that another station existed on G Division, situated at 36 Featherstone Street, between Bunhill Row and City Road south of Old Street.[1811] This station was an original police watchhouse, situated in the Parish of St. Lukes. Henry Jervis and Joseph Shackell were both Inspectors stationed at Featherstone Street.[1812] The other station on G Division at the time was Bagnigge Wells, or Kings Cross Road as we know it today,[1813] which was closed in favour of the new station which was built at 55 Old Street, not far from the old watch house.[1814] The combined strength of G Division was 346 officers including a reserve force, which was kept to deal with any civil disturbances.[1815]

The Receiver of the Metropolitan Police sought permission from the Home Office to purchase land to the east of the existing Old Street station, in Kingsland Road, Hoxton in 1860. A parcel of freehold land became available at the bottom end of Kingsland Road at a cost of £3,600, which was bought by the Receiver and a police station erected on the site. The station was attached to N Division, with an inspector in charge. This was a large division covering some sixty square miles.[1816]

Site of Kingsland Police Station, Hoxton

Hoxton Police (Robert Street) Station contained a Charge room, an Inspector's Office, a parade room, six cells, two water closets and a two-stall stable, which were all located on the ground floor. There were also nine rooms located in the basement, including four coal sheds. The Commissioners made a conscious decision to help with lodgings in an effort to maintain standards of health and hygiene. They duly built accommodation for both single and married police officers. Hoxton had two further floors above the ground floor, which housed one married inspector and his family, and 37 single constables in very cramped conditions. The cost of building the station was £3,609, and it became operational in 1861.[1817] In effect this made the Commissioners of Police one of the largest landlords in London, as it seemed sensible that if a station was built then accommodation should be included. Furthermore, the cost of accommodation could be deducted from pay, therefore defraying the daily costs of policing. There were two inspectors, eight sergeants and 84 constables attached to the station in 1864.[1818] A reserve constable was posted each day for 12 hours to man the Robert Street watch house.[1819]

In 1872 Hoxton Police Station was directly connected to Scotland Yard by the telegraphic network, with the call sign 'HX'. In 1873 it was designated an Inspector station.[1820]

On 1st July 1880 Hoxton Police Station was transferred from N to G Division, with its address shown as 17 Kingsland Road, Shoreditch.[1821] The following year the Census recorded Inspector Henry Parker in charge of the station. He resided there with his wife Caroline and son. Also on the premises were thirty-two single constables, who lived in the section house.[1822]

Also living at the section house, but stationed at Kingsland Road Police Station, was Constable David Garner, aged 22 years from Whittlesea in Cambridgeshire. He later found fame when he was involved in an armed incident and was shot at by a burglar William Wheatley early on the morning

Hoxton (Robert Street) Police Station 1861-1908

of 18th July 1884. Wheatley and another man had attempted to break into a furrier at 46 New North Road, when they were discovered by police. The suspects could not be found straight away. However, after several hours Wheatley was discovered by Constable Garner, who went to arrest him. It was at his point that Wheatley produced a gun and fired three shots. Two missed, but the third went straight through the constable's thigh. Garner, bleeding heavily, managed to hold onto Wheatley, and help was close at hand as Inspector Maynard and a local fireman came to his assistance. A short distance away Constable 462G William Snell tackled the other burglar, who also pulled a gun and shot the officer in the stomach. Snell was not thought to be seriously injured at the time, and managed to capture the suspect with the aid of passers-by.

While they were being taken to Kingsland Road Police Station a crowd of about twenty people demanded that the officers give up the prisoners to them. The police resisted the demand, but not before several of the crowd had successfully managed to land a number of blows on the prisoners.[1823] Constable Snell was later taken to hospital where the bullet was removed, but he was unwell for some time. In 1894 Snell, by then a sergeant, was pensioned off and died soon afterwards, the shooting having hastened his death.[1824]

In 1888 records also show that certain designated stations were used as 'places appointed for receiving persons drowned or dead, and at which drags and other apparatus was kept.' Hoxton Police Station was a designated mortuary.[1825]

Much has been written about the police culture and comradeship of police officers and their families. Their social life very often focused on the police station, which usually had its own social club, athletics section, police band, billiards table, library and recreation room. To engender team spirit and comradeship, competitions were organised amongst the work force. For example, the G Divisional Billiards championship took place at Hoxton Police station on 15th July 1898. There were 48 entrants. This handicapped event was won by Police Sergeant Wiltshire, who received a monetary prize. Such events helped to reinforce the culture and notion of the police family.[1826]

In 1898 there was another fatal injury to a local police officer. Police Constable James Baldwin was on patrol in Hoxton when he attempted to arrest a drunken man. During this process

1799 Metropolitan Police Orders dated 6th August 1965.
1801 Metropolitan Police Orders dated 26th February 1965.
1802 Metropolitan Police Orders dated 26th March 1965.
1803 Metropolitan Police Orders dated 31st October 1974.
1804 Metropolitan Police Orders dated 1st July 1975.
1805 content.met.police.uk/Borough/Hounslow/Contact accessed 18th January 2013.
1806 MPS (2018) Freedom of Information request: MPS Assets.
1807 John Back Archive (1975).
1808 B. Brown. (1996) 'Policing old Hackney', in *Peeler* magazine (Friends of the Metropolitan Police Museum).
1809 Metropolitan Police Lamp Reports 1837: Hoxton Police. Guildhall Library.
1810 65.107.211.206/victorian/history/police.html accessed 12th March 2002.
1811 *The Police and Constabulary List* 1844 p3.
1812 Ibid.
1813 Ibid.
1814 Ibid.
1815 See Old Street Police Station.
1816 Metropolitan Police Orders 12th January 1864.
1817 Metropolitan Police General Orders 1873.
1818 John Back Archive (1975).
1819 Metropolitan Police Orders dated 11th January 1864.
1820 Metropolitan Police General Orders 1873.
1821 Metropolitan Police Orders 1st July 1880.
1822 Census 1881.
1823 Gould, R. Waldron, M. (1986) *London's Armed Police*. Arms and Armour Press.
1824 www.policememorial.org.uk/Forces/Metropolitan/metroll.htm accessed 12th March 2002.
1825 *Dickens's Dictionary of London, 1888*. Old House Books. pp132-3.
1826 *Police Review*, July 1898.

the drunk produced a knife, and a violent struggle ensued. Constable Baldwin was stabbed, and died from his injuries.[1827]

In 1908 the station was no longer required for police purposes, and was leased to a Mr. Davis for 21 years at an annual rental of £110 for the first seven years, and £120 for the remainder.[1828]

The old station at Hoxton was vacated once City Road Police Station was opened. It was considered unsuitable for further use as a police station, and the interest was purchased by the London County Council.[1829]

Hunter Street Police Station

Hunter Street, Brunswick Square (1837-1895)

53-57 Judd Street (1895-1940)

E Division (1837-1940)

An old building, known to the public for many years as 'Hunter Street' Police Station, came into use in 1837 when the police officers transferred from George Street watch house in St. Giles. This move came about when premises situated in Hunter Street and Compton Street were found and leased. The lease period was seventy-one years, in accordance with the wishes of the owners, the Governors of the Foundling Hospital, who were paid an annual ground rent of £15.

The station was regarded as a quaint station, and had a basement, ground and first floor. It was fitted with a reserve room, charge room, four cells, mess room, recreation room, library, boot room and scullery. Entry to the station was by a long, dark narrow passage. Upstairs there was section house accommodation for 26 single constables. These single officers paid some £67 per year for their rent to the Receiver.

Hunter Street Police Station was originally shown as being located on E Division. The freehold to the site was eventually purchased in 1888 at a cost of £3,221.

Police Sergeant 11E Lucey taken between 1871 and 1883

The picture left shows Police Sergeant 11E Lucey, complete with whiskers, who was attached to Hunter Street Police Station. The photographers Timms, who took the picture, were situated close by. The sergeant is still on duty, as he is wearing his duty armlet on his left arm. The photograph can be dated to between 1871 and 1883, as he is wearing the new-styled uniform introduced in 1870 but does not have a whistle, which was not issued until 1883. Additionally, the sergeant is holding white gloves issued for ceremonial events like Trooping the Colour or a Royal Jubilee, so the likelihood is that the photograph was taken prior to or after such an event. Only specially-selected police officers were permitted to attend ceremonial, processions and other events, such as strikes or demonstrations, which required a large numbers of police officers. They were called Reserve Officers, and were introduced by the Metropolitan Police in 1870. They made up 10% of the police establishment, and ranged from inspectors (who were paid four shillings per week extra), sergeants (three shillings) and constables (one shilling and sixpence). Reserve Officers of Sergeant and Constable rank were required to wear the letter 'R' beside their divisional letter. They were supplied with a better grade of uniform for these events. The Sergeant above was probably a Reserve Officer, but his whiskers hide the rest of the letter 'R'. Reserve Officers posts were abolished in December 1913.[1830]

The photograph below shows a unit of mixed Reserve and ordinary officers from E Division performing duty at an industrial dispute on Humberside in 1911. The Hull dock strike was policed by many different Police forces including the Metropolitan Police, who were sent to the docks to deal with the national strike of stevedores, railwaymen, carters and other transport workers who brought much of the country to a standstill. Military detachments prepared to assist the police. Riots broke out in response to fears of widespread famine, and at least two men were shot dead.[1831]

E or Holborn Division on attachment to the Police at the Hull Dock Strike of 1911

The dispute started in early September, when about 10,000 Welsh miners came out on strike in sympathy with the dockers, who were also on strike. Throughout the autumn of 1910 serious rioting broke out in the Rhondda and Aberdare Valleys of South Wales, where the coal strike began in earnest. Units of the Metropolitan Police were sent by train to quell the disorder and rioting. The photograph below shows a contingent of E Division officers, in their greatcoats at Clydach Vale.

A Unit of E Division wearing their great coats, photographed at Clydach Vale

Meanwhile, the general health of the police officers and their families residing in police accommodation at Hunter Street was of serious concern. Senior officers considered that many of the buildings were substandard and very damp. To improve the general health of those residing at the station, and to relieve the cramped conditions, four beds were removed in 1882 and a further five more in 1883, allowing for a greater living area per officer.

Hunter Street was demolished in 1895 to make way for a modern police station. The freehold to the site was purchased in 1888, at a cost of £3,221.[1832] In 1890 the Receiver had also purchased 53, 55 and 57 Judd Street, which possibly explains the fact that Hunter Street Police Station was shown with an address in Judd Street. The new station was built of red brick and Portland stone, and had five floors.[1833]

Hunter Street Police Station 1890-1940

There was accommodation for a married inspector, and fifteen married and fifteen single constables. The police station had ten cells, which were fitted with the latest sanitary improvements. At the back of the station there was a yard with sufficient space for a prison van to visit. There was also a covered parade and drill shed, which was 45 feet long and 16 feet wide. The buildings were constructed from the designs and drawings of John Butler, the Metropolitan Police Surveyor, by the builder, Mr. J.O. Richardson, of Peckham. In 1898 and 1902 land was purchased in Hunter Street and Compton Street in order to build a new section house to accommodate single police officers.[1834]

In 1908, 59 Judd Street was purchased in order to extend the station's site, (Hunter Street stands at the junction with Judd Street). In October 1911[1835] new section house accommodation was made available for one married inspector, at 3s a week, and 80 unmarried men at 1s per week.[1836]

The address of the police station was no longer in Hunter Street, even though it continued with its name; Hunter Street Police Station was actually shown as 53-57 Judd Street, Brunswick Square, WC1.[1837] In 1934 the station was closed for extensive refurbishment together with the Section House, and later reopened, between August 1939 and August 1940, as a temporary police station whilst Gray's Inn Road Police Station was being reconstructed.

Macnaghten Section House taken around 1948

After this the building became Macnaghten Section House, a purpose-built residence for single police officers. The picture above shows the building around 1948. Accommodation for police officers in London had always been a problem. Even in Victorian times, accommodation was constructed or bought by the Receiver and rented out to single officers and their families, although in recent years accommodation was provided free of charge. Macnaghten Section House, which remained in service until the 1980s, stands as a fine example of a residence for single officers.

In recent years the police ceased to use the building, and sold it to the local authority who converted it to sheltered accommodation for the homeless.

Hyde Park Police Station

City of Westminster

Hyde Park, Old Police House, W2 2UH (1902-1974)

A Division (1902-1974)

Royal Parks Constabulary (1974-2004)

Metropolitan Police Royal Parks Operational Command Unit (2004 to Present)

Central West Basic Command Unit territory (2018 to Present)

Within A Division's boundaries were the central London Royal parks, including Hyde Park up to Kensington Palace. Originally part of Henry VIII's hunting forests, there was a treeless area to the east of the park that was used for military reviews and other events, and it became a venue for public leisure and sporting events. It was the location of Oliver Cromwell's becoming entangled with the harness of his bolting horse. The social scene of horse riding by day was contrasted with the situation at night, when crime became prevalent. One of the hunting parties of King George II was robbed. It was later, in 1851, the location of the Great Exhibition.

It was shopkeepers who first had the idea of holding an organised public meeting in the park. In July 1855 they applied to the Commissioner, Sir Richard Mayne, for permission to hold a protest about a Sunday Trading Bill. Mayne refused, but a few months later, in October 1855, a carpenter gathered a small crowd interested in hearing him expressing his opinions. He had not asked permission, and no official notice was taken, so he returned the following Sunday, again without incident.

The following three weeks saw speakers – and crowds – escalating, and a strong police presence was then deployed to prevent them recurring. In 1859 there was a large meeting that expressed sympathy for Napoleon's invasion of Italy, and then another meeting in 1862 to pledge loyalty to Garibaldi, but it was in 1866 that Speakers' Corner really became established.

In that year the Reform League unsuccessfully applied to hold a meeting at the park. There was serious rioting when police tried to stop the meeting from taking place, and a tree

---

1827 www.policememorial.org.uk/Forces/Metropolitan/metroll.htm accessed 12th March 2002.
1828 Metropolitan Police Surveyor's Records 1924.
1829 Ibid.
1830 Metropolitan Police Orders dated 12th December 1913.
1831 Mercer, *1988 Encyclopaedia of the 20th Century*, p155.
1832 *The Police Review and Parade Gossip*, 18th January 1895.
1833 Ibid.
1834 Ibid.
1835 Metropolitan Police Orders dated 28th October 1911.
1836 Metropolitan Police Property Schedule 1924.
1837 *Kirchner's Police Index* 1931.

was set on fire, reducing it to a stump, forever giving that location – the starting point of many later protest marches and demonstrations – the soubriquet 'Reformer's Tree'. When the Reform League applied again for permission to hold a meeting, permission was granted for the location known as the Meeting Ground at the north-east corner of the park, 150 yards away from Reformer's Tree. This then became 'Speakers' Corner'.

In August 1866 it was proposed that 'the system of appointing constables for special service in the Parks under the charge of the Board of Works should be forthwith abolished and that, in future, the protection of the parks should be confined exclusively to the Metropolitan Police Force.'[1838] The Metropolitan Police started formally to patrol inside the park in 1867, operating from a part of the magazine barracks of the Household Cavalry.

In 1889 an iron shelter was provided for the protection of police officers on duty at meetings. This was located in the kitchen garden of the Ranger's Lodge, approximately where the hallway of the current police station is situated. In 1899 approval was given for the building of a new police station.

The land for the new station had been leased from 31 December 1898 with a condition that the agreement would lapse if the police were no longer to be employed by the Commissioners of Hyde Park. The Receiver was obliged to build a station, which would be the property of the Crown, within five years. A temporary station was erected in 1900, and a new station opened on 10th March 1902.[1839]

Above: Hyde Park Police Station, from 1902 and Below: Rear aspect

In the early years of World War Two, Hyde Park was among many police stations to form a pig club. This was intended to help the nation's food shortages during the war. Constable G.R. Plumb described how he returned from war service with the RAF in 1949, was posted to Hyde Park, and took up one share in the pig club for £80. The club owned 50 pigs, housed in four sties made available by the Ministry of Works. Constables Huxley and Plumb drove around the West End collecting swill in a converted 1933 Austin 16 truck, purchased pigs and straw from markets, and took pigs for slaughter to Islington. The club was wound up in 1954.[1840]

Park keepers were employed in the Royal Parks in 1872 and were given police powers within the parks themselves, but the Metropolitan Police retained overall responsibility for Hyde Park, particularly in relation to major demonstrations. The Royal Park keepers became the Royal Parks Constabulary (RPC) in 1974. In April 2004 the Metropolitan Police took over the duties of the RPC for policing the 17 Royal parks within the Metropolitan Police District, and instituted a Royal Parks Operational Command Unit.

Hyde Park's police observation box, erected 1902

Ilford Police Station

The London Borough of Redbridge
House, Ilford Hill, Essex (1840-1861)
40 High Road, Ilford (1861-1995)
270-294 High Road, Ilford (1995 to Present)
K Division (1840-1965)
J Division (1965-1985/86)
Ilford Division (1985/86-2018)
Basic Command Unit East Area (EA) (2018 to Present)

In 1840 the Metropolitan Police moved out into Ilford. They firstly occupied a small brick-built house on the north side of Ilford Hill, near the junction of Mill Place. This was on the opposite side of the road to where the next police station was to be built in 1861. The small brick-built house is often referred to as Little Ilford Police Station.[1841] In 1844 William Richardson was the Inspector in charge of the station, with the area being called Great Ilford, Barking.[1842] Richardson was an experienced man, having been recruited into the Thames River Police in 1814 some fifteen years before the start of the Metropolitan Police.[1843] Ilford Police Station was then on K or Stepney Division.[1844]

The Home Office gave authority in 1860 to lease a site for a new police station with a ground rent of £13 13s 0d, which was paid annually to the owner, the Marquis of Salisbury. Later that same year the police station was erected at a cost of £1,744. On the first floor of the building there was accommodation for one married inspector and four constables.[1845]

Records show that in 1864 Ilford Police Station had one inspector, four sergeants and nine constables working from that building.[1846]

In 1873 the station name changed from Little Ilford to Great Ilford, and was supervised by an inspector. The station was linked to Scotland Yard (Commissioner's Office) by telegraph or wire.[1847]

By 1888 the number of officers at the station had risen to one inspector, seven sub-inspectors, ten sergeants and seventy-three constables.[1848]

Ilford Police Station 1861-1995

One of the many events which took place annually on K Division was the Ilford Police Station's Fete and Athletics Day. This was an event for all the family. The thirteenth annual fete of the Ilford Police took place in 1897 on the local sports ground in the presence of a large number of spectators. The profits from the Athletics Day was divided between the Metropolitan Police Orphanage, the Ilford Philanthropic Society and the Ilford Infectious Hospital Convalescent Fund. The band of the K Division Police, by kind permission of Supt. Creswell Wells, played during the afternoon, and in the evening the Band of the Ilford Volunteers rendered selections. Dancing took place, and the proceedings ended with a grand display of fireworks by Mr S.W. Hayden. There was also a cricket match between the residents (148 runs) and Police (82 runs).[1849]

In 1900 the freehold of the police station was purchased from the Marquis of Salisbury for £500.[1850] Additional land adjoining the site was bought in 1902, and new married quarters and a section house were built for occupation in November 1906.[1851]

In 1914 the Metropolitan Police Special Constabulary were formed to assist the regular police in its daily task of policing the division. Limehouse Police Station was the Headquarters station for K Division, and the remainder of the division consisted of Poplar, the Isle of Dogs, East Ham, West Ham, Forest Gate, Plaistow, Canning Town, North Woolwich, Ilford, Barking and Chadwell Heath.[1852] Special Constables were appointed and posted to Ilford Police Station from the headquarters station, where the newly-appointed Commanders Captain J.R. McLean and his assistant Mr. H.W. Castle were based.[1853]

Much of Ilford's responsibility during this time of war was to guard vulnerable points on the division, however K Division would often supply aid to neighbouring divisions. For example, J Division was particularly large, and quite remote in places. It also had a number of reservoirs, pumping stations, and railway bridges which were considered vulnerable, and often Special Constables from Ilford walked to Hog Hill in Chigwell, which was one of the most elevated spots in Essex, to guard the two reservoirs. The Special Constables from Ilford performed this duty from 2.00am-6.00am without complaint for two years. Unless they were cyclists, theirs was a long walk there and back.[1854]

1838 *Hyde Park Police Centenary Booklet* 1967.
1839 Metropolitan Police Surveyor's Property Register.
1840 *Hyde Park Police Centenary Booklet* 1967.
1841 John Back Archive (1975).
1842 *The Police and Constabulary List* 1844. Parker, Furnivall and Parker, London.
1843 Ibid.
1844 Ibid.
1845 John Back Archive (1975), and Elliott, B. (1993) *A History of the Police Stations of J Division 1886-1986*.
1846 Elliott, B. (1993) *A History of the Police Stations of J Division 1886-1986*.
1847 Metropolitan Police General Orders 1873.
1848 *Kelly's Directory* 1888.
1849 *Police Review*, August 1897.
1850 Elliott, B. (1993) *A History of the Police Stations of J Division 1886-1986*.
1851 Metropolitan Police Surveyor's records (undated).
1852 Reay, W. T. (1920) *The Specials*. Billing and Son, Guildford, Surrey.
1853 Ibid.
1854 Ibid.

Ilford Special Constabulary in the yard at the rear of the station c1916

Metropolitan Police Special Constable Walters

The post-war photograph above shows Special Constable Walters of K Division Special Constabulary proudly showing his medals and awards. He rescued a person from a fire in 1877 and won 'the Nine Stone' boxing belt for being champion of England in June 1881. Additionally, he won a Special Constabulary Cup and Special Constabulary long service medal with bar for services during the Great War. Walters must have been a dedicated officer to receive the special award of a trophy.[1855]

Some major reconstruction to the internal part of the building to put right some faults at a cost of £23,000 took place in 1939, but few details are known.[1856]

In 1939, the Government established a Police War Reserve in order to supplement the reduction in number of the regular police officers and Special Constabulary being called-up for active service in the Armed Forces. One such person was William Dunn, a carpenter living with his wife and daughter in Ilford, Essex, and who, at the age of 31 years, joined the M.P. War Reserve on 28th October 1940.[1857] He became Police Constable 729K/24093 Dunn, and after initial training at Peel House in London was posted to Ilford Police Station for street duties. Each War Reserve officer was given an individual and separate warrant number from the regular police officers.

Constable 729K William Dunn

In March 1944 the Government, after a review of available manpower, decided that Special Constables and War Reserves under the age of 35 years on 1st January 1944 were liable for call-up for service with the Armed Forces, or transference to Industry. William Dunn had by this time found himself in that category, and resigned from the Police on 31st May 1944[1858] and joined the Royal Artillery as a Gunner.

Ilford remained a station on K Division until the 1965 Local Government re-organisation, which saw a significant change in boundaries which had last been set in 1933. In the same year both Ilford and Chadwell Heath Police Stations transferred for the first time to J Division; Chadwell Heath was no longer the furthest Metropolitan station in the east, because Romford was transferred into the MPD from Essex Constabulary.[1859]

By the late 1980s a review of police station stock showed that the old Ilford Police Station was no longer suitable for modern police purposes, so arrangements were made for a new station to be planned. At the other end of the High Road, leading towards Seven Kings, a parcel of land was purchased and arrangements were made for building a new larger police station.

The new £5 million Ilford Police Station opened in June 1995,[1860] at the opposite end of the main shopping area in Ilford, at 270-294 High Road. A lounge within the building was dedicated to Police Constable Phillip Waters, who was shot and fatally wounded whilst on duty in April 1995 answering a call to an address at Mayfair Avenue, Ilford. A monument has also been erected at the scene of the shooting.

Ilford Police Station 1995 to present

The old police station at 40 High Road, Ilford was closed to the public in 1995, but continued to be used for police purposes for a number years. Finally it was put up for sale.

The new station is within yards of the site of two cottages which served as a 'police station' for the Bow Street Mounted Patrol, which preceded the Metropolitan Police, nearly two hundred years before.[1861]

Imber Court

By Chris Forester

Metropolitan Police Orders announced the appointment of Lt. Colonel Percy Robert Laurie, DSO to the post of Deputy Assistant Commissioner. His duties were stated to

'act generally as assistant to the Assistant Commissioner of 'A' Department in the work of supervision of the Metropolitan Police Administration and to take direct charge of the Mounted Branch of the force.' [1862]

The appointment of an officer of this rank to control and direct the Mounted Police was to transform the duties and operations of the Branch and consolidate its role as a principal

An early mounted police officer

and specialised agency to deal with public order, thus ensuring its survival to the present day. Laurie's remit was also to help raise the morale of the force as there had been strikes by the workforce in 1918 and 1919. The then 39 years old Percy Laurie (later Sir Percy Laurie) was eminently qualified to undertake the all the tasks required of him and had been strongly recommended to the Home Office for the post by no less a personage than Brigadier General Sir William Horwood, his most recent military Commanding officer and soon to be the incumbent Commissioner.

Percy Laurie's most recent military posting had been as Provost Marshal in Germany and responsible for policing a now destroyed and bankrupt city. His experiences were to aid him in his new post. As a long serving cavalryman in the prestigious Royal Scots Greys Regiment he would be expert in organising a large body of men such as the Mounted Branch. This part of the police had for some years been in decline, both men and horses were all in need of retraining and in many cases retirement! After making several much needed changes to routine stable and operational patrol work he turned his attention to training, both of horses (remounts) and men. Until 1887 remounts and recruits to the Mounted Branch had been trained 'On the job' from Rochester Row Police Stables; This training commitment had impeded the day to day operational work of the Branch and under the auspices of an earlier innovator, Captain George H. Dean the Adam & Eve Mews site at Kensington High Street had been opened. This location had been opened to enable a reserve section to be created to concentrate on just training and dealing with sick or injured horses. By 1919 Adam & Eve Mews had become untenable due to increasing traffic on the surrounding roads and a lack of turn out facilities for the sick horses.

The choice of Imber Court as the new training centre may have been suggested by Major W. H. Smith who had run the Munitions and Inventions Department (MID) on this site from 1915 to 1919. The MID had been a secret testing ground for many weird and wonderful inventions, one of which was an embryo helicopter. At the cessation of hostilities the shrewd and far sighted Major had purchased the whole estate from the owner Lord Michaelham. The old manor house at Imber Court had now fallen down and after its demolition Smith created a new trading and housing estate and sold the residue –some 38 acres to the Metropolitan Police in 1920 as a mounted training establishment, headquarters and later in 1929 a Metropolitan Police Athletic Association (MPAA) Sports ground.

From 1919 Imber Court was purpose-built as a Mounted Branch training establishment for both horses and men. It was also to become the headquarters of the Mounted Branch. Utilising some existing buildings a headquarters building, stabling, garaging, four sets of married quarters, a section house, an entrance lodge, a pavilion and grounds man's cottage were constructed or renovated.[1863] The police architect G. Mackenzie Trench designed the Imber Court Sports Club.

The opening of the Clubhouse at Imber Court in June 1929

Laurie spared no expense in equipping the site with all the latest innovative aids. An electric grooming machine (based on a Hoover) was purchased and found to be of limited use. Proper saddle soap was brought in along with redesigned saddles and the adoption of the 'Universal Reversible Port Mouthpiece' bit. This bit was that standard military bit designed to fit virtually any animal that could be ridden or harnessed, from llamas to camels, mules and horses. The stables themselves were built of Major Smith's invention, The Triangular Brick'. The brick was based on moulding triangular bricks on site and the whole stable was built with them. Whilst extremely strong in construction as many builders will testify after trying to drill into them their basic flaw was that they were hollow and damp could track right up to the roof. Smith's company was named 'TRIANCO' and after the failure of the Triangular Brick it went on to pioneer central heating boilers. The Mounted Branch had been run down during the war as most of its own horses had been requisitioned for the war effort and there was now a dire need to replenish the stock.

1855 Kennison, P. (2001), private correspondence.
1856 Metropolitan Police Surveyor's records (undated).
1857 Metropolitan Police Orders dated 31st October 1940.
1858 Metropolitan Police Orders dated 21st March 1944.
1859 John Back Archive (1975).
1860 Metropolitan Police Orders dated 24th May 1995.
1861 Ilford Police Station publicity material.
1862 Metropolitan Police Surveyor's Records (undated).
1863 Census 1881.

Laurie wasted no time in purchasing 43 horses from the army which were surplus to requirements. He personally selected the horses himself making journeys to studs in Yorkshire to view and make purchases.[1864]

During the 1930s Colonel Laurie again took advantage of the opportunity to purchase what were known as the Glebe lands or 40 acres for horse gallops. This area too changed when the new river was pushed through in 1980 to 1983.

As the years passed the training regime became routine, much of which endures to this day. From 1971 women were introduced to the Mounted Branch and during the mid 1980s civilian trainers and grooms were to supplant the serving remount training officers at Imber Court. Apart from the recruit instructors and supervisory staff the Mounted Training Establishment is now virtually completely civilianised.

In 1923 Laurie was to create another institution that lasted until the 1990s; that of the annual horse show at Imber Court. This spectacle was to be attended by royalty downwards. The cream of society would attend and participate in Coaching and Jumping events whilst police forces from all over Great Britain would compete for a variety of cups donated by scions of industry. This show was financed and arranged by the shrewd Colonel Laurie and his myriad of society contacts. Seating and tentage was loaned free by a local tent manufacturer, flowers would be borrowed from the Royal Parks Nurseries. The Catering and bars would be done by various local people and ground and gate staffing by officers and their families who 'Volunteered'. Stabling for the many horses and men would be within the Imber Court site or at nearby Hampton Court stables. These last were literally unchanged from Henry VIII days. This show whilst never making a great profit always broke even. The event acted a showpiece for the Metropolitan Police Service and enabled its Commissioner to invite many influential guests. For the men of the Branch it also acted as a bonding exercise with many advantages for training horses and officers in the skills required on the street.

Final rehearsal at Imber Court of the combined Mounted Branch and Traffic patrol display for the international Horse show

But what of the Sports and Social Club? After the General Strike in 1926 the Daily Mail set up the Police Fund in thanks for the work done by the Police in keeping London going during the Strike.

This fund was to finance the building of the Clubhouse designed by Mackenzie Trench the Police architect. The original MPAA clubhouse had been established in the 'Eagle Hut' in Aldwych. This had been built as a social centre for Canadian troops during the first war. At the end the MPAA had taken it over as their office. The new Clubhouse had been built and was opened on 11th June 1929 when the MPAA held the opening ceremony which was attended by Percy Laurie who with his many contacts managed to get Prince George (later King George VI) as guest of honour.

Originally it was possible to stay overnight in the clubhouse and over the next few years the Clubhouse would be extended and improved. In the 1970s major improvements took place and a new frontage was put on the old lodge house and entrance were demolished with the car park now fully covered. More upgrading took place in 1998 when the interior of the Club was gutted and enhanced with new bars and meeting rooms.

The Clubhouse in 2013 at Imber Court, originally designed by G. Mackenzie Trench

In 2000 Esher, Thames Ditton and Molesey became part of the Surrey Police area and Imber Court became isolated from the MPD. Thirteen years on and in spite of the attentions of avaricious developers it is still part of the Metropolitan Police.

Isle of Dogs Police Station

Newby Place, Poplar (1830-1868)
126 Manchester Road (1864-1973)
240A West Ferry Road (1973-2002)
160-174 Manchester Road, E14 3BN (2002-2013)
K Division (1830-1933)
H Division (1933-1985/86)
Limehouse Division HL (1985/86-1993)
Tower Hamlets OCU (1993-2018/19)
Basic Command Unit Central East (CE) (with the London Borough of Hackney) (2018/19 to Present)

Prior to the introduction of the New Police, the Isle of Dogs was patrolled by the Bow Street Horse Patrol from its station at Maryland Point near Stratford in London. The Parish Watchmen also patrolled the Isle of Dogs, although in winter the approaches to the 'Island' were often impassable. The watchmen were situated at the watch house in Newby Place, near Poplar Church.

In May 1863 the Home Office approved the leasing of a site on which to build a new police station on the Isle of Dogs. This was the first station to be built there. The site was located at 126 Manchester Road, and was situated at the southern end of the Isle of Dogs. It was leased for 79 years from the Commissioners of Greenwich Hospital. The Receiver was required to pay ground rent on the land amounting to £18 per year. A new station was built on the site at a cost of £1,500 19s 6d, and it comprised a ground and first floor. On the ground floor was an inspector's office, a reserve room, a charge room, a mess room, a cleaning room, a clothing room, a scullery and a drying room. There were also three cells, three water closets and two coal cellars. The first floor provided accommodation for eleven single constables in two rooms, a married constable who had two rooms and a married Inspector who had three rooms. The Receiver obtained £31 4s per year rent for providing the rooms on the premises.[1865]

Isle of Dogs Police Station 1864-1973

Records show that in May 1865 the new police station was located, and occupied, in the interior district of K Division. It replaced the policing from Poplar, even though the latter station remained until 1868.

Policing the dock area was undertaken by a number of different police forces. The West India Dock Company Police were set up in 1802 when the docks first opened, followed later in 1838 by the East India Dock Police. In 1871 the Great Eastern Railway Police were responsible for crime with the opening of the Millwall Docks Line to Glengall Grove and its later extension to North Greenwich (Island Gardens).

In the 1881 Census the station address was recorded as 126 Manchester Road, Poplar, London. The inspector in charge was Thomas L. Proctor, who resided there with his wife. Constable Smith also lived at the station with his wife and son. There were six single constables also in residence.[1866] Towards the end of the century the Home Office gave their approval for the freehold purchase of the station, which was bought for £600 in September 1899.[1867]

In 1909 the two Dock Police Forces were amalgamated to form part of the Port of London Authority Police. In 1923 the Great Eastern Railway Police were absorbed into the London and North-Eastern Railway Police, but were completely withdrawn after the General Strike of 1926 when the North Greenwich line was closed.

Isle of Dogs Police Office 1973-2002

In June 1933, as part of general boundary revisions to ensure economy and efficiency, the Isle of Dogs was transferred to H or Whitechapel Division from K or East Ham Division.[1868]

Limehouse Division, on which the Isle of Dogs police is located, has always been famous for its public houses. These include places like the City Arms, the Vulcan, the Magnet and Dewdrop, the Tooke Arms and the Waterman's Arms. Police stations were often sited near public houses, and the Waterman's was located behind the Isle of Dogs Police Station, in Saunderness Road.[1869]

In 1960 the Island Police Station appears to have been relegated to the status of police office, with the issue of an Order instructing that the station should be closed from the hours of 10.00pm-6.00am (night duty). A telephone connection was maintained from the office, with its Sub-Divisional station at Limehouse where all calls were routed.

Further boundary changes in 1965, which occurred as a result of Local Authority revisions, established the Isle of Dogs (HI) as a Sectional Station of Limehouse Sub-Division (HH) within the newly-formed London Borough of Tower Hamlets. The night closure order was rescinded as from Monday, 16th May 1966.

By now the old Isle of Dogs Police Station had outlived its usefulness, and the Receiver looked around for another suitable site on which to build a new station. Between 1963 and 1974 no less than three separate parcels of land were purchased in the vicinity, but Government cutbacks meant that none could be built on in the foreseeable future. Accordingly a temporary police office, in portakabins, was constructed on the former Westwoods site at 240A West Ferry Road, E14, and it became operational on Friday, 26th October 1973. In the meantime the old station was demolished to make way for the George Green Centre.

Isle of Dogs Police Station 2002 to present

A new station was eventually built on the Isle of Dogs in 2002. The address was shown as Manchester Road, Isle of Dogs, London E14 3BN.

The front counter access to the public closed in 2013, but as of 2019 the building has been retained and is still in use by the police.[1870]

1864 John Back Archive (1975).
1865 Ibid.
1866 The H Division Handbook 1968/69.
1867 MPS station closures since 2010 Information Rights Unit MSP, accessed 6th May 2019
1868 www.british-history.ac.uk/report.aspx?compid=45433 accessed 8th January 2013.
1869 en.wikipedia.org/wiki/Isleworth accessed on 8th January 2013.
1870 Metropolitan Police Surveyor's Records.

Isleworth Police Station

The London Borough of Hounslow
Worple Road (1873-1931)
T Division (1873-1931)

'The village of Isleworth is situated on the banks of the Thames, at the distance of eight miles and a half from Hyde Park Corner. It lies within the hundred, to which it gives name. The parish is bounded on the south by the river Thames; on the east, north, and west, principally by Brentford, Heston, Twickenham, and Feltham. It touches also in some parts (upon Hounslow-heath) Bedfont, and Hanworth'. [1871]

The main route in London covers many communities. In Kensington it is 'High Street', in Hammersmith 'King Street', in Chiswick it's the 'High Road', in Brentford it's the 'High Street', and is Isleworth's 'London Road', and as it passes into Hounslow it again becomes 'High Street'. Previously this formed part of the 'King's Highway' to Windsor,[1872] and is still an important thoroughfare today.

In 1845 a police section house was brought into service in Isleworth. This was a constable's station house, and did not have any facilities for detaining prisoners or charging suspects for crimes. The house was owned by Mr George Wiles and Mrs Salways of Richmond on a yearly renewable rent of £17 (later increased to £20). It was a small single-storey brick and tile house which had been painted some two years before. There were three rooms with a kitchen and scullery, but one room was used for police business as a reserve room. There were also some premises in the rear which were in a poor state of repair, and needed renovation.[1873] A constable paid one shilling a week to rent the rooms at the house. The buildings in the rear were probably for stabling a horse for use by the constable on his patrols.

By 1862 a proper, much larger station house was being rented in Isleworth where charges were taken, but prisoners had to be conveyed to nearby station at Staines because there were no cell facilities. This was a police station and section house rented from Mr James Hugh Wiles of Ickenham Road, Isleworth on three yearly contracts for £40 per year. The accommodation consisted of a charge room, reserve room and kitchen with cooking facilities. Outside there were four coal vaults to store fuel. There were a further six rooms for residential purposes. This was now a sergeant-supervised police station.[1874] The contract was renewed in 1870 for three years, whilst surveyors considered purchasing a piece of land on which to build a proper station.

The inspector from Brentford would patrol not only his own section on horseback but also go as far as Staines, visiting Heston, Hounslow, Stanwell and Isleworth.

Isleworth was a station on T or Kensington Division, and had one sergeant and eight constables posted there with two constables who worked the day shift and six on night duty.[1875] The old station had accommodation for two married officers and their families, and was probably a horse patrol station with stables in a rear yard. There were two sets of married quarters, with one being slightly larger than the other. The larger accommodation was occupied by the sergeant, and the weekly rent was five shillings and four shillings respectively.[1876]

Land was purchased in Worple Road, Isleworth in 1869, and it is likely that it was the result of a compulsory purchase. The address of the old station is unknown, and it is unlikely to have been on the same site since the old station was given up by the police in order to occupy the new station later. Plans were drawn up and the front of the station would face Byfield Road. The building consisted of a purpose-built police station with one set of married quarters. It also had a charge room, store, kitchen, scullery, drying room, four coal cellars and three cells. There was sufficient space for three sets of married quarters, one for the station sergeant and two others for married constables and their families. The new police station was built on land purchased as freehold, and it came into service in 1873.[1877]

The local police gather outside Isleworth Police Station c1887

The rather old picture above shows the police of Isleworth with their inspector, who is seated front-centre outside their station in the 1880s.

The address of the station in Police Orders of 20th June 1884 was shown as Worple Road, Isleworth.[1878] Together with Hounslow, Isleworth was a sectional station to Brentford, and in 1914 Station Sergeant J. Blake, three sergeants and 30 constables were located there.[1879]

Isleworth Police Station 1873-1931

Isleworth became an important station during both world wars after a contingent of the MSC was formed in 1914 and stationed there. An office and changing room was made available for them to arrange duties and parade in.

In the picture on the following page the side and rear view of the station can be seen. Its shows that access to the rear of the station could made be through the yard gate, and access into the residential part of the station was through the small side door where the cycle is situated.

The station closed at 6.00am on Monday, 1st June 1931 and all business was transferred to Hounslow Police Station. The building was later sold privately and it still stands today.

Side aspect of Isleworth Police Station c1906

Islington Police Station

The London Borough of Islington
Watch House at Islington Green (1829-1852)
277 Upper Street, Islington (1952-1992)
2 Tolpuddle Street, Islington (1992 to Present)
N Division (1830-1958)
G Division (1958-1965)
N Division (1965-1985/86)
Kings Cross Road Division ND (1965-1992)

A watch house at Islington Green was rebuilt in 1797 after the old one had fallen into decay.[1880] It was located at the corner of the green where Hugh Middleton's statue now stands. Previously there had been a place of detention near St. Mary's Church Street, Upper Street. It had a cage and a whipping post attached.[1881] In 1828 the Parish employed fourteen officers to prevent nuisances during the night, and for other duties during the day. These included six constables and six headborough.[1882]

In 1829 the policing of Islington came within the Metropolitan Police.[1883] The 12th Company of the New Police marched into the Parish of St. Mary's Middlesex from their headquarters in Whitehall Place on 1st February 1830[1884] and took over the watch house with its front room, charge room and two cells. It was still in operation in 1840.[1885] It belonged to the Receiver of the Metropolitan Police, and was shown located within the N or Islington Division, although the Headquarters were situated at Kingsland, or Stoke Newington as it is now known. Divisional Superintendent James Johnson was in charge, and his supervisory responsibilities included travelling by horse to the surrounding stations of Hackney Old Town, Robert Street, Hoxton and Islington.[1886]

By 1852 the station on the green was no longer suitable for police purposes, so they were to be relocated to 277 Upper Street, next to the Town Hall, where a new site was leased for a period of 21 years.[1887] The building on the site was unsuitable until it was rebuilt, so a temporary station was established in the Section House at Bird's Buildings. The freehold became available and was purchased by the police in 1857, although work was not completed on the new station until 1858 at a cost of £3,256, plus an additional £2,000 for the freehold.[1888]

Once complete it had eight cells, a charge room and Inspector's office on the ground floor. The basement was used for the constables' uniform storage, and the usual drying room and cooking facilities for the officers. The station strength was reported as two inspectors, nine sergeants, and 89 constables.[1889]

By 1864 there were two inspectors, nine sergeants and eighty-nine constables at the station.[1890] There was also one horse, which was ridden alternately by the inspectors on duty.

Islington Police Station 1858-1992

In 1871 the address of the Police station was shown as 277 Upper Street. At this time the constables from this station were only a short walk from the fields surrounding Canonbury Manor. There was open farmland after crossing Highbury Cross (Highbury Corner). This meant that much of the officer's work at that time related to the licensing of animals and their associated diseases.

1871 Metropolitan Police Surveyor's Records.
1872 Metropolitan Special Police Order 1862.
1873 Metropolitan Police Orders dated 4th February 1871.
1874 Metropolitan Police Orders dated 26th March 1873.
1875 Metropolitan Police Orders dated 28th July 1870.
1876 *Kelly's Hertfordshire and Middlesex Directory* 1915.
1877 Vestry Minute Book 1777-1811, 119, information from Mr J.C. Connell.
1878 *The History of Middlesex* (1995) p84.
1879 Ibid.
1880 10 Geo. IV c.44.
1881 Brown, B. (1992) 'The Station on the Green' in *Islington History Journal*.
1882 Ibid.
1883 Ibid.
1884 Ibid.
1885 John Back Archive (1975).
1886 Brown, B. (1992) 'The Station on the Green' in *Islington History Journal*.
1887 *Kelly's Directory* 1864.
1888 Brown, B. (1992) 'The Station on the Green' in *Islington History Journal*.
1889 Ibid.
1890 Metropolitan Police General Orders 1873.

The Islington Vestry occupied premises next door to the police station, and the relationship between the two parties was not always harmonious. On one occasion, the Vestry asked the Superintendent of Police to remove the airbricks in the police station wall to prevent the foul air from the cells polluting the Vestry Hall. The Superintendent later retaliated by asking the Vestry to brick up windows in their property which overlooked the parade area in the station yard where constables were drilled every morning, so as to prevent undesirable persons looking at his officers.

Officers who worked at the local station often lived nearby, and the Receiver of the Metropolitan Police had purchased or rented houses for this purpose. They were located at 14 Chapel Street, 28 Colebrook Row and 20 Camden Street (now Camden Walk). These three premises were given up in 1837 in favour of a much larger property at Bird's Buildings in Lower Road,[1891] now called Essex Road.

Telegraph communications using the code 'IN' were established in 1872, although from 1965 onwards these were reversed to become November India (NI).[1892]

Records show that Islington (Upper Street) was supervised by an Inspector.[1893] In 1881 the officer in charge was Inspector Bateman, who resided at the station with his wife and two children. There were thirty-nine single police officers and women who appear to have been servants/cleaners.[1894] In 1888 St. Mary's Islington ceased to be located in Middlesex, and instead became part of London County Council (LCC). There were now four inspectors, twelve sergeants and 120 constables on Islington Sub-Division.[1895]

The newspapers often reported details of crimes and unusual incidents, particularly acts of heroism, which had taken place in various parts of London. In 1894 the *Daily News* reported that a new and very young Constable 325J Pipes had fame thrust upon him. On his first day of service he was alone, just before dawn, when he saw a man trying to leave a house through a window in Grosvenor Road, Canonbury. The constable stopped the man, who put up a vicious fight, cutting the officer with a knife, causing serious injuries to his hands and beating him with his fists.

At North London Magistrates' Court the Stipendiary Magistrate, Mr. R.O.B. Lane, commended the officer for his great courage and resolution. The facts were reported to the Commissioner of Police of the Metropolis. As a result of the publicity, several members of the public sent rewards to the Court which totalled £25 10s 6d. The officer was allowed to retain this particular reward for his heroic act of courage. Constable Pipes was further rewarded for his heroism with £10 from the Bow Street Reward Fund. His assailant, Edward Purdoe, was later sentenced to three years' imprisonment for assault and house-breaking.[1896]

The picture at the top of the following paragraph shows Inspector Pocock, who served on N Division for a short period of time. He joined in 1882, but was medically discharged from the police with fourteen years service in April 1896. The inspector was retired medically because he had received an injury on duty in 1884 during the arrest of a drunken man who was assaulting his wife.

This incident caused a degenerative spinal injury, resulting in the officer's inability to walk. This situation was unlikely to improve. However, a gratuity was offered to the inspector by the Commissioner, which was not accepted because the injury was sustained in the line of duty, entitling the officer to his pension. The Commissioner persisted and paid the officer the gratuity, even though he knew the circumstances that caused the injury. Pocock made an appeal to the Home Secretary, but this was unsuccessful and the gratuity of £138 1s 5d was paid, nonetheless. His full pension was therefore forfeited as a result.

Inspector James Pocock

James H. Pocock was promoted to Sergeant in October 1887 and transferred to N Division. He served two months at Walthamstow, and then was selected for special duty at the Royal Gunpowder Factory, Waltham Abbey, where he remained for two years. He was then moved to Islington, at his own request. In April 1892 he arrested John Roxe, a notorious thief, for highway robbery with violence on an aged cabman in Liverpool Road. In October the same year he arrested William Holmes for attempting to murder his wife at Islington Green. Both men were later convicted. At his retirement he was presented with a handsome marble clock and a pair of bronzes as a mark of respect.[1897]

Police officers could retire on pension once they had completed 25 years' service. This was thought of as a waste of experienced officers. Retirement celebrations were a good chance for officers to meet back at the station to say farewell to a colleague. Divisional Superintendent McFadden made the presentations to two retiring officers at Upper Street Police Station (Islington) in October 1896. They were Constable Brewer, of the N Division Mounted Branch, and Constable Hutchings. Both received timepieces. Brewer had spent 19 years of his service at Islington Police Station.[1898]

Shortly before Christmas 1900 Constable 42N (Reserve) Stanton was on mounted duty in Upper Street, Islington when he was set upon by a gang of men who surrounded him, knocked him to the ground and started to kick him. The officer was then stabbed in the neck. A member of the public, Mr. Ambrose Harnett, came to the officer's assistance and the men ran off. As a token of their appreciation for the assistance rendered Sub-Divisional Inspector Mason, the officer in charge of Islington Police, made a presentation of a silver snuff box to Mr Harnett, in front of invited guests at the station.[1899]

Constable Charles Efford

The photograph on the left is of Constable 351H/95975 Charles Victor Efford, who was later stationed at Islington Police Station. He had joined the Metropolitan Police in August 1908 and was posted to H Division. However, in April 1920 he was transferred, on promotion, to Islington on N Division. He left the police through ill-health in April 1932, following 24 years' service. He died in March 1975. In this photograph he is still a constable of H Division.[1900] Even in ill-health Sergeant Efford 'made old bones', living to the age of nearly 90 years and drawing 43 years' police pension.

In 1904 there was extensive refurbishment to the station.

A new building was constructed at the rear of the premises, on the site of the old stables and parade shed. It became a new section house, and opened in October 1906.[1901] The parade room was relocated to the basement. There was now accommodation for forty-two single men. Further work included the front door and steps being relocated right in the next window recess. This enabled an entrance hall to be built, and also for a waiting room to be constructed to the right of the hall. There was now new accommodation in the police station for a married inspector to occupy four rooms, and accommodation for thirty-eight single men.[1902]

In June 1933, as part of extensive re-organisation, the station area was transferred from N or Islington to G or Finsbury Division instead. Additionally, in 1965 the boroughs of Islington and Finsbury combined under local Government reorganisation, causing a change of police boundary, and Islington became part of G Division.

During the Second World War Islington took a pounding throughout the bombing campaign. The police worked tirelessly throughout the action and sometimes paid the ultimate price. In 1940, War Reserve Constable Charles Henry Huck was killed by a bomb during an air raid when he left the shelter to go and investigate a fire.[1903]

In 1973 one of the co-authors, Constable Peter Kennison (later Inspector), was transferred from the Training School to his first posting at Islington Police Station. He remained there until 1977, when he transferred on promotion to Hackney Police Station. Below is the Training School photograph where PC Kennison is shown middle row, extreme right.

Photograph of the class passing out from Hendon Police Training School in January 1973

Superintendent David Swinden, another of the co-authors, finally closed this station in April 1992, when the new police station in Tolpuddle Street at the junction with Penton Street, Islington was opened.

This new Islington Police Station was officially opened in October 1992 by the then-Commissioner of Police, the late Sir (and Lord) Peter Imbert, accompanied by Lady Imbert, the Receiver of the Metropolitan Police District, Mr. Graham Angel, and the Mayor of the London Borough of Islington, Councillor Edna Griffiths.

The new police station was built on the site of an old country mansion named White Conduit House and gardens known as 'The Cockney Retreat'. This was a park where people could eat a 'hearty meal' or have a good pint of ale, or just wander through the various displays and exhibitions set up for the entertainment of all. The park was also used for political meetings, and in 1836 the Dorchester Labourers, known as the 'Tolpuddle Martyrs', were entertained to a dinner to celebrate their release.

Islington police station's front counter was temporarily closed for refurbishment in September 2020.

Islington Police Station 1992 to present

Kenley Police Station

The London Borough of Croydon
94-96 Godstone Road, Kenley CR3 0EB (1896-2013)
W Division (1887-1921)
Z Division (1921-1985/86)
Croydon Division ZD (1985/86-2013)

In May 1886 Home Office authorised the Receiver to purchase a freehold site at Kenley for the erection of a new police station for the sum of £419. The land was compulsorily purchased from a Mr William Taylor under a Bill presented in the House of Commons on 25th March 1887 by one of Her Majesty's Principal Secretaries of State under the Metropolitan Police Act, 1886, relating to lands in the Parishes of Leyton (Essex) and Coulsdon (Surrey).[1904] The transaction for the land purchase was completed in July 1887.[1905]

Kenley Police Station 1896 to present

1891 Census 1881.
1892 Ibid.
1893 *Police Review and Parade Gossip*, April 1894.
1894 *Police Review and Parade Gossip*, April 1896.
1895 *Police Review and Parade Gossip*, 9th October 1896.
1896 *Police Review and Parade Gossip*, 15th February 1901.
1897 Metropolitan Police Service Records.
1898 Metropolitan Police Orders dated 22nd October 1906.
1899 Metropolitan Police Surveyor's Records dated 1924.
1900 www.policememorial.org.uk/Forces/Metropolitan/metroll.htm accessed 12th March 2002.
1901 Metropolitan Police Orders dated 17th February 1919.
1902 Metropolitan Police Property Schedule 1924.
1903 Fido, M and Skinner, K (1999) *The Official History of Scotland Yard*, pp170-174.
1904 LB 804.
1905 Metropolitan Police Surveyor's records 1924.

The new station was erected and formed part of W or Clapham Division. The building was designed by the Metropolitan Police Surveyor, John Butler, and completed by his son, John Dixon Butler, who followed his father into the Surveyor's post. The Architectural Plans at the National Archives are dated 1895.[1906] The cost of the building was £3,789,[1907] and it consisted of a station together with three sets of separate married quarters.

It was taken into occupation by the Police and business commenced therein in July 1896.[1908]

At the formation of the new Z Division in 1921 Kenley was transferred from W to Z Division, and designated a Section Station of Croydon Division.[1909]

Kenley Police Officers in 1937

The photograph above was taken in 1937 when the officers received their Coronation medals, having being part of the ceremonies.

With the new local authority boundaries created in 1965, Kenley (ZK) continued to be a Sectional Station to Croydon Sub-Division, situated in the new London Borough of Croydon.[1910]

Kenley Police Station was closed in 2013, and the building then sold for £600,000 in February 2015.[1911]

Kennington Lane and Kennington Road Police Stations

Although Kennington Lane and Kennington Road are separate Police Stations, they have been included in the same part of the chapter due to their close inter-relationship.

Kennington Lane Police Station

The London Borough of Lambeth

10 Tower Street Watch House (1830-1871)

42 Lower Kennington Road (1871-1932)

L Division (1930-1932)

In 1838 there were three police stations covering the area, and prior to 1830 all were former parish watch Houses. They were at 10 Tower Street, Waterloo Road, Lambeth; High Street, Old Lambeth; and Christchurch, Blackfriars Road.[1912] The buildings were unsuitable to accommodate Police officers.

The Tower Street Watch House, a station on L Division at 10 Tower Street, was handed over to the Police together with the lease which still had 50 years to run. The premises were owned by Mr William Hadnut of William Street, Westminster Road. The annual rent was £65, and the records show that this was

'an old brick plaster and tile house with a covered yard with a parade ground. There is a small open yard at the back with three cells, water closet, coal store and dust hole. It contains 8 rooms including a scullery.'

The Metropolitan Police retained this old Watch House for some time, and they maintained it well as in 1844 it was whitened, coloured and repaired. In 1853 it was cleansed and painted whilst the outside was painted in 1857, 1860, 1864 and 1871. The Police Surveyors were concerned about the cell floors, which appeared to be deteriorating at the time of renting, whilst the drains were defective and had to be cleaned. The premises were generally clean, ventilation good and water in plentiful supply.[1913] In 1844 the station was important enough to be designated for supervision by an inspector.[1914] Just behind the Watch House, the Receiver purchased a house to use as a residence for Police Officers.

The Section House in Hertford Place, Webber Street adjoined the police station, and was also owned by Mr Hadnut who leased the premises for 50 years from 1834. 23 constables lived in the station, whilst one sergeant and five constables lived in the house. Both the house and Watch House were vacated in 1875.[1915]

In 1844 the estimated cost of erecting a new police station and police court at Kennington was £2,300. The Receiver was to be the copyholder, and a tenant of the Duchy of Cornwall.[1916] Prior to this, in 1842, it had been suggested that a Police Court be built for the Metropolitan Police District on a triangle of land bounded by Kennington Lane, Windmill Row and Kennington Road. This idea was abandoned after much public opposition.[1917]

At this time, L Division was led by Police Superintendent Samuel Dicken Corbet Grinsell, who had been appointed a Superintendent in the Force in 1833 and was based at Tower Street, Waterloo Place. Working with Grinsell were four Police Inspectors, D. Ferguson, J. Evans, William Stannard and William J. Topp. The inspectors operated from two stations; one at Tower Street and the other at High Street, Lambeth.[1918] All four inspectors were recorded on L Division in 1841 when Inspector Topp had replaced Inspector Joseph Wrangle on the latter's retirement in consequence of being 'worn out' in May 1841, on an annual pension of £108.[1919]

Many police officers were retired towards the end of their service and the cause for leaving shown as 'worn out', but this does not occur for the lower ranks in the present Police Service. However, the superintending ranks of the Metropolitan Police Service were not normally allowed to serve beyond the age of 55 years because of regulations laid down some time ago. It was stated that a superintendent was 'worn out' by the time he or she reached 55 years. This regulation was certainly in place at least until the mid-1990s.

The 1841 Census shows Superintendent Grinsell living in the Police accommodation at 9 Kennington Cross, with his family and eleven police constables.[1920] Superintendent Grinsell is an interesting person. On leaving the Police Service he moved from Kennington Cross to Hillingdon Heath, Hillingdon, Middlesex, and became the Deputy Bailiff at Brentford County Court. He later moved to Camden Square, Camberwell in Surrey, and was occasionally employed in the Surrey Zoological Gardens. It is not certain how he was employed at the time, but in July 1849 he found himself in debt and in Queen's Prison.[1921]

By 1849 there were four police stations on L or Lambeth Division, under the command of Superintendent Anthony Rutt.[1922] One was at Tower Street, Waterloo Road; one at Kennington Lane; one at High Street, Lambeth; and the other at Christchurch, near the old church.[1923] However, by 1864 the Division had only two stations: Tower Street (shown as

Kennington Lane Police Station 1871-1932

No. 58 in the National Census Return of 1841, the road was later renamed Morley Street in 1937), and Kennington Lane. The combined strength of the two stations in 1864 was four inspectors, 21 sergeants and 178 constables.[1924] In addition, a police constable was on duty in charge of the lock-up at Christ Church during the day; a stretcher was kept there, but no station duty was performed there.[1925]

In April 1865, the Vestry of the Parish of Lambeth notified the Police that the address of Kennington Lane Police Station was changing from 4 York Row to 8 Kennington Park Road.[1926] In 1868 the lease was extended for 63 years, with an annual rent of £127, and a new station was built on the site in 1870.

At various times in a police officer's career he may well find himself in a situation which could result in him being injured or, at worst, killed. This has been the reality since early times, when Constables enforced the law of the land, and many officers have lost their lives whilst trying to uphold the law. One such officer, in May 1851, was Police Constable Henry James Chaplin, who was attacked and struck with bricks by a disorderly crowd at Vauxhall Walk. The officer is buried in St. Mark's Churchyard, Kennington.[1927]

In 1868 it was decided to erect a new Kennington Lane Station to be designed by Frederick Caiger, Metropolitan Police Surveyor. The cost was calculated to be in the region of £8,000, but actually cost only £7,040. Three years later, in November 1871, the new station opened for business.[1928] A new detached Section House was built on the site of the station's rear yard, but facing onto Renfrew Road which ran down the side of the police station. There were objections by the local residents that the frontage line extended too far, but planning permission was given regardless.[1929] It was described as the 'Home for Recruits',[1930] and later as a 'Candidates Section House'.

This new Section House opened in October 1887 and was occupied by one inspector, 30 constables and 51 recruits.[1931] It ceased to house recruits when, in 1907, Peel House was opened in Regency Street.[1932]

The station at High Street, Lambeth was closed when the new Kennington Lane Police Station, whose address in 1880 was given as 42 Lower Kennington Lane, corner of Renfrew Road,[1933] was opened.[1934] In 1933 it was often referred to as 'Renfrew Road Section House'.[1935]

1906 MEPO 9/97.
1907 Metropolitan Police Surveyor's Book.
1908 Metropolitan Police Order dated 4th July 1896.
1909 Metropolitan Police Order dated 24th February 1921.
1910 Metropolitan Police Order dated 6th August 1964.
1911 Metropolitan Police Information Rights Unit accessed 25th January 2001.
1912 *Post Office London Directory* 1838.
1913 Metropolitan Police Surveyor's Report.
1914 *Kelly's Directory* 1844.
1915 *Kelly's Directory* 1875.
1916 John Back Archive (1975).
1917 *Survey of London Vol. XXVI St Mary Lambeth*, Part 2.
1918 *Police and Constabulary List* 1844.
1919 B. Brown, Metropolitan Police Historical Collection, date unknown.
1920 Census 1841.
1921 *London Gazette* 20th July 1849 p2324 and 24th July 1849 p2347.
1922 *Post Office London Directory* 1849.
1923 Ibid.
1924 Metropolitan Police Order dated 11th January 1864.
1925 John Back Archive (1975).
1926 Ibid.
1927 Fido, M. and Skinner, K. (1999) *The Official Encyclopaedia of Scotland Yard*.
1928 Metropolitan Police Order dated 4th November 1871.
1929 MBW/BA/36558.
1930 *The Builder*, 6th November 1886 p686.
1931 Metropolitan Police Order dated 8th November 1887.
1932 MEPO 2/2584.
1933 John Back Archive (1975).
1934 Brown, B. Metropolitan Police Historical Collection, date unknown.
1935 MEPO 2/2584.

Detective Sergeant Benjamin Leeson described how he joined the Metropolitan Police in December 1890 and was taken to Kennington Lane Section House, a Police barracks and school of instruction. The courses there varied from three to five weeks in length, and every morning after breakfast the recruits were taken to Wellington Barracks for two hours of foot drill. Leeson also described his fellow recruits as being a mixed lot, consisting of farm labourers, ploughmen and waggoners from every county in the British Isles.[1936] At the end of the course they were marched from Kennington to New Scotland Yard to be sworn in. They were issued with two complete uniforms, described as good but poorly-made, and then posted to various Police divisions.[1937]

In 1869 Superintendent Charles Webb was in charge of L or Lambeth Division, and was based at Kennington Lane Police Station. An inspector was in charge at 58 Tower Street, Waterloo.

In 1881 a report on Kennington Lane Police Station described it as an important station which had been recently built; it was a large site, although on low-lying land. The basement had been under water, but steps were being taken to check the flooding[1938] and some considerable alterations were made to the building in 1912. Inside there were two sets of married quarters, and part of the main building was a Police Section House.

The new Police Section House erected on the site of the old Kennington Lane Police Station, which closed in 1932, became known as Gilmore House.[1939]

Kennington Road Police Station

London Borough of Lambeth

Kennington Road (1874-1939)

49-51 Kennington Road SE1 7QA (1955-2017)

L Division (1874-1932)

M Division (1932-2018)

A new station was built, to the designs of Frederick Caiger, Metropolitan Police Surveyor, in Kennington Road and this opened in August 1874.[1940] In 1879 L Division comprised of just two stations, Kennington Lane and Kennington Road, with Superintendent James Brannan in charge.[1941]

Kennington Road Police Station 1874-1939

A report in 1881 report described the Kennington Road station as having the single men living in one block and married men living in the building containing the administration. At the time of the report the accommodation housed two married inspectors, two single sergeants and forty-eight constables. This was a new station which had been built only six years earlier, but they criticized the same mess room and stressed the need for more cells to be built.[1942] This was carried out, and they were brought into use in 1890.[1943]

Superintendent Brannan was still in charge in 1891. At Kennington Lane he was assisted by Chief Inspector Chisholm and Inspectors T. Padgett, T. Green, J. Hill, W. Whatley, G. Bartle, J. Barrett, T. Neal and C. Easter. The following inspectors were at Kennington Road: H. Garland, J. Jackson, G. Lowe, G. Payne, G.M. Lennett and T. Martin.[1944] The address of Kennington Road Police Station was 47 Kennington Road.[1945]

In 1893 Inspector H. Garland, mentioned above, retired. He had served at Kennington Road for twelve years and, as often happened when officers retired, there was a presentation. The report was as follows:

"A gratifying testimony to the appreciation in which Insp, Garland, of the L Division was held by the inhabitants of Lambeth has been supplied on his retirement, after holding the position for 12 years. His unvarying courtesy and integrity in discharging his duties had earned for him popularity and respect, and led the leading trade-men of the district to offer him a token of their esteem. The presentation took place at the Horse and Groom, Westminster Bridge road, where, after a capital dinner, the host Mr Douglas Hart, who presided, handed Insp. Garland a purse containing 100 guineas and a gold Albert chain... The presentation was accompanied by a testimonial on vellum." [1946]

In June 1892 the Home Office approved the purchase of the freehold of the station at 47 Kennington Road for £6,000 from the freeholder, a Mr. W. Stock, although the transaction was not completed until March 1893.[1947]

In 1928 Superintendent Thomas Abbott was in charge of L Division, based at Kennington Lane Police Station. The division also included Kennington Road, Battersea, Clapham, Lavender Hill and Nine Elms Police Stations.[1948]

By 1930 Superintendent Ernest Brind was in charge of L Division.[1949] During a reorganisation of Police boundaries of No. 4 District in 1932, Kennington Road Police Station was transferred from L to M or Southwark Division.[1950] Seven years later, in 1939, Kennington Road Police Station was closed for reconstruction and all business was transferred to a temporary station at Gilmore House, Renfrew Street.[1951]

The Old Kennington Road Station was demolished and drawings prepared for the erection of a new station, but the outbreak of World War II prevented further action. During the War the London Fire Brigade utilised the site to hold an emergency water supply for use during the air raids.[1952]

In 1949 the freehold of the adjoining properties, 49-51 Kennington Road, were purchased for £1,500 in order to increase the site on which the new station to would be erected.[1953]

The new Sub-Divisional Police Station at Kennington Road, M Division, designed by J. Innes Elliott, Metropolitan Police Chief Architect and Surveyor, was built and eventually opened for business in October 1955. The temporary police station at Gilmore Section House was closed.[1954]

The reorganisation of local authority boundaries in 1965 moved Kennington Road Sub-Divisional Station (LK) back to L Division, within the London Borough of Lambeth.[1955]

In October 1980 Police Constable Frank O'Neill was fatally stabbed at Lower Marsh whilst attempting to arrest a suspect using a forged prescription. A plaque to his memory was placed in the foyer of Kennington Police Station and unveiled by the Commissioner, Sir David McNee, in May 1981.

The areas policed by Kennington Road and Clapham Police Stations were amalgamated in January 1994 to form the new

Vauxhall Division. Kennington Road, normally referred to as Kennington Police Station was closed for public enquiries by 2019.

Kennington Police Station from 1955

Kensington Police Station

Royal Borough of Kensington and Chelsea

1 Church Court (known as Church Street by 1832) (1830-1873)

78 Kensington High Street (1873-1956)

72 Earls Court Road (1956 to Present)

T Division (1830-1886)

F Division (1886-1965)

B Division (1965-1993/94)

Part of Brompton OCU (1993/94-2018/19)

Part of Central West BCU (2018-19 to Present)

The first police station appears to have been located at 1 Church Court, Kensington, where the rate book shows the police station for 1830. It was perhaps linked to premises at 1-2 High Street, where a lease was taken out for 21 years from September 1838 from the landlord, a Mr. T. Cade of Marchmont Street, Brunswick Square. The freehold was bought for £670 in 1855. It became a substantial brick-and-slate-built house with its own yard and four cells.[1956] In 1844 Inspector Thomas B. Smith was in charge, having been promoted in 1838.[1957] As the map below of the area shows, the station was located between the Vestry Hall and St. Mary Abbots church.

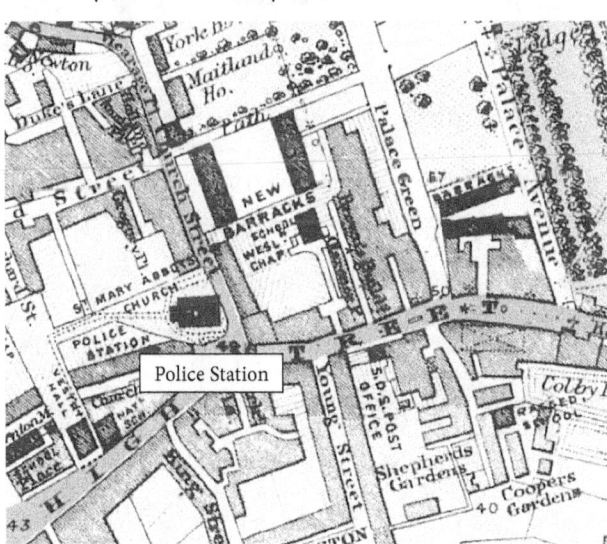

Kensington Police Station shown on an 1863 map

One of Kensington's Superintendents, Edward Tarlton, had a tragic end to his career. He had been born in Ireland in 1812. He applied to join the Metropolitan Police and was accepted in 1836 with warrant no. 11677. Some ten years later he married Louisa Hannah Purdie from Islington. Louisa was very attached to her parents, who resided at 17 Upper Park Street, Islington, and visited them often. In 1851 he was living with his wife and their five daughters at 7 Upper Crown Street, Westminster and travelled to Stoke Newington each day for his duty as an Inspector after being promoted from Sergeant on A Division. He finally moved his family to Hackney in 1851. Tarlton was a hardworking and conscientious police officer who seemed destined for promotion, and by 1857 he had indeed been promoted to Superintendent of T (Kensington) Division. His time at Hackney saw his wife give birth to a son in 1853, whom he called Edward Pitt Tarlton, named after his younger brother Pitt, a V Division Inspector attached to Chelsea Police Station.

Tarlton was a strong family man, and his only son was the apple of his father's eye. The family had moved to the Superintendent's quarters at 152 Hammersmith Bridge Road, a fine house suitable for a Superintendent of this busy division and his family. As the Divisional Superintendent he was heading murder investigations, dealing with suspicious deaths or taking control of fires, using reserves of police from the section house when necessary. He appeared before the local courts frequently, and was a well-known and respected senior police officer in the neighbourhood.

Tarlton and his family then experienced a series of tragic events that spelled disaster for the whole family. In December 1860 his wife Louisa (then aged just 41 years) had returned to Upper Park Street, Islington to nurse her sick mother Hannah (aged 59), when tragically and mysteriously both mother and daughter died within the same hour. This tragedy left him to bring up his daughters Ann (21), Susannah (19), Louisa (14) Emily (12), and son Edward Pitt (8), and it fell to the eldest, Ann, to help her father, together with a house servant, to bring up the rest of the family.

In early November 1862 Inspector Searle of T Division submitted a bill for expenses to Tarlton which the

---

1936 In 1874 a survey of recruiting, over a two period, showed that of those who had joined the Force, 31% came from land jobs, 12% from military service and 5% from other police jobs. The remainder mostly carried out manual jobs. The majority of recruits and serving officers at that time came from outside London. www.friendsofmethistory.co.uk/timeline accessed 9th January 2008.

1937 Leeson, B. *Lost London*. Stanley Paul (1934).

1938 Metropolitan Police Surveyor's Report 1881.

1939 Metropolitan Police Orders dated 24th April 1939.

1940 Metropolitan Police Orders dated 6th August 1874.

1941 *Post Office Directory* 1879.

1942 Report on the Condition of Police Stations 1881.

1943 Metropolitan Police Orders dated 5th March 1890.

1944 *Kelly's Sydenham, Norwood & Streatham Directory* 1891.

1945 John Back Archive (1975).

1946 *Police Review*, 1893 Vol. 1.

1947 John Back Archive (1975).

1948 *Post Office Directory* 1928.

1949 *Police Almanac* 1930.

1950 Metropolitan Police Orders dated 1st January 1932.

1951 Metropolitan Police Orders dated 24th April 1939.

1952 John Back Archive (1975).

1953 Ibid.

1954 Metropolitan Police Orders dated 25th October 1955.

1955 Metropolitan Police Orders dated 6th August 1964.

1956 Metropolitan Police Property Register.

1957 *The Police and Constabulary List* 1844.

Superintendent failed to sign to signify that he had seen and authorised its payment. Instead, the bill was forwarded to the Commissioner Sir Richard Mayne accidentally. Mayne was not best pleased and immediately called for the Inspector to appear before him at Scotland Yard. On hearing the evidence he found that Searle had spoken truthfully about the circumstances, but recommended to Tarlton that Searle should be transferred to another station as soon as a position became available.

It appears that word had got back to the Commissioner about the running of the division, as within a month Assistant Commissioner Captain Labalmondiere stipulated that he wanted to conduct an inspection. He duly arrived on 1st December and, whilst it is unknown what he discovered, within four days Tarlton had been placed on leave and his deputy, Inspector John Mitchell, put in charge. Tarlton's daughter Susannah had also died on 5th December and his son Edward also became seriously ill, with little chance of survival. Two weeks later, on 19th December 1862 Tarlton's own medical condition became worse and on his doctor's advice was prescribed bed rest. Superintendent Tarlton was then placed on sick leave, and Police Orders confirmed that Inspector Mitchell was temporarily placed in charge of the division. This series of events had left Tarlton severely depressed and confined to bed. In fact, so serious was the situation that Inspector Mitchell's wife went to help out at the Tarlton family home in Bridge Road.

Mary Ball had been resident in the Tarlton household for about three months helping out as the housekeeper. Tarlton and the housekeeper had helped to look after his ailing daughter during her long illness. She noticed how Tarlton was despondent and heartbroken at the loss of his wife and daughter. At about 7.00pm on 2nd January 1863 the housekeeper found that Tarlton had cut his own throat with a razor. Tarlton died, according to police records, having taken his own life with the bland comment in Police Orders explaining that Tarlton had 'committed suicide' with a reference in other internal documents that his police account had 'insufficient funds'.

An inquest took place on Saturday evening at the Sussex Arms public house, Bridge Road. Mr Alfred Bird, the Coroner, had known Tarlton extremely well. So upset were Bird and other witnesses in viewing the body that evening, which had been kept in the cool cellar of the public house, that proceedings had to be delayed in order that those who were distressed could compose themselves. During the inquest, evidence was heard from Tarlton's doctor that he had been suffering from an inflamed stomach and chronic bronchitis, from which he could not recover, and that he had said that 'he wanted to be put at the bottom of a pond'. The jugular had been severed, and this was the cause of his demise, leaving the coroner to record a verdict of 'death due to temporary insanity'.

Superintendent Tarlton held a contingency account which was used for paying the officers under his command and for other financial matters. His Clerk Sergeant and the man who organised the finances for the division was Sergeant 2T Thomas Hindes from Beccles in Suffolk, who had joined in 1853. Hindes would travel with his Superintendent on a Wednesday to Scotland Yard to collect a cheque paid into the Bank of England and converted into cash.

On 7th January 1863, as a consequence of checking the accounts prior to a new Superintendent being transferred to the Division, the Receiver's Office found errors in the accounts and seized them. Sergeant Hindes was immediately suspended from duty 'as a consequence of the errors found in the late Superintendent's accounts' and his pay was stopped. Checking and re-checking these accounts took some considerable time.

In the meantime, Sir Richard Mayne decided to move a substantive Superintendent into T Division, and Beckerson was duly transferred from L Division on 19th January. Sergeant Hindes was called before the Commissioner to explain himself, but it was not until 23rd April that he was finally dealt with. All this time was spent at home with his wife Eliza and his large, family worrying about his likely fate. During his suspension there would have been concerns that this would end in the criminal courts as misappropriation of police funds. The Commissioner fined Hindes one month's pay, on top of losing 11 weeks' pay on suspension, and stated:

'The sergeant was, I believe, unconscious of the very serious nature of the offence he was committing, and was certainly acting under the express orders of his Superintendent at the time'.

But after all this tragedy and misfortune there was some fair play in the end, as the matter was not held against him and Hindes was promoted to Inspector in January 1864 and transferred to D Division. By 1879 he had become Divisional Superintendent at Woolwich Dockyard (and Arsenal), and in March 1889 he retired on pension and remained resident in Plumstead. In the meantime, Tarlton's family had to vacate their police house, probably by 19th January 1863, and were scattered around London with the remaining daughters all finding suitors and having their own families.

Kensington Police Station 1873-1956

Ten years later, when Chief Inspector Thomas Bocking from Kensington retired in 1873, it was a time of change in policing the area. One development was the demolition of Jennings' Buildings, a wooden-built 'rookery' slum housing a thousand poor families, whose inhabitants had kept Mr Bocking and his officers busy for many years. One local magistrate said Jennings' Buildings was 'a lawless neighbourhood and the police were compelled to use a great deal of severity.'[1958] The local newspaper commented that Mr Bocking 'was not only respected by the inhabitants [of Kensington], but by the roughs themselves.' Jennings' Buildings was near Kensington Palace and the parish church, so one can imagine the animosity that might be felt towards the residents of the block by the better-off residents of Kensington.

The Metropolitan Police also took responsibility for keeping order within workhouses in this period. A constable was sworn in 1866 to help keep order at Kensington workhouse, and was issued with a warrant from the Commissioner which would be returned when not needed.

But another event in 1873 was the opening of a new police station, the address now being recorded as 78 Kensington High Street, adjacent to St Mary Abbott Church, Kensington Church Street, at a total cost of £11,000. The building work was delayed by legal issues, and the Receiver eventually made an undertaking to Kensington Parish that there would be strict compliance with the design of the building as set out by the famous Victorian architect Sir Gilbert Scott, who lived locally at Courtfield Gardens, South Kensington.

In 1901 a section house for single officers had been built at the rear of the premises at Kensington Church Court, accommodating 30 officers. In 1942 the section house was converted for use as offices, and after a period of being rented out they were taken back into police use in 1969 as a Traffic Wardens' centre and, in due course, a base for the Diplomatic Protection Group.

A new police station at 72 Earls Court Road was opened on 14th September 1956, boasting double windows to combat traffic noise. It had been built on a site purchased for £10,250 before the Second World War, with construction delayed because of hostilities and post-war austerity. The total cost eventually reached £230,000, housing a new District Headquarters and, with its own separate entrance, a section house for 67 officers. The section house featured a billiards room, common rooms, a library, a hobbies room and a residents' dining room. The District Headquarters had previously been at Great Scotland Yard, and the new premises provided offices for the District Commander, with the District Detective Chief Superintendent, the District Superintendents of the Women Police, Mounted Branch and Traffic Division, a map room and a conference room.[1959]

In an exemplary initiative to improve public relations and understanding of police work, a public open day at the station was hosted by Commander Gordon Maggs in August 1970. Guests included Prince Richard of Gloucester, who opened the event, and Jack Warner, the actor who played PC George Dixon in the TV series Dixon of Dock Green. The Metropolitan Police band was present, playing under the direction of their Director of Music, Major Williams.

It was on Kensington's ground in 1973 that an incident occurred which resulted in the award of a George Medal to PC Peter Slimon. There have been 138 George Medals awarded to Metropolitan Police officers since the medal's inception in 1940, 59% of them in connection with war time activities. In PC Slimon's case he witnessed an armed bank robbery taking place, and, having possession of a police firearm himself because of his Diplomatic Protection Group duties, he challenged the robbers, and was wounded in the subsequent exchange of gunfire which resulted in the death of one of the robbers. PC Slimon's citation published in the London Gazette mentions his 'outstanding resolution, devotion to duty, and courage of a very high order.'

Inexplicably, and despite the undoubted bravery shown by police officers on the streets of modern-day London, no George Medal was awarded to a Metropolitan Police officer from 1992 until the actions of off-duty PC Charlie Guenigault were recognised in 2018 after he confronted terrorists in an

Kensington Police Station, opened 1956

incident at London Bridge on 3rd June 2017. PC Slimon's actions also remind us of the courage required to challenge armed and dangerous criminals, notwithstanding the fact that officers themselves may be armed. The death of criminals engaged in their unlawful activities must surely be regarded as an occupational hazard for them, despite the obligation to refer such cases, without further comment, to the Independent Office for Police Conduct.

A section house in Gore Lane, Kensington was in use from 1836 until 1857.

Kentish Town Police Station

Junction Place (1832-1896)
10-12A Holmes Road NW5 3AE (1896 to Present)
N Division (1933-1965)
E Division (1965-1985/86)
Kentish Town Division (1985/86 -1993)
London Borough of Camden OCU (1993-2018)
Central North BCU (together with Islington) 2018 to Present)

Kentish Town Police Station Lamp

Most police stations have a standard lamp at the front of the building. A number of differing designs have been used and shown left is Kentish Town's lamp, which is still in use today. Commissioner Sir Peter Imbert revamped many station lamps some years ago.

Records show that in 1844 the inspector in charge of Kentish Town Police Station was Inspector Aggs. He had been an inspector for fourteen years, having joined the division at its start in 1830.[1960] The station was in fact the Old Watch House, which was designated as a station located on S or Hampstead

---

1958 Jennifer Davis, 'Policing of the Poor' in *Police Review*, 7th February 1986.
1959 *Police Review*, 31 August 1956.
1960 *The Police and Constabulary List of 1844*, Monograph No. 3, the Police History Society.

Division. The building was located in Junction Place, and was a brick-and-slate-built house consisting of a charge room and two cells. It belonged to the Receiver of the Metropolitan Police and remained in service until 1853, and given up in 1860.

In 1853 a police station was erected at the cost of £2,081. The land was leased from General Sir D. Leighton KCB of Charlton Kings, Gloucester, for 90 years, with a ground rent of £30 which was payable annually. The officer in charge of the Division, at the time, was Superintendent Edward Worels, whilst Chief Inspector William Odell was responsible for the station and deputy to the Superintendent in the event that he went on leave. The division also had a further thirteen inspectors, with George Gilby being favoured as the Reserve Inspector. It is interesting to note that there was accommodation on the premises for twenty-one unmarried men who paid over £54 per year for their quarters. This more than covered the annual ground rent the Receiver paid for the building.

Under the divisional re-organisations of 1865 Y or Highgate Division was formed, with Kentish Town Police Station becoming the Divisional Headquarters for this new division. The new division stretched from Highgate in the south to Enfield in the north, and even in those early days each station was connected by telegraph.[1961]

In 1881 Edward Worells, the divisional superintendent, resided at 1 Lawford Road, Kentish Town, which was a short distance from the station. He lived there with his wife and three children.[1962] Worells had transferred from K to Y Division as a superintendent in June 1876. He had joined the service in May 1847 (warrant no. 24450) after leaving his job as a watchmaker. He became a sergeant within three years, an inspector within a further five years and superintendent ten years later. The inspector in charge of the station in 1881 was John Golder aged 33, who resided there with his family.[1963]

In 1888 the Divisional strength numbered 727 officers, with William J. Huntley being the Superintendent in charge, assisted by 46 inspectors, 73 sergeants and 607 constables.[1964] Huntley remained Superintendent until 2nd November 1891, when he retired on pension.[1965]

In December 1889 the Receiver purchased the freehold of the station at a cost of £1,200, although a yearly sum of one shilling per annum was payable to the Midland Railway, because station windows overlooked some of the tracks.

In 1892 more land was acquired to accommodate prison vans, and the new station at 12 Holmes Road, Kentish Town, was occupied in April 1896.[1966] Architect Richard Norman Shaw, who designed the old New Scotland Yard on the Embankment, designed the building. The building is now listed as of architectural and historical interest.

Further divisional re-organisation in 1933 saw Kentish Town transferred from Y to N Division. From 1958 until 1962 the London Probation Service was allowed offices on police premises at 12 Holmes Road. The Metropolitan Police District (MPD) was split into four Districts, each with a District Headquarters. Kentish Town was located on 3 District, with Stoke Newington being the Headquarters. Each station on the district was linked via a private telephone line, replacing the old telegraph system, to headquarters at CO or Scotland Yard. This was a secure non-public line. Kentish Town was also linked to other stations through this network. These were Albany Street (D), Caledonian Road, Hampstead (S), Holloway and Hornsey on Y Division.

A section house at 10 Holmes Road was opened in December 1964 to accommodate 108 men. In 1965 the Local Authority re-organisation saw Kentish Town become a sub-divisional station on E Division. After the re-organisation, E Division moved to 2 District.[1967]

Kentish Town Police Station 1896 to present

In 2002 Kentish Town was shown within the London Borough of Camden at 12A Holmes Road, Kentish Town, London, NW5 3EA. As of 2019 the station has remained open to the public 24 hours a day 7 days a week.[1968]

Kew Police Station

The London Borough of Richmond

96 North Road Kew (1914-1933)

V Division (1914-1932)

The freehold title to a vacant site was purchased at 96 North Road, Kew in 1912, when a station and two sets of married quarters were built.[1969] Originally, when it was brought into service in 1914,[1970] like Barnes Kew was a sectional station on V or Wandsworth Division to Richmond. It remained a station on V Division until 1932.

Kew Police Station 1914-1933

In 1929 a police call box – V6 – was erected on the south-west corner of North Road and High Park Avenue, on the

Kilburn Police Station 1891-1940

forecourt of the police station. The box was taken down in 1960.[1971] There was another box, V8, situated in Kew at the southeast corner of the junction with Kew Road and The Avenue, Kew and that was removed in July 1959.[1972]

Kew Police Station closed in April 1933 as part of police re-organisation under the new commissioner, Lord Trenchard, but it was retained for other police purposes by the Receiver.

Kilburn Police Station

The London Borough of Brent
Kilburn Lane, Kilburn (1851-1870)
11-13 High Road, Kilburn (1870-1891)
38 Salusbury Road (1891-1914)
38 Harvist Road, Willesden (1914-1917)
38 Salusbury Road (1917-1938)
Closed business transferred to Harrow Road Police Station
(Section House 1940) (destroyed by WW2 bomb)
36 Salusbury Road (1965-1967)
2 Harvist Road, Kilburn (1967-1977)
Albert Road, NW6 (1977-1980)
38 Salusbury Road NW6 6NJ (1980 to Present)
X Division (1870-1938)
Q Division (1969-1993)
The London Borough of Brent OCU (1993-2018)
Brent BCU (North West) (2018 to Present)

By 1851 there was a police station at Kilburn Lane.[1973] Kilburn was also served by successive stations at 11-13 High Road (1870-1891), and Salusbury Road from 1891 until it closed in 1938.[1974] Salusbury Road Police Station existed before other public buildings were erected next to it in 1894.[1975]

Kilburn Police Section House, at 5&6 Kempshall Terrace Kilburn, was a brick and slate building which had been repaired and adapted for occupation. The premises were leased from Henry and John Childs from December 1870 until December 1891. On the ground floor of one of buildings there was a reserve room, a charge room and 2 cells, and a kitchen in the basement. In the other building the ground floor consisted of a mess room and a brushing room. The basement had a washing room and a kitchen.[1976]

Police also rented a coach house and stable at 23 Bridge Street, Kilburn from June 1871 until June 1892, from Peter Mudie, Esq of Bridge Crescent, Kilburn.[1977]

At 11-13 High Road, Kilburn a portion of land and the houses thereon were leased from Mrs Jane Roy of Marl Hill, Carisbrooke, Isle of Wight at an annual rental of £107. The lease was from 1870 until Christmas 1891. The houses were converted for use by Police and this new police station was taken into use on 12th February 1872.[1978]

1961 John Back Archive (1975).
1962 Census 1881.
1963 Ibid.
1964 *Dickens's Dictionary of London* (1888) pp197-199.
1965 Curator's List of Divisional Superintendents.
1966 Metropolitan Police Orders dated 25th April 1896.
1967 John Back Archive (1975).
1968 uat01.nonlive.camden.pfiks.com/contact-police-stations accessed 31st October 2019.
1969 Metropolitan Police Surveyor's Records 1924.
1970 *Kelly's Directory* 1914.
1971 Site locations for Metropolitan Police telephone boxes and telephone posts for V Division.
1972 Ibid.
1973 HO 107/1700/135/3, pp332 sqq.
1974 *Kilburn and Willesden Directory* (1872-1940).
1975 Ibid.
1976 Metropolitan Police Surveyor's Book 1845.
1977 Ibid.
1978 Metropolitan Police Orders dated 10th February 1872.

In June 1889, a freehold plot of land was purchased from the Ecclesiastical Commissioners for England for the sum of £960 for the erection of a new police station. It had a frontage of 80 feet in Salusbury Road, Kilburn, at the junction of Mortimer Road. The land then extended for a length of 160 feet along Mortimer Road. In December 1889 the conveyance for the site was received from the Home Office.[1979] The conditions imposed were that if the Receiver wished to dispose of this property at any time, or make use of land other than for police, county or municipal purposes, six months notice must be given to the Ecclesiastical Commissioners who had the right to re-purchase.

In order to provide for the more efficient performance of the duties at Ealing, Acton and Hanwell, portions of Brentford, Shepherds Bush and Chiswick sub-divisions of T or Hammersmith Division, were transferred to X or Kilburn Division. The boundaries were then revised accordingly,[1980] and Harrow Road became the headquarters station from 1888.

The new police station and the section house were completed in 1891/2 at a cost of £5,905,[1981] and the station was opened in December 1891.[1982] The single men's quarters at the new station were ready for occupation in March 1892. The lodging assessment was at 1s each per week for the 20 single Constables.[1983]

In 1890 X Division was under the command of Superintendent George Carr, and at Kilburn were Inspectors Joseph W. Cooper (warrant no. 52151), W. Redstone, N. Mansfield and A. McDonald.[1984] Cooper joined the police in 1869 and was shown on X Division located at Kilburn in 1891, where he resided in the married quarters with his wife and 5 children in the newly-opened police station. He had to move from the premises when he retired in 1899 after 30 years service. By 1893 Cooper had been promoted to Sub-Divisional Inspector. In 1893 X Division was now under the command of Superintendent James Cuthbert, and at Kilburn were Inspectors N. Manfield, A. McDonald and George Hodder.[1985]

In September 1893 Constable 196 Craney, X Division, was patrolling his beat in Victoria Road, Kilburn when his attention was drawn to a woman outside no. 18 who stated the house was on fire. The officer entered the building and went to the top floor where the occupant was desperately trying to put out a fire which had started when a paraffin stove had been accidentally knocked over. The officer put out the fire and rendered first aid to the occupant who had sustained burns to his hands. The occupant was not insured so was unlikely to have been compensated for any damage to the property.[1986]

Superintendent Cuthbert was still in charge of X or Kilburn Division in 1895, and assisted by Sub-Divisional Inspector George Bridgen.[1987] In 1898 Inspector William Bell, taking over from Cooper, was the officer in charge of Kilburn Police Station and its area which was a sectional station to Harrow Road. Between 1895 and 1898 Harlesden Sub-Division was created and Willesden became a sectional station with Harrow.

The picture above right shows Inspector Charles Taylor of Kilburn with his cycle together with the Station Sergeant in about 1910. Taylor stayed at Kilburn until about 1917.[1988] The Secretary of State sanctioned the use of pedal cycles for patrol duty especially in outer lying stations in 1904, and an allowance was paid to police officers who supplied and maintained their own machines. The sum of 10d per day was paid to Chief Inspectors and Sub-Divisional Inspectors who were authorised by the Divisional Superintendent. Cleaning and maintaining the cycle was the responsibility of the officer concerned and was to be carried out in their own time. Each Wednesday cycles would be inspected by the Sub-Divisional Inspector or Station Officer (at the same time as pay parade), and the details were recorded in the station Occurrence Book. Inspectors and Station Sergeants were paid 8d per day whilst for Sergeants and Constables the daily rate was 6d.

Inspector Charles Taylor with his Station Sergeant in the yard at Kilburn

Supervision using a cycle was made easier although Inspectors still had their horses. Serious damage to a cycle which was caused in the normal course of daily police work was paid for from official funds, but if the damage was due to neglect then no compensation would be allowed.[1989] Kilburn was a sectional station to Harrow Road in 1903. Taylor stayed at Kilburn until about 1917.[1990]

By 1918 the Superintendent of X Division was James William Olive,[1991] and at that time there were just four stations at Kilburn, Harrow Road, Willesden Green and Harlesden. At Kilburn there were three Inspectors Charles Taylor, Arthur Macer and Thomas Brain.[1992] The address of Kilburn Police Station in 1924 was shown as 38 Salusbury Road.[1993]

The boundaries of Divisions north of the Thames were revised again in effect from 1st December 1933.[1994]

Kilburn Station was closed at 6am 1st March 1938, and all business was transferred to Harrow Road.[1995] The station was converted into a section house, and on the outbreak of the war in 1939 it became a Group Reserve Centre.

On the 6th November 1940 the station received a direct hit by three high incendiary bombs and it was completely demolished. Fourteen out of the eighteen people on duty were killed. Kilburn continued to be policed from Harrow Road which was the Divisional Headquarters of X Division until 31st March 1965.[1996]

Constable Don Light was on duty at Kilburn Station Police that night in 1940 when the station was destroyed. Describing in 1971 what happened that night he said,

'I was returning to the station having dealt with a fire. It was a terrible night, with bombs falling all over the place. The whole ground seemed to be alight. When we were about twenty yards from the station, which was the Group Reserve Centre, we heard a couple of 'crumps' and threw ourselves flat. I looked up to see what was like a million red-hot coals flying into the air. There were blokes from all over London who came to help, but it was no good. The bomb fell directly on the station. There was only one person alive when I went in and he died within minutes. There were 14 killed out of 18 on duty.' [1997]

Among those who died on that day were Police Constables 119605 John Brown, 124990 Clifford Davies, 094375 Charlie

Summers (Re-engaged pensioner) and 124285 Charles MacInnes, and War Reserve Constables (warrant no. 07717) George Borham, (warrant no. 23425) Leonard Bowes, (warrant no. 07737) Thomas Coe, (warrant no. 22374) Thomas Craven, (warrant no. 07753) Llewellyn Davies, (warrant no. 07787) Gerard Harvey, (warrant no. 07859) George Smith and (warrant no. 22586) George Wallis.[1998] In addition Mr Robert Vose, station cleaner, also died that night.[1999]

A new police station, a prefabricated building at 36, Salusbury Road, NW6, was used from 1st April 1965.[2000] Kilburn then became a sectional station of Harlesden (QH) Sub-Division in the newly-formed London Borough of Brent.

Kilburn Police Station 1980-2017

Kilburn Police Station (temporary) 1965-1967

The freehold of a house at 2 Harvist Road was obtained in 1967. The CID moved from the temporary station into this house in 1969. The Receiver purchased the premises of the fire station and the mortuary which were next to the Kilburn site in 1970 with a view to erecting a new police station on the now enlarged site at Harvist Road.[2001]

Kilburn Police Station 1967-1977

In May 1977 Kilburn Police moved to a building in Albert Road, NW6 and the pre-fabricated building was vacated and shut for police purposes. This was a quarter of a mile from the one at 2, Harvist Road. The Albert Road premises were to be used for about two years until a permanent police station was rebuilt at the site of Harvist Road junction with Salusbury Road.[2002]

On 20th March 1980 the new Kilburn Police Station was opened by the Home Secretary, William Whitelaw, before an invited audience of local dignitaries. The Commissioner, Sir David McNee, invited the Home Secretary to unveil a plaque commemorating the event.[2003] Another guest at the opening was retired Station Sergeant William Watson who was on duty in 1940 in Harrow Road when the bomb fell on Kilburn.

A number of his friends were amongst those persons killed on that night.

In 1980 the new station became the divisional headquarters and Harlesden Division was renamed Kilburn Division under the command of Chief Superintendent George Wise. The new station cost £1,000,000 and took three years to build.[2004]

In 2001 Kilburn was located at 38 Salusbury Road, with the station code (QK). The station was open 24 hours a day every day of the year, and was also a station for the detaining and charging of prisoners.

King Street Police Station

City of Westminster
22 King Street, Westminster (1847-1899)
A Division (1847-1899)

King Street no longer exists as a street, but once ran parallel to the modern Parliament Street at the south end of Whitehall. In 1847 a police station was built at 22 King Street, on the corner of Gardiner's Lane, with the police taking up possession at Christmas that year. It was a substantial station, costing £7,626 10s 10d, with 13 rooms, including a charge room, offices for a superintendent and two inspectors, a library, and living accommodation for two inspectors and four sergeants. A section house for 104 single officers fronted on to Gardiner's Lane. There were stables for 16 horses, with rooms for the

1979 J. Back Archives circa 1965.
1980 Metropolitan Police Orders dated 28th December 1889.
1981 J. Back Archives circa 1965.
1982 Metropolitan Police Orders dated 18th December 1891.
1983 Metropolitan Police Orders dated 24th February 1892.
1984 *Kilburn and Willesden Directory* 1890.
1985 *Kilburn and Willesden Directory* 1893.
1986 *Police Review and Parade Gossip*, 18th September 1893.
1987 *Kilburn and Willesden Directory* 1895.
1988 *Kelly's Directory* 1910-1917.
1989 *Police Review and Parade Gossip*, 9th September 1904.
1990 *Kelly's Directory* 1910-1917.
1991 James William Olive was the first officer to join as Constable and attain the rank of Deputy Commissioner. He served a total of nearly 53 years, and was probably one of the longest serving officers. He was one of the founder members of the Metropolitan Police Minstrels, which raised money to support the Police Orphanage.
1992 *Kilburn, Willesden and Cricklewood Directory* 1918-1919.
1993 Metropolitan List of Police Stations 1924.
1994 Metropolitan Police Orders dated 28th November 1933.
1995 Metropolitan Police Orders dated 23rd February 1938.
1996 J. Back Archives circa 1965.
1997 *The Job*, 29th January 1971.
1998 Metropolitan Police Orders dated 7th November 1940.
1999 Listed on the memorial plaque at Kilburn Police Station unveiled on 21st May 2010.
2000 Metropolitan Police Orders 26th March 1965.
2001 J. Back Archives circa 1965.
2002 NSY Press Release dated 18th May 1977.
2003 NSY Press Release dated 20th March 1980.
2004 *Kilburn Times*, 28th March 1980.

grooms, and two sheds for horse-drawn vans. By 1894, a scheme to widen Parliament Street meant that the police station had to be demolished, and the station was replaced by Cannon Row.

King Street Police Station 1847-1899

The officers pictured at the front of the station below are, from left to right, Sub-Divisional Inspector Cousins, Reserve Inspector Pashley, Chief Inspector Winkler (Marlborough Street Court), Chief Inspector Horsley (House of Commons), Superintendent Beard, Chief Inspector Rose, Chief Inspector Robinson, Inspector Hobden, Inspector German, Inspector Scantlebury, Inspector Stratton, Inspector Lowe and Local Inspector Baldock (in doorway).

Great Scotland Yard and King Street were the only two stations on A Division in 1849, but by 1886 Rochester Row and Hyde Park had been transferred to A Division, which then became known as Westminster rather than Whitehall. In the early days, the Superintendent of A Division took a pre-eminent position by coordinating reports from his counterparts of other divisions, and clerks from the division often helped out their colleagues in the headquarters at Great Scotland Yard. In due course, however, the Metropolitan Police headquarters became completely separated organisationally from A Division.

The policing of Whitehall and Parliament Square often takes place under the gaze of politicians and people of influence. State occasions and processions pass through the ground with world-famous pomp and pageantry. Incidents that might not be publicised had they occurred elsewhere in London sometimes become magnified because of the location where they occurred. Officers often had a good view of historic events.

In March 1863 Police Sergeant 57A James Swinden (warrant no. 20847),[2005] stationed at King Street Police Station, was selected to be in charge of eleven police constables and sent to Windsor. They were there to control the crowds outside the castle on the occasion of the wedding of HRH the Prince of Wales to Princess Alexandra of Demark.[2006] They were complimented on their work during the time they were there.[2007]

Sergeant Swinden had joined the Metropolitan Police in 1843 at the age of 21 years, having previously been a gardener in his home village of Speen in Berkshire. By 1851, James was a young constable living in the police 'barracks' at 18 Northumberland Street, Westminster. On the night of the national census on 30th March 1851, he was one of 39 single police constables living there in the section house.[2008] In May 1857 he married Fanny Rounswell, and by 1863 was promoted to Sergeant and posted to King Street Police Station. He lived with his wife at 10 Barton Street, Westminster, but unfortunately by 1867 he had died of bronchitis.[2009] He was one of 61 serving police officers who died that year. At that time London was not a very healthy place to live. In those days authority was given, within the Force, for a subscription to be held for his widow.[2010] His wife, Fanny, originally from Sudbury, went on to marry Police Sergeant John Measures from Huntingdon, who later became an inspector.

One officer who was familiar with policing in Westminster was Inspector Daniel Bradstock (warrant no. 20585). He was appointed in charge of the Division for a period when Superintendent Walker was on sick leave in January 1864. By that time the inspector had 21 years' service and had clearly risen to a position where he exercised great responsibility. On 2nd June 1868 he was tragically murdered on duty by an insane prisoner who had been detained at the police station.

Some police stations acquired pets as a form of mascot. In a cemetery for cats and dogs off Bayswater Road is the grave of Topper, a mongrel who appears to have inhabited King Street Police Station. According to the *Strand* magazine of 1893, the dog was 'of thoroughly dissipated habits' and eventually ate himself to death, perhaps because he was spoiled by the officers at the station.[2011] Topper is seen in the picture of King Street above, being held by a sergeant on the first floor.

King Street mascot Topper the dog

King Street Police Station was notified as vacated in Police Orders of 23rd March 1899, when officers in due course transferred to the new Cannon Row, perhaps with a period of being accommodated at Great Scotland Yard.

Kings Cross Road Police Station

The London Borough of Islington
Euston Road, Kings Cross (1829-1845)
76 Kings Cross Road WC1X 9QG (1845-1992)
G Division (1829-1965)
N Division (1965-1985/86)
Kings Cross Road Division ND (1985/86-1992)

There were two watch houses in the Kings Cross area. The first was at Rosoman Street, Sparfields and was set up in 1813. On the formation of the Metropolitan Police in 1829 the building was improved, with a large lofty room on the first floor and two strong cells, one for males and one for females.

The watch house closed in 1842 and they moved to premises in Bagnigge Wells Road (King's Cross Road). There was a second watch house at Clerk's Well, in Ray Street.[2012]

In 1829 when Sir Robert Peel introduced his new police force a 'new' police station was set up in an exhibition hall under the column erected to George IV that stood at the junction of the present Euston Road (formerly New Road), York Way (formerly Maiden Lane), and Grays Inn Road (formerly Grays Inn Lane). It was opposite the smallpox hospital, which is now the site of Kings Cross Railway Station, on the corner of Maiden Lane.[2013]

The picture below shows the old station at Kings Cross Police Station being demolished in 1845. The old station became a beer house, but the building became an obstruction to traffic because happy and drunken customers overflowed into the road outside and it was soon closed.[2014]

Kings Cross Police Station 1829-1845

In 1860 the Metropolitan Railway Company purchased the land, on which the Bagnigge Wells Road Police Station now stands, from the New River Company. The tunnels for London's first underground railway from Paddington to Farringdon were then excavated, and the station, built above them at ground level once the tunnelling had been completed, became known as the 'Clerkenwell' police station, later renamed as Kings Cross Road and was later renamed 'Kings Cross Road' Police Station.[2015] In 1864 the station complement consisted of two inspectors, fourteen sergeants and 169 constables. As this was the divisional headquarters there was also a Superintendent. There were a further two Inspectors located at the station, one attached to the reserve detachment and another who was responsible for the van service which transported prisoners to court and prison. There were three further sergeants and thirty constables attached to the reserve. The van service detachment consisted of two sergeants and five constables. There were six horses housed in the large stable, five for the van service and one for the Superintendent.[2016]

By 1868, the building had become somewhat overcrowded and a new police station was built on the same site. The address was shown as 76, Kings Cross Road. It was opened in January 1870,[2017] although they had used the new cells since the previous October.[2018]

Kings Cross Road Police Station 1870-1992

In 1888 twenty three Inspectors, forty six sergeants and 480 constables assisted Superintendent Charles Hunt, who was in charge of the Division.[2019] The station telegraphic code in 1893 was Gold Delta (GD).[2020]

Police officers are very often rewarded for their bravery, and in April 1894 a ceremony was held to honour Constable 47GR Joyce who was given a cheque for £5 from the Bow Street magistrate Sir John Bridge for saving the lives of two men in a serious fire in Northampton Street, Clerkenwell. The officer in charge of the station, Superintendent Hammond, attended the ceremony and thanked the Commissioner for the reward on the constable's behalf.[2021]

In July 1897 'a cowardly outrage' was committed upon a police officer in Clerkenwell when Constable 329G John Moore was patrolling Warner Street, and a gang of 'roughs' suddenly attacked him. The Constable drew his truncheon to defend himself, but was quickly overwhelmed and knocked to the ground. One of the gang grabbed the officer's truncheon from him, and hit him on the head until the Constable became insensible. He was taken to the Royal Free Hospital, where he was detained and treated for his serious injuries. Later that year a James Daley was sentenced to nine months'

2005 Metropolitan Police Divisional Records: A Division.
2006 Swinden, D.R. (1992) 'Police in London during the early 19th Century', University of London (unpublished).
2007 Letter sent by the Clerk to the Justices, Guildhall Windsor to Sir Richard Mayne, Commissioner, Metropolitan Police dated 16th March 1963. National Archives, MEPO 3/37.
2008 Census 1851.
2009 Register of Deaths of Serving Metropolitan Police Officers (1829-1889). National Archives MEPO4/2.
2010 Metropolitan Police Orders dated 26th March 1867.
2011 *Sunday Express*, 17th July 1994.
2012 John Back Archive (1975).
2013 Ibid.
2014 Bird, M. (1992) unpublished research. New Scotland Yard, London.
2015 John Back Archive (1975).
2016 Metropolitan Police Orders dated 11th January 1864.
2017 Metropolitan Police Orders dated 10th January 1870.
2018 Metropolitan Police Orders dated 27th October 1869.
2019 *Dickens's Dictionary of London* (1888) pp197-199.
2020 Metropolitan Police General Orders 1893.
2021 *Police Review*, April 1894.

imprisonment with hard labour, and John Saunders was fined 40 shillings, or in default, one month's imprisonment for the attack on the officer.[2022]

The police station is situated next door to Clerkenwell Magistrates Court where Charles Dickens, at one time was a Court reporter. One of his books, *Oliver Twist*, was written against the background of the 'Rookeries' (places of low morals and deprivation) in the vicinity of the Court.[2023]

In 1913 the station was enlarged to accommodate extra staff. The building was re-built to include two sets of married quarters and accommodation for 53 unmarried men.[2024]

Plans were prepared in 1939 to erect a new police station on the existing site but with the outbreak of the Second World War the plans were abandoned. Land at the rear of the station, known as Percy Yard, was used during those war years for growing vegetables. The freehold was purchased in 1955, for £2,500, to provide extra car parking space.[2025]

In 1960 Kings Cross was EK, or Echo Kilo, as it was a station on E or Holborn Division under the supervision of Superintendent Wharton.[2026]

It remained an operational police station until 1992 when a new police station was opened at Tolpuddle Street, Islington. The old police station is still used for non-operational police purposes. It is also a Grade II listed building.

Kingsbury Police Station

The London Borough of Brent
5 The Mall, Kingsbury (1973-1977) (temporary building)
5 The Mall Kingsbury (1977-2012)
19 Kingsbury Trading Estate, Barningham Way, Kingsbury

A temporary police office was established on this site during the petrol strike in the 1970s. The official date of the opening of the building was 23rd July 1973 and it took the code 'QY'. The address was 5, The Mall, Kingsbury, and it was situated by the side of the cadet training centre.

Kingsbury Police Station 1973-1977

The permanent police station was built, and became fully operational and opened in 1977. Superintendent Ken Wright said at the time:

'There has been a long felt need to provide the people of Kingsbury with a better service. It's a long way to Wembley and this arrangement is obviously more convenient.' [2027]

By 2000 the Metropolitan Police had left the cadet training centre and the local authority planning committee agreed to a change of use for the site, and for the 106 separate rooms to be turned into a hostel for the homeless. It had also become prime land for further building. In December 2009 the local authority received a further application to demolish the existing buildings. This was approved and in 2012 the area of 1-3 The Mall was a large building site.[2028]

Kingsbury Police Station 1973-2012

Meanwhile the small area, at the edge of the building site on which the Kingsbury Police Station was sited remained untouched and in 2010 it was closed to the public and the site disposed of.[2029]

In 2012 a police office was built in Kingsbury which housed the Safer Neighbourhoods team located at Unit 19, Kingsbury Trading Estate, Barningham Way, Kingsbury.[2030]

Kingston Police Station

London Road, Kingston (1840-1968)
5-7 High Street Kingston (1968-1993)
V Division (1840-1993)
London Borough of Kingston BCU (1993-2018/19)
SW BCU (together with Merton, Richmond and Wandsworth) (2018/19 to Present)

In 1777 the Corporation of Kingston was granted permission to raise money to build watch houses and to recruit 14 constables[2031] who also lit the street lamps. In 1835 the Corporation applied for the Metropolitan Police boundary to extend to Kingston, but at this stage it was declined.

From 13th January 1840, the MPD was extended out to Kingston parish and beyond. The new Kingston Sub-Division, under an inspector, comprised three sergeants and 16 constables who were responsible for the town, together with the hamlet of Hook and Chessington parish. Two constables were deployed in Long Ditton, Thames Ditton and West Molesey, while a solitary constable patrolled East or Upper Molesey parish and another in the hamlet of Claygate.[2032]

When the Metropolitan Police Act extended the boundaries to Kingston, initially the first police inspector in Kingston occupied an office located in the town hall until new premises were found elsewhere. A building was rented in London Road, Kingston in 1840, belonging to Mr William Walker at £50 per year for a period of 21 years[2033] as a station on V or Wandsworth Division.

Of the three sergeants posted with the inspector, two were mounted patrols and lodged in the section house.[2034] The watch house in Kingston was returned to the parish authorities on 7th April 1840 as it was no longer required.

Inspector Richard Dowsett had been appointed as inspector in 1814 for the horse patrol, and was incorporated into the division as the inspector in charge of Kingston in 1844. He was an experienced officer, and remained in charge until retirement in 1850.[2035] Pension records show that Dowsett was 60 years old, having completed 35 years' service when he retired, and was classified as being 'worn out'. His annual pension was £95 per year (when a constable's typical pension was £27 per year).[2036]

On 6th July 1840, at the Central Criminal Court, Thomas John Simms was tried for simple larceny at the Bird in Hand public house at Hampton Wick. The crime involved stealing three spoons value 12 shillings, silver sugar tongs value 3 shillings, a brooch valued at three shillings and a one shilling coin, the property of James Atkins. Sergeant 23V William George Worfall was on duty as station officer at Kingston when the prisoner was brought in and property handed over. Simms was found guilty and sentenced to seven years' transportation.[2037]

Thomas Bicknell, the Divisional Superintendent, was stationed at Waterside, Wandsworth and had been in charge of the division since 1840. He remained there until 1855, when he retired, suffering with vertigo, on pension of £166 pa with 24 years' service. In 1851 Septimus Fenn (who had been a constable at Deptford in 1841) replaced Dowsett (the former horse patrol inspector) as the inspector in charge of the station, which was shown as being located in Norbiton Street. Fenn remained there until 1855, when he was promoted to Divisional Superintendent replacing Bicknell. In turn, his place was taken by Inspector James Rapsey in the same year, who remained the officer in charge until 1861.[2038] Whilst doing duty at Kingston, the unfortunate Rapsey, now aged 41 years, received a serious chest injury whilst on duty and was quickly pensioned off.[2039] After retirement he moved to Brixton, and was cared for by his wife and family but sadly died of his injuries shortly afterwards. Whilst there would have been remuneration for Mrs Rapsey, this was by no means a forgone conclusion since she needed to apply to the Commissioner for an annual award, which needed to be sanctioned by the Home Department. This was an annual figure, usually about £40. By 1871 Eliza Rapsey had moved away from Brixton and was residing with her 24-year-old daughter in Hackney, without her other five children.[2040]

In 1862 a report was sent to Commissioner Sir Richard Mayne concerning the condition of the police station at Kingston, which had been badly damaged by fire, recommending an urgent need for new premises. Land in London Street belonging to Mr Edward Ward of Claremont Square, Pentonville was leased from 1863 for 100 years, at an annual rental of £30. This land was suitable[2041] for a purpose-built police station, and the Metropolitan Police surveyor, Charles Reeves, set about arranging the plans and building works, and their organisation.

During the 1860s there was an augmentation of personnel generally, and this was reflected with additional staff for Kingston, who increased to one inspector, five sergeants and 31 constables.[2042]

In 1861 Inspector Joseph Armstrong replaced pensioned Inspector Rapsey as the inspector in charge of Kingston. Originally from Brighton, Armstrong was ably assisted by Sergeant John Ayre from Devon. Armstrong remained there until 1870 when he retired to Kingston on pension. He died in 1902, aged 95.[2043] Ayre resided with his wife in Albert Road, just a few doors away from his Inspector, who lived at number 159.[2044] Clearly Inspector Armstrong thought a lot of Sergeant Ayre, who, on his recommendation, was promoted to inspector in 1863, allowing Ayre to remain on V Division until 1871, when he himself retired to live in Sunbury.[2045]

The photograph right was taken in Kingston in 1868, and shows a local police officer who is on duty. It was common in those days to wear whiskers – but this caused a problem with identifying the police officer from his collar number in case of complaint by a member of the public. This was rectified when the collar number was also shown in the centre of the helmet plate as well as on each side of the officer's collar.

An early Kingston Police officer taken in 1868

The inspector's task was not an easy one, and at Kingston he did not undertake any station duty, this being was left to the station sergeants. Instead he had to patrol on horseback, visiting the Kingston, Ditton, Epsom, Hampton and Sunbury areas. There were four sergeants at the station who assisted him; one sergeant with one acting sergeant performed day duty with nine constables who covered the foot beats in the town area. There was also one sergeant and one acting sergeant, together with twenty constables, who covered the night beats.

The inspector had to visit each police station in the area and sign the occurrence book to ensure that all was running well. Additionally, two sergeants at Kingston were required to also patrol both nine and twelve-hour tours of duty alternately

2022 *Police Review*, July 1897.
2023 John Back Archive (1975).
2024 Metropolitan Police Surveyor's Records, and Metropolitan Police Orders dated 28th April 1913.
2025 John Back Archive (1975).
2026 *Police and Constabulary Almanac* 1960.
2027 New Scotland Yard press release dated 5th August 1977.
2028 London Borough of Brent, Committee Report. Planning, Agenda Item 5, 16th March 2010.
2029 Freedom of Information request: MPS assets disposed of since 2010 (2019).
2030 content.met.police.uk/Team/Brent/Kenton accessed 3rd July 2012.
2031 *The Job*, 13th August 1971.
2032 Metropolitan Police Correspondence.
2033 MEPO 5/3 (10/44).
2034 MEPO 2/76.
2035 *Kelly's Directory* 1851.
2036 Pension Records 1840-1858.
2037 Old Bailey Proceedings Online, July 1840, trial of Thomas John Simms (t18400706-1881).
2038 *Kelly's Directories* 1855-1860.
2039 The Metropolitan Police Roll of Honour at www.policememorial.org.uk, accessed 12th March 2002.
2040 Census 1861 and 1871.
2041 MEPO 5/51.
2042 Metropolitan Police Orders dated 11th January 1864.
2043 *Police Review and Parade Gossip*, 20th June 1902.
2044 Census 1861.
2045 Census 1871.

Kingston Police Station 1864-1968

every night from 9.00pm. Instructions were given that the sergeants should 'take care of their horse', as it could be an arduous and difficult duty.[2046] In all, there were five horses stabled at the station, and two constables per shift would cover the main highways on horseback in and out of Kingston. One horse each belonged to the inspector and the two sergeants. In addition to other duties, one constable was designated the 'groom', and it was his job to ensure the horses were properly fed and looked after. It was important that each of the constables and sergeants employed on mounted patrol were able to be drilled in proper horsemanship. One of the sergeants at Kingston in 1870 was George Robbins, who was practising mounted drill on the drill ground in accordance with regulations. Whilst maintaining his horse he was killed instantly when he was kicked in the chest.[2047]

The station area boundary commenced at

'Kingston Vale immediately West of the 'Robin Hood Public House' by right of Kingston Hill to Warren road, thence in a straight line to the bridge over the London and South Western Railway (Kingston Branch) by Dickerage Lane, and right of same to Kingston Head, thence in a straight line to the London and South Western Main Line, and then by centre of Hoggsmill Stream to Uwell Road [sic], 'by centre of same to Park Avenue by right to London road, by right to High Street, south west, by right of same to Mongers Lane, by right of same to Reigate Road, to Fir Tree Road, by right of same to Tattenham Corner, then by Metropolitan Police District Boundary to Headley Road and Epsom Common to Ashstead Woods, by northeast side of same to Telegraph Hill to Star Lane, continuing by Metropolitan Police District Boundary to River Thames at West Molesey, by centre of same to Half Mile Tree at Lower Ham Road, thence following the boundary of the Parish of Ham eastward to starting point (taking the centre of Molesey and Kingston Bridges.' [2048]

A magnificent new and substantial station designed by Charles Reeves, the Metropolitan Police Surveyor, was brought into service in London Road, Kingston on land rented from Edward Ward in June 1864. It included section house accommodation for single officers,[2049] and also one set of married quarters[2050] for the inspector in charge. However, when this station came to the end of its serviceable life, it will be seen there were great hurdles to overcome and a sequence of unfortunate events which led to delays in securing a suitable new police station site in Kingston.

Rear Yard aspect of Kingston Police station

Whilst stationed at Kingston in 1881 constable Fred Atkins (warrant no. 61462) disturbed a burglar in a house on Kingston Hill. These were dangerous times for a constable on his own, as Atkins found out because the burglar was armed and he fired at the officer a number of times trying to escape. The officer was hit three times and died the following day; the burglar made good his escape.[2051]

In 1881 a review of all Metropolitan Police accommodation for the Secretary of State showed that Kingston was a well-built tenement, with the inspector and his family occupying two quarters. The station cell space was inadequate, since they could hold few prisoners when on Derby Day they could be expected to hold at least 20 prisoners. There were 13 single constables who occupied the section house, but there were no locks on the door between the inspector's rooms and the section house. Recommendations in the 1881 report included separating both the married and single quarters, building in a toilet on the upper floor, placing better lighting to the cells area, and putting in buzzers into each cell.[2052]

Kingston on Thames Police Station was a main station, and Sub-Divisional Inspector Alfred Rushbridge (warrant no. 49827) was in charge in 1891. He was supported by four inspectors, five sergeants and 60 constables.[2053] Rushbridge did not reside at the station, but lived at May Cottage on Avenue Road, Kingston. He remained in charge until 1894, when he retired having joined the force in 1868, a total 26 years' service.[2054] His replacement, Inspector Henry Trott (warrant no. 63063), had joined V Division in 1893, but just a year later he was promoted to Sub-Divisional Inspector in charge of Kingston Sub-Division.[2055]

The rear entrance to the station taken in 1906

Kingston Sub-Division was responsible for hosting the 14th Annual Garden Party and Sports Day in 1895, held in Woodbines Park, with funds going to the Metropolitan Police and City Orphanage at Twickenham. This event was attended by the divisional senior officers, including Superintendent David Saines, whose responsibility was to give out the prizes to the winners at the end, and Chief Inspector Pryke, who was a judge seeing to fair play. This was a heavy responsibility, which fell to Inspector Trott who arranged for the club secretary, Sergeant Collins, to help. The garden party was a well-attended event, with the police officers, their wives and children taking the day off to be present. On this Monday it rained, but this did not stop the enjoyment of the participants and the races going ahead. In the Tug-of-War, the Kingston and Surbiton Fire Brigade beat the Kingston team. There was a balloon race during the day, the divisional police band was in attendance, and after dark, once dancing had finished, there was a firework display.[2056]

Sub-Divisional Inspector Trott retired in 1897 after completing 25 years' service,[2057] and his place was taken by Sub-Divisional Inspector Edward West (warrant no. 63737), who remained until 1902, when he was promoted to Chief Inspector and transferred to K or Bow Division, north of the River Thames in the East End. West eventually became a respected superintendent and took charge of W Division.[2058] Residing with West were his wife Emma and their five children. The section house also had eight single constables in residence in 1901.

December 1890 was recorded as the coldest in 150 years, and in 1894 the centre of Kingston was flooded in November, followed by a very severe winter. The wet weather made drying the police boots and shoes a problem, since those not living at the station (where there was a drying room) often did not have facilities for keeping their footwear dry. In such extreme inclement weather, supervising sergeants would give orders for the patrolling police officers to remain in the station, and they would only go out in an emergency.

One of the acute problems police face in their daily work, was (and still is) the risk of injury which they receive in the execution of their duty. In October 1895 Station Sergeant William Mace (warrant no. 59515) at Kingston was dealing with a prisoner in the charge room when he was violently assaulted by him. Once the prisoner was restrained and placed in a cell Mace was seen by the divisional surgeon, who placed him on the sick list. His injuries were so severe that the police medical officer decided that Mace could not carry on as a police officer, and retired him after 22 years' police service. This was very disappointing for Mace as it was likely he could have been further promoted, but such was the esteem in which the local townsfolk held the officer a collection was made on his behalf. A quantity of gold and silver coins were presented to him, together with an engraved pocket watch. There was a presentation at the station for Mace, who heard tributes from his colleagues and from Mr Greenwood, who represented the Kingston Committee.[2059]

2046 Metropolitan Police Orders dated 11th January 1864.
2047 The Metropolitan Police Roll of Honour at www.policememorial.org.uk accessed 12th March 2002.
2048 *The Police and Constabulary List* 1871.
2049 Metropolitan Police Orders dated 21st September 1864.
2050 Metropolitan Police Surveyor's Records 1924.
2051 The Metropolitan Police Roll of Honour at www.policememorial.org.uk accessed 12th March 2002.
2052 Report on Condition of Stations 1881.
2053 *Kelly's Directory* 1891.
2054 *Kelly's Directory* 1894 p2203.
2055 Ibid, and *Kelly's Directory* 1895.
2056 *Police Review and Parade Gossip*, 16th August 1895.
2057 MEPO 3/340.
2058 MEPO 4/346.
2059 *Police Review and Parade Gossip*, 25th October 1895.

Retirement through injury at Kingston c1908

Rear aspect of Kingston Police Station in 1908

The picture above shows a retirement on V Division around 1908 of an officer invalided out of the service, as denoted by the crutches, with the pensioned officer and his wife to the right of the clock. To the left of the clock is the mayor, divisional Superintendent Robinson and Chief Inspector James Smith.[2060]

There were many police officers who were recruited from the army before they joined. This often meant that they remained part of the military reserve. Henry Edwin Flack joined V or Wandsworth Division in August 1896 as Constable 155V, warrant no. 81488, where he remained for three years until he applied to return to the military and join the Boer War campaign in South Africa. He left his Irish wife Martha and ten-year-old son and returned to the colours. Fortunately he survived this harsh war. On his return in 1902 he became constable 406V, based at Kingston Police Station. He saw his entire service on V Division. Flack lived at 126 Clifton Road, Kingston and retired in August 1921 (his army service counting towards his police service) after 25 years. Aged 47, he was entitled to an annual pension of £153 13s 5d.

One of the principle policing problems in Kingston was the Cattle Fair held once a year, in November. There was also a weekly fair held on Wednesdays, Thursdays and Saturdays.[2061]

Motor Car accident on Kingston Hill in 1903

The picture above shows a very early car accident on Kingston Hill in 1903. These were still a rare thing, but their speed often caused accidents and Kingston Hill posed its difficulties, especially with stopping or braking. Because of the rarity of such an event the cameras were soon on scene, and people, including the police constable, posed for the picture.

The photograph on the previous page shows the rear aspect of the station including a high protective wall and the rear entrance door through which all police officers with a key would be able to pass through. On the top floor of the main building one can see where the station inspector and his family lived. Children could often be seen playing in the station yard.

A rather strange case arose at Kingston in 1904, when a Metropolitan Police sergeant residing at the police station with his family applied to the Kingston Board of Guardians for assistance in paying nearly 16 shillings a week for the detention of his wife, who was an invalid and in the County Asylum at Brookwood. The sergeant's take home pay was a mere £2 per week, and from this he had to employ a housekeeper to look after the children. During a hearing where the sergeant was questioned regarding every detail of his expenditure down to the last penny, the Board made a recommendation that the sergeant should pay eight shillings per week and they would pay the remainder.

The case of rent allowance was also being considered in Parliament at the time especially poignant when the wages were so low.[2062]

In the picture on the right is Sergeant 5VR Brooks, stationed at Kingston, smartly-dressed in his double-breasted greatcoat with whistle chain hanging from the second button down, and also showing his cape which is draped over the fence behind.

Another retirement occurred in 1904 when a very popular officer, Inspector Challingsworth of Kingston Police Station, completed his service. Challingsworth, who was the court inspector, was received by the mayor who on behalf of the Justices presented him with a gold Albert fob watch and medallion. There were speeches and also the presentation of a certificate of appreciation for services given to them during his service on the sub-division.[2063] A short time later another presentation took place, this time by Mr Sticklands of the Esher bus conductors and drivers, who expressed their gratitude and gave him an ebony walking stick in appreciation of his 25 years' police service.[2064]

Sergeant 5 VR Brooks stationed at Kingston

Inspector William Bryce took charge of the sub-division in West's place until 1910, when his place was taken by Sub-Divisional Inspector David Thompson.[2065] David Thompson, who had been a respected and hard-working inspector on W or Clapham Division. Thompson was not in charge of Kingston for long. He had been born in Northumberland, and his wife Alice was from Norfolk; their three sons and four daughters resided in the cramped and unsanitary police station accommodation at Kingston living above the police station itself. Their children ranged between 14 years and one year old.[2066]

By 1912 the station was proving to be inadequate for police purposes, being too small for current use. Even the divisional surgeon recorded that the sanitary conditions were appalling. The Commissioner sent a request to the Receiver to search for a new plot of land, and a site was found in Richmond Road. Purchased in June 1914, the land was not developed, probably because of the commencement of World War One. Yet when war finished, and the subsequent post-war depression, even this land was considered too small to be of use. In August 1914 the boundaries of Wandsworth, Battersea, Wimbledon and Kingston Sub-Divisions were redrawn. This re-organisation created the Earlsfield Sub-Division.[2067]

In 1913 Thompson's position as Sub-Divisional Inspector was taken by Race Thomas Hooper (warrant no. 78043). Unlike in Victorian times, where he might have been assisted by sergeants, these positions were taken by junior inspectors, these being Inspectors Henry Winter and William Grimmett. They would deal with the day-to-day workings of the station and its ground, rather than the whole sub-division of Kingston, Ditton, Epsom, Surbiton and East Molesey. Also in support were two station sergeants, nine section sergeants and 76 constables. There was also one detective sergeant and two detective constables attached to the station.[2068] Hooper remained in charge until 1921, when he retired on pension.[2069] The sub-divisional inspectors at Kingston, Richmond and Wimbledon were the only SDIs on V Division who were authorised as mounted officers, and each was allocated a horse for that purpose.[2070]

During 1915 Constable 2VR Welton retired from Kingston after 25 years' service. Welton had made his name stopping speeding motorists, and in ten years had dealt with 2,000 cases which had raised £2,000 in fines imposed. Some of his most notable 'captures' were Prince Henry of Battenburg, the Duke of Westminster, Earl Lonsdale, Viscount Curzon, and Winston Churchill MP.[2071]

In the same year Sergeant Kempster and Constable Freeman of Kingston were investigating a theft in the town centre by two guardsmen. They scoured the area and saw both men cross Home Park. On seeing the two suspects, who had now crossed the river, they gave chase on their pedal cycles. A search took place and they were both found hiding in the undergrowth and were arrested.[2072]

Another serious incident occurred later in 1915 when Constable Frederick Daniel Kennett, who was on his patrol in Kingston, stopped two men he wished to speak to. Soon both attempted to escape, and in the process seriously assaulted the officer. Kennett hung on to one of his assailants, who was continually striking him, whilst the other made off. Miss Gladys Avis answered the officer's call for assistance and, not being able to help in any other way, pulled out his whistle and blew it as hard as she could. This attracted a number of people, including other police officers at the police station. A soldier came over together with a retired naval officer and helped the constable, who lapsed into unconsciousness as they held the prisoner before the police arrived. Kennett was placed on the sick list after seeing the Divisional surgeon, who sent him home. At Kingston Magistrates' Court Kennett and all the people who came to the officer's aid where thanked for their courage and helpfulness.[2073]

On 2nd February 1929 V Division was chosen for an experiment using new police boxes on the Richmond Sub-Division (which also included Barnes and Kew), soon to be a familiar sight all over London until the 1960s. A later generation knew them only as Dr Who's TARDIS. 'Time travel' was soon extended to the rest of V Division in October 1930 (Wimbledon), March 1931 (Kingston) and in April 1931 (Wandsworth).[2074]

After WWII a review was undertaken and it was decided that V Division would be increased in size with the transfer of Esher Sub-Division, which included stations at Cobham, and Oxshott from the Surrey Constabulary, on 1st April 1947. Oxshott was not used operationally by the Metropolitan Police, however.[2075]

An opportunity arose to exchange the purchased land with another available site called 'Meadowland' on Berrylands Road, Surbiton on which a section house could be built, but this did not happen as after World War II it was developed as married quarters instead.[2076] Attempts were made to purchase another site on which a station could be built in St. James Road, behind the Guildhall, however the onset of World War Two prevented completion of the sale.[2077] On 23rd September 1940 the station suffered a near miss when a stack of bombs fell nearby, with one high-incendiary bomb demolishing some shops on the same side of the road.[2078]

Once the war had finished fresh attempts were made to restart the purchase of the Fairfield West site, but town planning proposals made it unacceptable for the corporation. Instead, co-operation with the corporation secured a site in Thames Street for the police,[2079] and the freehold was purchased July 1955.[2080] As the development of the Thames Street site was nearing its final stages the corporation again intervened, and a revised town plan meant the new proposals for the station became unacceptable. An exchange of lands were finally agreed in 1964 and freehold purchased in 1965, enabling a new station to be built.

At Kingston Superintendent T.E. Thomas and Chief Inspector F.L. Sharp were in charge of the sub-division in 1965.[2081]

The Local Government Act 1963 (introduced in 1965) caused the Metropolitan police to revise its divisional boundaries in line with those of the new local authorities. The intention was that Kingston be designated as the Divisional Headquarters, however during the planning, development and building stage,

2060 *Kelly's Directory* 1908.
2061 *Kelly's Directory* 1913.
2062 *Police Review and Parade Gossip*, 12th August 1904 p386.
2063 *Police Review and Parade Gossip*, 1st July 1904 p323.
2064 *Police Review and Parade Gossip*, 8th July 1904 p335.
2065 Census 1911.
2066 Ibid.
2067 Metropolitan Police Orders dated 27th August 1914.
2068 *Kelly's Directory* 1913.
2069 MEPO 4/346.
2070 Metropolitan Police Orders dated 27th September 1919.
2071 *The Police Chronicle*, 30th April 1915.
2072 *The Police Chronicle*, 3rd September 1915.
2073 *The Police Chronicle*, 10th September 1915.
2074 Brown, B. 'When Victor Bowed Out', *Police Review*, 29th October 1985.
2075 Ibid.
2076 Back, J. (1975) Kingston Police Station.
2077 Ibid.
2078 Kingston Library resources (www.rbksch.org/museum) accessed 9th February 2012.
2079 LB 660/67/1.
2080 LB660/-/0 Part 2.
2081 Metropolitan Police Stations 1965.

which would take a further three years, Putney Police Station became the temporary divisional HQ, until Wimbledon became available.[2082]

The divisional staff included senior officers moved between these two stations until the new station became occupied in April 1968, with Chief Superintendent Peter Jackson was in charge and Chief Inspector Bill Stevens as his deputy in 1968. Crime problems for the division included cycle thefts, underage drinking, drug offences which the Chief Inspector stated 'comes from the hippies which exist in encampments along the Thames'. There was a new Chief Inspector's suite, a new modern collator's office and a juvenile bureau at the station which also boasted a social club, volunteer cadet scheme and sea cadets squad located on the training ship HMS *Trafalgar* moored on the Thames.

The new station, designed by J. Innes Elliott in association with Kingston Architects Brewer, Smith and Brewer, was built on the banks of the Hogsmill at Clatern Bridge. It was an architectural challenge, being built adjoining the Guildhall and the Coronation stone on really poor wet land that needed 50ft deep piles from the basement in order to support the structure. The Hogsmill river was often liable to flooding, and precautions had to be taken to ensure that flooding in the basement was kept to a minimum. The building, fronted in Portland stone, cost £254,503 to build.[2083]

Kingston Police Station 1968 to present

Kingston Police Station (VD) was now located at 5-7 High Street, Kingston, and the existing station at 22 London Road (VK) was closed, being quickly rented out as offices to a local company.[2084] In 1986 the old police station, which had been listed as of special architectural interest, was put up for sale by the police and purchased by Garfunkels restaurant.[2085]

In 1980 Kingston and Esher divisions were amalgamated, making one of the largest divisions in the Metropolitan Police District. The new division incorporated New Malden, Esher, Cobham, Surbiton and East Molesey into Kingston Sub-Division on V Division.[2086]

In 2000 the only station open 24 hours a day on Kingston Borough[2087] was Kingston itself, which was also the centre for detaining, processing and charging prisoners for court.

In 2019 the station was retained for police purposes as the headquarters station for the London Borough of Kingston.[2088]

Knights Hill or Lower Norwood Police Station

The London Borough of Lambeth
59 Knights Hill, Lower Norwood (1886-1930)
P Division (1886-1930)

In September 1870 the Police leased property in Knights Hill, Lower Norwood, until March 1879 from a Mrs Mary Buck for the sum of £1,000. After adaptation and repair, occupation was taken up in March 1872. It became a Police Station on P Division. The building was described in a report of 1881 as 'a cottage in a large garden, pleasantly situated. Two cells have been added.'[2089] Knights Hill Police Station was often referred to as Lower Norwood.

In 1886 the Receiver purchased a small cottage, built in 1854, at 59 Knights Hill, between Ernest Avenue and Knights Hill Square, and when renovated three cells were included in the building. The site on which the building stood was fairly large, with a frontage of approximately 50 feet and a depth of 120 feet.[2090] In June that year the police station became operational, and in 1891 Inspector Scantlebury was in charge.[2091]

It was part of Norwood Sub-Division. The station was very small and cramped; up until 1929 the one CID Officer at the station had to use one of the cells as an office.

The staff included one station sergeant, seven sergeants, 21 constables and one CID officer, and at the closure of the station the work and all staff were transferred to Gipsy Hill Police Station.

In the preceding years the station had not been particularly busy. In 1927 there had been only eighteen arrests; in 1928 thirty-two, and in 1929 nineteen. However, most of their work came as a result of the close proximity of a tram station and omnibus depot. It became very convenient for their staff to hand in items of lost property to the police station. In 1929 some 4,000 items of lost property were handed in.[2092]

Knights Hill Station closed in June 1930 after exactly 44 years of service.[2093]

With its closure, one of the new Police telephone boxes was placed on the forecourt of the old station. This provided a free direct line to Gipsy Hill Police Station, where a garage had been built to house its first motor car – a Jowett – to be used when required for answering calls from Knights Hill and the wider district.[2094]

The site of the old police station was at one time considered as a possibility for a detached section house for single Police officers.[2095]

To mark the closure of Knights Hill Police Station, the *Crystal Palace District Advertiser* printed the following words:

'West Norwood can pride itself on its good behaviour, surely, when a police station can be closed down.'[2097]

In 1938 the property came under the hammer at the London Auction Mart, and was purchased for £1,000 by 70-year-old Mr Walter Booth, who had lived in Norwood as a boy some 50 years previously when it was just a village. He bought the property as an investment, and although he was not sure what he was going to do with the old police station he thought he would turn the cells into a garage.[2098]

Knights Hill Police Station 1886-1930

Sadly, the old building was destroyed by a V1 flying bomb in 1941, and there are now modern commercial buildings on the site of the old police station.

Knockholt Police Station (PT)

Main Road, Knockholt (1895-1947)

The Bungalow, Chevening Lane (1947 to Present)

Kent County Constabulary (1895-1947)

P Division (1947-1969)

Transferred to Kent County Constabulary (1st April 1969)

In the eighteenth century, Knockholt village was on the main stagecoach road from London to Rye, with its fair share of problems from highwaymen, but in 1836 a new road between Pratts Bottom and Dunton Green by-passed the hills around Knockholt and removed through traffic from the village. Even the modern railway line, which still contains a small station called Knockholt, followed this trend by coming no closer than two miles to the village. Still within the M25 motorway, its relative quietness and position on the borders between Greater London and Kent has contributed to changes in jurisdiction for the village over the years.

In 1857 the newly-formed Kent County Constabulary policed the village as part of its Sevenoaks division. On 27th May 1895 the constabulary opened a new police station in Knockholt, from where responsibility was also taken for Chelsfield and Cudham. Sergeant Alfred Thompson was in charge, with the inappropriately named Constable A. Fright. Within months, bicycles had been introduced for patrolling rural beats.

Knockholt Police Station c1895-1947

In 1929 the parishes of Knockholt, Cudham and Chelsfield passed from Bromley Rural District to Orpington Council, but remained, for policing purposes, part of Kent County Constabulary's jurisdiction. World War II saw much activity, especially from the RAF at nearby Biggin Hill, and plans to amalgamate Knockholt and other parts of Orpington Rural District into the Metropolitan Police District were delayed by the war. Knockholt received more than its fair share of bombs, crashed aircraft and security scares during WWII, with the Battle of Britain being played out in the sky overhead. Security was such that on one occasion a PC Kitney was on his cycle patrol at night near the RAF Station at Biggin Hill when even he was accidentally arrested on suspicion of being a German spy!

The local population valued the service given by their Police, and presented the occupants of The Bungalow, then the police station in Chevening Lane, with a brass coalscuttle engraved 'Presented to Knockholt Police. For Vigilance'.

Eventually Knockholt changed police forces and became part of the Metropolitan Police District on 1st April 1947. Transfer of policing responsibility was one thing; local authority jurisdiction was much more emotive. When the London Borough of Bromley was created on 1st April 1965, Knockholt would remain under the eye of the Metropolitan Police, but the inhabitants had no wish to become part of a London borough. 72% of the inhabitants signed a petition against becoming part of the London Borough of Bromley, and Knockholt was transferred, along with its policing, back to Kent on 1st April 1969.

Lavender Hill Police Station

London Borough of Wandsworth

176 Lavender Hill (1896 to Present)

V Division (1896-1923)

W Division (1923-1993)

Borough of Wandsworth OCU (1993 to 2018/19)

SW BCU with Richmond, Kingston and Merton

(2018/19 to Present)

It was not until 1892 that there was a particular need for a police station to be built in the area around Lavender Hill. The station that covered the area was located near the parish boundary and was considered too far away. The size of the local population had greatly increased, and news had reached the Commissioner that a very influential petition was being prepared.

2082 Metropolitan Police Orders dated 6th August 1964.
2083 'The June Sampson Feature', *Surrey Comet*, March 1998.
2084 Metropolitan Police Orders dated 29th March 1968.
2085 'The June Sampson Feature', *Surrey Comet*, March 1998.
2086 Metropolitan Police Orders dated 4th February 1980.
2087 Metropolitan Police Authority (2000) Police Station opening hours Committee; MPA Reports 9th November.
2088 Freedom of Information request: MPS assets (2019).
2089 Report on the Condition of Police Stations 1881.
2090 MEPO 2/2584.
2091 *Kelly's Sydenham, Norwood and Streatham Directory* 1891.
2092 PC Roger Hickman, *The Beat*, p17.
2093 Ibid.
2094 Ibid.
2095 MEPO 2/2584.
2096 *Crystal Palace District Advertiser*, 30th June 1930.
2097 *News Chronicle*, 11th April 1938.
2098 LB690/1/1.

A new Police Magistrate's Court had been built in the area (South Western Police Court, at 176a Lavender Hill), and with this in mind a site next door was found and soon purchased for £3,000. It was located at the corner of Latchmere Lane and Lavender Hill.[2099]

The new station was designed by John Butler, the Metropolitan Police Surveyor, and was ready for occupation in March 1896. As was usual, the station was built with accommodation in mind for married and single officers. The design allowed for a married inspector and his family in one set of rooms, and also a Section House for 22 single officers.[2100]

Lavender Hill Police Station 1896-1962

The station was put under the supervision of Sub-Divisional Inspector John Concannon, who was transferred from Battersea.[2101] Concannon did not stay long at Lavender Hill, possibly of his own choice through seeking another posting elsewhere. By 1898 he was transferred to N or Islington Division, north of the River Thames.[2102]

Changes in divisional and sub-divisional boundaries during re-organisations often meant that supervision would also change, occasionally quite frequently. For example, in 1924 the address was published as 176 Lavender Hill, SW11, and shown on L Division. Re-organisation of 4 District boundaries in 1931 saw the area transferred to W or Clapham Division.

The rear yard view showing the boundary wall, coal store and the back gates in 1907

Lavender Hill Station was renovated in 1936.

Between 1957 and 1960 Lavender Hill was a station on W or Tooting Division, under the charge of Superintendent A.H. Jones.[2103] It was a sub-divisional station, where prisoners were housed and charges were taken and dealt with.[2104]

Within a few years the old station was no longer suitable for its purpose, and a temporary station was brought into service at Theatre Street at the junction with Lavender Hill. Before being demolished in February 1962[2105] the station had been gutted of all its equipment, which was removed to the temporary station.

Lavender Hill Police Station 1963 to present

Battersea Police Station became the sub-divisional station following the closure, however in December 1963 the new Lavender Hill Station was opened for operational purposes[2106] and the temporary station was closed. Its status was as sectional station to Battersea (WA).[2107]

In 2001 Lavender Hill was a station on Wandsworth Operational Command Unit (OCU), with charging facilities and where prisoners were taken and dealt with under the Police and Criminal Evidence Act 1984. The OCU Commander was Superintendent Brian Wade, who was assisted by Superintendent V. Marr, and the Sub-Divisional Superintendent was J. Long.[2108]

Restricted opening hours were in place in 2009, with the station being closed at night and only open from 7.00am until 11.00pm daily.[2109] By 2010 the station was reduced to office status only.[2110]

As of 2019 Lavender Hill remains in the possession of the Metropolitan Police.[2111]

Lee Road Police Station

The London Borough of Lewisham
258A Lee Road, SE12 (1850-2003)
(Renumbered in 1909 as 418 High Road)
P Division (1850-2003)

The roads around London were divided into four divisions and were patrolled by the Bow Street Horse Patrol. The first Division was responsible for that area of North West Kent which today is south east London, and one of its stations was situated at Lee Green. The Horse Patrol was embodied into the Metropolitan Police in 1836, and formed the nucleus of what is today the Mounted Branch.[2112]

With the extension of the Metropolitan Police District under the Metropolitan Police Act, 1839, a new police station for Lee was proposed. This would cover part of Charlton, part of Lewisham, Kidbrooke, Mottingham and Eltham, all of which had been taken over by the Metropolitan Police.[2113] A new station, designed by Metropolitan Police Surveyor Charles Reeves was erected in 1850 on land belonging to Lord Northbrook at 258A Lee Road, at a cost of £1,265 12s 1d. It was leased at a ground rent of £7 14s per annum from Lady Day in 1850 to Lady Day in 1911.[2114]

By January 1864 the station's address was shown as Lee Green, Lee,[2115] and had a complement of one inspector, two sergeants, two acting sergeants, 26 constables and two horses.[2116]

As the area around Lee was expanding in the late 1880s consideration was given to the building of a larger station. With this in view, the freehold of the existing police station site was purchased in May 1889 for the sum of £660. The freehold of the adjoining property, 258 High Road, known as 'Ivy Cottage', was purchased in October 1901 for £400 from the Board of Lewisham Guardians, and the leasehold from a Mrs Mitchell for £800.[2117] The stables to the rear of the site were used as a temporary police station during the rebuilding.

Lee Road Police Station 1903-2003

The new police station, also designed by John Dixon Butler, was erected on the combined sites and opened March 1903.[2117] In 1909 the station address was 418 High Road, as a result of renumbering premises in the High Road.[2118]

The new local authority and police boundaries changed in April 1965, and Lee Road Police Station was transferred from R to P Division in the new London Borough of Lewisham.[2119]

From time to time police stations needed to be fumigated after infestations of various vermin. One such occasion was in 1939 at Lee Road Police Station, when the CID office was infested with bugs. The officers had seized some stolen bed linen from a local pawnbroker's shop. At the same station in 1940 they had lice in one of the cells, and in 1948 they were overrun with mice in the food store of the police canteen.[2120] Lee Road station was no different from other police stations in London when dealing with prisoners and property, which was not always very clean.

In March 1980 Lee Road (PE) and Sydenham Police Stations were reduced in status and had a 24-hour counter service. All other matters were transferred to the Divisional Station at Catford.[2121] In 1982 Area Traffic Patrol Officers were using the premises.[2122]

The police station, land and outbuildings were sold in 2003 and the premises are now flats called 'Met. Apartments'.[2123]

Leman Street Police Station

The London Borough of Tower Hamlets
Wellclose Watch house (1696-1829)
Denmark Street, Ratcliff Highway (1829-1849)
Leman Street, Goodmans Field (1849-1861)
Leman Street, Whitechapel (1861-1891)
96 Leman Street (1891-1967)
74 Leman Street (1970-1993)
H Division (1829-1993)
Tower Hamlets OCU (1993-2018/19)
Basic Command Unit Central East (CE) (with The London Borough of Hackney) (2018/19 to Present)

The police stations of the East End of London have always held significant importance in policing history. Most areas had a watch house, although Whitechapel had two as a consequence of its infamous reputation. One police station or watch office was located in Lambeth Street, Whitechapel (now Crowder Street) some fifty yards from the junction with the Highway, and not far from Leman Street.[2124] It had been there since 1792. Two other watch houses were taken over by police in the East End of London. These were Denmark Street Watch House at St. George's-in-the-East and Chapel Yard, Spitalfields.

St George's Watch House, Denmark Street, pre-1829

2099 Metropolitan Police Orders dated 29th February 1896.
2100 Ibid.
2101 *Post Office Directory* 1898.
2102 *Police and Constabulary Almanac* 1957 and 1960.
2103 *Police and Constabulary Almanac* 1960.
2104 Metropolitan Police Orders dated 16th February 1962.
2105 Metropolitan Police Orders dated 13th December 1963.
2106 Metropolitan Police List 1966.
2107 *Police and Constabulary Almanac* 2001.
2108 Metropolitan Police Authority (MPA) Committee reports accessed 15th February 2009.
2109 cms.met.police.uk/met/boroughs/wandsworth/index accessed 29th January 2010.
2110 MPS Assets (2019) Freedom of Information request.
2111 MEPO 5/25.
2112 MEPO 2/76.
2113 MEPO 2/26.
2114 Metropolitan Police Orders dated 20th June 1864.
2115 John Back archive (1975).
2116 Ibid.
2117 Metropolitan Police Orders dated March 1903.
2118 John Back archive (1975).
2119 Metropolitan Police Orders dated 6th August 1964.
2120 MEPO 2/2619.
2121 Metropolitan Police Orders dated 12th March 1980.
2122 Metropolitan Police Orders dated 1st October 1982.
2123 leeforum.org.uk/wp-content/uploads/2019/06/Lee-Neighbourhood-Development-Plan-Version-15.pdf accessed 8th December 2019.
2124 *The H Division Handbook* 1968/69.

Lambeth Street Watch House had been set up together with six constables from Thames Division, who were employed by a magistrate. Lambeth Street Police Court, Whitechapel was set up by Order of Council on 10th November 1840 to hear charges as a Petty Sessional Court. Another police watch house was located in Wellclose Square.

Wellclose Watch House, Wellclose Square, pre-1829

In 1844 H or Whitechapel Division was policed from the old watch house situated in Chapel Yard, Spitalfields, which had been leased for 40 years in 1840 from the Rev. C. Wheeler. It was a station with two cells. The Receiver was required to pay all taxes and rates, although the provision of insurance is recorded as not being needed. The Chapel Yard Watch House was the oldest of the watch houses, and was located near the site of the present post office in Whitechurch Lane, in the yard of Whitechapel Church.[2125] It had a ground, first and ground floor with two cells. Annual rent was £11 14s, payable to the Parish Authorities. The building only remained in service until 1880. It was shown as a station on H Division, and it housed seven married constables who had two rooms each paying a total £55 18s rent annually.[2126]

When studying police orders from 1829 the name 'Watch House' was used, later becoming a 'Police House', then 'Police Office' and, by 1840, a Police Station.

This station served as the divisional headquarters for some time. The officer in charge of the division was William F. Pierse, who had been promoted to the rank of Superintendent on 6th March 1835. He was assisted by Joseph Lewis and Henry Harris, who were both Inspectors.[2127] Pierse remained as Superintendent until his death in 1846, when Superintendent W. Medlicott took over. Medlicott remained until 3rd February 1849, when he was disciplined, reduced in rank to Inspector and transferred to A Division.[2128] The rules for each rank were strict, and discipline was harsh. In those days there was no right of appeal, even if the officer had been unfairly treated.

The Metropolitan Police took over the old watch house site located in Denmark Street, Ratcliffe Highway in 1829 for £11 14s annual rent, and used the building until a new station (called Leman Street Police Station) was built in 1847 in Goodman's Fields near Mansell Street, E1. The old watch house was entrusted to the Receiver of the Metropolitan Police by Act of Parliament. The freehold to Denmark Street Watch House was purchased July 1885 at a cost of £120. The building had a ground and first floor with two cells.[2129] The officer in charge of the station was Inspector John Donigan, who had been promoted to Inspector in 1841.[2130]

Records show that Superintendent J. Stead took over the Division in 1849, assisted by four Inspectors. The oldest serving on the Division was Henry Harris (in 1844 he was attached to Chapel Yard, Spitalfields), then Daniel Forbes, Thomas Ellis and William Miller.[2131] They were all shown as located at Leman Street Police Station in Goodman's Fields. By 1855 the senior Divisional Inspector was William Miller, with four new inspectors: George Marsh, Albert Gernon, Henry Barny and Philip Brine.[2132]

In published records Leman Street was designated the Headquarters station of H or Whitechapel Division, with other stations at Chapel Yard and London Docks.[2133]

In 1870 records show H Division having 273 personnel, consisting of one superintendent, six inspectors, twenty-five sergeants and 241 constables. The division had seven officers posted to detective duties. In 1881 the station held 53 single constables, and the records also show there were six prisoners in the cells.[2134]

Leman Street Police Station 1891-1967

The address of Leman Street Police Station was published in Police Orders in 1884 as 76 Leman Street, Whitechapel, although strictly speaking its address was 74-78, Leman Street, Whitechapel E1.

Records also show that during 1886 the Home Office authorized the purchase of freehold land, formally known as the Garrick Theatre site, which adjoined the police station, for the sum of £2,000. A decision had been made to rebuild the station. Furthermore, the Metropolitan Police purchased 16 Tenter Street in 1887.

A temporary police station was brought into operation at 64 Leman Street during the rebuilding process on 27th March 1890. The new station was built by 1891, and occupation and police business commenced there in March. Demolition of the old theatre was entrusted to Mr. Base, who salvaged materials from the Garrick at a cost of £66 15s paid to the Receiver.[2135]

Early records also show that there was a police station located a short distance from the section house on the corner of Mile End Road and Stepney Green,[2136] although details appear sparse. Mile End Road Police Station was situated at 102 Mile End Road and was a police section house, although the census refers to the building as being a police station.

The building may have been used as a police office, except

the occupants are referred to as boarders. Sergeant Joseph Roskelly from Sampson in Cornwall was an unmarried resident at the section house, although it was a designated constable station.[2137] There were nineteen other residents at the section house.[2138]

In 1881 the inspector residing at Leman Street Police Station at the time was Adam Marsh, who lived there with his wife and family.[2139] Ten years later Sergeant Hugh Fanning was the senior officer in charge. He was aged 35 years, came from Ireland and was accompanied by sixteen single residents.[2140]

The Metropolitan Police Property Records of 1912 show that an ambulance shelter was located outside the Royal Mint, which was situated opposite the Tower of London in Royal Mint Street. The shelter was on land belonging to the London Borough of Stepney, which required no rental from the police. The Royal Mint had its own police guard, which in 1876 consisted of one sergeant and six constables. In 1881 Sergeant William Durrant resided in Royal Mint House Entrance Gate with his wife and five children.[2141] By the turn of the century there were two sergeants and ten constables. The sergeants supervised the police constables, four on day duty whilst two patrolled at night.[2142]

Royal Mint Police of H Division c1906

One of the responsibilities of the superintendent in charge of the division was to provide officers to police the Royal Mint. The 1907 postcard above shows the complete complement on the steps outside the Royal Mint building. The Royal Mint guard were Metropolitan Police officers from H Division attached to Leman Street Police Station, and a direct telephone line was fitted from Royal Mint station to Leman Street Police Station. The same constable is present in both the photograph of the band and the Royal Mint Police. Seated second right, next to the band sergeant, is PC 243H, with a chest full of medals. On the Royal Mint card he is located in the back row, situated third from the right. One of his medals is the distinctive Kedeve star, which meant that he saw service in Egypt in the 1880s.

The H Division Police Band c1913

At the bottom of the preceding column is a photograph of the H Division Police band located at Leman Street Police Station. The two senior officers in the middle are the only police officers wearing their duty flat hats, whilst all the rest have special bandsman's hats and badges. Many police officers in bands learnt to play instruments in the services before they joined the police. The picture was taken about 1913.

In January 1919, after being demobbed from the Seaforth Highlanders, Peter (Jock) Beveridge joined the Metropolitan Police.[2143] Originating from Fife in Scotland, Beveridge later became a celebrated detective. After eight weeks' training at Eagle Hut in the Strand he was posted to Leman Street.[2144] Beveridge resided at the section house with 98 other single officers. He remembered being advised to keep his food locker secured, although he considered this advice a little unnecessary, but soon found out that when someone ran short they would help themselves.[2145]

On each floor of the section house there were a number of cubicles with wooden walls, which stopped about two feet from the ceiling. In each cubicle there was an iron bedstead, a hard chair and a steel locker with a few shelves for clothes. At intervals down the corridor gas lamps spluttered so that only certain cubicles were reasonably well lit.[2146]

By now Leman Street was a divisional station, with a section house located in Tenter Street at the back of the station together with seven sets of married quarters. In August 1947 Leman Street lost its divisional status when Arbour Square became the Headquarters for H Division. In the review of police and local authority boundaries in 1965, Leman Street was shown as a sub-divisional station situated in the London Borough of Tower Hamlets.

In the late 1960s a new station for Leman Street was planned. The cost was estimated at £400,000. On 9th December 1967 Leman Street Police Station was closed and its police officers were transferred. Building work commenced, and meanwhile the area was policed from Commercial Street and Bethnal Green Police Stations. Doubtless the station's strength was distributed at the other two stations during rebuilding work. Bethnal Green Police Station assumed sub-divisional status during this process.

2125 Ibid.
2126 Metropolitan Police Surveyor's Records.
2127 *The Police and Constabulary List* 1844, Parker, Furnivall and Parker.
2128 Metropolitan Police Service Records.
2129 Metropolitan Police Surveyor's Records.
2130 *The Police and Constabulary List* 1844. Parker Furnivall and Parker.
2131 *Police Office London Directory* 1849.
2132 *Kelly's Directory* 1855.
2133 Metropolitan Police Orders dated 11th January 1864.
2134 Census 1881.
2135 John Back Archive (1975).
2136 Ramsey W. G. (1999) *The East End (Then and now)*, Basildon, p218.
2137 Metropolitan General Orders 1873.
2138 Census 1881.
2139 Ibid.
2140 Census 1891.
2141 Ibid.
2142 Metropolitan Police orders dated 9th February 1876 and Metropolitan Police General Orders 1893.
2143 Beveridge, P. (1957) *Inside the CID*. Evans Brothers, London.
2144 Ibid.
2145 Ibid.
2146 Ibid.

The new station was completed and ready for occupation at 6.00am on 9th March 1970, when all staff were transferred back to Leman Street. The station code was reported as 'HD', and the telegraphic code was revised to the letter 'H'.

Leman Street Police Station 1970-1995

In 1974 the Irish Republican Army left a bomb at the Tower of London, resulting in one fatality and a number of people being injured. Between 24th January 1986 and 15th February 1987 there was a protracted industrial dispute at the News International Building at Wapping. The police played a prominent part in keeping the peace. The dispute was policed 24 hours a day, and aid from other divisions were directed from the purpose-built operations room at Leman Street Police Station.

On 12th October 1992 Sector or Geographic Policing commenced at Leman Street. This was a new form of policing, which involved consulting the public to assess policing priorities.

On Tuesday, 7th November 1995 Leman Street Police Station closed to the public, however the building was retained for operational purposes. Simultaneously Bethnal Green Police Station, situated at 458 Bethnal Green Road, also closed, and policing of both stations was transferred to the new purpose-built station at 12 Victoria Park Square, London, E2 9NZ. Both stations amalgamated into Whitechapel Division, although the new station retained the name Bethnal Green Police Station, and its station code became 'HT'. On 17th May 1996 the Commissioner Sir Paul Condon QPM (now Lord) officially opened the new police station.

As of 2019 Leman Street Police station has been retained for operational purposes.[2147]

Lewisham Police Station

The London Borough of Lewisham
Rushey Green (1841-1871)
Vicarage Terrace (1871-2004)
43 Lewisham High Street (2004 to Present)
P Division (1840-1985/86)
Lewisham Division (1985/86-2018)
Basic Command Unit South East (SE) (2018 to Present)

Prior to the formation of the Metropolitan Police in 1829 there existed the Lewisham Cage. This was a small octagonal building that stood on Watch House Green (where the island between Lewis Grove and High Street is today), close to the stocks and whipping post, and very likely on the spot now occupied by the post office. It was used for the temporary imprisonment of petty offenders – at least it was until the day when some unfortunates set fire to their straw bedding, and were burnt to death before the key could be found.[2148]

Lewisham's first police station was believed to have been located at Rushey Green, close to the site of Marks and Spencer's. The second station was next to the almshouses, also in Rushey Green and opposite George Lane.[2149] The building was situated next door to John Thackeray's Almshouses, and served as the police station by 1841. Prior to 1817 the building had almost certainly been the original parish workhouse.[2150] The Metropolitan Police Surveyor reported that the lease on these premises expired at Michaelmas 1864. They were then retained on the basis of a yearly lease until disposed of.[2151]

In the early 1850s the Lewisham Police Station moved from its site opposite George Lane to a house just north of the Black Horse in Rushey Green, and again in the mid-1870s to one opposite Ladywell Road. All three were existing buildings that were converted so that they could be used as stations. The first purpose-built police station in the area was the one at Sydenham, on part of the present site and which opened in 1848.[2152]

Lewisham Police Station, Rushey Green, c1841-1871

In 1864 the inspector at Lewisham was also responsible for patrolling the neighbouring police stations of Sydenham, Beckenham, Bromley and Farnborough. At that point Lewisham was part of R or Greenwich Division. There was one horse at Lewisham, which was ridden alternately by two sergeants on station duty.[2153]

In December 1864 the Commissioner directed that superintendents (in communication with the Police Surveyor) of several divisions should make immediate efforts to obtain sites whereon police stations may be erected. Lewisham was one of those divisions in need of a new police station.[2154]

Lewisham Police Station, Vicarage Terrace, 1871-2004

Meanwhile, in 1865 Police boundaries changed and an inspector residing at Lee Green Police Station was responsible not only for that station but also Lewisham and Sydenham. Now known as the Lee Sub-Division, it was part of P or Camberwell Division.[2155] The Superintendent of P Division was Thomas Butt. He was assisted by Chief Inspector James Davis, and Detective Inspector Daniel Hunt was in charge of the Criminal Investigation Department.

In October 1869 this all changed again when Sydenham, Lewisham and parts of Penge Police Section were formed into a new Sydenham Sub-Division.[2156]

In March 1870 a Mr Wiston of 45 Manor Road, Lewisham wrote to the Commissioner requesting that a police station should be built in the Lewisham area, as the one at Blackheath Road, Greenwich was too far away. In June that year a letter was received from a Mr Joshua Liddiard offering premises at 3&4 Vicarage Terrace, Lewisham for Police purposes on a long rental. At about the same time James C. Corbett of Lewisham Bridge wrote that the Police should purchase the site on the corner of Lady Well Park for a police station, as one was needed in the neighbourhood. In September 1870 Home Office authority to lease 3&4 Vicarage Terrace for Police purposes from the trustees of the Morden College Estate was received.[2157] The lease was for 30 years at £44 per annum.[2158]

In September 1871 the Metropolitan Police Surveyor, Frederick Caiger, reported that the old station at Rushey Green would be surrendered and that the new station at Vicarage Terrace, Lewisham was to be taken into possession and duties to commence there forthwith.[2159] The premises consisted of a brick-and-slate house with a charge room, basement (which housed the cooking kitchen and mess kitchen for the Section House), a ground floor day room, two cells and a two-stall stable.[2160]

A notice was received in August 1880 from the Lewisham Board of Works that the address of the station would be 233-235 High Street, Lewisham, SE.[2161]

In 1881 there was a Report on the condition of Metropolitan Police Stations and it stated that the aforementioned two houses which served as Lewisham Police Station were of 'somewhat unstable construction', and that they were not well adapted to the purpose for which they are being used. These houses were occupied by a married inspector, one married constable and seven single constables. The married officers lived in one house with their families, while the other was being used by the single men and administration. The report also went on to say that the kitchen and mess room were too small and unsatisfactory. It had also found that the two cells were very often insufficient for the number of prisoners

2147 MPS Information Rights Unit (2019) MPS Assets.
2148 Coulter, J. (1994) *Lewisham: History and Guide.* Alan Sutton, p105.
2149 John Back Archive (1975).
2150 Coulter, J. (1994) *Lewisham: History and Guide.* Alan Sutton, p30.
2151 John Back Archive (1975).
2152 Coulter, J. (1994) *Lewisham: History and Guide.* Alan Sutton, p52.
2153 Metropolitan Police Orders dated 11th January 1864.
2154 Metropolitan Police Orders dated 31st December 1864.
2155 Metropolitan Police Orders dated 28th October 1865.
2156 Metropolitan Police Orders dated 30th September 1869.
2157 John Back Archive (1975).
2158 MEPO4/234.
2159 Metropolitan Police Orders dated 29th September 1871.
2160 Metropolitan Police Surveyor's Report.
2161 John Back Archive (1975).

detained. The Secretary of State had ordered that only one person should be confined in a cell at one time.[2162]

By 1891 it appears that Superintendent T. Butt was still in charge of P Division, and Inspector Butcher was responsible for operations at Lewisham Police Station.[2163] However, by 1899 Superintendent G. Carr had taken over the Division and there were two Station Sergeants, Albert Bright and Charles R. Butler stationed at Lewisham.[2164]

The population of Lewisham expanded in the late 1880s, and a larger police station was required. In November 1894 the Home Office authorised the Receiver to commence negotiations for the purchase of a portion of the site of Lewisham House for the erection of a police station.[2165] Lewisham House, which stood on the corner of Ladywell Road, was a large red-brick mansion, built or rebuilt in 1680. The house was pulled down in 1894 and the area that it covered, including the garden, became the site of the new police station, a fire station (1898), some shops and the Coroner's Court.[2166] The freehold site was purchased in March 1895 from Messrs Routh, Stacey and Castle of 14 Southampton Street, Bloomsbury for the sum of £1,500. In October 1897 the Home Office approved Messrs Hart's tender of £7,467 for the construction of the new police station.[2167]

The new Lewisham Police Station, designed by John Dixon Butler, was built in the Queen Anne style[2168] and was opened for business in January 1899.[2169] Sub-Divisional Inspector Fraser and Inspectors Lane and Austin were transferred from Catford Police Station as a result of Lewisham being made the Sub-Divisional Station instead of Catford.[2170]

In April 1965 the new local authority boundaries, as defined in the London Government Act, 1963, meant that Lewisham (PL), designated the Sub-Divisional Station, with Deptford (PP) and Brockley (PK) were now within the new London Borough of Lewisham.[2171]

In July 1973 Lewisham Police Station was listed as a building with special architectural interest by the Department of the Environment.[2172]

Temporary closure of the station took place in 1982, and a temporary station was established at Brockley.[2173] A temporary police station located at 300 Lewisham High Street (PL) closed on 26th September 1983.[2174]

In October 2002 the Metropolitan Police Authority authorised the sale of the old Lewisham Police Station, it having been made redundant by the building of the new one.[2175]

In 2001 the site of the new Lewisham Police Station was the subject of an archaeological evaluation by Pre-Construct Archaeological Ltd of Brockley. The area examined was bounded in the north by St. Stephens Grove, to the east by Lockmead Road, to the west by Lewisham High Street and to the south by residential and retail buildings. No significant archaeological deposits had survived on the site.[2176]

The building of the new Lewisham Police Station was controversial. Lewisham Council objected to the site of the new station and refused planning permission, but lost on appeal. The Council had felt that, as this site was right in the centre of Lewisham, it would have been better utilised for 'livelier retail or entertainment use'.[2177] In addition, Lewisham was one of four police stations in the south east of the Metropolitan Police District that was completed under the Private Finance Initiative (PFI). This is the Metropolitan Police's partnership with the private sector, formed to develop better-equipped police stations and to replace some of the existing properties which are ageing and no longer suitable.[2178]

The private sector partner was Equion, which not only provides the building, services and maintains it, but also takes over some of the Metropolitan Police's civilian staff and employs them to provide back-up services. Equion, part of the Laing group, is contracted to do this for 25 years from 2003 in return for rent (technically a 'unity charge'). At the end of the term the police station remains the property of Equion.[2179]

The new Lewisham Police Station was formally opened in April 2004 by the Metropolitan Police Commissioner Sir John Stevens and Toby Harris, Chair of the Metropolitan Police Authority.[2180] It was built at the cost of £33.2 million by Lang O'Rouke. The architects for the project were Raymond Smith Partnership and Clifford Tewe & Gale.[2181]

Lewisham Police Station 2004 to present

Police officers working at the Ladywell site and at Catford Police Station were transferred to the new 'state-of-the-art' Lewisham Police Station in November 2003 prior to the formal opening. The station contains 36 cells, a new gym, a purpose-built training suite, stables for 26 horses, a Scientific Support Unit and a Serious Crime Group.[2182] It is currently open 24 hours a day, and is the base of the Senior Management Team.

Leyton Police Station

London Borough of Waltham Forest
501 Lea Bridge Road, Leyton (1861-1891)
215 Francis Road, Leyton (1891-2013)
N Division (1840-1886)
J Division (1886-1985/86)
Leytonstone Division (1985/86-1993/94)
Leyton OCU (1993/94-2013)

Lea Bridge Road Police Station was the name of the first station in the Leyton area. It was situated on the site of the current multi-storey Police Section House, which still stands today, located on the north side of the main road about half a

Lea Bridge Road Police Station 1861-1891

mile south of the Bakers Arms at the junction with Shrubland Road. In the early days it was often referred to as Walthamstow Police Station, even though it was in Leyton.[2183]

In 1867 the Receiver of the Metropolitan Police purchased a freehold parcel of land in the Lea Bridge Road at a cost of £620. In November 1868 the new police station at 501 Lea Bridge Road opened at a cost of £4,139. This was a brick-built station house with a ground and first floor. The ground floor consisted of a charge room, a day room, a mess room, a brush room, a washroom scullery, a drying room, four cells, four stalls (stables), three water closets and four coal sheds. The first floor provided accommodation for ten single constables paying 1/- per week rent, one single constable paying 3/- per week, one married sergeant paying 5/6d per week, and one married Inspector paying 5/6d per week rent.[2184]

The picture below shows Lea Bridge Toll House, situated near the Anglers Public House about 1865. The constable was posted to the toll from Lea Bridge Road Police Station to assist the toll-keeper to ensure that the necessary tolls were paid.

The Lea Bridge Toll House c1865

In 1871 Lea Bridge Road Police Station was shown situated in an area known as Leyton Street, and was one of the more important and substantial stations in the area.[2185] In 1881 the Inspector in charge of the station was Henry Craggs, who resided there with his large family. He had two daughters and three sons. Inspector Craggs was from Chelsea, and at the time was aged 35 years. His wife Sarah was aged 38 years, and came from Brighton in Sussex. Also resident at the station was Constable John Cook, his wife Ann and their son. There were also ten single constables living at the station at the time.[2186]

Leyton Police Station 1891-1940

The formation of J or Bethnal Green Division in 1886 encompassed part of Lea Bridge Road Sub-Division. There was no station at Leyton, and policing of the division operated from either Leytonstone (Harrow Green) or Lea Bridge Road stations. In 1894 the officer in charge of the station was recorded as Station Sergeant Henry Pratchett.[2187] Located next door to the police station was a station cottage (seen to the left of the picture above). This was occupied by a serving police officer, William Denford, and his family.[2188]

In 1887 freehold land was purchased at a cost of £420, on which to build a new station. The Home Office approved the purchase in Francis Road, Leyton, at the corner of Morley Road. The station was built at a cost of £4,355, and was ready for occupation in January 1891.[2189] It included section house accommodation for fifteen single men. The building was a two-storey brick-built station house. Leyton Police Station was a sub-divisional station of Wanstead Section.

Leyton Police Station retirement c1900

The picture above shows a retirement at Leyton Police Station between 1898 and 1901. The recipient is shown with his gifts: a beautiful mantle clock, which is flanked by flowerpots. Police officers served for 25 years before they were eligible for a pension, and only a very few stayed after this time.

Police officers bonded together in many ways. Not only did they work together, they also lived and played together.

2162 Report on the Condition of the Metropolitan Police Stations 1881.
2163 *Kelly's Sydenham, Norwood and Streatham Directory* 1891.
2164 *Kelly's Lewisham, Brockley & Catford Directory* 1899.
2165 John Back Archive (1975).
2166 Leland L Duncan (1908). *History of the Borough of Lewisham*. The Blackheath Press, London.
2167 John Back Archive (1975).
2168 B. Cherry & N. Pevsner (1983). *Buildings of England - London: 2 South*. Penguin Books.
2169 Metropolitan Police Orders dated 28th January 1899.
2170 Metropolitan Police Orders dated 14th December 1905.
2171 Metropolitan Police Orders dated 6th August 1964.
2172 John Back Archive (1975).
2173 Metropolitan Police Orders dated July 1882.
2174 B. Brown.
2175 www.mps.gov.uk/committees/f/2004/040923/14.htm accessed 18th November 2005.
2176 Deeves, S. *Archaeological Evaluation Report* July 2001.
2177 Aldous, T. *The Guide*. November 2003.
2178 www.met.police.uk/lewisham/new_station.htm accessed 18th November 2005.
2179 Aldous, T. *The Guide*. November 2003.
2180 www.laing.com/equion_news_511.htm accessed 9th March 2006.
2181 Aldous, T. *The Guide*. November 2003.
2182 Ibid.
2183 Mead, B. (undated) Welcome Pack, Chingford Division.
2184 Metropolitan Police General Orders dated November 1868.
2185 The Metropolitan Police Annual Report for 1871.
2186 Census 1881.
2187 *Kelly's Directory* 1894.
2188 Ibid.
2189 Metropolitan Police Orders dated January 1891.

Senior officers were concerned that single police officers would develop bad habits if they were not kept occupied. Competitive sports were encouraged, whether it was football, rugby or cricket. Each station had a variety of sports teams. Leyton had a reputation for having a good swimming team, which was helped by having a municipal pool not far away.

The successful Life Saving Team from Leyton Police Station in 1904

The above group is the Life Saving Class of Leyton Swimming Club taken in 1904. These are the successful medallion holders, with their medals shown in the centre. The back row comprises Constable 509J Budd, Constable 607J Waters, Constable 258J Ping, Constable 553J Boyling, Sergeant 78J Allen (Hon. Sec.), Constable 299J Mapeley, Constable 560J Hopker. Front (left to right) Constable 97J Barker, Mr. T. Minett (non-police instructor) Mr. W. Wire (non-police instructor) and Constable 364J Palmer.

Once the new station had been built, the Lea Bridge Road site was rebuilt to provide accommodation for more single police officers. The new section house at Lea Bridge Road was occupied in April 1908, and provided accommodation for twenty-six unmarried men at 1s per week rent.[2190]

It appears that Lea Bridge Road Police Station was re-opened in February 1913 after refurbishment, and included two sets of married quarters.[2191]

Up until July 1927 there was no Leyton division as such, because its status was as a sectional station to Wanstead Sub-Division. Records show the status of both stations were altered; Wanstead became a sectional station, whilst Leyton was enhanced to sub-division. Accordingly, Sub-Divisional Inspector Farrell was transferred to Leyton from Wanstead to take up supervisory duties.[2192]

Setting off the maroons in the yard at Leyton Police Station to commemorate the end of WW1

The photograph below left taken in the yard at Leyton shows Constable 509J Ernest Budd (warrant no. 84134) on the left. He had joined the Metropolitan Police on 20th June 1898 and retired on 24th June 1923 after 25 years' service. It would seem he remained at Leyton Police Station for some time – probably all his service. The picture features Constable Budd together with the station inspector (in flat hat) and another constable. The Inspector is setting off the maroons as a mark that peace had been signed in 1918. Constable Budd is also shown in the retirement group photograph shown on the previous page, as the fifth from the left in the back row.

In August 1927 the section house was converted into two sets of married quarters.[2193] On re-organisation in 1933 Leyton remained a sub-divisional station, but with Leytonstone as the sectional station. The address of the station was published as 215 Francis Road, Leyton, part of J Division with Hackney Police Station being the Divisional Headquarters. Lea Bridge Road Police Station was closed in August 1933.[2194]

By 1939 the station required rebuilding, as it was no longer adequate for policing purposes. The premises were vacated on Sunday, 26th March 1939 and personnel were transferred to the previously-closed Lea Bridge Road Police Station, situated at 501 Lea Bridge Road. The old station was demolished, and a new much bigger one was built in its place.

There were a number of problems with the building of the new station. The site was 'V'-shaped, with Francis Road and Morley Road forming an acute angle. Furthermore, the station had to be three times larger than it was previously. To overcome these problems the architect Julian Leathart FRIBA designed the intersection of the two wings by curving the frontage rather than slicing off the corner. He included a large lower ground floor, and designed in the fenestration of the top floor, which tends to give the impression of a two-floored building. The coming of war meant that late Air Raid Precautions had to be designed into the building.

The cells were built to receive natural light, with exterior glass bricks forming part of the external walls. The general contractors were Messrs Pitchers Ltd of 57 Ashburton Grove, N7. The new station was quickly built, and was ready for occupation in August 1940.[2195]

Lea Bridge Road Police Station had served the area well, having previously been an N Division station covering Walthamstow and Leyton from 1868 to 1904. In later years Lea Bridge Road Police Station became married quarters, as well as a section house. It was then demolished, and a new multi-storey Police section house built in its place called Lea Bridge Road Section House.

There has always been a number of mysteries concerning the station at Leyton. Firstly, why was a station built with no licensed premises in its vicinity? This is usually a pre-requisite; for example, Stoke Newington was built between two public houses. The second question relates as to why the current Leyton Police Station has no blue lamp outside, when the old station had? The third and perhaps most perplexing question is why was the station built in such an out-of-the-way location, in a quiet side street and not in the main High Street?

In the early 1900s various editors of local newspapers called the siting of the original station 'as in the wilderness', and its location caused much anger and frustration. Rumours (which have absolutely no factual basis whatsoever) gave the reason for siting as the land being bequeathed to the Receiver with the stipulation that only a police station could be built there, and no other building. This raised interesting possibilities that perhaps the benefactor was concerned at the lack of police presence in the area, or perhaps the donor just liked the police. The answers to these problems will perhaps never be known.[2196] What tends to dispel this theory is that Metropolitan Police Surveyor's records show the various amounts of money paid for the site and building.

Leyton Police Station 1940-2013

Special constables have always provided a support function to the regular police. They hold the office of constable, and special constables are sworn into service by Justices of the Peace or Magistrates within the area they police, and are provided with a warrant card as proof of holding that office. A surviving card from Ernest Alfred Levey, for instance, shows that he had been sworn in by two Justices in the district of Beacontree, Essex.

In 1963 further restructuring of the London Boroughs filtered through to police re-organisations in 1965. Part of Local Government boundary revisions identified Leyton within the London Borough of Waltham Forest. Furthermore, the station was upgraded to Divisional Headquarters for J Division, replacing Hackney Police Station.[2197]

As from 1st April 1965 the telegraphic code for Leyton became Juliet Delta (JD), located within the London Borough of Waltham Forest.

In 1969, Leyton Police Station became the Headquarters for J Division, moving from Hackney. This was a popular move, and placed commanders in charge of the old divisions which were renamed Districts.[2198]

In 1975 a new station at Chigwell (Brook Parade) was built to accommodate headquarters functions, and these were transferred. In 1986 Leyton and Leytonstone formed the new Leyton Division.

In 1999, under the latest re-structuring arrangements and re-organisation of the Metropolitan Police, individual Borough Commanders replaced the 3 Area Headquarters management structure, which was abolished. The new Borough Commanders (now Chief Superintendents) took up their posts, and today Leyton remains within the London Borough of Waltham Forest and therefore part of North East (NE) Basic Command Unit.

The Leyton police station was closed in 2013 and sold in 2014 for £1.25M.[2199]

Leytonstone Police Station

London Borough of Waltham Forest
High Road, Harrow Green, Leytonstone (1878-1913)
470 High Road, Leytonstone (1913-2007)
N Division (1840-1929)
J Division (1929-1985/86)
Leytonstone Division (1985/86-1993/94)
Leyton OCU (1993/94-2007)

Leytonstone Police Station Lamp

Situated on a main route out of London to Colchester was a small hamlet called Leyton Stone. About midway between Maryland Point (near Stratford) and Leyton Stone travelling East was located the tiny village of Salts Green (1777), later renamed Harrow Green on account of a nearby inn called Le Harrow.[2200]

Before 1872 the area of Walthamstow and Low Leyton was policed from Lea Bridge Road Police Station. Police records make reference to the building of a new station at Leytonstone, although originally the name of the new station was Harrow Green Police Station.[2201]

The police sought a suitable house in the Harrow Green area to use as a police station. In 1878 they found a suitable house called Maria Cottage, in Harrow Green, Leytonstone, which could be leased for the purpose. An agreement was reached with the owners to lease the house initially for seven years, but with options for fourteen or twenty-one years if necessary. Leytonstone (Harrow Green) station was occupied by police and shown located on N Division with a call sign of Lima Echo (LE).[2202]

The lease to the station was terminated in 1892 after 14 years, when it was retained on an annual basis. The station at Harrow Green (Leytonstone) was small by today's standards, but it included a charge room, a reserve room, two coal sheds, two cells and a water closet. It was a place where constables paraded for duty, and prisoners were charged for court. It was located on the west side of the Leytonstone Road, just south of Cathall Road, Harrow Green.

As far back as the mid-1880s the police decided that because of local expansion in population a more suitable premises should be sought. The local people were happy with the location of the station, and a row brewed up over police plans to close the local station and re-site it some distance away. The editors of several local papers joined in the argument, stating,

---

2190 Metropolitan Police Orders dated 27th April 1908.
2191 Metropolitan Police Orders dated February 1913.
2192 Metropolitan Police Orders dated 20th July 1927.
2193 Metropolitan Police Surveyors Records.
2194 Metropolitan Police Orders dated 27th July 1933.
2195 Metropolitan Police Orders dated August 1940.
2196 Leyton Police Station cited in *Three District Magazine* (1960).
2197 Back, J. (1975) The Metropolitan Police Museum, Charlton.
2198 Fido, M and Skinner, K. (1999). *The Official Encyclopedia of Scotland Yard*, p277.
2199 Metropolitan Police Information Rights Unit accessed 25th January 2019.
2200 Ramsey, G (1997) *The East End Then and Now*. Heronsgate, p368.
2201 Metropolitan Police Orders dated 20th November 1872.
2202 Metropolitan Police General Orders 1893.

Harrow Green Police Station High Road, Harrow Green, Leytonstone 1878-1913

'We do not know if the police authorities are still determined to persevere in their utterly mad project in doing away with Harrow Green Police Station and placing one in the wilderness. We should fancy the condemnation of the whole intelligent public... blundering... preposterous notion... silly and gigantic muddle at Harrow Green.' [2203]

The wilderness referred to by the papers was a small plot of land three-quarters of a mile away off the High Road, Leyton, situated in what some observers described as 'the better class residential area of Leyton'.[2204]

On the completion of the new Leyton Police Station built at 215 Francis Road, the former building was re-opened as married quarters for a police officer at a weekly rental of 2/-. In 1892 instructions were issued to re-open the station, as a result of strong local representation. Accordingly, force instructions stated that Harrow Green (Leytonstone) re-opened on 9th May 1892. With the formation of the new J or Bethnal Green Division, Leytonstone was transferred from N to J.[2205]

Soon the area of Leytonstone became a popular location for people, and this caused a significant increase in population. By 1908 concern was expressed as to the suitability of the old station and its ability to cope with the pressure of the increase in inhabitants. Accordingly, permission was given to purchase a parcel of land located at 470 High Road, Leytonstone, with sufficient space for a back entrance in Cobden Road. The freehold was secured in 1908. A new station was built on the site and opened in February 1913.[2206] It also included two sets of married quarters. Rent for one set of quarters was shown as 8/6d per week, whilst the other set cost 8/- per week.

Leytonstone Police Station, 470 High Road, Leytonstone, 1913-2007

Leytonstone had an ambulance shelter which was located at a public house called the Old Red Lion at 640 High Road, Leytonstone. Mr. E.W. Greenwood is shown as being the person responsible for said shelter,[2207] which probably housed a wooden two-wheeled cart known as a hand ambulance. Locating an ambulance at such a place appears to have assisted police officers conveying drunken persons back to the police station. This facility was withdrawn on 13th August 1929.

In 1931 Leytonstone was shown as still located on J Division, but Hackney had superseded Bethnal Green as the divisional headquarters. Re-organisation in 1965 made Leytonstone (JS) a sectional station of Leyton Sub-Division.

In the early 1960s concern had been expressed at senior level regarding the effectiveness of police to fight crime and deal with disorder. The solution to this dilemma was to form a 'squad' of suitable constables, sergeants and inspectors. The name of this squad was the Special Patrol Group (SPG). The SPG were organised throughout the Metropolitan Police District in 1961.[2208] The SPG were a centrally-based, highly mobile unit introduced to combat serious crime which could not be dealt with by divisions due to increasing shortages in manpower.[2209] Leytonstone was considered a suitable station to house one of the new mobile patrols.

Constable 161281 David Leonard Donaldson

The picture right shows Constable 161281 David Leonard Donaldson, who transferred from C Division in March 1973 to A8(2) Department – the SPG and Leytonstone Station.[2210] It was during this period with the SPG that Constable 563CO Donaldson found a skill in detecting crime, because he became a Temporary Detective Constable in March 1975 and a Detective Constable in 1978, at which point he was posted to Bow Police Station. He successfully studied for the promotion exam and became a sergeant in October 1979, when he returned to uniform duties. Sergeant Donaldson stayed in uniform for a year and transferred back to detective duties as a Detective Sergeant 2nd Class, from Kentish Town to Barkingside Police Station. He was twice commended by the Commissioner for the Metropolis. He became a uniform inspector in June 1990 and ended his distinguished career in 1996 after returning to the CID, having been seconded to the recently-formed National Criminal Intelligence Service (NCIS) in 1993[2211]

Daily our police act with courage and bravery. One officer attached to Leyton Police Station was Constable John Barrett, who in July 1965 kept observation on a stolen Mini saloon car with false numberplates in Drayton Road, Leytonstone. On seeing a person return to the vehicle he challenged him, but the driver ignored the officer's warning and tried to knock down the officer as he attempted to make an arrest. The officer jumped on the bonnet of the vehicle as it sped through the back streets of Leytonstone. It crashed after travelling some distance, severely injuring the officer. The driver decamped, leaving the officer lying injured on the road, however Constable Barrett was able to direct other officers to the suspect, who was hiding nearby. Later at the Old Bailey

Constable John Barrett receiving his British Empire Medal from Field Marshall Earl Alexander of Tunis in 1966, and Right: British Empire and Police Long Service Medals

the driver was imprisoned for a variety of offences including grievous bodily harm, theft of a number of motor vehicles and marine equipment from Southampton. Constable Barrett was commended for his bravery by His Honour Judge Griffith-Jones, and was later awarded the British Empire Medal for Gallantry. The picture below shows Constable Barrett being awarded his medal by Field Marshall Earl Alexander of Tunis.

The British Empire Medal is shown above, together with Constable Barrett's Police Long Service and Good Conduct Medal, which is received after 22½ years' unblemished service. The Queen had normally awarded these medals personally, but wrote to Constable Barrett apologising for not being able to on this occasion.[2212]

Leytonstone Police Station was closed in 2007 and the property sold.[2213]

Limehouse Police Station

Newby Place Poplar (1830-1873)
Poplar East Dock Road (1873-1879)
15 Piggott Street (1879-1897)
27 West India Dock Road (1897-1993)
K Division (1830-1965)
H Division (1965-1985/86)
Limehouse Division HH (1985/86-1993/94)
Tower Hamlets OCU (1993/94-2018/19)
Basic Command Unit Central East (CE) (with The London Borough of Hackney) (2018/19 to Present)

Limehouse Police Station Lamp

Records show that a watch office became the first police station in the area, located not far from Limehouse in Newby Place, Poplar next to Poplar Church (see also Poplar Police Station). The station at Newby Place was shown located on K or Stepney Division, whose headquarters were situated at Arbour Square.

A new K Division Section House was opened in East India Dock Road in May 1869, for occupation by single police officers.[2214] The first police station in Limehouse was opened in April 1879,[2215] and was located at 15 Piggott Street, Limehouse on K Division. Instructions stated that occupation of the new station should be taken up immediately. Piggott Street is located at the bottom of Burdett Road and Commercial Road (A13). Land had been leased on 11th August 1878 from Mr. Henry Spicker of Laummas House, Hackney Common, at a cost of £32 per year. The lease was variable for 7, 14 or 21 years. The house was altered for police purposes at a cost of £304 19s, and was reported fit for occupation in 1879.

On the ground floor was a charge room, a reserve room, a kitchen, a scullery, two cells and two water closets. The first and second floors contained living accommodation for police officers. The lodging assessment for those fortunate enough to receive subsidised housing was shown as one married sergeant at 3/9d and one married constable at 2/6d per week. Augmentation of the station strength was published at the same time, and was set to increase by four 3rd Class inspectors, one sergeant and three constables.[2216] At 10 Piggott Street lived Inspector Thomas Reid, his wife Emily and six children. Reid had been born in Ireland in 1845. Constable George Wayman, his wife and two children occupied rooms above the station, together with Police Divisional Surgeon Robert Kemp and his wife Sarah.[2217]

Limehouse Police Station 1879-1897

2203 *Express and Independent*, 27th November 1886.
2204 Leathart, J. 'Leyton Police Station' in *The Builder*, 3rd January 1941.
2205 Metropolitan Police Orders dated 22nd July 1886.
2206 Metropolitan Police Orders dated March 1913.
2207 Metropolitan Police Surveyor's Records dated 1924.
2208 Fido, M and Skinner, K. (1999) *The Official Encyclopedia of Scotland Yard*, p252.
2209 Ibid.
2210 Metropolitan Police Service Records (undated).
2211 Ibid.
2212 Personal correspondence of Mr John Barrett BEM.
2213 Metropolitan Police Information Rights Unit accessed 25th January 2019.
2214 Metropolitan Police Orders dated 13th May 1869.
2215 Metropolitan Police Orders dated 16th April 1879.
2216 Ibid.
2217 Census 1881.

In April 1886 the Home Office approved the purchase of a freehold site, known as The Cooperage, in West India Dock Road, Limehouse on which to build a police station. The site was purchased in 1887, and at the same time an adjacent property at 7 Birchfield Street was also purchased. The cost of building the new station was shown as £4,250, and its address was 27 West India Dock Road. It included a section house. The Birchfield Street site was recorded as having one set of married quarters. The new station was ready for occupation in May 1889, and had sub-divisional status.

On 28th May 1897, just a day after the opening of the new Limehouse Police Station, there was the grand opening of the Blackwall Tunnel. The police were required to make arrangements for the tunnel opening, but this was marred by an unfortunate accident to Superintendent Beard of A Division, who sustained a fractured arm caused by being thrown from his horse during the event.[2218] In October 1897 Constable Beveridge, a Limehouse Police Officer,[2219] was singled out for his bravery. It was recorded that he was presented with a marble clock, bronze ornaments, and a purse of money by the inhabitants of Limehouse in recognition of his courageous conduct in stopping two runaway horses a few weeks earlier, and thereby preventing what might have been a most serious accident.[2220]

Limehouse Police Station 1897-1940

With the opening of the new station came a change in the boundaries. Poplar, Limehouse and Isle of Dogs section become Limehouse Sub-Division. During further re-organisation in 1933 Limehouse, Poplar, Bow and the Isle of Dogs stations were transferred from K or East Ham Division to H or Whitechapel Division.

Plans were made during the 1930s to build a new police station and section house (Harold Scott Section House), which would hold 130 single officers and several sets of married quarters, on the existing site. The freehold purchase of 29 West India Dock Road (a dilapidated old cottage) was completed on 26th September 1935 at a cost of £200. In 1931 records show that Limehouse was the Sub-Divisional Headquarters for K or Bow Division, to which the Divisional Superintendent was attached.

Further freehold purchases were made; 31-37 West India Dock Road and 1,3&5 Birchfield Street. The houses at 33-37 West India Dock Road were adapted to become the temporary police station during building work. Because of the outbreak of war in 1939, part of the building work was left incomplete, however there was sufficient completed work for administrative business to commence on Saturday, 10th August 1940. The station and section house were completed after the war.

Limehouse Police Station 1940 to present

In 1958 co-author Superintendent Swinden, as a young constable, lived in the section house for the first few months of his service, whilst stationed at West Ham Police Station. He then moved to Normal Kendall Section House at the rear of East Ham Police Station. This was his official home for the next four years.

The revision of boundaries in 1965 designated Limehouse Police Station (HH) to remain as a sub-divisional station, with both Poplar (HP) and the Isle of Dogs (HI) stations becoming sectional stations. All were shown located in the new London Borough of Tower Hamlets.

In 2002 the station address was shown as 29 West India Dock Road, Limehouse.[2221]

As of 2019 the police station and section house are still owned by the police for operational purposes, however the front counter was shut in 2017.[2222]

Limes Farm Police Office

Epping Forest District Council
Limes Avenue, Chigwell IG7 5NT (1972-2000)
J Division (1972-2000)
Essex Police (from 2000)

In 1972 another new estate was being built on the borders of Chigwell and Barkingside. This was called Limes Farm, and contained 1,000 houses. It was felt that due to the large numbers of people living there a police office should be opened to the public at limited times. A Police house called Limes Farm Police Office was opened in May 1972,[2223] with a call sign of 'JT'.

In 2000 all three properties, Debden, Marks Gate and Hainault, were handed over to Essex Police. The Limes Farm site is currently (2019) known as the Limes Farm Community Office and the police office is closed.

Loughton Police Station

Epping Forest District Council
Cage Green Cottage, Loughton (1840-1872)
158 High Road, Loughton (1872-2000)
K Division (1840-1865)
N Division (1865-1886)
J Division (1886-2000)
Essex Police (from 2000)

The police arrived in Loughton in 1840, when a 'police residence' was established at Cage Green Cottage. It was situated on the cricket field, nearly opposite the War Memorial where the village cage was placed.

The Old Police Station, Cage Green Cottage, 1840-1872

In a special report dated 24th November 1859 Superintendent Howie, the chief officer of K or Stepney Division, reported on the suitability of the current station house located at Loughton in Essex. He felt that the station was badly situated and inadequate for police purposes, being some distance from the new railway. The Commissioner had informed his Divisional Superintendents to be vigilant in locating suitable sites for the building of police stations. Superintendent Howie reported that a suitable parcel of land had become available at the corner of Forest Road and the High Street, Loughton. The freehold owner, Mr. Doyle, was leasing the land for 99 years, with an annual ground rent of £11.

In November 1860 Home Office approval was granted to build a station on the site. The land was sold to the Metropolitan Police in 1872 for the sum of £330.[2224]

Accordingly, a police station was built on the land and included a ground and first floor. The living space was cramped, as records show that on the first floor there were six rooms and four single constables who resided in just one communal room. A married constable occupied another three rooms, and a married sergeant and his family occupied a further two rooms.[2225] Records also indicated that the station, which was located on K or Stepney Division, had a strength of two sergeants and seven constables.[2226]

Loughton Police Station 1872-1964

In October 1884 there was a revision of the station boundaries, together with the formation of three new divisions, namely W, X and Y. During these changes Loughton transferred to N or Islington Division. In 1886 formation of the new J Division took place, and saw Loughton transfer from N.[2227] In 1898 the location of the police station was shown in the High Road. Station Sergeant Harry Clarke was in charge, and there were three other sergeants and fourteen constables.[2228]

The station address of Loughton Police Station has changed over time, even though the station itself never moved. For example, in 1864 it was shown as High Road, Loughton, although police records in 1924 show[2229] the address as Forest Road, but in July 1931 the Urban District Council of Loughton notified the officer in charge of Loughton Police Station that, as of the 29th of that month, the location and address would be changed to 158 High Street.[2230] The station house was shown to have been originally built with one set of married quarters.[2231]

The picture below shows the local police escorting a parade through the town in about 1910. Behind is the old station house. On no less than two occasions Loughton Police Station was nearly consumed by fire. On 16th January 1906, when the station was not yet 50 years old, a fire broke out in adjacent premises, however the police alerted the fire brigade who put out the fire in good enough time. The same thing occurred on 9th June 1937, with the same result. No damage was caused to the station on either occasion.[2232]

Police from Loughton escorting a band through the High Street c1910

In the 1930s the Commissioner of the Metropolis reported twice that Loughton Police Station was inadequate for current policing needs, but it was not until 1957 that something was done about it.[2233]

In the mid-1930s the Metropolitan Police introduced wireless-equipped radio cars, which were used to patrol the division on increasingly-busier trunk roads, although they were not delivered immediately to each police station.[2234]

2218 *Police Review and Parade Gossip*, May 1897
2219 This is not the same Constable Beveridge who was posted to Leman Street Police Station in 1919.
2220 *Police Review and Parade Gossip*, October 1897.
2221 www.met.police.uk/contact/phone.htm accessed 23rd March 2002.
2222 MPS station closures since 2010; Information Rights Unit MSP accessed 6th May 2019.
2223 Metropolitan Police Orders dated 1st May 1972.
2224 Metropolitan Police Surveyor's Records (undated).
2225 Ibid.
2226 Metropolitan Police Orders dated 11th January 1864.
2227 Metropolitan Police Orders dated 22nd July 1886.
2228 *Kelly's Directory of Essex* 1898.
2229 Metropolitan Police Property Records 1924.
2230 John Back Archive (1975).
2231 Metropolitan Police Property Records 1872.
2232 John Back Archive (1975).
2233 Ibid.
2234 Elliott, B. (1991). 'History of Loughton and Chigwell Police'. Chigwell and Waltham Abbey History Society.

An amazing incident occurred in Loughton in 1930 that demonstrates the dedication and commitment to duty that police officers have. Early on the morning of 11th July, Constable 273J Alfred Charles James saw a man with a motor car which had been reported stolen to police. He approached the vehicle and spoke to the man, who offered an explanation as to the ownership of the vehicle with which the officer was not satisfied. Constable James then told the man that he was under arrest, but the motorist produced a gun, placed the muzzle against the officer's body and threatened to shoot him. There was a struggle in the street, but some members of the public nearby who were alerted to the commotion came to the officer's assistance and together they managed to overpower the man, who was arrested. Such brave meritorious actions were recognised that year, when the King bestowed on Constable James the award of King's Police Medal.[2235]

The Police were served by motor vans which had been distributed to divisional stations, which for Loughton meant a drive from Hackney Division. Additionally, to improve communications between both Police and public a system of Police Boxes were installed at major road junctions throughout the Metropolitan Police District. There were four shown located on Loughton section (JO), and three for Claybury (JY). These were Box by Woodford Railway station (JY), Box at Roding Lane near railway bridge, Buckhurst Hill (JO), Box at Epping New Road junction with Rangers Road (JO) Box 7 at Roding Road junction with Valley Hill (JO), Box 9 at Goldings Hill opposite England Lane (JO), Box at Hainault Road near the Bald Hind Public House (JY), and lastly Box in the village, Chigwell Road, by Vicarage Lane (JY).[2236]

It was common practice to post a constable on station security, usually for the purposes of diverting casual members of the public from troubling the Station Officer (the sergeant). During time of war this principle did not change, and the constable positioned himself behind the wall of sandbags which ringed the front door to the station. On 12th May 1941 War Reserve PC 1084J Albert Hinds and recalled police pensioner Constable Samuel Jordan 133JR, who had retired in 1933 after 25 years' loyal service, were standing near the front door to Loughton Police Station. At roughly the same time three men were passing along the High Road to take up Air Raid Precautionary duties further up the road when a huge explosion occurred. An anti-aircraft shell exploded right outside the station, leaving a 3ft diameter hole in the road and killing two of the passing men and War Reserve Police Albert Hinds. The shell probably came from one of the anti-aircraft guns protecting the small arms factory at Enfield. Constable Jordan lost an arm in the explosion, and in consequence was retired medically unfit with an enhanced pension. He died in 1987 in his mid-eighties.[2237]

Loughton was a sectional station of Woodford Sub-Division, and shown as a station on 3 District (the District HQ was located at Macnaghten Section House), whilst the Divisional Headquarters was shown at Hackney Police Station.[2238]

Needless to say, the war intervened rendering the building of a new station at Loughton unimportant. However, in September 1957 Estates Branch recommended that 2,4&6 Forest Road should be purchased and demolished to make way for a larger station. In February 1958 the freehold to these properties were acquired for £11,500. However, both 2 and 4 Forest Road were occupied by Messrs. Ingle (Furnishing), who still had leasehold status on the addresses. Negotiations for the leasehold commenced, resulting in Ingles vacating the premises on 19th October, at which point the leasehold was purchased for £7,500.[2239]

Local Government boundary changes and police re-organisation designated Loughton (JO) as a sectional station to Barkingside Sub-Division, situated in Chigwell Urban District Council area. The new three-storey police station was built and came into operational use at 6.00am on 2nd November 1964.[2240]

Loughton Police Station 1964-2016

In April 2000 Loughton Police station was handed over to Essex Police as part of the boundary changes that coincided with the introduction of Borough-based policing in the Metropolitan Police. The station was closed to the public in 2016, although is still used for police operational purposes.[2241]

Marble Arch Police Station

City of Westminster

Marble Arch, Oxford Street W1H 7EJ (1851-1950)

A Division (1851-1908)

D Division (1908-1950)

Marble Arch, at the north end of Park Lane, had a set of accommodation similar to Wellington Arch and was first used by the police in 1851, again primarily for traffic control. There was a gap some time prior to 1886 when the upper rooms were not used, but in 1887 officers were again allowed to reside there. It was transferred to D Division on 18th September 1908. The police became more overtly responsible for controlling the traffic flow through London from 1841, when the Commissioners rather reluctantly took on the responsibility for fixing the location of cab ranks. In 1869 the police had been given licensing responsibilities, and by the 1880s and 1890s the streets were as congested with horse-drawn traffic as they are by motor vehicles today.

Marble Arch Police Station 1851-1950

The first traffic signal was a gas-lit device in Bridge Street near the Houses of Parliament, inspired by a railway signal, but when it exploded the system of using police officers on point duty regained support until a more efficient electric system was introduced.

The introduction of computer-coordinated traffic lights has been assisting London's traffic flow since the 1970s. GATSO cameras, named after a Dutch rally driver Maurice Gatsoides who invented automatic cameras to improve his driving performance, have been introduced to enforce speed limits and compliance with traffic signals progressively since 1988. Another use of technology has been the widespread use of CCTV. All of these developments have transformed the way in which London's traffic is controlled and some traffic laws enforced.

Marks Gate Police Station

The London Borough of Barking and Dagenham

78 Rose Lane, Romford, Essex RM6 5JU

London Borough of Barking and Dagenham OCU

(1996 -2020)

Marks Gate is part of the area known as Little Heath and originally referred to as an entrance into Hainault Forest. Dagenham council built an estate at Marks Gate in the late 1950s and much of the housing remains in municipal ownership. The area is situated to the south of Whalebone Lane North.

In 1996 an extended end of terrace house was used as a police station for the police to serve the local housing estate. It did not have facilities to act in detaining and the charging of prisoners. Essentially it was used as a base for local police officers and a reference point for the public. The station is situated near the border with the London Boroughs of Redbridge and Havering at 78, Rose Lane, Romford, Essex.

Marks Gate Police Station 1996-2013

As a result of electoral boundary changes in 1994 the area of Marks Gate changed. Revisions meant that Barkingside Police gave up this remote site located on the north side of the A12, mid way between Barley Lane and Whalebone Lane.

Because of the remote nature of the station to Marks Gate it was decided to locate a detached police office on the Estate called Marks Gate Police Station. The police office was closed to the public in 2013.[2242] In 2017 the station was still a base of operational police officers but closed to the public.

Marylebone Lane Police Station

Marylebone Lane Watch House (from pre-1829)

69 Welbeck Street (1859-1892)

50 Marylebone Lane (1892-1977)

19 Seymour Street (1977-c.2017)

D Division (1829-1985)

Part of No. 8 Area (1985/86-c.1993)

Part of No. 1 Area (Central) (c.1993-c.2017)

The original D Division in 1829 was centred on Marylebone, with its boundaries comprising, in modern terms, the area north of Oxford Street, west of Portland Place, east of Edgware Road, and encompassing Regent's Park.

Marylebone Lane was one of the two original watch houses on D Division taken over by the Metropolitan Police in 1829, and referred to as being 'vested in the Receiver by Act of Parliament'.[2243] There was also a separate Marylebone police office in Marylebone High Street that had been established under the Middlesex Justices Act of 1792, which we would refer to nowadays as a magistrates' court.[2244] This office opened after the office at Shadwell had closed.[2245]

Number 69 Welbeck Street was leased for 60 years from Michaelmas 1857, providing accommodation right through to Marylebone Lane, and a station was then built in 1859. The ground floor had a Superintendent's office, an Inspector's room, a charge room and twelve cells. The 69 Welbeck Street frontage was to maintain the appearance of a private residence, with a private entrance 'for the superior officers only'.

1863 map showing the location of Marylebone Lane police station

2235 *Police Review and Parade Gossip*, 9th January 1931.
2236 Elliott, B. (1991) 'History of Loughton and Chigwell Police'. Chigwell and Waltham Abbey History Society.
2237 Ibid.
2238 *The Police and Constabulary Almanac* 1957.
2239 John Back Archive (1975).
2240 Ibid.
2241 www.guardian-series.co.uk 31st March 2016, accessed 28th June 2019.
2242 Metropolitan Police Information Rights Unit 22nd March 2017, accessed 25th January 2019.
2243 Metropolitan Police Property Registers.
2244 Bernard Brown (undated). 'A Short History of D Division'.
2245 International Centre for the History of Policing, Crime and Justice, The Open University.

Marylebone Lane Police Station 1892-1977

A new police station was erected in 1892 at 50 Marylebone Lane W1, purchased in 1892 at a cost of £6,935. This was, in turn, replaced by a more modern building at 19 Seymour Street W1 in 1977. This building remained in use until approximately 2017, and by 2019 it had been sold and converted into flats.

The policing of Lord's cricket ground was part of the Division's responsibility, and indeed the demands of coping with those who steal from Oxford Street, one of the busiest shopping centres in the world.

The Metropolitan and City Police Orphanage

Fortescue House, London Road (1870-1874)

Wellesley House, Strawberry Hill, Twickenham (1874-1937)

Metropolitan and City Police Orphans Fund, 30 Hazlewell Road, Putney, SW15 6LH (1937 to present)

Lt. Col. Sir Edmund Y.W. Henderson, KCB, Commissioner of Police of the Metropolis from 1869 to 1886, was widely known as the founding father of the charity we know today as the Metropolitan and City Police Orphans Fund. Established in 1870, the fund can be safely attributed to his reputed kindness, sympathy and understanding. After all, Henderson himself knew the conditions of service of the 8,800 constables and sergeants serving in London in 1870. He would appreciate, too, that if a constable died from injuries received in the course of duty, his widow received an annuity of £15 plus £2 10s 0d for each child, and that in any other case she received a gratuity of £31 and nothing else. He also knew that any police accommodation would need to be vacated, often with indecent haste, rendering the situation even more desperate.[2246]

This was not the first home which catered for the dependent children of deceased policemen, as unofficial premises existed at the Home for Destitute Orphans of Police which had been established at Brighton. Privately-owned, it relied on subscriptions from both inside and outside the Police Service. By 1870, of the 28 children accommodated in the Home, 17 were from the London area.[2247]

The Metropolitan Police Orphanage was opened in October 1870 with 20 children, however by 1871 it was renamed to include the City of London Police and granted Royal Patronage the same year.[2248]

Its original home was Fortescue House, London Road, Twickenham (long since demolished), the former home of Earl Fortescue. Admission was confined to children orphaned after 1st January 1870, and was limited to two from each family. However the number of orphaned children rose rapidly, and to cater for these ever-increasing numbers Bath House, London Road, (opposite Fortescue House and since demolished) was taken on lease to accommodate 40 of the younger children. Yet this was still not enough. Within three years, there were 115 orphans eligible for accommodation. In 1874 Wellesley House, Hampton Road, Twickenham was also purchased. With accommodation for at least 200 children, later extended to house a further 60, Wellesley House was occupied on 25th September 1874, where the Orphanage was to remain for the next 63 years.[2249]

During the 67 years of its existence 2,807 boys and girls passed through the Institution, as it became known under the rules.

A group of children from the Orphanage

By 1878, however, there were 1,000 orphaned children, only 200 of who could be given Orphanage accommodation. It was clear the institution could not fulfil its purpose, and a new dimension was necessary. Thus, in 1883 a compassionate allowance at the rate of £2 12s 0d per child per annum became payable for children for whom there was no accommodation, and between that year and 31st December 1969, some £1,369,320 was paid to 5,243 widows in respect of 10,728 orphaned children. So, in the course of 100 years, benefit in kind or in cash was been bestowed on 13,535 children.

The Dining Hall

Metropolitan and City Police Orphanage: the main entrance

But this new dimension demanded increased income. A boat race on the Thames in 1871 from Putney Bridge to Barnes Bridge between crews from T and TA Divisions saw a collection on the towpath which yielded £4 1s 7d, typical of several Herculean fundraising efforts. The Police Minstrels, who raised over £200,000 before being disbanded in 1933, were by far the biggest benefactors. But periods of recurring adversity added aggravations. 609 children were orphaned in the two world wars, 283 in the first and 326 in the second, and a further 170 through the influenza epidemic of 1919. In 1919, 1,275 children received benefit, the highest annual total in the history of the charity.[2250]

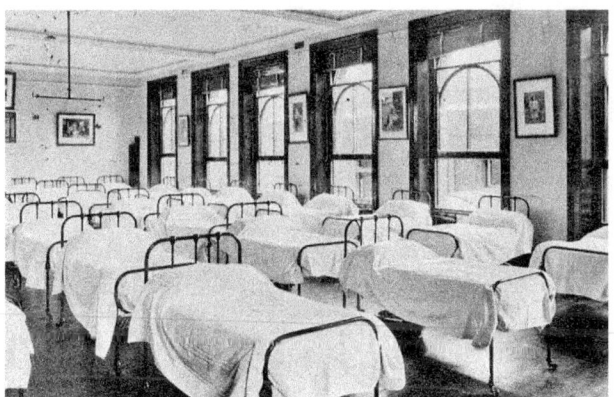

A dormitory at the Orphanage

In 1874 the Baroness Burdett Coutts made an interest-free loan of £3,000 to build a new wing in order to house 60 additional children. It was opened in 1882 by HRH the Prince of Wales, later King Edward VII, and named the Burdett Coutts Wing.

The late Henry Whiting, founder of the Police Relief Fund, afterwards the Bow Street Reward Fund and the Metropolitan and City Police Relief Fund, gave generously during his lifetime. On his death in 1895 his widow and daughter erected a striking clock to his memory in the Orphanage, overlooking the grounds. It still survives, as does a wall-plaque beneath, commemorating the occasion.[2251]

The late Alexander Mann of Richmond, Surrey, who died in 1917, bequeathed the residue of his estate to the Orphanage. His memory is permanently enshrined in the Alexander Mann Bequest, which appears in the annual balance sheet, as does the Twells Memorial Fund founded in 1880 by the late Mrs G. Twells of Enfield with a donation of £500 in memory of her husband.[2252]

The Orphanage's War Memorial Hospital that was built in the grounds of the Orphanage on subscriptions from members of the two Forces in memory of 387 colleagues who gave their lives in the First World War still exists and functions as a hospital. It was opened in 1923 by HRH the Prince of Wales, subsequently the Duke of Windsor.[2253]

The introduction of the 1921 Police Pensions Act probably hastened the closure of the Orphanage, as it gave the widow of a constable and sergeant who had completed at least five years' service an annual pension and an allowance per child to stay at home. The numbers dwindled, and following a vote of the trustees the Orphanage shut in July 1937. On closure the Fund was set up and today it is a registered charity.

Since that time there have been small increases whenever possible, and, following a further increase in the minimum rate of police subscriptions from 3d to 5d weekly from January 1963, the allowance has gradually been increased to £168 per child per annum, the amount payable at 31st December 1969.

2246 www.met-cityorphans.org.uk/history/index3.php accessed 30th March 2012.
2247 Ibid.
2248 Ibid.
2249 Ibid.
2250 Ibid.
2251 Ibid.
2252 Ibid.
2253 Ibid.

During 1969 a total of 357 children received benefit, and at 1st January 1970, 303 children were in receipt of monthly allowances.[2254]

The charity supports the children of serving or former police officers from the Metropolitan and City Police who contributed to the fund and are now either deceased or retired on pension, and are so incapacitated that they are unable to contribute materially to the family upkeep. Applicants can apply to the fund for compassionate allowance etc, and each case is considered on merit by the management board. If you would like to donate please visit www.met-cityorphans.org

The Metropolitan Police (Hayes) Sports Club

London Borough of Bromley

The Warren, Croydon Road, Bromley, Kent (1935 to Present)

The house and lodge at what is now The Warren Police Sports Club was built in the Flemish style by Walter Maximilian de Zoete on land leased, in 1882, for 60 years from Dame Julia Lennard, the wife of Colonel Sir John Farnaby Lennard, a prominent landowner in the district. The de Zoete family, as their name suggests, came from Holland, and became prominent merchants and then stockbrokers in the City of London. Walter's father Samuel was at one time chairman of the Stock Exchange. Walter was a keen golfer, playing in the first amateur golf championship at Hoylake in 1885, and was also interested in antiques and works of art.

The house was named Warren House after the wooded valley to the west of the house known locally as 'the warren' because of rabbits, which locals would catch with ferrets and polecats. A lane bordering the club is named Polecat Alley for similar reasons.

In 1885 Walter de Zoete gave up his interest in the property to banker Martin R. Smith, a great philanthropist and entertainer who extended the premises by adding a billiards room, a new wing, two cottages and a summer house. The main house had twelve bedrooms on the first floor, five staff bedrooms and provided employment for a butler, housekeeper, cook, two footmen, a hall boy, maids, governesses, coachmen and 18 gardeners.

The two cottages housed the head gardener and the watchman, a Mr Wilkins, whose duties had previously been carried out by police constables. In the north-east corner of the grounds is Julian's Wood. Julian, who died in the First World War, was the youngest of Mr Smith's four sons. Carnations began to be cultivated there in 1899, no doubt through the skill of the head gardener Charles Blick. Two of Martin Smith's daughters married into the Hambro banking family, Sir Edward Hambro living nearby in Hayes Place. The game 'bumplepuppy', an early version of swingball, was played in the garden near the house.

Martin Smith died in 1908, and his son Everard sold the house for £15,000 at auction by John Wood and Sons of Grosvenor Square London in 1909. Sir Robert Laidlaw MP, a wealthy businessman whose company Whiteway & Laidlaw were known as the Selfridges of India, planted the trees and rhododendrons that add so much beauty to the grounds.

During the First World War Sir Robert gave the house to the British Red Cross Society for use as a 50-bed hospital, which continued until 1916, the year in which Orpington hospital was opened to treat wounded soldiers from the war. Sir Robert died in 1915, and in 1920 the house was sold to Edwin Preston of West Wickham for £19,500. Mr Preston was interested in growing flowering shrubs and rare plants. He changed the name from Warren House to The Warren.

Conditions were harsh for police officers in those days. Police pay had been 25-35 shillings per week in 1890, and started at 30s per week in 1914. An increase of 13s per week was given in 1918. In 1906 officers had one rest day per fortnight, and received ten days annual leave. The Desborough Committee, set up after Police Strikes of 1918 and 1919, started to improve pay and conditions, and recognised the need for welfare and sports facilities. In 1926 the Mayor of Bromley asked for gifts towards the purchase of a sports ground for the police of P Division, particularly as a sports ground at Thames Ditton was situated too far away to benefit local officers. Mr Preston, whose home was later to become that sought-after sports ground, was himself a contributor to the fund.

In 1934 Mr Preston sold the house to Gordon Ralph Hall-Caine MP of Maidenhead, but he did not take up residence, and it was then bought by the Receiver for the Metropolitan Police District, with assistance from Lady Margetson, the wife of the then Deputy Commissioner, Sir Philip Margetson. The sports club had previously been renting 18 acres at Monks Orchard, Beckenham. Extensive work was needed to convert the house into a clubhouse with a playing field. The large ground floor rooms became dining rooms, one of which had a fine dance floor, and the club was officially opened on 13th June 1935 by the Commissioner, Lord Trenchard.

During the Second World War the stables became a Home Guard base, and many pilots from Biggin Hill were entertained there.

Over the years a number of projects have improved the facilities. Six tennis courts were laid over the old sunken gardens, followed later by two squash courts to complement the football and cricket pitches, and picturesque bowling green. In 1974 the stables were refurbished to accommodate a unit of the Mounted Branch, who stayed until the stables were closed in 1997.

The Warren Sports Club in 2007

The Hobbit sports pavilion and its facilities were opened in 1984, which released space in the main building for offices and a conference room. Then in 1989 the Coney Suite was opened as a popular functions room that can accommodate 300 people, or 200 for a formal dinner. The original drawing room became a members' bar.

This fine house and gardens continues to form a recreational facility for serving and retired members of the Metropolitan Police Service and their families.

Mill Hill Police Station

11-12 Deans Drive, Edgware NW7 (1910-1997)
London Borough of Barnet
S Division (1966-1993)
Borough of Barnet OCU (1993-1997)

The freehold of a vacant site at 11-12 Deans Drive, Edgware NW7 was purchased by the Receiver in 1910. Adjacent property fronting Victoria Road was for use as dwelling houses only.[2255]

The building was a temporary structure of prefabricated sections with a sloping roof. It was principally made of wood and glass, and finished off with a bitumen roof. The station was erected in about 1965 as a temporary police office.

Mill Hill Police Office 1965-1997

In 1966 Mill Hill (SH) was a sectional station to West Hendon (SW) Sub-Divisional station.

The station was closed in 1997, and the functions and police officers transferred to the newly-completed Colindale Police Station.[2256]

Mitcham Police Station

The London Borough of Merton
The Causeway, Lower Green Mitcham (1867-1965)
58 Cricket Green, Mitcham, Surrey CR4 4LA
P or Camberwell Division (1841-1856)
W or Clapham Division (1856 -1965)
V Division (1965-1993)
London Borough of Merton OCU (1993-2018)
South West BCU (SW) (from 2018-20)

The London to Dorking Turnpike, which was established in 1755, passed through Mitcham and had a tollgate situated at Figges Marsh. In reports from 1738 it was considered that travel over Putney Heath was dangerous by both day and night, and this did not change for some time. Even 60 years later Jerry Abershaw, a local highwayman, was sentenced to death and hanged for his deeds. The current police station overlooks Mitcham Cricket Green, and is probably the most famous village cricket green in the world as the game has been played there for more than 250 years. It was the cradle of cricket, providing some of the most famous cricketers of their day. Lord Nelson and Lady Hamilton would drive over to watch matches. Some matches used to attract 6,000 spectators, and the famous W.G. Grace played on the green.

Records show that as early as 1841 there was a police station in Mitcham, under the control of Superintendent Andrew McLean of P or Camberwell Division.[2257] Mr Simpson of

The Green Mitcham with the Town Hall

Church Street, Mitcham was the owner, but Mr Pocock of 17 Lincolns Inn Fields handled the renting of the premises to the Metropolitan Police. The station house was not purpose-built, and consisted of a brick-and-tile house containing seven rooms, with a stable at the rear. There were also two cells, and the conveniences were located at the back in its long garden.

In 1840 P Division (Camberwell) was enlarged to include the Parishes of Croydon, Streatham, Morden, Mitcham, Carshalton, Wallington, Beddington, Woodmansterne, Sutton, Cheam, Banstead, Farleigh, Addington, Coulsdon and Warlingham. New police stations were established at this time at Streatham, Mitcham and Croydon.[2258]

Between 1844 and 1849 Henry Maude, the Brixton Road inspector, was responsible for visiting Mitcham regularly for the purposes of supervision[2259] and usually did so on his horse. The lock-up or cells had been rented and were returned to the owner in December 1868, although no reason was given for this. The Police were responsible for good maintenance of the station both inside and out, so to maintain a smart, white station exterior it was repainted in 1858, 1863 and 1868.

The rent for the Police officers residing at the address was 2s per week for the one married constable, whilst the seven single constables were charged 1s per week rent. It would appear that the married constable was in charge of the daily running of the station up until 1864, when Mitcham Police Station, still on P (or Walworth) Division, became a sergeant-designated station. It had two sergeants and one acting sergeant, with three patrols covered by three constables by day and eleven beats covered by eleven constables during the hours of darkness. The acting sergeant was distinguishable by having two stripes instead of three on each upper arm. The inspector from Carshalton would also visit Mitcham on horseback to sign and check relevant books at the station. The inspector would record his visit in the Occurrence Book in order to show other senior officers that visits had been made. This was a practice carried out by all senior officers, and at times with 'Royalty' visiting.

2254 www.met-cityorphans.org.uk/history/index6.php accessed 6th November 2013.
2255 Metropolitan Police Surveyor's Records, 1912.
2256 MPS Station Closures and Reduced Opening Hours 1997-2000.
2257 *Kelly's Directory* 1843.
2258 Brown, B. (date unknown) 'Metropolitan Police in the County of Surrey'.
2259 *Kelly's Directory* 1849.

In 1856 Mitcham had been removed to W (Clapham) Division, under the charge of Divisional Superintendent William Hayes. In 1873 the Police leased property suitable for a police station from William Simpson of Church Street, Mitcham on a yearly tenancy of £25. This was a sergeant-designated station. In the same year, General Orders issued to all superintendents instructed them to establish a Thieves Register at each station. This contained the name and antecedents of each convicted criminal or suspected person known to be residing in the station area. The register was made available to all those Police officers wishing to view it.[2260] Other books held at stations were called Felony Books, and these were the equivalent to modern-day Crime Books. Reports of crimes were entered into Felony Books.

Constables were earning £52 per annum in 1871, whilst their hours of duty was First Relief 6.00-9.00am, Second Relief 9.00am-3.00pm and 7.00-10.00pm, and Night duty 10.00pm-6.00am.[2261] One day's leave was granted every 14 days, and annual leave for a constable was seven days per annum. For sergeants this was ten days, and inspectors fourteen days.

In 1877 the freehold for land situated at The Causeway, Lower Mitcham, was purchased by the Receiver at a cost of £650. The area was being developed, and greater numbers of people were moving from the Home Counties to Mitcham. This meant that the status of the station was upgraded to an Inspector's Station.

A new Mitcham Station was built in the Victorian style on the purchased land, with two sets of married quarters and a section house situated at the rear. The station also boasted a charge room, inspector's office, cell, and association cell. In the station yard was a parade shed, and an ambulance shelter for the hand ambulance. The station had accommodation for one sergeant and six constables.

In 1878 this was still a station on W or Clapham Division. In 1881 records show that, during a review of cell space, the two cells there were deemed inadequate for the number of prisoners being dealt with, so recommendations were made for a further cell to be added, although the station was considered to be very dilapidated.[2262] In the same year the station was linked by the telegraph via Streatham to its headquarters at Brixton. Any messages for the Commissioner's Office would be passed on from there. The telegraphic code used to identify the station was Mike Charlie (MC), although this was changed later in the 1930s during the Trenchard re-organisation.[2263]

Elias Harris was the sergeant in charge in 1878, and he supervised 19 constables situated at the Causeway, Lower Mitcham.[2264] The following year the station remained sergeant-supervised, with Superintendent William Wiseman in overall charge.[2265]

Surveyors' records in 1881 stated that:

'This Station is dilapidated and the construction of it has been under consideration for years. It should now be taken in hand. The arrangement of the married and single men is bad. The Station is also occupied by One married Constable and six single Constables.' [2266]

Only minimum work was carried out, as arrangements for a new station had been made. By 1881 Mitcham had become an Inspector-Station, still on W Division.

Inspector Robert Butters was in charge of the station in 1891, assisted by four sergeants and 22 constables.[2267] By 1894 Mitcham and Tooting had become a Sectional Station of Streatham.[2268]

In 1919 PC David Davies went down a sewer at Mitcham to investigate the whereabouts of two missing workmen. Davies knew that the fumes generated in the sewers could be lethal, however he progressed with caution. After a short while he found both men collapsed, having become overcome by the fumes. With little regard for his own safety he pulled both out of the sewer. For this brave action he was awarded the King's Police Medal, a rare award.

After 1924 the address of the station changed to 58 The Causeway, Lower East Street (later Lower Green East) a station on W Division. The old-style station required modernisation, and the influx of new residents of Mitcham meant that a new station was needed. Adjacent to the station some prime land became available and inquiries by the Metropolitan Police Surveyors' Department revealed five partly-demolished cottages were up for sale. In 1936 48-56 Lower Green East, Mitcham were purchased from H.W. Harding of St Clements, Romsey, Hants for £1,750.[2269]

In 1938 a telephone line was established between the Police station and the Fire Brigade station. The onset of deteriorating relations with Germany meant there was a likelihood of war, and other priorities meant that a new police station was not built immediately – in fact there was a wait of nearly thirty years before the new station was built at all. In 1939 the address of the station was shown as 58 Lower Green East, with Superintendent M. Miller from Tooting Police Station[2270] in charge.

In 1954 PC John Richard Bailey (warrant no. 128776) was awarded the George Medal for bravery, courage and determination in effecting the arrest of a dangerous criminal in Mitcham who used a firearm to resist capture.

Mitcham Police Station 1965 to present

The current Mitcham Police Station, shown above, was built in 1965 and is located at 58 Cricket Green, Mitcham, Surrey. Built in the modern design over three floors, this station is similar to Albany Street and Holloway Police Stations in north London.

Mitcham Police Station Lamp

Generally, each station has a different blue Police lamp situated at the front, a feature that originated in Victorian London to denote a police station. The lamp shown left was originally built as part of the station in 1965, and was restored as part of a revamp of police station lamps in 1978.

Mitcham Police Station was still open in 2012 with unrestricted opening hours. In 2019 the station was still in the possession of the Metropolitan Police for operational purposes.[2271]

Molyneux Street or John Street (Crawford Place) Police Station

1 Molyneux Street and adjoining buildings (1849-1904)
John Street, Crawford Place (1904-1933)
D Division (1849-1933)

In 1836, D Division comprised Marylebone Lane and 5 Little Harcourt Street, Marylebone, and, perhaps as a replacement for these premises, John Street Police Station and section house was built and occupied in 1848. The John Street site (called Molyneux Street, Edgware Road) was eventually the result of amalgamated freehold purchases at 1 Molyneux Street, 8-10 John Street, 41-43 Horace Street, 1,3&5 Molyneux Street and the Horse and Groom public house. The station came into use in 1849, and an inspector was in charge. The building occupied the corner plot and was situated opposite the Union Almshouse, a short distance from Edgware Road, as we see in the map below.

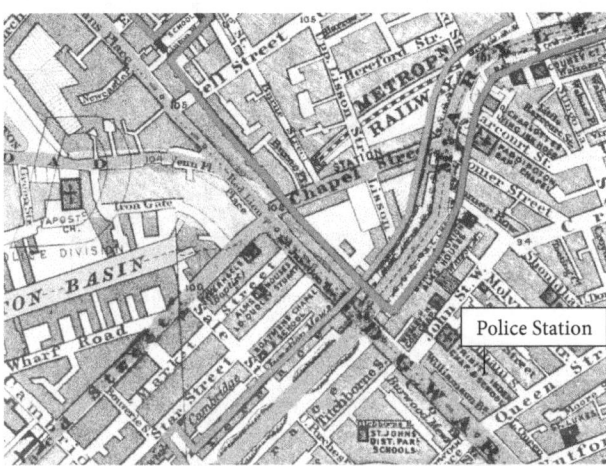

1863 map showing the location of Molyneux Street Police Station

A new police station was then built, and its opening announced in Police Orders of 4th July 1904. It was renamed Crawford Place in Police Orders of 8th February 1913, and was closed on 28th November 1933.

John Street Police Station 1904-1933

John Street also housed, at no. 32, the Shaftesbury Society and Ragged School Union from 1914. The Society (now known as Livability) is a large Christian-based charity that works with disabled people and communities to achieve social inclusion, empowerment and justice.

The Ragged School Union was formed by Lord Shaftesbury in 1844 and was a great force for establishing free education for poor children. As the police stations, and officers in them, upheld the law in London during and after Victorian times, it must have been apparent to many of them that poverty, lack of educational opportunities and the state of local communities would often be the background from which offenders launched into a life of crime. It is a reminder that the police service does not uphold the law in isolation from other features of society.

Morden Police Office

The London Borough of Merton
4 Crown Parade, Crown Lane Morden Surrey (1995-c2018/19)
V Division (1995-1993)
Wimbledon OCU (1993-2018/19)

Morden is situated at the southern end of the Underground's Northern Line, and as an expanding area it was decided to locate a Police Office in Crown Parade.

Morden Police Office, 1995 to present (from the Merton Messenger, July 1995)

In 1961 DC Peter George Bridgwood was killed while on night duty, driving the CID car between stations, when he lost control and collided with a lamp standard in the early hours of the morning at Morden.[2272] This was a tragic story, but sadly not an uncommon one.

It was shown in the records that Morden Police Station was opened in 1995 and situated at 4 Crown Parade, Crown Lane, Morden, Surrey, SM5 5DA. It appears to have office status, and in 2009 was open Mondays to Fridays 8.00am to 4.00pm.[2273]

In 2013 the police station front counter was closed to the public. In 2019 the Morden Police office was still leased but not owned and occupied by the Metropolitan Police with its front counter no longer open.[2274]

2260 *Commissioner's Annual Report* 1972.
2261 MEPO 2/135.
2262 Metropolitan Police Surveyor's Records 1888.
2263 Metropolitan Police General Orders 1893
2264 *Kelly's Directory* 1878 p144.
2265 *Post Office Directory* 1879.
2266 Metropolitan Police Surveyor's Records 1881.
2267 *Kelly's Directory* 1891 p1373.
2268 *Kelly's Directory* 1894.
2269 Metropolitan Police Surveyor's Records.
2270 *Post Office Directory* 1939.
2271 MPS (2019) Freedom of Information request: MPS assets.
2272 www.met.police.uk/history/remembrance4.htm accessed 4th January 2010.
2273 MPA website accessed 15th February 2009.
2274 MPS (2018) Freedom of Information request: MPS assets.

Muswell Hill Police Station 1904-2014

Muswell Hill Police Station

Fortis Green Road (1904-2014)
Y Division (1904-1993)
Hornsey OCU (1993/94-2014)

In 1899 the Metropolitan Police searched for a site for a new police station in the east Finchley area. The Surveyor reported that a suitable site had been found midway between Finchley and Muswell Hill railway stations, at Fortis Green. Authority was given by the Home Office for the purchase of this land, which was situated at the junction with Fortis Green Road and Fortis Green Crescent in the parish of Hornsey, at a cost of £2,500. The sale was completed on 25th June 1900.[2275] A further application for capital to build a new station was authorised by the Home Office on 7th March 1900, with a stipulation that the new station was to cost no more than £2,700.[2276] Tenders were invited and the successful builder completed the new station for occupation in September 1904.[2277]

The records show that an annual rental of 1/- was paid to Messrs. Mann, Crossman and Paulin "in respect of light and air easement". Apart from the station, two sets of married quarters and section house accommodation were provided. There were quarters for the inspector and his family, together with room for ten single constables in the section house.[2278]

The station has on occasions been known as Fortis Green Police Station. The above photograph was taken in 1907, and there is no visible police station lamp, as it was installed later.

A brief insight into the personal arrangements can be seen when inspecting the Y Divisional Seniority Records. On arrival at the station from the Training School, the officer's details were entered into a variety of police ledgers. These were created to ensure that all officers were paid correctly and received appropriate courses and training. It was important to ensure that all constables were trained in first aid so that they could help save lives on the street.

Station Inspector 88268 Axten became an authorised cyclist, having arrived at the station on promotion at the end of October 1922. It had long been recognised that there were not enough inspectors at sub-divisional stations, and even the men began to recognise station sergeants.[2279] Axten was responsible for inside duties, however on occasions he would leave the station on his cycle and supervise the sub-division. He had joined the police on 24th February 1902, giving up his job as a fitter. After training he was posted to the police station, supplied with a uniform and other items of equipment. This would have included a police whistle. Each whistle was numbered and the number, in this case 8162, logged on his records. He had been promoted in August 1908 to sergeant and in December 1912 to station sergeant. In 1922 he was made up to inspector.[2280] The increased administrative obligations of superintendents and sub-divisional inspectors who ran stations meant that the rank of inspector was to be split into classes. These were chief inspectors, 1st and 2nd Class inspectors. Axten was a 2nd Class inspector.

Prior to the revision of station signal codes, Muswell Hill Police Station had been shown as 'MU',[2281] however in the 1930s this was altered to 'YM'.

During the early 1960s economies required the station to be shut for the night shift from 10.00pm-6.00am, commencing on Sunday, 11th September 1960. Initially this closure was for an experimental six months, and required outside duties to be performed by those on the night shift.[2282] A telephone was installed in a container in the window of the station for use by members of the public and police officers as part of what was called the 'Telephone box system'. This telephone was connected to the sub-divisional police station, whilst telephone calls from the public were diverted by the GPO to Hornsey Police Station. Records also show that night closures for certain police stations were ordered, although from 16th April 1968 Muswell Hill Police Station was removed from the list and would cease to close at night.[2283]

Re-organisation in 1965 designated Muswell Hill (YM) as a sectional station to Hornsey (YR) Sub-Division within the newly-formed Borough of Haringey.

In 1998 Muswell Hill was an operational station without designated charging facilities,[2284] but by 1999 it was no longer open to the public.[2285] The building was retained by the police for use as offices, but in February 2014 was sold[2286] and acquired by the Acorn property Group, who have converted the property into top end luxury flats in what is called now called 'Station House'.[2287] The price for the police station was £3.525M.[2288]

New Malden Police Station

The London Borough of Kingston

128 Malden Road KT3 6DD (1887-1993)

V Division (1887-1993)

London Borough of Kingston BCU (1993-1998)

On 30th July 1886 the Superintendent of V or Wandsworth Division reported that a Mr. J. King of Cromwell House, Maiden Road, New Malden in Surrey, had a plot of land for sale on the corner of Maiden and Burlington Roads. The asking price was £600, and it was well situated for a police station, 'exactly in the position required'.

New Malden was a fast-growing neighbourhood, and in the course of a few years became a populous area. The Police Surveyor recommended the purchase of the site in August 1886, and in the October Home Office approval was received for negotiations to be entered into with the vendor. The freehold site was purchased on 28th January 1887 for the sum of £550. Plans were drawn up and a builder obtained to construct the new police station. The cost of erecting the new station was £3,306 3s 10.

New Malden Police Station 1881-1998

The new station at New Malden, on V Division, was occupied by the police and business started there on 1st August 1881. The premises were built with two sets of married quarters, which were rented to police officers who were married with children. The lodging assessment was one married inspector at 5s 6d per week and one married constable at 3s per week.[2289]

In 1901 Sergeant William Ough (warrant no. 66554), aged 40 years, resided at the station with his wife Jane and two sons. Ough had joined the police in 1882, and he resigned on pension in 1907. Also living at the station in 1901 was Constable Thomas Adams, his wife Elizabeth and their two children.[2290]

Rear aspect to New Malden Police station circa 1908

The photograph above shows the rear aspect to the station. To the right is the cell block with iron bars on the windows. Behind the block (where the coal bunker can be seen) was a large charge room, where the station sergeant would take and record all prisoners brought in. He would remove and itemise all their personal items of property and place them safely in paper envelopes, which were methodically sealed for safe-keeping until the prisoner was taken to court or given bail.

A communication was received at the station dated 28th March 1911 from the Maldens and Coombe Urban District Council, decreeing that the number 128 should be marked on the premises. The address of the station thus became 128 Malden Road, New Malden, Surrey.

The Secretary of State authorised a re-organisation of the Force, designed to relate police boundaries to the new local

2275 John Back Archive (1975).
2276 Ibid.
2277 Metropolitan Police Orders dated 10th September 1904.
2278 Metropolitan Police Surveyor's Records 1924.
2279 Fido, M. and Skinner, K. (1999) *The Official Encyclopaedia of Scotland Yard*.
2280 Metropolitan Police Y Divisional Seniority Register (revised 1922).
2281 Metropolitan Police General Orders 1898.
2282 Metropolitan Police Orders dated 10th September 1960.
2283 Metropolitan Police Orders dated 7th May 1968.
2284 *Police and Constabulary Almanac 1998*.
2285 www.met.police.uk/contact/phone.htm dated 12th March 2002.
2286 MPS Stations closed since 2010: Freedom of information request (2017).
2287 www.acornpropertygroup.org/development/station-house-muswell-hill accessed 8th June 2019.
2288 MPS Information rights unit (2019) Land and property sold by the MPS for over £1M over the last 10 years.
2289 Metropolitan Police Orders dated 31st August 1881.
2290 Census 1901.

authority boundaries created by the London Government Act 1963. The new local authority and police boundaries were introduced on 1st April 1965, and New Malden (VN) was designated a sectional station of Kingston (VD) Sub-Division, situated in the new London Borough of Kingston-upon-Thames.[2291]

In February 1980 there were further boundary changes on V District, with a reduction of divisions from three to two when Kingston and Esher Divisions were amalgamated. The new division was named Kingston Division, and incorporated New Malden, Esher, Cobham, Surbiton and East Molesey Sub-Divisions. There was no change to the sub-divisional boundaries.[2292]

The station was shut in 1998 and boarded up, but after a while it was sold to J.D. Wetherspoons who have turned the old station into a public house named The Watchman.[2293]

A new police community office was opened as a contact point soon after the police station was shut. This is located at the CI Tower, St George's Square, High Street, New Malden KT3 4DN (from 1998), and as of 2019 was open to the public between 12.30 and 5.30pm, six days a week.

New Scotland Yard

City of Westminster

Victoria Embankment, SW1A 2HZ (1890-1967)

1 Broadway SW1H 0BG (1967-2016)

35 Victoria Embankment SW1A 2JL (from 2016)

The first headquarters of the Metropolitan Police was at Great Scotland Yard, but running a rapidly expanding organisation from a relatively small house soon became difficult. In the mid-1870s, *The Times* commented;

'Innumerable books are piled up on staircases so that they are almost impassable, piles of clothing, saddles and horse furniture, blankets and all manner of things are piled up in little garrets in a state of what outside Scotland Yard would be called hopeless confusion.'[2294]

So it was not surprising that more buildings in the vicinity were taken into use. By 1887 the police were using numbers 3, 4, 5, 21 and 22 Whitehall Place, and numbers 8 and 9 Great Scotland Yard. Within the yard itself, the police used numbers 1-2 Palace Place as a prisoners' property store and Surveyor's offices. There was a freestanding building that had variously been used to hold stores, the Public Carriage Office, and CID offices. This building was also known as PCO – Police Central Office.

From 1870, the search began for a new headquarters. The completion of Victoria Embankment had created a stretch of land reclaimed from the River Thames, and when a project to build the Grand National Opera House on part of this ground collapsed through lack of funds, the building was then completed in the form of the now famous New Scotland Yard, designed by architect Norman Shaw.

The building provided 140 offices, of which 40 were for the Criminal Investigation Department, with the Commissioner enjoying a turret office overlooking the river. The police took over the building in 1890. The old headquarters 4 Whitehall Place was eventually sub-let before being sold.

The interior of the Norman Shaw building featured a memorial to the Metropolitan Police staff who lost their lives in the two World Wars

Five years later, the police built another building in matching style, known as Scotland House, with a connecting bridge to the original Shaw building. Cannon Row Police Station completed the complex. An extension of the north part of the Norman Shaw building was completed in 1940 and was first used by Combined Operations in World War Two under Lord Louis Mountbatten, before eventually reverting to Metropolitan Police use, and becoming known as the Curtis Green building, after the architect, William Curtis Green.

This building became in due course, the new Cannon Row police station, a Diplomatic Protection Group base, and eventually, in November 2016, New Scotland Yard after the Broadway building was sold for redevelopment.

The 1967 Broadway building was a modern office block for its time, with some floors apparently needing reinforcement to take the weight of the

New Scotland Yard, the famous Norman Shaw building on Embankment SW1 1890-1967. This North building was built first, followed by the South extension

New Scotland Yard, Broadway, 1967-2017

thousands of paper files of Criminal Records Office. The reluctance of some people to leave the iconic Norman Shaw building was soon replaced by Broadway developing its own status and fame, assisted by the revolving New Scotland Yard sign, symbolising the constant 24-hour patrolling watchfulness and made of copper, an architectural pun.

By 2016, the interior of the building had been transformed by computers replacing old-fashioned paper-based administration. Flexible office working removed the need for individual offices, and, in a time of enormous financial constraint, the Broadway site was sold, and the staff transferred into a refurbished Curtis Green building which then took on the name of New Scotland Yard along with the revolving sign.

New Southgate Police Station 1889-1990

New Southgate Police Station

Garfield Road, New Southgate

Y Division (1889-1985)

Edmonton Division (1985-1990/91)

The London Borough of Enfield

New Southgate Police Station Lamp

In June 1886 land was purchased freehold for the building of a Police station at New Southgate, at a cost of £1,000. Records reported that the new station was located on Y Division, and police business commenced in May 1889.[2295] It was situated at the junction of Betsyle Road and Garfield Road. Considerable road and housebuilding appears to have shortened Betsyle Road, because it now lies some distance from the station which is at the junction with the High Road and Garfield Road, New Southgate.

New Southgate was part of Y Division's divisional boundary changes.[2296] As such re-organisation involved re-allocating personnel, Dr. Hugh Scott of Colney Hatch was appointed as Divisional Surgeon to New Southgate.

In May 1889 a request was made by Southgate Local Board to erect a hut on wheels, which would stand in the yard of the station and contain a fire hose. For this an annual rent of 1/- was paid. This was followed in 1905 by a fire escape ladder, which attracted a fee of 5/- per year until it was removed in 1907. The hut was extended in 1909, but by 1929 it was no longer required for the fire hose when it was removed. The Special Constabulary occupied the hut from January 1930.[2297]

In 1930 New Southgate was shown as a Sectional Station of Wood Green, but when local Government boundaries were re-organised in April 1965 it was shown as a Sectional Station of Edmonton Sub-Division. It was designated YN. New Southgate was one of the police stations which were closed at night between 10.00pm and 6.00am.[2298] A telephone for public and police use was installed in a pillar near the front door of the station. This temporary closure later became permanent.[2299]

New Southgate Police Station was given the status of police office, and re-opened to the public for limited periods.[2300] The area was then policed as a neighbourhood unit from Southgate Police Station.

By 1990 the station was still owned by the police, but was closed for operational purposes although various area squads used its offices. The station was closed and by 1992 ceased to be owned by the Metropolitan Police.[2301]

Nine Elms Police Station or Battersea Park Road Police Station

The London Borough of Wandsworth

143 Battersea Park Road (1878-1921)

147 Battersea Park Road (1921-1993)

L Division (1921-1965)

W Division (1965-1921)

L Division (1921-1965)

W Division (1965-1993)

Borough of Wandsworth OCU (1993-2018/19)

SW BCU with Richmond, Kingston and Merton

(2018/19 to Present)

Brought into service in 1878,[2302] a police station at Nine Elms was rented for £38 per year from Mrs Amelia Bird of Kenley. Its address was 143 Battersea Park Road, and the original contract was for 21 years. This was a conventional large Victorian house with basement, ground and first floor. The building required some conversion from an ordinary residential house, and alterations costing £449 ensured the building was suitable

2291 Metropolitan Police Orders dated 6th August 1964.
2292 Metropolitan Police Orders dated 1st February 1980.
2293 www.newmaldenpeople.co.uk/New-Weatherspoon-pub-New-Malden/story-15122381-detail/story.html accessed 14th February 2012.
2294 Weinreb & Hibbert.
2295 Metropolitan Police Orders dated 22nd November 1888.
2296 Metropolitan police Orders dated 4th May 1889.
2297 Metropolitan Police Surveyors Records.
2298 Metropolitan Police Orders dated 25th November 1960.
2299 Metropolitan Police Orders dated 4th August 1961.
2300 Metropolitan Police Orders dated 3rd May 1968.
2301 Police and Constabulary Almanac 1992.
2302 Metropolitan Police Orders dated 13th August 1879.

Nine Elms Police Station Lamp

for Police purposes. For example, there was room for two cells, a charge room, a reserve room and store on the ground floor, whilst the basement contained a kitchen and two day rooms. There is evidence that twelve single constables lived in somewhat cramped circumstances above the station, and a married constable resided in the basement. At the time this cost the married constable £37 16s per annum. Freehold to the premises was obtained in January 1878, and by August 1879 the premises were suitable for occupation.[2303]

Police Orders reported that the building was to be occupied at once, and that the lodging assessment was 3s per week for one married constable whilst the five single constables paid 1s per week each.[2304]

In 1881 Constable Frederick Petherick, his wife and their daughter occupied married quarters at the station, in addition to five single constables who occupied the Section House.[2305]

The Surveyor's report of 1881 showed that at the time of the inspection it was occupied by one married constable and five single constables, and that the conditions were of some concern.

They described the building as

'An ordinary dwelling-house, to which some cells, &c. have been added. It is quite unsuited for its present occupation. The married woman has her washing boiler in the men's mess room.'[2306]

By 1887 the Home Office had decided to authorise the freehold purchase of the site and house together with an adjoining property. The cost of the police station came to £1,550.[2307]

Nine Elms Police Station 1925 to present

Next to the police station in the picture above remnants of the old Victorian Nine Elms Police Station can be seen, and its frontage suggest it was called 'Scotties'.

Police Orders in 1893 confirmed that the station had been fitted with a telegraph and that its call sign was 'Bravo Papa' (BP).[2308] Receiving and sending telegraphs was a responsible position, and was carried out by an 'intelligent constable' who would assist the inspector in charge and had been carefully instructed in the use of the instrument. The station was shown as a Sectional station of Clapham.[2309]

This was shown in 1912 as a station on W or Brixton Division, with the address of 143&145 Battersea Park Road;[2310] it was not called Nine Elms until some time later, in fact until 1923.

It consisted of a station and section house, with the latter replaced and three sets of married quarters built in its place. Nine Elms was designated a station on L or Kennington Division in February 1921, when Z Division was formed and there was a revision of boundaries.[2311] The name change occurred in 1923, when notice was given that Battersea Park Road Station would in future be known as Nine Elms.[2312] A new station was built on the site and occupied for police purposes on 24th August 1925,[2313] although operational matters actually commenced in December 1925.[2314]

Re-alignment of borough boundaries under the Local Government Act 1963, introduced in April 1965, saw Nine Elms being transferred to W or Tooting Division as a Sectional station.[2315]

In 1972 the status of the station was downgraded and Nine Elms became a Police office.[2316] Notice was given in 1977 that Nine Elms would cease to operate as a Police station, and that the premises would be taken over by other departments of the MPS.[2317]

Police search dog Jake and his handler PC Bob Crawford received the Blue Cross Medal for heroism, bravery, and dedication being displayed by the animal at a special award ceremony held by the Blue Cross Animal Hospital in Victoria.

PC Crawford proudly showing off his dog Jake and the Blue Cross medal won

The award, which was presented by actress Felicity Kendal in 2007, was in recognition for their work during the London bombings in July 2005. Jake, a cocker spaniel, and PC Bob Crawford, based at Nine Elms Police Station, were responsible for searching the bus at Tavistock Square and also the Underground tunnel at Russell Square for secondary devices in order that the injured could be evacuated.[2318] The station accommodates dog handlers and other Divisional units for operational purposes but is no longer open to the public.

Nine Elms remains an asset of the Metropolitan Police in 2019 housing part of the dog section.[2319]

Norbury Police Station

The London Borough of Croydon
1516 London Road, Norbury (1925-2013)
W Division (1925-1921)
Z Division (1921-2013)

The area of Norbury was created around the railway station

on the London Road which expanded in the 1930s, and is now indistinguishable from Thornton Heath and the fringes of Streatham (Lambeth) and Mitcham (Merton).[2320]

Superintendent West of W Division submitted a report and plan dated 20th July 1910 for the consideration of the Commissioner for the purchase of a suitable site at Norbury, with a view to securing a piece of land while cheap and the erection of a new station, at a later period, in this rapidly-growing district.

The LCC was erecting 800 workmen's houses on their Norbury Estate and a working-class colony was springing up there; other areas surrounding the site were also available for building purposes. The superintendent felt that it would in time be necessary to have a police station at this spot to relieve Streatham and Thornton Heath Sections. The distance from Streatham was about 1½ miles, from Thornton Heath 1¼ miles, and about two miles from Mitcham Station.[2321]

The Commissioner, in a memorandum to the Home Office dated 6th August 1910, suggested that a site be acquired in the Norbury area for the erection of a new police station.[2322]

On 30th December 1911 a freehold site at Norbury for the erection of the new station was purchased for the sum of £900. The land, which was owned by the Master, Fellows and Scholars of Pembroke College, Cambridge was on lease to the North Surrey Golf Club.[2323]

In September 1912 two local officers, Police Constables 73 Preston and 186 Bevans, sought and were given permission to cultivate the new site on the understanding that they risk the loss of crops when building operations commenced; the officers agreed to pay the Local Authority for any rates that were demanded.[2324]

Norbury Police Station 1925-2013

Discussions on the erection of the new police station took place in June 1913, and plans and working drawings for the new station were approved in October 1915 by the then Commissioner, Sir Edward Henry.[2325] It seems that the officers enjoyed nearly three seasons on the site.

The new police station at Norbury was taken into occupation and business commenced on 17th August 1925. The station included five sets of married quarters.[2326] The Thornton Heath Sub-Division became known as the Norbury Sub-Division, and Sub-Divisional Inspector Pullen was transferred to Norbury.[2327]

On January 1928 the address for the police station was changed to 1516 London Road, Norbury.[2328]

In October 1931 Thornton Heath Police Station was closed to the public and the area, for policing purposes, was divided between Croydon, South Norwood and Norbury Stations.[2329]

A plot of land adjoining Norbury Police Station was purchased freehold for the sum of £575 from a Mr B.G. Utting on 17th November 1938, with a view to further development of the station.[2330] It was recognised that Norbury was totally inadequate for a Sub-Divisional Station, and plans were made to bring it up to near Home Office standards. In the meantime the war intervened, and it was not until 1962 that the building was finally ameliorated and alterations carried out.[2331]

In April 1965, with the creation of the new London Borough of Croydon, Norbury (ZN) remained a Sub-Divisional Station with South Norwood as its Sectional Station.[2332] In 1968 Norbury Police Station became an 'Inspector Unit' with Inspector Derek Bainbridge in charge.[2333]

Norbury Police Station closed in 2013 and was sold the following year for £940,000.[2334]

North Fulham Police Station

London Borough of Hammersmith and Fulham

Crown Road (later named 353 Lillie Road) (1887-1938)

T Division (1887-1909)

B Division (1909-1938)

The land for North Fulham Police Station was purchased in September 1885 at the cost of £1,350, and the construction of the new police station cost £2,559.[2335] It was situated at Crown Road at the junction of Lillie Road. The new station was designed by John Butler, the Metropolitan Police Surveyor, and was opened in October 1887.[2336] The police station was known locally as the 'Jubilee Police Station' because Queen Victoria celebrated her Diamond Jubilee that year.

2303 MEPO 5/50 (376).
2304 Metropolitan Police Orders dated 13th August 1879.
2305 Census 1881.
2306 Metropolitan Police Surveyor's Records 1881.
2307 LB450.
2308 Metropolitan Police General Orders 1893.
2309 *Kirchner's Almanac* 1907.
2310 Metropolitan Surveyor's Records 1912.
2311 Metropolitan Police Orders dated 24th February 1921.
2312 Metropolitan Police Orders dated 21st September 1923.
2313 Metropolitan Surveyor's Records 1924.
2314 Metropolitan Police Orders dated 7th December 1925.
2315 Metropolitan Police Orders dated 6th August 1965.
2316 Metropolitan Police Orders dated 29th December 1972.
2317 Metropolitan Police Orders dated 29th November 1977.
2318 Ibid.
2319 MPS Assets (2019) Freedom of Information request.
2320 Pevsner, N and Cherry, B. (1983) *London: 2. South*. Penguin, Harmondsworth. p225.
2321 MEPO 2/1872.
2322 Ibid.
2323 LB 808.
2324 MEPO 2/1872.
2325 Ibid.
2326 Metropolitan Police Surveyor's Records 1924.
2327 Metropolitan Police Orders dated 14th August 1925.
2328 LB 808.
2329 Metropolitan Police Orders dated 9th October 1931.
2330 LB 808.
2331 Ibid.
2332 Metropolitan Police Orders dated 6th August 1964.
2333 *Croydon Midweek*, 22nd October 1968.
2334 Metropolitan Police Information Rights Unit 22nd October 2017, accessed 25th January 2019.
2335 Metropolitan Police Surveyor's Book.
2336 Metropolitan Police Orders dated 22nd October 1887.

In October 1893 a presentation took place at North Fulham Police Station. This was not to a retiring police officer, which was the normal practice, but to a member of the public. A handsome marble timepiece, subscribed for by the police of the sub-division, was made to Mr W.R. White, an employee of the London Road Car Company. It was for rendering assistance to Constable 121T Timpson when he was brutally assaulted by a number of 'roughs' in Lillie Road, Fulham on 18th July 1893.[2337]

In April 1894 two new cells were added to the existing three, at a cost of £698.[2338]

In the national census of 1911 there were ten constables residing in North Fulham Police Station. The census form was completed and signed by Inspector William Bamsey, although he was living elsewhere with his family.[2339]

In 1928 the police station was a sectional station to Walham Green, and the address was 353 Lillie Road.[2340]

On 1st January 1938, at 6.00am, North Fulham Police Station in Lillie Road was closed and all business transferred to Walham Green.[2341] The building was used for police purposes during the war years from 1939 until 1944, when it was closed.[2342]

North Woolwich Police Station

The London Borough of Newham
Albert Road, North Woolwich E16 2JJ (1904-2013)
K Division (1904-1985/86)
East Ham Division (1985/86-1993/94)
Plaistow Division (1993/94 -2013)

North Woolwich has had a police station in Albert Road since November 1873, when Police Orders gave instructions for the opening of a new Station on K or Stepney Division.[2343] The station was built with single accommodation for four constables and married quarters for the sergeant. It was located on the corner of Albert Road and Station Street, on the opposite side of the road from its present location, some six roads east.[2344]

During upgrading of police buildings at the turn of the century, Police Surveyors felt that a new station was required in North Woolwich. They looked around for land for sale and found that John and Annie Clare owned a site large enough for a police station. Negotiation with the Home Office commenced for the grant of authority to purchase the freehold site at a cost of £2,050, and this was approved in March 1881. The land was purchased in June 1894,[2345] and the new station opened in December 1904.[2346] It housed one married constable and ten single men, paying 4/6d and 1/- per week respectively.[2347]

North Woolwich Police Station 1904-2013

In 1912 there was a dock strike, and detachments of police were drafted in to ensure essential supplies were transported from the docks to their destinations. The event was marked by photographers taking pictures of goods being transported, mounted police and foot duty escorts.

K Division on duty at the Dock Strike of 1912

The picture above shows two inspectors, three sergeants and 22 constables (two dressed in plain clothes) taken by photographers G.L. Shotter of 340 Barking Road, East Ham. This photographer was prolific in taking pictures of the dispute. This picture appears to have been taken in the Victoria and Albert Docks at North Woolwich.

The picture below shows mounted officers from Woodford on J Division. Duty at such disputes involved long hours at work, especially for mounted officers who often paraded at their stations, then tended and fed their horses before riding them to the docks. Often these officers worked twelve-hour days or longer, but they were compensated with overtime pay. This meant that to be selected for such duty was extremely lucrative.

Mounted officers in London's Docks during the 1912 strike

In 1927 the section house at North Woolwich was closed for renovation and refurbishment, but re-opened in January the following year.

North Woolwich Police Station was badly damaged during the 1939-45 war, and there were four casualties. It remained an operational building in spite of the damage.[2348]

During the re-organisation of Local Authority Boundaries in 1965 North Woolwich was shown as a sectional station to East Ham Sub-Division.

In 2013 the North Woolwich Police was closed to the public and the property was then offered for sale.[2349]

Northwood Police Station 1911-2013

Northwood Police Station

The London Borough of Hillingdon

2 Murray Road, Northwood (1911-2019)

X Division (1961-1993/94)

Hillingdon (XS) Division (1993/94-2019)

At the turn of the 20th century Northwood, which until then had been just a village, began to expand. The arrival of the Metropolitan railway gave easier access to the capital, and more residents were moving into the area. Northwood was sparsely policed, and in 1905 Superintendent Olive of X Division sent a report to the Commissioner drawing his attention to the subject. This led directly to an increase in police strength at Ruislip Police Station of one sergeant and two constables[2350] to patrol the Northwood area. There was no police station at Northwood at this stage.[2351]

A plot of freehold land in Northwood, situated at the corner of Murray and Maxwell Roads, was purchased from a Mr L.T. Simmons in December 1906 for £1,000. This land had originally been part of the Eastbury Estate, which had been split up and sold in plots for the building of houses. The Receiver had intended to erect four cottages for police officers to reside in on this site. However, a letter signed by four magistrates living in Northwood was received, requesting that a police station with cell accommodation should be provided at Northwood, and not just cottages.[2352]

Unfortunately, the owners of the land and houses around and adjacent to the Receiver's site did not take kindly to there being a police station in their midst. In May 1908 they petitioned the Commissioner, suggesting that the tone of the neighbourhood would be lowered and the value of their property would drop considerably. They even suggested that the police station should be erected to the east of the railway, in the poorer part of the town where it was most needed.

Nevertheless, in spite of all objections a contract was signed on 7th September 1909 between the Receiver and a local builder, Mr Charles Keasley, for the erection of a new station at Northwood, to include four sets of married quarters, for the sum of £4,793. The building was designed by the Metropolitan Police Surveyor, John Dixon Butler. The new station was built and ready for occupation in July 1911.[2353]

Northwood Police Station is one of only two stations in the whole of London that had a white 'POLICE' light sign outside the building. The local authority would not allow a normal blue lamp, perhaps due to the pressure of local residents who did not want the police station in the first place. However, a blue lamp was installed later. The other police station was Bow Street, opposite the Royal Opera House in Bow Street, London.

The citizens of Northwood had not ceased in their fight against the new police station, and several actions for damages were instituted against the Receiver. In fact, two actually reached the King's Bench Division in the High Court. On

2337 *Birmingham Daily Post*, 27th October 1893.
2338 Metropolitan Police Surveyor's Book.
2339 Census 1911.
2340 *Post Office Directory* 1928.
2341 Metropolitan Police Orders dated 29th December 1937.
2342 MEPO 2/6199.
2343 *K Division Handbook* 1967.
2344 *Bacon's London Atlas* 1888.
2345 *K Division Handbook* 1967.
2346 Metropolitan Police Orders dated 10th December 1904.
2347 Metropolitan Police Surveyor's Records.
2348 *Police at War* (1947). HMSO.
2349 www.met.police.uk Information Rights Unit dated 18th February 2018, accessed 25th January 2019.
2350 Metropolitan Police Orders dated 12th February 1906.
2351 John Back Archive c1975.
2352 Ibid.
2353 Metropolitan Police Orders dated 29th July 1911.

counsel's advice, minimal costs for damages were paid to the plaintiffs and there the matter finally ended, and the presence of the police station was accepted by one and all.[2354]

In 1911 Police Constable William Munday and his wife Ellen and their two teenage children were living in four rooms at the police station.[2355]

There are rumours of a ghost in the police station. Apparently a sergeant hanged himself in the married quarters in the 1920s, and it is said that his ghost occasionally walks from the cells to the station office.[2356]

In October 1927 the local Council informed police that the postal address of the station would be 2 Murray Road, as the entrance was in that road, and that the married quarters should be shown in Maxwell Road, as it was a corner site.[2357]

Special Constables leaving the station on patrol in the 1920s

In the reorganisation of police boundaries, as a result of the creation of new London boroughs with effect from 1st April 1965, the Northwood Police Station became a section station of Uxbridge Sub-Division in the new London Borough of Hillingdon.[2358]

In 1973 Inspector George Rowland was in charge of the station.

In 2008 Northwood Police Station was designated a British listed building, Grade II, under the English Heritage System.[2359] There was special architectural interest as a notable example of a police station by John Dixon Butler, Metropolitan Police Surveyor and Architect, in an old English style, a response to the particularities of the location. Also, the style was subtly expressed and the building is equal in architectural quality to the best of the domestic suburban development with which it sought to be in keeping. Lastly, it was in a good state of preservation with interior and subsidiary features of interest including front doors, vestibule screen, front desk, staircase, post lamp and 1930s police call box.

Grade II listed Northwood Police Station has been vacated and closed. The front counter service at Northwood Police Station came to an end when the volunteers locked up at 1.00pm on Tuesday 5th February 2019. The remainder of the building was scheduled to be operationally shut down from 15th February 2019 and put up for sale.[2360]

Norwood Green Police Station

The London Borough of Ealing
Frognal Green, Heston (1874-1890)
190 Norwood Road, Southall (1890-2008)
T Division (1839-1865)
X Division (1865 -1985/86)
Southall Division XS (1985/86-2008)

In 1854 mention was made of there being a station at Heston on T Division.[2361] There is no information available as to where that station was situated, or indeed what type of station it was.

However, on 9th October 1872 Superintendent W. Fisher of T Division reported on the availability of a nearly new house at 1 Harewood Villas, Frognal Green, Heston which was suitable for a sectional police station. The premises comprised six rooms, and were owned by a Henry Rowe of Norwood Green. They were situated on the road from Southall to Heston. Water was supplied from a well on the premises, and there was suitable accommodation available for a married sergeant. The rent of this house was £20 per annum.

The police surveyor inspected the premises on 1st November 1872 and reported them suitable for police purposes. The Home Office sanctioned the lease of the house on 23rd November 1872 for a term of seven years, commencing 24th June 1873.

In January 1874 Heston (Norwood Green) was ready to be opened for public business.[2362]

The weekly rent for the resident married sergeant was four shillings.[2363] The premises were fairly small; apart from the living accommodation, it only allowed for a charge room and a reserve room.

On 15th July 1880 the Home Office authorised the extension of the lease for a further seven years at a rent of £22 per annum. The lease was further extended from 1887, until these premises were finally given up on 24th June 1890 when a new station opened.

In 1881 the police station at Norwood Green was described as a small cottage in the general line of the houses in the village, occupied by a police inspector. The report also stated that the premises were not fit for permanent occupation, and that the frontage was too narrow.[2364]

Norwood Green Police circa 1890s

In 1886 Inspector John Arnett was in charge.[2365] Later that year, on 22nd November 1886, the agent for the Earl of Jersey, who owned the nearby Osterley Estate, offered a piece of land opposite the station to the Receiver. The asking price was £215 freehold, and this was purchased on 19th April 1888 with a view to the erection of a new station at some future date.[2366] This piece of land was originally the site of Manor Farmhouse and occupied by a Thomas Walton. It is not certain when the building was demolished prior to 1886.[2367]

A new station, the present one, was built on the new site at a cost of £2,714.[2368] It was taken into occupation on 16th June 1890.[2369] In 1894 Norwood Green was a sectional station on T Division, and Superintendent Charles Hunt was in charge of the Division. In 1911 Police Sergeant Arthur Springthorpe was living in four rooms in Norwood Green Police Station with his wife Ada and their two sons.

Norwood Green Police Station 1890-2008

You will note that on the roof of the station is one of the air raid sirens which were placed on police stations in the metropolis in preparation for the oncoming likelihood of war. It appeared that in May 1938 the Home Office placed the responsibility on the Commissioner of operating the public air raid warning system in London. To start with, and to enable coverage across the Metropolitan Police District adequately and so that the sirens could be heard within a mile radius, it was decided that 154 police stations should have a siren. Less powerful sirens, which covered a half-mile radius, were to be placed on 227 Police Boxes. Work commenced in June 1939, and eventually the final figures were increased to 205 police stations and 246 police boxes.[2370]

As a result of experimental night closure of certain police stations in 1960, Norwood Green was one of those affected.[2371] A telephone connected to the sub-divisional station was installed in a pillar in the front garden of the station. This was to allow members of the public to call police when the station was closed. The station remained closed at night until February 1968, when it re-opened 24 hours a day.[2372]

With the reorganisation of the local authority boundaries in April 1965, Norwood Green Police Station was transferred from T to X Division as a sectional station on Southall Division, situated in the London Borough of Ealing.[2373]

When Southall Police Station was being rebuilt in 1973, Norwood Green Police station assumed sub-divisional status.[2374] The senior officers and administration staff were transferred to Norwood Green, and housed in a temporary building built in the station yard. However, in December 1975 the new police station at Southall (XS) was ready for business, and Norwood Green (XW) reverted to sectional status.[2375]

In 1972 Police considered rebuilding Norwood Green Police Station on the existing land, which would have to be extended. A provisional date was set for April 1977, and the estimated cost to be about £150,000. The project was shelved.[2376]

By 2007 the police station was no longer considered viable and fit for purpose, with the Metropolitan Police Asset Management Report suggesting that it should be sold in favour of a new building. In 2008 all operational and administrative offices and staff were moved out of the station, and the building boarded up.

In 2010 Simon Williams Commercial property consultants marketed and sold the old station for development.[2377]

Norwood/Gipsy Hill Police Station

The London Borough of Lambeth
6 Gipsy Hill, Norwood (1859-1940)
66 Central Hill SE19 1DT (1940 to Present)
P Division (1859-1921)
Z Division (1921-1965)
L Division (1965-1985/86)
Streatham Division (1985/86-2018/19)
Part of Central South AS BCU (from 2018/19)

In 1853 the Home Office gave authority for a search to be made for a site for new police station. The need for a new one was due to the start of transferring the Great Exhibition from Hyde Park to Crystal Palace in August 1852. By March 1854 a suitable site had been found in Gipsy Hill, and was leased for a period of 92 years from Mrs Mary Scott of Norfolk Terrace, Fulham Road[2378] with a ground rent of £26.[2379] The new Police Station would be very near the Exhibition site, but the building of the station was delayed during the following months because the contractors complained that the price of building materials had soared since tendering.[2380] Queen Victoria formally opened the Exhibition in June 1854.

A new Police Norwood Sub-Division was formed when the station was opened for business. The building was designed by Charles Reeves, Metropolitan Police Surveyor, and erected a

2354 John Back Archive c1975.
2355 Census 1911.
2356 Metropolitan Police Heritage Archives.
2357 John Back Archive c1975.
2358 Metropolitan Police Orders dated 6th August 1964.
2359 www.britishlistedbuildings.co.uk accessed 21st December 2010.
2360 www.northwoodresidents.co.uk accessed 27th October 2020.
2361 Metropolitan Police Order dated 11th January 1864.
2362 Metropolitan Police Order dated 31st January 1874.
2363 John Back Archive c1975.
2364 Metropolitan Police Report Condition of Police Stations 1881.
2365 *Kelly's Directory* 1886.
2366 John Back Archive c1975.
2367 British History online accessed 16th July 2012; Southall Borough Library Norwood Valuations 1821.
2368 Metropolitan Police Surveyor's Register p174.
2369 Metropolitan Police Orders dated 28th June 1890.
2370 Metropolitan Police Heritage Archives.
2371 Metropolitan Police Orders dated 5th August 1960.
2372 Metropolitan Police Orders dated 30th April 1968.
2373 Metropolitan Police Orders dated 6th August 1964.
2374 Metropolitan Police Orders dated 20th March 1973.
2375 Metropolitan Police Orders dated 5th December 1975.
2376 John Back Archive c1975.
2377 www.sitesetserver2.co.uk/properties.php accessed 3rd December 2012.
2378 Metropolitan Police Surveyor's Records.
2379 Ibid.
2380 MEPO 5/28 (169).

at a cost of £2,461.[2381] The station was built of substantial brick-and-slate, and had 16 rooms, a kitchen, offices, four cells, a three-stall stable, a loft, and two water closets. There were also dung and dust pits, as well as five coal vaults.[2382] An inspector was appointed for duty at the station,[2383] and by 1864 the strength of officers at Norwood comprised two inspectors, eight sergeants and 59 constables. One horse was to be ridden by either of the two inspectors alternately on duty.[2384]

In 1876 a Mrs E.M. Dowling requested permission to place a small window in the party wall adjoining Norwood (later called Gipsy Hill) Police Station, and this was granted. It will be noted that at this time the station was commonly known as Gipsy Hill rather that by its official name of Norwood.[2385] A later Police Order quoted the address of the station as 6 Gipsy Hill, Norwood.[2386] It was not until 1926 that the official name of the station changed to Gipsy Hill.[2387]

In 1881 a report mentioned the close proximity of the station to Crystal Palace, and commented that the basement was occupied by the mess, and the upper rooms were badly arranged into single men's sleeping rooms and a married quarter. It was at that time occupied by one married inspector and 21 single constables.[2388]

Policing at the Crystal Palace Exhibition caused additional work for the Police of Gypsy Hill, so to ease the burden extra officers were allocated to police the Exhibition and Inspector John Fyfe was posted to the site, along with other officers.[2389]

The Census record of 1891 showed that there were still twenty single officers living at the station,[2390] with Inspector Ellams being the officer in charge.[2391]

Gipsy Hill Police Station 1859-1940

The formation of Z (Croydon) Division in 1921 meant that Gipsy Hill was transferred from P to Z.[2392]

On the evening of 30th November 1936, at about 7.40pm, a serious fire occurred at the Crystal Palace, Sydenham. The first officer on the scene was Police Constable Parkins, who called the Penge Fire Brigade; Inspector Hussey of Z Division and Police Constable Wollard then arrived. The fire spread rapidly, and within half an hour the whole Palace was in flames. Police estimated that a crowd of at least 100,000 people had gathered to watch. The mass of people, and a large number of vehicles, caused the inspector to request aid from other police stations. Eventually Superintendent White, two chief inspectors, seven senior divisional inspectors, 21 inspectors, 62 sergeants, 651 constables and five mounted police were in attendance.[2393]

In 1936 it was decided to rebuild Gipsy Hill Police Station in a different location, as the existing site, which fronted on Gipsy Hill, was small and on the side of a steep hill. The freehold of that site had been compulsory purchased in the beginning, and the agent for the freeholders informed the Receiver that they would not sell any additional land voluntarily. In these circumstances another site called Highland House was found, situated on the corner of Central Hill and Highland Road (now Vicars Oak Road). The property was not on the market at that time, but the Ecclesiastical Commissioners were prepared to draw up a 999-year lease and sell for £3,750. Negotiations were concluded in 1937, and a new police station was erected.[2394]

Gipsy Hill Police Station 1940-2013

The modern building was designed by G. Mackenzie Trench, Metropolitan Police Architect and Surveyor, and built by Gibson of Croydon. The design of the new station had been exhibited at the Royal Academy in 1938. It was and still is an imposing structure, in multi-coloured brick and stone with green Starreburg tiling on the roof. Because World War II was ongoing, the new station was not officially opened,[2395] but instead went straight into service at 16 Central Hill in April 1940.[2396] The freehold of the property was bought later, in 1953, for £1,000.[2397] During the Second World War the station was badly damaged by a flying bomb, but there were no Police casualties and the station remained operational.

Meanwhile the old police station was converted into Police flats in 1948; it is now owned by the local authority, and called Gipsy Hill House.

The local authority boundaries changed in 1965, and this resulted in Gipsy Hill Police Station (LG) becoming the sectional station to Streatham Sub-Division (LS) on L Division, within the London Borough of Lambeth.[2398] In 1975 the address of was noted as 66 Central Hill, SE19.[2399]

Gipsy Hill Police Station's front counter was closed to the public in 2013.[2400]

Notting Dale Police Station

Royal Borough of Kensington and Chelsea
St Clement's Road (1868-1897)
Re-designated 58 Sirdar Road (1897 to Present)
X Division (1868-1886)
F Division (1886-1965)
B Division (1965-1993/94)
Part of Brompton OCU (1993/94-2018/19)
Part of Central West BCU (2018/19 to Present)

The modern police station, at 58 Sirdar Road (known as St Clement's Road before 1897) was taken into use on 14th October 1968, replacing an earlier station on the site that had opened in 1876 and had cost £4,881 to build. New cells were added ten years later, in 1886. At the official opening of the new station in 1968, one of the guests was 87-year-old retired PC

Richard Jago, who had joined the Metropolitan Police in 1919 and remembered living in the earlier police station. PC Jago had been brought up to London as a servant in the household of a wealthy family from his native Cornwall, enlisted in the Duke of Cornwall's Light Infantry for the First World War, and then joined the Metropolitan Police, where he described the training as 'making sure that you could read and write'. The uniform consisted of a thick serge jacket with a stiff collar, rather than any shirt and tie, and this became very hot in the summer. Crime was low, and arrests were mainly drunks, who were transported to the station by means of a hand barrow. Transport consisted of three horses, and twenty officers would parade for night duty. The old Notting Dale was described by Mr Jago as hardly a prestige building. 'It was a terrible place. We lived in little boxes at the top, and the basement where we ate was dark and damp.'[2401]

The architect's plan of Notting Dale Police Station 1868-c1968

The Potteries district of Notting Dale had been described in the *Daily News* of January 1893 under the title 'A West End Avernus' (a mythical entrance to the underworld). The reporter used lurid language to describe the social conditions there, concluding that he had 'never seen anything in London more hopelessly degraded and abandoned in life than these wretched places.'[2402] There were eleven common lodging houses there, accommodating 723 people. The death rate in 1896 was found by a Dr Dudfield to be 42.6 per 1,000 living population, compared to 18.1 for the whole of London of the time. The lodging houses were inspected twice per week by the police.

Mary Osbourne (born 1928) lived nearby, and described life in her childhood for *The Story of Notting Dale*:

'We had an area what got flooded and ratty through the summer. We had so many bugs you'd be glad to come out in the summer and sit on the step to get away from them. They'd be crawling up the walls everywhere and them times you had that thick brown paper and inside you could see the larvae. You'd have bets on what one was going to reach the top first. The bugs were in abundance and you would paraffin the bed. They were always buying stuff to get rid of the bugs but you never did.'

She described how the Local Authority had, despite the protests of her father, a totter, insisted on fumigating their furniture when they were being re-housed from Windsor House, Sirdar Road as late as 1951. They had also lived in Bangor Street where '...people helped one another. If you were ill they would order the food. They'd order the food, take it to the family and then go out and collect it, and their first stop use to be Notting Dale police station. They had a basin and everybody would drop in.'

Street betting was also something that the police there had to deal with:

'We'd get the gamblers at night and then the police would come. We'd have the gamblers standing around the lamppost and there would be a boy there and he'd clap the clapper. My brother done it one night and as he clapped the clapper the policeman got hold of my brother and slapped his face. So me mum come out of the house and she, down she went, took my brother away, my Jim it was, and she's hit the copper back and she had to run and the police chased her. She couldn't come out for about a week because every time he was there and they asked the kids 'do you know that lady?' and they'd say no. If they asked anybody they'd say she only just moved there, we don't know her. They used to call the policeman Lightning because he was quick, so she said

Notting Dale Police Station 1968 to present

2381 *Survey of London*. Volume 26, p187.
2382 Metropolitan Police Surveyor's Records.
2383 Metropolitan Police Orders dated 26th January 1859.
2384 Metropolitan Police Orders dated 11th January 1864.
2385 MEPO 5/48 (342).
2386 Metropolitan Police Orders dated 20th June 1884.
2387 Metropolitan Police Orders dated 26th March 1926.
2388 Metropolitan Police Report Condition of Police Stations 1881.
2389 Census 1881.
2390 Census 1891.
2391 *Kelly's Sydenham, Norwood and Streatham Directory* 1891.
2392 Metropolitan Police Orders dated 24 February 1921.
2393 Metropolitan Police Historical Collection.
2394 LB 802.
2395 *West Norwood Times*, 19th April 1940.
2396 Metropolitan Police Orders dated 5th April 1940.
2397 LB 802.
2398 Metropolitan Police Orders dated 6th August 1964.
2399 Metropolitan Police Orders dated 1st August 1975.
2400 Metropolitan Police Information Rights Unit 22nd October 2017, accessed 25th January 2019.
2401 'All Change at the Dale', newspaper item by Simon Frodsham, Metropolitan Police Heritage Centre.
2402 *Survey of London* p346.

to him 'you're not like lightning today are you? You're more like bleedin' thunder' and she smacked his face and ran.'[2403]

When the new Notting Dale was opened in October 1968, in addition to constables, the establishment included three station sergeants, six section sergeants for patrolling, a detective inspector and CID officers. It was a good example of the scheme for extended responsibility for local policing that was a policy of the time.

Community relations of a different perspective were represented by the later location of the Community Liaison Officer and Juvenile Bureau at Notting Dale, currently the base of an active Safer Neighbourhood Unit.

Notting Hill Police Station

Royal Borough of Kensington and Chelsea
69 Ladbroke Road (1854-1906)
101 Ladbroke Road (1906 to Present)
T Division (1854-1865)
X Division (1865-1886)
F Division (1886-1965)
B Division (1965-1993/94)
Part of Brompton OCU (1993/94-2018/19)
Part of Central West BCU (2018/19 to Present)

In the early 19th century, the clay of the Notting Hill area made it a centre for brick making and potteries in the area that later became the Norlands Estate. Pig farming came to the area in the 1820s.

A police station and section house for then T Division was erected in 1854, at a cost of £1,425, at 69 Ladbroke Road W11 on land leased for 50 years from June that year. The building boasted a reserve room, library, charge room, mess, four cells, two WCs, a urinal, and 'pits for dung and dust'.[2404]

Notting Hill Police Station 1854-1906

When the current station at 101 Ladbroke Road was opened in 1906, the former police station was converted into married quarters and was used as such from 1907 until 1939.

Kensington and Notting Hill were amalgamated into the Kensington Sub-Division of F Division on 20th August 1939.

Later, the larger houses in the area became multi-occupied, and Notting Hill eventually became one of the centres for Afro-Caribbean settlement in London after the Second World War. Tensions between white racist youths and the immigrant community resulted in perceptions that the police were not taking racist assaults seriously, and protests about the situation led up to the Notting Hill race riots in 1958. A series of attacks on black people led to the arrest of ten white youths immediately before the riots erupted, and their trial, that took place after the riots, led to exemplary sentences of five years' imprisonment to act as a deterrent.

Notting Hill Police Station 1906 to present

The following year, 1959, saw the start of the Notting Hill Carnival, intended by Claudia Jones as a positive celebration of black culture. This event gradually increased in size to become the largest regular public order commitment for the Metropolitan Police, attracting over one million people to the streets of Notting Hill on the last Sunday and Monday of each August. Rioting after the 1976 carnival saw police officers trying to protect themselves with dustbin lids, prior to the introduction of public order shields and protective uniform and equipment.

In 1985 the moving music floats were persuaded to adopt a set route rather than adopting random and sometimes conflicting paths through narrow streets. Greater control over the static sound systems, street trading, close-down times and alcohol sales have gradually made the event more manageable and attractive to sponsors. Public safety and street crime remain important issues in terms of policing the event, so that exuberant enjoyment can take place, but with some ability to control things when the need arises.

The scale of the event has long since been taken over by the Metropolitan Police as a whole rather than managed by the local Division. More recently, the large houses in some parts of Notting Hill have attracted a more wealthy residential population.

Old Street Police Station

The London Borough of Hackney
Old Street, St. Lukes (1833-1852]
53 Old Street (1852-1906)
337 Old Street (1906-1973)
G Division (1833-1973)

There have been three police stations located in the Old Street area. Two were located in Old Street itself, whilst another was situated at 58 Featherstone Street, Finsbury in the Parish of St.

Old Street Police Station 1906-1973

Lukes, just north of Bunhill Fields.

This station was originally named Old Street, St. Lukes Police Station, and was not only an operational police station but also a section house. It was leased in December 1833 for 21 years from Mr. William Mouls of Newington Butts, Lambeth. The building consisted of an old brick-and-tile house with a small yard, four cells, two water closets and a dirt hole. This station was vacated in 1852 in favour of Old Street Police Station situated not far away, where all police business was transferred.

The Metropolitan Police Surveyor was interested in some land, which became available for lease in 1850 in Old Street, St. Lukes on the north side of the road just east of Goswell Road in Finsbury. The site was considered suitable for the building of a police station. The arrangements for the lease ensured that the owners Messrs H.B. Ray and R.J. Olives (Trustees) would receive £52 10s per year ground rent, and that the lease would run for 70 years expiring in 1920. The Receiver was required to pay the rates and deal with any repairs, although no insurance was required to be paid by the police.

In 1852 a station was built at 55 Old Street, Finsbury, in the parish of St. Lukes, on the north side opposite the junction with Norway Street some distance from Goswell Road. This was the first station to be located in Old Street. The station cost a total of £2,400 and included a basement, ground, first and second floors. On the first and second floors, 32 constables resided in cubicles under cramped conditions. A married sergeant occupied two rooms on the first floor. The net income of £92 6s 0d meant a profit of just under £40 for the Receiver.

In 1862 the station was shown as located on G or Finsbury Division. In 1873 G Division comprised only two stations, Old Street and Kings Cross Road. Both were stations with inspectors in charge, covering an area of just over one square mile.[2405]

In 1881 a married constable, Charles Denlow from Yarmouth in Norfolk, and his wife and son lived at the station with 31 single constables.[2406]

Records also show that the freehold title to the site was obtained in December 1900. These included buildings located at 335, 337 & 339 Old Street, together with 1a, 2a, 4, 6, 8 & 10 Hoxton Street. Furthermore, land on which the Weavers and Porters Almshouses stood was also purchased. A builder's yard and adjacent almshouses cost the Receiver £16,500 and £11,300 to buy.

Old Street Police station was built at a cost of £11,120, whilst the court building was more expensive to construct at £16,680. The builders were Grover and Son, Wilton Works, New North Road, Islington. The whole Old Street Court complex, including the land purchases and buildings, had cost the Receiver £82,209, which was a large amount of money in those days.

The facilities at the station and courthouse were considerable. For example, there was one large association cell which could take anything up to twenty prisoners, whilst there were five single cells for men and four cells for women. There was also an inspectors' room and a charge room on the ground floor. Records indicate that an inspector (married) paid rent of 9/6 per week for a medium-sized room on the first floor, whilst 37 single constables paid 1/- per week rent.

The new police station and court were completed in January 1906.[2407] In 1924 a telephone line was installed as part of air raid precautions in the event of war, and the station remained open until 1973.[2408] It was considered no longer useful as a police station, and the building was taken over by the court.[2409]

2403 Notting Dale Urban Studies. Interview of Mary Osbourne by Sharon Whetlor for 'The Story of Notting Dale' at www.historytalk.org/Notting%20Dale/nd%20maryosbourne.pdf
2404 Metropolitan Police Property Register.
2405 Metropolitan Police General Orders 1873.
2406 Census 1881.
2407 Metropolitan Police Orders 6th January 1906.
2408 Metropolitan Police Orders 6th July 1973.
2409 John Back Archive (1975).

Orpington Police Station (PN)

London Borough of Bromley
The Walnuts, BR6 0TE (1983-2017)
P Division (1983-1985/86)
Orpington Division PN (1985/86-1993/94)
Bromley & Orpington OCU PY (1993/94-2017)

The town of Orpington spent its early life as a village smaller than St Mary Cray, but the introduction of a railway station with a good service to London soon created a rapid expansion of housing development. For many years the town was policed from St Mary Cray Police Station, which lived under the perpetual state of being intended for replacement by a new station in Orpington. St Mary Cray was referred to as the 'temporary' sub-divisional headquarters in the 1965 re-organisation, and Orpington finally received its brand-new police station in the then-new Walnuts shopping centre in December 1983.

Orpington Police Station 1983-2017

The architecture of the police station reflects the times in which it was planned. Offices had become the largest use of space, particularly on the upper floors, and the constant changes of use made it worthwhile to have internal walls that could easily be moved. The custody suite was purpose-built for its time, and a trend to emphasise public service and community links meant that there was little taste for copying the more fortified appearance of some other London police stations that had been designed to withstand riots.

All divisions at this time also had their own purpose-built command and control rooms, with computerised links from New Scotland Yard to transfer details of 999 emergency calls to a series of control monitors that could also deal with telephone calls, local radio traffic and other communications tasks. As the rise in telephone use has grown over the years, so the number of emergency and non-emergency call traffic has increased dramatically. The lone station telephonist may have known the surrounding area well, but the modern trend is for more distant call centres, operated under contract, that can use large numbers of staff to aim for better standards of efficiency and flexible working to meet this particular form of demand.

Orpington police station was sold, demolished and re-developed as flats and a medical centre in 2017.

Paddington and Paddington Green Police Stations

City of Westminster
Church Place, Paddington (1830-1840/41)
Hermitage Street, Paddington (c.1841-1865)
6 (later 62) Harrow Road (including 31 Dudley Grove) (1864-1971)
2-4 Harrow Road (1971-2016)
88 Church Street NW8 (from 2016)
T Division (1829-1865)
X Division (1865-1886)
F Division (1886-1933)
D Division (1933-1985/86)
Part of No. 8 Area (1985/86-c.1993)
Part of No. 1 Area (Central) (c.1993-c.2018)
Part of Central West Basic Command Unit (c.2018 to Present)

An early Paddington police station existed, vested with the Receiver by Act of Parliament, and was probably the station referred to in about 1832[2410] as T Division's Church Place, Paddington which was given up in 1840. The Property Register recorded this building as being substantial, with three cells, a coal cellar, a charge room, a WC and a small yard, but noted that 'the cells are not warmed and the floors are decaying'. There is confusion between identifying some early stations, especially Paddington and what later became Harrow Road, as both had addresses in the same road but at differing ends. In 1841 a station at Hermitage Street (called Hermitage Street, Paddington) was situated at the junction with Bishops Row, Paddington with Inspector William Wiggins in charge as a station of D or Marylebone Division.[2411]

This substantial station backed on to the almshouses, and was right opposite the Paddington vestry hall. The station was given up in 1865 when the replacement at 6 Harrow Road became available.[2412]

1863 map showing Hermitage Street Police Station, Paddington

A police station was built in Dudley Grove, immediately opposite the old station in the stretch of Harrow Road west of the hall, in 1864. There were 88 rooms, 17 WCs, 16 coal cellars, 12 pantries, 12 sculleries, five cells and three dust shafts. Both the vestry hall, which later became the town hall, and the police station were afterwards substantially enlarged, giving some dignity to an already run-down neighbourhood at the price of being separated from many of Paddington's later public buildings nearer Bayswater.

Business was transferred to the new police station in 1865 – to 6 Harrow Road W2, the address being referred to as no.

62 in 1924,[2413] including 31 Dudley Grove. It was built as a station, section house and a complex of 66 model dwellings, at a cost of £8,617 after the land had been purchased for £2,875.

Paddington Police Station 1864-1971, and Below, the rear yard of the station showing married quarters and the station prisoner transport

Alterations to remove the triangular-shaped gables on its roof were made and it closed in 1971, being replaced by a large complex.

Paddington had been part of F Division in 1909 and transferred to D Division in 1933. In the picture at the top of the next column one can see the police station to the right, and the section house and model dwellings to the left. There was a separate door into the accommodation part, and these buildings were essentially separate.

The most striking change was the construction in the mid-1960s of the flyover across Edgware Road and its linking in 1970 with the elevated Westway, which ran parallel to a widened and realigned Harrow Road along the southern edge of Paddington Green. Buildings at the junction of Harrow

Paddington Police Station after alterations

and Edgware Roads, including the Metropolitan Theatre of Varieties, were partly replaced by the large Paddington Green Police Station at the north corner and the towering London Metropole hotel at the south.

The old town hall, police station, and houses of Dudley Grove were also demolished, to allow Harrow Road to pass closer to the church. Modern road building has reinforced the separation of Paddington Green from the south part of the parish, where Edgware Road, except near Praed Street, is much more imposing and uniform than it is between the flyover and Maida Vale.[2414] The stark new concrete police station and yellow-brick blocks of Gilbert Sheldon House contrast with many converted mid-19th century houses, those of the old Devonshire Terrace having shop fronts built over their gardens, and with J. Turner & Son's former boot factory of c.1865 at the corner of Cuthbert Street. Similarly, the shopping parade and towers of Hall Place contrast with a late 19th-century red-brick range near Maida Avenue.[2415]

On 23rd March 1971 the new Paddington Green station was opened on a site that included the former Metropolitan Palace of Varieties. The new building, which cost £1.4m, was hailed at the time as the most modern in the world.

Dominated by the A40 Marylebone flyover, it was at the time by far the largest station complex ever built by the Metropolitan Police. It accommodated a section house, but more significantly the recruits selection and careers information centre, and became the first police building entered by many officers during their service.

Building work had started in January 1968 on the new Paddington Green Police Station situated at 2-4 Harrow Road. Designed to be defensible against attack, the station also accommodated a secure custody area set aside for terrorist prisoners and high-risk suspects.

The cells are described as:

'The walls are a cheery yellow, a colour designed to give an illusion of space. The chair and the thick mattress are an equally bright blue. Daylight filters in through a perspex domed window

2410 Return of Mops (1832) Metropolitan Police.
2411 *The Police and Constabulary List* 1844.
2412 *Kelly's Directory* 1865.
2413 Metropolitan Police Property Schedule, February 1924.
2414 'Paddington: Paddington Green' in *A History of the County of Middlesex: Volume 9: Hampstead, Paddington* (1989), pp185-190 via www.british-history.ac.uk/report.aspx?compid=22663&strquery= police accessed 3rd December 2012.
2415 Ibid.

in the ceiling; there's air-conditioning, a private WC and basin, a desk, storage for clothes and books and even access to music and films. It could be any superior budget hotel, and it's in a great location – just ten minutes from London's Oxford Street.'

Paddington Green Police Station 1971-2018

There are 2 inch-thick steel doors, with sound-deadening materials in the walls, and a CCTV camera monitoring system that follows your every move (except perhaps those using the en-suite facilities). They have been refurbished at a reported cost of £490,000. Suspects could potentially stay for up to 28 days, although in reality they stay less than six hours in the main. For the longer-stay customers, this is reflected in that beds have a thick mattress and, instead of a police blanket, detainees get a soft duvet.' [2416]

In 2016 the Mayor's Office for Policing and Crime (MOPAC) decided to redevelop the site and to create a front counter facility from the financial proceeds. This resulted in the building being closed, and a Safer Neighbourhood Base being established at 88 Church Street, NW8 in a busy market area on the eastern side of Edgware Road.

Church Street Safer Neighbourhood Base 2018 to present

Peckham Police Station

The London Borough of Southwark
177 High Street, Peckham (1847 to Present)
P Division (1830-1932)
L Division (1932-1965)
M Division (1965-1985/86)
Peckham Division (1985/86-2018/19)
Central South AS OCU (from 2018/19)

Prior to the arrival of the Metropolitan Police in Peckham the watchmen worked from a Watch House at the corner of High Street and Hill Street.[2417]

In the year 1847 a property known as The Clock House, situated at 177 High Street, Peckham was leased from a Mr Henry Thomas Perkins to be used for Police purposes.[2418] The building had previously been occupied by the wealthy Dalton family, and was formerly part of their fine mansion. It was subsequently used a nunnery.[2419] The lease ran from Michaelmas of that year to Michaelmas 1903, with a rent of £103 10 0d per annum. A year later, in 1848, the old Peckham Watch House was surrendered to the parochial authorities as being no longer required.[2420]

In 1864 Peckham Police Station was recorded as being on P (Camberwell) Division. The station strength was two inspectors, seven sergeants, 69 constables and three horses. One horse was shared by the two inspectors, and another shared by the two sergeants when on duty; alternatively at either of the two stations of Peckham or Brixton.[2421]

Peckham Police Station 1847-1893

In 1880 the address of the station was shown as The Clock House, High Street, Peckham.[2422] In 1881 a report was made on the condition of all the Met's police stations. Peckham was described as

"a fine property with large area. The principal building is an old Manor House, occupied as quarters for single men and one married man. The arrangement is inconvenient. There is another block, containing the administration and some sleeping rooms, not well arranged." [2423]

During the 1880s it was decided to rebuild Peckham Police Station, as the present one was considered unsuitable for the district which had grown up around it. With this in mind, the owner of the property, Mr Perkins, was approached to consider selling his freehold interest to the Receiver. He was not interested, so the Receiver, using his powers under the Metropolitan Police Act 1886, was given approval by the Home Office on 11th September 1889 to acquire compulsorily the freehold of the Peckham Police premises. In May 1890 at the High Court of Justice, Mr Lumley Smith QC official referee, heard the case Perkins v The Receiver of Police to assess the

in the ceiling; there's air-conditioning, a private WC and basin, a desk, storage for clothes and books and even access to music and films. It could be any superior budget hotel, and it's in a great location – just ten minutes from London's Oxford Street.'

Paddington Green Police Station 1971-2018

There are 2 inch-thick steel doors, with sound-deadening materials in the walls, and a CCTV camera monitoring system that follows your every move (except perhaps those using the en-suite facilities). They have been refurbished at a reported cost of £490,000. Suspects could potentially stay for up to 28 days, although in reality they stay less than six hours in the main. For the longer-stay customers, this is reflected in that beds have a thick mattress and, instead of a police blanket, detainees get a soft duvet.' 2416

In 2016 the Mayor's Office for Policing and Crime (MOPAC) decided to redevelop the site and to create a front counter facility from the financial proceeds. This resulted in the building being closed, and a Safer Neighbourhood Base being established at 88 Church Street, NW8 in a busy market area on the eastern side of Edgware Road.

Church Street Safer Neighbourhood Base 2018 to present

Peckham Police Station

The London Borough of Southwark
177 High Street, Peckham (1847 to Present)
P Division (1830-1932)
L Division (1932-1965)
M Division (1965-1985/86)
Peckham Division (1985/86-2018/19)
Central South AS OCU (from 2018/19)

Prior to the arrival of the Metropolitan Police in Peckham the watchmen worked from a Watch House at the corner of High Street and Hill Street.2417

In the year 1847 a property known as The Clock House, situated at 177 High Street, Peckham was leased from a Mr Henry Thomas Perkins to be used for Police purposes.2418 The building had previously been occupied by the wealthy Dalton family, and was formerly part of their fine mansion. It was subsequently used a nunnery.2419 The lease ran from Michaelmas of that year to Michaelmas 1903, with a rent of £103 10 0d per annum. A year later, in 1848, the old Peckham Watch House was surrendered to the parochial authorities as being no longer required.2420

In 1864 Peckham Police Station was recorded as being on P (Camberwell) Division. The station strength was two inspectors, seven sergeants, 69 constables and three horses. One horse was shared by the two inspectors, and another shared by the two sergeants when on duty; alternatively at either of the two stations of Peckham or Brixton.2421

Peckham Police Station 1847-1893

In 1880 the address of the station was shown as The Clock House, High Street, Peckham.2422 In 1881 a report was made on the condition of all the Met's police stations. Peckham was described as

"a fine property with large area. The principal building is an old Manor House, occupied as quarters for single men and one married man. The arrangement is inconvenient. There is another block, containing the administration and some sleeping rooms, not well arranged." 2423

During the 1880s it was decided to rebuild Peckham Police Station, as the present one was considered unsuitable for the district which had grown up around it. With this in mind, the owner of the property, Mr Perkins, was approached to consider selling his freehold interest to the Receiver. He was not interested, so the Receiver, using his powers under the Metropolitan Police Act 1886, was given approval by the Home Office on 11th September 1889 to acquire compulsorily the freehold of the Peckham Police premises. In May 1890 at the High Court of Justice, Mr Lumley Smith QC official referee, heard the case Perkins v The Receiver of Police to assess the

62 in 1924,[2413] including 31 Dudley Grove. It was built as a station, section house and a complex of 66 model dwellings, at a cost of £8,617 after the land had been purchased for £2,875.

Paddington Police Station 1864-1971, and Below, the rear yard of the station showing married quarters and the station prisoner transport

Alterations to remove the triangular-shaped gables on its roof were made and it closed in 1971, being replaced by a large complex.

Paddington had been part of F Division in 1909 and transferred to D Division in 1933. In the picture at the top of the next column one can see the police station to the right, and the section house and model dwellings to the left. There was a separate door into the accommodation part, and these buildings were essentially separate.

The most striking change was the construction in the mid-1960s of the flyover across Edgware Road and its linking in 1970 with the elevated Westway, which ran parallel to a widened and realigned Harrow Road along the southern edge of Paddington Green. Buildings at the junction of Harrow

Paddington Police Station after alterations

and Edgware Roads, including the Metropolitan Theatre of Varieties, were partly replaced by the large Paddington Green Police Station at the north corner and the towering London Metropole hotel at the south.

The old town hall, police station, and houses of Dudley Grove were also demolished, to allow Harrow Road to pass closer to the church. Modern road building has reinforced the separation of Paddington Green from the south part of the parish, where Edgware Road, except near Praed Street, is much more imposing and uniform than it is between the flyover and Maida Vale.[2414] The stark new concrete police station and yellow-brick blocks of Gilbert Sheldon House contrast with many converted mid-19th century houses, those of the old Devonshire Terrace having shop fronts built over their gardens, and with J. Turner & Son's former boot factory of c.1865 at the corner of Cuthbert Street. Similarly, the shopping parade and towers of Hall Place contrast with a late 19th-century red-brick range near Maida Avenue.[2415]

On 23rd March 1971 the new Paddington Green station was opened on a site that included the former Metropolitan Palace of Varieties. The new building, which cost £1.4m, was hailed at the time as the most modern in the world.

Dominated by the A40 Marylebone flyover, it was at the time by far the largest station complex ever built by the Metropolitan Police. It accommodated a section house, but more significantly the recruits selection and careers information centre, and became the first police building entered by many officers during their service.

Building work had started in January 1968 on the new Paddington Green Police Station situated at 2-4 Harrow Road. Designed to be defensible against attack, the station also accommodated a secure custody area set aside for terrorist prisoners and high-risk suspects.

The cells are described as:

'The walls are a cheery yellow, a colour designed to give an illusion of space. The chair and the thick mattress are an equally bright blue. Daylight filters in through a perspex domed window

2410 Return of Mops (1832) Metropolitan Police.
2411 *The Police and Constabulary List* 1844.
2412 *Kelly's Directory* 1865.
2413 Metropolitan Police Property Schedule, February 1924.
2414 'Paddington: Paddington Green' in *A History of the County of Middlesex: Volume 9: Hampstead, Paddington* (1989), pp185-190 via www.british-history.ac.uk/report.aspx?compid=22663&strquery= police accessed 3rd December 2012.
2415 Ibid.

amount of compensation to be paid to Mr Perkins for the compulsory purchase of the buildings and land at Peckham which had been rented for Police purposes. The sum awarded was £4,000 and the purchase of the freehold was completed on 11th September 1890.[2424]

The National Census in 1891 recorded that there were nineteen single officers living at the station; Police Sergeant Joseph Daniel and eighteen constables.[2425]

The new station, designed by John Butler, Metropolitan Police Surveyor, was opened in November 1893[2426] and cost £8,788 to build.[2427] The new building was built on the same site as the old one, at the corner of Peckham High Street and Meeting House Lane. Prior to the building of the new station the Vestry indicated that they were unhappy that the new police station was not only replacing the old one, but also that the boundary was too far out at the corner of the road. They had gained a road widening at this junction and the new police station, in spite of having a single-storey front, was coming out over the building line. The Vestry was told that the Council were unable to alter the plans.

Peckham Police Station 1893-2017

An interesting point of note is that on 3rd January 1898, the parish of St. Giles, Camberwell granted permission for the display of a notice board outside the police station upon the nominal payment of 1s 0d per annum.[2428]

Charles Booth's *Inquiry into the Life and Labour of the People in London*, undertaken between 1886 and 1903, was one of several surveys of working class life carried out in the 19th century. Booth and his researchers walked with Police Officers in various parts of North and South London, and in October 1899 records show that Police Constable Dolby of Peckham Police Station conducted the researchers around his beat. Dolby had been in the Force for about eight years, and had been stationed at Peckham in all that time. He had been 'marked out' for promotion, and was hoping to be promoted to Sergeant within the year. He was described as 'a good fellow, capable and honest'. He was one of the few 'cockneys' in the force, having born in Fore Street, City.[2429]

In 1932 there was a reorganisation of Police boundaries and Peckham was transferred from P Division to L or Lambeth Division.[2430] By 1939 the Division was under the command of Superintendent M. Purbrick.[2431]

With a view to the future and possible erection of another new station for Peckham, the derelict properties of 180-188 Meeting House Lane, which adjoined the station site, were purchased on 1st September 1938 from a Miss Clayton for the sum of £1,700 freehold. This project never got off the ground, and in 1976 it was reported that it was no longer in the Building Programme.

More boundary changes in 1964 moved Peckham (MM) as a Sub-Divisional Station on M Division with East Dulwich (ME) and West Dulwich (MW) as its Sectional Stations, all situated in the new London Borough of Southwark.[2432]

In 1973 it was said that the police station would be demolished and a new one built at the cost of £500,000.[2433]

In 1985 Peckham Police Station was closed for major building work. Staff were relocated to Camberwell Police Station until March 1988. HRH Princess Alexandra reopened the extended Peckham.[2434]

Peckham Police Station is the base for four Safer Neighbourhood Teams.[2435]

Penge Police Station

London Borough of Bromley

175 High Street (formerly Beckenham Road) (1875-2015)

P Division (1875-1985/86)

Bromley Division (1985/6-2015)

It was in October 1867 that the overseers of the hamlet of Penge drew the attention of the Metropolitan Police Commissioner in strong but polite terms to the fact that they were contributing over £3,000 per annum to the Metropolitan Police rate, and had been begging for a police station for four years 'consequent on the growing poverty and want of employment of the lower classes in this locality.'

The local police had identified a site at the corner of Green Lane and Dulwich Road, Penge, and a year later Home Office approval came through to lease the premises. A temporary police station became operational on 2nd May 1870, and was part of a new Sydenham Sub-Division where Inspector Ings took charge not only of the police station and the officers, but also the horse previously ridden by the sergeant. The new police station at Penge was built for £788 10s 5d, and occupied on 17th May 1872, with its address clarified as 175 Beckenham Road, Penge (in 1879 renamed High Street, but keeping the same number).

The original lease belonged to Mr Cree Jew, Lower Tulse Hill, Brixton to run from September 1868 to 29th September 1958 with an annual rental of £130. Later the lease passed to Mr Henry Chandless of Henrietta Street, Covent Garden, from whom the freehold was bought for £1,617 in January 1899.

2416   dailymail.co.uk/home/moslive/article-1287132/Inside-terror-cell-The-London-police-station-housed-failed-July-21-bombers-Guantanamo-Bay-prisoners.html accessed 3rd December 2012.
2417   'The Story of Peckham'. London Borough of Southwark, No. 3 2nd Ed (1983) p.12.
2418   John Back Archive (1975).
2419   John Beasley, Local historian.
2420   John Back Archive (1975).
2421   Metropolitan Police Orders dated 11th January 1864.
2422   John Back Archive (1975); HO45/9675/A46779.
2423   Metropolitan Police Report Condition of Police Stations 1881.
2424   John Back Archive (1975).
2425   Census 1891.
2426   Metropolitan Police Orders dated 22nd November 1893.
2427   London Metropolitan Archives GLC/AR/BR/22/004837.
2428   HBR/JD 5th January 1959.
2429   booth.lse.ac.uk accessed 11th April 2008.
2430   Metropolitan Police Orders dated 1st January 1932.
2431   *London Directory* 1939.
2432   Metropolitan Police Orders dated 6 Aug 1964.
2433   *South London Press*, 7th August 1973.
2434   John Beasley, Local historian.
2435   Metropolitan Police Estate. Asset Management Plan 2007.

Penge Police Station 1872-2015

The building featured a reserve room (later the mainstay of the communications for police stations until the Command and Control project of the 1980s), an office and three cells. In the basement was a washing room, a cooking kitchen, a drying room, brushing room, a water closet and five cellars. The supplies of coal and coke were organised by a series of contracts throughout the Metropolitan Police District. Penge was in south east London for these purposes, the contractor in 1884 being Messrs Corrall & Co. of Forest Hill.

The rear of Penge Police Station, showing the stable and hay loft

Lockers were provided for food, but were found, in 1881, often also to contain a miscellany of boot polish and other equipment. Officers needed somewhere to dry their wet uniforms and to store their boots, and uniform lockers remain to this day a major accommodation issue in the basements of police stations.

Penge and Beckenham became part of Southend Village (ie Catford) Sub-Division on 1st January 1932, but both were transferred to Bromley Sub-Division on 1st April 1965 when Divisional boundaries were changed to match the new London Boroughs.

Penge station was closed at night from October 1960, but re-opened in May 1966 to survive for a period as one of the oldest police stations still to be operational.

By 2015 Penge Police Station had closed, replaced by a Safer Neighbourhood base at Charles Dickens Terrace, 190 Maple Road, which itself was closed by 2019.

Penge Safer Neighbourhood Base 2015-2019

Pinner Police Station

The London Borough of Harrow
Cottages, Pinner (1840-1899)
Waxwell Rise, Pinner (1899 to Present)
T Division (1840-1899)
X Division (1899-1965)
Q Division (1965-1993)
Borough of Harrow OCU (1993-2018/19)
North West (NW) BCU with Barnet and Brent
(2018/19 to Present)

Pinner today is a fairly genteel and prosperous outer London, "Metroline" suburb. Going back in history, however, Pinner was a small village 13 miles from London.[2436] A parish constable was responsible for early policing at least as far back as 1510. At that date the Manor Court Rolls show that Richard Rede was elected as constable of Pinner in place of John Clarke. One of their duties at that time was to ensure that all boys over the age of 12 years had bows and arrows.[2437]

In 1840 one sergeant and seven constables and a horse patrol were set up in Pinner, together with another four constables and a horse patrol in the town of Harrow. The area was part of an extended T or Paddington Division. All charges at the two stations had their cases heard at Pinner.

In 1903 Pinner was a sectional station of Willesden. In the picture below, taken in 1903, Sub-Divisional Inspector Smith from Harrow Road, Willesden is seated in the centre, flanked to his right by the original inhabitant of the station, Station Sergeant 68X John Moore (four stripes on arms). To the Inspector's left was Acting Sergeant 452X Tooth (two stripes on arms). Other officers include PC 557X Barber, to the left of door, and Constable 160X Thomas Westwood, standing in the doorway to the right. Standing to the right of the door are Constable 123X Isaac Mitchell and the unfortunate horse patrol, Constable 583X William Batchelor, who sports his riding boots and cutlass. He was later to be medically retired from the Force after one of the police horses in the stable bit off the thumb on his right hand in May 1902.[2438] The stable block is shown to the far right of the photo.

Pinner Police Station 1903

As Pinner grew in size in the 19th century, the need for a police station increased. Before the arrival of the police station birth, drunks, and disorderly prisoners were housed in a cage near the present Pinner Metropolitan Line Station. It is hard to say how needed the station was in those far off days but Pinner was, and still is, one of London's quieter locations.

In a local case in 1893 held at the court it was pointed out to the Justice of the Peace by the defence that there had been no charges for being drunk for ten years at Pinner. However, the local JP was quick to point out that this was mainly due to the fact that Pinner had no 'lock-up'.

On 4th January 1892 a memo from the Commissioner's office stated:

'A Sergeant's station with telegraphic communication is needed at Pinner where there are indications of a development of building operations. With a station on the Metropolitan Railway, an extensive suburb will doubtless grow up. At present there is no station nearer than Harrow and Ruislip, each over 3 miles distant.'

The locals had been petitioning for a police station for some time and in the spring of 1898 the *Harrow Gazette* stated:

'Thirty years ago the inhabitants of Pinner met in vestry and petitioned Scotland Yard for a police station. This requirement is about to be granted. The contractor's office and a quantity of bricks have been delivered on the site for the purpose.' [2439]

It was reported to the Commissioner that there was no station nearer than Harrow and Ruislip, each about 3½ miles distant. A police station at Pinner was originally proposed in a Commissioner's Memorandum dated 4th January 1892, which noted housing development in the area and with a Station on the Metropolitan Railway an extensive suburb will doubtless grow up. On 30th March 1892 the Police Surveyor recommended the purchase of a plot of land at the corner of the main Pinner Road and Waxwell Rise. The freehold to this land, on which the station now stands, was eventually purchased on 29th September 1893 from a J. Healey Lea, and the Home Office also kindly added £35 for the provision of a fence and gate to show the property's boundary.

The plans by John Dixon Butler are dated August 1897, and were approved on 27th September.[2440] The station was built between 1898 and 1899 by Fassnidge and Sons of Uxbridge, costing £3,165 8s and 2d to erect.[2441] The station was originally shown as being at Waxwell Rise, High Road, Pinner, though it was later to be renumbered 1 Waxwell Lane on 13th March 1939.

The police station consisted of a lobby, waiting room, inspector's office, charge room, parade room and three cells. The stable had stalls for two horses and an attached ambulance shed. The Pinner Gas Company supplied the gas, and the Colne Valley Water Company supplied the water.[2442] The site had previously been used as a penning area for stray animals which was called the Pinner Pound.

The building was described in a recent report by English Heritage:

...as a picturesque composition in the Domestic Revival manner, occupying a prominent corner site. The elevations have gables of different heights with deep eaves and bargeboards, some with decorative timber framing. Steep pitched roofs and tall stacks. Windows are mainly multi-pane timber sashes; those at ground floor within stone mullions, some with ogee carving to lintels. The front (south) elevation has a broad central gabled bay and a porch to the side with a moulded stone arch bearing a crenellated sign reading POLICE. There was an original

---

2436 A milestone opposite Pinner Police Station, which still stands outside the Oddfellows Arms, states "London 13 miles".
2437 Ware, Edwin M. (1956) *Pinner in the Vale*.
2438 *Harrow Gazette*, 10th May 1902.
2439 *Harrow Gazette*, 7th May 1898.
2440 Metropolitan Police Archives.
2441 Met Police Property Register for Pinner Police Station, page 218.

Pinner Police Station 1899 to present

plank door with cover fillets and brass furniture. Brick ramp and steps with metal railings are not of special interest. The east elevation has paired asymmetrical gables; the angle of the right-hand bay has a curved mullioned window above which is a deep moulded stone corbel. The single-storey cell block has a three-light mullioned window. The west elevation has paired asymmetrical gables and a single-storey WC block with a gablet; entrance to right (originally serving the married quarters) has ogee lintel and door similar to main entrance. The rear (north) elevation has a small tile-hung gable and full-width glazing to ground-floor parade room, with double doors. The roof has a steel platform, originally mounting a WWII air-raid siren. The basement has metal ventilation grilles and stone steps down to the entrance. The rear (west) elevation of the cell block retains one original cell window with cast-iron frame, set high up in the wall; those to the other two bays have been enlarged. Small brick extension at north end is not of special interest.[2443]

As one enters the station through the glazed timber lobby, probably dating from the 1930s, there are surviving features that include a simple stair with stick balusters and chamfered newel posts, some doors and surrounds and a cell door. Glazed brick dados also survive in the parade room which have been painted over.[2444]

Outside there is a stable block consisting of a single storey with hayloft above, designed in similar style and materials to the police station. The building exterior consisted of rendered gable to the front (east) elevation, chimney on the north and an outshed, originally a shed for a horse-drawn ambulance but now WCs, on the south side. The front elevation, which originally had a stable door to the right, has been re-modelled at ground floor level and now has paired sash windows and an entrance to left.[2445] This is now a canteen area.

Next to the stable is a brick boundary wall with a tall gate pier with pyramidal stone cap. Sections of perimeter fence to the east and west remain, with long and short close-boarding and timber piers. The small garden to the front elevation is enclosed by low stone bollards connected by a single iron rail; the western bollard has the original cast-iron police lamp-post and lantern. A signal lamp of uncertain date has been fixed to a pole mounted on the fence on Elm Park Road and another on the south-west corner of the building.[2446]

Police Orders of 1899 show, in the Buildings and Fixtures section, the following announcement:

'X (Division) The new Police Station at Pinner is to be taken into occupation by Police and business commenced therein 1st prox. The lodging assessment will be as follows; – 1 married sergeant at 4s per week.' [2447]

The *Pinner Gazette* was happy to report the station finally open on 1st May 1899, under the headline 'The New Police Station' writing thus:

'The police authorities entered into occupation on Monday. The building is of prepossessing appearance and the interior arrangements have all been carried out with admirable circumspection. Station Sergeant Moore, who has for some months past been stationed at Harrow, is the officer in charge.' [2448]

Station Sergeant 68X John Moore (warrant no. 62681), was the first resident at Pinner Police Station in 1901. He was aged 43 years at the time, originally from Melton Mowbray in Leicestershire. Living at the station with him were his wife Kate,[2449] aged 38, as well as their three children, John aged 14, a railway parcels boy, Henry aged 9, and George aged 4. Crime and punishment was in John's family, as his father Henry Moore was Superannuated Warder at Oakham Prison.[2450] Sergeant Moore was fully six feet tall, with grey eyes and dark, greying hair.[2451] He retired to 22 Bedford Road, Kempston, Bedfordshire with a pension of £69 11s 6d in 1903. His pay at the end of his service in 1903 was £2 10s 6d a week, plus his accommodation in the station.

Station Sergeant 68X John Moore

Sergeant Moore's retirement was fully reported in the local press in 1903.[2452] Inspector Smith made a speech on behalf of the Superintendent, praising his efforts during the "trials and difficulties that he had had to contend with." He concluded that though "there had not been much crime in the district," Sergeant Moore's "promptitude had always been exerted with good result."

The ink on the front of Station Sergeant Moore's new Occurrence Book could hardly have been dry when the police station had its first 'customer', who was brought into the charge room on 11th May 1899. It arose from probably the most infamous public order outrages ever seen in leafy Pinner. The cause of the commotion was the Headstone Spring Races Riot. The incident was sensational news in the press for many weeks, and it led directly to the cancellation of what had been a traditional event.

The *Wealdstone Harrow and Wembley Observer* reported the event with the headline 'Riot at Headstone Races yesterday – Many Injured'. The paper was scathing in its reporting on the behaviour of the race goers. It reported:

'There was a large gathering of persons at the Headstone Spring races yesterday, when a serious riot occurred in which many persons were badly injured. Unfortunately with the growth of the local races in popularity, the foreign and objectionable crowd from London has become each year in greater evidence, and yesterday it is safe to say that a more unruly, objectionable, and disgraceful mob has never been seen on any racecourse. Blackguards of the worst and lowest type, in fact the scum of civilisation came into the district. The police were totally inadequate to deal with the rough element.' [2453]

Serious violence took place after a dispute of the result of one of the races and the event was stopped by the police. The race official, Mr. Drury, had all the windows of his house smashed, however he responded by threatening the 'maddened crowd' with a gun. Only nine police officers were on duty, and they struggled to control a crowd of London roughnecks with 1,500 people attending the event.

The *Harrow Gazette* described the day as 'Rampant ruffianism,'[2454] and that "organised gang of London scoundrels could do anything they wanted." Ginger beer bottles, poles and stones were being thrown around. The rioters then made their way back to Harrow Metropolitan Station. The mob sang ribald songs and swore at, and insulted passengers. The station bookstall was overturned and scattered, a porter was cuffed and a lady had a watch taken from her breast.

One arrest was made on the day, and it proved to be Pinner's first prisoner and later surrounded the case of Metropolitan Police v Charles Wilson (alias Williams).

The same paper reported thus on the arrest, under the headline 'The First Charge'.

'This morning at Pinner Police Station, before Mr C.R. Nugent, the first police case was heard, and arose from the riot at Headstone races yesterday. Charles Wilson, who refused his address, was charged with attempting to pick pocket at the Headstone Races yesterday. Police evidence was given, and the prisoner was remanded to Edgware on Wednesday.' [2455]

At his subsequent trial Mr. Wilson, who gave his address as Whitehorse Street, Stepney denied the charge, but was convicted and sentenced to six weeks' hard labour.

The arresting officer, Constable 384X, had had difficulty in effecting the arrest. He told the court that a large man in the road had tried to rescue the prisoner. He had managed to place Wilson in a trap, which took him to Pinner. On the way to the station the prisoner threatened to throw the policeman out of the trap, while the crowd threw sticks and stones at the police transport.

Police Constable 469X Thomas Piner

The appropriately-named PC 469X Thomas Piner[2456] (left) would have almost certainly been on duty on the day of the Pinner Races Riot. Constable Piner must have been quite a character. He was born on 11th March 1857 in Burnham, Bucks, and was a mere 5ft 8in tall and had joined the force at Great Scotland Yard on 5th February 1877 at the tender age of 19 years. He was tattooed on both arms with Britannia and crossed flags, and a ballad girl and crossed flags on his right arm and on his left was his initials, T.P., and the words "faith, hope and charity". He had been around a bit, having transferred around the Metropolitan Police area frequently, serving on D, K, H, A and X Divisions, however his last 14 years service were spent at Pinner. He lived at West End, Pinner with his wife Elizabeth and their ten children.[2457]

Giving evidence at court must have been amusing, as he would have taken the Oath and explained that he 'was Constable Piner attached to Pinner Police station'. Sometimes bored Divisional clerks, whose jobs it was to post officers from headquarters stations, amused themselves with such antics.

The *Harrow Gazette* records PC Piner's retirement in 1902. He was presented with a "handsome 8 day clock with barometer and thermometer combined" by Inspector Smith. He had been involved in a number of arrests over the years. In August 1899 together with Constable Batchelor he arrested three youths for robbing an orchard belonging to a Mr Elkington of Ruislip. He also felt George Halford's collar, after catching him red-handed pulling up a farmer's potatoes. The prisoner kicked Constable Piner in the leg, and for these he was given seven days' imprisonment for the theft but also received one month imprisonment for assaulting Piner.

By 1908 Pinner was a sectional station to the newly-created sub-division of Harlesden, and Sub-Divisional Inspector Smith was still in charge.[2458]

Waxwell Lane entrance to the station c1908. The scene is little changed today except that the lamps, the dog kennel and the washing have all been removed

A plan dated 1942 notes that the station was "ameliorated in 1936", and showed alterations to the layout of the building with only the northern cell still in use with the other two now serving as a surgeon and matron's room and a detention room.

A telephone room was inserted between the parade room and Inspector's room, incorporating what was originally a store room. Over the years, the charge room and waiting room were reduced in size and an interview room added. Changes were also made to the layout of the entrance lobby and waiting room. On the upper floor the larder was converted to a third bedroom, and a bicycle shed added to the rear of the cell block (subsequently converted to a generator room and later rebuilt). The stable has been converted to a canteen and the ambulance shed to WCs. The plan also shows the layout of the vegetable garden which once occupied the land to the west of the building.

2442 Met Police Property Register for Pinner Police Station, page 218.
2443 English Heritage (2013). Letter confirming Listed building status of Pinner Police Station dated 25th January.
2444 Ibid.
2445 Ibid.
2446 Ibid.
2447 Metropolitan Police Orders 29th April 1899.
2448 *The Pinner Gazette*, 6th May 1899.
2449 Census 1901.
2450 Census 1881 and 1871.
2451 Metropolitan Police Pension record for Sgt John Moore.
2452 *Harrow Gazette*, 25th July 1903.
2453 *Wealdstone Harrow and Wembley Observer*, May 1899.
2454 *Harrow Gazette*, 13th May 1899.
2455 Ibid.
2456 Metropolitan Police Pension records for PC Thomas Piner.
2457 Census 1891 and 1901.
2458 *Kelly's Directory* 1908

By 1942 the first floor corridor had been extended eastwards, the two northern rooms had been subdivided, the larder and scullery had been enlarged and several cupboards reconfigured. The partition in the north west room was later relocated to its present position. The basic original layout of two bedrooms to the north and a living room to the south, flanked by a scullery and larder, remains discernible despite the later alterations. The ground floor layout remained as shown on the 1942 plan, with some change of use of rooms, and cells and the parade room has been encroached upon by the central store room and later subdivided into two irregular spaces, completely compromising its plan form and strongly affecting its character.

In 1962 a real bonus for the local constabulary arrived with the introduction to the event of the 'Walkie Talkie' (better known now as personal radios), which were reported to have been a big success. Another success that year was the use of the Interview Room at Pinner Police Station by a representative of Harrow Council and the Showman's Guild to arbitrate disputes. The cells ceased to be used around 1964.

Having served intermittently as offices since 1976, the police station reopened in July 2002 on a part-time operational basis.

In 2012 Pinner Police Station housed two Safer Neighbourhood teams and was still open to the public, though it was staffed by Volunteers. In 2013 was awarded Grade II listing status.

As of 2019 the station is still open, a base for the Safer Neighbourhood Team and the police cadets. It operates restricted public opening hours and services, and is still run by Police Volunteers.

Plaistow Police Station

The London Borough of Newham
Barking Road, Plaistow (1864-1914)
444 Barking Road (1914-2017)
K Division (1865-2017)

Plaistow Police Station Lamp

The Old Watch House known as the Old Cage, which was situated in the local area, was surrendered to the parochial authorities as being no longer required for police purposes in April 1851.

The Metropolitan Police decided to build a police station on K or Stepney Division in Barking Road, and it was called Barking Road New Station.

This station was built in 1862 and cost £1,729. Ground rent of £21 per annum was paid to the owner, Mr. Benjamin Bosher of 12 Duke Street, Manchester Square. The leasehold was purchased for 100 years, and was set to expire in 1962, however it was essential for the freehold to be purchased and this occurred in May 1899 at a cost of £880.[2459]

The ground floor of the station had five main rooms. They were an Inspector's office, a charge room, a mess room, a library, and a kitchen and drying room. There were also two cells. The basement was for the storage of coal and had one room, which was used as a cleaning room. On the first floor there was accommodation for one married sergeant and six constables.[2460]

Refurbishments prior to 1891 led to an extra cell being built.

In the same year the station was inspected, and a report stated that the accommodation was badly arranged. It showed that one married Inspector occupied two sets of quarters at the station. This was considered unsuitable and was to be rectified. Five constables were reported as occupying the single men's accommodation.

The cell space was reported as being insufficient for its needs, so the station drying room was converted to take prisoners. The station had ventilation and heating problems, and there was a bad smell from the sewers. Often both men and women prisoners shared the same sanitary arrangements.[2461]

Early reference was made to the new station when details appeared in Police Orders that "the Police of K Division are to take charge of and occupy the new Police Station and Section House" with effect from September 1864. Instructions stated that:

"the horse of the mounted constable now stabled at West Ham Station is to be removed to Barking Road Station." [2462]

West Ham Sub-Division had to surrender some of its area, during re-alignment of the station boundaries, to Barking Road Police Station, together with three constables for reserve duty. These were selected by the Superintendent for transfer. Furthermore, the officers who policed this section (both sergeants and constables) were now to parade and take up duty at the new station. Barking Road new station was shown as being a station in the exterior district of K or Stepney Division.

Barking Road Police Station, Plaistow, 1864-1912

On 14th August 1869 the name of the station was changed to Plaistow Police Station.[2463]

In November 1874 instructions were given for two new sub-divisions to be formed. These were called West Ham Sub-Division and Plaistow Sub-Division respectively. This re-organisation saw the separation of Plaistow and North Woolwich into one division, leaving West Ham on its own.[2464] The instruction noted that the Inspector would now be stationed at Plaistow.[2465]

In 1881 Eccles Golding, aged 36 years from Sligo, Ireland was the inspector in charge of the station. He resided there with his wife Adelaide, aged 33 years from Fressingfield in Suffolk, and his daughter Anne aged 11 years, born in Hackney, Middlesex. They lived there with nine single constables.[2466]

In 1884 Plaistow Police Station was located at 386 Barking Road at the junction with New Barn Street, and shown to have one Inspector, nine sergeants, 57 constables and three horses. The freehold of the property was purchased in 1899.[2467]

The picture at the top of the next column shows the station strength on the date shown and was taken in the yard of the station. The picture includes officers of the Criminal Investigation Department, who are dressed in plain clothes, and senior officers. Notice they are all wearing their ceremonial dress, including their medals.

A picture taken in the yard of Plaistow Police Station on 15th July 1908

At the turn of the century there was a need to update the housing stock of police stations within the metropolis, and the station at Plaistow was identified as one for re-siting. Accordingly, in August 1908 the freehold of the premises a short distance away from the old station was acquired. The site was located at 444, 446 & 448 Barking Road, and was purchased for £2,360. Tenders were accepted for the building and a new station was constructed after all the houses were demolished. There were problems with the building of Plaistow Police Station because a number of restricted covenants stated that the building could only be of a certain height and specification, which created difficulties for the planners. These problems were soon overcome, and an acceptable plan was agreed and implemented.[2468]

The opening of the new station was in September 1912. It had two sets of married quarters, for which rent cost 9/- and 6/6d respectively, whilst thirty unmarried men could be housed at 1/- per week each.[2469]

Plaistow Police Station 1912-2017

During World War One London was bombed by German Gotha bombers and Zeppelins. On the night of 19th-20th May 1918, K Division was bombed for the last time during that conflict, killing three people and injuring several others.[2470]

The picture left features two officers of Plaistow Police Special Constabulary, and was taken during the First World War. Notice the Special Sub-Inspector is riding a motorcycle and sidecar, with the Inspector being chauffeured.

A motorcycle and sidecar used for supervision during WWI at Plaistow

In September 1919 the old station house was leased to a branch of the Westminster Bank for 80 years on an annual rental of £70, however in August 1935 the building came up for public auction and was sold to Ironstone Freeholds for the sum of £2,250.[2471]

The section house was refurbished and re-opened in November 1924.

Local Government re-organisation in 1965 shows that Plaistow (KO) was designated as a sectional station of East Ham (KE) Sub-Division situated in the London Borough of Newham.

Plaistow Police Station was closed to the public in December 2017.[2472]

Plough Corner Police Station

The London Borough of Havering

Plough Corner, Romford (1924-2000)

Essex Police (1924-1965)

K Division (1965-2000)

This was a small detached police station, which was originally a pair of houses used for accommodating two police officers and their families. It was situated just north of Gallows Corner flyover in Straight Road, Romford. The station was built near a public house in 1924 called The Plough, hence its name. These are shown to the left of the direction sign in the picture overleaf. The station was located near a most important traffic point, at the junction with the A12 at Gallows Corner.

2459 Metropolitan Police Surveyor's Records.
2460 Ibid.
2461 Metropolitan Police Sanitation Inspection Report 1891.
2462 Metropolitan Police Orders dated September 1864.
2463 John Back Archive (1975); Metropolitan Police Orders dated 14th August 1869.
2464 Metropolitan Police Orders dated November 1874.
2465 Ibid.
2466 Census 1881.
2467 Metropolitan Police Orders dated 20th June 1884.
2468 John Back Archive (1975).
2469 Metropolitan Police Surveyor's Records; John Back Archive (1975).
2470 Reay, Col. W.T. (1920) *The Specials*, Billing and Sons, p215.
2471 Metropolitan Police Surveyor's Records.
2472 www.met.police.uk Information Rights Unit dated 18th February 2018, accessed 25th January 2019.

Gallows Corner junction in the 1930s showing the police station on the left

In the early 1930s the station strength was shown as one sergeant and four constables.

Aid was frequently called from other parts of the division to man the post during the summer months. It was estimated that the local population was about 1,000 persons.[2473]

Plough Corner Police Station 1924-2000

The photograph above of the station was taken in 1925. In addition to the station, the houses provided accommodation for police officers and their families. One famous occupant was Sergeant Woodgate, who is the Essex Police Historian. During his early service in Essex he lived in one of the houses shown in the photograph, and later published an extensive account of policing in the County of Essex.

The station was closed in December 1968, and then used as a police office until March 1970.[2474] Prior to closing it for good in 2000[2475] it housed officers from the Juvenile Bureau (or Youth and Communities Section) for K Division for some time. Today the junction is extremely busy, being on the main routes to Colchester (A12) and Southend (A127). The nearest police station is Romford Police Station, as Harold Wood has been sold for redevelopment. (see Harold Wood)

Plumstead Police Station

The London Borough of Greenwich
2-6 High Street (1893-1988)
295 Plumstead Road (1988-1991)
200 Plumstead High Street (1991-1993)
R Division (1893-1993)
Borough of Greenwich OCU (1993-2018)
South East (SE) BCU (together with Bexley and Lewisham) (2018 to Present)

Plumstead was not included into the Metropolitan Police area until 1839, when it became part of R Division[2476] and permission was given for the Police to take over from the local Parish Watch. In the 1840s Plumstead consisted of market gardens, brick-fields, chalk pits and tile kilns. A part of the Woolwich Arsenal was situated in the parish in the 1840s. By the 1850s the population in Plumstead had grown three-fold, mainly due to the North Plumstead Railway which was built in 1849.[2477]

Plumstead had its own Cage, originally named Cage Road situated at Lakedale Road (as it is now then known),[2478] situated at the junctions with the Brewery.[2479] Prisoners who were arrested and detained in the Cage overnight by the Police were taken the next morning to the local court, which were undertaken by local Justices of the Peace at the Castle Public House in Powis Road, Woolwich Town.

Revisions to Police boundaries occurred in 1863, when R Division saw Eltham transferred from the Lee to the Shooters Hill Sub-Division which was also responsible for the sections east of the Plumstead parish at Erith and Bexley Heath.[2480]

Officers from Woolwich were used, together with re-enforcements which were hastily drafted in, to deal with the battle of Plumstead Common in 1878. Attempts to acquire the Common for the Metropolitan Board of Works caused major disturbances in the area.

Police officers from Woolwich Watch House patrolled the environs of Plumstead until plans were approved in the late 1880s for a station to be built there.

John Butler, Metropolitan Police Surveyor, designed Plumstead Police Station and plans were approved by the Home Office in 1890, taking into consideration the substantial increase that had occurred of people moving into the area, and dwellings being subsequently erected. It was built by Lathey Bros, who provided the lowest estimate from the thirteen bids tendered.[2481] A piece of land had been found in Plumstead High Street at the corner of Riverdale Road in 1891 belonging to Mr. Wilson, and this was purchased for £1,140. The station, which was built for £4,120, was opened in August 1893.[2482]

The view to the rear of Plumstead Police Station, with the garden in the foreground and the parade shed in the distance on the left

Pevsner described Plumstead Police Station being located in 1893 'at the corner of Riverdale Road, are the only buildings which stand out in Plumstead, High Street.'[2483]

Taking charge of the new station was Inspector Walshe, who had been transferred from Blackheath Road, and Sergeant Hudson.[2484] The boundaries of the Woolwich and Belvedere Sub-Divisions were altered in August 1893 to coincide with the building of the new Sectional Station at Plumstead. Given the address 216 Plumstead High Street, SE18, it was accorded the status of Sectional Station of Woolwich Sub-Division.[2485]

In 1897 Inspector Hocking was in charge of the station, where he stayed for at least two years. Sub-Divisional Inspector

Plumstead Police Station 1893-1988

Goodhall at Woolwich was in overall charge of the Sectional Station until 1898, when his place was taken by Sub-Divisional Inspector Sara. By this time the Sub- Divisional strength stood at four inspectors, 20 sergeants and 98 constables.[2486] The telegraph was installed into the station with the code sign Papa Sierra (PS).[2487] Accommodation for eight constables was provided in the Section House above the station, at a cost of 1 shilling a week each.[2488]

There was for some years a Fixed Traffic Point in Plumstead High Street at the junction with Cage Lane, Lakedale Road, which was manned between 8.00am and 1.00am in all weathers. This Fixed Point was withdrawn when the new station was built, although a new Point was established later outside Plumstead Railway Station.

Records show that in 1915 Sub-Divisional Inspector Gadd, and Inspectors Henry Jarvis and Charles Butt, were resident at the Station together with their respective families.

In 1965, under Local Government re-organisation Plumstead (RP), remained the Sectional Station of Woolwich (RW), situated in the new London Borough of Greenwich.[2489]

Major re-organisation in 1980 through the Metropolitan Police service saw R Division renamed R District. The old station was demolished in March 1988 and a temporary Police Office was opened at 295 Plumstead High Street to cope with the routine day-to-day police station duties. The Police office

2473 Essex County Constabulary: *Police Stations and Police Houses Register* (c1930).
2474 MEPO 11.
2475 Verified by a telephone call to Romford Police Station on 21st February 2002.
2476 History of Greenwich on intranet.aware.mps/BOCU_eh/Greenwich accessed 5th March 2008.
2477 Brown, B (undated). 'Not Quite a Century: The Story of Plumstead Police Station'.
2478 Hadaway, D. (1990) 'The Metropolitan Police in Woolwich'.
2479 Hyde, R. (1987) *The A-Z of Victorian London*. London Topographical Society.
2480 Brown, B (undated). 'Not Quite a Century: The Story of Plumstead Police Station'.
2481 *The Builder*, 11th June 1892 p.467.
2482 Metropolitan Police Orders dated 18th August 1893.
2483 *Buildings of England (South)*, Cherry and Pevsner. 1983.
2484 Brown, B (undated). 'Not Quite a Century: The Story of Plumstead Police Station'.
2485 *Kirchner's Police Index* 1931
2486 Brown, B (undated). 'Not Quite a Century: The Story of Plumstead Police Station'.
2487 Ibid.
2488 Metropolitan Police Orders dated 18th March 1893.
2489 Metropolitan Police Orders dated 6th August 1964.

Plumstead Police Station 1991 to present

remained in use until 1991, when the officers moved to the new station. In the meantime, prisoners were taken to Woolwich for processing and detention for court. Other functions such as administration and support were distributed throughout the Division.

Plans were drawn up by the Metropolitan Police Property Services Department with designers Damond Lock Grabowski for a police station and divisional headquarters to be built on the site of the old station. Work commenced in 1988, and was completed in April 1991 at a cost of £2.5M.

The new Plumstead Police Station was opened by the Princess Royal. Its three-storey building includes a charge room, 12 cells, two detention rooms, a restaurant, billiard room and space for 50 cars. Officers at the Station have since 1991 worn the two-letter code 'RW' on their shoulders. At roughly the same time a new maximum-security prison was opened on Plumstead Marshes, and was named Belmarsh. The station complement on occupation of the new building consisted of one chief superintendent, who is the Borough Commander, one superintendent, three chief inspectors, eleven inspectors, 17 sergeants and 75 constables. Supporting them were 54 members of the civil staff and 33 traffic wardens. The new address was 200 Plumstead High Street, SE18 1JY.

As of 2019 Plumstead remains in the hands of the Metropolitan Police.[2490]

Ponders End/Enfield Highway Police Station

The London Borough of Enfield
204-214 High Street, Ponders End
N Division (1864-1865)
Y Division (1865-1886)
N Division (1886-1888)
Y Division (1888 – 1933)
N Division (1933-1993)
Borough of Enfield OCU (1993-2012)

The area of Ponders End before 1969 was known as Enfield Highway. In January 1864 details showed Enfield Highway Police Station, as it was then known, as a being located on N or Islington Division. When the new Y or Highgate Division was formed, Enfield Highway Police Station was transferred from N to Y Division.[2491] The expansion of the police areas and revision of boundaries in June 1886 meant that Enfield Highway was transferred back to N or Islington Division.

Enfield Highway Police Station 1868-1968

The freehold title to a parcel of land was purchased in 1866 for £520 in order to build a new police station. The land was located at 198 Hertford Road, Enfield Highway, and plans were completed by the Surveyor who instructed a building company to complete the work. The new police station was opened in March 1868[2492] at a cost of £2,525. The station was built with a loft to the first floor, whilst on the ground floor there was a charge room, three cells and an office. In the yard was a two-stall stable. An inspector supervised the station.[2493]

The boundaries between Chingford and Enfield Highway were again revised when Chingford Police Station was built on Kings Head Hill in March 1888. This revision meant that Enfield Highway was transferred to Y Division.

The N Division group responsible for the Royal Small Arms Factory at Enfield Lock in 1915

The photograph above shows a unit of Y Division officers performing special duty at the Royal Small Arms Factory, Enfield Lock in 1915. The special duty included factory security in times of war under the Emergency Powers legislation. The reason for taking this picture is unclear as it appears to be some special occasion, particularly as some are wearing their medals and decorations. The inspector (seated with the flat cap in the centre front), two sergeants and eleven constables were posted to a small station within the small arms factory. Later in the war women special constables took over the security of policing the small arms factory. This enabled the male officers to supplement the war effort, either by joining the ranks or returning to normal station duties. The women shown located there in December 1916 were Sub-Inspector Buckpitt, Sergeants R. Green, M. Johnson, A. Moore and G. West, Corporal K. Canter, Constables, M. Beaney, E. Boyes, E. Buckingham, E. Daniels, A. Everfield, A. Ayre, D. Gardiner, C. Gosling, K. Kaye, C. Knight, N. Little, A. Mackay, E. Mouland, S. Pernull, E. Pickard, M. Read, E. Tolfield, A. Wheeler and A. White.[2494]

The Metropolitan Police Surveyor, R.G. Strachan, included in his records that Enfield Highway Police Station was situated at 198 Hertford Road, Enfield Highway. In 1926 there were alterations made to the station, and one set of the married quarters was converted for operational purposes. Alterations and additions were completed in September 1926.[2495]

The station remained on N Division until the boundary revision was completed north of the River Thames in July 1933. Enfield Highway (now located on N or Stoke Newington Division) was transferred back to Y or Wood Green Division. It would appear that a rationalisation of stations and divisional boundaries, especially divisional headquarters stations, were also completed at the same time.

In 1962 there had been concern expressed that the old station had come to the end of its operational life, and efforts should be made to build a new, modern station. The Metropolitan Police Surveyor noted that suitable freehold land, on which to build a police station in Ponders End, had become available and should be purchased at a cost of £41,000. In fact efforts had been made since 1956 to obtain a suitable parcel of land, to no avail. Home Office consent preceded the purchase in November 1962. Tenders were invited to build the new police station, and the contract was awarded to Messrs. Robert Hart and Sons Ltd for £130,685. The Local Authority boundary review of April 1965 placed Enfield Highway within the London Borough of Enfield. The station at 204-214 High Street, Ponders End, Enfield was completed for use in July 1969.

The opening of the new station in July replaced the old station in Enfield Highway.[2496] There was no formal opening ceremony to mark the occasion, but in June 1970 there was a station open day where invited local dignitaries and members of the public were shown around the new station. The station housed traffic wardens and the Regional Crime Squad office, in addition to members of the CID and uniform branch. However by 2010 the police station operated within a reduced number of hours as its future was being decided given austerity measures introduced to save money.

Ponders End Police Station 1969-2012

In 2012 it was vacated and put up for sale. It fetched £1.115M and sold to the London Borough of Enfield.[2497]

Poplar Police Station

The London Borough of Tower Hamlets

Newby Place (1830-1873)

East India Dock Road (1873-1897)

191-193 East India Dock Road (1897-1993)

2 Market Way, Chrisp Street (1975-1993)

K Division (1830-1933)

H Division (1933-1993)

Tower Hamlets OCU (1993-2018/19)

Basic Command Unit Central East (CE) (with the London Borough of Hackney) (2018/19 to Present)

The first police station in Poplar belonged to the Parish authorities and was situated on the west side of Newby Place, Poplar (next to Poplar Church) and opposite Montague Place, not far from the entrance to the Blackwall Tunnel and the Isle of Dogs. The introduction of the New Police in 1829 saw many of these old stations handed over to the Metropolitan Police for their use. The address was shown as 1 Church Papage, whilst next door at No. 2 was a section house with eight rooms for single constables. The premises at 1-4 were leased from 1840 for 40 years from Mr. Beckwish of 9 Lad Lane.

In 1844 Poplar Police Station at Newby Place was shown on K or Stepney Division, and one of the first inspectors in charge was Charles May, who had been appointed in 1839. Boundary revisions were published in Police Orders, restating that Poplar Police Station was to remain located on K Division.[2498]

In 1863 William Henry Keens joined the police at Poplar. He assisted other officers to recover bodies from the River Thames when the Princess Alice sank off Blackwall Point in 1878. Constable Keens served in the force for 25 years, and when he retired the ratepayers publicly presented him with a clock and a purse of gold. It was not unusual for there to be an advertisement placed in the local paper asking the public to subscribe to the testimonial of a retiring officer. Constable Keens went on to receive his police pension for 47 years, until 1935 when he died aged 91 years, whilst living in Grundy Street, Poplar. Very few officers manage to draw pension for many more years than they served in the Force.[2499]

In June 1868 buildings had been leased to the Metropolitan Police at 193&195 East India (Dock) Road, Poplar for the purposes of carrying on the business of a police station. The station was originally called East India Road Police Station. It was also sometimes referred to as Susannah Street Police Station. The station consisted of a basement, a ground floor and a first floor. On the ground floor there was a charge room, five cells, a day room, a library and four water closets whilst in the basement there were five rooms including a drying room, a mess room, a bathroom, and there were also three coal sheds. Located in the yard was a two-stall stable. The Receiver insured the station against loss or damage amounting to £1,800 per year. In 1869 the station was altered, at a cost of £1,343, with the permission of the owner.

The relationship between the owner Mrs Simons and the police soured, resulting in a rather strange course of events and eventual recourse to litigation on the part of the owner.

The police station business, including noise and constant activity, had been the cause of trouble and nuisance between the police and the owner. Mrs. Simons was not happy with her tenants, and she sued them in the High Court. Under the terms of the lease the Lessee (the police) should do nothing which might cause the Lessor (Mrs Simons) any nuisance, annoyance, damage or disturbance, and if done this would amount to a breach of the covenant. The Lessor applied for a notice to eject the police from the station.

It appears this situation arose because Mrs. Simons was no longer satisfied with the terms and conditions of the original lease. The owner probably felt insufficiently compensated for the supply of this prime accommodation, and felt she could obtain a better deal with new tenants.

2490 MPS Information Rights Unit (2019) Freedom of Information: MPS assets.
2491 Metropolitan Police Orders dated 28th October 1865.
2492 Metropolitan Police Orders dated 11th March 1868.
2493 Metropolitan Police General Orders 1873.
2494 Heyneman, J. (1925) *The Pioneer Policewoman*. Chatto and Windus, London.
2495 Metropolitan Police Property Manifest 1924.
2496 Metropolitan Police Orders dated 19th September 1969.
2497 MPS Information Rights Unit (2019) Freedom of Information: Land or property sold by the MPS for over £1M.
2498 Metropolitan Police Orders dated 11th January 1864.
2499 *East End News*, 30th April 1930.

Poplar Police Station 1897-1971

The police, ever fearful of the consequences of publicity arising from the court action, attempted to settle the matter out of court. Negotiations commenced, resulting in an out-of-court agreement. The action was finally settled with the police surrendering the present lease and replacing it with a fresh one costing £50 per year. All costs were borne by the police. They felt they had headed off a significant problem, because if the owner had won the case the court was empowered to eject the police from the station forthwith. Considerable embarrassment was avoided in this instance, although later the police would encounter the difficult Mrs Simons again.

Protracted negotiations to secure the freehold for the station from Mrs Simons commenced in 1891. After a lengthy process the freehold was eventually secured on 26th June 1892, at a cost of £2,000. The records show that these drawn-out negotiations included a threat by the police to take out a compulsory purchase order on the land in order to secure it.

In 1873 records show Poplar to be a station connected by wire to Scotland Yard, and also in the command of an Inspector.[2500] In 1881 there were eleven single constables in residence together with Sergeant Joseph Plummer, his wife and their daughter.[2501]

The address of the station was published in Police Orders on 20th June 1884 as 195 East India Dock Road, Poplar. The station became a sectional station of Limehouse Sub-Division after re-organisation and a change of divisional name. (Limehouse was transferred from K or Stepney Division to K, East Ham Division).

In 1888 Poplar Police Station was shown as a receiving house for drowned or dead bodies. Equipment for dragging the Thames including a hand cart (ambulance) was often kept at public houses near canals or on the Thames.[2502]

On 23rd April 1897 the Home Office authorised the Receiver to accept the lowest tender to build a new police station and section house on the site of the old station. At this stage negotiations secured the leasehold of premises next door to the old station, 191-193 East India Dock Road, Poplar. The successful builders were Messrs. Willmott & Son, who secured the contract for £9,985. They commenced building the station and completed the administrative section and married quarters next door at 193 East India Dock Road for occupation in March 1899.

The section house was occupied in March 1899. It had space for twenty-one single men, who paid 1/- per week each for rent. The rent for the married quarters cost 5/6d per week, and instructions stated that it was for use by a married inspector.

Records also show that the leasehold for 68A East India Dock Road, Poplar had been secured as the Superintendent's residence from the leaseholder Mr. C.J. Anderson of 26 Lower North Street, Poplar from 25th March 1918 for an annual rental of £60. The police property manifest records that contracts were exchanged for transfer of the lease on 18th October 1929 to Dr. Fisher costing £400.

In 1933 Poplar was transferred from K or East Ham to H or Whitechapel Division. The freehold to 191-193 East India Dock Road, Poplar was secured and was purchased in January 1960 for £10,500. A review of policing demands had been completed entitled the Dixon Report. This concluded that Poplar Police Station should be extended; however, the work was never completed.

The Local Authority boundary reviews of 1965 located Poplar (HP) as a Sectional station of Limehouse (HH) Sub-Division, which was situated in the new borough of Tower Hamlets. A review of H Division on 1st January 1970 reduced the status of Poplar to that of a Police Office.

In November 1971 Poplar Police Office was shut and boarded up. All police functions were transferred to Limehouse Police Station. The local population did not like to see their station close, and in 1973 pressure was brought on the police at Limehouse to re-open the old station. Concern had been expressed from both the residents and stallholders of the nearby Chrisp Street market that the nearest police station was some three miles away at Limehouse.

Poplar Police Office 1975 to present

On market days the increase in visitors caused public order and crime problems which were not easily solved locally. Agreement was reached that a police presence should be kept in Poplar, but the old police station was considered unsuitable. Negotiations were made to lease an empty shop from the Greater London Council at 2 Market Way, Chrisp Street at an annual rent of £1,050. Arrangements were made to convert the shop into a police office, and this was opened in May 1975.

The front counter was closed in 2013, however as of 2019 the building was still retained for operational purposes by the Metropolitan Police.[2503]

Potters Bar Police Station

London Borough of Barnet

High Road, Potters Bar (1871-1886)

The Causeway, Potters Bar (1886-1993)

S Division (1871-1993)

Borough of Barnet OCU (1993-2011)

In 1851 Constable James Harrod, with his wife and family of seven children resided at 95 High Road, Potters Bar village. Harrod would patrol the High Road on foot or by horse, by day and night. It was likely that this cottage was an old horse patrol station, which had a separate stable in the garden.

In 1871 constable George Fossket, his wife and family occupied a police house in Potters Bar at 90, The High Road.[2505] William Parish, his wife and family also resided nearby in Potters Bar in Holly Bank Cottage at the same time as Fossket.[2506] By 1881 a married inspector, his wife and family occupied Holly Bank cottage at Potters Bar. A married constable also occupied another part of the cottage, obviously in cramped conditions.

Local Potters Bar history records shows that in 1891 William Parish from Norfolk living at Potters Bar Police Station. His occupation was shown as 'Metropolitan Police Constable',[2506] and he was 50 years old residing with his wife Elizabeth.

The cottage was described as having no running water, and the well in the garden was polluted. The cesspool had been sited near the well, into which it seeped. A stable had been erected in the garden, and a suggestion was made that a cell should be constructed as it was needed to house prisoners. There was no waiting area for people wishing to see the constable or report matters. There was also an administrative office where the inspector would make his daily reports. The station was designated as being on Y or Highgate Division at this time.[2507]

In 1891 the officer in charge at Potters Bar was 45-year-old Inspector John Geater from Glemham in Suffolk, who resided there with his wife Sophie and their four children.[2508] A short distance away in Laurel Cottage lived Constable Charles Moore, his wife and five children.[2509] The 1901 Census shows Constable William Chandler living in the High Street, Potters Bar.

As a matter of interest, the boundary marks of the Metropolitan Police area (denoted by white posts erected with a City of London crest on) can be seen at Potters Bar in Hatfield Road, and in Church Road and also at Colney Heath Lane, South Mimms; and London Road, London Colney Hertfordshire. Potters Bar Police Station was situated very close to the boundary.[2510]

Potters Bar Police Station 1871-1886

A cottage in Southgate Road, Potters Bar had been leased from Mr. C. Woodward, the licensee of the White Swan Inn on Bell Bar, Hatfield, on an annual rental of £30. It was occupied for police purposes in 1871 and a stable was erected in the garden. In 1880 it was reported that the cottage had no cell space, and there had been calls for some to be provided. The cottage housed a married inspector with his family, and also a married constable, but the married constable and his family were moved out to make way for more space for the workings of the station.

2500   Metropolitan Police General Orders 1873.

2501   Census 1881.

2502   *Dickens's Dictionary of London* (1888) Moretonhampstead. pp132-133; T.A.Critichley (1967) *The History of the Police of England and Wales* 1967 Constable Publications. p42.

2503   Information Rights Unit MSP: MPS Station Closures Since 2010 accessed 6th May 2019.

2504   Census 1871.

2505   Ibid.

2506   www.pbhistory.co.uk/buildings/police.html accessed 2nd February 2012.

2507   Metropolitan Police Report Condition of Police Stations 1881.

2508   Census 1891.

2509   Ibid.

2510   Martin, S. (1970) 'The Policing of Finchley Through the Ages'.

The Vestry – the parish-based forerunner of the local authority – did not confine itself to church affairs after 1835. It often discussed the water supply, and in 1887 it complained about the increased police rate and questioned the necessity of having 22 policemen at Potters Bar.[2511]

Freehold to a site situated at the Causeway, Potters Bar was purchased in 1886, which at this time showed the station as situated on Y or Highgate Division, but a station and one set of married quarters were not erected until 1897. The station call sign for the telegraph published in Police Orders in 1893 was Papa Bravo (PB), but by the 1920s these were changed to Sierra Papa (SP).[2512]

Potters Bar was a sectional station to the sub-divisional station at Enfield on Y or Highgate Division in 1899. It remained there until about 1937, when it transferred to S or Hampstead Division as a sectional station on Barnet Sub-Division. Potters Bar was allocated a squad of special constables to make up for the call-up of regular officers to the colours[2513] in WW1.

The address of the police station was shown as The Causeway, Potters Bar, Hertfordshire. In 1925 the Station Sergeant was David Partner, assisted by Sergeants Hubert Porter and Phillip Phillips. James Cryan and Stephen Church were Acting Sergeants, assisted by 14 constables.[2514]

The station was renovated in 1938. In 1947 the station was still part of S Division, with the station code of 'SP' and a sectional station of Barnet Sub-Division.[2515]

Potters Bar Police Station 1886–2011

After divisional boundary changes in 2000, Potters Bar transferred from S Division. The Hertsmere area of the Metropolitan Police covering Potters Bar, South Mimms, Borehamwood, Bushey and its surrounding villages were transferred to the Hertfordshire Constabulary and Potters Bar is now part of J Division, station code 'J3' within Hertfordshire.

The station was sold in 2011.

The Hertfordshire Officers who patrol the Potters Bar area now parade out of Borehamwood Police Station. Officers from the Potters Bar Community Team and Probationer Training Unit are the only officers now based at Potters Bar.[2516]

Putney Police Station

London Borough of Wandsworth
Richmond Road (1874-1893)
Chestnut Cottage, Upper Richmond Road (1893-1909)
215-219 Upper Richmond Road (1909-1993)
V Division (1874-1885)
W Division (1885-1893)
V Division (1893-1909)
W Division (1909-1993)
Borough of Wandsworth OCU (1993-2006)

Putney was part of the manor of Wimbledon, situated next to the River Thames and remaining quite rural; although by the 18th century it had become gentrified and remained so until the mid-20th century. The first Putney Bridge was built in 1725, and rebuilt in its current form in 1886.

Demand for a police station in Putney prompted a letter to be written by a Mr Hare that offered a site in Upper Richmond Road, Putney, on a 99-year lease from Christmas 1868.[2517] It is not clear whether this option was taken up, but the new police station was rented for 99 years at 9 shillings a week from James Dean, a builder of River Street, Putney[2518] and brought into service in August 1873. The station, located on V or Wandsworth Division, housed a married sergeant, a married constable and six single constables.[2519] The sergeant was placed in charge, and ensured that police officers were properly supervised.[2520]

Putney Police Station's address in 1880 was noted as Chestnut Cottage, Upper Richmond Road,[2521] and was numbered 191 a year later.[2522]

Constable Charles Edwards (warrant no. 61607), who joined in 1877, resided there with his wife and three children and occupied the married quarters at the station in 1881.[2523] He retired in 1902.

By 1881 the status of the station was enhanced and an inspector was placed in charge.[2524] An inspection by Metropolitan Police Surveyors in 1881 found that this was:

'A modern and substantial Station. The married and single men's quarters are not separated. Ablution room, inconveniently placed, can only be reached by passing through the mess rooms.'[2525]

It was occupied by one married inspector, one married constable and six single constables.[2526]

Whilst on duty at Putney in 1883, Constable William Silvey was on his patrol when he stopped a passing wagon from which he could hear noises, but whilst searching the wagon he lost his footing and fell, fatally injuring himself.[2527]

By 1885 Putney had been relocated to the new W or Clapham Division, although a change back to V Division occurred in 1893 when it became a Sectional Station of Wandsworth.[2528] The station was linked to a telegraph, which made communication to Scotland Yard easy. The call sign for Putney in 1893 was Papa Yankee (PY). Standardisation of telegraph, telephone and later radio call signs relating to the police station areas along divisional lines was not completed until the 1930s.

The increase in population during the latter part of the century placed extra demands on policing the area, and so plans were made to enlarge the station. Attempts were made to purchase the freehold title, and this was purchased successfully from Mr John Temple Leader for £363 in 1899.[2529]

Between 1902 and 1904 the addresses adjacent to the station were purchased at a cost of £1,600, and were renumbered 215-219 Upper Richmond Road in 1904.[2530] There is evidence that the vendor sold the buildings to the Police reluctantly, because an attachment was made to the deeds that the vendor was to be given first refusal if the premises were sold later. It was not uncommon for potential police station premises to be the subject of compulsory purchase at this time, so a desired residence could be lost to an owner if the Police required it.

Yet the Police did not rush to design and build a new station on the site to the obvious frustration of the previous owner. Instead, they sub-let 219 until 1909 to a Mr R. Waller, for an annual rental of £40. The family continued to live at the address into the 1920s, when the annual rental was increased to £48 by 1924.[2531]

Putney Police Station 1903-2006

There was a large contingent of Metropolitan Police Special Constabulary at Putney Police Station, and during the First World War this was the Headquarters. The Division lost no fewer than 1,657 regular men to the Colours during the war. The Specials attached here knew that they would be kept active, being assigned to man vulnerable points, of which V Division had a great number. These included the reservoirs, gas works, electric light works, power stations, the Sopwith Aviation Factory, an aqueduct and all had to be guarded. Unpleasant assignments also included the local sewage works, which saw Specials performing their four hours' duty mostly without complaint. During air raids the Specials withdrew to air raid shelters, which had become numerous in Wandsworth, and ensured the good order and safety of the civilians seeking shelter.

In June 1916 the local population were upset about foreigners living and trading amongst them, and regularly the Police, together with the Special Constabulary, had to defend people's lives and protect their property in Putney. In December 1917 German air raids saw two bombs dropped on Putney in Lower Common Road, and two people were killed. This was the furthest west of this night's attack.[2532]

The V Division Special Constabulary also supervised food queues, national registration work and Election stations where citizens recorded their votes. They involved themselves in Police lectures, ambulance training, and rifle shooting within the Division. The Specials also had the most efficient drill instructor, Sergeant Major F.W. Eggleton, a champion ex-army swordsman of the army gymnastic staff. He regularly gathered the Division on Wimbledon Common for drill musters and to put them through their paces.[2533]

Percy Laurie Section House SQ 20, with accommodation for 101 single police officers, was built in the 1930s at a cost of £90,000.

Simultaneously, a new police station was built which replaced Wandsworth as the Divisional Station, becoming fully operational in July 1935.[2534] Wandsworth was relegated to Sectional Station, with Putney as the Sub-Divisional Station. The picture below shows the rear of Putney Police Station in 1908 with the parade shed on the right, together with the station's garden where potatoes and tomatoes seem to be growing. The rear of the station is shown in the background.

Above: The rear gardens of the Police station in 1907, and Below, the rear of the station showing parade shed to the right

2511 www.british-history.ac.uk/report.aspx accessed 9th November 2011.
2512 Metropolitan Police General Orders 1893.
2513 Col. W. T. Reay (1919) *The Specials – How They Served London*.
2514 www.pbhistory.co.uk/buildings/police.html.
2515 Police Property List 1947.
2516 Ibid.
2517 MEPO 5/53 (419).
2518 MEPO 03/234.
2519 Metropolitan Police Orders dated 30th August 1873.
2520 *Kelly's Directory* 1875 p1989.
2521 MEPO 5/54 (441).
2522 MEPO 5/53 (419).
2523 Census 1881.
2524 *Post Office Directory* 1881 p1970.
2525 Metropolitan Police Surveyor's Records 1881; MEPO 02/234.
2526 Ibid.
2527 National Roll of Honour dated 2002.
2528 *Police Office Directory* 1894 p2203.
2529 LB664/-/0.
2530 Ibid.
2531 Metropolitan Police Surveyor's Records 1924.
2532 Col. W. T. Reay (1919) *The Specials – How They Served London*.
2533 Ibid.
2534 Metropolitan Police Orders dated 27th June 1935.

Putney Police Station was struck by German bombs on 9th September 1940, killing Station Sergeant Wilfred John Chilcott, aged 46, who was on duty at the time.[2535]

During the Local Government re-organisations of the 1960s, Putney, designated call sign (VD), was transferred (with Wandsworth) to W Division and re-designated (WP). Both stations were located within the London Borough of Wandsworth. In 1981 the orientation between Putney and Wandsworth changed. The station areas were amalgamated, and Putney Division of W District was now called Wandsworth Division, with the main headquarters function being established back at Wandsworth. The chief superintendent, superintendent and part of the admin were located at Wandsworth, whilst the chief inspector (admin) and the Process Section retained at Putney.[2536]

A Police Office was opened at Jubilee House, 230-232 Putney Bridge Road, Putney on Wandsworth Sub-Division in May 1978. Known as Putney Bridge Office, it was given the telegraph designation 'WB'. The opening hours were Mondays to Saturdays between 10.00am and 12 noon, and 3.00 to 5.00pm. Designated a Sectional Station it was opened when needed, such as for the Oxford and Cambridge Boat Races or the Head of River Boat Race.[2537]

This office was not open for long, and was closed in 1983.[2538] The station was retained on leasehold and reopened, although by 2013 the front counter public access was closed again.[2539]

Percy Laurie Section House was sold to developers during the 1990s as part of the section house closure programme. The scheme to reduce bed spaces for single officers also ended any automatic obligation by the Police to provide single accommodation.

The original Putney Police Station was shut in 2006 and sold off.

In 2010 Putney Police Office was set up and located in Putney High Street, adjacent to the Odeon Cinema.

As of 2019, a police office is open at 325 Tildesley Road, Putney Heath, and is a Safer Neighbourhoods Unit.[2540]

Radlett Police Station

The London Borough of Barnet
Watling Street Radlett 1946 -1967)
77 The Oakway, Watling Street (1967-1980)
S Division (1946-1980)

Radlett is a small village situated between St. Albans and Borehamwood in Hertfordshire, and in 2020 has just over 8,000 inhabitants. Records show that in 1932 a police station existed in Radlett village as a station of S or Hampstead Division,[2541] although there are no firm details of where and for how long the station remained open. The station was closed during WW2 1939-1945.

In 1946, following the end of World War II, a police station was opened by the Metropolitan Police in Radlett, although again its exact location is also unknown.

By the 1960s the Commissioner considered establishing a police office in Watling Street, Radlett which would serve as a base for officers who were responsible for the area, and would be open at certain times of the day to cater for local enquiries. A shop front that had previously been an electrical shop was leased, initially for seven years, and in November 1967 a new police office opened at 77 The Oakway, Watling Street, Radlett. The front clear glass to the building was replaced with obscured panes and billboards for recruiting and local information when the station opened.

The call sign of the station at that time was Sierra Echo (SE), and it was a sectional office as part of West Hendon Sub-Division. In 1973 the lease expired and it was renewed for a further another seven years.

Radlett Police Office 1967-1980

In the 1980s Radlett Police Station was situated opposite Park Road next to the fire station at 193 Watling Street, Radlett, Hertfordshire. The call sign had changed to SR prior to 1998.

The station was transferred to Hertfordshire Police in 2000, and by 2012 no police station existed in Radlett.

Rainham Police Station

The London Borough of Havering
3 New Road, Rainham, Essex (1935-2011)
Essex Police (1935-1965)
K Division (1965-2011)

Essex Police Helmet Plate Badge c1901-1936

In 1850 there was one constable posted to Rainham, and was long overdue an addition of four constables. The constable would have either been supplied with a cottage/house or had to find accommodation in the area for himself and his family. Constable 38 George Johnson, who had joined in January 1859, was the local village constable in 1861.[2542] In 1891 there were extensive boundary changes with the Essex Constabulary, which resulted in

Rainham Police Station 1935-2011

Rainham becoming a station within the Orsett Division.[2543] This station at 3 New Road, Rainham was built in 1935 by the Essex Constabulary, and transferred to the Metropolitan Police during boundary changes in 1965.

The station did not have charging facilities, and therefore all prisoners had to be transferred to Hornchurch Police Station.

Rainham Police Station was vacated in 2011,[2544] and sold for £801,000 that year.[2545]

Richmond Police Station

The London Borough of Richmond
Princes Street (1841-1871)
35 George Street (1971-1993)
V Division (1841-2013)
The London Borough of Richmond OCU (1993-2013)

From early mediaeval times until the 19th century, the maintenance of law and order in Richmond was largely the responsibility of the Lord of the Manor through his Court Leet. The Court Leet was presided over by the Steward of the Manor or his deputy. The Steward was the judge, with all administrative matters such as the empanelling of the jury and the election of officials being handled by the bailiff.[2546]

The elected officials of the court were the constable, headborough (chief of the ten men who made up the jury of frankpledge) and the aleconner, who was the forerunner of the present day Public Protection Officer, responsible for the quality of the ale and beer, and also for ensuring that they were sold to the proper weight and measure. Richmond, Ham and Kew each had their own officials. The constable was responsible for supervising the 'Watch and Ward' under the Statute of Westminster 1285. This was the forerunner of our police service, the 'Ward' being daytime patrols and the 'Watch', night-time ones. The constable was also responsible for inspecting alehouses and suppressing gaming houses, the apprenticing of poor children, the supervising of the settlement or removal of vagrants and beggars, the welfare of the poor, the collecting of taxes, the supervision of military arms supply and military training, and ensuring the upkeep of the local means of punishment. In other words, he was the equivalent of the local council and the police. It was a considerable undertaking and a highly-unpopular job.[2547]

In 1631 Edward Monday 'obstinately refused to perform his office'. The court records show that the constable was not exempt from being brought before the Steward for failing to carry out his duties, and was subject to punishment. In Richmond in those duties relating to the poor were dealt with by the parish constable.[2548] The law and order situation was somewhat confused in Richmond by the fact that the manor covered three parishes, each with their own vestry that had the duty to elect constables and maintain law and order. Presumably there was a working agreement as to the duties that were undertaken by the manor constables and those by the parish constables. In practice it appears that the parish constable was responsible for the 'social' and 'military' aspects of the work. In 1651 the constable presented to the vestry certain strangers and inmates who had crept into the parish and were likely to be a charge on the parish. In July 1654

'several persons were ordered to remove tenants out of their houses, or give a bond to the Churchwardens, to save the Parish against expenses to be incurred for their relief.'

and Thomas Raymond was ordered

'to remove his wife's mother out of the parish within a fortnight.'[2549]

A small watchhouse and lock-up can be seen in the Prospect of Richmond map of 1726, standing in the wide part of George Street near the junction with Duke Street. By 1730, there was a new watch house with

'a convenient house... to contain the two fire engines adjacent to it.'[2550]

In 1768 the Parish Trustees appointed two able-bodied men to watch and patrol the streets, by 1772 there were six men on regular watch and that number was doubled in 1783. In 1785 saw the introduction of a 'nightly watch' within the said parish.'[2551]

It appears not to have been a success because in 1785 a further Act was passed 'for making new provisions for the relief of the poor... and watching the streets...' and the trustees were replaced by Vestrymen. This was a much better system, and the first meeting of the newly-constituted body was held at the Greyhound Inn in George Street. Thereafter they met at the Parish Room in the churchyard.[2552] New offices were built, and the first meeting held at the corner of Vineyard Passage and Paradise Road took place on 11th April 1791.

The Vestry's time was largely taken up by the relief of the poor, and by provision of a new workhouse on Pest House Common in Queens Road to replace the one in Petersham Road. The old workhouse occupied Rump Hall in Petersham Road (then Lower Road), which the vestry had leased for some 30 years. However, they also had a duty to maintain law and order in the town, and one of their first acts in this direction was on 24th April 1786 when they ordered

'that the surveyor give notice to the inhabitants who leave out carriages... in the streets, highways...that if they cause such obstructions in future this Vestry must be obliged to levy the penalties upon them for their neglect'.

In 1787 the beadles were sent to remove the stage of a mountebank and threatened to prosecute him, while Robert Tasker, another Richmond resident, was let off with a caution for allowing his swine to roam the streets.[2553]

2535 www.policememorial.org.uk/Forces/Metropolitan/Metropolitan_Roll_1940-1945.htm accessed 3rd February 2010.
2536 Metropolitan Police Orders dated 4th August 1981.
2537 Metropolitan Police Orders dated 28th April 1978.
2538 Metropolitan Police Orders dated 15th February 1983.
2539 MPS Assets (2019) Freedom of Information request.
2540 Ibid.
2541 Police and Constabulary Almanac 1932.
2542 Essex Record Office Q/Apr. 12 Distribution List.
2543 Woodgate, J. (1985) The Essex Police, Lavenham, Suffolk.
2544 www. Metropolitan Police. Information Rights Unit, Police Stations Closed since 2010, accessed 10th June 2019.
2545 Ibid.
2546 www.richmond.gov.uk/home/leisure_and_culture/local_history_and_heritage/local_studies_collection/local_history_notes/law_and_order_in_richmond.htm accessed 31st January 2012.
2547 Ibid.
2548 www.richmond.gov.uk/local_history_and_heritage/law_and_order_in_richmond.htm accessed 31st January 2012.
2549 Ibid.
2550 Ibid.
2551 Ibid.
2552 Ibid.
2553 Ibid.

Richmond Police Station 1871-1912

In 1793 the Vestry had to deal with problems caused by an influx of emigrants from France. There was a

'complaint… that some idle and disorderly persons have of late made a practice of assaulting and grossly abusing several of the foreigners resident in the town without cause… it is ordered that the beadles be particularly attentive in the discovery of such persons'

These people would then be taken before the magistrates. The magistrates were appointed by the county, and the two resident in Richmond had a seat on the Vestry. Offenders were taken before one of them sitting in his own home; throughout the latter part of the 18th century there is frequent mention of offenders being taken before Sir William Richardson at his home on Richmond Hill (later known as Doughty House).[2554]

In 1794 John Thatcher, apprehended by the Sergeant of the Night for stealing malt from Edward Collins' brewery, was taken before the magistrate and later sentenced at the Guildford Assizes to seven years' transportation. Offenders were generally sent by the magistrates to Southwark Jail to await the Assize, which could be held in one of several different towns in Surrey including Reigate, Dorking and Guildford. Sentences included transportation for stealing and hanging for murder. The vestry was empowered to send men to Bridewell Gaol for failing to maintain their wives and families, and to the House of Correction at Kingston for embezzlement and assault. They did not punish blindly as Edward Brown and George Barley discovered in 1829 when, having expressed their regret at having obstructed and assaulted one of the watchmen, and made a public acknowledgement of their misdemeanour by circulating a handbill, all further proceedings against them were suspended.[2555]

One of the first tasks of the reorganised vestry in 1785 had been to order the erection of a watch house. On 30th December 1793 it adopted Mr. Justice Bonding's system of watching and laid down a rota of 'beats' to be walked by the watchmen.[2556]

Originally set up in 1805 to patrol the local area on horseback up to 16 miles around London, the new Bow Street horse patrols were stationed at North Cheam, Croydon, Sutton, Merton, Wimbledon, Robin Hood Hill, Kingston and Ditton Marsh which were all far beyond the MPD when it was first established.

By 1829 the watch was in its final years. Barnes had been the only part of the present borough to come within the Metropolitan Police area when Wandsworth or V Division was formed in 1830. But Richmond was added to the MPD on 13th January 1840 and the Vestry was relieved of its duty in that direction, other than collecting the Police Levy. They did not completely give up their responsibilities however, and reminded the police in February 1840

'to suppress the nuisances which occur on Shrove Tuesday in every year occasioned by a football being kicked through the public streets and thoroughfares of this parish to the great annoyance of all persons desirous of passing quietly through the same and to the detriment of the shopkeepers in Richmond.'[2557]

In 1849 the Vestry Hall was enlarged, and the police court was added. The watch house had been closed in 1841 when the police station, in two converted cottages in Princes Street (the cottages were demolished in 1966 to make way for Waitrose's supermarket in Sheen Road), was opened.

In 1851, residing at the station in one of the cottages (the section house for single police officers) was Constable Michael Madigan from Ireland, who lived there with Constables Henry Upton, Edward Bourke, and Merrick Perfse. In the other cottage was Constable John Jukes and his wife Elizabeth. Tragically, the 30-year-old Madigan fell into the Thames whilst out on his patrol, got into difficulties and drowned.[2558]

The station was later moved to a new building at 35 George Street. The land had been purchased in 1867 for £3,300 from Mr Vialls, and the new large purpose-built police station, constructed at a cost of £3,884 4s 2d, was opened in 1871. The station ground floor consisted of a charge room, inspector's office, four cells, drying room, mess room, library and smoking room. Outside was a parade shed, ambulance shed, and a four-stall stable with loft. In the basement there was a clothes room, recreation room, kitchen, lavatory, and bathroom. One married inspector and his family occupied six rooms at a weekly rent of 6/6d. Ten single constables also resided upstairs at the station, and they paid one shilling a week rent which was stopped from their pay.

In 1864 a re-organisation of the Metropolitan Police divisions took place, with Richmond being authorised as an inspector station. To assist the inspector were three sergeants and 30 constables split into a day and night shift, whose sole responsibility was for the area of Richmond. The inspector was also responsible for Twickenham and Barnes, and he was instructed not to do station duty as that would be done by one of the sergeants. The inspector's duty was continual patrolling in all weathers and at all times. Inspectors could choose their patrol times as they saw fit, which would overlap shift changes. The Divisional Superintendent often made unannounced visits, which could catch the inspector out if he was not careful. There were two horses, one for the inspector and the other for the mounted sergeant who would patrol the sub-division but not go beyond Richmond.[2559]

Rear aspect of Richmond Police Station with officers by the scullery

The two pictures above and below show the rear of the police station at Richmond. The picture above shows two officers enjoying the sunshine during their meal break, outside what was probably their mess room. It was important for all police stations to have a rear access through which prisoners could be transported on foot or in a prison van in and out of the station, out of the view of the public.

The rear gate and yard of Richmond Police station

There were two inspectors at the station, and one was more senior than the other. In 1878 John Pearman became inspector in charge of Richmond Police Station, and he was assisted a year later by Inspector William Jones. In 1891 Inspector Charles Pearn (warrant no. 64842) from Cornwall, with only eleven years service, became a sub-divisional inspector and took over charge of the station at Richmond, still on V Division, and he was assisted by a strength of three sergeants and 22 constables.[2560] Pearn was destined for far higher rank, and by 1901 was a Chief Inspector at Stoke Newington. In 1907 he had become Divisional Superintendent of J or Bethnal Green Division, from where he retired in 1910.[2561]

The Richmond Murder Mystery

In October 2010 a human skull was found in the garden of television presenter Sir David Attenborough in Park Road, Richmond which was later linked to a most notorious Richmond murder that took place in March 1879.[2562]

This was the second time police at Richmond station were asked to investigate this alleged murder. The Richmond mystery started when a box which had been seen floating in the Thames near Barnes Bridge settled along the foreshore. A man named Wheatley kicked it, only to discover there were bones, flesh and body parts inside. A passing man by the name of Kennison (a distant relative of one of the authors) was asked to mind the box whilst the finder went to the police station to report the matter, but Mr Kennison himself summoned a local constable before Wheatley returned. Sergeant 5V Childs verified the contents of the box as being body parts, before removing them to the mortuary and referring to the coroner. There was no clue as to whose remains these were at that time. Other body parts which had been hidden in an allotment not far away and in other places were eventually discovered.[2563]

2554 www.richmond.gov.uk/local_history_and_heritage/law_and_order_in_richmond.htm accessed 31st January 2012.
2555 Ibid.
2556 Ibid.
2557 Ibid.
2558 Metropolitan Police Roll of Honour (www.policememorial.org.uk) accessed 12th March 02.
2559 Metropolitan Police Special Police Orders 1864.
2560 *Kelly's Directory* 1891.
2561 *Kelly's Directory* 1907 and Census 1901.
2562 www.thisislocallondon.co.uk/news/8484943.Murder_mystery/ accessed 14th February 2012.
2563 www.oldbaileyonline.org/browse.jsp?id=t18790630-653&div=t18790630-653&terms accessed 14th February 2012.

On Saturday, 22nd March 1879 a Mr Porter, Mr Church and Mr Hughes, a solicitor, went to Richmond Police Station and saw Inspector Pearman to report Mrs Julia Martha Thomas, who lived at 2 Vine Cottages, Richmond, missing. Inspector Pearman and the men went immediately to Vine Cottages, and when no-one answered the door the inspector broke in. It later transpired that Mr Porter had unknowingly helped to dispose of stolen property having sold it on, which had come into the hands of one Catherine Webster, whom he knew, and who had told him an aunt had died and left the property to her.[2564]

In truth, Webster was a 29-year-old maid who had been employed by the missing Mrs Thomas, and had pushed her down the stairs and strangled her. She then disposed of the body by cutting it up, burning some of it in the grate of the fire and then placing some of the parts in a box which she threw into the Thames off Barnes Bridge.[2565]

Left: Victim Mrs Thomas, and murderer Kate Webster (right)

Inspector Creswell Wells (later a famous Superintendent of K and A Divisions) gave evidence at Webster's Old Bailey trial regarding plans he had drawn for the Treasury Counsel conducting the prosecution. Wells was an expert in this regard. As he was not recorded as an inspector on V Division he may have been attached to Scotland Yard. Inspector John Dowdell, a Scotland Yard detective, had travelled to Wexford in Ireland, where Webster was believed to be, and had arrested her for murder and theft of property. On the journey back she made a statement incriminating Mr Church in the murder, an allegation she repeated at Richmond Police Station in front of Inspectors William Jones and John Pearman the next day. Inspector Pearman had found a carpet bag in the basement of the cottage containing a variety of body parts, a razor and blood-stained clothing. In the fire grate he also discovered a chopper, charred bones and other body materials. The victim's head was missing.[2566]

At the end of her trial at the Old Bailey Webster was found guilty of murder. She claimed that she was pregnant in order to escape punishment. A panel of medical experts was convened and they examined Webster, reporting back to the judge that she was not 'with child'. She was sentenced to death and executed, only confessing to the priest shortly beforehand that it was she and no-one else who killed Mrs Thomas.[2567]

Only in 2010, with the discovery of the skull in David Attenborough's garden, was the riddle regarding the whereabouts of Mrs Thomas' head solved.

The Tragic and Suspicious Death of Sub-Divisional Inspector George Henry Dixon

Richmond's 50-year-old Sub-Divisional Inspector George Henry Dixon (warrant no. 52444) was found drowned in a few inches of water of the River Thames after going missing on duty in suspicious circumstances at Hampton Court in 1893. Foul play was suspected, and an inquiry was launched by detectives. The investigation revealed that the inspector came on duty on 2nd March 1893 arriving at Richmond from Hampton station. He made his customary round of the sub-division on his horse, calling at Bedfont, Twickenham and Teddington, arriving at Hampton at 10.00pm, although he soon found that he had lost some disciplinary papers relating to an officer at Twickenham. He remained at the station for a further hour, and on telling Station Sergeant George Smith he would return in an hour he left the station. He was last seen hurriedly making his way to Hampton Court Palace, where he would have had to pass the recreation ground next to the Thames – the place where his body was found two days later.

The officer never reached the Palace. Dixon was a keen police officer, and prior to his disappearance he had an altercation with navvies working on an adjacent water works.

At the inquest held at the Red Lion public house, one witness who lived near the recreation ground stated that she had 'heard a man's scream in some distress' coming from the recreation ground at 11.15pm, which also woke her housekeeper. No further cries were heard, although heavy footsteps came past the house from the direction of the recreation ground soon afterwards. Dixon was found 2-3ft from the bank, lying face down in 16 inches of water with his cap over his face and his arms embedded in the mud. The inquest concluded that he did not commit suicide.[2568] Dixon's funeral took place on 11th March, when his coffin was carried by men of the division.

A large body of men were in attendance at Hampton Cemetery where he was buried. Dixon was born and bred at St. Georges in the East End of London. In the 1891 census he was resident at 11 Smith Street, Mile End Old Town, where he resided with his wife Louisa Ann and their five children. Dixon had been an Inspector on Y Division, but had come to V Division from H or Whitechapel Division. Dixon had joined the Metropolitan Police in February 1870 He remained only for a very short period in Whitechapel – from 1888 until 1891 – from where he had been promoted to Sub-Divisional Inspector and transferred to Richmond. Dixon was present in the East End of London during the Jack the Ripper murders, and may have had more than a suspicion on the likely suspects.

In 1891 there were seven inspectors attached to Richmond section, with Dixon's predecessor Sub-Divisional Inspector John Pryke in charge of the area. He was supported by Inspectors Richard Feaver and Arthur How who were in charge of the station, and together with three sergeants, three acting sergeants and 38 constables[2569] dealt with the day-to-day running of the station and neighbourhood. The Divisional Surgeon appointed to Richmond Police station was James Adams MD, who resided at 3 The Terrace.[2570]

The photograph right shows Constable 1169V James Frank Dellar (warrant no. 78885), who was born at Homerton, East London. He joined the Metropolitan Police at Richmond in 1893, but a year later was transferred to A or Westminster Division. Within a year he was again transferred, this time to S or Highgate Division, but returned to V or Wandsworth Division in March 1901, where he stayed until 1920, serving at Kingston

Constable 1169V James Frank Dellar

until he retired. Dellar resided with his wife, son and daughter at 106 Elm Road, Kingston.[2571] By 1911 the family had moved to larger premises, and a further son and daughter had been born in the meantime.[2572] The photograph, taken on his return to V Division, shows him with three medals – the 1897 Queen's Jubilee medal, the 1902 Coronation medal and the 1911 Coronation medal.

In 1895 the old Vestry Hall, which in 1859 had witnessed the enquiry into the poisoning of Isabella Bankes and, on 31st March 1879, the beginning of the prosecution of the arch-murderess Kate Webster, having outlived its usefulness and been replaced for all except its magisterial duties by the new Town Hall in Hill Street (Richmond became a borough in 1890), was pulled down and replaced by a new magistrates' court and mortuary, which opened in October 1896. This building was greeted with mixed feelings. According to one local paper:

'The universal opinion (that) the exterior... is not exactly calculated to inspire respect mingled with admiration, (whilst) the interior is very well adapted to for its purpose... No money (has been spent on its outside) ornamentation.'

In 1903 it was decided to improve the cell area of the station by providing better drainage and heating for prisoners detained there. These alterations cost £963 18s.

A well-known police officer on Richmond Sub-Division retired in March 1904, and to mark the occasion there was a ceremonial leaving party. Police Sergeant Henry Burrows (warrant no. 63381) was entertained at the station, where Divisional Superintendent Saines presented him with a marble clock and made a speech.[2573] These arrangements would have normally taken place on a Wednesday after 2.00pm, when the men had been paid. Afterwards there was a party where the divisional band played music and food and drink was available.

By 1905 it was felt that the single officers residing in the section house should get more privacy, so cubicles were erected around each bed space at a cost of £67.[2574]

The present location in Red Lion Street was a site acquired by the Council in 1912 for £1,625. The land, situated at 8 Red Lion Street, Richmond was purchased from the council in the same year and the police set to work to build a station, section house and two sets of married quarters.[2575] The picture below is an historic one, showing the Royal Flying Corps (RFC) and Richmond Police football teams in November 1916, playing a match in aid of the British Sportsman's Ambulance Fund. The RFC won 6-1. The game was played in Old Deer Park, Richmond at the back of the police, and was kicked off by the Solicitor General Sir George Cave. The event was attended by many spectators and dignitaries.

Royal Flying Corps verses Richmond Police station teams raise money for the British Sportsman's Ambulance Fund

In 1919 the sub-divisional station of Richmond (VR) was a station on V or Wandsworth Division, with its sectional stations being Barnes and Kew. Inspectors were still in charge of the station. In 1924 the old police station at 35 George Street, Richmond was sold to Express Dairies for £12,000.[2576]

Kew closed as a police station in 1932, although the area was still policed from Richmond. Between 1955 and 1960 Superintendent Rawlings was in charge of the sub-division. His place was taken by Superintendent Mulchay MM.

Richmond Police Station 1912-2013

In 1965 Richmond became a sub-division on T Division as police divisions started to match the boundaries of local authorities. The call sign for the station altered to 'TR'. Within T Division were the London Boroughs of Richmond-upon-Thames and Hounslow, and the Urban Districts of Staines and Sunbury-on-Thames. The divisional headquarters changed to Hounslow, situated at 5 Montague Road, Hounslow. By 1969 Superintendent R.H. Anning was in charge of the station and his deputy was Chief Inspector F.J. Attwood.[2577] The sub-division remained on T Division throughout the 1980s.

In 1989 the Richmond and Twickenham Police divisions amalgamated to form the Richmond-upon-Thames division. A review of police station opening times saw the station open Mondays to Fridays from 9.00am to 5.00pm.[2578] In the meantime Richmond Police Station still remained in the ownership of the Metropolitan police, and in 2011 its opening times were extended to 8.00am to 8.00pm.

2564 www.oldbaileyonline.org/browse.jsp?id=t18790630-653&div=t18790630-653&terms accessed 14th February 2012.
2565 www.thisislocallondon.co.uk/news/8484943.Murder_mystery/ accessed 14th February 2012.
2566 www.oldbaileyonline.org/browse.jsp?id=t18790630-653&div=t18790630-653&terms accessed 14th February 2012.
2567 www.thisislocallondon.co.uk/news/8484943.Murder_mystery/ accessed 14th February 2012.
2568 *The Police Review and Parade Gossip*, 9th October 1893.
2569 *Kelly's Directory* 1891.
2570 Ibid.
2571 Census 1901.
2572 Census 1911.
2573 *The Police Review and Parade Gossip*, 6th May 1904.
2574 Metropolitan Police Surveyor's Records.
2575 Metropolitan Police Surveyor's Records 1924.
2576 Ibid.
2577 *Police and Constabulary Almanac* 1969.
2578 Metropolitan Police Authority. Police Station opening hours Committee; MPA Reports 9th November 2000.

In 2012 a new police office opened at Sovereign Gate, 18-20 Kew Road Richmond. The front counter at a new police base – Sovereign Gate – officially opened to the public on Wednesday, 8th February 2012 and replaced the front counter at Richmond Police Station.

To reflect the needs of the public, Sovereign Gate's front counter operates from 8.00am to 8.00pm every day. Members of the public who need to report crimes outside of these hours were encouraged to go to Twickenham Police Station, open 24 hours a day.

Sovereign Gate is also the new base for South Richmond and Kew Safer Neighbourhoods Team, both formerly situated at Richmond Police Station. Additionally it is a Regional Learning Centre, where officers from the borough and other areas of south west London will receive training in matters such as emergency life support.

Richmond Police Station continues to operate as a base for some of the borough's other police departments, including the CID.

The then Borough Commander, Chief Superintendent Clive Chalk, said:

'I am pleased to announce the opening of Sovereign Gate's front counter which, with its external lift, split-level counters and hearing loops, is much more modern and accessible to the public than Richmond Police Station was.' [2579]

Richmond Police Station was vacated and sold in October 2013 for £2.7M to SnowFinch LLP.[2580]

Rochester Row Police Station

City of Westminster
63 Rochester Row, SW1P (1845-1993)
B Division (1845-1886)
A Division (1886-1985/86)
No. 8 Area (1985/86-1993)

In the first days of the Metropolitan Police, the new B Division took over the watch house at New Way, off Tothill Street in Westminster. This had a reserve room, three cells, a parish engine house, charge room, Superintendent's office and a small yard used for parading officers. The Property Register noted that

'the whole premises need thorough repair, and [it is] intended for demolition for Westminster Improvement Schemes.' [2581]

Rochester Row Police Station 1845-1993

In 1845, a new police court (at no. 69), station and section house (nos. 63-7) was built in Rochester Row, this new building replacing the old watch house, the section houses in Cowley Street and Great Smith Street, and the old Westminster police court at Queen's Square, Pimlico.[2582] Originally, the part of Westminster lying to the south and west of Buckingham Palace and Knightsbridge had been part of B Division before it became co-terminous with the Borough of Kensington and Chelsea.

A Superintendent's residence for A Division and three sets of living quarters were established in 1906 at 68 Vincent Square that backed on to Rochester Row. Two sets of annuity charges, representing the money spent on erecting the buildings, were payable to the University Life Assurance Society based at 25 Pall Mall, this being the Receiver, John Wray's, address. The Receiver had in fact been a founder member of the Society, and used its investment capacity to fund several police buildings.[2583]

Rochester Row became a busy station on A Division, with stables for Mounted Branch and, at one point in the 1980s, a special custody complex for terrorists until this was replaced by a unit at Paddington Green. The station closed in 1993, replaced by Belgravia.

Rodney Road Police Station

The London Borough of Southwark
1 Flint Street, Walworth (1829-1932)
P Division (1829-1921)
M Division (1921-1932)

A brick-and-slate house was rented from Mr Golden of Boyce House, Whetstone as a police station and section house at Lockfields, Walworth on P Division. It had a small garden, a charge room and three cells for prisoners. It was painted in 1846, 1852, 1861, 1866 and 1869, at a total cost of £128. Its constant use meant that it became dilapidated and in need of repairs inside to the woodwork and cells, and the drains into the common sewer. The surveyors reported that there was plenty of water leaking into both the kitchen and the three cells. The cost of insurance was set at £25 per year.[2584]

A memorandum from the Commissioner dated August 1871 was enquiring about Lockfields, one of the chief stations of P Division. A further memo from the Commissioner in January 1872 stated that he proposed to have a police station at Lockfields, Walworth. In June 1872 premises at Park House, Walworth, were leased from Mr Thomas H Golden at £105 per annum.[2585] In May 1873 the building was ready for public business, and was known as Rodney Road Police Station.[2586] The station strength on opening was two station sergeants and five constables.[2587]

In August 1880 a notice was received from the Clerk to the Vestry, Vestry Hall, Walworth Road, that the address of the police station would be 1 Flint Street.[2588]

The 1881 Report of the Condition of Police Stations indicated that Rodney Road Police Station consisted of an administrative block that was currently occupied by one inspector and four constables and had three cells.[2589]

It was quite separate from another house occupied by married families, in which the distribution of the accommodation among the various families was bad. Compulsory purchase powers relating to the premises were obtained in February 1889. The station was rebuilt in 1892 at a cost £7,648, of which the freehold was £2,700.[2590] The lowest tender by Garlick and Horton was accepted.[2591]

Inspector Philip McCarthy was a notable officer, whose service in the Police was merited by an article in the *Police Review and Parade Gossip*. He retired from Rodney Road in

1908 having been there for six years, and during his service he specialised in cruelty cases against children and animals. He also concentrated on vagrancy patrols to ensure that only valid cases merited assistance, and the professional vagrant was moved on. He left to become an Inspector for the Royal Society for the Prevention of Cruelty to Children.[2592]

Rodney Road Police Station 1873-1932

By 1921 Rodney Road Police Station was on L Division, but was transferred to M (Southwark) Division[2593] where it remained until it was closed in January 1932.[2594] In December 1933 consideration was given to selling the property. It was described as a substantial building occupying a corner site in a very poor neighbourhood. When in use there had been a Section House, which formed part of the station, for 19 men, but it had not been occupied since the station closed and it was suggested that the building be sold.[2595]

In 1991 it was noted that the old police station was now part of the English Martyrs Roman Catholic Infants School.[2596]

Roehampton Police Station

The London Borough of Wandsworth

Roehampton Lane (1871-1908)

8-10 Medfield Street, Roehampton Lane (1908-1929)

117 Danbury Avenue (West Putney Police Office) (1967-1993)

V Division (1871-1993)

Borough of Wandsworth OCU (1993-2018/19)

SW BCU with Richmond, Kingston and Merton

(2018/19 to Present)

In 1871 a cottage was leased for seven years from Miss Snow of Wimbledon for the sum of £22 per annum.[2597] By 1881 a small cottage acted as the station in Roehampton, and housing two married constables and their families.[2598] A station in Roehampton was brought into service in 1894 to cope with demand and the increased density in population. Expansion in the area particularly necessitated the Divisional Superintendent to reconsider the boundaries within his division. A suitable site with three cottages was found, and although originally rented they were purchased later, in 1908.

The address of these was 6,8&10 Medfield Street, Roehampton Lane, SW15. Roehampton became a station, in a loose sense of the word, on V or Wandsworth Division,[2599] because as records show each cottage comprised just accommodation with three sets of quarters but not necessarily having other features like cells, charge room or station office for visitors. Although originally called a station, this was one of low status and it became a sectional station (with Wandsworth Common, Wimbledon, and Putney) to Wandsworth, which of course was not only a sub-divisional station but also the divisional headquarters as well. The postal address to which correspondence and inquiries were directed was no. 8.[2600]

In 1871 Widows and Orphans boxes were sanctioned to be placed at the front of police stations in order to support orphaned children and to help towards the cost of the Metropolitan Police and City Orphanage at Strawberry Hill.

Roehampton Police Office 1967 to present

The station was still in Roehampton in the 1930s, but today Roehampton Police Station is little more than an office and is situated at 117 Danebury Avenue, London, SW15. This is between Putney Heath and Richmond Park Golf Club. The office was formally a flat on the ground floor, however it has

2579 content.met.police.uk/News/Sovereign-Gates-Front-Counter-Officially-Opens/1400006512411/1257246745756 accessed 9th December 2012.
2580 MPS (2018) Freedom of Information Request: Land and property sold by the MPS for over £1M.
2581 Metropolitan Police Property Registers.
2582 Brown, B. 'Following in Footsteps', in *The Job*, 15th May 1987.
2583 Reynolds, J. (undated) 'The Receiver for the Metropolitan Police District: A Short History'.
2584 Metropolitan Police Surveyor's Records.
2585 Metropolitan Police Surveyor's Records.
2586 MEPO 5/52.
2587 Metropolitan Police Orders dated 12th June 1873.
2588 MEPO 5/52.
2589 Metropolitan Police Report Condition of Police Stations 1881.
2590 *Ten Year Report 1884-1893*.
2591 *The Builder*, 1891.
2592 *The Police Review and Parade Gossip*, June 1908.
2593 Metropolitan Police Orders dated 24th February 1921.
2594 Metropolitan Police Orders dated 1st January 1932.
2595 MEPO 2/2584.
2596 Richard Sharp, letter dated 15th February 1991.
2597 Metropolitan Police Surveyor's Report 1881 (MEPO 04/234).
2598 Ibid.
2599 Metropolitan Police Surveyor's Records 1912.
2600 Metropolitan Police Surveyor's Records 1924.

wheelchair access, a feature built into the office when it was constructed in the 1960s. In 2010 the office – now called West Putney Police Office – is still in use, although it has the police blue façade. A new police office was also located at 325 Tildesley Road, Roehampton, London, SW15 3BB in 2010.

Romford Police Station

The London Borough of Havering
South Street, Romford (1892-1965)
19 Main Road, Romford (1965 to Present)
Essex Police (1892-1965)
K Division (1965-2018)
Basic Command Unit East Area (EA) (2018 to Present)

The Bow Street Horse patrols were formed in 1777 and patrolled the turnpike roads out of London. They were under the jurisdiction of the Bow Street Magistrates. These horse patrols were stationed at various places on the outskirts of London. Romford formed part of the 4th Division, with further patrols situated at Enfield, Lea Bridge Road, Woodford, Loughton, Epping, Stratford and Ilford.[2601]

In 1805 a single horse patrol was stationed in Romford Town. There were patrols at Romford Road (Maryland Point) and two in Ilford.[2602] In 1830 the nearest Metropolitan Police Boundary was the Bow Bridge, which marked the boundary between Middlesex and Essex, although by 1840 when the boundary moved it stopped short of Romford.[2603] The horse patrols were incorporated into the Metropolitan Police in 1837, so Romford was policed by them until 1840, when the Essex Police were formed.

In 1839 the Parish of Romford sent a testimonial to the Metropolitan Police Commissioner asking to be included into the MPD, but this was ignored. Romford became a station included within Brentwood Division of the Essex Police under the newly-appointed Captain McHardy.[2604]

Romford Town has always been a busy location, and certainly in policing terms it was one of the busiest stations in Essex. Questions have been asked whether Romford should have become the divisional headquarters, but for reasons that have been unexplained it was located at Brentwood instead. In 1841 the town had a population of over 5,000, half the size of Romford. Superintendent Marsingale was the first officer in charge of the division, having joined the force on 31st March 1841 as an inspector. Marsingale had been a schoolmaster from Norton in Somerset.[2605]

The station strength was one superintendent and four constables. These were Constable 45 James Barnard (who had joined in November 1840 and resigned in April 1841), Constable 17 Joseph Copsey, Constable 63 Cracknell and Constable 96 F. Lambert. Constable Lambert, who had also seen service at Romford, was previously a cornfactor from Dunmow in Essex,[2606] and had joined the Essex Constabulary in September 1841. He could have had a problem, perhaps with discipline or even drinking, as by May 1843 he had been transferred to four different stations – Orsett, Rainham, Averley and Stifford.[2607]

In 1844 the Superintendent (First Class) in charge of the Division was Thomas Coulson, who had previously been attached to Chelmsford Headquarters,[2608] having been appointed on 22nd April 1840.[2609] It was a thriving town, heralded for its leather works, brewery and busy cattle market. Added to this was a workhouse designed to cater for 500 people. Romford was regarded as a 'detached' police station, and records show that Inspector John Haydon, who had been appointed in November 1840, was the officer in charge.[2610]

The Essex Constabulary was formed in 1840 and had been responsible for this area since that time. Its headquarters were shown at Brentwood, under the supervision of Superintendent Edward Davis. In the same year one inspector and three constables were posted to Romford, where a building was acquired as a police station in the High Street.[2611] The parishes of Havering, Hornchurch and Romford were policed by eight constables – an area of over 12,000 acres.[2612] In early 1861 Romford had a station strength of one inspector and seven constables. The officer in charge was Inspector William Gilpin, who joined in July 1854. The other officers were Constable 1 William Dennis, Constable 54 William Cousins, Constable 126 James Manning, Constable 31 James Parslow (who was posted to Romford in May 1859 and had 20 years service – see also Collier Row Police Station), Constable 63 James Danes and Constable 45 William King. James seemed to be a popular first name for the constables at this station. There was a vacancy for one more constable at this time.

In 1881 James Farrow was the Sergeant of police at Romford, and he was assisted by Constables Charles Archer, George Emmery, Benjamin Free, William Spalding, John Mount, Alfred Lazell, and Charles Harrington.[2613] The police operated from the Liberty Hall, Market Place, Romford.[2614]

Romford Police received notoriety in 1885 when a tragic incident occurred. Inspector Simmons, his wife Mary and their two children resided near the station at a house in the South Street Gas works. He had been posted to the station in 1881, and was then aged 34 years having been born in Holloway, north London.[2615] He was on patrol together with another officer when they spotted a well-known burglar called David Dredge on the road between Romford and Hornchurch. After a failed attempt by the officer to gather re-enforcements, the inspector returned to the vicinity and confronted Dredge, who was with two other men. The taller man of the group pulled a gun and shot Simmons, who died four days later.

The funeral of Inspector Simmons took place on Tuesday, 27th January and was attended by an enormous crowd. Simmons was buried at Oldchurch cemetery. In attendance were the Chief Constable Major Poyntz and Assistant Chief Constable Raglan Somerset, and every county and divisional superintendent and 140 inspectors, sergeants and constables also attended the funeral. The Metropolitan Police also sent 100 officers to the ceremony as a token of respect.[2616]

A nationwide hunt took place and, with the incentive of a reward, eventually Dredge and another man called James Lee (who had tried to pawn a gun in Euston) were tried, convicted and hanged in April 1885. It was widely believed at the time that Lee was in fact innocent and wrongly convicted.[2617] This was an example of a high-profile case which resulted in police officers on the outer fringes of the Metropolitan Area being allowed to carry revolvers.

Inspector Simmons was succeeded by Inspector Thomas J. Cooper, aged 42, born at Alresford in Essex. He was promoted from sergeant to fill the vacancy, and transferred from Rayne Road Station near Bocking with his wife and two children.[2618] One of Inspector Cooper's main problems in Romford was the policing of the Salvation Army. Organised along military lines, their headquarters were at Holm Lodge, Romford. Cooper had to report disturbances to the local magistrates, who were concerned that the banging of drums and singing caused a nuisance. In any event the police often protected the Salvationists, who would be followed by ever-increasing groups of the lower classes bent on violence if they got the opportunity.[2619]

Romford was described as the busiest town in Essex, and its station as hardly adequate for policing the town. Romford had a strength of one inspector, one sergeant and eleven constables.[2620] The original Romford Police Station in the High Street remained in use until it was no longer suitable for police purposes. In 1891 it was agreed to build a new police station and Court House at South Street, Romford.[2621]

Romford Police Station 1892-1965

The new police station was finished and occupied in 1892, although the courthouse was not built onto the rear of the station until the 1930s.[2622] Rather than walk the prisoners through the streets of Romford, the magistrates moved to buildings in South Street which now house the County Court.[2623]

In 1894 the introduction of the new telephone system meant that Chelmsford, Romford, Brentwood and Chadwell Heath were all connected to the telephone network, and they could directly communicate with each other.[2624]

Romford Police Station became the Divisional Headquarters in 1916. In the same year the newly-promoted Superintendent W.T.J. Howlett took charge at the station, where he was a well-respected, keen and conscientious senior officer. William Howlett lived with his parents at Little Maplestead before becoming a cornfactor's assistant.[2625] He joined the Essex Constabulary in 1886 and was promoted Acting Sergeant in January 1894.[2626] Obviously other senior officers recognised his skills, and by 1922 he was promoted to Deputy Chief Constable of Essex and transferred to Essex Police Headquarters at Springfield, Chelmsford. The town of Romford was expanding as people moved out from London because of the growth of the railways.

When the First World War started in August 1914 many policemen voluntarily joined the colours and fought for their country. Superintendents had to decide on minimum numbers of officers required to police each area, and to send remaining officers for war service. The county of Essex was indeed vulnerable to aerial attack by German bombers and Zeppelins, and resources were stretched to the limit.

Superintendent W.T.J. Howlett, later Deputy Chief Constable (1866-1926)

During the war Romford Division of Essex Constabulary was one of the first stations in the county, if not the country, to receive women Special Constables. Manning levels had been reduced, and special constables were used extensively to supplement the numbers of regular police. In 1917 Romford Justices asked for female Special Constables to patrol the town. Authority was given in June 1918 to pay two women 5 shillings a day, with 3s 8d per month boot allowance and deductions of 1/3d for insurance. The picture above, taken in 1918, shows Women Special Constable 2478 Dora Jordan, who is also shown in the second photograph overleaf of a group of officers. They were well accepted by the regular officers, even though they were not permanent nor did they have any police powers. Their appointment was terminated in October 1919.

Woman Special Constable 2478 Dora Jordan

When recruiting for the force commenced in 1919, Fred Joslin, a war veteran and farmworker, together with 21 other former soldiers, signed up and joined the Essex Constabulary. Joslin was posted to Romford Police Station, where he lived in single officer's quarters. A resident housekeeper there cooked all single officers' meals.

2601 MEPO 14/40.
2602 Brown, B. (1990) 'Romford Police 'The Anniversary of a Change' in the *Romford Record*, Romford and District Historical Society.
2603 Ibid.
2604 Ibid.
2605 Woodgate, J. (1985) *The Essex Police*, Lavenham, p138.
2606 Ibid.
2607 Essex Record Office Q/Apr. 12: Distribution List.
2608 Essex Record Office Q/Apr. 1: Distribution List.
2609 *The Police and Constabulary List 1844*. Parker, Furnival and Parker, London.
2610 Ibid.
2611 Scollan, M. (1993) *Sworn to Serve*. Phillimore, Chichester.
2612 Woodgate, J. (1985) *The Essex Police*. Lavenham.
2613 Census 1881.
2614 Ibid.
2615 Ibid.
2616 Woodgate, J. (1985) *The Essex Police*. Lavenham.
2617 Scollen, M. (1993) *Sworn to Serve*. Phillimore, Chichester.
2618 Census 1881.
2619 Ibid.
2620 Woodgate, J. (1985) *The Essex Police*. Lavenham.
2621 *3 Area Magazine*, 1975.
2622 Woodgate, J. (1985) *The Essex Police*. Lavenham.
2623 Ibid p67.
2624 Scollen, M. (1993) *Sworn to Serve*. Phillimore, Chichester.
2625 Census 1881.
2626 *The Police Review and Parade Gossip*, 12th January 1894.

In 1922 a demonstration involving 2,000 unemployed men marched to Romford to persuade the Poor Law Guardians to increase the poor rate to 9 shillings a week.[2627] Inspector Hyde and his constables from Romford were overwhelmed by the sheer numbers of people, but the personal intervention of the Chief Constable, who drove to Romford, prevented a serious disturbance when he managed to influence the Guardians to agree the change and bring rates into line with Metropolitan workhouse unions.[2628] In the same year Romford Division was successful at cricket, and celebrated the fact with a photograph of the whole division, with the Divisional Cricket Team proudly displaying their trophy.

The Cricket Team at Romford in 1922. Seated in front was Superintendent Howlett, himself a very keen cricketer

The picture below shows Constable Havers, located at the extreme right of the second row from the top. He had joined the service in October 1913 and, after initial training, had been posted to Brightlingsea. However he was soon called-up during the First World War and joined as a Royal Military Police Officer. He was injured in September 1917, eventually returning to Romford Division in April 1918 where he served with Superintendent Howlett for the next ten years.[2629]

Romford Division 1918 with Superintendent Howlett at centre

In front of Havers (in plainclothes) is Detective George H. Totterdell. By the 1950s he had become one of the most respected and celebrated detectives of the Essex Police. Totterdell was born on 2nd July 1892, the son of a village constable at Eastwood near Southend. Totterdell's father had entered the police service when his former employer, Lord Rookwood of Down Hall, Harlow, who was recognised as the father of the Essex Police, recommended him.[2630]

Detective Totterdell was involved in many famous cases during his service. He assisted in the murder inquiry of Constable George Gutteridge, who was gunned down at Howe Green on the Romford to Ongar Road on 27th September 1927. G.H. Totterdell became the first Detective Superintendent of the Essex Police, and followed in the footsteps of Detective Inspector Hyde (later responsible for the Criminal Investigation Department for the whole force),[2631] who is in the same picture, seated to the right of Superintendent Howlett, who later became Deputy Chief Constable of the Essex Constabulary. It is perhaps a less common facet of life today than in previous years that police officers died 'in service', or shortly after commencing retirement, but that is exactly what happened to Deputy Chief Constable Howlett. He died suddenly on 12th June 1926, just six weeks after he retired. He received a full police funeral, where the whole of Romford Division and Senior Officers of the Constabulary turned out to escort the horse-drawn hearse. His passing was a sad loss to the Service and to the community of Romford.

Detective Superintendent Totterdell

The funeral procession of Superintendent Howlett in 1926

The picture below shows the rare internal view of Romford's cellblock area. This is the view a prisoner would receive when taken from the custody office to the cellblock after having been booked in or charged with a criminal offence. It shows the cell passage to the cells. The cell passage was of painted brickwork whilst inside each cell glazed tiles were used from

A typical cell at Romford Police Station in the 1920s

floor to ceiling to enable quick cleaning. In the case of drunken or dirty prisoners it was necessary to mop up debris quickly from the stone floors or walls. There were few comforts for prisoners who were allowed blankets and a mattress usually of horse hair which was hard and robust to cope with the constant usage. There was also little for the prisoners to damage or harm themselves with. Often people arrested for serious matters decide to end it all rather than suffer or face the consequences, therefore the police practice of taking possession of articles like matches, belts and knives has been sensible since the first prisoners were detained at stations.

It was usual for constables to walk up to twenty miles a day in rural areas. Patrolling could be more effective by using a bicycle. The photograph below shows Sergeant Havers in the rear yard of Romford Police Station with his police-issue bicycle. Often police officers could be issued with cycles which were hired, or they could purchase their own and claim cycle mileage allowance in order for them to patrol their beats. The cycle allowance was 1d per mile. The cycle proved a cheaper and more effective option than hiring a horse and cart, especially when dealing with the problem of 'scorchers', as they were called at the time, who rode furiously along the county's roads.[2632]

Sergeant Havers at Romford in 1920

Supervising sergeants were often issued with pedal cycles in order to perform their duty, yet they were required to keep them clean at all times. The cycle above certainly looks very new and clean. It would have been housed in the cycle rack in the rear yard. Inspectors had traditionally been allocated a horse and trap for supervisory purposes.

In 1930 the strength of Romford Police Station consisted of one superintendent, two inspectors, five sergeants and 45 constables. There were also 13 sets of married quarters, however all 21 single men lived nearby in rented lodgings.[2633]

The station was described as somewhat old-fashioned, but on a restricted site in an excellent position. There were four cells which the surveyor reported were in some ways inadequate for purpose, with the heating and lighting in need of replacement as they were obsolete.[2634] The surveyor suggested that a new site should be sought, but this not followed up.[2635] The superintendent resided in accommodation at the station.

The population at the time was estimated at 27,000, and covered an area of 29 square miles.[2636]

By 1949 the Romford Division was divided into sub-divisions. Romford Division also included other stations such as Plough Corner, and police officers stationed in Collier Row and Rydal Mount, Havering.[2637]

Essex Police Orders in 1951 gave instructions for the amalgamation of Brentwood and Romford Divisions, under the control of the Superintendent at Brentwood. The Essex Police still had a horse located at Romford, however instructions were given in the following manner:

'The county horse should be transferred to Brentwood from Romford for the use of the Superintendent.' [2638]

The Local Government Act 1963 created the Greater London Council, and together with the Police Act 1964 changed policing boundaries. It was unacceptable for a county force to police a metropolitan area. The Essex Constabulary moved out of Romford on 1st April 1965. There had been a ballot of staff, and out of 229 officers and men 139 chose to say behind and transfer to the Metropolitan Police.[2639] The cadets were also given the option to transfer.

John George Smith, who became an Essex Police Cadet on 12th November 1962, transferred to the Metropolitan Police Cadets as 21958 on 1st April 1965. He become a constable, with warrant number 155158, in August 1965 and after training school was posted to Hackney Police Station as PC212, G Division. Constable Smith gained much experience at many stations during his service, but he remained longest in Traffic Division at TDJ Rigg Approach, Leyton. He took promotion to sergeant and retired from Barkingside Police Station as an inspector after thirty years' service.

Sergeant (later Inspector) John George Smith

2627 Scollen, M. (1993) *Sworn to Serve*. Phillimore, Chichester.
2628 Ibid.
2629 Havers family history records.
2630 Totterdell, G. H. (1956) *Country Copper*. Harrap, London.
2631 Ibid.
2632 Scollan, M. (1993) *Sworn to Serve*. Phillimore, Chichester.
2633 Essex County Constabulary: Police Stations and Police Houses Booklet (c1930) Essex Police Museum, Police Headquarters, Springfield, Chelmsford, Essex.
2634 Ibid.
2635 Ibid.
2636 Ibid.
2637 *3Area Magazine*, 1975.
2638 *Essex Police News and Views*, 1965.
2639 Brown, B. (1990) 'Romford Police – Anniversary of Change, in the *Police History Society Journal* No. 7.

The re-organisation of boundaries meant that the existing stations of Romford (KR), Collier Row (KL), Upminster (KU), Hornchurch (KC), Harold Hill (KA), Rainham (KM) and Plough Corner (KP) were transferred to the Metropolitan Police District.²⁶⁴⁰

Romford Police Station and the courthouse were demolished, soon after the Metropolitan Police took over the policing of the division in 1965. The Metropolitan Police occupied the newly-built Police Station at 19 Main Road, Romford almost as soon as they arrived.²⁶⁴¹ The modern police station was built next to the new Magistrates' Court, and was opened officially in November 1965.²⁶⁴² Romford was to be the Divisional Headquarters for K Division, although whilst the operational side commenced on 1st April the divisional staff did not move from East Ham until 28th November 1965.²⁶⁴³

The new divisional station was opened and the existing station in South Street ('KR') was closed. The new station at Romford was given the code Kilo-Delta ('KD') to mark its headquarters status. Simultaneously, East Ham changed its telegraphic code to 'KE'.²⁶⁴⁴

Romford Police Station 1965 to present

In 1990 Romford Police Station was shut to allow for modernisation, which cost £3million. The refit was estimated to take some time, therefore the headquarters staff and Criminal Investigation Department were relocated to rented buildings at Blackburn House, Eastern Road, Romford.²⁶⁴⁵ After 18 months of building work, which took place alongside operational police duties, the then-Commissioner Sir John Stevens re-opened the new station. The Borough of Havering Police Headquarters then returned to Main Road and the rented accommodation was vacated. The refit was designed to bring new improved technology to the station with state-of-the-art computers with on-screen mapping etc. Recent CCTV coverage of the town means that officers can now target areas and video crimes and arrests for later use as evidence.²⁶⁴⁶

Romford Police Station operates 24 hours, seven days a week.

Rotherhithe Police Station

The London Borough of Southwark
23 Paradise Street, Rotherhithe (1836-1965)
99 Lower Road, Rotherhithe (1965-2013)
R Division (1883-1929)
M Division (1929-2013)

In the early 1800s there were two Watch Houses covering the Rotherhithe area; one had been built in Trinity Street (now Rotherhithe Street), and the other in Church Street (now St. Marychurch Street).²⁶⁴⁷ The original Watch House was in Church Passage but it was moved to the entrance of the new burial ground on the opposite side of Church Street.²⁶⁴⁸ This was to keep watch over the new graves, and prevent bodysnatchers from removing bodies after burial and selling them to hospitals for medical research. As early as 1839 Rotherhithe Parish became part of M (Southwark) Division.

Old Watch House, St Marychurch Street

On 1st March 1836 the Home Office gave authority for taking over premises at Paradise Street, Rotherhithe, for Police purposes from Mr. John Gaitskell at a rent of £75 per annum for 21 years. The building dated back to 1814, and the solid mahogany double doors had brass handles in the shape of a lion's head, modelled, it is said, on those of Bermondsey Abbey.²⁶⁴⁹ The Watch House was closed when the new building was taken over by Police, and further authority was given to renew the lease on 14th February 1857 for 50 years, at £100 per annum. The building was insured for £2,000.²⁶⁵⁰

Rotherhithe Police Station 1836-1965

In 1864 Rotherhithe Police Station was shown on M Division together with Stones End (Southwark) and Bermondsey Police Stations. The total number of officers at Rotherhithe was 117.²⁶⁵¹ The following year Rotherhithe was shown on R (Greenwich) Division.²⁶⁵²

The 1881 Report stated that it was

"An old house with evidences of having been a first-class residence. The bedrooms are lofty, but the basement, in which is the mess, is very bad indeed, in a sanitary point of view. The outbuildings, including the cells, are dilapidated and unsatisfactory and require reconstruction."

The accommodation at that stage was occupied by one single sergeant and thirty-nine single constables.[2653]

One evening in 1881 the original two lion-head brass door knockers were removed, without authority, from the front doors of the police station. An investigation followed, but the door furniture had disappeared. In 1952, nearly seventy years later, Police Constable Hynds was called to a house not far from the old police station where an elderly lady showed the officer two lion-head brass knockers. They had been carefully wrapped in tissue paper, and had been found under the floorboards of the house. Apparently her father had removed the knockers from the police station door as a 'dare' whilst drinking with others in a local public house, and had been too scared to return them. On his death bed he told his daughter what had happened, and told her where he had hidden them.[2654]

Home Office authority was granted to surrender the old lease of the property on 11th April 1882 and to take out a new one for a period of 99 years at a rental of £110 per annum once renovations were completed.[2655]

Rotherhithe moved back to M Division in 1883, and joined the three other Sub-Divisions of Southwark, Bermondsey and the new Sub-Division of Grange Road. By then the number of Police Officers had reduced to 73.[2656] The address of the station was shown as 22 Paradise Street, Rotherhithe.[2657] In 1905 the lodging assessment for each of the thirty-one single officers living at Rotherhithe was one shilling a week.[2658]

In March 1907 Police Constable Conrad Scott was presented with the Royal Humane Society Award for rescuing a woman who had been thrown into the Surrey Canal by her boyfriend.[2659] This was one of the awards made by the Society to those persons who, at personal risk, save, or endeavour to save, life from drowning.

In 1924 the freehold of 99 Lower Road was purchased for £5,000 from the Port of London Authority. The property was a gentleman's residence called Landale Lodge, comprising a very large house and grounds, and was leased to Mr George Blake. A local doctor, Alfred Salter, wanted the site to build a sanatorium for curing tuberculosis, which was rife in the area,[2660] but the Home Office wanted it for Police purposes. Evidence was placed before the Right Honourable Edward Shortt, and the award was in favour of the Police.[2661] The building was used for a time as living quarters for police officers, but was eventually demolished and flats erected. These were completed in 1953, situated at the rear of the new station, and were named Landale House.[2662]

In 1965 Rotherhithe Police Station was shown as a sectional station to Tower Bridge Police Station.[2663]

A new sectional police station at Rotherhithe was opened at 99 Lower Road, SE16 in September 1965, and the old station at 23 Paradise Street was closed.[2664] The old building was extensively refurbished by Dormer Builders Ltd of Manor Mount, Forest Hill, after buying the freehold, to provide 6,000 sq ft of commercial office accommodation. The three-storey building, which is Grade II listed, retained its railings and wrought iron archway from which used to hang the blue lamp.[2665]

Rotherhithe Police Station 1965-2013

In 1980 Robert Horne Computer Services paid almost £250,000 for the restored Victorian office building.[2666]

In 2013 the front counter of Rotherhithe Police Station closed to the public, although the station was retained for operational purposes.[2667]

Ruislip Police Station

The London Borough of Hillingdon
Cottage, Ickenham Road (1840-1869)
17 High Street (1869-1961)
The Oaks, Manor Road (1961-2013)
T Division (1840-1865)
X Division (1865-2013)

In the 1840s, when the Metropolitan Police took over Ruislip, they moved into an old cottage on the Ruislip Park Estate in Ickenham Road, near the junction of Clark Avenue, Ruislip.[2668]

2640 Scollen, M. (1993) *Sworn to Serve*. Phillimore, Chichester.
2641 *3 Area Magazine*, 1975.
2642 Ibid.
2643 MEPO 14/40.
2644 Ibid.
2645 www.met.police.uk/contact/phone.htm accessed 3rd February 2002.
2646 *The Job*, 1990.
2647 'Police Stations in Rotherhithe: A Short History'. PC Chris Lorden.
2648 Beck, E.W. (1907). *A History of the Parish of St Mary Rotherhithe*. Cambridge University.
2649 *Guardian*, 30th July 1963.
2650 MEPO 5/9.
2651 Metropolitan Police Orders dated 11th January 1864.
2652 Metropolitan Police Orders dated 28th October 1865.
2653 Surveyor's Report 1881.
2654 Hynds, Len. Letter to *London Police Pensioner*, June 2009.
2655 MEPO 5/9.
2656 Metropolitan Police Orders dated 22th October 1883.
2657 Metropolitan Police Orders dated 20th June 1884.
2658 Metropolitan Police Orders dated 3rd May 1905
2659 www.historybytheyard.co.uk accessed 20th January 2008.
2660 'Police Stations in Rotherhithe: A Short History'. PC Chris Lorden.
2661 LB468.
2662 'Police Stations in Rotherhithe: A Short History'. PC Chris Lorden.
2663 Metropolitan Police Orders dated 6th August 1964.
2664 Metropolitan Police Orders dated 3rd September 1965.
2665 *South London Press*, 15th April 1977.
2666 *Estates Gazette*, 11th October 1980.
2667 MPS (2019) Freedom of Information request: Station closures broken down by year.
2668 *Hillingdon Mirror*, 19th June 1979.

Ruislip Police Station 1869-1961

The cottage was held on a £10 yearly tenancy from a Mr Clark. The cottage was later owned by Mr J. Spinks. It was a brick-and-tile property with a large garden, scullery and two stables. The sergeant living in the quarters paid rent and taxes for the use of the garden.[2669]

The cottage of the horse patrol was on the north side of what is now called King Edwards Road, about 100 yards from Church Avenue. It is likely the horse patrol station was given up in 1869 when the new Ruislip Police Station became operational at 17 High Street.

Police records in 1864 show that Ruislip was a station on T or Kensington Division, but it was premises without cells or a charge room.[2670] Then in 1865, with the formation of three new divisions, Ruislip transferred to the newly-formed X or Paddington Division.[2671]

The Police Surveyor reported in May 1869 on the dilapidated condition of the station, and suggested that it should be given up as soon as more suitable premises could be found.

Superintendent Hugh Eccles of X Division also reported in June 1869 on the dangerous state of the existing police station. He further reported on a seven-roomed house at 17 High Street, Ruislip belonging to a Mr. Richard Ewer of Hill Farm, Ruislip as being ideal for the purpose. The Surveyor inspected the premises and reported there would be accommodation available for a married sergeant and constable, and a room which could be appropriated as a charge room. It would require stabling and cells to be provided. The property could be leased at a rent of £20 per annum.[2672] The lease was for 21 years, from Michaelmas 1869 to Michaelmas 1890, with the option to purchase for £500 within three years. The Receiver was responsible for repairs and paying the taxes and insurance.[2673] Police eventually purchased the freehold of the property in 1873.[2674]

In December 1869 the Surveyor reported that the newly-leased premises were ready for occupation by Police.[2675] The first floor and parts of the ground floor were occupied as police quarters until 1935, when the sergeant who lived there with his family retired and moved out, allowing the whole of the building to be converted for police use.[2676] The ground floor rooms were altered to become the front office, charge room and communication room. The upstairs rooms became the canteen and CID office. A room above the stables became the Special Constabulary office. The station had its own water well in the yard. The cells were used as a decontamination centre, and were never again used for prisoners. From that date until 1961 Ruislip was without cells, and prisoners were conveyed to Uxbridge.[2677]

When police moved out of the old police station cottage into the new property in 1869, the old cottage was converted into tea rooms. However, in the 1911 census[2678] there is reference to an address of Old Police Station, Ruislip, where we find John Weatherly, a bricklayer and builder, living with his wife Grace and their seven children. The cottage was probably the old police station. It was eventually demolished in 1926.

A police report in 1881 described the property acquired in 1869 with one married inspector in occupation, but reported that it was 'an ordinary dwelling in a small village with cells and stables added.'[2679]

By 1902 Ruislip Police Station was often referred to as Ruislip Village Police Station.[2680] A freehold piece of land and shop, opposite the station, was acquired late in 1906 for £850 by the Receiver, with a view to one day erecting a new station.[2681] The shop was let at 15s 6d per week including rates and taxes.[2682]

In 1908 Police Constable George Rolfe was fatally injured when he accidentally collided with a man while cycling to work at Ruislip.[2683] In 1911 Police Sergeant John Dunford, his wife Eliza and their two children were living in four rooms at the police station.[2684]

Superintendent Olive of X Division reported in May 1912 that some 6,000 acres of land lying between Ruislip and Northwood were to be converted into a Garden City. The increase in the population would mean an increase in the number of police at Ruislip, and a new police station would therefore need to be built. Plans were drawn up for the new station, but the outbreak of the 1914-18 war stopped any building.[2685]

In 1924 the address of Ruislip Police Station, together with one set of married quarters, was shown as 1 West End Road, Ruislip.[2686] In March 1928 a strip of the frontage outside Ruislip Police Station was sold to Middlesex County Council for £72 12s 0d.[2687]

In 1934 a property called 'The Oaks' was purchased at a cost of £4,500. The site was next to the undeveloped site previously bought by police in 1906. Parts of this property were sold off as surplus to requirements. Once again war intervened, this time the 1939-45 conflict. Building was very slow after the war, but eventually five sets of married quarters and a new Ruislip Police Station were built on the site.[2688] In 1940 two War Reserve Constables, Alexander Bruce and Thomas Oswald Bell Cockburn, were killed in a bomb explosion during an enemy raid at Ruislip.[2689]

Ruislip Police Station sandbagged up during WWI

The new sectional police station at The Oaks, Manor Road, Ruislip was finally opened for business 30th October 1961. At the same time, the existing station at 17 High Street was closed.[2690] The old station, with its beautiful little front garden adding colour to the High Street, was sold in 1963 and demolished to make way for offices and shops,[2691] and the builders had great trouble filling in the well at the rear.[2692] Up until about 1935 the well was in full use, pumping up clear water.[2693]

In 1965 Ruislip became a section station of Uxbridge Sub-Division when the new London Borough of Hillingdon was created.[2694] In 1968 further changes enhanced the status of Ruislip, when it became a Sub-Division, with Uxbridge and Northwood sectional stations on the division.[2695]

Ruislip Police Station 1961-2013

In 1993 Police Constable Michael Robert Perry was unfortunately killed when his patrol car crashed into a tree while responding to an emergency call at Ruislip.[2696]

Ruislip Police Station was finally closed to the public in 2013.[2697]

Sanderstead (Hamsley Green) Police Station

The London Borough of Croydon

Village of Sanderstead (1849-1898)

P Division (1849-1898)

Sanderstead is an old village south of Croydon, whose identity is preserved by the surrounding golf courses and open spaces.[2698]

2669 Metropolitan Police Heritage Centre Archives.
2670 Metropolitan Police Orders dated 11th January 1864.
2671 Metropolitan Police Orders dated 28th October 1865.
2672 John Back Archives c1975.
2673 List of Police Stations 1873 (MEPO4/234).
2674 X Division Surveyor's List 1924.
2675 *Commissioner's Annual Report* 1870.
2676 *Hillingdon Mirror*, 19th June 1979.
2677 Metropolitan Police Heritage Centre Archives.
2678 Census 1911.
2679 Metropolitan Police Report: Condition of Police Stations 1881.
2680 *Post Office London Directory* 1902.
2681 John Back Archives c1975.
2682 X Division Surveyor's List 1924.
2683 Metropolitan Police Book of Remembrance.
2684 Census 1911.
2685 John Back Archives c1975.
2686 X Division Surveyor's List 1924.
2687 John Back Archives c1975.
2688 Ibid.
2689 Metropolitan Police Book of Remembrance.
2690 Metropolitan Police Orders dated 27th October 1961.
2691 Jephcote, J. (1969) 'Histories of Police Stations in Hillingdon'.
2692 *Hillingdon Mirror*, 19th June 1979.
2693 Metropolitan Police Heritage Centre Archives.
2694 Metropolitan Police Orders dated 6th August 1964.
2695 Metropolitan Police Orders dated 6th December 1968.
2696 Metropolitan Police Book of Remembrance.
2697 Information Rights Unit 10th June 2018, accessed 25th January 2019.
2698 Pevsner, N and Cherry, B. (1983) *London: 2. South*. Penguin, Harmondsworth p227.

In 1849 there was a station on P or Camberwell Division situated here, until 1865. It was a sergeant-designated station.[2699] The Police rented a two-stall stable from Captain Wigzell at an annual rental of £10.

In 1888 a station at Sanderstead was shown as a constable-station, located on W or Clapham Division, with no telegraphic communications had been linked to the main station. In 1894 Sanderstead was shown as a sectional station of Croydon. Frederick Bonner, the Croydon Sub-Divisional Inspector, would visit periodically to check that matters at Sanderstead were in good order.[2700]

By 1898 Sanderstead Police Station was no longer in existence, with Kenley replacing it as the sectional station.[2701]

Shadwell Police Station

London Borough of Tower Hamlets
King David Lane, Juniper Street (1850-1908)
10-24 King David Lane (1908-1933)
K Division (1850-1880)
H Division (1880-1933)

Shadwell is situated in the Parish of St. Paul within the Borough of Stepney. In 1848 negotiations commenced for the lease of a corner site in King David Lane, Shadwell, next to St. Paul's Leather Works in Juniper Street (later Juniper Road), owned by the Trustees to the Shadwell Estate. The 64-year lease commenced at Christmas 1848 and expired in 1912. The terms included that rates taxes and repairs were the responsibility of the Receiver, who should also insure the property for four-fifths its value. The annual ground rent was £21.[2702]

A new station was built in 1850 at a cost of £1,790, but within five years three more cells were added at a cost of £694 10s. The premises were insured at the Law Office for £1,200.[2703]

Shadwell Police Station 1850-1908

In 1873 Shadwell Police Station was considered important enough to be designated as under the Supervision of an Inspector, and was linked to the Commissioner's Office by means of an electric telegraph.[2704]

Shadwell was a station on K Division, however by July 1880 boundary revisions meant that it was transferred to H Division.[2705] The station was home to one married inspector, who paid 5s per week rent for three rooms, one married constable who had two rooms and paid weekly rent of 3s, and thirteen constables who resided in cubicles in rooms which held between five and eight to a room.[2706]

In 1881 Constable Charles Thorndell and his wife Louisa occupied the two rooms. There were seven prisoners in the station at the time these records were made. The inspector in charge of the station was John Le Cocq, who resided there with his wife Catherine, who was ten years older than her husband. Inspector Le Cocq was aged 35 years, and had been born in Alderney in the Channel Islands.[2707] There were also thirteen single constables resident at the station.[2708]

In 1885 the cells to the station were revamped at a cost of £694.[2709] The health of those working at the station was a primary concern, particularly amongst senior officers. A review of the drainage system raised further concerns regarding disease, and led to a complete upgrading of the water and other drains, costing £513 in 1896.[2710] The freehold to the site was purchased in February 1889 for £1,1777 from the Estate of Lady Glamis, a relative of the late Queen Elizabeth, the Queen Mother.

In March 1896 Inspector Smith of R Division was promoted to Sub-Divisional Inspector in charge of Shadwell Police Station[2711] He replaced Inspector Payne,[2712] who had been at the station for about three years. There were five inspectors posted to the station,[2713] and the sub-divisional inspector was the most senior of them all.

A further purchase of surrounding land at a cost of £2,500 from the same estate in 1905 meant that the old station could be demolished and a new one built in its place.[2714] Although the station was situated between 9 and 19 King David Lane,[2715] police records show the address as 10-24 King David Lane.[2716]

There were four stations on H Division in 1907. These being Leman Street, Commercial Street, Stepney and Shadwell.[2717]

A huge new police station was built at a cost of £12,668, and opened in December 1908. There was residential accommodation for two married officers and 36 unmarried men.[2718]

Shadwell Police Station 1908-1933

On the ground floor of the station there was a large inspector's office, CID office, telegraph room, charge room, matron's room and ten cells. There were six male cells, and three cells specifically for women. The last cell was an association cell or 'drunk tank', which could house up to ten drunken and rowdy prisoners at a time. In the basement was a parade room, where the constables would be paraded by the sergeant. This would involve a formal inspection to see if the officers were clean and tidy. They also needed to produce their appointments, which included their notebook, truncheon and whistle. Often the inspector on duty would supervise the parade of men coming on duty. Any officer who was not correctly dressed or equipped would be disciplined. In the basement was a mess room or canteen, where the constables and other officers could prepare their meals and refreshments. As the station had a large number of single officers, a resident library and recreation room were included. The recreation room even had a skittle alley, which provided a source of amusement and competition amongst the men.[2719]

Shadwell Police Station was closed for police purposes in 1933,[2720] as a result of a large-scale divisional re-organisation implemented by the Commissioner Lord Trenchard. It was felt that the nearby stations of Leman Street and Limehouse could absorb the additional area and workload without any problems. The original section house had closed in 1931,[2721] and was replaced by a large new section house suitable for 60 single police officers[2722] in 1938.[2723]

The new accommodation for single men (which also included a flat) took up part of the station yard and six residences in King David Lane.[2724] This Section House was initially called Shadwell Section House, however it was later renamed Moylan House in memory of a previous Receiver of the Metropolitan Police.

King David Lane (Moylan) Section House in 2002

In September 1971 the Section House was improved, and it would appear the flat was converted into single accommodation as six extra single rooms were built. Residents were moved to other accommodation while the building works were being carried out. Lifts were put in (or upgraded) to all floors during the building works.[2725] There was a small yard with ten car parking places. It remained in service with the address of 10 King David Lane, London E1 until it became no longer suitable for police purposes, and in September 1993, as part of the scheme to dispose of properties to generate much-needed income, Moylan House was sold to Mount Anville Construction Company, Elmscote House, Rickmansworth for £462,500.[2726]

Today the site belongs to London University and is used as accommodation for students.

Shenley Police Station

London Borough of Barnet

Harris Lane (1849-1859)

Cottage and stabling, Harris Lane (1859-1871)

Harris Lane, Shenley (1871-1957)

0S Division (1849-1957)

Evidence of the village cage or lockup can still be seen at Shenley by the village pond, at the junction of London Road and Cage Bond Road. This was a brick or stone construction, and was used for a long time. Finchley cage was made of wood and brick and was still in use in the 1860s, but prior to 1815 the cage or lockup was used at Highgate instead, as it appears to have been the nearest.[2727] In the picture below the old cage can be seen behind the three children in the foreground.

The Old Cage at Shenley c1905

A police station has been recorded on Shenley Hill (now Harris Lane), Hertfordshire since 1849,[2728] and until the present day two stations have remained very close to each other. Buildings were rented in Shenley from Mr. Edward Osman, a local builder, for £15 per year. The buildings located

2699 *Kelly's Directories* 1849-1865.
2700 *Kelly's Directories* 1880-1890.
2701 Metropolitan Police Surveyor's Records p62.
2702 Metropolitan Police Surveyor's Records.
2703 Ibid.
2704 Metropolitan Police General Orders 1873.
2705 *The H Division Handbook 1968/69*.
2706 Metropolitan Police Surveyor's Records.
2707 Census 1881.
2708 Ibid.
2709 Metropolitan Police Surveyor's Records p62.
2710 Ibid.
2711 *The Police Review and Parade Gossip*, 27th March 1896.
2712 *The Police Review and Parade Gossip*, 11th December 1893
2713 Ibid.
2714 Census 1881.
2715 Ibid.
2716 Metropolitan Police Surveyor's Records.
2717 *Kirchner's Almanac* 1907.
2718 Metropolitan Police Orders dated 10th December 1908.
2719 Ibid.
2720 Brown, B. (1998). 'H Division 1830-1899'.
2721 Metropolitan Police Orders dated 2nd March 1931.
2722 Metropolitan Police Surveyor's Records, LB364.
2723 Metropolitan Police Orders dated 29th December 1938.
2724 Land Registry for Shadwell Tithe No. 102204.
2725 Metropolitan Police Surveyor's Records, 19th February 1973.
2726 Metropolitan Police Surveyors Records, LB364.
2727 'The History of Ballards Lane' by C.O. Banks, printed in the *Finchley Press* of 1927/8 (C/603/LF).
2728 *Post Office Directory* 1849 p1528.

in Harris Lane consisted of four rooms, an outhouse and a four-stall stable were converted into a police station and section house which was in use between 1852 and Christmas 1858.[2729] Sergeant William Floyd was located there with his wife and four children in 1851.[2730]

This cottage became no longer suitable for use as a station and section house as it was probably too small, so the police looked around the local area for further accommodation. They found suitable buildings of brick and slate locally, which were then converted into a police station and section house for single officers.

Accommodation was rented in 1859 on an annual rent of £15. The owner, Mr Rainsford, a barrister of 36 Lincolns Inn Fields provided the building with five rooms, a scullery, fuel house, kitchen and a one-stall stable. Surveyors reported that it was in a good state of repair and had good water supply.[2731]

Supervision of Shenley occurred by the patrolling inspector from Barnet riding out on horseback from his station and visiting South Mimms, Whetstone and Shenley. He would record his visit in the Occurrence Book so that the divisional superintendent could be assured that supervision of the constables and sergeants was strictly carried out.

Whilst Shenley was a station where prisoners were taken and charged, they could not remain there in custody as there were no facilities to detain them. They were transferred by station transport to Barnet instead after charging, and the Barnet station officer would be responsible for detention and transfer to the local magistrates' court.[2732] Another cottage and stabling was purchased for £400 in 1871 from Mr. Cordell of Shenley, and this remained operational until 1892.[2733]

Land was purchased in Harris Lane (a cottage and stabling), including ground at the rear, in 1885 and 1892[2734] to extend the station, which was on S Division.

The old police station as it is today

Sub-Inspector William Girling (warrant no. 56536) was the inspector who was resident with his family in 1891. He had joined the police in 1873, and stayed at Shenley until 1899 when he retired on pension with 26 years' service.

There was one substantive sergeant and one acting sergeant attached to the station, and two day-time constables patrolling the vicinity and four night beats, who would be supervised by the sergeant patrolling on horseback.[2735]

The station call sign, published in Police Orders in 1893, was Sierra Echo (SE), but by the 1920s this changed to Sierra Yankey (SY).[2736]

In 1901 42-year-old Station Sergeant Richmond Young resided there with his family, wife Mary and their daughters Eliza and Angeline. Constable William Lancaster also resided in Harris Lane, not far from the station he worked at with his wife Ellen and two sons and three daughters.[2737] Constable Reuben Fordham and his family lived in New Road, Shenley; Constable Sackville Bobyer with his family lived next door to Constable John Houndsome and family in Grove Place, and Constable Daniel Murphy in Bay Cottages.[2738] Scotsman Constable William Jones, his wife and seven children could not find accommodation sufficiently large enough in the village, so the farmer at Limes Farm rented a house to them.[2739]

The picture below was taken in 1902, and shows the station strength with the inspector wearing a flat kepi (chin-strap down) and riding boots flanked by Station Sergeant Richmond Young (four stripes) on the right and on the left by the section sergeant.

A picture taken in the rear yard at Shenley Police Station c1902

Note also the two acting sergeants at each end with two stripes on their arms. There were also eight constables, plus two men in plain clothes. The man in the flat straw hat appears to be a detective, whilst the man in a cloth cap probably was the groom who tended the horses. He also was the reserve constable, able to fill in any vacancy where necessary. The picture was likely to have been taken on Coronation Day in 1902 as a mark of celebration for the new King.

In 1914 Sergeant Thomas Henry Harris was in charge of the station, assisted by two acting sergeants and twelve constables.[2740]

Shenley Police Station was shut on 6th March 1957, with staff and business transferred to the newly-built pre-fabricated buildings at Borehamwood.[2741]

The picture at the top of the following column shows the last police officer at Shenley, Constable Neal, walking past the station when it became a police office in 1967. In 2000 the area of Shenley was ceded to the Hertfordshire Constabulary and the Metropolitan Police withdrew.

Constable Neal walks past the Shenley Police Office in 1967

Shepherds Bush Police Station

London Borough of Hammersmith and Fulham

142 Starch Green Road, later renamed 87 Askew Road (1884-1963)

253-258 Uxbridge Road (1963 to Present)

T Division (1884-1933)

F Division (1933-2018)

Basic Command Unit Central West (CW) (2018 to Present)

Land in Askew Road, W12 was considered suitable for a police station and was purchased by the Receiver in June 1881 at a cost of £1,107. The new station was built between 1883 and 1884, and was designed by the Metropolitan Police Surveyor, John Butler. Although the architectural plans are retained at the National Archives, they are not available for consultation by the public. This is a policy laid down in respect of any police building still being used for police purposes.[2742]

Shepherds Bush Police Station 1884-1963

In 1884 a new sub-division was formed on T Division known as Shepherds Bush. At the same time a new police station was opened in February of that year.[2743] The address of the new station was 142 Starch Green Road, but later in 1887 it was renamed 87 Askew Road. The cost of the land was £1,457 and the construction of the building cost £4,589.

By 1888 the boundaries of Hammersmith and Shepherds Bush Sub-Divisions were altered in consequence of the opening of Ravenscourt Park, Hammersmith.[2744] In 1896 Inspector Thomas Neal was in charge of Shepherds Bush Police Station.[2745]

In 1924 Shepherds Bush was a sub-division under the command of the divisional commander, Superintendent William Newman at Hammersmith. There were two inspectors, Edward Pinks and George Rhodes, both based at Shepherds Bush.[2746]

In 1933 there was a reorganisation of divisions north of the Thames, and Shepherds Bush was transferred from T to F Division.[2747]

From 1937 onwards ideas were put forward to erect a new police station in the Shepherds Bush area to replace Notting Dale and Shepherds Bush Police Stations. Many sites in the Uxbridge Road were examined, but none were found to be suitable. The war years intervened and afterwards a suitable site was at last found. After protracted negotiations with the freeholder, construction got under way.[2748]

The new station at 252-258 Uxbridge Road was completed and opened in July 1963.[2749] At the same time, the old station at Askew Road was closed and later sold to the London Borough of Hammersmith for redevelopment.[2750]

Shepherds Bush Police Station 1963 to present

2729 Metropolitan Police Surveyor's Records.
2730 Census 1851.
2731 Metropolitan Police Surveyor's Records.
2732 Metropolitan Police Special Police Order 1869.
2733 Metropolitan Police Surveyor's Records.
2734 Metropolitan Police Surveyor's Records 1912, p29.
2735 Ibid.
2736 Metropolitan Police General Orders 1893.
2737 Census 1901.
2738 Ibid.
2739 Ibid.
2740 *Kelly's Directory* 1914.
2741 Metropolitan Police Orders dated 4th March 1957.
2742 MEPO 9/144.
2743 Metropolitan Police Orders dated 22nd February 1884.
2744 Metropolitan Police Orders dated 7th June 1888.
2745 *Kelly's West Kensington and Hammersmith Directory* 1896/97.
2746 *Kelly's Hammersmith and Shepherds Bush Directory* 1924/25.
2747 Metropolitan Police Orders dated 28th November 1933.
2748 John Back Archive circa 1975.
2749 Metropolitan Police Orders dated 5th July 1963.
2750 John Back Archive circa 1975.

Shepherds Bush Police Station has had its share of police officers being fatally injured whilst on duty or travelling to or from duty. In 1930 Constable Henry Falshaw-Skelly died in a motorcycle accident whilst travelling to duty at the station. Then in 1993 Constable Noel Charles Frick was killed in a road accident whilst on motorcycle surveillance duty at Shepherds Bush. In 2002 Constable Nicholas Hill was also killed in a motorcycle accident, at Barnes, whilst travelling to duty at Shepherds Bush Police Station.[2751]

The most tragic case in recent times was the murder of three police officers in 1966, known as the Shepherds Bush Murders. Police Constable Geoffrey Roger Fox, Detective Sergeant Christopher Tippett Head and Temporary Detective Constable David Stanley Bertram Wombwell were all shot dead, without warning, as they were questioning three suspects in a van parked suspiciously outside Wormwood Scrubs Prison in Braybrook Street.[2752]

The outrage from the press and public over the shooting of the three police officers in such a cold-blooded way while they were carrying out their lawful duty sparked calls for the reinstatement of the death penalty.

As a result of these horrendous murders it should be remembered that Sir Billy Butlin, the holiday camp owner and philanthropist, immediately sent a cheque for £100,000 to the Commissioner, Sir Joseph Simpson KBE. From that gesture, with the help of Lord Stonham, was born the Police Dependants' Trust.[2753] The Trust, together with the National Police Fund, provides financial support to help ease some of the pressures that police families experience when a police officer has been killed or injured on duty.

The Braybrook Suite at Hammersmith Police Station (FS) was named after the officers in 1996.[2754]

Shepherds Bush Police Station's front counter and charging facilities were withdrawn in January 2013, however the station has been retained for other policing purposes and officers continue to patrol from the building.[2755] The front counter was reopened in 2016 whilst the refurbishment of Hammersmith Police Station takes place until at least 2020.[2756]

Shepperton Lock Police Station

The London Borough of Spelthorne
Shepperton Lock (1966-1992)
Thames Division

Following the extension of River Police patrols to Staines, authority was given to rent a piece of land from the Thames Conservancy on a lease for 21 years at a nominal rent of £1 per annum from September 1965. The intention was to erect a small hut and landing stage to provide Thames Division with a new station at Shepperton Lock.[2757]

A new sectional station for Shepperton Lock was introduced into service at 6.00am on Monday, 4th April 1966. The station would be open from 6.00am to 10.00pm daily, and had a telegraph code of 'UP'.[2758]

A mutual arrangement with the lock-keeper enabled one patrol boat during the summer months to occupy a berth just above the lock alongside the river wall. This arrangement was regularised with the Thames Conservancy Board with an agreement to run as from 1st November 1972 for a permanent mooring above the lock for a Thames launch.

The advantage of having permanent berths available above and below Shepperton Lock proved most valuable. It obviated the need for duty boats passing through the lock at the beginning and end of a patrol, an operation which takes at least 15 minutes in each direction. The time saved over the years in not having to 'lock through' may well have resulted in the saving of life, or the prevention of injury to persons or damage to property.

Shepperton Lock Police Office 1965-1992

In 1967 Hampton station was opened on the river island known as Platt's Eyot (pronounced eight and sometimes spelt 'eit').[2759] Hampton was shut in 1978 and Shepperton Lock in 1992. There are just mooring facilities located there today.

Shooters Hill Police Station

The London Borough of Greenwich
Well Hall Road (1852-1915)
Shooters Hill (1915-1993)
R Division (1852-1993)
Borough of Greenwich OCU (1993-2001)

The 1st Division of the Bow Street Horse Patrol Station was situated on Shooters Hill near the present Brook Hospital,[2760] on the site of the Fox on the Hill Inn. The Police established themselves on a very famous thoroughfare originally called Watling Street which was built by the Romans. After some correspondence between the Commissioner and the Board of Ordnance at Woolwich (as both Lords of the Manor of Eltham and owners of the land), favourable consideration for a new police station was given in Old Dover Road, Shooters Hill.

The station was originally given the name Old Dover Road Police Station, even though it was situated on Shooters Hill. Naming a station like this often belies its real location.

Shooters Hill Police Station 1852-1915

Land was leased from the owners on favourable terms amounting to 5s per year ground rent, and the new station was built in 1852 at a cost of £1,513 6s 6d. It was a standard station house, which consisted of a basement, ground and first floor.

Shooters Hill Police Station 1915-2001

The station was small by today's standards, and consisted of a charge room, two cells, library, mess room, three-stall stable and hay loft.

A married inspector was resident, occupying four rooms for which he paid 4s per week rent. There was room for seven single constables in the section house, each paying a nominal 1s per week rent.[2761] In the interests of hygiene, on the first floor was a bath and clothes room; a rare but necessary feature. The police station backed onto Eltham Common, and by 1888 the fire station, also originally manned by police officers, was situated next door.

In 1864 Shooters Hill was an important station and had an inspector in charge. There were two sergeants and a further two acting sergeants, who performed station and patrol day and night duties.[2762] There was also a total of 14 constables. One acting sergeant also supervised the day duty of four constables, whilst the other was responsible for the night duty and eight constables. Two horses were available for supervision, one ridden by the inspector in charge, whilst the sergeant, who would supervise not only his own station area but also those of Bexley and Erith, took the other.[2763] There were some boundary alterations in 1865 because of the creation of three new Divisions, W, X and Y.

In 1881 a further re-organisation saw Shooters Hill Sub-Division being absorbed into what became known as Belvedere Sub-Division.[2764] Inspector Meering was transferred from Shooters Hill to Belvedere to join three other inspectors. There was an address change in 1884 to Shooters Hill Road, Shooters Hill,[2765] and the station's telegraph call sign in 1893 was Sierra Hotel (SH).[2766] Shooters Hill was occupied in 1893 on an annual tenancy of seven shillings.[2767]

In 1908 there was a revision in the lodging assessment for the married quarters, which rose to 5s per week.[2768] As far back as 1905 the Receiver of the Metropolitan Police had decided to return the land leased (including the station) back the original owners and move from the site. Some land to the west of the present station owned by the War Office was strongly favoured, and discussions commenced indicating that they were prepared to sell the freehold to the Police.[2769] The Receiver initially agreed to rent the land, at a nominal cost of

2751 met.police.uk/history/remembrance2 accessed 17th October 2012.
2752 Fido, M. & Skinner, K. (1999) *The Official Encyclopedia of Scotland Yard*.
2753 *The Times*, 19th June 1980.
2754 Fido, M. & Skinner, K. (1999) *The Official Encyclopedia of Scotland Yard*.
2755 shepherds-bush.blogspot.co.uk/2012/11/shepherds-bush-police-station-to-close.html accessed 22nd October 2013.
2756 www.mylondon.news 29th May 2019, accessed 3rd July 2019.
2757 Shepperton Lock Police Station History (John Back Archive).
2758 Metropolitan Police Orders dated 1st April 1966.
2759 Budworth, G. (1997) *The River Beat*.
2760 Hadaway, D. (1990) 'The Metropolitan Police in Woolwich'.
2761 Metropolitan Police Surveyors' Records.
2762 Metropolitan Police Orders dated 11th January 1864.
2763 Ibid.
2764 Metropolitan Police Orders dated 8th October 1881.
2765 Metropolitan Police Surveyors' Records.
2766 Metropolitan Police General Orders 1893.
2767 Metropolitan Police HC Document.
2768 Metropolitan Police Surveyors' Records.
2769 Ibid.

1s per annum, but purchased the land for £629 in June 1912.[2770] The old station was given up once instructions had been received to move next door, and the Police took possession of the new station on 12th May 1915.[2771] It had the call sign Romeo Hotel (RH).

The station had a large yard, and boasted a beautifully laid-out garden with a palm tree, although Tooting often won the garden competition and Eltham only had window boxes.

In 1973 a detective constable had his finger blown off whilst opening a letter at the station. Such was public concern at the time, and given the positive image the local Police had, the detective received many gifts and letters of sympathy. Many officers were on duty and sent to assist during the bomb outrage at the Kings Arms public house in Woolwich. All the officers pitched in together.

The station came up for sale around 2001, initially in the region of £340,000, but following outrage by the public, who thought the premises were undervalued, the price was raised. The property later sold for over £1 million, and the site is now occupied by luxury flats.[2772]

In 2006 Shooters Hill Safer Neighbourhood Team was established, with two sergeants, two constables and three police community support officers, although they were stationed elsewhere. They are located at 31 Herbert Road, Woolwich.[2773]

Sidcup Police Station (RS)

London Borough of Bexley
High Street, Sidcup (1842-1902)
87 Main Road, Sidcup (1902-2012)
R Division (1842-2012)

Located in the south eastern part of the London Borough of Bexley, Sidcup had been covered by the Bow Street horse patrols from as early as 1805, and when the Metropolitan Police took over these patrols in 1836 two horse patrol 'stations' were rented at Sidcup from a Mrs Mauney of Footscray. Sidcup officially became part of the Metropolitan Police District in January 1840, when R (Greenwich) Division was extended to cover approximately the same area covered by the London Borough of Bexley today.[2774]

A police station was set up in the village of Footscray to cover the villages of the Crays (ie St Mary Cray, St Paul's Cray, North Cray and Footscray), Chislehurst and Sidcup, and their prisoners were sent to the magistrates at Locks Bottom (see London Borough of Bromley).

In 1842 the Receiver took out a 61-year lease from Thomas Norfolk Brewery of Deptford on a house in High Street Sidcup, adjoining the Black Horse public house, to form a police station with two cells, a mess kitchen, a charge room, a wash house and a yard at the back with two stables and two water closets. In 1845 a survey found that the cleanliness was good, but the drainage was very bad. The cesspool needed emptying, and the water was unfit for use because the cesspool was near to the well. It was also felt that a dustbin and water butt was required.

By 1850 the opening of a police station in St Mary Cray had enabled the territory to be split, and by 1855 magistrates attended Sidcup Police Station itself on the second Monday of each month to hear charges. Sergeant Robert Saunders was the officer in charge at Sidcup, with seven constables.

In March 1865, Sidcup section, which had been part of Lee Sub-Division, was placed under Bromley Sub-Division that also then took in Beckenham, Farnborough and the Crays. In 1873, Chislehurst was split from Sidcup to become a Section in its own right.[2775]

Sidcup Police Station 1842-1902

A comprehensive survey of the condition of Metropolitan Police stations in 1881 found that one of the walls of the sleeping rooms was damp, that the mess accommodation was not sufficient, and that a significant amount of work was required to make the premises satisfactory.

The last Sidcup Police Station originated from a decision on 24th January 1896 to purchase land on Main Road for the sum of £620, and a newly-built station, at a cost of £8,062 14s, was opened on 13th October 1902. There was accommodation for a married inspector, assessed for rent at 5s 6d per week, for a married constable at 3s, and for six single officers at 1s per week. As times had moved on, provision was not only made for an inspector's office, there was also a waiting room for the public, a telegraph room, a parade room, a day room, mess room and kitchen. It was before the days of the London Ambulance Service, and an ambulance shed was provided at the new station.

Sidcup Police Station 1902-2012

From 24th January 1906, Sidcup became the sub-divisional headquarters, taking in Chislehurst and St Mary Cray stations, an arrangement that lasted until 1932 when St Mary Cray and Chislehurst were transferred to P Division, with Sidcup remaining on R Division as part of Eltham Sub-Division.

The reorganisation of local authority and police boundaries on 1st April 1965 split Sidcup from Chislehurst & Sidcup Urban District Council, and brought it into the new London Borough of Bexley for local authority purposes. Sidcup Police

Station remained on R Division as part of the Bexleyheath Sub-Division (later division).

Front elevation of Sidcup Police Station in 1908

Run as a Chief Inspector unit from 1965, a further reorganisation on 30th March 1987 removed the chief inspector (one of the authors being the last Chief Inspector serving there in that role) and brought the Sidcup sergeants and constables within the responsibility of the Chief Inspector (Operations) and Inspectors at Bexleyheath, who then had teams of sergeants and constables parading for duty at each station within the borough. Three home beat officers did remain permanently at Sidcup, however.

In March 2012 the station closed, with officers being accommodated in Marlowe House Sidcup.

Safer Neighbourhood base at Marlowe House, Sidcup

By 2009, a Safer Neighbourhood Team had established an office in the North Cray Neighbourhood Centre, thereby providing a police service in the same building as Local Authority-related services. This was located at Davis Way, North Cray, but the premises were closed by 2019. In 2009, the Colyers Safer Neighbourhood Team had established an office in The Howbury Centre, Slade Green Road, Erith, where the Local Authority also based a pupil referral unit.

Somers Town Police Station

Phoenix Street, Somers Town (1829-1850)
Platt Street (1850-1869)
23 Platt Street (1869-1946)

S Division (1829-1869)
Y Division (1869-1946)

Somers Town is located north of the Euston Road between the railway stations of Euston and St. Pancras. The northern end borders Camden Town. There has been a police presence in Somers Town for some considerable time, with a watch house located in Phoenix Street, Somers Town before 1829. Records show that in 1840 Inspector-in-charge George Billers was promoted and transferred there. The watch house, which had belonged to the Old Parochial Watch, consisted of a small room and two small cells.[2776]

Somers Town has a significant place in police history, as this area saw the first Metropolitan Police officer to be killed on duty. On 29th June 1830, some nine months after the first police parade had taken place, Police Constable Grantham, attached to Somers Town, was patrolling his beat when he came across two drunken Irishmen quarrelling over a woman. After stepping between the two men to prevent a continued breach of the peace, both men and the woman turned on him. This resulted in Constable Grantham being knocked to the ground, where he received a blow to the temple and died a few minutes later. Enquiries in the area, after the event, reported that Constable Grantham got very much what he deserved and was not liked in the small neighbourhood.[2777]

The original Somers Town Police Station was described as 'an old straight-built house in a dilapidated state'.[2778] In 1849 Metropolitan Police Commissioner Sir Richard Mayne wrote a 'requisition report' to the Divisional Superintendent regarding the poor conditions and state of Somers Town Police Station. He instructed that a new site should be found on which to build a new station. The old watch house was closed in 1850.[2779] The station was relocated to Blenheim Cottages in Park village, with a rent of £20 per annum. However, this was soon unfit for habitation and notice was served on Sergeant Gatesby, the officer in charge of the station at the time, to quit on 22nd June 1860. The house contained two cells and a charge room.

Much of the neighbouring land had been taken up with building large railway stations and goods yards, so the small watch house was no longer deemed suitable for policing the expanding area. In those days Somers Town Police Station was shown as a station on S or Hampstead Division. The division radiated from Somers Town to the south, with Kentish Town as the Divisional Headquarters, to Barnet in the northwest.

The Receiver of the Metropolitan Police decided that a purpose-built police station should be built in Somers Town, and so enquiries were made to find a suitable site for this purpose. A site located at 23 Platt Street, not far from Brill Row (later the Pancras Road), seemed appropriate, and contracts were drawn up to lease the site from December 1849. This was on a 99-year lease from the Company of Brewers of Addle Street, East Central. Once the contracts had been signed the annual ground rent payment was fixed at £20 per year.

Somers Town Police station was transferred from S Division and re-designated as a station on Y Division.[2780] The police station was erected in 1851 at a cost of £3,488.

2770 John Back Archive (1975).
2771 Metropolitan Police Orders dated 13th April 1915.
2772 Private correspondence.
2773 www.met.police.uksaferneighbourhoods/boroughs/Greenwich/saferneighbourhoods.htm accessed 12th December 2006.
2774 Brown, Bernard. 'The History of Sidcup Police Station'.
2775 Metropolitan Police Orders dated 10th March 1865 and 15th October 1873.
2776 MEPO 45/2632.
2777 Cobb, Belton (1961). *Murdered on Duty*. W. H. Allen, London.
2778 Metropolitan Police Surveyor's Manifest (1882).
2779 MEPO 45/2632.
2780 John Back Archive (1975).

The accommodation comprised a traditional Victorian-style station house. It had a basement, ground, first and second floors. The ground and first floor were used for police business, whilst rooms on the second floor housed single officers. There were three public rooms, which are shown as an inspector's office, reserve room and public waiting room. The station also had a library, parade room and eight cells on the ground floor, with a kitchen, mess room and a coal store in the basement. The terms of the lease stipulated that the station was to be insured for £2,800 at the Law Office.[2781]

In 1873 Inspector Gould from Enfield Police Station conducted the novelist Charles Dickens on a fact-finding journey around Somers Tow, which at the time had the reputation of being a very unsavoury place indeed.

Somers Town Police Station was designated a station under the command of an Inspector, and was connected by wire to the Commissioner's Office.[2782]

In 1881 the station was still shown as a station on Y or Highgate Division. Records show that there was accommodation for a maximum of 33 single constables, who paid between them a total of £104 annual rent to the Receiver. They lived in the section house above the station. On the night the 1881 census was taken 32 single constables were in residence, and five prisoners occupied the eight available cells.[2783] Conditions at the station were less than satisfactory when police surveyors inspected the premises in the same year. They found some of the cells and parts of the basement were very dark.

In 1904 alterations reduced the numbers accommodated at the station from 33 to 22 single constables. Cubicles for privacy were built into the residential rooms, at a cost of £129.[2784]

In 1881 Police Constable Francis Carlin, a 47-year-old man from Co. Tyrone, Ireland lived at 37 Middlesex Street with his wife Jane, their three daughters and two sons.[2785] One of their sons was to become one of the most celebrated detectives of his day. Francis Carlin was born in 1871 in Kentish Town, St. Pancras and followed his father's footsteps into the police, although his father had higher aspirations for him.[2786] At 15 years old Carlin worked in a coal factor's office, but after four years he left that job to join the police. After three weeks of foot drill Carlin became a constable on K Division, and was posted to Plaistow Police Station on 15th December 1890.[2787] Carlin patrolled Plaistow, Canning Town and Poplar. Later he became one of the so-called 'Big Four' Detective Superintendents responsible for high-profile murder enquiries, such as the cases of Thompson and Bywaters, the Crumbles, the Norman Thorne murders and the Fahmy affair.[2788]

Arthur Henry Bishop (second from left) under arrest for the murder of Frank Edward Rix, a butler of Mayfair

Another one of Detective Superintendent Carlin's cases involved Arthur Henry Bishop, who is shown seated between two detectives in the picture above. Here he is under arrest for the murder of Frank Edward Rix, a butler for whom Bishop worked as a pantry boy. Bishop attacked and killed Rix with an axe late one night at a Mayfair residence. Detective Superintendent Carlin is shown at extreme right. Bishop was later convicted of murder and was hanged at Pentonville Prison on 14th August 1925.

Posting the notice of execution of Arthur Henry Bishop on 14th August 1925

To the left is the main gate outside Pentonville Prison when the notice of execution of Bishop was posted on the door. Bishop was hanged by Robert Orridge Baxter[2789] of Balfour Street, Hertford, the favoured and principal hangman at the time. He was assisted by Henry Pollard, Edward Taylor and Robert Wilson who were all experts at their trade.[2790]

The photograph of the constable on the right was taken before the First World War, probably in 1912, by a commercial photographer near to Somers Town Police station. It shows the constable with white gloves, which usually denotes that he was attending a ceremonial event. He is wearing three medals, which are the 1897 Jubilee medal and the Coronation medals of 1902 and 1911. All Metropolitan and City of London Police who were either on normal duty or at the Coronation in 1911 were entitled to the Coronation Medal. Many other police forces were also represented, and they were awarded medals as well. As these medals were personalized with each officer's name it took time to collate all the information, and they were not issued until 1912.

E Division Police Constable, 1912

In 1919 Constable William Rawlings (later Deputy Commander) joined the Metropolitan Police, and after training was posted to Somers Town Police Station. Constable

541Y Rawlings was met by Sub-Divisional Inspector Pacey, who did not use their names but called the officers by their collar numbers. This practice continues even today. Rawlings was allocated a cubicle in an upstairs dormitory. He was quoted as saying the accommodation was 'dark and not too clean', and mentioned that he was often bitten at night. A policeman's widow used to come in and cook a meal every day for the single men who slept in the upstairs dormitory. They all sat on long benches at a wooden table in the basement for their meals.[2791]

The police station was very badly damaged by a parachute mine on 17th April 1941.[2792] There were no casualties. In 1945 a decision was taken not to rebuild the station, but to return the site to the owners as it was, although the lease had several more years to run.

Somers Town Police Station closed in June 1946, and all police business was transferred to Caledonian Road Police Station.[2793]

Somers Town Police Station 1851-1946

However this was only a temporary closure, as the 1970s picture of Somers Town Police Station above shows. It was clearly rebuilt after the war, and the owners rented the building out for other purposes. It appears the front of the station was undamaged from German bombing and the rear of the station was reconstructed. This sad picture of this once gracious Victorian police station is the only known surviving example.

(South) Mimms Police Station

London Borough of Barnet

Old St Albans Road (1840-2000)

S Division (1840-1993)

Borough of Barnet OCU (1993-2000)

Transferred to Hertfordshire Police (2000)

The parish of South Mimms was added to the Metropolitan Police in 1840. A police station which consisted of a brick-and-tile house with stable was initially rented from Mr. Edward Whalley for £11 per year, and was brought into service in 1844 on S Division. This was located near to the tollgate in South Mimms, and a sergeant was placed in charge. It was prudent to situate stations near turnpikes and toll-houses, since patrolling constables could obtain useful information and intelligence on crime which may have been committed on passersby. The toll-house keepers would also inform the police of people who evaded paying the toll. Local residents resented paying the toll, and often got into trouble.

Repairs were made prior to occupation, as the accommodation was in a sad state. The freehold to the building and land in Old St. Albans Road was purchased in 1846. The station (now called Blackhorse Lane) consisted of four rooms, with a charge room, coal shed, a little garden and small stable,[2794] and opened in 1847. As was the norm, there was one substantive sergeant and one acting sergeant posted to the station. The sergeant would be attached to the night duty, where he would supervise the seven night duty constables on horseback. There were two horses attached to the station, with the other horse being used by the reserve constable.[2795]

The station was small, and there was only sufficient space for one set of married quarters when it was rebuilt in 1870. Rent of 3/3d per week was charged to the married officer in 1871.[2796]

South Mimms Police Station 1871-2000

Sub-Inspector Lewis Skeats (warrant no. 48679) and his wife Mary resided at the station in 1891. Skeats had joined the police in 1867, and by 1885 was an inspector on S or Hampstead Division. He retired in 1892 on pension. In 1899 James Wheller was the station sergeant in charge, assisted by two acting sergeants, one section sergeant and eleven constables.[2797] Inspector Frederick Leggatt, aged 45 years, his wife, their son and three daughters lived at the station in 1901.[2798]

In 1905 a further set of four cottages were purchased for accommodation in the High Road, South Mimms. In the 1920s the station call sign changed to Sierra Mike (SM), and it was a sectional station of Barnet.

2781 Metropolitan Police Surveyor's records.
2782 Metropolitan Police General Orders 1873.
2783 Census 1881.
2784 Metropolitan Police Surveyor's records 1924.
2785 Census 1881.
2786 Carlin, F. (1925). *Reminiscences of an Ex-Detective*. Hutchinson and Co., London.
2787 Ibid.
2788 Ibid.
2789 Fielding, S. (1990) *The Hangman's Record. Vol. Two: 1900-1929*.
2790 Ibid.
2791 Rawlings, Deputy Commander William Benjamin OBE, MC. (1961) *A Case for the Yard*. John Long, London. pp331-33.
2792 Howgrave-Graham, H.M. CBE (1947) 'The Metropolitan Police at War' (HMSO).
2793 Metropolitan Police Orders dated 21st June 1946.
2794 Metropolitan Police Surveyor's Records.
2795 Metropolitan Police Special Orders 1869.
2796 Metropolitan Police Orders dated 4th February 1871.
2797 *Kelly's Directory* 1899.
2798 Census 1901.

The picture right shows a rather stern-looking Station Sergeant 84S William Baker (warrant no. 77760), posing in the garden of the station. Baker was the officer in charge of South Mimms Police station between 1912 and 1919. Baker, from Woodford in Essex, had joined as Constable 226W in June 1892, and by 1901 was still a constable located in Southwark. Having decided to seek promotion to better himself, Baker soon progressed to sergeant and then to station sergeant at South Mimms.

Station Sergeant William Baker c1919

By 1911, Baker then aged 43 years, his wife Mary and his son John William Baker occupied four rooms at the station.[2799] It was likely that there were about seven constables attached to the station, for whom he had responsibility. He retired with an exemplary record aged 51 years in January 1919 (once the war had finished), with 27 years' service, and was awarded an annual pension of £121 15s. He lived to a ripe old age and died, aged 79 years, in 1948.

South Mimms station strength in 1894

In 1925 sergeants Leonard Worth, Frederick Jardine and Charles Haines were shown to be based at South Mimms, assisted by nine constables.

The station was further renovated in 1938. Records show that the station was situated in the Old St. Albans Road, South Mimms, Hertfordshire in 1947.

The station was transferred in 2000 to Hertfordshire Police, who decided to shut it down and put it up for sale. In the meantime, the buildings of this famous old station deteriorated into a very sad state of repair. South Mimms Police Station still exists today as a residential premises.[2800]

South Norwood Police Station

The London Borough of Croydon
83 High Street (1873-1988)
11 Olive Grove (1988-2013)
W Division (1873-1921)
Z Division (1921-1985/86)
South Norwood Division & OCU (1985/86-2013)

As the London population continued to grow in the early 1800s, local residents started to feel that they needed their own police station. The population of the area tended to congregate around the railway station at Norwood Junction.[2801]

In October 1871 Mr Haynes wrote on behalf of the residents of South Norwood to the District Police Superintendent, Captain Baynes. Haynes suggested that suitable premises in High Street, South Norwood, near the junction of Station Road, were available for conversion into a police station.[2802] The property was obtained in 1872 on a 99-year lease from Charles Pawley of Kirkdale, Sydenham, at a ground rent of £19 10s 0d. Alterations to the property cost £1,200. The freehold on the property was purchased in 1899 for the sum of £740.[2803]

A report in 1881 on the condition of Metropolitan Police stations describes South Norwood as two adjoining ordinary dwelling-houses united as a police station. The quarters were occupied by one married sergeant, one married constable and eight single constables but these were not well arranged and the mess room was not being used.[2804]

The new police station opened in December 1873. The assessment for rent was one married sergeant at 4s a week, one married constable at 3s a week, and eight single constables at 1s a week.[2805]

South Norwood Police Station 1873-1988

In 1884 the new address of the police station was reported as 83 High Street, South Norwood.[2806] South Norwood was a sectional station of Thornton Heath, where Sub-Divisional Inspector William Lemmey was in charge.[2807]

In 1921, following the formation of the new Z Division, South Norwood was transferred from W to Z.[2808]

In 1960 it was recommended that South Norwood Police Station should be rebuilt. The old building had outlived its usefulness. A new site near to the existing station was sought. A possible site, 193/195 Selhurst Road, was earmarked for development, but the Planning Committee of the County Borough of Croydon turned down a planning application on the grounds that it was a residential site and it would be seriously detrimental to the area for a station to be built there. The Receiver then found an alternative site at Nos. 1-11 Olive Road. The freehold-combined properties were purchased between 1964 and 1969 for the sum of £36,250. The site was later let to the London Borough of Croydon as a public car park in September 1969.[2809]

In 1961 the top floor of the police station ceased to be married quarters,[2810] and the space was instead used for administrative matters. In 1968 South Norwood Police Station became an 'Inspector Unit', with Inspector George in charge.[2811]

In September 1985 districts, formerly called divisions, were abolished and the Metropolitan Police was re-organised into new eight-area structures. South Norwood (ZN) became part of the new 4 Area South, with the following Divisions: LD, LK, LM, VM, ZD, ZN and ZP.[2812] This meant that police officers at South Norwood ceased to wear the single 'Z' letter, and changed to having a two letter 'ZN' Divisional (Norbury) code on their shoulders.[2813]

The new police station at 11 Olive Grove was opened on 21st November 1988 by Lord Lane, and Chief Superintendent Sally Hubbard took possession of the new station. It then became the Divisional Headquarters (ZY), and all officers on the division changed their shoulder letters to 'ZY'.

South Norwood Police Station 1988-2013

By 1994 the Metropolitan Police Service was restructured again, from eight areas to five. South Norwood became part of 4 Area, with headquarters based in Sidcup.

In April 2000 the Metropolitan Police restructured into borough-based policing within the local authority boundaries. South Norwood, New Addington, Kenley, Norbury and Croydon were all administrated under Croydon Borough Police.[2814]

In 2013 the South Norwood Police Station closed, and was sold in 2014 for the sum of £2,300,000.[2815]

Southall Police Station

The London Borough of Ealing

North Road, Southall (1908-1927)

250 High Street (1927-1975)

67 High Street (1975-2017)

X Division (1908-1985/86)

Southall Division XS (1985/86-1993/94)

Hillingdon OCU XH (1993/94-2018/19)

West Area BCU WA (from 2018/19)

On 25th October 1905 the Commissioner sent a memorandum to the Receiver instructing him to purchase a property known as Elm Lodge, Southall for use as a police station. This property situated at 67 High Street was purchased early in 1906, freehold for the sum of £1,750, and the premises adapted for police purposes.[2816] The temporary police station was opened on 17th August 1908.[2817]

In 1911 Southall Police Station was shown as being situated in North Road, with Sergeant Barnett in charge together with three other sergeants and fifteen constables there on the day of the census.[2818]

Southall Police Station 1908-1927

In 1917 it was decided to build a permanent station to replace the temporary station. Plans were drawn up and submitted to the Home Office for approval, but because the 1914-18 War was still in progress it was temporarily shelved until its aftermath, and the new station was completed in 1927.

It opened for business on 11th June 1927.[2819] The new station was designed by Mackenzie Trench, the Metropolitan Chief Architect and Surveyor. The building covered an area of 51ft by 36ft. It was described as a fine building:

'The entrance doors were in oak, and when open reveal a neat lobby, the floor of which is mosaic and the walls are faced with monastic tiles. Another feature is the heavy moulded brick cornice which surrounds the building'.

The builders were Messrs A. & B. Hanson Ltd of Southall.[2820]

A reorganisation of divisions in 1933 moved Southall as a sectional station on Ealing Sub-Division.[2821] Then in 1965 a

2799 Census 1911.
2800 www.pbhistory.co.uk/buildings/police.html accessed 2nd February 2012.
2801 Pevsner, N and Cherry, B. (1983). *London 2. South*. Penguin, p230.
2802 www.met.police.uk/croydon/history.htm accessed 11th August 2007.
2803 Metropolitan Police Surveyor's Records.
2804 Metropolitan Police Report: Condition of Police Stations 1881.
2805 Metropolitan Police Orders dated 5th December 1873.
2806 Metropolitan Police Orders dated 20th June 1884.
2807 *Kelly's Directory* 1895.
2808 Metropolitan Police Orders 24th February 1927.
2809 Moore C. and Gerrard Derek *A History of South Norwood Police Station*. Printed by the New Police Station Builders.
2810 Ibid.
2811 *Croydon Midweek*, 22nd October 1968.
2812 Metropolitan Police Orders dated 29th August 1985.
2813 Brown B. (1998) 'Policing Old Norwood'.
2814 www.met.police.uk/croydon/history.htm accessed 11th August 2007.
2815 Metropolitan Police Information Rights Unit 21st January 2018, accessed 25th January 2019.
2816 John Back Archive (1975).
2817 Metropolitan Police Orders dated 22nd August 1908.
2818 Census 1911.
2819 Metropolitan Police Orders dated 8th June 1927.
2820 *The Times*, 1927.
2821 Metropolitan Police Orders dated 28th November 1933.

Southall Police Station 1927-1975

further reorganisation took place, and Southall (XS) found itself a sectional station to Greenford Sub-Division within the London Borough of Ealing.

In 1969 an additional freehold piece of land adjacent to the station at 1 North Road was purchased for later development of the site. In 1970 plans were drawn up for the rebuilding of the station. The old station was to be demolished, and its personnel were housed whilst rebuilding took place in temporary accommodation at the rear of the station, as the new station was to be erected on the site of the old one. The senior officers and the administration staff were moved to hutted accommodation at the rear of Norwood Green Police Station.

Work commenced on 1st October 1973, with an estimated completion date of 31st December 1975. The whole operation, which the Home Office said in 1970 should cost no more that £204,725, eventually came to £640,218.[2822] The building was designed by Brewer, Smith and Brewer in association with J. Innes Elliot, the Metropolitan Police Chief Architect and Surveyor. It was built by Miller Buckley Construction. The five-storey building is entirely brick-clad with a reinforced concrete frame.[2823]

Southall Police Station 1975-2017

The new Southall Police Station was opened for business on 8th December 1975, and formally opened in December 1976 by Sir Robert Mark, Commissioner of the Police of the Metropolis, assisted by the Mayor and Mayoress of Ealing, Councillor and Mrs John Wood. Leading representatives of the Indian, Sikh, Muslim and Pakistan communities were also present.[2824]

In 2017 the police station was closed to the public,[2825] but as of 2019 had been retained for police operational purposes.

Southgate Police Station

The London Borough of Enfield
Chase Side Old Southgate 1865-1993
59 Crown lane as (New) Southgate 1993 -2020
N Division (1859-1865)
Y Division (1865-1985/86)
Edmonton Division (1985/86-1993)
Borough of Enfield OCU (1993-2018)
North Area NA BCU 2018 together with Haringey
(2018 to Present)

In 1859 the Metropolitan Police purchased land in Chase Side, Old Southgate for £285. The site was considered suitable for the building of a new police station and section house. Tenders were invited to build the new station, which was finally completed in 1861[2826] at a cost of £1,528. The building comprised ground and first floors, with a charge room, office, mess, four cells and two water closets located on the ground floor. In the yard was a three-stall stable for horses. Land was also purchased at the rear of the station to allow access into Crown Land.[2827]

The Commissioner approved Constable 214 Kirby (Acting Sergeant) to be employed on station duties at Southgate as from April 1864.[2828]

Southgate Police Station 1861-1970

In 1873 Southgate was a station situated on Y or Highgate Division.[2829] The picture above shows the old Southgate Police Station in Chase Side. It was built from traditional brick. In 1881 records show that Inspector Thomas E. Maher[2830] was the officer in charge of the station, although in 1873 it had been a sergeant designated station.[2831] Inspector Maher resided there with his wife Jael and their five children. There were six single police officers also resident at the station at this time.[2832]

Local people and dignitaries who arranged parties and events often treated the police and their families. One such event took place in Southgate, where Sub-Inspector Lambert from Southgate, whilst competing in an obstacle race at the Annual Police Party of Mr Cory Wright JP on 20th July 1897, collided violently with one of the obstacles, breaking his leg. He was taken to the Great Northern Hospital, where he was detained.[2833]

By 1909 the area within the Southgate Parish had become well populated, with a number of new houses being built. In fact, the population had trebled between 1899 and 1909.[2834]

Consideration was given in 1965 to replacing the police station, which was no longer suitable for modern policing requirements. The contract to build a police station, women police hostel and two sets of married quarters was awarded to Messrs Chas. S. Foster and Sons for the sum of £152,000.[2835] The new station was opened in 1970 together with the hostel at 59 Crown Lane, Southgate[2836] The station was built with a charge room and cell accommodation, although today they are rarely used as custody arrangements have been reorganised. The station code is 'YS'. The new station was located about 100 yards away from the Victoria Underground line at Southgate.

Once built, New Southgate Police Station was given the status of police office, and only open to the public for limited periods.[2837] The area of New Southgate was then policed as a neighbourhood unit from Southgate Police Station.

Southgate Police Station 1970 to present

Since 1970 Southgate Police Station has been the home of the Y Division Youth and Community Section, who occupy the hostel accommodation. This was not an ideal building for the administration of youth justice in the boroughs of Enfield, and Haringey (within the old Y Divisional boundary), as each room had a sink and wardrobe as standard.

As of 2019 Southgate Police Station remains in the hands of the Metropolitan Police for operational purposes.[2838]

Southwark/Stones End Police Station

The London Borough of Southwark

Montaque Street, Stones End (1844-1870)

50 Blackman Street, Borough (1870-1940)

23 Borough High Street (1940-2017)

M Division (1830-1985/86)

Southwark Division & OCU MD (1985/86-2018/19)

Central South BCU AS (from 2018/19)

In February 1830 the 11th Company of the Metropolitan Police – known as M (Southwark) Division – took over the policing of this area. There were two police stations, one at Guildford Street, a former Watch House, and the other at 4&5 Southwark Bridge Road (which had been built between 1814 and 1819).[2839] M Division consisted of one superintendent, four inspectors, 16 sergeants and 163 constables.[2840] As a result of taking over the old system of policing, the Metropolitan Police found that they had some 50 surplus Watch Boxes remaining in the area. These were later auctioned in six lots in 1830.[2841]

In 1832 a cholera epidemic killed two M Division officers out of a total of thirteen Metropolitan Police officers who died that year; eleven of them dying between 20th July and 18th September 1832.[2842] The return of a further epidemic in 1849 killed ten police constables and one sergeant.[2843] A total of 27 Metropolitan Police officers died, 26 of them between 5th July and September 1849.[2844]

The first purpose-built police station for the Southwark area was designed by the newly-appointed Metropolitan Police Surveyor, Charles Reeves, and erected in 1844 in Montague Street, Stones End at a cost of £4,435. The name Stones End was chosen because it marked the end of the paved footway from the City. Montague Street became the name of the station in 1856. Montague Street still exists but under another name; Stones End Street.[2845] This new police station replaced the Southwark Bridge Road Station.

In 1840 Superintendent William Murray was shown in charge of M Division. Murray was one of the first superintendents appointed at the start of the Metropolitan Police in 1829.[2846] He remained in charge until 1845.

Southwark Police Station was called Stones End and was the Divisional Station of M Division. In 1849 the command of the division was now in the hands of Superintendent Samuel Evans. There was one other station on the division at Paradise Street, Rotherhithe, near Mill Pond Bridge. There were four inspectors; John Yates, George Hornsby, Philip Froud and

2822 John Back Archive c1975.
2823 *Building Design*, 10th May 1974.
2824 *The Job*, 10th December 1976.
2825 Metropolitan Police Information Rights Unit 10th June 2018, accessed 25th January 2019.
2826 Opened 20th September 1861 (Metropolitan Police Order dated 19th September 1861).
2827 John Back Archive c1975.
2828 Metropolitan Police Orders dated 27th April 1864.
2829 Metropolitan Police General Orders 1873.
2830 Census 1881.
2831 Metropolitan Police General Orders 1873.
2832 Census 1881.
2833 *Police Review* July 1897.
2834 John Back Archive c1975.
2835 Ibid.
2836 Metropolitan Police Orders dated 12th June 1970.
2837 Metropolitan Police Orders dated 3rd May 1968.
2838 MPS (2019) Freedom of Information request: MPS Assets.
2839 Brown. B. 'The Metropolitan Police in the County of Surrey' in *Police History Society Journal*, 1994.
2840 Brown, B. 'M Division 1830-1899', December 1998.
2841 Brown, B. *The Job*, March 1988.
2842 Metropolitan Police Returns of Deaths Register 1829-1846.
2843 Brown, B. *The Job*, March 1988.
2844 Metropolitan Police Returns of Death Register 1829-1860.
2845 John Back Archive c1975.
2846 *Police and Constabulary List* 1844.

John Richard Cowlin. There were fourteen sergeants and 143 constables stationed there.²⁸⁴⁷ There was also one horse, which was ridden by the superintendent.²⁸⁴⁸

In December 1867 it was decided to look for a larger site for a new police station at Stones End, and in January 1868 premises in Blackman Street, Borough were obtained. The landlord was Alfred Cox of Somerset, and the lease for 90 years from 1868 at £500 per annum.²⁸⁴⁹ This is the site of today's station. It was estimated that the cost of the new building would be in the region of £10,000,²⁸⁵⁰ and during the building of the new station Superintendent Joseph Dunlop was in charge of the division.²⁸⁵¹

The new station was built to the design of Frederick Caiger, Metropolitan Police Surveyor, and Southwark Station was taken into use in July 1870.²⁸⁵² The address in 1880 was shown as 50 Blackman Street, Borough.

Southwark Police Station 1870 -1940

The 1881 Report states that:

"This establishment consists of two blocks; one is for married people only and is well designed. In the other there are married and single men's quarters kept separate, but not sufficiently distinct from the administrative portion. The bedrooms are not well planned. The water closets and urinals are in an underground cavity and deficient in light and air. The site lies low and the basement has been flooded; but steps have been taken to remedy this. More cells are required."

There were seven cells at the station, and during the twelve-month period between October 1879 and October 1880 there were a total of 397 prisoners in excess of the number of cells.²⁸⁵³ To deal this problem five new cells were added a short time later at a cost of £951.²⁸⁵⁴

The Police strength in 1883 showed an increase, as there were now eight inspectors, 23 sergeants and 187 constables, with Superintendent Harnett was in charge of the division. This included not only Southwark, but also Bermondsey, Grange Road and Rotherhithe.²⁸⁵⁵ In 1896 Grange Road and Southwark Sub-Divisions were amalgamated into one Sub-Division, called Southwark.²⁸⁵⁶

It was in 1889 that the County of London (LCC) was created, and M Division police stations at Blackman Street (later renamed Borough High Street), Borough (new station being built), Bermondsey Street, Rotherhithe and Grange Road ceased to be within the County of Surrey.²⁸⁵⁷

Sub-Divisional Inspector May

The picture on the left is of Sub-Divisional Inspector May who took over the Borough Sub-Division, which included Upper Grange Road, Bermondsey Police Station, in 1911.

At Southwark Police Station in June 1893 a presentation took place to honour a retiring officer. This was a normal occurrence at stations throughout the country, particularly when the officer had completed at least his 25 years' service. On this occasion ex-Inspector Henry Bealing, who retired on pension after 25 years' service, was presented with a handsome marble clock, suitably engraved, by Superintendent Neylan on behalf of the officers and men of the division. Many officers and men were present, including Chief Inspector Darling and Inspectors Robinson and Cleave.²⁸⁵⁸

Charles Booth's Social History Project records that in March 1900 they visited Southwark Police Station in Borough High Street and interviewed Superintendent H. Wyborn, who was described as a:

"strong, tall, rather portly man, between 50 and 60: vigorous with a short reddish beard turning grey. He is the only police superintendent who has Mr Booth's map (1887-89) hung up framed in his office." ²⁸⁵⁹

The fact that the map, which described the social conditions in London, was on display was of credit to Wyborn.

Southwark Police outing c1910

The picture above shows Southwark station's annual outing, circa 1910. When travelling outside the Metropolitan Police area the officers had to be appropriately dressed, and the officers in the photograph are shown wearing suits, ties, straw hats and even flowers in their lapels. Fifth from the left is Sub-Divisional Inspector Frederick May. Note that they are using a covered open-sided charabanc, which was probably hired locally at very reasonable rates; these vehicles were open to the elements and very cold. This outing was only for the men; the married women stayed at home to look after the children. The two drivers, in white coats, are shown on the left.

To mark the occasion of the Coronation of the King in 1911 the police station was dressed up with flowers, bunting and floral decorations. Below shows the effort that a number of constables and their families put into dressing the outside of the station.

Southwark Police Station dressed for the 1911 Coronation

Senior officers encouraged the playing of sports to keep their officers fit for duty, but sport was an ulterior motive for competition and being the best. Shown below, M Division won the Metropolitan Police Divisional Football Competition for 1912/13. This was a prestigious trophy to win, as the senior officers could boast about their divisional achievements to their compatriots. To mark the occasion the senior officers would get together as seen above. The Superintendent, Donald Waters, is shown behind the player with the ball, whilst to his left is Sub-Divisional Inspector May. Waters had become the Divisional Superintendent in 1900, taking over from Superintendent Walter T. Wren on the latter's retirement.

M Division Football Team

The Police had needed more space, and moved into the Old Court Building situated at 298 Borough High Street. In fact the premises were entirely used for Police purposes, and had been converted to take the family of the superintendent, the divisional offices, stores and the gymnasium.[2860]

On 21st July 1920, with an eye to future expansion of the Southwark Police Station site, the freehold of the building at 323 Borough High Street plus those of the adjoining properties, Nos. 319 and 321, were purchased for the sum of £15,000.[2861]

There were sports events which were held annually usually at the Police Sports Grounds. The picture below was taken at the M Division Sports Day, and their particularly successful Tug-of-War team is shown in action.

M Division Sports Day

In 1928 Superintendent William A. Ewart was in charge of M Division,[2862] but by 1930 Superintendent Henry Mann had taken over. The stations of the division were then at Southwark, Carter Street, Deptford, Grange Road, Rodney Road, Rotherhithe and Tower Bridge.[2863]

In 1938 plans were drawn up for a new divisional headquarters and sub-divisional police station for Southwark to be erected on the site of the existing building.

In October 1938 Southwark Police Station was closed for rebuilding, and all business transferred to a temporary station at 298 Borough High Street.[2864] Some property was moved to other temporary premises in Montague Place, opposite the old police station.[2865] The new station opened in September 1940, although the divisional headquarters temporarily remained in the old building.[2866]

On 18th February 1957 the Borough of Southwark wrote to the Receiver requesting permission to erect an historical sign – a bronze plaque on the wall of Southwark Police Station facing Borough High Street, with the following wording:

"Here was 'Stones End' where 'Town Street' met the old Turnpike Road. One of the parliamentary forts, erected to defend London during the Civil War, stood here."

Permission was readily granted and the sign was affixed to the wall of the police station in July 1958.[2867]

2847 *Post Office Directory* 1849.
2848 John Back Archive (1975).
2849 MEPO 4/234.
2850 John Back Archive (1975).
2851 *Police Almanac* 1869.
2852 Metropolitan Police Orders dated 20th July 1870.
2853 Metropolitan Police Surveyor's Report 1881.
2854 Metropolitan Police Surveyor's Records.
2855 Metropolitan Police Orders dated 22nd October 1883.
2856 Metropolitan Police Orders dated 15th October 1896.
2857 Brown, B. 'Met Police in the County of Surrey'. Date unknown.
2858 *Police Review & Parade Gossip*, 26th June 1893 p.309.
2859 www.boothlse.ac.uk accessed February 2010.
2860 Metropolitan Police Surveyor's Records 1924.
2861 John Back Archive (1975).
2862 *Post Office London Directory* 1928.
2863 *Kirchner's Police Almanac* 1931.
2864 Metropolitan Police Orders dated 20th October 1938.
2865 *Evening News*, 14th October 1938.
2866 Metropolitan Police Orders dated 12th September 1940.
2867 John Back Archive (1975).

In 1974 the stables at Southwark Police Station were closed when new stabling accommodation for the Mounted Branch was opened at 'The Warren', the Police Sports' Club at Hayes, Kent.[2868] Re-opening of the station took place in October 1983.[2869]

Southwark Police Station 1940-2017

Southwark Police Station's front counter closed in June 2013, but the station was retained for operational reasons.[2870]

St. Ann's Road Police Station

289 St. Ann's Road (1885-2014)
N Division (1885-1965)
Y Division (1965-1985/86)
Tottenham Division YT (1985/86-1993)
The London Borough of Haringey OCU (1993-2014)

The growth of population in this area of Tottenham (previously called the waste of the Manor of Tottenham) caused police to consider building a new police station there. They searched for suitable land, and found an available plot owned by Mr. R. Bushfield. The Receiver negotiated the purchase of the freehold title of the land in St. Ann's Road, Woodbury Down and Tottenham for £1,088.

Once purchased, the police surveyors designed a new large brick-and-tile police station on the land. It was an impressive two-storey building, and included a section house for twelve single constables. Just a year later, in 1885, the new St. Ann's Road Police Station was opened.[2871] The cost of building the station had been £3,222.[2872]

St. Ann's Road Police Station 1885-2014

The building was designed with an inspector's office, a charge room, a store, a waiting room, two cells, an association cell (often called the drunk tank as it could hold a number of drunken men), a kitchen, a scullery, a drying room, a boot room and a brushing room, all located on the ground floor. The first floor had a mess room, a food locker room, a clothes room and a day room. The second floor contained three large rooms for the single constables, and also a bathroom and lavatory. In the loft a room was built to accommodate three constables. In the station yard was a parade shed, an ambulance shed, seven water closets, a urinal, two coal cellars and a coke cellar.[2873] The land acquired enabled a large station yard to be laid to the side of the station. This would later be used as a District Traffic Garage.

There seemed to be a problem for the previous owner of the site, Mr. Bushfield, because the building of the station prevented access or further development of other land owned by him. In 1886 the Metropolitan Police gave permission for a right of way to be given to the public for access to land in Hermitage Road. Additionally, certain monies had to be paid by the police for the right of way over the land, which was jointly owned by the Tottenham Vestry and the Lord of the Manor. In the case of the Lord of the Manor this was done via the Trustees of the Settled Estate of Sir William M. Curtis (Bart), the previous Lord of the Manor of Tottenham, and was not properly settled until 1888.

The address of the station was shown as 289 St. Ann's Road, London N15.[2874] In 1904 the Metropolitan Police paid Tottenham Urban District Council £197 as a proportion of the cost to make up Hermitage Road. In June 1895 a telephone line was installed in the station, paid for by Tottenham Council at 5s per annum.[2875]

Permission was granted for a fire engine kept on standby to be located in the yard of the station.[2876] In 1907 the station was designated a sectional station of Wood Green.[2877]

In 1924 the single officers were moved out, and extensive structural alterations converted the accommodation into two sets of married quarters, which were quickly occupied.[2878] A district traffic garage was built at St. Ann's Road in 1936, beside the North Eastern Fever Hospital occupying a substantial site next door. A garage unit was built to house traffic police and their vehicles. It also became a workshop for repair and maintenance of police vehicles.[2879]

St. Ann's Road police pictured in the yard in 1912

The photograph above was taken in the yard of St. Ann's Road Police Station, and shows the station complement with their medals. The picture above shows those on duty and who were present at the Coronation of King George V. This occasion was marked by the award of a medal, which took time to prepare for presentation, and the officers received the award later. The picture appears to have been taken in 1912, when those who had performed duty at the Coronation in 1911 received their medals. The names of those who took part were collected and presented to the Home Department in order that the name, rank and division could be inscribed around the rim of the award.

King George V's Police Coronation medal was only struck in silver, and had a red ribbon with three vertical blue lines. They were awarded to the City of London Police, Metropolitan Police, County and Borough Police, the Police Ambulance service, London Fire Brigade, Royal Irish Constabulary, Scottish Police, St. Johns Ambulance Brigade and St. Andrews Ambulance Corps, and 109 were awarded to Park Keepers of the Royal Parks.[2880] There were 19,783 medals awarded to the Metropolitan Police and 1,400 to the City of London Police.[2881]

Coronation medal 1912

The call sign for St. Ann's Road was Sierra India (SI),[2882] and this was changed in the 1930s to November Alpha when it was the sectional station to Stoke Newington.[2883] Later it was changed again to Yankee Alpha (YA), when the station was transferred to Y Division.

Since the introduction of the Police and Criminal Evidence Act 1984 a requirement was placed on the police in respect of prisoner's rights and identification evidence. To this end, in the early 1990s there were some structural alterations made to the station, mainly to the rear, which included a purpose-built Identification Suite (ID) which could deal with identification parades in a more effective and professional manner. The new ID Suites served the whole area.

In 1998 the station was still open to the public,[2884] but was shut a year later for operational purposes.[2885] Records show that by 2001 charges were no longer taken there,[2886] and in 2014 St. Ann's Road Police Station was sold for £3.4M to Citystyleliving (Muswell Hill) Ltd.[2887]

St. John's Wood Police Station (formerly Portland Town Police Station)

London Borough of Camden

New Street, Portland Town (renamed in 1918 as
   St. John's Wood) (1896-1965)

Newcourt Street, St. Johns Wood (1965-1993)

S Division (1896-1965)

D Division (1965-1985/86)

Marylebone Lane Division DM (1985/86 -1993)

London Borough of Camden OCU (1993-2013)

In 1849 the Commissioner leased land in the Portland Town area on which a police station was built at a cost of £2,655.[2888]

In 1864 Portland Town Police Station was located on S or Hampstead Division. It was a station supervised by an inspector,[2889] although there were actually two inspectors posted there.[2890] The supervising inspector was supplied with a horse to perform his duty, while instructions were given for the duty inspector to patrol Willesden as well their own station area.[2891] There were five sergeants and 62 constables attached to the station.[2892]

Portland Town was a charging station, and cells for the detention of prisoners were attached.[2893] The station had been connected to the private wire network so contact could be maintained with Scotland Yard,[2894] and the station call sign was Papa Tango (PT).[2895]

In 1877 Inspector Richard Pope was the inspector in charge of the station.[2896] St. John's Wood Sub-Division had been previously called Portland Town, but had been renamed because of difficulties and confusion with mail deliveries between Portland in Dorset and Portland Town in London. The name change took place in August 1918.

In 1896 there were severe problems with the drainage, and extensive works to rectify them cost a staggering £2,049.[2897]

St. John's Wood Police Station (formerly Portland Town) 1896-1972

2868 Metropolitan Police Orders dated 24th May 1974.
2869 John Back Archive (1975).
2870 MPS (2019) Freedom of Information request. Station closures broken down by year.
2871 John Back Archive (1975); Metropolitan Police Orders dated 25th November 1885.
2872 Metropolitan Police Surveyor's Records 1884.
2873 Ibid.
2874 *Kitchener's Almanac* 1931.
2875 Metropolitan Police Surveyor's Records 1924.
2876 Ibid.
2877 *Kirchner's Almanac* 1907.
2878 Metropolitan Police Surveyor's records 1924.
2879 John Back Archive (1975).
2880 Cole, H. N. (1977) *Coronation and Royal Commemorative Medals 1887-1977* p31-32.
2881 Mackay, J. (eds) *Medal News Yearbook 1995*. Token Publishing, Honiton.
2882 Metropolitan Police General Orders 1893.
2883 *Police and Constabulary Almanac* 1957 and 1960.
2884 *Police and Constabulary Almanac* 1998.
2885 www.met.police.uk/contact/phone.htm accessed 12th March 2002.
2886 *Police and Constabulary Almanac* 2001.
2887 MPS Information rights unit (2019) Land and property sold by the MPS for over £1M over the last 10 years.
2888 Metropolitan Police Property Register pp159/60.
2889 *Police and Constabulary Almanac* 1864.
2890 Metropolitan Police Orders dated 11th January 1864.
2891 Ibid.
2892 Ibid.
2893 Ibid.
2894 Metropolitan Police General Orders 1873.
2895 Metropolitan Police General Orders 1893.
2896 *Police Office London Directory* 1877.
2897 Metropolitan Police Property Register pp159/60.

Freehold to the property in New Street, St. John's Wood was purchased in 1893 for £910.[2898] The vendors were the Trustees of the Will of the Noblest William Henry Cavendish Scott, 4th Duke of Portland.[2899] The station was built and ready for occupation in 1896,[2900] and included an inspector's office, a charge room and four cells. There was also a parade shed in the yard, and two stables for horses. Accommodation above the station included a section house for single officers.[2901]

Reconstruction work in the section house took place in 1905, and saw the construction of 33 cubicles for single officers, at a cost of £203.[2902] Gas was laid on in 1906.[2903]

At the beginning of the First World War, Portland Town (St. John's Wood) Police Station was the home to a Company of the S Division Metropolitan Police Special Constabulary (MPSC). They were a dedicated band of men, who helped to fill the void left by departing police officers who had joined the colours to fight. Although not fitted with uniforms until 1916, many of the Special Constabulary wore a duty armlet on their own plain clothes until that time.[2904]

Senior officers of the S Division Special Constabulary during WWI

Portland Town Special Constabulary 1916

The picture above, taken in the yard at Portland Town, shows the supervising officers of the station's Special Constabulary. In the centre (third from right at front) is Chief Inspector Dr. E. Climson Greenwood, flanked to the left by Inspector (later Chief Inspector) F.S. Bristowe, who compiled a fascinating account of life as a member of the Special Constabulary at Portland Town from 1914 until 1919. The inspectors are seated, whilst the sergeants are standing behind.

Following rioting in Camden Town after the sinking of the Lusitania by a German U-boat, the officers of S Division Special Constabulary considered it important for their men to wear uniforms as it was impossible to distinguish them from ordinary civilians. Uniforms were therefore issued after 18th May 1916.[2905]

The division was particularly well organised, and the picture at the top of the next column shows its leadership. The two men seated with canes are (from left to right) Commander R.A. Simson OBE and Assistant Commander C. Wharton Collard, who were stationed at Divisional Headquarters at Albany Street. Top left of the picture, and in charge of Portland Town SC, was the Police Divisional Surgeon Dr. E. Climson Greenwood. He was sworn into the MSC on 17th August 1914 as an Inspector. He became a Chief Inspector in November 1915, and an Acting/Assistant Commander in February 1919. Working from left to right along the back row is Chief Inspector J.T. Ash of West Hampstead MPSC, next is Chief Inspector Cross of Finchley, followed by Chief Inspector Levick of Golders Green.

The Special Constabulary on S Division formed a rifle club, and individual stations competed against each other on a number of occasions. Portland Town Rifle Club was formed in December 1914, with Sub-Inspector Scott nominated as President. Soon there was a working membership of some 113 officers.[2907] In January 1915 a weekly Silver Spoon competition was instituted, but later on the competitions were held monthly. Some 44 spoons were competed for, and four members each succeeded in winning a set of six spoons, which were engraved with the dates they were won.[2907]

On 7th March 1918 a bomb dropped by a German aeroplane destroyed 11,12,&13 New Street, killing six people. This was forty yards from the police station at Portland Town. The King and Queen, accompanied by the Commissioner Sir Edward Henry, visited the scene and station, where they were presented to Chief Inspector Climson Greenwood. The records show the awarding of a merit certificate to Special Constable J.R. Hodge, stationed at Portland Town, who performed 305 duties and attended 44 emergency calls.[2908]

In August 1918 Portland Town Police Station was renamed St. John's Wood Police Station,[2909] and in 1931 it was still recorded on S or Hampstead Division.[2910] The following year the London County Council informed the Commissioner about a change of road name, with New Street being changed to New Court Street.[2911]

During the Metropolitan Police re-organisation in 1964, St. John's Wood was transferred to D Division, where its call sign was changed to Delta Sierra (DS).

In 2013 the station was vacated and put up for sale, selling a year later for £8,555,555 to a property developed who converted the site into residential flats.[2912]

St. Mary Cray Police Station (PM)

London Borough of Bromley

Cottages, High Street, St Mary Cray (1851-1896)

79 High Street, St Mary Cray (1896-1988)

R Division (1840-1865)

P Division (1865)

R Division (1865-1932)

P Division (1932-1985/86)

Orpington Division (1985/86-1988)

The River Cray gave its name to a number of villages along its course towards the Medway, St Mary Cray being the most southerly of the Crays. As early as 1653 a parish constable,

St Mary Cray Police Station 1896-1988

George Burton, was put in custody for the manslaughter of a George Dixon, who had been put in the stocks for being drunk.

The problem of highwaymen caused the Bow Street horse patrols to visit the Crays, but in January 1840 the area became part of R Division of the Metropolitan Police when three constables patrolled St Mary Cray, then with a population of 470.

In October 1851 St Mary Cray received its first police station where Sergeant John Bovis was in charge of five constables on a site in the High Street leased from Mr J. Ayre, the proprietor of the adjacent Black Boy inn. An old lock-up at Crayford was given up to a Mr Barnes.

Kelly's 1855 *Directory of Kent* referred to the Crays as:

'four highly respectable villages... in beautiful countryside... with paper mills... Interspersed with numerous elegant seats and noble mansions.'

The area today is far more notable for its density of social housing.

Sidcup and St Mary Cray were initially part of Lee Sub-Division, but were transferred to P Division's Bromley for a few months from March until October 1865. In 1873 an Inspector Samuel Higgins was in charge, and remained so until 1890.

One of the most serious cases he would have dealt with was that of Joseph Waller, a former constable, who was sent to the Maidstone assizes charged with the murder of an elderly couple on St Paul's Cray Common in October 1880. Waller, like many prisoners, scratched a drawing on his cell wall: a picture of a cottage and a gallows was accompanied by a signed inscription:

'Joseph Waller, charged with the wilful murder of Edward and Elizabeth Ellis, shot down with a revolver by me.'

The police station, with six rooms, a charge room, a kitchen and two cells was officially described as 'dilapidated' in 1887, and a new replacement building was finally completed on 14th September 1896 at a cost of £3,597 10s 2d at a freehold site which became known as 79 High Street, St. Mary Cray, Kent. Allocated with a telegraphic code of 'SC' in 1893, it was a station of R Division.

2898 Metropolitan Police Property Schedule 1924.
2899 Metropolitan Police Property Register pp 159/60.
2900 Metropolitan Police Orders dated 5th September 1896.
2901 Op cit.
2902 Ibid.
2903 Ibid.
2904 Bristowe, F. S. (1919) 'Souvenir of St. Johns Wood Special Constabulary'.
2905 Ibid.
2906 Ibid.
2907 Ibid.
2908 Ibid.
2909 Metropolitan Police Orders August 1918.
2910 Kirchner's Police Index 1931.
2911 Metropolitan Police Property Schedule 1924.
2912 MPD (2018) MOPAC Police station closures broken down by year.

Ten years later, St Mary Cray became part of the Sidcup Sub-Division, and from 1st January 1932 was returned to P Division as part of Bromley Sub-Division. The house next door, 81 High Street, once a shop, was purchased in 1939 with a view to the land providing the means to extend the police station. These plans never came to fruition, and despite the erection of a temporary wooden building the accommodation became more and more cramped.

In April 1965, St Mary Cray became a sub-divisional headquarters within the new London Borough of Bromley, and, after Orpington Police Station was opened in December 1983, St Mary Cray's station became a police office, finally closing in January 1988. The community felt the loss of the police station very keenly, and after a period of campaigning a new police office was opened in September 1994.

A rare view of the rear of St Mary Cray Police Station showing to the left the original four cottages that formed the first police station there. Note the washing hanging at left and the cultivated gardens

Cray Police Office 1994 to present

Staines Police Station (and Spelthorne)

The London Borough of Hillingdon
London Road, Staines (1841-1872)
2 London Road, Staines (1872-1999)
22 Kingston Road Staines (1999- 2000)
T Division (1840-1999)
Transferred to the Surrey Constabulary

In the 1830s, the parishioners of Staines requested that a corps of the Metropolitan Police be placed on permanent duty in the town. The fame of the force, largely composed of former Bow Street horse patrol and dismounted Bow Street patrols and military men, was spreading outwards from London to the suburbs, where residents felt the need for effective policing.

Bounty hunters in the style of the Wild West would, it appears, have been encouraged to aid law and order. Following an incident in January 1819 when postman James Harris, conveying mail between Chertsey and Staines, was 'feloniously stopped in the highway and robbed of his watch, and was also cruelly beaten by the robber or robbers', the General Post Office in London offered a £20 reward to 'whoever shall apprehend the person or persons guilty of the said robbery.'[2913]

As early as 1805 the men of the Bow Street horse patrols had set up horse patrol stations on the Staines Road at Hounslow Heath, at Bedfont and on the Bath Road at Colnbrook in Berkshire. These original horse patrols were absorbed into the Metropolitan Police in 1839, and in January 1840 the New Police established station houses in the parishes of Staines and Sunbury.

Staines was placed under the T or Kensington Division (Brentford Sub-Division), whose complement of three sergeants and 15 constables patrolled the parishes of Staines (population 2,486), Stanwell (population 1,386 with Colnbrook), Ashford (population 4,518), Bedfont, West Bedfont, Hatton, Laleham, Littleton, Shepperton (population 847) and Upper Halliford.[2914]

The old 'parish cage' – probably little more than a single brick-built cell with a solid door and barred window – stood on the junction of the High Street and Thames Street in Staines. It was demolished in 1830.[2915]

Nighttime foot patrols were introduced, followed by horse patrols which operated on main roads within a 16-mile radius of central London. Until the 1830s, the Bow Street Runners had a station in London Road, Staines, at the junction with Swinburn Lane, now non-existent, which led to Stanwell Moor. The station was manned by a captain, a corporal and five troopers or townsmen. One of their jobs was to control the local and farm traffic along the London and Kingston Roads, and along the High Street towards Staines Bridge, so that the streets were clear when the fast mail coaches were due through.

The Runners had already disbanded by 1839 when two constables and four headboroughs, nominated by the 'leet jury and sworn in before the Lord of the Manor at his court leet', were tasked with keeping the peace. The Metropolitan Police took over the area a few years later.

In 1841 a substantial brick-and-slate building in Staines containing seven rooms with a yard was rented by the Receiver from Mr South of Staines on an annual rent of £33. The station was shown as part of T Division. There was a kitchen, charge room and cells on the ground floor. The agreement was that the police would have it painted regularly, and the station was whitened usually every four years. Records show that this was done in 1868 and 1871. When surveyed in 1845, the station was said to be in a good, clean condition with plenty of water and good ventilation.[2916]

Staines Police Station 1872-1999

Thames Division operated patrol boats as far as Staines Bridge. The Marine Police had been financed by the West India Company in the 1790s, when numerous rogues were stealing from ships on the Thames. The marine police set up their base at Wapping, and Thames Division still has its headquarters there to this day.

The officers in charge at Staines in 1851 (the year Surrey Constabulary was formed) were Inspector George Bailey and Sergeant Walter Lee. The nearest railway station to Staines was at West Drayton, opened by the Great Western Railway in June 1838, from which incidentally a branch line ran to Staines by way of Colnbrook between 1885 and 1965. A decade later, in August 1848, the London and South Western Railway extended their Richmond branch to Datchet with stations at Staines and Ashford, the latter for some years carrying the suffix (Middlesex) to differentiate its namesake in Kent.[2917]

Staines Police Station Yard and rear entrance to the building

In 1861 Constables Henry Ing, Patrick Roche, Richard Williams, Joseph Burbridge and Charles Brill were resident in the section house at the station. Sergeant Charles Simpkins, his wife and their three children were resident at the station. Sergeant William Atter, Constables Charles Brooks and William Prideaux also lived at the station at this time.

The old station survived until November 1998, when it was replaced by the present modern building in Kingston Road.

Sunbury was transferred from V to T Division in October 1865, and ever since then Staines and Sunbury have been closely associated. The latter was served by the Thames Valley Railway from November 1864 as part of the Shepperton Branch, Upper Halliford, however it only dates from 1944, when it was opened for war workers.[2918]

Despite Staines now being within the jurisdiction of the Metropolitan Police District, one Jasper Adams still held the ancient office of High Constable. The Sunbury section, then part of the V or Wandsworth Division, was within the vast Kingston Sub-Division and was located at No. 19 Thames Street. Four sergeants and 21 constables were responsible for the parishes of Sunbury (population 1,863), Teddington, Hampton Court, Hampton Wick, Feltham and Hanworth.[2919]

The old two-cell Staines Police Station dating from 1841 in London Road was replaced in 1872, at a cost of £3,932. The new station had four cells, and four stalls for the horse patrols. The town now had a population of 3,469, while the parish itself numbered 3,659 souls.[2920]

The rear yard of Staines Police Station circa 1908 showing gardening plot

The old Bow Street patrol office was the first building to be occupied in Staines by the Metropolitan Police. Then, in 1865, a building almost opposite – the site of a candle factory – was taken over. It soon became clear that a purpose-built station was required, and for the sum of £500 Nightingale's Field was purchased. The new station, built at a cost of over £4,000 and opened in 1876, served Staines for over 100 years. Meanwhile, during its construction a temporary move into yet another building was deemed necessary. This was where Kingston Road School was later built. Spelthorne's new police station is on the same site.[2921]

Under the Summary Jurisdiction Act 1879 the old station was used as an occasional courthouse until January 1883, when this function passed to the new station.[2922]

2913 Whitling, D. (1999) 'A History of Policing in Spelthorne' Metropolitan Police.
2914 Brown, B. (1989) 'Policing Old Spelthorne'.
2915 Whitling, D. (1999) 'A History of Policing in Spelthorne' Metropolitan Police.
2916 Metropolitan Police Surveyor's Records ESB London.
2917 Brown, B. (1989) 'Policing Old Spelthorne'.
2918 Spelthorne History sheet.
2919 Brown, B. (1989) 'Policing Old Spelthorne'.
2920 Ibid.
2921 Whitling, D. (1999) 'A History of Policing in Spelthorne' Metropolitan Police.
2922 Brown, B. (1989) 'Policing Old Spelthorne'.

Although Staines was a nearly new police station, there were problems with sanitation and design. In 1881 an inspection found the well in the yard was contaminated with sewage, and instructions were given to isolate the cesspool and dig a new well to provide drinking water. The station contained the inspector and sergeant with their respective families, although these rooms were not considered sufficiently private enough and they were not self-contained. The men would parade inside the station in the charge room, but this was no longer workable as numbers of officers on parade often interfered with the station inspector or sergeant dealing with prisoners. It was recommended that a suitably-sized parade shed was constructed in the yard for this purpose.[2923]

An amusing story is told about the Victorian building. One of the men working on the construction of the cells was bricklayer 'Socky' Bolton. On their completion he celebrated in time-honoured manner, and was then arrested for being drunk, thus becoming the first-ever occupant of the cells. The next day he had to walk to Bedfont for the Petty Sessions alongside a mounted police officer, where he was fined a shilling, plus a shilling costs. He then had to walk home again.[2924]

Neither Ashford or Stanwell were apparently large enough communities to warrant their own police stations, although not too far away there was a station at Bedfont, which was then a sub-division of Staines.

In 1890 Staines had a resident inspector, two other inspectors, three sergeants and twenty constables. Sunbury had two inspectors, two sergeants and seventeen constables.[2925]

In 1894 the various parishes were placed under the jurisdiction of Urban Districts. Sunbury UDC took in an area of 2,659 acres, which in 1911 had a population of 4,606, while Staines UDC, with a population of 6,756, covered an area of 1,918 acres. In addition, a Staines Rural District was also created, comprising a vast 17,964 acres with a population of 21,932 stretching as far north as Harlington and including a detached portion at Hanworth.[2926]

Staines Police Station celebrations for the 1911 Coronation

Prior to the Great War the Staines section had been part of the Bedfont Sub-Division, but in January 1917 assumed sub-divisional status to include Bedfont, Harlington and Sunbury sections. In 1926, the year of the General Strike, Staines was under the charge of Sub-Divisional Inspector Alfred Harwood who had under him ten sergeants and 32 constables. The old Rural District Council ceased to exist after 1929, leaving just the two urban districts, Littleton Parish passing from Sunbury to Staines UDC.[2927]

Retired Staines police officer Fred Lipscombe, who was spoken to by the author of the History of Policing in Spelthorne when he was aged 92, clearly remembered 1932 when he was posted to Staines once his probation finished. As an Eastender he felt it was a punishment to be sent out into the country, but he married a local girl and stayed. The six-footer with army experience was considered an excellent candidate for the Met, which only recruited physically fit, disciplined men of at least 5ft 10in in height. In those days, the whole eight-hour shift had to be spent on the beat. Constables ate their sandwiches sitting in a police box, after booking off by phone. They were not allowed back to the station except for necessary reports, and at some point, even in the middle of the night, a sergeant would make sure they were still on the beat, whatever the weather.

'Decent people weren't out at night in those days... So anyone abroad after midnight was probably up to no good! On the 11pm to 7am beat, officers were expected to pass lengths of black cotton over doorways and alleyways, and check before they booked off that the thread was intact, to ensure no-one had been that way. If the cotton was broken, the building was checked out.'[2928]

Fred was one of the first Metropolitan Police radio telegraphy (RT) operators in the new patrol cars, known as 'Bean' cars.[2929] They were little more than a framework with an engine and transparent screens to keep the weather out, said Fred. He had learned Morse Code in the army, and after brushing up his skills went out with the drivers on the division. Later, during the War, he also accompanied an Assistant Commissioner around London as his personal operator.[2930] Other memories of the War include arresting Canadian soldiers, one of the soldiers was a huge Red Indian, billeted in Windsor Great Park, who came to Staines to get drunk. He also has memories of the 'razor gangs' who got into bloody fights after a boozy day at the Kempton Park races.

Awards ceremony at Staines early 1930s

The 1930s saw a major upheaval of police boundaries, resulting in the closure of both Bedfont and Sunbury Police Stations in June 1932, followed in December 1933 by Hampton being transferred from Twickenham Sub-Division to Staines, in lieu of Hounslow.[2931]

A deputation was made to Scotland Yard by members of Sunbury-on-Thames Urban District Council concerned over the closure of their police station, but the Home Secretary decided that there was adequate policing in the area. In July 1936 a Dr. Who TARDIS-type police box was installed in front of the closed station. A plan was mooted for a new police station at Feltham, which was deferred due to the war, and a temporary station opened in November 1953 as a part replacement for Bedfont under the jurisdiction of the Staines Sub-Division.[2932]

In April 1965, with the creation of the GLC, a further revision of Staines boundaries occurred when Feltham passed to the

Hounslow Sub-Division with Staines once again reduced to a mere sectional station on Twickenham Sub-Division along with Hampton, upon the closure of Harlington. Up until this date the Thames Division had only patrolled upstream as far as Teddington Lock hut (although in the early 1800s the Marine Police had patrolled to Staines Bridge), but they were now authorised to patrol up to Staines Bridge, new moorings and a police station being taken into use at Shepperton Lock.[2933]

As Staines and Sunbury were beyond the GLC, the urban districts were now administered by Surrey Council instead of Middlesex. In November 1974 the Metropolitan Police assumed responsibility for the former British Airports Authority Police at Heathrow. The new division now included Staines, and from October 1980 also Sunbury (having reopened in January 1966); both stations returning to what was then T District in December 1984.[2934]

Staines Police Station 1998 to present

An unusual anomaly occurred in May 1988 when a small section of Felix Lane, Shepperton was handed over to the Metropolitan Police from the Surrey Police. At least a mile into the MPD, the area had traditionally been patrolled by Surrey, but with realignment of the Thames tributaries over the years it gradually found itself on the Middlesex side of the river. In January 1989 the Staines and Sunbury sections were amalgamated as the Spelthorne Division, taking its name from the ancient Hundred. Instead of wearing the divisional letters 'TW' (Twickenham) on officers' shoulders, they then used the letters 'TG' (Staines). One might ask why the letters 'TS' were not used. 'TS' was in fact the station code for Staines up until 1946 when it was adopted for the new Training School Division, although this went out of use in 1993.[2935]

With the introduction of sector policing in 1992/93, two new sector offices were opened in Shepperton and Ashford. In April 1995, however, part of the latter sector was reduced in size when Poyle and Colnbrook in Middlesex were taken over by Berkshire County Council, and policing passed to the Thames Valley force.[2936]

Late in 1998 the long-awaited new station, on the site of the former Kingston Road School, opened its doors to police and civil staff. The official opening ceremony, conducted by the Metropolitan Police Commissioner Sir Paul Condon, was planned for 24th April 1999. In recent years, new police offices had been opened for the convenience of Shepperton and Ashford residents. Officers could quickly call on various specialist units not too far away to ensure effective policing – there was a traffic unit at Hampton, dog patrols based at West Drayton and Teddington, a fully equipped helicopter with heat-seeking equipment based at Fairoaks airport, and the Thames Division at Shepperton. Large numbers of officers could be called in from surrounding divisions in an emergency, and Spelthorne also sent officers all over the Metropolitan Police area to help when required.[2937]

Spelthorne had its own scenes of crime officer (SOCO), crime prevention officer (CPO) and schools' officers on division. Staines had a dedicated officer to look after vulnerable people with problems of a domestic, racist or homophobic nature. Partnership schemes with the local council and businesses sought to reduce crime.

In 2000, boundary changes which were discussed as long ago as the 1960s came into force and from April 2000 the entire Spelthorne division was placed under the jurisdiction of the Surrey Police, albeit officially still part of Middlesex. The white 'coal-posts' bearing the City of London crest no longer marked the boundary between the County Constabulary and the MPD, whose jurisdiction ended after 160 years. The transfer occurred a year after the new super station and area headquarters was built at Staines, so the Surrey Constabulary were gifted a modern state-of-the-art purpose-built station and headquarters.[2938]

Stanwell Police House (Station)

The London Borough of Hillingdon
Stanwell Village (1845-1866)
T Division (1845-1866)

The parish of St. Mary's, together with its church and churchyard at Stanwell, is famous as containing many notable burials. Several houses are listed, including Dunmore House on the village green built in 1719 by John, Earl of Dunmore. This is a very fine building, with a galleried hall and a worthy accompaniment to any village. Arundel House at the east end of the village was originally a police station in the middle of the 19th century. The building originated between 1620-1640, but extensive alterations leave little of the original features visible. These never included glazed windows, but some of the interior walls contain bricks larger than normal, which were an answer to the brick tax instituted to finance the Napoleonic wars.[2939]

2923 Metropolitan Police Report: Condition of Police Stations 1881.
2924 Whitling, D. (1999) 'A History of Policing in Spelthorne' Metropolitan Police.
2925 Ibid.
2926 Brown, B. (1989) 'Policing Old Spelthorne'.
2927 Ibid.
2928 Whitling, D. (1999) 'A History of Policing in Spelthorne' Metropolitan Police.
2929 Bean Cars were made in factories in Dudley, Worcestershire, and Coseley, Staffordshire, England, between 1919 and 1929. For a few years in the early 1920s Bean outsold Austin and Morris althoughtheir success was not sustainable (source: Wikipedia, accessed 23rd October 2013).
2930 Whitling, D. (1999) 'A History of Policing in Spelthorne' Metropolitan Police.
2931 Brown, B. (1989) 'Policing Old Spelthorne'.
2932 Ibid.
2933 Ibid.
2934 Ibid.
2935 Ibid.
2936 Ibid.
2937 Whitling, D. (1999) 'A History of Policing in Spelthorne' Metropolitan Police.
2938 Brown, B. (1989) 'Policing Old Spelthorne'.
2939 Grigg, F.C. (date unknown) 'Stanwell the Village that would not die'. (accessed Hounslow Library).

In 1845 an additional police station (in fact the sergeant's house) was established in Stanwell Village which was rented yearly at a cost of £14 14s from Mr W. Hall of Kingsland. This was a common brick-and-slate house in good condition with a small garden. In the yard was a two-stall stable with hay loft. Also at the station was a scullery, and accommodation consisting of four rooms rented at a cost of 2/6d per week.

Sergeant George Bigarlsford, his wife and their family lived at the station in 1851. The police station was still there in 1866. Living in Stanwell in retirement was pensioner ex-Metropolitan Police Superintendent William Durkin, aged 53, and his wife, aged 33, who lived together on the village green.

The police officers from the horse patrol were housed there, and there was a cupboard originally with an exterior entrance which used to house drunken prisoners overnight. On one occasion a prisoner was found to have suffocated after a very hot night, as a result of which ventilation holes were drilled over the interior door, and these are still visible today.[2940]

This horse patrol station was given up on Christmas Eve 1868, along with Colnbrook when the new Bedfont Police Station opened.[2941]

In 1901 35-year-old Sergeant Harry England from Radlett in Hertfordshire and his wife Annie and five children lived at Stanwell Moor, to the north west of the former police station. The police station had been shut in 1866.[2942]

Stoke Newington (Kingsland) Police Station

High Street, Kingsland Road (1832-1866)
33 High Street (1866-1993)
N Division (1832-1965)
G Division (1965-1985/86)
Stoke Newington Division GN and Hackney OCU
(1985/86-2018/19)
Central East CE BCU (from 2018/19)

Stoke Newington was included in the Metropolitan Police District in 1829/30. The Vestry[2943] declared satisfaction with the new police declaring that

"...they were better than the watch, although Cut Throat Lane, Lordship Lane, Woodberry Down and the north parts of Green Lanes were insufficiently policed." [2944]

The numbers of watchmen were gradually reduced from twenty-five in 1828 to twelve in 1834. In 1829 their swords were removed and by 1830 their pistols were declared unnecessary.[2945] Prior to the building of a police station at Stoke Newington there was an old Watch House and Parish Pound situated in Stoke Newington Church Street just behind the Red Lion Public House.[2946] The station was the Divisional Headquarters and housed the officer in charge of the division.

In 1845 Superintendent James Johnston was responsible for the vast N or Islington Division. At the Divisional Headquarters a Divisional Clerk Sergeant assisted the Superintendent. The Superintendent was issued with a horse and accordingly a Constable was appointed as groom to ensure that the senior officer could supervise the division.[2947] The officer in charge at Kingsland Station was Inspector Daniel Howie.[2948] Apart from Kingsland Johnston supervised, Church Street Hackney, Robert Street, Hoxton, Islington Green, Islington (the previous Divisional Headquarters), Green Street, Enfield Highway, Lordship Road, Stoke Newington, Hornsey, Tottenham near Scotland Green, Edmonton near the Old Church, Enfield, Cheshunt, Walthamstow and Waltham Abbey.[2949] In 1850 Johnston was still the officer in charge, and five Inspectors namely Joseph Mellish, George Thatcher, Edward Tarlton, John Pascoe and James Coward assisted him.[2950]

Land was purchased at 33 High Street, Stoke Newington in 1864 on which to build a police station.[2951] The new station was built at a cost of £5,678, and was opened in 1866.[2952] The station was built next to one public house called The Victoria and seven doors away from another.[2953] This new station was called Kingsland Police Station, and must not be confused with Kingsland Road Station, which was built in 1866 and situated at the junction with Robert Street, Hoxton.

The station had four floors containing 36 rooms. Originally the Superintendent of the Division occupied a room on the ground floor, but later he moved to the first floor together with his headquarters staff.

Stoke Newington Police Station 1866-1990

In 1873 records show that communication by wire had been established with Scotland Yard and that the operational management of the station was in the hands of an Inspector.[2954] In 1881 there were forty single constables residing at the station together with the Station Inspector George Dudman, and his large family. Inspector Dudman was born in Lugershall in Wiltshire in 1832 and lived at the station with his wife, Louisa and their seven children. They had five daughters and two sons. Records show that there were four prisoners in the cells (two males and two females) at the time details was taken.[2955] In 1888 the officer in charge of the Division was Superintendent William J. Sherlock, (who had been an Inspector at Hackney in 1881) and his headquarters were re-located to Stoke Newington Police Station. He had a divisional strength of 37 inspectors, 66 sergeants and 536 constables.[2956] A new coach house and stables were erected in February 1889 with eight stalls. The station had a charge room, six cells and in the yard was a parade shed. At one stage there were 41 single constables living in cramped conditions on the second floor of the station. In 1886, however, there were only 38 constables living there.

Stations were often the focus of sporting and social activities and also for annual events for the officers and their families who lived or worked at or near police stations. For example, on 16th August 1894 the second N Division Annual sports day took place at the "To te tum" sports ground in Stamford Hill. It was well attended, although it rained all day. The sports day was attended by Superintendent McFadden accompanied by his wife, who supplied and later presented all the prizes. Also in attendance were Chief Inspector Parsons and Sub-Divisional Inspector Nean. Additionally the N Division Police Band played tunes all afternoon.[2957]

Often sad or tragic events happened and the death of any police officer even of natural causes was of great distress to those who knew the officer. It was reported that a single officer Constable Patrick McGowan aged 44 years, was found dead in his section house bed at Stoke Newington on 6th January 1898. The cause of death was later established as consumption (pulmonary tuberculosis), which was a fairly common cause of death at the turn of the 20th century. Constable McGowan a popular member of the station, received a traditional police funeral. His remains were buried at Abney Park cemetery on 9th January 1898, and 200 members of the force attended in uniform to pay their last respects. The police station band played the Funeral March en route to the cemetery. His supervisory officers, Inspectors Ford and Osgood and Sub-Divisional Inspector Thorpe headed the procession.[2958]

Stoke Newington Police 2nd football team in 1914 with trainers

Other events took place at the station involving recreation or sport. The photograph above shows a Stoke Newington football team in 1914. The police have always enjoyed playing competitive sports, encouraged by senior officers who were not only keen to maintain an active and fit police force, but also to re-enforce the bond of comradeship and loyalty, often referred to today as meaning the 'Police Culture'. Playing sport for the Force, rather than the station, ensured time off from active duty. Many individual clubs were being run in the Metropolitan Police including football, boxing, rugby, cricket etc; however

"It was not until after the war that the Home Office made a grant which enabled the different games clubs throughout the Metropolitan Police to join together into one general association and shoulder the burden of the upkeep of the ground that was bought." [2959]

At the rear of Stoke Newington Police Station a new section house for 72 officers was built. It opened in December 1913.[2960] Some additional married quarters were also built and these opened in August 1914.[2961]

In 1929 the Metropolitan Police celebrated their centenary with a parade in Hyde Park, an inspection by HRH The Prince of Wales, and a march past Buckingham Palace. Superintendent Pearce, (the Divisional Superintendent) stationed at Stoke Newington, was in attendance together with the No. 3 District Chief Constable Major M. Tomlin OBE. With them were eight Inspectors, 32 Sergeants and 240 constables taken from the whole division. Over 12,000 officers, members of the Criminal Intelligence Department and Special Constabulary attended the ceremony.[2962]

In the 1970s and '80s policing in Stoke Newington and Dalston became the scene of black confrontation with the police. Black people regarded the police with suspicion and distrust, and when highly publicised cases of deaths in police custody occurred, then the 'closed and secretive' nature of policing provoked public annoyance and anger. Over a period of time Stoke Newington Police Station and its police officers developed a reputation of apparent racist conduct. Asseti Sims died in 1970, Michael Fereira in 1978, Colin Roach in 1983, Tunay Hassan (at Dalston) in 1987 and Trevor Monerville in 1987.[2963] In the meantime in 1981 there were major riots and unrest in the Stoke Newington area, near JJ's Café in Sandringham Road.[2964]

Stoke Newington Police Station 1990 to present

2940 Grigg, F.C. (date unknown) 'Stanwell the Village that would not die'.
2941 Brown, B. (1989) 'Policing Old Spelthorne'.
2942 *Post Office Directories* 1845-1867.
2943 The Church Vestry often concerned themselves with the safety of their parishioners and expressed their opinions to the Watch Committee when necessary. Sometimes members of the Vestry were also representatives of the Watch Committee.
2944 *The Victorian County of Middlesex* (1995) p201.
2945 Ibid.
2946 John Back Archive (1975).
2947 Metropolitan Police Orders dated 11th January 1864.
2948 *The Police and Constabulary List* 1844 p3.
2949 Ibid.
2950 *Kelly's Directory* 1850.
2951 Metropolitan Police Orders dated 21st December 1866.
2952 Ibid; and John Back Archive(1975).
2953 Ordnance Survey Map (Stoke Newington) 1868.
2954 Metropolitan Police General Orders 1873.
2955 Census 1881.
2956 *Dickens's Dictionary of London*, 1888. Old House Books, Moretonhampstead, pp132-3.
2957 *Police Review*, August 1894.
2958 *Police Review*, January 1898.
2959 Tomlin, M. (1936) *The Police and the Public*. p45.
2960 Metropolitan Police Orders dated 20th December 1913.
2961 Metropolitan Police Orders dated 3rd August 1914.
2962 *The Metropolitan Police Centenary Programme* 1929.
2963 Keith, M. (1993) *Race, Riots and Policing*. UCL Press, London.
2964 Ibid p37.

A new station in Stoke Newington was planned as far back as 1938, and efforts to start rebuilding on the old site also came to nothing in 1976.[2965] A new £5.25 million police station, in a very modern style, was built on the old site whilst normal operational policing continued at the same time.

The station opened in April 1990.[2966] The three storey building took two and half years to complete, using 134,000 bricks, 560 tons of steel and 4000 cubic metres of concrete. New police stations are designed in such a way as to be modern and pleasing to the eye, but also resilient enough to withstand a siege or a bomb blast. In fact entrances can be sealed off and there are certain protections and shutters behind windows which afford better security.[2967]

In 1995 a Service restructuring exercise reduced the Areas to five from eight. This meant that Leman Street ceased to be Area HQ, when Stoke Newington Police Station became attached to 3 Area (North East) Headquarters located at Edmonton Police Station. The further changes in 1998 meant no change for Stoke Newington Police Station.[2968]

In 2019 the station was still a contact point and in the possession of the Metropolitan Police.[2969]

Streatham Police Station

The London Borough of Lambeth
High Road, Streatham (1868-2013)
W Division (1865-1932)
Z Division (1932-1965)
L Division (1965-1985/86)
Streatham Division & OCU LS (1985/86-2013)

In 1865 Streatham Police Station was show in records on W (Clapham) Division.[2970] In June 1867 the Home Office authorised the acceptance of the tender submitted by a Mr Higgs in the sum of £3,117 for the erection of a new police station at Streatham.[2971] The freehold of the site had been purchased for £1,800 the previous year.[2972]

The new station was opened in July 1868, and was described as no more than 'a Policeman's cottage'.[2973] By 1879 Streatham had become an inspector's station, under the overall command of Superintendent William Wiseman. W Division at that time was comprised of Brixton, Clapham, Croydon, Streatham, Mitcham, Sutton, Banstead, Tooting and Carshalton.[2974] In the animated picture below you can clearly see the old station at Streatham on the left-hand side. It is a typical Victorian two-storey police station, with two chimneys.

Streatham Police Station 1868-1912

A report in 1881 stated that the men use the kitchen at Streatham Police Station as a mess room, the clothes room as a sitting room and the married and single quarters were mixed. The accommodation housed one married inspector, one married sergeant and eleven single constables. All of these issues were unsatisfactory. In addition, the report stated that the public could see into the cell passage and 'sometimes give trouble'.[2975]

In 1884 the address of Streatham Police Station was shown as High Road, Streatham.[2976] By 1891, with Clapham still on W Division, Superintendent S.T. Lucas was in charge, assisted by Sub-Divisional Inspector J. Janes and Inspector Worth.[2977]

Streatham's first mounted officer was Police Constable 759W Edward Jeffrey, who joined the Police in 1902 and then resigned through ill-health in 1918 with 'traumatic arthritis of wrist'. He died in 1939.[2978]

In August 1908 the freehold of the Streatham Old Branch Post Office was purchased for £2,000, with a view to rebuilding the police station situated at the corner of Streatham High Road and Shrubbery Road. In October 1909 Commissioner Sir Edward Henry, in a memorandum to the Receiver, informed him that the question of rebuilding the police station was a pressing one, as the current building was no longer adequate for the important and growing district in which it was situated. The existing station had been built 40 years before, when Streatham was just a village. The population had grown from 33,000 in 1901 to 60,000 in 1909, and the station was sited on the main London to Brighton road. It received many callers and, as there was no waiting room, chaos often reigned in the Front Office. In short, the present building was too small for present-day requirements and the rebuilding could no longer be delayed.

Streatham Police Station 1912-2013

The new station designed by John Dixon Butler, the Metropolitan Police Surveyor, was completed in two stages. The administrative part was opened for business in July 1912[2979] and the new Police Section House was ready for occupation in April 1913. Residential accommodation was provided for 30 single men at 1/- per week each. There were also two sets of married quarters. The building was designed as a cube over three storeys. At the third floor level the stone cornice was used to create a large stone pediment as a simple decorative device on the three visible sides of the building. The address was 101 High Road, Streatham, SW16. There was a commemorative foundation stone by the main door in Shrubbery Road.[2980] During the rebuilding, the day-to-day business was conducted from a temporary police station in the old Post Office at the rear of the premises.[2981]

In 1928 Superintendent Charles R. Clark was in charge of W Division. Streatham Police Station and ten other stations were under his command.[2982]

Following the revision of Police boundaries in 1931,

Streatham was transferred from W (Brixton) Division to Z (Croydon) Division. Streatham was the Sub-Divisional Station, with Gipsy Hill as its Sectional Station. Sub-Divisional Inspector Murrells was transferred from Gipsy Hill to Streatham.[2983]

In 1963 it was decided to acquire additional land at Streatham to provide a new site for the station to be built between the years 1966 and 1970, so land to the rear of 103-113 Streatham High Road was purchased freehold for the sum of £5000 in January 1964.[2984]

The revision of local authority boundaries in 1965 moved Streatham and its Sectional Station from Z to L Division, in the London Borough of Lambeth.[2985]

The police station was closed in 2013, and in 2015 sold for £4,249M.[2986]

Sunbury Police Station

The London Borough of Hillingdon

10 Thames Street, Sunbury (1840-1892)

189 Staines Road, Sunbury (1892-1998)

V Division (1840-1864)

T Division (1864-1985/86)

Staines /Spelthorne Division /OCU (1985/86-1998)

The Metropolitan Police Force was extended to its present limits by virtue of the Metropolitan Police Act 1839. No. 10 Thames Street, Sunbury (previously called 'Belle View') was acquired from Monday, 13th January 1840 as a sectional police station under the Kingston Sub-Division, and part of V or Wandsworth Division. The station, held on a yearly tenancy from a Mr Roe of Brentford, was described as a brick-and-tile built house with a two-stall stable, two cells, a small rear garden, and eight rooms in all. The landlord was responsible for all rates and taxes.[2987]

There were 21 constables and four sergeants working from Sunbury, deployed as follows: three constables in Teddington (housed privately), three constables in Hampton (housed in section house), two constables in Hampton Court (housed privately), two constables in Hampton Wick (housed privately), three constables in Feltham and Feltham Hill (housed privately), one constable at Hanworth (housed privately) one constable in Ashford (housed privately).[2988]

There were two sergeants, six constables and two horse patrol sergeants housed in the section house at Sunbury Police Station, on Thames Street, who patrolled Sunbury and Upper Halliford. The early police constables were former parish constables and were not used to the discipline of the New Police. Many were dismissed from the force, such as Constable Daniel Brian, dismissed on 22nd February 1840 'for being drunk and assaulting Mr J Turner Esq of Sunbury and other misconduct'; on 30th March 1840 Constable Charles Smith and Constable Thomas Yates were released 'for being in The Goat public house Upper Halliford at 2am and tossing for gin and water when on duty'.[2989] In August 1840 Constable Francis Masters was 'convicted by the Staines magistrates and committed for 21 days' hard labour for attempting to stab his sergeant when drunk'.[2990] The sergeant was likely to have been 31-year-old Robert Graham McIntyre from Perthshire, who resided at the station with his wife, a local lady from Sunbury, and their three children in 1851.[2991]

The police station at Sunbury is shown in 1842 as being part of V or Wandsworth Division,[2992] and by 1844 it was designated a sergeant station.[2993]

The distribution of the Force in Police Orders 11th January 1864 again shows Sunbury as a station of V Division, however due to the formation of three new Divisions Sunbury was transferred to T or Kensington Division.[2994]

The house had been altered to provide two cells, two stables, eight rooms and a small back garden. Officers based there covered Teddington, all the Hamptons, Feltham and Hanworth. This was not a suitable arrangement, as the premises were cramped and unsuitable. Records show that in 1861 30-year-old Sergeant Charles Simpkins from Walton-on-Thames, his wife and three children resided at Sunbury Police Station. Five unmarried constables, all under 23 years old, also resided at the station.[2995] In 1864 a sergeant was in charge with three constables by day, whilst during the hours of darkness an acting sergeant and twelve constables patrolled.[2996]

At Christmas 1875 the station was taken on a five-year lease from the landlord, who was now a E.R. Fisher Esq of Farncombe, Guildford at a rate of £35 per annum. The Receiver of the Metropolitan Police District had to pay all rates, taxes and repairs.[2997]

In 1881 an inspection of Sunbury stated that it was a dilapidated station and in urgent need of replacement, although plans were already underway to find a site on which to build a purpose-built police station in the area.

In June 1880 Home Office approval had been given for the purchase of a site at 189 Staines Road for the sum of £300 from a Mr. Baker. The new station was taken into use accordingly,[2998] and immediately upgraded to an inspector-supervised

2965 John Back Archive (1975).
2966 *The Job*, 13th April 1990
2967 Fido, M. and Skinner, K. (1999) *The Official Encyclopedia of Scotland Yard*.
2968 www.met.police.uk/contact/phone.htm accessed 12th March 2002.
2969 MPS (2018) Freedom of Information request: MPS Assets.
2970 Metropolitan Police Orders dated 28th October 1865.
2971 John Back Archive (1975).
2972 Metropolitan Police Surveyor's Records.
2973 Metropolitan Police Orders dated 17th July 1868.
2974 *Post Office London Directory* 1879.
2975 Report on the Condition of Police Stations 1881.
2976 Metropolitan Police Orders dated 20 June 1884.
2977 *Kelly's Sydenham, Norwood and Streatham Directory* 1891.
2978 Metropolitan Police Archive.
2979 Metropolitan Police Orders dated 26th July 1912.
2980 Planning Committee. Chief Executive Office, Lambeth 7th December 1999.
2981 John Back Archive (1975).
2982 *Post Office London Directory* 1928.
2983 Metropolitan Police Orders dated 9th October 1931.
2984 John Back Archive (1975).
2985 Metropolitan Police Orders dated 6th August 1964.
2986 Metropolitan Police Information Rights Unit 22nd October 2017, accessed 25th January 2019.
2987 Brown, B. (1987) Private correspondence to Mr Hayes architect of 10 Thames Street (The old police station).
2988 Ibid.
2989 Ibid.
2990 Ibid.
2991 Census 1851
2992 *Kelly's Directory* 1842 p1042.
2993 *Kelly's Directory* 1844 p1373.
2994 Metropolitan Police Orders dated 28th October 1875 and 'Sunbury Station History' in John Back Archive (1975).
2995 Census 1861.
2996 Metropolitan Police Special Police Orders 1st January 1864.
2997 Metropolitan Police Orders dated 28th October 1875 and 'Sunbury Station History' in John Back Archive (1975).
2998 Metropolitan Police Orders dated 23rd December 1882.

Sunbury Police Station 1882-1998

The well and parade shed in the yard at Sunbury

station.[2999] The old building was used as an occasional courthouse for some time after the present Sunbury Police Station in Staines Road East opened at Christmas, 1882.[3000]

Police officers were housed in rented accommodation all over the areas covered by the sections and sub-divisions, and there would be little doubt that much of their work was done from home as they could hardly be expected to walk to and from their stations every day. There were only a couple of horses available in each area; a stables with a flat above were built at the Victorian Staines Police Station, which was later turned into stores and canteen, and can still be seen by the rear gates in the photograph below. A stable building in the rear yard at Sunbury was demolished when horses were phased out, and room was needed for vehicles to drive in and out. In the nineteenth century and into the early years of the twentieth, a sergeant – or possibly an inspector – lived in at the police station together with a few constables. They and their families had just two rooms, if they were lucky. The constables' wives were expected to do all the cleaning and chores, and allotments were provided at the rear to provide fresh vegetables. Water had to be carried from the yard, and the toilets were of course outside.

responsible to the Sub-Divisional Inspector at Hampton, Thomas Neal. Constable James Watson and family, Constable Edward Rudge and family also lived at Sunbury Police Station in 1901. In 1911 alterations were made to the station.

At the end of WWI a commemoration photograph (below) was taken outside Sunbury Police Station to mark the end of hostilities, and this is shown below. At the back, from left to right, are constables Newman, Fry, Baker and Judd. Next row forward (L-R) are constables Hitchcock, Newnham, Smith, Archer, Axleton, Strutt, George and Adams. The next row forward (L-R) Constable Cookie, Acting Sergeant (APS) Porter, an unidentified sergeant, Sergeant Muggeridge, Station Sergeants Newman and Barnard, Sergeant Bligh, APS Clapham, Constable Proops. Seated on the ground (L-R) constables Chambleton, Titheridge, Kennough and Budmead.

Sunbury Police Station strength celebrating the end of the War in 1919

A building in the rear yard of the station

In 1891 Constable Jabez Lamb and his family lived at the police station. Also resident at the same time were constable James Watson and family. The officer in charge was Irishman Inspector James Donnolly, who also lived there in 1891 with his wife Kate and two children.

In 1894 Maurice Elms was an inspector at Sunbury,

In 1921 the premises next door at 187 Staines Road was purchased with a large area of land. Two sets of quarters were built to accommodate married officers and their families. Further land was purchased freehold in 1936.

In due course the Commissioner announced certain police station closures, often an unpopular move. Accordingly, Bedfont and Sunbury Stations were closed at 6.00am on Wednesday, 1st June 1932, and all business transferred to Harlington and Staines stations respectively.[3001] This caused a furious outrage, with members of Sunbury-on-Thames Urban District Council making representations on 25th April 1932 to the Deputy Commissioner, the Hon. Sir Trevor Bigham, at Scotland Yard. A further deputation from the Council was seen by the Commissioner, Air Vice Marshall Sir Philip Game, on 15th July 1937. Questions were asked in the House of Commons by the local Member of Parliament, Sir Reginald Blaker, on 15th April 1932 regarding the closure of Sunbury Police Station, with the Home Secretary replying that the area, as far as he was aware, was adequately policed.[3002]

A retirement group at Sunbury circa 1910

The station was later altered into two sets of married quarters (from three), with one dwelling on the first floor for an inspector and one on the ground floor for a constable.

Although the station was closed to the public for business, certain rooms to the rear were used by the local police for parading and refreshment purposes. Office accommodation was also used by members of the Special Constabulary. A police box was erected in the front entrance lobby of the station for the use by the public.

In 1965 the two sets of married quarters were taken out of use altogether. Alterations were made to the interior, and an extension was built on the side of the station at the cost of £14,000. The station was re-opened for police business as a sectional station on 11th January 1966.

The station remained in use until after 1992, but shut in 1998. It was transferred to the Surrey Constabulary in 2000.

Surbiton (Tolworth) Police Station

1 Ditton Road, Tolworth (1888-1974)

299 Ewell Road (1974-1993)

V Division (1888-1985/86)

Kingston Division /OCU (1985/86-1993)

London Borough of Kingston BCU (1993-2011)

The Portsmouth Road, which had been turnpiked by the Surrey & Sussex Trust in 1718, boasted no fewer than six stagecoach services on the Portsmouth to London route serving Kingston, bearing such colourful names as The Independent, The Economist, The Rocket, The Regulator, The Nelson and of course The Royal Mail.

Although, Kingston parish was beyond the Metropolitan Police District until 1840, the area had, since 1805, been patrolled by the Bow Street horse-patrols, who had stations situated on Robin Hood Hill, Kingston Market and Ditton Marsh. These were placed under the jurisdiction of the Metropolitan Police as part of V Division in October 1836.

The horse patrol constables were each paid four shillings daily. They wore a uniform consisting of blue trousers with blue double-breasted greatcoat bearing yellow metal buttons over a scarlet waistcoat, wellington boots with steel spurs, and tall black leather hat. To complete the uniform, the protective leather stocks were available as a guard against garrotting. Not all of the uniform was provided free. The spurs, greatcoat and hats had to be paid for out of the patrolmen's wages.

A horse harness and loaded pistol completed the equipment. Although the pistol was supplied, no officially-sanctioned means of carrying spare ammunition was available until pouches were added to the saddles from December 1852.[3003]

The parish constable of Kingston at that time was Mr. R.W. Cooke.[3004]

When V or Wandsworth Division was formed in May 1830 it came no nearer to Kingston-upon-Thames than the parish boundary on Putney Heath. The old stagecoaches gradually dwindled after the opening of the London & Southampton Railway from Nine Elms to Woking Common on 21st May 1838, with intermediate stations at Esher and Kingston. The latter was, in fact, some distance from Kingston-upon-Thames, in the hamlet of Surbiton, and was renamed Surbiton & Kingston station in July 1863, after Kingston received its own branch the same year. A further branch, at first horse-drawn, opened to Hampton Court serving Thames Ditton in 1849.

V Division stretched at that time as far east as Vauxhall Bridge until cut back to Battersea in October 1865, the whole of which was at that time in the parish of Surrey. The roads through Surbiton prior to the introduction of Turnpike Trusts were, for most of the winter months, virtually impassable. The first road to be turnpiked west of Kingston was built by the Great Kingston Trust to Petersfield in 1749, who erected a toll-gate at Sandown Farm.[3005]

This was followed by the Epsom Trust in 1755, who erected a toll-gate at Talworth Court (as spelt), and finally, in 1811, the Leatherhead Trust erected a toll-gate in Hook Road at its junction with Ditton Road by The Maypole public house. In order to stop the evasion of tolls, the Epsom Trust erected a new toll-house and gate on the corner of Ewell Road/Ditton Road. After the turnpike system was given up in 1883, the site was purchased by the Metropolitan Police on 22nd May 1886.

A communication dated 15th December 1885 was received from the Secretary of State for the Home Department, authorising the Receiver to purchase a freehold plot of land in the Ewell Road, Surbiton from Mr. M. Bryant for the sum of £640, for the purpose of building a police station. The freehold title to land was obtained by the Receiver, and the transaction was completed on 22nd May 1886. In the meantime, plans were drawn up for the new police station and when built cost £3,107 15s 5d.[3006]

The station finally opened on 7th December 1888, its telegraphic station code being 'SA'; Kingston was 'KT' and Ditton 'DT'. The new station was on V or Wandsworth Division, and had been ready for occupation on 28th August,[3007] however there was a delay in the building since it was not occupied for police purposes until 10th December. As was usual, the Receiver stipulated what rent was due to the Commissioner by the occupants of the accommodation in order that this would be taken from their weekly pay. The married inspector

2999 *Kelly's Directory* 1881 p1909.
3000 Whitling, D. (1999) 'A History of Policing in Spelthorne', Metropolitan Police.
3001 Metropolitan Police Orders dated 30th May 1932.
3002 'Sunbury Station History' in John Back Archive (1975).
3003 www.eppingforestdc.gov.uk/Library/Leisure/MUSEUM/collections/PEELERSPROGRESS.pdf accessed 9th February 2012.
3004 Ibid.
3005 Metropolitan Police Correspondence.
3006 'Surbiton Police Station' in John Back Archive (1975).
3007 Metropolitan Police Orders dated 23rd August 1888.

Surbiton Police Station 1888-1974

was charged 5s 6d, whilst the married constable paid just 3s. The station was built on the site at 1 Ditton Road, Tolworth together with two sets of married quarters.[3008]

In 1891 Inspector Robert McFadden was in charge of Tolworth Police Station, as it was then called. He was supported by another inspector, William Pickett, three sergeants and 19 constables.[3009]

The 1907 *Kelly's Directory of Surrey* shows that Surbiton had three station sergeants, four sergeants and 30 constables, but unfortunately does not name the officers in charge, as it does at Winters Bridge, Ditton which was in the charge of Station Sergeant Willie Tilby, who had three sergeants and 20 constables under him. Included as part of the Kingston Sub-Division was Molseley (opened as 'MY' in September 1902) and Epsom ('EM'), the latter being transferred to W Division in February 1921, when Z Division was formed.

Rear aspect of Tolworth (Surbiton) Police Station c1908

The new Kingston bypass, now known as the A3, opened through Tolworth and Hook in 1929, bringing with it suburban development. New railway stations served the new communities at Hinchley Wood (1930), Berrylands (1933), Tolworth (1939) and Chessington North and South (1939). There was a fixed point box located at Surbiton railway station on land owned by the Surbiton Urban District Council.[3010]

This was replaced in December 1930 by a telephone box located inside the station yard. Southern Railway did not insist on any rent from the police for the purpose. Surbiton finally became a separate borough in 1936, the same time as neighbouring Malden and Coombe.

Police boxes were introduced throughout Kingston Sub-Division in March 1931, and this more efficient means of communication finally led to the closure of Ditton Police Station two years later. Kingston had been the V Division headquarters, but in July 1935 this was moved to Putney.

The Surrey Constabulary had only been formed in 1851. In that year white coal posts had been erected about 16 miles around the metropolis bearing the City of London arms, which were re-sited at the MPD boundary a decade later.

One of these posts, at the former turnpike at Sandown Park, was part of a series extending from the Thames at Sunbury over to the MPD boundary on Erith Marshes in Kent, ceased to be the extent of V Division in April 1947, when the Esher and Cobham sections were transferred to the Metropolitan Police from Surrey. The former urban district has, since 1974, been part of Elmbridge, and since 1980 part of Kingston Sub-Division.

Police officers and their families still lived at the station up until the 1950s. Constable David Osborne and his wife Barbara resided there for nine years in 1954. Their daughter aged two years moved in with them, and in 1959 their son Richard was born there. They lived on the top floor. Constable Osborne worked at the station in the administration unit for a while, but also worked at Esher and Kingston – not moving far.[3011]

One notable officer who was stationed at Surbiton was Detective Sergeant Ray Purdy, who was killed on duty in the 1950s by Gunter Podola, a burglar who he had arrested for blackmail. It was a notebook which Purdy had taken from Podola that eventually led to his arrest and conviction. Constable Osborne and his family knew Ray Purdy well, and it was a shocking event to happen for all police officers, as many of them face danger and sometimes pay the ultimate price. Podola was sentenced to death and was hanged at Wandsworth in 1959. Purdy was given a service funeral paid for by the police. Purdy's widow lived at Berrylands Road, Surbiton, and there was a call to grant Mrs Purdy a special grant in recognition of the price paid by her husband in the line of duty. She was awarded £10 10s 8d per week, and this included a special allowance for her two children who had lost their father.[3012]

On 9th May 1962 Surbiton saw the very last trolleybus route to operate in London. This route, the 601 from Twickenham to Tolworth, had a direct replacement in the present bus route 281.

In 1965 there was a revision of boundaries within the Metropolitan Police District because of the municipal boundary changes. Surbiton (VS) was designated a sub-divisional station, with East Molesey (VE), Esher (VH) and Cobham (VC) as its sectional stations situated in Esher (Surrey).[3013]

In April 1968 Surbiton acquired its own traffic garage in Hollyfield Road, although V District had been the first to be abolished in 1985 when the area was split between the two divisions of Kingston and Wimbledon. Surbiton then became part of the new No. 5 (South West) Area on Kingston Division, which changed its code letters from 'VD' to 'VK'.

Discussions had taken place during the 1970s as to the urgency of rebuilding Surbiton Police Station, however difficulties were being encountered in acquiring adjacent properties or land to the existing station. The plan was to build a much bigger police station, with all the equipment necessary for policing, such as computerisation. There was a lack of suitable space where a much larger new sub-divisional station could be built.

Surbiton Police Station 1977-2012

Because of financial cutbacks the project was shelved in 1974, and temporary accommodation was sought in the vicinity of the existing station. In the meantime, the freehold of Old St Matthew's School, 299 Ewell Road, Surbiton was obtained in July 1974' which was about 100 yards away from the old station. Building works to adapt the school house for police purposes was started, costing £120,000,[3014] although this took longer than anticipated and the new station was not opened until the end of December 1977, with a police order that stated;

'On 19th December, a new (temporary) sectional Police Station will be opened at Surbiton (VS). The address of the new Station is 299 Ewell Road Surbiton, Telephone numbers will remain unaltered.' [3015]

The station was much bigger, with plenty of space, although it had been a purpose-built school.

In 1980 there were further re-organisations to V District, which reduced the divisions from three to two when Kingston and Esher Divisions were amalgamated. The new division was known as Kingston Division, and incorporated New Malden, Esher, Cobham, Surbiton and East Molesey Sub-Divisions. There was no change to the sub-divisional boundaries or the contact telephone numbers.[3016]

From 2000 Surbiton was subject to restricted opening hours under a review by the Metropolitan Police Authority of police station opening times.[3017] This situation lasted until 2012, when Surbiton was opened Mondays to Fridays from 10.00am until 6.00pm, being closed on Saturdays and Sundays.[3018]

Surbiton Police Station was shut in 2011 and the building put up for sale.[3019] It was sold in December 2011 the building was sold for £1.5M to a property developer.[3020] A police office in Ewell Road has been opened instead.

Sutton Police Station

The London Borough of Sutton

84 High Street, Sutton (1854-1906) (sold 1908)

1 (later no. 6) Carshalton Road, Sutton (1906-2020)

P Division (1854-1888)

W Division (1888-1965)

Z Division (1965-1985/86)

Epsom Division (1985/86-1993/94)

Epsom & Sutton OCU (1993/94-2018/19)

South Area BCU SN (from 2018/19)

Sutton village, which lies between the Green and the north end of the High Street and the parish church, was transformed when the main Brighton Road passed through the High Street between 1775 and 1809. The coming of the railway in 1847 added to the expansion saw it grow from a village with a population of 1,304 in 1841 into a town which by 1881 had 10,334 residents.[3021]

3008 Metropolitan Police Surveyor's Records 1924.
3009 *Kelly's Directory* 1891.
3010 Metropolitan Police Surveyor's Records 1924.
3011 *London Police Pensioner* No. 114, September 2004.
3012 hansard.millbanksystems.com/written_answers/1959/jul/23/detective-sergeant-r-purdy accessed 27th April 2012.
3013 'Surbiton Police Station' in John Back Archive (1975).
3014 'New Home Opens', *The Job*, 6th January 1978.
3015 Metropolitan Police Orders dated 16th December 1977.
3016 Metropolitan Police Orders dated 1st February 1980.
3017 Metropolitan Police Authority (2000) Police Station Opening Hours Committee; MPA Reports 9th November.
3018 www.allinlondon.co.uk/directory/1252/101922.php accessed 14th February 2012.
3019 www.surbitonpeople.co.uk/Surbiton-Police-Station-grabs/story-13312500-detail/story.html accessed 14th February 2012.
3020 MPS Freedom of information request (2018) Police Station Closures by Year Since 2010.
3021 Pevsner, N and Cherry, B. (1983) *London. 2: South*. Penguin, Harmondsworth p654.

In 1827 there was a station of the Second Division of the Bow Street Horse Patrol at Sutton. The Patrol was formed in 1805, and policed the main turnpike roads in and out of London. It came under the jurisdiction of the Bow Street Magistrates, and complemented the famous Bow Street Runners and Foot Patrols which operated in the central area.

The Receiver purchased a site at 84 High Street, Sutton in 1852 for the erection a police station, which was finally built and ready for occupation in 1854.[3022] In 1864 Sutton Police Station formed part of P or Camberwell Division. It was a Sectional Station of Carshalton Sub-Division, and was split into two beats.

Sutton Police Station 1854-1908

The strength was two sergeants, eleven constables and one horse. The Mounted Sergeant had to perform three hours' duty at the station, and patrol on horse or foot for nine hours a day; he also had to look after his horse.[3023]

On the formation of three new divisions – W or Clapham, X or Paddington, and Y or Highgate, Sutton was one of several stations transferred to form the new W Division.[3024]

Between 1877 and 1882 Inspector Walter Goodall was posted in charge of the station.[3025] By 1897 Inspector Walter Northover was in charge.[3026]

In October 1886 the Superintendent of W Division drew attention to the inconveniences and inadequate facilities at Sutton Police Station. His report in August 1887 stated that the station was small and cramped, and must, at no distant date, be reconstructed or rebuilt. In September 1894 certain modifications, especially to the drainage system, were carried out. By March 1905 the situation had become acute, and the Home Office forwarded a letter to the Commissioner from the Receiver recommending that additional ground, space or a new site should be acquired with a view to the provision of a new police station for Sutton.[3027]

If the station was small and cramped, then the fact that Inspector William Holdaway, his wife Emily, their six children aged between 1 year and 20 years, one married constable and five single constables were all living at the station must have caused the superintendent to request larger premises.[3028] Further staffing at the station consisted of five sergeants and 48 constables in 1891.[3029]

On 29th June 1905 a letter was received from the Secretary of State at the Home Office approving the purchase of a freehold property known as 'Sutton Court', at a price not exceeding £2,650, as a site for a new police station at Sutton. The purchase was completed on 10th October 1905. On 29th August 1906 the Home Office sanctioned the sale of a portion of this Police site at Sutton, facing Sutton Court Road, to the Surrey Standing Joint Committee for the sum of £800. This parcel of land was required for the provision of a courthouse for the use of the Justices of the Epsom Division.[3030]

Sutton Police Station 1908-2004

The new police station at 1 Carshalton Road, Sutton was open for business in December 1908. The lodging assessment at married quarters at the station was one set of quarters at 10s per week and another set of quarters at 4s 6d a week. The ten unmarried men were each charged one shilling a week each.[3031]

The old police station was sold in 1908 to Dendy Napper, miller and corn merchant, who had a shop next door to the old premises. In fact, behind the old station stood a windmill, which later became Napper's steam flour mills. After purchasing the old station he extended his shop across the front of the old building.[3032]

The boundaries of P, W and Z Divisions were revised in October 1931. Thornton Heath Station was closed, and Streatham and Wallington Stations were transferred from W to Z. Sutton was designated a sub-divisional station of W Division, with Epsom and Banstead as its sectional stations.[3033] At the time Sub-Divisional Inspector S.C. Lawrence was in charge of the station.[3034]

In October 1933 notification was received at Sutton Police Station from the local authority that in future the address of the premises would change from No. 1 to No. 6 Carshalton Road West.[3035]

By 1936 the station was in need of refurbishment due to the wear and tear of the previous twenty-eight years; this was duly carried out.

With the reorganisation of local authority boundaries in 1965, Sutton (ZT) was designated a sub-divisional station of Z Division with Wallington (ZW) as its Sectional Station, both being situated in the new London Borough of Sutton.[3036]

In 1975 the United Reformed Church in Carshalton Road was bought by Police for £130,000 to be used for future extension to the police station next door. It was immediately demolished, for short term use as a Police car park.[3037]

Between 1980 and 1983 the station call sign was Zulu Tango (ZT).[3038]

With effect from January 1980, Epsom and Sutton Divisions were amalgamated. The new division was known as Epsom Division, with its headquarters at Epsom Police Station. Sutton Police Station was re-designated a sub-divisional, but retained charging facilities.[3039]

In 1988 the station was given a £650,000 facelift. An

outbuilding was demolished, and a new two-storey extension built to accommodate staff.[3040]

It was decided that a new police station was necessary and planning permission was sought and given in 1996, but the finances were just not available to go ahead at this stage. It was two years later that tenders to build were invited.[3041] Whilst all this was taking place, a group of conservationists campaigned to save the old Sutton Police Station, a Grade II-listed building. Their campaign, together with the need for additional local authority accommodation, saved the building and a new police station was built next to the old one.

The new Sutton Police Station was built under the Public Financial Initiative (PFI), and was officially opened in March 2004 by Commissioner Sir John Stevens and the Borough Police Commander, Joe Royle. The new station has much better accommodation for staff, and includes 30 cells and a state-of-the-art Custody Suite for dealing with prisoners. At the opening Sir John said:

"The new police station will provide improved facilities for officers and also a more pleasant environment for members of the public who visit." [3042]

The new station building is dedicated to Police Constable Patrick Dunne, who sadly died in 1993 having been shot and killed when responding to a report of gunfire in Clapham. His name on the front of the building is a fitting memorial to this brave officer.

Sutton Police Station 2003 to present

In 2010, Sutton Police Station was open 24 hours a day.[3043] In 2013 Cross Point House was opened as a contact point for the public.

Sydenham Police Station

The London Borough of Lewisham

Dartmouth Road (1848-1966)

179 Dartmouth Road (1966-2013)

P Division (1848-1985/86)

Catford Division (1985/86-2000)

Lewisham OCU (2000-2013)

A police station was erected at Sydenham in 1848 at a cost of £1,231 3s 10d.[3044] The landlord at the time was Robert Harrild of Sydenham, and the lease was from 1848 for a period of 75 years, at £10 per annum.[3045] The plans were drawn up and signed by Charles Reeves, Metropolitan Police Surveyor.[3046]

In a letter dated 11th February 1853, Home Office authority was given to purchase a site for £350 if the Crystal Palace Co. would build a station and the Receiver rent it, but this was not acceptable for the firm. Eventually a plot of land was leased

Sydenham Police Station 1848-1966

near Crystal Palace from a Mr Nicholls on a 99-year lease, at £16 10s per annum. Home Office authority was granted in January 1854, and there was an estimated outlay of £2,080 for the building.[3047]

In June 1855 John Thomas Fox, aged 21 years, joined the Metropolitan Police as a constable. His warrant number was 33705. As warrants issued started at No. 1 in 1829, you can see just how many officers had joined the Metropolitan Police Force since its inception. Fox had been recommended by submitting testimonials as a suitable candidate from a Mr John Scott of Limehouse and a Mr J. Harris. By 1861 Fox was living in Brockley Lane, Sydenham with his wife and four children.

In 1871 Fox, now a Police Sergeant, was living at the Sydenham Police Station with his wife and three of their children. There were also ten constables and one prisoner, a 67-year-old female named Mary Alden.

Writing in his diary at about this time, Sergeant Fox recorded the following:

"19.1.1877 – Apprehended a woman for highway robbery."

3022 Letter to R.P. Smith from Metropolitan Police, 24th December 1858.
3023 Metropolitan Police Orders dated 11th January 1864.
3024 Metropolitan Police Orders dated 28th October 1865.
3025 *Kelly's Directories* 1877-1882.
3026 *Pile's Sutton Streets Directory* 1897.
3027 MEPO 2/347.
3028 Census 1891.
3029 *Kelly's Directory* 1891.
3030 LB 696.
3031 Metropolitan Police Orders dated 5th December 1908.
3032 Berry P. *Sutton in Old Photographs* 1994.
3033 Metropolitan Police Orders dated 9th October 1931.
3034 Pile's Directory: Sutton and District 1931.
3035 LB 696.
3036 Metropolitan Police Orders dated 6th August 1964.
3037 *Wallington & Carshalton Times*, 12th June 1975.
3038 MEPO 14.
3039 Metropolitan Police Orders dated 28th December 1979.
3040 *Sutton Guardian*, 4th August 1888.
3041 *Sutton & Banstead Independent*, 11th February 1898.
3042 *Sutton Post*, 24th March 1904.
3043 www.met.police.uk accessed 10th October 2010.
3044 MEPO 2/26.
3045 MEPO 4/234.
3046 London Metropolitan Archives MBO/Plans 140.
3047 MEPO 5/3 (10).

This was at a time when robbers on horseback terrorised the lanes and byways of Sydenham. Other entries in the diary showed monetary awards made to him between 1860 and 1878. One such reads:

"2/6d Stopping a man with 15 fowls."

Fox was promoted to Inspector (3rd Class) in August 1878, when station sergeants were upgraded. He then retired on a pension of £76 in 1881.

By 1864 there were two sergeants and 17 constables posted to Sydenham Police Station, which was then shown as being on R Division. The inspector at Lewisham Police Station had the responsibility for patrolling and supervising Sydenham, Beckenham, Bromley and Farnborough Police Stations. The mounted sergeants at Sydenham, Beckenham, Bromley and Farnborough were each to patrol, either on horse or on foot, for at least nine hours out of every 24, and care for the welfare of their horses.[3048]

Sydenham then became part of P Division in 1865,[3049] and later became the Sub-Division which was responsible for Sydenham, Lewisham and part of Penge. An Inspector Ings was placed in charge of the station and directed to ride the horse belonging to the sergeant, who became dismounted.[3050]

In 1881 there was a report which criticised the cramped conditions of the station. It also drew attention to the unsanitary condition of the inspector's quarters, himself and his family (six persons) having to sleep in one room.[3051]

The address of the station was 114 High Street, Sydenham,[3052] and the freehold of the premises was purchased in February 1890. It was at about this time that Inspector J. Broadbridge was the inspector.[3053] Inspector Swan was there in 1935,[3054] and by January 1937 the address of the station had been changed to 179 Dartmouth Road.

In April 1941, during World War II, the shop next door to the station was completely destroyed and the station badly damaged by a parachute mine.[3055] Police Constable 115732 Charles Henry Moore, formerly 463C and later to become 463P, was on duty and killed in this incident.[3056] Moore lived at 4 Trilby Road, Forest Hill, London and was pronounced dead at South East Hospital Mortuary. The picture below shows PC Moore posing in his garden in full uniform (without duty armlet).

Constable Charles Henry Moore killed by parachute mine in 1941

There were five other casualties as well.[3057] The police station was then closed for business due to the damage, and work was transferred to a temporary station at 'The Towers', Sydenham Rise.[3058] The repaired station reopened for business in October 1947.[3059] In January 1948 the freehold was purchased for 181 Dartmouth Road so that the station could be extended.[3060]

In 1950 the Receiver purchased the freehold of sites in Willow Way in order to erect married quarters. On 31st March 1960 more freehold sites were purchased, thus forming the nucleus of the police station, section house and married quarters. Finally, in June 1964 an exchange of lands was completed with the Church Authorities to adjust the boundary where it adjoined Holy Trinity Hall.[3061]

In April 1965, under the new local authority boundaries, Sydenham and Lee Road became Sectional Stations to Catford Division.[3062]

The new Sydenham Police Station at 179 Dartmouth Road, designed by J. Innes-Elliott, was taken into operational use on 7th March 1966 and the old station was closed.[3063]

Sydenham Police Station 1966-2013

By 1980 Sydenham Station, together with Lee Road, had been reduced in status to a Police Office where a 24-hour public counter service only was provided. All administration and operational matters were then undertaken by the divisional station at Catford.[3064]

In 2013 the station was closed and the building sold for £1,455,000.[3065]

Teddington Police Station

The London Borough of Richmond
High Street Teddington (1873-1881)
Church Road, Teddington (1881-1998)
18 Park Road (1998 to Present)
T Division (1873-1985/86)
Richmond upon Thames Division / OCU TW
 (1985/86-2018/19)
South West BCU SW (from 2018/19)

In 1873 at station was situated at Teddington which was designated as being on T or Kensington Division, and Sergeant Edward Wilkins was in charge.[3066] Teddington remained a sergeant station until the late 1870s, when an inspector was placed in charge.

A new larger station at Church Road, Teddington was built in 1881, and with the promotion of more sergeants to inspector rank every station on T Division, including Teddington, became an inspector station.[3067] Upstairs was accommodation for the family of the inspector in charge of the station. The photograph below shows the rear of the station including a garden, where the inspector and his family were allowed to grow their own vegetables etc. The photograph below that shows another aspect of the station, which included a rounded elevated wall to the left of the station which was put in place to afford protection to the occupants either from Fenian bomb attacks or provide additional security.

In 1894 Teddington, together with Sunbury and Twickenham, were sectional stations to Hampton Sub-Division.[3068]

In 1924 Teddington Police Station was listed as a station on T or Hammersmith Division. It was located at 52 Church Road, Teddington, at the junction of Luther Road, and the freehold to the site had been purchased in 1880. The station had been built with two sets of married quarters, but a re-allocation of space meant that only one set was acceptable.[3069]

Above: Teddington Police Station 1881-1998, and Below: rear aspect c1908

A police call telephone – Box T28 – without air raid warning siren, was erected on 20th July 1936 at the junction with Kingston Road, 30 yards south of Bushey Park Road. It was removed in March 1970.[3070]

Teddington's protective wall against bombs

The photograph below shows a retirement of two police officers from Teddington Police Station. Each have been awarded two expensive ornate mantle clocks, which would have been purchased from contributions made by the officers and men of the sub-division. The sub-divisional inspector for Hampton, John Kempin, whose sub-divisional station was Teddington, presided over the retirement arrangements. Here he is seen with his flat cap standing behind the clock in the centre of the picture behind the two police officers who were retiring. Arrangements would have included the taking of this ceremonial photograph, which would have been presented to the officers later, together with the station band who would have played music. In the canteen food would have been prepared by the wives and daughters of the men to mark the occasion, with the likelihood that beer would have been consumed.

Teddington Police station retirement celebrations c1910

In 1932 Teddington became a sectional station to Twickenham together with a downgraded Hampton, which also lost its sub-divisional status.[3071] After WWII the headquarters of T Division became Ealing, and Teddington (TT) remained under the supervision of Superintendent A.R. Thomas.[3072]

A site had been purchased in 1950 at Park Road and Park Lane, on which there was an old building called Teddington Lodge which was demolished to make way for the new police station.[3073] The call sign of the station was 'TT' from 1960 until at least the mid-1980s.

3048 Metropolitan Police Orders dated 11th January 1864.
3049 Metropolitan Police Orders dated 28th October 1865.
3050 Metropolitan Police Orders dated 30th September 1869.
3051 Report on the Condition of Police Stations 1881.
3052 Metropolitan Police Orders dated 20th June 1884.
3053 *Kelly's Sydenham, Norwood & Streatham Directory* 1891.
3054 *Kelly's Sydenham & Forest Hill Directory* 1935.
3055 John Back Archive (1975).
3056 www.policememorial.org.uk accessed 19th August 2007.
3057 Home Office (1947) 'Metropolitan Police at War'.
3058 Metropolitan Police Orders dated 7th July 1941.
3059 Metropolitan Police Orders dated 3rd October 1947.
3060 John Back Archive (1975).
3061 Ibid.
3062 Metropolitan Police Orders dated 6th August 1964.
3063 Metropolitan Police Orders dated 4th March 1966.
3064 Metropolitan Police Orders dated March 1980.
3065 Metropolitan Police Information Rights Unit 22nd October 2017, accessed 25th January 2019.
3066 *Kelly's Directory* 1873.
3067 *Kelly's Directory* 1881.
3068 *Kelly's Directory* 1894
3069 Metropolitan Police Surveyor's Records 1924.
3070 Site Locations for Metropolitan Police Telephone boxes and telephone posts for V Division.
3071 *Kelly's Directory* 1932 p744.
3072 *The Police and Constabulary Almanac* 1946 p93.
3073 www.twickenham-museum.org.uk/tour_detail.asp?TourID=60 accessed 30th March 2012.

A new modern police station at 18 Park Road was built at Teddington and in 1998 was situated on 5 Area. This was a fully-operational station, with charging facilities under the Police and Criminal Evidence Act. No longer was Teddington a station on T Division, but was now located within the new Borough Operational Command Unit of Richmond-on-Thames. It was now sub-divisional station to Twickenham (the Borough Headquarters), where Borough Commander Chief Superintendent J. Hurst was in charge.[3074]

Teddington Police Station 1998 to present

In 2000 Teddington was subject of a review of police station opening times. which were restricted to Monday to Friday 9.00am until 5.00pm.[3075] By 2012 the opening hours of the station had been varied to 10.00am-5.00pm, Monday to Friday, and 11.00am-2.00pm on Saturdays.[3076]

In 2019 Teddington Police Station was still in police ownership.[3077]

Thamesmead Police Station

The London Borough of Greenwich
Tavy Bridge (1973-1987)
90 Tittmus Road (1987-1993)
R Division (1973-1985/86)
Woolwich Division (1985/86-1993/94)
Plumstead OCU (1993/94-2018/19)
South East BCU SE (from 2018/19)

By the 1960s London's housing problem had become critical and long-term solutions were needed. Launched by Sir William Fiske as the Woolwich-Erith Project it was funded by the Greater London Council in 1966. It had to overcome many obstacles such as pollution from the nearby sewage works, drainage and building on peat land.

The estate was built to house up to 60,000 residents, many taken from East end slum clearances and who had been housed in pre-fabricated buildings in nearby Belvedere. The Thamesmead Estate was built on Erith Marshes in the early 1960s, and is situated between Abbeywood and the Thames. The estate is a riverside development of high and low-rise blocks covering some 130 acres, and which effectively became a new town. Originally planned as a development of 100,000 people and dubbed 'the town of the 21st Century', the initial stages were built of pre-formed concrete blocks, which proved to be hard to maintain and prone to cause damp and condensation. Its name soon became synonymous with crime, disorder and a variety of other social problems.

The marsh was drained into a series of lakes that are inter-connected by a number of canals. The fishing is excellent and provides some measure of relief to the starkness of the early development. By the 1970s Thamesmead should have been completed, but by 1974 just 12,000 people were resident and the project was shelved temporarily. Eventually, after a re-think, the use of concrete was dropped, and the planners reverted to old 18th century brick, and the building of high-rise blocks was halted.

Today, Thamesmead is a town of more than 30,000 people and is still only half completed. In 1973 a second station or police office was established in South Thamesmead (RA), and shown as operating for Police purposes. This was located in the precinct at the Tavybridge Centre, but closed in 1987.

Thamesmead Police Station, Tavybridge Centre, 1973-1987

Another Thamesmead Police Station was opened as a new sub-divisional station with the designation RT in June 1987, and replaced two smaller stations in the area.[3078] The station was located at 90 Titmus Avenue.

The stations to close were Thamesmead (RA) and Titmuss Avenue (RT). These were a complex of portacabins as is shown below. There was a transfer of staff from Plumstead Police Station to the new building, and these consisted of the CID, Collator, Crime Desk, Scenes of Crime Officer, and also the Metropolitan Police Special Constabulary (MSC). Thamesmead Police Station is located within the London Borough of Greenwich.

Thamesmead Police Station, 90 Titmus Avenue, 1987-2010

In 2008 the station was still in use, and housed the Safer Neighbourhood Teams. In the same year the Neighbourhood Policing Team in the area was designated the Thameside Moorings Team and consisted of one sergeant, two constables and five police community support officers. They held regular drop-in surgeries at the nearby Thamesmead Leisure Centre.

In 2010 Thamesmead Police Station was closed and disposed of.[3079]

Thornton Heath Police Station

The London Borough of Croydon

80 Parchmore Road, Thornton Heath (1887-1931)

W Division (1887-1921)

Z Division (1921-1931)

The area of Thornton Heath developed in the late 19th Century, and with the increase in population there was a need for a police station to be built in that area. The freehold title to a site located in Thornton Heath was purchased in 1885, and Thornton Heath Police Station, consisting of a station and section house designed by John Butler, was opened on 5th November 1887[3080] at 80 Parchmore Road, on the junction with Heath Road. The cost of the freehold in 1885 was £400 and the erection of the building was £2,811. The architectural drawings held by National Archives are dated 1886.[3081]

The station was closed in October 1931[3082] when Norbury took responsibility for the area. In 1933 an internal police report looked at what should be done with the old station. They described it as a fairly large building, occupying a large site in a commanding corner position in a fairly good class neighbourhood. Part of the building was used as a section house for ten men and was still occupied. To convert the whole building into a section house was considered but there was doubt that it would justify the cost, but it certainly wasn't viable to retain the building as a section house for just ten men. The sale of the building and land would have raised a substantial sum of money, but the building was retained.

In July 1935 the then Metropolitan Police Architect and Surveyor, G. Mackenzie Trench, drew up plans to convert the building and land into a district traffic garage for 28 Police vehicles and suitable accommodation for Police staff, and it was re-opened on 10th August 1936 as 4 Area District Garage (DG4). When the new traffic patrols took to the road, a new batch of divisional numbers 767Z to 834Z were introduced.

After a period of closure again after the traffic officers moved out, the premises were re-opened in April 1990 to house Area Dog section and Territorial Support Group.[3083]

Tooting (and Lower or South Tooting) Police Station

The London Borough of Wandsworth

Lower Tooting (1842-1889)

204 Mitcham Road (1889-1939)

251 Mitcham Road (1939 to Present)

V Division (1842-1865)

W Division (1865-1993)

Borough of Wandsworth OCU (1993-2018/19)

SW BCU with Richmond, Kingston and Merton

(2018/19 to Present)

The earliest records for Tooting Police Station are shown in 1842, when a station located at Lower Tooting is recorded as having a sergeant in charge and being located on V or Wandsworth Division.[3084] The station was located at the Broadway, Lower Tooting, and the turning where the station was located was called Salvador. Both this station and that in the Broadway at Amen Corner have in the past been referred to as South Tooting Police Station.

In 1864 the station strength was shown as one sergeant and fourteen constables. Two horses were stabled at the station, with one being ridden alternately by the two station sergeants and the remaining horse, in the charge of either the mounted inspector or the sergeant, patrolled the neighbourhoods of Battersea, Merton and Tooting from Wandsworth.[3085] The shift system was different at Merton and Tooting, with both the acting sergeants and sergeants on section duties changing from night to day duties on a monthly basis.

In 1865 three new divisions were formed and Tooting moved to W or Clapham Division.[3086] The new landlord was George Houghton of 40 St. Johns Park Villas, Haverstock Hill, who leased them a building for 21 years from Michaelmas, 1870 at £45 per annum.

The status of the station was raised in 1881 when an inspector was placed in charge replacing the sergeants. Inspector Joseph Ashley, his wife and four children occupied the married quarters above the station, and three single constables lived in rooms nearby.[3087] Metropolitan Police Surveyors reported in the same year that it was occupied by one married inspector and three single constables. Additionally, they made the comment that this was

'a poor class of dwelling. Two cells have been built in the back yard. The arrangements of the occupation are very bad indeed. The men's ablution room is the women's wash-house. The men's bedroom door is opposite that of the Inspector's daughter.' [3088]

The address of the station was published as The Broadway, Lower Tooting.[3089] In 1889 the superintendent of the division was asked about any problems with cell space, and the two cells at Tooting were considered sufficient for current prisoner numbers.[3090]

Between 1881 and 1885 there was a significant push by the Commissioner to replace the sergeant-designated stations with those of inspectors, and whilst not completely successful the majority of stations had an inspector in charge. All the stations on W or Clapham Division were now inspector-designated, with the exception of Sanderstead which was too small for even a sergeant to be in charge; therefore a responsible constable was selected to take over. Tooting's call sign for the telegraph was Tango Golf (TG).

A new venue was being sought for a station because the old one was no longer suitable. A site a short distance away in Mitcham Road was found, and purchased by the Receiver at a cost of £480 in 1886.

Plans were drawn up for a station and tenders were put out for a builder. The station was built at a cost of £3,149 and came into service in May 1889.[3091] It was relatively small, and designed to accommodate about a dozen police officers. No longer called Lower Tooting, the name became Tooting Police Station and later the address was shown as 204 Mitcham Road.[3092] With the building of the new station there was a change in status. Tooting became a sectional station of Streatham, remained so until the 1920s.

3084   *Post Office Directory* 1842.
3085   Metropolitan Police Orders dated 11th January 1864.
3086   Metropolitan Police Orders dated 28th October 1865.
3087   Census 1881.
3088   Report on the Condition of Police Stations 1881.
3089   Metropolitan Police Orders dated 20th June 1884.
3090   Metropolitan Police Receiver's List 1888.
3091   Metropolitan Police Orders dated 25th May 1889.
3092   Metropolitan Police Surveyor's Records 1912.

Tooting Police Station 1889-1939

Tragic events occur from time to time, and the dangers of policing can become much more noticeable when a police officer is killed in the line of duty. In 1930 Tooting Constable Arthur Laws, who was on night duty, attempted to stop a stolen car that was being driven without lights when he was knocked down and killed.[3093]

The rear of the station showing the back gate and boundary wall

In 1937 Sub-Divisional Inspector A. Robertson DCM was the officer in charge of the sub-division, with Mitcham being a sectional station.[3094]

Changes in divisional station boundaries during the 1930s caused the Police to re-think the importance of the area, and plans were made to create a new much larger police station and divisional headquarters in Tooting, built on a substantial piece of land. A site 150 yards away was purchased in 1931, although a station and adjoining section house was not completed until 1939.[3095] Designed by G. Mackenzie Trench, Police Chief Architect and Surveyor, the new station was built to front two streets, Mitcham Road and Ascot Road.

Almost immediately the old station was put up for sale by local estate agents. The new station was built with a section house to accommodate 80 single officers plus stables, which were located in the basement, garages and administrative offices. Built with three canteens (senior officers', sergeants' and constables' dining rooms) to be served by one kitchen provided the architect with the problem of service and inter-communication. The problem was solved by placing the canteens in a row, and providing a continuous counter through each room. The new station was designed to provide the six police stations of the Borough of Wandsworth that made up W Division with headquarters support. The station was also built with 12 flats for married officers and their families.

In 1957 Chief Superintendent W.E. Davis was in charge of the whole division, assisted by Superintendent T. Evans as Staff Officer. The functions of the CID were also localised, with Detective Superintendent F. Close also being located within the headquarters station at Tooting. Normal day-to-day policing of Tooting Sub-Division was supervised by Superintendent J. Lawlor, who also took responsibility for Mitcham Police Section.[3096]

Tooting Police Station 1939 to present

In 2002 the station was open from 8.00am until 8.00pm, however by 2009 the hours had been extended until 11.00pm daily.[3097] By 2019 the freehold Tooting Police Station was still in the possession of the Metropolitan Police,[3098] but was closed in October 2020 and bought for £8.25m by property developers Telereal Trillium in March 2021 to be turned into flats. Designed by Gilbert MacKenzie Trench, the building was listed as being of special architectural or historic interest in April 2021.

Tottenham Police Station

The London Borough of Haringey
Tottenham village (1839-1865)
Scotland Green (1865-1914)
398 High Road (1914-1993)
N Division (1839-1865)
Y Division (1865-1993)
Haringey OCU (1993-2018/19)
Basic Command Unit North Area (NA) with the London Borough of Enfield (2018/19 to Present)

In January 1859 the Home Office authorised the purchase of a freehold site for £550 for a new police station in Tottenham. The station cost £1,966 to build, and had four cells on the ground floor. On the first and second floors there was accommodation for twelve constables and one married inspector.

In 1864 the address of the station was shown as 'near Scotland Green, Tottenham', and was a station on N or Islington Division.[3099] That year the Commissioner gave approval for Acting Sergeant, Constable 337N Bacon to be posted to Station Duties at Tottenham Police Station. Records also show that there was an inspector in charge of the station, with four sergeants to assist him.[3100]

In 1873 Tottenham was a station under the supervision of an inspector and shown as part of Y or Highgate Division.[3101] By 1881 Tottenham Police Station was shown with the address High Road, Tottenham, and had accommodation for one married inspector and his family and 13 single constables.[3102] However there were only eleven single constables in residence when the census was taken that year. The officer in charge of the station was Inspector George Carr, who resided there with his wife and four children.[3103] The records show that in 1893 the call sign for the station was Tango Mike (TM).[3104]

Tottenham Police Station 1864-1914

In 1904 Constable Leonard Russell collapsed and died whilst arresting a man in Tottenham for drunkenness.[3105]

It is not often that events in other parts of Europe have repercussions in London, and especially not in Tottenham, but this was the case in 1909. In 1907 there was a failed attempt to blow up the President of France; instead the bomber blew himself to pieces. His two companions (one of whom was his brother) fled France and found refuge in England. On 23rd January 1909 they decided to rob the Schnurmann Rubber Factory in Chestnut Road, Tottenham. This incident and its aftermath became known as the Tottenham Outrage. One conspirator had left the factory after finding the work too hard, but suggested it would be a soft target when the wages were delivered on a Saturday. The subsequent robbery was a farce, except that a number of shots were fired and the thieves managed to escape with the money. The shots alerted two police officers at Tottenham Police Station, Constable 510 Newman and Constable 403 Tyler, who jumped into a passing car to give chase. The section house above the station also turned out to help even though they were off duty.

There was a hue and cry, with a number of police officers and members of the public following the robbers. Several times the robbers turned, and on one occasion shot and killed a young lad, Ralph Joscelyn, who was running towards the car to evade being hit by the multitude of bullets. The two constables in the car attempted to head off the conspirators, but when confronted one took careful aim and shot Constable Tyler straight through the head. He died instantly. The chase lasted more than two hours, covering a distance of six miles, and saw a huge number of rounds of ammunition fired by the conspirators. Whilst trying to scale a fence one of the conspirators shot himself in the head. He was not killed outright, but stayed alive for an agonising three weeks before he died in hospital. The other made off and eventually took refuge in the bedroom of a nearby house, where he shot himself when the room was stormed by police.[3106]

The 'In Loving Memory' card shown below was produced to mark the deaths of Constable Tyler, aged 30 years, and Ralph Joscelyne, aged 10 years. The conspirators also wounded twenty-one other people during their attempt to escape.

The picture below shows the funeral procession of Constable Tyler and Master Ralph Joscelyne through the streets of Tottenham on their way to Abney Park cemetery. Both were buried in the same place on 29th January 1909.

3093 The National Police Roll of Honour accessed March 2002.
3094 Map of Districts and Divisions dated 1937.
3095 Metropolitan Police Orders dated 21st June 1939.
3096 *Police and Constabulary Almanac* 1957.
3097 Metropolitan Police Authority (MPA) Committee Reports accessed 15th February 2009; cms.met.police.uk/boroughs/wandsworth/09contact_us/index.
3098 MPS Assets (2019) Freedom of Information request.
3099 Metropolitan Police Orders dated 27th April 1864; John Back Archive (1975).
3100 Metropolitan Police Orders 11th January 1864.
3101 Metropolitan Police General Orders 1873.
3102 Metropolitan Police Surveyor's Records 1881.
3103 Census 1881.
3104 Metropolitan Police General Orders 1893.
3105 www.policememorial.org.uk/Forces/Metropolitan/metroll.htm accessed 12th March 2002.
3106 Gould, R. W. and Waldron, M. J. (1986) *London's Armed Police*. Arms and Armour Press, Hampstead, London.

A collection totalling £1,055 was raised by the public for Constable Tyler's widow. She invested the money and lived off the interest, which she added to the £15 per year police-granted pension. The wages bag with £80 was never found, but it was said that the owners of the cottage where one conspirator was cornered found it in the chimney flue and lived for some time on the proceeds. Constable Tyler received the posthumous award of the newly-instituted King's Police Medal.[3107]

Constable Tyler's carriage flanked by officers

In time Tottenham station became too small for policing requirements, and a larger building was required. It was in 1910 that the Commissioner of Police, Sir Edward Henry, visited the station and wrote, "The accommodation here – residential and administrative – is inadequate and unsatisfactory." Accordingly, a year later in 1911 steps were taken to acquire the adjacent freehold sites of 394-396 High Road, Tottenham, which included several cottages located at the rear. The building of a new police station then became a priority. The adjoining were purchased for the sum of £1,500.[3108]

The new building provided accommodation for 31 single men, and was erected and opened in May 1914.[3109] Surveyor's records indicate that the station was refurbished in 1936.[3110]

Mr Gilbert Bowles (second left), Commandant of Y Division Special Constabulary, pictured in 1937 at Tottenham with other officers

The picture above shows a line up of four officers taken in 1937, one a regular officer and three members of the Metropolitan Police Special Constabulary. The taller man in the centre without medals is the sub-divisional inspector for Tottenham Police Station, who was almost certainly responsible for the Y Division Special Constabulary. To the left of him is the Special Commandant for Y Division, Mr. Gilbert Humphrey Bowles MBE. The commandant is proudly showing his MBE, which was the likely reason for the picture. The two remaining special officers are Mr Coucher (Special Chief Inspector attached to Tottenham Police Station) and Mr Woodhouse (Special Inspector attached to Edmonton Police Station).

In 1960 Superintendent S.A. Palin was the officer in charge of the station, and the call sign was Yankee Tango (YT).[3111] The station was then refurbished in 1975,[3112] and again in 1990.[3113]

In 1985 a tragic incident occurred on the Broadwater Farm Estate in Tottenham. On 5th October police searched the address of Mrs Cynthia Jarrett in Thorpe Road, Tottenham as a result of the arrest of her son Floyd. During the search Mrs Jarrett collapsed and died. Community leaders at Tottenham Police Station made complaints the following day and, perceiving a lack of action, a breakaway group of people began to congregate and demonstrate outside the police station. This resulted in a disturbance where the windows of the station were broken. A police inspector driving past the Broadwater Farm Estate was set upon by two youths on a motorcycle, causing injury to the officer and damage to the car. Police responding to an emergency call to the estate were surrounded. Officers with riot equipment attended, but were ill-prepared for what happened next. Under sustained attack some time later, Constable Keith Blakelock, attached to Tottenham Police Station, was stabbed to death by the angry crowd. Later in the evening the crowd dispersed and a murder enquiry commenced.[3114]

Tottenham Police Station 1914 to present

In 1998 the station was shown as a designated charging station,[3115] however by 2002 it had become the Borough Police Headquarters for Haringey and was open to the public 24-hours a day, seven days a week.[3116]

In 2019 Tottenham Police Station was still retained for operation purposes by the Metropolitan Police.[3117]

Tottenham Court Road Police Station

London Borough of Camden

56 Tottenham Court Road (1876-c.2001)

E Division (1876-1886)

C Division (1886-c.1910)

D Division (c.1910-1933)

C Division (1933-1965)

E Division (1965-19931)

Camden OCU 1993-2002

At various times part of C, D or E Divisions, Tottenham Court Road was located just within the boundary of the London Borough of Camden.

Tottenham Court Road Police Station may have partly

replaced George Street in about 1895.

A station at 56 and 58 Tottenham Court Road was built in 1900 and demolished in 1940. The premises comprised a police station, section house and three sets of married quarters. The replacement station was built on the site and opened in 1940.

Tottenham Court Road Police Station 1900-1941

The oral history project of the Friends of the Metropolitan Police Historical Collection contains an interview with an officer who had served at this station in 1919, during a police strike, when the branch secretary of the police union (as it then was) wrongly told officers coming to the police station for early turn duty that all officers at Tottenham Court Road were already out on strike. The officers then returned to their homes and were dismissed, along with hundreds of other officers. This harsh treatment was a reflection of the discipline of the times, but their grievance was exacerbated by the fact that the branch secretary's information about other officers being on strike was false. One sergeant, Fred Hillier, kept his officers at the police station and would not let them return to their homes because he feared that they would be dismissed as strikers. At that time police officers often had part-time jobs, such as acting as doormen at night clubs and theatres, but this practice was stopped by the Commissioner Lord Trenchard.

Tottenham Court Road Police Station 1942-c2002

The interviewed officer remembered 142 officers on the strength at the police station, with sometimes up to 50 officers parading for night duty. Every crossing along Oxford Street was controlled by a police officer, and it would not be surprising that that level of police cover has led to reminiscences of how frequently officers were seen on the beat.

In 1941 there was a change of sub-divisional inspector at Tottenham Court Road. Sub-Divisional Inspector Gavin (warrant no. 113487), who had been at the station when it was bombed, was transferred to West End Central, and SDI Osborne (warrant no. 113848) replaced him.

The station accommodated part of the Regional Crime Squad at one point, and by the late 1990s featured a public enquiry counter but no custody suite. It was put up for sale by the then Metropolitan Police Authority in 2000/01.

Tower Bridge Police Station

The London Borough of Southwark

Tooley Street (1904-1999)

M Division (1904-1993)

Southwark OCU 1993-1999

On 2nd May 1898 the Home Office authorised the Receiver to acquire a site in Bermondsey for the erection of a new police station for that locality.[3118]

In March 1900 a freehold site was subsequently purchased, for the sum of £10,000 from the Corporation of the City of London. This was known as the Tooley Street and Queen Elizabeth Street site. A month later, in April 1900, the Home Office sanctioned a proposal that a new police court for the Southwark District be erected in lieu of the existing court. A parcel of land next to the police station site was purchased freehold on 30th September 1901 for £8,161.[3119]

Tenders were put out to various firms for the construction of a combined Police station and court at Bermondsey. The tender submitted by Messrs Grover and Sons for providing the foundations for the proposed buildings at a cost of £3,874 was accepted. The main contract was awarded to Messrs John Mowlem & Co., of Grosvenor Wharf, Millbank, Westminster, whose tender for the construction was £39,446.[3120] The Police Architect and Surveyor, John Dixon Butler, was responsible for the design of the buildings.

The building was described by Pevsner as:

"Quite spectacular of its date, with a large broken pediment and an outward-curving balcony, and a doorway with a curved hood on elongated brackets." [3121]

3107 Gould, R. W. and Waldron, M. J. (1986) *London's Armed Police*, Arms and Armour Press, Hampstead.
3108 John Back Archive (1975).
3109 Metropolitan Police Orders dated 16th May 1914 and Metropolitan Police Surveyor's Records 1924.
3110 Metropolitan Police Surveyor's Records 1924.
3111 *Police and Constabulary Almanac* 1960.
3112 Metropolitan Police Orders dated 28th November 1975.
3113 Metropolitan Police Surveyor's Records (undated).
3114 Fido, M and Skinner, K. (1999) *The Official Encyclopaedia of Scotland Yard*.
3115 *Police and Constabulary Almanac* 1998.
3116 www.met.police.uk/contact/phone.htm accessed 12th March 2002.
3117 MPS Information Rights Unit (2019) MPS assets.
3118 John Back Archive (1975).
3119 Ibid.
3120 Ibid.
3121 *Pevsner Buildings of England: London South.* Penguin 1983 p602.

Tower Bridge Police Station 1888-1974

The new police station at 209 Tooley Street, Tower Bridge, shown on the left of the picture above, opened in December 1904.[3122] In 1905 William Hopkins was appointed the first Sub-Divisional Inspector for Tower Bridge on M (Southwark) Division. He remained there until 1910, when he was promoted to Chief Inspector on J or Hackney Division.[3123] Henry Nichols took over from Hopkins and remained until 1917.

The Police purchased the freehold to the court in 1925.[3124]

On the creation of the London Borough of Southwark in 1965 Tower Bridge Police Station (MT) remained a sub-divisional station, with Rotherhithe as its section station.[3125]

During another revision of Police boundaries in 1980 Tower Bridge Division was amalgamated with Southwark Division.[3126] The station was reduced to station officer status in 1983.[3127]

Tower Bridge Police Station was closed in 1999. Tower Bridge Magistrates' Court and the former police station building are currently Grade III listed. The court closed in June 2013,[3128] and the police station was shut in February 2014 when it was sold to The Ministry of Justice for £6.975M.[3129]

The building is now the luxury Dixon, Tower Bridge hotel, named after its architect.

Trenchard House Section House

City of Westminster

19-25 Broadwick Street (c.1930-2004)

Trenchard House was a large section house in Broadwick Street on West End Central's ground. Their social and athletic club held a concert there on 10th March 1949 featuring Tommy Trinder, Edmundo Ros and his Rumba band, Jon Pertwee, the magician George Braund, Len Marten, Arthur Haynes & Frederick Ferrari from the BBC show 'Stand Easy', and various other accomplished entertainers. This was a reflection, perhaps, of a form of police social life that has largely disappeared, and of a good relationship between the police of the West End and the entertainers in London's theatres.

Trenchard House Section House 1930s-2004

Trenchard Section House, at 19-25 Broadwick Street was purpose-built in the 1930s to provide individuals with single rooms for 214 officers, with shared bathroom/shower facilities. Other facilities in the building included catering, bar and common room areas, squash courts and gymnasium facilities, as well as laundry facilities.

In 2004 the Metropolitan Police announced that it had sold the section house to the national regeneration agency English Partnerships, who provide affordable homes for sale, for groups such as key workers and first-time buyers. The premises had been unoccupied since 1999 and were considered no longer required for its original purpose of housing single police officers.

Twickenham Police Station

The London Borough of Richmond
London Road, Twickenham (1854-1858)
45 London Road (1858-1947)
41 London Road (1947-2018)
18 Park Road (2018/19 to Present)
T Division (1854-1993)
The London Borough of Richmond OCU (1993-2018)
South West (SW) BCU (2018/19 to Present)

Land and a property in Twickenham was rented from Miss Ward of Disraeli Road, Ealing by the Receiver in 1854 on a ground rent of £17 per annum. The rental agreement was for 94½ years, with the rates, taxes, insurance and repairs being borne by the Receiver.

In 1858 a purpose-built police station was built on the site at a cost £1,230. The station consisted of a ground floor with an inspector's office, three cells, a urinal, coal cellars, a library, mess room, kitchen, lavatory and boot room. Upstairs on the first floor was a section house which consisted of single room in which five single constables lived. They paid a weekly rent of 1 shilling up until at least 1911, which was deducted from their pay.

Also residing in four rooms upstairs originally was the station sergeant and his family, however later his place was taken by the inspector and his family. The inspector paid 4 shillings a week for these rooms, which also included a scullery.[3130]

Twickenham Police Station 1858-1947

In 1864 Twickenham Police Station was situated at 45 London Road, but this was later changed to No. 41 and was shown as a station on V or Wandsworth Division as a sectional station together with Barnes Police Station of Richmond. The Inspector at Richmond was instructed not to do station duty, but his purpose was to patrol for supervisory purposes.

Contractors were paid to repaint the outside of the station in 1869, and in 1872 the inside of the station was whitewashed.[3131]

Rear aspect to the station c1908

Twickenham had two sergeants, one for day duty and the other for night duty, and 14 constables. There were four day-beats and nine night-beats covered by the constables.[3132] The extra constable was the reserve, and required to undertake a variety of extra jobs such as covering for a constable who had made an arrest. The Commissioner suggested that when the sergeants were on patrol then the station could be closed. Twickenham had facilities for charging prisoners and holding them in cells.[3133]

Parade shed and station yard c1908

3122 Metropolitan Police Orders dated 9th December 1904.
3123 *Kelly's Directories* 1905-1911.
3124 Metropolitan Police Surveyors' Records.
3125 Metropolitan Police Orders dated 6th August 1964.
3126 Metropolitan Police Orders dated 22nd January 1980.
3127 Metropolitan Police Orders dated 25th October 1983.
3128 www.london-sel.co.uk/news/view/4637 accessed 10th October 2010.
3129 MPS (2019) Freedom of Information request: Land and property sold in the last 10 years for over £1M.
3130 Metropolitan Police Surveyor's Records.
3131 Ibid.
3132 Metropolitan Police Special Police Orders 1864.
3133 Ibid.

In 1873 Twickenham was a station of T or Kensington Division, and a sergeant was designated as in charge.[3134]

The freehold to the property was purchased in 1902 by the police for £550.[3135] Twickenham Police Station was then situated at 41 London Road and included a section house for single police officers, although this accommodation was converted and given up in favour of one set of married quarters in 1924.[3136]

In 1920 the freehold to a site at 60-88 Grosvenor Road, Twickenham, at the rear of the old police station, was purchased by the Receiver. The site also fronted onto the High Street with the purchase of 41-45 London Road (odd numbers) in 1929. The police station had rear access into the yard through Grosvenor Road with the further purchase of Caroline Cottages.[3137]

In 1936 the Metropolitan Police introduced police boxes on to T Division, and Box T32 was erected on 20th July. The police call box was situated at The Green (Staines Road), south side, ten yards west of Knowle Road. The box was removed in March 1970.[3138] In 1939 an air raid warning-dedicated telephone was installed in the station, the cost being borne by Twickenham Borough council.[3139] It was later removed when no longer needed.

In 1965 Twickenham (TW) was a sub-divisional station, with Superintendent Brough in charge.[3140]

Two officers from Twickenham who lost their lives whilst on duty were Constable Matthew John Allen, who died in a crash in Twickenham while responding to an emergency call in 1992, and Constable Kulwant Singh Sidhu, who was killed when he fell through a glass skylight pursuing suspects across a roof in Twickenham in 1999.[3141] It was this last case that brought the Commissioner at the time, Sir John Stevens, to face trial at the Old Bailey on charges relating to health and safety. In a prosecution considered by many to be at best pedantic, but a reflection of the Health and Safety Executives policies, the Commissioner was acquitted. Later the law was changed to remove a chief officers' personal liability for health and safety law infringements.

Twickenham Police Station 1947 to present

In 2000 Twickenham became the subject of a review by the Metropolitan Police Authority and was designated a station to remain open 24 hours a day. It was also a charging station within the terms of the Police and Criminal Evidence Act where officers could detain, process and charge prisoners for court.[3142]

In 2019 Twickenham Police Station was still in police ownership.[3143]

Upminster Police Station

The London Borough of Havering
233 St Marys Lane, Upminster, Essex (1929-2010)
Essex Police (1929-1965)
K Division (1965-1993)
Havering OCU 1993-2010

There was a system of parochial police in Upminster with which the residents were happy. From 1829 the New Police began to spread out from London into the surrounding areas and shires. In 1834 Upminster increased its number of parish constables to three, however by 1842 this was increased to eight.[3144] In the following year the numbers were reduced to five (two blacksmiths, a butcher, a farmer and a carpenter). This was due in part to what was referred to at the time as the 'hungry Forties', when people were driven elsewhere to seek better conditions.

In 1840 the Essex Police was formed, and by 1851 there was an increase in the force by four constables of which one was posted to Upminster.[3145] No station was built as the area was still very rural. Often the police house where the village constable lived acted as the focal point for enquiries. By 1861 the strength had risen to two constables, namely Constable 72 Alexander McFadden (joined April 1852 and had probably been at Upminster since then), and Constable 171 George Digby (joined April 1859).[3146] In 1881 Constable Isaac Boreham lived in a cottage in the village with his wife Mary Jane.[3147]

The Essex Police, like the Metropolitan Police, sought to employ efficient constables. In early 1886 Constable Drew was the local officer in Upminster, however he was brought before the Chief Constable in a somewhat embarrassing situation. The constable could not account for his uniform greatcoat, belt and gloves which he had been wearing on night duty. These items had been found in a field in the early morning. The constable, apart from being the butt of jokes throughout the county, was ordered to resign his position.[3148]

In 1886 Constable J. Webb became the village policeman and stayed for ten years. On his transfer a grateful public presented him with a marble clock.[3149]

In 1891 (and again in 1900) the chief constable set about reducing the size of the two largest county divisions, Colchester and Brentwood.[3150] At the turn of the century, in 1900, because of boundary revisions Upminster became a station within Brentwood Division.[3151] A new officer, Constable Beasley, arrived in 1901 and quickly established himself as a hard-working and vigilant officer. In 1912 he was promoted to sergeant and remained until 1917, when he was transferred to Harwich to assist the war effort.[3152]

In 1910 the Essex Standing Committee recommended the purchase of a semi-detached house with adjoining piece of land on Cranham Road, for not more than £640. However later that year a double-fronted house was purchased for £750. There was plenty of room on which to build a lock-up for the purpose of detaining drunks and disorderly persons.

Later Upminster Police Station was an end of terrace house built in 1928.

The 1930s review of the Essex Police building stock showed that one sergeant and four constables were stationed there. Five police houses were built there in 1929, and there was a recommendation to build four more. The population was shown as 7,000 persons.[3153]

In 1965 the station was extended by including 225 St. Mary's

Lane, when it transferred to the Metropolitan Police, and 62-64 St. Lawrence Road.

Upminster Police Station 1929-2010

The address of the present station is 233 St. Marys Lane, Upminster, Essex. In 2002 Upminster Police Station was open from 12 noon until 8.00pm Mondays to Fridays for enquiries from the public. The Community Constables who police the local area were stationed there, however emergency calls were dealt with from Hornchurch.[3154]

Upminster Police Station was shut and sold in 2010 for £1,100,00.[3155] The property has since been demolished, and new houses erected on the site.

Upper Holloway Police Station (also known as Archway Police Station)

The London Borough of Islington

Zoffany Street, N7 (1870-1933)

Y Division (1870-1933)

In 1869 it was proposed that a new sub-division be formed at Upper Holloway and a new police station erected. A site was purchased in 1870 where a temporary station operated until 1873.

Upper Holloway Police Station was situated at Scholefield Road at the corner of Zephany Street (now Zoffany Street, N7) within the Parish of St. Mary, Islington. In 1886 the Receiver purchased the freehold title to the land at a cost of £750 from Mr R.D. Lown, a master builder residing at Bartholomew Road, Islington. The station was built at a cost of £2,992 and was taken into service in November 1887. Upper Holloway was shown as a station on Y Division.[3156]

Upper Holloway Police Station 1887-1933

The station was a typical three-storey Victorian police station house. On the ground floor of the building there were a Charge Room, an Inspectors' Office, a waiting room, a store, an association cell (often called the drunk tank) and three other cells. On the ground floor there was also a kitchen, a scullery, a brushing room, a clothes room, a drying room, a boot room, eight WCs and a urinal. In the yard there was also a parade shed and hand ambulance shed. The first floor had a Day room, a mess room, a food locker room and a lavatory. Eight single men lived on the first floor and twelve on the second floor. In the yard were a parade shed and a hand ambulance hut.

Being a London police officer very often had its dangers, especially the risk of assault or even death. On 4th October 1896 a constable stationed at Upper Holloway Police Station was severely wounded by a violent assailant. It was reported that a George Chamberlain in Upper Holloway assaulted Police Constable 302Y William Haynes. He stabbed the officer in the head with a knife. This action left the officer unconscious and allowed the prisoner to escape. He was captured later and taken before the magistrates at North London Magistrates' Court in Stoke Newington, and dealt with later at a higher court.[3157]

In 1905 permission was granted for Islington Borough Council to leave a mobile fire escape between 7.00am until 9.00pm each day in the station yard positioned opposite the yard gates for ease of access. This ladder was placed there by the Fire Brigade in case of fire in buildings with a number of storeys. This service attracted a rental of 5 shillings per annum. The escape was removed in April 1907.[3158]

3134 Metropolitan Police General Orders 1873.
3135 Metropolitan Police Surveyor's Records.
3136 Metropolitan Police Surveyor's Records 1924.
3137 *The Police List* 1947.
3138 Site Locations for Metropolitan Police telephone boxes and telephone posts for V Division.
3139 Metropolitan Police Surveyor's Records.
3140 Metropolitan Police Stations 1965.
3141 Metropolitan Police Roll of Honour (www.policememorial.org.uk) accessed 12th March 2012.
3142 Metropolitan Police Authority (2000). Police Station opening hours Committee; MPA Reports 9th November.
3143 MPS (2018) Freedom of Information request: MPS Assets.
3144 'The Story of Upminster' by the Upminster Local History Group, Book 11. 1960. p22.
3145 Brown, B. (1990) 'Romford Police: The Anniversary of a Change' in the *Romford Record*. Romford and District Historical Society.
3146 Essex Record Office Q/Apr. 12 – Distribution List.
3147 Census 1881.
3148 Woodgate, John (1985) *The Essex Police*. Terence Dalton Ltd, Lavenham.
3149 'The Story of Upminster' by the Upminster Local History Group, Book 11. 1960. p23.
3150 Woodgate, John (1985) *The Essex Police*. Terence Dalton Ltd, Lavenham.
3151 Ibid.
3152 Ibid. p25.
3153 Essex County Constabulary: Police Stations and Police Houses Register (c1930).
3154 Local enquiry of the station officer, 26th July 2002.
3155 Metropolitan Police Information Rights Unit 22nd October 2017, accessed 25th January 2019.
3156 John Back Archive (1975).
3157 *Police Review and Parade Gossip*, October 1897.
3158 Metropolitan Police Surveyor's Records 1924.

A retirement at Upper Holloway Police Station in 1910

The picture above shows the retirement of a constable in 1910 from Upper Holloway Police Station. The officers and men include two Inspectors (one Station and one Sub-Divisional) two Station sergeants (identified with four bars on each upper arm) four sergeants and 37 constables. The officer retiring has been awarded a handsome marble clock for his mantle-piece and probably a purse of money. Retirement presents came from collecting subscriptions from the officers and men at the station. The Metropolitan Police did not contribute except perhaps in the provision of a pension after 25 years' loyal service and also the provision of a certificate of service, which was provided in lieu of a reference.

During World War One the police station at Upper Holloway was considered to be a Special Constabulary station. The photograph below shows the entire Special Constabulary of Upper Holloway (46 in number), in about 1914, in the yard at the rear of the station. This is an early photograph as none of the special constables has been issued with uniforms and are wearing their civilian clothes with their duty armlets. They were asked to complete four hours a week duty, which was unpaid. It was generally difficult to distinguish between ranks, but in the front row a number are wearing an additional band on the opposite arm to the duty armlet signifying either a Sergeant or Inspector.

Special Constabulary, Upper Holloway, 1914

The war volunteers were disbanded in 1918 when the war was over although some would have carried on if needed. Those who had served during the war were rewarded with a medal.

The police station was closed in 1933, but the building still stands although not used for police purposes. In 1936 the Islington Borough Council purchased the title for £1,800 and it is still in use today as offices for the council.

In 2003 a Police Sector Office was shown located at Gill House, Highgate Hill, Upper Holloway, London N19. It is for police use only and has no facilities for the public.[3159]

Victoria Park Police Station

The London Borough of Hackney
184 Wick Road, Homerton (1888-1936)
N Division (1832-1886)
J Division (1886-1936)

A freehold site within the Parish of St. John, Hackney with an address of 184 Wick Road, Hackney Wick, Homerton was purchased by the Metropolitan Police in 1888 from the executors of the late Mr J. Fenton for a freehold price of £850. Plans were immediately made for a police station on the site, and these were passed in 1889. Victoria Park Police Station was built at a cost of £3,739, and was completed for occupation in September 1890, and included a section house to accommodate ten single officers.

The station was built with a charge room, inspector's office, waiting lobby, parade room and four cells on the ground floor. In the yard at the rear was a two-stall stable, together with a loft for the storage of hay and feed. Also in the yard was a hand ambulance shed, which housed the wooden handcart on which drunken or ill people would be conveyed to a police station or doctor. There were two further floors to the station, with the first floor housing single constables quarters and the second floor in the roof having a day room and library.

There were extensive refurbishments made in 1912, which cost the sum of £1,326.[3160] Her Majesty owns much of this area in Hackney and the Crown Estate administers the land on her behalf. This not only includes Victoria Park but also many of the properties surrounding it. The Crown Estates lease out land and properties to tenants and ensure their general maintenance and upkeep.

During the Victorian era it became a custom for people to take walks, push prams or take their children to play in the local parks. On a Sunday, for example, people would congregate at the bandstand and listen to bands playing. The picture right was taken between 1864 and 1870, and shows an off duty sergeant of H Division. He was probably attached to Church Street Police Station located at the bottom end of Bethnal Green Road. Sergeants lived as close as possible to the stations where they were attached, and often accommodation was found for them or they organised rented housing nearby.[3161] He is dressed in the new style of uniform which replaced the swallow tailcoat and top hat introduced in 1829. This blue serge uniform had an eight-button tunic, and a cox-comb helmet which displayed the number of the officer in the centre of the helmet plate.

Police Sergeant taken near Victoria Park, 1870

At the southern edge of Victoria Park lies the boundary between Hackney and Bethnal Green Sub-Divisions. This boundary ran through the centre of the Regents Canal. Regularly people fell or jumped into the canal.

Victoria Park Police Station

On 8th July 1898, at 5.00am, Constable George Lees, stationed at nearby Victoria Park Police Station, was on patrol in London Fields when he saw a man by the name of George Johnson from Clapton jump into the canal from the Cat and Mutton Bridge. The constable ran to the bridge, discarding his bullseye lamp and helmet and, according to witnesses, jumped into the canal to rescue the man. In those days it was a criminal offence to attempt suicide, and this was the intent of Johnson who was desperate, unemployed and starving. A fearful struggle took place, and the men disappeared twice under the water. The constable eventually got the man to the bank. A witness had heard Johnson say he would drown the constable if he did not let go.

Johnson was charged and appeared at North London Magistrates' Court where, after hearing the evidence, the magistrate recorded that a commendation should be awarded to Constable Lees and that his superiors should hear of his brave conduct. Johnson's plight was made worse, because having failed to commit suicide then prison was the likely punishment.[3162]

During duty one evening in 1900 Constable George Stephen Funnell and other officers came across a fire raging out of control in a public house. He quickly found out that there were three women trapped in the premises, and went to their aid. It was in the process of rescuing them that he was severely injured. Once the women had been rescued he was taken to hospital where he died from his injuries.[3163]

In 1924 Victoria Park Police Station was shown as a station on J Division, where it was a sectional station to Hackney Sub-Division.

In January 1936 the station strength was shown as one Inspector White (warrant no. 109701), one Station Sergeant Hitchcock (warrant no. 108279), three sergeants and six constables.

In August 1936 Victoria Park Police Station was shut, and all staff transferred to Hackney Police Station.[3164] In 1937 the building and land were sold to the Hackney Wick Agency and Garages of 10 Riseholme Street, Hackney Wick for £1,850.[3165]

Vine Street Police Station

City of Westminster

10 Little Vine Street (later renamed Piccadilly Place and Vine Street) (1829-1940; 1971-1997)

C Division (1829-1985/86)

No. 0 Area (1985/86-1993/94)

No. 1 Area (1993/94-1997)

The original St James's parish watch house at 10 Little Vine Street (later Piccadilly Place and 10 Vine Street) was taken over in 1829 as the original C Division headquarters. It was

---

3159 www.islington.gov.uk/community.asp?sectionis?=1190 accessed 4th June 2003.
3160 John Back Archive (1975).
3161 Metropolitan Police General Orders 1829 and 1871.
3162 *Police Review* July 1898.
3163 www.policememorial.org.uk/Forces/Metropolitan/metroll.htm accessed 12th March 2002.
3164 Metropolitan Police Orders 8th January 1936.
3165 Metropolitan Police Surveyor's Records (undated).

rebuilt in 1868-69, enlarged in 1897 and extended into the former Man in the Moon public house to accommodate administrative functions in 1931. When West End Central was opened in 1940 Vine Street became the Aliens' Registration Office.

Vine Street Police Station 1868-1997

The merging of the two divisions of Vine Street and Great Marlborough Street into West End Central caused much work for the one station, and Vine Street re-opened in 1971 to overcome the anomaly where two Divisions, CD1 and CD2, had been created for West End Central, each with its own command structure.

A small back street near Piccadilly Circus, Vine Street was the centre for the policing of Boat Race celebrations in the 1930s and, with Marlborough Street and Bow Street, enjoys the prestige of featuring in the famous Monopoly board game. Its final closure in November 1997 brought to an end the premises' long association with policing.

In 1914, Constable 356C Foreman, a single man who had been a police officer for seven years, was stopped by pickets on his way to Vine Street from Bow Street section house. It was the day of a police strike that had been called to protest against police pay and conditions. PC Foreman defied the pickets and went on parade at Vine Street, where 13 of 35 officers due to parade were absent. The superintendent took the parade and warned the officers that they could expect opposition from pickets. The first officer in the file being marched out refused to lead the others on to the street, but Constable Foreman saw that the pickets were from B rather than C Division and, using his high opinion of his own division, threatened the pickets with his truncheon, saying "No-one from B Division is going to tell me what to do!"

The dispute was settled by a pay increase of 13 shillings per week and the grant of widows' pensions of 10 shillings per week, but the First World War intervened.[3166] There were further police strikes in 1918 and 1919, the year that the Police Federation was formed.

Wallington Police Station

The London Borough of Sutton
84 Stafford Road (1915-2012)
W Division (1915-1933)
Z Division (1931-1993)
Borough of Sutton OCU (1993-2012)

In a list of 'Parishes and Places' the hamlet of Wallington is mentioned; it was included when the Metropolitan Police District was extended in 1839. The Parish of Beddington is linked with the hamlet, and was policed by three police constables from Croydon Police Station on P Division.

Petty Sessions were held at Croydon, and the Parishes of Addington, Beddington and Chaldon were aligned with the Hundreds of Wallington. The two magistrates listed were Sir Henry Bridges of Beddington and Robert G. Loraine of Wallington.[3167]

When three new divisions were formed in 1888 – W or Clapham, X or Paddington, and Y or Highgate – Croydon was transferred from P to W Division.[3168]

There was an increase of strength for one constable for special beat patrol for the Wallington area, authorised in 1904.[3169] In 1905 the Wallington Parish Council requested the provision of a police station in the area of Beddington and Wallington, so authority was sought for a suitable site to be purchased for the purpose of erecting a pair of police cottages.

In 1906 the Beddington Parish Council requested the provision of a police station in the area of South Beddington,[3170] and after protracted negotiations a freehold site was purchased on 9th July 1912 in Stafford Road.

It is quoted by the Local Authority that "Stafford Road is an old highway leading from the South End of Sutton to Croydon."[3171] An extract from a letter dated 10th May 1913 from the Local Authority said "Wallington is, and I should say must always remain, a fairly quiet neighbourhood. There is no Section House at the Carshalton Police Station, which the new station at Wallington will replace…"[3172]

The administrative portion of the new police station at Wallington was staffed and business commenced on 24th May 1915.[3173]

Wallington Police Station 1915-2012

On 7th June 1915 the two married quarters at Wallington Police Station were occupied. The lodging assessment of one was set at 9s 6d a week, and the other at 9s a week.[3174]

The Police received notice from the Beddington and Wallington Urban District council concerning the numbering of buildings, in which it stated that Wallington Police Station was numbered 84.[3175]

The boundaries of P, W and Z Divisions were revised in 1931, when Streatham and Wallington sub-divisional stations were transferred from W to Z Division.[3176]

A reorganisation of the Force designed to relate Police boundaries to the new local authority boundaries in 1965 meant that Wallington became a sectional station to Sutton Sub-Division on Z or Croydon Division.[3177]

Property at 16-18 Stanley Park Road was purchased in 1965 for the purpose of erecting a new police station, however when the building committee convened in 1971 it was recommended that on the completion of Sutton's new station, Wallington should be removed from the building programme and reduced in status to that of a police office.[3178]

Like many old police stations where there is a possibility of either closure or restricted opening times, the local population feel that they will not receive the service and support previously given. When Wallington Police Station was in danger of complete closure in 1977 the local newspaper reported a strong feeling locally against the closure after its 62 years of service.[3179] This was repeated in 1991, when it was again proposed that the station should be closed.[3180]

In 1987 the station was visited by an elderly lady on the eve of her 100th birthday. She was Kate Blanche Gosling, one of Hertfordshire's first police women, with a warrant number of 303, and who had served in the Police nearly 80 years previously. She was given the opportunity to see how the Police Service had changed during the intervening years.[3181] She died in 1994 aged 107 years.

In March 2012 Wallington Police Station was put up for sale and fetched £701,000.[3182] A Safer Neighbourhoods office was opened as a contact point for the public at Crosspoint House, 28 Stafford Road, Wallington in 2013, but in May 2019 this was shut and proposals for a Safer Neighbourhoods office to be opened at Wallington Fire Station has been made in the meantime.[3183]

Waltham Abbey Police Station

Epping Forest District Council

Highbridge Street, Waltham Abbey, Essex (1840-1876)

Sun Street, Waltham Abbey (1876-2016)

N Division (1840-1886)

J Division (1886-1987)

Barkingside Division 1987-1993

Redbridge OCU 1993-2000

Essex Police (2000-2016)

In 1840 Waltham Abbey was incorporated into the Metropolitan Police Area and the old time watchmen and the new police replaced the existing three town constables, who remained in the town but mainly in an honorary role. The station strength consisted of four sergeants, one mounted constable and nine other constables. All lived in private accommodation locally. Several outlying local hamlets had their own constable.[3184] White-painted cast iron posts mark the northern boundary of the Metropolitan Police, which are said to have been present since 1666.[3185] The pay for a constable from 1829 until 1869 was £1 1s, for which they worked every day of the week for 12 hours each day.[3186] Such was the demand from the police that a number of officers were retired as being worn out. Police Sergeant 15N Henry Sturgeon was retired from Waltham Abbey in 1872 under precisely these circumstances.

Waltham Abbey Police Station 1840-1876

The station was located at Highbridge Street, opposite the Abbey Church and was small, badly-constructed and lacked rear windows. Furthermore, the earth closets in the cells together with bad ventilation provided an almost constant stench, which was aggravated in summer. This station, shown above, remained in use until 1876.

In 1864 the Commissioners gave instructions for superintendents to take steps to erect a police station at Waltham Abbey, which almost certainly came about as a result of complaints from prominent local citizens who wrote to the Commissioners about the small station already in use which was no longer suitable for use as a police station.

Superintendent Green proposed two suitable sites to the Commissioners, with one located in Sun Street, a one-acre orchard which eventually became the favoured location. This was purchased from Mr. Richard Clayton Brown for the sum of £400. Almost immediately, a section of the site was sold to Mr. Chetwood for the sum of £25 in September 1872. A new building was constructed on the site for the sum of £3,570.[3187]

3166   Best, C.F. (undated) 'C' or St James's – A History of Policing in the West End of London.
3167   MEPO 2/76.
3168   Metropolitan Police Order dated 28th October 1865.
3169   Metropolitan Police Order dated 16th June 1904.
3170   MEPO 2/811.
3171   LB 816.
3172   MEPO 2/811.
3173   Metropolitan Police Order dated 22nd May 1915.
3174   Metropolitan Police Order dated 5th June 1915.
3175   LB 816.
3176   Metropolitan Police Order dated 9th October 1931.
3177   Metropolitan Police Order dated 6th August 1964.
3178   LB 817.
3179   *Wallington and Carshalton Advertiser*, 4th August 1977.
3180   *The Advertiser*, 29th March 1991.
3181   *Sutton & Banstead News*, 12th November 1987.
3182   MPS (2018) Freedom of information request: Police station closures by year.
3183   www.thisislocallondon.co.uk/news/17657546.mp-tom-brake-in-talks-to-open-base-at-wallington-fire-station accessed 2nd November 2019.
3184   Elliott, B. (1987) *The Abbey*.
3185   Ibid.
3186   Ibid.
3187   Ibid.

One room downstairs provided the operation accommodation, whilst the remainder provided living space for one sergeant and his family, one constable and his family and four single constables. The constables shared one room upstairs. Privacy was at a premium. To the right of the entrance was the operational room, which contained three cells, a meal room or canteen, which was communal. The premises had been opened in 1876 and charges for accommodation were levied on the occupants as 4s a week for the sergeant, 3s for the constable and 1s a week for the single officers.³¹⁸⁸ It was common to hire a servant to look after the single constables, but often the married constable's wife took on this obligation.³¹⁸⁹

Annual leave was allowed for officers at a rate of fourteen days for inspectors, ten days for sergeants and seven days for constables, although leave of absence was sometimes allowed without pay on Form 139 for the Assistant Commissioner's approval, together with any other applications for leave for more than three days at a time.

One of the main responsibilities of the divisional superintendent was to ensure the safe policing of the Royal Small arms factory at Enfield Lock and the Royal Gunpowder factory at Waltham Abbey. Responsibility for security of the gunpowder factory commenced in April 1860.³¹⁹⁰ In 1869 there was a police station on both sites.³¹⁹¹ The gunpowder factory required an inspector to be in charge, whilst down the road at the other site a sergeant was in command. The duties of the inspector were that he should visit the small arms factory daily. The rules for running these factories were strict, and it was the responsibility of police to ensure their security.³¹⁹²

In 1869 the strength for such duties was one inspector, four sergeants and twenty constables. There were two sergeants stationed at each factory, with the gunpowder factory having thirteen constables and the small arms factory seven.³¹⁹³ By 1874 the gunpowder factory strength had been reduced by two constables.³¹⁹⁴

In 1886 J Division was formed which included Waltham Abbey. An electric telegraph was installed at the lock in 1883, which connected it to Waltham Abbey station.

In 1893 records show that one chief inspector, three sergeants and nine constables were the established strength of the small arms factory, although the chief inspector was based at the gunpowder factory.

Waltham Abbey Police Station 1876-2016

Deaths in harness were common, and often the men died young. One such case occurred in 1876, when Acting Sergeant Jepthah Farrow, who was stationed at the Royal Gun Powder Factory at Waltham Abbey, died. He had spent ten of his fifteen years service there, but had also seen duty at Sun Street station. He died at the age of 39 years, having succumbed to a lingering illness where he was on sick leave for four months. He left a widow and two children both under eight years old.³¹⁹⁵ Being ten years short on his pension his family may have received a gratuity, but an application would have been made to the Secretary for the Home Department. They would have had to vacate any police residence they occupied.

Records show that in 1888 a police station was located at Mott Street, High Beech.³¹⁹⁶

In January 1908 some ten or so constables from Waltham Abbey Police Station were involved in the pursuit of two Russian anarchists who had killed two innocent people (one a constable) and wounded 25 others. The chase stared in Tottenham, and ended six miles away some two hours later. Both anarchists committed suicide rather than be captured. This became known as the Tottenham Outrage (see Tottenham Police Station).³¹⁹⁷

In 1911 the police horse patrol was removed from Waltham Abbey Police Station. The reason for their withdrawal was unknown, although the introduction of the telegraph in 1907 and the increased use of bicycles would have rendered them inefficient. The stables were converted into a parade room, a role it performed for the next forty years. The section house for four constables was withdrawn in 1913.³¹⁹⁸

The Great War saw the introduction of the Metropolitan Police Special Constabulary, and Waltham Abbey Police Station was given strength of some 50 Specials, far outnumbering the number of regular officers. At the beginning of the War specials wore armbands denoting they were on duty, with differing colours signifying what rank they were, eg blue, yellow and red. Uniforms didn't arrive until three years after the War started. Their duties included air raid warnings and war hospital postings at the Town Hall, where the local Red Cross had set up a 32-bed ward. The dangers to Waltham Abbey by German bombers and Zeppelins were apparent. Not only was the Royal Small Arms factory a target, but so was the Royal Gun Powder Factory nearby. So too were the barges of gunpowder which were en-route along the River Lea, supervised by police officers from the gunpowder factory, destined for the Woolwich Arsenal, to be made into bombs and munitions.³¹⁹⁹

After the War had finished people were commemorating the fallen at the Cenotaph a year after, on the eleventh hour of the eleventh day. Waltham Abbey joined in the observation by firing a maroon into the morning sky thirty seconds before the hour, and again two minutes beyond – a tradition which continued until the 1970s.³²⁰⁰

In 1923 the Metropolitan Police ceased to police the Royal Gun Powder Factory, and the twenty or so officers were dispersed throughout London. In 1929 a fire brigade siren was erected on the roof of Waltham Abbey Police Station after a member of the Town Council sent a request. A charge of five shillings per year was charged for the sirens use on police premises by the Receiver of the Metropolis.³²⁰¹

The Great Depression of the 1930s hit police officers very badly when a mandatory deduction of 5/- a week was withdrawn from constables and 6/3d from sergeants, regardless of rate of pay in 1931. Police constables who earned at least 78s were particularly hard hit. The following year saw a further deduction of 3/6d and 11s respectively.³²⁰²

On 1st August 1933, along with Walthamstow and Chingford, Waltham Abbey left N Division and joined J Division, the headquarters station being located at Bethnal Green in the East End of London. The divisional boundary changes were reported in 1933. The Order shows the most senior officer,

Inspector Alexander Robertson (warrant no. 105743) as earning 129s per week at that time, whilst the most junior constable, Leslie Welham (warrant no. 120488) earned 74s per week.[3203]

In 1937 a commemorative medal was struck to mark the coronation of King George VI. Traditionally all Metropolitan Police officers received a coronation medal, but this was to change and only limited numbers were produced two of which were awarded to Sergeant James Styles and Constable Albert Clare at Waltham Abbey Police Station. Also in 1937, the 999 emergency telephone system was introduced, which meant the change of the station's telegraphic code from 'WY' to 'JA'.[3204]

By 1939 there were 25 officers working at Waltham Abbey Police Station, serving a population of some 7,000 people. The onset of trouble in the wake of the Munich crisis saw the return to duty of many retired officers as War reserve, a precaution in the event of war. Special constables were also recruited as war reserve officers, and supplied with special badges of office.[3205] Up until the war the Metropolitan Police had been responsible for security at the gunpowder factory, which had since been taken over by the War Department Police.[3206] In January 1940 a huge explosion rocked the little town of Waltham Abbey. This was due to the levels of unskilled operators who had been recruited to work at the factory. Another major explosion took place three months later. This occurred in the mixing house killing five people and injuring fifteen more. This explosion was said to have been heard as far away as Brighton, and caused severe damage to the centre of Waltham Abbey – even damaging the Police Station.[3207]

Noddy bikes or Velocettes were introduced to Waltham Abbey from late 1959 and remained until the 1970s.[3208]

In 1960 Constable Robert Kent's efforts to improve the garden at the station won him the first-ever police station garden competition, which the station won a further three times. Later that year, as part of an experiment, the station was shut for night duty to visitors although a cabinet was installed in the front of the station for enquirers to contact Walthamstow Police Station by telephone.

Boundary changes in April 1965 ceded Chingford to Waltham Holy Cross Urban District Council, and under the authority of Waltham Abbey Police Sub-Division. Manpower was shown as one inspector, five sergeants, 35 constables and two officers from the CID.[3209]

In January 1984 a new police lamp was fitted to the wall outside the station to replace the lamp that had been removed in 1954.

A site for a new police station had been earmarked in Highbridge Street, previously the superintendent's residence of the Royal Gunpowder Factory. It had been purchased by the Metropolitan Police in 1975 for £75,000. Vandalism and theft had made the building dangerous, and refusals to demolish the existing building were given by the Local Authority. Demolition was finally agreed in January 1977. Part of the site was sold off, causing problems of access to the remaining site.

In 1987 Waltham Abbey was relocated onto the new Epping Forest Sub-Division, together with Loughton and Chigwell, as part of Barkingside Division. The aim was to relocate borders so that the division fell within the boundaries of the new local authority.[3210]

On 1st April 2000 Waltham Abbey Police Station was handed over to Essex Police as part of a rationalisation process in making borough and council boundaries co-terminus with police borders.

The station front counter was closed in 2011, and finally the station closed completely in 2016.

Walthamstow Police Station

London Borough of Waltham Forest
Vestry House, Church End, Walthamstow (1840-1870)
360 Forest Road, Walthamstow (1892-2012)
N Division (1840-1886)
J Division (1886-1993)
Waltham Forest OCU 1993-2012

Walthamstow Police Station Lamp

In 1829 the general area of Walthamstow was patrolled by the Metropolitan Police horse patrol. A building of brick-and-slate with six rooms had been leased from Mr. Leberty of the Castle Inn, Walthamstow for a rent of £17 per annum. This building was used to house the officer and his family, and also to stable the horse.

In 1840 the police officers moved into premises at Vestry House, Church End, Walthamstow[3211] (this building is now the Vestry museum). This was a two-storey building made of brown stock brick, and had been constructed in 1730 (and extended in 1756) by order of the Vestry.[3212] The extension provided extra room for the large number of paupers in Walthamstow at the time. It was this space that was used by the police from 1841 until 1870, when the police were transferred to Lea Bridge Road.[3213]

There were four sergeants, seventeen constables and one mounted constable. The station inspector from Enfield Highway Police Station – some distance away – supervised them.[3214]

3188 Metropolitan Police Orders dated 10th January 1876.
3189 Elliott, B. (1987) *The Abbey*.
3190 Ibid.
3191 *Metropolitan Police Commissioner's Annual Report* 1869.
3192 Metropolitan Police General Orders 1873.
3193 *Metropolitan Police Commissioner's Annual Report* 1869.
3194 *Metropolitan Police Commissioner's Annual Report* 1874.
3195 Elliott, B. (1987) *The Abbey*.
3196 Elliott, B. (1993) 'A History of the Police Stations of J Division 1886-1986'.
3197 Gould, R. and Waldren, M. (1986) *London's Armed Police* Arms and Armour Press, London.
3198 Elliott, B. (1987) *The Abbey*.
3199 Ibid.
3200 Ibid.
3201 Ibid.
3202 Ibid.
3203 Metropolitan Police Orders dated 27th July 1933.
3204 Elliott, B. (1987) *The Abbey*.
3205 Ibid
3206 Ingleton, R. (1994) *The Gentlemen at War Policing Britain 1939-45*. Cranborne, Maidstone, Kent.
3207 Ibid.
3208 Elliott, B. (1987) *The Abbey*.
3209 Metropolitan Police Orders dated April 1965.
3210 Ibid.
3211 Elliot, B (1992) 'History of the Police Stations of J Division 1886-1986' p11.
3212 www.lbwf.gov.uk/leisure/vestry/vest_hist.stm accessed 6th May 2002.
3213 Ibid.
3214 Mead, B. (undated) Welcome Pack: Chingford Division.

The station provided accommodation for a single internal cell in which to house one prisoner, whilst outside there was a lock-up attached to the east wall of the building.³²¹⁵

In 1864 the Commissioner approved the transfer of Walthamstow to N or Islington Division³²¹⁶ and the employment of Police Sergeant 57N Turner on station duties at the police station.³²¹⁷ Even today the lock-up can still be seen, complete with Victorian graffiti written on the walls by the prisoners.³²¹⁸

Walthamstow Police Station 1840-1870

However, these premises were not ideal for police use and a new building was opened in November 1868³²¹⁹ in Lea Bridge Road, on the corner of Shrubland Road. Once vacated, the old station building was taken over for use as an armoury by the Walthamstow Volunteers.³²²⁰

In 1886 Bethnal Green took over as the headquarters station for N Division.³²²¹

In August 1889 the Home Office sanctioned the purchase of a plot of land at the junction of Clay Street (Forest Road) and Greenleaf Road, Walthamstow as suitable for a police station. The freehold site was obtained for the sum of £435.³²²² It opened for business in December 1892.³²²³

Walthamstow Police Station 1892-1941

From December 1898 until December 1906 various communications were received from The Overseers of the Poor of the Parish of Walthamstow, Walthamstow Urban District Council and certain individuals complaining of the shortage of police in the area. In 1891 there were seventy officers of all ranks performing duty in the parish. In December 1892 the Superintendent requested a further augmentation of two sergeants and 22 constables to add to his overworked officers at the station, but only five more constables were granted.³²²⁴ In 1899 the strength had risen to ninety officers.³²²⁵

This was the station built in 1892, and substantially reconstructed in 1941.

There had been a population explosion during that period, and the numbers had risen from 46,000 to an estimated 80,000 persons in 1899. Many new houses were built during this period, with newcomers attracted to the area by the twenty-minute train service journey to London. Fares were cheap, and the Great Eastern Railway issued workmen's return tickets to London at 0004 hours for 2d, and then up until 0800 hours for 4d.³²²⁶

In 1907 the station was connected to the public telephone network. In 1929 a motor van was delivered to the station – the first police transport for the area.³²²⁷

Just prior to WWII it was decided to reconstruct the station on the original site purchased in 1890. The new station at 360 Forest Road, Walthamstow was built for the sum of £26,815, and work was completed in 1941.³²²⁹ In effect, the size of the station was doubled to its right with the building of a new entrance hall and gabled extrusion. Walthamstow division suffered only one casualty during the war, when Constable 620J Bentley was killed during an enemy air attack in March 1941.³²³⁰

A variety of additional requirements brought on by the onset of war caused a certain amount of disruption at the station. The addition of air raid sirens, a certain amount of target hardening and the building of a cleansing centre connected to air raid precaution measures, meant that the contract to rebuild the station could not be completed until 1943.³²³¹

Walthamstow Police Station 1941-2012

In 1971 more space was required for the increase in numbers of police officers, however it was decided that rebuilding Chingford Police Station was a better option.³²³² In 1977 Walthamstow transferred its divisional offices to Chingford,³²³³ when it became a sectional station.³²³⁴ In 2013 the station was closed and sold for £1m to E17 Met Ltd.³²³⁵

In 2002, to help them police the busy Walthamstow Town Centre – which boasted the longest street market in Europe – a purpose-built police office was set up at 193 High Street, Walthamstow.

The station was staffed by one sergeant, seven permanent constables and five other constables drawn from the core relief team.³²³⁵ The office did not have cells or interview facilities, but the unit made a large number of arrests each year and prisoners were taken to the nearest police station for processing.³²³⁶ The market area is covered by a number of closed-circuit television cameras in an effort to stamp out crime through the Walthamstow Retail Anti-Crime Partnership. In 2017 the office was closed.³²³⁷

Walthamstow Town Police Office 2002-2017

Walton Street Police Station

Royal Borough of Kensington and Chelsea

60-62 Walton Street (1851-2009)

B Division (1851-2003)

Kensington and Chelsea OCU (2003-2009)

Walton Street Police Station was added to B Division in 1851, the same year when the major development of creating Victoria Street was implemented. There was a lease from a Mr W. Delferier from Michaelmas 1849.[3238] The station was connected to the Metropolitan Police telegraph network with the code 'WS' in December 1871.[3239]

Walton Street was seen as a good location for a police station. It was just to the south of Brompton Road, and its rear yard could be accessed from Yeoman's Row, a cul-de-sac that ran south from Brompton Road and ended in the alleyway (Glynde Mews) that connected to Walton Street itself. The police commitment to the area was confirmed with the purchase of the freehold of the site at 60-62 Walton Street on 31st May 1894. Plans were started for a new police station.

The files relating to the development are an interesting reflection of how the police operated in those days. The Receiver would write formal letters to the Commissioner about relatively small details. At times, the Receiver's office acted almost as if it were a separate organisation. Letters were exchanged about giving access to the roof for police families, and running a pipe from the kitchen so that they might have hot water for a bath. The Receiver stated that the plumbing cost of £20 would need to be referred to the Secretary of State, that the police officers should pay an extra 6d in rent for the extra facility, and that it would be important that washing should not be hung out within the view of the well-kept garden of an expensively-rented house in Egerton Terrace. After the rent details had been published, perhaps waiting deliberately, the Commissioner then suggested that the Receiver might not wish to undertake the extra administrative effort and submissions to have the rent changed again for the sake of the extra 6d per week.

The local division were not given access to the plans, but they made up a sketch plan on the basis of which they made their representations. They thought that it would be desirable for the surgeon's room to be big enough to accommodate a hand ambulance. Superintendent Isaac objected to plans for the detention room to be practically in the charge room,

Yeoman's Row, showing the rear of Walton Street Police Station on the left

3215 Elliot, B (1992) 'History of the Police Stations of J Division 1886-1986'.
3216 Mead, B. (undated) Welcome Pack: Chingford Division.
3217 Metropolitan Police Orders dated 27th April 1864.
3218 www.lbwf.gov.uk/leisure/vestry/vest_hist.stm dated 06.05.02.
3219 Metropolitan Police Orders dated 5th November 1868.
3220 www.lbwf.gov.uk/leisure/vestry/vest_hist.stm dated 06.05.02.
3221 Mead, B. (undated) Welcome Pack: Chingford Division.
3222 John Back Archive (1975).
3223 Metropolitan Police Orders dated 24th December 1892.
3224 Mead, B. (undated) Welcome Pack: Chingford Division
3225 John Back Archive (1975).
3226 Elliot, B (1992) 'History of the Police Stations of J Division 1886-1986'.
3228 Mead, B. (undated) Welcome Pack: Chingford Division.
3229 John Back Archive (1975).
3230 Mead, B. (undated) Welcome Pack: Chingford Division.
3231 Ibid.
3232 Ibid.
3233 Ibid; also John Back Archive (1975).
3234 Metropolitan Police Orders dated 7th January 1977.
3235 Freedom of Information Request Information Rights Unit property sales Data 2008-2018.
3236 Metropolitan Police Orders dated 7th January 1977.
3237 www.walthamforestecho.co.uk (2nd September 2017).
3238 List of Metropolitan Police Stations 1873 (MEPO 4/234).
3239 Bernard Brown.

Walton Street Police Station 1851-2009

because a detention room was 'intended for the occupation of persons of the better class who …should not be treated as the ordinary prisoner and …subject to the vile language used by low class prisoners waiting to be charged, which is sometimes of a shocking nature'. By October 1907 the Commissioner was writing to the Receiver about the delay, stating that he would 'be greatly obliged if consideration of the plans were dealt with a pressing matter'.[3240]

The basements of the police station and section house were connected by means of a passageway running underneath the police station yard.

One part of the development was completed on 18th December 1895, and the next stage was ready for occupation in April 1911. The first floor accommodated offices for the superintendent, a chief inspector, the divisional clerks and the CID. On the ground floor were the inspectors' office, the charge room, six cells and an association cell. In the yard was an ambulance shed for the hand ambulances that were used by the police officers of the day for taking people to hospital, or drunks to the station.

In the days when the rank of sub-divisional inspector existed, quarters were provided (April 1905 until 1910) for him at 47 Ovingdon Street, Chelsea. A new section house at Yeoman's Row was taken into use on 14th February 1910.

Walton Street became absorbed by another sub-division, when Chelsea was opened at Lucan Place in 1939. More recently it had been used as a base for the Diplomatic Protection Group, and was put up for sale and disposed of with 64 Yeoman's Row in 2009 and sold to Walton Street properties for £17.25M.[3241]

Wandsworth Police Station

The London Borough of Wandsworth
Bridge Field, Wandsworth (1830-1833)
The Plain, Wandsworth (1832-1864)
Love Lane, Wandsworth (1864-1883)
146 High Street (1883 to Present)
V Division (1830-1965)
W Division (1965-1993)
Borough of Wandsworth OCU (1993-2018/19)
SW BCU with Richmond, Kingston and Merton
(2018/19 to Present)

This station is not to be confused with Wandsworth Common Police Station situated in Trinity Road, Tooting, which is dealt with separately. Records show that from 2nd May 1830 provision was made for Police premises to be leased for three years in Bridge Field, Wandsworth on an annual rent of £52.[3242] It is uncertain whether this was for use as a police station, detached office or for accommodation, however further references give an address as 10 Love Lane.[3243]

Documentation relating to the cleaning of Metropolitan Police Stations in 1832 shows a Station located at The Plain, Wandsworth, being a station on V Division,[3244] where the superintendent had his offices. In those earlier days there was only a Wandsworth designation, and a divisional letter had not yet been brought into use. However by 1840 Wandsworth was shown as part of V or Wandsworth Division.

Later references also show that Wandsworth had a Watch House, and that as of 25th June 1850 it was no longer used for Police purposes.[3245] This was probably the one in The Plain. Wandsworth was not apparently under Metropolitan Police jurisdiction until 1839, disputing the claim made earlier that the boundary extended to cover the Parishes of Battersea, Wandsworth, Barnes, Mortlake, Wimbledon, Merton and Tooting. Prior to this policing was carried out locally by the Parish Constable aided by paid constables from the watch house premises, and they were said to be very efficient in their duties. Wandsworth was also the place where Petty Court sessions were introduced at the same time, and a list of magistrates together with their addresses were published.[3246] Another building was used, also located in Love Lane, and was brought into service in 1864. The property was leased from Mr Joseph Langton for a duration of 21 years at an annual rent of £85.[3247]

Wandsworth Police Station was referred to as Wandsworth, Love Lane and it retained its divisional headquarters status as well being an operational station. It had three cells, a recreation room and large stables accommodating up to 15 horses. In the yard were a van house and a coal shed. The station strength in 1864 was two inspectors, seven sergeants and 52 constables. The station had a superintendent's office, and a divisional office occupied by the divisional clerk. Instructions were issued that the mounted inspector or sergeant was also to patrol Battersea, Merton and Tooting.[3248]

Wandsworth Police Station 1864-1883

The prisoner transport van was stationed at Love Lane, as well as a hand cart for the removal of drunken prisoners from the street. The divisional Criminal Investigation Department occupied the whole of the second floor after those single constables were moved out in 1878 to live at Bay Cottage next door.[3249] In 1881 the cottage was still occupied, but arrangements were being made move the occupants out. This was given up in March 1884.[3250]

The section house, called Bay Cottage, housed ten single constables, with the head constable being George Dowty, aged 34, from Wiltshire.[3251]

The Metropolitan Police Surveyor's concern with regard to the poor state of the station was evident in their 1881 report, in which it said that:

'This station has for years been abandoned as a police dwelling on account of its dilapidated condition and because it was infested with vermin. A site for a new station was purchased about 1874, and the constables have been located in a small cottage not far off as a temporary expedient, but the erection of the new station is not begun.'[3252]

The police station and courthouse stood where Armoury Way now stands, and was demolished in 1892. The old station remained occupied until 1883, when it was vacated.[3253]

The station also had a recreation room, where there was a billiard table for the use of off duty officers. The Commissioner instructed that Wandsworth should receive a new billiard table in 1870, and Battersea was allocated a variety of games for its recreation room.[3254]

Wandsworth Police Station 1883 to present

Often police officers would be assaulted in the execution of their duty, a risk at that of which officers were most aware. Whistles were issued (from 1881 onwards) to each officer to summon help; three short blasts and a constable on a neighbouring beat would hurry to render assistance. Drunken males were often a problem as they could be violent, and Constable Joseph Eite was kicked and died whilst trying to arrest a person for drunkenness in 1868.[3255] The lack of a sufficient number of Police was often the cause of increased assaults on officers, and 1881 saw the sad death of Inspector John Pearman, who had been at Wandsworth since 1877, who perished from wounds which he received following an arrest.[3256]

Inspector John Bussain
Promoted 1830
Address: The Plain Police Station at Wandsworth

Inspector Richard Turner
Promoted 1830
Address: Princes Street Police Station at Richmond

Inspector Richard Dowset
Appointed Inspector in 1814
Address: London Road Police Station at Kingston

3240 MEPO 2/726.
3241 Freedom of Information Request Information Rights Unit Property Sales Data 2008-2018.
3242 MEPO 5/3.
3243 MEPO 5/54(441).
3244 Distribution and Return of Wool Mops for Cleaning Stations on each Division, dated 1st July 1832,
3245 MEPO 5/7.
3246 MEPO 2/76.
3247 Metropolitan Police Surveyor's Records.
3248 Metropolitan Police Orders dated 11th January 1864.
3249 Metropolitan Police Surveyor's Records.
3250 Report on the Condition of Police Stations 1881.
3251 Census 1881.
3252 Report on the Condition of Police Stations 1881.
3253 Metropolitan Police Surveyor's Records 1864.
3254 Metropolitan Police Orders dated 15th July 1869.
3255 National Police Roll of Honour, 2002.
3256 Ibid.

A postcard of Wandsworth High Street showing the position of the police station

Inspector James Shepherd
Promoted in 1837
Address: Milman Road, Chelsea

Inspector Henry Creed
Promoted 1842
Address: Clapham Common, Clapham

What is clear from the listing above is that the most experienced and longest-serving Inspector was Richard Dowsett, who had most likely been a Bow Street Horse Patrole Inspector prior to being posted to Kingston, a Thames-side posting.

Boundary revisions between Wandsworth and Clapham were included in the changes in borders between B, L and V Divisions in 1863.[3257] From 1864 Wandsworth was designated a station on V Division, and that it was a place where Police duties were to be carried out including the parading of police officers, charges taken and prisoners detained in cells.[3258] The station must have been important, as it was shown as having a strength of two inspectors, seven sergeants and 52 constables. It contained stables to house the horses, which were used by sergeants and inspectors for supervision purposes. Two sergeants at the station would take it in turns to ride one horse on the sub-division, whilst either the inspector or the remaining sergeant was to use the other to patrol further afield including visiting Battersea, Merton and Tooting.[3259]

Superintendent Butt reported the problems of policing in Wandsworth in his annual report to the Commissioner, but indicated that crime had dropped by 20% between 1869 and 1871, that vagrancy offences had also fallen by 70% and that there were far fewer complaints of begging. Other issues related to leaving washing out during the night and the control of public houses and beer houses.[3260]

The photograph at the top of the next column shows the large rear yard of the station; a separate section house was later built further away.

The huge rear yard of the station

In 1868 Wandsworth Sub-Division was divided in two and a separate sub-division of Battersea was created; Inspector Egerton from Wandsworth was transferred to Battersea to take charge of this newly-created area. Some 22 horses were stabled at the station, including six which were used for prisoner van transportation from the court to prison.

The division had expanded to include Wandsworth, Battersea, Merton, Barnes, Richmond, Kingston, Ditton and Epsom.[3261] Firearms were stored at the station, and Wandsworth is shown to have had then second-issue revolvers, which were distributed on 19th November 1868. Ten rounds of ammunition were issued for each weapon.[3262]

The picture below shows the rear aspect of the station and the access to the main building. By the mid 1870s the old station house was considered no longer suitable for carrying out the duties of policing, and suggestions were offered about finding a larger site on which to build a bigger and more up-to-date police station. Some available land located on higher ground seemed perfect for the job, as it would offer better access for the prison van to facilitate the transport of prisoners, and on 6th April 1875 the freehold was purchased for £2,000.

A rear view of the station showing access to the main building

The picture below shows another aspect, with the parade shed where the constables would form up prior to coming on duty and be inspected by the sergeant. During the parade the constables would produce their appointments, their notebook, handcuffs, truncheon and whistle for inspection. Any constable unable or who produced defective appointments would become the subject of a disciplinary charge. Any important local intelligence would also be disclosed and noted down, such as stolen cars or details of persons wanted.

Wandsworth's Parade Shed in the rear yard

Interestingly, part of the premises had formerly belonged to the Lord of the Manor.[3263] Building started on the new police station in 1882, and by Christmas Eve 1883 the administration section of the building was suitable for occupation. The address was recorded as West Hill, Wandsworth,[3264] formerly the site of 'Sword House'.

A substantial station was built on the site at a cost of £10,738 3s, and contained accommodation for V Division's headquarters. Superintendent Charles Digby took charge of the station and, as married quarters of five rooms had been built on the first floor, these were occupied by him and his family.

In addition, thirty-four single constables resided on both the first and second floors. With the constant comings and goings of the divisional superintendent and his family, the constables needed to behave themselves at all times otherwise serious disciplinary issues would have arisen. Later, in 1881, Digby and his wife and daughter moved from the station to Thurnhill Villa, Rose Hill Road, Wandsworth;[3265] special Police dwellings for senior officers. In 1888 Digby was assisted by David Saines as Chief Inspector and George Earwaker as Reserve (mounted) Inspector.

Wandsworth Sub-Divisional Inspectors

William Gillies (1893-1895)
Edward Mckenna (1895-1905)
James Andrews (1905-1906)
Walter Cleave (1906-1908)
William Brice (1908-1910)
Charles Hodges (1910-1914)
William Barham (1914-1917)

By 1893, because of the appointment of large numbers of inspectors the Commissioner decided that there should be a more senior inspector between the chief inspector and the ordinary station inspector, so he appointed sub-divisional inspectors on promotion. These were usually responsible, trusted and experienced inspectors, and they were easily distinguishable by having two stars on either side of their tunic collar. Whilst all stations on Wandsworth division had inspectors, Sub-Divisional Inspector William Gillies took charge of Wandsworth, Wandsworth Common, Wimbledon, Putney and Roehampton.

Sometimes when an officer takes action in the line of duty unfortunate circumstances which could lead to tragic events may occur. In 1896 Constable Edwin Stone died of a heart attack whilst arresting a violent prisoner at Wandsworth.[3266]

In 1907 the address of the station was shown as High Street, Wandsworth. It was a station on V Division, and was also the divisional headquarters. A sectional station was also shown at Wandsworth Common. The division, together with L, M, P, R and W, formed the Southern District, which was under the supervision of a chief constable stationed at New Scotland Yard.[3267]

The ranks of the Police at Wandsworth were swelled by large numbers of the Special Constabulary, who as citizens held down essential jobs but also volunteered their services free to supplement dwindling Police numbers. In June 1916, for example, the Wandsworth men joined the regular officers in saving the lives of enemy aliens (usually people of German or European extraction) and protecting their property from public wrath.

A revision of boundaries in 1914 between Wandsworth and Richmond Sub-Divisions resulted in a new station at Kew being opened.[3268] Further revisions established the sub-division of Earlsfield, which meant that there were boundary alterations at Wandsworth, Battersea, Wimbledon and Kingston. A new division was formed in 1921 named Z or Croydon Division, which led to further alterations to W or Wandsworth divisional boundaries.[3269] In 1937 Wandsworth was a sectional station of Putney (VD).[3270]

3257 Metropolitan Police Orders dated 21st October 1863.
3258 Metropolitan Police Orders dated 11th January 1864.
3259 Ibid.
3260 *Commissioner's Annual Report* 1971 p68.
3261 Metropolitan Police Orders dated 13th July 1868.
3262 Metropolitan Police Orders dated 10th March 1869.
3263 John Back Archive (1975); LB 670.
3264 Metropolitan Police Orders dated 20th June 1884.
3265 Census 1881.
3266 The National Police Roll of Honour dated 2002.
3267 *Kirchner's Almanac* 1907.
3268 Metropolitan Police Orders dated 29th January 1914.
3269 Metropolitan Police Orders dated 24th February 1921.
3270 Districts and Divisions Map 1937.

A review of Police buildings took place in 1959, and it was recommended that even though Wandsworth was built in 1883 and was old, it was not recommended for rebuilding until at least 1974.³²⁷¹ In line with the creation of Local Authority Boundary changes taking place in London under the London Government Act 1963, the status of Wandsworth as a station was reduced to that of sectional station to Putney Sub-Division. The station was shown as being located on W or Tooting Division at this time,³²⁷² and this was still the case in 1966.³²⁷³

Its divisional administration of chief superintendent, superintendent and a portion of the general administrative staff was transferred to Wandsworth Police Station. Chief Inspector Admin, together with the Process Section, remained at Putney.³²⁷⁴

In 1981 Putney Division was re-designated as a sub-divisional station and absorbed into W Division.

In 2009 records show that a police office had been established in the Arndale Shopping Centre, Wandsworth, and that it was open Mondays to Saturdays. Although fixed opening hours are not available these appear to be the same as the shopping centre itself.³²⁷⁵

The main Wandsworth station was still retained for police purposes as of 2019.³²⁷⁶

Wandsworth Common (Trinity Road) Police Station

The London Borough of Wandsworth
Wandsworth Common (1873-1883)
76 Trinity Road (1883-1993)
V Division (1873-1923)
W Division (1923-1993)
Borough of Wandsworth OCU (1993-2012)

This station was shown on the corner of Trinity Road, Upper Tooting, SW17, and situated at the junction with St. Nicholas Road. Often the station has been referred to as Trinity Road Police Station; this was a road that stretched from East Hill, Wandsworth, straight through Wandsworth Common to Balham. The station was situated at the Balham end of the road. In 1873 Wandsworth Common was shown as a station of V or Wandsworth Division, and had a sergeant in charge.

In 1878 additional premises were leased until 1886 from Mr H.P. Rainbow of Broderick Road. These were to be used as a section house, with living accommodation for an inspector, a sergeant and five constables.

The two-storey premises in Broderick Road, Wandsworth Common, cost £50 per year to rent, and there were stipulations in the contract that the premises were not to be used for cells or a lock-up, and that no other buildings were to be erected on the site.³²⁷⁷ This meant that this was not a police station, and that prisoners were transferred to Wandsworth for charging.

Metropolitan Police Surveyors reported in 1881 that the premises for use as a police station at Trinity Road were occupied by one married inspector and five single constables and that the station was:

'an ordinary dwelling house in a suburban road, ill-adapted to the requirements. The men wash in the inspector's scullery and a proper station would be a great advantage.' ³²⁷⁸

Freehold to the site was purchased in 1882, and a police station built and occupied in 1886. It also contained a section house which was built at the location. The station was built in about 1890, and was constructed using a plum brick, with egg-and-dart mouldings to string courses and a stone staircase.

Wandsworth Common Police Station 1883-2012

Records show that in 1893 the station was situated on V or Wandsworth Division, and was connected to the telegraph system. In fact both Wandsworth and Wandsworth Common Police Stations had been connected to the telegraph system on 23rd September 1886, and were awarded the code Whiskey Charlie (WC).³²⁷⁹ During Trenchard's reforms of the 1930s, the oddity for this station was that it retained the same telegraph code and was probably the only station in the Metropolitan Police to do so.

The picture below shows the rear yard aspect.

Rear yard of the station

During 1885 the sub-inspector at Wandsworth Common was Nathan Thompson Lee, born in 1824 at Strelton in Cumberland, who had joined the Police in 1868. He had come to note as a self-taught amateur woodworker, winning 23 prizes for his exhibited works at various industrial schools in London. His distinguished Police career was marked with a full-page tribute in the *Police Review and Parade Gossip* of 1895. Amongst his many commendations were the 'clever capture' of two house-breakers at Hampton Wick, and the arrest of a local notorious ruffian, Patsy Ryan. The article reports that he was promoted to sergeant on the strength of these arrests, and transferred to Arbour Square on H Division in London's East End. What was unique in Mr Lee's service was the fact that he did not miss one hour's duty through sickness. He received substantial gifts for his loyal service, together with an oil painting of himself in uniform painted by a local artist. After two years at Wandsworth Common Inspector Lee was transferred to Battersea, where he saw out his service.³²⁸⁰

In 1924 Wandsworth Common was a station on W or Brixton Division, and no longer V Division. In 1925 a strip of surplus land with a frontage was sold to Messrs Frost for £230. The address of the police station was shown as 76 Trinity Road in 1931.

A fixed-point box was erected in Alma Terrace, but in June 1932 it was removed to Wandsworth Police Station and replaced with Telephone Box No. 37.[3281]

The station was given a substantial rebuild in 1937. Its telegraphic call sign was Whiskey Charlie (WC), and it was shown as a sectional station to Balham (Cavendish Road) in the same year.

A rear view of the main building in 1907

During the 1960s the status of the station was shown as sectional to the sub-divisional station situated at Balham.[3282] In May 1971 application was received by Wandsworth Council from the Surveyor of the Metropolitan Police for another rebuilding of the station. Plans submitted requested that a bigger station was required for Policing purposes, and rebuilding was to include the adjoining site in Upper Tooting Park.[3283]

Wandsworth Common Police Station amalgamated with Earlsfield Police Station in January 1974 and adopted the status of Police office, being open from 8.30am until 11.30pm when the station would close. Outside of opening hours a telephone link to Tooting Police Station was available free of charge to provide immediate contact for callers.[3284]

In 2007 Wandsworth Common Police Station was still in use as a Police Office, and housed the newly-introduced Safer Neighbourhood Teams which consisted of one sergeant, two constables and five Police Community Support Officers.[3285]

In February 2012 the freehold site and station was put up for sale and fetched £1.53M.[3286]

Wanstead Police Station

The London Borough of Redbridge

Various houses in Wanstead (1840-1886)

Spratt Hall Road, Wanstead (1886-2013)

N Division (1840-1886)

J Division (1886-1993)

Redbridge OCU (1993-2013)

The general area of Walthamstow, Wanstead and Low Leyton were patrolled by the Metropolitan Police Horse Patrol. A total of one sergeant and three constables from the station at

Wanstead Police Station Lamp

Great Ilford policed Wanstead in 1840. In 1845 a station and section house were occupied in Wanstead Broadway. The premises were leased from Mr. A.J. Cooper of the George Inn, Wanstead on a yearly lease of £20. Records show that it was small, but it had a charge room and a kitchen. Stables were available at the rear at an additional cost of £10 per annum.

In 1864 Wanstead was shown as a station where constables paraded for duty. Charges were not taken and the building did not have cells. There was one sergeant in charge together with an acting sergeant, who split night and day duty between them. Two constables worked the day shift, whilst seven constables took over during the hours of darkness.[3287] An inspector supervised Wanstead from nearby (Little) Ilford Police Station.[3288]

The police were still occupying the property as a temporary police station in 1867. Records showed that as from that date

"The police of N Division are to take charge of and occupy the house at Wanstead Broadway, recently taken as a temporary police station. All prisoners charged at this station are to be conveyed to Walthamstow Police Station, to be kept there in safe custody after charges have been preferred." [3289]

In 1877 Wanstead was a minor station of N or Islington Division, and was designated a station with a sergeant in charge.[3290] The following police sergeants and police constables were appointed to perform station duty at Wanstead temporary station, in periods of 12 hours each: PS2N Phillips, PS1N Lucas, PC124N Howe and PC271N Gardener.[3291]

After the Broadway building had been occupied police found a number of other buildings for use as a temporary police station. For example, at 1 George Lane a rather dilapidated two-stall stable in the yard of the George and Dragon public house was used to house police horses, for an annual rent of £40.

3271 John Back Archive (1975); LB 670.
3272 Metropolitan Police Orders dated 6th August 1964.
3273 Metropolitan Police List 1966.
3274 Metropolitan Police Orders dated 4th August 1981.
3275 Metropolitan Police Authority (MPA) Committee reports accessed 15th February 2009 cms.met.police.uk/boroughs/wandsworth/09contact_us/index.
3276 MPS Assets (2019) Freedom of Information request.
3277 Metropolitan Police Surveyor's Records 1878.
3278 Report on the Condition of Police Stations 1881.
3279 Metropolitan Police General Orders 1893.
3280 *Police Review and Parade Gossip*, 1st March 1895.
3281 Metropolitan Police Surveyor's Records 1924.
3282 *Police and Constabulary Almanac* 1960.
3283 'Police Station rebuilding' in *Balham and Tooting News*, 14th May 1971.
3284 'Police Stations combine' in *Wandsworth Borough News*, 4th January 1974.
3285 www.met.police.uk/wandsworth/saferneighbourhoods.htm accessed 3rd September 2007.
3286 MPS (2018) Freedom of Information request: Police station closures broken down by year.
3287 Metropolitan Police Orders dated 11th January 1864.
3288 Ibid.
3289 Metropolitan Police Orders dated 11th March 1867.
3290 *Police Office London Directory* 1877.
3291 John Back Archive (1975).

In 1881 Constable John Creasey lived at the station. He was 41-years-old, and resided there with his wife Elizabeth (aged 36 years) and their four children.[3292]

Police Orders in June 1884 showed the new address of the station as 1 Tenterden Terrace, Nightingale Lane, Wanstead.[3293] These premises were rented for £25 per annum.[3294]

A freehold site was purchased in 1885 for the sum of £700 for the erection of a new police station in Spratt Hall Road, at the junction of Chaucer Road, Wanstead. It was built for the sum of £2,366. The new station opened in September 1886.[3295]

The accommodation included space for one married inspector, who lived in four rooms on the first floor and two rooms on the second floor above the police station. A married constable lived in three rooms on the ground floor of the stable block and two rooms on the first floor.[3296] By 1890 there were four Inspectors – James Ware, Thomas Groves, John Gillies and George Rolfe – one sergeant and sixteen constables posted to the station.[3297]

Wanstead Police Station 1886-2013

On 1st January 1897 a retirement presentation took place, and the newly-retired Sub-Divisional Inspector Alexander Wallace of J Division, now stationed at Hackney but formerly at Wanstead, was presented with a handsome saddle, bridle and riding whip as a mark of respect by a number of the residents of Wanstead.[3298]

Wanstead was a sectional station to Leyton in 1930.[3299] Wanstead Police Station was refurbished in 1935.[3300]

In 1957 Barkingside, Claybury, Loughton and Wanstead were sectional stations to Woodford Sub-Division. Superintendent A.L. Barratt, who was located at Woodford, was in charge of the station. Wanstead was situated on J or Hackney Division, which supervised by Chief Superintendent H.E. Howlett.[3301] In 1960 Wanstead's call sign was Juliet November (JN).[3302]

In July 2000 Wanstead (with Chadwell Heath Police Station) was a sub-divisional station of Ilford Division, however because of boundary changes it became part of the Borough of Redbridge.

The police station was sold on 12th March 2014 to a private resident for £1,653,000. The building has since been converted into residential accommodation, and two additional houses have been built on the site in keeping with surrounding properties.

Waterloo Pier Police Station

City of Westminster
Tower Lifeboat Station, Victoria Embankment
Thames Division (1873-2006)
Royal National Lifeboat Institution (2006 to Present)

The Marine Police on the River Thames was established in 1798, before the Metropolitan Police, and installed a floating police station, the former warship *Port Mahon* alongside Somerset House to become its upstream station (the middle station being Wapping and the lower station at Blackwall). Waterloo Pier was rented in 1873 to replace the old warship, and the location covered not only the incidents that might occur in the river near Westminster, but also the unfortunate trend for depressed people to throw themselves into the river from Waterloo Bridge.

Waterloo Pier Police Station 1873 to present

The spectacular reduction in crime from the London docks when the Marine Police was first established gave way to a steadier pace of patrolling the river, but the dangers of the river are sometimes seen when boats collide.

In 1878 the paddle steamer *Princess Alice* was near Woolwich on a 'moonlight trip' back to London Bridge from Gravesend when she collided with the *Bywell Castle*, a much larger vessel used for carrying coal that was being accompanied by a Thames river pilot. Confusion over how they should pass each other led to the *Princess Alice* being cut in two and it rapidly sunk, with the loss of over 650 lives.

The river police were only using rowing boats at the time, but the inquiry into the disaster recommended their being supplied with steam launches so that they could be more effective at dealing with such rescue emergencies in the future.

In August 1989 the *Marchioness* pleasure boat was sunk by the dredger *Bowbelle* near Cannon Street railway bridge with the loss of 51 lives, providing another example of the importance of careful seamanship when small boats use the same river as much larger vessels.

The RNLI was asked to consider extending their life-saving operations to the River Thames, the first time that the RNLI had been asked to cover a river rather than a coastline. They established a station at Waterloo Pier in 2002. Work to complete the transition of the pier to an RNLI station was completed in 2006. The RNLI Tower Pier is their busiest station and is staffed 24 hours per day. Their operations are also based at Teddington and Chiswick.

Wealdstone Police Station

The London Borough of Harrow
74 High Street (1908-1933)
78 High Street (1933-2011)
S Division (1909-1933)
X Division (1933-1965)
Q Division (1965-1993)
Borough of Harrow OCU (1993-2011)

Wealdstone Police Station Lamp

Wealdstone Police Station opened in 1909, but prior to this the area was served by the police station at Edgware (Little Stanmore).[3303] In the 1880s, the London and North Western Railway was promoting a bill through Parliament for the construction of a railway line from Harrow to Stanmore. It was thought that a new line would attract a considerable amount of people to the area.

Shown taking part on the usual weekly pay parade in the picture below is Sergeant Frederick Bolsover (warrant no. 83843), shown with flat cap back row sixth from left, who joined the police in April 1898. He went onto become a station sergeant, and retired from X Division in April 1923 after completing 25 years. Service.[3304] Also in the picture are (front row) Constables Swan, Palethorpe, Alfred Wasp, Taylor, Sergeant Boyce, Sergeant Stewart, Constables William Chidgey, Howland; (back row) Constables Parker, Chapman, William Larcombe, Turner, and Albert Sands, Sergeant Bolsover, Constable Mills, Sergeants Pameter and Lanning, and Constable Soper. Officers used to collect their pay at (Little) Stanmore on a Wednesday.

Wealdstone and Stanmore Police (S Division) pay parade, 1907

In anticipation of greater numbers of people coming to the district, the Receiver of the Metropolitan Police bought an area of land opposite the Seven Balls public house in Weald Lane, at the junction with Hay Lane, on 15th April 1887.[3305] These roads are now renamed Kenton Lane and Gordon Avenue respectively. The site is now a car showroom, while the pub still survives.

By 1904 the proposed railway had never materialised, and the area around Stanmore remained as rural as ever. By this time, the population of Wealdstone had greatly increased due to several large factories being built in the area. With this in mind the Commissioner decided that the Harrow Weald site should be abandoned in favour of a new police station in Wealdstone.[3306] The Harrow Weald site was eventually sold for £875 on 24th September 1934 to a Mr N.H. Sagar.

The site for the station was the four cottages called Mary's Place between the Board School and The Case Is Altered public house. The cottages were purchased for £2,200 and then demolished.[3307] The work on the new station began in late 1907, with the foundation stone being laid in 1908, and the station became fully operational on 22nd February 1909[3308] at a cost of £7,768.[3309] The first occupant of the station was Inspector Chapman, who lived above the station, and Sergeant Lanning was his assistant.[3310]

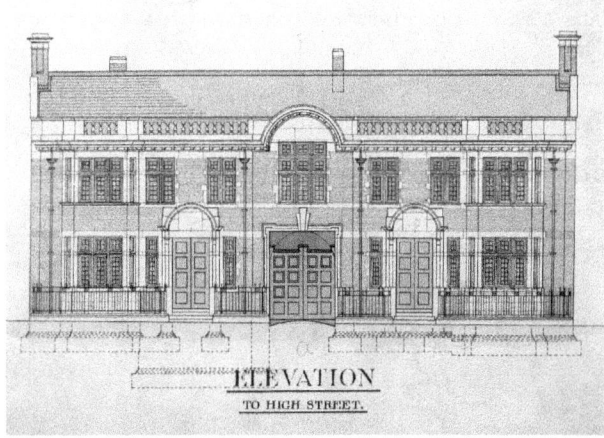

Front elevation plans for Wealdstone Police Station

The picture below shows Wealdstone Police Station in 1907. Once the buildings were pulled down construction of a new station and court building commenced. The Case is Altered Public House is clearly visible on the right of the photograph.

Site of Wealdstone Police Station, 1907

3292   Census 1881.
3293   Elliott, B. (1993) 'A History of the Police Stations of J Division 1886-1986'.
3294   John Back Archive (1975).
3295   Metropolitan Police Orders dated 22nd September 1886.
3296   Metropolitan Police Surveyor's Records.
3297   *Kelly's Directory* 1890.
3298   *Police Review*, January 1897.
3299   *Kirchner's Police Index* 1930.
3300   Metropolitan Police Surveyor's Records.
3301   *Police and Constabulary Almanac* 1957.
3302   *Police and Constabulary Almanac* 1960.
3303   Linwood, Jean. 'Wealdstone Police Station: A Brief History' in *Stanmore & Harrow Historical Society Newsletter*), Autumn 1994.
3304   Metropolitan Police Pension Records.
3305   Metropolitan Police Property register and map for Harrow Weald, dated 15th April 1887, page 158.
3306   Linwood, Jean. *Stanmore & Harrow Historical Society Newsletter*, Autumn 1994.
3307   Metropolitan Police Property Register for Wealdstone, p165.
3308   Metropolitan Police Orders dated 20th February 1909.
3309   Metropolitan Police Property Register for Wealdstone, p165.
3310   'My Diary' by Plato. Undated newspaper article held by Harrow Archives written after receiving an interesting letter from Mr Stanley Lanning of 110 College Road on policing in Wealdstone.

The station, which is now a Grade II-listed building,³³¹¹ was built with an integral magistrates' court, and was described by the Scotland Yard architect J. Dixon Butler as "stone dressed in red brick with a central archway flanked by mullion bays." The right-hand entrance was the police station, the left-hand entrance the magistrates' court. The court comprised two courtrooms, a magistrates' room, waiting room, clerk's office, strong room, women's waiting room, warrant office, solicitor's room and a store.³³¹² The court was operational until 25th June 1935, when court business transferred to the newly-built Harrow Magistrates' Court at Rosslyn Crescent, Harrow. That court closed in 2011.

Wealdstone Police Station and Court c1910

Wealdstone Police Station 1910-2014

When the court opened, the first sitting was reported by the local newspaper under the heading 'Wealdstone Petty Sessions – First Sitting'. Mr Montague Sharpe of the Middlesex Quarter Sessions attended to officially declare the building open.³³¹³ Twelve justices sat in the first session, among them Sir William Gilbert, the famous composer of Gilbert and Sullivan fame, who was a local JP. Also present was the local police chief, Superintendent T. Williams.

The very first case to be heard in the new court was a case of 65-year-old Thomas Jeffs of Wembley, who was charged with misconduct and using obscene language. Constable 404X told the court that Mr Jeffs had called him a "Swede gnawer". He had reacted violently to being arrested and was conveyed to the police station on a tram, where he had to be held down. During the hearing Jeffs clashed with his own solicitor. Later in the proceedings Mr Montague Sharpe observed that he was an excitable man, but being as this was the first ever case at Wealdstone Court a fine would suffice. After being fined 5 shillings Mr Jeffs then swore at the chairman, who increased the fine to one pound and fourteen shillings.

The police station section of the building comprised an inspector's office, charge room, waiting room, telegraph room, four cells, ambulance shed, store, coal room, heating and WCs. Later, from 1948 until 1964, the station shared the building with the Middlesex County Library.³³¹⁴

In March 1909 the local newspaper³³¹⁵ reported the playing of the annual Harrow Police v Harrow Firemen football match at Mr Atkins' field. Terrible weather of rain and snow had affected the pitch, which was in a "shocking condition". Having sold a large number of tickets for the match, the terrible weather restricted the size of the crowd to only twenty hardy souls. 6ft 10in JP, Mr Brian Piers Lascelles, the chairman of the local council, attended to kick off the match. The police led the game 2-0 with five minutes to play, when the referee abandoned the match. The fireman had put in a "plucky" performance, though they had only been able to field ten men.

The police team was Woodward; Saw and Gibson; Jackson, Lewendon and Rush; Moore, Windsor, Kessell, Tible (Captain) and Taschner, with the secretary and linesman being Constable Thompson. The holders of the challenge cup were the Fire Brigade. The trophy was present at the match in the custody of fire chief, Captain Leader, but the report does not make clear whether it was actually awarded to the police due to the abandonment. The match was followed by a dinner with singing and speeches, which was attended by the Divisional Superintendent Olive, as well as Inspector McCondach. Much mutual respect was exchanged between the police and the Fire Brigade. It was said that "Harrow Police are an excellent set of fellows".

Wealdstone Police Station and Court building were appropriately situated right next to The Case is Altered public house. This court replaced the courthouse located next to the Chandos Arms in Edgware.

In November 1933 Wealdstone was transferred from S or Hampstead Division to X or Kilburn Division when it became a sectional station to Harrow. When the new courthouse opened in 1935 the police moved into the old court building, and the CID took over some of the accommodation.

The most momentous day in the history of Wealdstone Police Station was without question 8th October 1952, when a rail disaster took place at Harrow & Wealdstone Station at 8.19am.³³¹⁶ The Perth to Euston overnight sleeper crashed into the back of the stationary Tring to Euston train. Seconds later the London to Liverpool train ran into the wreckage, and 112 people died in Britain's second-worst rail tragedy.

Aside from the 112 fatalities, there were an additional 167 taken to hospital and a further 183 people treated for injuries at the site. Casualties were taken to eight local hospitals. Edgware General Hospital had 40 doctors, 250 nurses and four operating theatres mobilised to help deal with the casualties. Police officers were drafted in from the surrounding area from Acton, Hampstead, Hendon, Hounslow, Golders Green, Ealing, Southall and Teddington Police Stations to help. Some 40 officers came from the Metropolitan Police Driving School from Hendon.

Police Sergeant 39X Morgan witnessed the crash as he stepped off the number 30 bus outside the station. He ran 300 yards to Wealdstone Police Station to inform the station officer. By 9.05am Chief Superintendent David Illesley arrived from Harrow Road Police Station to take charge of the police operation at the scene, and set up a control point on Platform 7. By 9.30am 137 police officers were on the scene, as well as 18 police vehicles. Chief Inspector Ivan Bray took charge of matters at Wealdstone Police Station.

The police mobile canteen finally arrived at 4.00pm, which was long after the US Air Force canteen from Ruislip had arrived at the station to help feed the rescue workers. Wealdstone Police Station was overwhelmed by enquiries from relatives, and a long queue formed outside the station. Extra phone lines had to be brought in to cope with the volume of calls. Overnight 100 officers continued to help with the police operation, which continued for some days afterwards. Valuable lessons were learned by the police in dealing with major incidents as a result of the crash.

In 1954 Acting Sergeant 713X Eddie Phillips was attached to the station. In the picture right he is seen in the yard at Wealdstone, in front of the wireless patrol car.

Another boundary change in 1964 saw Wealdstone become a sectional station to Edgware, when it became part of Q Division and took on the call sign 'QW'. Further re-organisation in 1976 saw 'QW' return to Harrow, and Pinner (QP) and Edgware (QE) revert to office status. A chief inspector assisted by an inspector took charge.

Acting Sergeant 713X Eddie Phillips

The station closed in 2011 and was boarded up for several years. In May 2014 it was sold for £950,000 to a developer.[3317] There were applications to make extensions and new buildings at the site in 2016 and 2017, but these were both refused.

The old station is currently on the Historic England, 'At Risk' Register, describing the state of the building as 'fair'.[3318] Squatters broke in and occupied the site in 2016. At the time of writing, a new planning application has been approved by Harrow Council to turn the building into six one-bedroom flats, a 'financial and professional services office' and a cafe. The building will remain unaltered externally, with great attention being paid to the roof and new windows. Plans show the cell/charge room area will become a one-bedroom flat, with the three cells becoming a dressing room, a storage room and a utility room, with the cell tiles being retained.[3319]

Welling Police Office

London Borough of Bexley

60-62 High Street, Welling, Kent (1967-2000)

R Division (1967-2000)

Welling was originally one of the bases for the Bow Street horse patrol in 1827,[3320] but proposals for a police office were put forward many years later in March 1965 because of the growth in the local population and the two-mile distance from Bexleyheath Police Station. The office opened at 60-62 High Street, Welling in April 1967.[3321]

By 2000 the Welling office had closed, but a Safer Neighbourhood Team for the East Wickham ward was established within the grounds of a local secondary school in Falconwood, the Harris Academy, The Green, Welling. In premises that had seen better days, perhaps because they were once portacabins containing classrooms, the location was good for a police presence within the school and was equipped with the Aware internal Metropolitan Police computer system. It was replaced by premises at 135-137 Bellegrove Road, Welling.

Welling Police Office 1967-2000

In 1870 Superintendent James Griffin reported that there were three sheep stolen on R Division. Two of them were taken away by boat, and remained undetected. The third, however, was found to be missing at 6.30am on 4th December 1870, when one of the shepherds employed by Mr Bean of Danson's Park, Welling went with the gamekeeper, Mr William Robins, and knocked up PC110R Bromage, who had just finished night duty.

Safer Neighbourhoods Unit, Bellegrove Road, Welling 2019

In an incident that would later resemble part of the training of the Dog Section, they found the thief's tracks and, after 300 yards, the sheep's entrails. One hundred yards later they found the animal's head and part of the carcass. They lost the track at a road, but later picked it up again on a footpath towards

3311 English Heritage List, (Listed Buildings), Entry Number 1245418.
3312 Metropolitan Police Property Register for Wealdstone, p165.
3313 *Harrow Gazette*, 10th March 1909.
3314 Linwood, Jean. 'Wealdstone Police Station, A Brief History' in *Stanmore & Harrow Historical Society Newsletter*, Autumn 1994.
3315 *Harrow Gazette*, 10th March 1909.
3316 'Harrow & Wealdstone 50 years on. Clearing up: the aftermath' by Peter Tatlow.
3317 MPS (2018) Freedom of Information: Police Station Closures broken down by year.
3318 Historic England (ref 1245418).
3319 Harrow Council Planning Application Ref P0954/19.
3320 MEPO 2/25 and LB557.
3321 Metropolitan Police Orders dated 28th April 1967.

Sidcup. Three miles away from the sheepfold, the scene of the crime, they found a labourer, James Gilbert, with twenty pounds of mutton in a canvas bag under his bed. Gilbert was not known to have a criminal record, but he was sentenced to 12 months' imprisonment at his trial at Maidstone. The gamekeeper Mr Robins and PC Bromage were each rewarded by the Commissioner for their 'tact and vigilance'. The shepherd, Mr Bean, was not rewarded, perhaps because it had been his duty to look after the sheep in the first place. Nor was any mention made about any part played by the gamekeeper's dog.[3322]

Wellington Arch Police Station

City of Westminster
Hyde Park Corner (1831-1992)
A Division (1831-1992)

In the middle of Hyde Park Corner stands Wellington Arch, built in 1828 at the same time as Buckingham Palace, and, since the 1960s surrounded by a busy one-way traffic scheme. Inside the arch was a small police station, used primarily as a base for observing and controlling traffic, particularly before the advent of computer-controlled traffic management schemes. Wellington Arch was at one time referred to as the Triumphal Arch, the landlord being shown as Her Majesty's Commissioners of Woods and Forests. It was described as a section house and had four box rooms, a kitchen and boot-cleaning room.

Officers inside the Wellington Arch

Wembley Police Station

The London Borough of Brent
167 Harrow Road, Wembley (in 1950 renamed 551 High Street (1910-1971)
603 Harrow Road (1971 to Present)
X Division (1910-1965)
Q Division (1965-1993)
Brent OCU 1993-2018
Basic Command Unit. North West (NW) (2018 to Present)

In December 1893 the occupant of Newton Villa, East Lane, Wembley, Middlesex wrote a letter to Willesden police station drawing attention to the need for adequate police protection in the Wembley area. Wembley Urban District Council had also been asking for better police coverage. The various new railways were bringing large numbers of vagrants to the area.[3323]

In April 1900, the Home Office sanctioned an increase in the Force of two Constables for fixed point duty at the bridge on the main road at Sudbury and Wembley railway station. This had been suggested by the Sub-Divisional Inspector at Harlesden and supported by the Superintendent X Division. The fixed point was to be manned from 9.00am to 3.00pm daily, and it marked the boundary between Harlesden and Harrow police sections.[3324]

Wembley Urban District Council made a further request in 1902 for more Police in the area, especially as they were contributing nearly £1000 a year to the police rate. The police then installed a 'fixed point box' with telephonic communication with the police station at Harlesden. This replaced the two fixed point men on the railway bridge at Sudbury and Wembley Railway Station. The box was erected in 1903 and was manned continuously until the new Wembley Police Station was opened in 1910.[3325]

Early in 1904 a search was made in the Wembley area for a site for a new police station. Some land, with a frontage to the Harrow Road junction of Ranelagh Road, was purchased in February 1905, by the Receiver, with the authority of the Home Office, for £1200.[3326] This freehold piece of land formed part of the Curtis Estate. The police station was built and opened for business in February 1910.

Wembley Police Station 1910-1971

In 1923 the Football Association Cup Final was held at the then newly-opened Wembley Stadium. The organisers had not planned for such an overwhelming interest in the venue. Whilst the venue could accommodate up to 120,000 persons an additional 150,000 people turned up to watch the game. Fans stormed the gates and eventually there were about 200,000 persons on the pitch. A number of mounted police officers were on the pitch trying to move the crowds back but one police horse stood out from the crowd. A large grey horse named Billy, with its rider Constable George Scorey, became known as the 'White Horse' when shown on black and white film of the event. The crowd were eventually forced back to the touchline by the police horses. Billy died in 1930, and one of his hooves was polished, mounted and presented to Constable Scorey. When the newly rebuilt Wembley Stadium was opened in 2007 fans poured into the venue via a footbridge named 'White Horse' a lasting tribute to Billy.[3327]

The picture shows on the top of the next column Sergeant Walter Wheaton (warrant no. 99308) of Wembley at the British Empire Exhibition in 1924. A temporary police station was opened within the grounds at Wembley. There were plenty of opportunities for officers at Wembley Police Station to take part in special events at Wembley. This not only included football matches but exhibitions to showcase British and Commonwealth products. Wheaton retired from X Division in 1935.

Sergeant Walter Wheaton

Wembley District Garage was built and the police station was reconstructed during the years 1935/36. The postal address at the time was 167 High Road, Wembley but later, in 1951, it was renumbered 551 High Road, Wembley. A freehold strip of land was purchased in July 1958 between the police station and 6 Ranelagh Road for £905 with a view to extending Wembley Police Station in the future.

The Home Office gave its authority in 1960 to purchase land to provide headquarters offices for the proposed new Q Division. It was thought that the new Harrow Police Station could be enlarged to accommodate a divisional station. A site at Sudbury Hall, Harrow Road, Wembley was offered for sale by auction in May 1961. The proposed Q Division covered most of Harrow and Uxbridge Divisions, on which Wembley was the innermost section. The site of Wembley Police Station and the district garage in 1960 was too small for a divisional station so the Sudbury Hall site was purchased in June 1961 for £90,000. This was large enough for the erection of a new Divisional Headquarters Station with room at the rear for a section house to accommodate 100 single police officers.[3328]

The reorganisation of the Force took place on the 1st April 1965,[3329] with the new London Borough of Brent coming into existence. Wembley was designated the Divisional Headquarters, but pending the completion of the new Station the Divisional Headquarters was accommodated at Harrow Old Police Station, 76, West Street, Harrow-on-the-Hill. Stage one was completed at the Wembley site when the new section house opened in February 1965.[3330] The address was 603, Harrow Road, Wembley. Stage two, the new Wembley Police Station, was completed and opened in June 1971.[3331]

On the opening of the new Wembley Police Station the old station became a traffic warden centre. The Police Headquarters for Q Division, moved into the two top floors of the new Wembley Police Station in 1971.

In 2001 a review of the whole estate was undertaken by the Metropolitan Police Authority (MPA) in conjunction with the Property Services Department. It stipulated that substantial renovation was required at Wembley Police Station costing in the region of £9,788,000 which included £740,000 for a new communications infrastructure and also included central charging facilities and headquarters functions at the station. Other functions carried out at Kilburn were also added to the new plans.[3332] In 2003 work commenced which included converting the old police section house which was then to be renamed Sudbury House after an old building situated nearby in the 1880s. The new accommodation provided five floors of office space and catering facilities for police officers and support staff, but new demands increased the costs of the project which also needed to reflect diversity and disabilities policies.[3333]

In 2004 Wembley Constable Pirthi Ralpal Singh Bedi, aged 24, was killed in a traffic accident and the conference room at Wembley Police Station was dedicated to his memory.[3334]

In 2010 Wembley became one of the stations to be a pilot, along with Kilburn and Acton, for the introduction of video conferencing along with Kilburn and Acton as a result of many different languages being spoken in Brent. The police team wished to change the policy in respect of linguistic matters and needed to collaborate with the Ministry of Justice, the Legal Services Commission, the Law Society, the Criminal Law Committee and the Crown Prosecution Service with a view to gaining wide acceptance on the principle of interpreters through video conferencing and to removing any possible legal obstacles.[3335]

In 2012 the old Wembley Police Station had become an Indian restaurant. The new police station is open 24 hours a day, seven days a week.

West Drayton Police Station

The London Borough of Hillingdon
Station Road, West Drayton (1965-2010)
X Division (1963-1993)
Hillingdon OCU 1993-2010

In 1959 the Commissioner approved the search for a site in West Drayton on which to build a police station. Initially the council declined approval of land found by the Surveyors to the north and along Bath Road in 1961, on the grounds that this was green-belt land and subject to restrictions.

3322   *Report of the Commissioner of Police of the Metropolis* 1870 C 358.
3323   *Wembley History Society Journal*, Vol V No 1 1980 p8.
3324   Ibid.
3325   Ibid.
3326   Ibid.
3327   www.news.bbc.co.uk/dna/place-lancashire/plain/A31655757 accessed 18th March 2013.
3328   *Wembley History Society Journal*, Vol V No.1 1980 p10.
3329   Metropolitan Police Orders dated 6th August 1964.
3330   Metropolitan Police Orders dated 19th February 1965.
3331   Metropolitan Police Orders dated 4th June 1971.
3332   www.mpa.gov.uk/committees/x-f/2001/010619/25/ accessed 21st June 2012.
3333   www.mpa.gov.uk/committees/x-f/2003/030710/17/?qu=wembley&sc=2&ht=1 accessed 21st June 2012.
3334   *Harrow Times*, 20th January 2005.
3335   www.mpa.gov.uk/committees/x-resources/2009/091105/07/?qu=wembley&sc=2&ht=1 accessed 21st June 2012.

Wembley Police Station 1971 to present

This refusal delayed any planning and construction, but despite the obstruction the Commissioner went ahead and, with Home Office approval, purchased some land originally part of Drayton Hall for the sum of £12,500.

This site and plans for a station were approved, and in January 1964 the Home Office approved expenditure of initially £83,500 – but later upgraded to £87,500 – to build the police station at West Drayton. In the meantime, representations were made to the Commissioner over the delay in the building of the much-needed station because vandalism and hooliganism had greatly increased in the area. Plans were drawn up and contractors hired to build the station, which was completed in 1965.

West Drayton Police Station 1965-2010

When the station at Harlington was closed the same year, policing of the area was transferred to the newly-opened West Drayton. Changes in borough boundaries within the Greater London Council meant that Hillingdon Borough included West Drayton.[3336] The 'Police' sign made of stone from the portico at Harlington was removed from the building when it was closed and taken to West Drayton, where it was placed in the driveway.

Records show that the police station was located in Station Road, West Drayton, Middlesex. It was incomplete when built, as it was not supplied with the traditional police blue lamp to the front of the building. In 1969 Yiewsley Tenants Association wrote to the police complaining about the lack of a lamp, which they stated would 'show passers-by that here was a police station'.

When the Airport Division was introduced in July 1970 this sectional station came under the control of Heathrow.

In 2000 West Drayton station ('XE') was a temporary station, with limited opening hours, on Hillingdon Borough. It was still open in 2009, again with restricted opening times, and had no charging facilities so prisoners were taken to Uxbridge for detention and charging.

The front counter was finally closed in 2010, and West Drayton Police Station was sold in 2014 for £2,200,000.[3337]

A new purpose-built custody facility opened in 2011, located at Unit 3, Polar Park, Bath Road, West Drayton.

West End Central Police Station

City of Westminster
27 Savile Row (1940 to Present)
C Division (1940-1985/86)
No. 8 Area (1985/86-1993/94)
No. 1 Area (1993/94-2018/19)
Central West BCU (2018/19 to Present)

A famously busy station, West End Central – sometimes known as Savile Row – was opened on 14th July 1940 as a purpose-built police station to replace Great Marlborough Street and Vine Street stations. The new station's location was the subject of comment, and there was some resistance to the idea that Savile Row would be associated with something other than the purchase of gentlemen's fine suits. It was pointed out that 'the Commissioner too has paid for a Savile Row address', and the controversy may have contributed to the station becoming known not by the name of the street in which it is located but as 'West End Central'.

Just over two months after its occupation, on 14th July 1940, a parachute mine fell on its front doorstep and killed three officers, injuring 22, and reduced the brand new station to a shell. It was re-occupied in December 1940, and was counted amongst the ten Metropolitan Police stations 'knocked out', as distinct from being heavily-damaged, during World War Two.[3338]

On 15th December 1941 King George VI and Queen Elizabeth paid a morale-boosting visit to the station. Ralph Kirker, a West End Central officer, misjudged the timing of his meal in the canteen and, contrary to carefully-laid plans, was eating his meal when he was interrupted by the royal party's arrival. The officer described the kindly comments from the Queen, but noted that the faces of the senior officers looked distinctly less gracious. He waited with some trepidation for repercussions about this unplanned incident, but was relieved not to hear any more about it![3339]

Always at the centre of policing the vice-related crime of the West End, the station dealt with many street prostitutes, particularly before the Street Offences Act of 1959 changed the system from the routine but ineffective fining of prostitutes to a system of cautioning and then liability for imprisonment.

Temptations to corruption can only be combatted by eternal vigilance, preferably in the context of a legal framework that is effective and practical in matching public morality. In 1921 Sergeant Horace Josling accused a fellow sergeant, George Goddard, of taking bribes from illegal bookmakers. Later there were anonymous letters that also accused Goddard of taking bribes from club and restaurant owners who permitted gaming, erotic cabarets and prostitution on their premises, including a notorious Kate Meyrick of the Cecil Club in Gerrard Street, Soho. Horace Josling's case was not accepted and it was he, rather than Goddard, who ended up being dismissed. Chief Constable Frederick Wensley later used the Flying Squad to raid the Cecil Club and prosecuted Kate Meyrick. He also prosecuted Goddard, using Goddard's assistant as a witness against him. When Goddard was sent to prison, Horace Josling, an honourable man, was thoroughly vindicated.[3340]

During the Second World War the vice scene in Soho thrived. 'Bottle parties', where patrons brought their own alcohol to otherwise unlicensed clubs, became havens for prostitutes and organised crime, and the Clubs Office was introduced to focus policing operations to control them. 'Near beer' joints (selling malt liquor with insufficient alcohol to need licensing) and brothels proliferated, and card games were often organised to fleece visitors to Soho who rarely realised that the other members of the card game were collaborating against them.

By the late 1940s the Messina brothers were organising marriages of convenience for French prostitutes and had started to organise a thriving vice trade, some of the proceeds of which were channelled back to Malta, the country to which Giuseppe Messina had moved from Sicily.

West End Central Police Station 1940 to present

The 1950s saw Bernard Silver charging exorbitant rents to prostitutes where they plied their trade. He and eight others were prosecuted for living on the earnings of prostitution in 1956 on the basis that the rents they charged were eight times the normal market rent, but they were acquitted on legal grounds by direction of the trial judge. Silver was, however, eventually convicted in 1974 at the beginning of a sustained effort from the Metropolitan Police which saw convictions for prominent pornographer James Humphreys, a reorganisation of responsibility for policing pornography away from a central CID branch at Scotland Yard, and a drive against police corruption.

Since then, changes to licensing laws and close collaboration with Westminster City Council have significantly reduced the various manifestations of Soho's vice trade.[3341] The reduction of police corruption in the 1970s and 1980s, both in this area and more generally, has been one of the significant unsung achievements of the Metropolitan Police Service.

In 2019 West End Central featured a local operational control room and acted as a base for local West End neighbourhood teams.

West Ham Police Station

London Borough of Newham

44a West Ham Lane, Stratford (1850-1895)

64-66 West Ham Lane, Stratford (1895-1969)

18 West Ham Lane, Stratford (1969-2017)

K Division (1840-1993)

Newham OCU 1993-2017

West Ham Police Station Lamp

The presence of the Metropolitan Police in West Ham dates back to 1840. The Metropolitan Police took over the old watch houses, and although one was known to exist at Stratford its precise location is unknown. There also appears to have been a Metropolitan Police Horse patrol operating from a rented house at Maryland Point, Leytonstone Road owned by Mr. Curtis of the Broadway, Stratford.[3342] The 1841 Census shows a number of police officers living in private lodgings in and around the Stratford area.[3343]

The first police station was built in 1850 at 44a West Ham Lane, at the corner of Langthorne Street, at a cost of £1,297 10s 8d. Occupation of the building commenced in March 1851. It contained eleven rooms, three cells, and stables for two horses. Prisoners were detained and charged at West Ham, and retained for court the next day. The three cells were of a particular size and specification, and often situated near to the charge room or Inspector's Office for ease of supervision. Prior to 1890 the cell space was increased from three to five cells.

The Census took place in March 1851, just as the police officers moved into the new police station, now recorded as being at 48 West Ham Lane.[3344]

West Ham Police Station 1851-1895

3336 Metropolitan Police Orders dated 8th November 1965.
3337 Information rights unit dated 21st January 2018, accessed 25th January 2019.
3338 Howgrave-Graham, H.M. (1947) *The Metropolitan Police at War*.
3339 'West End Central: Commemorating the Official Opening' (after refurbishment, 2007) Metropolitan Police.
3340 Fido, M. and Skinner, K (1999) *The Official Encyclopedia of Scotland Yard*. Virgin, London.
3341 'Eight Area Clubs and Vice Unit – A Brief History'. Metropolitan Police.
3342 Metropolitan Police Surveyor;s Records.
3343 Census 1841.

Above the ground floor a section house was built to accommodate twelve single constables.[3345] The site had been leased for 71 years from Thomas Henry Golden of 16 Bassett Road, North Kensington, with a ground rent of £16 per annum. The freehold title, according to Police Surveyors, could be purchased for £390, and authority for the purchase of the freehold title was sanctioned by the Home Office in November 1864.

Police Orders in April 1864 reported re-organisation in divisional boundaries, and recorded that portions of Bow and Poplar Sub-Divisions would be formed into a new division. This was called West Ham Sub-Division, and was located on K or Stepney Division. Instructions noted that police duty should be carried on there where police officers paraded for duty, charges were taken and prisoners housed in the cells. Records show that two new inspectors, Arthur Mason and William White, were posted to the station.[3346] The strength of the station was shown as two inspectors, six sergeants and 51 constables, with one horse which was to be ridden by the two inspectors on their alternate tours of duty.[3347]

Officers from West Ham patrolled a lot further than their current boundary, and often made their way on foot to Canning Town and Forest Gate.[3348]

The photograph right of a West Ham sergeant was taken between 1870 and 1883. Police Orders in March 1869 gave authority for police officers to wear whiskers or beards. Previously it had been felt that whiskers would obscure the collar numbers on uniforms, which this example nearly does. In the event that members of the public wished to complain, or preferably to bring to light good police work, it was important that each constable or sergeant should be identifiable.

West Ham Sergeant 1870-1883

The officer is not wearing a whistle and chain, which were introduced in 1883. The photograph, which was taken at a studio in Stratford, shows the sergeant with ceremonial white gloves and best No. 1 uniform, a sign that he was required to perform duty in central London, possibly in connection with Royalty, at an event such as Trooping the Colour at Buckingham Palace.

Police Orders gave instructions for two new sub-divisions to be formed. These were West Ham and Plaistow respectively. This saw the breaking up of Plaistow and North Woolwich into one division, leaving West Ham on its own. The orders noted that the inspector would be stationed at Plaistow.[3349]

The strength of both stations in 1874 was recorded as follows:

Inspectors: West Ham 1; Plaistow 1
Sergeants: West Ham 7; Plaistow 9
Constables: West Ham 66; Plaistow 57
Horses: West Ham 1; Plaistow 3

In 1880 the address of the station was shown as West Ham Lane, corner of Langthorne Street. In 1891 an inspection was carried out which reported that the accommodation for two sergeants was now occupied by thirteen single constables. The station had ventilation problems, and it was considered too small, so more ground space was required. There were several unhealthy stations where from time to time typhoid would break out, often due to unsanitary conditions. There were several outbreaks of this disease at Bow Road Police Station between 1883 and 1891. Furthermore, the section house was inspected in 1891 and found to be overcrowded, having at least two more occupants than it should have had. A recommendation was made for larger premises to be built.

In 1881 there were twelve constables living at the station. The head constable was shown as Benjamin Coleman, aged 35 years, from Sarre in Kent.[3350]

In 1888 parts of West Ham and Ilford Sub-Divisions were taken away to form a new division called Forest Gate.

Sub-Divisional Inspector Thompson, assisted by Inspector William Rooks, was in charge in 1890, with eleven sergeants and 92 constables.[3351] That year the Metropolitan Police Surveyor, J. Dixon Butler, recommended the purchase of a freehold site located at 64-66 West Ham Lane on which to build the new police station. The parcel of land was purchased from Mr. S.R. Bastard for the sum of £950. A station and section house were built at a cost of £6,393, and occupation was taken up in July 1895.[3352] The old station became a lodging house when police moved out.

In 1891 senior police officers agreed that there was insufficient cell space in the metropolis to cope with the demand. There were 531 cells located in London's police stations, and this number was considered woefully insufficient. The standard size for cell space was 6x9x9ft, giving 486 cubic feet of space, although there were some slightly larger cells which had a capacity of between four to six persons in what was described as rather unsanitary conditions. It was recommended that each prisoner should have not less than 600 cubic feet of space. Cells were often without independent lighting, although heating would come from the basement coal boiler, which often overheated the cells.[3353]

West Ham Police Station 1895-1969

Sir Edward Bradford, the Metropolitan Police Commissioner, visited the station on 28th May 1895 and declared himself very satisfied with the new building.[3354] The old premises at 48 West Ham Lane were leased in 1897 to the Rev. Augustus Scott-White at a yearly rent of £20. A small two-storey cottage was erected in the station yard which housed the sub-divisional inspector and his family. It was used as married quarters until 1967, when it was converted to office accommodation.[3355]

The first sub-divisional inspector to take charge of the new station was Inspector K. Quigley, who was assisted by

Inspector H. Titcombe as his deputy.[3356]

In 1901 Inspector Murray became sub-divisional inspector, followed by Inspector Arthur Ferrett in 1910. By this time West Ham also had Detective Inspector Albert Yeo and three other inspectors – John Simmonds, John Harding and Frank Bookson. The working strength also included six station sergeants, nine sergeants and 127 constables.[3357]

The following list shows all the sub-divisional inspectors at West Ham between 1920 and 1949, when the rank was abolished:

C. Brailey	29th March 1920
J. Parson	21st February 1921
J Bradley	17th July 1922
A. Thompson	20th August 1923
A. Sawyer	26th August 1929
J. Crowley	2nd October 1933
A Barnes	18th April 1938
W. Watts	4th August 1943

William Watts, West Ham's last sub-divisional inspector, was appointed Superintendent in charge of the sub-division on 1st July 1949.[3358]

On 1st June 1933 all of K Division west of the River Lea became H Division, meaning that Limehouse, Bow, Poplar and the Isle of Dogs were transferred to H.

Everyday police officers patrol the streets of Britain and deal with all sorts of situations, events and incidents. The only difference between these was their scale of seriousness. Today police officers have the benefit of radios and communication, so that in the event of trouble help can be called immediately. From the early 1880s until the late 1960s the only communication which would attract the attention of another officer in times of distress would be three blows on his police issue whistle.

Police officers often deal with uncertainty, and their experience and good humour ensures the minimum of conflict. Police officers often risk their lives in the routine exercise of their duty, and this is a factor, which they readily accept as part of the job. The bravery of Britain's civilian police has been well documented, yet today bravery shown in the past is often forgotten in the mists of time, and when faced with formidable opposition his only protection is recourse to a medium sized wooden truncheon. Whilst danger is always present, it is not often that an officer comes near to death, nor is it a common occurrence for firearms to be used, yet both these events happened simultaneously on 2nd January 1898 near West Ham Court, in Stratford not far from the police station.

A builder by the name of John Jolly was involved in shooting Constable George Hill near the court which was witnessed by Constable Bateman, who was standing nearby. Furthermore, Constable Bateman turned around and saw the assailant pointing his firearm in his direction. The prisoner was arrested and taken before the magistrates, where he was remanded for trial for the felonious shooting of Constable Hill with intent to murder. The officer survived the incident after the removal of a bullet.

Police history shows that retirement very often occurred after 25 years' service, although an officer could work until he had 30 years' pensionable service. In the last part of the 19th century there was widespread concern that many good men were taking their pensions early, with 98% retiring at 25 years.[3359]

Even senior police officers like Sub-Divisional Inspector Henry Pipe, attached to West Ham Police Station, took his pension at 26 years' service. He had been the officer in charge of the police station, and as a mark of respect all the serving officers turned up at his retirement to bid him farewell.[3360] Henry Pipe was from Woodbridge in Suffolk and was married to Eliza, also from Suffolk. They had four sons. In 1881 he was the sergeant at Stoke Newington Police Station, residing not far from his place of work at 2 Stoke Newington Common, Hackney.[3361]

Very often presents to the retiring policemen would be given, both from the officers at the station and also from local traders and publicans. The event would be captured with a photograph, which was given to the retiring officer. Many officers left before their time because discipline was very strict, and as one error of judgment meant a lost pension, officers retired whilst they were eligible for a pension. Correspondence highlighted the dilemma regarding wastage, but it appears that no early solution was forthcoming.[3362]

The photograph below, taken about 1908, shows a typical retirement scene on a police sub-division. The two officers retiring are seated to the left, with two local dignitaries occupying the seats opposite.

The presentation of gifts to retiring officers c1908

They are proudly showing the presents that have been bought for them by their colleagues, which in this case consist of two expensive mantle clocks. Usually the whole station was present in the picture, several in plain clothes due to the nature of shift

---

3344 Census 1851.
3345 Metropolitan Police Surveyor's Records.
3346 Metropolitan Police Orders dated April 1864.
3347 Ibid.
3348 'West Ham Police Station' (1970) author unknown. Met Police Heritage Centre.
3349 Metropolitan Police Orders dated November 1874.
3350 Census 1881.
3351 'West Ham Police Station' (1970) author unknown. Met Police Heritage Centre.
3352 Metropolitan Police Orders dated 6th June 1895.
3353 *Metropolitan Police Sanitation Inspection of Police Stations* 1891 by The Chief Medical Officer.
3354 'West Ham Police Station' (1970) author unknown. Met Police Heritage Centre.
3355 Ibid.
3356 Ibid.
3357 Ibid.
3358 Ibid.
3359 *Police Review*, 11th March 1898 p112.
3360 *Police Review*, May 1897.
3361 Census 1881.
3362 Op cit.

work. In the centre is the divisional superintendent, who is wearing the ornate uniform. Traditionally the officer in charge of the station would give an account of the officer's service to the gathered audience, a custom that still takes place today.

In May 1908 another officer retired from the Force after just over 26 years' service. He was Inspector C. Lanktree, who was at that time the tallest officer in the Metropolitan Police, his height being 6ft 5½in.[3363]

Re-organisation in 1933 made West Ham a sub-divisional station of K or East Ham Division, with Forest Gate becoming its sectional station. With the distribution of station codes, which were introduced to improve communication, West Ham was allocated 'KW' or Kilo Whiskey.[3364]

Constable David Swinden, attached to West Ham Police Station, 1960

The picture left shows co-author David Swinden as a young constable in The Mall, London, in 1960. The occasion was the visit of the President of France, General Charles de Gaulle. Police officers from the outer divisions were sent to assist officers on the central divisions. Note the black helmet plate badge with white centre, which was worn together with the No. 1 uniform. The jacket was buttoned all the way to the top, and the officer's number was worn on both sides of the collar. A snake-hook belt was also provided, to be worn outside the jacket. The officer would have been wearing white gloves.

In 1961 a most tragic incident occurred on West Ham Police Station Division, whilst David Swinden was stationed there as a police constable. This incident involved the unfortunate death of two colleagues. Mr John Hall had been arrested, and was being interviewed in the CID Office at the police station when he produced an automatic weapon and escaped. Sergeant Frederick Hutchins and Constable Charles Cox, who were both unarmed, gave chase together with a number of other police officers, and close to the station the two above-named officers caught up with Hall, who turned and pointed his weapon and shot them both. A little further away Hall was confronted by Inspector Philip Pawsey, who he calmly shot and killed as the inspector also tried to stop him from escaping from custody. Hutchins died later in hospital, whilst Cox survived his terrible injuries. Later that day Hall turned the weapon on himself, and he too died of his injuries.

Both Pawsey and Hutchins received the posthumous Queen's Police Medal for Gallantry, and Constable Cox was awarded the George Medal. Constable Leslie England, who was also involved in the chase, received the British Empire Medal.[3365] A plaque was unveiled in the foyer of the West Ham Police Station by Sir David McNee, Metropolitan Police Commissioner, in 1981. In the picture at the top of the following column the Commissioner is flanked on the right by the officer in charge of the station, Chief Superintendent Redgewell. To the left are Les England (in uniform) and Charlie Cox.

In 1964 Local Authority re-organisation designated West Ham (KW) as a sectional station within the London Borough

Uneviling the plaque to commemorate the brave officers who lost their lives in 1961, with Charlie Cox (second left) and Les England (first left)

of Newham. By the 1960s the station was unsuitable for further use, and was condemned as it fell below the standards required by the Home Office.

Another site was chosen some 200 yards away, on which the Stratford Conference Centre had stood until it was destroyed by a German air raid in 1941. The land was owned by the Methodist Church, who sold the plot to the Metropolitan Police for £7,000.

West Ham (later renamed Stratford Police) Station 1969-2017

The new station was ready for occupation by the late summer of 1969. It cost £165,000, and the address was recorded as 18 West Ham Lane. The old police station was no longer required and was occupied by local community groups.

In February 1994 West Ham was renamed Stratford Police Station, and was allocated the station code 'KS'. When borough-based policing was introduced later in 2000, Stratford Police Station became the borough headquarters,[3366] until the new police station was built at Forest Gate. West Ham Police Station was closed to the public in 2017.[3367]

West Hampstead Police Station

The London Borough of Camden
99 West End Lane (1883-1972)
21 Fortune Green Road, West Hampstead (1972 to Present)
S Division (1883-1965)
E Division (1965-1993)
London Borough of Camden OCU (1993-2018)
Central North BCU (together with Islington) (2018 to Present)

In 1880 a portion of land, situated in the Parish of St. John Hampstead, was identified as suitable for a police station. The land was located in West End Lane, close to West Hampstead Railway Station, and was leased from Mr. Thomas Bale to the Metropolitan Police for £40 per annum. However, in March 1882 the Receiver of the Metropolitan Police purchased the title from G.H. Essington and others at a cost £715. Plans were soon made to erect a large station on the site, and this was built at a cost of £3,971. When the station was occupied a new sub-division of S Division was established and named West Hampstead.

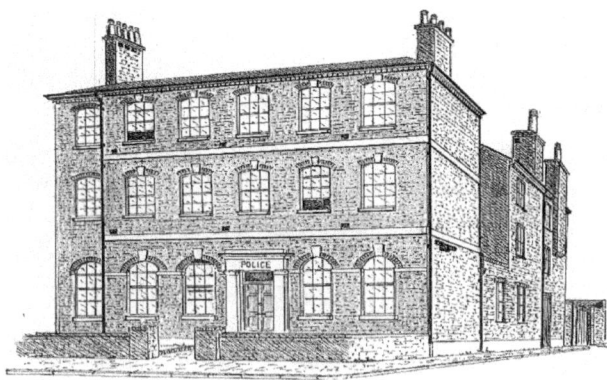

West Hampstead Police Station

The station was built with a charge room, inspector's office, waiting room and three cells on the ground floor. One of the cells was an association cell, meaning that it could hold a larger number of prisoners than the single cells. The station also had a basement, and a first floor.

There appears to have been a clause in the title deeds stating that the building could only be used for a police station or residence, and for no other purpose. Furthermore, any alterations which affected the near neighbours could only be made with the permission of the Cotton family, who resided next door. The address of this station was shown as 90 West End Lane, West Hampstead, and it was a station located on S or Hampstead Division. The station was opened on 1st January 1883. A married constable, inspector and six single constables occupied married quarters at the station.

Police Orders in March 1893 amalgamated several sub-divisions, and both Portland Town and West Hampstead were combined to form Portland Town Sub-Division.

By 1935 there were plans laid to construct a new station in the area, and in October 1939 recommendations by Estates Branch to purchase 92 West End Lane, next door to the existing station, and plans to build a station on the enlarged site were considered. However, due to the war and economies this proposal was turned down. It was felt that if reconstruction was to take place this could be done on the old station site, and that extra space provided by the section house would be sufficient.

In the 1965 Local Government boundary changes saw West Hampstead, along with Hampstead Sub-Division, transferred from S to E Division into the newly-formed London Borough of Camden.

In 1972 a new station and stables were opened at 21 Fortune Green Road, West Hampstead, and the old station was closed.

West Hampstead Police Station 1972 to present

In 2019 there were limited opening hours for members of the public,[3368] although the police station remained in the possession of police as an operational station.

West Hendon Police Station

London Borough of Barnet
West Hendon Broadway, Edgware Road NW9
S Division (1964-1993)
Borough of Barnet OCU (1993-2013)

In 1963/64 it was decided to include in the Metropolitan Police Building Programme for that year a new station in place of the present one at Willesden Green at the junction of High Road, Willesden Green and Huddlestone Road, as it was considered no longer adequate for the functions of a modern police service. A site was sought in the Hendon area as proposed by the Dixon Committee Report, roughly doubling its area in size. It was to serve as a sub-divisional station.[3369]

A suitable plot of land known as Beach's Fairground on West Hendon Broadway opposite the Old Welsh Harp public house came on to the market. This freehold piece of land was purchased at auction by the Metropolitan Police in 1961 for the sum of £92,500. It had a frontage to Brent Park Road. It was previously used as part of the winter quarters of a fairground and a permanent caravan site.

The planning stage was slow, and a number of restrictions were imposed by the planning officer and the local authority to specify the height of the building fronting West Hendon Broadway to be four-storey, to allow sufficient space at the frontage. This was to allow for future road development in the Broadway by the Ministry of Transport, and to provide for a 20ft deep area to Brent Park Road to be landscaped.[3370]

3363 *Police Review*, May 1908.
3364 John Back Archive (1975).
3365 Fido, M. and Skinner, K. (1999) *The Official Encyclopaedia of Scotland Yard*. Virgin, London.
3366 *Police and Constabulary Almanac* 2001.
3367 Information Rights Unit dated 18th February 2018 accessed 25th January 2019.
3368 uat01.nonlive.camden.pfiks.com/contact-police-stations accessed 31st October 2019.
3369 Metropolitan Police Surveyor's memo; John Back Archive (1975).
3370 Ibid.

Police stations were designed to ensure that the public entrance was well-defined, and visible from a reasonable distance along a public transport route. The station yard needed to provide for the security of prisoners in transit, good vehicular access, and direct access from the yard into the charge room. Provision was also made to ensure that catering delivery and refuse collection could be facilitated easily. A 45ft frontage to West Hendon Broadway was to provide a landscaped forecourt to ensure a pleasant introduction to the main entrance, and thereby encourage the public to use the police service. Suitable parking for visitors' and police private cars was also created. The entrance to the station yard was located at the back of the site to ensure ease of vehicular access and the avoidance of congestion at the road junction. The boiler house, refuse collection areas, garage and stores were dealt with by ensuring that single out-buildings were built surrounding the yard space. The building was designed on a modular basis.[3371]

Permission was necessary from the Home Office to sell off the surplus land on the site to Hendon Borough Council, and this was received on 8th February 1963. The sale was completed on 12th November 1963, and the £55,000 realised from the sale saved on costs for the future building work. In the meantime, tenders were requested from suitable building companies to erect the new station. Prospectuses were sent out outlining the planning requirements and expectations regarding the final form of the building. In February 1964 the Home Office approved the acceptance of the tender of Messrs H. Fairweather & Co. Ltd for £153,557 4s 8d for the construction of the new station.

Police Orders of 1st August 1964 stated:

"Under the boundary changes to be implemented on 1st April 1965, a new sub-division comprising West Hendon, Hendon, Mill Hill, Elstree and Borehamwood Police Stations, is to be formed and the new station at West Hendon is to be the sub-divisional headquarters. The station will be situated in the new London Borough of Barnet."

The new West Hendon (SW) police station, part of S Division with the postal address of West Hendon Broadway, Edgware Road, was opened and taken into operational use at 6.00am on 1st April 1964.[3372]

Willesden Green Police Station did not in fact close, and was not replaced when West Hendon was opened. It remained functioning long afterwards as a station on Q Division, with station code 'QL'.

In 1966 there were three stations which were sub-divisional stations with superintendents in charge, and these were Golders Green, West Hendon and Barnet.[3373] The first officer in charge was Superintendent G.H.K. Woolard, who was succeeded by Superintendent W.L. Rees. Chief Inspectors T.B. Hunt and J.F. Marriott supported the supervisory staff.[3374]

In the original designs they failed to ensure that there was space for the mounted section and the housing of police horses necessary for public order events and other functions. As a result, Metropolitan Police surveyors arranged for the building of a set of stables on the site. Once constructed, a Police Order was issued that stated:

'New stabling accommodation for Mounted Branch at West Hendon Police Station (SW) (later SV) will be taken into operational use at 6 am on Monday, 29th February, at which time the stables at Harlesden Police Station (QH) will be closed.'[3375]

The station was shut in 1997 and the functions and police officers transferred to the newly-completed Colindale Police Station,[3376] although for a time Simpson Hall, Aerodrome Road, Colindale was used for front counter enquiries until the new station was finalised.

West Hendon Police Station 1964-2013

By 2013 the building had been renamed Julian Headon House, and in April of the same year was sold for £3.250M to Torah Vocheseed Buildings Ltd.[3377]

West Wickham Police Office

London Borough of Bromley
9 High Street, West Wickham, Kent (1974 to Present)
P Division (1974-1993/94)
Bromley & Orpington OCU (PY) (1993/94-2018/19)
South Area (SN) BCU (2018/19 to Present)

As long ago as 1606, the parish of St John the Baptist, West Wickham had stocks installed at Norwood Cross, Wickham Street, outside The Swan public house, where a large tree, known as the 'Stocks Tree', survived well into the twentieth century, only to be blown down in 1968. In a document dated December 1839 a lock-up is mentioned as located in West Wickham, where petty sessions (the equivalent of modern magistrates' court hearings) were also held. Later, West Wickham's police strength was shown as two constables accommodated in private lodgings.

This was despite proposals for a local police station dating from 1887, when a vacant freehold site in Grosvenor Road was acquired for £480. The site was still in possession of the Metropolitan Police in 1924, and it was many years before police premises were finally established. In 1955 a police office for West Wickham was suggested on Glebe Way, and the matter was resurrected in 1963. Eventually, negotiations commenced for the leasehold of 9 High Street, West Wickham which, after conversion, finally opened on 18th March 1974.

West Wickham Police Office 1974 to present

Westcombe Park Police Station 1885-2012

In 1918 PC James Hardy was severely injured by an armed poacher in Ruffets Wood, West Wickham. Despite his injuries, the officer succeeded in arresting the man, and his bravery was recognised by an announcement that he would be awarded the King's Police Medal for gallantry. On the very day before the investiture ceremony, however, PC Hardy was killed in a cycling accident, and never saw the medal that he had been awarded. PC Hardy's name appears amongst many other officers who have died on duty on the National Roll of Honour that can be seen at www.policememorial.org.uk The Police Roll of Honour Trust, a charity now incorporated by Royal Charter, maintains the records of officers who have died on duty, building on work originally undertaken by Lancashire Police Sergeant, now retired, Anthony Rae. The Roll is available in book form from www.MangoBooks.co.uk

The Roll of Honour at New Scotland Yard was introduced after discussions in 1935 between the Police Federation and the Commissioner, Lord Trenchard, as a means to recognise the heroic death of PC James Thomson KPM, who was killed by a cement lorry that was running uncontrolled down Barnet Hill. PC Thomson remained in the road, clearing pedestrians from the danger, but was himself killed by the approaching lorry.

On 27th July 1950 the Metropolitan Police War Memorial book, also in the form of a Roll of Honour, was dedicated in Westminster Abbey in the presence of the King and Queen. The Roll contains 1,076 names of Metropolitan Police officers and civil staff who lost their lives during the two world wars, either serving in His Majesty's armed forces, or as the result of enemy action at home.

Westcombe Park Police Station

The London Borough of Greenwich

11-13 Coombedale Road (1885-2012)

R Division (1885-1993)

Borough of Greenwich OCU (1993-2012)

Local residents whose income exceeded £10 per annum paid for policing this part of Charlton in 1812. The 'Charlton Guard', as they were called, were raised because of local concerns about criminals frequenting the area. The Guard were provided with a lantern, rattle and firearm, and kept watch from 8.00pm-5.00am. They were paid the sum of 4s per night, but soon ceased to patrol. The Guard were again raised in 1827, now paid only 2/6d per night, but instructed to watch against resurrectionists and kept guard in Charlton Churchyard during the night.[3378]

A new station was considered to supplement those of Blackheath Road and East Greenwich because of the huge increase in population into the area. Accordingly, a new police station was built and occupied at 9&11 Coombedale Road, Westcombe Park in 1885,[3379] on land purchased from Mr. John Pound for £950. Rather than 'East Greenwich' the new station was called 'Westcombe Park' instead, and was occupied for Police purposes in December 1893.[3380]

In 1891 the inspector in charge of the station was George Hocking, who supervised six sergeants and 36 constables[3381] Hocking resided nearby with his family at 2 Farmdale Road.[3382]

The station was renumbered in 1925 so that the address changed slightly to 11-13 Coombedale Road. Westcombe Park had a call sign Whiskey Papa (WP).[3383]

3371 Metropolitan Police Surveyor's memo and John Back Archive.
3372 Metropolitan Police Orders dated 26th March 1965.
3373 Metropolitan Police List 1966.
3374 Ibid.
3375 Metropolitan Police Orders dated 6th February 1970.
3376 MPS Station Closures and Reduced Opening Hours 1997-2000.
3377 MPS (2018) Land and property sold for over £1M in the last 10 years.
3378 Hadaway, D. (1985) 'Westcombe Park Police Station Centenary 1885-1985'.
3379 Metropolitan Police Orders dated 13th November 1885
3380 MEPO 5 no.55 – OS451.
3381 *Kelly's Directory* 1891.
3382 Hadaway, D. (1985) 'Westcombe Park Police Station Centenary 1885-1985'.
3383 Metropolitan Police General Orders 1893.

The rear yard of the station in 1911 showing the cell block on the left

During World War I Charlton and Greenwich were bombed three times each, Blackheath seven times, and Woolwich, with its military targets, six times.[3384] Westcombe Park Special Constables performed lookout duty to spot enemy bombers and Zeppelins. They would take turns to stand at the top of Severndroog Castle, at the top of Shooters Hill, and using binoculars would pass information via the telephone on top of the Central Observation Station at Spring Gardens.[3385]

Anti-German feeling was rife during the war, and there were concerns that residents were passing information about targets to the enemy in Belgium and Germany. Police Orders dated 4th September 1914 instructed that Constables should visit every pigeon loft and release the birds, so that they could be monitored by the Officers and see if they flew off in the direction of Holland and Belgium.[3386]

The Second War started with the issuing of Defence of the Realm Regulations that included blackout instructions, and the Police prosecuted people if the blackout regulations were not properly adhered to. The players and staff of Charlton Athletic Football Club were all enrolled as War Reservists and sent to the emergency Police Station in the basement of Charlton House. When SPS 20R Harold White arrived to take charge of the contingent he found the basement filled with coal, however the unit was posted to main station a year later when the air raids had stopped.[3387]

Westcombe Park station survived the war, but often when police officers returned at the end of their shift they would find some of their numbers were not present, and stayed behind to find their colleagues who had been injured or killed in bombing raids. Some fourteen R Division Officers were killed in air raids during the war, and a further 23 whilst serving in the RAF or Royal Navy.

The cell area is believed to be haunted by a ghost ever since a prisoner hung himself there, however since an annex was added in 1990 there have been no further sightings.[3388]

Station office counter facilities were withdrawn from Westcombe Park in June 1999. Later, in November, the Millennium Policing Team moved into the station to oversee the celebrations and take responsibility for the Dome and the Greenwich Peninsula.[3389] When the Millennium Team moved out it left the station as the Greenwich Sector base.

In 2012 the station was closed and the site disposed of,[3390] and fetched £770.000.[3391]

Whetstone Police Station

The London Borough of Barnet
Church End (1873-1889)
1230 High Road, Whetstone (1989-1960)
170 High Road, Whetstone (1960-2014)
S Division (1873-1993)
Borough of Barnet OCU (1993-2014)

In 1815 the vestry asserted that a place of confinement was absolutely necessary, and planned for cages to be erected at Whetstone and near the stocks at Church End, suggesting that the earlier cage was no longer in use. There was still no agreement with Friern Barnet, but a brick cage was built at Church End close to the Queen's Head.[3392] Pupils of the National School had to pass the cage, and in 1860 the prisoners' behaviour led the vestry to demand its closure, but the Metropolitan Police insisted on keeping it: 143 persons had been confined there during the previous five years. The cage was eventually removed in 1880.[3393]

Three police forces operated in the mid-19th century: the parish constable, the Metropolitan Police, and the Bow Street horse patrol. The patrol, revived in 1805 to safeguard the turnpike roads out of London,[3394] was first recorded in Finchley in 1818. By 1828 its Third Division operated as far as Whetstone, and in 1836 four constables worked from Finchley (Highgate) and two from Whetstone.

The two patrols at Whetstone were No. 49 Bow Street Horse Patrol Smith, whose beat included patrolling, walking or riding from Barnet to Archway/ Highgate, a distance of six miles twice a day, and from the 8th milestone to the 9th milestone four times a day. No. 50 Davis patrolled in the opposite direction, either riding walking or patrolling the Finchley New Road from the police station to Grand Junction Gate, also a distance of six miles, and from the 3rd to 4th milestone four times a day[3395] The distance travelled each day by each patrol was 20 miles on average, and they would look out for coaches, carts and riders travelling from the north down the main highway towards London looking for crime, criminals or victim of robbery and violence. Their duty was to prevent and deter highway robberies. Their greeting was 'Bow Street Horse Patrol', which was reassuring to travellers. The patrol would seek information from the tollgate keepers, who would provide intelligence on the movements of individuals. When the two patrols met up on patrol or back at the station they would exchange the information which would also be passed onto other patrols at Finchley (Highgate).

There was also still a Bow Street horse patrol station on the Great North Road in 1851, which was occupied by four men. There were then eleven other policemen from the Metropolitan Police residing in the parish.[3396]

From 1840 Finchley was included in the Metropolitan Police District.[3397] The freehold to a building and land at Whetstone,

Westcombe Park Police Station photographed in the 1970s

High Street was purchased in 1851.[3398] A substantial brick with slate-roof police station was built at Whetstone, on the east side of the main road on land purchased for £72 in 1851. The station included one set of married quarters which had been developed for occupation in the same year. The station also had three cells space for prisoners, who were dealt with by one sergeant and a further acting sergeant. The other accommodation consisted of eight rooms with scullery and mess room on the first floor. Outside there were two coal pens, two water closets, a two-stall stable, with dung and dust pens.[3399]

There was a total of 12 constables posted to the station, with four on the day shift and seven on night duty together with a floating constable on double relief duties.[3400] This relief officer would cover for an officer who was absent, or remain at the station ready to collect prisoners from another station with the trap and convey them to Barnet or to the court. The weekly rent for the two married men's accommodation was 3/4d, whilst the two single constables paid each.[3401]

In 1855 Sergeant Ralph Norman was shown in charge of the police and horse patrol station.[3402]

Whetstone Police Station 1889-1965

In 1865[3403] the vestry requested more police,[3404] and in 1873 a police station was opened in Church End, in a rented house. In 1871 two married officers and their families resided at Whetstone, respectively paying 3/- and 2/9d per week rent.[3405] By 1881 Constable William Chennell (warrant no. 59752), his wife and daughter lived in married quarters above the station until 1900, when they had to vacate their lodgings on retirement.

Wentworth Lodge in Ballards Lane was bought in 1886 and a station was opened on the site in 1889, closed in 1965, and rebuilt shortly afterwards.

Officers and constables (including new recruits) of each division were to be instructed in drill formations, and for S and Y Divisions the drill ground was located at Finchley. This took place regularly each week on Wednesdays, between 12.30 and 2.00pm. Each police officer was issued with a drill manual which showed the drill formations in which they were to be instructed. There was mounted and foot drill, although superintendents were excluded from both.

The officer appointed for taking charge of drill was normally an inspector. No drill classes were taken in inclement weather, during very hot periods or during the winter. Drill classes which would be postponed would be notified to stations by the drill instructor using the telegraph system. The inspector provided a return to the superintendent of those attending drill, including the dates and hours involved. In turn, the superintendent was required to notify the Commissioner quarterly giving the numbers attending drill.

The Superintendent of No. 3 District oversaw the general riding drill to ensure that all sergeants and inspectors were suitably trained. Even those recommended for promotion would not be advanced until they had passed the necessary examination in foot drill. For riding lessons police officers would be relieved of their normal duties and be taught by the inspector of the B Division Reserve, although no expenses or allowances would be granted.[3406]

A drill training ground was needed by the local superintendent in order to drill his men as part of their training, and in order to ensure that police officers remained a disciplined group. The training consisted of not only foot drill or marching of groups of men, but of horsemanship, where mounted police officers of all ranks would be put through their paces on horseback. At Whetstone a drill ground was found, owned by Mr. G.R. Hey of Blue House Farm, Whetstone. Commencing from May 1880 the annual rent was £30, however by 1885 this had been dropped to £10 per annum. Mounted drill sessions numbering more than five annually would cost £2 extra for each occasion.

Whetstone Station, which also housed a married inspector and his family, was in a lamentable state. The well in the garden had become polluted from a nearby leaking sewer pipe, and was in need of connection to mains water supply immediately. Conditions were cramped, with the married constable and his family being moved out and these rooms reallocated.[3407] The three cells were no longer enough to house prisoners at the station, and a further additional cell was required.[3408]

From 1888 until 1891 the inspector at Whetstone was Thomas Bissett, who was sub-inspector when he came to S or Hampstead Division in 1888. He was initially based at Albany

3384 Hadaway, D. (1985) 'Westcombe Park Police Station Centenary 1885-1985'.
3385 Ibid.
3386 Ibid.
3387 Ibid.
3388 Greenwich-History of Greenwich intranet.aware.mps/BOCU_eh/ Greenwich accessed 5th March 2008.
3389 Brown, B. (2001) 'Romeo- Law and Order in Old Greenwich' (part 2 1900-2000) in *Bygone Kent* Vol. 22 No 3.
3390 MPS Information Rights Unit (2019) Freedom of Information: stations sold by the MPS since 2010.
3391 www.google.com/search?q=sale+of+Westcombe+park+police+ station&rlz=1C1SVEC_enGB520GB536&oq=sale+of+Westcombe+ park+police+station&aqs=chrome..69i57.12044j0j4&sourceid= chrome&ie=UTF-8 accessed 6th November 2019.
3392 www.british-history.ac.uk/report.aspx?compid=22507&strquery= police accessed 9th November 2011.
3393 Ibid.
3394 Babington, Anthony. *A House in Bow Street*. 1969.
3395 Martin, S. (1970). 'The policing of Finchley through the ages'.
3396 www.british-history.ac.uk/report.aspx?compid=22507&strquery= police accessed 9th November 2011
3397 *London Gazette*, 13 October 1840, p2250.
3398 Metropolitan Police Surveyor's Records 1912.
3399 Metropolitan Police Surveyor's Records.
3400 Metropolitan Police Special Police Order 1869.
3401 Metropolitan Police Surveyor's Records.
3402 *Kelly's Directory of Herts, Essex and Middlesex* 1855.
3403 OS Map 6", Mdx. VI. SE. (1867-73 edn.); ex inf. New Scotland Yd. rec. officer.
3404 B.L.H.L., P.A.F. 1/9.
3405 Metropolitan Police Orders dated 4th February 1871.
3406 *Metropolitan Police Instruction Manual* 1873.
3407 Metropolitan Police hygiene Inspection report of Police Premises 1880 p70.
3408 Ibid.

Street, Regents Park, but later moved to Whetstone. Whilst at Whestone, Bissett was summoned to a burglary which took place at the jeweler's shop of Mr John Walker of High Road, North Finchley. At about 4.00am the owner was disturbed by a noise in his shop and, going downstairs, he found the shutters broken open and a portion of the window cut or broken out. The glass appeared to have been cut with a diamond glass-cutter. Missing from the display were several pocket watches, which bore the owner's private mark, and several pins, with a total value of £80.

The police were called and the inspector arrived soon after, whereby a search of the local area was made for suspects without any trace. The inspector recorded the details and immediately telegraphed the details to Scotland Yard and the various divisions for circulation. From there constable 196M Albert Hatton at Stones End Police Station duly recorded the details in his notebook during parade before leaving the station on his beat. Once in Blackfriars Road he was passing Mr. Hyams' shop on the same day and saw a man offering to pledge (pawn) a watch to the shop owner. The constable decided to inquire about the watch and immediately, on inspecting it, found that it corresponded with the description that had been circulated. The constable asked a man now identified as George Baker to account for the possession of the watch, and immediately the suspect offered to take the constable back to his lodging and show him a receipt. Once outside the shop the suspect ran off, quickly followed by the police officer. The chase lasted some distance before the officer caught Baker, who struggled ferociously for about 20 minutes. Supported by a passing carman and an officer of L Division, Baker was subdued and arrested.

The property was identified by Inspector Bissett who visited Stones End Police Station as that stolen from the shop that day. The prisoner was released into the charge of the inspector, and handcuffed to be taken back to Whetstone for charging. There were commendations for Inspector Bissett and Constable Hatton from the chairman of the bench for their prompt action and vigilance, which resulted in the arrest of Baker.

Bissett retired from the police in May 1891 and moved to Whitstable in Kent. He had received the 1887 Jubilee medal for his part in the Queen's celebrations. Unusually, he was able to return twice more as a re-joiner for brief periods, and took part in the 1897 Jubilee celebrations and the 1902 Coronation, for which he was allowed a clasp in 1897 and a Coronation medal in 1902. Because he was part of the reserve he was allowed a seven-day re-joiner in 1897 and a 28-day re-joiner in 1902, despite being 60 years old at the time.[3409] Copies of the medals are shown below.

The 1887 Jubilee medal, the 1897 Jubilee (bar) and the 1902 Coronation medals awarded to Inspector Bissett

The station call sign for the telegraph published in Police Orders in 1893 was Whiskey Echo (WE), but by the 1920s this was changed[3410] to Sierra Tango (ST).

In 1911 the local council wanted to widen the road, and compulsorily purchased a strip of land approximately 20x20ft from the frontage in Friern Barnet Lane.[3411] A new site for the police station had been purchased in Friern Barnet Lane that same year, but this was considered too small for use and was rebuilt in 1938.

Ten years later, in 1948, adjoining premises at the corner of High Road and Friern Barnet Lane were bought, and in 1960 a new station opened there and the old one closed.[3412] The address of the new station was 170 High Road.

Whetstone Police Station 1960-2014

In 2012 the station was open from 0700 to 2200 daily, except Public Holidays.

In March 2014 the station was vacated and put up for sale, fetching £4.150M. The purchaser was Alma Primary.[3413]

Willesden Green Police Station

The London Borough of Brent
96 High Road, Willesden Green (1896-2013)
X Division (1896-1965)
Q Division (1965-1993)
Brent OCU (1993-2013)

The arrival of the Metropolitan railway to the area in 1879 at Willesden Green, and then onward to Harrow the following year, increased the population, and so additional new police stations were needed. The old Willesden police station was renamed Harlesden to avoid any confusion.

The new Willesden Green Police Station was built by Messrs Higgs and Hill for the sum of £3,444, and was designed by the Metropolitan Police Surveyor, John Dixon Butler. It was built on waste land by the High Road, Willesden Green, at the corner of Huddlestone Road and opposite St Andrew's Church.[3414] The freehold for the site had been purchased in 1893. The new police station was opened for business at Willesden Green on X Division in July 1896.[3415] The staff at the station consisted of one Sergeant and two Constables. This meant a twice-daily cycle ride to Harlesden Police Station to receive orders from the divisional inspector.

By 1918 Willesden Green Police Station was under the command of Superintendent James Olive, stationed at Harrow Road Police Station. Inspector William George Cole was responsible for Willesden Green.[3416]

In the 1930s it was said that a local fishmonger used to drive his van into the station yard every week where local residents used to queue up to buy their fish.[3417]

Willesden Green Police Station 1896-2013

In October 1956 the town clerk of the borough of Willesden wrote to New Scotland Yard asking whether police would be interested in erecting a new police station in a proposed civic centre at the High Road junction of Brondesbury Park, Willesden. (This new civic centre was built and comprises a library, cinema and a restaurant). The offer was declined as it would not be sufficiently central location for a new police station, and that a site at Staples Corner would be better placed in relation to adjoining police stations.[3418]

In 1965, when the new local authority boundaries were created Willesden Green Police Station formed part of the new Q Division. It became a sectional station to Harlesden in the new London Borough of Brent.[3419]

In 1978 the station was slimmed down when the Metropolitan Police restructured the divisions, but in April 1985 the station was upgraded into a fully operational station.[3420]

In 1995 Willesden Green police were presented with the Vicountess Byng of Vimy Perpetual Trophy for winning the large garden category in the Metropolitan Police gardens competition.

In October 1995 the station closed leaving only a portakabin in the rear yard as a station office. A temporary office site was opened for police business in Neasden Lane, on the old 'McNichols' site. Meanwhile, the police station was completely renovated and staff then moved back into the premises.

The police station was closed in 2013 and then sold in 2014 for £2.550M.[3421]

Wimbledon Police Station (and Merton)

Bow Street Horse Patrole Station:
  The Ridgeway Wimbledon Village (1790-1844)
Merton Police Station, P Division (1841-1842)
Merton Police Station, V Division (1843-1871)
Wimbledon Police Station, V Division (1872-1993)
Borough of Merton OCU (1993-2018/19)
South West (SW) BCU (together with Kingston and Richmond) (2018/19 to Present)

In 1790 a new Watch House was taken over in Wimbledon Village. The stocks were situated next to it. There was also a pillory near Wimbledon Common..[3422] In 1804 local households and shopkeepers agreed to pay for a Wimbledon Watch who would patrol the village streets and 'cry the hour'. This scheme was discontinued after two years when the Beadle (Town Crier) was appointed Watchman and Constable of the Night.[3423]

Early records show that in 1840 Thomas Hunt Dann combined his work as a miller with that of the Parish Constable (even though a Metropolitan Police Horse Patrol existed in the village), and one day he ran from his mill having witnessed an illegal duel between Lord Cardigan and Earl Tuckett. Dann arrested them both, although Cardigan had been the better shot having injured Tuckett. Cardigan was later brought before his peers in the House of Lords, only to be acquitted. Duelling on the Common was a regular pursuit, having over time involved some very famous people including the Duke of Wellington in 1829 and William Pitt in 1798.

In 1760 Sir John Fielding, the Bow Street magistrate, had developed a plan for mounted patrols to deal with the plague of highwaymen infesting the Metropolitan area's turnpike roads. The plan was so successful that the original Horse Patrol of eight men was strengthened to more than 50 in 1805. The Bow Street Horse Patrol could then provide protection cover on all the main roads within 20 miles of Charing Cross, and they were a regular sight in Merton.

There was no immediate Wimbledon Police Station built in 1829 when the Metropolitan Police came into being, although the 2nd Division of the Bow Street Horse Patrol took responsibility for patrolling the area.

Records show that a station house existed just off Wimbledon Lane as early as 1844,[3424] although this had been the original Bow Street Horse patrol station.

Records held by the Metropolitan Police show that in 1845 they had taken control of a double cottage belonging to the Horse Patrol at 1 Brickfield Crescent on the Ridgeway (now 1 Oldfield Road and 3a The Ridgeway), Wimbledon village. This is directly opposite what is now known as Lingfield Road. Today Wimbledon Lane continues into Wimbledon Hill Road, but in the 1860s the lane stretched from Wimbledon Village down the hill through the Broadway and into Merton Road, continuing onto High Street, Merton.[3425]

The Horse Patrol was under the supervision of Inspector William Richardson, who was responsible for the stations at Croydon, Sutton, Merton (Millers Mead), North Cheam, Wimbledon (Village), Kingston, Robin Hood Hill and Ditton Marsh.[3426]

3409 Private correspondence from David Collett.
3410 General Orders 1893.
3411 Metropolitan Police Surveyor's Records 1912 and 1924.
3412 www.british-history.ac.uk/report.aspx?compid=22507&strquery= police accessed 9th November 2011.
3413 MPS (2018) Land and property sold for over £1M in the last 10 years.
3414 *Willesden Chronicle*, April 1895.
3415 Metropolitan Police Orders dated 11th July 1896.
3416 *Kilburn, Willesden and Cricklewood Directory* 1918-1919.
3417 Centenary Document MPHC Archive: Retired Police Officer 1984.
3418 John Back Archive c1965.
3419 Metropolitan Police Orders dated 6th August 1964.
3420 *Kilburn Times*, 22nd March 1985.
3421 Metropolitan Police Information Rights Unit 20th January 2018, accessed 25th January 2019.
3422 Metropolitan Police Intranet.
3423 Ibid.
3424 *Police and Constabulary List* 1844.
3425 *Bacon's London Atlas* 1862
3426 Brown, B. (date unknown) 'The Metropolitan Police in the County of Surrey'.

The Horse Patrol was incorporated into the Metropolitan Police in 1836, and the Magistrates at Bow Street relinquished control of them.

Wimbledon Police Station 1790-1844

The police station house is shown above; the terraced house behind acted as further residential accommodation. The building was made of brick, with a slate roof, and had three bedrooms and a small garden at the rear. It had a walled garden, which can be seen at the front of the house. Also situated in the garden was a one-stall stable for a horse. Access was from the Ridgeway, where the single-storey stable has now been converted into living accommodation and can clearly be seen from the main road.

The Metropolitan Police Surveyors decided to renovate the building by converting several rooms to accommodate several single constables. The first record of a professional police officer living in Wimbledon at Oldfield Road was Sergeant Pinegar, who lived at the station.

The local court records show they were kept busy dealing with men drunk and disorderly, costermongers, obstructing the Broadway, owners of dangerous dogs and a man from Tooting driving a carriage without lights and trying to bribe a policeman not to report him.

Merton Police Station 1805-1831

There was another police station used by the Bow Street Horse Patrol which was taken over by the Metropolitan Police. This was referred to as Merton Police Station, and was situated at 2 and 3 Millers Mead, Colliers Wood at the end of Merton High Street. These were a pair of whitewashed cottages at the front of Wandle Park, just inside the Parish of Wimbledon. This ceased operation in 1831, when the cottages were sold to Moses Barton Legg.[3427] Until then cottages with a stable were part of V (Wandsworth) Division,[3428] and senior Officers came on horseback to supervise the area from the nearby headquarters. It was likely that the original occupant was retained by the Metropolitan Police and transferred to another station to carry on his normal duties as part of the mounted patrol. The cottages were demolished in the 1970s.[3429]

In 1845 a double cottage was let for use as a police station and section house in Merton Road, and was originally the Horse Patrol Station. Leased from Mr F. Bower of Merton Park, it was in a sad state of repair when it was taken over by the Metropolitan Police. The building was in need of repair both inside and out, and had not been painted inside for at least five years. The cottages had originally been painted white outside, and other colours which by now are indistinct. The buildings were vacated on 22nd June 1869, when notice was sent to the superintendent that better premises had been secured[3430] in the Broadway.

Police stations would only be able to provide limited accommodation for a small number of police officers. Where none was provided, the officers needed to find lodgings near the station. Further accommodation was required, and surveyors needed to look for accommodation nearby. Premises were found in Larkhall Lane that offered room for one sergeant and eight constables.

Records show that in 1845 Mr Sankey offered the property on a yearly rental, although these premises were in a very poor state of repair. Once renovated the police officers were able to move in.

In 1864 General Police Orders published a re-organisation of police stations, supervision and their strengths. It shows Merton, as it was then known, to have four day beats and ten night beats. One acting sergeant supervised the four day beat constables, whilst the substantive sergeant was responsible for the ten night duty constables. The strength for the station was one sergeant and 15 constables.[3431]

This was by comparison a small station, and accordingly there were no cells to house any prisoners there. No charges were taken there either, meaning that any prisoners would be arrested and taken to Merton to inform the station officer, and then walked to Battersea where they would be charged and housed. Merton (together with Tooting) was a sub-divisional station of Battersea. The mounted inspector or sergeant at Wandsworth would supervise generally and patrol Tooting, Merton and Battersea. The night and day duty sergeants would swap shifts every month. Because there was no additional space, when the Commissioner informed divisional superintendents in July 1869 that they should install recreation and games rooms with billiard tables at main stations, none could be installed at Merton – a situation which changed in 1871 when they moved to a new bigger building.[3432]

In 1860 rifle ranges had been built by the National Rifle Association (whose patron was Queen Victoria) on Wimbledon Common for practice. Preparations were made for a Royal procession to Wimbledon when Queen Victoria opened the National Rifle Association ranges. Bunting and flags lined the route, together with a great number of enthusiastic onlookers. PC William Skinner, stationed at Wandsworth, was sent to Wimbledon as part of a serial[3433] of Police to guard the Common, the ranges and other important areas. A sad incident soured the occasion when a man fell to his death from a ladder while putting up bunting.[3434] PC Skinner had another job, which was to look after the rifle which the Queen used as the first person to fire a shot on the ranges. She scored a bullseye. Annual shooting meetings were held there until the increase in population made it too dangerous to stage the event, and so it was transferred to Bisley in 1890. Police officers were regularly seconded from V Division to help with crowds and prevent crime elsewhere in London.

One of the problems for Merton involved cattle plague. There were six police officers situated on the exterior boundary of the division at Wimbledon, Tooting, Kingston, Richmond and Barnes. One officer during daylight hours was located at White Houses, Wimbledon Common to inspect cows being brought to market in London.[3435]

In March 1870 a piece of land was leased until 1919 for £5 per year,[3436] as well as a newly-leased building (later located in the Broadway) to act as a police station and section house in South Wimbledon.

In the 1881 census the address of the station was recorded as 24 Merton Road, although at No. 23 lived Constable David Cuthbert, his wife Mary and their daughter Ada.[3437] This was described as a house adapted for Police purposes, which had one married inspector, one married constable and eight single constables resident there.[3438] It was located just beyond the site of the future Victoria Crescent (made in 1887 to celebrate the Queens Golden Jubilee). It was staffed by one sergeant (as it was designated a sergeant station for supervision purposes) and eight constables, who resided in the Section House above. The premises were leased for 50 years in 1869 on an annual rental of £120 from the owner Mr James Couch of Oakfield Lodge, South Wimbledon.[3439]

It is often the case that police stations took on the name of the road they were located in, which has caused confusion as the station was often quoted as 'Merton Road Police Station' even though it was in the Parish of South Wimbledon. Superintendent Charles Digby had overall supervision of the division.[3440]

This was also a large brick-and-slate house which was repaired and adapted when it was occupied, although Police Orders contradict this and state it was erected and purpose-built. Alterations costing £566 were made to the building in order to ensure that it was suitably converted into a station, with appropriate accommodation, for Police purposes.

The station had a charge room, living room, kitchen, scullery, reading room and two cells. In the yard was a two-stall stable for horses. There was also an inspector's office on the ground floor.[3441] Merton was shown as being on V (Wandsworth) Division in 1871, but by time the new station was occupied in 1872 it had been renamed Wimbledon. The rooms upstairs were allocated to accommodate one sergeant and nine constables. In 1878 Sergeant Benjamin Peake was in charge. Because of development in the town centre, the address was changed to show that it was located at 21 Broadway, Wimbledon.

In line with the general re-organisation in 1881, all the stations on the division were made inspector stations, although there were not sufficient inspectors to go round. A promise to increase the establishment of inspectors was made by the Home Office, and in the intervening period substantial numbers of station or Clerk sergeants were promoted to inspector to cover all the stations necessary.

By 1881 Inspector John Rogers resided at the station with his wife and daughter. The inspector was designated as attached to V Division, and probably did duty at the station although he may also have been attached to another station on the division. The 37-year-old inspector and his family resided there until 1888. Another inspector was attached to the station by the name of John Fuller. The two inspectors would cover both the day and night shift between them. Also living at the station was Constable David Cuthbert and his family, living in married quarters next door. Eight single constables also resided in the section house. Thomas Miles, a 25-year-old from Greenwich, was designated Head Constable, and he would have been charged with ensuring good order at the section house.[3442]

Wimbledon Police Station 1860-1900, the gabled building by the lamp post

When the station was inspected in 1881 the surveyors were very concerned that the single constables did not have sufficient washing arrangements. They said that 'the single men are washing in the cook's sink in the kitchen', seemingly concerned that washing and preparing food should not use the same sink. Clearly standards of hygiene were being established, since disease amongst the Police Service often meant sick leave and absence from the station, or even death.

The Commissioner had issued instructions regarding feeding arrangements at stations where officers lived in section houses. Thomas Miles, as the senior constable at Wimbledon, would have been made responsible for the mess room and the need to comply with the rules and regulations as laid down. The Commissioner issued instructions that, where there was a section house, arrangements should be made to establish a mess. This in effect created a canteen for sergeants and constables only. No senior officer, in this case Inspector Rogers, was allowed to be a part of the scheme.

3427 Montague, A. 'Colliers Wood: A Pictorial History'.
3428 *Post Office Directory* 1841.
3429 Montague, A. 'Colliers Wood: A Pictorial History'.
3430 Metropolitan Police Surveyor's Records.
3431 Metropolitan Police General Orders 1864.
3432 Metropolitan Police Orders dated 15th July 1869.
3433 A serial of police officer usually comprised of one inspector, three sergeants and 30 constables.
3434 Forrester, C. (1996) 'Skinner's Horse' in *The Peeler* Vol 1 pp7-11.
3435 *Commissioner's Annual Report* 1869.
3436 MEPO 234.
3437 Census 1881.
3438 Report on the Condition of the Metropolitan Police Stations 1881.
3439 Metropolitan Police Surveyor's Records.
3440 MEPO 234.
3441 Metropolitan Police Surveyor's Records.
3442 Census 1881.

The mess would employ a caterer, who would ensure that dinners, and often breakfasts, could be made for those who were members. Membership was to be paid for at a minimum of 1d per week, or more if the members of the mess agreed. A suitable mess officer was appointed, and he would arrange for the collection of monies (usually each Monday) so that he could attend shops and markets on a Tuesday and collect the necessary provisions for the rest of the week. Bills from reputable tradesmen only were to be paid for on Tuesdays. The mess monies were collected also to buy plates, cutlery, pots, pans and tablecloths. Such property belonged to the mess, and when a member left he no longer retained any interest in any of the utensils. The ovens and cookers needed would be provided to the mess 'at cost' by the Receiver. The meals would be arranged so that every member was able to sit down at the same hour. If a member was called out for something urgent his meal would be put in the oven and kept warm until he could return. A printed scale of charges was put on display in the mess, and to ensure good order the most senior mess officer had a duty to report to the inspector if a sergeant was absent at any time, or if there was any bad language or behaviour by a constable. Police officers were not to become cooks, unless the officer was still able to perform his normal duties.

Most mess officers managed matters extremely well, however occasionally senior officers learnt through bitter experience when police officers managed the financial affairs of messes badly. For example, some mess officers found it difficult not to treat the mess account as their own, and in effect embezzled monies from their colleagues. There was also the issue that some traders could be coerced into providing provisions for free. Some traders, especially at markets, found it difficult not to curry favour with the Police by giving away produce, especially at the end of the day, although the rules suggested that the lowest prices were to be obtained. Accounts had to be presented to the inspector or superintendent each week, and he would sign as supervising. Vouchers for payment by tradesmen would be presented to the inspector, who would pay from the petty cash account. Occasionally gratuities of food and drink were received in stations, and before these could be accepted a report was made to the inspector.

In 1885 the station transferred to W (Clapham) Division and placed in the charge of an inspector. The Home Office's promise to increase supervisory strength of inspectors had materialised by 1888, when 27 inspectors were posted to V Division to provide cover for the ten police stations. There were now sufficient inspectors on the division to have two per station. By 1888 Wimbledon had been connected to the telegraph, and had direct communication not only with Scotland Yard but to its surrounding stations as well.[3443] Wimbledon had a direct link to the superintendent at the divisional headquarters at Wandsworth. The station code used to identify the station was Whiskey Bravo (WB).[3444]

In 1893 the sub-divisonal inspector in charge was Edward Bonner, although the following year a re-organisation saw the station losing its sub-divisional status and become a sectional station of Wandsworth, along with Wandsworth Common, Putney and Roehampton.

In 1894 the station was considered too small for Police purposes, and a plot of land was found in Queen's Road. The freehold was purchased in 1896 for £500. In the meantime the Metropolitan Police Surveyors designed a new police station and appointed contracted builders to construct it.

The station cost £8,033, and was built with room for modern accoutrements including a telegraph room, charge room, inspector's office, library, mess room, three cells and an association cell. The yard also boasted a parade room, wash house and an ambulance shed. There was also a two-stall stable, and room for 15 constables to live.[3445]

The V Division despatch van

The photograph above shows the V Division despatch van in the station yard at Wandsworth. This was the headquarters station, and formed the base from which the horses and men employed were allocated to either the prison van or despatch van. A groom at the station was responsible for the welfare of all the horses kept at there. The superintendent and inspector's horses needed to be available at a moment's notice, and this was part of the groom's job.

The police officer above would collect correspondence, papers and Police packages from and to headquarters. The van would travel between all the sub-divisional stations and park in the yard, where he would take despatch bags into the front office, and the station officer would confirm receipt of the bag coming in and ensuring the outward bag was made up ready for onward transmission. The van was a secure internal system, that ensured that only the correctly-authorised people saw the sensitive nature of some of the correspondence. Even today the Police still run its own internal despatch network between stations in London.

The United Kingdom became embroiled in a distant war with the Boers in South Africa and, in company with many other police officers (especially if they had served in the forces before joining the Police), a considerable number wanted to rejoin their old units and fight the cause. 20-year-old George William Draper, PC837 attached to Wimbledon Police Station, had applied to join the Wiltshire Regiment as a private on short service for the duration of the conflict. While a number of police officers were sadly killed in the war, Draper survived the conflict and rejoined the Police at Queen's Road in 1902, with his discharge papers saying that his conduct was very good.

Later, in 1900, the station was completed and fit for occupation,[3446] yet by 1905 its sub-divisional status had been lost again. There was a stable in the yard and accommodation above the station for a section house for single constables. The old station that had been given up in the Broadway, at the corner of Victoria Crescent, became a jeweller's shop in 1987.

In 1907 the Wimbledon Section showed a station strength as two inspectors, nine sergeants and 82 constables. In February of the same year the Superintendent authorised two constables from the station to be attached to the reserve, and one constable to be the warrant officer responsible for overseeing that all arrest warrants sent to the station were carried out and the subjects brought before the court.[3447]

In 1908 V Division had established Wimbledon as a sub-divisional station under Inspector William Hart. The address was shown as 15 Queen's Road, South Park Road, Wimbledon. In 1912 a hand ambulance was stationed at the Grove Hotel in Wimbledon for drunks or injured members of the public.

The old station in the Broadway was retained until 1919. The re-organisation had attached two sectional stations to Wimbledon, these being Putney and Roehampton.[3448] William Hart stayed until 1911, when his place was taken by William Barnham. In 1914 Race Hooper was the sub-divisional inspector, until 1917.[3449] The duty of sub-divisional inspectors was an important one, and equal to that carried out by superintendents today.

In WWI Wimbledon, still a station located on V (Wandsworth) Division, formed part of No. 3 District that included L, M, P and R Divisions. Like all the other London stations, Wimbledon Police Station displayed recruiting posters on billboards at the front of the building. This helped to encourage ordinary working men to enlist as special constables. At each of the 180 police stations across the capital a unit of special constables were formed. A Group was one sergeant and nine men. A Squad was one sub-inspector and three Groups, and a Company was one inspector, three Squads and one Group.[3450]

The response to the campaign was overwhelming, with large numbers of men doing their day job, coming home, having their food and going out to their stations for duty. But it appears that in the early days, while the Home Office were trying to provision the specials, they left them short; understandable as they were fighting a war as well. The indignant specials resorted to their own means of obtaining funds, and produced their owns means of raising funds by privately producing postcards for sale to the public.

There was a very strong unit of special constables at Wimbledon. Lectures on subjects, ambulance training and rifle shooting were some of the tasks undertaken by the Wimbledon Special Constabulary. Apart from guarding vulnerable points, specials could be seen conducting people towards air raid shelters during bombing raids.[3451]

By 1915 observation posts had been established on the division, and Wimbledon's specials kept observation from the roof of the station not only to give an early warning of Zeppelins and Gotha bombers, but also to extinguish any suspicious lights during the blackout.[3452] It was thought at the time that some of those sympathetic to the German cause deliberately left their lights on to provide an indication of a target.

The Wimbledon Special Constabulary Rifle Team winners of 1916

The picture bottom left shows Wimbledon's Sub-Divisional Special Constabulary rifle shooting team in 1916. They had won the divisional shooting contest, and proudly display their cup and team. The picture shows V Division on the collar of their greatcoats, which had recently been issued. Notice also that the sergeants have what appear to round strips rather than chevrons, and then only on one arm. This was a distinction that was later changed, but for the meantime it served to distinguish regular police officers from special constables, who were temporary.

Some of the very first Women Police came to do duty at Wimbledon during the war. The superintendent of V Division was presented with a letter of introduction written by the Commissioner of Police, instructing that two women police from the Women Police Service (formally the Women Police Volunteers) should do duty at Wimbledon. The Women's Local Government Association had arranged for six women police to be paid for. Two were posted to Paddington, two to Wimbledon and two to Marylebone. The posts were purely unofficial, however the superintendent was reported to be 'glad to have their assistance'.[3453] The picture right shows the uniform that the women wore. Note they also wore the duty armlet denoting they were on duty. Times were changing for women, especially since there was a drive in recognition for the good work carried out by those women who replaced men in factories during the war.

A Women Police Service Officer attached to the Metropolitan Police at Wimbledon

Police officers were in a protected occupation, meaning they did not need to apply to join the forces and fight in the First World War. However no obstruction was placed in the path of officers wishing to apply to join the armed services. One such person who applied for a short service application was Enoch John Pierce from Wimbledon Police Station. In May 1915 he applied to join the Army Service Corps as a butcher, which had been his former trade before joining the Metropolitan Police. Pierce was 25 years old, a single man and lived at the station. The application, together with the declaration, was signed by Pierce, and needed to be sworn in the presence of a

3443 *Kelly's Directory* 1888.
3444 Metropolitan Police General Orders 1893.
3445 Metropolitan Police Surveyors Records.
3446 Metropolitan Police Orders 27th September 1900.
3447 Metropolitan Police Divisional Records for V Division.
3448 *Kirchner's Police Almanac* 1907.
3449 *Kelly's Law Directories* 1908-1917.
3450 Reay, W. (1919) *The Specials*. Heinemann, London p29.
3451 Ibid p91.
3452 Ibid p177.

magistrate. The magistrates in Wimbledon witnessed the Oath and countersigned the Army Form B 2505. Pierce notified his sergeant in a report, and this was passed to the inspector and then to the divisional superintendent for information. A date would be notified later when Pierce needed to report to Aldershot Barracks in Surrey.

In 1928 there was a change of sub-divisional inspector (today's superintendent) who was responsible for the sub-division. This had been Sub-Divisional Inspector Albert Cavendish (warrant no. 86359), who had represented the rank of inspector on the Central Committee of the Police Federation from 1922-23. As a constable he had arrested Mrs Pankhurst, the suffragette who had presented him with a button badge bearing the words 'Votes for Women' and a sprig of heather as a keepsake in acknowledgement of his kindness and forbearance. He was retiring on grounds of ill-health after 28 years' service, and moved to the coast at Hove in Sussex. His place was being taken by Sub-Divisional Inspector Aylett, on promotion from Peckham Police Station.[3454]

The picture below was taken in the yard of Wimbledon Police Station and shows the inspector of Wimbledon Sub-Division with his station sergeant (to his left) and his men. This picture was taken around 1923, probably for a ceremonial event, although no-one is wearing the armlet denoting he was on duty. Only about one third of the station strength of constables is shown in the picture.

Wimbledon Police mid-1920s

Harry Green was a constable at the station during the 1930s and he recorded his experiences whilst living there. He wrote:

"A wooden partition separated each officer from its neighbour about 6 feet high. The beds were made of iron with pallet mattresses filled with straw. There were two gas lamps for illumination over the passage that separated the two lines of bunks. A man going on early turn would have to cook his breakfast, (prepare) his sandwich and make a flask of tea before Parade time at 5.45am. There were no traffic signals and no pedestrian crossings. Traffic was controlled by a PC on Point Duty at Alexandra Road, The Grove, Hartfield Road Level Crossing and Skew Arches at Raynes Park. Trolley Buses went from Wimbledon to Kingston." [3455]

The station address in 1928 was shown as 15 Queen's Road, South Wimbledon.[3456] Because stations were in operation 24 hours a day, 365 days a week they needed redecoration from time to time. They were generally re-painted every three or four years, however Surveyors planned ahead and in 1937 Wimbledon was re-fitted and the station greatly improved. The sub-divisional inspector was W.F. Kendall during 1937.

During World War II Wimbledon town was bombed on a regular basis, possibly because bombs which were not dropped on London by German planes could be dropped on their way home on useful well-lit targets. Sandbags were placed around the front of the station, usually to door height, and this acted as a protection barrier for those at work. At the front of the station there was either a regular officer, war reserve constable or special constable on guard duty.

On 15th August 1939 Merton High Street and the Kingston Road area was bombed heavily, killing 14 and injuring a further 59 people. Bombing continued until May 1941, however by far the worst night was 6th November 1940, when 67 bombs fell on central Wimbledon within an hour. Remarkably, only four people were killed and thirteen injured.

An incident occurred which was to seriously affect the supervision of the sub-division. Wimbledon suffered from Flying Bomb attacks in 1944, when on 19th June at 6.30am a V1 fell on Wimbledon Hill outside Emerson Court, killing three people. Two of the deceased were Police inspectors from Wimbledon; Reserve Inspector 0100478 Alfred John Giles and Inspector 114157 Bernard Sylvester.[3457] This was a most unfortunate incident, as one was driving the other home from the night shift when the flying bomb struck. The police station, however, escaped any damage during the war.

Contingency plans had been prepared by Scotland Yard to evacuate staff to less dangerous surroundings in the Wimbledon area. It was thought that even though it had been the subject of bombing attacks it may have been safer than central London, especially since the south turret of the headquarters building had been struck and seriously damaged by German bombs on 11th May 1941. A large school near Wimbledon Common had become available, and this was later leased by the Metropolitan Police Receiver for this purpose[3458] and staff from the Receivers' Office was relocated there. In fact many local people, particularly women, sought to work for the Receivers' Office.

After the war there was a recruiting drive to enlist more special constables, and a 9,000 more men were required to help combat very high levels of crime, including robberies, assaults and burglaries. However, because of the shortfall in numbers, applications were invited for the first time from women in 1950.

Wimbledon Police Station 1900 to present

During the 1950s there was a recruitment drive and accommodation was sought and purchased to house police officers and their families in the Metropolitan Police area. This policy had a significant impact on Wimbledon, since a number of premises or areas of land were purchased. For example

Lantern House, The Downs, Wimbledon was purchased in 1951 for £15,000, with 18 married quarters created. In 1953 a further 18 flats were created at Dunarden, 15 Inner Park Road, when it was bought for £5,000.[3459]

In 1954 the Home Office suggested that Wimbledon Police Station needed refurbishment and extending because it was unfit for current purposes, however it took a further 32 years to achieve any sort of renovation. Between 1955 and 1978 plans were drawn up, and a number of properties surrounding the station were purchased including 2 South Park Road (previously an ambulance station) and 17,19,21&23 Queen's Road. These were also probably obtained by compulsory purchase.

The lamp shown left is the one outside Wimbledon Police Station as can be seen from the picture of the station opposite. The Wimbledon lamp, which is not unique, shares its design with Claybury, Gerald Road, Greenford and Lewisham.

Superintendents took over the supervision of important stations from sub-divisional inspectors when all those in the rank were promoted to chief inspector in the 1930s.

In 1957 Superintendent C. Rackham was in charge at Wimbledon, also having responsibility for New Malden.[3460] By 1960 Wimbledon (VM) had replaced Rackham and Superintendent W.H. Porter was in charge.[3461]

In 1965 Wimbledon, Mitcham, Merton and Morden were merged into the London Borough of Merton, and simultaneously Wimbledon Sub-Division was re-organised. This meant that the administrative jurisdiction of the County of Surrey was removed, with the formation of the London County Council. Consequentially, this resulted in the re-alignment of the police sub-divisions of Mitcham, Wimbledon and New Malden sections were reduced to conform to the new borough boundaries. New Malden was removed completely from the division.

In 1968 a tragic incident occurred, when PC George Arthur Dale was killed when his Police patrol car went out of control and crashed at Wimbledon.[3462] A year later, in 1969, PC Michael John Davies was off duty but, after identifying himself to warn a man on Wimbledon Common, he was attacked and stabbed to death.[3463] Such events underline the fact that policing is dangerous, risky and unpredictable.

In 1980 the Metropolitan Police Divisions in Surrey (AD, T, V and Z) were all renamed Districts, however in 1984 the Metropolitan Police District was split into 8 Areas. There was some confusion on V District, since for a time it was being administered by both W and Z Divisions, which were located on different areas. To resolve the problem Wimbledon Division was dissolved completely in September 1985, and the responsibility split between the two Areas (4 Area South and 5 Area South West).[3464] Districts were dissolved in 1986, leaving the individual stations as divisions.

During 1984 the Met's own Surveyor's Department sought contractors to complete the building works. This was not just building an extension, but refurbishing the whole station at a cost of £1.5Million. John Mowlems contractors were hired to complete the work in three stages; the extension, the alterations to the old building, and finally the work in the station yard.

In the 1980s the stables at the Queen's Road Station were demolished to make way for additional car parking and an extension. The section house was subsequently closed, converted into administrative offices and the residents rehoused.

After the introduction of the Police and Criminal Evidence Act 1984, certain stations on divisions were designated by the Commissioner as authorised to take charges, and Wimbledon was a charging station for these purposes.[3465]

Wimbledon Police Station, with new extension completed in 1987

The extension of the existing station shown in the picture above beside the old station was opened in October 1987 by the Mayor of Merton, Councillor Harold Turner, with a state-of-the-art spacious computerised Control Room, a good-sized crime investigation office, more cells and charging facilities, more accommodation for the support and civil staff, and better canteen and recreation facilities. Also from the picture above one can see that the station has been substantially enlarged, with modern accommodation being built next to and attached to the old station.

In 1992 there was a change in name and station codes for the Division. The 4 Area station that had been on Z Division was now called Merton Division and Wimbledon became 'ZM', Mitcham 'ZC' and Morden Police Office 'ZE'.[3466]

Wimbledon became the divisional OCU headquarters for the Borough of Merton in 1998.[3467]

3453 Allen, M.S. (1925) *The Pioneer Police Women* p145.
3454 *The Police Review and Parade Gossip*, 27th April 1928.
3455 Quoted by PC Harry Green Constable at Wimbledon in the 1930s in the Chief Superintendent's speech for the opening of the new station extension dated 1st October 1987.
3456 *Post Office Directory* 1928.
3457 Metropolitan Police Roll of Honour dated 2002.
3458 Browne D. (1956) *The Rise of Scotland Yard* p359.
3459 Metropolitan Police Surveyor's Records.
3460 *Police and Constabulary Almanac* 1957.
3461 *Police and Constabulary Almanac* 1960.
3462 www.met.police.uk/history/remembrance4.htm accessed 4th January 2010.
3463 Ibid.
3464 Brown, B. 'The Metropolitan Police in the County of Surrey'.
3465 *Police and Constabulary Almanac* 1998.
3466 Metropolitan Police Orders dated 12th February 1992.
3467 Ibid.

Wimbledon itself is a busy and vibrant town centre with a thriving day- and night-time economy. The borough is perhaps best known for the two weeks in summer when a large number of visitors and sports enthusiasts from around the world attend the famous Wimbledon Tennis Championships.[3468] To deal with this, and the usual wide range of policing challenges, the borough has a total of 435 personnel including police officers, police community support officers and police staff.

In 2017 the Mayor of London proposed to sell off Wimbledon Police Station and move the front counter to Mitcham Police Station, however this decision met with very strong local resistance and this proposal was shelved.[3469] In 2019 the station is still in the operational control of the Metropolitan Police.[3470]

Winchmore Hill Police Station

The London Borough of Enfield
687 Green Lanes, Winchmore Hill
Y Division (1915-1993)
Borough of Enfield OCU (1993-2013)

Winchmore Hill Police Station Lamp

The Winchmore Hill area grew in size in the early 1900s with the development of a number of housing projects, and with the influx of large numbers of people came the justification for the building of a police station. The Metropolitan Police looked around for a site, which it obtained from the London Brick Company in the vicinity of Compton Road. This land originally formed part of the Highfield House Estate. The freehold land was purchased for the sum of £1,215 on 8th January 1907.

The new station was built and came into use in December 1915.[3471] and included two sets of married quarters (rent at 10s per week), cells and a charge room. The code signal for the station was 'WV'. When constructed in 1915 Winchmore Hill was also listed as having an ambulance shelter, which housed the hand ambulance for the conveyance of sick and injured people.

Winchmore Hill Police Station 1915-1998

In 1931 Winchmore Hill was a sectional station on Y or Highgate Division, although the divisional headquarters was located at Kentish Town Police Station. The sub-divisional station appears to have been Enfield.

During the re-organisation of 1933, Winchmore Hill Police Station was shown as a sectional station of Wood Green Sub-Division at 687 Green Lanes. Further reorganisation in 1964 saw the station re-assigned to Edmonton Sub-Division as a sectional station situated in the Borough of Enfield.

The station closed in 1998 and was sold to Choudray devlopment group in 2013.

Wood Green Police Station

The London Borough of Haringey
347 High Road (1866-1908)
Y Division (1866-1993)
Haringey OCU (1993-2018/2019)
Basic Command Unit North Area (NA) (with the London Borough of Enfield) (2018/9 to Present)

Wood Green Police Station Lamp

Wood Green Police Station opened on 10th September 1866,[3472] locationed on Y Division. Freehold land at 347 High Road, Wood Green had been purchased the previous year. The picture below shows the front view to the station, which was designated a sergeant-supervised station in 1873.[3473]

A new division – J or Bethnal Green – was formed in 1886, which meant boundary changes for the surrounding divisions. This Order stated that Y Division was composed of Kentish Town, Somers Town, Caledonian Road, Holloway, Highgate, Hornsey, and Enfield, with stations also at Wood Green, Southgate and Potters Bar.[3474]

Wood Green became a sub-division on 4th May 1889. By the turn of the century it was felt that the present station was not large enough for current requirements, so land adjacent was purchased in 1903 from Mr. C.L. Finch. The address of the purchased property was shown as 343 and 345 High Road, Wood Green. The new station was completed and occupied in April 1908.[3475] Two sets of married quarters and accommodation for eleven constables were included above the station.[3476]

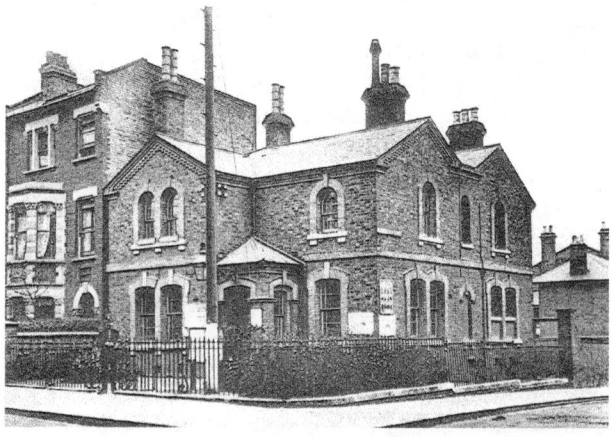

Wood Green Police Station 1866-1908

Religion played a part in the culture of policing. The International Christian Police Association (ICPA)[3477] was formed by Miss Catherine Gurney OBE,[3478] who had also formed the Police Institute, located at 1a Adelphi Terrace, Adam Street, Strand. The Police Institute, which was affiliated to the ICPA, was like an exclusive club for police officers and their families. It had a reading room, writing room with library, restaurant and bed and breakfast cost 3/6 in 1924.[3479] Miss Gurney was a very influential person with respect to the police, because she was not only Hon. Sec. of the Institute but also on the boards of the Seaside Home at Brighton, Hove, the Northern Convalescent Home, Harrogate, Provincial Police Orphanage, Redhill, and the Northern Police Orphanage at Harrogate.[3480] Most police divisions had ICPA representatives, which were usually ladies who volunteered for the post. Officers from Y Division had Miss Bridger of 48 Mercers Road, Tufnel Park as their delegate. Funds were collected from charitable donations and publications. For 6d one could purchase a small pocket-size almanac and diary.

Inspector Horace Elphick (warrant no. 87670) was attached to E Division but seconded to the Law Courts in the Strand. He had joined the Metropolitan Police in August 1901, and was a devout Christian and keen member of the ICPA. When he retired from the police in 1927[3481] he continued to raise funds for the charity, and published a pamphlet entitled 'The Experiences of a London Police Officer', priced at one shilling. Inside were Elphick's experiences with other police officers or members of the public, together with words of wisdom and extracts from the Bible.[3482] The Catholic Guild was formed in 1913 by a group of officers who found themselves meeting after mass at Westminster Cathedral.[3483]

It was realised in 1919 that members of the Special Constabulary could have a role in peacetime. Between 1919 and 1934 a Special Constabulary Reserve was maintained, numbering 10,000 men. In 1926 the General Strike caused the Government to ask for further volunteers. Some 61,000 responded to the call, and recruitment to the Special Constabulary was suspended for some time.[3484]

1919, and was awarded to members of the Special Constabulary for nine years' unpaid service with a minimum of 50 hours duty per year. War service counted as triple time. At the time of taking the picture on the right Yalden was a chief inspector, and has completed either 27 years' continuous service or more probably earned at least one clasp during World War I.

Special Constables were often not trusted by their regular colleagues, because they were seen as strike breakers. This occurred in both 1918 and 1919, because during the police strike and demonstrations they carried on performing beat and station duties against the express wishes of those who were attempting to get a better deal for police officers.[3485]

In 1929 the sub-divisional inspector in charge of the station was William Abbey. He had joined the police on 28th November 1898, and was given the warrant number 84628. He had been promoted to sergeant in September 1912, station sergeant in January 1921 and inspector in February 1924. He was further promoted to sub-divisional inspector in January 1929. Registers at the station show that he was also an authorised cyclist, and had been so since March 1922.[3486]

Special Chief Inspector William Yalden, and Below: Metropolitan Police Special Constabulary medal issued during WWI

Entrance Declaration for William Yalden

The application above relates to William Yalden of 82 Victoria Road, Alexandra Park, who applied to join the reserve on 16th May 1926. It appears that Yalden had already been a member of the MPSC before re-applying as a reserve. The medal he is wearing is the Special Constabulary Long Service Medal with two bars. This medal was instituted on 30th August

3468 Metropolitan Police Orders dated 12th February 1992.
3469 The Mayor's Office for Policing and Crime and Metropolitan Police Service (2017). 'Public Access and Engagement Strategy'.
3470 MPS (2019) Freedom of Information request: MPS Assets.
3471 Metropolitan Police Orders dated 11th December 1915.
3472 Metropolitan Police Orders 10th September 1866.
3473 General Orders 1873.
3474 Metropolitan Police Orders dated 22nd July 1886.
3475 Metropolitan Police Orders dated 18th April 1908
3476 John Back Archive (1975).
3477 The International Christian Police Association was formed in 1883 by Ms Gurney, who encouraged the formation of associations from all over the Empire. She was awarded the OBE in recognition for her devotion and organisational skills in establishing the ICPA.
3478 Fido, M and Skinner, K. (1999) *The Official Encyclopaedia of Scotland Yard.* Virgin, London p40.
3479 *The Policeman's Pocket Almanac and Diary* 1924.
3480 Ibid.
3481 Metropolitan Police Service Records.
3482 Elphick, H. (1927) *The Experiences of a London Police Officer.* International Christian Police Association, London WC1.
3483 Fido, M and Skinner, K. (1999) *The Official Encyclopaedia of Scotland Yard.* Virgin, London p35.
3484 Ibid.
3485 Ibid
3486 Metropolitan Police Y Divisional Seniority Register (revised 1922).

During the boundary revisions of 1933 the status of Wood Green was enhanced and it became the divisional headquarters for Y Division.

On 1st April 1934 the Police telephone box system was extended to include Wood Green Sub-Division, which involved the delivery to the station of a fully-equipped police van with first aid apparatus to deal with serious accidents.[3487]

Wood Green had suffered with a number of fatalities since the beginning of the Second World War. In 1941 Special Constable Bertie Mazetti died when he collided with a lorry whilst cycling to duty at Wood Green during the blackout. In 1944, Constable Frederick Ernest Clarke was killed by enemy action when a long-range V2 rocket exploded in Wood Green.[3488] Tragically, in 1950 Constable Samuel Lock was cleaning a police issue pistol at the station when it accidentally discharged itself, killing him instantly.[3489] In 1967 Constable James Brian May was directing traffic at a busy road junction in Wood Green when he was struck by a vehicle and died of his injuries.[3490]

Wood Green Police Station 1908 to present

In 1998 Wood Green was part of 2 Area (North West) and was a designated charging station, however by 2002 it had become a borough-based station, operational 24 hours a day, seven days a week.[3491]

In 2019 the freehold Wood Green Police station was retained for operational purposes by the Metropolitan Police.[3492]

Woodford Police Station

The London Borough of Redbridge
Various rented houses (1840-1871)
1 Mornington Road, Woodford Wells, Essex (1871-1968)
590 High Road, Woodford Green, Essex (1968-2013)
K Division (1840-1886)
J Division (1886-1993)
Redbridge OCU (1993-2013)

Policing the Woodford area prior to the formation of the Metropolitan Police in 1829 was left very much to the Bow Street Horse Patrol and the locally-recruited and not-very-able Parish constables. The Horse Patrols were formed in 1805 to combat the many highway robberies taking place on the roads around London. Recruits were taken from married ex-Cavalrymen aged between 30-65 years old who were paid 4s per day.[3493] It took a further ten years, until 1839, for the Metropolitan Police borders to take in Woodford.[3494]

In 1836 there were fifteen horse patrol stations, numbered from 51-65, in the Fourth Division. There were three horse patrols responsible at three different places (called stations) in the Woodford area. Station 54 was rented for £15 per year from Mr. P. Mallard. This station was occupied by Constable John Emerson, who was a 46-year-old Leicestershire man who had joined the horse patrol in 1823. Station 55, which was also rented from Mr. Mallard, was occupied by Constable John Marlow, aged 32 years, and his family. Marlow came originally from Sussex, and had joined the Horse Patrol from the Metropolitan Police in 1833. Station 56 was situated at Snakes Lane, and was rented from Lady Thynne. Constable William Fair, aged 35 years and born in Jamaica, was also recruited to the Horse Patrol from the Metropolitan Police, in September 1833. Constable Fair was responsible for patrolling between Woodford and the thirteen-mile post at Abridge, whilst the two patrols covered the New Road as far as Walthamstow.[3495]

The general description and exact location of the first police station at Woodford is not known, however they were usually the same buildings which were used by the Parish Constables and vacated when the borders of the Metropolitan Police District was extended.

In 1840 the station was known as Woodford Police Station, although a Woodford Bridge Police Station situated near Chigwell, Essex is also shown. Records show that Woodford was in the outer district of K Division, and was one of only three stations able to take charges. The station strength comprised of one sergeant and five constables, with supervision by the inspector coming from Ilford Police Station. The sergeant at Woodford was also responsible for supervising the three constables at Loughton. Records show that the four officers all lived in private lodgings.

A little further away, the Receiver of the Metropolitan Police acquired two houses in Abridge and Epping. These were both Horse Patrol stations, and the Epping station was called Holly Wall Station. It consisted of a brick-and-slate house with a small garden and a stable. It was shown as a station on K Division, and was rented from Mr. Payton of Copt Hall, Loughton. The premises were given up in 1853. The house in Abridge had no name, but was almost identical to the Epping property and was rented yearly from Mr. Chinery of Loughton for an undisclosed rent.[3496]

A likely location for the station was a single-storey premises referred to as Woodford Goal, situated in what was later the High Road outside the property named 'Elmhurst'. This structure was positioned close to the excavation cut in modern times to build the North Circular Road, where it joins the start of the M11 motorway, above and a short distance from Charlie Brown's roundabout.

In 1855 Charles Reeves, the Metropolitan Police Surveyor, reported that the Receiver had been given permission by the Home Office to lease land and premises to be used for police purposes at Woodford in Essex. Temporary accommodation had been found, which was reported at the time to be of indifferent character and lacking in cell and stable facilities.

Mr. Wood offered the Metropolitan Police a plot of land with a frontage to Woodford Green, together with a 60-year lease and ground rent of £10 per annum. The local superintendent reported that the site was suitable for the police building, and permission was given by the Home Office for leasing the land in November 1855. The temporary accommodation cost £39 per year to rent, and stable boarding cost 4/- per week.[3497]

In 1864 Woodford Police Station was shown to have an available strength of two sergeants and ten constables, and was shown as a station on K or Stepney Division where charges were taken, although there were still no cells available.[3498]

Directions were given by the Commissioner to build a new station in December 1864. Records show a suitable site was found in Woodford on land belonging to the Earl of Cowley, which was held in trust from the Estate of the Earl of Mornington. Their agents, Messrs. Glaisse and Bristowe, negotiated for a 99-year lease from mid-summer 1867 to 1966 costing £52 10d per year, with restrictions. The Receiver of the Metropolitan Police was responsible for the repair of the building, the payment of all taxes and the provision of insurance of three-quarters the value of £2,500 with the London Assurance Office.[3499]

In October 1865 re-organisation meant that Woodford was transferred to N or Islington Division.[3500]

Work started on the new station in 1870, and it included a basement, a ground floor and a first floor. The ground floor was built with a charge room, a reserve room, an inspector's office, a day room, stores, three cells, four stalls (stables) and two water closets. The first floor provided residence for four single constables and for a married sergeant, who paid 2/3d per week rent. The station opened in March 1871 and was supervised by the sergeant in charge.[3501] The address of the station was later given as 1 Mornington Road, Woodford Wells, Essex.[3502]

Woodford Police Station 1871-1968

Further re-organisation, and the creation of a new sub-division at Woodford were reported in 1873.[3503] This allowed for one mounted inspector to be stationed at Woodford together with six sergeants, two at Woodford (one mounted) two at Loughton (one mounted) and two at Waltham Abbey. Some 53 constables covered the division, including 18 at Woodford with one on detective duties, two mounted constables and five reserve constables. (Reserve constables were trusted reliable officers who could be sent anywhere to deal with public order problems. They were paid slightly more than ordinary constables.) The remaining distribution was shown as ten constables for Loughton including one mounted constable; 14 constables for Waltham Abbey; one mounted officer and six constables for Chigwell, and five constables for Chingford. All the officers were split into ten sections, with five sections patrolling during the day and five sections patrolling at night.[3504]

Soon after this an augmentation of Woodford Sub-Division saw an increase of one inspector and one horse. Records show that accommodation upstairs at the station was revised to provide rooms for the inspector, who was married. The sergeant was removed, and five rooms were allocated to the station inspector and his family.

In 1884 the address of the station was reported as Woodford Wells. When J or Bethnal Green Division was formed on 1st August 1886 Woodford was transferred to the new division as a sub-divisional station.[3505]

One of the most rewarding social events, which have taken place at all stations since the police were formed, was that of an officer's retirement after exemplary service. In May 1894 over 50 constables and sergeants congregated at Woodford Police Station for the retirement of Inspector William Pearman, whose testimonial took the form of a handsome marble clock, which had been inscribed to recognise the twenty-six years' service which he had given to the Force. In his speech Inspector Pearman congratulated the police officers present, and stated that the superintendent would find it hard to find finer officers anywhere else on the division.[3506]

The Metropolitan Police obtained the freehold to the station in 1898.[3507]

Records show that in 1924 there was one fixed point box, located in the High Road, Woodford on a site owned by Messrs W. and S. Single.[3508] This dated from an agreement of 27th April 1907. In 1925 this box was removed to the junction of High Road, South Woodford with Grove Road, and was re-sited on land owned by the Ministry of Transport. Furthermore, it was reported that in George Lane, Woodford, on land owned by the Woodford Urban District Council, were premises designated as an ambulance shelter.[3509] This was probably for the handcart used to convey ill, injured or drunken people to a place of recovery.[3510]

Divisional alterations in December 1926 reported Woodford Sub-Division as being responsible for policing Woodford, Loughton, Claybury and Barkingside. In 1931 records show that Woodford Sub-Division was attached to J or Hackney Division.[3511] In 1933 Wanstead, Barkingside, Claybury and Loughton were shown as sectional stations to Woodford after re-organisation. Chingford and Waltham Abbey were now shown on N or Islington Division.

In the mid 1930s Police Boxes were placed at major road junctions to facilitate communications. These boxes were intended to be used by both police officers ringing in and also by members of the public. There were two police boxes

3487 Metropolitan Police Orders 1st April 1934.
3488 www.policememorial.org.uk/Forces/Metropolitan/metroll.htm accessed 12th March 2002.
3489 Ibid.
3490 Ibid.
3491 www.met.police.uk/contact/phone.htm accessed 12th March 2002.
3492 MPS Information rights unit (2019) MPS Assets.
3493 Elliott, B. (1987) 'The Abbey – Policing Since 1840'.
3494 John Back Archive (1975).
3495 Elliott, B. (1987) 'The Abbey – Policing Since 1840'.
3496 Metropolitan Police Surveyor's Records (undated).
3497 Ibid.
3498 Metropolitan Police Orders dated 11th January 1864.
3499 Metropolitan Police Surveyor's Records (undated).
3500 Metropolitan Police Orders dated October 1865.
3501 Metropolitan Police General Orders 1873.
3502 Metropolitan Police Surveyor's Records (undated).
3503 Metropolitan Police Orders dated 18th October 1873.
3504 Elliott, B. (1987) 'The Abbey – Policing Since 1840'.
3505 Elliott, B. (1993) 'A History of the Police Stations of J Division 1886-1986'.
3506 *Police Review,* May 1894.
3507 Metropolitan Police Surveyor's Records (undated).
3508 The Metropolitan Police Surveyor's Records 1924.
3509 Ibid.
3510 Elliott, B. (1987) The Abbey – Policing Since 1840.
3511 *Kirchner's Almanac* 1931.

on Woodford Division. These were located at the junction of Epping New Road and High Beach Road (Box 38), and on Epping Road near the Wake Arms junction (Box 40),[3512] both on Woodford Section.

Some of the police boxes were also fitted with air raid warning sirens. They were simply furnished and contained first aid facilities and a single non-dial telephone in a cabinet, which opened from outside or inside as required. There was also a fixed table with a drawer and a hard oval stool to enable the officer to sit and write reports and take refreshments. In wintertime a small electric heater was used to heat the box, which also had an interior light and interconnected telephone bell and flashing light. Some later boxes were made of concrete, and situated on new housing estates.[3513]

In 1965 Local Government boundary changes caused a status change for Woodford (JF), which was reduced to a sectional station to Barkingside (JB) and situated within the new London Borough of Redbridge.[3514]

By 1962 the station, which despite alterations including absorbing the married accommodation within the station, was reported as being inadequate for current policing needs.[3515] A new leased site was found at 94-100 High Road, Woodford that was situated on the south west corner of Chestnut Walk. Tenders were invited for the new station, which Messrs Hawkins Bros. (Gosport) Limited won the contract at a cost of £95,856. Work commenced in June 1967, and the station was ready for occupation by the end of 1968.[3516] Renumbering of properties in the High Road meant that the station was now located at 509 High Road, Woodford Green, on the main A11 trunk road to Newmarket.[3517] The location of the new station was about 400 yards north east of the old station.

Woodford Police Station 1968-2013

In October 1974 the Metropolitan Police purchased the freehold to the new station for £30,000.[3518]

The police station is now closed to the public, but is still used for police purposes.

Woolwich Police Station

The London Borough of Greenwich

William Street (1847-1910)

29 Market Street (1910-2014)

R Division (1847-1993)

Borough of Greenwich OCU (1993-2014)

The original Watch House and Cage used by the Parish Constable and his Watchmen were situated at the north end of Rope Yard Rails on the corner of the High Street, not far from Cannon Row.[3519] Woolwich Parish petitioned the Home Secretary for an extension of the Metropolitan Police limits in February 1839 because of the lawlessness of the local area, and being of the opinion that the local Watch could no longer cope with the situation.

The Metropolitan Police arrived in Woolwich on 13th January 1840, not only taking over the duties of the Watch but also the Watch House. The Watch House was shown as a station on R Division of the Metropolitan Police, and such was its importance that an inspector was posted in charge. The areas of Woolwich, Wickham, Plumstead and part of Charlton were taken over by the Metropolitan Police.

The Police quickly realised the scale of the task when they arrived, because they considered the resources inadequate and began looking for a suitable site on which to build a larger Police station house. In 1841 the University Life Office leased land to the Metropolitan Police for 80 years, at an annual cost of £68 14s.

The new two-storey station house was built by the Receiver at a cost £1,374 and was shown as a station on R Division in 1841.[3520] In 1844 Inspector George Clifford, who had been promoted the year before, was shown in charge of the station and sub-division at High Street, Woolwich.[3521] There was another inspector of R Division by the name of Roger Howard, who had been promoted in 1839 and who was stationed not far away in charge at Woolwich Dockyard.[3522]

The dockyards had been taken over by R Division in 1841, and possession of Woolwich Arsenal occurred in 1844 when it was removed from the responsibility of the Dockyard Police. A contingent of local police officers provided gate and perimeter security and also guarded the main magazine, which included the onerous task of guarding the magazine hulks moored offshore.[3523] Occasionally there would be accidents when munitions exploded, causing serious damage and loss of life. In September 1845 an explosion killed seven workers, and another in December 1855 killed a further four more. Officers from Woolwich would be required to send assistance, help with first aid, and clear up the damage.[3524]

From time to time outside Police Forces would ask the Metropolitan Police for assistance in dealing with disorder or public unrest. In December 1843 an illegal prize-fight between Tass Parker and the Tipton Slasher was taking place at Greenhithe in Kent, and disorder was expected. The Police at Woolwich were asked to supply assistance, and sent six officers immediately. However, when disorder broke out amongst the 300 supporters they, with local officers, were not enough to quell the trouble. A further three mounted police and a troop of Dragoons[3525] augmented the numbers and soon established order.[3526]

The original Watch House was eventually surrendered back to the Parish Authorities in 1848.[3527]

In 1856 £260 was allocated in order to add four extra cells to those already present at the station.[3528] Such was the importance relating to the security of dockyards that a senior police officer was placed in charge, and those early officers that had showed aptitude were quickly promoted. For example, Charles F. Field was promoted from constable or sergeant to inspector in 1833 (less than five years after the Police commenced) and posted in charge of Deptford Dockyard.

Records show that in 1873 there was still an inspector in charge of the police station at Woolwich, William Street, which was later renamed Calderwood Street.[3529] William Street was situated between Powis Street and Brewer Street, and the Police Station was next door to Woolwich Town Hall. The court building appears to have been owned by the Receiver for

Woolwich Police Station 1847-1910

the Metropolitan Police.³⁵³⁰

The military authorities were anxious not to have officers with local connections, and put the Commissioners under great pressure to provide dockyard security outside London. It wasn't until 1860 that the Metropolitan Police took over responsibility for Woolwich, Portsmouth, Devonport, Chatham and Sheerness, and Pembroke, using a special detachment of Police from London.³⁵³¹

The established strength of the station rose in 1864, with numbers totalling two inspectors, five sergeants and 34 constables. There were eight day beats and 21 by night to cover.³⁵³²

The Special Constabulary has often augmented the Police during times of local disorder and riot. The forerunners of the IRA were causing mayhem on the mainland in 1867, so there was a recruitment drive which supplemented the Police with an additional 5,000 men. Yet the finest hour for the Special Constabulary was during the First World War, when large numbers of civilians supplemented their Police. Woolwich was issued with six Adams breech-loading revolvers in November 1868, together with 60 rounds of ammunition.³⁵³³

Woolwich Docks were a bigger operation than those of Greenwich in 1869, when records show that it had an establishment of one superintendent, 14 inspectors, 22 sergeants and 136 constables, making this by far the largest number in any of the dockyards in England and Wales.³⁵³⁴

Woolwich Police Station photographed from Upper Market Street in 1911

3512 Op Cit.
3513 Ibid.
3514 Elliott, B. (1993) 'A History of J Division 1886-1986'.
3515 Ibid.
3516 Ibid.
3517 Ibid.
3518 Ibid.
3519 Hadaway, D. (1990) 'The Metropolitan Police in Woolwich'.
3520 Metropolitan Police Surveyor's Records.
3521 *The Police and Constabulary List* (1844) Parker, Furnival and Parker, London.
3522 Ibid.
3523 Hadaway, D. (1985) *Eltham Police Station; The First Hundred Years.* Latter Books, Sussex.
3524 Hadaway, D. (1990) 'The Metropolitan Police in Woolwich'.

One of the greatest tragedies to befall not only Woolwich, but the country as a whole, was the collision of two ships in the Thames off Tipcock Pier in September 1878. The *Bywell Castle* collided with the *Princess Alice*, a paddle steamer, resulting in the deaths of 590 men women and children. Officers from Woolwich and the Thames Division worked tirelessly to identify bodies, ensure the safekeeping of a deceased's property, and notify the next of kin.[3535]

The freehold to Woolwich (William Street) was purchased in December 1890 at a cost of £5,000. This was a traditional 16-room Police station house over three levels, with basement, ground floor and first floor. On the ground floor there was a charge room, fodder room (for the horses) and inspector's office that were all public rooms and therefore liable for rent to paid by the public. There were also five cells and a two-stall stable. There were two rooms on the ground floor, occupied by Inspector Elias Ford, his wife and five children,[3536] paying 5s and 6d per week rent. In addition there were twelve single constables stationed in the section house, each paying 1s per week rent,[3537] their number being reduced to eleven in 1883. In 1879 the annual rent for the whole property was increased to £83 14s 2d.[3538]

The call sign for Woolwich Police Station was Whiskey Lima (WL).[3539] When the magistrates in 1893 instructed that a boy should receive a birching (a thrashing with a wooden birch), the offenders would have to return at the allotted time to Woolwich Magistrates' Court and were introduced to Sergeant Gilham, the huge 22-stone gaoler. Gilham was the 'official boy bircher', who would go easy on new offenders whilst regulars would be spared no mercy – nor expect any.[3540]

The Refused Charge Book for the early part of the 20th century still survives, and much space was devoted to the stealing of growing vegetables and fruit. Charges were declined in many circumstances, presumably at the instigation of a station officer with a sense of proportion.

There was a suggestion in 1903 that a new police station should be built next door to Woolwich Police Court, but this was not to be. In July 1904 a site at 29 Market Street, Woolwich was compulsorily purchased from the Trustees of the Ogilby Estate on which to build a new police station, because the old one was no longer suitable.

In August 1910 the new sub-divisional station of Greenwich on R Division was opened for business, with living accommodation comprising of one set of married quarters and a section house with space for 25 single constables.[3541] Previously the Police were only entitled to one day off per fortnight, but in 1910 this became one day off a week.[3542] The new station had all the amenities and services with piped flowing water, electricity and gas, together with surface and foul water drains. The basement contained the parade room, billiard room, lost property store and male toilets. The first floor of the station contained a large charge room, three cells, a detention room and the inspector's office, whose only door led into the charge room. The general front office could be entered through the lobby from Market Street, which took the visitor to the front counter. A substantial part of the ground floor station was taken up with the canteen, senior officer's dining room, servery and kitchen.

The first floor contained the detective inspector's office, the CID office, collator's office, women police office and women sergeant's office. The offices of the superintendent, chief inspector, admin inspector, plan drawer, the women staff rest room, and general administration were situated on the second floor. Alterations were implemented in January 1969.

Woolwich Police Station 1910-2014

During the First World War German bombers, airships and Zeppelins targeted the areas of Charlton, Greenwich and Woolwich, sometimes with great success. On the night of 2nd September 1916 Captain William Leefe Robinson shot down at Cuffley the airship Schütte Lanz 11, piloted by Captain Wilhelm Schramm, who had been born and had lived in London with his family at 9 Victoria Road (now Way), Charlton, and Wilhelm's father had worked in an executive position at the nearby German firm of Siemens. The searchlights at Woolwich had seen Schramm's airship hovering over East London and the Thames, and when the heavy guns opened up the barrage forced it north to its fate. Schramm would have known the connection with Woolwich Arsenal and the gunpowder factory at Waltham Abbey, so it is likely that because of the barrage he went in search of the powder works instead.

This was the first German airship to be shot down in the war, and Captain Robinson was awarded the VC (shown left) for his success.

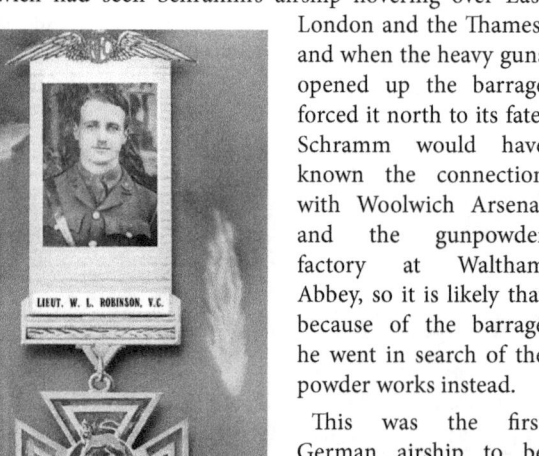

Lieutenant Robinson together with his Victoria Cross

The formation of the women police

had its roots in Woolwich when the National Union of Women Workers of Great Britain and Ireland informed the Metropolitan Police Commissioner that it had raised a Women's Patrol Committee (Woolwich Branch), a voluntary patrol, to safeguard the morals of women munitions workers. The women would patrol in pairs, were dressed in black and wore red embroidered numbers on duty armlets.

It was not until 1922 that an official Women Police were introduced into the Metropolitan Police and given powers of arrest. Those early volunteers laid the foundation for the modern day Women Police. Woolwich was called 'RW', and one of the famous Women Police Officers of her time was Winifred Gould, who was born on 24th July 1905 and joined the Metropolitan Police on 24th August 1931. She retired eventually on 3rd December 1962 on a medical discharge, following a vehicle accident on duty. Her warrant number was 257, and her uniform collar number was 18. Winifred also had a strong family connection to Police work, from her grandfather in Hampshire to her father who, by contrast, had joined the Metropolitan Police in 1887. Her father had retired after thirty-two and half years of service. George Gould was an R Division officer who drew his pension for twenty-nine years and died in 1948. It is worth noting that Winifred would apparently be the first Policewoman at Woolwich to have the power of arrest; she also became a CID officer. Winifred entered Peel House on 15th June 1931 and, as previously stated, joined the Force two months later.[3543]

Woman Police Constable 108 M.P. Steere, taken in 1921

The picture above shows the sort of uniform Winifred would have worn when she joined. Her first posting was to Hyde Park Station, under the tutorship of Women Patrol Annie Matthews, and later posted to Bow Street, Paddington and Hammersmith to gain wider experience. She was then transferred to Blackheath Road Police Station on 4th December 1934, where she worked with Women Patrol Emily Walsh. Winifred was transferred to Woolwich Police Station on 21st June 1937. Her further training included a short period at Vine Street to learn how to take 'sex offence statements'. Winifred also worked from time to time at Lewisham Garage, dealing with speeding against the new 30 mile per hour limit. This was a plain-clothes role for the two officers, one male and one female. It appears Winifred was the first woman to issue a summons on Shooters Hill Road and take it before the court. She had been in company with Police Sergeant MacAndrew. She was referred to as the original 'Gertie the girl with the gong'.[3544]

A newspaper article from 8th December 1953 reported the following:

'On Monday, before Mr A. A. Pereira, WOMAN DETECTIVE COMMENDED.

'Woman Detective Winifred Gould attached to Blackheath Road Police Station for 'her plucky conduct in effecting the arrest of two men who were charged with being concerned in stealing a child's tricycle valued at £7 15s 2d from outside a shop in New Cross.'

It goes on to describe the struggle between Winifred, the two men (one aged 29 the other 25) and the shopkeeper. Both offenders had been drinking, and were aggressive and threatening. The magistrate fined them £10.[3545]

Another such cutting, apparently from a paper in December 1948, refers to 'ARREST OF A 'PRAM THIEF'', where Winifred and one other woman officer were deployed undercover to investigate the thefts from perambulators. The location was the Welfare Centre in Chevening Road, Greenwich. A woman from Spearman Street, Woolwich, was arrested as a result. Winifred gave the following evidence:

"The female suspect on being arrested said "Please can't you forgive me this time? I promise not to do it again. Here is the purse." At the Police Station she confessed to stealing £2 from the perambulator the previous November."

Winifred continued that the arrested woman "had three sons – boys of 16, 15 and 6 years of age. Her husband gave her £5 a week, out of which she paid 11s 9½d rent, and the two elder boys paid her £1 and 10s respectively." [3546]

3525 The term 'Troop' would have been used for a number of members of cavalry regiments at the time and would have consisted of approximately 40 men (information supplied by the 1st The Queen's Dragoon Guards Regimental Museum curator in Cardiff.
3526 Hadaway, D. (1990) 'The Metropolitan Police in Woolwich'.
3527 MEPO 5/23 (128).
3528 Hadaway, D. (1990) 'The Metropolitan Police in Woolwich'.
3529 Ibid.
3530 'Premises in the occupation of the Metropolitan Police' (1898), Metropolitan Police Surveyor's Department.
3531 Moylan, J. F. (1929) *Scotland Yard*. Puttnams, London p217.
3532 John Back Archive (1975).
3533 Metropolitan Police Orders dated 28th January 1869.
3534 Report to the Commissioner of the Police 1869.
3535 Hadaway, D. (1990) The Metropolitan Police in Woolwich.
3536 Census Records 1881.
3537 Metropolitan Police Surveyor's Records.
3538 Ibid.
3539 Metropolitan Police General Orders 1893.
3540 Hadaway, D. (1990) 'The Metropolitan Police in Woolwich'.
3541 Metropolitan Police Surveyor's Records.
3542 Hadaway, D. (1990) 'The Metropolitan Police in Woolwich'.
3543 Sculley, R., 'The Warren, Win the Rebel'. Spring 1977 p32.
3544 Ibid p35.
3545 Court report dated 8th December 1953.
3546 Court report, newspaper unknown, believed December 1948.

The woman was bound over at the Woolwich Court for seven offences of similar type, and fined £10 with 21 days to pay the magistrate, Mr L.A. Stevenson. Winifred, who certainly was a character, liked to refer to herself as 'Old Win the Rebel'.[3547] She is certainly remembered with affection, as it is people who populate the space and time within the police stations – not the buildings.

In 1960 RW was a sub-divisional station with Superintendent H.R. Abbott in charge.[3548]

By 2001 Woolwich had been relegated to office status and was located at 29 Market Street, but under the Police and Criminal Evidence Act it was no longer a charging station.[3549]

In December 2014 Woolwich Police Station was sold for £2.202M to Woolwich Arsenal Investments.[3550]

Worcester Park Police Office

The London Borough of Sutton

154 Central Road, Worcester Park (1971 to Present)

Z Division (1971-1993)

Borough of Sutton OCU 1993 – 2018/9

Borough of Sutton BCU Area South BCU (with Croydon and Bromley) (2018/19 to Present)

When the Metropolitan Police District was extended in 1839 the Liberty of Worcester Park was one of the places mentioned. Being under the jurisdiction of Richmond Police Station on V Division, it had the strength of one constable.[3551]

In November 1966 it was found that a number of areas near the outskirts of the Metropolitan Police District had no police station within easy reach, so it was decided that small neighbourhood Police Units should be formed. One of these areas consisted of parts of North Cheam and Worcester Park.

A site was found and Home Office authority was granted, but because of the protracted negotiations regarding a right of way the owner withdrew his offer. Other properties were sought, but it was not until 1970 that a suitable site came on the market. The lease was obtained for a vacant shop with living accommodation above which was tenanted.[3552]

On Tuesday, 13th April 1971 a Police Office was opened at 154 Central Road, Worcester Park, Surrey, on Sutton Sub-Division.[3553] It was opened by Chief Superintendent Frederick Jarvis from Sutton Police Station.[3554]

Worcester Park Police Officer 1971 to present

Inspector John Mower, the Unit Commander at Sutton, said:

"We hope local people will make full use of the Office and call in any time on any matter concerning the Police. It will save them a longish return journey to the Station at Sutton." [3555]

The Police Office was open from 10.00am to 2.00pm on Monday to Friday,[3556] but in 2017 closed for public access. It is still retained as an operational building in 2019.[3557]

3547 Sculley, R. 'The Warren, Win the Rebel', Spring 1977 p31.
3548 *The Police and Constabulary Almanac* 1960.
3549 *The Police and Constabulary Almanac* 2001.
3550 MPS Information Rights Unit (2019) Freedom of Information: Land and property sold by the MPS for over £1M.
3551 MEPO 2/76.
3552 LB 844.
3553 Metropolitan Police Order dated 8th April 1971.
3554 *Sutton and Cheam Herald*, 15th April 1971.
3555 *Sutton and Cheam Herald*, 8th April 1981.
3556 www.met.police.uk accessed 10th October 2010.
3557 MPS (2018) Freedom of information request: Police station closures broken down by year.

Chapter 5.
Thames Division

The police of the Thames Division were formed before the Metropolitan Police were established; the Thames Police Preventative Force was established in June 1798, because vast wealth was pouring into the Port of London and it was established that:

"...there were no fewer than 10,000 thieves, footpads, prostitutes and pilferers at work on the jetties, quays that lined the riverside and that the plunder and pillage represented an annual loss of over half a million pounds." [3558]

With the formation of the Metropolitan Police in 1829, the River Police became a division of the Met. The first station to open near the Thames was Wapping, followed by an office at Greenwich, which had an establishment of one hundred constables. Police were recruited not only to stem the tide of crime on the river, but also to deal with the frequent robberies on the roads leading into the metropolis and thefts in the dockyards at Deptford and Woolwich.

The division extended practically through the whole navigable area of the River Thames. This stretched from Teddington Lock in the west to Dartford Creek, Kent and Rainham, Essex in the east.[3559] The following stations, description and events of the Thames Division relate mainly to the east of Tower Bridge as these places are located within north and north-east London.

Thames – Blackwall Police Station

The head of the Thames River Police in 1844 was shown as Mr. James Christopher Evans, who was appointed as Superintendent in 1798.[3560] Evans had considerable experience of the River Thames and of managing the River Police. He was assisted by 21 inspectors. In the early days of the River Police the stations were shown as ships which were moored in strategic places. For example, at Wapping in 1844 a floating station was located off Wapping Stairs; the ship Royalist was shown moored off Somerset House, Strand Lane (although this was re-located eastwards later), and the Scorpion off the Folly House, Blackwall in Poplar.[3561] Folly House was a famous riverside public tavern, noted not only for its pleasure gardens but also for its famous resident, mistress of Charles II Nell Gwynne, who died in 1687. It stood between Stewart Street and the River Thames.

Additionally, the Thames Police shared the police station located at London Docks with H or Whitechapel Division. The station ship Royalist was leased from Mr. John Hards of Greenwich, Kent, and the Receiver paid for all outgoings. In July 1880 a mooring agreement was reached with the conservators of the River Thames, who stipulated that the ship could be moored near the Saltings between Greenwich and Blackwall.[3562]

Records show that in 1844 there were seven inspectors attached to Blackwall station. These were William Leonard, who was promoted in 1837, George Webb, Richard White, Thomas Benjamin Walker, John Judge, George Maddox and Thomas Grimstone, all promoted to inspector in 1840.[3563]

In the early days of the Metropolitan Police, H Division sergeants and constables were under the direct supervision of the Inspectors of Thames Division.[3564] This was a sensible step, considering their experience given they had been formed thirty-one years before Peel's new model.

There were fifteen boats attached to Thames Division, eleven being kept for duty with four in reserve. These were rowing boats. By 1864 the strength of Thames Division was 25 Inspectors and 86 constables. In the intervening period there had been a change of ship at Blackwall, with the *Royalist* having been moved from off Somerset House down to what was now considered to be an out of the way place for policing purposes, off the Folly House, Blackwall.[3565] The vessel was facetiously called the 'Abode of the Bliss', named after Inspector 'Daddy' Bliss who resided there with six single constables.[3566] John Bliss was the inspector in charge, but it is doubtful that he lived in the vessel. Bliss was married and also had a son, which would have meant very cramped conditions for all on the floating station. In 1881 records show that he lived at 62 Brunswick Road, Bromley with his wife Maria and son William. Bliss was born in 1843 in London (Middlesex).[3567]

Blackwall Police Station, Pierhead, Blackwall, 1875-1894

Above is the hulk of the *Royalist*, which was a designated police station with an inspector in charge.[3568] Records show

---

3558 Colquhoun, P. (1875) *A Treatise of the Police of the Metropolis.*
3559 Richardson, A. (1957) *Nick of the River.* Harrap, London.
3560 Sleigh, A.W. (1844) *The Police and Constabulary List 1844.* Parker, Furnival and Parker, London.
3561 Ibid.
3562 Metropolitan Police Surveyor's Records (undated).
3563 Sleigh, A.W. (1844) *The Police and Constabulary List 1844.* Parker, Furnival and Parker, London.
3564 John Back Archive (1975).
3565 Budworth, G. (1997) *The River Beat.* Historical Publications, London.
3566 Ibid.
3567 Census 1881.
3568 Metropolitan Police General Orders 1873.

that in 1873 it was situated off Strand Lane.³⁵⁶⁹ The constables of Thames Division were divided into four watches, each of six hours duration, thereby ensuring a boat came in to the station every two hours and allowing for a fresh crew to take their place out on patrol.³⁵⁷⁰

In November 1875 District Superintendent A.C. Howard proposed a new location for the floating station at the Pierhead, Blackwall, located at the west entrance of the east India Dock Wall Road. This site afforded good access for a land or water approach, and also gave a complete view down Bugsby's Reach and again up Blackwall Road to Greenwich.³⁵⁷¹ The call sign of the station was Romeo Tango (RT).³⁵⁷²

In 1877 Inspector 1st Class Wootton was shown in charge of the *Royalist*, assisted by Inspectors 2nd Class George Roberts and Thomas Pridmore.³⁵⁷³ The 2nd Class inspectors were in fact sergeants. It appears that efforts to relocate the station came to nothing, and little was done until 1887 when a number of new sites were proposed. A site located at 19 Coldharbour Lane, E14 was purchased freehold in May 1891, at a cost of £4,000. Blackwall was designated as a receiving house or mortuary for dead bodies taken from the Thames.³⁵⁷⁴

A new station called Thames Blackwall was built on the site, together with four sets of married quarters. It was taken into service on 4th February 1895.³⁵⁷⁵ In 1894 the *Royalist* was taken out of service when the new Blackwall station became operational.³⁵⁷⁶

Blackwall Police Station 1894-1998

Lodging costs for the married Inspector was assessed at 5/6d per week whilst the three married Constables each paid 3/- weekly. At the location beside Browns Wharf, the jetty belonged to the Thames Conservancy, and the Receiver of the Metropolitan Police had to pay £1 per year for the privilege of mooring a coal hulk there.³⁵⁷⁷

London Police escorting good from the dockyards during the strike of 1912

In 1912 a national dock and transport strike severely tested the resolve of the police in London. As the image bottom left shows, convoys leaving the docks had to be escorted by large numbers of police, many of who were brought in from outside the Borough to help. The police displayed an even-tempered attitude and earned the respect of the striking workers.

By 1924 the Port of London Authority had taken over leasing the mooring and control of the Jetty. Under the agreement, the annual rental of the mooring still cost £1 per year, but use of the Jetty amounted to £4 4s 0d per year. A clause in the agreement stipulated that if the PLA, who were the conservators of the Jetty, gave notice in writing to the Metropolitan Police for the jetty's removal, then the Receiver would ensure this was done. Furthermore, rental of £1 per year was also charged by the PLA for piles and a boom, which were on licence from the conservators.³⁵⁷⁸

A group of Thames Police pictured at Blackwall Police Station in 1909

This photograph above, taken in 1909 at Blackwall Police Station, shows nine constables and two sergeants, with the senior sergeant having four bars to his stripes. The Thames Division uniform was different from normal Metropolitan Police issue uniforms, because the type of duty was not normal foot duty. In those days the launches were not all motorised, and getting about on the Thames often relied on rowing everywhere. The waterproof short coats and trousers, rather than the normal police duty issue full-length great coat, kept the police officers dry whilst rowing and protected them from inclement weather in the open boats.

The station had been sold into private hands prior to 1998. By 2016 the police station had been sold to Coldharbour (Blackwall) Management Limited, who made extensive repairs and renovations to the property. In 2019 the name and address had been varied to read Coldharbour E14 (East Side) River Police Station. It is a Grade II listed property, recorded in 1973.

Thames – Wapping Police Station

Wapping Police Station was the Headquarters of the Thames Division, and was opened on the site of the present station in 1798.³⁵⁷⁸ As well as a Police Department at the station there was also a Judicial Department, all under the control of a resident Magistrate Captain John Harriott. The Thames River Police were soon heralded as extremely good at their job, earning praise from merchants and ship owners alike. By 1800 they received statutory authority, and were frequently called upon to assist other law enforcement officers in their duties.

In 1839, some ten years after the commencement of the Metropolitan Police, the Thames River Police were absorbed into the London Police and the Judicial Department became the Thames Police Court. The first officer in charge of the

River Police was Superintendent James Evans, who completed fifty years' unbroken service when he retired on pension in 1848.[3579] He had joined in 1798 as an assistant surveyor, and handed over command to his son, Superintendent John Christopher Evans. Charles Dickens noted that a picture of James Evans hung in the charge room of the station.[3580]

By 1844 the court had moved near to Arbour Square, Stepney where two magistrates sat daily except for weekends, from 10.00am until 5.00pm. Records show that the magistrates at Thames Police Court were Mr. William Ballantine of 89 Cadogan Place, off Eaton Square, and William J. Broderip of 2 Raymond Buildings, Grays Inn. The clerk was Edward William Symonds. Thames Police Court boundaries were fixed by order of the Council dated 10th December 1842, and included all in the eastern entrance of the London Docks, north side of the dock area to Fox's Lane, High Street Shadwell, Ratcliff Highway, Cannon Street, Cannon Street Road, Whitechapel Road, Mile End Road, Grove Road, Eastern Counties Railway, along it to the River Lea, to River Thames and back to the eastern entrance of the London Docks.[3581]

On 9th January 1843 a letter from the Home Office to the Receiver recommended that the lease to the station should be extended and a new police station established on the site.[3582] In 1844 the established Thames Division strength of Inspectors was twenty-one, with nine posted to Wapping Police Station. These included William Judge (appointed 1817), John Gaskin (appointed 1826), William Isbester (appointed 1827), Joshua Judge (promoted to Inspector in 1831), James Christopher Evans, Charles Henry Falconer and Thomas Fox, all appointed in 1833. John Joseph Lewis and James Robert White were appointed in 1834.[3583]

Later, a system of 1st and 2nd Class Inspectors were introduced, as only inspectors were legally able to board boats and inspect their contents. The 2nd Class Inspector wore the badge of rank for a sergeant, i.e. three chevrons on each forearm. Third Class Inspectors were also introduced at some later stage.

In 1863 the lease was renewed, costing £100 per annum instead of the previous sum of £80 for a term of either fourteen or twenty-one years. The strength of the Division was shown as 111 officers of mixed rank, which included seventeen inspectors (Second Class), who were employed in the boats. The Division kept some fifteen boats, eleven being in use with four kept in reserve.[3584]

Land was leased from the Governors of Bridewell in 1867 on which to build the new station at Wapping. The lease was set for sixty years from Christmas 1867, expiring at Christmas 1927. The Receiver had to pay the rates and costs of repair for the new station, which included painting the inside of the building every seven years and the outside every three years. The Governors of Bridewell stipulated that the premises were to be insured for a sum of £3,000 annually.[3585] The station included a Superintendent's Office, which was located on the first floor with a charge room, a reserve room, two cells and two water closets on the ground floor. In the basement were the shipwrights' office and two coal cellars. On the second floor was accommodation for one married Inspector, who occupied two rooms with a third room downstairs on the ground floor for a weekly rent of 5/6d. There was also room for seventeen constables on both the first and second floors of the accompanying Section House. They paid one shilling per week rent. The station was occupied by the Police of Thames Division in January 1871, and had cost £3,490 to build.[3586] In 1877 Inspector 1st Class Isaac Hill was shown in charge of the station, assisted by Inspectors 2nd Class Charles Marler and William Robson.[3587] More is mentioned of William Robson later.

The Thameside of Wapping Police Station as drawn by Whistler in the 1880s

The print shown above was sketched by Whistler, the famous Victorian artist, and shows the Thames at Wapping. It pictures the police station on the extreme right.

A report from the Surveyor prompted the need for a new pile and girders costing some £25 10s in order to protect the police boats from barges drifting down on the ebb tide.[3588] Suitable protection had been afforded to the station when Aberdeen Wharf was operating, however now that the location had been vacated the boats and piles were no longer present leaving the location vulnerable.

On 1st November 1880 the Divisional Superintendent drew attention to the bad state of the foreshore at Wapping and the need for repairs. A barge load of shingle was purchased for £14 10s, and the cost of repair was £4. A granite causeway was built in October 1883 for the sum of £25 in order to facilitate the launching of the boats.[3589]

3569 Metropolitan Police General Orders 1873.
3570 Budworth, G. (1997) *The River Beat*. Historical Publications, London.
3571 John Back Archive (1975).
3572 Metropolitan Police General Orders 1893.
3573 **Post Office London Directory** 1877.
3574 *Dickens Dictionary of London* (1888). Devon, pp132-133.
3575 Metropolitan Police Surveyor's Records (undated).
3576 Budworth, G. (1997) *The River Beat*. Historical Publications, London.
3577 Metropolitan Police Surveyor's Records (undated)
3578 Ibid.
3579 John Back Archive (1975).
3580 Fido, M. and Skinner, S. (1999) *The Official Encyclopedia of Scotland Yard*. Virgin, London.
3581 Sleigh, A.W. (1844) *The Police and Constabulary List 1844*. Parker, Furnival and Parker, London.
3582 Ibid.
3583 Ibid.
3584 John Back Archive (1975).
3585 Metropolitan Police Surveyor's Records (undated).
3586 John Back Archive (1975).
3587 *Post Office London Directory* 1877.
3588 Metropolitan Police Internal Report dated 1878.
3589 John Back Archive (1975).

Wapping Police Station 1871 to present (street-side)

In 1881 Constable William Snell, a 28-year-old from Margate in Kent, was a resident of the section house at High Street Thames Police Station.[3590] Constable Snell was to later find fame, when in 1884 he was shot in the stomach by an armed burglar in Hoxton. By April 1885 the increased use of firearms by burglars led to authority for police to be armed with revolvers.[3591]

Chief Inspector George Steed (warrant no. 40880) joined the London Police in 1861. As Superintendent of Thames Division, one responsibility was to identify for the Coroner dead bodies found in the river. Steed had a working relationship with the photographer Louis Gumprecht of 11 Cannon Street Road, whose job it was to photograph the dead bodies found in the Thames by the Thames police. Later Gumprecht retired and his business was taken over by Joseph Martin, who using Gumprecht's materials and cards, became famous as the official photographer for the police, taking the picture of Jack the Ripper's victims in the east end.[3592]

Chief Inspector George Steed became Superintendent of Thames Division after transfer from Limehouse in 1883

Inspector 2nd Class William Robson lived at Wapping Police Station in 1881 with his wife, and records showed the address to be 255, High Street, Wapping.[3593] Tragically, Robson gave his life for the job he loved. He was accidentally drowned in 1884 when his police boat was hit by a steam tug whilst visiting river patrols at Charlton.[3594] Robson is remembered in the UK Police Roll of Honour.[3595]

In May 1888 the premises adjacent to the station were leased for use as a boathouse. Accommodation was provided for one married inspector at a cost of 5s 6d per week, and one married constable for a weekly rent of 3s. The freehold for the station and the boathouse was purchased in April 1891 for the sum of £8,290.[3596] Records show that in 1888, Superintendent George Skeats was in charge of the Division assisted by 49 inspectors, four sergeants and 607 constables.[3597]

Wapping Police Station was given the designated call sign Tango Alpha (TA).[3598]

In 1904 the Superintendent of Thames Division reported to the Commissioner on the unsuitability of the current station, accommodation and workshops at Wapping, and suggested that a new, more modern station should be erected. This was agreed, and by March 1907 plans for a new station were accepted and tenders invited for building the new station. The bid by Messrs. Lawrence and Sons was accepted, and by August demolition of the old police station had started. The station, section house, married quarters and administration section were ready for occupation by 28th February 1910. The section house was built to house 27 single men at a weekly rent of 1s, whilst the two sets of married quarters attracted rental of 9s 6d and 7s 6d respectively per week.[3599]

Constable 212 Howe, Thames Division

The picture on the left shows Constable 212 Thames Division Howe in his uniform. Constable Howe joined the service with warrant number 96885 on 17th May 1909. He was originally posted to H Division as 425, but transferred to Thames Division on 13th June 1912. He was promoted on 18th March 1916, when he became Sergeant 12 of the 4th Division Chatham Dockyard Police. Howe left the Dockyard Police on 9th October 1922, when he was posted to K Division. He then became a Station Sergeant on 29th June 1923. When World War Two broke out he was retained as a pensioner, and then further pensioned on 25th September 1945.

There is a great difference in type, style and make up of this uniform compared to the standard Metropolitan style. The flat cap shows an anchor badge with chinstrap up. The number of the constable is clearly shown on the lapels of the greatcoat he is wearing. Note also that he is wearing a collar (detachable) and tie. Later, in order to avoid being strangled with their own ties, Metropolitan Police officers wore detachable ties.

On 27th April 1920 a Bill called the Metropolitan Police Order Confirmation Act 1920 was passed in Parliament allowing the compulsory purchase of 102 High Street, Wapping to allow the station to be enlarged and improved. This property was located adjacent to the station and belonged to the Bridewell and Bethlehem Royal Hospital. The freehold was purchased for the sum of £5,605 on 5th January 1921.[3600]

The standard river police rowing boat was called a 'galley', and they were in use from 1789 until 1925. These open clinker built boats were 8.2 metres long and carried a surveyor or Inspector in the stern who operated the rudder strings whilst three oarsmen rowed the craft.[3601] The men were out in all weathers, and all too often literally worked to death.[3602] The rowing boat was replaced in 1925 by engine-powered patrol boats.[3603]

The rare picture on the next page shows Station Sergeant 5/83458 Albert Ernest Porter of Thames Division, who joined the Metropolitan Police in 1898. The Station Sergeants wore four bars instead of three. He is shown with his three medals – the 1898 Jubilee Medal, the 1902 Coronation Medal and the 1911 Coronation Medal. Porter became a sergeant in September 1908, and was pensioned in 1924 after 26 years' service, retiring as a Station Sergeant. He received his pension for 29 years and died on 12th March 1953.

On 25th March 1922 a licence was issued from the Port of London Authority which authorised rental of eleven single piles, seven double piles, booms, a causeway, a slipway, a gridiron and campshedding. Also included were a raft, an overhanging runway and an overhanging girder, together with two overhanging windows. This cost the Receiver £15 rent per annum. On 29th September 1923 a further licence was issued from the Port of London Authority to place six lifesaving chains on an iron ladder on the river frontage at an annual rental of £1.[3604]

Staton Sergeant 5 Porter, Thames Division

Wapping has always been the headquarters for Thames Division. At various times the Division has been supervised by a variety of ranks. For example, in 1937 Chief Inspector J. Brown was the officer in charge,[3605] however twenty years later an officer two ranks senior headed the Thames Division. In 1957 Chief Superintendent C.L. McDonough GM commanded the Division, with Superintendent H. Morley being responsible for the station and its patrols.[3606] Thames formed part of No. 3 District, which also included E, G, H, J and K Divisions. The District Headquarters was located at Macnaghten Section House, 55 Judd Street, WC1. Commander H.J. Evans was in charge, together with Deputy Commander W.C. Batson[3607] (see also Barking and Dagenham for further information).

Wapping Police Station 1871 to present (Thames-side)

It was felt that in order to further improve the facilities of the Divisional Headquarters for Thames Division, more land would be needed in the future. Accordingly, two parcels of land were acquired, the first being the freehold site of the Morocco and Eagle Sufferance Wharves at 82-84 Wapping High Street. This was purchased for the sum of £53,500 in February 1965.

This purchase was intended primarily for the construction of a new boat repair yard. The second purchase occurred when the freehold interest of the old Aberdeen Wharf at 94-96 Wapping High Street became available for the sum of £50,000. Plans had been laid for the complete rebuilding of Wapping Police Station, scheduled to commence in 1971/72, and this second parcel of land was required in order to complete the task.[3608]

However, in 1978 a radical policy re-think in respect of Thames Division occurred together with substantial financial cutbacks, and it was decided not to re-build the new station.

Wapping Police Station is now a Grade II listed building because of its architectural importance, and it cannot be demolished. The pontoon on the river is used to land the twenty or more bodies a year which are pulled from the 54-mile stretch of the Thames between Staines and Dartford. Waterloo Pier had also been used to land dead bodies, but public concern at this site was deemed to be too disturbing so the practice ended. Whilst the station does have cells, they are considered unsuitable for the detention of prisoners so they are transferred to Whitechapel Police Station.

The station is still in use today for parading of police officers and the housing of boats.[3609] The call sign of the station is Uniform Delta (UD).[3610] In 2002 Wapping Police Station was shown as closed to the public but retained for operational purposes,[3611] although prisoners arrested are taken to other land-based stations. In 2019 both the boatyard, including the workshops, and the police station continued to remain open and operational.[3612]

3590 Census 1881.
3591 Gould, R. and Waldron, M. (1986) *London's Armed Police*. Arms and Armour Press, London.
3592 Joseph Martin's mortuary photographs of the Whitechapel victims were of Martha Tabram, Mary Ann Nichols, Annie Chapman, Elizabeth Stride, Mary Kelly, Alice McKenzie and Frances Coles.
3593 Metropolitan Police Orders dated 20th June 1884.
3594 Fido, M. and Skinner, S. (1999) *The Official Encyclopedia of Scotland Yard*. Virgin, London.
3595 A tribute to police officers who died in service in the form of a roll of honour has been compiled and updated as part of a research project by Sergeant Anthony Rae, Lancashire Constabulary (formerly of the Metropolitan Police).
3596 Metropolitan Police Surveyor's Records (undated).
3597 Kelly London Directory 1888.
3598 Metropolitan Police General Orders 1893.
3599 John Back Archive (1975).
3600 Metropolitan Police Surveyor's records (undated).
3601 Ibid.
3602 Ibid.
3603 Fido, M. and Skinner, S. (1999) *The Official Encyclopedia of Scotland Yard*. Virgin, London.
3604 Metropolitan Police Surveyor's Records
3605 *The Police and Constabulary Almanac* 1937.
3606 *The Police and Constabulary Almanac* 1957.
3607 Ibid.
3608 John Back Archive (1975).
3609 *The Police and Constabulary Almanac* 2001.
3610 Ibid.
3611 www.met.police.uk/contact/phone.htm accessed 23rd March 2002.
3612 MPS (2019) Freedom of Information request: MPS Assets.

Chapter 6.
The Royal Dockyard Divisions

The Naval Dockyards have had a long history, with Chatham dating back to the 1570s. The London area boasted the most prestigious engineering and shipbuilding industries in the land. There were four Royal Docks and 160 private yards in London, most of which were located between London Bridge and the Woolwich Ferry. Since the 16th Century this stretch of river equipped England with most of its battleships, merchant ships, fishing boats and barges.[3613]

A dedicated Dockyard Police Force had been introduced in 1831, and by 1834 they had taken over control of all Royal Naval Dockyards.[3614] However, they were not to last very long in London. The key posts and authority for the Police of the dockyards had traditionally rested with former naval officers, who perhaps did not understand the function of security as it was common knowledge that vast quantities of stores were being regularly misappropriated. The Admiralty had noticed the success of the New Police introduced in the metropolis in 1829, and the former was concerned that the law enforcers employed in dockyards had not been totally satisfactory. Using members of the workforce as watchmen, or having porters, rounders, warders, watchmen and later wardens was obviously a problem.[3615] The Admiralty resolved to consider a better system, and following considerable discussions decided to introduce a more efficient force based on the Metropolitan Police model.

Unlike the force they replaced, the full powers of a constable were granted to the Police of the new Dockyard Force but this was found to be unworkable. Powers extending beyond the dockyards were more appropriate, since it was often necessary to search the houses of suspected workers for stolen property. Search warrants were easily obtained, as the Naval Superintendents were also ex Officio Magistrates by virtue of their appointment.[3616]

The Metropolitan Police had for some time been responsible for patrolling the Royal Naval dockyards at Greenwich and Woolwich on R Division, and this gave them a special expertise which had helped to make them successful. Because of this experience, especially during strikes and industrial unrest, including in wartime, Police were later seconded under special arrangements that ensured the security of all the royal dockyards. Many of these dockyards had no outer walls, and these yards provided an open invitation for thieves to steal timber and other supplies meant for HM ships.

Woolwich Dockyard, because it was located in London, was policed from 1841 until 1916 by the Metropolitan Police. Other dockyards were gradually taken over by the London Force and policed from 1860 onwards. These included Devonport (until 1934), Chatham (until 1932), Portsmouth (until 1933), Rosyth (from 1914 to 1926), and Pembroke Docks (until 1926).

The picture at the top of the following column shows a Metropolitan Police inspector in the uniform of the time, which included a top hat. This style of uniform was replaced by a different one in 1865 which included a helmet with a reef helmet plate.

Superintendent Mallalieu from R Division (Woolwich) had experience in the supervision of London Dockyards. He was asked to review the old dockyard system and make recommendations to the Admiralty on the efficiency of the Dockyard Force. He concluded that the Dockyard Force 'gained much from giving little', so they were inefficient and ineffective. This led to the disbanding of the dedicated Dockyard

Metropolitan Police Dockyard Inspector at Portsmouth, 1860-65

Police and replacing them with Metropolitan Police officers in December 1860.[3617] This move saw the spread of Met officers extend beyond the metropolis to other Royal Dockyards and War Department premises throughout the UK. There were other advantages which were seen by Mallalieu relating to the interchange ability of the workforce. It was a distinct advantage to have a mobile force where individuals could be transferred to other Dockyard Divisions at a moment's notice.

Following a force-wide re-organisation in operations and supervision of the Metropolitan Police in 1859, five new exclusive Dockyard Divisions were established, detaching them from supervision of Land Divisions. They were given a one year trial. Each was set up with a Superintendent in charge and consisted of Woolwich, Portsmouth, Devonport, Chatham and Pembroke. Rosyth joined this group in 1914.

Recruits who joined the Police and were then subsequently posted to the dockyards or military stations were required to swear a separate oath to the Queen. This was different to the oath sworn by police officers appointed to the Town Divisions located in London. The oath for the dockyards etc varied to include duty outside London at any War Department establishment, which included an area some 15 miles outside their place of duty. In other words, an officer could swear two separate oaths during his service.

Superintendent Mallalieu made periodic and unannounced visits for supervisory purposes. He became the founding father of all the Dockyard Divisions by introducing new methods and differing working conditions. He was an extremely thorough man who neglected nothing,[3618] and soon made a number of changes by establishing a new system of stations, beats and patrols. He improved the shift pattern system, and based his style of policing on making stations of the docks, hospitals or buildings located within. He placed an inspector in charge of each, and added support staff to equal that in a police station. He also established Woolwich as the Divisional Headquarters, and introduced training for police officers as firemen; all unmarried constables had to live in the dockyard and to receive educational instruction.[3619] This group of officers were often kept on reserve to be used when needed. In January 1871 instructions were given to ensure not only the security of dockyards, but also that under no circumstances was information about naval dockyards to be given to persons connected with the press.[3620]

There is a general perception that Police of dockyards wore different uniforms, helmets and accoutrements to their town-based counterparts in the metropolis, but the Dockyard police wore the distinctive garter helmet plate showing the fouled anchor and divisional number. Each Dockyard allocated its own collar numbers and inter-dockyard transfers usually required a new one.

The uniform of a dockyard constable showing rolled cape, lamp and spring-loaded truncheon case

The picture on the left also shows the Police Officer/Fireman dressed in a double-breasted coat and long boots. He also has a bull's-eye lamp attached to his belt, a rolled cape under his left arm and a truncheon in a leather case. The only difference from town-based Divisions was in the badge detail. The badge shown below which was issued in about 1870 shows the Queen's crown, whilst underneath the 'fouled anchor' indicates his membership of a Dockyard Division. Below this is shown the Divisional number, which was allocated on arrival at Divisional Dockyard Headquarters once the Officer was posted. The only difference to the town-based Divisions was that the anchor would be replaced by the Divisional letter.

In 1863 a new Instruction Book with a cream cover was published and issued to 7,254 constables in the Force. Additional copies were supplied to inspectors and sergeants, and for placing in reading rooms.[3621] A special smaller, black-covered Instruction Book for Police Officers posted to dockyards and War Department stations was introduced in 1873.

This contained the instructions to all ranks on the efficient running of the Royal Dockyards, and in 1890 was reprinted with a blue cover and containing other details. Since the Police had been given extra powers at dockyards information on duties performed there were also included and copies were issued to the 203 constables at Woolwich, 182 constables at Portsmouth, 154 constables at Devonport, 116 constables at Chatham and 32 constables at Pembroke.

Generally, when the Metropolitan Police took over any dockyard they occupied existing buildings or ships for duty and accommodation. It was the responsibility of the Admiralty to make the necessary arrangements for Police accommodation, although the Metropolitan Police surveyors attended from time to time to see if the police officers were housed in adequate accommodation. If not they would render any repairs or alterations with the permission of the Dockyard Captain Superintendent. Police officers and their families paid a reduced rent if they lived within the docks.

Woolwich Dockyard or 1st Division

Superintendents
Alexander Thompson 1842-1863
Kingston Mark (joined 1835) 1862-1864
Robert Bray 1862 (from N temporary during the suspension and supervision of Supt Mark)
Alexander Thompson (from Pembroke) 1865-1871
Thomas E. Hindes (joined 1853) 1871-1889 (retired)
Robert W. Congdon (44172) (joined 1863) 1889-1894 (retired)
Josiah C. Hobbins (44292) (joined 1863) 1895-1903 (retired)
John Devine OBE (64460) (joined 1880) 1903-1924 (retired)

Chief Inspectors
Colin Forbes 1863, Deptford Dockyard
Philip Brine 1863-1865, Royal Arsenal
Thomas Carnelly (1843), 1865-1877 Royal Arsenal
John Pethers 1867 (died same year) Deptford (on promotion from Chatham)
Philip Beare (1844) 1867-1869 (retired), Deptford Dockyard
Clement Gosby 1885
Daniel Collins 1869
William Capon 1878
Robert. W. Congdon (1863) 1883-1889
Charles Woonton (44275) (1863) 1888-1892 (retired)
George Harding (1860) 1890-1897 (retired)
John Willmott (40960) (1861) 1885-1894 (retired)
George Cavell (43696) (1863) 1891-1894 (to Chatham)
James Tait (54915) (1871) 1898-1903 (retired)
Thomas Rogers 1902-1904 (transferred to Chatham)
James Haynes (64246) (1880) 1904-1909 (retired)
Joseph Spry (62359) (1878) 1902-1903 (to Chief Inspector, Woolwich)

3613 Weightmand, G and Humphries, S. (1983) *The Making of Modern London 1815-1914*. Sidgewick and Jackson, London.
3614 Ibid.
3615 Salter, A.R. (1983) 'The Protection of Chatham Dockyard Throughout the Ages'. Gillingham Local History Series No.12. Kent County Library.
3616 Ibid.
3617 Ibid.
3618 Ibid.
3619 Ibid.
3620 Metropolitan Police Orders dated 31st January 1871.
3621 Metropolitan Police Orders dated 22nd January 1863.

Woolwich Royal Arsenal c1910

Owen Webb (78058) (1892) 1915-1917
Frederick Spencer 1914-1915
Henry Morgan 1914
Frederick Wright (74225) 1889-1920
Albert Saunders (80946) 1896-1923 (retired)

Sub-Divisional Inspectors
Michael Money 43163 (j1862) 1869-1888
Alfred Chatterley 70947 (j1885) 1908-17 (retired)
Adam Llewellyn 65822 (1881-1906)
Thomas Evans 1903-06
James Haynes (64246) (1880) 1903-1904
 (to Chief Inspector, Woolwich)
Francis Shorthouse (70825) (1886) 1910-1912 (retired)
Elias Thomas (78684) (1893) 1917-1923 (retired)
James Shorthouse (74225) 1885-1923 (retired)
SDI Walter Mcintyre (80525) 1926 (Royal Arsenal
Joseph Spry (62359) (1878) 1903-1904 (retired)
Charles Ferrier (79438) 1894-1920 (retired)
Willie Smith (80236) (1895) 1917-1923 (retired)

Woolwich Dockyard was protected by the Metropolitan Police from 1841 until 1926. In the early days of the Metropolitan Police it was the responsibility of the Division on which the dockyard was located to provide the manpower and supervision for dockyards. This meant that Woolwich Dockyard became the responsibility of R Division, which policed the Thameside area of Greenwich, Woolwich, Plumstead and Blackheath. Regular supervisory visits were made by the Divisional Superintendent, who would sign the visitors' book as a mark of his supervision. The dockyard was a designated Inspector Station and therefore an inspector was in overall charge of day to day operations.

Responsibility for the policing of Woolwich Arsenal passed to the dockyards in 1844, and from this date the old-style Dockyard Police were replaced. The picture above shows the front gate of the Royal Arsenal. A contingent of local police officers provided gate and perimeter security; they also guarded the main magazine, which included the onerous task of guarding the magazine hulks moored off shore.[3622] Records show that Inspector Roger Howard of R Division was in charge at Woolwich Dockyard, having been stationed there in 1844. Howard had been promoted to Inspector in 1839,[3623] and was an early recruit.

The stations located within the dockyard between 1860 and 1907 consisted of Woolwich Royal Arsenal, Woolwich Dockyard, Deptford Victualing Yard, Naval Store Depot, West India Dock, Powder and Cordite Magazines and Railway depot, Plumstead Marshes, Floating magazine Thalia, and the Royal Military Repository Woolwich Common.[3624]

Living conditions for police officers of all ranks and their families was interesting. Woolwich Dockyard, for example, provided married quarters in the factory gate for police officers and their families. However, the gate would have been locked after bell ringing and the key to be let in was kept at the main gate.[3625] Only the main gate had sufficient space for a Section House for use by the twenty single officers. This was to ensure proper supervision of daily activities by the Superintendent, who resided in the Main Gate House at Woolwich. Two days would be set aside during the week when washing and drying clothes could take place. Married men, even when off duty, needed to be in their quarters by 10.00pm in order that they became a reserve should a fire or other emergency take place.[3626] All reports of missing persons or property lost or stolen would have been forwarded to R Division or sent direct to the Commissioner's Office (CO).[3627]

The Dockyard Police were responsible for receiving, housing in police cells and escorting naval prisoners from ships at Sheerness, Woolwich and Chatham for onward conveyance to Lewes gaol. Records showing the expiry of sentence details were kept by police so that they were aware of the release date.[3628] Policing in the dockyards was different from policing in the town divisions. For this reason it was difficult to get serious incentives for deserving 2nd Class constables to transfer to the Royal Arsenal, Woolwich. The Commissioner made offers in Police Orders to entice extra committed constables for duty at the dockyard.[3629]

One of the less attractive features of policing in the Dockyard Division were the dangers that existed in dockyards. Occasionally there would be serious accidents when munitions exploded, causing serious damage, fire and loss of life. In September 1845 an explosion killed seven workers, and another in December 1855 killed four more. Police Officers from Woolwich would have been required to send assistance, help with first aid, and to clear up the damage.[3630] This meant that not only were Police required for security purposes, but they were employed also as fire watchers and were at all times required to remain vigilant over the threat of fire. They later became part of the Dockyard Fire Brigade, which was often a mix of all professions within the dockyards. In the very first year there was a Fire Brigade established, and such was the professionalism and efficiency that they were able to put out some 26 small fires.[3631]

Woolwich Dockyard was used as a training base to teach Divisional Police Officers on transfer their dockyard duties and responsibilities. Once competent and if confirmation of the transfer was agreed, those who passed would be transferred to other Dockyard Divisions at the expense of Commissioner. Regular notices for volunteers were posted in Police Orders to encourage volunteers to sign up to dockyard duties.[3632]

It was in a police officers' interest to ensure that provisions were not stolen or removed from the yards without authority. It was the responsibility of the Police to detect crime and, on occasions, failure to prevent a crime on their beat rendered them liable to discipline. For instance, a large quantity of sugar had been stolen from a naval store at Woolwich in April 1863 and suspicion fell on Constable 89 Wright and Constable 88 West, who were both in the vicinity at the time. The subsequent and very rigorous inquiry by the Dockyard Superintendent produced evidence to Sir Richard Mayne, the Commissioner, which exonerated both officers.[3633] It was not uncommon at this time to suspend police constables from duty without pay during their suspension, or even make them pay a fine if they failed to discover a crime committed on their beat while they were on duty. Any suspended officer was required to hand in his appointments, truncheon, note book, whistle and handcuffs, etc.

Instructions were regularly issued, alerting all Police of the names of officers of ships moored in the docks or harbour so they would be able to give visitors reliable information when they were visiting those officers, ships etc.[3634]

Alexander Thompson was the first Police Superintendent of the dockyard, from 1842 until 1863, and was an experienced and respected officer. He was transferred to Pembroke Dockyard, but was not there for long as he was recalled back to Woolwich following concerns that the new Superintendent was not up to the job. In charge of the dockyard in 1863 was Superintendent Kingston Mark,[3635] whose name at times was frequently reversed in Police Orders. The Superintendent's residence was in the main gate, and he lived there with his wife and five children. Superintendent Mark had been the subject of Police discipline the year before, when he was suspended from duty and his command taken over by ex-Dockyard Superintendent Mott of N Division. This must have been a huge embarrassment to Mark, because he still resided at the dockyard, and while he was suspended he received no pay. He appeared at Scotland Yard following an inquiry, where he was found at fault and the Commissioner fined him one week's pay and reprimanded him for a failure in supervision.[3636] Mark was re-instated and advised by the Commissioner that any further infractions would mean losing his command. Kingston Mark had joined the Metropolitan Police in 1835 and became a Dockyard Police Officer as an Inspector in 1858, when he joined Woolwich. He had been highly regarded, as he only spent four years as an Inspector and was then promoted straight to Superintendent. Mark retired in 1864 when Thompson returned for a short while before he too retired.

Inspector James Gill, his wife and child lived in the Factor Gate, where two sergeants and their families also resided. The Superintendent had been aware that Inspector Kell had been unwell for some time. The Police physician had asked the Dockyard Superintendent for his views on the continued employment of his inspector. Inspector Kell, who had joined the Metropolitan Police in 1836, had been stationed at the Royal Arsenal for some time and had become unwell and unable to do duty. This meant that another officer had to take responsibility for the inspector's duties. Kell was later retired, the reason stated being that he was 'worn out'.[3637]

There were a number of general health problems which came with working in the Dockyards Divisions. These mostly seem to have been rheumatism, and for those working as Water Police the constant rolling had led to a number of cases of vertigo. Considering the openness and location of dockyards with their equally damp atmospheres and windy conditions, it would have been hardly surprising that many police officers resorted to these as reasons for retiring early.

The main entrance the Royal Naval College, Greenwich

The photograph above shows the main gate at the Royal Naval College which had to be manned by Police for security purposes, as can be seen. Police were required to check the

---

3622   Hadaway, D. (1985) *Eltham Police Station; The First Hundred Years* Latter Books, Sussex
3623   *The Police and Constabulary List* (1844) Parker, Furnival and Parker, Whitehall.
3624   *Kirchner's Almanac* 1907.
3625   Wynne, H. (1998) 'Extracts taken from the Metropolitan Police Orders 1873 (Dockyard Divisions)'. Friends of the Ministry of Defence Museum.
3626   Ibid.
3627   Ibid.
3628   Ibid.
3629   Metropolitan Police Orders date 5th January 1859
3630   Hadaway, D. (1990) 'The Metropolitan Police in Woolwich'.
3631   *Commissioner's Annual Report* 1871
3632   Metropolitan Police Orders dated 2nd February 1863
3633   Metropolitan Police Orders dated 30th April 1863
3634   Metropolitan Police Orders dated 10th November 1862
3635   *Police and Constabulary Almanac* 1864
3636   Metropolitan Police Orders dated 11th September 1862
3637   Metropolitan Police Orders dated 6th January 1864

passes of people entering and leaving the establishments and to detain any goods or persons who were responsible for illegal removal.

Police wives often worked for the Metropolitan Police in the dockyards in a number of capacities since they did not have to travel far, being able to earn some pin money and raise their children at the same time. The senior officers realised that this relationship was beneficial to both sides, especially since police officers' wives were generally not allowed to work. For example, the wife of Constable 140 Archer was employed to clean the single constables' bedrooms and the family-occupied apartments in the Main Gate.[3638] It also appears that employing Police wives in the mess[3639] was a condition of occupation of some of the married quarters, rather than a voluntary matter.[3640]

The Superintendent would have been aware of tragic events taking place in his dockyard especially, for example, the death of a police officer. Such was the case for Superintendent Thomson, who by this time had been transferred from Pembroke Dockyard to Woolwich. In 1865 Constable George Sykes died from his injuries whilst attempting to release a brig that had become stuck in the mud at Woolwich Dockyard.[3641] In the same year Inspector Brine also died following a long illness.

By 1866 the dockyard was replenishing its stock of fire engines, and new steam engines were being issued to replace manual ones. The steam engine replaced three manual engines and these were returned to the store keeper as instructed.[3642] Steam-driven fire engines were far more powerful and efficient compared to the hand-pumped versions.

During 1868 the War Department Stores called back the firearms which it had issued to the Metropolitan Police Dockyards. It did allow twelve guns per Division to be kept.[3643] Cutlasses which had been issued to sergeants and constables were also withdrawn and returned to Stores.[3644]

In 1869 Woolwich Dockyard had by far the largest complement of men, with a total of 173. In addition to one Superintendent there were 14 inspectors, 22 sergeants and 136 constables.[3645] The War Department owned houses in Czar Street, Deptford, which was near the dock gates and where police officers were housed at a nominal rent. Instructions were issued that these houses were to be vacated should the War Department require their use for the public service at any time.[3646]

The Royal Dockyard at Deptford had been a responsibility for R Division to police, but in 1871 it was sold off to become the Foreign Cattle Market. Police deployed there were withdrawn and posted to dockyard duties elsewhere. In the same year, Woolwich Dockyard extended its security to take in the Army Service Corps barracks, also known as the Grand Depot Stores, where one sergeant and three constables were added to the Sub-Divisional strength.[3647] Other duties for the constables consisted of escorting railway wagons across the rifle range to the gate leading to the Magazines. This was a precarious and dangerous undertaking. There was an elaborate system of crossing the ranges which involved a constable hoisting a small red flag and sounding a bugle, which would then be acknowledged at the shooting point in the same manner. Once the trucks and escorts had arrived, the constable would sound the bugle once more to announce the successful crossing.[3648]

One of the greatest fears in the dockyards was fire, especially with some highly flammable material being stored which included immensely volatile munitions and explosives.

The Dockyard strength at Woolwich in 1873 consisted of one superintendent, twelve inspectors, 21 sergeants and 125 constables.[3649] Special Fire Brigade training sessions were introduced, and these were attended not only by Metropolitan Police officers but also suitably trained dockyard workers who had particular skills. All police officers were members of the Brigade, and the equipment was issued into their control and supervision. All Police at the yards were trained in fire drills and the use of engines, ladders and pumps. The picture below shows the Royal Arsenal Dockyard Police with their Superintendent, Chief Inspector and Inspector.

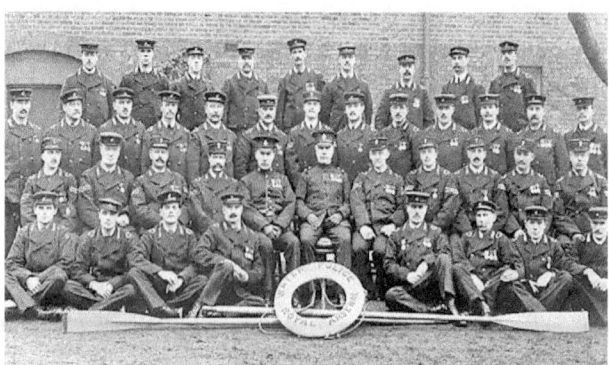

The Water Police of the Royal Arsenal with the Superintendent shown in the centre

There was no reserve of men waiting on standby at the dockyards for a fire like the Fire Brigades of today, however there was a person who was allocated the task of keeping the steam engine fire stoked up and ready to go just in case. In the event of a fire all trained officers would make their way as quickly as possible to the scene and operate under the instructions of the Superintendent or his deputy. There was constant vigilance regarding fires, and inspections of buildings would take place to see if any fires had been left on when the work force had gone home.[3650] The Fire Brigade at the Woolwich Dockyard was tested early in 1864, when a powder magazine exploded on Erith Marshes, which was adjacent to the Thames. The devastation resulted in a breach of the Thames wall and the Police who responded to the call 'worked tirelessly in relays to shore up the breach and prevent serious flooding.'[3651] Furthermore, a serious fire broke out at Plumstead several years later and such was the level of professionalism displayed that a Letter of Commendation was sent to the Commissioner of Police from the Inspector of Works, Royal Arsenal, Woolwich, which bore testimony to the job well done in extinguishing the fire.[3652]

In the same year, during the introduction of the Dockyard Divisions, the Royal Arsenal Sub-Divisional New Stores Depot was also established. This was the land-based Police Section, who were supported by their own Marine Police as shown in the picture above. Very often their duties were extremely dangerous, and included having to escort gunpowder barges from Waltham Abbey Gunpowder Works through the various canals to the River Thames. The gunpowder was for delivery to the various munitions depots in Plumstead, Woolwich and beyond.

Uniform security was considered important enough for a chief inspector to be placed in charge at the Arsenal, together with one sergeant and four constables. The sergeant resided at No. 1 Cottage a short distance away, and his tour of duty was from 7.00am until 7.00pm each day. No. 2 cottage was occupied by a constable, who took over duty for the remaining 12-hour tour. The constables were split into one for day duty, 2.00pm until 10.00pm, and the remaining two constables from

10.00pm until 6.00am, to guard the entrance gates. The gates were visited by the chief inspector at least once during the day or night, and by an ordinary inspector during each tour of duty.[3653]

The picture below shows a group of women involved in the manufacture of munitions at Woolwich. They wore a sort of uniform made of a lint-based product that reduced any friction that might cause an explosion.

A group of women worker at the Royal Arsenal

Checking passes both in and out of the dockyards, apprehending people on the premises illegally, stopping and recording the details of visitors, preventing loitering and the controlling of prostitutes in or near dockyards were some of the duties of the gate constables. Many females worked in the Royal Arsenal and they could only enter with the necessary authority.

In 1865 the Commissioner's attention was drawn to the fact that 'a number of Police residences at Woolwich Dockyard were occupied illegally by unauthorised personnel'. The system of monitoring the occupation of Police premises in Dockyard Divisions at Woolwich had become rather lax, and when a number of sergeants and constables moved away the premises granted for Police occupation were handed over to relatives or members of their family, who were not wives or children. Other Police rooms were taken over illegally by some police officers whose families had grown too large. Those who had taken charge of these premises were given three months' notice to vacate their own premises or comply with the regulations.[3654]

Officers were reminded that they should also immediately report any damaged lamps or leaking gas pipes in order to prevent fire and explosion. In 1870 George Potts, a dockyard constable, went missing on duty and a search was made of his beat at Woolwich Dockyard. Tragically, he was found floating in the dock having drowned. The reason for this was uncertain, although foul play was not ruled out. Sadly the death of a serving police officer was not uncommon during these times, and he was one of 42 Metropolitan Police officers who died in service that year.[3655] The duties and responsibilities of the Dockyard Police were many and varied.

The picture at the top of the following column shows the Royal Dock gate at Woolwich, and as can be seen there was a constant movement of supplies through the gate. Passes and supply papers would need to be checked by the constables on gate duty before any visitors would be allowed in.

A glimpse of life can be found when looking at Superintendents' reports. In 1875 the report to the Commissioners by Superintendent Hindes states that there had been 38,171 persons who had visited the Royal Arsenal,

The Royal Dockyard, Woolwich

some 5,572 admission passes had been handed out and eleven small fires had been found and put out without loss or injury. Another of the obligations of Night Duty constables stationed at dockyards was the daily lighting and extinguishing of gas lamps situated within the yards.[3656] Hindes further comments on the newly-formed Fire Brigade, when he confirms that it had been a great success with the men being efficient, 'maintaining their drills and keeping their fire plants in excellent order'.[3657]

One of the problems which beset the Police in Dockyard Divisions were the number of common women loitering nearing the vicinity, since it was necessary for them to have a medical examination under the Contagious Diseases Acts. However, the Superintendent reported that 54 fewer women were proceeded against than in the previous year.[3658]

Records show that in 1877 Thomas Hindes was still the Superintendent in charge, and he was assisted by Thomas J. Carnelly as Chief Inspector. The Inspectors were Robert Congton, John Cronk, James Tunbridge, John Willmott, George Godfrey, William Payne, Edward Coffey, Donald Taylor, Henry Parker, James McElliott and Michael Money.[3659]

3638 Metropolitan Police Orders dated 4th October 1864.
3639 The Mess was the latter-day canteen where one of the duties was cooking for single men in the section house. This was often undertaken by Mess women - the wives of police officers who would have received either a reduction on the rent paid for married quarters or wages.
3640 Metropolitan Police Orders dated 4th January 1864.
3641 National Police Roll of Honour (www.policememorial.org.uk) accessed 12th March 2002.
3642 Metropolitan Police Orders dated 6th November 1866.
3643 Metropolitan Police Orders dated 22nd May 1868.
3644 Ibid.
3645 *Commissioner's Annual Report* 1869.
3646 Metropolitan Police Orders dated 3rd September 1868.
3647 *Commissioner's Annual Report* 1871.
3648 Wynne, H. (1998) 'Extracts taken from the Metropolitan Police Orders 1873 (Dockyard Divisions)'. Friends of the Ministry of Defence Museum.
3649 Metropolitan Police General Orders and Regulation 1873.
3650 Metropolitan Police Instructions. Dockyards and Stations of the War Department 1873.
3651 Metropolitan Police Orders dated 25th October 1864.
3652 Metropolitan Police Orders dated 7th August 1869.
3653 Metropolitan Police Orders dated 22nd February 1869.
3654 Metropolitan Police Orders dated 24th July 1865.
3655 *Commissioner's Annual Report* 1870.
3656 Metropolitan Police Instructions. Dockyards and Stations of the War Department 1873.
3657 *Commissioner's Annual Report* 1875.
3658 Ibid.
3659 *Commissioner's Annual Report* 1869.

The Metropolitan Police Surveyors inspected the premises to which police officers were posted, or in which they resided. The same was true even if they did not own the buildings, as it appears that they were responsible for comfort and safety. In 1881 they inspected the Woolwich Division Victualing Yard at Deptford, and reported that one married inspector, three single sergeants and twelve single constables resided there. Many of the buildings occupied by dockyard Police Officers were very old and suffered from neglect. An inspection took place of the inspector's quarters in Greenwich Naval College and it was noticed that damp had penetrated the walls; ventilation was poor and sunlight did not reach the basement rooms.[3660]

It occasionally transpired that army deserters, once identified, were returned under escort by soldiers to their various regiments, although often these duties were delegated to the dockyard Police Officers. In October 1893 the non-police escort party from the Royal Horse Artillery collected a prisoner from Holloway Gaol and escorted him back to Woolwich Dockyard. They travelled by train to Woolwich Arsenal Station, and on arrival decided to refresh themselves in The Bull public house, taking their prisoner with them. A short while later a problem arose when the escorted prisoner escaped. When Gunner Pennant realised this he came rushing out from the public house, aimed his rifle and fired at the fleeing escapee, fortunately missing hitting him. Discharging a firearm in a public place is not only against the law, but allowing a prisoner to escape as well are both offences in breach of army discipline. They were court-martialed and punished heavily,[3661] although they were not discharged from the army.

Some police officers attached to the dockyards had complained that such work was boring and monotonous for most of the time, and for this reason they did not want to stay. So there was a need to offer incentives for Police Constables to remain. Promotion in dockyards was also a bone of contention, since it appears to have been very slow.[3662] There was also less chance of arresting people for crimes than would be the case if stationed on Division, and crime arrests might be rewarded with extra pay or expenses.

The work was at times difficult and dangerous. In 1893 two brothers, Richard and John Crawley, were part of a team of labourers engaged in discharging grain into a barge when a dispute arose over the size of grain sacks. There was a dispute between the supervisors and labourers, who said that they were too large to be carried by them. A crowd assembled and two Metropolitan Police dockyard Constables, PCs Gundrey and Butcher, attempted to resolve the dispute only for the two brothers and the crowd to attack the officers. Amidst calls from the crowd for them to be thrown into the river, a boat was sent across just in case the crowd carried out its chant. Later, when the brothers were arrested, they were charged with assaulting the two constables and taken before the court. Richard was sent to prison for four months with hard labour, while his brother was imprisoned for two months.[3663]

During the First World War a number of bombs were dropped by Zeppelins and aircraft on the Royal Dockyard. Four bombs landed in the Royal Arsenal causing minimal damage and three others fell in the dockyard itself, while one struck the hospital and a further two hit the Artillery barracks.[3664] There was a considerable amount of traffic both in and out of the dockyard, and in 1918 Constable Edward William Swan was killed when he was run over by an army lorry whilst on point duty there.[3665] In 1924 Superintendent J. Devine was in charge of the dockyard supervising 170 police officers,[3666] an increase in strength of eleven since 1873.

In true tradition, many police officers over the years, have been involved in some acts of outstanding bravery, none more so than in 1919 when extreme danger occurred as a munitions train caught fire at Woolwich Arsenal. PC 92939 Percy Carr, PC 93291 William Mewton and PC 78028 William Monnery, all stationed at the Royal Arsenal, managed to extinguish fires in two adjacent trucks of a 26-truck ammunition train standing beside a magazine at Woolwich Arsenal. Carr had run immediately to the nearest fire hydrant, connected the hose and then ran it down to the train. Two trucks were by then alight, and both Mewton and Monnery (the older officer who took charge) played the hose on the burning trucks until the flames went out. Hot ammunition and fuses continued to be discharged, even after the fire was put out. The officers could have been killed at any time, as they had to reach the fires by approaching through a hail of exploding bullets and fuses. For extinguishing the fire and preventing a far greater tragedy all three were awarded the well-deserved King's Police Medal.[3667]

Police pay rises in the early 1920s and the creation of the Police Federation made the Metropolitan Police Dockyard contingents very expensive, and the Admiralty and the War Department tried to consider ways of minimising the cost. It was decided that with effect from 1st January 1927 the security of Woolwich should be transferred to the Marine Police. This was a special force drawn from Military backgrounds. Sub-Divisional Inspector (80525) MacIntyre and his deputy Inspector (86374) Michael Lofus together with three station sergeants, eight sergeants and 55 constables were transferred to other Divisions within London.[3668]

Portsmouth Dockyard or 2nd Division

Superintendents
James Mott 1861-1863, Customs
Henry Guy (1836)1863-1869 (retired) (from Woolwich)
Archibald Macdonald 1869-1882 (died in service of cancerous tumour)
George Godfrey (Acting Supt) 1882-1883
Robert Martin 1883-1885
William Ventham (1863) 1888-1895 (retired) (originally dockyard PC at Pembroke)
James Carter 1898-1907 (retired)
James Last 1910-1914 (retired)
Frederick Spencer 1915-1923 (retired)
David Sewell 1924-1928 (retired)
John George Parsons (87860) 1928-1933 (retired)

Portsmouth Dockyard remained in the control of the Metropolitan Police from October 1860 until 1934, when they were replaced by a dedicated Dockyard Force. The Police were not only responsible for the dockyard but also for Gosport Victualing Yard; Gunboat Yard, Haslar; Haslar Naval Hospital; Gun Wharf, Portsmouth Naval Depot; Portland Magazines; Priddys Hard; Floating Magazines, Portsmouth Harbour; and the Magazine at Marchwood[3669] These were referred to as War Department (Military) Stations, located in the dockyards. The instruction to supervise the dockyards took effect from 7th November 1862. At the same time there was an increase of police officers at Portsmouth by one sergeant and twelve constables.[3670] Some of the first constables transferred to Portsmouth from London Divisions (all unmarried) consisted of Constables Neale, Blackman, Ely, Costello, Cogger, Peacock, Rayment, Savage, Lock, Clarke, Childs, Christmas and Stribling.

Superintendent Henry Guy had been asked by the Commissioner to compile a list of married police officers who resided outside the dockyard and who lived more that five minutes away. The Commissioner noticed that 23 constables and sergeants lived over a mile away from the dockyard. Concerned that they may not be able to make it back to the dockyard (in their own time for which they were not paid) should a fire alarm occur, the Commissioner reminded Guy and the other superintendents that in future not to allow a married officer to reside more that one mile from the dockyard.[3671]

In 1869, when Portsmouth was being established, the dockyard strength included four 1st Class inspectors, one detective sergeant, four water sergeants, seven 1st Class sergeants, 106 1st Class constables, 24 2nd Class constables and one 3rd Class constable.[3672] Later this was adjusted, and became one superintendent, seven inspectors, 24 sergeants and 133 constables. Records show that Henry Guy remained the Superintendent until 1869,[3673] when Sir Thomas Paisley, Admiral Superintendent of the dockyard, was replaced. The Admiral highly commended Superintendent Guy and his men for their tact and ability together with Inspector Sherlock of the Water Police, who was always prompt with assistance.[3674] Sherlock was a trusted and responsible police officer, who was in charge of duties outside the dockyard that not only included the Water Police but also the Detective Police, contagious disease prevention duties, prisoner transport and apprehension of stragglers, deserters and disorderly seamen and marines.[3675] The strength at Portsmouth in 1873 was one superintendent, eight inspectors, 24 sergeants and 127 constables.[3676]

By 1877 Mr. Archibald McDonald was the Superintendent, assisted by Robert Martin as Chief Inspector. The inspectors were Daniel Godden, William Jones, William Connell, George Morsman, George Coppen, Joseph Wooton, John Camac and William Briggs.[3677]

The Dockyard Police were responsible for the supervision of Royal Navy Hospitals, and Haslar was a designated Inspector Station with an office situated near the entrance gate. The inspector was responsible for patrolling the hospital at least once each shift, to supervise and take charge of the front gates, and compile daily reports to the Superintendent.[3678]

Women and children of seamen and marines were allowed to visit the hospital for treatment and to use the dispensary. Passes for medicine would be inspected at the main gate prior to anyone leaving the hospital grounds.[3679] Visitors were allowed to visit the museum, and to inspect the building and the grounds at allotted times. Those visitors were allowed in after verification and once they had signed the visitors' book. Visitors to patients were stopped and often searched in an effort to find tobacco, fruit, cake or alcohol of any kind, as none of these were permitted by the Captain Superintendent and confiscated.

Passes issued by the Medical Examiner for others to enter would be collected and returned to the Captain Superintendent. Any strangers, people of known bad character or those discharged for misconduct were not allowed to enter the yards. When dockyard workers and male nurses left the hospital at midday and in the evening, the inspector in charge would be present and decide whether anyone should be searched or not. Constables supervised smoking arrangements of the building, since smoking only took place in the outer airing ground and the back of the hospital square between 10.00am and 12 noon and 1.00 until 3.00pm.

The picture right shows the bell which was sounded on the instructions of the Admiral Superintendent, normally for calling dockyard trades to work, to dinner, and when to vacate the yard. At other times the bell would be used to alert people to a fire in the yard and rung only with special authority.[3680]

The dockyard bell which was sounded calling people to work

There was also a list of duties for Police minimum staff manning the Main Gate, Factory Gate and East Gate to the Dockyard. For example, staffing of the Main Gate at Portsmouth consisted of one inspector, one sergeant and two constables, with similar arrangements for the other gates. The inspector was required to be present at all times, unless relieved by the sergeant. The constables' function in all instances was to stop and question all strangers, visitors and others before they were allowed in or out.[3681] An inspector, or sergeant acting for him whilst he was away, was also responsible for duties outside the gates meaning, supervision of the Water Police, detectives, duties under the Contagious Diseases Prevention Act, conveyance of prisoners to Lewes Gaol and apprehension of disorderly Sailors and Marines.[3682] The inspector would be on duty from 8.00am until 6.00pm, and was responsible for parading the Dockyard Police Officers for duty at their fixed hours, inspecting their appointments, reading out the list of absentees from the dockyard and any other relevant information. He would then supervise Police employed at the wharves, landing places, railways and afloat and inspecting the Police Ship and cells.[3683] The inspector also needed to complete entries in the occurrence book of matters

3660 Metropolitan Police Inspection of Police Premises 1881 p105.
3661 *The Police and Parade Gossip*, 30th October 1893.
3662 *The Police and Parade Gossip*, 26th January 1894 p40.
3663 *The Police and Parade Gossip*, 30th October 1893 p527.
3664 *The Daily Mail Map of Zeppelin and Aeroplane Bombs on London 1914-1918*.
3665 National Police Roll of Honour (www.policememorial.org.uk) accessed 12th March 2002.
3666 *The Policeman's Pocket Almanac and Diary* 1924.
3667 HO45/11016/372290.
3668 Metropolitan Police Orders dated 23rd December 1926.
3669 *Kirchner's Almanac* 1907.
3670 Metropolitan Police Orders dated 12th November 1862.
3671 Metropolitan Police Orders dated 25th September 1868.
3672 Metropolitan Police Orders dated 17th July 1869.
3673 *Police and Constabulary Almanac* 1864.
3674 Metropolitan Police Orders dated 10th April 1869.
3675 Metropolitan Police Orders dated 30th August 1865.
3676 Metropolitan Police General Orders and Regulation 1873.
3677 *Police Office London Directory* 1877.
3678 Ibid.
3679 Wynne, H. (1998) 'Extracts taken from the Metropolitan Police Orders 1873 (Dockyard Divisions)'. Friends of the Ministry of Defence Museum.
3680 Ibid.
3681 Metropolitan Police Instructions. Dockyards and Stations of the War Department 1873 p40.
3682 Ibid.
3683 Ibid.

connected with his duties, compile the daily report to the Superintendent by 8.00am, and attend the Divisional Office when required to do so. The conveyance of prisoners to gaol with the appropriate constable acting as escort was another feature of dockyard life. Prisoners were transferred along the coast from Portsmouth to Lewes by train. Expenses were paid to Police in advance.[3684]

The picture left shows a Dockyard Police Officer circa 1870, complete with summer-wear ceremonial gloves. They were required to wear gloves all year round, wearing thick dark woollen gloves in winter.[3685] There was no discretion in those days for supervisors to instruct their staff to wear shirt sleeve order during hot weather. They generally wore a t-shirt underneath a tunic which buttoned up to the neck.

Portsmouth Dockyard had a long reputation for losing or having property stolen from its stores. This came to light in 1796 through Colquhoun's review of the Police of the Metropolis, and asserted that nearly one million pounds sterling was lost in time of war, and half that in peacetime, through fraud, plunder or pillage. Ensuring the security of property over such an extensive and complicated site as Portsmouth was a big problem for the Dockyard Police. Inspector Horne was rewarded with £5 on the personal directions of Sir Richard Mayne, the Chief Commissioner, for his actions in discovering stolen property being removed from the dockyard.[3686]

Dockyard constable c1870
Below: Dockyard helmet plate 1880-1902

Honesty was always the best policy, but lying to a senior officer was always unforgivable and treated harshly. Police officers worked seven days a week and had no day off. Senior officers also had to be vigilant when presented applications for leave based on the uncorroborated facts on family matters. For example, Constable 48 Boxall attached to the dockyard sought leave to visit his dying mother. He was sacked when it was found that this was not the case,[3687] and she was not in imminent danger of death. Not the first example nor would it be the last of a Police officer wanting leave and giving a dubious reason.

In 1875 the Superintendent in charge submitted to the Commissioner in his annual report that 29 cases of embezzlement had been detected, with convictions obtained in each case and all outstanding property recovered.[3688] The Dockyard Fire Brigade and Police Officers had been vigilant in 1875 as there were no reports of fires in the dockyard, but they helped fight three fires in the neighbourhood.[3689]

Portsmouth Dockyard c1915

The picture above shows a view across the dockyard taken after the Semaphore Tower had been burnt down in 1913.

By 1879 the strength at Portsmouth had increased to 202 Police officers and a new Section House built near Unicorn Gate to accommodate two inspectors, two married sergeants and 35 single constables. It was occupied in the same year.[3690] Inspector Connell was a dockyard officer through and through. He retired from the dockyard after 43 years' Police service, having spent 21 years at Portsmouth, the last ten years of which he was in charge of the Clarence Victualling Yard, Gosport. Inspector Connell was a trusted officer and had also been responsible for the police arrangements on the many occasions the Queen and her entourage passed through the yard,[3691] often on the way to Osborne House on the Isle of Wight. The photograph below shows the Section House contingent in 1914.

Unicorn Dockyard Section House 1914

43-year-old Inspector Coppen was originally from Linton in Kent, resided at the Royal Naval Hospital at Haslar with his wife Sarah and their six children.[3692] Coppen had joined the Police in 1868 and within three years was a Dockyard Inspector, a rank in which he remained until he retired in 1894.

There was a social side to policing, which was not only reflected in the Dockyards Divisions but on the London Divisions as well. The Police family included the wives, children and the officer's other relatives. For example, a social club was in place at most police stations, and Christmas parties for the children have long been a tradition, even up to today. In 1894, the fifth annual Portsmouth Dockyard event for the children of Police took place. This not only included the children of serving Dockyard Police, but also Police orphans and children of retired police officers. The show lasted three hours, and took place in the dining hall of the Workman's restaurant near Unicorn Gates. Entertainment included Herr Wingard, a magician. A bun, an orange and sweets were provided to each child as they left.[3693]

The issuing of a Police Order in 1894 that prevented Dockyard Police from working in yards where their relatives were also employed caused considerable concern among the police officers. The effect of this order, originating from the Home Secretary, suggested that Dockyard police officers would be re-assigned to other postings if found working with or near relatives. In Portsmouth and Gosport this affected some 50-60 police officers alone, and such was their concern that Assistant Commissioner A.C. Howard had to visit to dispel anxieties. The result was that a liberal interpretation was applied to the general satisfaction of those affected.[3694]

The picture below shows the Dockyard Fire Brigade with fire engines, ladders, and divers in their breathing equipment. Notice that there is very little specialist equipment for fire fighting. Superintendent Carter, in flat kepi, is standing proudly fourth from the left.

Superintendent Carter and his Dockyard Fire Brigade in 1902

Inspector Michael Money resided at 4 Dockyard Extension Police Station with his wife Sarah in 1881. Money, originally from Ireland, was 40-years-old and his wife was eight years younger. Money had joined the Police in 1862, and by 1869 had become an Inspector at Woolwich Dockyard where he stayed until 1881, when he was transferred to Portsmouth in the same rank. He was promoted to Chief Inspector at Portsmouth in 1888. On retiring from the Dockyard Police in June 1894 he was presented with a cheque, a handsome gilt clock and ornaments commemorating his 32 years' service.[3695] Money had been transferred at a time when the serving Superintendent, Archibald Macdonald, was quite unwell and it was felt that Money could support the ailing Macdonald, who was Superintendent of the dockyard in 1869 until his death in 1882 from a cancerous tumour.

The picture at the top of the following column shows the Haslar Naval Hospital gates with police officers at their posts.

In March 1895 Superintendent Ventham also retired, moving a short distance to St. Denys, Southampton. Ventham originally started at Pembroke as a Constable in 1863 and had worked his way up the ranks. He had been in charge of the dockyard at Portsmouth for seven years. The Commissioner moved Superintendent Carter (shown below) from Chatham Dockyard to take his place. Ventham was held in very high regard by his men. Although he was a strict disciplinarian, he was also described as being courteous and obliging to all

The Haslar Naval Hospital was a busy place, and only people who had business inside were allowed in by police

he had contact with. He spoke two foreign languages, French and German; a great asset bearing in mind the many different nationalities he would meet in the course of daily business in the dockyard.[3696]

Sport amongst the police officers was always encouraged by senior officers, and the differing sporting events also provided constant entertainment for off-duty officers, some of whom, from the dockyard in Portsmouth, took part in a game of cricket against Portsmouth Borough Police. The Dockyard Police won by three runs,[3697] but in the return match a short while later the Borough Police won by six runs, making matters all square.[3698]

One of the Dockyard gates at Portsmouth, Unicorn Gate is shown below.

Unicorn Gate, Portsmouth Dockyard at leaving time

3684 Ibid.
3685 Metropolitan Police General Orders and Regulation 1873.
3686 Metropolitan Police Orders dated 15th February 1865.
3687 Metropolitan Police Orders dated 13th December 1860.
3688 *Commissioner's Annual Report* 1875.
3689 Ibid.
3690 *Commissioner's Annual Report* 1879.
3691 *Police and Parade Gossip*, 12th January 1894.
3692 Census 881.
3693 *Police and Parade Gossip*, 19th January 1894.
3694 *Police and Parade Gossip*, 11th May and 18th May 1894.
3695 *Police and Parade Gossip*, 22nd June 1894.
3696 *Police and Parade Gossip*, 1st March 1895.
3697 *Police and Parade Gossip*, 31st August 1894.
3698 *Police and Parade Gossip*, 7th September 1894.

In May 1895 Inspector Chubbock also served notice of his intention to retire after 25 years of service. He was presented with a 'handsome marble timepiece' as a token of esteem and goodwill.³⁶⁹⁹ Chubbock had joined in 1869 and been a Dockyard Inspector from 1888 until he retired.

One of the first presentations that Superintendent Carter attended was of the retirement of a constable who had completed 38 years in the Police. This was a considerable length of service by the standards of the day.

Constable F. Lane retired on pension and Carter presented him with a silver-mounted walking cane and a pipe. Kind words were expressed by Inspector Goss, Chief Inspector Last and Det. Sergeant Smallbridge.³⁷⁰⁰

The picture right shows Superintendent Carter dressed in his ceremonial uniform and with his medals. Carter was the Superintendent at Portsmouth from 1898 until he retired in 1905. Before his appointment he had been Chief Inspector at Portsmouth from 1895, after being transferred from Pembroke where he had served as the officer in charge. Carter had joined the Woolwich Dockyard as Inspector in 1885, where he progressed well and earned the respect of his superiors.

Superintendent Carter 1898-1907

The picture below shows the sergeants of Portsmouth Dockyard in receipt of their 1897 Jubilee medal, which they are proudly displaying.

Portsmouth Dockyard sergeants posing with their medals in 1897

Police officers were trained in fire fighting techniques, and those who were either on or off duty had to go and help put out any fire that should occur. Whilst there was no standing brigade available at Portsmouth it depended solely on availability. One police officer or another member of the dockyard workforce was normally posted to the fire engine and remained with it in case an alarm was sounded. The Dockyard Inspector General was responsible for overseeing the safety of all people working within the docks. He recognised the efficiency of the Police Fire Brigade when he commended Inspector Rogers and his police officers for their promptitude in extinguishing a potentially serious fire in the Haslar Hospital in 1896.³⁷⁰¹ Inspector Rogers was a prominent and respected Dockyard Inspector, later becoming Sub-Divisional Inspector in 1897 and Chief Inspector at Woolwich. He was also a member of the Dockyard Cricket Club, whose annual luncheon was held in the Recreation Room at Marlborough Gate and which was attended by 60 people in November 1896. The Chairman Superintendent Carter was presiding, with Chief Inspector Last and Inspectors Short, Rogers and Butler also in attendance.³⁷⁰² Speeches were normally made by the various officers of the Club.

Portsmouth and Gosport Dockyard Police in 1902

The picture above shows Portsmouth and Gosport Police circa 1902; Superintendent James Carter is seated in the centre of the second row.

In 1908, whilst out on inquiries, Detective Sergeant Alfred Barton was found drowned in the dockyard,³⁷⁰³ another case of an unexplained death on duty which almost never ended in prosecution.

The photograph below shows PC443 Charles Burton who, in 1916, was presented with the Royal Humane Society Medal by Rear Admiral Superintendent A.A. Weymouth.³⁷⁰⁴ Constable Burton, whilst on night duty the November before, had jumped fully clothed into the tidal basin to rescue a stoker (who is standing to the right of the table) had fallen overboard from his vessel which had been moored alongside the quay. He was further rewarded by Sir John Dickenson, Magistrate at Bow Street, with a reward of £10 from the Hero Reward Fund. In the photograph, Superintendent Frederick Spencer is standing facing the recipient after having given his speech, still holding his notes in his hand. The medal shown above is the bronze version as given to PC Burton.

RHS medal

The 1916 award ceremony for Constable Burton

Saturday 20th December 1913 was a particularly memorable day in the life of the dockyard, as what occurred then had serious consequences for years to come. A fire, which quickly got out of hand, broke out and destroyed one of the central features which dominated the skyline and helped guide ships into the docks. The Semaphore Tower was completely destroyed. An investigation into the cause of the fire was undertaken by Superintendent Last, who reported the results to the Admiral Superintendent. The investigation required a report from witnesses and workers who were in the area prior to the fire breaking out. All the facts were taken down, and anyone who could be blamed for the fire would be the subject of disciplinary action by the Admiral Superintendent. Artists and illustrators were busy attempting to recreate the scene in order to sell the images as postcards to an interested public, such as the card shown below.

An artist's impression of the fire at Portsmouth Dockyard in 1913

All the dockyard Police were summoned together with other workers from the dockyard to fight the fire and it took some considerable time to put out. The charred remains of the Semaphore Tower are evident in the picture below, which was taken by a local photographer the next day. Access to take such pictures was strictly regulated, as this was an embarrassment to the authorities. There is a slim chance that the picture was taken by a workman, dock worker, sailor or even a police officer and then sold on later.

The aftermath of the dockyard fire, showing charred timbers and ruins of the Semaphore Tower

Portsmouth was a very busy port and there was much to see and supervise. In 1905 Portsmouth Dockyard was responsible for building and launching the Dreadnought Class battleships, a prelude to an arms race with Germany that ended with the start of the First World War. Thousands of workers were needed to help towards the war effort.

Vigilance was an essential skill for the many police officers who were sent to the dockyards to supplement the dwindling numbers. It had been felt that Germany would spy on British efforts to get ahead in this race, and police officers were constantly aware of the threat. Arrests were made on a number of occasions.

The patrol of a Dockyard Constable on duty at Portsmouth c1910

Dockyard sergeant c1904

The picture on the left shows a Dockyard officer wearing the 1887 Jubilee medal with bar (1897) and the 1902 Coronation Medal. On the table is the officer's helmet with its badge.

In 1924 Portsmouth Dockyard Police had the largest complement of men with 211 officers, sergeants and constables, with Superintendent D. Sewell in charge.[3705] By 1932 the dockyard strength was reduced, with six constables being transferred to town divisions back in the Metropolitan Police area.[3706] The remaining Metropolitan Dockyard Police were all transferred back to London in 1933.

The cup shown right is the Metropolitan Police Portsmouth Challenge Cup, which was presented in 1922 by the Admiral Superintendent to the winning sports team from the Dockyard.

3699 *Police and Parade Gossip*, 17th May 1895.
3700 *Police and Parade Gossip*, 31st May 1895.
3701 *Police and Parade Gossip*, 29th May 1896.
3702 *Police and Parade Gossip*, 27th November 1896.
3703 National Police Roll of Honour (www.policememorial.org.uk) accessed 12th March 2002.
3704 Metropolitan Police Orders dated 15th February 1916.
3705 *The Policeman's Pocket Almanac and Diary* 1924.
3706 Metropolitan Police Orders dated 26th January 1932.

Devonport Dockyard or 3rd Division

Superintendents
Robert Bray 1860-61 (transferred to R)
John Baxter 1861-1869
William Wakeford 1869-1891 (retired). Transferred to Devonport as Inspector in 1860; 1869-1891 Customs Inspector Pembroke; 1860-1865 later; 1865-1867 Superintendent at Pembroke
Josiah Hobbins 1891-1894
Edwin Smith 1897-1905
George Dixson 1910-1913
Thomas Evans (68285) 1913-1918 (retired)
Albert Keys 1923 (retired)
David Sewell 1923-1924 (to Portsmouth)
Owen Webb 1924-1930 (retired)

Chief Inspectors
William Crook (1840) 1868-1876
William Ventham 1877-1878 (PC 18 at Pembroke in 1862)
J. Willmott 1885-1888 (to Woolwich)
George Harding 1891-1894
Charles Wall 1894-1899
George Dixson 1901-1903 (transferred to Portsmouth)
William Tett (transferred from M to C/I) 1902-1905
Albert Keys 1910-1917
Down (1911)
Alford Hunt (86548) 1927 (later Superintendent N Division)

Devonport is situated in the docks at Plymouth. The police responsibility at Devonport not only included the Devonport Dockyard – South and Devonport Dockyard – North but also Keyham Factory Yard, Stonehouse Victualling Yard, Stonehouse Naval Hospital, Gun Wharf, Floating Magazines, Hamoaze, Turnchapel Coal Depot and St. Georges Halland, the Royal Magazine at Bull Point.[3707] These all had inspectors in charge, whilst sergeants took responsibility for Stonehouse Naval Hospital and Gun Wharf. The picture below is the Naval Barrack gate. A number of constables had been sent for duty at Devonport, but all were quickly promoted or reallocated different roles. PCs Anniss (later Inspector at Portsmouth), Chaplin, Bates and Looker were all promoted to sergeant, whilst PCs Huxtable, Pearn and Angear were re-assigned to the Water Police.[3708] In 1862 eight constables were transferred to Devonport from London as part of the increase in establishment.

Devonport Dockyard gate

Duty at Royal Hospitals varied slightly from other hospitals, but generally this involved ensuring strangers, vagrants and other undesirable folk were not permitted entry. Female searchers were employed on the front gate to search women and children. No patient was allowed to leave without a discharge pass being issued, and these would be inspected at the front gate before the bearer was allowed to leave. Women, children and families of the navy and marines were allowed to enter to attend the dispensary or for advice from the medical attendant.[3709]

Gratuities were allowed to Police for good detection and police work. In 1860 the magistrate, in essence the Dockyard Admiral Superintendent, awarded a sergeant a sum of money as a gratuity for his diligence in discovering stolen property being removed from the dockyard.[3710] All the authorities were keen to ensure the success of the newly-installed Police, and rewards were granted to police officers, in addition to extra pay and free accommodation, to lure them to work in the dockyards. Sergeants Brown and Anniss of the Devonport Police shared a large reward of £12 7s 8d each, which was the residue of a fine of £50 imposed by the Navel Dockyard Superintendent on Richard Pascoe.[3711] Such rewards provided a valuable incentive to police officers to be diligent in their duties.

The picture below is of the Royal William Yard Gate, Devonport. In 1864 Superintendent John Baxter,[3712] who was in charge of the dockyard, had the sad task of dealing with dockyard constable Charles Pearce, who had been on normal patrol in a Police launch when he fell into the estuary and drowned.[3713]

Royal William Yard gate

Baxter was followed by Superintendent William Wakeford in 1869, who remained in charge of Devonport for 22 years until he retired. This was the longest period of time spent not only as a Superintendent in the same post, but also without a move to another dockyard. Wakeford clearly had the confidence of the Commissioner, who had decided to leave him in situ.

The fortunes of people can change in an instant, especially when some failure of duty was discovered. In August 1873 Inspector Bradley was suspended from duty. An investigation was carried out by Superintendent William Wakeford who submitted a report that was forwarded to the Commissioner Edmund Henderson. It was not known exactly what Bradley did, but it was serious enough for him to be dismissed from the Force on 30th August. Bradley and his family were required to immediately vacate their subsidised lodgings in the dockyard.[3714] There would have been a great deal of sympathy amongst his fellow police officers, and to be sacked in this way was very harsh especially given his circumstances. Often a collection was raised amongst the officers and families to tide them over.

This Victorian shaving mug measuring 12cm across and bearing the fouled anchor of the Dockyard Police was unearthed in the garden of a house once occupied by a Dockyard Constable in 1890. It shows that even the dockyards produced china-ware for their own purposes.

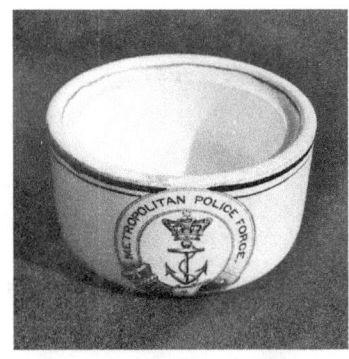

In 1869 the Dockyard Police established strength was one superintendent, eight inspectors, 20 sergeants and 133 constables. One inspector was responsible for the duties outside the yards and he was stationed in the Police Reserve Room at St. Georges Hall, Stonehouse. Care was to be taken in inspecting the ships held in reserve by the Admiralty and located in the estuary at Hamoaze. The inspector was also to ensure at least three visits to the ships by the Water Police in each 24-hour period, although going aboard would only be undertaken if something irregular was going on.[3715] The Water Police had their own station aboard the hulk *Leda*, which was also fitted out as a residence for officers and men.[3716] This had replaced the unserviceable and condemned ship *Igeria*, which had been removed. Inspector Anniss and his family occupied four of the stern cabins, whilst Sergeant Angear was instructed to live in No. 1 Suite which consisted of three cabins with one entrance.[3717] There were 17 houses in Pitt Street, Portsea which were the property of the War Department and because of a shortage of living accommodation for Police these were handed over for their use until such times as they were required again for public service.[3718]

A new steam fire engine was delivered to the dockyard to replace one of the manual engines, and to ensure the fire engine was properly looked after the Commissioner instructed Superintendent Strength on the deployment arrangements for the new engine once it was delivered.[3719]

Dockyard Constable 96 Hollins was handsomely rewarded for his courageous conduct in the rescue of RN Lieutenant Macauley's brother-in-law from drowning when he fell into the dock basin. Hollins received a solid silver watch and chain as a reward.[3720]

In November 1867 Superintendent Baxter retired from the dockyard on an annual pension of £153 6s.[3721] A constable would receive an annual pension in the order of £30. In 1877 Baxter was succeeded by William Wakeford, who was assisted by Chief Inspector William Ventham with Silas Anniss, Edwin Smith, Henry Smale, Neil McCrimmon, Leonard James, Aubrey Hann, Thomas Wonnall and William Potts as inspectors.

In 1894 Inspector C. Wall was promoted to Chief Inspector,[3722] being replaced in 1899 by Sub Divisional Inspector Moorman.[3723]

The Devonport Police Dockyard Social Club took its annual outing to Oakhampton in Devon on 10th July and a good time was had by all. This outing by charabanc (an open-topped long wheel-based bus) included not only the police officers, but often their wives and children as well. Only those officers who were off duty were able to take advantage of the trip.[3724]

In August 1906 Superintendent Edwin Smith retired on pension from Devonport. Smith had joined the Metropolitan Police in July 1865 from his native Nottingham, and he commenced 41 years of duty. He was originally drafted to Woolwich Dockyard Division and within two years was promoted to Sergeant and transferred to Pembroke Dockyard in Wales. Two years later he was back at Woolwich, where he remained until 1887 when he was promoted to Inspector. On promotion he was transferred to Devonport Dockyard, and in 1886 he was recommended for promotion again. As a Chief Inspector he was posted to Chatham, moving to Sheerness in 1893. Only one year later he was once again promoted and sent to Devonport.

Superintendent Edwin Smith

Promoted to Sub-Divisional Inspector was Inspector Wedlock, who stayed in situ.[3725] Sergeant Rothnie was transferred to detective duties, and Inspector Burch was promoted to Sub-Divisional Inspector.[3726]

In 1911 Inspector Alfred Sly retired on pension after 27 years' service in Devonport Dockyard. Inspector Sly had a very strong connection with Devonport, since his father (who had five sons, all of whom joined the Metropolitan Police) spent all of his service stationed at the dockyard. Sly's father had also been a Dockyard Police Officer.

Sub-Divisional Inspector Alfred Sly in 1911

3707 *Kirchner's Almanac* 1907.
3708 Metropolitan Police Orders dated 3rd November 1860.
3709 Wynne, H. (1998) 'Extracts taken from the Metropolitan Police Orders 1873 (Dockyard Divisions)'. Friends of the Ministry of Defence Museum.
3710 Metropolitan Police Orders dated 17th December 1869.
3711 Metropolitan Police Orders dated 7th January 1863.
3712 *Police and Constabulary Almanac* 1864.
3713 National Police Roll of Honour (www.policememorial.org.uk) accessed 12th March 2002.
3714 Metropolitan Police orders dated 2nd August 1873.
3715 Wynne, H. (1998) 'Extracts taken from the Metropolitan Police Orders 1873 (Dockyard Divisions)'. Friends of the Ministry of Defence Museum.
3716 Ibid.
3717 Metropolitan Police Orders dated 31st March 1865.
3718 Metropolitan Police Orders dated 3rd September 1868.
3719 Metropolitan Police Orders dated 30th December 1866.
3720 Metropolitan Police Orders dated 8th September 1869.
3721 Metropolitan Police Orders dated 4th November 1867.
3722 *Police and Parade Gossip*, 9th November 1894.
3723 *Police and Parade Gossip*, 21st April 1899.
3724 *Police and Parade Gossip*, 19th July 1895.
3725 *Police and Parade Gossip*, 28th April 1899.
3726 *Police and Parade Gossip*, 16th June 1899.

The picture below shows the horse-drawn steam fire engine at Devonport in 1903. Inspector John Wedlake, on the left, had overall responsibility for the engine. The Brigade consisted of police officers, dockyard workers and labourers. In the upper centre of the picture is a member of the Dockyard Water Police who is wearing a flat hat, and there are ten civilian members all wearing an assortment of hats.

Devonport Dockyard Fire Brigade in 1903

The dockyard strength had been increased by four constables at that time, so it was felt by the men that there was no reason not to allow their leave. Weekly leave days could not be accumulated, so they were lost.[3727] This must have been resolved, since nothing further was reported about the problem in the paper.

Devonport Dockyard Band in 1912

The picture above shows the Devonport Police Band in 1912, with the Dockyard Superintendent George Dixson in the centre. To his right is Chief Inspector Albert Keys, who later took Dixson's place as Superintendent. Many police officers learnt to play an instrument, as it meant that they would be present at every ceremonial event or even playing at the local bandstand on a Sunday afternoon. Senior officers encouraged this, since it promoted team spirit and a sense or camaraderie. In the same way, sport was also promoted amongst the constables and sergeants as it was prestigious for senior officers to have the winning team. Games played between Police teams included football, rugby, cricket, hockey, tug of war and swimming. There was even a water tug of war event.

The picture at the top of the following column shows the Devonport Police Rifle Team, who in 1913 won the cup shown on the table following an open rifle shoot. The five man winning squad consisted of Sergeant Frewin, (back row standing left to right) Constable Lack, Constable Hill, Clerk Sergeant Wakefield and Station Sergeant Thompson (seated front row left). Superintendent Evans is shown seated front left. The cup was presented by the wife of Admiral Superintendent Stokes. In the prelude to the First World War such competitions were encouraged, especially at the Dockyard Divisions since there were times when police officers would need to be armed, especially on sentry duty.

Devonport Dockyard Rifle Team in 1913

Following the events of the First World War when the Germans employed mustard gas and other similar substances to overcome their opponents, the Government and Police developed anti-gas schools to teach their officers the dangers associated with gas attacks. They were particularly concerned that German bombers or Zeppelins could deploy gas bombs, especially on dockyards, and cripple their operations. They taught them about the substances that were available to be used and how to use the Household Respirator. The picture below shows the school at Devonport, with their gas masks and respirators correctly deployed.

Devonport Dockyard Gas Training School

By 1924 Devonport had 198 police officers, with Superintendent Owen Webb in charge.[3728] Webb retired in 1930 and was not replaced as Superintendent.

In 1934 instructions arrived for the vacation of the Devonport Dockyard by the Metropolitan Police and control to be handed over to the newly-appointed Marine Police. By 20th August 1934 Inspector (97240) Turner, two station sergeants, three sergeants and 23 constables had left the dockyard and returned to London[3729] after handing over duties to their replacements. Thus ended the long association between the Metropolitan Police and Devonport dockyard.

The Gatehouse at Chatham taken between 1865 and 1870, showing the Constables wearing cox-comb helmets with badges

Chatham (and Sheerness) Dockyard or 4th Division

Superintendent

Thomas Richardson 1863-64 Customs. Demoted to Inspector and transferred away from the dockyard to N Division. He never returned

John Strength (joined 1842) 1864-1871

John Smith 1872-1886 (died in post)

George Godfrey (1860) 1886-1894 (retired). Inspector at Woolwich 1873 -1881. Chief Inspector Portsmouth 1881 -1885

G. Hornsby 1897-1900. Transferred on promotion from K or Bow Division (No previous dockyard experience)

William. Smith 1902-1910. Chief Inspector at Chatham 1893-1907 (to Sheerness Dockyard from Chatham)

William Tell 1910-1919/ Transferred from M to C/I to Devonport 1902-1910. No previous dockyard experience

Charles E. Sly (74318) 1920-1929. Chief Inspector at Chatham 1914-15 and later Chief Inspector at Pembroke in 1917

Chief Inspector

John Kane 1927-1932 (last senior officer to leave Chatham Dockyard). Transferred to Devonport

Chatham Dockyard was located in the county of Kent, on the Thames and situated outside the jurisdiction of the Metropolitan Police, although the London Police took control over Chatham from December 1860 until 1932. Once the Metropolitan Police had left in 1932 the security for the dockyard was handed over to the Royal Marine Police,[3730] a substantially cheaper option.

Prior to this, duties at Dockyard Divisions meant officers had to ensure the security and protection of property owned by the government by preventing theft and burglary. Records show that security at the dockyard in 1574 was undertaken by 'men with mastiff dogs who patrolled the boundary hedges at night'.[3731] Later, in 1628, porters were recruited to man the gates and take charge of the keys when not in use.[3732] Experience had been gained when Samuel Pepys, the famous diarist who became the Secretary to the Admiralty, saw the depredations taking place at Deptford and Woolwich Dockyards.[3733] The porters stayed until 1686, when they were joined by rounders and warders.[3734]

3727 *Police and Parade Gossip*, 24th July 1896.
3728 *The Policeman's Pocket Almanac and Diary* 1924.
3729 Metropolitan Police Orders dated 7th August 1934.
3730 Brown, B. (1992) 'The Maritime duties of London's Bobbies' in *Bygone Kent* vol.13 no.4.
3731 Salter, A.R. (1983) 'The Protection of Chatham Dockyard throughout the Ages'. Gillingham Local History Series No. 12. Kent County Library.
3732 Ibid.
3733 Ibid.
3734 Ibid.

This marked the first organised protection of Chatham Dockyard, a factor which continued unbroken until 1983 when the yards closed.

Lieutenant William Hubbard (RN) was the first superintendent in charge at Chatham, in 1838, and he originally took charge of Dockyard policing until the Admiralty felt that a more efficient form could be developed. The Superintendent's Divisional Headquarters were situated at Chatham Dockyard, whilst the police stations were located at Chatham Dockyard, Sheerness Dockyard, Upnor Powder Magazines, Sheerness Gun Wharf, Royal Naval Hospital Chatham, Chatham Gun Wharf, Chattenden Naval Ordnance, Powder Magazines Chattenden, Submarine Mining Establishment, Field Park, Chatham, Field Park and Upnor and Brennan's Factories, Chatham.[3735] Initially, Inspector Burke was promoted to Chief Inspector and placed in charge of Sheerness Dockyard.[3736]

Superintendent F.M. Mallalieu was best placed to supervise the Chatham Dockyard, as he had become the R Divisional Superintendent back in October 1835 and was experienced in the supervision of dockyards; R Division was responsible for Woolwich and Deptford docks. His experience with the dockyards made him the natural advisor, especially when the Metropolitan Police were given security responsibilities for all the Royal dockyards.

In 1859, in addition to his own Divisional responsibilities Mallalieu took operational charge of Chatham from Lieutenant Thomas Pearse, who was at that time the director of the Dockyard Police. Many ex-Dockyard Police were retained by the Metropolitan Police and allowed to keep their uniforms as they were similar to the Metropolitan Police's swallowtail coats, but they had to pay to have their collars altered and buttons replaced.[3737] Sergeants had been allocated numbers from 26R to 39R, whilst Constables started at 243R to 301R.[3738] The numbering of police officers later changed and the Divisional letter was removed.

In March 1861 Mallalieu gave up charge of R Division but kept his responsibilities for the Dockyards by becoming Inspecting Superintendent, a position he kept until January 1870 when he was retired on pension for being 'worn out'.[3739] In fact, he had been seriously ill for some time, and once pensioned he did not live very long to enjoy his retirement. Because of R Division's association with the dockyards of Woolwich and Deptford it was felt that this Land Division should have an experienced Dockyard Superintendent in charge. Accordingly Superintendent Bray was transferred from Devonport Dockyard to take over from the departing Mallalieu.[3740] It was clear that apart from his Divisional responsibilities Bray was also in charge of Chatham while Mallalieu established his Dockyard Divisions throughout the country. In 1863 Bray handed over to Superintendent Richardson, who then took control.[3741]

In the early days, apart from Chatham and Sheerness Dockyards which were supervised by inspectors, sergeants were responsible for Chatham (Melville) Naval Hospital and Chatham Gun Wharf. Married and single residents of dockyards who were off duty had to hold themselves in a general state of readiness for action at all times. In other words, they were a sort of instant reserve that the Superintendent could call on at any time. Permission was required in advance from the Superintendent or his deputy for Police to be absent from the dockyard for more than three hours.[3742] Off duty Police were to be in their residences by 11.00pm, except when coming off duty at 10.00pm when the time of 11.30pm was allowed, as this was the time for gas to be shut off at the meter.[3743] The probable reason for this was to prevent fire. One particular responsibility for the early shift at Gun Wharf, Chatham was the extinguishing of the gas street lamps.[3744] Police Orders published the lighting-up times and gave instructions for the time at which those lamps should be put out, and a designated police officer would walk around and turn the gas taps off.

Mallalieu gave the Dockyard Superintendents permission to suspend inspectors, sergeants and constables from duty. He also authorised them to hear minor disciplinary infractions against sergeants and constables, which he stipulated could be dealt with locally and with a maximum deduction of up to one day's pay. Appeals against this punishment could be made in writing by the defaulter to the Commissioner or to Inspecting Superintendent Mallalieu who would hear the appeal when visiting the dockyard concerned.[3745]

To ensure that proper order and supervision was maintained, the senior police officers were given married quarters in main parts of the dockyards. For example, at Sheerness the main gatehouse was occupied by Inspector Court and his family, whilst Inspector Still was located in rooms a short distance away.[3746] Inspector Still was an original dockyard officer at Chatham who was taken on after 1860 by the Metropolitan Police, although he retired on a medical pension in 1865, the Chief Police Medical Examiner having described the reason for Inspector Still's retirement as being 'worn out'.[3747] His pension was paid for by the Admiralty, and amounted to £79 2s which was less than the pension that a retiring Metropolitan Inspector leaving under similar circumstances would receive.

Inspector Payne was stationed at Sheerness, and his quarters were situated on the Police Ship the *Etna*, where he was expected to reside with his wife and family.[3748] Police officers stationed on ships (*Etna*, *Juno* and *Leda*) were not normally charged for the rent of their cabins and this was waived by the War Department. Those police officers with accommodation ashore were required to pay rent on an agreed scale.[3749]

A commendation was received by the Commissioner from Rear Admiral Hall when he was replaced as Admiral Superintendent of Sheerness Dockyard in 1869. He praised the work of Chief Inspector Burke and his men for the zealous and satisfactory manner in which they carried out their duties at the dockyard.[3750]

A new uniform had been introduced into the Metropolitan Police in 1863, with the stovepipe top hats being replaced with a cox-comb helmet with a badge containing the officer's divisional number and anchor. On either side of the officer's collar was his divisional number together with a fouled anchor and Queen's crown. Notice also that the anchor denoting dockyard duty is shown above the number.

Smoking was strictly forbidden in dockyards, except for concessions that had been made by the Captain Superintendent for workmen at Chatham and Sheerness Dockyards. The instructions were for Police to ensure that these concessions, which operated only during dinner time and in places allocated, were not abused by them. The supply and sale of alcohol was also strictly regulated and banned from sale in any premises. Supply in the canteens was agreeable, with permission and under certain circumstances.[3751]

All storehouse and timber shed keys would be deposited with the Superintendent or his deputy when working hours finished, and they would have been responsible for their safety. Access to these premises would normally be gained only in the event of a fire.[3752]

Regulations were established by the Captain Superintendent to ensure that fire engines, with their boilers left on, and fire-fighting equipment were readily available at all times. Inspections by Police of the rope store and spinning loft were also important, although daily reviews were replaced by Saturday evenings and prior to public holiday's reviews only.[3753] At the front gate of Sheerness Dockyard was a sign on the wall which stated that 'Lucifer' matches must not be taken into the dockyard. Inside the yards, all fires in foundries or anywhere else were to be extinguished before workers could leave to go home.

In 1863 a new slaughterhouse for the killing of oxen was erected by the Admiralty at Sheerness. The security was immediately handed over to the Dockyard Police at Chatham.[3754]

Discipline was strict, and failing to comply with instructions was a serious matter. Constable 103 Doust had settled himself at the dockyard and was happy in his duties there. However he was transferred without warning, and instructed in Police Orders to move to Pembroke Dockyard from Chatham. He took great exception to the move and refused to go, and quickly appeared before Commissioner Sir Richard Mayne, who ordered that he be required to resign forthwith.[3755] Arguing with senior officers, especially the Commissioner, lost Doust his job.

The picture right shows PC69 George Collins, who joined the Metropolitan Police in 1865. The photograph was taken at Sheerness in 1869 when he was appointed to the Dockyard Police there. He is shown proudly wearing his new uniform, with a cox-comb helmet and his number in the plate as can be seen from the illustrated helmet plate above. Collins had been attached to the Water Police, and the winter weather had been extremely wet and cold. He tragically died in January 1874 of bronchitis, having been confined to the Melville Hospital, Chatham for 23 days. Police Orders report the death unsympathetically, saying: 'Pay to 14th'.[3756] No entry of the death was recorded in the Commissioner's Annual Report for that year, which would have been the usual practice.

PC Rogers of Chatham Dockyard c1881, wearing the star pattern helmet plate.

As can be seen from the list of Police Officers in Dockyard Divisions leaving the police at this time, many retired on grounds of ill health – mainly from bronchitis, one of the many causes of death as it rapidly developed into pneumonia.

In 1864 scandal rocked the dockyard when Superintendent Richardson was bizarrely suspended from duty.[3757] Details are sketchy, but this was a serious enough situation to put ex-Dockyard Superintendent Mott (now in charge of N Division) temporarily in charge of the dockyard whilst the matter was investigated. The result of the disciplinary inquiry was that Richardson was reduced in rank to inspector and removed to N Division, away from the Dockyard so that he received closer supervision from Superintendent Mott.[3758] Mott knew only too well about being suspended, as the previous year Commissioner Sir Richard Mayne had seen fit to briefly suspend him for failing to follow an agreed line of route for a Royal procession between Hyde Park and Marble Arch.[3759] Harsh discipline prevailed not only for the lower ranks, but for supervisory officers as well.

On promotion from Portsmouth Dockyard John Strength took over as Superintendent to replace the disgraced Richardson.[3760] Superintendent Strength, a Dockyard officer through and through, was obviously held in high regard when he was chosen to take over this prestigious posting. He had joined the police in 1842, and by 1860 was a Dockyard Inspector at Portsmouth. Just four years later he was promoted to Superintendent.

In January 1868 instructions had been issued to the Superintendent to allocate two constables to a detached post in the newly-built extension to the Sheerness Dockyard. This was the Royal Engineers Establishment that was situated in

PC 69 George Collins of Sheerness Dockyard

3735   *Kirchner's Almanac* 1907.
3736   Metropolitan Police Orders dated 10th June 1869.
3737   Brown, B. (1992) 'The Maritime duties of London's Bobbies' in *Bygone Kent* vol.13 no.4.
3738   Ibid.
3739   List of Superintendents, Met Police Heritage Centre.
3740   Ibid
3741   Police and Constabulary Almanac 1864.
3742   Wynne, H. (1998) 'Extracts taken from the Metropolitan Police Orders 1873 (Dockyard Divisions)'. Friends of the Ministry of Defence Museum.
3743   Ibid
3744   Metropolitan Police Orders dated 20th December 1862.
3745   Metropolitan Police Orders dated 3rd December 1860.
3746   Metropolitan Police Orders dated 4th January 1865.
3747   Metropolitan Police Orders dated 15th November 1865.
3748   Metropolitan Police Orders dated 24th September 1866.
3749   Metropolitan Police Orders dated 3rd September 1868.
3750   Metropolitan Police Orders dated 7th April 1869.
3751   Wynne, H. (1998) 'Extracts taken from the Metropolitan Police Orders 1873 (Dockyard Divisions)'. Friends of the Ministry of Defence Museum.
3752   Ibid
3753   Ibid
3754   Metropolitan Police Orders dated 19th June 1863.
3755   Metropolitan Police Orders dated 29th June 1863.
3756   Metropolitan Police Orders dated 15th January 1874.
3757   Metropolitan Police Orders dated 13th January 1864.
3758   Metropolitan Police Orders dated 4th February 1864.
3759   Metropolitan Police Orders dated 9th March 1863.
3760   Metropolitan Police Orders dated 4th February 1864.

the extension works, and was to be visited once in each shift during the night.[3761]

There had been some problems with housing police officers and their families at Chatham. The Admiralty had been kind enough to loan a number of quarters to the Police, and the Commissioner decided that any new incumbents should be charged an enhanced rental for these premises.

In order to ensure that proper importation of goods from foreign destinations took place and that any prohibited materials were confiscated, a number of police officers of varying ranks from superintendent to constable were made customs officers. These functions were added to their normal duties, at no extra pay. Proper declaration could now be allowed to be made by travellers, sailors and other people when coming ashore, or when challenged by those in authority. Ordinary Police sometimes came across boats and ships carrying suspicious goods, but these could only be searched and items seized by a police officer with a Royal Customs warrant. In 1869 there was a staff totalling 128 police officers, comprising one superintendent, seven inspectors, fourteen sergeants and 106 constables. Within two years the strength had increased to 160 police officers.

Constable George Potts was found drowned in the docks at Chatham on 15th August 1870,[3762] although his death was not treated as suspicious at the time. Many people could not swim, let alone Dockyard Police, so even if they fell into the water they could get into difficulties very quickly. Dockyards are dangerous places, and many Dockyard police officers perished in this way either by accident, suicide or murder.

John Smith was the Superintendent in 1877, Joseph King the Chief Inspector, and the Inspectors were William Oaks, James Atkins, Thomas Borsberry, Charles Hallett, William Capon and Josiah Hobbins (later himself to become a Superintendent in the Dockyard Divisions). John Smith was aged 49 at the time of the 1881 census, and these records show he was from Warbstow in Cornwall. He lived at the dockyard with his wife Lavinia, aged 50, interestingly from Devonport in Devon, together with their six children. The Superintendent knew his men, and when he took charge of Chatham he inherited a number of old Dockyard Police who had been there for some years. He drew to the attention of the Commissioner an injustice which Old Dockyard police officers were likely to suffer; the fact that even if they were to complete 40 years service, they would not be entitled to a pension of the same order as his other Metropolitan Dockyard police officers retiring with 24 and 28 years' service.[3763] The Commissioner resolved the problem by requesting the Admiralty to supplement the pension of these old Dockyard Police.

Sadly, Superintendent Smith died in office in November 1886, and such was the regard in which he was held that a memorial from his men was erected in the old cemetery next to Gillingham Church, where it can be seen today. John Smith was succeeded by William Wakeford.

Above is Superintendent 44292 Josiah Hobbins in full uniform. In 1881 he was an Inspector aged 35 years, residing in the Dockyard with his wife Fanny and their five children. Hobbins had been born in Portsmouth in 1846, and within a year of joining the Metropolitan Police on C Division in 1863 he joined the Dockyard Divisions. Hobbins had been to America by the time he was 12 and worked on ships as a cabin boy. Such were his survival skills and tenacity that he lived through the traumas of being shipwrecked twice.

His first dockyard posting was to Woolwich from 1864-1867. In 1866 he became Acting Sergeant, due mainly to his skill with a cutlass which resulted in his becoming the Divisional Instructor. In 1867 he became a Sergeant and transferred back to his home town of Portsmouth. Whilst there he served most of his time in the Water Police and was commended on a number of occasions, even occasionally receiving a reward for his services. On one occasion he was lowered into the burning hold of HMS *Argus* to locate the fire.

1870 saw his rapid promotion to Inspector, and then being posted to Thames Division for a short period. He also held a Customs Warrant, enabling him to act as an Excise Officer. In 1874 he transferred to Chatham, where he re-wrote Dockyard Standing Orders.[3764]

Superintendent Josiah Hobbins

The 1871 census shows that 33 single constables lived in a Section House within the dockyard, but a number of others lived on ships. These not only included ten single constables, but also a married constable by the name of William Huggin, his wife Louisa and their two children. Louisa's job title was described as the 'ship's cook to mess', which meant that she prepared the meals for the ten single constables as well as for her family.

Inspector William Oaks had been an inspector in the original old Dockyard Police at Chatham before the London Police took control in 1860. He had spent some time at Chatham and was very experienced in matters at the dockyards. However, it was felt that a change was necessary, so he was transferred to Sheerness in 1869. He was a senior Inspector who could be trusted and was well-regarded; however, an incident occurred at Sheerness just after his transfer which brought his judgement into question by the Commissioner, Sir Richard Mayne.

The Commissioner felt from a report submitted to him that a navy rating, who had obstructed the police during an incident, should have been arrested. Oaks, who was present at the time, was cautioned for this error,[3765] a fact which would have been recorded on the Inspector's defaulter's sheet. Oaks remained for another 10 years at Sheerness when he retired with 19 years Metropolitan Police service. As an old dockyard Inspector his pension before 1860 was paid by the Admiralty.

Superintendent Smith had the sad task of dealing with deaths on duty, and this was a particular problem for Dockyard Police since an accidental fall into a dock was often fatal. Such was the case in 1879 when PC William Stevens Nazer fell from the quayside whilst on patrol and drowned.[3766] PC John Beer was retired on pension in 1887, but subsequently died of injuries he received whilst serving as a Dockyard Constable at Chatham.[3767]

The picture on the following page shows Chatham Dockyard senior officers and men in 1896. This was the year that Superintendent Godfrey retired, and he is seated in the centre in plain-clothes wearing a bowler hat. He is flanked either side by Chief Inspectors Smith and Cavell.

In 1892 the Dockyard Superintendent had been replaced

Senior officers and men of Chatham Dockyard in 1896

by William Wakeford, however by 1897 Superintendent G. Hornsby was in charge and Chief Inspector W. Smith his deputy.[3768] Chief Inspector Smith had been a Dockyard Inspector at Portsmouth Dockyard, and successfully passed a stiff examination for the post in 1893.[3769] He was later promoted to Dockyard Superintendent on Hornsby's retirement in 1910. Smith was assisted by Chief Inspector Cross, Sub-Divisional Inspector R. Hayter and Inspectors T. Bamber, C Bryant, J Green and J. Judge. Sergeant Charles Stubbington retired from the Police at Chatham Dockyard, having completed 26 years' service. On behalf of the officers and men of Chatham Dockyard Division, Superintendent Godfey presented the Sergeant with a beautiful clock to mark his retirement.[3770]

In 1899 the respected Chief Inspector William Kemp, stationed at Chatham Dockyard, retired with 28 years' service, his last three years having been spent there. Such was the esteem with which this officer was held that his retirement was published in the *Police Review and Parade Gossip*. The comments about him were positive and complementary, including his having remained for all of his service on Division but never having been a Dockyard Officer. Kemp

Chief Inspector William Kemp in 1899

had attained 25 years' service and was expected to retire, but he wanted to stay so he had been transferred to a less favourable and possibly quieter posting out of London to a Dockyard Division.[3771]

In 1895 a rather strange event occurred referring to voting principles by Police in the Dockyard Division at Chatham. The Liberals had protested on the grounds that for single police officers who resided in cubicles in the Section House, it did not constitute a residence of separate occupation. This meant that these officers were struck off the voters register and therefore could not vote in General Elections.[3772]

In 1917 the Superintendent had another unpleasant task to perform; the investigation into the death of a Dockyard Constable on duty. During a rather stormy night duty Constable Michael Donovan, whilst on patrol, fell into the dock and drowned.[3773] An investigation tried to establish

3761 *Metropolitan Police Orders* dated 31st January 1868.
3762 *Commissioners' Annual Report* 1870 p14.
3763 *Commissioners' Annual Report* 1874 p99.
3764 *Police Review and Parade Gossip*, 15th September 1911 p438.
3765 Metropolitan Police Orders dated 23rd November 1869.
3766 National Police Roll of Honour (www.policememorial.org.uk) accessed 12th March 2002.
3767 Ibid.
3768 Salter, A.R. (1983) 'The Protection of Chatham Dockyard throughout the Ages'. Gillingham Local History Series No. 12. Kent County Library.
3769 *Police Review and Parade Gossip*, 20th November 1893.
3770 *Police Review and Parade Gossip*, 11th December 1893.
3771 *Police Review and Parade Gossip*, 4th August 1899.
3772 *Police Review and Parade Gossip*, 11th October 1895.
3773 National Police Roll of Honour (www.policememorial.org.uk) accessed 12th March 2002.

whether this tragic event was an accident or not, but there appears to have been insufficient evidence to justify a full-scale murder investigation.

By 1924 Chatham had 164 police officers, with Superintendent C. Sly in charge.[3774] On 26th January 1932 instructions were issued for the removal of the Metropolitan Police contingent with effect from 1st February 1932.[3775] Chief Inspector Kane and Inspector Harold Nightingale led their men, including two station sergeants, 22 sergeants and 49 constables, from the dockyard, their places being taken by the Marine Police. Some of the dockyard officers such as Chief Inspector Kane were transferred to other dockyard duties at Devonport and Portsmouth.

The 600-acre Chatham Naval Dockyard site was eventually closed in March 1984.[3776]

Pembroke Dockyard or 5th Division

Pembroke Dockyard became the responsibility of the Metropolitan Police in December 1860, where they remained until 1926. Initially Inspector Thompson was transferred from K Division to take up the position as Acting Superintendent, together with 10 constables who were taken from a variety of divisions, on 15th December 1860. To supplement the strength, later in the month two inspectors and four sergeants, all on promotion, were transferred two weeks later.

This was by far the smallest dockyard and operationally this was an Inspector-designated station, although in reality a chief inspector was in charge. In addition to the chief inspector there was one other inspector who acted as deputy, three sergeants and 21 constables. Inspector Alexander Thomson, who had considerable experience of dockyard duty, had been transferred as Acting Superintendent from K Division in January 1861 by the following year had been and placed in charge of the dockyard. In the meantime Thomson had been promoted to Superintendent[3777] and remained in command until replaced by Superintendent William Wakeford succeeded him in 1865. Wakeford was himself replaced by Superintendent Archibald Macdonald in 1867. Macdonald lasted two years when he transferred to Portsmouth in 1869 and Pembroke Dockyard supervision reverted to chief inspector level, probably to save money. His deputy was Inspector Daniel Collins,[3778] who was promoted to Chief Inspector in 1869. His deputy was Inspector George Harding.

The overall police responsibility was for Pembroke Dockyard, Hobbs Point.[3779] It was recognised by senior officers at the dockyard that there was a significant amount of property belonging to the Admiralty that was being stolen, so Superintendent Alexander Thompson encouraged his officers to stop and search workers leaving the premises. Rewards were recommended for good police work.

One of the exceptional police officers at Pembroke at the time was PC 18 Ventham, who would later become one of the dockyard's most famous senior officers. Ventham had learnt all the duties, including the art of a Dockyard Constable, and worked hard at it. He became a respected constable because he was able to apprehend offenders and confiscate stolen property. He was often recognised by the Commissioner, and in December 1862 rewarded with 10 shillings for his diligence.[3780] The following month another good piece of police work at the docks was rewarded by Superintendent Thompson, when he recommended a reward to four of his Constables. PC 9 Goddard, PC 20 Tunbridge, PC 14 Thomas and PC 27 Emerson were each presented with 5 shillings.[3781]

The constables and sergeants were paid in accordance with the class they were in. There were four classes of constable, 1st to 4th Class, and their pay was 25s per week for 1st Class, 23s for 2nd, 21s for 3rd and 19s for 4th. Only 1st Class constables were on Water Police duties; detectives in the dockyards were paid 30s per week.[3782] There were no 4th Class constables, because becoming a Dockyard Constable would mean an automatic advance in class. This was an incentive which attracted constables to the dockyards.

The postcard above shows workers leaving to go home after a day's work at the Pembroke Dock.

So keen was the Commissioner to encourage constables and others to move to the dockyard he offered incentives such as double pay for nine days, which attracted PCs Bonbery and Edwards of R Division, who transferred to Pembroke in 1860.[3783] So desperate was the Commissioner that he asked for a constable from each division except R to present himself at Scotland Yard with reports of who was willing to transfer.[3784]

Police Orders showed that Sergeants Wakeford of A Division and Collins, R Division, (both later Superintendents) who were transferred at the same time did not receive the extra pay, but they were promoted to Inspector later in December as their reward.[3785] Both these officers became senior officers within the dockyards, and remained there for the duration of their service.

In 1864 Inspector Wakeford was placed in charge of the dockyard during Superintendent Thomson's absence through ill-health. Once Thomson returned from his period of sickness he was transferred back to Woolwich to take charge there, on the retirement Superintendent Kingston Mark.[3786] Wakeford retained supervision of Pembroke on his promotion to Superintendent, and had to move from his police premises into the more prestigious Superintendent's accommodation vacated by Thomson and his family.

Police pay was a weekly responsibility of those in charge of dockyards. Estimates of pay, returns and pay sheets had to be prepared the previous week and sent to the Executive Officer (usually an Inspector but later a Superintendent) at Scotland Yard for checking and ratification. These would be agreed and Superintendents would personally attend the bank in their area and draw monies, which they would carry in a secure case back to the dockyard. Often they would be on horseback and accompanied by another member of the dockyard staff to provide extra security. Once back at the dockyard the Administration Sergeant would ensure that pay packets were prepared and that monies distributed as instructed. A pay parade would take place once per week and police officers (on or off duty) would attend to collect their pay at a certain hour. When they had been paid they had to personally sign their names on the pay list on receipt of their pay. In the early days police officers would receive their pay from a wooden cup, as their pay would all be in coins as there was no paper money available, although later this gave way to pay packets, but in any event the police officers had to individually check that their pay or contents were correct. Any later accusation that their pay was short was viewed very dimly.

Duties at the dockyard included pursuing and apprehending stragglers and deserters from the Navy, and the conveyance of naval prisoners to either the County Prison at Haverfordwest or the Naval Prison at Lewes in Sussex. The Chief Inspector made daily reports to the Captain Superintendent at the dockyard.

In 1871 Pembroke became the centre for an epidemic of smallpox which caused the dockyard senior officer to ensure that all his men were vaccinated against the virus.[3787] A number of fires occurred in the dockyard during the year, and a small fire was discovered in the saw pits of the largest building in the yard in December. The result was that the fire was extinguished within ten minutes, but had it not been discovered for another half an hour the whole building would have been destroyed.[3788] Rewards for preventing crimes and discovering stolen property was a significant and well-publicised fact of working in the dockyards. Recommendation for a reward was made at the discretion of the Superintendent once a report had been made to him. Inspector Crook and Sergeant Ingar were rewarded with 10 shillings each for preventing the theft of government property from the dockyard in 1864.[3789]

Police officers in dockyards had to acquaint themselves from time to time with the names and faces of senior commissioned officers of the army and navy and senior dockyard officers, and salute them whenever they were in port and wearing their swords.[3790]

Senior officers from Scotland Yard would pay periodic visits for inspection purposes. In September 1893 the Assistant Commissioner, A.C. Howard, inspected the Police stationed at Pembroke Dockyard and was pleased to see the constables put through their paces on the drill square by Inspector Young.[3791] The dockyard now had 33 police officers stationed there, with Chief Inspector Kane was in charge.[3792]

The senior officers at Pembroke are above proudly displaying the new fire engine which they had taken delivery of in 1924. Notice that the engines were no longer horse-drawn, but had a steam engine. They were now fully mechanical and had large water pipes powered by the engine so that sufficient water could be played on to a fire.

The picture at the top of the following column shows Constable William Shepherd (warrant no. 100865), who joined the Metropolitan Police in June of 1911 as PC 865N. He transferred to the 5th Division at Pembroke as PC 53 Dockyard (Water Police) in July 1914 just as the war was beginning. He was transferred to Chatham Docks in April 1915, and by 1919 he was moved as PC 214 at C Division, then as PC 122TA (Thames Division) in September 1924. He was pensioned from C Division as 355C in May 1935.

The Water Police wore different jackets to their land-based colleagues, which kept them warm and were mostly waterproofed. The constable's number was shown on the collar, and also showed the fouled anchor and crown denoting dockyard service. The flat cap was also a feature of the Water Police, and had a chin strap which could help keep it from blowing away in windy weather.

Constable William Shepherd photographed in 1914

In 1926 Inspector (89805) John Kane was transferred from Pembroke to Chatham. He had supervised the handover of responsibilities to the Marine Police and clearly done a good job in the eyes of his supervisors. Some 15 constables, six sergeants and the CID Officer were all transferred out at the same time. Later, as the Chief Inspector Kane was also to supervise the transfer of the Police from Chatham and later Devonport.

Rosyth Dockyard

The Government decided to build another Royal Dockyard as part of the War effort, and the authorities asked for the Metropolitan Police to continue its function and guard this dockyard in Scotland as part of their duties; they took control from 1914 until 1926. Their duties required policing both the Royal Rosyth Dockyard and the naval base. The Met were also responsible for Invergordon Dockyard.

3774 *The Policeman's Pocket Almanac and Diary* 1924.
3775 Metropolitan Police Orders dated 26th January 1932.
3776 Salter, A.R. (1983) 'The Protection of Chatham Dockyard throughout the Ages'. Gillingham Local History Series No. 12. Kent County Library.
3777 Metropolitan Police Orders dated 10th June 1869.
3778 *Kirchner's Almanac* 1907.
3779 Metropolitan Police Orders dated 10th November 1862.
3780 Metropolitan Police Orders dated 11th December 1862.
3781 Metropolitan Police Orders dated 1st August 1868.
3782 Metropolitan Police Orders dated 27th December 1860.
3783 Metropolitan Police Orders dated 8th December 1860.
3784 Metropolitan Police Orders dated 11th December 1860.
3785 Metropolitan Police Orders dated 3rd May 1864.
3786 Wynne, H. (1998) 'Extracts taken from the Metropolitan Police Orders 1873 (Dockyard Divisions)'. Friends of the Ministry of Defence Museum.
3787 *Commissioner's Annual Report* 1871.
3788 Ibid.
3789 Metropolitan Police Orders dated 12th October 1864.
3790 Metropolitan Police General Orders and Regulation 1873.
3791 *Police Review and Parade Gossip*, 9th October 1893.
3792 *The Policeman's Pocket Almanac and Diary* 1924.

The combined police of the Rosyth dockyard in 1918 with Superintendent Keys seated centre with flat hat

Chosen for its ideal docking facilities, Rosyth was not only designed to withstand attack but was positioned much closer to essential facilities such as the iron foundries and coal fields of the north. It was situated 16 miles inland from the mouth of the Firth of Forth and out of reach of most modern artillery, and was completed in March 1916.

The 1918 picture above shows Rosyth Dockyard Police with a mixture of Land Police (with helmets) and Water Police (with flat caps), and includes Superintendent Keys who is wearing his flat hat and sitting in the centre of the second row from the front.

Chief Inspector Charles Sly was initially placed in charge of the dockyard whilst a search was made for a suitable Superintendent to take overall control. Sub-Divisional Inspector James Keith was posted there together with Inspectors Henry Urban, John Wannop and John Sutherland. In 1915 the Officer in Charge was Albert Keys, who had been a Chief Inspector at Devonport before he was transferred on promotion to Rosyth.

Apart from duties on land, Rosyth also had a Water Police who patrolled in launches to detect crime and recover stolen Government stores.

Police fatalities were fairly commonplace in Dockyard Divisions, as they were dangerous places especially when dockyard personnel, visitors and police officers themselves may not have taken proper care. In 1916 Rosyth Dockyard Constable 100867 Herbert Archer, who had been on duty for seven hours, was awarded the King's Police Medal for rescuing a boy who could not swim from a caisson chamber at 5.20am on a very cold March morning. The boy had fallen into the dock some 40 feet below and Archer, having removed his helmet and outer clothing, jumped in. It was still dark but he found the boy after hearing splashing nearby. A rope was lowered and the Constable, holding the boy, was pulled up. However, the person pulling in the rope had to let go because of the weight and they plunged back into the icy water. The Constable, still holding of the boy, swam to the end of the caisson where they were helped out of the dock without further incident. Archer also received an award from the Carnegie Hero Trust Fund and the Royal Humane Society Medal and Certificate.[3793]

Other dangers existed, and in 1917 Constable Lawrence James Quibell was killed in a road traffic accident whilst on a training exercise with the fire brigade.[3794] By 1924 the complement of Police stood at 91 constables, with Chief Inspector R. Gadd in charge.[3795]

The Metropolitan Police dockyard contingent left Rosyth on 1st October 1926. Both Inspector (84294) Robert Allen and Inspector (92415) Thomas Pearce were returned to London Divisions, along with 51 constables, eight sergeants and one station sergeant.[3796]

3793 HO45/10954/306338.
3794 National Police Roll of Honour (www.policememorial.org.uk) accessed 12th March 2002.
3795 The Policeman's Pocket Almanac and Diary 1924.
3796 Metropolitan Police Orders dated 24th September 1926.

Chapter 7.
Police Uniforms, Badges and Equipment

In this chapter we deal generally with police uniforms, headgear and accoutrements for male and female police officers. We recognise that at the same time many subjects covered, such as tipstaves, whistles, buttons caps and helmets deserve individual books in their own right.

Over the course of time there have been many experiments carried out to find suitable garments for police officers which would stand the test of time in all types of weather. In the beginning, the only real precedent was the army and many commissioners turned to military outfitters to fulfil their requirements.

Police Orders issued to stations would inform the officers and men regarding changes of uniform including equipment, helmets, plates and so forth. Because there were no illustrations included in the published orders, much of what we know now has to be gleaned not only from the detail of these instructions, but also from rare photographs taken at the time. Other documentation, for example from the Home Office, also exists, from which we can draw useful information. In the end much is open to debate and interpretation. For example, there is a commonly-held misconception that the second helmet plate, issued between 1870 and 1875[3797] with the laurel wreath removed, was only issued to dockyards and not to divisions. The evidence, taken from old dated photographs, although contested and presented below, tends to dismiss this claim. Research into uniforms cannot be exhaustive, as new information from archives on this subject is surfacing online regularly.

1829-1864

On Tuesday 29th September 1829 at 6.00am the first Metropolitan Police officers took to the streets, clothed in a uniform based very much on the civilian attire of the period. Initially, Home Secretary Sir Robert Peel favoured a military-style jacket of red like those of the Horse Patrol, but it was eventually decided that a non-military style of uniform should be provided and the first men were fitted in the grounds of the Foundling Hospital in Bloomsbury.

A clothing return from 1830 established what should be worn and when it would be replaced. This instruction was for sergeants and constables only and consisted of

'1 greatcoat, 1 cape, 1 badge, 1 coat, 2 pairs of trousers, 2 pairs of boots, 1 hat cover, 1 stock [neckware], 1 embroidered collar, 1 number to hat cover, 1 button brush and stick. The coat, trousers, boots and hat were to be changed every second year. The pay was stated to be £1 2s 6d per week for a Sergeant and 19/- for a Constable.'[3798]

Before the formation of the Metropolitan Police, police (watchmen) buttons were made of pewter. By the mid-19th Century nickel buttons were introduced. This was followed by brass with the front dipped in chrome, known as dipped silver.

A pre-1844 Metropolitan Police button with oak leaves and crown

Some buttons were made of chrome on nickel silver, but this proved too costly.

Although the first police officers were issued with a uniform which was meant to be more civilian than military, the military influence regarding the helmet prevailed.

The tunic issued in 1844 featured eight gilt buttons with a crown and the words 'POLICE FORCE' in the centre, on a dark blue swallowtail coat. Inside the coat tail was a pocket for the rattle and truncheon. To guard against being strangled, a four-inch leather stock was worn inside the stand collar. The trousers and coat were of blue felt cloth. The trousers were so thick that it was said they could stand up on their own accord. The greatcoat was also of dark blue cloth, double-breasted with stand-up collar and detachable cloth cape.[3799]

The stovepipe top hat was six and three-quarter-inches tall, with a two-inch wide brim. Black three-quarter-inch braid was stitched around the base with a knot worn over the left ear. The top hat was seven inches wide and seven-and-a-half inches front to back. The brim was two inches wide, and was piped in black braid. Hat covers were issued for use in bad weather. The top consisted of black leather which had a half-inch overlap onto black beaver skin.[3800] The inside was reinforced with cane side stays to protect the wearer from head injuries.

Metropolitan Police constable c1860s

3797 Even this second plate is open to debate, since there is evidence to suggest that the coxcomb helmet was fitted with a Maltese Cross badge at some stage.
3798 *The Standard*, 16th August 1830.
3799 Taylor, M.B. and Wilkinson, V. (1989) *Badges of Office*. Hazel and Co. Henley on Thames.
3800 Ibid.

Following complaints from the public that it was impossible to tell whether a policeman was on or off duty, a duty armlet was issued in 1830. This was two inches wide, with eight horizontal blue-and-white alternating stripes and was to be worn on the left arm above the cuff.

In the picture right the constable is wearing the new white metal divisional numbers and single divisional letter, which indicates that this was a later photograph taken around the early 1860s.

Almost immediately the officers and men were unhappy at the inferior quality of the garments, which they said were sold to them at exorbitant prices. These concerns were immediately raised with the Commissioners, because each man was required to pay for his own clothing. His dress coat cost £1 7s 6d, greatcoat £1 15s, trousers 12s 9d, hat 12s and boots 12s. Payment for his entire uniform was thus £4 19s 3d, for which two shillings (10p) per week was deducted from his wages,[3801] making it nearly one year before the monies due had been paid.

As a matter of urgency the Commissioners examined the clothing which was supplied, and they were determined to placate their own men's concerns. They set about to alter the arrangements about uniforms, and instructions were given to the clothing contractors, Charles Hebbert military clothiers of 8 Pall Mall East, Westminster, to supply them with new and better quality clothing forthwith.

Founded in 1815, the firm was originally known as Hebbert & Hume of Leicester Square, London and from 1826 had moved to Pall Mall. From 1830 the company was known as Charles Hebbert, and then in 1852 Charles Hebbert & Co. In 1843 they were described as 'Army clothiers', and by 1863 'Army clothiers, cap & accoutrement maker',[3802] although by this time Hebbert had lost the Metropolitan Police contract. Hebbert was a very enterprising man,[3803] who outwitted his competitors by offering the police a made-to-measure service and even set up a store to accept the return of uniforms from men who had resigned. This enterprise involved Hebbert in losses at first, but eventually provided a very lucrative business.[3804]

The replacement of defective clothing was undertaken before Christmas 1830. These instructions to Hebbert and Co. included that:

'The private men are to have cloth of a better quality, the Serjeants are to wear the same description of costume as at present worn by Inspectors, the Inspectors are to wear a pattern the Superintendents now possess, the Superintendents' clothes are to be decorated with the acorn and laurel leaf embroidered insilver on the collar, and the collar and cuffs are to be edged with a narrow silver lace; all to wear chin straps to their hats, 'a la militaire', The inscription upon the button is to be altered; instead of 'Police Force' it is to be 'Metropolitan Police'. The total number of men now in the service amounts to 3,540, and about Christmas two more divisions are to be added.' [3805]

After 1841 the hats of superintendents and inspectors were made one inch taller for constables and sergeants. A tunic was issued to superintendents in 1843, and an example of their button is shown at the top of the following column.

In the 1850s constables began altering their top hats in a number of ways. Some filled the hat with old clothing or newspaper, because in their experience the hat offered little protection when attempting to quell a riot or demonstration. Others altered their hats by cutting the brims, or even resorting to wearing their own private, better quality top hats. Instructions were issued forbidding the altering of any

Victorian button issued for inspectors and above

hats, and the wearing of non-issue hats with leather tops was also forbidden. As can be seen from the photograph on the previous page, the hat was stitched down the side and officers were reminded to wear the hat straight so that this stitching, together with the knot, was over the left ear. It was popular fashion at the time with men wearing top hats to tilt them slightly, hence the commissioner's instructions. The top hat also was fitted with a wide chin strap, although none survive today with it still attached.

In 1838 constables, sergeants and inspectors were permitted to wear suitable tunic belts. These were 2½ inches wide with a brass buckle. Belts had been originally issued for use with a great coat so as to carry a lantern, however not with a tunic. The Victorian button shown right was introduced in 1830, and shows the Metropolitan Police within a garter belt.

Victorian Metropolitan Police silvered button

Senior officers wore braided tunics which did not require crested (eg raised) buttons. It is clear that in some forces they adopted black buttons for their jackets as a distinction from the lower ranks. The most common use of black buttons was on greatcoats and raincoats.[3806] In 1843 superintendents' tunics were made single-breasted, with a hook-and-eye front that had a stand collar. There were no shoulder straps, although later uniforms showed a twisted braid on each shoulder. The front was edged with two rows of plain black braid and the cuffs, were embellished with the Austrian knot.[3807]

Many officers, sergeants, inspectors and superintendents needed to patrol their divisions on horseback, although no special riding clothes were provided until 1839 when the mounted branch was formed.

In 1853 sergeants were issued with armlets with two narrow blue lines which were to be worn on the right arm.

Greatcoats were issued to all police officers. They were dark blue, double-breasted frock coat pattern with straight fronts and a stand-up collar. Down either side of the front were four black Victorian Crown buttons. There was also one small Victorian Crown button underneath each side of the collar, so as to attach the cape. Instructions were given in 1853 that the coats were to be buttoned uniformly on one side and sides changed once a month.

The badge of office for constables which was worn on the coat collar consisted of a white embroidered crow's toe containing the divisional letter and number. These were later replaced with metal numbers and a letter.

In 1859 the uncomfortable stock collar was reduced to two inches. During the summer (and until 1861), white trousers were worn, but they were not standard issue and were purchased by the police officers at their own expense. Sergeants were distinguished through the numbers on their collars from one to sixteen, and the fact they wore the duty armlet on their right cuff. Duty armlets were withdrawn on 1st July 1968.

A pre-1863 constable's tunic

Changes to the old uniform began at the end of 1863 and the new issues were not completed until 1865, meaning that some officers were wearing both types of clothing whilst others had completely new uniforms.

1864-1870

Police officers were obliged to wear their uniform at all times and were even, on occasions, required to sleep in them during an emergency. The top hat was heavy, uncomfortable and cumbersome. It afforded no ventilation, a factor made worse in hotter weather.

Superintendents, inspectors and sergeants could not easily be distinguished from constables. Those officers, many of whom were from military backgrounds, soon became conscious of their ranks and pressed for their uniforms to be distinguished from more junior officers.[3808] A cox-comb helmet modelled on the German (Prussian) military 'pickelhaube', and standard issue for the British army, replaced the by-now unserviceable top hat in 1864. The military-style helmet described by *Punch* as an 'upturned escutcheon urn' was introduced, probably because many of the senior officers were ex-military and the Army and various militias had copied the Prussian helmet in 1854. The helmet, with its ventilation tab at the front, allowed cooler air to circulate inside, making it more comfortable to wear. The cox-comb helmet was issued only to constables, sergeants and inspectors. These were made of dark blue pressed felt. They had an overall length of eleven-and-a-half inches and a height of eight inches, with the width surmounted by a comb. The brim was two inches wide front and back, which was slightly turned down. A three-quarter inch black leather band was fitted around the base. There was a similar but wider band inside the helmet for the head to rest against. Weighing eleven-and-a-half ounces, it was fitted with a black leather chin strap two-and-a-half inches wide, which was worn to the point of the chin.[3809]

The 1864 wreath-type helmet plate

The 1864 helmet[3810] plate (shown left) consisted of a laurel wreath-type in japanned black, bearing a Victoria crown and garter ribbon. The ribbon contained the words 'METROPOLITAN POLICE' in raised letters, and a square buckle. The centre was made of black leather. Constables' and sergeants' helmet plates bore the divisional letter above the number, which was fastened through the black leather centre. In the case of inspectors, a much larger divisional letter was shown.

Introduced first into the dockyards, the distribution was phased into the London land divisions gradually from 1st February 1865. Inspectors and superintendents wore the same helmet plate, except that it was silvered. The dockyard was recognised by its 'fouled anchor', which was worn in the centre of the plate by inspectors and superintendents, whilst their divisional 'town' colleagues had a large divisional letter instead.

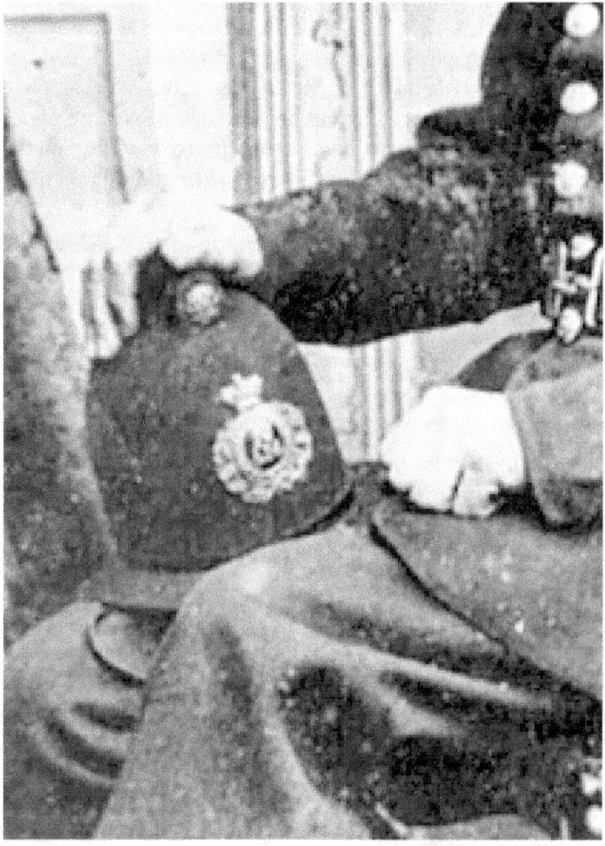

The new helmet introduced from 1864

Superintendents and inspectors were each issued with a kepi. This was the standard pill-box type, with ventilation holes on both sides. The peak was made of patent leather. The superintendents wore an embroidered button surrounded by black scroll embroidery on the crown of the kepi. An

3801 *The Standard*, 30th August 1830.
3802 Burt, D. (2008) Hebbert and Co. information at www.authentic-campaigner.com/forum/showthread.php?14899-24-October-1864-Invoice-from-Hebbert-%28sic%29-Pall-Mall-East&s=0c9c50605555 63c5a2994b2ae34b4254 accessed 24th July 2013.
3803 Hebbert also supplied military clothing and equipment to the Confederate forces together with Tait and Co.
3804 Howard, G. (1953) *Guardians of the Queen's Peace*. Oldmans, London. p129.
3805 Ibid.
3806 Ripley, H. (1983) *Police Buttons*. R. Hazell & Co.
3807 Fairfax, N. and Wilkinson, V.L. (undated) 'History of Metropolitan Police Uniforms and Equipment'. Vol. 2. p24.
3808 Ibid, p23.
3809 Ibid.
3810 There is an image of this helmet in Appendix 1 of *The Official Encyclopedia of Scotland Yard*.

The black Victorian button with garter

embroidered black oak-leaf braid was fitted around the kepi, with the peak being kept horizontal. Inspectors wore something similar with a knitted button to the crown, plus a band made of embroidered black braid around with a peak at a 45 degree angle. Initially there was no badge to the front, but later a knitted crown was added.

In 1864 acting sergeants were also introduced, and together with sergeants were given a distinctive badge of office. For sergeants this was a three-bar silver lace (Russia Braid) chevron, whilst acting sergeants had a two-bar silver lace chevron, both to be worn on the upper arm. Worsted chevrons were worn on greatcoats; although the chevrons were initially worn on the upper right arm, within a few months they were worn on both arms.

Truncheons for inspectors, sergeants and constables were carried in a leather case which consisted of a black leather tube sewn with a single seam. These were convex shaped with a bucket-style bottom to accommodate the rounded end of the truncheon. There was a loop strap for attachment to the belt, and a clip-down leather lid with a spring inside the tube.[3811] These were withdrawn in 1887 when a truncheon pocket was fitted in the trouser leg.

A double-breasted greatcoat with a stand-up collar and blunted ends was issued to all ranks in 1864. This was made of dark blue cloth, and buttoned both sides. There were five composition black buttons on either side in parallel rows, and the rear of the coat had two pleats sewn in.

An instruction was given in 1860 regarding the issue of leather belts to constables and sergeants. Recommendations on a police-issued leather belt to help carry a police cape were made by the Commissioners, stating that these could be supplied by Messrs. Bramston and Co. of Kings Cross at a cost of 2/6d.[3812] A double thickness belt was issued for the first time in 1864 to inspectors, sergeants and constables for wear with a tunic. This was made of leather with a snake-clasp, although belts had been issued for use with a greatcoat as far back as 1847. This belt lasted until 1973.

Tunics were of dark blue cloth for inspectors to constables, similar to the old swallowtail, except that the tail was shortened and the front lengthened to correspond. There were eight metal buttons to the front, and to the rear one button over each of the two slits. Instructions were issued in 1864 that armlets issued to sergeants should be worn on the left arm. Inspectors were instructed to have a small piece of silver lace on the collar, while constables and sergeants wore white metal numerals and letter(s) on each collar replacing the crow's toes with embroidered numerals and divisional letter.

The suppliers of uniform and equipment to the Metropolitan Police in 1864 were R.T. Tait and Co. of 10 Essex Street, Strand, and they had been the contractors since 1859.[3813] The advertising picture from Taits from the same year shown below depicts a constable wearing a cox-comb helmet with wide brim front and back, together with a Maltese Cross helmet plate badge.[3814] He is wearing an eight-button jacket with a snake-buckle belt, from which hangs a truncheon case. This obviously was a preliminary design by Taits, as it is uncertain whether a Maltese cross plate was ever issued by them for use by the police.[3815]

In the same year an instruction was issued regarding chin straps on helmets which stated that they should be worn at all times, and that the strap should not be worn beneath the under lip, but on the extreme point of the chin. It was also not to be worn in the crown of the helmet.

Swords were also worn by some police officers, but usually these were originally the horse patrol and later the mounted police. Suppliers of swords, rattles and truncheons were often military suppliers first, and these included Charles Hebbert of Pall Mall, William Mills of 120 High Holborn, R.S. Garden of 29 Piccadilly and William Parker, founded in 1790 based at 233 Holborn (this business was taken over by the son-in-law in 1886 when 'Field' was added to the company name.

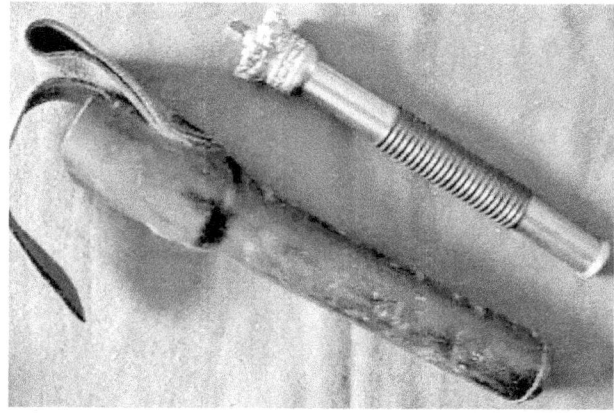

Victorian Tipstaff and belt holder

Taits advertising with Maltese crown plate

The picture above show a Victorian gilded brass tipstaff with a pouch or holster, sometimes also referred to as a frog. The holster has a loop where it is threaded onto the officer's/official's belt.

The tipstaff was the badge or insignia of office of a customs official, police officer, magistrate or other official working on behalf of the Crown. It represented the ancient symbol of authority under the Crown. For police, these were carried before the days of warrant cards,

Chief Inspector with tipstaff in the 1880s

which eventually replaced them.

The expression "I'll crown you" is derived from arrests made by police officers in plain-clothes or on detective duties, who on production of the tipstaff would say "I crown you" to validate an arrest. The tipstaff was made of hollow gilded brass, with an unscrewable gilded brass crown finial. To enable it to be held in the hand, an ebony (or even perhaps lignum vitae) grip was fixed to the tubular shank. The item shown is dated to around the 1860s, and was made by Tait & Co, Southwark Street in London. The company ceased trading in 1870 when it became insolvent. The tipstaff measures 18.5 centimetres long and weighs 159.8 grams, and fits into the pouch or holster which is spring-loaded to enable it to be quickly drawn to show proof of office. Originally issued to the Bow Street Runners, superintendents and inspectors purchased their own tipstaffs until 1867, when they became part of the official uniform. Parish Constables did have tipstaves, but after 1829 constables of the New Police did not. Tipstaves were withdrawn in 1887. Even today tipstaves are represented on the badges of office for Chief Officers, which consist of crossed tipstaves within a laurel wreath.

First mentioned in 1845, an experiment to trial whistles for police use was abandoned and only in 1869 was the naval flute pattern whistle introduced into dockyards. In 1873 Thames Division adopted the whistle. In 1884 whistles were introduced for outer divisions during the daytime, although rattles remained in use for night duty until 1886 when they were withdrawn. Matters remained the same until recently, when whistles have been withdrawn completely.

Early police buttons issued during the mid-19th century were originally made of pewter. These were replaced by brass versions which had the front dipped in chrome, known as 'dipped silver'. Some other buttons were produced made in chrome on nickel silver, but these proved costly and were abandoned. This chrome King's Crown button right has the garter belt and buckle removed in favour of two concentric circles, within which 'METROPOLITAN POLICE' is displayed. This denotes that this button is pre 1953, but post 1935.

Chrome button with King's crown produced between 1935 and 1953

1870-c1880

In 1870 the helmet was again remodelled, to a design which is recognisable today, and the cox-comb was discarded. Companies such as J.R. Gaunt of Birmingham (who made military headgear) were asked to present designs for police helmets and their plates. Their instructions included helmet plates for constables and sergeants, with inspectors and superintendents afforded a different plate entirely.

Gaunt's designs, taken from their pattern book, show that their original artwork was accepted with some modifications. The 'VR' (Victoria Regina) cypher – or more correctly the Guelphic crown – shown in the centre was removed in favour of the divisional letter and number. Gaunt's originally suggested a (Brunswick) star pattern of white plate, again with 'VR' cypher and filled-in Victoria crown for inspectors and sergeants, but this pattern was rejected for inspectors and issued instead to superintendents in 1875. Instead of

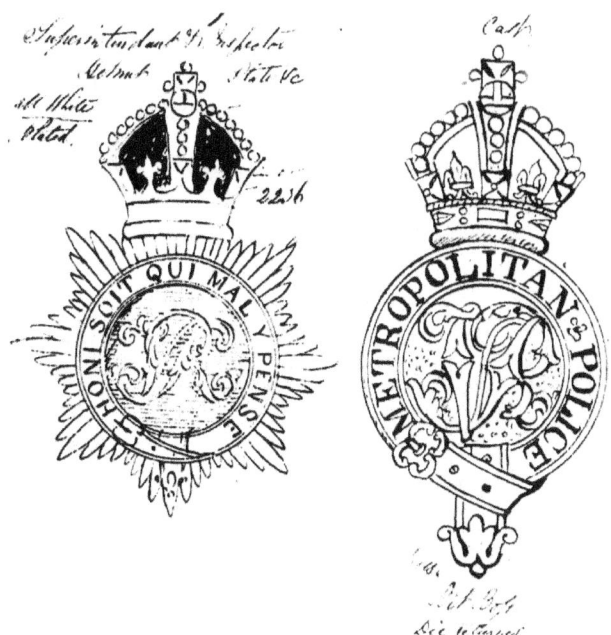

Left: Tait's original drawing for the senior officers helmet plate
Right: Tait's design for the constable's and sergeant's helmet plate

'METROPOLITAN POLICE' written in the garter the French 'HONI SOIT QUI MALY PENSE' is shown, which literally means 'shamed be he who thinks evil of it' and is the motto of the English chivalric Order of the Garter.[3816] This design of helmet plate for superintendents continued for many years.

The cox-comb helmet was withdrawn in 1870 and replaced with a more conical six panel helmet without comb (although the number of panels is subject to speculation; see below). The crown of the new helmet was strengthened by inserting twelve overlapping segments of cork, which were glued into place. There were six panels of blue cloth with raised seams, with two attached to each panel. The peak and brim were lowered, with the back enlarged to prevent rainwater dripping down the neck. The rim was finished in black patent leather trim. The crown was affixed with a metal

Constable 465 Y with new helmet and plate circa 1870

3811 Ibid p31.
3812 Metropolitan Police Orders dated 12th June 1860.
3813 *The Police and Constabulary Almanac* 1864.
3814 Whilst it is uncertain whether this plate was issued generally, a picture exists of a mounted Metropolitan Police officer wearing one.
3815 Metropolitan Police Orders dated 5th July 1864.
3816 en.wikipedia.org/wiki/Honi_soit_qui_mal_y_pense accessed 17th August 2013.

rose on the top of the ventilation holes. Two similar holes were made on either side of the helmet near the crown top. An ornamental black leather band three-tenths of an inch deep was pinned around the base. Inside the helmet American cloth and a leather band was fixed, together with a soft felt inner band for comfort.[3817] There were similar holes fitted near the crown to provide additional ventilation.

The helmet plate badge was also changed in 1870, although a further change occurred in 1880/81 when the star pattern plate was introduced.

Left: The 1870 new conical helmet and plate
Right: The new 1870 plate

The laurel wreath on either side of the badge had been removed, and instead of a Victoria crown, which was filled in, a hollowed one in japanned black appeared instead. The number and divisional letter was retained in the helmet plate, although the helmet itself has no discernible panels and appears to be made in at least one or, more probably, two sections. The helmet band masks the joins in the helmet. In the example above what can also be clearly seen is the divisional number and letter 'Y 465' in the centre of the helmet plate.

The plain belt buckle was removed and a more ornate version introduced, as can be seen in Gaunt's designs. Whilst station sergeants (and clerk sergeants) were recognised in 1871, they were not issued with a badge of office until 1875 when four Russia braid (silver lace) chevrons were introduced.

In 1870 the superintendent's uniform tunic of 1843 was amended, and four rows of black cord with drop loops and eyes, knitted buttons and olivets were added across the chest.[3818] At the rear, an Austrian knot was added to the back seams and crow's toes with two knitted buttons were sewn into the skirts. In 1875 two sets of eye braiding were added to the back seam embroidery, with shoulder cords being added in 1906.[3819]

The photograph right shows Superintendent Thomas Butt of P

Superintendent Thomas Butt of P Division with ceremonial helmet

Division, probably taken on promotion, in his fitted dress uniform dated circa 1881. Butt is wearing his duty helmet with plate with chain mail embellishments, riding breeches, riding boots, and sword. The collar of the tunic shows oak leaves either side, together with knotted shoulder cords. The cuffs of the tunic show an upturned 'V' formation which later changed to a more elaborate design, as can be seen from the uniform jacket below.

Superintendent's ceremonial helmet and plate as worn by Butt

Superintendent Smith of Chatham Dockyard

For comparison, the picture on the left shows how uniforms changed. Superintendent William Smith (warrant no. 52797) of Chatham dockyard is shown in a similar jacket, with more embellished forearms. He is also wearing the kepi with obvious 'slashed' peak rather than a helmet. Smith retired in 1910 after 40 years' service.

1880/81–1901/06

In 1880/81 the helmet and plate were modified again, to a shape and design that we would recognise today. In fact this particular plate remained in use until about 1906, even though Queen Victoria had died in 1901. The new headwear comprised six panels and a seven-pointed Brunswick star type badge with Victoria crown, introduced to replace the garter type. Again this was japanned black, and had 'METROPOLITAN POLICE' in raised letters around the circumference within the garter ribbon together with silvered divisional letter and numbers in the centre.

The Brunswick star issued in about 1880 to dockyards

Gaunts also quoted the Metropolitan Police for inspectors and superintendents to have chain mail as helmet furniture, together with a rose top that provided ventilation, but it appears that inspectors wore the 'Prussian' helmet except for ceremonial occasions. This helmet pattern remains the same today.

The 1864 greatcoat was also modified for chief constables

The new Brunswick star for divisional wear

Metropolitan Police helmet plate 1901-1935

to inspectors, to include the latest design called a Lancer front: top buttons which are 2½ inches to the point of the shoulders, and the bottom ones 5 inches apart. The coat had one rear pleat with four small composition buttons.

In 1871 the rank of Chief Inspector was introduced, although it had been used before this date for the CID. In 1886 the uniform for chief constables to superintendents was modified. The collar was edged with a half-inch black braid, with bullet eye embroidery within. The cuffs were made with black braid to a point with one row of eyes and one fan below, together with eight rows of tracing with small crows' toes.

Truncheon cases were withdrawn in 1887, when trousers included a pocket inside of the right trouser leg to place the truncheon out of sight. In the same year a number of senior inspectors were re-designated to the new rank of Sub-Divisional Inspector (SDI).

Armlet loops were sewn into the left sleeve of the jacket in 1895.

In 1897 a five-buttoned blue serge patrol jacket was introduced which had two breast pockets. This jacket was for summer wear, between May and September. In the same year a waist slit for a shoulder belt was added to the tunic. Epaulettes were added to the jacket much later in 1960. In the picture below Thomson, the famous ex-detective who was later promoted to superintendent, is shown in his superintendent's dress uniform, with oak leaf collars and cuffs. The front has crow's feet edging vertically on both sides. He has a stripe down the outside of each leg.

Superintendent James J. Thomson, E Division

1901/06-1935

Following the death of Queen Victoria in 1901 the Edward VII helmet plate was introduced, a slightly smaller plate featuring Imperial crown. Everything else remained the same.

Prior to 1906, embroidered badges of rank for chief constables (silver Victoria crown from 1886) and superintendents (silver Victoria crown from 1875) were worn on collars, but after 1906 they were changed to their epaulettes. In 1901 the crown was altered to an imperial crown, and for superintendents in 1908 an embroidered star was added to the crown.

The Home Office recommendations of 1934 included standardisation of buttons for all English and Welsh police forces. The most obvious effect was that chromium-plated buttons (which do not require polishing) began to be introduced. The report also recommended that forces should adopt a common basic design of button showing the Royal Crown and the title of the force.[3820]

The five-button tunic was replaced by a seven-button version in 1934.[3821] During the 1930s, the Royal College of Heralds informed the Metropolitan Police that its garter ribbon within the star and buttons had not been given proper authorisation to be worn on helmets. This caused some concern at the time, but led to swift and significant changes, not only relating to police headgear. In terms of the helmet plate, one change placed the 'Royal Cypher' of the reigning monarch in the centre of the badge, as shown below.

At the same time the Home Office established a panel of inquiry to standardise the police uniform. In 1935 the pattern of plate changed, because even though the George V plate had been in use for some 34 years the garter was removed. This was replaced by two plain rope-effect circles, which still retained the words 'METROPOLITAN POLICE'. This also afforded an opportunity to remove the divisional letter and numbers from the plate, and transfer them to the collar of the new 'dog collar' style tunic, the jacket being made of a lighter serge material. The cap badge right (top) is for a superintendent, while that below is for inspectors.

*Top: Superintendent's cap badge
Bottom: Inspector's cap badge, both 1935*

3817 Fairfax, N. and Wilkinson, V. L. (undated) *History of Metropolitan Police Uniforms and Equipment* Vol. 2. p33.
3818 Ibid p34.
3819 Ibid p35.
3820 Ripley, H. (1983) *Police Buttons*. R. Hazell & Co.
3821 Metropolitan Police Heritage Collection.

The belt was discarded for this uniform, as the design had a more draped appearance. The five-buttoned summer-wear serge patrol jacket was fixed with metal letters 'MP' on the epaulettes in 1932, although the collar still showed the officer's divisional letter and number on both sides. The jacket was replaced in 1934 with a seven-button version, but it was not until 1937 that all these replacements had been carried out. The

Metropolitan Police War Reserve cap badge

letters 'MP' were stitched down all around, probably from fear of injuring a prisoner during an altercation. The two breast pockets had a three-pointed flap with a central external pleat.

George V Metropolitan Police helmet plate with rope-effect circles

The eight-buttoned tunic was altered in 1934, when two extra buttons were added to the back of the coat and the inverted 'V' on each sleeve was removed leaving plain sleeves.

With the start of the WW2, three types of auxiliaries joined the police family to aid the war effort. These were categorised with titles of Reserves. The 1st Reserve were re-engaged pensioners from all ranks (previously retired Metropolitan Police). The 2nd Reserve were members of the Special Constabulary who volunteered for duty on a full-time basis, although existing members of the MSC could remain on their part-time basis. Lastly, the 3rd Reserve were men recruited for war service only, and they were referred to as War Reserves.

The helmet badge left shows the 'GVR' cypher within the double-circle centre, having had the garter ribbon removed. Such was the pressure to clothe and equip these reserves it soon became clear that no strict adherence to established patterns of distribution could be achieved. Those who were given clothing and equipment, whether or not they were officially entitled to have them, soon exchanged them with others and cooperated in times of need. This often occurred following damage and destruction of clothing after bombing or during rescue work. Helmets and helmet plates were only issued to 1st Reserves, whilst 2nd and 3rd Reserves were supplied with caps and cap badges. The reserve forces were also given patrol jackets, trousers, greatcoats, shoes, gloves and black woollen armlets (to denote they were on war service). In terms of letters and numerals, 1st and 3rd Reserves were supplied with those as for the regular service.

Meanwhile, all officers of the regular force were issued with steel helmets which clearly showed the word 'POLICE' in white at the front, along with badges of office. The 2nd Reserve had the letters 'SC', and the 3rd Reserve 'WR' above the word 'POLICE'.[3822] On 15th October 1940 the Secretary of State deemed it necessary to issue instructions relating to the wearing of steel helmets, which stipulated:

'It has accordingly been decided that the helmets of officers of, and above, the rank of Inspector shall be painted white, with the word POLICE painted in blue in the front, and above, it the appropriate badge of rank. The blue helmets of Sergeant will be marked by two horizontal white bands ½ wide and ½ apart, the lower band commencing at the base of the crown of the helmet and both bands encircling the helmet from the extremities of the word POLICE.' [3823]

A Special Constable's WW2 steel helmet

This instruction confirms that the steel helmet shown above is that of a sergeant in the Special Constabulary, while that below is one for a regular inspector.

Inspector's WW2 steel helmet

Wartime shortages meant that there were sometimes differences in, for example, the weight, colour and make up of certain materials for capes, belts and greatcoats. Each regular and reserve officer was issued with a haversack containing a respirator, and another rucksack containing special protective anti-gas clothing. These included a coat, trousers, galoshes and a hat cover.[3824]

Between 1944 and 1946 wound stripes and War service chevrons were authorised for members of the uniform branch and reserves. Wound stripes were made up of narrow braid one and a half inches long, coloured either gold or red. Gold marked each occasion in the current war when the holder was wounded, while red (one only to be worn) denoted injury to a member of the armed services in earlier wars. Inspectors and above wore their stripe above the inverted 'V' and sleeve embroidery on their respective tunics on their right side, while constables and sergeants wore theirs some six inches above the start of the same side sleeve.[3825]

In 1942 members of the Women's Auxiliary Police Corps (WAPC) were attested, and their wound stripe was worn four inches above the bottom of the right sleeve. Its members were afforded no police powers, but employed to take on clerical and driving duties. When the Corps was disbanded in 1946 many of its members applied to join the regular police force.[3826]

As Critchley asserts:

A Women's Auxiliary Police Corps, instituted in August 1939, for women between the ages of eighteen and fifty five. In the early part of the war the women were allowed to carry out only a restricted range of police duties which typically included the driving and maintenance of motor transport, and clerical, telephone, radio, and canteen work, but many were later attested as constables, so that their duties expanded over the whole range of law enforcement.

Women's Auxiliary Police Corps badge

Edward VIII Helmet plate (mock-up)

War service chevrons were issued for the same period as wound stripes.

1936

With the assent of Edward VIII to the throne in 1936 a new japanned helmet plate, again based on the seven-pointed star, was designed for police wear. The plate appears to have been made in brass before being blackened, and designed to include the raised words 'METROPOLITAN' occupying the top section and 'POLICE' being reversed around the bottom of the double-circle.

Those who had been issued with them needed to return the old 1935 George V helmet plate. It would appear that helmet plates were only issued to A and D Divisions before they were withdrawn. The helmet plate shown left is not authentic, as the badge should be bigger as the cypher overlaps the double-circle which should have had the rope effect.

The same situation occurred with police cap badges, where

Flat cap badge for constables and sergeants

three were designed for use. Firstly for constables and sergeants, secondly for inspectors, and lastly for superintendents. No special helmet plate was issued to officers of inspector and superintendent rank.

The helmet plates were withdrawn when King Edward decided to abdicate from the throne given his wish to marry Mrs Wallis Simpson.

Very few survive in the correct form as the illustration above shows. Instead, the title passed onto his younger brother, George VI. The Metropolitan Police then retained the 'GV' helmet plate badge until stocks of 'GVI' plates became available. The Edward VIII helmet plate is rare and very few have been seen; most are in private hands. The stock held by the Metropolitan Police were disposed of and probably melted down.

The flat cap badge shown below left was produced for superintendents, while the badge on the right was for wear by constables and sergeants.

Flat cap badge for inspectors

George VI helmet plate with cypher in the centre

1938-1954

When George VI came to the throne the helmet plate changed again, although retaining many of the features of previous plates. Again, the seven-pointed star pattern of japanned plate (black) and chromium (silver) plate with 'METROPOLITAN POLICE' around the circumference and King's Crown remained, but the centre which had contained the divisional letter and number was replaced by the George VI Royal cypher. These two helmet plates were of the same size; the black plates were meant for night duty and silver plates for day duty. It was felt that it would be easier to detect and arrest offenders at night with a darkened helmet plate. The plate seems to have not been replaced immediately in some divisions, and it took the authorities nearly a year after the Coronation to design, make and issue it to officers. Whilst the japanned version of the helmet plate was worn by constables and sergeants, a chromium version appears to have been worn by Inspectors and above for ceremonial dress helmet plate use from 1937 until 1954.

3822 Fairfax, N. and Wilkinson, V. L. (undated) *History of Metropolitan Police Uniforms and Equipment.* Vol. 2 p57.
3823 Instructions from the Home Secretary dated 15th October 1940.
3824 Fairfax, N. and Wilkinson, V. L. (undated) *History of Metropolitan Police Uniforms and Equipment.* Vol. 2 p57.
3825 Ibid p58.
3826 www.peoplescollectionwales.co.uk/Item/7743-lapel-badge-womens-auxiliary-police-corps-193#sthash.EIgJNR4D.dpuf accessed 28th July 2013.

Police officers had been issued with two 'dog collar' eight-button tunics, but in September 1948 one was reserved for ceremonial purposes only, being finally withdrawn in March 1973 after 109 years' use by the Metropolitan Police. White gloves were worn with the ceremonial tunic.

In 1949 a further change to the closed-neck, seven-button jacket was authorised when it was replaced by a five-button version with open neck which was to be worn for the first time by constables and sergeants. The entire replacement programme again took several years, finally being completed in 1952. The open-neck jacket with five buttons was worn with a blue shirt, which initially had detachable collars. Black ties were also issued for wear with the shirts. The jacket had two breast pockets that had three-pointed flaps and an external pleat. The serge jacket was also made up for summer wear, using a lightweight serge material. The issue of this jacket saw the removal of 'MP' from the epaulettes which were in use until 1959/60 when a four-pocket version was introduced. Numbers and divisional letter previously worn on each side of the collar were transferred to the epaulettes. In 1950 station sergeants and sergeants were issued with chromium-plated badges of rank for epaulettes of mackintoshes.

Perhaps one of the most famous female police officers was Annie Matthews (1890-1966), who joined the Women Police Service in 1918 and served for 30 years. Annie became a Women's Police Patrol no. 17 (warrant no. 64). In 1920 she was highly commended for her part in working under cover and infiltrating a gang responsible for distributing cocaine in Piccadilly. Her role in the discovery of evidence against the gang was very brave and highly dangerous.

Annie Matthews in Bather uniform

She was described following her retirement in 1950 by colleague Lilian Wyles as 'the perfect police woman', demonstrating 'strength, wisdom and immense charity in a rugged exterior'.

Annie is shown wearing the 'Bather' uniform, named after its originator Elizabeth Bather, which was issued to women police between 1946 and 1960. The new uniform was modelled on the Women Auxiliary Air Force uniform worn during WW2. The four-buttoned open-neck jacket with epaulettes and tie had two small upper (button-down) pockets, and below the belt were two larger pockets. It was accompanied by a tailored skirt and was an altogether smarter uniform. The cumbersome wide-brimmed bowler type helmet gave way to a more army service style with a lighter-weight peaked hat.

The hat shows the George VI cypher cap badge. The picture below contrasts the two styles of women police uniform. More detailed information on women police uniforms can be found in the chapter Women Police.

1952-2013

On the accession of Queen Elizabeth II to the throne, two specific changes took place to the design of the helmet plate. The St. Edward's crown was replaced by the Tudor crown, and the 'EIIR' cypher was introduced. The original plate issued in 1952 was of japanned black and it wasn't until 26th February 1965 that a chromium plate replaced it.

The new EIIR helmet plate issued in chrome in 1965

In the same year of the Queen's accession new badges of rank were issued. Chief Superintendents were issued with a new St. Edward's crown to accompany two stars. Superintendents grade one were also issued with the same crown, until 1959 when a star was added to their badge of rank. Superintendents grade two were issued with the St. Edward's crown from 1953 until 1959. Likewise, station sergeants were issued with the new crown in the same year. Cap badges with the new St. Edward's crown with royal cypher were issued to the ranks of commissioner down to inspectors. New St. Edward's buttons were also issued to the Commissioner down to Deputy Commander. In 1959 the first police reserve was disbanded.

Cape number

A belt was designed to be worn with the new open-neck four-button jacket in 1959, which had had a further two button-down pockets added to the lower part. This was fitted with a cloth belt with a two-pronged white metal buckle. The new jacket had four buttons to the front. Tunic jackets of inspectors and above differed from those of constables and sergeants only in that they had an inverted 'V' with button on each cuff. They also had bellows-style pockets with three pointed flaps rather than 'inpatch' pockets with three pointed

The two styles of uniform: 1920 and 1956

Chrome cape number for a sergeant

flaps.[3827] Shirt sleeve order (SSO) was introduced for the first time in 1960, where all sergeants and constables were allowed to wear SSO for certain duties without jackets during warm weather.

ERII Black resin greatcoat button

In 1968 inspectors and above were issued with a lightweight office jacket for wear whilst performing office duties. These light blue terylene cotton jackets were nicknamed 'ice-cream jackets', and displayed the badge of rank on dark blue epaulettes but these were later removed to either side of the lapels. These single-breasted jackets had three front St. Edward's crown buttons, two open-waist patch pockets and an open left breast pocket. Lightweight jackets were issued for summer wear in 1960.

In the same year open-neck greatcoats and Mackintoshes were issued to constables and sergeants, and the old 'oilskin' cape was replaced by the mackintosh cape. Cloth capes were retained by chief superintendents down to station police sergeants. Lightweight patrol jackets were issued to the ranks of and between chief superintendent and constable in 1960 for summer wear. Until 1960 issued trousers had been self-supporting, meaning that braces could be worn to hold them up, but in 1967 a leather belt was issued. The chromium badges were permitted for wear for bush-type shirts in 1961 and raincoats in 1962. In 1965 Traffic Division officers were issued with 'TD' as part of their shoulder number instead of divisional codes.

The duty armlet worn for about 100 years was discarded in 1968, and later versions of the tunic saw the armlet loops removed. In January 1970 the first British police officer to wear a turban was Kenya-born Special Constable Harbans Singh Jabbal at East Ham. White shirts replaced the original blue style with detachable collars in 1977.

In 1980 a new style tunic with no epaulettes or waist belt was introduced, including two breast pockets each with button and flap that had four silver buttons down front.[3828]

In 1980/81 a new helmet plate (shown right) was designed and issued. The new plate continued use of the seven-pointed star, but adopted the blue circle from the flat cap badge making the surround of the 'EIIR' coloured in blue, off-setting the silver of the surrounding star.

The design of the black resin greatcoat button is shown above. It shows the EIIR crown within a double-circle showing 'METROPOLITAN POLICE'.

The 1980/81 EIIR helmet plate

3827 Fairfax, N. and Wilkinson, V. L. (undated) *History of Metropolitan Police Uniforms and Equipment*. Vol. 2 p64.
3828 Metropolitan Police Orders dated 22nd August 1980.

Chapter 8.
Police Ranks

Since the formation of the Metropolitan Police there have been a number of different titles used for various ranks within the structure. As the size of the Force increased it was necessary to increase the number of supervisors. The Constable rank supports all those ranks above in the hierarchal structure. The history of the rank structure is as follows.

Constables/ Detective Constable

This is the basic rank at the front line of policing within the police service. Before the establishment of the Metropolitan Police in 1829, constables were the local magistrates. Local householders also served for a period of twelve months as the parish constable. In the early days they wore a re-enforced top hat which did not have any badge at all.

In 1829 the divisional numbers were stitched onto the collars, however when the uniforms changed in 1863 the top hat gave way to the 'Prussian helmet' and the plate attached had the divisional letter and number in the centre. The stitched numbers on the collar were replaced also with silvered metal. There were a number of different classes of constable, each being paid extra money as they moved up through the grades. The constable can be recognised by a number and divisional letter (or two letters which show a station designation), which are shown on either shoulder.

Metropolitan Police Constable 1865-1871

Oil skin and cloth capes were introduced for wear by constables and sergeants, and in 1882 a new pattern was issued with a wider skirt and lower neck.

In 1951 an open-neck tunic was introduced that showed the divisional letter and numbers on epaulettes.[3829] However, the ceremonial No. 1 dress uniform tunic was still in existence and showed the identification around the collar. Today a constable wears their divisional numbers and letters on the epaulettes on their shoulders.

Sergeant/ Detective Sergeant (2nd Class)

SERGEANT

The next rank above that of constable is sergeant. It is the first supervisory level in the command structure. This was the only military title adopted in 1829. The badge of rank is that of triple chevrons on the sleeves. They are also known as section sergeants, as they supervised eight to ten constables. The badge of office was changed in 1864 and consisted of three chevrons made of silver lace (Russia braid), together with worsted chevrons for greatcoats. At the start they were worn on the upper right arm only, but after a few months they were worn on both arms. Acting sergeants were introduced in 1864 to cope with the increasingly heavy work load of substantive sergeants. These constables who were considered responsible enough wore a pair of silver lace chevrons, usually on one upper arm.

From 1872 until 1875 there existed the post of schoolmaster sergeant. The post was created due to the high rate of illiteracy in the Force. Whilst today sergeants perform a range of duties within their rank, there have been divisions within the sergeant rank. Sergeants perform Custody Officer Duty when they are attached to charge rooms and Custody Suites. They can also be section sergeants, which requires them to perform duty out on the streets or section of the sub-division. Sergeants can also be attached to the Criminal Investigation Department (CID), but they wear no overt badge of rank because they operate mainly in plain clothes. Their identity and rank can be verified by disclosure of their warrant cards.

The rank of acting sergeants still exists on a temporary basis, and those nominated wear two stripes of the silver lace on each arm or cut-down metal sergeant's stripes for attachment to the epaulette.

Station Sergeant / Detective Sergeant (1st Class)

In 1868, owing to a lack of inspectors at that time, the senior sergeant was known as the station sergeant/clerk sergeant and deputised for the inspectors who were in charge of stations on the Division. When the Chief Inspector rank was created in 1869 on the division, the inspectors became 1st Class and 2nd Class inspectors, and then in 1878 station sergeants became 3rd Class inspectors.

The rank of clerk sergeant was created to be responsible for administrative work on a division and was introduced in 1875. Originally the sergeants added an extra bar to the three chevrons making a four-bar sergeant, however this was phased out in 1921 when a Tudor crown replaced the fourth bar. The

Station Sergeant pre-1921

picture left, dated 1902, shows a sergeant with four bars on each upper arm. The picture below shows the badge of rank post-1921.

From 1890 until 1973 the rank of station sergeant was unique to the Metropolitan Police, and replaced the short-lived rank of sub-inspector. The badge of rank was three chevrons, with a crown above.

Victorian Inspector's helmet plate for G Division 1880-1902

and superintendents' top hats were one inch taller than those worn by constables and sergeants.

By 1868 there were insufficient inspectors, so the rank of station sergeant was created between that of sergeant and inspector. In 1869 inspectors were graded in classes from one to four. In 1878 station sergeants were appointed for a short period of time as 3rd Class inspectors.[3832]

The inspector was responsible for the proper and efficient running of a police station. Inspectors wore the standard service pattern helmet, but instead of a number and division the centre of the plate contained a large divisional letter as shown in the illustration below.

Station Sergeant post-1921

In 1950 a chromium-plated badge of four stripes was allowed on epaulettes for bush type shirts (1961) and raincoats (1962).[3830] The rank was phased out in the 1970s when the last station sergeant retired.

Inspector/Detective Inspector/ Junior Station Inspector/Station Inspector/Sub-Divisional Inspector

INSPECTOR

This rank was introduced in 1829 as the next supervisory level above that of a sergeant.[3831] At that time, the next level above the inspector was the superintendent, who was in charge of the Division. In 1838 inspectors with constables and sergeants were permitted to wear suitable belts that were 2-and-half inch wide, with a brass buckle. In 1841 inspectors had an embroidered double-crow's toe containing the divisional letter sown onto the coat collar. The collar of the inspector's uniform showed silver oak leaves in the 1860s. The most able inspectors were promoted to superintendent, and the best sergeants to inspector. As can be seen from the 1864 picture right, there was very little elaboration on an inspector's uniform to denote the importance of the rank or set it apart from other ranks including that of superintendent. The inspectors'

Victorian Inspector pre-1864

The picture right shows an ordinary uniform inspector with kepi hat (introduced in 1865)[3833] without badge or any indications of rank on the jacket collar, but with medals and ceremonial gloves. The medals are the 1887 Silver Jubilee, the 1897 bar, and the 1901 Coronation medal. It appears that the picture was taken in a station yard outside the parade room.

Kepi hats were withdrawn from wear in 1908. Inspectors had a better standard of uniform than constables and sergeants, with one-inch black braid on the cap and four rows of black cord with drop loops on the shoulders on ceremonial uniforms.[3834] Dark blue caps with ventilation holes were introduced in 1906 and replaced the kepi.[3835]

Inspector c1906

From 1916 all inspectors, chief inspectors and sub-divisional inspectors wore a crown badge on the cap, although a simple metal crown had been unofficially worn prior to this date.[3836]

3829 Fido, M. and Skinner, K. (1999) *The Official Encyclopaedia of Scotland Yard.* Virgin, London.
3830 Fairfax, N and Wilkinson, V. (1969) 'Uniforms of the Metropolitan Police' (unpublished).
3831 Ibid.
3832 Ibid.
3833 Ibid.
3834 Ibid.
3835 Ibid.
3836 Ibid.

By 1919 the senior inspector was known as the station inspector. Both superintendents and inspectors replaced their braid for two stars (sub-divisional inspectors) and one star (inspectors) in 1921. In 1922, all inspectors badge of rank was required on mackintosh epaulettes and greatcoats.[3837] Lord Trenchard introduced the rank of junior station inspector for the graduates from the newly-formed Hendon College, but the rank was abolished in 1939. In the 1960s temporary inspectors wore only one star during their probationary period. The picture above shows an inspector with an ordinary plain flat cap without badge.

Inspector with flat hat without black braid peak

The picture right shows a sub-divisional inspector (SDI) in normal daily uniform plus spurs and a ceremonial sword. The SDI was first introduced in 1887, and a number of senior inspectors were re-designated. The picture shows the SDI with a star (introduced in 1904) located on each side of the collar and a hat badge on his cap, issued in 1906 for use during the day and at night. The cap had a black patent leather chin strap secured by two silk buttons on the sides.

Inspectors would generally be accomplished horsemen, because supervision at the turn of the century was often done on horseback, especially in the outer Divisions. They therefore had riding equipment, as shown in the photograph, and would also have their chin straps down to secure their flat cap during riding. This inspector is also displaying his service medals, starting from the left with the 1897 Jubilee, the 1901 Coronation and the 1911 Coronation medals. This meant that he took an active part in the celebrations and was on duty, almost certainly as part of a serial of officers policing the event. It is hard to judge whether the picture was taken for ceremonial purposes, although this is doubtful otherwise he would have worn his more ornate ceremonial tunic with embellishments.

Sub-Divisional Inspector c1916

The single star shown below is the badge of rank for a temporary Inspector issued in the 1930s. Two stars were introduced for SDIs in 1921, and all inspectors were now to wear one star on their collars of their tunics and on the shoulders of their greatcoats.

The current badge of rank for an inspector is two stars, and this is worn on the shoulders. The inspector's flat cap has black braid on the peak (as shown on the cap of the sub-divisional inspector opposite).

Chief Inspector/Detective Chief Inspector

CHIEF INSPECTOR

The rank of chief inspector was introduced first in the CID in 1868, and introduced to Divisions the following year. The inspector's uniforms, caps, kepis and other items of clothing remained the same for chief inspectors.

In Victorian times the rank was denoted with scrolled silver braid on both sleeves, and silver oak leaves on the collar. A silver Victorian crown for chief inspectors was introduced in 1871.

Victorian Chief Inspector in ceremonial dress with sword

Between 1875-76 the crown was displayed on each sleeve. The crown was again placed on the peaked hat in 1887, being replaced by a silver crown in 1896, an imperial crown in 1901 and a Tudor crown in 1911. In 1871 silver loops in bay leaf embroidery were introduced on the sleeves of the uniform, as shown in the picture right.

Some confusion exists, as both chief inspectors and superintendents wore crowns in their caps. The chief inspector had a smaller crown and a narrower peak. Superintendents were issued with these crowns, which they hold to the present day.

Mackintoshes were issued to chief inspectors in outer divisions in 1904, and inner divisions in 1914. The badge of rank was originally a crown, but this later became three stars. In the picture below the chief inspector is standing outside Buckingham Palace.[3838]

The chief inspector is the last inspecting and federated rank before the superintendent ranks. Shirts, collars and ties were issued to chief inspectors in 1947. Open-pattern jackets were also issued, as was a new pattern cap with black braid peak.

Victorian Chief Inspector's helmet plate, C Division

Superintendent/ Detective Superintendent

SUPERINTENDENT

The superintendent rank in 1829 was the highest rank below the two Commissioners. The title used by them was seen as non-military, and the same as used by orphanages, schools etc.

Between 1830 and 1843 a small piece of silver lace on the coat or the greatcoat collar denoted the badge of rank for superintendent.[3839] The tunic was single-breasted, having hook and eyes to enable them to be done up. They had no shoulder straps and the front was edged with two rows of plain black braid. There was an Austrian knot on the cuffs.

Later, the badge of rank became a Tudor crown. When the Metropolitan Police District was extended in 1840 to cover an area of just under 700 square miles (about six times its former size) an inspecting superintendent was appointed. His job was to travel around the District and save the Commissioners a great deal of routine supervision.[3840]

In 1872 superintendents wore kepi-style caps, which differed from the inspectors because it had a smaller peak. Whilst the peak for inspectors was horizontal, for superintendents it was slashed to a 45° angle.

Superintendent Grade 1, pre-1953

Victorian Superintendent's Helmet

The picture left shows a superintendent's helmet with chain mail surround and Victorian helmet plate badge bearing the letters 'VR'.

Superintendents were able to wear a kepi of the standard pill-box type, with ventilation holes which had a crown at the front, knitted buttons and surrounded by a black scroll embroidery. Kepis were replaced by caps in 1906.

Chief Inspector circa 1916

3837 Fairfax, N and Wilkinson, V. (1969) *Uniforms of the Metropolitan Police* (unpublished).
3838 Ibid.
3839 Ibid.
3840 Heron F.E. (1970) *A Brief History of the Metropolitan Police.* p17 (unpublished).

Grade 2 Superintendent's crown, pre-1953

The single crown above shows the St Edward's crown issued between 1953 and 1959 for Grade 2 superintendents. Prior to 1953 there were three grades of superintendent. Although designated by the Police Act 1964, which introduced two grades of superintendent, these grades had been in force since 1953.[3841] These were termed Class I and Class II and the same badge of rank was worn, i.e. the crown. Class I superintendents in the Metropolitan Police were often called chief superintendents (see below).

Grade 2 superintendents were abolished in 1959. At the same time, superintendents were required to remove the imperial crown in favour of the St. Edward's crown pattern. The Metropolitan Police superintendents Class I wore a crown and bath star later known as chief superintendents.[3842]

Chief Superintendent/ Detective Chief Superintendent

CHIEF SUPERINTENDENT

The first time the term 'Chief Superintendent' was used in the Metropolitan Police was in January 1866, when the Superintendent on A Division was recognised as the senior superintendent and officially designated Chief Superintendent. The term only lasted until February 1869 when it was discontinued.[3843]

In 1949 the rank of chief superintendent was reintroduced, initially to take charge of Divisions, which later became Districts. Divisions were divided into Sub-Divisions. It was phased out in 1995 as a formal rank, although it is currently used as recognition of seniority. The badge of rank is a crown above a star.

Divisional Chief Superintendent c1936

The senior officer of the Metropolitan Police above is wearing his ceremonial uniform, together with a sabre. His helmet shows the 1911-1935 Senior Officer's ornate helmet plate together with a braided chin strap. His ornate ceremonial uniform befits the rank of Chief Superintendent. It was probably taken around 1935 for the Jubilee celebrations. Additionally, he is wearing three medals, which from left to right are the Order of St. John of Jerusalem medal, the 1911 silver Coronation medal, and the 1937 Coronation medal. One noteworthy point from this photograph is the fact that he does not have a moustache or beard which was common at the time for most police officers. The badge of rank left is the old style (1930s) Chief Superintendent's insignia.

Chief Superintendent's insignia, pre-1953

The Superintendent shown below is John Michael Mulvaney KPM, who joined H Division of the Metropolitan Police as warrant number 54255 on 29th May 1871. He later rejoined H or Whitechapel Division as Divisional Superintendent from L or Lambeth Division where he had been a Chief Inspector on 8th November 1895. He remained there until he retired on 2nd September 1911 aged 61 years following 40 years' service. He was awarded the King's Police Medal on 5th January 1912 after he retired for distinguished service, most notably for his control of the Siege of Sidney Street. The picture of Mulvaney below shows him wearing a flat cap, introduced in 1906 with an embroidered crown at the front.[3844] He is wearing his ceremonial uniform jacket although not with his sword or ceremonial helmet as shown in the illustration above.

Superintendent John Michael Mulvaney, H Division

In 1960 summer wear (lightweight) jackets were introduced for superintendents. In 1968 a lightweight, light blue terylene cotton jacket was introduced for office duties. Today, Borough Police Commanders hold the rank Superintendent Grade I, but wear the crown and star attributed to the Chief Superintendent – a rank which was phased out in 1995. The additional star is to denote seniority over Superintendents (Grade II).

Chief Constable

Chief Constable, Deputy Commissioner and Assistant Commissioner

This rank was created in 1886, and in rank order is between Superintendent and Assistant Commissioner. It was given to the four District Superintendents placed in charge of all the Divisions within their District in 1869. The reason for creating the title was a matter of equivalence, bearing in mind that some of the Metropolitan Police Districts were larger than many provincial constabularies which were headed by Chief Constables.

In 1886 the first ever Chief Constable was appointed and he was put in charge of the CID at Scotland Yard. Later more Chief Constables were appointed and based at Scotland Yard until 1918, when they were

Chief Constable P.V. Sprules MBE

required to work from an office within their own separate District.[3845]

The picture left shows Chief Constable P.V. Sprules MBE in 1939, who was attached to 4 District Headquarters. This is a rare picture of a Metropolitan Police Chief Constable, and shows him wearing a non-ceremonial uniform. His badge of rank shows crossed tipstaves in a bay leaf reef, the same for deputy commander. He is shown wearing a collar and tie, open neck jacket with waistband and breast pockets. He is also wearing shoes rather than boots.

The picture right shows Chief Constable John Hughes Ashley (warrant no. 78923) who joined the Metropolitan Police on 28th July 1893 and retired on 7th August 1932 as Chief Constable of the CID after a famous and distinguished career at Scotland Yard of nearly 40 years. In February 1919 when Detective Sergeant at Scotland Yard, he was commended and rewarded 7/6 for detective ability. The picture below shows him in full ceremonial uniform, including medals. As Detective Superintendent, Ashley joined the 'Big Four' top Metropolitan Police Detectives (Frederick Wensley, Arthur Neil, Francis Carlin and Albert Hawkins), making it the 'Big Five'. Each of the Big Five were responsible for the detection of serious crime in the various sections of London.

John Hughes Ashley, Chief Constable, Metropolitan Police in 1932

The creation of the rank of Deputy Assistant Commissioner in 1928 was seen as more senior than the rank of Chief Constable and rendered the rank superfluous, leading to its abolition in 1946.

Deputy Commander

The post was created in 1946 when the rank of Chief Constable was abolished, as a deputy to the new rank of Commander.[3846]

The badge of rank for Deputy Commander was crossed

tipstaves in a bay leaf wreath, which were later used for Commanders. When the re-grading took place in the late 1960s, most Deputy Commanders were re-graded as Commanders. The rank was abolished when those not re-graded retired.

In the picture above Deputy Commander Walter Batson is shown in conversation with another officer; a Chief Superintendent. The image shows the differences between those ranks. The headgear and badge of office are the same, except for the front material of the peak. The Deputy Commander has silver oak leaf fringe, while on the right the Chief Superintendent has silver braid instead. Other than the shoulder badges of rank, then, the only real difference are the two white material strips called gorgets which are situated down each side of the lapel.

Commander

The rank is between Chief Superintendent and Deputy Assistant Commissioner. It is the lowest rank of Chief Officer, conferring membership of the Association of Chief Police Officers (ACPO). It was introduced in 1946 to take charge of the four Districts of London. It is held to be the equivalent to Assistant Chief Constable rank. The rank of Commander today dropped the star, leaving the crossed tipstaves in a bay leaf wreath.

3841 Fairfax, N and Wilkinson, V. (1969) *Uniforms of the Metropolitan Police* (unpublished).
3842 Devlin, J. D. (1966) *Police Procedure, Organisation and Administration.* Butterworths, London.
3843 Ibid.
3844 Fairfax, N and Wilkinson, V. (1969) *Uniforms of the Metropolitan Police* (unpublished).
3845 Metropolitan Police Orders dated 16th November 1918.
3846 Metropolitan Police Orders dated 15th March 1946.

The uniform of a Commander

When the rank was introduced the badge of office was similar to Deputy Commander, but with the cloth star later used for Deputy Assistant Commissioners. In the late 1960s the Divisions were renamed Districts and the majority of the Chief Superintendents were promoted to Commander. The four original Districts were renamed Areas, and a Deputy Assistant Commissioner was placed in charge of each.

The badge of rank for a Commander is cross batons on a laurel wreath.[3847] Two silver braid strips on an embroidered band are stitched onto the collar either side. The hat is embellished with laurel silvered braiding to the front of the cap.

Deputy Assistant Commissioner

Chief Constable, Deputy Commissioner and Assistant Commissioner

The rank was introduced in 1919[3848] and was used to head departments at New Scotland Yard. In 1925 the silver star was added to the crossed batons.

In 1933 the four Chief Constables in charge of each of the four districts were replaced by four Deputy Assistant Commissioners (DACs). The DAC's rank was seen as a grade senior to the Chief Constable rank it replaced. In March 1946, on each of the four Districts of the Metropolitan Police the title of DAC was changed to Commander, and that of Chief Constable to Deputy Commander.[3849] Then in 1969 the DACs replaced the Commanders in each area, and the DAC's deputy, a Commander, took on an inspectorial role over the Districts, which were now commanded by Commanders.

In 1976 the DACs took over more of an operational and administrative role.[3850]

In 1995 it was considered that it was not necessary for there to be the two ranks of DAC and Commander to occupy the position between Superintendents and Assistant Commissioners. The title has been given to some Commanders, however, to reflect higher responsibilities. The badge of rank is cross batons on a laurel wreath and one bath star.

Assistant Commissioners

The rank was first authorised in 1856,[3851] with initially two Assistant Commissioners which was increased to three in 1884.[3852]

The number of Assistant Commissioners were further increased to four in 1909[3853] and to five in 1933.[3854]

The Assistant Commissioners were in charge of major headquarter departments at New Scotland Yard. In recent years, some of the Assistant Commissioners have been moved from New Scotland Yard and put into operational command positions. The badge of rank, which has remained consistent (save for the crown), is the cross batons on a laurel leaf and a crown. The illustration below is the current badge of rank, introduced in 1953 and up until 2000 was also used for the Deputy Commissioner.

Deputy and Assistant Commissioners c1946

Deputy Commissioner

The fifth Assistant Commissioner post was created in 1933[3855] and allowed the Force to use one of the Assistant Commissioners as a Deputy to the Commissioner, usually Assistant Commissioner 'A' Department. The rank was officially introduced in 1919 with a new pattern of uniform, and marked the first time that the Commissioner and the Assistant Commissioner had a service uniform. Until 2000 the post holder wore the badge of rank of an Assistant Commissioner, but now has cross batons on a laurel wreath, and small stars and a crown.

Commissioner

COMMISSIONER

The Crown appoints the Commissioner, who heads the Metropolitan Police. When the Met was first formed there were two Commissioners, but only one from 1856.[3856] The badge of rank is cross batons on laurel wreath, one crown and a bath star. Below is the older commissioner's badge of rank, which shows an imperial crown rather than a Tudor crown as worn today.

There are two types of rank for Commissioner, one having metal insignia whilst the other is of fabric construction. Furthermore, the insert to the Tudor crown is now shown in blue rather than red. The metal embellished epaulette was for wear during inclement weather and for use on mackintoshes or florescent jackets etc. The fabric epaulette is for normal day wear with a tunic, and changed when Sir Ian Blair was Commissioner.

Pre-1953 badge of office

The picture on the opposite page shows the Metropolitan Police Commissioner Sir Joseph Simpson in his full ceremonial dress and medals, taken around 1960.

Sir Joseph Simpson tragically died in 1967 whilst still serving. His death can be attributed to over-work, as he was a reforming Commissioner but at the same time was a policeman, having risen through the ranks. He was the third Commissioner to die in service.

Police Ranks

*Sir Joseph Simpson,
Commissioner 1958-67*

The Commissioner is regarded as the lead senior police officer in the country because they have general responsibilities outside of the Metropolitan Police District. These include Counter Terrorism, Diplomatic and Royal Protection.

3847 Fido, M. and Skinner, K. (1999) *The Official Encyclopaedia of Scotland Yard.* Virgin, London.
3848 Police Act 1919.
3849 Heron F.E. (1970) *A Brief history of the Metropolitan Police* p17 (unpublished).
3850 Metropolitan Police Orders dated 2nd July 1976.
3851 Metropolitan Police Act, 1856.
3852 Metropolitan Police Act, 1884.
3853 Police Act 1909.
3854 Metropolitan Police Act, 1933.0
3855 Ibid.
3856 Metropolitan Police Act, 1856.

Chapter 9.
Women Police

On 17th May 2019 a service was held at Westminster Abbey to celebrate the centenary of Metropolitan Women Police. The religious service formed part of a period of recognition and reflection of how the role of women police officers has changed over the years, echoing to some degree the attitudes of society generally.

During World War One, when so many men were recruited to the armed forces, women became far more involved in undertaking what had previously been regarded as 'men's work'. In September 1914 Margaret Damer Dawson and Nina Boyle founded a uniformed organisation called the Women Police Volunteers, later Women Police Service (WPS), but others also independently developed plans for women to undertake policing.

The nucleus of the first Metropolitan Women Police was organised by the National Union of Women Workers (NUWW; now the National Union of Women) Women's Police Committee.

The Commissioner, Sir Edward Henry, gave permission for each group to patrol the streets, issued them with identity cards and asked police officers to assist them when required. The women tended to concentrate on deterring prostitution and vice-related matters. Other forces asked the WPS to supply policewomen, and this resulted in Grantham Police formally attesting Mrs Edith Smith in 1915 as the first woman to possess legal police powers.

When the 1916 Police, Factories (Miscellaneous) Act was passed, it included a section allowing for the employment of women on police duties. The Commissioner immediately announced that with Home Office permission he was going to employ a few women patrols, part-time.

They wore the blue and white armlets of constables on their left arm. Since Mrs Sophia Stanley, the first woman in charge, could not spare the necessary time to run the training course, Miss Dorothy Peto (who was later to become Superintendent in charge of the women in 1930) came from Bristol to London to carry through the class instruction. Bristol was a centre for training women patrols and women police, and Dorothy Peto had observed the London training system earlier, with her colleagues Miss Joseph and Mrs Gent. Patrol committees in the south of England were encouraged to send their patrol leaders for short courses, while longer training was also available at Bristol for women who wanted to secure appointments to police forces.

In her memoirs Dorothy Peto related how, in 1918, the new Commissioner, Sir C. Nevil Macready, asked for reports from his divisional superintendents about the work of the voluntary patrols, and on the basis of those reports decided to introduce an experimental system of paid part-time employment of women on police duties. He invited Sophia Stanley to select suitable candidates from amongst her voluntary patrols and to arrange for their training. This took place in Great Smith Street, Westminster in a committee room belonging to the National Union of Trained Nurses, of which Flora Joseph was the Honorary Secretary. The selected women attended training classes in the daytime and went out on street duty in the evenings. Dorothy Peto often accompanied them on patrol and saw how they worked. They were employed for four hours a day, six days a week, in Hyde Park, the West End and at main railway stations such as Victoria, King's Cross, Euston, Paddington and Waterloo.

The new female recruits needed to be aged 35-38, at least 5' 4" in height, educated, physically fit and with no dependent children. These patrols would come under the command of Superintendent Sophia Stanley within the Metropolitan Police structures, and would be paid 30 shillings plus a War bonus of 12 shillings per week. The first 21 women signed their year's contract and then started to patrol the streets of London in February 1919. By 1920 they numbered 112. They had no police power of arrest.

Lilian Wyles (warrant no. 23) became the first woman to join the CID as a detective in December 1922, rising to Detective Inspector (First Class) in 1935 and a specialist statement taker for victims of sexual offences. She wrote an autobiography titled *A Woman at Scotland Yard* (Faber 1952), a pioneer for the involvement of female officers dealing with rape and other sexual crimes. Other women performed dangerous and delicate operations by going under cover against drug dealers. In 1920 a Parliamentary committee chaired by Major Sir John Baird was set up and recommended that female officers should be given powers of arrest and better pay, but the 'Geddes axe' in 1922 (an attempt to reduce public sector employees under Sir Eric Geddes) recommended the disbandment of the women police patrols. After a campaign by Lady Astor MP and others this resulted in a compromise reduction of their numbers to 20, but in 1923 they were given power of arrest and were properly referred to as Constables.

By 1931 their strength had built up to more than 50 and a new branch – A4 – was created, under Miss Dorothy Peto, to deal with Women Police matters. New conditions of service were introduced which required women officers to resign on marriage.

After World War Two, the women police establishment was raised to 300 and the 1931 prohibition on matrimony was dropped. The separate establishment, which effectively limited the number and ranks of female officers, remained in place until 1972, when women police were integrated into the rest of the Metropolitan Police Service with their work of dealing with children, missing persons, female offenders and sexual offences no longer being regarded as specialist duties exclusively to be undertaken by women. This responded to legislation requiring male and female employees to be treated equally. Their hours of duty were raised from seven to eight hours per shift, and their pay was made equal with that of their male counterparts. In 1990 the ranks of female officers were no longer designated as 'Woman Detective Sergeant', for example, and their warrant numbers were allocated in the same series as their male counterparts.

Within police stations, the offices that had once been allocated to women police became available for other purposes. Posts within the CID and in the rank structure reserved for female officers were abolished. The high standards and demands of dealing with specialist women police duties were remembered with nostalgia, pride, and sometimes regret by the many female officers who then undertook general police duties alongside their male counterparts without a counter-balancing training for male officers in dealing with children and care proceedings. There was no longer an internal maximum limit for the number of female officers.

The emphasis then shifted to monitoring, encouraging and mandating equality of opportunity and advancement into specialist duties and higher ranks, with various officers creating their own special place in history when they became one of the first women to break into what had until then been various exclusively male sections of the organisation.

This process reached an important milestone when Dame Cressida Dick was appointed as the first female Commissioner in 2017.

In 1957 Shirley Becke (later Commander) and Barbara Kelley were appointed Detective Inspectors for general CID duties on Division. The first woman was appointed to the Flying Squad in 1959. The women were trained as firearms officers in 1989, and by 2003 the Flying Squad was led by a woman.

Commander Shirley Becke

Shirley Cameron Becke OBE, QPM, Commander Metropolitan Police

Born Shirley Jennings in 1917 at Chiswick to a gas engineer, her life demonstrated skill, aptitude and ability. She distinguished herself in many ways, achieving a number of firsts. Initially she was the first woman ever to qualify as a Higher Grade Gas Engineer, then during her police career as the most senior women police detective, then as the most senior woman police officer in the country and the first woman to reach Chief Officer rank as Commander in 1969.

Educated at Westminster Technical Institute, Shirley Jennings found work at the Gas Light and Coke Company (later North Thames Gas Board) from where she joined the Metropolitan Police in 1941, warrant no. 478. She only intended to stay in the police for the duration of the War, however WPC Jennings joined as 55C.

In 1942 she showed aptitude before her probationary period ended, being posted into plain clothes with allowance and was commended by the Commissioner for shutting down undesirable premises.

Later, in 1945, she joined the CID at West End Central Police Station, becoming Detective Constable. Further commendations followed in 1946 in two matters for alertness in a case of housebreaking, one for persistence in a case of demanding money with menaces, and another in 1948 for two cases whilst attached to COC1 for perseverance in a case of uttering false bank notes, a case of receiving. In November 1945, after an undercover operation to unmask the killers of Reuben 'Russian Robert' Martirosoff, she posed as the wife of one of the missing suspects. Her skill, courage and daring uncovered the suspects' location, and their arrest, prosecution and later led to their execution.

Rapid promotions followed: Detective Sergeant in 1952, Detective Inspector in 1957, and Detective Chief Inspector in 1959. A year later he was promoted to Superintendent, and returned to uniform duties taking command of Women Police in South West London.

In 1966, as Superintendent she transferred to New Scotland Yard A Department, in charge of Administration and Operations. Promotion to Chief Superintendent saw her transfer to Scotland Yard's A4 (Women Police Department).

In 1972 she was awarded the Queen's Police medal. A year later the Women Police department was abolished, and women officers joined their male counterparts as equals.

In 1974 she transferred to the Metropolitan Police Inspectorate, finally retiring in April that year, and in retirement becoming a Regional administrator and deputy chairman between 1976 and 1983 in the Women's Royal Voluntary Service.

Shirley Jennings had met and married Justice Becke, a chartered accountant (later to become the Reverend Justice Becke MBE) in 1954, becoming the first head of the Women Police to be married.

She died in 2011 aged 94 in Chichester, Sussex, her husband having predeceased her. Shirley Becke's funeral took place in September 2011 at Chichester Cathedral.

In life she showed herself as an outstanding, skilful and resourceful person, earning the respect of all her junior officers and senior colleagues. She certainly helped in the struggle for women's equality within the police service.

*

In October 2018, female officers numbered:
Commander and above: 5
Chief Superintendents: 11
Superintendents: 47
Chief Inspectors: 63
Inspectors: 263
Sergeants: 863
Constables: 6,628

Other firsts for women officers:

1918 Superintendent Sophia Stanley led the first women police patrols

1922 Lillian Wyles joined the CID

1947 Woman Detective Sergeant Alberta Watts awarded King's Police and Fire Service Medal for gallantry for acting as a decoy on Tooting Bec Common where women were being attacked and robbed. This was the first award of gallantry made to a Women Police Officer

1955 Women Police Constables Ethel Bush and Kathleen Parrott each receive the George Medal for acting undercover to catch a male attacker in Croydon where physical injury was sustained. This was the first George Medal to be awarded to women police

1959 First women officer appointed to the Flying Squad

1968 Sislin Fay Allen became the first black police women

1969 Shirley Becke becomes the first female Commander

1971 The first women officers selected as specialist dog handlers were constables Lyn Nicholson and Sandra Kertzen

1973 Inspector Sheila Ward became the first female inspector to command a street duty relief, at King's Cross Road Police station

1983 Alison Halford became the first female to take operational control of a police station (Tottenham Court Road)

1998 First two women officers become Deputy Assistant Commissioners

2007 Helen Ball become the first female officer to Head Operation Trident, which tackles London's gang problem

2009 First female officer takes charge of the Specialist Crime Directorate

2014 In April 2017 Dame Cressida Dick became the Commissioner of the Metropolitan Police

In February 2017 Cressida Dick QPM was appointed as the first woman Commissioner to take charge of the Metropolitan Police Service, which she had joined as a Constable in 1983. She was appointed a Superintendent in Thames Valley Police in 1995, and returned to the MPS as a Commander in 2001. After further promotions to Acting Deputy Commissioner, she became a Director General in the Foreign Office in 2015 before her welcome and historic return to Scotland Yard as Commissioner. She was awarded the QPM in 2010 and the CBE in 2015, before being made Dame Commander of the British Empire in September 2019.

Dame Cressida Dick is to date the most successful woman police officer of all time, rising to the most senior police rank. She is also the most senior Association of Chief Police Officers (ACPO) within the UK. This is because there are portfolios only associated with the status of the Metropolitan Police Commissioner not held by any other Chief Officer such as Royalty and Diplomatic protection. The Commissioner is directly accountable to the Home Secretary and the public nationally amongst many others (the Mayor's Office for Policing and Crime, the Mayor of London, Londoners), whereas smaller police forces are only accountable to residents and their local Police and Crime Commissioner or police authority. Below is an example of the Commissioner's headgear and rank insignia. The rank of Commissioner is worn on the shoulders like male officers.

The sometimes random risk of injury and death in the police service does not discriminate.

In 1944 WPC Bertha Gleghorn of C Division became the first female officer to be killed on duty, when a wartime flying bomb exploded at Tottenham Court Road Police Station. She was one of 207 Metropolitan Police officers to have lost their lives on duty during World War Two.

Jane Arbuthnot lost her life when she was killed by an IRA bomb outside Harrod's store, Knightsbridge, in 1983.

Yvonne Fletcher was shot and killed by 'diplomats' from the Libyan People's Bureau in St. James's Square in 1984.

Nina MacKay was stabbed to death whilst on Territorial Support Group duties at Forest Gate in 1997.

In 1994 Gail Pirnie collapsed and died of heart failure during a baton training course.

Nor have the ranks of female officers been without their courageous heroes. In 1947 Alberta Watts (née Law) was awarded the King's Police and Fire Service Medal for her courage whilst acting as a decoy on Tooting Bec common, chasing a suspect and grappling with him despite her injuries.

In 1964 Margaret Cleland was awarded the George Medal for her bravery in dealing with a prolonged rooftop rescue of a 20-month child from his deranged father.

Developing and maintaining modern standards of equality of opportunity inevitably requires constant vigilance, but the pioneers of women policing would no doubt be gratified to see the progress that has been made, and the esteem with which their modern-day sisters regard them.

Women Police uniforms

From 1919 Women Police had their own separate Department which later became CO-A4, and their identity as Women Police ceased with the Equal Pay Act 1970 which forbade less favourable working conditions and introduced equality. The Metropolitan Police dragged their feet with the Act, which was not being implemented until 1973 when women were distributed amongst Divisions and CO Departments. Uniforms for police men and women in the past reflected their gender, with women's uniforms passing through seven distinct uniform changes. Today there are moves towards creating more gender neutral uniforms and headgear.

The Stanley Uniform 1919-1931

The very first Metropolitan Police uniform issued to women in 1919 was very similar to that worn by the men. The various women police organisations throughout the country operating before 1919 had differing designs.

The Metropolitan Police uniform issued to women constables and sergeants resembled a colonial design, with its 6-button tunic with its high neck design and large collar numbers. The uniform was referred to as the 'Stanley Uniform', named after Superintendent Sophia Stanley, the first women police superintendent. These uniforms, which were fitted by Harrod's, were made from a coarse material and were uncomfortable to

Women Police

Lillian Wyles in her 1919 Stanley uniform

wear.

The tunic was single-breasted and tapered down at the front, with two large deep flapped button-down pockets either side below the belt. It had six white metal buttons down the front. Like the men, they wore a whistle and chain looped from the second button-down to an internal waist pocket. The belt was also similar in design to the men, made of black tanned leather joined with a looped snake's head-clasp.

The collar identified the officer, with a number and the letters 'MP' for Metropolitan Police.

In the example right Sergeant Lillian Wyles, who was the twenty-third woman police officer to join the Metropolitan Police, displays her collar number of '4'. On joining she was made a sergeant and given responsibility for a third of London which included Central London and the East End. She had a very successful police career.

The women constables and sergeants also wore a duty armlet on their left forearm like the men, signifying their 'On duty' status. They were issued with a domed wide-brimmed hat, which curved down with a thick black glossy band above its rim, which most likely acted as a chin strap and could be worn down to ensure the hat remained in place. On top of the hat was a felt button, which finished off the headgear. Experience had taught police during WW1 that a substantial hat was needed for protection, and the Metropolitan Police adopted a design of headgear so as to provide ample defence from any blows to the head.

Above the band in the centre was a black painted Brunswick star-patterned plate with a King's Crown, with circular garter-type and dropped-down loop. Like the men, their collar number (without the 'MP') appeared in small white metal numbers within the centre. The garter belt and buckle within the plate holds the words 'METROPOLITAN POLICE' around the circumference, and the badge was smaller in design than their male counterparts.

The 1919-1935 women star-pattern police hat badge

Officers of inspector rank and above had the same badge, but the centre had a guelphic script 'GvR' for George V, as shown below. Rather than a number in their collars, inspectors wore a single star either side of the collar to denote the rank of Inspector.

The officers also wore also a long, mid-calf length skirt of the same material as the jacket. To cover the ankles they wore black boots with a one-inch heel and black woollen stockings. The uniform changed again in 1931 to a more comfortable one.

The 1919-1931 Senior Women Police Brunswick star

To distinguish the upper ranks from constables etc, those above inspector rank wore a different style jacket which had an open neck with folded-down lapels. Under the jacket they wore a high-collared white cotton shirt and black tie. The jacket had three black buttons down the front, and the pockets had a black button as well.

The Stanley (remodelled) 1931-1946

In 1931 a newer uniform was introduced which dispensed with the high-neck collar, leather belt and boots. The uncomfortable old uniform was substituted for a more aggregable uniform which had a more pleasing look.

In came an open-neck jacket with lapels, a white shirt and black tie. Shoes replaced the clumpy boots. This uniform jacket, which now had four white metal buttons down the front, also had two larger tapered jacket pockets either side. The snake's-head belt clasp was replaced with a chrome oblong buckle with a single pin. A fitted material belt drew the waist in and substituted the previous leather binding.

The 1931 uniforms for inspectors, sergeants and constables

The headgear remained very much the same, with a domed re-enforced hat, except that the brim was wider and flatter. The polished band at the top of the brim was removed, as was the stitched leather brim edging and the felt button on the top.

The black painted Brunswick star-pattern helmet plates for all ranks were also replaced. For inspectors and above these were replaced a white metal star pattern version, whilst a chrome white metal circular badge was worn for constables and sergeants. Both designs had a King's Crown of George V. This design of uniform lasted until 1946.

The Bather Uniform (1946 -1968)

The two women officers shown at the top of the following column are wearing what became known as the Bather uniform, after its originator Elizabeth Constance Bather OBE (1904-1988). This style was worn from 1946 until 1968.

Bather was first a Women's Auxiliary Air Force (WAAF) officer and later police officer, who was the first woman to be promoted to Chief Superintendent when the rank was introduced in 1949.

In 1945 she joined the Metropolitan Police as a chief inspector, and a year later succeeded Superintendent Dorothy Peto as Superintendent and Head of the Women Police A4 Branch.

Bather attempted to feminise the force, re-designing the uniform in 1946. She was a forward-thinking officer who allowed women to wear make-up on duty. She also allowed married women to join, and let serving officers marry without having to resign.

Also retained was the white cotton shirt and tie of the previous 1931 design, however the jacket was completely remodelled. The uniform jacket which continued with an open-neck collar had four white metal buttons that fastened the uniform.

The Bather uniform: Inspector rank and above on the left, and below on the right

Two breast pockets and two large expandable satchel pockets fitted externally were added below the waist, with a white metal buttons.

Epaulettes fastened with a small white metal button were introduced on each shoulder that included small white metal letters and numerals for identification.

A belt made of the same material as the uniform was fastened by a white metal buckle. The whistle was placed in the left-hand breast pocket with the chain looped around the top button.

The cap badge of a white metal circular design, with King's Crown of a belted circular type, changed to the same design worn by the men. The circle became simplified, losing the belt and drop loop.

For officers above the rank of inspector, women police wore a white metal small star-pattern King's Crown design,

Left: The 1931-35 GV cap badge for constables and sergeants
Right: Cap badge for inspectors and above

denoting George V up until 1931, although the example above dates from 1937.

The white metal cap badge for women constables, sergeants and inspectors consisted of the King's Crown small circular design, with 'GR VI' in the centre and 'METROPOLITAN POLICE', which was issued for all ranks. The badge became circular and differed from the George V badge, with the buckled belt being removed.

The Geo VI replacement cap badge 1937-53

Woman constable wearing trench coat

The photograph of the constable on the left shows the ankle-length double-breasted mackintosh or trench coat, with detachable epaulettes and button over flap down lapels.

In the example below showing Superintendents Bather (left) and Peto, the King's Crown star-pattern hat badge was worn for ranks above inspector. Bather often tilted her hat to the left at what was often described as a 'jaunty angle' – much admired in the forces.

Superintendents Bather (left) and Peto of the Women Police

The Norman Hartnell design (1968-1973)

In 1968 the fashion designer and Royal favourite, Norman Hartnell was asked to redesign the uniform and cape, but not the hat, which became the responsibility of Mme Simone Mirman, who worked closely with Hartnell on many other projects. Mme Mirman was a Parisian-born Milliner who, like Hartnell, was a favourite of Princess Margaret, the Queen Mother and Queen Elizabeth. She was noted for her high 'off the face' hats, with her pillar-box design becoming the pattern for women police.

The uniform style was to encompass elegance, comfort and utility. A long-sleeve white cotton shirt with epaulette loops on each shoulder allowed for black epaulettes to be inserted for shirt-sleeve wear. The sleeves could also be folded up in hot weather. The shirt was worn with a bow tie which was introduced for the first time, and fastened with a collar stud.

The skirt became knee-length rather than below the knee, and either tights or stockings were worn. The women wore a double-breasted boxed

Sislin Allen, the first female black constable in 1968, in the Hartnell uniform

Recruiting poster 1971 with constable in jacket and hat

design jacket with six white metal buttons. Two white metal buttons fastened the epaulette to the jacket shoulders. Just to finish off the look, the top part of the lapel collar was edged in a soft black crushed velvet.

A cape fastened with a chain was also designed for wear over the uniform during inclement weather, replacing the greatcoat. The design was eye-catching but short-lived, lasting only until 1973.

The Surrey (1972-1978)

In 1972 the Surrey Women Police Uniform was adopted by the Metropolitan Police, after the Constabulary had issued it to their own women officers and constables in 1970. When the new uniform was introduced in October 1970 by the Surrey Police, the press described the new uniform as including a "semi-fitted jacket, neat long-sleeve blouse, modish three-quarter length cape and a Robin Hood-style hat."[3857] This was meant to give women officers a more feminine appearance, keeping in step with modern fashion.

This style of uniform was issued to women officers, special constables and cadets.

Small changes had been made to the Norman Hartnell uniform, mainly to the jacket. The six-button double-breasted jacket was replaced by a four white metal button version.

3857 *Daily Mail*, 29th October 1970.

All the permutations of women police uniform wearing the Surrey design

The 1953 to present cap badge

The main change, however, was to the headgear. A floppy-brimmed dark hat folded at the rear had a white cover for summer wear and a dark crown for use in winter.[3858] Outside the cover, a diced or checkered cap band was introduced. To the front and on top of the diced band was the Force standard-issue cap badge, with Queen's Crown as issued to the men, as shown above, issued to constables and sergeants including cadets and special constables. Inspectors and above were issued with the small star-pattern hat badge, in line with their male counterparts. The standard-issue small white metal chromed buttons, as also worn by the men, was included in the women's uniform.

Retained was the long-sleeve shirt and cape designs. The bow tie was produced with a clip on the new version, and the collar stud was discarded. The skirt was of the classic A Line style with a tight-fitting waist. An experimental trouser suit was also brought in to aid women officers working in the Special Patrol Group, Traffic and Dog Sections. The picture right shows a patrol constable with her trousers and cape. The old style raincoat was replaced by a slightly shorter version.

A constable with cape and trousers in the Surrey style

Short-sleeve shirts were introduced into the women police uniform, as shown by the photograph opposite.

The Butcher (Boy) uniform (1978-1985)

In 1978 a new 'mix & match' uniform was designed by Mansfield Originals (Women's Clothing) of Great Titchfield Street, London W1.

This became known as the 'Butcher Boy' (sometimes also referred to as Baker Boy or Smurf type) uniform, however this name was more associated with the hat created again by Mme Simone Mirman. This uniform style was a firm favourite of HRH Princess Anne.

This Butcher boy concept became the fashion statement in the late 1970s, which included the 'off the face pattern' with wide, rigid stitched brim. At the top of the cap there was a button fitted that fastened the 12 panels together in a stylish manner. The white shirt was re-designed to have a more prominent collar, particularly to include the clip-on cravats issued for the first time, which replaced bow ties.

Constable in shirt sleeve order with handbag

Side view of the Butcher Boy hat design

To the front of the cap a black oval flap was introduced to enable the cap badge to be inserted above the checkered band. There were concerns, however, from women officers that whilst the cap was a design feature and comfortable, it afforded little head protection especially in public order situations. In the 1970s the black and white diced 'Sillitoe' chequered hat band was added to the cap. The skirt was designed with inverted pleats, enabling officers to chase offenders easily, whilst the jacket now had a belt.

Front elevation of the Butcher boy cap

The jacket and skirt were popular but the hat was later discarded by those officers on division in favour of the original, and more popular, Surrey design headgear. Those officers in Training School were not given a choice, and issued the Butcher boy-style hat. In 1976 women were given permission to be dressed in trousers on duty for normal wear. This was particularly helpful for use on night duty, and for getting in and out of vehicles.

The Bowler (1985 – Present day)

In 1985, along with many other forces the Metropolitan Police introduced the 'Pathfinder' bowler hat design for women, made by Compton and Webb of Witney in Oxfordshire. Alongside their sister company Christys, CW Headdress has been one of the foremost suppliers of ceremonial and protective headwear for the men and women of the police and armed forces since 1900.[3859]

The picture on the following page shows the two types of uniform, one with trousers the other with a skirt. The bowler was also sometimes known as the 'pathfinder' and was issued to female officers of all ranks including Special Constables, Police and Community Support officers (PCSOs), and cadets as well.

The outer material is made from a black wool, and is banded with the usual blue-and-white, chequered band. The hat is fitted with a thick, two-inch wide brim which is made from black wool with ventilation eyelets positioned at both sides. On the interior it has a leather sweat forehead-patch, and it is fully lined with a re-enforced, padded black foam. The inner crown is fitted with a pad of black foam. The interior is also fitted with public-order black chinstrap, fitted on both sides at four points on the rim, allowing for it to be worn up or down. The bowler weighs 334g.

This headgear is still in use as of 2019, although options for a more gender-neutral hat are available in some forces. The

3858 *Reading Evening Post*, 30th May 1973.
3859 www.cwheaddress.com accessed 26th November 2019.

The round chrome hat badge was replaced by the small star-pattern enamelled hat badge on the bowler hat. Retained was the checkered hat band. The uniform itself changed little, with the same design of jacket, belt and epaulettes. Officers of superintendent rank and above have silvered rank designs situated under the hat badge to differentiate them from rank-and-file officers.

Dame Cressida Dick CBE, QPM, Commissioner Metropolitan Police

In February 2017 Dame Cressida Dick QPM was appointed as the first woman Commissioner to take charge of the Metropolitan Police Service, which she had joined as a Constable in 1983. She was appointed a Superintendent in Thames Valley Police in 1995, and returned to the MPS as a Commander in 2001. After further promotion to Acting Deputy Commissioner, she became a Director General in the Foreign Office in 2015 before her welcome and historic return to Scotland Yard as Commissioner. She was awarded the QPM in 2010 and the CBE in 2015 before being made Dame Commander of the British Empire in September 2019.

Dame Cressida Dick is to date the most successful woman police officer of all time, rising to the most senior police rank. She is also the most senior Association of Chief Police Officers (ACPO) within the UK. This is because there are portfolios only associated with the status of the Metropolitan Police Commissioner not held by any other Chief Officer, such as Royalty and Diplomatic Protection. The Commissioner is directly accountable to the Home Secretary and the public nationally amongst many others (the Mayor's Office for Policing and Crime, the Mayor of London, Londoners), whereas smaller police forces are only accountable to residents and their local Police and Crime Commissioner or police authority.[3861]

The Bowler design headgear with uniform skirt and trousers

bowler differs from the Butcher boy since it is reinforced and offers more physical protection, something that its predecessor did not do. This is in line with the protection afforded in the male 'Custodian' helmet produced by the same company, which is required to satisfy the bump cap safety standard (EN812:2012)[3860] that ensures a reduced chance of injury.

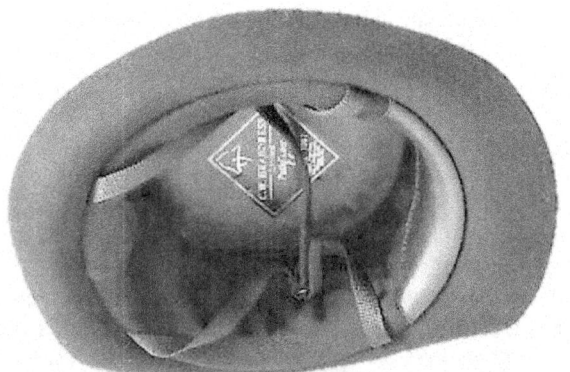

An internal view of the Women Police Bowler hat, showing protection

3860   Information courtesy Lisa Maycock at CW Headdress, 26th November 2019.
3861   Metropolitan Police Authority - the Commissioner of Police of the Metropolis, archived 14 August 2011 at the Wayback Machine.

Chapter 10.
Metropolitan Police Divisions: A History 1829-2019

When the Metropolitan Police was first established in 1829, it was divided into territorial Divisions, headed by a Superintendent. Officers wore the letter signifying their Division and their Divisional number on their uniforms. A variation of this tradition still exists today, but Divisions have been replaced by twelve Basic Command Units covering the Metropolitan Police District (MPD). A photograph of an epaulette of a uniformed officer may therefore reveal the part of London in which they were serving, but the details have changed over the years. To help to understand which parts of London were involved, the following guide describes a rather complicated situation in more detail.

From 1829 until 1985/86 there would typically be one letter to indicate the Division or, from around the early 1970s when Metropolitan Police Divisions were re-classified as Districts, the District involved. In 1985/86 Districts were abolished and officers wore a two-letter Divisional code on their uniforms (eg AD for Cannon Row). In 1993-94 Divisions were reclassified as Operational Command Units, but the two letter codes remained.

Since 2018/19 officers wear the two-letter code of their Basic Command Unit (eg CW for Central West). Divisions are used in this chapter as the historic basis of the analysis, but the situation is complicated not only by a large number of police reorganisations, but also by parishes and local authority areas that have changed over the years. The Divisions in semi-Inner London have been very susceptible to changes, whilst the outskirts of the Metropolitan Police District (MPD) have sometimes been affected by the MPD limit of 12-, later 15-mile distance from Charing Cross, as set out in Section 2, Metropolitan Police Act 1839, not corresponding neatly with local authority areas.

The term 'Division' progressively dropped out of police terminology from the mid-1990s, being replaced by 'Operational Command Unit' or 'Borough' before 'Basic Command Units' were introduced. Station codes are quoted

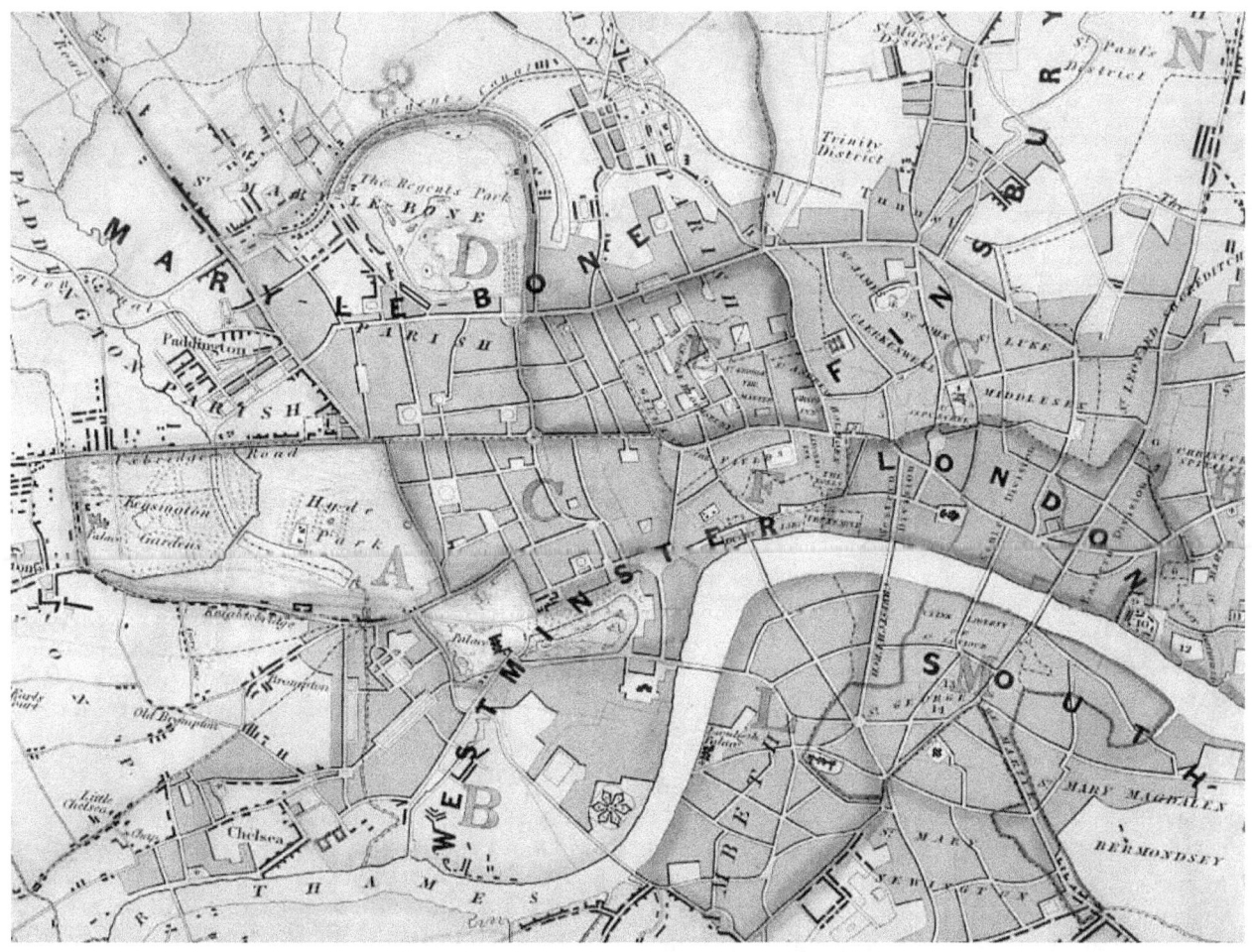

Central London Divisions, 1837

Map of the Metropolitan Police District (MPD) c1866-70

on the basis that this may help identify where an individual officer would be serving. The issue of what ranks were held by officers in charge of Divisions or equivalent units is not described in these pages.

A Division

A Division was known as Whitehall Division from 1829, later as Westminster. It originally policed the vicinity of Whitehall, Trafalgar Square, Buckingham Palace and Hyde Park, and later took in Pimlico and Belgravia. For many years A Division officers policed the royal palaces before the introduction of the Royal Palaces Division and the Royalty and Diplomatic Protection Department.

Its stations comprised Great Scotland Yard, 2 Gardiner's Lane, King Street, Cannon Row (from 1902), and Wellington Arch. It policed Hyde Park from is earliest days. Rochester Row was transferred from B in 1886, so that A Division then extended west to Vauxhall Bridge Road. Gerald Road became A Division in 1965, extending the Division west to the Royal Albert Hall. Cannon Row, Rochester Row and Gerald Road were the three divisions within No. 8 Area from 1985/86. Belgravia, effectively amalgamating those three Divisions, became South Westminster and in due course an Operational Command Unit (OCU) within No. 1 Area (Central) in 1993-94, and part of Central West Basic Command Unit in 2018/19.

B Division

Originally B Division was named Westminster when it was formed on 21st September 1829, policing Pimlico and Belgravia with stations at New Way, Tothill Street and at Roberts Buildings (subsequently replaced by Cottage Road). From 1865 B Division's stations comprised Rochester Row,

Walton Street and Cottage Road (later Gerald Road). Chelsea became part of the Division in 1886. By 1910 North Fulham (closed 1938) and South Fulham (also known as Walham Green and Fulham during its life) were part of B Division. The 1965 reorganisation made the Division co-terminous with the Royal Borough of Kensington and Chelsea, comprising three sub-divisions of Notting Hill, Kensington and Chelsea. These three later became Divisions and part of No. 6 Area in 1985/86. Brompton (an amalgamation of Chelsea and Kensington) and Notting Hill (BH) became Operational Command Units on No. 1 Area (Central) in 1993/94, and part of the Central West Basic Command Unit in 2018/19.

C Division

C or St James's Division policed Mayfair and Soho when it was formed on 21st September 1829. The police stations were firstly at 10 Little Vine Street (subsequently Vine Street), Great Marlborough Street and, for a short time, Greek Street and Dean Street. Great Marlborough Street and Vine Street were replaced by West End Central in July 1940, with Vine Street reopening from 1971-1997. The Division took in Bow Street in 1965 so as to become responsible for the western side of the City of Westminster. The three sub-divisions of West End Central, Vine Street and Bow Street became Divisions in their own right, and were incorporated into No. 6 Area in 1885/86. They became Operational Command Units on No. 1 Area (Central) in 1993/94, and part of the Central West Basic Command Unit (CW) in 2018/19.

D Division

D Division policed Marylebone when it was established on 21st September 1829, with Oxford Street marking its boundary with C Division to the south. The police stations were initially at Marylebone Lane and 5 Little Harcourt Street (later Molyneux/John Street/Crawford Place). By 1841 D Division was responsible for Hermitage Street, Paddington, and by 1910 had been extended to include Tottenham Court Road. By 1933 Albany Street and St John's Wood stations were added, the territory shifting westward, as Tottenham Court Road moved to C, and Paddington then becoming D rather than F Division. In 1965 D Division boundaries were aligned with those of the City of Westminster and then comprised Harrow Road (DR), Paddington (DD), Marylebone Lane (DM) and St John's Wood (DD), which were incorporated into No. 6 Area in 1885/86, the first three becoming Operational Command Units on No. 1 Area (Central) in 1993/94, and part of the Central West Basic Command Unit in 2018/19.

F Division

F Division took the Covent Garden and Seven Dials area when it was established on 21st September 1829, operating firstly from a watch house near St Paul's church and later from Bow Street, until October 1869 when it was combined with E Division. From October 1869 until April 1886 there was no F Division.

In April 1886 a new F Division was established, based at Paddington, and included Notting Hill, Notting Dale and Kensington. In 1933 Chiswick and Shepherd's Bush moved from T to F Division, and Paddington transferred to D Division. At the time, Hammersmith, Fulham, Kensington and Paddington were all boroughs within the administrative county of London, whilst Acton and Brentford & Chiswick were Metropolitan Boroughs. In 1965 F Division became Fulham (FF), Hammersmith (FD) and Shepherd's Bush (FS) policing the same territory as the new London Borough of Hammersmith & Fulham. In 1985/86 these three had become Divisions in their own right, and then became part of No. 6 Area. In 1993/94 they had become two Operational Command Units, Hammersmith (FH) and Fulham (FF), within No. 1 Area (Central), and in 2018/19 the Borough of Hammersmith & Fulham became part of the Central West Basic Command Unit (CW).

G Division

G Division (Finsbury) was formed on 10th February 1830, policing the parishes of Clerkenwell, St. Luke's and part of Shoreditch. The police operated from watch houses in Bagnigge Wells and Rosoman's Street in Clerkenwell and Featherstone Street, St Luke's, but by 1865 were using purpose-built police stations at King's Cross Road and Old Street, with City Road being added in 1901. King's Cross Road transferred to E in June 1933, when Commercial Street, Islington and Dalston all moved to G Division. By 1958, G Division comprised City Road, Islington, Old Street and Commercial Street. After the April 1965 reorganisation, G Division policed the London Borough of Hackney, operating from City Road (GD), Old Street (GS), Hackney (GH), Dalston (GA) and Stoke Newington (GN). In 1985/86 the two Divisions of Hackney and Stoke Newington became part of No. 2 Area, and later Operational Command Units within No. 2 Area (North-West) in 1993/94. In 2018/19 the London borough of Hackney became part of Central East Basic Command Unit (CE).

H Division

H (Whitechapel) Division was created on 10th February 1830, with officers based at Chapel Yard/29 Church Street Spitalfields, Denmark Street, St George's East, and at Church Street in Whitechapel, covering the immediate built-up area to the east of the City of London. By 1849, Leman Street Goodman's Field replaced Denmark Street Police Station. In 1880 Arbour Square (also known as Stepney Arbour Street and Stepney East Arbour Street in subsequent years) and Shadwell transferred to H from K Division as London's policing demands expanded eastward and Divisional workloads were adjusted. By 1929 the H stations were Leman Street, Shadwell, Commercial Street (until around 1946), East Arbour Street Stepney (ie Arbour Square) and Wapping. Bethnal Green, Bow, Isle of Dogs and Poplar moved to H Division in 1933. The 1965 reorganisation made H Division co-terminous with the London Borough of Tower Hamlets with stations at Arbour Square (HD), Bow (HW), Commercial Street (GC), Leman Street (HL), Bethnal Green (HB), Limehouse (HH), Poplar (HP) and Isle of Dogs (HI). Tower Hamlets became part of No. 2 Area in 1985/86, No. 3 Area (North East) in 1993/94, and Central East (CE) Basic Command Unit in 2018/19.

J Division

J (Bethnal Green) Division was not created until April 1886, when Bethnal Green was joined with Hackney, Dalston, Leyton, Leytonstone, Loughton, Chigwell, Waltham Abbey and Woodford in a typical wedge-shape Division, with its headquarters in inner London, radiating out to the outskirts of the MPD. Much of the territory had previously been on N Division. By 1910, the stations on J (Hackney) were listed as Bethnal Green, Victoria Park, Dalston, Hackney, Wanstead, Woodford, Leyton, Leytonstone, Loughton, Claybury and Barkingside. In 1933, J Division lost Bethnal Green to H and Dalston to G, but gained Walthamstow (previously N) as a sub-division, encompassing Wanstead, Barkingside, Claybury and Loughton. In 1965 J Division became co-terminous with the London Boroughs of Waltham Forest and Redbridge, and Epping Forest District Council, the Sub-Divisions (later Divisions) being Leyton (JD), Leytonstone (JS), Walthamstow (JW), Chingford (JC), Waltham Abbey (JA), Ilford (JI), Chadwell Heath (JH), Wanstead (JN), Barkingside (JB), Woodford (JF), Claybury (JY) and Loughton (JO). In 1985/86 the three local authority areas became part of No. 1 Area, and in 1993/94 part of No. 3 Area (North-East). In 2000, Epping Forest was transferred to Essex Police. In 2018/19 the Waltham Forest was policed by the North East Basic Command Unit (NE), and Redbridge by the East Area BCU (EA).

K Division

K Division (Stepney) was formed on 10th February 1830 with stations at Arbour Square Stepney (from 1844), Mile End Road, Devon's Lane Bromley, Bethnal Green, Newby Place Poplar, Green Bank Wapping and King David Lane Shadwell. The boundary for the watchhouse in Newby Place Poplar also covered the Isle of Dogs, which in 1864 was a station on H Division. In 1839 the MPD was extended, and K Division then expanded eastward to include Barking, Dagenham, East Ham, West Ham, Great & Little Ilford, Loughton, Woodford, Woodford Bridge and Chadwell. By 1865, K Division stations were listed as Arbour Square, Shadwell, Poplar (Newby Place), Bethnal Green, Limehouse (from 1879), Isle of Dogs, Bow, West Ham, East Ham, Barking Road Plaistow, Barking, Ilford, Dagenham, Chadwell Heath, Barkingside and Chigwell. By 1873 Poplar Newby Place was replaced by Poplar (East India Dock Road), still on K Division. In 1880 Arbour Square and Shadwell were transferred to H, and Bow Road became the Divisional Headquarters for K Division rather than Stepney. In 1910 the K stations were Limehouse, Bow [Road], Forest Gate, Poplar, Isle of Dogs, Canning Town, North Woolwich, Blackwall, Plaistow, East Ham, West Ham, Barking, Ilford, Dagenham, Chadwell Heath, and Purfleet powder magazine.

In 1933 Limehouse, Poplar, Isle of Dogs and Bow transferred from K to H Division. The 1965 reorganisation that aligned many police boundaries to local authorities created an extension eastwards into Essex for K Division, which then took in the Urban Districts of Romford and Hornchurch in the form of the new London Borough of Havering, the Division then comprising Romford (KR, later KD), West Ham

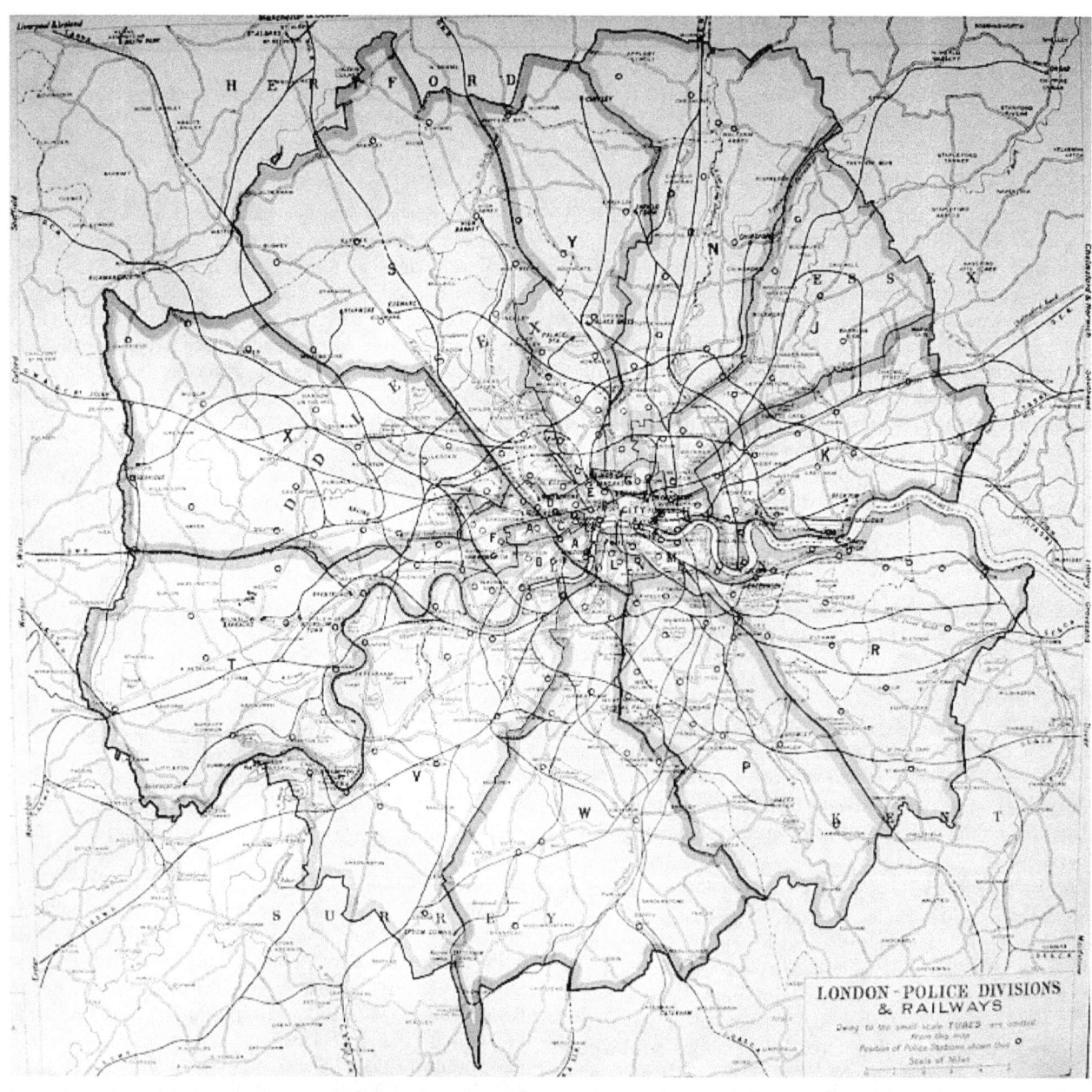

MPD 1910 (from Bacon map)

(KW), East Ham (KE), Plaistow (KO), North Woolwich (KN), Forest Gate (KF), Collier Row (KL), Harold Hill (KA), Plough Corner (KP), Hornchurch (KC), Rainham (KM), Upminster (KU), Dagenham (KG) and Barking (KG). K Division became part of No. 2 Area in 1985/86, and No. 3 Area (North East) in 1993/94. In 2018/19 Havering, and Barking & Dagenham were policed by East Area Basic Command Unit (EA), and Newham by North East BCU (NE).

L Division

L Division (Lambeth) was formed on 10th February 1830 with three bases, at Waterloo Road, High Street Old Lambeth and Christchurch Blackfriars Road. In 1865 the stations were listed as Kennington Lane, Tower Street (near the modern Westminster Bridge Road, opposite the junction with St George's Road) and Kennington Road (from 1874), Carter Street station in Walworth being transferred to L from P Division in 1886. By 1910 the stations were listed as Kennington Lane, Kennington Road, Carter Street and Rodney Road. In 1921 Wandsworth, Clapham and Battersea Park Road (Nine Elms) were transferred from W to L Division, with Carter Street and Rodney Road moving from L to M.

By 1925 the L Division stations were listed as Kennington Road, Kennington Lane, Battersea, Lavender Hill, Nine Elms and Clapham.

In 1932 a reorganisation transferred Brixton from W to L, Kennington Road from L to M, Camberwell and Peckham from P to L, Carter Street from M to L, Lavender Hill and Battersea from L to W, and Kennington Lane was closed. The L Division stations in 1958 were listed as Brixton, Clapham, Carter Street, Camberwell and Peckham.

In 1965 L Division became co-terminous with the London Borough of Lambeth, with stations at Brixton (LD), Kennington Road (LK), Clapham (LM), Balham/Cavendish Road (LB), Streatham (LS) and Gipsy Hill (LG). The London Borough of Lambeth became part of No. 4 Area in 1985/86, and an Operational Command Unit (OCU) part of No. 5 Area (South West) in 1993/94. In 2018/19 it became part of Central South (CS) BCU.

M Division

M Division (Southwark) was formed on 19th December 1829, operating from 4-5 Southwark Bridge Road and from Guildford Street, and by 1865 stations had been established at Southwark and Bermondsey (also known as Grange Road or Dunton Road). In 1880 Rotherhithe moved to M from R Division, and by 1883 M Division had four sub-divisions: Southwark, Bermondsey, Rotherhithe and Grange Road. In 1921 Carter Street transferred from L to M Division, which then comprised Southwark, Carter Street, Deptford, Grange Road, Rotherhithe and Tower Bridge. In 1932 Kennington Road became part of M, whilst Carter Street moved to L Division. The 1965 reorganisation made M Division co-terminous with the London Borough of Southwark, then comprising Southwark (MD), Tower Bridge (MT), Rotherhithe (MR), Carter Street (MS), Camberwell (MC), Peckham (MM), East Dulwich (ME) and West Dulwich (MW). In 1985/86 the London Borough of Southwark became part of No. 4 Area, and in 1993/94 part of No. 4 Area (South East). In 2018-19 it formed part of Central South (CS) BCU.

N Division

N Division (Islington), formed on 10th April 1830, was first based at Islington Green, Kingsland Road, Robert Street Hoxton, Jerusalem Square (off Well Street) Hackney; from 1832 Church Street Old Tower, later renamed Mare Street, and Stoke Newington. In 1839 the Metropolitan Police District was extended so that N Division then included Edmonton, Enfield, Tottenham, Chigwell, Chingford, Leyton, Cheshunt, Waltham Cross, Walthamstow and Wanstead. This was an enormous area compared to later territory of the Division, and various reorganisations took place until it became established as the London Borough of Islington in 1965. In 1865 a smaller N Division (Islington) comprised Islington, Hoxton, Kingsland, Hackney, Walthamstow, Waltham Abbey, Loughton, Woodford, Wanstead and Chigwell. A new Y (Highgate) Division was formed on that date, which took over Tottenham, Hornsey, Edmonton, Enfield and Cheshunt. The 1886 reorganisation that introduced the new J (Bethnal Green) Division also involved transfer of territory from N, so that J Division then took over Chigwell and Loughton. By 1910, N Division comprised Islington, Highbury Vale, Stoke Newington, St Ann's Road, Walthamstow, Tottenham, Edmonton, Chingford, Waltham Abbey (including the Royal Gunpowder Factory), Lea Bridge Road, Enfield Highway, Enfield Lock (Small Arms Factory), Cheshunt and Goffs Oak. Caledonian Road, Kentish Town, Holloway and Somers Town were added in 1933, but Islington was transferred to G Division, and N lost much of its outer London territory. Also in 1933, Cheshunt, Enfield Highway/Ponders End, Tottenham and Edmonton were moved to Y Division. Walthamstow Chingford and Waltham Abbey moved to J Division. In 1958 N Division was listed as comprising Stoke Newington, Caledonian Road, Holloway, Highbury Vale and St Ann's Road.

The 1965 reorganisation made N Division co-terminous with the London Borough of Islington, so that it then comprised King's Cross Road (ND), Caledonian Road (NC), Islington (NI), Holloway (NH) and Highbury Vale (NV). The borough became part of No. 1 Area in 1985/86, No. 2 Area (North West) in 1993/94 and Central North (CN) Basic Command Unit in 2018/19.

O Division

It is very rare for the Divisional letter O to appear on a Metropolitan Police uniform. Apart from Jack Warner's fictional *Dixon of Dock Green* TV programme character who wore the letter O from 1955-76, there were four occasions when Metropolitan Police officers wore that Divisional letter. The letter was used for re-engaged pensioners who temporarily supplemented the strength required for celebrations for the 1887 and 1897 Jubilee celebrations. Additionally the Coronations of 1902 and 1911 also included re-engaged trustworthy pensioners at their original rank with O Division. In May 1935 and May 1937, recruits from the Training School were temporarily posted to an O Division and wore that letter to police the Silver Jubilee procession of King George V and the Coronation of King George VI.

P Division

P (Camberwell) Division was formed on 13 May 1830, based at East Lane in Walworth, Camberwell Green, Brixton Washway and Christchurch watch house off Blackfriars Road. When the MPD was extended in 1839, the Division then took in the extra locations of Lewisham, Addington, Banstead, Croydon, Carshalton, Cheam, Mitcham, Sutton, Merton, Morden and Wallington. In 1865 a new W Division was formed, which covered some of the western territory previously on P, eg Banstead, Brixton, Croydon, Carshalton, Mitcham, Sutton and Tooting, leaving P Division to police Camberwell, Walworth/Carter Street, Rodney Road (from 1873), Peckham, Dulwich, Norwood (Gipsy Hill), Sydenham, Lewisham, Beckenham, Bromley and Farnborough, which included some areas earlier policed by R Division.

In 1889 when the London County Council was formed Mitcham was shown as being on P Division, but by 1912 it had become part of V Division. By 1910 P Division comprised Camberwell, Peckham, Lewisham, Southend Village Catford, Brockley, Penge, Bromley, Beckenham, East Dulwich, West Dulwich, Farnborough, Sydenham, Knights Hill (Lower Norwood) and Norwood. When the new Z (Croydon) Division was formed in 1921, South Norwood, Gipsy Hill and Knights Hill moved from P to Z.

In 1932 St Mary Cray and Chislehurst moved from R to P Division, and Camberwell and Peckham transferred to L Division. Orpington Urban District Council was moved entirely into the MPD in 1946.

By 1958 P Division was listed as Lewisham, West Dulwich, East Dulwich, Brockley, Sydenham, Catford, Penge, Beckenham, Bromley, Chislehurst, St Mary Cray and Farnborough. The 1965 reorganisation aligned P Division to the two London Boroughs of Lewisham and Bromley: Catford (PD), Lee Road (PE), Sydenham (PS), Lewisham (PL), Deptford (PP), Brockley (PK), Bromley (PR), Beckenham (PB), Penge (PG), St Mary Cray (PM), Chislehurst (PC), Farnborough (PF) and Knockholt (PT), until its transfer to Kent in 1969.

In 1985/86 the four Divisions of Lewisham (PL), Catford (PD), Bromley (PR) and Orpington (PR) became part of No. 3 Area, and in 1993/94 Catford (PD), Lewisham (PL) and Bromley & Orpington (PY) became part of No. 4 Area (South East). In 2018/19, the borough of Lewisham became part of the South East Basic Command Unit (SE) Bexley and Greenwich, and the borough of Bromley became part of South Area BCU (SN) with Croydon and Sutton.

Q Division

Q Division was formed in 1965 to police the new London Boroughs of Brent and Harrow and part of Hertfordshire, covering Wembley (QD), Harlesden (QH), Willesden Green (QL), Kilburn (QK), Harrow (QA), Pinner (QP), Edgware (QE), Wealdstone (QW), and Bushey (QB). In 1985-86 the three Divisions of Kilburn (QK), Wembley (QD) and Harrow (QA) became part of No. 7 Area. In 1993/94 it was part of No. 2 Area (North West). In 2000 Bushey was transferred to Hertfordshire Police, and in 2018/19 the boroughs of Brent and of Harrow became North West BCU (NW) with the London Borough of Barnet.

R Division

R (Greenwich) Division was founded on 13th May 1830, the same date as P, T and V Divisions. The first bases were at Orchard Lane (replaced by Blackheath Road from 1836) and Paradise Street Rotherhithe. As the MPD was extended in 1839, the Division also took responsibility for Beckenham, Bexley, Bromley, Chislehurst, Crayford, Downe, Eltham, Erith, Farnborough, Footscray, Hayes (Kent), Keston, Orpington/St. Mary Cray, Plumstead, Charlton and Woolwich. In 1865 Beckenham, Bromley and Farnborough were transferred to P, leaving R Division to police Blackheath Road, Deptford, Woolwich, East Greenwich/Park Row, Rotherhithe, Shooters Hill (formerly Old Dover Road), Bexley, Erith, Lee, Eltham, Sidcup and St Mary Cray. Plumstead had its own police station on the Division from 1893, and Westcombe Park was built in 1885. Lee Road was on R Division in 1910.

By 1925 Deptford and Rotherhithe had transferred to M. In 1932 St. Mary Cray and Chislehurst moved from R to P Division. The 1965 reorganisation made R Division co-terminous with the two London Boroughs of Greenwich and Bexley, comprising Greenwich (RD), Westcombe Park (RK), Woolwich (RW), Eltham (RM), Shooters Hill (RH), Plumstead (RP), Bexleyheath (RB), Belvedere (RB), Erith (RE) and Sidcup (RS).

The Divisions of Greenwich (RD, later RG), Woolwich (RW), and Bexleyheath (RY) became part of No. 3 Area in 1985/86, and, as Operational Command Units, part of No. 4 Area (South East) in 1993/94. In 2018/19 the boroughs of Bexley and Greenwich were part of the South East BCU (SE).

S Division

S (Hampstead) Division was formed in April 1830 with bases at Albany Street Regent's Park, Phoenix Street Somers Town, Junction Place Kentish Town, Salisbury Street Portman Market, and Heath Street Hampstead. In 1839 the Division was extended to include Finchley, Hendon, Willesden, Edgware, Barnet, Stone Bridge (Harlesden), Edgware Road (8-mile stone), Chipping Barnet (later High Barnet), Bushey, South Mimms, Aldenham, Shenley, Elstree and Totteridge. High Street Highgate was added to the Division in 1841. Highgate transferred to Y Division in 1865, when the stations were listed as Albany Street, Portland Town (later St. John's Wood), Hampstead, Whetstone, Barnet, Mimms, Shenley, Hendon, Edgware and Bushey. By 1920 Finchley and Shenley were also listed, and by 1925 Golders Green, Finchley and Shenley appear. In 1933 Wealdstone moved from S to X Division, Potters Bar went from Y to S, and Albany Street and St. John's Wood transferred from S to D Division. A new station at Radlett was opened around 1946 at a time when the outer boundaries of the MPD were adjusted, with Watford district then being wholly moved to Hertfordshire.

The 1965 reorganisation made S Division co-terminous with the London Borough of Barnet and the Hertsmere district of Hertfordshire that covers Potters Bar, South Mimms, Borehamwood, Bushey, Aldenham, Bushey and Elstree. Hampstead was transferred to E Division as it was located within the Borough of Camden. The S Division stations and their codes were Golders Green (SG), Finchley (SF), West Hendon (SW), Hendon (SN), Mill Hill (SI), Elstree (SL), Boreham Wood (SR), Barnet (SA), Whetstone (ST), South Mimms (SM) and Potters Bar (SP).

In 1985/86 this territory, organised as Golders Green (SG), Hampstead (SH) and Barnet (SA) Divisions became part of No. 7 Area, and in 1993/94 Barnet & Hertsmere (SA), West Hendon (SV) and Golders Green (SG), became Operational Command Units within No. 2 Area (North West). Hertsmere was transferred to Hertfordshire Police in 2000. In 2018/19 the London Borough of Barnet became part of North West Basic Command Unit (NW) with the boroughs of Brent and Harrow.

T Division

T (Kensington) Division was established on 13th May 1830, based at 1 Church Court Kensington, Church Place Paddington, Brook Green Hammersmith, Front Street Old Brentford, Acton and Chiswick. Then, as the MPD expanded in 1839, the Division also took in Harrow, Hanwell,

Metropolitan Police Divisions

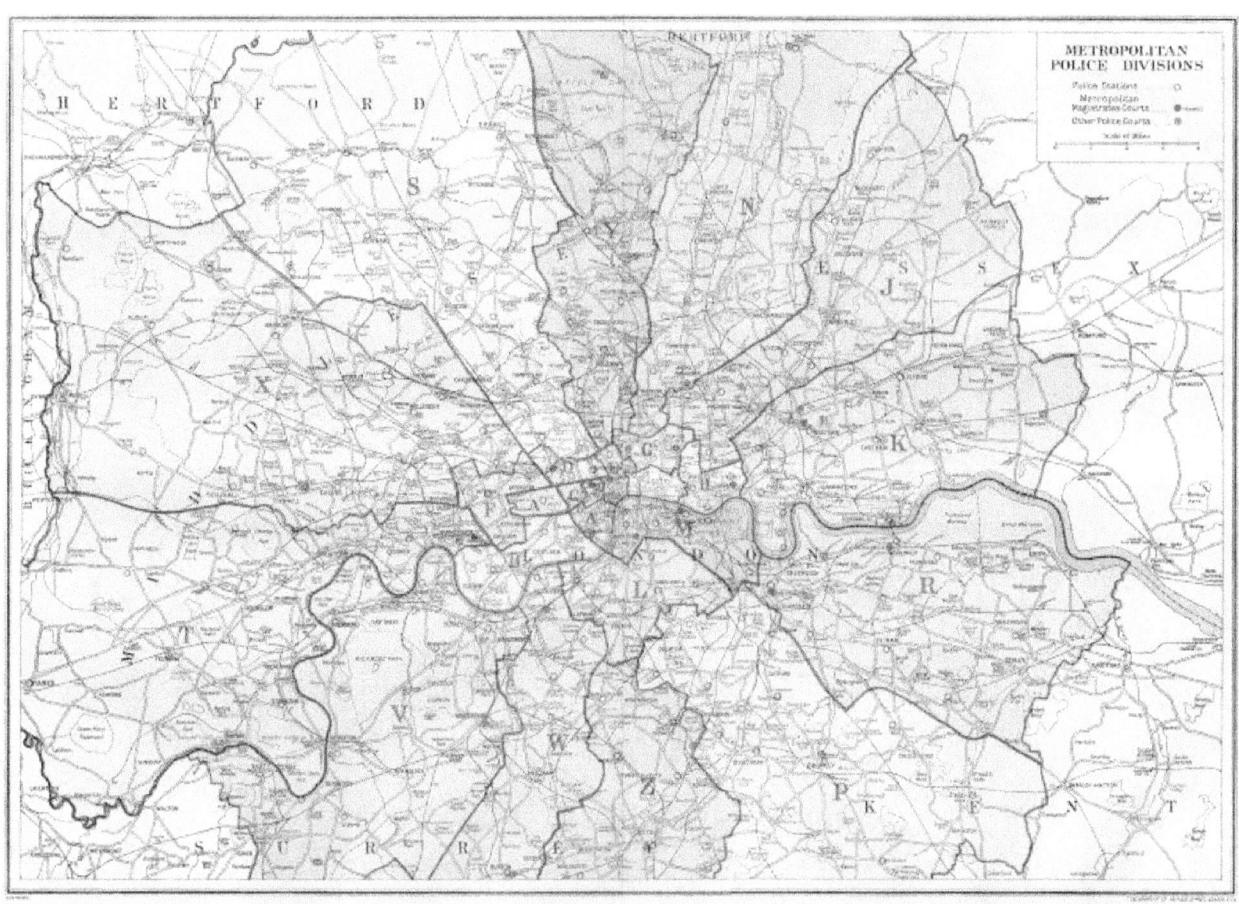

Geographia map of the MPD in 1933

Greenford, Pinner, Hillingdon, Uxbridge, Ruislip, Staines, Feltham, Isleworth, Ashford (Middlesex), Cowley, West Drayton, Hayes (Middlesex) and Shepperton. In 1865 the new X (Paddington) Division was formed and included Hillingdon and Acton, with Harrow transferring to it. T Division then comprised Kensington, Hammersmith, Chelsea, Fulham, Chiswick, Ealing (transferred to X in December 1865), Brentford, Hounslow, Harlington, Staines, Sunbury, Hampton, Twickenham, Isleworth and Heston (later Norwood Green). In 1886 a new F Division took over Paddington.

By 1910 Shepherd's Bush and Teddington had been added to T (Hammersmith) Division, and by 1925 the stations were listed as Hammersmith, Shepherds Bush, Chiswick, Bedfont, Harlington, Staines, Brentford, Hounslow, Isleworth, Norwood Green, Hampton, Sunbury, Teddington and Twickenham. In 1933 Acton and Ealing moved to T Division, whilst Shepherd's Bush transferred from T to F Division. By 1958 the T stations were listed as Acton, Ealing, Brentford, Southall, Hanwell, Norwood Green, Hounslow, Twickenham, Teddington, Hampton, Staines, Sunbury, Feltham, Bedfont and Harlington.

The 1965 reorganisation made T Division co-terminous with the London Boroughs of Hounslow and Richmond-upon-Thames, together with Elmbridge, a borough otherwise part of Surrey. The stations were then Hounslow (TD), Feltham (TF), Brentford (TB), Chiswick (TC), Teddington (TT), Hampton (TM), Richmond (TR), Barnes (TN), Staines (TE), Twickenham (TW) and Sunbury (TY). The four Divisions – Richmond, Chiswick, Hounslow and Twickenham (but not Staines) – became part of No. 5 Area in 1985/86, and OCUs as part of No. 5 Area (South West) in 1993/94. In 2000 Staines and the borough of Spelthorne were transferred to Surrey Police. In 2018/19 the London Borough of Hounslow became part of West Area BCU (WA), whilst Richmond was taken over by South West BCU (SW).

V Division

V (Wandsworth) Division was formed on 13th May 1830, operating from The Plain Wandsworth, Clapham Common and 1-2 Milman's Row Chelsea. In 1842 Lower Tooting, Salvador[3862] joined the division. That part of Chelsea, known as 'World's End', was apparently regarded, until 1865, as being easier to police from Wandsworth than from Kensington. Nine years later the Division was extended to include Wimbledon, Epsom, Kingston, Hook, Chessington, Ditton, Hampton, Sunbury, Mortlake, Ewell, Richmond, Worcester Park, Merton, Lower Tooting, Barnes and Twickenham. In 1865 a new W Division was formed to include Tooting, and T Division took over Twickenham. V Division then consisted of Wandsworth, Battersea, Wimbledon, Merton, Barnes, Richmond, Kingston, Ditton, Epsom, Hampton Court Palace, and Kew Gardens. In 1874 Putney was added to the division, remaining there until 1885 when it transferred to W Division. Putney returned to V Division in 1893 but then returned to W Division in 1909.

In 1910 the V stations were Wandsworth, Wandsworth Common (Trinity Road), Battersea, Lavender Hill, Kingston, Wimbledon, Ditton, Epsom, Putney, New

---

[3862] Salvador was a village in Lower Tooting named after a famous philanthropic family who were patrons of those less famous than themselves.

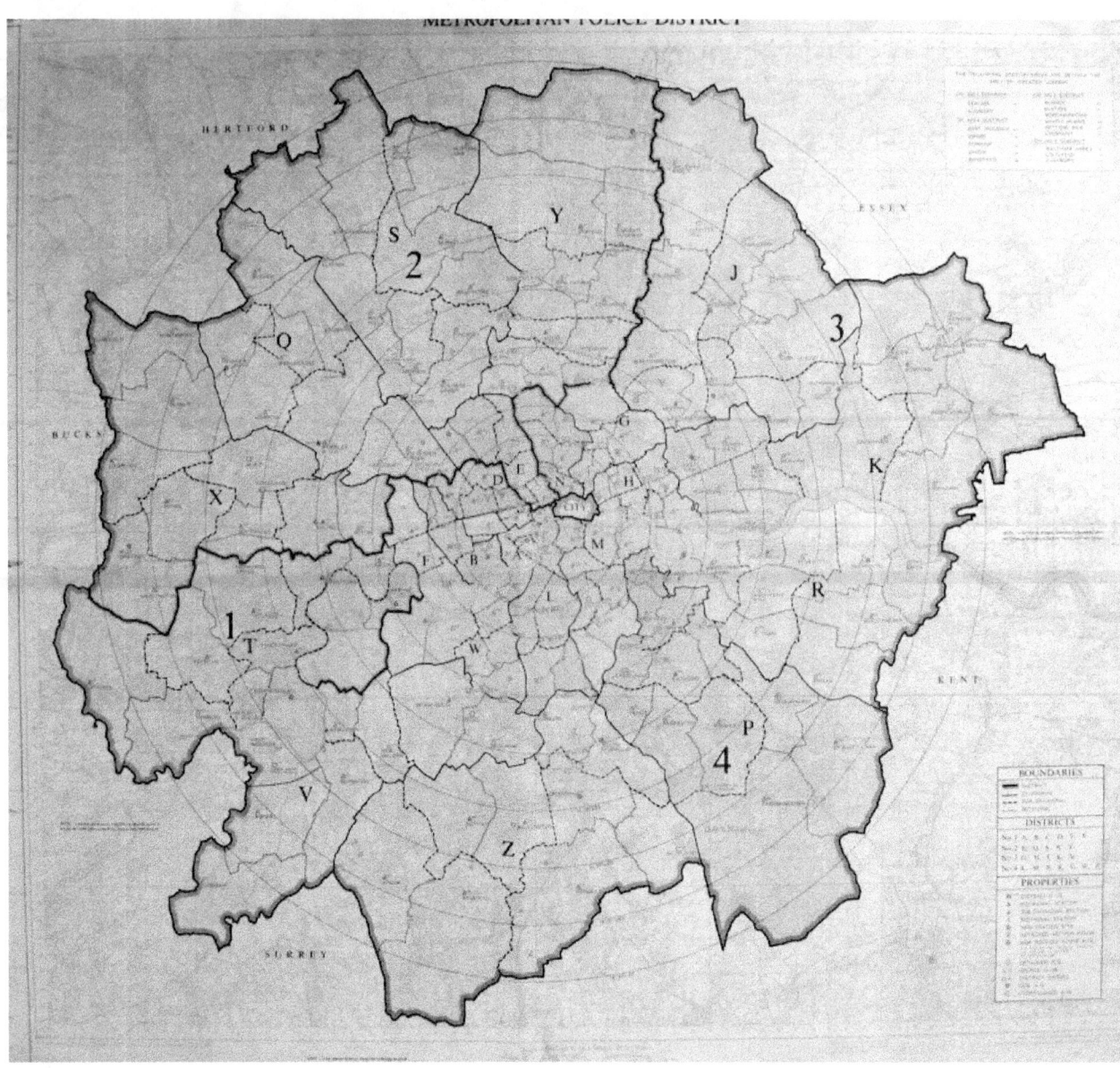

The Metropolitan Police District in 1965

Malden, Roehampton, Surbiton (formerly known as Tolworth), Richmond, Barnes and East Molesey. Mitcham was transferred to V from P by 1912. By 1923 Wandsworth Common and Epsom had transferred to W Division, while Lavender Hill and Battersea had moved to L. In 1946 the outer boundaries of the MPD were adjusted to simplify the issue of financial contributions from local authorities that were only partly within the MPD. At that point Cobham was transferred to V Division from Surrey. In 1958 V Division was listed as Wandsworth, Putney, Barnes, Richmond, Kingston, Wimbledon, New Malden, Surbiton, East Molesey, Esher and Cobham.

The 1965 reorganisation made V Division co-terminus with the London Borough of Merton, the Royal Borough of Kingston-upon-Thames and part of the Elmbridge district of Surrey, the stations being Kingston (VK), New Malden (VN), Wimbledon (VD), Mitcham (VM), Cobham (VC), Surbiton (VS), East Molesey (VE) and Esher (VH). Wandsworth moved to W Division.

In 1985/86 the former V Division, renamed as a District, was split, with Wimbledon Division (ie the Borough of Merton) becoming part of No. 4 Area, and Kingston and Elmbridge being part of No. 5 Area. In 1993/94 Merton (ZM), Kingston (VK), Battersea (WA) and Wandsworth (WW) were all included as Operational Command Units within No. 5 Area (South West). Elmbridge was transferred to Surrey Police in 2000, and in 2018/19 Kingston, Merton, Wandsworth and Richmond became South West BCU (SW).

W Division

W (Clapham) Division was announced as a new Division in Police Orders of 28th October 1865, to cover Clapham, Brixton, Streatham, Croydon, Sanderstead, Carshalton, Mitcham, Sutton, Banstead and Tooting. In 1883 Battersea Park Road had joined the division, and by 1910 Balham/Cavendish Road, Kenley, Thornton Heath and South Norwood had been added as well. In 1884 Putney joined the division, remaining until 1893 when it returned to V Division. Putney returned to W Division in 1909, where it remained until 1993. Earlsfield was included in 1914 as a new station.

In 1921, when the new Z (Croydon) Division was formed, Wandsworth, Clapham and Battersea Park Road (Nine Elms) were transferred to L Division. Brixton became L Division headquarters in 1932, when Lavender Hill and Battersea moved from L to W. In 1958 the W stations were listed as Battersea, Lavender Hill, Earlsfield, Wandsworth Common

(Trinity Road), Tooting, Mitcham, Sutton, Banstead and Epsom. The 1965 reorganisation matched W Division with the London Borough of Wandsworth, comprising Tooting (WD), Earlsfield (WF), Wandsworth Common (WC), Putney (WP), Wandsworth (WW), Battersea (WA), Lavender Hill (WL) and Nine Elms (WN).

In 1985/86 these became part of No. 5 Area, and in 1993/94, in the form of two OCUs, Battersea and Wandsworth, part of No. 5 Area (South West). In 2018/19 they became part of South West BCU (SW).

X Division

The first X Division was a temporary arrangement, for the policing of the International Exhibition from February to December 1862.

X (Paddington) Division was one of three new Divisions created as part of the October 1865 reorganisation to police Paddington, Notting Hill, Notting Dale (from 1868), Harrow Road, Acton, Hanwell, Hillingdon, Harefield, Harrow, Willesden (later Harlesden), Greenford and Ruislip. In April 1886 a new F Division took over Paddington, Notting Hill, Notting Dale and Kensington, and in 1899 Pinner joined the division. By 1910, X (Kilburn) Division stations were listed as Kilburn, Harrow Road, Pinner, Southall, Greenford, Uxbridge, Harlesden, Northwood, Hayes, Willesden Green, Ealing, Harefield, Wembley, Acton, Ruislip, Harrow and Hanwell.

In 1933 Wealdstone moved from S to X Division. In the same year Acton, Southall and Ealing moved from X to T Division. In 1958 the stations on X were listed as Harrow Road, Kilburn, Willesden Green, Harlesden, Wembley, Greenford, Harrow, Wealdstone, Pinner, Ruislip, Northwood, Harefield, Uxbridge, Hayes and Northolt.

The 1965 reorganisation made X Division co-terminous with the London Boroughs of Ealing and Hillingdon, comprising Ealing (XD), Acton (XA), Greenford (XG), Southall (XS), Norwood Green (XN), Ruislip (XR), Northwood (XN), Hayes (XY), Harlington/West Drayton (XT) and Uxbridge (XU). Pinner became QP Wealdstone QW and Harrow QA when they moved from X to Q Division.

In 1985/86 X Division became part of No. 6 Area, whilst the three Divisions of Kilburn (QK), Wembley (QD) and Harrow (QA) became part of No. 7 Area. In 1993/94 Hillingdon (XH) became an OCU within No. 5 Area (South West), and Southall (XS) an OCU on No. 2 Area (North West). In 2018/19 Ealing, Hillingdon and Hounslow became the West Area BCU (WA).

Y Division

Y (Highgate) Division was the third new Division created in 1865, to police Highgate, Somers Town, Kentish Town, Caledonian Road, Tottenham, Hornsey (from N Division), Southgate, Enfield Town, Enfield Highway (later Ponders End), Edmonton, Cheshunt and Holloway (a new police station from 1874). Cheshunt, Edmonton and Enfield Highway/Ponders End were transferred from Y to N in 1886, and in 1910 the stations on Y Division were listed as Highgate, Kentish Town, Enfield, Somers Town, Hornsey, East Barnet, Caledonian Road, Wood Green, Potters Bar, Holloway, New Southgate, Southgate, Upper Holloway and Muswell Hill, with Winchmore Hill added to the list by 1925.

In 1933 Kentish Town, Holloway, Caledonian Road and Somers Town transferred from Y to N Division, counterbalanced by Cheshunt, Enfield Highway/Ponders End, Tottenham and Edmonton moving to Y Division from N. Upper Holloway was closed at that point. The list of stations in 1958 were Highgate, Hornsey, Muswell Hill, Wood Green, Tottenham, Edmonton, Winchmore Hill, Southgate, Enfield, Enfield Highway, Cheshunt and Goffs Oak.

The 1965 reorganisation made Y Division match the boundaries of the London Boroughs of Haringey and Enfield, together with most of Broxbourne District Council area, the stations comprising Wood Green (YD), Tottenham (YT), Hornsey (YR), Muswell Hill (YM), Highgate (YH), St Ann's Road (YA), Edmonton (YE), Winchmore Hill (YW), Southgate (YS), New Southgate (YS), Enfield (YE), Enfield Highway (YI) and Cheshunt (YC).

In 1985/86 the Divisions Hornsey (YR), Tottenham (YT), Edmonton (YE) and Enfield (YF) became part of No. 1 Area, and in 1993/94 Tottenham and Hornsey became part of No. 2 Area (North West), whilst Enfield and Edmonton were then No. 3 Area (North East). In 2000 policing Broxbourne was transferred to Hertfordshire Police. In 2018/19 the London Boroughs of Enfield and Haringey became the North Area Basic Command Unit (NA).

Z Division

Z Division (Croydon) was created in 1921 to reflect the growing importance of Croydon that had previously been policed as part of W Division. The new division included Croydon, Kenley, Thornton Heath, South Norwood, Gipsy Hill (from P Division), and Knights Hill (Lower Norwood). Norwood/Gipsy Hill and Norbury had been added to the Z Division list of stations by 1925, while Streatham and Wallington were transferred from W to Z in October 1931. The Warlingham district was transferred to Kent in 1947 as the result of changes made in the Police Act 1946. The stations on Z in 1958 were Croydon, Streatham, Gipsy Hill, Norbury, South Norwood, Kenley and Wallington.

The 1965 reorganisation made Z Division co-terminous with the London Boroughs of Croydon and Sutton, plus the Epsom and Ewell borough council area of Surrey, comprising Croydon (ZD), Kenley (ZK), Norbury (ZN), South Norwood (ZS), Sutton (ZT), Wallington (ZW), Epsom (ZP) and Banstead (ZB).

In 1985/86 three Divisions – Croydon (ZD), South Norwood (ZN) and Epsom (ZP) – became part of No. 4 Area, and in 1993/94 Epsom & Sutton (ZP), Croydon (ZD) and South Norwood (ZN) were OCUs within No. 4 Area (South East). In 2000 Epsom was transferred to Surrey Police, and in 2018/19 the London Boroughs of Sutton, Croydon and Bromley comprised the South Area (SN) Basic Command Unit.

Airport Division

The Metropolitan Police took responsibility for policing Heathrow airport in November 1974 when it became a District (equivalent to a former Division) in its own right, comprising Heathrow and parts of West Drayton and Staines. It was known as Airport Division/District with a code of AD and a telegraphic code of ID. It became part of No. 6 Area with code ID in 1985/86, an OCU in No. 5 Area (South West) in 1993/94, and from 2002 has been policed by Specialist Operations at New Scotland Yard, currently the Aviation Policing Command.

A map of the eight Areas introduced in 1985/86

Appendix A.
Metropolitan Police Warrant Numbers 1829–2019

When joining the Police Service Police Officers are given an individual warrant number which remains with them for ever. This is a general guide indicating the year in which the officer joined the Service. In recent years warrant numbers have been allocated at the recruitment stage, but the officer may not formally be attested as a Constable until later.

Women Police Officers formally joined the Metropolitan Police in 1919, and were allocated separate warrant numbers up until the end of 1992. Thereafter both male and female officers were given a six figure warrant number.

YEAR	MALE OFFICERS Start	Finish	FEMALE OFFICERS Start	Finish
1829	1	1590		
1830	1591	5680		
1831	5681	7145		
1832	7146	8100		
1833	8101	9098		
1834	9099	10130		
1835	10131	11277		
1836	11278	12333		
1837	12334	13454		
1838	13455	14550		
1839	14551	15805		
1840	15806	17889		
1841	17890	19019		
1842	19020	19888		
1843	19889	20931		
1844	20932	21751		
1845	21752	22772		
1846	22773	23994		
1847	23995	25075		
1848	25076	26454		
1849	26455	27295		
1850	27296	28154		
1851	28155	29900		
1852	29901	30746		
1853	30747	32012		
1854	32013	33213		
1855	33214	34323		
1856	34324	35345		
1857	35346	36633		
1858	36634	37702		
1859	37703	38602		
1860	38603	40126		
1861	40127	41180		
1862	41181	43505		
1863	43506	44581		
1864	44582	45647		
1865	45648	46869		
1866	46870	47941		
1867	47942	49153		
1868	49154	51382		
1869	51383	52319		
1870	52320	53466		
1871	53467	55018		
1872	55019	56399		
1873	56400	57488		
1874	57489	58561		
1875	58562	59819		
1876	59820	61042		
1877	61043	62114		
1878	62115	63173		
1879	63174	64172		
1880	64173	65149		
1881	65150	66159		
1882	66160	67354		
1883	67355	68830		
1884	68831	69957		
1885	69958	71048		
1886	71049	72224		
1887	72225	73144		
1888	73145	74142		
1889	74143	75054		
1890	75055	76480		
1891	76481	77318		
1892	77319	78187		
1893	78188	79227		
1894	79228	80147		
1895	80148	80903		
1896	80904	81811		
1897	81812	83496		
1898	83497	84741		
1899	84742	85895		
1900	85896	86986		
1901	86987	88150		
1902	88151	89422		
1903	89423	90387		
1904	90388	91356		
1905	91357	92760		
1906	92761	94152		
1907	94153	95313		
1908	95314	96457		
1909	96458	97734		
1910	97735	99563		
1911	99564	100928		
1912	100929	102128		
1913	102129	103574		
1914	103575	104647		
1915	104648	105205		
1916	105206	105209		

YEAR	MALE OFFICERS Start	Finish	FEMALE OFFICERS Start	Finish
1917	105210	105212		
1918	105213	105235		
1919	105236	108413	1	125
1920	108414	111242	126	161
1921	111243	112137	162	168
1922	112138	112268	169	181
1923	112269	112531	182	183
1924	112532	113555	184	191
1925	113556	115085	192	221
1926	115086	116068	222	229
1927	116069	117122	230	231
1928	117123	118042	232	236
1929	118043	119309	237	241
1930	119310	120633	242	251
1931	120634	121959	252	264
1932	121960	122676	265	268
1933	122677	123179	269	279
1934	123180	123898	280	286
1935	123899	124677	287	300
1936	124678	125442	301	316
1937	125443	126591	317	350
1938	126592	127433	351	373
1939	127434	128336	374	421
1940	128337	128340	422	464
1941	128341	128342	465	505
1942	128343	128343	506	525
1943	128343	128343	526	535
1944	128344	128345	536	545
1945	128346	128347	546	551
1946	128348	130122	552	606
1947	130123	132418	607	677
1948	132419	134162	678	741
1949	134163	135258	742	819
1950	135259	136624	820	943
1951	136625	137505	944	1031
1952	137506	138816	1032	1110
1953	138817	139849	1111	1246
1954	139850	141157	1247	1346
1955	141158	142540	1347	1432
1956	142541	144298	1433	1527
1957	144299	145873	1528	1616
1958	145874	147251	1617	1689
1959	147252	148595	1690	1756
1960	148596	149657	1757	1813
1961	149658	150882	1814	1884
1962	150883	152097	1885	1953
1963	152098	153317	1954	2047
1964	153318	154373	2048	2126
1965	154374	155588	2127	2226
1966	155589	156962	2227	2322
1967	156963	158570	2323	2452
1968	158571	159825	2453	2540
1969	159826	161018	2541	2638
1970	161019	162175	2639	2765
1971	162176	163210	2766	2864
1972	163211	164320	2865	2980
1973	164321	165326	2981	3086
1974	165327	166626	3087	3319
1975	166627	168094	3320	3607
1976	168095	170080	3608	4143
1977	170081	171503	4140	4600
1978	171504	172751	4601	4916
1979	172752	174488	4917	5394
1980	174489	176305	5395	5946
1981	176306	178761	5947	6382
1982	178762	180947	6383	6718
1983	180948	182422	6719	6913
1984	182423	183493	6914	7063
1985	183494	184560	7064	7270
1986	184561	186018	7271	7562
1987	186019	187426	7563	8069
1988	187427	189205	8070	8590
1989	189206	190569	8591	9018
1990	195570	191671	9019	9343
1991	191672	192583	9344	9701
1992	192584	193264	9702	9994
1993	193268	194414		
1994	194415	195606		
1995	195607	196678		
1996	196679	197745		
1997	197746	198855		
1998	198856	200199		
1999	200200	201453		
2000	201454	202648		
2001	202649	205107		
2002	205108	208350		
2003	208351	217921		
2004	217922	220926		
2005	220927	220965		
2006	220966	224740		
2007	224741	226712		
2008	226713	229031		
2009	229032	232026		
2010	232027	232537		
2011	232545	233246		
2012	232923	234583		
2013	234584	235946		
2014	235947	239347		
2015	238348	250283		
2016	241727	243608		
2017	243415	244859		
2018	244853	251760		
2019	251761	255709		

Appendix B.
Section Houses

Accommodation for police officers was sometimes provided on the upper floors of police stations. In small stations on the outskirts of London, an officer sometimes lived at the station with his family. For single officers, the accommodation was called section houses, a 'section' meaning part of a Division, in the same way in which Sergeants were called 'Section Sergeants'. Section houses were spread throughout London, sometimes named after senior police officers, Home Secretaries or Receivers. Each had an identification code starting SQ. Female single officers sometimes lived in police hostels.

Missing numbers in the SQ series refer to section houses, like Beak Street, that had been closed or converted for other purposes. The list below originates from 1991.

Section Houses

- SQ1 **Stoke Newington** 3 Victorian Road N16 8HP
- SQ4 **Ede House** 146 Mare Street E8 3SQ
- SQ5 **Elizabeth House** Winchester Place N6 5HJ
- SQ6 **Elliott House** Molyneux Street W1H 6BY
- SQ7 **Finchley** Amberden Avenue N3 3DG
- SQ9 **Gilmour House** 42 Kennington Lane SE11 4LS
- SQ10 **Harold Scott House** 1 Birchfield Street E14 8ED
- SQ11 **Kentish Town** 10A Holmes Road NW5 3AD
- SQ12 **Lea Bridge Road** 497 Lea Bridge Road, E10 7ED
- SQ13 **Macnaghten House** Compton Place WC1H 9SD
- SQ14 **Maurice Drummond House** Catherine Grove SE10 8BT
- SQ15 **Moylan House** 10 King David Lane E1 0EJ
- SQ16 **Nightingale Lane** 3-5 Nightingale Lane SW4 9AF
- SQ17 **Norman Kendal House** 4 High Street, East Ham E6 6EL
- SQ18 **Olive House** 30 Canonbury Park South N1 2HL
- SQ19 **Robert Mark House** 6-16 Bryanston Street W1H 7AN
- SQ20 **Percy Laurie House** 215 Upper Richmond Road SW15 6SH
- SQ22 **Philip Game House** Ixworth Place SW3 3QJ
- SQ23 **Ravenscourt House** 3 Paddenswick Road W6 0UE
- SQ24 **Paul Breen House** 185 Dartmouth Road SE26 4RJ
- SQ25 **Trenchard House** Broadwick Street W1 0DF
- SQ26 **Trevor Bigham House** 41 Ascot Road SW17 9JJ
- SQ28 **Wembley** 603-605 Harrow Road HA0 2EQ
- SQ30 **Willesden** 229-231 Willesden Lane NW2 5RP
- SQ31 **Brentford** 5 St Paul's Road, Brentford TW8 0NB
- SQ34 **Northumberland Park** 143 Northumberland Park N17 0TR
- SQ35 **Paddington Green** 2 Harrow Road W2 1XL
- SQ36 **Kensington** 72 Earls Court Road W8 6EQ
- SQ38 **Goldhawk House** 292 Goldhawk Road, Hammersmith W12 9PF
- SQ39 **Douglas Webb House** 546 Sipson Road, West Drayton UX7 0JB
- SQ40 **Sir Ranulph Bacon House** 8 Sylvan Hill, Upper Norwood SE19 2QG
- SQ40 **Beak Street** 40 Beak Street W1F 9RQ
- SQ40 **Ambrosden House** 1 Ambrosden Avenue SW1P 1QQ

Hostels

- SQ50 **Putney** 215 Upper Richmond Road SW15 6SH
- SQ55 **Northwood** 2 Murray Road, Northwood HA6 2YN
- SQ59 **Barnes** 1 Beverley Road SW13 0LX

Acknowledgements

The authors are particularly indebted to friends and colleagues who advised, directed and discussed the research, yet still remained interested. Particular gratitude and thanks are also extended to Mr Julian Jephcote (retired police officer and historian), whose knowledge and pictures were invaluable. Phillip Barnes-Warden (with Paul Dew and Neil Paterson, all from the Metropolitan Police Historical Collection) provided essential assistance and reliable information including pictures, often at short notice. Bernard Brown (retired Metropolitan Police Sergeant) again deserves an extra mention, because it has been his consistent historical research and work of that has made our task easier - thank-you. The Metropolitan and City Police Orphans Fund, formerly the Metropolitan and City Police Orphange, kindly allowed us to reprint material from their website. Also requiring special mention is the late John Back, whose research from 1970s in the Metropolitan Archives provided us with valuable material.

Our thanks also go to:

Dave Allen, Friend of Bow Street Police Station

Phil Anderson, Metropolitan Police Officer retired

Helen Barnard, Friend of the Metropolitan Police Collection

John Barnie, Chief Executive Metropolitan Police Trading Service

S. Barson

Maggie Bird, Curator Metropolitan Police Museum

Dr Melvyn Brooks, contributor

Ken Butler, Friend of the Metropolitan Police Collection

David Capus, Records Management Branch

Sioban Clark, Friend of the Metropolitan Police Historical Collection

Professor Linda Clarke, Middlesex University

David Collett, Historian and police medal collector

Tony Cooper, Property Service Department

Jeff Cowdell, former Police officer Staffordshire Police and badge collector

Bill Davison, Metropolitan Police Surveyor

Tony Dawson, Metropolitan Police retired

Jack Edwards

Bryn Elliott, Contributor on Waltham Abbey

Chris Forester, retired Police officer and Friend of the Metropolitan Police Collection

Anna Gardiner, MPS Historic Collection

Charles Griggs, Chief Superintendent Metropolitan Police

Stuart Grist, contributor

Alex Hart, serving Metropolitan Police officer and police history enthusiast

Janice Horne, family historian who gave details about Inspector Charles Brown

Neville (Spike) Hughes, retired Metropolitan Police officer (who sadly passed away in 2008)

Stuart Inglis, contributor

Claire Johnson, PC Metropolitan Police

Trefor Jones, Epsom Historical Society

Dee Jupp, Merton Borough

Dick Kirby, retired Metropolitan Police Detective Sergeant

Nicholas Long, retired Metropolitan Police officer

Nick Mackay, Police officer with the Border Agency

Dave Moss, Metropolitan Police Sergeant

Ken Moxley, retired Metropolitan Police officer

Chris Newman, Sheerness Historian

Barry Nicholson, retired Metropolitan Police officer, historian and researcher Met Police Historic Collection

Dr Jonathan Oates, Archivist at London Borough of Ealing

Hazel Ogilvie, Harrow Central Librarian who gave permission to use Harrow pictures

Camilla O'Hare, Head of income generation, Metropolitan Police

Simon Ovens, Chief Superintendent and Police medal collector

Barnaby Palmer, Police history researcher

Adrian Phipps, Property Service Department

John Player

George Plumb, Specialist Police badge collector

Bill Prowse

Peter Reed, Webmaster of the Epsom and Ewell Historical Explorer

Ray Seal, Curator Metropolitan Police Historic Collection

Nigel Short, contributor

Peter Simmons

Jon Simpson, Superintendent Metropolitan Police

Keith Skinner, Police history researcher

Dr Clare Smith, Curator at Metropolitan Police Heritage Collection

Barbara Street

Jude Swinden, title contributor

Roger Vaughn, specialist photograph collector

Neil Watson, for researching and writing about the London Borough of Harrow's Police stations.

Dave Wilkinson, historian and helmet plate/badge collector

Victor Legender Wilkinson, Chief Superintendent Metropolitan Police (retired)

The staff of Brent Central Library

Essex Police Museum

The staff of the *Job* magazine

The London Borough of Hackney Archives

The staff of the London Borough Libraries of Bexley, Bromley, Croydon, Greenwich, Lambeth, Lewisham, Merton, Sutton, Southwark and Wandsworth

Old Enfield Charitable Trust

The staff of Hillingdon Central Library

The staff of Hammersmith and Fulham Libraries

And lastly our gratitude and appreciation goes to our publisher Adam Wood of Mango Books, who took on the challenge of putting together the research dating from before 2003 until 2021.

Index of Police Stations and Other Buildings

Abbey Wood Police Station 23, 37
Addington Police Office/New Addington Police Station 21, 39
Albany Street Police Station 17, 20, 40, 150, 160, 242, 276, 344, 477, 480
Aldenham Police (Station) 18, 41
Ambrosden House Section House 3, 41, 487
Arbour Square Police Station and
  Thames Police Court 36, 42, 61, 64, 117, 118, 259, 267, 384, 421, 477
Ashford and Ashford Police Cottages 26, 44

Balham/Cavendish Road Police Station 32, 44, 128, 129, 384, 479, 482
Banstead Police Station 4, 35, 45, 108, 113, 114, 352, 358, 483
Barking Police Station 33, 46, 95, 118, 227, 478
Barkingside Police Station 34, 48, 119, 121, 266, 271, 321
Barnes Police Station 34, 50, 369
Battersea Police Station 51, 256
Beak Street Section House 15, 53, 487
Beckenham Police Station (PB) 19, 53
Bedfont Police Station 29, 54, 148, 350
Belgravia Police Station 58, 158
Belvedere Police Station 18, 59
Bethnal Green Police Station 60, 259, 260
Bexleyheath Police Station 18, 61, 389
Biggin Hill Police Station 19, 63
Borehamwood Police Station 18, 63, 160, 308, 398
Bow Road Police Station 44, 64, 154, 394
Bow Street Police Station 20, 66, 73, 213
Brentford Police Station 29, 68
Brixton Police Station 30, 32, 73
Brockley Police Station 32, 76
Bromley Police Station (PR) 19, 77
Bushey Police Station 18, 78

Caledonian Road Police Station 29, 79, 335
Camberwell Police Station 35, 80, 295
Canning Town Police Station 33, 83
Cannon Row Police Station 84, 91, 280
Carshalton Police Station 35, 86, 374
Carter Street/Walworth Police Station 35, 86, 119, 341, 479, 480
Catford and Southend Village Police Stations 32, 89
Chadwell Heath Police Station 34, 90, 228, 386
Chalkhill Police Station 19, 91
Charing Cross Police Station 68, 86, 91
Chelsea Police Station 92, 239
Cheshunt Police Station 22, 94
Chigwell and Claybury Police Stations 22, 95
Chingford Police Station 96, 304, 378
(Chipping) Barnet Police Station 18, 99,
Chislehurst Police Station (PC) 19, 78, 102
Chiswick Police Station 29, 103, 149
City Road Police Station 24, 106, 224
Clapham Police Station 30, 32, 108, 238
Clark's Buildings (later George Street Police Station) 67, 109
Cobham Police Station 34, 109
Colindale Police Station 18, 111, 209, 275, 398
Collier Row Police Station 26, 112, 318

Commercial Street Police Station 112
Croydon Police Station 21, 39, 113, 374

Dagenham Police Station 117
Dalston Police Station 24, 119, 172
Dean Street Police Station 121
Debden Police Office 22, 121
Deptford Police Station 32, 122, 168
Ditton Police Station (aka Thames Ditton and Long Ditton) 34, 123, 356
North Dulwich Police Station 35, 124
East Dulwich Police Station 35, 125
West Dulwich Police Station 35, 90, 125, 126

Ealing Police Station 21, 126
Earlsfield Police Station 128, 385
East (New) Barnet Police Station 18, 129
East Greenwich Police Station 23, 130
East Ham Police Station 33, 132, 268
East Molesey Police Station 34, 133
Edgware Police Station 25, 133, 139
Edmonton Police Station 22, 49, 96, 108, 136, 352, 366
Elstree Police Station 18, 138
Eltham Police Station 23, 139, 168
Enfield Police Station 22, 141, 334
Epsom Police Station 35, 142, 358
Erith Police Station (RE) 19, 144
Esher Police Station 34, 146
Ewell Police Station 31, 147

Farnborough Police Station (PF) 19, 147, 360
Feltham Police Station 29, 148
Finchley Police Station 18, 149
Forest Gate Police Station 33, 133, 153
Fulham Police Station (aka Walham Green, South Fulham) 104, 155, 177

Gardiner's Lane Police Station 157
Gerald Road Police Station 157
Goffs Oak Police Station 22, 159
Golders Green Police Station 18, 159
Grange Road Police Station (Bermondsey) 35, 160
Gray's Inn Road Police Station 20, 161, 225
Great Marlborough Street Police Station 161
Great Scotland Yard 3, 162, 241, 246, 280, 299, 476
Greek Street Police Station 163
Greenford Police Station 21, 163
Greenwich Police Station 130, 164

Hackney Police Station 24, 169, 235, 264, 265, 270, 321, 373
Hainault Police Office 22, 173
Ham Police Station (Office) 34, 174
Hammersmith Police Station 24, 38, 174, 330
Hampstead Police Station 20, 177, 205
Hampton Police Station 34, 178
Hanwell Police Station 21, 181
Harefield Police Station 26, 182

Harlesden Police Station (formerly named Willesden)........19, 183, 398, 402
Harlington Police Station 26, 57, 186
Harold Hill Police Station 26, 187
Harrow (Northolt Road) Police Station........25, 187
Harrow (West Street) Police Station........25, 188
Harrow Road Police Station........192, 243, 388, 402
Hayes and Gould's Green Police Stations 26, 194
Heathrow Airport Division SO18 ....26, 195
Hendon: The Peel Centre 18, 200
Hendon Police Station........18, 205
Highbury Vale Police Station........29, 209
Highgate Police Station........25, 210, 219
Hillingdon and Uxbridge Police Stations 26, 211
Holborn Police Station 21, 68, 161, 214
Holloway Police Station........29, 210, 214, 276
Hornchurch Police Station........26, 217, 311
Hornsey Police Station 25, 218, 278
Hounslow Police Station........29, 220, 232
Hoxton (Kingsland Road) Police Station........24, 222
Hunter Street Police Station........21, 161, 224
Hyde Park Police Station........225

Ilford Police Station 34, 46, 50, 90, 95, 117, 226, 385, 412
Imber Court........35, 146, 228
Isle of Dogs Police Station........230
Isleworth Police Station........29, 232
Islington Police Station........29, 210, 233

Kenley Police Station 21, 235
Kennington Lane Police Station........31, 236
Kennington Road Police Station........109, 236
Kensington Police Station 9, 239
Kentish Town Police Station 21, 210, 241, 410
Kew Police Station........34, 242
Kilburn Police Station........19, 185, 243
King Street Police Station........157, 245
Kings Cross Road Police Station 29, 107, 247
Kingsbury Police Station........19, 248
Kingston Police Station 31, 248
Knights Hill or Lower Norwood Police Station........32, 254
Knockholt Police Station (PT)........19, 255

Lavender Hill Police Station........255
Lee Road Police Station........32, 256
Leman Street Police Station 43, 61, 257
Lewisham Police Station........32, 76, 260, 360
Leyton Police Station........96, 262, 266
Leytonstone Police Station........265
Limehouse Police Station........36, 227, 267, 307
Limes Farm Police Office 22, 268
Loughton Police Station 22, 268

Marble Arch Police Station 270
Marks Gate Police Station........119, 271
Marylebone Lane Police Station........271
Metropolitan and City Police Orphanage........10, 34, 175, 227, 251, 272, 317
Metropolitan Police (Hayes) Sports Club........19, 274
Mill Hill Police Station........18, 275
Mitcham Police Station........33, 275, 364, 410
Molyneux Street or John Street (Crawford Place) Police Station........277
Morden Police Office........33, 277, 409
Muswell Hill Police Station........25, 211, 278

New Malden Police Station........31, 279
New Scotland Yard........84, 85, 86, 98, 137, 156, 163, 214, 238, 242, 280,
........292, 383, 399, 403, 464, 467, 483
New Southgate Police Station........22, 281, 339, 483

Nine Elms Police Station or Battersea Park Road Police Station........44, 281
Norbury Police Station........21, 282
North Fulham Police Station........24, 155, 156, 283
North Woolwich Police Station........33, 284
Northwood Police Station 26, 189, 285
Norwood Green Police Station........21, 128, 286, 338
Norwood/Gipsy Hill Police Station........32, 254, 287
Notting Dale Police Station........190, 288
Notting Hill Police Station........290

Old Street Police Station........24, 104, 290
Orpington Police Station (PN)........19, 292, 346

Paddington and Paddington Green Police Stations........292, 477
Peckham Police Station 35, 81, 294, 408
Penge Police Station........19, 190, 261, 295
Pinner Police Station 25, 188, 297
Plaistow Police Station........33, 84, 132, 300, 334
Plough Corner Police Station 26, 301
Plumstead Police Station........23, 302, 362
Ponders End/Enfield Highway Police Station........22, 304, 377
Poplar Police Station........267, 305
Potters Bar Police Station........18, 307
Putney Police Station........254, 308

Radlett Police Station........18, 310
Rainham Police Station 26, 310
Richmond Police Station........34, 174, 311, 418
Rochester Row Police Station 30, 229, 316
Rodney Road Police Station........35, 88, 316
Roehampton Police Station........317
Romford Police Station........26, 302, 318
Rotherhithe Police Station 35, 322
Ruislip Police Station 26, 183, 285, 323

Sanderstead (Hamsley Green) Police Station........21, 325
Shadwell Police Station........43, 326
Shenley Police Station........18, 327
Shepherds Bush Police Station........24, 177, 329
Shepperton Lock Police Station........26, 330
Shooters Hill Police Station........23, 330
Sidcup Police Station (RS)........19, 332
Somers Town Police Station........20, 21, 99, 333
(South) Mimms Police Station........18, 335
South Norwood Police Station........21, 336
Southall Police Station........21, 287, 337
Southgate Police Station 22, 338
Southwark/Stones End Police Station........35, 127, 339, 402
St. Ann's Road Police Station 25, 342
St. John's Wood Police Station
(formerly Portland Town Police Station)........21, 343
St. Mary Cray Police Station (PM) 19, 292, 344
Staines Police Station (and Spelthorne) 26, 346, 354
Stanwell Police House (Station) 26, 349
Stoke Newington (Kingsland) Police Station 24, 350
Streatham Police Station........32, 352
Sunbury Police Station 26, 348, 353
Surbiton (Tolworth) Police Station 31, 355
Sutton Police Station........35, 46, 357, 418
Sydenham Police Station........32, 257, 359

Teddington Police Station........35, 360
Thamesmead Police Station 23, 362
Thornton Heath Police Station 21, 283, 363
Tooting (and Lower or South Tooting) Police Station 363
Tottenham Police Station 25, 218, 364, 376
Tottenham Court Road Police Station........366, 468

Index

Tower Bridge Police Station 35, 161, 323, 367
Trenchard House Section House 368, 487
Twickenham Police Station 34, 315, 316, 369

Upminster Police Station..26, 370
Upper Holloway Police Station (aka Archway Police Station) 29, 371

Victoria Park Police Station 24, 372
Vine Street Police Station 53, 214, 373

Wallington Police Station 35, 374
Waltham Abbey Police Station 22, 96, 375
Walthamstow Police Station 98, 263, 377, 385
Walton Street Police Station 379
Wandsworth Police Station 30, 34, 85, 380
Wandsworth Common (Trinity Road) Police Station................................384
Wanstead Police Station 34, 385
Waterloo Pier Police Station 386

Wealdstone Police Station 25, 387
Welling Police Office...19, 389
Wellington Arch Police Station 390
Wembley Police Station 19, 390
West Drayton Police Station 26, 187, 391
West End Central Police Station...162, 392, 467
West Ham Police Station 33, 128, 153, 155, 268, 393
West Hampstead Police Station 21, 397
West Hendon Police Station..18, 111, 397
West Wickham Police Office..19, 398
Westcombe Park Police Station 23, 399
Whetstone Police Station 18, 176, 400
Willesden Green Police Station 19, 398, 402
Wimbledon Police Station (and Merton) 33, 403
Winchmore Hill Police Station 22, 410
Woodford Police Station 34, 95, 412
Woolwich Police Station 23, 414
Worcester Park Police Office..35, 418

Index of Dockyard and Marine Policing

Thames – Blackwall Police Station 419
Thames – Wapping Police Station 42, 420

Woolwich Dockyard or 1st Division....240, 414, 424, 425, 433, 434, 437, 439
Portsmouth Dockyard or 2nd Division 430, 441, 443

Devonport Dockyard or 3rd Division...436
Chatham (and Sheerness) Dockyard or 4th Division 422, 433, 439
Pembroke Dockyard or 5th Division 427, 428, 437, 441, 444
Rosyth Dockyard...445

Index of Basic Command Units

Central East CE.................1, 2, 24, 35, 42, 60, 64, 106, 230, 257, 267, 305, 350
Central North CN 1, 2, 20, 29, 40, 214, 241, 397, 479
Central South AS............................1, 2, 31, 35, 44, 73, 86, 287, 294, 339, 479
Central West CW 1, 2, 24, 30, 58, 91, 92, 94, 174, 192, 208, 225, 239,
....288, 290, 292, 329, 392, 475, 476, 477
East Area EA........................2, 25, 34, 46, 48, 96, 117, 217, 226, 318, 478, 479
North Area NA 2, 22, 24, 136, 141, 218, 338, 364, 410, 483
North West NW 2, 19, 20, 21, 25, 29, 63, 99, 111, 133, 183, 187, 188,
....243, 297, 390, 412, 477, 479, 480, 483
North East NE 2, 22, 24, 25, 33, 34, 35, 108, 153, 265, 352, 477,
....478, 479, 483
South Area SN 2, 19, 21, 45, 53, 63, 77, 78, 102, 113, 141, 169, 357, 398,
....480, 483

South East SE............ 2, 18, 19, 21, 22, 32, 35, 59, 76, 123, 132, 139, 260, 302,
....362, 479, 480, 483
South West SW 2, 28, 30, 32, 34, 50, 106, 275, 357, 360, 369, 403, 409,
....479, 481, 482, 483
West Area WA 2, 21, 26, 28, 37, 103, 106, 148, 220, 337, 481, 483

Essex Police..............................2, 22, 25, 94, 112, 173, 187, 217, 268, 301, 310,
....318, 370, 375, 478
Hertfordshire Police.................3, 64, 79, 95, 308, 310, 328, 335, 335, 480, 483
Kent Constabulary 3, 32, 59, 63, 122, 164, 255, 345, 389, 398
Surrey Constabulary 3, 30, 34, 35, 45, 109, 110, 111, 133, 142,
....146, 253, 346, 349, 355

Index of Uniform

Equipment 7, 21, 30, 72, 327, 383, 395, 425, 427, 447-457
Badges 27, 28, 72, 142, 185, 196, 197, 310, 377, 396, 408,
.... 421, 422, 425, 435, 440, 447-457, 458, 459, 460, 461, 462, 463, 464,
.... 469, 470, 471, 472, 473, 474,

Buttons 28, 160, 197, 355, 372, 408, 440, 447-457, 460, 461
Headgear 7, 46, 47, 99, 144, 167, 193, 196, 198, 208, 249, 310, 372, 396,
.... 424, 425, 435, 440, 441, 447-457, 460, 461
Tunics 28, 160, 197, 372, 383, 432, 447-457, 458, 460, 461, 464, 468, 469

Index of Women Police

ALLEN, Mary (Constable, Harlesden) 185
ALLEN, Sislin Fay (Constable, Croydon) 116, 468, 471
ARBUTHNOT, Jane (Constable, Women Police) 468
BATHER, Elizabeth (Chief Superintendent) 456, 470, 471
BECKE, Shirley Cameron (Commander) 467, 468
BUSH, Ethel (Constable, Women Police) 468
CHAMBERS, S. (Constable, Harlesden) 185
DAWSON, Margaret Damer (Constable, Harlesden) 185, 466
DICK, Dame Cressida (Commissioner) .... i, 467, 468, 474
GLEGHORN, Bertha (Constable, Women Police) 468
GOSLING, Kate (Constable, Sutton) 375
GOULD, Winifred (Constable, Woolwich) 417
HALFORD, Alison (Chief Superintendent, Women Police) 468
HUBBARD, Sally (Chief Superintendent, South Norwood) 337
JORDAN, Dora (Constable (Specials), Romford) 319
KELLEY, Barbara (Detective Inspector, Women Police) 467
KERTZEN, Sandra (Constable, Women Police) 468
MATHEWS, Annie (Constable, Woolwich) 417, 456
MOUNCE, M.R. (Woman Sergeant (Specials), Commercial Street) 113
NICOLSON, Lyn (Constable, Women Police) 468
PARROTT, Kathleen (Constable, Women Police) 468
PETO, Dorothy (Superintendent, Women Police) 14, 466, 470, 471
SEWELL, Beryl (Constable, Hendon) 207
SMITH, Edith (Constable, Women Police) 466
STANLEY, Sophia (Superintendent, Women Police) 466, 468
Training 12, 14
Uniforms 468-474
WALSH, Emily (Constable, Woolwich) 417
WARD, Sheila (Inspector, Women Police) 468
WATTS, Alberta (Detective Sergeant, Women Police) 468
WILSON, Eleanor (Constable, Hendon) 207
Women Police 15, 62, 116, 153, 185, 207, 241, 339, 407, 416, 416, 417,
.... 456, 466-474
WYLES, Lilian (Detective Inspector, Women Police) 456, 466, 468, 469

Index of Officers Named in this Book

ABBEY, William (Sub-Divisional Inspector, Wood Green) 411
ABBIS, George (Assistant Commissioner, Peel House (Training)/
   City of Westminster) 14
ABBIS, George (Chief Constable, Feltham) 148
ABBOTT, H.R. (Superintendent, Woolwich) 418
ABBOTT, Thomas (Superintendent, Kennington) 238
ABBERLINE, Frederick George (Detective Chief Inspector,
   Commercial Street) 113
ACOTT, Bob (Detective Chief Inspector, Chelsea) 93
ADAMS (Constable, Sunbury) 354
ADAMS, C. (Superintendent, Ealing) 127
ADAMS, Thomas (Constable, New Malden) 279
ADAMS, Wilfred John (Constable, Dagenham) 118
AGGS (Inspector, Kentish Town) 241
ALDERTON (MSC Sub-Inspector, Finchley) 151
ALDRIDGE, William (Constable, Deptford) 122
ALDRIDGE, William (Inspector, Ditton) 124
ALLEN, Mary (Constable, Harlesden) 185
ALLEN, Matthew John (Constable, Twickenham) 370
ALLEN, Robert (Inspector, Rosyth) 446
ALLEN, Sislin Fay (Constable, Croydon) 116, 468, 471
ALLEN, George (Inspector, Barking) 46
ALLEN (Sergeant, Leyton) 264
ALLINSON, Tom (Station Sergeant, Bushey) 79
ALMOND, Dave (Superintendent, Forest Gate) 155
ANDERSON, Charles (Constable, Brentford) 72
ANDREWS, Henry (Sub-Divisional Inspector, Ealing) 127
ANDREWS, James (Sub-Divisional Inspector, Wandsworth) 383
ANDREWS, William (Constable, Bedfont) 55
ANGEAR (Constable, Devonport) 436, 437
ANNING, Raymond H. (Superintendent, Richmond) 315
ANNIS, Arthur (Superintendent, Golders Green) 160
ANNISS (Sergeant, Devonport) 436
ANNISS, Silas (Inspector, Devonport) 436, 437
APPLEGATE, George (Constable, Brixton) 74
ARBUTHNOT, Jane (Constable, Women Police) 468
ARCHER (Constable, Sunbury) 354
ARCHER (Constable, Woolwich) 428
ARCHER, Charles (Constable, Romford) 318
ARCHER, Herbert (Constable, Rosyth) 446
ARMSTRONG, Joseph (Inspector, Kingston) 249
ARNETT, John (Inspector, Norwood Green) 286
ARNOLD (Sergeant, Harrow) 188
ARNOLD, Edmund (Inspector, L.B. Camden) 20
ARNOLD, Thomas (Superintendent, Arbour Square) 36, 43
ARNUP, Frederick (Constable, Greenwich) 165
ARTHERTON, William (Constable, Barnet) 101
ASH, J.T. (Chief Inspector (Specials), St. John's Wood) 344
ASHLEY, Joseph (Inspector, Tooting) 363
ASHLEY, John Hughes (Chief Constable) 463
ASHWELL, H. (Inspector, Hammersmith) 175
ASKEW, Austin (Sub-Divisional Inspector, Hackney) 170
ATKINS, Fred (Constable, Kingston) 251
ATKINS, James (Inspector, Chatham) 249, 442
ATTER, William (Sergeant, Staines) 347
ATTWOOD, F.J. (Chief Inspector, Richmond) 315
AUBYN, George (Constable, Holloway) 215
AUNGER, Henry (Inspector, L.B. Camden) 20
AUSTIN, William (Inspector, Catford) 89
AXLETON (Constable, Sunbury) 354
AXTEN (Station Inspector, Muswell Hill) 278
AYLAND, Edwin (Constable, Hoxton) 222
AYLETT (Sub-Divisional Inspector, Wimbledon) 408
AYLETT, T.W.C. (Superintendent, East Ham) 133
AYRE, John (Sergeant, Kingston) 249
AYRE, A. (Constable (Specials), Ponders End) 304

BACCHUS, Ernest (Superintendent, Fulham) 156
BACON (A/Sergeant, Tottenham) 364
BACON, William (Sergeant, Greenwich) 165
BAILEY, Bill (Sergeant, Hendon) 204
BAILEY, George (Inspector, Staines) 347
BAILEY, John Richard (Constable, Mitcham) 276
BAINBRIDGE, Derek (Inspector, Norbury) 283
BAKER, William (Station Sergeant, South Mimms) 336
BAKER (Constable, Sunbury) 354
BALDOCK (Inspector, Westminster) 246
BALDRY, Jim (Constable, Hendon) 207

Index

BALDWIN, James (Constable, Hoxton) 223
BALL, Helen (Deputy Assistant Commissioner, Women Police) 468
BALLANTYNE (Superintendent, Balham) 45
BALM, L.R. (Chief Superintendent, Golders Green) 160
BAMBER, T. (Inspector, Chatham) 443
BAMSEY, William (Inspector, North Fulham) 284
BARBER (Constable, Pinner) 297
BARHAM, William (Sub-Divisional Inspector, Wandsworth) 383
BARKER (Constable, Leyton) 264
BARNARD (Station Sergeant, Sunbury) 354
BARNARD, James (Constable, Romford) 318
BARNES, A. (Sub-Divisional Inspector, West Ham) 395
BARNETT, George (Inspector, Harlesden) 186
BARNHAM, William (Sub-Divisional Inspector, Wimbledon) 407
BARNY, Henry (Inspector, Leman Street) 258
BARRATT, A.L. (Superintendent, Wanstead) 386
BARRETT, Alfred J. (Superintendent, Greenwich) 168
BARRETT, J. (Inspector, Kennington) 238
BARRETT, John (Constable, Leytonstone) 266
BARRETT, Stephen (Sergeant, West Dulwich) 126
BARRETT, T. (D/Chief Superintendent, Hendon) 203
BARRETT, William (Inspector, Bedfont) 56
BARTLE, G. (Inspector, Kennington) 238
BARTON, Alfred (Detective Sergeant, Portsmouth) 434
BARTON, Henry (A/Sergeant, East Barnet) 130
BASSETT, Henry (Constable, Ashford) 44
BASSOM, Arthur (Superintendent, Bexleyheath) 11
BATCHELOR, William (Constable, Pinner) 297, 299
BATEMAN (Constable, West Ham) 395
BATEMAN (Inspector, Islington 234
BATES (Constable, Devonport) 436
BATHER, Elizabeth (Chief Superintendent) 456, 470, 471
BATSON, Walter C. (Deputy Commander, Barking /Marine: Wapping) ... 48
BAXTER, (Superintendent, Bexley) 18
BAXTER, John (Superintendent, Devonport) 436
BAYNES, Captain H. (District Superintendent, Brockley/Brixton/
 Belvedere/Croydon) 59, 74, 76, 114, 336
BEALING, Henry (Inspector, Southwark) 340
BEANEY, M. (Constable (Specials), Ponders End) 304
BEARD (Superintendent, Limehouse) 268
BEARD (Superintendent, Westminster) 246
BEASLEY (Constable, Upminster) 370
BECKE, Shirley Cameron (Commander, Women Police) 467, 468
BECKERSON (Superintendent, Kensington) 240
BECKERSON, Robert (Superintendent, Brentford) 70
BEDI, Pirthi Ralpal Singh (Constable, Wembley) 391
BEER, John (Constable, Chatham) 442
BELIENIE, Frank (Constable, Hillingdon and Uxbridge) 213
BELL, Edward (Inspector, L.B. Camden) 20
BELL, William (Inspector, Harrow Road) 192
BELL, William (Inspector, Kilburn) 244
BENNER, Frederick (Constable, Hillingdon and Uxbridge) 213
BENTLEY (Constable, Walthamstow) 378
BENTLEY, P. (Special Constable, Brentford) 72
BERRETT (Detective Inspector, Brixton) 75
BEVANS (Constable, Norbury) 283
BEVERIDGE (Constable, Leman Street) 259
BEVERIDGE (Constable, Limehouse) 268
BICKNELL, Thomas (Superintendent, L.B. Wandsworth/Kingston) 249
BIGARLSFORD, George (Sergeant, Staines) 350
BIGHAM, Trevor Sir (Deputy Commissioner, Sunbury) 354
BILLERS, George (Inspector, Barnet) 99
BILLERS, George (Inspector, Camden) 333
BINGHAM, William (Inspector, Hounslow) 220
BIRDSEYE, Jonathon (Constable, Collier Row) 112
BISSETT, Thomas (Inspector, Whetstone) 401-402
BLACKMAN (Constable, Portsmouth) 430

BLACKWELL, William Henry (Station Sergeant, Hendon) 204
BLAKE, Charles (Sergeant, Brentford) 70
BLAKE, J. (Station Sergeant, Isleworth) 232
BLAKELOCK, Keith (Constable, Tottenham) 366
BLIGH (Sergeant, Sunbury) 354
BLISS, John (Inspector, Marine: Blackwall) 419
BLUEKWILL, John (Constable, Bedfont) 56
BOBYER, Sackville (Constable, Shenley) 328
BOCKING, Thomas (Chief Inspector, Kensington) 240
BOLSOVER, Frederick (Sergeant, Wealdstone) 387
BOND, Joseph (Sergeant, Erith) 144
BONNER, Edward (Sub-Divisional Inspector, Wimbledon) 406
BONNER, Frederick (Sub-Divisional Inspector, Croydon) 115, 326
BONNYMAN, G. (Inspector, Fulham) 156
BOOKSON, Frank (Inspector, West Ham) 395
BOREHAM, Isaac (Constable, Upminster) 370
BORHAM, George (War Reserve Constable, Kilburn) 245
BORSBERRY, Thomas (Inspector, Chatham) 442
BOWES, Leonard (War Reserve Constable, Kilburn) 245
BOWLES, Gilbert Humphrey (Commandant, Tottenham) 366
BOXALL (Constable, Portsmouth) 432
BOYCE (Sergeant, Wealdstone) 387
BOYES, E. (Constable (Specials), Ponders End) 304
BOYLE, James (Sub-Divisional Inspector, Hammersmith) 175
BOYLING (Constable, Leyton) 264
BRACEY, Ivan (Constable, Elstree) 139
BRADFORD, Sir Edward (Commissioner) 80, 394
BRADLEY (Inspector, Devonport) 436
BRADLEY, J. (Sub- Divisional Inspector, West Ham) 395
BRADSTOCK, Daniel (Inspector, Westminster) 246
BRAILEY, C. (Sub-Divisional Inspector, West Ham) 395
BRAIN, Thomas (Inspector, Kilburn) 244
BRANNAN, Jas (Superintendent, Kennington/Carter Street) 87, 238
BRANWHITE, C. (Inspector, Carter Street) 87
BRAY (Superintendent, Chatham) 440
BRAY, Ivan (Chief Inspector, Wealdstone) 388
BRAY, Robert (Superintendent, Devonport) 425, 436
BREED, Francis (Sergeant, Chingford) 97
BRENNAN (Inspector, Acton) 38
BREWER (Constable, Islington) 234
BREWER, Harold (Station Sergeant, Croydon) 115
BRIAN, Daniel (Constable, Sunbury) 353
BRICE, William (Sub-Divisional Inspector, Wandsworth) 383
BRIDGE, Sir John (Commissioner, Kings Cross Road) 247
BRIDGEN, George (Sub-Divisional Inspector, Kilburn) 244
BRIDGWOOD, Peter George (Detective Constable, Morden) 277
BRIGGS, William (Inspector, Portsmouth) 431
BRIGHT, Albert (Station Sergeant, Lewisham) 262
BRILL, Charles (Constable, Staines) 347
BRIND, Ernest (Superintendent, Kennington) 109, 238
BRINE, Philip (Inspector, Woolwich) 425
BRINE, Philip (Inspector, Leman Street) 258
BRISTOW, Fred (Station Sergeant, Harlington) 186
BRISTOW, Thomas (Sergeant, Brentford) 69
BRISTOWE, F.S. (Inspector (Specials), St.John's Wood) 344
BROAD, Philip R. (Chief Superintendent, New Scotland Yard /
 City of Westminster) 14
BROADBRIDGE, J (Inspector, Sydenham) 360
BROKENSHIRE (Chief Superintendent, Edmonton) 138
BROKENSHIRE, F. (Chief Inspector, Barnet) 102
BROMAGE (Constable, Sidcup) 389-390
BROOKS (Sergeant, Kingston) 252
BROOKS, Charles (Constable, Staines) 347
BROUGH (Superintendent, Twickenham) 370
BROUGHTON, George (Constable, Harefield) 183
BROWN (Sergeant, Devonport) 436
BROWN (Station Sergeant, Acton) 38

BROWN, Charles (Inspector, Harrow Road) 192-193
BROWN, F.C. (Superintendent, Balham) 129
BROWN, Ivan L.A. (Chief Superintendent, Forest Gate) 155
BROWN, J. (Chief Inspector, Thames: Wapping) 423
BROWN, John (Constable, Kilburn) 244
BROWN, Lawrence (Constable, City Road) 108
BROWING, Thomas (Inspector, Barnet) 101
BROWN, William (Inspector, Brentford) 69
BROWNING, George (Chief Inspector, Harlesden) 184
BROWNSCOMBE, Henry (Sub-Divisional Inspector,
  Hillingdon and Uxbridge) 213
BRUCE, Alexander (War Reserve Constable, Ruislip) 325
BRYANT, C. (Inspector, Chatham) 443
BRYCE, William (Inspector, Kingston) 252
BUCHANAN, Arthur (Superintendent, Peel House (Training)
  /City of Westminster) 14
BUCKINGHAM, E. (Constable (Specials), Ponders End) 304
BUCKPITT (Sub-Inspector (Specials), Ponders End) 304
BUCKS, John (Constable, Brentford) 70
BUDD, Ernest (Constable, Leyton) 264
BUDMEAD (Constable, Sunbury) 354
BULLIVENT (Acting Inspector, Hillingdon and Uxbridge) 212
BULLIVENT, Edward (Inspector, Hampton) 180
BULLOCK, R. (Divisional Commander (Specials), Chingford) 97
BUNDOCK, A.M.F. (Superintendent, Barnet) 102
BURBRIDGE, Joseph (Constable, Staines) 347
BURCH (Sub-Divisional Inspector, Devonport) 437
BURCHELL, Fred (Constable, Brentford) 72
BURKE (Chief Inspector, Chatham) 440
BURROWS, Henry (Sergeant, Richmond) 315
BURTON, Charles (Constable, Portsmouth) 434
BURTON, Clement (Inspector, Bromley) 77
BUSH, Ethel (Constable, Women Police) 468
BUSH, George (Inspector, Bedfont) 55
BUSHNELL, William (Inspector, L.B. Richmond) 30, 34
BUSSAIN, John (Inspector, Wandsworth) 381
BUTCHER (Constable, Woolwich) 430
BUTCHER (Inspector, Lewisham) 262
BUTFOY, Abia (Constable, Dagenham) 118
BUTLER (Inspector, Portsmouth) 343
BUTLER, Charles R. (Station Sergeant, Lewisham) 262
BUTT (Superintendent, Wandsworth) 382
BUTT, Charles (Inspector, Plumstead) 303
BUTT, Charles (Station Sergeant, Acton) 38
BUTT, Edward (Superintendent, L.B. Wandsworth) 30, 34
BUTT, Thomas (Superintendent, Lewisham/Camberwell) 81, 87, 261, 452
BUTTERS, Robert (Inspector, Mitcham) 276
BYRNE, M.J. (Superintendent, Golders Green/Finchley) 153

CALAMINUS, M. (Superintendent, Heathrow) 199
CAMAC, John (Inspector, Portsmouth) 431
CANTER, K. (Corporal (Specials), Ponders End) 304
CAPLIN, John William (Constable, Hayes and Gould's Green) 195
CAPON, William (Inspector, Chatham) 425, 442
CAPP, Joseph (Inspector, Hillingdon and Uxbridge) 212
CARLIN, Francis (Detective Superintendent, Somers Town) 334, 463
CARNELLY, Thomas J (Chief Inspector, Woolwich) 425
CARR, G. (Superintendent, Lewisham) 262
CARR, George (Inspector, Hornsey/Tottenham) 218, 364
CARR, George (Superintendent, Kilburn) 244
CARR, Percy (Constable, Woolwich) 430
CARSON, Cornelious (Superintendent, Hackney) 173
CARTER, James (Superintendent, Portsmouth) 430, 433-434
CARTER, John (Divisional Superintendent, Barnet/Edgware) 99, 133
CARTER, John (Superintendent, L.B. Camden /Albany Street) 20, 40
CASTLE, H.W. (Assistant Commander (Specials), Ilford) 227
CATHCART, John (Inspector, Catford) 89

CAUSBY (Sub-Divisional Inspector, Bow Road) 65
CAVELL, George (Chief Inspector, Chatham) 425, 442
CAVENDISH, Albert (Sub-Divisional Inspector, Wimbledon) 408
CAWDWELL (Constable, Bow Street) 68
CHALLINGSWORTH (Inspector, Kingston) 252
CHAMBERLAIN, Richard (Sergeant, Bedfont) 56
CHAMBERS, S. (Constable, Harlesden) 185
CHAMBLETON (Constable, Sunbury) 354
CHANDLER, William (Constable, Potters Bar) 307
CHAPLIN (Constable, Devonport) 436
CHAPLIN, Henry James (Constable, Kennington) 237
CHAPMAN (Constable, Wealdstone) 387
CHECKLEY, Richard (Inspector, L.B. Camden) 20
CHEESEMAN, Thomas King (Sergeant, Acton) 38
CHENNELL, William (Constable, Whetstone) 401
CHEYNEY, William (Sub-Divisional Inspector, Chiswick) 105
CHIDGEY, William (Constable, Wealdstone) 387
CHILCOTT, Wilfred John (Station Sergeant, Putney) 310
CHILDS (Constable, Portsmouth) 430
CHILDS (Sergeant, Richmond) 313
CHILDS, James (Constable, Banstead) 45
CHIN, Frank (Sub-Divisional Inspector, Croydon) 115
CHISHOLM (Chief Inspector, Kennington) 238
CHRISTIE, John (Constable, Gould's Green) 194
CHRISTMAS (Constable, Portsmouth) 430
CHRISTMAS, Jesse (Constable, Camberwell) 82
CHUBBOCK (Inspector, Portsmouth) 434
CHURCH, Stephen (Acting Sergeant, Potters Bar) 308
CLACKETT, Sidney Charles (Constable, East Ham) 132
CLAPHAM (Acting Sergeant, Sunbury) 354
CLARE, Albert (Constable, Epping Forest) 377
CLARK, Charles H. (Superintendent, Brixton) 75
CLARK, Charles R. (Superintendent, Streatham) 352
CLARK, George (Constable, Dagenham) 117
CLARK, Leonard (Inspector, Holloway) 216
CLARK, Charles R. (Superintendent, Streatham) 352
CLARKE (Constable, Portsmouth) 430
CLARKE, C. (Superintendent, Hounslow) 222
CLARKE, Frederick Ernest (Constable, Haringey) 412
CLARKE, Harry (Station Sergeant, Loughton) 269
CLARKE, Leonard Francis (Special Constable, Greenwich) 168
CLARKE, William James (Inspector, Hornsey) 219
CLAYDEN, William (Constable, Brentford) 72
CLEAVE (Inspector, Southwark) 340
CLEAVE, Walter (Sub-Divisional Inspector, Wandsworth) 383
CLELLAND, D. (Chief Inspector, Golders Green/Finchley) 153
CLEMENT, William (Inspector, L.B. Camden) 20
CLIFFORD, George (Inspector, Woolwich) 414
CLIFFORD, John (Chief Inspector, L.B. Camden) 20
CLOSE, F. (Detective Superintendent, Tooting) 364
CLOUGHTON, Arthur (Constable, Barnet) 101
COBBAN, Jock (Constable, Hendon) 207
COCKBURN, Thomas Oswand Bell (War Reserve Constable, Ruislip) ... 325
COE, Thomas (War Reserve Constable, Kilburn) 245
COFFEY, Edward (Inspector, Woolwich) 429
COGGER (Constable, Portsmouth) 430
COLE, George (Constable, Dalston) 120
COLE, Harry (Constable, Carter Street) 89
COLE, Thomas (Inspector, Barnet) 100
COLE, William (Constable, House of Parliament) 8
COLE, William George (Inspector, Willesden Green) 402
COLEMAN, Benjamin (Constable, Newham) 394
COLLIER, John (Inspector, Croydon) 114
COLLINS (Sergeant, Kingston) 251
COLLINS, Daniel (Inspector, Pembroke) 425, 444
COLLINS, George (Constable, Chatham) 441
COLLINS, John (Sub-Divisional Inspector, Carter Street) 88

Index

COLLINS, W. (Superintendent, Catford) 90
COLMAN, Richard (Sergeant, L.B. Croydon) 21
CONCANNON, John (Sub-Divisional Inspector, Lavender Hill)............ 256
CONDON, Sir Paul (Commissioner) 260, 349
CONGTON, Robert (Inspector, Woolwich) 429
CONNELL, Patrick (Constable, Hornsey) 219
CONNELL, William (Inspector, Portsmouth) 431, 432
COOK, Edward (Inspector, Hillingdon and Uxbridge) 212
COOK, John (Constable, Leyton) 263
COOK, John (Inspector, L.B. Camden) 20
COOK, William (Constable, Barking) 46
COOKE, George Samuel (Constable, Harrow) 190
COOKIE (Constable, Sunbury) 354
COOMBS, Ernest (Sergeant, Catford) 89
COOMBS, Thomas (Superintendent, Hammersmith) 176
COOPER, Ellis (Constable, Barnet) 101
COOPER, James J. (Sergeant, Harrow) 188
COOPER, Joseph W. (Inspector, Harlesden/Kilburn) 184, 244
COOPER, Thomas J. (Inspector, Romford) 318
COOPER, William D. (Inspector, Hackney) 169
COPE (Constable, Hackney) 172
COPPEN, George (Inspector, Portsmouth) 431-432
COPPING, Arthur (Sub-Divisional Inspector, Chiswick)........................ 105
COPSEY, Joseph (Constable, Romford) 318
CORDEN, Alfred (Sergeant, Hendon) 207
CORNISH, George (Detecive Chief Inspector, Charing Cross) 92
CORNWELL, David (Inspector, Esher) 146
COSTELLO (Constable, Portsmouth) 430
COSTER, Vincent (Sub-Divisional Inspector, Bromley) 77
COTTAGE, Herbert (Constable, Brentford) 72
COUCHER (Chief Inspector (Specials), Tottenham) 366
COULSON, Thomas (Superintendent, Romford) 318
COURT (Inspector, Chatham) 440
COUSINS (Sub-Divisional Inspector, King Street) 246
COUSINS, Edwin (Constable, Greenwich) 165
COUSINS, William (Constable, Romford) 318
COWARD, James (Inspector, Stoke Newington) 350
COWLIN, John Richard (Inspector, Southwark) 340
COX, Charles (Constable, Brentford) 69
COX, Charles (Constable, West Ham) 396
COX, John (Sergeant, Brentford) 71
CRABB, Richard (Constable, Greenwich) 165
CRACKNELL (Constable, Romford) 318
CRAGGS, Henry (Inspector, Leyton) 263
CRANEY (Constable, Kilburn) 244
CRAVEN, Thomas (War Reserve Constable, Kilburn) 245
CRAWFORD, Bob (Constable, Earlsfield) 282
CRAYFOURD, William (Superintendent, Fulham) 156
CREASEY, John (Constable, Wanstead) 386
CREED, Henry (Inspector, Wandsworth) 382
CROFT, Harry (Inspector, Brockley) 76
CRONIN, P. (Chief Inspector, Hammersmith) 175
CRONK, John (Inspector, Woolwich) 429
CROOK (Inspector, Pembroke) 445
CROOK, William (Chief Inspector, Devonport) 436
CROSS (Chief Inspector, Chatham) 344, 443
CROSS (MSC Chief Inspector, Finchley) 152
CROSTAN, William (Sub-Divisional Inspector, Greenwich) 166
CROWLEY, J. (Sub-Divisional Inspector, West Ham) 395
CRUISE, George (Inspector, L.B. Camden/West Ham) 20
CRYAN, James (Acting Sergeant, Potters Bar) 308
CUNDELL, John (Sub-Divisional Inspector, Finchley) 134, 151
CURL (Constable, Hendon) 208
CURRY, John (Station Sergeant, Holloway) 216
CUTHBERT, David (Constable, Wimbledon) 405
CUTHBERT, James (Superintendent, Ealing/Kilburn) 127, 244

DACE, C.J. (Superintendent, Golders Green) 160
DALE, George Arthur (Constable, Wimbledon) 409
DANES, James (Constable, Romford) 318
DANIEL, Joseph (Sergeant, Camberwell) 81
DANIEL, Joseph (Sergeant, Peckham) 295
DANIELS, E. (Constable (Specials), Ponders End) 304
DANIELS, William (Inspector, Hillingdon and Uxbridge) 213
DARLING (Chief Inspector, Southwark) 340
DAVIES, Clifford (Constable, Kilburn) 244
DAVIES, David (Constable, Mitcham) 276
DAVIES, Joseph (Inspector, Holloway) 215
DAVIES, Llewellyn (War Reserve Constable, Kilburn) 245
DAVIES, Michael John (Constable, Wimbledon) 409
DAVIS, Edward (Superintendent, Romford) 318
DAVIS, James (Chief Inspector, Camberwell/Lewisham) 81, 261
DAVIS, W.E. (Chief Superintendent, Tooting) 364
DAVEY, William John (Constable, Acton) 38
DAWSON, Margaret Damer (Constable, Harlesden) 185, 466
DAY, Ashley (Constable, Acton) 39
DE MAID, William (Inspector, L.B. Camden) 20
DEAN, Thomas (Constable, Deptford) 122
DEATH, Joseph (Inspector, Forest Gate) 154
DEEKS, Alfred Edward (Inspector, Ealing) 127
DELLAR, James Frank (Constable, Richmond) 314
DENFORD, William (Constable, Leyton) 263
DENLOW, Charles (Constable, Old Street) 291
DENNIS, William (Constable, Romford) 318
DEVINE, John (Superintendent, Woolwich) 325
DICK, Dame Cressida (Commissioner) ....i, 467, 468, 474
DICKENS, Charles (Constable, Brockley) 76
DICKINSON (Chief Superintendent, Edmonton) 138
DICKSON, James (Inspector, Barkingside) 48
DIGBY, Charles (Superintendent, Erith) 145
DIGBY, Charles (Superintendent, Wimbledon) 383, 405
DIGBY, Edwin (Sub-Divisional Inspector, Brentford) 71-72
DIGBY, George (Constable, Upminster) 370
DINGLE, William (Inspector, Harlesden) 185-186
DIXON, George Henry (Sub-Divisional Inspector, Richmond) 314
DIXON, Thomas (Inspector, Barking) 46
DIXSON, George (Superintendent, Devonport) 436, 438
DODD (Superintendent, Finchley) 150
DOLBY (Constable, Peckham) 295
DOLPHIN, Samuel (Sergeant, Hayes and Gould's Green) 194
DONALDSON, David Leonard (Constable (later Inspector),
    Leytonstone) 266
DONNOLLY, James (Inspector, Sunbury) 354
DONOVAN, Michael (Constable, Chatham) 443
DOUGLAS, James (Inspector, Greenwich) 164-165
DOUST (Constable, Chatham) 441
DOVER, Harold (Detective Sergeant, Cobham) 110
DOWDELL, John (Detective Inspector, Richmond) 314
DOWLING, Maurice G. (Superintendent, L.B. Lambeth) 32
DOWN (Chief Inspector, Devonport) 436
DOWSETT, Richard (Inspector, L.B Wandsworth/
    Wandsworth) 30, 34, 249, 382
DOWTY, George (Constable, Wandsworth) 381
DRAPER, George William (Constable, Wimbledon) 406
DREW (Constable, Upminster) 370
DUCKETT, John (Constable, Brentford) 69
DUDLEY, Gregory (Inspector, L.B. Camden) 20
DUDMAN, George (Station Inspector, Stoke Newington) 350
DUGUID, James (Constable, Brentford) 72
DUNFORD, John (Sergeant, Ruislip) 325
DUNLEAVY, G. (Inspector, Carter Street) 87
DUNLOP, Joseph (Superintendent, Southwark) 340
DUNN, Leonard (Constable, Greenwich) 167-168
DUNN, William (War Reserve Constable, Ilford) 228

DUNNE, Patrick (Constable, Sutton) 359
DURGAN, Edward (Inspector, L.B. Camden) 20
DURKIN (Superintendent, Ealing) 126
DURKIN, William (Superintendent, Stanwell) 250
DURLEY, John (Inspector, Dagenham) 118
DURRANT, William (Sergeant, Leman Street) 259
DUTCHESS, James (Inspector, L.B. Camden) 20
DYER, Frederick (Sergeant, Catford) 89

EAMES, John (Inspector, Hillingdon and Uxbridge) 212
EARWAKER, George (Reserve Inspector, Wandsworth) 383
EASTER, C. (Inspector, Kennington) 238
EATON, John (Constable, Harrow) 191
ECCLES (Acting Superintendent, Acton) 38
ECCLES, Hugh (Superintendent, Hillingdon and Uxbridge/
    Harlesden/Ruislip) 184, 212, 324
EDGAR, Nat (Constable, Harrow Road) 194
EDHOUSE (Sergeant, Fulham) 156
EDWARDS (Constable, Pembroke) 444
EDWARDS, Charles (Constable, Putney) 308
EFFORD, Charles Victor (Constable, Islington) 234
EGERTON, Samuel (Inspector, Battersea) 52, 382
EITE, Joseph (Constable, Wandsworth) 381
ELLAMS (Inspector, Gipsy Hill) 288
ELLIS, Benjamin (Inspector, Finchley) 150
ELLIS, Ernest (Constable, Hammersmith) 175
ELLIS, Thomas (Inspector, Leman Street) 258
ELLIS, Truman (Constable, Barnet) 100
ELLISON, William (Inspector, Acton) 38
ELMS, Maurice (Inspector, Sunbury) 354
ELPHICK, Horace (Inspector, Wood Green) 411
ELY (Constable, Portsmouth) 430
EMERICK (Sub-Divisional Inspector, Fulham) 156
EMERSON (Constable, Pembroke) 444
EMERSON, John (Constable, Woodford) 412
EMMERY, George (Constable, Romford) 318
EMSLEY, Ernest George (Constable, Hackney) 173
ENDICOTT, Bowden (Constable, Great Marlborough Street) ... 162
ENGLAND, Harry (Sergeant, Stanwell) 350
ENGLAND, Leslie (Constable, West Ham) 396
EVANS, H.J. (Commander, Marine: Wapping) 423
EVANS, J. (Inspector, Kennington) 236
EVANS, James (Inspector (later Superintendent), Marine: Blackwall/
    Wapping) 421
EVANS, John Christopher (Superintendent, Marine) 419, 421
EVANS, Samuel (Superintendent, Barnet) 99, 339
EVANS, T. (Superintendent, Tooting) 364
EVANS, Thomas (Superintendent, Devonport) 426, 436, 438
EVERFIELD, A. (Constable (Specials), Ponders End) 304
EWART, William A. (Superintendent, Southwark) 341

FABIAN, Robert (Detective Inspector, Cannon Row) 9
FAIR, William (Constable, Woodford) 412
FAIRFAX, Frederick (Detective Constable, Croydon) 116
FALCONER, Charles Henry (Inspector, Marine: Wapping) ... 421
FALSHAW-SKELLY, Henry (Constable, Shepherds Bush) 330
FANNING, Hugh (Sergeant, Leman Street) 259
FARLEY, Frederick (Constable, Bedfont) 55
FARRELL (Sub-Divisional Inspector, Waltham Forest) 264
FARRER, William (Constable, Brentford) 72
FARROW, James (Sergeant, Romford) 318
FARROW, Jepthah (Acting Sergeant, Waltham Abbey) 376
FAULKNER, Thomas (Sub-Divisional Inspector, Brentford) ... 72
FEAVER, Richard (Inspector, Richmond) 314
FEAVER, William (Sub-Inspector, Barnes) 50
FENN, Septimus (Divisional Superintendent, Kingston) 249
FENN, Septimus (Superintendent, L.B. Wandsworth) 51

FERGUSON, D. (Inspector, Kennington) 236
FERRETT, Arthur (Inspector, West Ham) 395
FIELD, Charles F. (Inspector, Woolwich) 414
FILBEE, William (Sergeant, Harefield) 183
FISH, Alex (Chief Superintendent, Harrow) 192
FISHER, William (Superintendent, Chiswick/
    Norwood Green/Hammersmith) 104, 174, 286
FITT, Percy (MSC Inspector, L.B. Hounslow) 29, 221
FITT, William E. (Superintendent, Hackney/Hendon) 171
FLACK, Henry Edwin (Constable, Kingston) 252
FLANAGAN, John (Inspector, East Dulwich) 125
FLETCHER (Sergeant, Cobham) 110
FLETCHER, Yvonne (Constable, Bow Street) 68, 368
FLETT, A. DFC (Superintendent, Harrow) 191
FLOYD, William (Sergeant, Shenley) 328
FLYNN, Thomas (Inspector, Banstead) 45-46
FOINETT, Thomas (Superintendent, Ealing) 127
FORBES, Daniel (Inspector, Leman Street) 258
FORD (Inspector, Stoke Newington) 351
FORD, Elias (Inspector, Woolwich) 416
FORD, James (Sub-Divisional Inspector, Carter Street) 88
FORDHAM, Reuben (Constable, Shenley) 328
FOREMAN (Constable, Vine Street) 374
FORMAN, Frederick (Constable, Brentford) 70
FOSSKET, George (Constable, Potters Bar) 307
FOSTER, Frederick (Sub-Divisional Inspector, Bedfont) 56
FOWLER, James (Constable, Hornchurch) 217
FOWLES (Constable, Hendon) 201
FOX (Inspector, Camberwell) 82
FOX, Geoffrey Roger (Constable, Shepherds Bush) 330
FOX, John Thomas (Sergeant, Sydenham) 359-360
FOX, Thomas (Inspector, Marine: Wapping) 421
FOXALL, Frederick George (Superintendent, L.B. Camden) ... 20
FRASER (Sub-Divisional Inspector, Lewisham) 262
FRASER, D. (Acting Superintendent, Brixton/Camberwell) ... 74, 81
FRASER, W. (Sub-Divisional Inspector, Catford) 89
FREE, Benjamin (Constable, Romford) 318
FREEMAN (Constable, Kingston) 253
FRENCH, William (Constable, Hillingdon and Uxbridge) 213
FREWIN (Sergeant, Devonport) 438
FRICK, Noel Charles (Constable, Shepherds Bush) 330
FRIGHT, A. (Constable, Knockholt) 255
FROUD, Philip (Inspector, Southwark) 339
FRY (Constable, Sunbury) 354
FRY, Alan (Deputy Assistant Commissioner, Fulham) 157
FRY, Len (Constable, Hendon) 206
FULLER, John (Inspector, Wimbledon) 405
FULLER, Uriah (Constable, Hornchurch) 217
FUNNELL, George Stephen (Constable, Victoria Park) 373
FYFE, John (Inspector, Gipsy Hill) 288

GADD (Sub-Divisional Inspector, Plumstead) 303
GADD, R. (Chief Inspector, Rosyth) 446
GAME, Philip, Sir (Commissioner, Sunbury) 355
GANE, William George (War Reserve Constable, Harlesden) ... 186
GARDE, William R. (Inspector, Arbour Square) 42
GARDENER (Constable, Wanstead) 385
GARDINER, D. (Constable (Specials), Ponders End) 304
GARLAND, H. (Inspector, Kennington) 238
GARNER, David (Constable, Hoxton) 222-223
GASKIN, John (Inspector, Thames: Wapping) 421
GATESBY (Sergeant, Somers Town) 333
GAVIN (Sub-Divisional Inspector, Tottenham Court Road) ... 367
GAYLOR, Charles (Constable, Brentford) 72
GAYNOR, Arthur (Sergeant, Greenwich) 165
GEATER, John (Inspector, Potters Bar) 307
GENTRY, George (MSC Commander, L.B. Hounslow/Chiswick) ... 28, 105

Index

GEORGE (Constable, Sunbury) 354
GEORGE, Inspector (South Norwood) 337
GERMAN (Inspector, Westminster) 246
GERNON, Albert (Inspector, Leman Street) 258
GIBSON (Constable, Wealdstone) 388
GIBSON (Sergeant, Chadwell Heath) 90
GIBSON, MacAlan (Sub-Divisional Inspector, Holloway) 216
GIBSON, W.C.E. (MSC Commander, L.B. Hounslow) 28
GIFFORD, Stephen W.T. (Sub-Divisional Inspector, Edgware) 134
GILBY, George (Inspector, Kentish Town) 242
GILES, Alfred John (Reserve Inspector, Wimbledon) 408
GILHAM (Sergeant, Woolwich) 416
GILL, James (Inspector, Woolwich) 427
GILLETT, William (Superintendent, Hackney) 169
GILLIES, John (Inspector, Wanstead) 386
GILLIES, William (Sub-Divisional Inspector, Wandsworth) 383
GILPIN, William (Inspector, Romford) 318
GIRLING, William (Sub-Inspector, Shenley) 328
GLASBY, H.S. (Sub-Divisional Inspector, Peel House (Training) /
   City of Westminster) 13
GLEGHORN, Bertha (Constable, Women Police) 468
GLEN, Simeon Oscar (War Reserve Constable, Hammersmith) .. 176
GODDARD (Constable, Pembroke) 444
GODDARD, George (Sergeant, West End Cenral) 392
GODDARD, Harry (Constable, Hammersmith) 175
GODDEN, Daniel (Inspector, Portsmouth) 431
GODDEN, J. (Inspector, Epsom) 143
GODFREY, George (Inspector, Woolwich) 429
GODFREY, George (Superintendent, Chatham) 439, 442
GOLDER, John (Inspector, Kentish Town) 242
GOLDING, Eccles (Inspector, Plaistow) 300
GOOD (Inspector, Finchley) 153
GOODALL, Walter (Inspector, Sutton) 358
GOODHALL (Sub-Divisional Inspector, Plumstead) 303
GORDON (Constable, Hendon) 208
GORE (Special Inspector, Hendon) 206
GOSLING, C. (Constable (Specials), Ponders End) 304
GOSLING, Kate (Constable, Sutton) 375
GOSS (Inspector, Portsmouth) 434
GOULD (Inspector, Somers Town) 334
GOULD, George (Constable, Woolwich) 417
GOULD, Winifred (Constable, Woolwich) 417
GRACE, Herbert (Sub-Divisional Inspector, Barnet) 101
GRANTHAM (Constable, Somers Town) 333
GRAY, William (Constable, Finchley) 151
GREEN (Constable, Hackney) 170
GREEN (Superintendent, Waltham Abbey) 375
GREEN, Harry (Constable, Wimbledon) 408
GREEN, J. (Inspector, Chatham) 443
GREEN, R. (Sergeant (Specials), Ponders End) 304
GREEN, T. (Inspector, Kennington) 238
GREEN, Thomas (Station Sergeant, Epsom) 143
GREEN, W.F. (Superintendent, Dagenham) 118
GREENHOFF, Edward (Constable, Canning Town) 83
GREENHOFF, George (Constable, Canning Town) 83
GREENWOOD, Dr. E. Climson (Chief Inspector (Specials),
   St.John's Wood) 344
GRIFFIN, James (Superintendent, Sidcup/East Greenwich) ... 10, 130, 389
GRIMMETT, William Gilbert (Sub-Divisional Inspector,
   Harlesden/Kingston) 186
GRIMSTONE, Thomas (Inspector, Thames: Blackwall) 419
GRIMWOOD, William E. (Superintendent, L.B. Camden) 20
GRINSELL, Samuel Dicken Corbet (Superintendent, Kennington) .. 236
GROSCH (Inspector, Hammersmith) 176
GROVER, George (Sergeant, Harefield) 183
GROVES, Thomas (Inspector, Wanstead) 386
GUNDREY (Constable, Woolwich) 430

GURNEY, Eddy (Constable, Dagenham) 119
GURNEY, William (Detective Inspector, Hammersmith) 176
GUTTERIDGE, George (Constable, Romford) 320
GUY, Henry (Superintendent, Portsmouth) 430, 431
HAGARTY, Edward (Sergeant, Bedfont) 56
HAINES, Charles (Sergeant, South Mimms) 336
HALE, Hubert (Sergeant, Edgware) 134
HALFORD, Alison (Chief Superintendent, Women Police) 468
HALFORD, Henry John (Constable, Enfield) 142
HALL, Charles (Constable, Bromley) 78
HALL, William (Constable, Harrow) 191
HALLETT, Charles (Inspector, Chatham) 442
HAMMOND (Superintendent, Kings Cross Road) 247
HANCOX, Charles Francis (Sergeant, Fulham) 156
HANKERVILLE (Sergeant, Chigwell) 96
HANN, Aubrey (Inspector, Devonport) 437
HANNAFORD, R.C. (Superintendent, Ealing) 127
HANNANT, S. (Superintendent, L.B. Camden) 20
HARDING, George (Inspector, Pembroke) 444
HARDING, George (Chief Inspector, Devonport) 425, 436
HARDING, John (Inspector, West Ham) 395
HARDY, James (Constable, West Wickham) 399
HARMON, George (Inspector, Hammersmith) 176
HARNETT (Superintendent, Southwark) 340
HARPER, William John (Constable, Harrow Road) 193
HARRINGTON, Charles (Constable, Hornchurch/Romford) 318
HARRINGTON, William ((Havering) 217
HARRIS, Dennis (Sergeant, Edgware) 135
HARRIS, E. (Inspector, Hammersmith) 175
HARRIS, Elias (Sergeant, Mitcham) 276
HARRIS, Henry (Inspector, Commercial Street/Leman Street) ... 112, 258
HARRIS, Thomas Henry (Sergeant, Shenley) 328
HARRISON, John (Sergeant, Edmonton) 136
HARROD, James (Constable, Potters Bar) 307
HART, William (Sub-Divisional Inspector, Wimbledon) 407
HARVARD, Roger (Inspector, L.B. Camden) 20
HARVEY, Gerald (War Reserve Constable, Kilburn) 245
HARWOOD, Alfred (Sub-Divisional Inspector, Staines) 348
HARWOOD, Joseph (Constable, Brentford) 72
HASTIE, James (Constable, Deptford) 122
HATTON, Albert (Constable, Whetstone) 402
HAVERS (Sergeant, Romford) 320-321
HAWKINS, Albert Victor (Constable, Ealing) 128, 463
HAYDON, John (Inspector, Romford) 318
HAYERS (Sub-Divisional Inspector, Bow Street/Charing Cross) .. 67
HAYES, William (Superintendent, Mitcham) 276
HAYNES, Henry (Sergeant, Epsom) 143
HAYNES, James (Chief Inspector, Woolwich) 425, 426
HAYNES, William (Constable, Kings Cross Road) 371
HAYTER, R. (Sub-Divisional Inspector, Chatham) 443
HEAD, Christopher Tippett (Detective Sergeant, Shepherds Bush) .. 330
HEAD, George (Inspector, Enfield) 142
HEMS, David James (Sergeant, Hackney) 173
HENDERSON, Sir Edmund (Commissioner, Sidcup) .. 10, 114, 272, 436
HENRY, Sir Edward (Commissioner) 12, 85, 128, 156, 158, 159, 178,
   .... 283, 344, 352, 366, 466
HERBERT, Gray (Constable, Barnet) 101
HERRING, D. (Superintendent, Tower Hamlets) 36
HERWIN, Henry (Sub-Divisional Inspector, Bedfont) 56
HIGGINS, Samuel (Inspector, St Mary Cray) 345
HILL (Sergeant, Devonport) 438
HILL, A. (Inspector, Epsom) 143
HILL, George (Constable, West Ham) 395
HILL, Isaac (Inspector, Marine: Wapping) 421
HILL, J. (Inspector, Kennington) 238
HILL, Nicholas (Constable, Shepherds Bush) 330

499

HILL, Thomas (Inspector, Chadwell Heath) 90
HILL, Thomas (Sub-Divisional Inspector, Greenwich Eltham) 140, 166
HILLIER, Fred (Sergeant, Tottenham Court Road) 367
HINDES, Thomas (Sergeant, Kensington) 240
HINDES, Thomas (Superintendent, Woolwich) 425, 429
HINDS, Albert (War Reserve Constable, Loughton) 270
HISLOP, David (Detective Superintendent, Chelsea) 93
HITCHCOCK (Constable, Sunbury) 354
HITCHCOCK (Station Sergeant, Victoria Park) 373
HITCHCOCK, Edward (Constable, Brentford) 70
HITCHCOCK, James (Retired Sergeant, Greenford) 164
HITE (Special Constable, Hendon) 206
HOBBINS, Josiah (Superintendent, Devonport/Chatham) 425, 436, 442
HOBDEN (Inspector, Westminster) 246
HOCKING (Inspector, Plumstead) 302
HOCKING, George (Inspector, Westcombe Park) 399
HODDER, George Robert (Inspector, Harlesden/Kilburn) 184-185
HODGE, J.R. (Constable (Specials), St.John's Wood) 344
HODGES, Charles (Sub-Divisional Inspector, Wandsworth) 383
HOLDAWAY, William (Inspector, Carshalton) 86, 358
HOLDEN, Brian Bernard Joseph (Constable, Ealing) 128
HOLLIER, Zachariah (Sergeant, Bushey) 78
HOLLINS (Constable, Devonport) 437
HOLLOWAY, William James (Inspector, Croydon) 115
HOLMES, Albert (Constable, Barnet) 100
HOOPER, Race Thomas (Sub-Divisional Inspector, Kingston/
   Wimbledon) 253, 407
HOPE, William (Constable, Brentford) 72
HOPKER (Constable, Leyton) 264
HOPKINS, Henry (Inspector, Edmonton) 136
HOPKINS, William (Sub-Divisional Inspector, Tower Bridge) 368
HORNE (Inspector, Portsmouth) 432
HORNSBY, G. (Superintendent, Chatham) 439, 443
HORNSBY, George (Inspector, Southwark) 339
HORSLEY (Chief Inspector, City of Westminster) 246
HORSLEY, D.C. (Superintendent, Cobham) 110
HOUNDSOME, John (Constable, City of Westminster/Shenley) ... 100, 328
HOW, Arthur (Inspector, Richmond) 314
HOWARD, A.C. (Assistant Commissioner, Portsmouth/
   Pembroke) 420, 433, 445
HOWARD, A.C. (Superintendent, Thames) 420
HOWARD, Johnny (Constable, Hendon) 208
HOWARD, Roger (Inspector, Woolwich) 414, 426
HOWE (Constable, Marine: Wapping) 422
HOWE (Constable, Wanstead) 385
HOWELL, H.W.C. (Chief Inspector, Harrow) 191
HOWIE (Superintendent, Loughton) 269
HOWIE, Daniel (Inspector, Stoke Newington) 350
HOWLETT, H.E. (Chief Superintendent, Wanstead) 386
HOWLETT, William T.J. (Superintendent, Romford) 319-320
HUBBARD, Sally (Chief Superintendent, South Norwood) 337
HUCK, Charles Henry (War Reserve Constable, Islington) 235
HUDSON (Chief Inspector, Feltham) 148
HUDSON (Sergeant, Plumstead) 302
HUGGIN, William (Constable, Chatham) 442
HUGHES, Joseph (Inspector, Bedfont) 56
HUGHES, Nevil (Constable, Dagenham) 119
HUGHES, Samuel (Superintendent, Harrow Road) 192
HUMPHREY, Simon (Superintendent, Finchley) 153
HUNT, Alfred (Chief Inspector, Devonport) 436
HUNT (Chief Superintendent, Edmonton) 138
HUNT, Charles (Inspector, Croydon) 114
HUNT, Charles (Superintendent, Hammersmith) 175
HUNT, Charles (Superintendent, Kings Cross Road) 247
HUNT, Charles (Superintendent, Norwood Green) 287
HUNT, Daniel (Detective Inspector, Lewisham) 261
HUNT, Ernest Frank (War Reserve Constable, Battersea) 53
HUNT, Robert (Assistant Commissioner, Forest Gate) 155
HUNT, T.B. (Chief Inspector, West Hendon) 398
HUNTLEY, William J (Superintendent, Kentish Town) 242
HURST, J. (Chief Superintendent, Teddington) 362
HUTCHESON, Ian (Superintendent, Heathrow) 199
HUTCHINGS (Constable, Islington) 234
HUTCHINS (Station Sergeant, Acton) 38
HUTCHINS, Frederick (Sergeant, West Ham) 396
HUXLEY (Constable, Hyde Park) 226
HUXTABLE (Constable, Devonport) 436
HYDE (Detective Inspector, Romford) 320
HYNDS, Len (Constable, Rotherhithe) 323

ILLESLEY, David (Chief Superintendent, Wealdstone) 388
IMBERT, Sir Peter (Commissioner) 137, 155, 157, 235, 241
ING, Henry (Constable, Staines) 347
INGAR (Sergeant, Pembroke) 445
INSTANCE, Frederick (Inspector, Acton) 38
ISAAC (Superintendent, Walton Street) 379
ISBESTER, William (Inspector, Marine: Wapping) 421

JACKSON (Constable, Wealdstone) 388
JACKSON, J. (Inspector, Kennington) 238
JACKSON, John (Sub-Divisional Inspector, Greenwich) 166
JACKSON, Peter (Chief Superintendent, Kingston) 254
JACOBS, Joseph (Constable, Brentford) 69
JAGO, Richard (Constable, Notting Dale) 289
JAMES, Alfred Charles (Constable, Loughton) 270
JAMES, Leonard (Inspector, Devonport) 437
JAMES, Thomas George (Superintendent, Fulham) 156
JANES, James (Sub-Divisional Inspector, Balham/Streatham/
   Clapham) 45, 352
JARDINE, Frederick (Sergeant, South Mimms) 336
JARVIS, Frederick (Chief Superintendent, Sutton) 418
JARVIS, Henry (Inspector, Plumstead) 303
JASPER, Thomas (Constable, Barnet) 101
JEAKS, Charles (Inspector, Hillingdon and Uxbridge) 212
JEFFREY, Edward (Constable, Streatham) 352
JENKINS (Inspector, Dalston) 120
JENKINS, Charles (Constable, Barnet) 101
JENNER (Constable, Cobham) 110
JERBURGH-BONSEY, H. (Assistant Commandant, Hackney) ... 28, 172
JERVIS, Henry (Inspector, Hoxton) 222
JEWELL (Inspector, Brockley) 76
JEWELL, George (Station Sergeant, East Barnet) 130
JIGGINS, John (Constable, Hammersmith) 175
JOHNSON, George (Constable, Battersea) 52
JOHNSON, George (Constable, Rainham) 310
JOHNSON, James (Superintendent, Islington) 233
JOHNSON, M. (Sergeant (Specials), Ponders End) 304
JOHNSON, R.A.S. (Chief Superintendent, Fulham) 157
JOHNSTON, James (Superintendent, Stoke Newington) 350
JONES, A.H. (Superintendent, Lavender Hill) 256
JONES, William (Constable, Shenley) 328
JONES, William (Inspector, Portsmouth) 431
JONES, William (Inspector, Richmond) 313-314
JORDAN, Dora (Constable (Specials), Romford) 319
JORDAN, Samuel (Constable, Loughton) 270
JORDON (Constable, Hendon) 201
JORDON, Carlos (Constable, Ealing) 127
JOSLIN, Fred (Constable, Romford) 319
JOSLING, Horace (Sergeant, West End Cenral) 392
JOYCE (Constable, Kings Cross Road) 247
JUDD (Constable, Sunbury) 354
JUDGE, J. (Inspector, Chatham) 443
JUDGE, John (Inspector, Marine: Blackwall/Wapping) 419, 421
JUDGE, Joshua (Inspector, Marine: Wapping) 421

Index

JUKES, John (Constable, Richmond) 313

KANE, John (Chief Inspector, Pembroke/Chatham) 439, 444, 445
KAYE, K. (Constable (Specials), Ponders End) 304
KEATING, James (Superintendent, Bethnal Green) 60-61
KEENS, William Henry (Constable, Poplar) 305
KEIL, Frederick Henry (Sergeant, Hackney) 173
KEITH, James (Sub-Divisional Inspector, Rosyth) 446
KELL (Inspector, Woolwich) 427
KELLEY, Barbara (Detective Inspector, Women Police) 467
KELLY, James (Constable, Acton) 38
KEMP, Edward (Sergeant, Ashford) 44
KEMP, William (Inspector, Chatham) 443
KEMPIN, John (Sub-Divisional Inspector, Teddington) 361
KEMPIN, John Henry (Inspector, Hampton) 180
KEMPSTER (Sergeant, Kingston) 253
KENDALL, Sir Norman (Assistant Commissioner, East Ham) 132
KENDALL, W.F. (Sub-Divisional Inspector, Wimbledon) 408
KENNEDY, John (Constable, Hornsey) 218
KENNETT, Frederick Daniel (Constable, Kingston) 253
KENNISON, Peter (Constable (later Inspector), Islington) 66, 173, 235
KENNOUGH (Constable, Sunbury) 354
KENTH, Piara Singh (Constable, Ealing) 128
KENTISH, William (Constable, Hillingdon and Uxbridge) 213
KENT, Robert (Constable, Waltham Abbey) 377
KERTZEN, Sandra (Constable, Women Police) 468
KESSELL (Constable, Wealdstone) 388
KEYS, Albert (Superintendent, Rosyth/Devonport) 436, 438, 446
KIDD, Albert (Sergeant, Bedfont) 56
KILLEN, Tom (War Reserve Constable, Holloway) 216
KING (Inspector, Haringey) 219
KING (Inspector, Hendon) 201
KING, A.T. (Chief Inspector, Hendon) 202
KING, Alan (Sergeant, Chingford) 98
KING, Joseph (Chief Inspector, Chatham) 442
KING, William (Constable, Romford) 318
KIRBY (Acting Sergeant, Southgate) 338
KIRKER, Ralph (Constable, West End Cenral) 392
KITCH, John B. (Superintendent, Fulham) 156
KITNEY (Constable, Knockholt) 255
KNELL, George (Detective Constable, Finchley) 150
KNIGHT, C. (Constable (Specials), Ponders End) 304
KNIGHTON, Harry (Inspector, Catford) 89
KNIGHTS, W. (Inspector, Epsom) 143
KNOTT, W. (Inspector, Epsom) 143

LABALMONDIERE (Deputy Commissioner, Kensington) 240
LACK (Constable, Devonport) 438
LAMB, Jabez (Constable, Sunbury) 354
LAMB, Thomas (Inspector, Barking) 46
LAMBERT (Sub-Divisional Inspector, Southgate) 339
LAMBERT, F. (Constable, Romford) 318
LANCASTER, William (Constable, Shenley) 328
LANCE, J. (Inspector, Hammersmith) 175
LANE, Charles (Inspector, Catford) 89
LANE, F. (Constable, Portsmouth) 434
LANKTREE, C. (Inspector, West Ham) 396
LANNING (Sergeant, Wealdstone) 387
LARCOMBE, William (Constable, Wealdstone) 387
LAST (Chief Inspector, Portsmouth) 434
LAST, James (Superintendent, Portsmouth) 430
LAVER, John (Sergeant, Bedfont) 55
LAWLOR, J. (Superintendent, Tooting) 364
LAWRENCE, S.C. (Sub-Divisional Inspector, Sutton) 358
LAWS, Arthur (Constable, Tooting) 364
LAY, William (Station Sergeant, Harefield) 183
LAZELL, Alfred (Constable, Romford) 318

LE COCQ, John (Inspector, Shadwell) 326
LEE, Charles Richard (Detective Sergeant, Hackney) 172
LEE, Nathan Thompson (Sub-Divisional Inspector,
  Wandsworth Common) 384
LEE, Walter (Sergeant, Staines) 347
LEE, Walter (Sub-Divisional Inspector, Greenwich) 166
LEECH (Sub-Divisional Inspector, Finchley) 150
LEES, George (Constable, Victoria Park) 373
LEESON, Ben (Detective Sergeant, Commercial Street/Kennington) .. 238
LEGGATT, Frederick (Inspector, South Mimms) 355
LEMMEY, William (Sub-Divisional Inspector, Croydon) 336
LENNETT, G.M. (Inspector, Kennington) 238
LEONARD, William (Inspector, Marine: Blackwall) 419
LEVEY, Ernest Alfred (Special Constable, Leyton) 265
LEVICK (Chief Inspector (Specials), Golders Green) 344
LEVY, James (Sergeant, Brentford) 69
LEWENDON (Constable, Wealdstone) 388
LEWIS, Henry (Station Sergeant, Elstree) 138
LEWIS, Jack (Constable, Bromley) 78
LEWIS, John Joseph (Inspector, Wapping) 112
LEWIS, Joseph (Inspector, Leman Street/Commercial Street) ... 258, 421
LEWIS, Ronald (Special Constable, Greenwich) 168
LIGHT, Don (Constable, Kilburn) 244
LINDBURN (Constable, Hendon) 207
LINDENBERN (Constable, Hendon) 208
LINGE, R. (Superintendent, Harlesden) 186
LINKINS, Herbert (Special Sub-Inspector, Greenwich) 168
LINVELL, James (Constable, Bromley) 77
LIPSCOMBE, Fred (Constable, Staines) 348
LITTLE, N. (Constable (Specials), Ponders End) 304
LITTLEJOHNS (Sub-Divisional Inspector, Hammersmith) 175
LLOYD, Samuel (Sergeant, Acton) 37
LOCK (Constable, Portsmouth) 430
LOCK, Samuel (Constable, Haringey) 412
LOCKE, William (Constable, Greenwich) 168
LOCKWOOD, Arnold (Chief Superintendent, Dagenham) 119
LOFUS, Michael (Inspector, Woolwich) 430
LONG, J. (Superintendent, Lavender Hill) 256
LOOKER (Constable, Devonport) 436
LOWE (Inspector, Westminster) 246
LOWE, G. (Inspector, Kennington) 238
LOWE, William Bowler (Constable, Greenford) 164
LOXTON (Superintendent, Barnet/AlbanyStreet) 40, 99
LUCAS (Sergeant, Wanstead) 385
LUCAS, Stephen T (Superintendent, Croydon/Streatham) 114-115, 352
LUCEY, William (Sergeant, Hunter Street) 234
LUMMUS, Frederick (Sub-Divisional Inspector, Belvedere) 59
LUSCOMBE, Samuel Henry (Constable, Hendon) 205
LUXTON (Inspector, Hanwell) 182
LYNCH, Patrick (Constable, Cobham) 110

M'KELVIE (Constable, Holloway) 215
MABER, Edward (Station Sergeant, Chingford) 97
MacANDREW (Sergeant, Woolwich) 417
MacDONALD, Archibald (Chief Inspector, Pembroke) 430, 433, 444
MACDONALD, D.C. (Deputy Commander, Hendon) 202
MACE, William (Station Sergeant, Kingston) 251
MACER, Arthur (Inspector, Kilburn) 244
MacINNES, Charles (Constable, Kilburn) 245
MacINTYRE (Sub-Divisional Inspector, Woolwich) 430
MACKAY, A. (Constable (Specials), Ponders End) 304
MACKAY, Nina (Constable, Barkingside) 468
MACKAY, Sidney (Chief Superintendent, Barkingside) 49-50
MacKINNON (Chief Superintendent, Edmonton) 138
MACKINTOSH (Constable, Hampton) 180
MACMILLAN, William (Sub- Divisional Inspector, Harlesden) 185
MACREADY, C. Nevil (Commissioner, Women Police) 466

MADDOX, George (Inspector, Marine: Blackwall) 419
MAGGS, Gordon (Commander, Kensington) 241
MAHER, Thomas E. (Inspector, Southgate) 338
MALLALIEU, Francis M (Superintendent, Greenwich/Chatham) 164
MALLIN, Henry William (Sergeant, Peel House (Training)
  /City of Westminster) 13-14
MANN, Henry M. (Superintendent, Southwark/Carter Street) 88, 341
MANNERS MSC (Commander, L.B. Hounslow) 28
MANNING, James (Constable, Romford) 318, 319
MANSFIELD, N. (Inspector, Kilburn) 244
MAPELEY (Constable, Leyton) 264
MARGETSON, Sir Philip (Deputy Commissioner) 274
MARK, Kingston (Superintendent, Pembroke) 444
MARK, Kingston (Superintendent, Woolwich) 425, 427
MARK, Sir Robert (Commissioner) 338
MARKHAM, Edward (Chief Superintendent, Edmonton) 138
MARLER, Charles (Inspector, Marine: Wapping) 421
MARLOW, John (Constable, Woodford) 412
MARQUARD, Courtney Henry (Inspector, Brentford) 69
MARR, V. (Superintendent, Lavender Hill) 256
MARRIOTT, J.F. (Chief Inspector, West Hendon) 398
MARSH, Adam (Inspector, Leman Street) 259
MARSH, George (Inspector, Leman Street) 258
MARSHALL, 'Ginger' (Constable, Hendon) 208
MARSINGALE (Superintendent, Romford) 318
MARTIN (Chief Superintendent, Edmonton) 138
MARTIN, George (Special Sergeant, Greenwich) 168
MARTIN, Robert (Chief Inspector, Portsmouth) 430, 431
MARTIN, T. (Inspector, Kennington) 238
MASON (Sub-Divisional Inspector, Islington) 234
MASON, Allen (Constable, Cobham) 110
MASON, Arthur (Inspector, West Ham) 394
MASON, William (Chief Inspector, Clapham/Croydon) 108, 114
MASTERS, Francis (Constable, Sunbury) 353
MATHEWS, Annie (Constable, Woolwich) 417, 456
MATTHEWS, Terrence (Inspector, Golders Green) 160
MAUDE, Henry (Inspector, Mitcham) 20, 275
MAY, Charles (Inspector, Poplar) 305
MAY, Frederick (Sub-Divisional Inspector, Southwark/Fulham) 156, 340
MAY, James Brian (Constable, Wood Green) 412
MAYNARD (Inspector, Hoxton) 223
MAYNE, Sir Richard (Commissioner) 5, 114, 139, 149, 150, 225, 240,
  .... 289, 333, 427, 432, 441, 442
MAZETTI, Bertie (Constable (Specials), Wood Green) 412
McADAM MSC (Commandant, L.B. Hounslow) 29
McCARTHY, Philip (Inspector, Rodney Road) 316
McCONDACH (Inspector, Wealdstone) 388
McCRIMMON, Neil (Inspector, Devonport) 437
McCULLOCK (Constable, Hendon) 201
McCULLOCK, Percy (Station Sergeant, Acton) 38
McDONALD, A. (Inspector, Kilburn) 244
McDONALD, Archibald (Superintendent, Portsmouth) 431
McDONOUGH, C.L. (Chief Superintendent, Marine: Wapping) 423
McELLIOTT, James (Inspector, Woolwich) 429
McFADDEN (Divisional Superintendent, Stoke Newington/
  Islington) 234, 351
McFADDEN, Alexander (Constable, Upminster) 370
McFADDEN, Robert (Inspector, Surbiton) 356
McGOWAN, Patrick (Constable, Stoke Newington) 351
McGRAW, Robert (Constable, Fulham) 156
McHUGO, Christopher H. (Superintendent, East Greenwich) 130
McINTYRE, Robert Graham (Sergeant, Sunbury) 353
McKENNA, Edward (Sub-Divisional Inspector, Wandsworth) 383
McLEAN, Alexander (Superintendent, Camberwell) 80
McLEAN, Andrew (Superintendent, Croydon/Mitcham) 114, 275
McLEAN, Capt. J.R. (Commander, Ilford) 227
McLEAN, Geoffrey (Assistant Commissioner, Edmonton) 137

McNEE, Sir David (Commissioner) 102, 116, 238, 245, 396
MEADON, Arthur (Constable, Barnet) 101
MEAPHAM, A.G. (Chief Inspector, Hampton) 181
MEASURES, John (Sergeant, King Street) 246
MEDLICOTT, W. (Superintendent, Leman Street) 258
MEE, William (Inspector, L.B. Camden) 20
MEEHAN, Leslie Edwin Vincent (Constable, Greenwich) 168
MEERING, Andrew (Superintendent, Belvedere) 331
MELLISH, Joseph (Inspector, Stoke Newington) 350
MELTON, Robert (Constable, Camberwell) 82
MERCHANT, W.J. (Superintendent, Dagenham) 119
MEWTON, William (Constable, Woolwich) 430
MILES, Sidney George (Constable, Croydon) 115
MILES, Thomas (Constable, Wimbledon) 405
MILLARD, Oliver (Inspector, Harlesden) 186
MILLER (Inspector, Gray's Inn Road) 161
MILLER, J.J. (Chief Superintendent, Hendon/Peel House) 13, 200
MILLER, William (Inspector, Leman Street) 258
MILLS (Constable, Wealdstone) 387
MILNER, Ernest (Detective Constable, East Barnet) 130
MITCHELL, Frederick (Sub-Divisional Inspector, Harrow Road) 192
MITCHELL, Isaac (Constable, Pinner) 297
MITCHELL, John (Inspector, Kensington) 240
MITTALL, Robert (Sergeant, Ditton) 123
MOBLEY, John (Inspector, Harrow Road) 192
MOFFATT, T. (Inspector, Hammersmith) 175
MONAGHAN, L. (Sergeant, Hillingdon and Uxbridge) 212
MONEY, Michael (Chief Inspector, Portsmouth/Woolwich) 426, 429, 433
MONK, Richard (Chief Superintendent, Brixton) 76
MONNERY, William (Constable, Woolwich) 430
MOORE (Constable, Wealdstone) 388
MOORE, A. (Sergeant(Specials), Ponders End) 304
MOORE, Bert (Chief Superintendent, Heathrow) 199
MOORE, Charles (Constable, Potters Bar) 307
MOORE, Charles Henry (Constable, Sydenham) 360
MOORE, John (Constable, Bedfont) 55
MOORE, John (Constable, Kings Cross Road) 247
MOORE, John (Station Sergeant, Pinner) 297, 298
MOORMAN (Sub-Divisional Inspector, Devonport) 437
MORGAN (Sergeant, Wealdstone) 388
MORGAN, Henry (Chief Inspector, Woolwich) 426
MORGAN, James (Inspector, Hammersmith) 174
MORLEY, H. (Superintendent, Marine: Wapping) 423
MORRIS (Chief Superintendent, Edmonton) 138
MORSLEY, James (Sub-Divisional Inspector, Bedfont) 56
MORSMAN, George (Inspector, Portsmouth) 431
MORTLOCK (Sergeant, Hornsey) 219
MOTT, James (Superintendent, Chatham/Woolwich) 56, 427, 430, 441
MOULAND, E. (Constable (Specials), Ponders End) 304
MOUNCE, M.R. (Woman Sergeant (Specials), Commercial Street) 113
MOUNT, John (Constable, Romford) 318
MOUNTIFIELD, William Steggles (Sub-Divisional Inspector,
  Holloway) 215
MOWER, John (Inspector, Worcester Park) 418
MUGGERIDGE (Sergeant, Sunbury) 354
MULCAHY, M.M. (Superintendent, Richmond/Hampton) 181
MULES, Thomas (Inspector, Acton) 38
MULVANY, John Michael (Divisional Superintendent) 462
MUMFORD, John Oran (Sub-Divisional Inspector, Brentford) 71
MUNDAY, William (Constable, Northwood) 286
MURPHY, Daniel (Constable, Shenley) 328
MURRAY (Inspector, West Ham) 395
MURRAY, William (Superintendent, Southwark) 339
MURTON, Robert (Constable, Hillingdon and Uxbridge) 213
MUSTO (Constable, Carter Street) 88
MYERS, Arthur Needham (War Reserve Constable, Hammersmith) 176

Index

NAZER, William Stevens (Constable, Chatham) ... 442
NEAL (Constable, Shenley) ... 328
NEAL, T. (Inspector, Kennington) ... 238
NEAL, Thomas (Inspector, Shepherds Bush) ... 329
NEAL, Thomas (Sub-Divisional Inspector, Sunbury) ... 354
NEALE (Constable, Portsmouth) ... 430
NEAN (Sub-Divisional Inspector, Stoke Newington) ... 351
NEVILLE, John (Sergeant, Bedfont) ... 56
NEWLANDS, Hugh (Reserve Inspector, Harrow Road) ... 192
NEWMAN (Constable, Sunbury) ... 354
NEWMAN (Constable, Tottenham) ... 365
NEWMAN (Station Sergeant, Sunbury) ... 354
NEWMAN, Ernest (Constable, Hornsey) ... 219
NEWMAN, Sir Kenneth (Commissioner) ... 19, 108, 209
NEWMAN, William (Superintendent, Hammersmith) ... 176
NEWMAN, William (Superintendent, Shepherds Bush) ... 329
NEWNHAM (Constable, Sunbury) ... 354
NEWNHAM, Alfred (Sub-Divisional Inspector, Acton/Ealing) ... 38, 127
NEYLAN (Superintendent, Southwark) ... 340
NICHOLS, F. (Sub-Divisional Inspector, Battersea) ... 53
NICHOLS, Henry (Sub-Divisional Inspector, Tower Bridge) ... 368
NICOLSON, Lyn (Constable, Women Police) ... 468
NIGHTINGALE, Harold (Inspector, Chatham) ... 444
NOCK, Henry (Constable, Brentford) ... 72
NORMAN, Ralph (Sergeant, Whetstone) ... 401
NORRIS, William (Sergeant, East Barnet) ... 130
NORTHOVER, Walter (Inspector, Sutton) ... 358
NOTT-BOWER, Sir John (Commissioner) ... 88
NUTT, Robert (Sub-Divisional Inspector, Barnet) ... 100

O'BRIAN, Nassau Smith (Superintendent, L.B. Camden) ... 20
O'CONNOR, Michael (Chief Superintendent, Edmonton) ... 138
O'LEARY, William (Constable, Hillingdon and Uxbridge) ... 213
O'NEILL, Frank (Constable, Kennington) ... 32, 238
OAKS, William (Inspector, Chatham) ... 442
ODELL, Francis (Sub-Divisional Inspector, Carter Street) ... 88
ODELL, William (Chief Inspector, Kentish Town) ... 242
OGDEN, S.M. (Sub-Divisional Inspector, Peel House (Training) ... 13
OLIVE, James (Superintendent, Acton/Harrow/Kilburn/Northwood/Ruslip/Willesden Green) ... 38, 285, 325, 402
OLIVER (Station Sergeant, Hendon) ... 207
OLIVER, John (Chief Inspector, Finchley) ... 153
OLLETT, Albany J. (Inspector, Battersea) ... 52
ORR (Sub-Inspector, Hendon) ... 206
ORWIN, Leigh (Superintendent, Heathrow) ... 199
OSBORNE, David (Constable, Surbiton) ... 356-357
OSBOURNE (Sub-Divisional Inspector, Tottenham Court Road) ... 367
OSGOOD (Inspector, Stoke Newington) ... 351
OTWAY, Charles (Inspector, Hillingdon and Uxbridge) ... 212
OUGH, William (Sergeant, New Malden) ... 279
OVERY (Inspector, Dalston) ... 120
OWEN, Frederick (Acting Sergeant, Greenford) ... 163
OWEN, Henry (Constable, Bromley) ... 8

PACEY (Sub-Divisional Inspector, Somers Town) ... 335
PACKER, Albert Ernest (Constable, Greenwich) ... 168
PADDICK, Brian (Commander, Balham) ... 45
PADGETT, T. (Inspector, Kennington) ... 238
PAGE, Tom Alec (War Reserve Constable, Finchley) ... 152
PAINE, Charles (Constable, Harefield) ... 183
PALETHORPE (Constable, Wealdstone) ... 387
PALIN, S.A. (Superintendent, Tottenham) ... 366
PALMER (Constable, Leyton) ... 264
PALMER, William (Station Sergeant, Bromley) ... 7
PAMETER (Sergeant, Wealdstone) ... 387
PARISH, William (Constable, Potters Bar) ... 307
PARKER (Constable, Wealdstone) ... 387
PARKER, Henry (Inspector, Hoxton) ... 222
PARKER, Henry (Inspector, Woolwich) ... 429
PARKINS (Constable, Gipsy Hill) ... 288
PARLETT, Samuel (Sub-Divisional Inspector, Croydon) ... 115
PARROTT, Kathleen (Constable, Women Police) ... 468
PARSLOW, James (Constable, Collier Row/Romford) ... 112, 318
PARSON, J. (Sub-Divisional Inspector, West Ham) ... 395
PARSONS (Chief Inspector, Stoke Newington) ... 351
PARSONS (Sergeant, Edmonton) ... 136
PARSONS, John Georege (Superintendent, Portsmouth) ... 430
PARSONS, William (Sergeant, Dagenham) ... 117-118
PARTNER, David (Station Sergeant, Potters Bar) ... 308
PASCOE, John (Inspector, Stoke Newington) ... 350
PASHLEY (Reserve Inspector, King Street) ... 246
PATERSON, Thomas (Constable, Ealing) ... 127
PAWLEY (Inspector, Epsom) ... 143
PAWSEY, Philip (Inspector, West Ham) ... 396
PAYNE (Inspector, Chatham) ... 440
PAYNE (Sub-Divisional Inspector, Shadwell) ... 326
PAYNE, Edward (Superintendent, Carter Street) ... 87
PAYNE, G. (Inspector, Kennington) ... 238
PAYNE, G.F. (Sub-Divisional Inspector, Hendon) ... 206
PAYNE, Jimmy (Constable, Bedfont) ... 57
PAYNE, William (Inspector, Woolwich) ... 429
PEACOCK (Constable, Portsmouth) ... 430
PEAKE, Benjamin (Sergeant, Wimbledon) ... 405
PEARCE (Superintendent, Stoke Newington) ... 351
PEARCE, C. (Divisional Superintendent, Edmonton) ... 137, 138
PEARCE, Charles (Constable, Devonport) ... 436
PEARCE, James Walter (Acting Sergeant, Harrow) ... 190, 191
PEARCE, Nicholas (Detective Inspector, Gardiner's Lane) ... 8, 157
PEARCE, Nicholas (Superintendent, Dagenham) ... 117
PEARCE, Thomas (Inspector, Rosyth) ... 446
PEARMAN, John (Inspector, Richmond) ... 313-314
PEARMAN, John (Inspector, Wandsworth) ... 381
PEARMAN, William (Inspector, Redbridge) ... 413
PEARN (Constable, Devonport) ... 436
PEARN (Inspector, East Dulwich) ... 125
PEARN, Charles (Inspector, Epsom) ... 143
PEARN, Charles (Sub-Divisional Inspector, Richmond) ... 313
PERNULL, S. (Constable (Specials), Ponders End) ... 304
PERRY, James (Chief Inspector, Camberwell) ... 81
PERRY, Michael Robert (Constable, Ruislip) ... 325
PERRY, William (Inspector, Harlesden) ... 185
PETHERICK, Frederick (Constable, Nine Elms) ... 282
PETO, Dorothy (Superintendent, Women Police) ... 14, 466, 470, 471
PHILLIPS (Sergeant, Wanstead) ... 385
PHILLIPS, Eddie (Acting Sergeant, Wealdstone) ... 389
PHILLIPS, Phillip (Acting Sergeant, Potters Bar) ... 308
PHILLIPS, William (Sub-Divisional Inspector, Catford) ... 89
PICKARD, E. (Constable (Specials), Ponders End) ... 304
PICKETT, Thomas Robert (War Reserve Constable, Hackney) ... 173
PICKETT, William (Inspector, Surbiton) ... 356
PIERCE, Enoch John (Constable, Wimbledon) ... 407-408
PIERSE, William F. (Superintendent, Leman Street) ... 258
PIKE, Francis (Detective Sergeant, Finchley) ... 150
PINEGAR (Inspector, Wimbledon) ... 404
PINER, Thomas (Constable, Pinner) ... 299
PING (Constable, Leyton) ... 264
PINKS, Edward (Inspector, Shepherds Bush) ... 329
PIPE, Henry (Sub-Divisional Inspector, West Ham) ... 395
PIPES (Constable, Islington) ... 234
PIRNIE, Gail ... 468
PLUMB, G.R. (Constable, Hyde Park) ... 226
PLUMMER, Joseph (Sergeant, Poplar) ... 306
POCOCK, James H. (Inspector, Islington) ... 234
POMEROY, Henry (Constable, Harrow) ... 190

PONTIN, Charles (Constable, Brentford) 70
POOLE, W.J. (Superintendent, Harrow) 191
POPE, Richard (Inspector, St. John's Wood) 343
PORTER (Acting Sergeant, Sunbury) 354
PORTER, Albert Ernest (Station Sergeant, Marine: Wapping) 422-423
PORTER, Hubert (Sergeant, Potters Bar) 308
PORTER, J. (Inspector, Carter Street) 87
PORTER, W.H. (Superintendent, Wimbledon) 409
POTTER, Charles (Sergeant, Harrow) 190
POTTER, Frank (Constable, Brentford) 72
POTTERILL, James (Constable, Ashford) 44
POTTS, George (Constable, Chatham/Woolwich) 429, 442
POTTS, William (Inspector, Devonport) 437
POWELL (Superintendent, Hammersmith) 176
POWELL, Bob (Constable, Cobham) 110
POWELL, H. (Inspector, Carter Street) 87
POWELL, James (Divisional Superintendent, Brentford) 71
POWELL, James (Superintendent, Cannon Row) 86
POYNTZ, Major (Chief Constable, Romford) 318
PRATCHETT, Henry (Station Sergeant, Leyton) 263
PRENDERGAST, Thomas (Sergeant, Croydon) 114
PRESTON (Constable, Norbury) 283
PRIDE (Inspector, East Dulwich) 125
PRIDEAUX, William (Constable, Staines) 347
PRIDMORE, Thomas (Inspector, Marine: Blackwall) 420
PROCTOR, Thomas L. (Inspector, Isle of Dogs) 231
PROOPS (Constable, Sunbury) 354
PROOPS, Goodman (Constable, Brentford) 72
PRYKE (Chief Inspector, Kingston) 251
PRYKE, John (Inspector, Eltham/Richmond) 140, 314
PULLEN (Sub-Divisional Inspector, Norbury) 283
PULLEN, Arthur (Sub-Divisional Inspector, Greenwich) 166
PURBRICK, M. (Superintendent, Peckham/Brixton) 75, 295
PURDY, Raymond (Detective Sergeant, Chelsea) 93-94, 357

QUIBELL, Lawrence James (Constable, Rosyth) 446
QUIGLEY, K. (Inspector, West Ham) 394
QUIGLEY, William (Inspector, Bethnal Green) 60
QUINCEY, H.C. (Superintendent, Croydon) 115

RACE, W.N. (Inspector, Carter Street) 87
RACEY, Henry (Constable, Barnet) 101
RACKHAM, C. (Superintendent, Wimbledon) 409
RAISHBROOK (Station Sergeant, Hendon) 207
RANDALL, Desmond (Sergeant, Cobham) 110
RANDALL, Ernest (Constable, Barnet) 100
RAPSEY, James (Inspector, Kingston) 249
RAWLEY, John (Inspector, L.B. Camden) 20
RAWLINGS (Superintendent, Richmond) 315
RAWLINGS, David (Sub-Divisional Inspector, Chiswick) 104-105
RAWLINGS, William (Constable, Somers Town) 334-335
RAYMENT (Constable, Portsmouth) 430
READ, Charles (Inspector, Hammersmith) 176
READ, M. (Constable (Specials), Ponders End) 304
REDGEWELL (Chief Superintendent, Newham) 396
REDSTONE, W. (Inspector, Kilburn) 244
REES, W.L. (Superintendent, West Hendon) 398
REEVES (Inspector, Fulham) 412
REID, Thomas (Inspector, Limehouse) 267
RENDALL, Joseph (Sergeant, Greenwich) 165
RHODES, George (Inspector, Shepherds Bush) 329
RICHARDS, David (Sub-Divisional Inspector, Ealing) 127
RICHARDS, W.H. (Constable, Edmonton) 137
RICHARDSON, Charles (Sub-Divisional Inspector, Brentford) 72, 220
RICHARDSON, Joseph Ernest (Constable, Dalston) 120
RICHARDSON, Thomas (Superintendent, Chatham) 439, 440, 441
RICHARDSON, William (Inspector, Wimbledon) 403
RICKENS, Arthur (Constable, Brentford) 72
RIDLEY, Albert (Constable, Hornchurch) 217
RIMMINGTON, Thomas (Constable, Brentford) 72
RIVETT, Frederick (Chief Inspector, Cannon Row) 86
ROADNIGHT, R. (Sergeant, Uxbridge) 212
ROBBINS, Edwin (Constable, Barnet) 100
ROBBINS, George (Sergeant, Kingston) 250
ROBBINS, Peter (Chief Superintendent, Hackney) 173
ROBERTS, George (Inspector, Marine: Blackwall) 420
ROBERTS, Norwell (Constable, Bow Street) 68
ROBERTSON, A. (Sub-Divisional Inspector, Wandsworth) 364
ROBERTSON, Alexander (Inspector, Waltham Abbey) 377
ROBINS, George (Sergeant, Carshalton) 86
ROBINSON (Chief Inspector, Westminster) 246
ROBINSON (Divisional Superintendent, Kingston) 252
ROBINSON (Inspector, Southwark) 340
ROBINSON, John (Constable, Holborn) 214
ROBSON, William (Inspector, Marine: Wapping) 421, 422
ROCHE, Patrick (Constable, Staines) 347
ROE MSC (Commander, L.B. Hounslow) 29
ROGERS, John (Constable, Edgware) 135
ROGERS, John (Inspector, Wimbledon) 405
ROGERS, R.E. MBE (Commander, Golders Green) 160
ROGERS, Thomas (Chief Inspector, Chatham/Woolwich) 425, 434, 441
ROLF, Francis (Sub-Divisional Inspector, Carter Street) 88
ROLFE, George (Constable, Ruislip) 325
ROLFE, George (Inspector, Wanstead) 386
ROOKS, William (Inspector, West Ham) 394
ROSE (Chief Inspector, Westminster) 246
ROSEN, James (Constable, Holloway) 216
ROTHNIE (Sergeant, Devonport) 437
ROWAN, Charles (Commissioner) 66
ROWBOTTOM (Inspector, Carshalton) 86
ROWLAND, George (Inspector, Northwood) 286
ROWLING, John (Sub-Divisional Inspector, Brentford) 71
ROYLE, Joe (Chief Superintendent, Sutton) 359
RUDGE, Edward (Constable, Sunbury) 354
RUDLING, Henry (Constable, Brentford) 72
RUFF (Sub-Divisional Inspector, Caledonian Road) 80
RUFF, Robert (Inspector, Finchley) 151
RUSH (Constable, Wealdstone) 388
RUSHBRIDGE, Alfred (Sub-Divisional Inspector, Kingston) 251
RUSSELL, Leonard (Constable, Tottenham) 365
RUTT, Anthony (Inspector, Arbour Square) 42
RUTT, Anthony (Superintendent, Kennington) 236

SAICH, George (Sergeant, Clapham) 108
SAINES (Divisional Superintendent, Richmond) 315
SAINES, David (Chief Inspector, L.B. Kingston/Kingston) 251, 383
SALLOWS, George (Sergeant, Bedfont) 56
SALTER, Charles (Sergeant, Bedfont) 55
SANDERSON, George (Constable, Uxbridge) 213
SANDFORD, John (Detective Sergeant, Chelsea) 93
SANDS, Albert (Constable, Wealdstone) 387
SARA (Sub-Divisional Inspector, Plumstead) 303
SAUNDERS. Albert (Chief Inspector, Woolwich) 425
SAUNDERS, Robert (Sergeant, Sidcup) 332
SAUNDERS, Thomas (Inspector, Barkingside) 48
SAVAGE (Constable, Harrow) 191
SAVAGE (Constable, Portsmouth) 430
SAVAGE, Frederick (Sergeant, Acton) 38
SAVILL, Jerry (Chief Superintendent, Heathrow) 199
SAW (Constable, Wealdstone) 388
SAWYER, A. (Sub-Divisional Inspector, West Ham) 395
SAWYER, William Rivers (Constable, Highgate) 210
SCAMMELL, Charles Lewis (Constable, Hanwell) 182
SCANTLEBURY (Inspector, Knights Hill/Westminster) 246, 254

Index

SCANTLEBURY, J. (Inspector, Hammersmith)....175
SCHUCK, M. (Superintendent, Fulham)....157
SCOREY, George (Constable, Wembley)....390
SCOTT (Sub-Inspector (Specials), St. John's Wood)....344
SCOTT, Conrad (Constable, Rotherhithe)....323
SCOTT, Harold (Commissioner)....194
SEAMAN, John (Constable, Brentford)....72
SEARLE (Inspector, Kensington)....239
SEARLE, Graheme (Chief Superintendent, Edmonton)....138
SELLARS, Albert Edward (Inspector, Hanwell)....182
SELMAN, Walter (Constable, Hayes and Goulds Green)....194
SERGEANT, William (Sub-Divisional Inspector, Hammersmith)....176
SEWELL, Beryl (Constable, Hendon)....207
SEWELL, David (Superintendent, Portsmouth)....430, 435, 436
SHACKELL, Joseph (Inspector, Hoxton)....222
SHARP, F.L. (Chief Inspector, Kingston)....253
SHARPLIN, George (Acting Sergeant, East Barnet)....130
SHAW, W.H. (Inspector, Croydon)....114
SHEPHERD, Arthur (Constable, Harrow)....191
SHEPHERD, James (Inspector, Chelsea)....382
SHEPHERD, William (Constable, Pembroke)....445
SHERLOCK (Inspector, Portsmouth)....431
SHERLOCK, William J. (Inspector, Stoke Newington)....350
SHERVINGTON, George (Chief Inspector, Fulham/Hammersmith)....156, 175, 176
SHERWOOD, Peter (Sergeant, Greenford)....164
SHORT (Inspector, Portsmouth)....434
SHORT, Joseph (Chief Inspector, Cannon Row)....86
SIDHU, Kulwant Singh (Constable, Twickenham)....370
SILVEY, William (Constable, Putney)....308
SIMMONDS, John (Inspector, West Ham)....395
SIMMONS (Inspector, Romford)....318
SIMPKINS, Charles (Sergeant, Staines/Sunbury)....347, 353
SIMPSON, Joseph KBE (Commissioner)....204, 330, 464-465
SIMS-KIRBY, J.L. (Superintendent, Haringey)....211
SIMSON, R.A. (Commander (Specials), St. John's Wood)....344
SKEATS, G. (Superintendent, Uxbridge)....212
SKEATS, George (Superintendent, Marine: Wapping)....422
SKEATS, Lewis (Sub-Inspector, South Mimms)....335
SKEGGS (Constable, Hendon)....201
SKENE, William (Superintendent, L.B. Camden)....20
SKINNER, William (Constable, Wimbledon)....404
SLIMON, Peter (Constable, Kensington)....241
SLY, Alfred (Inspector, Devonport)....437
SLY, Charles E. (Superintendent, Chatham//Rosyth)....439, 446
SMALE, Henry (Inspector, Devonport)....437
SMALLBRIDGE (Detective Sergeant, Portsmouth)....434
SMITH (Constable, Isle of Dogs)....231
SMITH (Inspector, Pinner)....297, 298, 299
SMITH (Sub-Divisional Inspector, Shadwell)....326
SMITH, A.D. (Superintendent, Greenwich)....166
SMITH, Ames (Constable, Hillingdon and Uxbridge)....212
SMITH, Charles (Constable, Sunbury)....353, 354
SMITH, Edith (Constable, Women Police)....466
SMITH, Edward (Constable, Brentford)....72
SMITH, Edwin (Superintendent, Devonport)....436, 437
SMITH, F. (Superintendent, Peel House (Training))....13
SMITH, George (Constable, Brentford)....72
SMITH, George (Station Sergeant, Richmond)....314
SMITH, George (Sub-Divisional Inspector, Catford)....89
SMITH, George (War Reserve Constable, Kilburn)....245
SMITH, Harry (Sub-Divisional Inspector, Bedfont)....56, 57
SMITH, James (Chief Inspector, Kingston)....252
SMITH, Jesse (Sergeant, Acton)....38
SMITH, John (Superintendent, Chatham)....439, 442
SMITH, John Albert (Constable, Harefield)....183
SMITH, John George (Cadet (later Inspector), Romford)....321
SMITH, Sydney (Inspector, Harlesden)....184
SMITH, Thomas B (Inspector, Kensington)....239
SMITH, Willie (Superintendent, Chatham/Devonport/Portsmouth)....426, 443, 452
SMITHERAM, Arthur (Inspector, Barnet)....101
SNELL, William (Constable (later sergeant), Hoxton/Thames: Wapping)....223, 422
SOLMAN, David (Superintendent, Forest Gate)....155
SOMERSET, Raglan (Assistant Chief Constable, Romford)....318
SOPER (Constable, Wealdstone)....387
SPALDING, William (Constable, Romford)....318
SPENCER, Frederick (Sub-Divisional Inspector, Carter Street)....88
SPENCER, Frederick (Superintendent, Portsmouth)....426, 430, 434
SPRINGTHORPE, Arthur (Sergeant, Norwood Green)....287
SPRUCES (Inspector, Finchley)....152
SPRULES, P.V. (Chief Constable)....463
SQUIRE, Stan (Commander, Barnet)....102
STANLEY, A.C. (Superintendent, Harrow)....191
STANLEY, Alick (Detective Sergeant, Holloway)....216
STANLEY, Sophia (Superintendent, Women Police)....466, 468
STANNARD, William (Inspector, Kennington)....236
STANTON (Constable, Islington)....234
STEAD, J. (Superintendent, Leman Street)....258
STEED, George (Inspector, Hampton)....180, 422
STEELE (Constable, Hendon)....201
STEGGLES, Richard W. (Superintendent, Camden)....20
STEPHENSON, Sir Paul (Commissioner)....199
STEVENS, Bill (Chief Inspector, Kingston)....254
STEVENS, Henry (Constable, Bromley)....78
STEVENS, Joseph (Constable, Banstead)....45
STEVENS, Sir John (Commissioner)....32, 262, 322, 359, 370
STEWART (Sergeant, Wealdstone)....387
STILL (Inspector, Chatham)....440
STONE, Edwin (Constable, Wandsworth)....383
STRATFORD, Frederick (Sergeant, Dagenham)....118
STRATTON (Inspector, Westminster)....246
STRENGTH, John (Superintendent, Chatham/Devonport)....437, 439, 441
STRIBLING (Constable, Portsmouth)....430
STRUTT (Constable, Sunbury)....354
STUBBINGTON, Charles (Sergeant, Chatham)....443
STURGEON, Henry (Sergeant, Waltham Abbey)....375
STURROCK, Wallace (Constable, Brentford)....72
STYLES, James (Sergeant, Epping Forest)....377
SUMMERS, Charlie (Constable, Kilburn)....244-245
SUMMERS, Raymond Henry (Constable, Holloway)....216
SUTHERLAND, A. (Station Sergeant, Finchley)....150
SUTHERLAND, John (Inspector, Rosyth)....446
SWAINE, James W. (Constable, Harlesden)....185
SWAN (Constable, Wealdstone)....387
SWAN (Inspector, Sydenham)....360
SWAN, Edward William (Constable, Woolwich)....430
SWINDEN, David Reginald (Superintendent, Ealing/ Hendon/ Islington/ East Ham/Limehouse/West Ham)....128, 132, 235, 268, 396
SWINDEN, James (Sergeant, King Street)....246
SYKES, George (Constable, Woolwich)....428
SYLVESTER, Bernard (Inspector, Wimbledon)....408
SYME, John (Inspector, Gerald Road)....158-159

TANNER, Richard (Inspector, Belvedere)....8
TARLING, James (Inspector, Brentford)....70
TARLTON, Edward (Superintendent, Kensington/Stoke Newington/Hackney)....30, 34, 239-240, 350
TARLTON, Pitt (Inspector, Chelsea)....30, 34, 239
TASCHNER (Constable, Wealdstone)....388
TAYLOR (Constable, Wealdstone)....387
TAYLOR, Charles (Inspector, Kilburn)....244
TAYLOR, Donald (Inspector, Woolwich)....429

TAYLOR, Thomas (Inspector, Hammersmith) 176
TAYLOR, W.M. (Chief Superintendent, Hendon) 202
TAYLOR, William (Constable, Hillingdon and Uxbridge) 213
TETT, William (Superintendent, Chatham/Devonport) 436, 439
THATCHER, George (Inspector, Stoke Newington) 350
THOBURN, George (Sergeant, Croydon) 114
THOMAS (Constable, Hendon) 201
THOMAS (Constable, Pembroke) 444
THOMAS (Inspector, Hornsey) 219
THOMAS, A.R. (Superintendent, Teddington) 361
THOMAS, David (Constable, Brentford) 72
THOMAS, Ian (Chief Superintendent, Camberwell) 83
THOMAS, T.E. (Superintendent, Kingston) 253
THOMPSON (Constable, Wealdstone) 388
THOMPSON, A. (Sub-Divisional Inspector, West Ham) 394, 295
THOMPSON, A.H. (Chief Superintendent, East Ham) 133
THOMPSON, Alexander (Superintendent, Woolwich/ Pembroke) 425, 427, 444
THOMPSON, Alfred (Sergeant, Knockholt) 255
THOMPSON, David (Sub-Divisional Inspector, Kingston) 252-253
THOMPSON, George (Constable, Uxbridge) 213
THOMPSON, Joseph (Station Sergeant, East Barnet) 130
THOMSON, James (Constable, West Wickham) 399
THOMSON, James J (Superintendent, L.B. Camden) 101
THOMSON, James Warrender (Constable, Barnet) 101
THORNDELL, Charles (Constable, Shadwell) 326
THORNTON (Chief Superintendent, Edmonton) 138
THORPE (Sub-Divisional Inspector, Stoke Newington) 351
THURSBY (Inspector, Fulham) 156
THURSEY, John (Inspector, Fulham) 156
TIBBLE, Stephen Andrew (Constable, Hammersmith) 177
TIBLE (Constable, Wealdstone) 388
TICKLE, E.J.E. (Superintendent, Cobham) 110
TICKNER, Frederick (Special Constable, Brentford) 72
TILBY, Willie (Station Sergeant, Esher/ Surbiton) 146, 356
TIMMINS, H. (Superintendent, East Ham) 133
TIMPSON (Constable, North Fulham) 284
TITCOMBE, H. (Inspector, West Ham) 395
TITHERIDGE (Constable, Sunbury) 354
TODD, William (Constable, Barnet) 100
TOLFIELD, E. (Constable (Specials), Ponders End) 304
TOMLIN, Major M. OBE (Chief Constable, Stoke Newington) 351
TONGE, John (Inspector, Hoxton) 222
TOOTH (Acting Sergeant, Pinner) 297
TOPP, William J. (Inspector, Kennington) 237
TOTTERDELL, George H. (Detective Superintendent, Romford) 320
TOTTEY, James Frederick (Constable, Greenwich) 168
TRENCHARD, Lord (Commissioner) ...... 5, 54, 100, 124, 130, 140, 160, 201, ... 243, 274, 276, 327, 367, 384, 399, 460
TROTT, Henry (Inspector, Kingston) 251
TROTT, Thomas George (Sub-Divisional Inspector, Finchley) 152
TROUNCE, Willian (Constable, Gardiner's Lane) 157
TUCKWELL, Alfred (Sergeant, Barnet) 99, 100
TUNBRIDGE (Constable, Pembroke) 444
TUNBRIDGE, James (Inspector, Woolwich) 429
TURK, Thomas (Inspector, Deptford) 122
TURNER (Constable, Wealdstone) 387
TURNER (Sergeant, Devonport) 438
TURNER (Sergeant, Walthamstow) 378
TURNER, George (Superintendent, Forest Gate/Bow Road) 65, 153
TURNER, James Axley (Sergeant, Uxbridge) 212
TURNER, James Oxley (Sergeant, Brentford) 69
TURNER, Richard (Inspector, Wandsworth) 381
TURNER, William (Constable, Barnet) 100
TURTON, Joshua (Constable, Hillingdon and Uxbridge) 212
TYLER (Constable, Tottenham) 365

UNDERWOOD, William (Superintendent, Hackney) 169
UNSTED, Edwin Carter (Sub-Divisional Inspector, Hampton) 180
URBAN, Henry (Inspector, Rosyth) 446

VARNEY, Eric (Station Sergeant, Edmonton) 137
VAUGHN, Philip (Constable, Brentford) 70
VENTHAM, William (Superintendent, Portsmouth/ Devonport) 430, 433, 436, 437, 444
VERONNE, Mark (Inspector, East Ham) 132
VINCENT, Barry (Superintendent, Edmonton /Forest Gate) 138, 155

WACHTER, Ernest (Constable, Brentford) 72
WADDELL, A. (Inspector, Carter Street) 87
WADE, Brian (Superintendent, Lavender Hill) 256
WADE, William T. (Sub-Divisional Inspector, Uxbridge) 212
WAKEFIELD (Sergeant, Devonport) 438
WAKEFORD, William (Superintendent, Devonport/ Chatham) 436, 437, 442-443, 444
WALKER (Superintendent, Cheshunt) 94
WALKER (Superintendent, Westminster) 246
WALKER, Ken (Constable, Fulham) 157
WALKER, Robert (District Superintendent, Greenford) 163
WALKER, Thomas Benjamin (Inspector, Marine: Blackwall) 419
WALL, Charles (Chief Inspector, Devonport) 436
WALL, Thomas (Superintendent, Peel House (Training)) 14
WALLACE, Alexander (Sub-Divisional Inspector, Wanstead) 386
WALLACE, John (Constable, Cobham) 110
WALLIS, George (War Reserve Constable, Kilburn) 245
WALLIS, Richard (Sub-Divisional Inspector, Brentford) 72
WALSH, Emily (Constable, Woolwich) 417
WALSHE (Inspector, Plumstead) 302
WALTERS (Special Constable, Ilford) 228
WALTERS, Donald (Sergeant, Greenwich) 166
WANNOP, John (Inspector, Rosyth) 446
WAPLING, George (Constable, Hornchurch) 217
WARD, Sheila (Inspector, Women Police) 468
WARE, James (Inspector, Redbridge) 386
WARING (Superintendent, Edmonton) 138
WARNE, J. (Station Sergeant, Finchley) 150
WARREN, 'Bunny' (Constable, Hendon) 208
WARREN, Sir Charles (Commissioner) 162
WASP, Alfred (Constable, Wealdstone) 387
WATERS (Constable, Leyton) 264
WATERS, Donald (Superintendent, Southwark) 341
WATSON (Superintendent, Edmonton) 138
WATSON, Archibald (Inspector, Acton) 38
WATSON, James (Constable, Sunbury) 354
WATSON, Neil (Constable, Harrow) 192
WATSON, William (Station Sergeant, Wembley) 245
WATTS, William (Sub-Divisional Inspector, West Ham) 395
WATTS, Alberta (Detective Sergeant, Women Police) 468
WAY, Andrew (Assistant Commissioner, Hendon) 202
WAYMAN, George (Constable, Limehouse) 267
WEAR (Constable, Barnes) 51
WEBB (Acting Superintendent, Hornsey) 218
WEBB, Charles (Superintendent, Kennington) 238
WEBB, George (Inspector, Thames: Blackwall) 419
WEBB, J. (Constable, Upminster) 370
WEBB, Joseph (Constable, Bedfont) 56
WEBB, O. (Sub-Divisional Inspector, Barnet) 101
WEBB, Owen (Superintendent, Devonport) 426, 436, 438
WEBB, Thomas (Constable, Barnet) 99
WEBB, Andrew (Chief Inspector, Croydon) 114
WEBBER, Tom (Constable, Barnet) 100
WEDLOCK (Sub-Divisional Inspector, Devonport) 437
WELHAM, Leslie (Constable, Waltham Abbey) 377
WELLER, Walter (Inspector, Uxbridge) 213

Index

WELLS (Superintendent, Bow Road) 65
WELLS, Arthur (Inspector, East Greenwich) 131
WELLS, Creswell (Superintendent, City of Westminster/Ilford/
 Richmond) 84-86, 227
WELLS, Sidney George (Constable, Bow Street) 85
WELTON (Constable, Kingston) 253
WENSLEY, Frederick (Chief Constable, West End Cenral) 392, 463
WEST (Superintendent, Brixton) 75, 283
WEST (Superintendent, Norbury) 283
WEST, Edward (Sub-Divisional Inspector, Kingston) 251, 252
WEST, G. (Sergeant (Specials), Ponders End) 304
WESTWOOD, Thomas (Constable, Pinner) 297
WHARTON (Superintendent, Islington) 248
WHARTON COLLARD, C. (Assistant Commander (Specials),
 St. John's Wood) 344
WHATLEY, W. (Inspector, Kennington) 238
WHEATON, Walter (Sergeant, Wembley) 390
WHEELER, A. (Constable (Specials), Ponders End) 304
WHELLAMS (Constable, Hendon) 206
WHELLER, James (Station Sergeant, South Mimms) 335
WHELLER, William James (Station Sergeant, Greenwich) 167
WHITE (Inspector, Victoria Park) 373
WHITE (Superintendent, Bethnal Green) 60
WHITE (Superintendent, Gipsy Hill) 288
WHITE, A. (Constable (Specials), Ponders End) 304
WHITE, Arthur Wilfred (War Reserve Constable, Ealing) 128
WHITE, H.G. (Superintendent, Battersea) 53
WHITE, J.H. (Superintendent, Cobham) 110
WHITE, James Robert (Inspector, Marine: Wapping) 421
WHITE, Richard (Inspector, Marine: Blackwall) 419
WHITE, William (Inspector, West Ham) 116
WHITING, Michael (Constable, Bow Street) 68
WHITMORE, James (Station Sergeant, Esher) 146
WHYTE, John (Constable, Hendon) 207-208
WIGGINS (Constable, Chingford) 97
WIGGINS, William (Inspector, Paddington) 292
WILCOX, George (Sub-Divisional Inspector, Fulham) 156
WILEY, George John (Special Constable, Ditton) 124
WILKES, Edward (Inspector, Caledonian Road) 80
WILKINS, Edward (Sergeant, Teddington) 360
WILKINSON, Tom Albert (Sub-Divisional Inspector, Barnet) 101
WILLIAMS (Chief Superintendent, Edmonton) 138
WILLIAMS (Superintendent, Golders Green) 159
WILLIAMS, Richard (Constable, Staines) 347
WILLIAMS, Thomas (Superintendent, Barnet) 101
WILLIAMSON, David (Superintendent, Hammersmith/
 Uxbridge/Brentford) 69, 174, 212
WILLIE, James (Constable, Brentford) 72
WILLIS, George (Inspector, Ealing) 127

WILLMOTT, John (Chief Inspector, Devonport/Woolwich) 425
WILLS, George (Inspector, Harrow) 127
WILSON, A. (Inspector, Epsom) 143
WILSON, Eleanor (Constable, Hendon) 207
WILSON, Henry (Sergeant, Erith) 144
WILSON, James (Superintendent, Croydon) 115
WILSON, W. (Superintendent, Cobham) 111
WILTSHIRE (Sergeant, Hoxton) 223
WINDSOR (Constable, Wealdstone) 388
WINKLER (Chief Inspector, Marlborough Street Court) 246
WINSHIP, Peter (Assistant Commissioner, Edmonton) 137
WINTER, Henry (Inspector, Kingston) 253
WINTERFLOOD, 'Stormy' (Constable, Hendon) 207
WISE, George (Chief Superintendent, Kilburn) 245
WISEMAN, William (Superintendent, Brixton/Clapham/Croydon) 276
WOLLARD (Constable, Gipsy Hill) 288
WOMBWELL, David Stanley Bertram (Detective Constable,
 Shepherds Bush) 330
WONNALL, Thomas (Inspector, Devonport) 437
WOOD, Henry (Chief Inspector, L.B. Camden) 20
WOODGATE, J. (Sergeant, Plough Corner) 302
WOODHOUSE (Inspector (Specials), Tottenham) 366
WOODS, Walter (Constable, Bedfont) 58
WOODWARD (Constable, Wealdstone) 388
WOOLARD, G.H.K. (Superintendent, West Hendon) 398
WOOLGAR, Robert (Constable, Chelsea) 92
WOOLMORE, Arthur (Constable, Barnet) 100
WOOTON, Joseph (Inspector, Portsmouth) 431
WOOTTON (Inspector, Marine: Blackwall) 420
WORELS, Edward (Superintendent, Kentish Town) 242
WORFALL, William George (Sergeant, Kingston) 249
WORTH (Inspector, Streatham) 353
WORTH, Leonard (Sergeant, South Mimms) 336
WREN, John (Constable, Hendon) 207
WREN, Walter T. (Superintendent, Southwark) 341
WRIGHT (Constable, Woolwich) 427
WRIGHT, Frederick (Inspector, Camberwell) 426
WYBORN, H. (Superintendent, Southwark) 340
WYLES, Lilian (Detective Inspector, Women Police) 456, 466, 468, 469

YALDEN, William (Chief Inspector (Specials), Wood Green) 411
YALLOP, Charles (Constable, Barnet) 101
YATES, John (Inspector, Southwark) 339
YATES, Thomas (Constable, Sunbury) 353
YEO, Albert (Detective Inspector, West Ham) 395
YOUNG (Inspector, Pembroke) 445
YOUNG, Alfred (Detective Constable, Hampstead) 178
YOUNG, Edward (Superintendent, Arbour Square) 42
YOUNG, Richmond (Station Sergeant, Shenley) 328

www.ingramcontent.com/pod-product-compliance
Lightning Source LLC
Chambersburg PA
CBHW080915230426
43667CB00016B/2689